PostgreSQL

PostgreSQL

The comprehensive guide to building, programming,
and administering PostgreSQL databases

Second Edition

Korry Douglas
Susan Douglas

DEVELOPER'S
LIBRARY

Sams Publishing, 800 East 96th Street, Indianapolis, Indiana 46240, USA

PostgreSQL, Second Edition

International Standard Book Number: 0-672-32756-2

Library of Congress Catalog Card Number: 2004097929

Printed in the United States of America

This product is printed digitally on demand.

Trademarks

Warning and Disclaimer

Bulk Sales

Sams Publishing offers excellent discounts on this book when ordered in quantity for bulk purchases or special sales. For more information, please contact

U.S. Corporate and Government Sales
1-800-382-3419
corpsales@pearsontechgroup.com

For sales outside of the U.S., please contact

International Sales
international@pearsoned.com

Acquisitions Editor
Shelley Johnston

Development Editor
Damon Jordan

Managing Editor
Charlotte Clapp

Project Editor
Dan Knott

Copy Editor
Linda Seifert

Indexer
Larry Sweazy

Proofreader
Wendy Ostermeyer

Technical Editor
Vince Vielhaber

Publishing Coordinator
Vanessa Evans

Multimedia Developer
Dan Scherf

Book Designer
Gary Adair

Page Layout
Jeff Henn

Contents at a Glance

Table of Contents

The Real Value in Free Software

These days, it seems that most discussion of open-source software centers around the idea that you should not have to tie your future to the whim of some giant corporation. People say that open-source software is better than proprietary software because it is developed and maintained by the users instead of a faceless company out to lighten your wallet.

I think that the real value in free software is education. I have never learned anything by reading my own code[1]. On the other hand, it's a rare occasion when I've looked at code written by someone else and haven't come away with another tool in my toolkit. People don't think alike. I don't mean that people disagree with each other; I mean that people solve problems in different ways. Each person brings a unique set of experiences to the table. Each person has his own set of goals and biases. Each person has his own interests. All of these things will shape the way you think about a problem. Often, I'll find myself in a heated disagreement with a colleague only to realize that we are each correct in our approach. Just because I'm right, doesn't mean that my colleague can't be right as well.

Open-source software is a great way to learn. You can learn about programming. You can learn about design. You can learn about debugging. Sometimes, you'll learn how *not* to design, code, or debug; but that's a valuable lesson, too. You can learn small things, like how to cache file descriptors on systems where file descriptors are a scarce and expensive resource, or how to use the `select()` function to implement fine-grained timers. You can learn big things, like how a query optimizer works or how to write a parser, or how to develop a good memory-management strategy.

PostgreSQL is a great example. I've been using databases for the last two decades. I've used most of the major commercial databases: Oracle, Sybase, DB2, and MS SQL Server. With each commercial database, there is a wall of knowledge between *my* needs and the *vendor's* need to protect his intellectual property. Until I started exploring open-source databases, I had an incomplete understanding of how a database works. Why was this particular feature implemented that way? Why am I getting poor performance when I try this? That's a neat feature; I wonder how they did that? Every commercial database tries to expose a small piece of its inner workings. The `explain` statement will show you why the database makes its optimization decisions. But, you only get to see what the vendor wants you to see. The vendor isn't trying to hide things from you (in most cases), but without complete access to the source code, they have to pick and choose how to expose information in a meaningful way. With open-source software, you can dive deep

---

[1] Maybe I should say that I have never learned anything *new* by reading my own code. I've certainly looked at code that I've written and wondered what I was thinking at the time, learning that I'm not nearly as clever as I had remembered. Oddly enough, those who have read my code have reached a similar conclusion.

into the source code and pull out all the information you need. While writing this book, I've spent a lot of time reading through the PostgreSQL source code. I've added a lot of my own code to reveal *more* information so that I could explain things more clearly. I can't do that with a commercial database.

There are gems of brilliance in most open-source projects. In a well-designed, well-factored project, you will find designs and code that you can use in your own projects. Many open-source projects are starting to split their code into reusable libraries. The Apache Portable Runtime is a good example. The Apache Web server runs on many diverse platforms. The Apache development team saw the need for a layer of abstraction that would provide a portable interface to system functions such as shared memory and network access. They decided to factor the portability layer into a library separate from their main project. The result is the Apache Portable Runtime—a library of code that can be used in *other* open-source projects (such as PostgreSQL).

Some developers hate to work on someone else's code. I love working on code written by another developer—I always learn something from the experience. I strongly encourage you to dive into the PostgreSQL source code. You will learn from it. You might even decide to contribute to the project.

—Korry Douglas

About the Authors

Korry Douglas is the director of research and development for Appx Software. Over the last two decades, he has worked on the design and implementation of a number of high-level, high-productivity languages and development environments. His products interface with many relational (and non-relational) databases. Working with so many different database products (Oracle, Sybase, SQL Server, DB2, PostgreSQL, MySQL, MSQL) has given him a broad understanding of the commonalities of, and differences between, databases.

Susan Douglas is the president and CEO of Conjectrix, Inc., a software company specializing in database technologies and security tools. Consulting to the end-user community has given her widespread database experience and a real appreciation for high-quality programs and flexible tools powerful enough to handle data well and intuitive enough to actually use.

Korry and his wife (and best friend) Susan raise horses in rural Virginia. Both are natives of the Pacific Northwest, but prefer the sunshine and open spaces offered by Virginia. They both telecommute, preferring to spend as much time as possible with their 200 or so animal friends (who never complain about buggy code, inelegant design, or poor performance). Susan is an avid equestrienne; Korry gets to clean the barn.

Acknowledgments

Thank you to our technical reviewer Vince Vielhaber. We appreciate his many hours spent poring over manuscripts exposing technical inaccuracies. His knowledge and expertise have been invaluable. We'd also like to thank Peter Eisentraut and Barry Stinson for reviewing the first edition of this book and Paul DuBois (of *MySQL* fame) for his guidance while we struggled for clarity in the first edition.

We would especially like to thank the developers of PostgreSQL for the years of development spent producing an excellent database. Without their devotion to the project, it wouldn't have evolved into the masterpiece we all know today.

Most of the books that we read are dedicated to various household members for the long hours devoted to their writing project rather than to family life. Instead, we have enjoyed the long hours of R&D spent together, interspersed with screaming (during breaks, on the roller coasters at King's Dominion—not at each other).

We Want to Hear from You!

As the reader of this book, *you* are our most important critic and commentator. We value your opinion and want to know what we're doing right, what we could do better, what areas you'd like to see us publish in, and any other words of wisdom you're willing to pass our way.

You can email or write me directly to let me know what you did or didn't like about this book—as well as what we can do to make our books stronger.

Please note that I cannot help you with technical problems related to the topic of this book, and that due to the high volume of mail I receive, I might not be able to reply to every message.

When you write, please be sure to include this book's title and author as well as your name and phone or email address. I will carefully review your comments and share them with the author and editors who worked on the book.

Email: opensource@samspublishing.com

Mail: Mark Taber
          Associate Publisher
          Sams Publishing
          800 East 96th Street
          Indianapolis, IN 46240 USA

Reader Services

For more information about this book or another Sams Publishing title, visit our website at www.samspublishing.com. Type the ISBN (excluding hyphens) or the title of a book in the Search field to find the page you're looking for.

Introduction

PostgreSQL is a relational database with a long history. In the late 1970s, the University of California at Berkeley began development of PostgreSQL's ancestor—a relational database known as Ingres. Relational Technologies turned Ingres into a commercial product. Relational Technologies became Ingres Corporation and was later acquired by Computer Associates. Around 1986, Michael Stonebraker from UC Berkeley led a team that added object-oriented features to the core of Ingres; the new version became known as Postgres. Postgres was again commercialized; this time by a company named Illustra, which became part of the Informix Corporation. Andrew Yu and Jolly Chen added SQL support to Postgres in the mid-'90s. Prior versions had used a different, Postgres-specific query language known as Postquel. In 1996, many new features were added, including the MVCC transaction model, more adherence to the SQL92 standard, and many performance improvements. Postgres once again took on a new name: PostgreSQL.

Today, PostgreSQL is developed by an international group of open-source software proponents known as the PostgreSQL Global Development group. PostgreSQL is an open-source product—it is not proprietary in any way. Red Hat has recently commercialized PostgreSQL, creating the Red Hat Database, but PostgreSQL itself will remain free and open source.

PostgreSQL Features

PostgreSQL has benefited well from its long history. Today, PostgreSQL is one of the most advanced database servers available. Here are a few of the features found in a standard PostgreSQL distribution:

- Object-relational—In PostgreSQL, every table defines a class. PostgreSQL implements inheritance between tables (or, if you like, between classes). Functions and operators are polymorphic.

- Standards compliant—PostgreSQL syntax implements most of the SQL92 standard and many features of SQL99. Where differences in syntax occur, they are most often related to features unique to PostgreSQL.

- Open source—An international team of developers maintains PostgreSQL. Team members come and go, but the core members have been enhancing PostgreSQL's performance and feature set since at least 1996. One advantage to PostgreSQL's open-source nature is that talent and knowledge can be recruited as needed. The fact that this team is international ensures that PostgreSQL is a product that can be used productively in *any* natural language, not just English.

- Transaction processing—PostgreSQL protects data and coordinates multiple concurrent users through full transaction processing. The transaction model used by PostgreSQL is based on multi-version concurrency control (MVCC). MVCC provides much better performance than you would find with other products that coordinate multiple users through table-, page-, or row-level locking.

- Referential integrity—PostgreSQL implements complete referential integrity by supporting foreign and primary key relationships as well as triggers. Business rules can be expressed *within* the database rather than relying on an external tool.

- Multiple procedural languages—Triggers and other procedures can be written in any of several procedural languages. Server-side code is most commonly written in PL/pgSQL, a procedural language similar to Oracle's PL/SQL. You can also develop server-side code in Tcl, Perl, even bash (the open-source Linux/Unix shell).

- Multiple-client APIs—PostgreSQL supports the development of client applications in many languages. This book describes how to interface to PostgreSQL from C, C++, ODBC, Perl, PHP, Tcl/Tk, and Python.

- Unique data types—PostgreSQL provides a variety of data types. Besides the usual numeric, string, and data types, you will also find geometric types, a Boolean data type, and data types designed specifically to deal with network addresses.

- Extensibility—One of the most important features of PostgreSQL is that it can be extended. If you don't find something that you need, you can usually add it yourself. For example, you can add new data types, new functions and operators, and even new procedural and client languages. There are many contributed packages available on the Internet. For example, Refractions Research, Inc. has developed a set of geographic data types that can be used to efficiently model spatial (GIS) data.

What Versions Does This Book Cover?

The first edition of this book covered versions 7.1 through 7.3. In this edition, we've updated the basics and added coverage for the new features introduced in versions 7.4 and 8.0. Throughout the book, I'll be sure to let you know which features work only in new releases, and, in a few cases, I'll explain features that have been deprecated (that is, features that are obsolete). You can use this book to install, configure, tune, program, and manage PostgreSQL versions 7.1 through 8.0.

Fortunately, the PostgreSQL developers try *very* hard to maintain forward compatibility—new features tend not to break existing applications. This means that all the features discussed in this book should still be available and substantially similar in later versions of PostgreSQL. I have tried to avoid talking about features that have not been released at the time of writing—where I *have* mentioned future developments, I will point them out.

Who Is This Book For?

If you are already using PostgreSQL, you should find this book a useful guide to some of the features that you might be less familiar with. The first part of the book provides an introduction to SQL and PostgreSQL for the new user. You'll also find information that shows how to obtain and install PostgreSQL on a Unix/Linux host, as well as on Microsoft Windows.

If you are developing an application that will store data in PostgreSQL, the second part of this book will provide you with a great deal of information relating to PostgreSQL programming. You'll find information on both server-side and client-side programming in a variety of languages.

Every database needs occasional administrative work. The final part of the book should be of help if you are a PostgreSQL administrator, or a developer or user that needs to do occasional administration. You will also find information on how to secure your data against inappropriate use.

Finally, if you are trying to decide *which* database to use for your current project (or for future projects), this book should provide all the information you need to evaluate whether PostgreSQL will fit your needs.

What Topics Does This Book Cover?

PostgreSQL is a *huge* product. It's not easy to find the right mix of topics when you are trying to fit everything into a single book. This book is divided into three parts.

The first part, "General PostgreSQL Use," is an introduction and user's guide for PostgreSQL. Chapter 1, "Introduction to PostgreSQL and SQL," covers the basics—how to obtain and install PostgreSQL (if you are running Linux, chances are you already have PostgreSQL and it may be installed). The first chapter also provides a gentle introduction to SQL and discusses the sample database we'll be using throughout the book. Chapter 2, "Working with Data in PostgreSQL," describes the many data types supported by a standard PostgreSQL distribution; you'll learn how to enter values (literals) for each data type, what kind of data you can store with each type, and how those data types are combined into expressions. Chapter 3, "PostgreSQL SQL Syntax and Use," fills in some of the details we glossed over in the first two chapters. You'll learn how to create new databases, new tables and indexes, and how PostgreSQL keeps your data safe through the use of transactions. Chapter 4, "Performance," describes the PostgreSQL optimizer. I'll show you how to get information about the decisions made by the optimizer, how to decipher that information, and how to influence those decisions.

Part II, "Programming with PostgreSQL," is all about PostgreSQL programming. In Chapter 5, "Introduction to PostgreSQL Programming," we start off by describing the options you have when developing a database application that works with PostgreSQL (and there are a *lot* of options). Chapter 6, "Extending PostgreSQL," briefly describes how to extend PostgreSQL by adding new functions, data types, and operators.

Chapter 7, "PL/pgSQL," describes the PL/pgSQL language. PL/pgSQL is a server-based procedural language. Code that you write in PL/pgSQL executes *within* the PostgreSQL server and has very fast access to data. Each chapter in the remainder of the programming section deals with a client-based API. You can connect to a PostgreSQL server using a number of languages. I show you how to interface to PostgreSQL using C, C++, ecpg, ODBC, JDBC, Perl, PHP, Tcl/Tk, Python, and Microsoft's .NET. Chapters 8 through 18 all follow the same pattern: you develop a series of client applications in a given language. The first client application shows you how to establish a connection to the database (and how that connection is represented by the language in question). The next client adds error checking so that you can intercept and react to unusual conditions. The third client in each chapter demonstrates how to process SQL commands from within the client. The final client wraps everything together and shows you how to build an interactive query processor using the language being discussed. Even if you program in only one or two languages, I would encourage you to study the other chapters in this section. I think you'll find that looking at the same application written in a variety of languages will help you understand the philosophy followed by the PostgreSQL development team, and it's a great way to start learning a new language. Chapter 19, "Other Useful Programming Tools," introduces you to a few programming tools (and interfaces) that you might find useful: PL/Java and PL/Perl. I'll also show you how to use PostgreSQL inside of bash shell scripts.

The final part of this book (Part III, "PostgreSQL Administration") deals with administrative issues. The final six chapters of this book show you how to perform the occasional duties required of a PostgreSQL administrator. In the first two chapters, Chapter 20, "Introduction to PostgreSQL Administration," and Chapter 21, "PostgreSQL Administration," you'll learn how to start up, shut down, back up, and restore a server. In Chapter 22, "Internationalization and Localization," you will learn how PostgreSQL supports internationalization and localization. PostgreSQL understands how to store and process a variety of single-byte and multi-byte character sets including Unicode, ASCII, and Japanese, Chinese, Korean, and Taiwan EUC. In Chapter 23, "Security," I'll show you how to secure your data against unauthorized uses (and unauthorized users). In Chapter 24, "Replicating PostgreSQL with Slony," you'll learn how to replicate data with PostgreSQL's Slony replication system. Chapter 25, "Contributed Modules," introduces a few open-source projects that work well with PostgreSQL. I'll show you how to query a PostgreSQL database using XML, how to configure and use TSEARCH2 (a full-text indexing and search system), and how to install and use PgAdmin III, a graphical user interface specifically designed for PostgreSQL.

What's New in the Second Edition?

The first edition of this book hit the shelves in February 2003—at that time, the PostgreSQL developers had just released version 7.3.2. Release 7.4 was unleashed in November 2003. In January 2005, the PostgreSQL developers released version 8.0—a major release full of new features. We timed the second edition of this book to coincide with the release of version 8.0 (the book will appear in bookstores a few months after 8.0 hits the streets). In this edition, we've added coverage for all of the (major) new features in 7.3, 7.4, and 8.0, including

- Installing, securing, and managing PostgreSQL on Windows hosts
- Tablespaces
- Schemas
- New quoting mechanisms for string values
- New data types (ANYARRAY, ANYELEMENT, VOID)
- The standards-conforming INFORMATION_SCHEMA
- Nested transactions (SAVEPOINT's)
- The new PostgreSQL buffer manager
- Auto-vacuum
- Prepared-statement execution (the PREPARE/EXECUTE model)
- Set-returning functions
- Exception handling in PL/pgSQL
- libpqxx, the new PostgreSQL interface for C++ clients
- New features in ecpg (the embedded SQL processor for C)
- New features in the ODBC, JDBC (Java), Perl, Python, PHP, and Tcl/Tk client interfaces
- npgsql—the PostgreSQL .NET data provider
- Other useful programming tools (PL/Java, pgpash, pgcurl, etc.)
- Point-in-time recovery
- Replication
- Using PostgreSQL with XML
- Full-text search

We hope you enjoy this book and find it useful. The PostgreSQL developers have done an incredible job of enhancing what was already a world-class database product. Now dig in.

I

General PostgreSQL Use

1

Introduction to PostgreSQL and SQL

POSTGRESQL IS AN OPEN-SOURCE, CLIENT/SERVER, relational database. PostgreSQL offers a unique mix of features that compare well to the major commercial databases such as Sybase, Oracle, and DB2. One of the major advantages to PostgreSQL is that it is open source—you can see the source code for PostgreSQL. PostgreSQL is not owned by any single company. It is developed, maintained, broken, and fixed by a group of volunteer developers around the world. You don't have to buy PostgreSQL—it's free. You won't have to pay any maintenance fees (although you can certainly find commercial sources for technical support).

PostgreSQL offers all the usual features of a relational database plus quite a few unique features. PostgreSQL offers inheritance (for you object-oriented readers). You can add your own data types to PostgreSQL. (I know, some of you are probably thinking that you can do that in your favorite database.) Most database systems allow you to give a new name to an existing type. Some systems allow you to define composite types. With PostgreSQL, you can add new *fundamental* data types. PostgreSQL includes support for geometric data types such as point, line segment, box, polygon, and circle. PostgreSQL uses indexing structures that make geometric data types *fast*. PostgreSQL can be *extended*—you can build new functions, new operators, and new data types in the language of your choice. PostgreSQL is built around client/server architecture. You can build client applications in a number of different languages, including C, C++, Java, Python, Perl, TCL/Tk, and others. On the server side, PostgreSQL sports a powerful procedural language, PL/pgSQL (okay, the language is sportier than the name). You can *add* procedural languages to the server. You will find procedural languages supporting Perl, TCL/Tk, and even the bash shell.

A Sample Database

Throughout this book, I'll use a simple example database to help explain some of the more complex concepts. The sample database represents some of the data storage and retrieval requirements that you might encounter when running a video rental store. I won't pretend that the sample database is useful for any real-world scenarios; instead, this database will help us explore how PostgreSQL works and should illustrate many PostgreSQL features.

To begin with, the sample database (which is called *movies*) contains three kinds of records: customers, tapes, and rentals.

Whenever a customer walks into our imaginary video store, you will consult your database to determine whether you already know this customer. If not, you'll add a new record. What items of information should you store for each customer? At the very least, you will want to record the customer's name. You will want to ensure that each customer has a unique identifier—you might have two customers named "Danny Johnson," and you'll want to keep them straight. A name is a poor choice for a unique identifier—names might not be unique, and they can often be spelled in different ways. ("Was that Danny, Dan, or Daniel?") You'll assign each customer a unique customer ID. You might also want to store the customer's birth date so that you know whether he should be allowed to rent certain movies. If you find that a customer has an overdue tape rental, you'll probably want to phone him, so you better store the customer's phone number. In a real-world business, you would probably want to know much more information about each customer (such as his home address), but for these purposes, you'll keep your storage requirements to a minimum.

Next, you will need to keep track of the videos that you stock. Each video has a title and a duration—you'll store those. You might own several copies of the same movie and you will certainly have many movies with the same duration, so you can't use either one for a unique identifier. Instead, you'll assign a unique ID to each video.

Finally, you will need to track rentals. When a customer rents a tape, you will store the customer ID, tape ID, and rental date.

Notice that you won't store the customer name with each rental. As long as you store the customer ID, you can always retrieve the customer name. You won't store the movie title with each rental, either—you can find the movie title by its unique identifier.

At a few points in this book, we might make changes to the layout of the sample database, but the basic shape will remain the same.

Basic Database Terminology

Before we get into the interesting stuff, it might be useful to get acquainted with a few of the terms that you will encounter in your PostgreSQL life. PostgreSQL has a long history—you can trace its history back to 1977 and a program known as Ingres. A lot has changed in the relational database world since 1977. When you are breaking ground with a new product (as the Ingres developers were), you don't have the luxury of using standard, well-understood, and well-accepted terminology—you have to make it up as you go along. Many of the terms used by PostgreSQL have synonyms (or at least close analogies) in today's relational marketplace. In this section, I'll show you a few of the terms that you'll encounter in this book and try to explain how they relate to similar concepts in other database products.

- **Schema**

  A *schema* is a named collection of tables. (see *table*). A schema can also contain views, indexes, sequences, data types, operators, and functions. Other relational database products use the term *catalog*.

- **Database**

  A *database* is a named collection of schemas. When a client application connects to a PostgreSQL server, it specifies the name of the database that it wants to access. A client cannot interact with more than one database per connection but it *can* open any number of connections in order to access multiple databases simultaneously.

- **Command**

  A *command* is a string that you send to the server in hopes of having the server do something useful. Some people use the word *statement* to mean *command*. The two words are very similar in meaning and, in practice, are interchangeable.

- **Query**

  A *query* is a type of command that retrieves data from the server.

- **Table (relation, file, class)**

  A *table* is a collection of rows. A table usually has a name, although some tables are temporary and exist only to carry out a command. All the rows in a table have the same shape (in other words, every row in a table contains the same set of columns). In other database systems, you may see the terms *relation*, *file*, or even *class*—these are all equivalent to a table.

- **Column (field, attribute)**

  A *column* is the smallest unit of storage in a relational database. A column represents one piece of information about an object. Every column has a name and a data type. Columns are grouped into rows, and rows are grouped into tables. In Figure 1.1, the shaded area depicts a single column.

  The terms *field* and *attribute* have similar meanings.

- **Row (record, tuple)**

  A *row* is a collection of column values. Every row in a table has the same shape (in other words, every row is composed of the same set of columns). If you are trying to model a real-world application, a row represents a real-world object. For example, if you are running an auto dealership, you might have a `vehicles` table. Each row in the `vehicles` table represents a car (or truck, or motorcycle, and so on). The kinds of information that you store are the same for all `vehicles` (that is, every car has a color, a vehicle ID, an engine, and so on). In Figure 1.2, the shaded area depicts a row.

  You may also see the terms *record* or *tuple*—these are equivalent to a row.

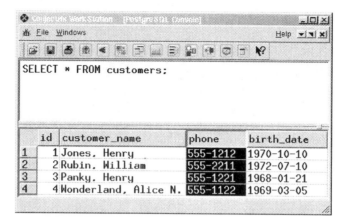

Figure 1.1 A column (highlighted).

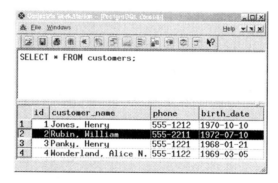

Figure 1.2 A row (highlighted).

- **Composite type**

  Starting with PostgreSQL version 8, you can create new data types that are composed of multiple values. For example, you could create a *composite type* named `address` that holds a street address, city, state/province, and postal code. When you create a table that contains a column of type `address`, you can store all four components in a single field. We discuss composite types in more detail in Chapter 2, "Working with Data in PostgreSQL."

- **Domain**

  A *domain* defines a named specialization of another data type. Domains are useful when you need to ensure that a single data type is used in several tables. For example, you might define a domain named `accountNumber` that contains a single letter followed by four digits. Then you can create columns of type `accountNumber` in a general ledger accounts table, an accounts receivable customer table, and so on.

- **View**

  A *view* is an alternative way to present a table (or tables). You might think of a view as a "virtual" table. A view is (usually) defined in terms of one or more tables. When you create a view, you are not storing more data, you are instead creating a different way of looking at existing data. A view is a useful way to give a name to a complex query that you may have to use repeatedly.

- **Client/server**

  PostgreSQL is built around a *client/server* architecture. In a client/server product, there are at least two programs involved. One is a client and the other is a server. These programs may exist on the same host or on different hosts that are connected by some sort of network. The server offers a service; in the case of PostgreSQL, the server offers to store, retrieve, and change data. The client asks a server to perform work; a PostgreSQL client asks a PostgreSQL server to serve up relational data.

- **Client**

  A *client* is an application that makes requests of the PostgreSQL server. Before a client application can talk to a server, it must connect to a postmaster (see `post-master`) and establish its identity. Client applications provide a user interface and can be written in many languages. Chapters 8 through 19 will show you how to write a client application.

- **Server**

  The PostgreSQL *server* is a program that services commands coming from client applications. The PostgreSQL server has no user interface—you can't talk to the server directly, you must use a client application.

- **Postmaster**

  Because PostgreSQL is a client/server database, something has to listen for connection requests coming from a client application. That's what the `postmaster` does. When a connection request arrives, the `postmaster` creates a new server process in the host operating system.

- **Transaction**

  A *transaction* is a collection of database operations that are treated as a unit. PostgreSQL guarantees that all the operations within a transaction complete or that none of them complete. This is an important property—it ensures that if something goes wrong in the middle of a transaction, changes made before the point of failure will not be reflected in the database. A transaction usually starts with a `BEGIN` command and ends with a `COMMIT` or `ROLLBACK` (see the next entries).

- **Commit**

  A *commit* marks the successful end of a transaction. When you perform a commit, you are telling PostgreSQL that you have completed a unit of operation and that all the changes that you made to the database should become permanent.

- **Rollback**

  A *rollback* marks the *un*successful end of a transaction. When you roll back a transaction, you are telling PostgreSQL to discard any changes that you have made to the database (since the beginning of the transaction).

- **Index**

  An *index* is a data structure that a database uses to reduce the amount of time it takes to perform certain operations. An index can also be used to ensure that duplicate values don't appear where they aren't wanted. I'll talk about indexes in Chapter 4, "Performance."

- **Tablespace**

  A *tablespace* defines an alternative storage location where you can create tables and indexes. When you create a table (or index), you can specify the name of a tablespace—if you don't specify a tablespace, PostgreSQL creates all objects in the same directory tree. You can use tablespaces to distribute the workload across multiple disk drives.

- **Result set**

  When you issue a query to a database, you get back a *result set*. The result set contains all the rows that satisfy your query. A result set may be empty.

Prerequisites

Before I go much further, let's talk about installing PostgreSQL. Chapters 21, "PostgreSQL Administration," and 23, "Security," discuss PostgreSQL installation in detail, but I'll show you a typical installation procedure here.

When you install PostgreSQL, you can start with prebuilt binaries or you can compile PostgreSQL from source code. In this chapter, I'll show you how to install PostgreSQL on a Linux host starting from prebuilt binaries. If you decide to install PostgreSQL from source code, many of the steps are the same. I'll show you how to build PostgreSQL from source code in Chapter 21.

In older versions of PostgreSQL, you could run the PostgreSQL server on a Windows host but you had to install a Unix-like infrastructure (Cygwin) first: PostgreSQL wasn't a native Windows application. Starting with PostgreSQL version 8.0, the PostgreSQL server has been ported to the Windows environment as a native-Windows application. Installing PostgreSQL on a Windows server is very simple; simply download and run the installer program. You do have a few choices to make, and we cover the entire procedure in Chapter 21.

Installing PostgreSQL Using an RPM

The easiest way to install PostgreSQL is to use a prebuilt RPM package. *RPM* is the *Red Hat Package Manager*. It's a software package designed to install (and manage) other software packages. If you choose to install using some method other than RPM, consult the documentation that comes with the distribution you are using.

PostgreSQL is distributed as a collection of RPM packages—you don't have to install all the packages to use PostgreSQL. Table 1.1 lists the RPM packages available as of release 7.4.5.

Table 1.1   **PostgreSQL RPM Packages as of Release 7.4.5**

Package	Description
postgresql	Clients, libraries, and documentation
postgresql-server	Programs (and data files) required to run a server
postgresql-devel	Files required to create new client applications
postgresql-jdbc	JDBC driver for PostgreSQL
postgresql-tcl	Tcl client and PL/Tcl
postgresql-python	PostgreSQL's Python library
postgresql-test	Regression test suite for PostgreSQL
postgresql-libs	Shared libraries for client applications
postgresql-docs	Extra documentation not included in the postgresql base package
postgresql-contrib	Contributed software

Don't worry if you don't know which of these you need, I'll explain most of the packages in later chapters. You can start working with PostgreSQL by downloading the postgresql, postgresql-libs, and postgresql-server packages. The actual files (at the www.postgresql.org website) have names that include a version number: `postgresql-7.4.5-2PGDG.i686.rpm`, for example.

I strongly recommend creating an empty directory, and then downloading the PostgreSQL packages into that directory. That way you can install all the PostgreSQL packages with a single command.

After you have downloaded the desired packages, use the `rpm` command to perform the installation procedure. You must have superuser privileges to install PostgreSQL.

To install the PostgreSQL packages, `cd` into the directory that contains the package files and issue the following command:

```
# rpm -ihv *.rpm
```

The `rpm` command installs all the packages in your current directory. You should see results similar to what is shown in Figure 1.3.

The RPM installer should have created a new user (named `postgres`) for your system. This user ID exists so that all database files accessed by PostgreSQL can be owned by a single user.

Each RPM package is composed of many files. You can view the list of files installed for a given package using the `rpm -ql` command:

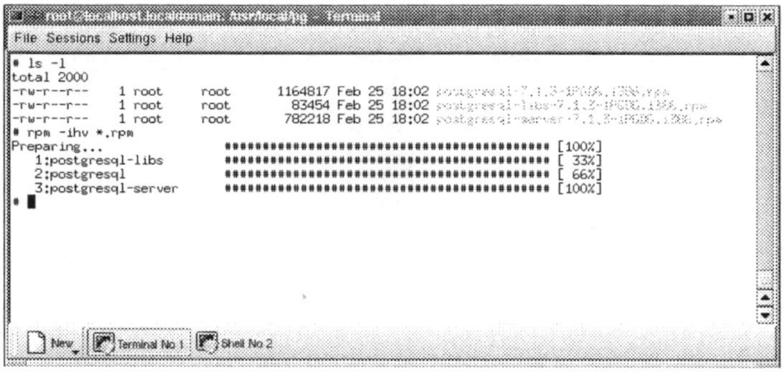

Figure 1.3   Using the `rpm` command to install PostgreSQL.

```
# rpm -ql postgresql-server
/etc/rc.d/init.d/postgresql
/usr/bin/initdb
/usr/bin/initlocation
...
/var/lib/pgsql/data
# rpm -ql postgresql-libs
/usr/lib/libecpg.so.3
/usr/lib/libecpg.so.3.2.0
/usr/lib/libpgeasy.so.2
...
/usr/lib/libpq.so.2.1
```

At this point (assuming that everything worked), you have installed PostgreSQL on your system. Now it's time to create a database to play, er, work in.

  While you have superuser privileges, issue the following commands:

```
# su - postgres
bash-2.04$ echo $PGDATA
/var/lib/pgsql/data
bash-2.04$ initdb
```

The first command (`su - postgres`) changes your identity from the OS superuser (root) to the PostgreSQL superuser (`postgres`). The second command (`echo $PGDATA`) shows you where the PostgreSQL data files will be created. The final command creates the two prototype databases (`template0` and `template1`).

  You should get output that looks like that shown in Figure 1.4.
You now have two empty databases named `template0` and `template1`. You really should not create new tables in either of these databases—a template database contains all the data required to create other databases. In other words, `template0` and `template1` act as prototypes for creating other databases. Instead, let's create a database that you *can* play in. First, start the `postmaster` process. The `postmaster` is a program that listens for

connection requests coming from client applications. When a connection request arrives, the `postmaster` starts a new server process. You can't do anything in PostgreSQL without a `postmaster`. Figure 1.5 shows you how to get the `postmaster` started.

Figure 1.4   Creating the prototype databases using `initdb`.

After starting the `postmaster`, use the `createdb` command to create the `movies` database (this is also shown in Figure 1.5). Most of the examples in this book take place in the `movies` database.

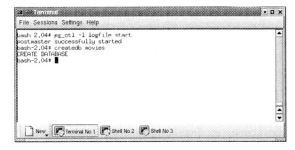

Figure 1.5   Creating a new database with `createdb`.

Notice that I used the pg_ctl command to start the postmaster[1].

The pg_ctl program makes it easy to start and stop the postmaster. To see a full description of the pg_ctl command, enter the command pg_ctl --help. You will get the output shown in Figure 1.6.

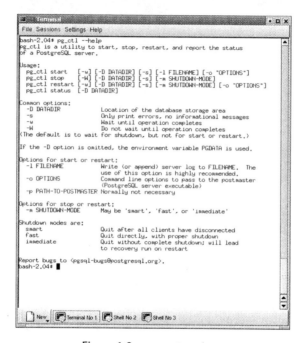

Figure 1.6 pg_ctl options.

If you use a recent RPM file to install PostgreSQL, the two previous steps (initdb and pg_ctl start) can be automated. If you find a file named postgresql in the /etc/rc.d/init.d directory, you can use that shell script to initialize the database and start the postmaster. The /etc/rc.d/init.d/postgresql script can be invoked with any of the command-line options shown in Table 1.2.

Table 1.2 /etc/rc.d/init.d/postgresql **Options**

Option	Description
start	Start the postmaster
stop	Stop the postmaster

---

[1] You can also arrange for the postmaster to start whenever you boot your computer, but the exact instructions vary depending on which operating system you are using. See the section titled "Arranging for PostgreSQL Startup and Shutdown" in Chapter 21.

Table 1.2 **Continued**

Option	Description
status	Display the process ID of the postmaster if it is running
restart	Stop and then start the postmaster
reload	Force the postmaster to reread its configuration files without performing a full restart

At this point, you should use the createuser command to tell PostgreSQL which users are allowed to access your database. Let's allow the user 'bruce' into our system (see Figure 1.7).

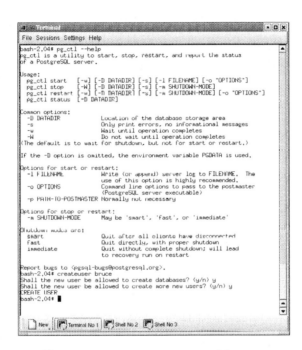

Figure 1.7   Creating a new PostgreSQL user.

That's it! You now have a PostgreSQL database up and running.

Connecting to a Database

Assuming that you have a copy of PostgreSQL up and running, it's pretty simple to connect to the database. Here is an example:

```
$ psql -d movies
Welcome to psql, the PostgreSQL interactive terminal.
```

```
Type:  \copyright for distribution terms
       \h for help with SQL commands
       \? for help on internal slash commands
       \g or terminate with semicolon to execute query
       \q to quit

movies=# \q
```

The psql program is a text-based interface to a PostgreSQL database. When you are running psql, you won't see a graphical application—no buttons or pictures or other bells and whistles, just a text-based interface. Later, I'll show you another client application that does provide a graphical interface (pgaccess).

psql supports a large collection of command-line options. To see a summary of the options that you can use, type psql --help:

```
$ psql --help
This is psql, the PostgreSQL interactive terminal.

Usage:
  psql [options] [dbname [username]]

Options:
  -a               Echo all input from script
  -A               Unaligned table output mode (-P format=unaligned)
  -c <query>       Run only single query (or slash command) and exit
  -d <dbname>      Specify database name to connect to (default: korry)
  -e               Echo queries sent to backend
  -E               Display queries that internal commands generate
  -f <filename>    Execute queries from file, then exit
  -F <string>      Set field separator (default: "|") (-P fieldsep=)
  -h <host>        Specify database server host (default: domain socket)
  -H               HTML table output mode (-P format=html)
  -l               List available databases, then exit
  -n               Disable readline
  -o <filename>    Send query output to filename (or |pipe)
  -p <port>        Specify database server port (default: hardwired)
  -P var[=arg]     Set printing option 'var' to 'arg' (see \pset command)
  -q               Run quietly (no messages, only query output)
  -R <string>      Set record separator (default: newline) (-P recordsep=)
  -s               Single step mode (confirm each query)
  -S               Single line mode (newline terminates query)
  -t               Print rows only (-P tuples_only)
  -T text          Set HTML table tag options (width, border) (-P tableattr=)
  -U <username>    Specify database username (default: Administrator)
  -v name=val      Set psql variable 'name' to 'value'
  -V               Show version information and exit
  -W               Prompt for password (should happen automatically)
```

```
-x                    Turn on expanded table output (-P expanded)
-X                    Do not read startup file (~/.psqlrc)
```

For more information, type \? (for internal commands) or \help (for SQL commands) from within psql, or consult the psql section in the PostgreSQL manual, which accompanies the distribution and is also available at http://www.postgresql.org. Report bugs to pgsql-bugs@postgresql.org.

The most important options are -U <user>, -d <dbname>, -h <host>, and -p <port>.

The -U option allows you to specify a username other than the one you are logged in as. For example, let's say that you are logged in to your host as user *bruce* and you want to connect to a PostgreSQL database as user *sheila*. This psql command makes the connection (or at least tries to):

```
$ whoami
bruce
$ psql -U sheila -d movies
```

Impersonating Another User

The -U option may or may not allow you to impersonate another user. Depending on how your PostgreSQL administrator has configured database security, you might be prompted for *sheila*'s password; if you don't know the proper password, you won't be allowed to impersonate her. (Chapter 23 discusses security in greater detail.) If you don't provide psql with a username, it will assume the username that you used when you logged in to your host.

You use the -d option to specify to which database you want to connect. If you don't specify a database, PostgreSQL will assume that you want to connect to a database whose name is your username. For example, if you are logged in as user *bruce*, PostgreSQL will assume that you want to connect to a database named bruce.

The -d and -U are not strictly required. The command line for psql should be of the following form:

```
psql [options] [dbname [username]]
```

If you are connecting to a PostgreSQL server that is running on the host that you are logged in to, you probably don't have to worry about the -h and -p options. If, on the other hand, you are connecting to a PostgreSQL server running on a different host, use the -h option to tell psql which host to connect to. You can also use the -p option to specify a TCP/IP port number—you only have to do that if you are connecting to a server that uses a nonstandard port (PostgreSQL usually listens for client connections on TCP/IP port number 5432). Here are a few examples:

```
$ # connect to a server waiting on the default port on host 192.168.0.1
$ psql -h 192.168.0.1

$ # connect to a server waiting on port 2000 on host arturo
$ psql -h arturo -p 2000
```

If you prefer, you can specify the database name, hostname, and TCP/IP port number using environment variables rather than using the command-line options. Table 1.3 lists some of the psql command-line options and the corresponding environment variables.

Table 1.3   psql **Environment Variables**

Command-Line Option		**Environment Variable Meaning**
-d <dbname>	PGDATABASE	Name of database to connect to
-h <host>	PGHOST	Name of host to connect to
-p <port>	PGPORT	Port number to connect to
-U <user>	PGUSER	PostgreSQL Username

A (Very) Simple Query

At this point, you should be running the psql client application. Let's try a *very* simple query:

```
$ psql -d movies
Welcome to psql, the PostgreSQL interactive terminal.

Type:  \copyright for distribution terms
       \h for help with SQL commands
       \? for help on internal slash commands
       \g or terminate with semicolon to execute query
       \q to quit

movies=# SELECT user;
 current_user
--------------
 korry
(1 row)

movies=# \q

$
```

Let's take a close look at this session. First, you can see that I started the psql program with the -d movies option—this tells psql that I want to connect to the movies database.

After greeting me and providing me with a few crucial hints, psql issues a prompt: movies=#. psql encodes some useful information into the prompt, starting with the name of the database that I am currently connected to (movies in this case). The character that follows the database name can vary. A = character means that psql is waiting for me to start a command. A - character means that psql is waiting for me to complete a command (psql allows you to split a single command over multiple lines. The first line is prompted by a = character; subsequent lines are prompted by a - character). If the prompt ends with a (character, you have entered more opening parentheses than closing parentheses.

You can see the command that I entered following the prompt: SELECT user;. Each SQL command starts with a verb—in this case, SELECT. The verb tells PostgreSQL what you want to do and the rest of the command provides information specific to that command. I am executing a SELECT command. SELECT is used to retrieve information from the database. When you execute a SELECT command, you have to tell PostgreSQL what information you are interested in. I want to retrieve my PostgreSQL user ID so I SELECT user. The final part of this command is the semicolon (;)—each SQL command must end with a semicolon.

After I enter the SELECT command (and press the Return key), psql displays the results of my command:

```
current_user
---------------
 korry
(1 row)
```

When you execute a SELECT command, psql starts by displaying a row of column headers. I have selected only a single column of information so I see only a single column header (each column header displays the name of the column). Following the row of column headers is a single row of separator characters (dashes). Next comes zero or more rows of the data that I requested. Finally, psql shows a count of the number of data rows displayed.

I ended this session using the \q command.

Tips for Interacting with PostgreSQL

The psql client has a lot of features that will make your PostgreSQL life easier.

Besides PostgreSQL commands (SELECT, INSERT, UPDATE, CREATE TABLE, and so on), psql provides a number of internal commands (also known as *meta-commands*). PostgreSQL commands are sent to the server, meta-commands are processed by psql itself. A meta-command begins with a backslash character (\). You can obtain a list of all the meta-commands using the \? meta-command:

```
movies=# \?
 \a             toggle between unaligned and aligned mode
 \c[onnect] [dbname|- [user]]
                connect to new database (currently 'movies')
 \C <title>     table title
 \copy ...      perform SQL COPY with data stream to the client machine
 \copyright     show PostgreSQL usage and distribution terms
 \d <table>     describe table (or view, index, sequence)
 \d{t|i|s|v}    list tables/indices/sequences/views
 \d{p|S|l}      list permissions/system tables/lobjects
 \da            list aggregates
 \dd [object]   list comment for table, type, function, or operator
 \df            list functions
 \do            list operators
```

```
\dT               list data types
\e [file]         edit the current query buffer or [file]
                  with external editor
\echo <text>      write text to stdout
\encoding <encoding>  set client encoding
\f <sep>          change field separator
\g [file]         send query to backend (and results in [file] or |pipe)
\h [cmd]          help on syntax of sql commands, * for all commands
\H                toggle HTML mode (currently off)
\i <file>         read and execute queries from <file>
\l                list all databases
\lo_export, \lo_import, \lo_list, \lo_unlink
                  large object operations
\o [file]         send all query results to [file], or |pipe
\p                show the content of the current query buffer
\pset <opt>       set table output
                     <opt> = {format|border|expanded|fieldsep|
                     null|recordsep|tuples_only|title|tableattr|pager}
\q                quit psql
\qecho <text>     write text to query output stream (see \o)
\r                reset (clear) the query buffer
\s [file]         print history or save it in [file]
\set <var> <value>  set internal variable
\t                show only rows (currently off)
\T <tags>         HTML table tags
\unset <var>      unset (delete) internal variable
\w <file>         write current query buffer to a <file>
\x                toggle expanded output (currently off)
\z                list table access permissions
\! [cmd]          shell escape or command
movies=#
```

The most important meta-commands are \? (meta-command help), and \q (quit). The \h (SQL help) meta-command is also very useful. Notice that unlike SQL commands, meta-commands don't require a terminating semicolon, which means that meta-commands must be entered entirely on one line. In the next few sections, I'll show you some of the other meta-commands.

Creating Tables

Now that you have seen how to connect to a database and issue a simple query, it's time to create some sample data to work with.

Because you are pretending to model a movie-rental business (that is, a video store), you will create tables that model the data that you might need in a video store. Start by creating three tables: tapes, customers, and rentals.

The tapes table is simple: For each videotape, you want to store the name of the movie, the duration, and a unique identifier (remember that you may have more than one copy of any given movie, so the movie name is not sufficient to uniquely identify a specific tape).

Here is the command you should use to create the `tapes` table:

```
CREATE TABLE tapes (
        tape_id        CHARACTER(8) UNIQUE,
        title          CHARACTER VARYING(80),
        duration       INTERVAL
);
```

Let's take a close look at this command.

The verb in this command is CREATE TABLE, and its meaning should be obvious—you want to create a table. Following the CREATE TABLE verb is the name of the table (`tapes`) and then a comma-separated list of column definitions, enclosed within parentheses.

Each column in a table is defined by a name and a data type. The first column in `tapes` is named `tape_id`. Column names (and table names) must begin with a letter or an underscore character[2] and should be 31 characters or fewer[3]. The tape_id column is created with a data type of CHARACTER(8). The data type you define for a column determines the set of values that you can put into that column. For example, if you want a column to hold numeric values, you should use a numeric data type; if you want a column to hold date (or time) values, you should use a date/time data type. tape_id holds alphanumeric values (a mixture of numbers and letters), so I chose a character data type, with a length of eight characters.

The tape_id column is defined as UNIQUE. The word UNIQUE is not a part of the data type—the data type is CHARACTER(8). The keyword 'UNIQUE' specifies a *column constraint*. A column constraint is a condition that must be met by a column. In this case, each row in the `tapes` table must have a unique tape_id. PostgreSQL supports a variety of column constraints (and table constraints). I'll cover constraints in Chapter 2.

The title is defined as CHARACTER VARYING(80). The difference between CHARACTER(n) and CHARACTER VARYING(n) is that a CHARACTER(n) column is fixed length—it will always contain a fixed number of characters (namely, *n* characters). A CHARACTER VARYING(n) column can contain a maximum of *n* characters. I'll mention here that CHARACTER(n) can be abbreviated as CHAR(n), and CHARACTER VARYING(n) can be abbreviated as VARCHAR(n). I chose CHAR(8) as the data type for tape_id because I know that a tape_id will always contain exactly eight characters, never more and never less. Movie titles, on the other hand, are not all the same length, so I chose VARCHAR(80) for those columns. A fixed length data type is a good choice when the data that you store is in fact fixed length; and in some cases, fixed length data types can give you a performance boost.

---

[2] You can begin a column or table name with nonalphabetic characters, but you must enclose the name in double quotes. You have to quote the name not only when you create it, but each time you reference it.

[3] You can increase the maximum identifier length beyond 31 characters if you build PostgreSQL from a source distribution. If you do so, you'll have to remember to increase the identifier length each time you upgrade your server, or whenever you migrate to a different server.

A variable length data type saves space (and often gives you better performance) when the data that you are storing is not all the same length and can vary widely.

The duration column is defined as an INTERVAL—an INTERVAL stores a period of time such as 2 weeks, 1 hour 45 minutes, and so on.

I'll be discussing PostgreSQL data types in detail in Chapter 2. Let's move on to creating the other tables in this example database.

The customers table is used to record information about each customer for the video store.

```
CREATE TABLE customers (
        customer_id   INTEGER UNIQUE,
        customer_name VARCHAR(50),
        phone         CHAR(8),
        birth_date    DATE,
        balance       NUMERIC(7,2)
);
```

Each customer will be assigned a unique customer_id. Notice that customer_id is defined as an INTEGER, whereas the identifier for a tape was defined as a CHAR(8). A tape_id can contain alphabetic characters, but a customer_id is entirely numeric[4].

I've used two other data types here that you may not have seen before: DATE and NUMERIC. A DATE column can hold date values (century, year, month, and day). PostgreSQL offers other date/time data types that can store different date/time components. For example, a TIME column can store time values (hours, minutes, seconds, and microseconds). A TIMESTAMP column gives you both date and time components—centuries through microseconds.

A NUMERIC column, obviously, holds numeric values. When you create a NUMERIC column, you have to tell PostgreSQL the total number of digits that you want to store and the number of fractional digits (that is, the number of digits to the right of the decimal point). The balance column contains a total of seven digits, with two digits to the right of the decimal point.

Now, let's create the rentals table:

```
CREATE TABLE rentals (
        tape_id     CHARACTER(8),
        customer_id INTEGER,
        rental_date DATE
);
```

When a customer comes in to rent a tape, you will add a row to the rentals table to record the transaction. There are three pieces of information that you need to record for each rental: the tape_id, the customer_id, and the date that the rental occurred. Notice that each row in the rentals table refers to a customer (customer_id) and a tape

---

[4] The decision to define customer_id as an INTEGER was arbitrary. I simply wanted to show a few more data types here.

(tape_id). In most cases, when one row refers to another row, you want to use the same data type for both columns.

What Makes a Relational Database Relational?

Notice that the each row in the rentals table refers to a row in the customer table (and a row in the tapes table). In other words, there is a relationship between rentals and customers and a relationship between rentals and tapes. The relationship between two rows is established by including an identifier from one row within the other row. Each row in the rentals table refers to a customer by including the customer_id. That's the heart of the relational database model—the relationship between two entities is established by including the unique identifier of one entity within the other.

Viewing Table Descriptions

At this point, you've defined three tables in the movies database: tapes, customers, and rentals. If you want to view the table definitions, you can use the \d meta-command in psql (remember that a meta-command is not really a SQL command, but a command understood by the psql client). The \d meta-command comes in two flavors: If you include a table name (\d customers), you will see the definition of that table; if you don't include a table name, \d will show you a list of all the tables defined in your database.

```
$ psql -d movies
Welcome to psql, the PostgreSQL interactive terminal

Type:  \copyright for distribution terms
       \h for help with SQL commands
       \? for help on internal slash commands
       \g or terminate with semicolon to execute query
       \q to quit

movies=# \d
         List of relations
   Name     | Type  |    Owner
-----------+-------+---------------
 customers | table | bruce
 rentals   | table | bruce
 tapes     | table | bruce
(3 rows)

movies=# \d tapes
              Table "tapes"

  Column   |         Type          | Modifiers
-----------+-----------------------+-----------
 tape_id   | character(8)          |
 title     | character varying(80) |
 duration  | interval              |
```

```
Indexes:
    "tapes_tape_id_key" UNIQUE, btree (tape_id)

movies=# \d customers
                Table "customers"
  Attribute   |          Type          | Modifier
--------------+------------------------+----------
 customer_id  | integer                |
 customer_name| character varying(50)  |
 phone        | character(8)           |
 birth_date   | date                   |
 balance      | numeric(7,2)           |
Index: customers_customer_id_key

movies=# \d rentals
          Table "rentals"
  Attribute  |     Type     | Modifier
-------------+--------------+----------
 tape_id     | character(8) |
 customer_id | integer      |
 rental_date | date         |

movies=#
```

I'll point out a few things about the \d meta-command.

Notice that for each column in a table, the \d meta-command returns three pieces of information: the column name (or Attribute), the data type, and a Modifier.

The data type reported by the \d meta-command is spelled out; you won't see char(n) or varchar(n), you'll see character(n) and character varying(n) instead.

The Modifier column shows additional column attributes. The most commonly encountered modifiers are NOT NULL and DEFAULT .... The NOT NULL modifier appears when you create a *mandatory* column—mandatory means that each row in the table must have a value for that column. The DEFAULT ... modifier appears when you create a column with a *default* value. A default value is inserted into a column when you don't specify a value for a column. If you don't specify a default value, PostgreSQL inserts the special value NULL. I'll discuss NULL values and default values in more detail in Chapter 2.

You might have noticed that the listing for the tapes and customers tables show that an index has been created. PostgreSQL automatically creates an index for you when you define UNIQUE columns. An index is a data structure that PostgreSQL can use to ensure uniqueness. Indexes are also used to increase performance. I'll cover indexes in more detail in Chapter 3, "PostgreSQL SQL Syntax and Use."

Depending on which version of PostgreSQL you're using, you may see each table name listed as "Table "public.*table-name*". The "public" part is the name of the *schema* that the table is defined in.

Adding New Records to a Table

The two previous sections showed you how to create some simple tables and how to view the table definitions. Now let's see how to insert data into these tables.

Using the `INSERT` Command

The most common method to get data into a table is by using the `INSERT` command. Like most SQL commands, there are a number of different formats for the `INSERT` command. Let's look at the simplest form first:

```
INSERT INTO table VALUES ( expression [,...] );
```

A Quick Introduction to Syntax Diagrams

In many books that describe a computer language (such as SQL), you will see *syntax diagrams*. A syntax diagram is a precise way to describe the syntax for a command. Here is an example of a simple syntax diagram:

```
INSERT INTO table VALUES ( expression [,...] );
```

In this book, I'll use the following conventions:

- Words that are presented in uppercase must be entered literally, as shown, except for the case. When you enter these words, it doesn't matter if you enter them in uppercase, lowercase, or mixed case, but the spelling must be the same. SQL keywords are traditionally typed in uppercase to improve readability, but the case does not really matter otherwise.

- A lowercase italic word is a placeholder for user-provided text. For example, the table placeholder shows where you would enter a table name, and expression shows where you would enter an expression.

- Optional text is shown inside a pair of square brackets ([]). If you include optional text, don't include the square brackets.

- Finally, ,... means that you can repeat the previous component one or more times, separating multiple occurrences with commas.

So, the following `INSERT` commands are (syntactically) correct:

```
INSERT INTO states VALUES ( 'WA', 'Washington' );
INSERT INTO states VALUES ( 'OR' );
```

This command would not be legal:

```
INSERT states VALUES ( 'WA' 'Washington' );
```

There are two problems with this command. First, I forgot to include the `INTO` keyword (following `INSERT`). Second, the two values that I provided are not separated by a comma.

When you use an `INSERT` statement, you have to provide the name of the table and the values that you want to include in the new row. The following command inserts a new row into the `customers` table:

```
INSERT INTO customers VALUES
(
  1,
  'William Rubin',
  '555-1212',
  '1970-12-31',
  0.00
);
```

This command creates a single row in the customers table. Notice that you did not have to tell PostgreSQL how to match up each value with a specific column: In this form of the INSERT command, PostgreSQL assumes that you listed the values in column order. In other words, the first value that you provide will be placed in the first column, the second value will be stored in the second column, and so forth. (The ordering of columns within a table is defined when you create the table.)

If you don't include one (or more) of the trailing values, PostgreSQL will insert default values for those columns. The default value is typically NULL.

Notice that I have included single quotes around some of the data values. Numeric data should not be quoted; most other data types must be. In Chapter 2, I'll cover the literal value syntax for each data type.

In the second form of the INSERT statement, you include a list of columns *and* a list of values:

```
INSERT INTO table ( column [,...] ) VALUES ( expression [,...] );
```

Using this form of INSERT, I can specify the order of the column values:

```
INSERT INTO customers
(
    customer_name, birth_date, phone, customer_id, balance
)
VALUES
(
  'William Rubin',
  '1970-12-31',
  '555-1212',
  1,
  0.00
);
```

As long as the column *values* match up with the order of the column *names* that you specified, everybody's happy.

The advantage to this second form is that you can omit the value for any column (at least any column that allows NULLs). If you use the first form (without column names), you can only omit values for trailing columns. You can't omit a value in the middle of the row because PostgreSQL can only match up column values in left to right order.

Here is an example that shows how to INSERT a customer who wasn't willing to give you his date of birth:

```
INSERT INTO customers
(
    customer_name, phone, customer_id, balance
)
VALUES
(
  'William Rubin',
  '555-1212',
  1,
  0.00
);
```

This is equivalent to either of the following statements:

```
INSERT INTO customers
(
    customer_name, birth_date, phone, customer_id, balance
)
VALUES
(
  'William Rubin',
  NULL,
  '555-1212',
  1,
  0.00
);
```

or

```
INSERT INTO customers VALUES
(
  1,
  'William Rubin',
  '555-1212',
  NULL,
  0.00
);
```

There are two other forms for the INSERT command. If you want to create a row that contains only default values, you can use the following form:

```
INSERT INTO table DEFAULT VALUES;
```

Of course, if any of the columns in your table are unique, you can only insert a single row with default values.

The final form for the INSERT statement allows you to insert one or more rows based on the results of a query:

```
INSERT INTO table ( column [,...] ) SELECT query;
```

I haven't really talked extensively about the SELECT statement yet (that's in the next section), but I'll show you a simple example here:

```
INSERT INTO customer_backup SELECT * from customers;
```

This INSERT command copies every row in the customers table into the customer_backup table. It's unusual to use INSERT...SELECT... to make an exact copy of a table (in fact, there are easier ways to do that). In most cases, you will use the INSERT...SELECT... command to make an altered version of a table; you might add or remove columns or change the data using expressions.

Using the COPY Command

If you need to load a lot of data into a table, you might want to use the COPY command. The COPY command comes in two forms. COPY ... TO writes the contents of a table into an external file. COPY ... FROM reads data from an external file into a table.

Let's start by exporting the customers table:

```
COPY customers TO '/tmp/customers.txt';
```

This command copies every row in the customers table into a file named '/tmp/customers.txt'. Take a look at the customers.txt file:

```
1       Jones, Henry     555-1212        1970-10-10      0.00
2       Rubin, William  555-2211        1972-07-10      15.00
3       Panky, Henry     555-1221        1968-01-21      0.00
4       Wonderland, Alison    555-1122        1980-03-05      3.00
```

If you compare the file contents with the definition of the customers table:

```
movies=# \d customers
                Table "customers"
   Attribute    |          Type          | Modifier
----------------+------------------------+----------
 customer_id    | integer                |
 customer_name  | character varying(50)  |
 phone          | character(8)           |
 birth_date     | date                   |
 balance        | numeric(7,2)           |
Index: customers_customer_id_key
```

You can see that the columns in the text form match (left to right) with the columns defined in the table: The leftmost column is the customer_id, followed by customer_name, phone, and so on. Each column is separated from the next by a tab character and each row ends with an invisible newline character. You can choose a different column separator (with the DELIMITERS 'delimiter' option), but you can't change the line terminator. That means that you have to be careful editing a COPY file using a

DOS (or Windows) text editor because most of these editors terminate each line with a carriage-return/newline combination. That will confuse the COPY ... FROM command when you try to import the text file.

The inverse of COPY ... TO is COPY ... FROM. COPY ... FROM imports data from an external file into a PostgreSQL table. When you use COPY ... FROM, the format of the text file is very important. The easiest way to find the correct format is to export a few rows using COPY ... TO, and then examine the text file.

If you decide to create your own text file for use with the COPY ... FROM command, you'll have to worry about a lot of details like proper quoting, column delimiters, and such. Consult the PostgreSQL reference documentation for more details.

Installing the Sample Database

If you want, you can download a sample database from this book's website: http://www.conjectrix.com/pgbook.

After you have downloaded the bookdata.tar.gz file, you can unpack it with either of the following commands:

```
$ tar -zxvf bookdata.tar.gz
```

or

```
$ gunzip -c bookdata.tar.gz | tar -xvf -
```

The bookdata.tar.gz file contains a number of files and will unpack into your current directory. After unpacking, you will see a subdirectory for each chapter (okay, for most chapters—not all chapters include sample code or sample data).

You can use the chapter1/load_sample.sql file to create and populate the three tables that I have discussed (tapes, customers, and rentals). To use the load_sample.sql file, execute the following command:

```
$ psql -d movies -f chapter1/load_sample.sql
```

This command drops the tapes, customers, and rentals tables (if they exist), creates them, and adds a few sample rows to each one.

Retrieving Data from the Sample Database

At this point, you should have a sample database (movies) that contains three tables (tapes, customers, and rentals) and a few rows in each table. You know how to get data *into* a table; now let's see how to view that data.

The SELECT statement is used to retrieve data from a database. SELECT is the most complex statement in the SQL language, and the most powerful. Using SELECT, you can retrieve entire tables, single rows, a group of rows that meet a set of constraints, combinations of multiple tables, expressions, and more. To help you understand the basics of the SELECT statement, I'll try to break it down into each of its forms and move from the simple to the more complex.

SELECT **Expression**

In its simplest form, you can use the SELECT statement to retrieve one or more values from a set of predefined functions. You've already seen how to retrieve your PostgreSQL user id:

```
movies=# select user;
 current_user
---------------
 korry
(1 row)

movies=# \q
```

Other values that you might want to see are

```
select 5;            -- returns the number 5 (whoopee)
select sqrt(2.0);    -- returns the square root of 2
select timeofday();  -- returns current date/time
select now();        -- returns time of start of transaction
select version();    -- returns the version of PostgreSQL you are using

select now(), timeofday();
```

> **Commenting**
>
> The -- characters introduce a comment—any text that follows is ignored.

The previous example shows how to SELECT more than one piece of information—just list all the values that you want, separated by commas.

The PostgreSQL User's Guide contains a list of all the functions that are distributed with PostgreSQL. In Chapter 2, I'll show you how to combine columns, functions, operators, and literal values into more complex expressions.

SELECT * FROM **Table**

You probably won't use the first form of the SELECT statement very often—it just isn't very exciting. Moving to the next level of complexity, let's see how to retrieve data from one of the tables that you created earlier:

```
movies=# SELECT * FROM customers;

 customer_id |    customer_name     |  phone    | birth_date | balance
-------------+----------------------+-----------+------------+---------
           3 | Panky, Henry         | 555-1221  | 1968-01-21 |    0.00
           1 | Jones, Henry         | 555-1212  | 1970-10-10 |    0.00
           4 | Wonderland, Alice N. | 555-1122  | 1969-03-05 |    3.00
           2 | Rubin, William       | 555-2211  | 1972-07-10 |   15.00(4 rows)
```

When you write a SELECT statement, you have to tell PostgreSQL what information you are trying to retrieve. Let's take a closer look at the components of this SELECT statement.

Following the SELECT keyword, you specify a list of the columns that you want to retrieve. I used an asterisk (*) here to tell PostgreSQL that we want to see *all* the columns in the customers table.

Next, you have to tell PostgreSQL which table you want to view, in this case, you want to see the customers table.

Now let's look at the results of this query. A SELECT statement returns a *result set*. A result set is a table composed of all the rows and columns (or *fields*) that you request. A result set may be empty.

You asked PostgreSQL to return all the columns in the customers table—notice that the columns are displayed (from left to right) in the order that you specified when you created the table. You may have noticed that the rows are returned in an (apparently) arbitrary order. That's an important thing to keep in mind: Unless you specifically request that PostgreSQL return rows in a particular order, you won't be able to predict which rows will come first[5]. This is a performance feature; if you don't care about row ordering, let PostgreSQL return the rows in the fastest possible way.

Making the Most of the psql Console

You'll be spending a lot of time using the psql console so it's a good idea to get to know it well. psql can do more than just send a command to the server and display the result. You can use bash-style tab completion to reduce the amount of typing you have to do. To use tab completion, just type in the first few characters of a word and then press the TAB key—psql will try to complete the rest of the word. Tab completion is smart. If you type in the first few characters of a command and then press TAB, psql tries to complete the command name. If you've already entered DROP DATABASE and then press TAB, psql shows you a list of databases; type in the first few characters of a database, press TAB, and psql completes the name of the database. If you press TAB in a context where psql expects to find a username (like DROP USER <TAB>), you'll see a list of users. psql can complete column names, data type names, domain names, aggregate names, function names, index names, table names, view names, database names, encodings, languages, schemas, and users.

You can also change the format that psql uses to display query results. By default, psql uses a format named aligned (each column is preceded by a column header and values are aligned within a grid). You can also choose unaligned, html, or latex format. To change the output format, use the command \pset format *format-name*. For example, to switch to html format, type in the command \pset format html. Once you're in HTML-mode, query results will include the HTML tags required to display the results in tabular form. You probably want to send HTML output to a file (rather than seeing all of the formatting commands in your terminal window). Use the \o *filename* command to route query results to the given *filename*. See the psql manual page ($ man psql) for complete details. Play around with the formatting options. Play around with tab completion. Change your psql prompt. psql packs a lot of power into an easy-to-use interface.

---

[5] Okay, some people probably could predict the order in which the rows will appear. Those people have way too much free time and consider a propeller to be fashionable headwear. They are also very good at inducing sleep.

SELECT `Single-Column` FROM **Table**

If you don't want to view all of the columns from a table, you can replace the * (following the SELECT keyword) with the name of a column:

```
movies=# SELECT title FROM tapes;
     title
---------------
 The Godfather
 The Godfather
 Casablanca
 Citizen Kane
 Rear Window
(5 rows)
```

Again, the rows are presented in an arbitrary order. But this time you see only a single column. You may have noticed that "The Godfather" appears twice in this list. That happens because our imaginary video store owns two copies of that movie. I'll show you how to get rid of duplicates in a moment.

SELECT `Column-List` FROM **Table**

So far, you have seen how to select all the columns in a table and how to select a single column. Of course, there is a middle ground—you can select a list of columns:

```
movies=# SELECT customer_name, birth_date FROM customers;
    customer_name     | birth_date
----------------------+------------
 Jones, Henry         | 1970-10-10
 Rubin, William       | 1972-07-10
 Panky, Henry         | 1968-01-21
 Wonderland, Alice N. | 1969-03-05
(4 rows)
```

Instead of naming a single column after the SELECT keyword, you can provide a column-separated list of column names. Column names can appear in any order, and the results will appear in the order you specify.

SELECT `Expression-List` FROM **Table**

In addition to selecting columns, you can also select expressions. Remember, an expression is a combination of columns, functions, operators, literal values, and other expressions that will evaluate to a single value. Here is an example:

```
movies=# SELECT
movies-#     customer_name,
movies-#     birth_date,
movies-#     age( birth_date )
movies-# FROM customers;
```

```
    customer_name      | birth_date |                 age
-----------------------+------------+-----------------------------
 Jones, Henry          | 1970-10-10 | 31 years 4 mons 3 days 01:00
 Rubin, William        | 1972-07-10 | 29 years 7 mons 3 days 01:00
 Panky, Henry          | 1968-01-21 | 34 years 23 days
 Wonderland, Alice N.  | 1969-03-05 | 32 years 11 mons 8 days
(4 rows)
```

In this example, I've selected two columns and an expression. The expression age(
birth_date) is evaluated for each row in the table. The age() function subtracts the
given date from the current date[6].

Selecting Specific Rows

The preceding few sections have shown you how to specify which columns you want to
see in a result set. Now let's see how to choose only the rows that you want.

First, I'll show you to how to eliminate duplicate rows; then I'll introduce the WHERE
clause.

SELECT [ALL | DISTINCT | DISTINCT ON]

In an earlier example, you selected the titles of all the videotapes owned by your video
store:

```
movies-# SELECT title from tapes;
     title
---------------
 The Godfather
 The Godfather
 Casablanca
 Citizen Kane
 Rear Window
(5 rows)
```

Notice that "The Godfather" is listed twice (you own two copies of that video). You can
use the DISTINCT clause to filter out duplicate rows:

```
movies=# SELECT DISTINCT title FROM tapes;
     title
---------------
 Casablanca
 Citizen Kane
 Rear Window
 The Godfather
(4 rows)
```

---

[6] Technically, the age() function subtracts the given timestamp (date+time) from the current date
and time.

You now have a single row with the value "The Godfather." Let's see what happens when you add the `tape_id` back into the previous query:

```
movies=# SELECT DISTINCT title, tape_id FROM tapes;
     title     | tape_id
---------------+----------
 Casablanca    | MC-68873
 Citizen Kane  | OW-41221
 Rear Window   | AH-54706
 The Godfather | AB-12345
 The Godfather | AB-67472
(5 rows)
```

We're back to seeing "The Godfather" twice. What happened? The DISTINCT clause removes duplicate rows, not duplicate column values; and when the tape IDs are added to the result, the rows containing "The Godfather" are no longer identical.

If you want to filter rows that have duplicate values in one (or more) columns, use the DISTINCT ON() form:

```
movies=# SELECT DISTINCT ON (title) title, tape_id FROM tapes;
     title     | tape_id
---------------+----------
 Casablanca    | MC-68873
 Citizen Kane  | OW-41221
 Rear Window   | AH-54706
 The Godfather | AB-12345
(4 rows)
```

Notice that one of the "The Godfather" rows has been omitted from the result set. If you don't include an ORDER BY clause (I'll cover that in a moment), you can't predict which row in a set of duplicates will be included in the result set.

You can list multiple columns (or expressions) in the DISTINCT ON() clause.

The WHERE Clause

The next form of the SELECT statement includes the WHERE clause. Here is the syntax diagram for this form:

```
SELECT expression-list FROM table WHERE conditions
```

Using the WHERE clause, you can filter out rows that you don't want included in the result set. Let's see a simple example. First, here is the complete customers table:

```
movies=# SELECT * FROM customers;

 customer_id |    customer_name     |  phone   | birth_date | balance
-------------+----------------------+----------+------------+---------
           3 | Panky, Henry         | 555-1221 | 1968-01-21 |    0.00
           1 | Jones, Henry         | 555-1212 | 1970-10-10 |    0.00
           4 | Wonderland, Alice N. | 555-1122 | 1969-03-05 |    3.00
           2 | Rubin, William       | 555-2211 | 1972-07-10 |   15.00
(4 rows)
```

Now pick out only those customers who owe you some money:

```
movies=# SELECT * FROM customers WHERE balance > 0;

 customer_id |    customer_name     |  phone   | birth_date | balance
-------------+----------------------+----------+------------+---------
           4 | Wonderland, Alice N. | 555-1122 | 1969-03-05 |    3.00
           2 | Rubin, William       | 555-2211 | 1972-07-10 |   15.00
(2 rows)
```

In this example, I've used a single condition to restrict the rows included in the result set: balance > 0.

When PostgreSQL executes a SELECT statement, it evaluates the WHERE clause as it processes each row. If all the conditions specified by the WHERE clause are met, the row will be included in the result set (if a row meets all the conditions in the WHERE clause, the row *satisfies* the WHERE clause).

Here is an example that is slightly more complex:

```
movies=# SELECT customer_name, phone FROM customers
movies-#   WHERE
movies-#      ( balance = 0 )
movies-#   AND
movies-#      ( AGE( birth_date ) < '35 years' )
movies-# ;
 customer_name |  phone
---------------+---------
 Jones, Henry  | 555 1212
(1 row)
```

In this query, I've specified two conditions, separated by an AND operator. The conditions are: balance = 0 and AGE(birth_date) < '34 years'[7]. As before, PostgreSQL reads each row in the customers table and evaluates the WHERE clause. If a given row is to be included in the result set, it must satisfy two constraints—balance must be equal to zero *and* the customer must be younger than 35 years of age. If either of these conditions is false for a given row, that row will not be included in the result set.

AND is one of the *logical operators* supported by PostgreSQL. A logical operator is used to combine *logical expressions*. A logical expression is an expression that evaluates to TRUE, FALSE, or unknown (NULL). The other two logical operators are OR and NOT.

Let's see how the OR operator works:

```
movies=# SELECT customer_id, customer_name, balance, AGE(birth_date)
movies-# FROM customers
movies-#   WHERE
movies-#      ( balance = 0 )
movies-#   OR
movies-#      ( AGE( birth_date ) < '35 years' )
movies-# ;
```

[7] I'll show you how to format various date/time related values in Chapter 2.

```
 customer_id | customer_name   | balance |                 age
-------------+-----------------+---------+------------------------------------
           3 | Panky, Henry    |    0.00 | 36 years 8 mons 29 days 23:00:00
           1 | Jones, Henry    |    0.00 | 34 years 10 days
           2 | Rubin, William  |   15.00 | 32 years 3 mons 10 days
(3 rows)
```

The OR operator evaluates to TRUE if *either* (or both) of the conditions is TRUE. The first row
(id = 1) is included in the result set because it satisfies the first condition (balance = 0).
It is included even if it *does not* satisfy the second condition. The second row (id = 2) is
included in the result set because it satisfies the second condition, but not the first. You can
see the difference between AND and OR. A row satisfies the AND operator if both conditions
are TRUE. A row satisfies the OR operator if either condition is TRUE (or if both are TRUE).

The NOT operator is simple:

```
movies=# SELECT * FROM customers
movies-# WHERE
movies-#     NOT ( balance = 0 )
movies-# ;
```

```
 customer_id |    customer_name     |  phone   | birth_date | balance
-------------+----------------------+----------+------------+---------
           4 | Wonderland, Alice N. | 555-1122 | 1969-03-05 |    3.00
           2 | Rubin, William       | 555-2211 | 1972-07-10 |   15.00
(2 rows)
```

NOT evaluates to TRUE if its operand is FALSE and evaluates to FALSE if its operand is
TRUE. The NOT operator inverts (or reverses) a test. Without the NOT operator, the previous example would have returned all customers where the balance column was equal
to zero. With the NOT operator, you get the other rows instead.

One other point that I should mention about the WHERE clause. Just because you
mention a column in the WHERE clause does not mean that you have to include the column in the result set. For example:

```
movies=# SELECT customer_id, customer_name FROM customers
movies-#     WHERE
movies-#     balance != 0
movies-# ;
```

```
 customer_id |    customer_name
-------------+----------------------
           4 | Wonderland, Alice N.
           2 | Rubin, William
(2 rows)
```

This example also shows a more common alternative to the NOT operator. The != operator means "*is not equal to.*" The != operator is not an exact replacement for NOT—it can
only be used to check for inequality, whereas NOT is used to reverse the sense of any logical expression.

NULL **Values**

Sometimes when you add data to a table, you find that you don't know what value you should include for a column. For example, you may encounter a customer who does not want to provide you with his or her birthday. What value should be recorded in the birth_date column for that customer? You don't really want to make up an answer— you want a date value that means "unknown." This is what the NULL value is for. NULL usually means that you don't know what value should be entered into a column, but it can also mean that a column does not apply. A NULL value in the birth_date column certainly means that we don't know a customer's birth_date, not that birth_date does not apply[8]. On the other hand, you might want to include a rating column in the tapes table. A NULL value in the rating column might imply that the movie was produced before ratings were introduced and therefore the rating column does not apply.

Some columns should not allow NULL values. In most cases, it would not make sense to add a customer to your customers table unless you know the customer's name. Therefore, the customer_name column should be mandatory (in other words, customer_name should not allow NULL values).

Let's drop and re-create the customers table so that you can tell PostgreSQL which columns should allow NULL values:

```
movies=# DROP TABLE customers;
DROP
movies-# CREATE TABLE customers (
movies-#        customer_id   INTEGER UNIQUE NOT NULL,
movies-#        customer_name VARCHAR(50)    NOT NULL,
movies-#        phone         CHAR(8),
movies-#        birth_date    DATE,
movies-#        balance       DECIMAL(7,2)
movies-#);
CREATE
```

The NOT NULL modifier tells PostgreSQL that the customer_id and customer_name columns are mandatory. If you don't specify NOT NULL, PostgreSQL assumes that a column is optional. You can include the keyword NULL to make your choices more obvious:

```
movies=# DROP TABLE customers;
DROP
movies=# CREATE TABLE customers (
movies-#        customer_id   INTEGER UNIQUE NOT NULL,
movies-#        customer_name VARCHAR(50)    NOT NULL,
movies-#        phone         CHAR(8)        NULL,
movies-#        birth_date    DATE           NULL,
movies-#        balance       DECIMAL(7,2)   NULL
movies-#);
CREATE
```

[8] I am making the assumption that the customers for your video store have actually been born. For some of you, that may not be a valid assumption.

Notice that a column of *any* data type can support NULL values.

The NULL value has a unique property that is often the source of much confusion. NULL is not equal to *any value*, not even itself. NULL is not less than any value, and NULL is not greater than any value. Let's add a customer with a NULL balance:

```
movies=# INSERT INTO customers
movies-#   VALUES
movies-#   (
movies(#      5, 'Funkmaster, Freddy', '555-FUNK', NULL, NULL
movies(#   )
movies-# ;
```

Now we have five customers:

```
movies=# SELECT * FROM customers;

 customer_id |    customer_name     |  phone   | birth_date | balance
-------------+----------------------+----------+------------+---------
           3 | Panky, Henry         | 555-1221 | 1968-01-21 |    0.00
           1 | Jones, Henry         | 555-1212 | 1970-10-10 |    0.00
           4 | Wonderland, Alice N. | 555-1122 | 1969-03-05 |    3.00
           2 | Rubin, William       | 555-2211 | 1972-07-10 |   15.00
           5 | Funkmaster, Freddy   | 555-FUNK |            |
(5 rows)
```

One of these customers has a NULL balance. Let's try a few queries:

```
movies=# SELECT * FROM customers WHERE balance > NULL;

 customer_id | customer_name | phone | birth_date | balance
-------------+---------------+-------+------------+---------
(0 rows)
```

This query did not return any rows. You might think that it should have customer number 2 (Rubin, William); after all, 15.00 is surely greater than 0. But remember, NULL is not equal to, greater than, or less than any other value. NULL is not the same as zero. Rather than using relational operators ('=', '!=', '<', or '>'), you should use either the IS or IS NOT operator.

```
movies=# SELECT * FROM customers WHERE balance IS NULL;

 customer_id |   customer_name    |  phone   | birth_date | balance
-------------+--------------------+----------+------------+---------
           5 | Funkmaster, Freddy | 555-FUNK |            |
(1 row)

movies=# SELECT * FROM customers WHERE balance IS NOT NULL;
```

```
customer_id |     customer_name      |  phone   | birth_date | balance
------------+------------------------+----------+------------+---------
          3 | Panky, Henry           | 555-1221 | 1968-01-21 |    0.00
          1 | Jones, Henry           | 555-1212 | 1970-10-10 |    0.00
          4 | Wonderland, Alice N.   | 555-1122 | 1969-03-05 |    3.00
          2 | Rubin, William         | 555-2211 | 1972-07-10 |   15.00
(4 rows)
```

The NULL value introduces another complication. If NULL is not greater than, equal to, or less than any other value, what would 'NULL + 4' mean? Is NULL + 4 greater than NULL? It can't be because that would imply that NULL is less than NULL + 4 and, by definition, NULL can't be less than another value. What does all this mean? It means that you can't do math with a NULL value.

```
movies=# SELECT customer_id, customer_name, balance, balance+4 FROM customers;

customer_id |     customer_name      | balance | ?column?
------------+------------------------+---------+----------
          3 | Panky, Henry           |    0.00 |    4.00
          1 | Jones, Henry           |    0.00 |    4.00
          4 | Wonderland, Alice N.   |    3.00 |    7.00
          2 | Rubin, William         |   15.00 |   19.00
          5 | Funkmaster, Freddy     |         |
(5 rows)
```

This query shows what happens when you try to perform a mathematical operation using NULL. When you try to add '4' to NULL, you end up with NULL.

The NULL value complicates logic operators as well. Most programmers are familiar with two-valued logic operators (that is, logic operators that are defined for the values TRUE and FALSE). When you add in NULL values, the logic operators become a bit more complex. Tables 1.4, 1.5, and 1.6 show the truth tables for each logical operator.

Table 1.4 **Truth Table for Three-Valued AND Operator**

a	b	a AND b
TRUE	TRUE	TRUE
TRUE	FALSE	FALSE
TRUE	NULL	NULL
FALSE	FALSE	FALSE
FALSE	NULL	FALSE
NULL	NULL	NULL

Source: PostgreSQL User's Guide

Table 1.5   **Truth Table for Three-Valued** OR **Operator**

a	b	a OR b
TRUE	TRUE	TRUE
TRUE	FALSE	TRUE
TRUE	NULL	TRUE
FALSE	FALSE	FALSE
FALSE	NULL	NULL
NULL	NULL	NULL

Source: PostgreSQL User's Guide

Table 1.6   **Truth Table for Three-Valued** NOT **Operator**

a	NOT a
TRUE	FALSE
FALSE	TRUE
NULL	NULL

Source: PostgreSQL User's Guide

I don't mean to scare you away from the NULL value—it's very useful and often necessary—but you do have to understand the complications that it introduces.

NULLIF() and COALESCE()

PostgreSQL offers two operators that can convert a NULL value to some other value or convert a specific value into NULL.

The COALESCE() operator will substitute a *default* value whenever it encounters a NULL. For example, pretend that you've added two more columns, male_lead and female_lead to the tapes table so that it looks like this:

```
movies=# SELECT * from tapes;
tape_id   |    title      |   male_lead      |  female_lead    | duration
----------+---------------+------------------+-----------------+----------
 AB-12345 | The Godfather | Marlon Brando    |                 | 02:55:00
 AB-67472 | The Godfather | Marlon Brando    |                 | 02:55:00
 MC-68873 | Casablanca    | Humphrey Bogart  | Ingrid Bergman  | 01:42:00
 OW-41221 | Citizen Kane  |                  |                 | 01:59:00
 AH-54706 | Rear Window   | James Stewart    | Grace Kelly     |
 AH-44289 | The Birds     |                  | Tippi Hedren    | 01:59:00
(6 rows)
```

You can use the COALESCE() operator to transform a NULL male_lead into the word 'Unknown':

```
movies=# SELECT title, COALESCE( male_lead, 'Unknown' ) FROM tapes;
     title      |     coalesce
----------------+-----------------
 The Godfather  | Marlon Brando
 The Godfather  | Marlon Brando
 Casablanca     | Humphrey Bogart
 Citizen Kane   | Unknown
 Rear Window    | James Stewart
 The Birds      | Unknown
(6 rows)
```

The COALESCE() operator is more talented than we've shown here—it can search through a list of values, returning the first non-NULL value it finds. For example, the following query prints the male_lead, or, if male_lead is NULL, the female_lead, or if both are NULL, 'Unknown':

```
movies=# SELECT title, COALESCE( male_lead, female_lead, 'Unknown' )
movies-#     AS "Starring"
movies-#     FROM TAPES;
     title      |     Starring
----------------+-----------------
 The Godfather  | Marlon Brando
 The Godfather  | Marlon Brando
 Casablanca     | Humphrey Bogart
 Citizen Kane   | Unknown
 Rear Window    | James Stewart
 The Birds      | Tippi Hedren
(6 rows)
```

You can string together any number of expressions inside of the COALESCE() operator (as long as all expressions evaluate to the same type) and COALESCE() will evaluate to the leftmost non-NULL value in the list. If all of the expressions *inside* COALESCE() are NULL, the entire expression evaluates to NULL.

The NULLIF() operator translates a non-NULL value into NULL. NULLIF() is often used to do the opposite of COALESCE(). COALESCE() transforms NULL into a default value—NULLIF() translates a default value into NULL. In many circumstances, you want to treat a numeric value and a NULL value as being the same thing. For example, the balance column (in the customers table) is NULL until a customer actually rents a tape: A NULL balance implies that you haven't actually done any business with the customer yet. But a NULL balance also implies that the customer owes you no money. To convert a NULL balance to 0, use COALESCE(balance, 0). To convert a zero balance to NULL, use NULLIF(balance, 0). When PostgreSQL evaluates an NULLIF(arg1, arg2) expression, it compares the two arguments; if they are equal, the expression evaluates to NULL; if they are not equal, the expression evaluates to the value of *arg1*.

The CASE Expression

The CASE expression is a more generic form of NULLIF() and COALESCE(). A CASE expression lets you map any given value into some other value. You can write a CASE expression in two different forms. The first form (called the *simple* form) looks like this:

```
CASE expression₁
    WHEN value₁ THEN result₁
    WHEN value₂ THEN result₂
    ...
    [ ELSE resultₙ ]
END
```

When PostgreSQL evaluates a simple CASE expression, it computes the value of $expression_1$ then compares the result to $value_1$. If $expression_1$ equals $value_1$, the CASE expression evaluates to $result_1$. If not, PostgreSQL compares $expression_1$ to $value_2$; if they match, the CASE expression evaluates to $result_2$. PostgreSQL continues searching through the WHEN clauses until it finds a match. If none of the values match $expression_1$, the expression evaluates to the value specified in the ELSE clause. If PostgreSQL gets all the way to the end of the list and you haven't specified an ELSE clause, the CASE expression evaluates to NULL. Note that $result_1, result_2, \ldots result_n$ must all have the same data type. You can see that NULLIF(balance, 0) is equivalent to

```
CASE balance
    WHEN 0 THEN NULL
    ELSE balance
END
```

The second, more flexible form of the CASE expression is called the *searched* form:

```
CASE
    WHEN condition₁ THEN result₁
    WHEN condition₂ THEN result₂
    ...
    [ ELSE resultₙ ]
END
```

When PostgreSQL evaluates a searched CASE expression, it first evaluates $condition_1$. If $condition_1$ evaluates to true, the value of the CASE expression is $result_1$. If $condition_1$ evaluates to false, PostgreSQL evaluates $condition_2$. If that condition evaluates to true, the value of the CASE expression is $result_2$. Otherwise, PostgreSQL moves on to the next condition. PostgreSQL continues to evaluate each condition until it finds one that evaluates to true. If none of the conditions is true, the CASE expression evaluates to $result_n$. If PostgreSQL gets all the way to the end of the list and you haven't specified an ELSE clause, the CASE expression evaluates to NULL.

Like the simple form, $result_1, result_2, \ldots result_n$ must all have the same data type. However, in the searched form, the conditions don't have to be similar to each other. For example, if you want to classify the titles in your tapes collection (and you're a big Jimmy Stewart fan), you might use a CASE expression like this:

```
movies=# SELECT
movies-#    title, male_lead, duration,
movies-#    CASE
movies-#      WHEN duration < '1 hour 45 min' THEN 'short movie'
movies-#      WHEN male_lead = 'James Stewart' THEN 'great movie'
movies-#      WHEN duration > '2 hours' THEN 'long movie'
movies-#    END
movies-# FROM
movies-#    tapes;
     title      |    male_lead     | duration |    case
---------------+------------------+----------+-------------
 The Godfather | Marlon Brando    | 02:55:00 | long movie
 The Godfather | Marlon Brando    | 02:55:00 | long movie
 Casablanca    | Humphrey Bogart  | 01:42:00 | short movie
 Citizen Kane  |                  | 01:59:00 |
 Rear Window   | James Stewart    |          | great movie
 The Birds     |                  | 01:59:00 |
(6 rows)
```

The ORDER BY Clause

So far, all the queries that you have seen return rows in an arbitrary order. You can add an ORDER BY clause to a SELECT command if you need to impose a predictable ordering. The general form of the ORDER BY clause is[9]

```
ORDER BY expression [ ASC | DESC ] [, ...]
```

The ASC and DESC terms mean ascending and descending, respectively. If you don't specify ASC or DESC, PostgreSQL assumes that you want to see results in ascending order. The expression following ORDER BY is called a *sort key*.

Let's look at a simple example:

```
movies=# SELECT * FROM customers ORDER BY balance;

 customer_id |    customer_name     |  phone   | birth_date | balance
-------------+----------------------+----------+------------+---------
           3 | Panky, Henry         | 555-1221 | 1968-01-21 |    0.00
           1 | Jones, Henry         | 555-1212 | 1970-10-10 |    0.00
           4 | Wonderland, Alice N. | 555-1122 | 1969-03-05 |    3.00
           2 | Rubin, William       | 555-2211 | 1972-07-10 |   15.00
           5 | Funkmaster, Freddy   | 555-FUNK |            |
(5 rows)
```

[9] PostgreSQL supports another form for the ORDER BY clause: ORDER BY expression [USING operator] [, ...]. This might seem a little confusing at first. When you specify ASC, PostgreSQL uses the < operator to determine row ordering. When you specify DESC, PostgreSQL uses the > operator. The second form of the ORDER BY clause allows you to specify an alternative operator.

You can see that this SELECT command returns the result set in ascending order of the balance column. Here is the same query, but in descending order:

```
movies=# SELECT * FROM customers ORDER BY balance DESC;

 customer_id |    customer_name    |   phone   | birth_date | balance
-------------+---------------------+-----------+------------+---------
           5 | Funkmaster, Freddy  | 555-FUNK  |            |
           2 | Rubin, William      | 555-2211  | 1972-07-10 |   15.00
           4 | Wonderland, Alice N. | 555-1122 | 1969-03-05 |    3.00
           3 | Panky, Henry        | 555-1221  | 1968-01-21 |    0.00
           1 | Jones, Henry        | 555-1212  | 1970-10-10 |    0.00
(5 rows)
```

This time, the largest balance is first, followed by successively smaller values.

You may have noticed something odd about how the ORDER BY clause handles the customer named Freddy Funkmaster. Recall from the previous section that NULL cannot be compared to other values. By its very nature, the ORDER BY clause must compare values. PostgreSQL resolves this issue with a simple rule: NULL is always considered larger than all other values when evaluating an ORDER BY clause.

You can include multiple sort keys in the ORDER BY clause. The following query sorts customers in ascending balance order, and then in descending birth_date order:

```
movies=# SELECT * FROM customers ORDER BY balance, birth_date DESC;

 customer_id |    customer_name    |   phone   | birth_date | balance
-------------+---------------------+-----------+------------+---------
           1 | Jones, Henry        | 555-1212  | 1970-10-10 |    0.00
           3 | Panky, Henry        | 555-1221  | 1968-01-21 |    0.00
           4 | Wonderland, Alice N. | 555-1122 | 1969-03-05 |    3.00
           2 | Rubin, William      | 555-2211  | 1972-07-10 |   15.00
           5 | Funkmaster, Freddy  | 555-FUNK  |            |
(5 rows)
```

When an ORDER BY clause contains multiple sort keys, you are telling PostgreSQL how to break ties. You can see that customers 1 and 3 have the same value (0.00) in the balance column—you have asked PostgreSQL to order rows using the balance column. What happens when PostgreSQL finds two rows with the same balance? When two sort key values are equal, PostgreSQL moves to the next sort key to break the tie. If two sort key values are not equal, sort keys with a lower precedence are ignored. So, when PostgreSQL finds that customers 1 and 3 have the same balance, it moves to the birth_date column to break the tie.

If you don't have a sort key with a lower precedence, you won't be able to predict the ordering of rows with duplicate sort key values.

You can include as many sort keys as you like.

LIMIT and OFFSET

Occasionally, you will find that you want to answer a question such as "Who are my top 10 salespeople?" In most relational databases, this is a difficult question to ask. PostgreSQL offers two extensions that make it easy to answer "Top *n*" or "Bottom *n*"–type questions. The first extension is the LIMIT clause. The following query shows the two customers who owe you the most money:

```
movies=# SELECT * FROM customers ORDER BY balance DESC LIMIT 2;

 customer_id |  customer_name   |  phone   | birth_date | balance
-------------+------------------+----------+------------+---------
           5 | Funkmaster, Freddy | 555-FUNK |            |
           2 | Rubin, William   | 555-2211 | 1972-07-10 |   15.00
(2 rows)
```

You can see here that I used an ORDER BY clause so that the rows are sorted such that the highest balances appear first—in most cases, you won't use a LIMIT clause without also using an ORDER BY clause. Let's change this query a little—this time we want the top five customers who have a balance over $10:

```
movies=# SELECT * FROM customers
movies-#   WHERE
movies-#     balance >= 10
movies-#   ORDER BY balance DESC
movies-#   LIMIT 5;

 customer_id | customer_name  |  phone   | birth_date | balance
-------------+----------------+----------+------------+---------
           2 | Rubin, William | 555-2211 | 1972-07-10 |   15.00
(1 row)
```

This example shows that the LIMIT clause won't always return the number of rows that were specified. Instead, LIMIT returns *no more than* the number of rows that you request. In this sample database, you have only one customer who owes you more than $10.

The second extension is the OFFSET n clause. The OFFSET n clause tells PostgreSQL to skip the first *n* rows of the result set. For example:

```
movies=# SELECT * FROM customers ORDER BY balance DESC OFFSET 1;

 customer_id |   customer_name    |  phone   | birth_date | balance
-------------+--------------------+----------+------------+---------
           2 | Rubin, William     | 555-2211 | 1972-07-10 |   15.00
           4 | Wonderland, Alice N. | 555-1122 | 1969-03-05 |    3.00
           3 | Panky, Henry       | 555-1221 | 1968-01-21 |    0.00
           1 | Jones, Henry       | 555-1212 | 1970-10-10 |    0.00
(4 rows)
```

In this case, we are viewing all the customers *except* the customer with the greatest balance. It's common to use LIMIT and OFFSET together:

```
movies=# SELECT * FROM customers
movies-#    ORDER BY balance DESC LIMIT 2 OFFSET 1;

 customer_id |     customer_name     |  phone    | birth_date | balance
-------------+-----------------------+-----------+------------+---------
           2 | Rubin, William        | 555-2211  | 1972-07-10 |   15.00
           4 | Wonderland, Alice N.  | 555-1122  | 1969-03-05 |    3.00
(2 rows)
```

Formatting Column Results

So far, you have seen how to tell PostgreSQL which rows you want to view, which columns you want to view, and the order in which the rows should be returned. Let's take a short side-trip here and learn how to change the appearance of the values that you select.

Take a look at the following query:

```
movies=# SELECT customer_id, customer_name, balance, balance+4 FROM customers;

 customer_id |     customer_name     | balance | ?column?
-------------+-----------------------+---------+----------
           3 | Panky, Henry          |    0.00 |    4.00
           1 | Jones, Henry          |    0.00 |    4.00
           4 | Wonderland, Alice N.  |    3.00 |    7.00
           2 | Rubin, William        |   15.00 |   19.00
           5 | Funkmaster, Freddy    |         |
(5 rows)
```

PostgreSQL inserts two lines of text between your query and the result set. These two lines are (obviously) column headings. You can see that the header for each of the first three columns contains the name of the column. What about the last column? When you SELECT an expression, PostgreSQL uses "?column?" for the field header[10].

You can change field headers using the AS clause:

```
movies=# SELECT customer_id, customer_name,
movies-#        balance AS "Old balance",
movies-#        balance + 4 AS "New balance"
movies-#  FROM customers;

 customer_id |     customer_name     | Old Balance | New balance
-------------+-----------------------+-------------+-------------
           3 | Panky, Henry          |        0.00 |        4.00
```

[10] Actually, if you SELECT a function (such as AGE() or SQRT()), PostgreSQL will use the name of the function for the field header.

```
1 | Jones, Henry           |     0.00 |     4.00
4 | Wonderland, Alice N. |     3.00 |     7.00
2 | Rubin, William        |    15.00 |    19.00
5 | Funkmaster, Freddy    |          |
```
(5 rows)

Notice that you can provide a field header for table columns as well as for expressions. If you rename a field and the query includes an ORDER BY clause that refers to the field, the ORDER BY should use the new name, not the original one:

```
movies=# SELECT id, customer_name,
movies-#        balance AS "Old balance",
movies-#        balance + 4 AS "New balance"
movies-#   FROM customers
movies-#   ORDER BY "Old balance";
```

```
customer_id |      customer_name    | Old Balance | New balance
-------------+-----------------------+-------------+-------------
           3 | Panky, Henry          |        0.00 |        4.00
           1 | Jones, Henry          |        0.00 |        4.00
           4 | Wonderland, Alice N. |        3.00 |        7.00
           2 | Rubin, William        |       15.00 |       19.00
           5 | Funkmaster, Freddy    |             |
```
(5 rows)

This section explained how to change the column headers for a SELECT command. You can also change the appearance of the data values. In the next section, I'll show you a few examples using date values for illustration.

Working with Date Values

PostgreSQL supports six basic date, time, and date/time data types, as shown in Table 1.7. I'll use the term *temporal* to cover date, time, and date/time data types.

Table 1.7 **PostgreSQL Temporal Data Types**

Data Type Name	Type of Data Stored	Earliest Date/Time	Latest Date/Time
TIMESTAMP	Date/Time	4713 BC	1465001 AD
TIMESTAMP WITH TIME ZONE	Date/Time	1903 AD	2037 AD
INTERVAL	Interval	–178000000 years	178000000 years
DATE	Date	4713 BC	32767 AD
TIME	Time	00:00:00.00	23:59:59.99
TIME WITH TIME ZONE	Time	00:00:00.00+12	23:59:59.99–12

I'll cover the details of the date/time data types in Chapter 2. You have already seen two of these temporal data types. The customers table contains a DATE column (birth_date):

```
movies=# \d customers
              Table "customers"

    Column       |         Type          | Modifiers
-----------------+-----------------------+-----------
 customer_id     | integer               | not null
 customer_name   | character varying(50) | not null
 phone           | character(8)          |
 birth_date      | date                  |
 balance         | numeric(7,2)          |
Indexes:
    "customers_customer_id_key" UNIQUE, btree (customer_id)

movies=# SELECT customer_name, birth_date FROM customers;
    customer_name     | birth_date
----------------------+------------
 Jones, Henry         | 1970-10-10
 Rubin, William       | 1972-07-10
 Panky, Henry         | 1968-01-21
 Wonderland, Alice N. | 1969-03-05
 Funkmaster, Freddy   |
(5 rows)
```

You've also seen the INTERVAL data type—the AGE() function returns an INTERVAL:

```
movies=# SELECT customer_name, AGE( birth_date ) FROM customers;
    customer_name     |             age
----------------------+-----------------------------
 Jones, Henry         | 31 years 4 mons 8 days 01:00
 Rubin, William       | 29 years 7 mons 8 days 01:00
 Panky, Henry         | 34 years 28 days
 Wonderland, Alice N. | 32 years 11 mons 13 days
 Funkmaster, Freddy   |
(5 rows)
```

Date/time values are usually pretty easy to work with, but there is a complication that you need to be aware of. Let's say that I need to add a new customer:

```
movies=# INSERT INTO customers
movies-#    VALUES
movies-#    (
movies-#      7, 'Gull, Jonathon LC', '555-1111', '02/05/1984', NULL
movies-#    );
```

This customer has a `birth_date` of `'02/05/1984'`—does that mean "February 5th 1984", or "May 2nd 1984"? How does PostgreSQL know which date I meant? The problem is that a date such as `'02/05/1984'` is ambiguous—you can't know which date this string represents without knowing something about the context in which it was entered. `'02/05/1984'` is ambiguous. `'May 02 1984'` is unambiguous.

PostgreSQL enables you to enter and display dates in a number of formats—some date formats are ambiguous and some are unambiguous. The DATESTYLE runtime variable tells PostgreSQL how to format dates when displaying data and how to interpret ambiguous dates that you enter.

The DATESTYLE variable can be a little confusing. DATESTYLE is composed of two parts. The first part, called the convention, tells PostgreSQL how to interpret ambiguous dates. The second part, called the display format, determines how PostgreSQL displays date values. The convention controls date input and the display format controls date output. Table 1.8 shows the DATESTYLE display formats.

Let's talk about the display format first. PostgreSQL supports four different display formats. Three of the display formats are unambiguous and one is ambiguous.

The default display format is named ISO. In ISO format, dates always appear in the form 'YYYY-MM-DD'. The next display format is GERMAN. In GERMAN format, dates always appear in the form 'DD.MM.YYYY'. The ISO and GERMAN formats are unambiguous because the format never changes. The POSTGRES format is also unambiguous, but the display format can vary. PostgreSQL needs a second piece of information (the convention) to decide whether the month should appear before the day (US convention) or the day should appear before the month (European convention). In POSTGRES format, date values display the day-of-the-week and month name in abbreviated text form; for example 'Wed May 02 1984' (US) or 'Wed 02 May 1984' (European).

The final display format is SQL. SQL format is ambiguous. In SQL format, the date 'May 02 1984' is displayed as '05/02/1984' (US), or as '02/05/1984' (European).

Table 1.8 DATESTYLE **Display Formats**

Display Format	US Convention	European Convention
ISO	1984-05-02	1984-05-02
GERMAN	02.05.1984	02.05.1984
POSTGRES	Wed May 02 1984	Wed 02 May 1984
SQL	05/02/1984	02/05/1984

As I mentioned earlier, the ISO and GERMAN display formats are unambiguous. In ISO format, the month always precedes the day. In GERMAN format, the day always precedes the month. If you choose POSTGRES or SQL format, you must also specify the order in which you want the month and day components to appear. You can specify the desired display format and month/day ordering (that is, the convention) in the DATESTYLE runtime variable:

```
movies=# SET DATESTYLE TO 'US,ISO';        -- 1984-05-02
movies=# SET DATESTYLE TO 'US,GERMAN';     -- 02.05.1984
```

```
movies=# SET DATESTYLE TO 'US,POSTGRES';        -- Wed May 02 1984
movies=# SET DATESTYLE TO 'US,SQL';             -- 05/02/1984

movies=# SET DATESTYLE TO 'EUROPEAN,ISO';       -- 1984-05-02
movies=# SET DATESTYLE TO 'EUROPEAN,GERMAN';    -- 02.05.1984
movies=# SET DATESTYLE TO 'EUROPEAN,POSTGRES';  -- Wed 02 May 1984
movies=# SET DATESTYLE TO 'EUROPEAN,SQL';       -- 02/05/1984
```

The convention part of the DATESTYLE variable determines how PostgreSQL will make sense of the date values that you enter. The convention also affects the ordering of the month and day components when displaying a POSTGRES or SQL date. Note that you are not restricted to entering date values in the format specified by DATESTYLE. For example, if you have chosen to display dates in 'US,SQL' format, you can still enter date values in any of the other formats.

Recall that the ISO and GERMAN date formats are unambiguous—the ordering of the month and day components is predefined. A date entered in POSTGRES format is unambiguous as well—you enter the name of the month so it cannot be confused with the day. If you choose to enter a date in SQL format, PostgreSQL will look to the first component of DATESTYLE (that is, the convention) to determine whether you want the value interpreted as a US or a European date. Let's look at a few examples.

```
movies=# SET DATESTYLE TO 'US,ISO';
movies=# SELECT CAST( '02/05/1984' AS DATE );
 1984-02-05

movies=# SET DATESTYLE TO 'EUROPEAN,ISO';
movies=# SELECT CAST( '02/05/1984' AS DATE );
 1984-05-02
```

In this example, I've asked PostgreSQL to display dates in ISO format, but I've entered a date in an ambiguous format. In the first case, you can see that PostgreSQL interpreted the ambiguous date using US conventions (the month precedes the day). In the second case, PostgreSQL uses European conventions to interpret the date.

Now let's see what happens when I enter an unambiguous date:

```
movies=# SET DATESTYLE TO 'US,ISO';
SET VARIABLE
movies=# SELECT CAST( '1984-05-02' AS DATE );
 1984-05-02

movies=# SET DATESTYLE TO 'EUROPEAN,ISO';
SET VARIABLE
movies=# SELECT CAST( '1984-05-02' AS DATE );
 1984-05-02
```

This time, there can be no confusion—an ISO-formatted date is always entered in 'YYYY-MM-DD' format. PostgreSQL ignores the convention.

So, you can see that I can enter date values in many formats. If I choose to enter a date in an ambiguous format, PostgreSQL uses the convention part of the current DATESTYLE to interpret the date. I can also use DATESTYLE to control the display format.

Matching Patterns

In the previous two sections, you took a short detour to learn a little about how to format results. Now let's get back to the task of *producing* the desired results.

The WHERE clause is used to restrict the number of rows returned by a SELECT command[11]. Sometimes, you don't know the exact value that you are searching for. For example, you may have a customer ask you for a film, but he doesn't remember the exact name, although he knows that the film has the word "Citizen" in the title. PostgreSQL provides two features that make it possible to search for partial alphanumeric values.

LIKE and NOT LIKE

The LIKE operator provides simple pattern-matching capabilities. LIKE uses two special characters that indicate the unknown part of a pattern. The underscore (_) character matches any single character. The percent sign (%) matches any sequence of zero or more characters. Table 1.9 shows a few examples.

Table 1.9   **Pattern Matching with the LIKE Operator**

String	Pattern	Result
The Godfather	%Godfather%	Matches
The Godfather	%Godfather	Matches
The Godfather	%Godfathe_	Matches
The Godfather	____ Godfather	Matches
The Godfather	Godfather%	Does not match
The Godfather	_Godfather	Does not match
The Godfather: Part II	%Godfather	Does not match

Now let's see how to use the LIKE operator in a SELECT command:

```
movies=# SELECT * FROM tapes WHERE title LIKE '%Citizen%';
 tape_id  |         title        | duration
----------+----------------------+----------
 OW-41221 | Citizen Kane         |
 KJ-03335 | American Citizen, An |
(2 rows)
```

---

[11] Technically, the WHERE clause constrains the set of rows affected by a SELECT, UPDATE, or DELETE command. I'll show you the UPDATE and DELETE commands a little later.

The `LIKE` operator is case-sensitive:

```
movies=# SELECT * FROM tapes WHERE title LIKE '%citizen%';
 tape_id | title | duration
---------+-------+----------
(0 rows)
```

If you want to perform case-insensitive pattern matching, use the `ILIKE` operator:

```
movies=# SELECT * FROM tapes WHERE title ILIKE '%citizen%';
 tape_id |        title        | duration
---------+---------------------+----------
 OW-41221 | Citizen Kane        |
 KJ-03335 | American Citizen, An |
(2 rows)
```

You can, of course, combine `LIKE` and `ILIKE` with the `NOT` operator to return rows that do not match a pattern:

```
movies=# SELECT * FROM tapes WHERE title NOT ILIKE '%citizen%';
 tape_id |     title     |   duration
---------+---------------+--------------
 AB-12345 | The Godfather |
 AB-67472 | The Godfather |
 MC-68873 | Casablanca    |
 AH-54706 | Rear Window   |
 OW-42200 | Sly           | 01:36
 OW-42201 | Stone         | 4 days 01:36
(6 rows)
```

Pattern Matching with Regular Expressions

The `LIKE` and `ILIKE` operators are easy to use, but they aren't very powerful. Fortunately, PostgreSQL lets you search for data using *regular expressions*. A regular expression is a string that specifies a pattern. The language that you use to create regular expressions is far more powerful than the `LIKE` and `ILIKE` operators. You have probably used regular expressions before; programs such as `grep`, `awk`, and the Unix (and DOS) shells use regular expressions.

The `LIKE` and `ILIKE` operators define two pattern-matching characters; the regular expression operator defines far more. First, the character "." within a regular expression operates in the same way as the "_" character in a `LIKE` pattern: it matches any single character. The characters ".*" in a regular expression operate in the same way as the "%" character in a `LIKE` pattern: they match zero or more occurrences of any single character.

Notice that in a regular expression, you use two characters to match a sequence of characters, whereas you use a single character in a `LIKE` pattern. The regular expression ".*" is actually two regular expressions combined into one complex expression. As I mentioned earlier, the "." character matches any single character. The "*" character matches zero or more occurrences of the pattern that precedes it. So, ".*" means to match any single character, zero or more times. There are three other repetition operators:

The "+" character matches one or more occurrences of the preceding pattern, and the "?" character matches zero or one occurrence of the preceding pattern. If you need to get really fancy (I never have), you can use the form "{x[,y]}" to match at least x and no more than y occurrences of the preceding pattern.

You can also search for things other than ".". For example, the character "^" matches the beginning of a string and "$" matches the end. The regular expression syntax even includes support for character classes. The pattern "[:upper:]*[:digit:]" will match any string that includes zero or more uppercase characters followed by a single digit.

The "|" character gives you a way to search for a string that matches either of two patterns. For example, the regular expression "(^God)|.*Donuts.*" would match a string that either starts with the string "God" or includes the word "Donuts".

Regular expressions are extremely powerful, but they can get awfully complex. If you need more information, Chapter 4 of the *PostgreSQL User's Manual* provides an exhaustive reference to the complete regular expression syntax.

Table 1.10 shows how to construct regular expressions that match the same strings matched by the LIKE patterns in shown in Table 1.9.

Table 1.10   **Pattern Matching with Regular Expressions**

String	Pattern	Result
The Godfather	.*Godfather	Matches
The Godfather	.^Godfather.*	Matches
The Godfather	.*Godfathe.	Matches
The Godfather	... Godfather	Matches
The Godfather	Godfather.*	Does not match
The Godfather	.Godfather	Does not match
The Godfather: Part II	.*Godfather	Does not match

Aggregates

PostgreSQL offers a number of aggregate functions. An *aggregate* is a collection of things—you can think of an aggregate as the set of rows returned by a query. An aggregate function is a function that operates on an aggregate (nonaggregate functions operate on a single row within an aggregate). Most of the aggregate functions operate on a single value extracted from each row—this is called an *aggregate expression*.

COUNT()

COUNT() is probably the simplest aggregate function. COUNT() returns the number of objects in an aggregate. The COUNT() function comes in four forms:

- COUNT(*)
- COUNT(expression)

- COUNT(ALL expression)
- COUNT(DISTINCT expression)

In the first form, COUNT(*) returns the number of rows in an aggregate:

```
movies=# SELECT * FROM customers;

 customer_id |    customer_name     |  phone   | birth_date | balance
-------------+----------------------+----------+------------+---------
           3 | Panky, Henry         | 555-1221 | 1968-01-21 |    0.00
           1 | Jones, Henry         | 555-1212 | 1970-10-10 |    0.00
           4 | Wonderland, Alice N. | 555-1122 | 1969-03-05 |    3.00
           2 | Rubin, William       | 555-2211 | 1972-07-10 |   15.00
           5 | Funkmaster, Freddy   | 555-FUNK |            |
           7 | Gull, Jonathon LC    | 555-1111 | 1984-02-05 |
           8 | Grumby, Jonas        | 555-2222 | 1984-02-21 |
(7 rows)

movies=# SELECT COUNT(*) FROM customers;
 count
-------
     7
(1 row)

movies=# SELECT COUNT(*) FROM customers WHERE customer_id < 5;
 count
-------
     4
(1 row)
```

You can see from this example that the COUNT(*) function pays attention to the WHERE clause. In other words, COUNT(*) returns the number of rows that filter through the WHERE clause; that is, the number of rows in the aggregate.

In the second form, COUNT(expression) returns the number of non-NULL values in the aggregate. For example, you might want to know how many customers have a non-NULL balance:

```
movies=# SELECT COUNT( balance ) FROM customers;
 count
-------
     4
(1 row)

movies=# SELECT COUNT(*) - COUNT( balance )  FROM customers;
 ?column?
----------
        3
(1 row)
```

The first query returns the number of non-NULL balances in the customers table. The second query returns the number of NULL balances.

The third form, COUNT(ALL expression) is equivalent to the second form. PostgreSQL includes the third form for completeness; it complements the fourth form.

COUNT(DISTINCT expression) returns the number of distinct non-NULL values in the aggregate.

```
movies=# SELECT DISTINCT balance FROM customers;
 balance
---------
    0.00
    3.00
   15.00


(4 rows)

movies=# SELECT COUNT( DISTINCT balance ) FROM customers;
 count
-------
     3
(1 row)
```

You might notice a surprising result in that last example. The first query returns the distinct balances in the customers table. Notice that PostgreSQL tells you that it returned four rows—there are four distinct values. The second query returns a count of the distinct balances—it says that there are only three.

Is this a bug? No, both queries returned the correct information. The first query includes the NULL value in the result set. COUNT(), and in fact all the aggregate functions (except for COUNT(*)), ignore NULL values.

SUM()

The SUM(expression) function returns the sum of all the values in the aggregate expression. Unlike COUNT(), you can't use SUM() on entire rows[12]. Instead, you usually specify a single column:

```
movies=# SELECT SUM( balance ) FROM customers;
  sum
-------
 18.00
(1 row)
```

Notice that the SUM() function expects an expression. The name of a numeric column is a valid expression. You can also specify an arbitrarily complex expression as long as that expression results in a numeric value.

[12] Actually, you can SUM(*), but it probably doesn't do what you would expect. SUM(*) is equivalent to COUNT(*).

You can also SUM() an aggregate of intervals. For example, the following query tells you how long it would take to watch all the tapes in your video store:

```
movies=# SELECT SUM( duration ) FROM tapes;
     sum
--------------
 4 days 03:12
(1 row)
```

AVG()

The AVG(expression) function returns the average of an aggregate expression. Like SUM(), you can find the average of a numeric aggregate or an interval aggregate.

```
movies=# SELECT AVG( balance ) FROM customers;
     avg
--------------
 4.5000000000
(1 row)
```

```
movies=# SELECT AVG( balance ) FROM customers
movies-#   WHERE balance IS NOT NULL;
     avg
--------------
 4.5000000000
(1 row)
```

These queries demonstrate an important point: the aggregate functions completely ignore rows where the aggregate expression evaluates to NULL. The aggregate produced by the second query explicitly omits any rows where the balance is NULL. The aggregate produced by the first query implicitly omits NULL balances. In other words, the following queries are equivalent:

```
SELECT AVG( balance ) FROM customers;
  SELECT AVG( balance ) FROM customers WHERE balance IS NOT NULL;
  SELECT SUM( balance ) / COUNT( balance ) FROM customers;
```

But these queries are *not* equivalent:

```
  SELECT AVG( balance ) FROM customers;
  SELECT SUM( balance ) / COUNT( * ) FROM customers;
```

Why not? Because COUNT(*) counts all rows whereas COUNT(balance) omits any rows where the balance is NULL.

MIN() **and** MAX()

The MIN(expression) and MAX(expression) functions return the minimum and maximum values, respectively, of an aggregate expression. The MIN() and MAX() functions can operate on numeric, date/time, or string aggregates:

```
movies=# SELECT MIN( balance ), MAX( balance ) FROM customers;
 min  | max
------+-------
 0.00 | 15.00
(1 row)

movies=# SELECT MIN( birth_date ), MAX( birth_date ) FROM customers;
    min     |    max
------------+------------
 1968-01-21 | 1984-02-21
(1 row)

movies=# SELECT MIN( customer_name ), MAX( customer_name )
movies-#   FROM customers;
        min         |         max
--------------------+----------------------
 Funkmaster, Freddy | Wonderland, Alice N.
(1 row)
```

Other Aggregate Functions

In addition to COUNT(), SUM(), AVG(), MIN(), and MAX(), PostgreSQL also supports the STDDEV(expression) and VARIANCE(expression) aggregate functions. These last two aggregate functions compute the standard deviation and variance of an aggregate, two common statistical measures of variation within a set of observations.

Grouping Results

The aggregate functions are useful for summarizing information. The result of an aggregate function is a single value. Sometimes, you really want an aggregate function to apply to each of a number of subsets of your data. For example, you may find it interesting to compute some demographic information about your customer base. Let's first look at the entire customers table:

```
movies=# SELECT * FROM customers;
```

customer_id	customer_name	phone	birth_date	balance
3	Panky, Henry	555-1221	1968-01-21	0.00
1	Jones, Henry	555-1212	1970-10-10	0.00
4	Wonderland, Alice N.	555-1122	1969-03-05	3.00
2	Rubin, William	555-2211	1972-07-10	15.00
5	Funkmaster, Freddy	555-FUNK		
7	Gull, Jonathon LC	555-1111	1984-02-05	
8	Grumby, Jonas	555-2222	1984-02-21	

```
(7 rows)
```

Look at the `birth_date` column—notice that you have customers born in three distinct decades (four if you count NULL as a decade):

```
movies=# SELECT DISTINCT( EXTRACT( DECADE FROM birth_date ))
movies-#    FROM customers;
 date_part
-----------
       196
       197
       198

(4 rows)
```

The `EXTRACT()` function extracts a date component from a date/time value. The DECADE component looks a little strange, but it makes sense to know whether the decade of the '60s refers to the 1960s or the 2060s, now that we are past Y2K.

Now that you know how many decades are represented in your customer base, you might next want to know how many customers were born in each decade. The GROUP BY clause helps answer this kind of question:

```
movies=# SELECT COUNT(*), EXTRACT( DECADE FROM birth_date )
movies-#    FROM customers
movies-#    GROUP BY  EXTRACT( DECADE FROM birth_date );
 count | date_part
-------+-----------
     2 |       196
     2 |       197
     2 |       198
     1 |
(4 rows)
```

The GROUP BY clause is used with aggregate functions. PostgreSQL sorts the result set by the GROUP BY expression and applies the aggregate function to each group.

There is an easier way to build this query. The problem with this query is that you had to repeat the `EXTRACT( DECADE FROM birth_date )` phrase. Instead, you can use the AS clause to name the decade field, and then you can refer to that field by name in the GROUP BY clause:

```
movies=# SELECT COUNT(*), EXTRACT( DECADE FROM birth_date ) AS decade
movies-#    FROM customers
movies-#    GROUP BY decade;
 count | decade
-------+--------
     2 |    196
     2 |    197
     2 |    198
     1 |
(4 rows)
```

If you don't request an explicit ordering, the GROUP BY clause will cause the result set to be sorted by the GROUP BY fields. If you want a different ordering, you can use the ORDER

BY clause with GROUP BY. The following query shows how many customers you have for each decade, sorted by the count:

```
movies=# SELECT
movies-#   COUNT(*) as "Customers",
movies-#   EXTRACT( DECADE FROM birth_date ) as "Decade"
movies-#  FROM customers
movies-#   GROUP BY "Decade"
movies-#   ORDER BY "Customers";
 Customers | Decade
-----------+--------
         1 |
         2 |    196
         2 |    197
         2 |    198
(4 rows)
```

The NULL decade looks a little funny in this result set. You have one customer (Freddy Funkmaster) who was too vain to tell you when he was born. You can use the HAVING clause to eliminate aggregate groups:

```
movies=# SELECT COUNT(*), EXTRACT( DECADE FROM birth_date ) as decade
movies-#   FROM customers
movies-#   GROUP BY decade
movies-#   HAVING EXTRACT( DECADE FROM birth_date ) IS NOT NULL;
 count | decade
-------+--------
     2 |    196
     2 |    197
     2 |    198
(3 rows)
```

You can see that the HAVING clause is similar to the WHERE clause. The WHERE clause determines which rows are included in the aggregate, whereas the HAVING clause determines which *groups* are included in the result set.

Multi-Table Joins

So far, all the queries that you've seen involve a single table. Most databases contain multiple tables and there are relationships between these tables. This sample database has an example:

```
movies=# \d rentals

           Table "rentals"
  Attribute   |     Type     | Modifier
--------------+--------------+----------
 tape_id      | character(8) | not null
 rental_date  | date         | not null
 customer_id  | integer      | not null
```

Here's a description of the `rentals` table from earlier in this chapter:

"When a customer comes in to rent a tape, we will add a row to the `rentals` table to record the transaction. There are three pieces of information that we need to record for each rental: the `tape_id`, the `customer_id`, and the date that the rental occurred. Notice that each row in the rentals table refers to a customer (`customer_id`) and a tape (`tape_id`)."

You can see that each row in the `rentals` table refers to a tape (`tape_id`) and to a customer (`customer_id`). If you SELECT from the rentals table, you can see the tape ID and customer ID, but you can't see the movie title or customer name. What you need here is a *join*. When you need to retrieve data from multiple tables, you *join* those tables.

PostgreSQL (and all relational databases) supports a number of join types. The most basic join type is a *cross-join* (or Cartesian product). In a cross join, PostgreSQL joins each row in the first table to each row in the second table to produce a result table. If you are joining against a third table, PostgreSQL joins each row in the intermediate result with each row in the third table.

Let's look at an example. We'll cross-join the `rentals` and `customers` tables. First, I'll show you each table:

```
movies=# SELECT * FROM rentals;
 tape_id  | rental_date | customer_id
----------+-------------+-------------
 AB-12345 | 2001-11-25  |           1
 AB-67472 | 2001-11-25  |           3
 OW-41221 | 2001-11-25  |           1
 MC-68873 | 2001-11-20  |           3
(4 rows)

movies=# SELECT * FROM customers;

 customer_id |    customer_name     |  phone   | birth_date | balance
-------------+----------------------+----------+------------+---------
           3 | Panky, Henry         | 555-1221 | 1968-01-21 |    0.00
           1 | Jones, Henry         | 555-1212 | 1970-10-10 |    0.00
           4 | Wonderland, Alice N. | 555-1122 | 1969-03-05 |    3.00
           2 | Rubin, William       | 555-2211 | 1972-07-10 |   15.00
           5 | Funkmaster, Freddy   | 555-FUNK |            |
           7 | Gull, Jonathon LC    | 555-1111 | 1984-02-05 |
           8 | Grumby, Jonas        | 555-2222 | 1984-02-21 |
(7 rows)
```

Now I'll join these tables. To perform a cross-join, we simply list each table in the FROM clause:

```
movies=# SELECT rentals.*, customers.customer_id, customers.customer_name
movies-#   FROM rentals, customers;
```

```
 tape_id  | rental_date | customer_id | customer_id |   customer_name
----------+-------------+-------------+-------------+---------------------
 AB-12345 | 2001-11-25  |           1 |           3 | Panky, Henry
 AB-12345 | 2001-11-25  |           1 |           1 | Jones, Henry
 AB-12345 | 2001-11-25  |           1 |           4 | Wonderland, Alice N.
 AB-12345 | 2001-11-25  |           1 |           2 | Rubin, William
 AB-12345 | 2001-11-25  |           1 |           5 | Funkmaster, Freddy
 AB-12345 | 2001-11-25  |           1 |           7 | Gull, Jonathon LC
 AB-12345 | 2001-11-25  |           1 |           8 | Grumby, Jonas
 AB-67472 | 2001-11-25  |           3 |           3 | Panky, Henry
 AB-67472 | 2001-11-25  |           3 |           1 | Jones, Henry
 AB-67472 | 2001-11-25  |           3 |           4 | Wonderland, Alice N.
 AB-67472 | 2001-11-25  |           3 |           2 | Rubin, William
 AB-67472 | 2001-11-25  |           3 |           5 | Funkmaster, Freddy
 AB-67472 | 2001-11-25  |           3 |           7 | Gull, Jonathon LC
 AB-67472 | 2001-11-25  |           3 |           8 | Grumby, Jonas
 OW-41221 | 2001-11-25  |           1 |           3 | Panky, Henry
 OW-41221 | 2001-11-25  |           1 |           1 | Jones, Henry
 OW-41221 | 2001 11 25  |           1 |           4 | Wonderland, Alice N.
 OW-41221 | 2001-11-25  |           1 |           2 | Rubin, William
 OW-41221 | 2001-11-25  |           1 |           5 | Funkmaster, Freddy
 OW-41221 | 2001-11-25  |           1 |           7 | Gull, Jonathon LC
 OW-41221 | 2001-11-25  |           1 |           8 | Grumby, Jonas
 MC-68873 | 2001-11-20  |           3 |           3 | Panky, Henry
 MC-68873 | 2001-11-20  |           3 |           1 | Jones, Henry
 MC-68873 | 2001-11-20  |           3 |           4 | Wonderland, Alice N.
 MC-68873 | 2001-11-20  |           3 |           2 | Rubin, William
 MC-68873 | 2001 11 20  |           3 |           5 | Funkmaster, Freddy
 MC-68873 | 2001-11-20  |           3 |           7 | Gull, Jonathon LC
 MC-68873 | 2001-11-20  |           3 |           8 | Grumby, Jonas
(28 rows)
```

You can see that PostgreSQL has joined each row in the rentals table to each row in the customers table. The rentals table contains four rows; the customers table contains seven rows. The result set contains 4 ⅄ 7 or 28 rows.

Cross-joins are rarely useful—they usually don't represent real-world relationships.

The second type of join, the *inner-join*, is very useful. An inner-join starts with a cross-join, and then throws out the rows that you don't want. Take a close look at the results of the previous query. Here are the first seven rows again:

```
 tape_id  | rental_date | customer_id | customer_id |   customer_name
----------+-------------+-------------+-------------+---------------------
 AB-12345 | 2001-11-25  |           1 |           3 | Panky, Henry
 AB-12345 | 2001-11-25  |           1 |           1 | Jones, Henry
 AB-12345 | 2001-11-25  |           1 |           4 | Wonderland, Alice N.
 AB-12345 | 2001-11-25  |           1 |           2 | Rubin, William
 AB-12345 | 2001-11-25  |           1 |           5 | Funkmaster, Freddy
```

```
AB-12345 | 2001-11-25 |            1 |          7 | Gull, Jonathon LC
AB-12345 | 2001-11-25 |            1 |          8 | Grumby, Jonas
```

These seven rows were produced by joining the first row in the `rentals` table:

```
tape_id  | rental_date | customer_id
---------+-------------+-------------
AB-12345 | 2001-11-25  |           1
```

with each row in the `customers` table. What is the real-world relationship between a `rentals` row and a `customers` row? Each row in the `rentals` table contains a customer ID. Each row in the `customers` table is uniquely identified by a customer ID. So, given a `rentals` row, we can find the corresponding `customers` row by searching for a customer where the customer ID is equal to `rentals.customer_id`. Looking back at the previous query, you can see that the meaningful rows are those `WHERE customers.customer_id = rentals.customer_id`.

Qualifying Column Names

Notice that this `WHERE` clause mentions two columns with the same names (`customer_id`). You may find it helpful to qualify each column name by prefixing it with the name of the corresponding table, followed by a period. So, `customers.customer_id` refers to the `customer_id` column in the `customers` table and `rentals.customer_id` refers to the `customer_id` column in the `rentals` table. Adding the table qualifier is sometimes required if a command involves two columns with identical names, but is useful in other cases.

Now you can construct a query that will show us all of the rentals and the names of the corresponding customers:

```
movies=# SELECT rentals.*, customers.customer_id, customers.customer_name
movies-#   FROM rentals, customers
movies-#   WHERE customers.customer_id = rentals.customer_id;

tape_id  | rental_date | customer_id | customer_id | customer_name
---------+-------------+-------------+-------------+---------------
AB-12345 | 2001-11-25  |           1 |           1 | Jones, Henry
AB-67472 | 2001-11-25  |           3 |           3 | Panky, Henry
OW-41221 | 2001-11-25  |           1 |           1 | Jones, Henry
MC-68873 | 2001-11-20  |           3 |           3 | Panky, Henry
(4 rows)
```

To execute this query, PostgreSQL could start by creating the cross-join between all the tables involved, producing an intermediate result table. Next, PostgreSQL could throw out all the rows that fail to satisfy the `WHERE` clause. In practice, this would be a poor strategy: Cross-joins can get very large quickly. Instead, the PostgreSQL query optimizer analyzes the query and plans an execution strategy to minimize execution time. I'll cover query optimization in Chapter 4.

Join Types

We've seen two join types so far: cross-joins and inner-joins. Now we'll look at *outer-joins*. An outer-join is similar to an inner-join: a relationship between two tables is established by correlating a column from each table.

In an earlier section, you wrote a query that answered the question: "Which customers are currently renting movies?" How would you answer the question: "Who are my customers and which movies are they currently renting?" You might start by trying the following query:

```
movies=# SELECT customers.*, rentals.tape_id
movies-#   FROM customers, rentals
movies-#  WHERE rentals.customer_id = customers.customer_id;
```

customer_id	customer_name	phone	birth_date	balance	tape_id
1	Jones, Henry	555-1212	1970-10-10	0.00	AB-12345
3	Panky, Henry	555-1221	1968-01-21	0.00	AB-67472
1	Jones, Henry	555-1212	1970-10-10	0.00	OW-41221
3	Panky, Henry	555-1221	1968-01-21	0.00	MC-68873

rows)

Well, that didn't work. This query showed you which customers are currently renting movies (and the movies that they are renting). What we really want is a list of *all* customers and, if a customer is currently renting any movies, all the movies rented. This is an outer-join. An outer-join preserves all the rows in one table (or both tables) regardless of whether a matching row can be found in the second table.

The syntax for an outer-join is a little strange. Here is an example:

```
movies=# SELECT customers.customer_name, rentals.tape_id
movies-#   FROM customers LEFT OUTER JOIN rentals
movies-#   ON customers.customer_id = rentals.customer_id;
```

customer_name	tape_id
Jones, Henry	AB-12345
Jones, Henry	OW-41221
Rubin, William	
Panky, Henry	AB-67472
Panky, Henry	MC-68873
Wonderland, Alice N.	
Funkmaster, Freddy	
Gull, Jonathon LC	
Grumby, Jonas	

rows)

This query is a *left outer-join*. Why left? Because you will see each row from the left table (the table to the left of the LEFT OUTER JOIN phrase). An inner-join would list only two customers ("Jones, Henry" and "Panky, Henry")—the other customers have no rentals.

A RIGHT OUTER JOIN preserves each row from the right table. A FULL OUTER JOIN preserves each row from both tables.

The following query shows a list of all customers, all tapes, and any rentals:

```
movies=# SELECT customers.customer_name, rentals.tape_id, tapes.title
movies-#   FROM customers FULL OUTER JOIN rentals
movies-#     ON customers.customer_id = rentals.customer_id
movies-#   FULL OUTER JOIN tapes
movies-#     ON tapes.tape_id = rentals.tape_id;
    customer_name      |  tape_id  |        title
-----------------------+-----------+-----------------------
 Jones, Henry          | AB-12345  | The Godfather
 Panky, Henry          | AB-67472  | The Godfather
                       |           | Rear Window
                       |           | American Citizen, An
 Panky, Henry          | MC-68873  | Casablanca
 Jones, Henry          | OW-41221  | Citizen Kane
 Rubin, William        |           |
 Wonderland, Alice N.  |           |
 Funkmaster, Freddy    |           |
 Gull, Jonathon LC     |           |
 Grumby, Jonas         |           |
                       |           | Sly
                       |           | Stone
(13 rows)
```

UPDATE

Now that you've seen a number of ways to view your data, let's see how to modify (and delete) existing data.

The UPDATE command modifies data in one or more rows. The general form of the UPDATE command is

```
UPDATE table SET column = expression [, ...] [WHERE condition]
```

Using the UPDATE command is straightforward: The WHERE clause (if present) determines which rows will be updated and the SET clause determines which columns will be updated (and the new values).

You might have noticed in earlier examples that one of the tapes had a duration of '4 days, 01:36'—that's obviously a mistake. You can correct this problem with the UPDATE command as follows:

```
movies=# UPDATE tapes SET duration = '4 hours 36 minutes'
movies-#   WHERE tape_id = 'OW-42201';
```

```
UPDATE 1

movies=# SELECT * FROM tapes;
 tape_id  |         title         | duration
----------+-----------------------+----------
 AB-12345 | The Godfather         |
 AB-67472 | The Godfather         |
 MC-68873 | Casablanca            |
 OW-41221 | Citizen Kane          |
 AH-54706 | Rear Window           |
 OW-42200 | Sly                   | 01:36
 KJ-03335 | American Citizen, An  |
 OW-42201 | Stone Cold            | 04:36
(8 rows)
```

Using the UPDATE command, you can update all the rows in the table, a single row, or a set of rows—it all depends on the WHERE clause. The SET clause in this example updates a single column in all the rows that satisfy the WHERE clause. If you want to update multiple columns, list each assignment, separated by commas:

```
movies=# UPDATE tapes
movies-#   SET duration = '1 hour 52 minutes', title = 'Stone Cold'
movies-#   WHERE tape_id = 'OW-42201';
UPDATE 1
movies=# SELECT * FROM tapes;
 tape_id  |         title         | duration
----------+-----------------------+----------
 AB-12345 | The Godfather         |
 AB-67472 | The Godfather         |
 MC-68873 | Casablanca            |
 OW-41221 | Citizen Kane          |
 AH-54706 | Rear Window           |
 OW-42200 | Sly                   | 01:36
 KJ-03335 | American Citizen, An  |
 OW-42201 | Stone Cold            | 01:52
(8 rows)
```

The UPDATE statement displays the number of rows that were modified. The following UPDATE will modify three of the seven rows in the customers table:

```
movies=# SELECT * FROM customers;

 customer_id |    customer_name    |  phone   | birth_date | balance
-------------+---------------------+----------+------------+---------
           3 | Panky, Henry        | 555-1221 | 1968-01-21 |    0.00
           1 | Jones, Henry        | 555-1212 | 1970-10-10 |    0.00
           4 | Wonderland, Alice N. | 555-1122 | 1969-03-05 |    3.00
           2 | Rubin, William      | 555-2211 | 1972-07-10 |   15.00
           5 | Funkmaster, Freddy  | 555-FUNK |            |
```

```
        7 | Gull, Jonathon LC    | 555-1111 | 1984-02-05 |
        8 | Grumby, Jonas        | 555-2222 | 1984-02-21 |
(7 rows)

movies=# UPDATE customers
movies-#   SET balance = 0
movies-#   WHERE balance IS NULL;
UPDATE 3
movies=# SELECT * FROM customers;

 customer_id |    customer_name     |   phone  | birth_date | balance
-------------+----------------------+----------+------------+---------
           3 | Panky, Henry         | 555-1221 | 1968-01-21 |    0.00
           1 | Jones, Henry         | 555-1212 | 1970-10-10 |    0.00
           4 | Wonderland, Alice N. | 555-1122 | 1969-03-05 |    3.00
           2 | Rubin, William       | 555-2211 | 1972-07-10 |   15.00
           5 | Funkmaster, Freddy   | 555-FUNK |            |    0.00
           7 | Gull, Jonathon LC    | 555-1111 | 1984-02-05 |    0.00
           8 | Grumby, Jonas        | 555-2222 | 1984-02-21 |    0.00
(7 rows)
```

DELETE

Like UPDATE, the DELETE command is simple. The general format of the DELETE command is

```
DELETE FROM table [ WHERE condition ]
```

The DELETE command removes all rows that satisfy the (optional) WHERE clause. Here is an example:

```
movies=# SELECT * FROM tapes;
 tape_id  |        title         | duration
----------+----------------------+----------
 AB-12345 | The Godfather        |
 AB-67472 | The Godfather        |
 MC-68873 | Casablanca           |
 OW-41221 | Citizen Kane         |
 AH-54706 | Rear Window          |
 OW-42200 | Sly                  | 01:36
 KJ-03335 | American Citizen, An |
 OW-42201 | Stone Cold           | 01:52
(8 rows)
movies=# BEGIN WORK;
BEGIN
movies=# DELETE FROM tapes WHERE duration IS NULL;
DELETE 6
```

```
movies=# SELECT * FROM tapes;
 tape_id  |   title     | duration
----------+-------------+----------
 OW-42200 | Sly         | 01:36
 OW-42201 | Stone Cold  | 01:52
(2 rows)

movies=# ROLLBACK;
ROLLBACK
```

Before we executed the DELETE command, there were eight rows in the tapes table, and six of these tapes had a NULL duration.

You can see that the DELETE statement returns the number of rows deleted ("DELETE 6"). After the DELETE statement, only two tapes remain.

If you omit the WHERE clause in a DELETE command, PostgreSQL will delete *all* rows. Similarly, forgetting the WHERE clause for an UPDATE command updates all rows. Be careful!

A (Very) Short Introduction to Transaction Processing

You might have noticed two new commands in this example. The BEGIN WORK and ROLLBACK commands are used for *transaction processing*. A transaction is a group of commands. Usually, a transaction includes one or more table modifications (INSERTs, DELETEs, and UPDATEs).

BEGIN WORK marks the beginning of a transaction. Inside of a transaction, any changes that you make to the database are temporary changes. There are two ways to mark the end of a transaction: COMMIT and ROLLBACK. If you COMMIT a transaction, you are telling PostgreSQL to write all the changes made within the transaction into the database—in other words, when you COMMIT a transaction, the changes become permanent. When you ROLLBACK a transaction, all changes made within the transaction are discarded.

You can see that transactions are handy in that you can discard your changes if you change your mind. But transactions are important for another reason. PostgreSQL guarantees that all the modifications in a transaction will complete, or none of them will complete. The classic example of the importance of this property is to pretend that you are transferring money from one bank account to another. This transaction might be written in two steps. The first step is to subtract an amount from the first account. The second step is to add the amount to the second account. Now consider what would happen if your system crashed after completing the first step, but before the second step. Somehow, you've lost money! If you wrap these steps in a transaction, PostgreSQL promises that the first step will be rolled back if the second step fails (actually, the transaction will be rolled back unless you perform a COMMIT).

I'll cover the transaction processing features of PostgreSQL in great detail in Chapter 3.

Creating New Tables Using CREATE TABLE...AS

Let's turn our attention to something completely different. Earlier in this chapter, you learned how to use the INSERT statement to store data in a table. Sometimes, you want to create a new table based on the results of a SELECT command. That's exactly what the CREATE TABLE...AS command is designed to do.

The format of CREATE TABLE...AS is

```
CREATE [ TEMPORARY | TEMP ] TABLE table [ (column [, ...] ) ]
  AS select_clause
```

When you execute a CREATE TABLE...AS command, PostgreSQL automatically creates a new table. Each column in the new table corresponds to a column returned by the SELECT clause. If you include the TEMPORARY (or TEMP) keyword, PostgreSQL will create a temporary table. This table is invisible to other users and is destroyed when you end your PostgreSQL session. A temporary table is useful because you don't have to remember to remove the table later—PostgreSQL takes care of that detail for you.

Let's look at an example. A few pages earlier in the chapter, you created a complex join between the customers, rentals, and tapes tables. Let's create a new table based on that query so you don't have to keep entering the same complex query[13]:

```
movies=# CREATE TABLE info AS
movies-#   SELECT customers.customer_name, rentals.tape_id, tapes.title
movies-#     FROM customers FULL OUTER JOIN rentals
movies-#       ON customers.customer_id = rentals.customer_id
movies-#     FULL OUTER JOIN tapes
movies-#       ON tapes.tape_id = rentals.tape_id;
SELECT
movies=# SELECT * FROM info;
      customer_name     | tape_id  |       title
------------------------+----------+---------------------
 Jones, Henry           | AB-12345 | The Godfather
 Panky, Henry           | AB-67472 | The Godfather
                        |          | Rear Window
                        |          | American Citizen, An
 Panky, Henry           | MC-68873 | Casablanca
 Jones, Henry           | OW-41221 | Citizen Kane
 Rubin, William         |          |
 Wonderland, Alice N.   |          |
 Funkmaster, Freddy     |          |
 Gull, Jonathon LC      |          |
 Grumby, Jonas          |          |
                        |          | Sly
                        |          | Stone Cold
(13 rows)
```

---

[13] Some readers are probably thinking, "Hey, you should use a view to do that!" You're right, you'll soon see that I just needed a bad example.

This is the same complex query that you saw earlier. I'll point out a few things about this example. First, notice that the SELECT command selected three columns (customer_name, tape_id, title)—the result table has three columns. Next, you can create a table using an arbitrarily complex SELECT command. Finally, notice that the TEMPORARY keyword is not included; therefore, info is a permanent table and is visible to other users.

What happens if you try to create the info table again?

```
movies=# CREATE TABLE info AS
movies-#    SELECT customers.customer_name, rentals.tape_id, tapes.title
movies-#      FROM customers FULL OUTER JOIN rentals
movies-#        ON customers.customer_id = rentals.customer_id
movies-#      FULL OUTER JOIN tapes
movies-#        ON tapes.tape_id = rentals.tape_id;
ERROR:  Relation 'info' already exists
```

As you might expect, you receive an error message because the info table already exists. CREATE TABLE...AS will not automatically drop an existing table. Now let's see what happens if you include the TEMPORARY keyword:

```
movies=# CREATE TEMPORARY TABLE info AS
movies-#    SELECT * FROM tapes;
SELECT
movies=# SELECT * FROM info;
  tape_id  |        title        | duration
-----------+---------------------+----------
 AD-12345  | The Godfather       |
 AB-67472  | The Godfather       |
 MC-68873  | Casablanca          |
 OW-41221  | Citizen Kane        |
 AH-54706  | Rear Window         |
 OW-42200  | Sly                 | 01:36
 KJ-03335  | American Citizen, An |
 OW-42201  | Stone Cold          | 01:52
(8 rows)
```

This time, the CREATE TABLE...AS command succeeded. When I SELECT from info, I see a copy of the tapes table. Doesn't this violate the rule that I mentioned earlier ("CREATE TABLE...AS will not automatically drop an existing table")? Not really. When you create a temporary table, you are hiding any permanent table of the same name—the original (permanent) table still exists. Other users will still see the permanent table. If you DROP the temporary table, the permanent table will reappear:

```
movies=# SELECT * FROM info;
  tape_id  |        title        | duration
-----------+---------------------+----------
 AB-12345  | The Godfather       |
 AB-67472  | The Godfather       |
```

```
MC-68873 | Casablanca        |
OW-41221 | Citizen Kane      |
AH-54706 | Rear Window       |
OW-42200 | Sly               | 01:36
KJ-03335 | American Citizen, An |
OW-42201 | Stone Cold        | 01:52
(8 rows)
```

```
movies=# DROP TABLE info;
DROP
movies=# SELECT * FROM info;
     customer_name      | tape_id  |       title
------------------------+----------+----------------------
 Jones, Henry           | AB-12345 | The Godfather
 Panky, Henry           | AB-67472 | The Godfather
                        |          | Rear Window
                        |          | American Citizen, An
 Panky, Henry           | MC-68873 | Casablanca
 Jones, Henry           | OW-41221 | Citizen Kane
 Rubin, William         |          |
 Wonderland, Alice N.   |          |
 Funkmaster, Freddy     |          |
 Gull, Jonathon LC      |          |
 Grumby, Jonas          |          |
                        |          | Sly
                        |          | Stone Cold
(13 rows)
```

Using VIEW

In the previous section, I used the CREATE TABLE...AS command to create the info table so that you didn't have to type in the same complex query over and over again. The problem with that approach is that the info table is a snapshot of the underlying tables at the time that the CREATE TABLE...AS command was executed. If any of the underlying tables change (and they probably will), the info table will be out of synch.

Fortunately, PostgreSQL provides a much better solution to this problem—the view. A *view* is a named query. The syntax you use to create a view is nearly identical to the CREATE TABLE...AS command:

```
CREATE VIEW view AS select_clause;
```

Let's get rid of the info table and replace it with a view:

```
movies=# DROP TABLE info;
DROP
movies=# CREATE VIEW info AS
movies-#   SELECT customers.customer_name, rentals.tape_id,tapes.title
```

```
movies-#      FROM customers FULL OUTER JOIN rentals
movies-#         ON customers.customer_id = rentals.customer_id
movies-#      FULL OUTER JOIN tapes
movies-#         ON tapes.tape id = rentals.tape_id;
CREATE
```

While using `psql`, you can see a list of the views in your database using the `\dv` meta-command:

```
movies=# \dv
       List of relations
 Name | Type |     Owner
------+------+---------------
 info | view | bruce
(1 row)
```

You can see the definition of a view using the `\d view-name` meta-command:

```
movies=# \d info
                    View "info"
  Attribute    |          Type          | Modifier
---------------+------------------------+----------
 customer_name | character varying(50)  |
 tape_id       | character(8)           |
 title         | character varying(80)  |
View definition: SELECT customers.customer_name,
                    rentals.tape_id, tapes.title
                FROM (( customers FULL JOIN rentals
                  ON ((customers.customer_id = rentals.customer_id)))
                FULL JOIN tapes
                  ON ((tapes.tape_id = rentals.tape_id)));
```

You can `SELECT` from a view in exactly the same way that you can `SELECT` from a table:

```
movies=# SELECT * FROM info WHERE tape_id IS NOT NULL;
 customer_name | tape_id  |     title
---------------+----------+----------------
 Jones, Henry  | AB-12345 | The Godfather
 Panky, Henry  | AB-67472 | The Godfather
 Panky, Henry  | MC-68873 | Casablanca
 Jones, Henry  | OW-41221 | Citizen Kane
(4 rows)
```

The great thing about a view is that it is always in synch with the underlying tables. Let's add a new `rentals` row:

```
movies=# INSERT INTO rentals VALUES( 'KJ-03335', '2001-11-26', 8 );
INSERT 38488 1
```

and then repeat the previous query:

```
movies=# SELECT * FROM info WHERE tape_id IS NOT NULL;
 customer_name | tape_id  |        title
---------------+----------+----------------------
 Jones, Henry  | AB-12345 | The Godfather
 Panky, Henry  | AB-67472 | The Godfather
 Grumby, Jonas | KJ-03335 | American Citizen, An
 Panky, Henry  | MC-68873 | Casablanca
 Jones, Henry  | OW-41221 | Citizen Kane
(5 rows)
```

To help you understand how a view works, you might imagine that the following sequence of events occurs each time you SELECT from a view:

1. PostgreSQL creates a temporary table by executing the SELECT command used to define the view.

2. PostgreSQL executes the SELECT command that you entered, substituting the name of temporary table everywhere that you used the name of the view.

3. PostgreSQL destroys the temporary table.

This is not what actually occurs under the covers, but it's the easiest way to think about views.

Unlike other relational databases, PostgreSQL treats all views as *read-only*—you can't INSERT, DELETE, or UPDATE a view.

To destroy a view, you use the DROP VIEW command:

```
movies=# DROP VIEW info;
DROP
```

Summary

This chapter has given you a gentle introduction to PostgreSQL. You have seen how to install PostgreSQL on your system and how to configure it for use. You've also created a sample database that you'll use throughout the rest of this book.

In the next chapter, I'll discuss the many PostgreSQL data types in more depth, and I'll give you some guidelines for choosing between them.

2

Working with Data in PostgreSQL

When you create a table in PostgreSQL, you specify the type of data that you will store in each column. For example, if you are storing a customer name, you will want to store alphabetic characters. If you are storing a customer's birth date, you will want to store values that can be interpreted as dates. An account balance would be stored in a numeric column.

Every value in a PostgreSQL database is defined within a data type. Each data type has a name (NUMERIC, TIMESTAMP, CHARACTER, and so on) and a range of valid values. When you enter a value in PostgreSQL, the data that you supply must conform to the syntax required by the type. PostgreSQL defines a set of functions that can operate on each data type; you can also define your own functions. Every data type has a set of *operators* that can be used with values of that type. An operator is a symbol used to build up complex expressions from simple expressions. You're already familiar with arithmetic operators such as + (addition) and - (subtraction). An operator represents some sort of computation applied to one or more operands. For example, in the expression 5 + 3, + is the operator and 5 and 3 are the operands. Most operators require two operands, some require a single operand, and others can function in either context. An operator that works with two operands is called a binary operator. An operator that works with one operand is called a unary operator.

You can convert most values from one data type to another. I'll describe type conversion at the end of this chapter.

This chapter explores each of the data types built into a standard PostgreSQL distribution (yes, you can also define your own custom data types). For each type, I'll show you the range of valid values, the syntax required to enter a value of that type, and a list of operators that you can use with that type.

Each section includes a table showing which operators you can use with a specific data type. For example, in the discussion of character data types, you will see that the string concatenation operator (||) can be used to append one string value to the end of another string value. The operator table in that section shows that you use the string concatenation operator to join two CHARACTER values, two VARCHAR values, or two TEXT values. What the table does *not* show is that you can use the string concatenation operator to append an INTEGER value to the end of a VARCHAR. PostgreSQL automatically converts the INTEGER value into a string value and then applies the || operator. It's important to keep this point in mind as you read through this chapter—the operator tables don't show all possible combinations, only the combinations that don't require type conversion.

Later in this chapter, I'll give a brief description of the process that PostgreSQL uses to decide whether an operator (or function) is applicable, and if so, which values require automatic type conversion. For a detailed explanation of the process, see Chapter 5 of the *PostgreSQL User's Guide* that came with your copy of PostgreSQL.

Besides the operators listed in this section, PostgreSQL offers a huge selection of functions that you can call from within expressions. For a complete, up-to-date list of functions, see the *PostgreSQL User's Guide*.

NULL **Values**

NULL values represent missing, unknown, or *not-applicable* values. For example, let's say that you want to add a membership_expiration_date to the customers table. Some customers might be permanent members—their memberships will never expire. For those customers, the membership_expiration_date is not applicable and should be set to NULL. You may also find some customers who don't want to provide you with their birth dates. The birth_date column for these customers should be NULL.

In one case, NULL means *not applicable*. In the other case, NULL means *don't know*. A NULL membership_expiration_date does not mean that you don't know the expiration date, it means that the expiration date does not apply. A NULL birth_date does not mean that the customer was never born(!); it means that the date of birth is unknown.

Of course, when you create a table, you can specify that a given column cannot hold NULL values (NOT NULL). When you do so, you aren't affecting the data type of the column; you're just saying that NULL is not a legal value for that particular column. A column that prohibits NULL values is *mandatory*; a column that allows NULL values is *optional*.

You may be wondering how a data type could hold all values legal for that type, plus one more value. The answer is that PostgreSQL knows whether a given column is NULL not by looking at the column itself, but by first examining a NULL indicator (a single bit) stored separately from the column. If the NULL indicator for a given row/column is set to TRUE, the data stored in the row/column is meaningless. This means that a data row is composed of values for each column plus an array of indicator bits—one bit for each optional column.

Character Values

There are three character (or, as they are more commonly known, string) data types offered by PostgreSQL. A string value is just that—a string of zero or more characters. The three string data types are CHARACTER(n), CHARACTER VARYING(n), and TEXT.

A value of type CHARACTER(n) can hold a fixed-length string of n characters. If you store a value that is shorter than n, the value is padded with spaces to increase the length to exactly n characters. You can abbreviate CHARACTER(n) to CHAR(n). If you omit the "(n)" when you create a CHARACTER column, the length is assumed to be 1.

The CHARACTER VARYING(n) type defines a variable-length string of at most n characters. VARCHAR(n) is a synonym for CHARACTER VARYING(n). If you omit the "(n)" when creating a CHARACTER VARYING column, you can store strings of any length in that column.

The last string type is TEXT. A TEXT column is equivalent to a VARCHAR column without a specified length—a TEXT column can store strings of any length.

Syntax for Literal Values

A *string value* is a sequence of characters surrounded by a pair of delimiters. Prior to PostgreSQL version 8.0, you had to use a pair of single quote characters to delimit a string value. Starting with version 8.0, you can also define your own delimiters for each string value using a form known as dollar quoting. Each of the following is a valid string value:

```
'I am a string'
'3.14159265'
''
```

You can also write these same string values using dollar quoting as follows:

```
$$I am a string$$
$$3.14159265$$
$$$$
```

The first example is obviously a string value. '3.14159265' is also a string value—at first glance it may look like a numeric value but the fact it is surrounded by single quotes tells you that it is really a string. The third example ('') is also a valid string: It is the string composed of zero characters (that is, it has a length of zero). It is important to understand that an empty string is not the same as a NULL value. An empty string means that you have a known value that just happens to be empty, whereas NULL implies that the value is unknown. Consider, for example, that you are storing an employee name in your database. You might create three columns to hold the complete name: first_name, middle_name, and last_name. If you find an employee whose middle_name is NULL, that should imply that the employee might have a middle name, but you don't know what it is. On the other hand, if you find an employee who has no middle name, you should store that middle_name as an empty string. Again, NULL implies that you don't have a piece of information; an empty string means that you do have the information, but it just happens to be empty.

If a string is delimited with single quotes, how do you represent a string that happens to include a single quote? There are four choices. First, you can embed a single quote within a string by entering two adjacent quotes. For example, the string "Where's my car?" could be entered as:

```
'Where''s my car?'
```

Two other alternatives involve an *escape* character. An escape is a special character that tells PostgreSQL that the character (or characters) following the escape is to be interpreted as a directive instead of as a literal value. In PostgreSQL, the escape character is the backslash (\). When PostgreSQL sees a backslash in a string literal, it discards the backslash and interprets the following characters according to the following rules:

```
\b is the backspace character
\f is the form feed character
\r is the carriage-return character
\n is the newline character
\t is the tab character
```

```
\xxx (where xxx is an octal number) means the character whose ASCII value is xxx.
```

If any character, other than those mentioned, follows the backslash, it is treated as its literal value. So, if you want to include a single quote in a string, you can *escape* the quote by preceding it with a backslash:

```
'Where\'s my car?'
```

Or you can embed a single quote (or any character) within a string by escaping its ASCII value (in octal), as in

```
'Where\047s my car?'
```

Finally, you can use dollar quoting. To write the string "Where's my car?" in dollar-quoted form, use this format:

```
$$Where's my car?$$
```

Notice that in this form, the embedded single quote doesn't cause any problems. When you write a string in dollar-quoted form, the single quote character has no special meaning—it's just another character. You may be thinking that dollar quoting just trades one special delimiter (a single quote) for another (two dollar signs). After all, what happens if you want to embed two consecutive dollar signs in a string value? OK, that's not very likely, but PostgreSQL doesn't just ignore the problem; it lets you define your *own* delimiters.

In its most simple form, a dollar-quote delimiter is just a pair of dollar signs. To define your own delimiter, simply include a *tag* between the two dollar signs at the beginning of the string and include the *same* tag between the two dollar signs at the end of the string. You get to choose the tag but be aware that tags are case sensitive. Here's a string written using a custom delimiter:

```
$MyTag$That restaurant's rated 3 $$$; it must be expensive$MyTag$
```

When you define your own delimiter, embedded single quotes lose their special meaning and so do consecutive dollar signs. You can define a custom delimiter for each string value that you write, but remember that you don't *have* to define a custom delimiter unless your string contains consecutive dollar signs.

To summarize, here are the four ways that you can embed a single quote within a string:

```
'It''s right where you left it'
'It\'s right where you left it'
'It\047s right where you left it'
$$It's right where you left it$$
```

Supported Operators

PostgreSQL offers a large number of string operators. One of the most basic operations is string concatenation. The concatenation operator (||) is used to combine two string values into a single TEXT value. For example, the expression

```
'This is ' || 'one string'
```

will evaluate to the value: 'This is one string'. And the expression

```
'The current time is ' || now()
```

will evaluate to a TEXT value such as, `'The current time is 2002-01-01 19:45:17-04'`.

PostgreSQL also gives you a variety of ways to compare string values. All comparison operators return a BOOLEAN value; the result will be TRUE, FALSE, or NULL. A comparison operator will evaluate to NULL if either of the operands are NULL.

The equality (=) and inequality (<>) operators behave the way you would expect—two strings are equal if they contain the same characters (in the same positions); otherwise, they are not equal. You can also determine whether one string is greater than or less than another (and of course, greater than or equal to and less than or equal to).

Table 2.1[1] shows a few sample string comparisons.

Table 2.1 **Sample String Comparisons**

Operator (θ)						
Expression	<	<=	=	<>	>=	>
`'string' θ 'string'`	FALSE	TRUE	TRUE	FALSE	TRUE	FALSE
`'string1' θ 'string'`	FALSE	FALSE	FALSE	TRUE	TRUE	TRUE
`'String1' θ 'string'`	TRUE	TRUE	FALSE	TRUE	FALSE	FALSE

You can also use pattern-matching operators with string values. PostgreSQL defines eight pattern-matching operators, but the names are a bit contrived and not particularly intuitive.

Table 2.2 contains a summary of the string operators.

The first set of pattern-matching operators is related to the LIKE keyword. ~~ is equivalent to LIKE. The ~~* operator is equivalent to ILIKE—it is a case-insensitive version of LIKE. !~~ and !~~* are equivalent to NOT LIKE and NOT ILIKE, respectively.

The second set of pattern-matching operators is used to match a string value against a regular expression (regular expressions are described in more detail in Chapter 1, "Introduction to PostgreSQL and SQL"). The naming convention for the regular expression operators is similar to that for the LIKE operators—regular expression operators are indicated with a single tilde and LIKE operators use two tildes. The ~ operator compares a string against a regular expression (returning True if the string satisfies the regular expression). ~* compares a string against a regular expression, ignoring differences in case. The !~ operator returns False if the string value matches the regular expression (and returns True if the string satisfies the regular expression). The !~* operator returns False if the string value matches the regular expression, ignoring differences in case, and returns True otherwise.

---

[1] You might find the format of this table a bit confusing at first. In the first column, I use the 'θ' character to represent any one of the operators listed in the remaining columns. So, the first row of the table tells you that `'string'` < `'string'` evaluates to FALSE, `'string'` <= `'string'` evaluates to TRUE, `'string'` = `'string'` evaluates to TRUE, and so forth. I'll use the 'θ' character throughout this chapter to indicate an operator.

Table 2.2 **String Operators**

Operator	Meaning	Case Sensitive?
||	Concatenation	*Not* applicable
~	Matches regular expression	Yes
~~	Matches LIKE expression	Yes
~*	Matches regular expression	No
~~*	Matches LIKE expression	No
!~	Does not match regular expression	Yes
!~~	Does not match LIKE expression	Yes
!~*	Does not match regular expression	No
!~~*	Does not match LIKE expression	No

Type Conversion Operators

There are two important operators that you should know about before we go much further—actually it's one operator, but you can write it two different ways.

The CAST() operator is used to convert a value from one data type to another. There are two ways to write the CAST() operator:

```
CAST(expression AS type)
expression::type
```

No matter which way you write it, the expression is converted into the specified type. Of course, not every value can be converted into every type. For example, the expression CAST('abc' AS INTEGER) results in an error (specifically, 'pg_atoi: error in "abc": can't parse "abc"') because 'abc' obviously can't be converted into an integer.

Most often, your casting requirements will come in either of two forms: you will need to CAST() a string value into some other type, or you will need to convert between related types (for example, INTEGER into NUMERIC). When you CAST() a string value into another data type, the string must be in the form required by the literal syntax for the target data type. Each of the following sections describes the literal syntax required by each type. When you convert between related data types, you may gain or lose precision. For example, when you convert from a fractional numeric type into an integer type, the value is rounded:

```
movies=# SELECT CAST( CAST( 12345.67 AS FLOAT8 ) AS INTEGER );
 ?column?
----------
    12346
```

Numeric Values

PostgreSQL provides a variety of numeric data types. Of the six numeric types, four are exact (SMALLINT, INTEGER, BIGINT, NUMERIC(p,s)) and two are approximate (REAL, DOUBLE PRECISION).

Three of the four exact numeric types (SMALLINT, INTEGER, and BIGINT) can store only integer values. The fourth (NUMERIC(p,s)) can accurately store any value that fits within the specified number (p) of digits.

The approximate numeric types, on the other hand, cannot store all values exactly. Instead, an approximate data type stores an approximation of a real number. The DOUBLE PRECISION type, for example, can store a total of 15 significant digits, but when you perform calculations using a DOUBLE PRECISION value, you can run into rounding errors. It's easy to see this problem:

```
movies=# select 2000.3 - 2000.0;
    ?column?
-------------------
 0.299999999999955
(1 row)
```

Size, Precision, and Range-of-Values

The four *exact* data types can accurately store any value within a type-specific range. The exact numeric types are described in Table 2.3.

Table 2.3   **Exact Numeric Data Types**

Type Name	Size in Bytes	Minimum Value	Maximum Value
SMALLINT	2	-32768	+32767
INTEGER	4	-2147483648	+2147483647
BIGINT	8	-9223372036854775808	+9223372036854775807
NUMERIC(p,s)	11+(p/2)	No limit	No limit

The NUMERIC(p,s) data type can accurately store any number that fits within the specified number of digits. When you create a column of type NUMERIC(p,s), you can specify the total number of decimal digits (p) and the number of fractional digits (s). The total number of decimal digits is called the *precision*, and the number of fractional digits is called the *scale*.

Table 2.3 shows that there is no limit to the values that you can store in a NUMERIC(p,s) column. In fact, there is a limit (normally 1,000 digits), but you can adjust the limit by changing a symbol and rebuilding your PostgreSQL server from source code.

The two approximate numeric types are named REAL and DOUBLE PRECISION. Table 2.4 shows the size and range for each of these data types, while Table 2.5 shows alternative names for the data types.

Table 2.4   **Approximate Numeric Data Types**

Type Name	Size in Bytes	Range
REAL	4	6 decimal digits
DOUBLE PRECISION	8	15 decimal digits

Table 2.5 **Alternate Names for Numeric Data Types**

Common Name	Synonyms
SMALLINT	INT2
INTEGER	INT, INT4
BIGINT	INT8
NUMERIC(p,s)	DECIMAL(p,s)
REAL	FLOAT, FLOAT4
DOUBLE PRECISION	FLOAT8

SERIAL, BIGSERIAL, and SEQUENCES

Besides the numeric data types already described, PostgreSQL supports two "advanced" numeric types: SERIAL and BIGSERIAL. A SERIAL column is really an unsigned INTEGER whose value automatically increases (or decreases) by a defined increment as you add new rows. Likewise, a BIGSERIAL is a BIG-INT that increases in value. When you create a BIGSERIAL or SERIAL column, PostgreSQL will automatically create a SEQUENCE for you. A SEQUENCE is an object that generates sequence numbers for you. I'll talk more about SEQUENCEs later in this chapter.

Syntax for Literal Values

When you need to enter a numeric literal, you must follow the formatting rules defined by PostgreSQL. There are two distinct styles for numeric literals: integer and fractional (the PostgreSQL documentation refers to fractional literals as floating-point literals).

Let's start by examining the format for fractional literals. Fractional literals can be entered in any of the following forms[2]:

```
[-]digits.[digits][E[+|-]digits]
[-][digits].digits[E[+|-]digits]
[-]digits[+|-]digits
```

Here are some examples of valid fractional literals:

```
3.14159
2.0e+15
0.2e-15
4e10
```

A numeric literal that contains only digits is considered to be an integer literal:

```
[-]digits
```

Here are some examples of valid integer literals:

```
-100
55590332
9223372036854775807
-9223372036854775808
```

[2] Syntax diagrams are described in detail in Chapter 1.

A fractional literal is always considered to be of type DOUBLE PRECISION. An integer literal is considered to be of type INTEGER, unless the value is too large to fit into an integer—in which case, it will be promoted first to type BIGINT, then to NUMERIC or REAL if necessary.

Supported Operators

PostgreSQL supports a variety of arithmetic, comparison, and bit-wise operators for the numeric data types. Tables 2.6 and 2.7 give some examples of the arithmetic operators.

Table 2.6   **Arithmetic Operators for Integers**

Data Types	Valid Operators (θ)
INT2 θ INT2	+ - * / %
INT2 θ INT4	+ - * / %
INT4 θ INT2	+ - * / %
INT4 θ INT4	+ - * / %
INT4 θ INT8	+ - * /
INT8 θ INT4	+ - * /
INT8 θ INT8	+ - * / %

Table 2.7   **Arithmetic Operators for Floats**

Data Types	Valid Operators (θ)
FLOAT4 θ FLOAT4	* + - /
FLOAT4 θ FLOAT8	* + - /
FLOAT8 θ FLOAT4	* + - /
FLOAT8 θ FLOAT8	* + - / ^

You use the comparison operators to determine the relationship between two numeric values. PostgreSQL supports the usual operators: <, <=, <> (not equal), =, >, and >=. You can use the comparison operators with all possible combinations of the numeric data types (some combinations will require type conversion).

PostgreSQL also provides a set of *bit-wise* operators that you can use with the integer data types. Bit-wise operators work on the individual bits that make up the two operands.

The easiest way to understand the bit-wise operators is to first convert your operands into binary notation-for example:

```
decimal 12 = binary 00001100
decimal  7 = binary 00000111
decimal 21 = binary 00010101
```

Next, let's look at each operator in turn.

The AND (&) operator compares corresponding bits in each operand and produces a 1 if both bits are 1 and a 0 otherwise. For example:

```
00001100 &     00000111 &
00010101       00010101
--------       --------
00000100       00000101
```

The OR (|) operator compares corresponding bits in each operand and produces a 1 if either (or both) bit is 1 and a 0 otherwise. For example:

```
00001100 |     00000111 |
00010101       00010101
--------       --------
00011101       00010111
```

The XOR (#) operator is similar to OR. XOR compares corresponding bits in each operand, and produces a 1 if either bit, but not both bits, is 1, and produces a 0 otherwise.

```
00001100 #     00000111 #
00010101       00010101
--------       --------
00011001       00010010
```

PostgreSQL also provides two *bit-shift* operators.

The left-shift operator (<<) shifts the bits in the first operand n bits to the left, where n is the second operand. The leftmost n bits are discarded, and the rightmost n bits are set to 0. A left-shift by n bits is equivalent to multiplying the first operand by 2^n—for example:

```
00001100 << 2(decimal) = 00110000
00010101 << 3(decimal) = 10101000
```

The right-shift operator (>>) >)>shifts the bits in the first operand n bits to the right, where n is the second operand. The rightmost n bits are discarded, and the leftmost n bits are set to 0. A right-shift by n bits is equivalent to dividing the first operand by 2^n:

```
00001100 >> 2(decimal) = 00000011
00010101 >> 3(decimal) = 00000010
```

The final bit-wise operator is the binary NOT (~). Unlike the other bit-wise operators, NOT is a unary operator—it takes a single operand. When you apply the NOT operator to a value, each bit in the original value is toggled: ones become zeroes and zeroes become ones. For example:

```
~00001100 = 11110011
~00010101 = 11101010
```

Table 2.8 shows the data types that you can use with the bit-wise operators.

Table 2.8 **Bit-Wise Operators for Integers**

Data Types	Valid Operators (θ)
INT2 θ INT2	# & | << >>
INT4 θ INT4	# & | << >>
INT8 θ INT4	<< >>
INT8 θ INT8	# & |

Date/Time Values

PostgreSQL supports four basic temporal data types plus a couple of extensions that deal with time zone issues.

The DATE type is used to store dates. A DATE value stores a century, year, month, and day.

The TIME data type is used to store a time-of-day value. A TIME value stores hours, minutes, seconds, and microseconds. It is important to note that a TIME value does not contain a time zone—if you want to include a time zone, you should use the type TIME WITH TIME ZONE. TIMETZ is a synonym for TIME WITH TIME ZONE.

The TIMESTAMP data type combines a DATE and a TIME, storing a century, year, month, day, hour, minutes, seconds, and microseconds. Unlike the TIME data type, a TIMESTAMP *does* include a time zone. If, for some reason, you want a date/time value that does not include a time zone, you can use the type TIMESTAMP WITHOUT TIME ZONE.

The last temporal data type is the INTERVAL. An INTERVAL represents a span of time. I find that the easiest way to think about INTERVAL values is to remember that an INTERVAL stores some (possibly large) number of seconds, but you can group the seconds into larger units for convenience. For example, the CAST('1 week' AS INTERVAL) is equal to CAST('604800 seconds' AS INTERVAL), which is equal to CAST('7 days' AS INTERVAL)—you can use whichever format you find easiest to work with.

Table 2.9 lists the size and range for each of the temporal data types.

Table 2.9 **Temporal Data Type Sizes and Ranges**

Data Type	Size (in bytes)	Range
DATE	4	-01-MAR-4801 BC 31 DEC-32767
TIME [WITHOUT TIME ZONE]	4	-00:00:00.00 23:59:59.99
TIME WITH TIME ZONE	12	-00:00:00.00+12 23:59:59.00-12
TIMESTAMP [WITH TIME ZONE]	8	-24-NOV-4714 BC 31-DEC- 5874897
TIMESTAMP WITHOUT TIME ZONE	8	-24-NOV-4714 BC 31-DEC- 5874897
INTERVAL	12	-178000000 YEARS +178000000 YEARS

The data types that contain a time value (TIME, TIME WITH TIME ZONE, TIMESTAMP, TIMESTAMP WITH TIME ZONE, and INTERVAL) have microsecond precision. The DATE data type has a precision of one day.

Syntax for Literal Values

I covered date literal syntax pretty thoroughly in Chapter 1; see the section titled "Working with Date Values."

You may recall from Chapter 1 that date values can be entered in many formats, and you have to tell PostgreSQL how to interpret ambiguous values. Fortunately, the syntax for TIME, TIMESTAMP, and INTERVAL values is much more straightforward.

A TIME value stores hours, minutes, seconds, and microseconds. The syntax for a TIME literal is

```
hh:mm[:ss[.µ ]] [AM|PM]µ
```

where hh specifies the hour, mm specifies the number of minutes past the hour, ss specifies the number of seconds, and µ specifies the number of microseconds. If you include an AM or PM indicator, the hh component must be less than or equal to 12; otherwise, the hour can range from 0 to 24.

Entering a TIME WITH TIME ZONE value is a bit more complex. A TIME WITH TIME ZONE value is a TIME value, plus a time zone. The time zone component can be specified in two ways. First, you can include an offset (in minutes and hours) from UTC:

```
hh:mm[:ss[.µ ]] [AM|PM] [{+|-}HH[:MM]]
```

where HH is the number of hours and MM is the number of minutes distant from UTC. Negative values are considered to be west of the prime meridian, and positive values are east of the prime meridian.

You can also use a standard time zone abbreviation (such as UTC, PDT, or EST) to specify the time zone:

```
hh:mm[:ss[.µ ]] [AM|PM] [ZZZ]
```

Table 2.10 shows all the time zone abbreviations accepted by PostgreSQL version 8.0.

Table 2.10 **PostgreSQL Time Zone Names**

Names	Offset	Description
FJST	–13:00	Fiji Summer Time
FJT	–12:00	Fiji Time
IDLW	–12:00	International Date Line, West
BST	–11:00	Bering Summer Time
NT	–11:00	Nome Time
NUT	–11:00	Niue Time
AHST	–10:00	Alaska-Hawaii Std Time
CAT	–10:00	Central Alaska Time
HST	–10:00	Hawaii Std Time

Table 2.10 **Continued**

THAT	−10:00	Tahiti Time
TKT	−10:00	Tokelau Time
MART	−09:30	Marquesas Time
AKST	−09:00	Alaska Standard Time
GAMT	−09:00	Gambier Time
HDT	−09:00	Hawaii/Alaska Daylight Time
YST	−09:00	Yukon Standard Time
AKDT	−08:00	Alaska Daylight Time
PST	−08:00	Pacific Standard Time
YDT	−08:00	Yukon Daylight Time
MST	−07:00	Mountain Standard Time
PDT	−07:00	Pacific Daylight Time
CST	−06:00	Central Standard Time
EAST	−06:00	Easter Island Time
GALT	−06:00	Galapagos Time
MDT	−06:00	Mountain Daylight Time
ZP6	−06:00	UTC +6 hours
ACT	−05:00	Atlantic/Porto Acre Time
CDT	−05:00	Central Daylight Time
COT	−05:00	Columbia Time
EASST	−05:00	Easter Island Summer Time
ECT	−05:00	Ecuador Time
EST	−05:00	Eastern Standard Time
PET	−05:00	Peru Time
ZP5	−05:00	UTC +5 hours
ACST	−04:00	Atlantic/Porto Acre Summer Time
AMT	−04:00	Amazon Time (Porto Velho)
AST	−04:00	Atlantic Std Time (Canada)
BOT	−04:00	Bolivia Time
CLT	−04:00	Chile Time
ECT	−04:00	Eastern Caribbean Time
EDT	−04:00	Eastern Daylight Time
GYT	−04:00	Guyana Time
PYT	−04:00	Paraguay Time
VET	−04:00	Venezuela Time
ZP4	−04:00	UTC +4 hours
NFT	−03:30	Newfoundland Standard Time
NST	−03:30	Newfoundland Standard Time
ADT	−03:00	Atlantic Daylight Time
AMST	−03:00	Amazon Summer Time (Porto Velho)

Table 2.10 **Continued**

ART	−03:00	Argentina Time
AWT	−03:00	Brazil Time
BRT	−03:00	Brasilia Time
BST	−03:00	Brazil Standard Time
CLST	−03:00	Chile Summer Time
FKST	−03:00	Falkland Islands Summer Time
GFT	−03:00	French Guiana Time
PYST	−03:00	Paraguay Summer Time
UYT	−03:00	Uruguay Time
WGT	−03:00	West Greenland Time
NDT	−02:30	Newfoundland Daylight Time
BRST	−02:00	Brasilia Summer Time
FKT	−02:00	Falkland Islands Time
FNT	−02:00	Fernando de Noronha Time
PMDT	−02:00	Pierre & Miquelon Daylight Time
UYST	−02:00	Uruguay Summer Time
WGST	−02:00	West Greenland Summer Time
AZOT	−01:00	Azores Time
EGT	−01:00	East Greenland Time
FNST	−01:00	Fernando de Noronha Summer Time
SET	−01:00	Seychelles Time
WAT	−01:00	West Africa Time
AZOST	+00:00	Azores Summer Time
EGST	+00:00	East Greenland Summer Time
GMT	+00:00	Greenwich Mean Time
UTC	+00:00	Universal Coordinated Time
UT	+00:00	Universal Time
WET	+00:00	Western Europe
ZULU	+00:00	Universal Time
Z	+00:00	ISO-8601 Universal Time
BST	+01:00	British Summer Time
CET	+01:00	Central European Time
DNT	+01:00	Dansk Normal Time
FST	+01:00	French Summer Time
MET	+01:00	Middle Europe Time
MEWT	+01:00	Middle Europe Winter Time
MEZ	+01:00	Middle Europe Zone
NOR	+01:00	Norway Standard Time
SWT	+01:00	Swedish Winter Time
WEST	+01:00	Western Europe Summer Time

Table 2.10 **Continued**

WETDST	+01:00	Western Europe Daylight Savings Time
BDST	+02:00	British Double Summer Time
CEST	+02:00	Central European Dayl. Time
CETDST	+02:00	Central European Dayl. Time
EET	+02:00	Eastern Europe, USSR Zone 1
FWT	+02:00	French Winter Time
IST	+02:00	Israel Time
MEST	+02:00	Middle Europe Summer Time
METDST	+02:00	Middle Europe Daylight Time
SST	+02:00	Swedish Summer Time
BT	+03:00	Baghdad Time
EAT	+03:00	East Africa Time
EAT	+03:00	Indian Antananarivo Time
EEST	+03:00	Eastern Europe Summer Time
EETDST	+03:00	Eastern Europe Daylight Time
HMT	+03:00	Hellas Mediterranean Time
MSK	+03:00	Moscow Time
IRT	+03:30	Iran Time
IT	+03:30	Iran Time
AMT	+04:00	Armenia Time (Yerevan)
AZT	+04:00	Azerbaijan Time
EAST	+04:00	Indian Antananarivo Savings Time
GET	+04:00	Georgia Time
MSD	+04:00	Moscow Summer Time
MUT	+04:00	Mauritius Island Time
RET	+04:00	Reunion Island Time
SCT	+04:00	Mahe Island Time
AFT	+04:30	Kabul Time
AMST	+05:00	Armenia Summer Time (Yerevan)
AZST	+05:00	Azerbaijan Summer Time
GEST	+05:00	Georgia Summer Time
IOT	+05:00	Indian Chagos Time
KGT	+05:00	Kyrgyzstan Time
MVT	+05:00	Maldives Island Time
PKT	+05:00	Pakistan Time
TFT	+05:00	Kerguelen Time
TJT	+05:00	Tajikistan Time
TMT	+05:00	Turkmenistan Time
UZT	+05:00	Uzbekistan Time
YEKT	+05:00	Yekaterinburg Time

Table 2.10 **Continued**

NPT	+05:45	Nepal Standard Time
ALMT	+06:00	Almaty Time
BDT	+06:00	Dacca Time
BTT	+06:00	Bhutan Time
DUSST	+06:00	Dushanbe Summer Time
KGST	+06:00	Kyrgyzstan Summer Time
LKT	+06:00	Lanka Time
MAWT	+06:00	Mawson, Antarctica
NOVT	+06:00	Novosibirsk Standard Time
OMST	+06:00	Omsk Time
UZST	+06:00	Uzbekistan Summer Time
YEKST	+06:00	Yekaterinburg Summer Time
CCT	+06:30	Indian Cocos (Island) Time
MMT	+06:30	Myanmar Time
ALMST	+07:00	Almaty Savings Time
CVT	+07:00	Christmas Island Time (Indian Ocean)
CXT	+07:00	Christmas Island Time (Indian Ocean)
DAVT	+07:00	Davis Time (Antarctica)
ICT	+07:00	Indochina Time
JAVT	+07:00	Java Time
KRAST	+07:00	Krasnoyarsk Summer Time
NOVST	+07:00	Novosibirsk Summer Time
OMSST	+07:00	Omsk Summer Time
WAST	+07:00	West Australian Std Time
JT	+07:30	Java Time
AWST	+08:00	Western Australia
BNT	+08:00	Brunei Darussalam Time
BORT	+08:00	Borneo Time (Indonesia)
CCT	+08:00	China Coast Time
HKT	+08:00	Hong Kong Time
IRKT	+08:00	Irkutsk Time
KRAT	+08:00	Krasnoyarsk Standard Time
MYT	+08:00	Malaysia Time
PHT	+08:00	Phillipine Time
ULAT	+08:00	Ulan Bator Time
WADT	+08:00	West Australian DST
WST	+08:00	West Australian Standard Time
MT	+08:30	Moluccas Time
AWSST	+09:00	Western Australia Time
IRKST	+09:00	Irkutsk Summer Time

Table 2.10 **Continued**

JAYT	+09:00	Jayapura Time (Indonesia)
JST	+09:00	Japan Std Time, USSR Zone 8
KST	+09:00	Korea Standard Time
PWT	+09:00	Palau Time
ULAST	+09:00	Ulan Bator Summer Time
WDT	+09:00	West Australian DST
YAKT	+09:00	Yakutsk Time
ACST	+09:30	Central Australia
CAST	+09:30	Central Australian ST
SAST	+09:30	South Australian Std Time
SAT	+09:30	South Australian Std Time
AEST	+10:00	Australia Eastern Std Time
DDUT	+10:00	Dumont-d'Urville Time (Antarctica)
EAST	+10:00	East Australian Std Time
EST	+10:00	Australia Eastern Std Time
GST	+10:00	Guam Std Time, USSR Zone 9
KDT	+10:00	Korea Daylight Time
LIGT	+10:00	From Melbourne, Australia
MPT	+10:00	North Mariana Islands Time
PGT	+10:00	Papua New Guinea Time
TRUK	+10:00	Truk Time
VLAT	+10:00	Vladivostok Time
YAKST	+10:00	Yakutsk Summer Time
YAPT	+10:00	Yap Time (Micronesia)
ACSST	+10:30	Central Australia Time
CADT	+10:30	Central Australian DST
CST	+10:30	Australia Central Std Time
LHST	+10:30	Lord Howe Standard Time, Australia
SADT	+10:30	South Australian Daylight Time
AESST	+11:00	Eastern Australia
LHDT	+11:00	Lord Howe Daylight Time, Australia
MAGT	+11:00	Magadan Time
NCT	+11:00	New Caledonia Time
PONT	+11:00	Ponape Time (Micronesia)
VLAST	+11:00	Vladivostok Summer Time
VUT	+11:00	Vanuata Time
ANAT	+12:00	Anadyr Time (Russia)
CKT	+12:00	Cook Islands Time
GILT	+12:00	Gilbert Islands Time
IDLE	+12:00	International Date Line, East

Table 2.10   **Continued**

KOST	+12:00	Kosrae Time
MAGST	+12:00	Magadan Summer Time
MHT	+12:00	Kwajalein Time
NZST	+12:00	New Zealand Standard Time
NZT	+12:00	New Zealand Time
PETT	+12:00	Petropavlovsk-Kamchatski Time
TVT	+12:00	Tuvalu Time
WAKT	+12:00	Wake Time
WFT	+12:00	Wallis and Futuna Time
CHAST	+12:45	Chatham Island Time
ANAST	+13:00	Anadyr Summer Time (Russia)
NZDT	+13:00	New Zealand Daylight Time
PETST	+13:00	Petropavlovsk-Kamchatski Summer Time
PHOT	+13:00	Phoenix Islands (Kiribati) Time
TOT	+13:00	Tonga Time
CHADT	+13:45	Chatham Island Daylight Time
LINT	+14:00	Line Islands Time (Kiribati)

I mentioned earlier in this section that an INTERVAL value represents a time span. I also mentioned than an INTERVAL stores some number of seconds. The syntax for an INTERVAL literal allows you to specify the number of seconds in a variety of units.

The format of an INTERVAL value is

```
quantity unit [quantity unit ...] [AGO]
```

The unit component specifies a number of seconds, as shown in Table 2.11. The quantity component acts as a multiplier (and may be fractional). If you have multiple quantity unit groups, they are all added together. The optional phrase AGO will cause the INTERVAL to be negative.

Table 2.11   INTERVAL **Units**

Description	Seconds	Unit Names
Microsecond[3]	.000001	us, usec, usecs, useconds, microsecon
Millisecond[3]	.001	-ms, msecs, mseconds, millisecon
Second	1	s, sec, secs, second, seconds
Minute	60	m, min, mins, minute, minutes

[3] Millisecond and microsecond can be used only in combination with another date/time component. For example, CAST('1 SECOND 5000 MSEC' AS INTERVAL) results in an interval of six seconds.

Table 2.11   **Continued**

Hour	3600	h, hr, hrs, hours
Day	86400	d, day, days
Week	604800	w, week, weeks
Month (30 days)	2592000	mon, mons, month, months
Year	31557600	y, yr, yrs, year, years
Decade	315576000	dec, decs, decade, decades
Century	3155760000	c, cent, century, centuries
Millennium	31557600000	mil, mils, millennia, millennium

You can use the EXTRACT(EPOCH FROM interval) function to convert an INTERVAL into a number of seconds. A few sample INTERVAL values are shown in Table 2.12. The Display column shows how PostgreSQL would format the Input Value for display. The EPOCH column shows the value that would be returned by extracting the EPOCH from the Input Value.

Table 2.12   **Sample** INTERVAL **Values**

Input Value	Display	EPOCH
.5 minutes	00:00:30	30
22 seconds 1 msec	00:00:22.00	22.001
22.001 seconds	00:00:22.00	22.001
10 centuries 2 decades	1020 years	32188752000
1 week 2 days 3.5 msec	9 days 00:00:00.00	777600.0035

Supported Operators

There are two types of operators that you can use with temporal values: arithmetic operators (addition and subtraction) and comparison operators.

You can add an INT4, a TIME, or a TIMETZ to a DATE. When you add an INT4, you are adding a number of days. Adding a TIME or TIMETZ to a DATE results in a TIMESTAMP. Table 2.13 lists the valid data type and operator combinations for temporal data types. The last column in Table 2.14 shows the data type of the resulting value.

Table 2.13   **Arithmetic Date/Time Operators**

Data Types	Valid Operators (θ)	Result Type
DATE θ DATE	-	INTEGER
DATE θ TIME	+	TIMESTAMP
DATE θ TIMETZ	+	TIMESTAMP WITH TIMEZONE

Table 2.13 **Continued**

DATE θ INT4	+ -	DATE
TIME θ DATE	+	TIMESTAMP
TIME θ INTERVAL	+ -	TIME
TIMETZ θ DATE	+	TIMESTAMP WITH TIMEZONE
TIMETZ θ INTERVAL	+ -	TIMETZ
TIMESTAMP θ TIMESTAMP	-	INTERVAL
TIMESTAMP θ INTERVAL	+ -	TIMESTAMP WITH TIMEZONE
INTERVAL θ TIME	+	TIME WITHOUT TIMEZONE

Table 2.14 shows how each of the arithmetic operators behave when applied to date/time values.

Table 2.14 **Arithmetic Date/Time Operator Examples**

Example	Result
'23-JAN-2003'::DATE - '23-JAN-2002'::DATE	365
'23-JAN-2003'::DATE + '2:35 PM'::TIME	2003-01-23 14:35:00
'23-JAN-2003'::DATE + '2:35 PM GMT'::TIMETZ	2003-01-23 09:35:00-05
'23-JAN-2003'::DATE + 2::INT4	2003-01-25
'2:35 PM'::TIME + '23-JAN-2003'::DATE	2003-01-23 14:35:00
'2:35 PM'::TIME + '2 hours 5 minutes'::INTERVAL	16:40:00
'2:35 PM EST'::TIMETZ + '23-JAN-2003'::DATE	2003-01-23 14:35:00-05
'2:35 PM EST'::TIMETZ + '2 hours 5 minutes'::INTERVAL	16:40:00-05
'23-JAN-2003 2:35 PM EST'::TIMESTAMP - '23-JAN-2002 1:00 PM EST'::TIMESTAMP	365 days 01:35
'23-JAN-2003 2:35 PM EST'::TIMESTAMP + '3 days 2 hours 5 minutes'::INTERVAL	2003-01-26 16:40:00-05
'2 hours 5 minutes'::INTERVAL + '2:34 PM'::TIME	16:39:00

Using the temporal comparison operators, you can determine the relationship between two date/time values. For purposes of comparison, an earlier date/time value is considered to be *less than* a later date/time value.

Table 2.15 shows how you can combine the various temporal types with comparison operators.

Table 2.15   **Date/Time Comparison Operators**

Data Types	Valid Operators (θ)
date θ date	< <= <> = >= >
time θ time	< <= <> = >= >
timetz θ timetz	< <= <> = >= >
timestamp θ timestamp	< <= <> = >= >

Boolean (Logical) Values

PostgreSQL supports a single Boolean (or logical) data type: BOOLEAN (BOOLEAN can be abbreviated as BOOL).

Size and Valid Values

A BOOLEAN can hold the values TRUE, FALSE, or NULL, and consumes a single byte of storage.

Syntax for Literal Values

Table 2.16 shows the alternate spellings for BOOLEAN literals.

Table 2.16   BOOLEAN **Literal Syntax**

Common Name	Synonyms
TRUE	true, 't', 'y', 'yes', 1
FALSE	false, 'f', 'n', 'no', 0

Supported Operators

The only operators supported for the BOOLEAN data type are the logical operators shown in Table 2.17:

Table 2.17   **Logical Operators for** BOOLEAN

Data Types	Valid Operators (θ)
BOOLEAN θ BOOLEAN	AND OR NOT

I covered the AND, OR, and NOT operators in Chapter 1. For a complete definition of these operators, see Tables 1.3, 1.4, and 1.5.

Geometric Data Types

PostgreSQL supports six data types that represent two-dimensional geometric objects. The most basic geometric data type is the POINT—as you might expect, a POINT represents a point within a two-dimensional plane.

A POINT is composed of an x-coordinate and a y-coordinate—each coordinate is a DOUBLE PRECISION number.

The LSEG data type represents a two-dimensional line segment. When you create a LSEG value, you specify two points—the starting POINT and the ending POINT.

A BOX value is used to define a rectangle—the two points that define a box specify opposite corners.

A PATH is a collection of an arbitrary number of POINTs that are connected. A PATH can specify either a closed path or an open path. In a closed path, the beginning and ending points are considered to be connected, and in an open path, the first and last points are not connected. PostgreSQL provides two functions to force a PATH to be either open or closed: POPEN() and PCLOSE(). You can also specify whether a PATH is open or closed using special literal syntax (described later).

A POLYGON is similar to a closed PATH. The difference between the two types is in the supporting functions.

A center POINT and a (DOUBLE PRECISION) floating-point radius represent a CIRCLE. Table 2.18 summarizes the geometric data types.

Table 2.18 **Geometric Data Types**

Type	Meaning	Defined By
POINT	2D point on a plane	x- and y-coordinates
LSEG	Line segment	Two points
BOX	Rectangle	Two points
PATH	Open or closed path	n points
POLYGON	Polygon	n points
CIRCLE	Circle	Center point and radius

Syntax for Literal Values

When you enter a value for geometric data type, keep in mind that you are working with a list of two-dimensional points (except in the case of a CIRCLE, where you are working with a POINT and a radius).

A single POINT can be entered in either of the following two forms:

```
'( x, y )'
' x, y '
```

The LSEG and BOX types are constructed from a pair of POINTs. You can enter a pair of POINTs in any of the following formats:

```
'(( x1, y1 ), ( x2, y2 ))'
'( x1, y1 ), ( x2, y2 )'
'x1, y1, x2, y2'
```

The PATH and POLYGON types are constructed from a list of one or more POINTs. Any of the following forms is acceptable for a PATH or POLYGON literal:

```
'(( x1, y1 ), ..., ( xn, yn ))'
'( x1, y1 ), ..., ( xn, yn )'
'( x1, y1, ..., xn, yn )'
'x1, y1, ..., xn, yn'
```

You can also use the syntax `'[( x1, y1 ), ..., ( xn, yn )]'` to enter a PATH literal. A PATH entered in this form is considered to be an open PATH.

A CIRCLE is described by a central point and a floating point radius. You can enter a CIRCLE in any of the following forms:

```
'< ( x, y ), r >'
'(( x, y ), r )'
'( x, y ), r'
'x, y, r'
```

Notice that the surrounding single quotes are required around all geometric literals—in other words, geometric literals are entered as string literals. If you want to create a geometric value from individual components, you will have to use a geometric conversion function. For example, if you want to create a POINT value from the results of some computation, you would use:

```
POINT( 4, 3*height )
```

The POINT(DOUBLE PRECISION x, DOUBLE PRECISION y) function creates a POINT value from two DOUBLE PRECISION values. There are similar functions that you can use to create any geometric type starting from individual components. Table 2.19 lists the conversion functions for geometric types.

Table 2.19 **Type Conversion Operators for the Geometric Data Types**

Result Type	Meaning
POINT	POINT(DOUBLE PRECISION x, DOUBLE PRECISION y)
LSEG	LSEG(POINT p1, POINT p2)
BOX	BOX(POINT p1, POINT p2)
PATH	PATH(POLYGON poly)
POLYGON	POLYGON(PATH path)
	POLYGON(BOX b) yields a 12-point polygon
	POLYGON(CIRCLE c) yields a 12-point polygon
	POLYGON(INTEGER n, CIRCLE c) yields an *n* point polygon
CIRCLE	CIRCLE(BOX b)
	CIRCLE(POINT radius, DOUBLE PRECISION point)

Sizes and Valid Values

Table 2.20 lists the size of each geometric data type.

Table 2.20 **Geographic Data Type Storage Requirements**

Type	Size (in bytes)
POINT	16 (2 * sizeof DOUBLE PRECISION)
LSEG	32 (2 * sizeof POINT)
BOX	32 (2 * sizeof POINT)
PATH	4+(32*number of points)[4]
POLYGON	4+(32*number of points)[4]
CIRCLE	24 (sizeof POINT + sizeof DOUBLE PRECISION)

Supported Operators

PostgreSQL features a large collection of operators that work with the geometric data types. I've divided the geometric operators into two broad categories (transformation and proximity) to make it a little easier to talk about them.

Using the transformation operators, you can translate, rotate, and scale geometric objects. The + and - operators translate a geometric object to a new location. Consider Figure 2.1, which shows a BOX defined as BOX(POINT(3,5), POINT(1,2)).

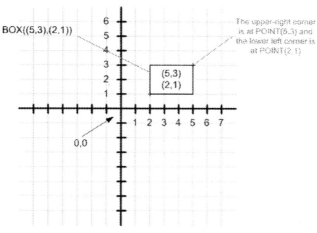

Figure 2.1 BOX(POINT(3,5), POINT(1,2)).

If you use the + operator to add the POINT(2,1) to this BOX, you end up with the object shown in Figure 2.2.

[4] The size of a PATH or POLYGON is equal to 4 + (size of LSEG * number of segments).

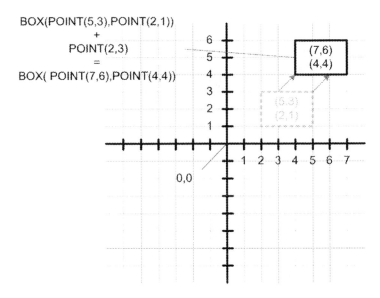

BOX(POINT(5,3),POINT(2,1))
+
POINT(2,3)
=
BOX(POINT(7,6),POINT(4,4))

(7,6)
(4,4)

(5,3)
(2,1)

0,0

Figure 2.2   Geometric translation.

You can see that the x-coordinate of the POINT is added to each of the x-coordinates in the BOX, and the y-coordinate of the POINT is added to the y-coordinates in the BOX. The - operator works in a similar fashion: the x-coordinate of the POINT is subtracted from the x-coordinates of the BOX, and the y-coordinate of the POINT is subtracted from each y-coordinate in the BOX.

Using the + and - operators, you can move a POINT, BOX, PATH, or CIRCLE to a new location. In each case, the x-coordinate in the second operand (a POINT), is added or subtracted from each x-coordinate in the first operand, and the y-coordinate in the second operand is added or subtracted from each y-coordinate in the first operand.

The multiplication and division operators (* and /) are used to scale and rotate. The multiplication and division operators treat the operands as points in the complex plane. Let's look at some examples.

Figure 2.3 shows the result of multiplying BOX(POINT(3,2),POINT(1,1)) by POINT(2,0).

You can see that each coordinate in the original box is multiplied by the x-coordinate of the point, resulting in BOX(POINT(6,4),POINT(2,2)). If you had multiplied the box by POINT(0.5,0), you would have ended up with BOX(POINT(1.5,1),POINT(0.5,0.5)). So the effect of multiplying an object by POINT(x,0) is that each coordinate in the object moves away from the origin by a factor x. If x is negative, the coordinates move to the other side of the origin, as shown in Figure 2.4.

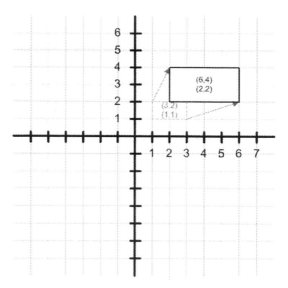

Figure 2.3   Point multiplication-scaling by a positive value.

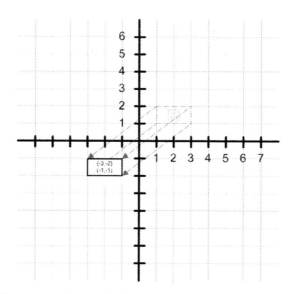

Figure 2.4   Point multiplication-scaling by a negative value.

The *x*-coordinate controls scaling. The *y*-coordinate controls rotation. When you multiply any given geometric object by POINT(0,y), each point in the object is rotated around the origin. When *y* is equal to 1, each point is rotated counterclockwise by 90° about the origin. When *y* is equal to −1, each point is rotated −90° about the origin (or 270°). When you rotate a point without scaling, the length of the line segment drawn between the point and origin remains constant, as shown in Figure 2.5.

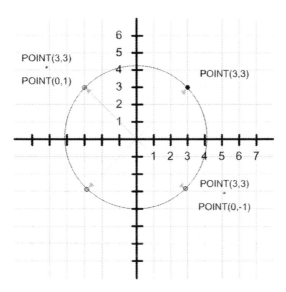

Figure 2.5   Point multiplication-rotation.

You can combine rotation and scaling into the same operation by specifying non-zero values for both the *x*- and *y*-coordinates. For more information on using complex numbers to represent geometric points, see http://www.clarku.edu/~djoyce/complex. Table 2.21 shows the valid combinations for geometric types and geometric operators.

Table 2.21 **Transformation Operators for the Geometric Types**

Data Types	Valid Operators (θ)
POINT θ POINT	* + - /
BOX θ POINT	* + - /
PATH θ POINT	* + - /
CIRCLE θ POINT	* + - /

The proximity operators allow you to determine the spatial relationships between two geometric objects.

First, let's look at the three containment operators. The ~ operator evaluates to TRUE if the left operand contains the right operand. The @ operator evaluates to TRUE if the left operand is contained within the right operand. The ~= returns TRUE if the left operand is the same as the right operand—two geographic objects are considered identical if the points that define the objects are identical (two circles are considered identical if the radii and center points are the same).

The next two operators are used to determine the distance between two geometric objects.

The ## operator returns the closest point between two objects. You can use the ## operator with the following operand types shown in Table 2.22.

Table 2.22 **Closest-Point Operators**

Operator	Description
LSEG$_a$ ## BOX$_b$	Returns the point in BOX$_b$ that is closest to LSEG$_a$
LSEG$_a$ ## LSEG$_b$	Returns the point in LSEG$_b$ that is closest to LSEG$_a$
POINT$_a$ ## BOX$_b$	Returns the point in BOX$_b$ that is closest to POINT$_a$
POINT$_a$ ## LSEG$_b$	Returns the point in LSEG$_b$ that is closest to POINT$_a$

The distance (<->) operator returns (as a DOUBLE PRECISION number) the distance between two geometric objects. You can use the distance operator with the operand types in Table 2.23.

Table 2.23 **Distance Operators**

Operator	Description (or Formula)
BOX$_a$ <-> BOX$_b$	(@@ BOX$_a$) <-> (@@ BOX$_b$)
CIRCLE$_a$ <-> CIRCLE$_b$	(@@ CIRCLE$_a$) <-> (@@ CIRCLE$_b$)
	-
	(radius$_a$ + radius$_b$)
CIRCLE$_a$ <-> POLYGON$_b$	-0 if any point in POLYGON$_b$ is inside CIRCLE$_a$ otherwise, distance between center of CIRCLE$_a$ and closest point in POLYGON$_b$
LSEG$_a$ <-> BOX$_b$	(LSEG ## BOX) <-> (LSEG ## (LSEG ## BOX))
LSEG$_a$ <-> LSEG$_b$	Distance between closest points (0 if LSEG$_a$ intersects LSEG$_b$)
PATH$_a$ <-> PATH$_b$	Distance between closest points
POINT$_a$ <-> BOX$_b$	POINT$_a$ <-> (POINT$_a$ ## BOX$_b$)
POINT$_a$ <-> CIRCLE$_b$	POINT$_a$ <-> ((@@ CIRCLE$_b$) - CIRCLE$_b$ radius)
POINT$_a$ <-> LSEG$_b$	POINT$_a$ <-> (POINT$_a$ ## LSEG$_b$)
POINT$_a$ <-> PATH$_b$	Distance between POINT$_a$ and closest points
POINT$_a$ <-> POINT$_b$	-SQRT((POINT$_a$.x - POINT$_b$.x)^2 + (POINT$_a$.y - POINT$_b$.y)^2)

Next, you can determine the spatial relationships between two objects using the left-of (<<), right-of(>>), below (<^), and above (>^) operators.

There are three overlap operators. && evaluates to TRUE if the left operand overlaps the right operand. The &> operator evaluates to TRUE if the leftmost point in the first operand is left of the rightmost point in the second operand. The &< evaluates to TRUE if the rightmost point in the first operand is right of the leftmost point in the second operand.

The intersection operator (#) returns the intersecting points of two objects. You can find the intersection of two BOXes, or the intersection of two LSEGs. The intersection of two BOXes evaluates to a BOX. The intersection of two LSEGs evaluates to a single POINT.

Finally, the θ# operator evaluates to TRUE if the first operand intersects with or overlaps the second operand.

The final set of geometric operators determines the relationship between a line segment and an axis, or the relationship between two line segments.

The θ- operator evaluates to TRUE if the given line segment is horizontal (that is, parallel to the x-axis). The θ| operator evaluates to TRUE if the given line segment is vertical (that is, parallel to the y-axis). When you use the θ- and θ| operators with a line segment, they function as prefix unary operators. You can also use the θ- and θ| operators as infix binary operators (meaning that the operator appears between two values), in which case they operate as if you specified two points on a line segment.

The θ-| operator evaluates to TRUE if the two operands are perpendicular. The θ|| operator evaluates to TRUE if the two operands are parallel. The perpendicular and parallel operators can be used only with values of type LSEG.

The final geometric operator (@@) returns the center point of an LSEG, PATH, BOX, POLYGON, or CIRCLE.

Tables 2.24 summarizes the proximity operators.

Table 2.24 **Proximity Operators for the Geometric Types**

Data Types	Valid Operators (θ)
POINT θ POINT	<-> << <^ >> >^ θ- θ| @
POINT θ LSEG	## <-> @
POINT θ BOX	## <-> @
POINT θ PATH	<-> @
POINT θ POLYGON	@
POINT θ CIRCLE	<-> @
LSEG θ LSEG	# ## < <-> <= <> = > >= θ# θ-| θ||
LSEG θ BOX	## <-> θ# @
BOX θ POINT	* + - /
BOX θ BOX	# && &< &> < <-> << <= <^ = > >= >> >^ θ# @ ~ ~=
PATH θ POINT	* + - / ~
PATH θ PATH	+ < <-> <= = > >= θ#
POLYGON θ POINT	~
POLYGON θ POLYGON	&& &< &> <-> >> << @ ~ ~=
CIRCLE θ POINT	* + - / ~
CIRCLE θ POLYGON	<->
CIRCLE θ CIRCLE	&& &< &> > <-> << <= <> <^ = > >= >> >^ @ ~ ~=

Table 2.25 summarizes the names of the proximity operators for geometric types.

Table 2.25 **Geometric Proximity Operator Names**

Data Types	Valid Operators (θ)
#	Intersection or point count(for polygons)
##	Point of closest proximity
<->	Distance between
<<	Left of θ

Table 2.25   **Continued**

>>	Right of θ
<^	Below θ
>^	Above θ
&&	Overlaps
&>	Overlaps to left
&<	Overlaps to right
θ#	Intersects or overlaps
@	Contained in
~	Contains
~=	Same as
θ-	Horizontal
θ|	Vertical
θ-|	Perpendicular
θ||	Parallel
@@	Center

Object IDs (OID)

An OID is a 32-bit, positive whole number. Every row[5] in a PostgreSQL database contains a unique identifier[6]—the object ID (or OID). Normally, the OID column is hidden. You can see the OID for a row by including the OID column in the target list of a SELECT statement:

```
movies=# SELECT OID, * FROM customers;
```

```
  oid  | customer_id |    customer_name     |  phone   | birth_date | balance
-------+-------------+----------------------+----------+------------+---------
 33876 |           3 | Panky, Henry         | 555-1221 | 1968-01-21 |    0.00
 33877 |           1 | Jones, Henry         | 555-1212 | 1970-10-10 |    0.00
 33878 |           4 | Wonderland, Alice N. | 555-1122 | 1969-03-05 |    3.00
 33879 |           2 | Rubin, William       | 555-2211 | 1972-07-10 |   15.00
 33889 |           5 | Funkmaster, Freddy   | 555-FUNK |            |    0.00
 33890 |           7 | Gull, Jonathon LC    | 555-1111 | 1984-02-05 |    0.00
 33891 |           8 | Grumby, Jonas        | 555-2222 | 1984-02-21 |    0.00
```

You can create a column of type OID if you want to explicitly refer to another object (usually a row in another table). Think back to the rentals table that you developed in Chapter 1. Each row in the rentals table contains a tape_id, a customer_id, and a rental date. The rentals table currently looks like this:

---

[5] By default, all tables are created such that every row contains an OID. You can omit the object IDs using the WITHOUT OIDS clause of the CREATE TABLE command.

[6] The PostgreSQL documentation warns that object IDs are currently unique within a database cluster; but in a future release, an OID may be unique only within a single table.

```
movies=# \d rentals
            Table "public.rentals"
  Attribute   |     Type     |  Modifier
--------------+--------------+-----------
 tape_id      | character(8) | not null
 rental_date  | date         | not null
 customer_id  | integer      | not null

movies=# SELECT * FROM rentals;
 tape_id  | rental_date | customer_id
----------+-------------+-------------
 AB-12345 | 2001-11-25  |           1
 AB-67472 | 2001-11-25  |           3
 OW-41221 | 2001-11-25  |           1
 MC-68873 | 2001-11-20  |           3
 KJ-03335 | 2001-11-26  |           8
(5 rows)
```

Each value in the tape_id column refers to a row in the tapes table. Each value in the customer_id column refers to a row in the customers table. Rather than storing the tape_id and customer_id in the rentals table, you could store OIDs for the corresponding rows. The following CREATE TABLE ... AS command creates a new table, rentals2, that is equivalent to the original rentals table:

```
movies=# CREATE TABLE rentals2 AS
movies-#     SELECT
movies-#         t.oid AS tape_oid, c.oid AS customer_oid, r.rental_date
movies-#     FROM
movies-#         tapes t, customers c, rentals r
movies-#     WHERE
movies-#         t.tape_id = r.tape_id
movies-#             AND
movies-#         c.id = r.customer_id;
```

This statement (conceptually) works as follows. First, you retrieve a row from the rentals table. Next, you use the rentals.customer_id column to retrieve the matching customers row and the rentals.tape_id column to retrieve the matching tapes row. Finally, you store the OID of the customers row and the OID of the tapes row (and the rental_date) in a new rentals2 row.

Now, when you SELECT from the rentals2 table, you will see the object IDs for the customers row and the tapes row:

```
movies=# SELECT * FROM rentals2;
 tape_oid | customer_oid | rental_date
----------+--------------+-------------
    38337 |        38333 | 2001-11-25
    38338 |        38335 | 2001-11-25
    38394 |        38393 | 2001-11-26
    38339 |        38335 | 2001-11-20
    38340 |        38333 | 2001-11-25
```

You can re-create the data in the original table by joining the corresponding `customers` and `tapes` records, based on their respective OIDs:

```
movies=# SELECT t.tape_id, r.rental_date, c.id
movies-#   FROM
movies-#     tapes t, rentals2 r, customers c
movies-#   WHERE
movies-#     t.oid = r.tape_oid AND
movies-#     c.oid = r.customer_oid
movies-#   ORDER BY t.tape_id;

tape_id  | rental_date  | id
---------+--------------+----
 AB-12345 | 2001-11-25  |  1
 AB-67472 | 2001-11-25  |  3
 KJ-03335 | 2001-11-26  |  8
 MC-68873 | 2001-11-20  |  3
 OW-41221 | 2001-11-25  |  1
(5 rows)
```

Here are a couple of warnings about using OIDs in your own tables.

The first concern has to do with backups. The standard tool for performing a backup of a PostgreSQL database is pg_dump. By default, pg_dump will *not* archive OIDs. This means that if you back up a table that contains an OID column (referring to another object) and then restore that table from the archive, the relationships between objects will be lost, unless you remembered to tell pg_dump to archive OIDs. This happens because when you restore a row from the archive, it might be assigned a *different* OID.

The second thing you should consider when using OIDs is that they offer no real performance advantages. If you are coming from an Oracle or Sybase environment, you might be thinking that an OID sounds an awful lot like a ROWID. It's true that an OID and a ROWID provide a unique identifier for a row, but that is where the similarity ends. In an Oracle environment, you can use a ROWID as the fastest possible way to get to a specific row. A ROWID encodes the location (on disk) of the row that it belongs to—when you retrieve a row by ROWID, you can bypass any index[7] searches and go straight to the data. An OID is just a 32-bit number—you can create an index on the OID column, but you could also create an index on any other (unique) column to achieve the same results. In fact, the only time that it might make sense to use an OID to identify a row is when the primary key[7] for a table is very long.

Finally, I should point out that OIDs can wrap. In an active database cluster, it's certainly possible that 4 billion objects can be created. That doesn't mean that all 4 billion objects have to exist at the same time, just that 4 billion OIDs have been created since the cluster was created. When the OID generator wraps, you end up with duplicate values. This may sound a little far-fetched, but it does happen and it is not easy to recover from. There really is no good reason to use an OID as a primary key—use SERIAL (or BIGSERIAL) instead.

---

[7] Don't be too concerned if you aren't familiar with the concept of indexes or primary keys. I'll cover each of those topics a bit later.

Syntax for Literal Values

The format in which you enter literal OID values is the same that you would use for unsigned INTEGER values. An OID literal is simply a sequence of decimal digits.

Size and Valid Values

As I mentioned earlier, an OID is an unsigned 32-bit (4-byte) integer. An OID column can hold values between 0 and 4294967295. The value 0 represents an invalid OID.

Supported Operators

You can compare two OID values, and you can compare an OID value against an INTEGER value. Table 2.26 shows which operators you can use with the OID data type.

Table 2.26   OID **Operators**

Data Types	Valid Operators
OID θ OID	< <= <> = >= >
OID θ INT4	< <= <> = >= >
INT4 θ OID	< <= <> = >= >

BLOBs

Most database systems provide a data type that can store raw data, and PostgreSQL is no exception. I use the term *raw data* to mean that the database doesn't understand the structure or meaning of a value. In contrast, PostgreSQL *does* understand the structure and meaning of other data types. For example, when you define an INTEGER column, PostgreSQL knows that the bytes of data that you place into that column are supposed to represent an integer value. PostgreSQL knows what an integer is—it can add integers, multiply them, convert them to and from string form, and so on. Raw data, on the other hand, is just a collection of bits—PostgreSQL can't infer any meaning in the data.

PostgreSQL offers the type BYTEA for storing raw data. A BYTEA column can theoretically hold values of any length, but it appears that the maximum length is 1GB.

The size of a BYTEA value is 4 bytes plus the actual number of bytes in the value.

Syntax for Literal Values

Entering a BYTEA value can be a little tricky. A BYTEA literal is entered as a string literal: It is just a string of characters enclosed within single quotes. Given that, how do you enter a BYTEA value that includes a single quote? If you look back to the discussion of string literal values (earlier in this chapter), you'll see that you can include *special characters* in a string value by escaping them. In particular, a single quote can by escaped in one of three ways:

- Double up the single quotes ('This is a single quote''')
- Precede the single quote with a backslash ('This is a single quote \'')
- Include the octal value of the character instead ('This is a single quote \047')

There are two other characters that you must escape when entering BYTEA literals. A byte whose value is zero (not the character 0, but the null byte) must be escaped, and the backslash character must be escaped. You can escape any character using the "\\ddd" form (where ddd is an octal number). You can escape any printable character using the "\\c" form. So, if you want to store a BYTEA value that includes a zero byte, you could enter it like this:

```
'This is a zero byte \\000'
```

If you want to store a BYTEA value that includes a backslash, you can enter it in either of the following forms:

```
'This is a backslash \\\\'
'This is also a backslash \\134'
```

If you compare these rules to the rules for quoting string literals, you'll notice that BYTEA literals require twice as many backslash characters. This is a quirk of the design of the PostgreSQL parser. BYTEA literals are processed by two different parsers. The main PostgreSQL parser sees a BYTEA literal as a string literal (gobbling up the first set of back-slash characters). Then, the BYTEA parser processes the result, gobbling up the second set of backslash characters.

So, if you have a BYTEA value such as This is a backslash \, you quote it as 'This is a backslash \\\\'. After the string parser processes this string, it has been turned into 'This is a backslash \\'. The BYTEA parser finally transforms this into This is a backslash \.

Supported Operators

PostgreSQL offers a single BYTEA operator: concatenation. You can append one BYTEA value to another BYTEA value using the concatenation (||) operator.

Note that you can't compare two BYTEA values, even for equality/inequality. You can, of course, convert a BYTEA value into another value using the CAST() operator, and that opens up other operators.

Large-Objects

The BYTEA data type is currently limited to storing values no larger than 1GB. If you need to store values larger than will fit into a BYTEA column, you can use large-objects. A *large-object* is a value stored *outside* of a table. For example, if you want to store a photograph with each row in your tapes table, you would add an OID column to hold a *reference* to the corresponding large-object:

```
movies=# ALTER TABLE tapes ADD COLUMN photo_id OID;
ALTER
```

Each value in the photo_id column refers to an entry in the pg_largeobject system table. PostgreSQL provides a function that will load an external file (such as a JPEG file) into the pg_largeobject table:

```
movies=# INSERT INTO tapes VALUES
movies-# (
movies(#   'AA-55892',
movies(#   'Casablanca',
movies(#   '102 min',
movies(#   lo_import('/tmp/casablanca.jpg' )
movies(# );
```

The lo_import() function loads the named file into pg_largeobject and returns an OID value that refers to the large-object. Now when you SELECT this row, you see the OID, not the actual bits that make up the photo:

```
movies=# SELECT * FROM tapes WHERE tape_id = 'AA-55892';


 tape_id  |   title    | duration | photo_id
----------+------------+----------+----------
 AA-55892 | Casablanca | 01:42:00 |   510699
```

If you want to write the photo back into a file, you can use the lo_export() function:

```
movies=# SELECT lo_export( 510699, '/tmp/Casablanca.jpg' );
 lo_export
-----------
         1
(1 row)
```

To see all large-objects in the current database, use psql's \lo_list metacommand:

```
movies=# \lo_list
    Large objects
   ID   | Description
--------+-------------
 510699 |
(1 row)
```

You can remove large-objects from your database using the lo_unlink() function:

```
movies=# SELECT lo_unlink( 510699 );
 lo_unlink
-----------
         1
(1 row)

movies=# \lo_list
   Large objects
```

```
ID | Description
----+-------------
(0 rows)
```

How do you get to the actual bits behind the reference OID? You can't—at least not with psql. Large-object support must be built into the client application that you are using. psql is a text-oriented tool and has no way to display a photograph, so the best that you can do is to look at the raw data in the pg_largeobject table. A few client applications, such as the Conjectrix Workstation, do support large-objects and can interpret the raw data properly, in most cases.

Network Address Data Types

PostgreSQL supports three data types that are designed to hold network addresses, both IP[8] (logical) and MAC[9] (physical) addresses. I don't think there are many applications that require the storage of an IP or MAC address, so I won't spend too much time describing them. The *PostgreSQL User's Guide* contains all the details that you might need to know regarding network data types.

MACADDR

The MACADDR type is designed to hold a MAC address. A MAC address is a hardware address, usually the address of an ethernet interface.

CIDR

The CIDR data type is designed to hold an IP network address. A CIDR value contains an IP network address and an optional netmask (the netmask determines the number of meaningful bits in the network address).

INET

An INET value can hold the IP address of a network or of a network host. An INET value contains a network address and an optional netmask. If the netmask is omitted, it is assumed that the address identifies a single host (in other words, there is no discernible network component in the address).

Note that an INET value can represent a network or a host, but a CIDR is designed to represent the address of a network.

Syntax for Literal Values

The syntax required for literal network values is shown in Table 2.27.

---

[8] IP stands for Internet Protocol, the substrate of the Internet.
[9] The acronym MAC stands for one or more of the following: Machine Address Code, Media Access Control, or Macaroni And Cheese.

Table 2.27   **Literal Syntax for Network Types**

Type	Syntax	Examples
INET	a.b.c.d[/e]	192.168.0.1_
		192.168.150.0/26_
		130.155.16.1/20
CIDR	a[.b[.c[.d]]][/e]	192.168.0.0/16_
		192.168/16
MACADDR	xxxxxx:xxxxxx	0004E2:3695C0
	xxxxxx-xxxxxx	0004E2-3695C0
	xxxx.xxxx.xxxx	0004.E236.95C0
	xx-xx-xx-xx-xx-xx	00-04-E2-36-95-C0
	xx:xx:xx:xx:xx:xx	00:04:E2:36:95:C0

Starting with version 7.4, you can also store IPv6 (colon-separated) addresses in an INET or CIDR value.

An INET or CIDR value consumes either 12 bytes or 24 bytes of storage (depending on the number of bits in the address). A MACADDR value consumes 6 bytes of storage.

Supported Operators

PostgreSQL provides comparison operators that you can use to compare two INET values, two CIDR values, or two MACADDR values. The comparison operators work by first checking the common bits in the network components of the two addresses; then, if those are equal, the address with the greatest number of netmask bits is considered the largest value. If the number of bits in the netmask is equal (and the network components of the addresses are equal), then the entire address is compared. The net effect (pun intended) is that 192.168.0.22/24 is considered greater than 192.168.0.22/20.

When you are working with two INET (or CIDR) values, you can also check for containership. Table 2.28 describes the network address operators.

Table 2.28   **Network Address Operators**

Operator	Meaning
$INET_1 < INET_2$ $CIDR_1 < CIDR_2$ $MACADDR_1 < MACADDR_2$	True if $operand_1$ is less than $operand_2$
$INET_1 <= INET_2$ $CIDR_1 <= CIDR_2$ $MACADDR_1 <= MACADDR_2$	True if $operand_1$ is less than or equal to $operand_2$
$INET_1 <> INET_2$ $CIDR_1 <> CIDR_2$ $MACADDR_1 <> MACADDR_2$	True if $operand_1$ is not equal to $operand_2$
$INET_1 = INET_2$ $CIDR_1 = CIDR_2$ $MACADDR_1 = MACADDR_2$	True if $operand_1$ is equal to $operand_2$
$INET_1 >= INET_2$ $CIDR_1 >= CIDR_2$ $MACADDR_1 >= MACADDR_2$	True if $operand_1$ is greater than or equal to $operand_2$

Table 2.28 **Continued**

$INET_1$ > $INET_2$ $CIDR_1$ > $CIDR_2$ $MACADDR_1$ > $MACADDR_2$	True if $operand_1$ is greater than $operand_2$
$INET_1$ << $INET_2$ $CIDR_1$ << $CIDR_2$	True if $operand_1$ is contained within $operand_2$
$INET_1$ <<= $INET_2$ $CIDR_1$ <<= $CIDR_2$	True if $operand_1$ is contained within $operand_2$ or if $operand_1$ is equal to $operand_2$
$INET_1$ >> $INET_2$ $CIDR_1$ >> $CIDR_2$	True if $operand_1$ contains $operand_2$
$INET_1$ >>= $INET_2$ $CIDR_1$ >>= $CIDR_2$	True if $operand_1$ contains $operand_2$ or if $operand_1$ is equal to $operand_2$

Sequences

One problem that you will most likely encounter in your database life is the need to generate unique identifiers. We've already seen one example of this in the *customers* table—the *customer_id* column is nothing more than a unique identifier. Sometimes, an entity that you want to store in your database will have a naturally unique identifier. For example, if you are designing a database to track employee information (in the United States), a Social Security number might make a good identifier. Of course, if you employ people who are not U.S. citizens, the Social Security number scheme will fail. If you are tracking information about automobiles, you might be tempted to use the license plate number as a unique identifier. That would work fine until you needed to track autos in more than one state. The VIN (or Vehicle Identification Number) is a naturally unique identifier.

Quite often, you will need to store information about an entity that has no naturally unique ID. In those cases, you are likely to simply assign a unique number to each entity. After you have decided to create a uniquifier[10], the next problem is coming up with a sequence of unique numbers.

PostgreSQL offers help in the form of a SEQUENCE. A SEQUENCE is an object that automatically generates sequence numbers. You can create as many SEQUENCE objects as you like: Each SEQUENCE has a unique name.

Let's create a new SEQUENCE that you can use to generate unique identifiers for rows in your customers table. You already have a few customers, so start the sequence numbers at 10:

```
movies=# CREATE SEQUENCE customer_id_seq START 10;
CREATE
```

The "\ds" command (in psql) shows you a list of the SEQUENCE objects in your database:

```
movies=# \ds
          List of relations
```

---

[10] I'm not sure that "uniquifier" is a real word, but I've used it for quite some time and it sure is a lot easier to say than "disambiguator."

```
      Name      |   Type    | Owner
----------------+-----------+------
 customer_id_seq | sequence | korry
(1 row)
```

Now, let's try using this SEQUENCE. PostgreSQL provides a number of functions that you can call to make use of a SEQUENCE. The one that you are most interested in at the moment is the nextval() function. When you call the nextval() function, you provide (in the form of a string) the name of the SEQUENCE as the only argument.

For example, when you INSERT a new row in the customers table, you want PostgreSQL to automatically assign a unique customer_id:

```
movies=# INSERT INTO
movies-#    customers( customer_id, customer_name )
movies-# VALUES
movies-#  (
movies-#    nextval( 'customer_id_seq' ), 'John Gomez'
movies-#  );

movies=# SELECT * FROM customers WHERE customer_name = 'John Gomez';
 customer_id | customer_name | phone | birth_date | balance
-------------+---------------+-------+------------+--------
          10 | John Gomez    |       |            |
(1 row)
```

You can see that the SEQUENCE (customer_id_seq) generated a new customer_id, starting with the value that you requested. You can use the currval() function to find the value that was just generated by your server process:

```
movies=# SELECT currval( 'customer_id_seq' );
 currval
---------
      10
```

The complete syntax for the CREATE SEQUENCE command is

```
CREATE SEQUENCE name
    [ INCREMENT increment ]
    [ MINVALUE min ]
    [ MAXVALUE max ]
    [ START start_value ]
    [ CACHE cache_count ]
    [ CYCLE ]
```

Notice that the only required item is the name.

The INCREMENT attribute determines the amount added to generate a new sequence number. This value can be positive or negative, but not zero. Positive values cause the sequence numbers to increase in value as they are generated (that is, 0, 1, 2, and so on).

Negative values cause the sequence numbers to decrease in value (that is, 3, 2, 1, 0, and so on).

The MINVALUE and MAXVALUE attributes control the minimum and maximum values (respectively) for the SEQUENCE.

What happens when a SEQUENCE has reached the end of its valid range? You get to decide: If you include the CYCLE attribute, the SEQUENCE will wrap around. For example, if you create a cyclical SEQUENCE with MINVALUE 0 and MAXVALUE 3, you will retrieve the following sequence numbers: 0, 1, 2, 3, 0, 1, 2, 3, ... If you don't include the CYCLE attribute, you will see: 0, 1, 2, 3, error: reached MAXVALUE.

The START attribute determines the first sequence number generated by a SEQUENCE. The value for the START attribute must be within the MINVALUE and MAXVALUE range.

The default values for most of the SEQUENCE attributes depend on whether the INCREMENT is positive or negative. The default value for the INCREMENT attribute is 1. If you specify a negative INCREMENT, the MINVALUE defaults to -2147483647, and MAXVALUE defaults to -1. If you specify a positive INCREMENT, MINVALUE defaults to 1, and MAXVALUE defaults to 2147483647. The default value for the START attribute is also dependent on the sign of the INCREMENT. A positive INCREMENT defaults the START value to the MINVALUE attribute. A negative INCREMENT defaults the START value to the MAXVALUE attribute.

Remember, these are the defaults—you can choose any meaningful combination of values that you like (within the valid range of a BIGINT).

The default SEQUENCE attributes are summarized in Table 2.29.

Table 2.29 **Sequence Attributes**

Attribute Name	Default Value
INCREMENT	1
MINVALUE	-INCREMENT > 0 ? 1_INCREMENT < 0 ? -2147483647
MAXVALUE	INCREMENT > 0 ? 2147483647
	INCREMENT < 0 ? -1
START	INCREMENT > 0 ? MINVALUE
	INCREMENT < 0 ? MAXVALUE
CACHE	1
CYCLE	False

The CACHE attribute is a performance-tuning parameter; it determines how many sequence numbers are generated and held in memory. In most cases, you can simply use the default value (1). If you suspect that sequence number generation is a bottleneck in your application, you might consider increasing the CACHE attribute, but be sure to read the warning in the PostgreSQL documentation (see the CREATE SEQUENCE section).

You can view the attributes of a SEQUENCE by treating it as a table and selecting from it[11]:

[11] There are four other columns in a SEQUENCE, but they hold bookkeeping information required to properly maintain the SEQUENCE.

```
movies=# SELECT
movies-#    increment_by, max_value, min_value, cache_value, is_cycled
movies-# FROM
movies-#    customer_id_seq;

 increment_by | max_value | min_value | cache_value | is_cycled
--------------+-----------+-----------+-------------+-----------
            1 |         3 |         0 |           1 | f
```

PostgreSQL provides three functions that work with SEQUENCES. I described the nextval() and currval() functions earlier; nextval() generates (and returns) a new value from a SEQUENCE, and currval() retrieves the most recently generated value. You can reset a SEQUENCE to any value between MINVALUE and MAXVALUE by calling the setval() function. For example:

```
movies=# SELECT nextval( 'customer_id_seq' );
ERROR:  customer_id_seq.nextval: reached MAXVALUE (3)

movies-# SELECT setval( 'customer_id_seq', 0 );
 setval
--------
      0
(1 row)

movies=# SELECT nextval( 'customer_id_seq' );
 nextval
---------
       1
```

Now that you know how SEQUENCEs work in PostgreSQL, let's revisit the SERIAL data type. I mentioned earlier in this chapter that a SERIAL is really implemented as a SEQUENCE (see the "SERIAL, BIGSERIAL, and SEQUENCES" sidebar). Remember that a SERIAL provides an automatically increasing (or decreasing) unique identifier. That sounds just like a SEQUENCE, so what's the difference? A SEQUENCE is a standalone object, whereas SERIAL is a data type that you can assign to a column.

Let's create a new table that contains a SERIAL column:

```
movies=# CREATE TABLE serial_test ( pkey SERIAL, payload INTEGER );

NOTICE:  CREATE TABLE will create implicit
         sequence 'serial_test_pkey_seq' for
         SERIAL column 'serial_test.pkey'
NOTICE:  CREATE TABLE/UNIQUE will create implicit
         index 'serial_test_pkey_key' for table 'serial_test'
CREATE
```

The CREATE TABLE command is normally silent. When you create a table with a SERIAL column, PostgreSQL does a little extra work on your behalf. First, PostgreSQL creates a SEQUENCE for you. The name of the SEQUENCE is based on the name of the table and the name of the column. In this case, the SEQUENCE is named serial_test_pkey_seq. Next,

PostgreSQL creates a unique index. We haven't really talked about indexes yet: for now, know that a unique index on the pkey column ensures that you have no duplicate values in that column. PostgreSQL performs one more nicety for you when you create a SERIAL column. The \d command (in psql) shows you this last step:

```
movies=# \d serial_test
                          Table "public.serial_test"
  Attribute |  Type   |                   Modifier
-----------+---------+-------------------------------------------------------
 pkey       | integer | not null default nextval('serial_test_pkey_seq')
 payload    | integer |
Index: serial_test_pkey_key
```

PostgreSQL has created a default value for the pkey column. A column's default value is used whenever you insert a row but omit a value for that column. For example, if you execute the command INSERT INTO serial_test(payload) VALUES(24307);, you have not provided an explicit value for the pkey column. In this case, PostgreSQL evaluates the default value for pkey and inserts the resulting value. Because the default value for pkey is a call to the nextval() function, each new row is assigned a new (unique) sequence number.

Arrays

One of the unique features of PostgreSQL is the fact that you can define a column to be an array. Most commercial database systems require that a single column within a given row can hold no more than one value. With PostgreSQL, you aren't bound by that rule—you can create columns that store multiple values (of the same data type).

The customers table defined in Chapter 1 contained a single balance column. What change would you have to make to the database if you wanted to store a month-by-month balance for each customer, going back at most 12 months? One alternative would be to create a separate table to store monthly balances. The primary key of the cust_balance might be composed of the customer_id and the month number (either 0–11 or 1–12, whichever you found more convenient)[12]. This would certainly work, but in PostgreSQL, it's not the only choice.

You know that there are never more than 12 months in a year and that there are never fewer than 12 months in a year. Parent/child relationships are perfect when the parent has a variable number of children, but they aren't always the most convenient choice when the number of child records is fixed.

Instead, you could store all 12 monthly balance values inside the customers table. Here is how you might create the customers table using an array to store the monthly balances:

---

[12] The relationship between the customers table and the cust_balance is called a parent/child relationship. In this case, the customers table is the parent and cust_balance is the child. The primary key of a child table is composed of the parent key plus a uniquifier (that is, a value, such as the month number, that provides a unique identifier within a group of related children).

```
CREATE TABLE customers (
        customer_id      INTEGER UNIQUE,
        customer_name    VARCHAR(50),
        phone            CHAR(8),
        birth_date       DATE,
        balance          DECIMAL(7,2),
        monthly_balances DECIMAL(7,2)[12]
);
```

Notice that I have added a new column named `monthly_balances`—this is an array of 12 DECIMAL values. I'll show you how to put values into an array in a moment.

You can define an array of *any* data type: the built-in types, user-defined types, even other arrays. When you create an array of arrays, you are actually creating a multidimensional array. For example, if we wanted to store month-by-month balances for the three previous years, I could have created the `monthly_balances` field as

```
monthly_balances DECIMAL(7,2)[3][12]
```

This would give you three arrays of 12-element arrays.

There is no limit to the number of members in an array. There is also no limit to the number of dimensions in a multidimensional array.

Now, let's talk about inserting and updating array values. When you want to insert a new row into the customers table, you provide values for each member in the monthly_balances array as follows:

```
INSERT INTO customers
(
customer_id, customer_name, phone, birth_date, balance, monthly_balances
)
VALUES
(
    8,
    'Wink Wankel',
    '555-1000',
    '1988-12-25',
    0.00,
    '{1,2,3,4,5,6,7,8,9,10,11,12}'
);
```

To INSERT values into an array, you enclose all the array elements in single quotes and braces ({}) and separate multiple elements with a comma. Starting with PostgreSQL version 7.4, you can use an alternate form to write an array value. To express the same array value in *constructor syntax* form, you would write:

```
ARRAY[1,2,3,4,5,6,7,8,9,10,11,12]
```

There are two advantages to the new array constructor syntax. First, the meaning is a bit more obvious when you're looking at a piece of unfamiliar SQL code. Second, if you write an array value expressed '{ *element_1*, *element_2*, ...}' form, you have to double up the quotes if the array contains string values. In array constructor form, you don't have to do that. The following array values are equivalent:

```
'{ ''Panky, Henry'', ''Rubin, William'', ''Grumby, Jonas'' }'
ARRAY[ 'Panky, Henry', 'Rubin, William', 'Grumby, Jonas' ]
```

Inserting values into a multidimensional array is treated as if you were inserting an array of arrays. For example, if you had a table defined as

```
CREATE TABLE arr
(
    pkey  serial,
    val   int[2][3]
);
```

you would INSERT a row as

```
INSERT INTO arr( val ) VALUES( '{ {1,2,3}, {4,5,6} }' );
```

Or, to write the same array value in constructor form:

```
INSERT INTO arr( val ) VALUES( ARRAY[ [1,2,3], [4,5,6] ] );
```

Looking back at the customers table now; if you SELECT the row that you INSERTed, you'll see:

```
movies=# \x
Expanded display is on.

movies=# SELECT
movies-#    customer_name, monthly_balances
movies-#  FROM customers
movies-#  WHERE customer_id = 8;
-[ RECORD 1 ]----+-------------------------------------

customer_name    | Wink Wankel

monthly_balances | {1.00,2,3,4,5,6,7,8,9,10,11,12.00}
```

To make this example a little more readable in book form, I have used psql's \x command to rearrange the display format here. I have also edited out some of the trailing zeroes in the monthly_balances column.

You can retrieve specific elements within an array:

```
movies=# SELECT
movies-#    customer_name, monthly_balances[3]
movies-#  FROM customers
movies-#  WHERE customer_id = 8;
 customer_name | monthly_balances
---------------+------------------
 Wink Wankel   |            3.00
(1 row)
```

---

[13] The PostgreSQL documentation refers to a contiguous range of array elements as a slice.

Or you can ask for a range[13] of array elements:

```
movies=# SELECT
movies-#    customer_name, monthly_balances[1:3]
movies-#  FROM customers
movies-#  WHERE customer_id = 8;
 customer_name |      monthly_balances
---------------+-------------------------
 Wink Wankel   |  {"1.00","2.00","3.00"}
(1 row)
```

The index for an array starts at 1 by default. I'll show you how to change the range of an index in a moment.

You can use an array element in any situation where you can use a value of the same data type. For example, you can use an array element in a WHERE clause:

```
movies=# SELECT
movies-#    customer_name, monthly_balances[1:3]
movies-# FROM customers
movies-# WHERE monthly_balances[1] > 0;
 customer_name |      monthly_balances
---------------+-------------------------
 Wink Wankel   |  {"1.00","2.00","3.00"}
(1 row)
```

There are three ways to UPDATE an array. If you want to UPDATE all elements in an array, simply SET the array to a new value:

```
movies=# UPDATE customers SET
movies-#    monthly_balances = '{12,11,10,9,8,7,6,5,4,3,1}'
movies-# WHERE customer_id = 8;
```

If you want to UPDATE a single array element, simply identify the element:

```
movies=# UPDATE customers SET monthly_balances[1] = 22;
```

Finally, you can UPDATE a contiguous range of elements:

```
movies=# UPDATE customers SET monthly_balances[1:3] = '{11,22,33}';
```

Now, there are a few odd things you should know about arrays in PostgreSQL.

First, the array bounds that you specify when you create a column are optional. I don't just mean that you can omit an array bound when you create a column (although you can), I mean that PostgreSQL won't enforce any limits that you try to impose. For example, you created the monthly_balances column as a 12-element array. PostgreSQL happily lets you put a value into element 13, 14, or 268. The array_dims() function tells the upper and lower bounds of an array value:

```
movies=# SELECT array_dims( monthly_balances ) FROM customers
movies-#    WHERE
```

[14] The PostgreSQL documentation warns that you can't expand a multidimensional array.

```
movies-#      customer_id = 8;

array_dims
------------
 [1:12]
```

You can increase the size of an array by updating values adjacent to those that already exist[14]. For example, the monthly_balances column for customer 8 (Wink Wankel) contains 12 elements, numbered 1 through 12. You can add new elements at either end of the range (array subscripts can be negative):

```
movies=# UPDATE customers SET
movies-#      monthly_balances[13] = 13
movies-#  WHERE
movies-#      customer_id = 8;
UPDATE 1

movies=# SELECT array_dims( monthly_balances ) FROM customers
movies-#  WHERE
movies-#      customer_id = 8;
 array_dims
------------
 [1:13]

movies=# UPDATE customers SET
movies-#      monthly_balances[-1:0] = '{ -1, 0 }'
movies-#  WHERE
movies-#      customer_id = 8;
UPDATE 1

movies=# SELECT array_dims( monthly_balances ) FROM customers
movies-#  WHERE
movies=#      customer_id = 8;
array_dims
------------
 [-1:13]
```

Note that you can expand an array only by updating elements that are directly adjacent to the existing elements. For example, customer number 8 now contains elements -1:13. We can't add an element 15 without first adding element 14:

```
movies=# UPDATE customers SET
movies-#      monthly_balances[15] = 15
movies-# WHERE
movies-#      customer_id = 8;
ERROR:  Invalid array subscripts
```

Next, the syntax for inserting or updating array values is a bit misleading. Let's say that you want to insert a new row in your customers table, but you only want to provide a balance for month number 3:

```
movies=# INSERT INTO customers
movies-# ( customer_id, customer_name, monthly_balances[3] )
movies-# VALUES
movies-# ( 9, 'Samuel Boney', '{300}' );
```

This appears to work, but there is danger lurking here. Let's go back and retrieve the data that you just inserted:

```
movies=# SELECT customer_name, monthly_balances[3]
movies-#    FROM customers
movies-#    WHERE
movies-#       customer_id = 9;
 customer_name | monthly_balances
---------------+------------------
 Samuel Boney  |
```

Where'd the data go? If you SELECT all array elements, the data is still there:

```
movies=# SELECT customer_name, monthly_balances
movies-#    FROM customers
movies-#    WHERE
movies-#       customer_id = 9;
 customer_name | monthly_balances
---------------+------------------
 Samuel Boney  | {"300"}
```

The array_dims() function gives you a pretty good hint:

```
movies=# SELECT array_dims( monthly_balances ) FROM customers
movies-#    WHERE
movies-#       customer_id = 9;

array_dims
------------
 [1:1]
```

According to array_dims(), the high and low subscript values are both 1. You explicitly INSERTed the value 300 into array element 3, but PostgreSQL (silently) decided to place it into element 1 anyway. This seems a bit mysterious to me, but that's how it works.

The final oddity concerns how PostgreSQL handles NULL values and arrays. An array can be NULL, but an individual element cannot—you can't have an array in which some elements are NULL and others are not. Furthermore, PostgreSQL silently ignores an attempt to UPDATE an array member to NULL:

```
movies=# SELECT customer_name, monthly_balances
movies-#    FROM
```

```
movies-#       customers
movies-#    WHERE
movies-#       customer_id = 8;
-[ RECORD 1 ]----+------------------------------------
id               | 8
customer_name    | Wink Wankel
phone            | 555-1000
birth_date       | 1988-12-25
monthly_balances | {1.00,2,3,4,5,6,7,8,9,10,11,12.00}

movies=# UPDATE customers SET
movies-#    monthly_balances[1] = NULL
movies-# WHERE
movies-#    customer_id = 8;
UPDATE 1
```

You won't get any error messages when you try to change an array element to NULL, but a SELECT statement will show that the UPDATE had no effect:

```
movies=# SELECT customer_name, monthly_balances
movies-#    FROM
movies-#       customers
movies-#    WHERE
movies-#       customer_id = 8;
-[ RECORD 1 ]----+------------------------------------
id               | 8
customer_name    | Wink Wankel
phone            | 555-1000
birth_date       | 1988-12-25
monthly_balances | {1.00,2,3,4,5,6,7,8,9,10,11,12.00}
```

If you keep these three oddities in mind, arrays can be very useful. Remember, though, that an array is not a substitute for a child table. You should use an array only when the number of elements is fixed by some real-world constraint (12 months per year, 7 days per week, and so on).

Column Constraints

When you create a PostgreSQL table, you can define column constraints[15]. A *column constraint* is a rule that must be satisfied whenever you insert or update a value in that column.

It's very important to understand that when you define a column constraint, PostgreSQL won't ever let your table get into a state in which the constraints are not met. If you try to INSERT a value that violates a constraint, the insertion will fail. If you try to UPDATE a value in such a way that it would violate a constraint, the modification will be rejected.

You can also define constraints that establish relationships between two tables. For example, each row in the rentals table contains a tape_id (corresponding to a row in

---

[15] You can also define table constraints. A table constraint applies to the table as a whole, not just a single column. We'll discuss table constraints in Chapter 3, "PostgreSQL SQL Syntax and Use."

the tapes table). You could define a constraint to tell PostgreSQL that the rentals.tape_id column REFERENCES the tapes.tape_id column. I'll discuss the implications of a REFERENCES constraint in a moment.

Needless to say, column constraints are a very powerful feature.

NULL/NOT NULL

Let's start with the most basic column constraints: NULL and NOT NULL. You've already seen some examples of the NOT NULL constraint (in Chapter 1):

```
CREATE TABLE customers (
        customer_id    INTEGER UNIQUE NOT NULL,
        name           VARCHAR(50)    NOT NULL,
        phone          CHAR(8),
        birth_date     DATE,
        balance        DECIMAL(7,2)
);
```

I have specified that the customer_id and name columns are NOT NULL. The meaning of a NOT NULL constraint is pretty clear: The column is not allowed to contain a NULL value[16]. If you try to INSERT a NULL value into the customer_id or name columns, you will receive an error:

```
INSERT INTO customers VALUES
(
    11,
    NULL,
    '555-1984',
    '10-MAY-1980',
    0
),

ERROR:  ExecAppend: Fail to add null value in not null
                attribute customer_name
```

You'll also get an error if you try to UPDATE either column in such a way that the result would be NULL:

```
UPDATE customers SET customer_name = NULL WHERE customer_id = 1;

ERROR:  ExecReplace: Fail to add null value in not null
                attribute customer_name
```

The opposite of NOT NULL is NULL. You can explicitly define a NULL constraint, but it really doesn't function as a constraint. A NULL constraint does not force a column to contain *only* NULL values (that would be pretty pointless). Instead, a NULL constraint simply

---

[16] A column that has been defined to be NOT NULL is also known as a mandatory column. A column that can accept NULL values is said to be optional.

tells PostgreSQL that NULL values are allowed in a particular column. If you don't specify that a column is mandatory, it is considered optional.

UNIQUE

The UNIQUE constraint ensures that a column will contain unique values; that is, there will be no duplicate values in the column. If you look back to the previous section, you'll see that you specified that the customer_id column should be UNIQUE. If you try to INSERT a duplicate value into a UNIQUE column, you will receive an error message:

```
movies=# SELECT * FROM customers;

 customer_id |    customer_name      |  phone   | birth_date | balance
-------------+-----------------------+----------+------------+--------
           1 | Jones, Henry          | 555-1212 | 1970-10-10 |    0.00
           2 | Rubin, William        | 555-2211 | 1972-07-10 |   15.00
           3 | Panky, Henry          | 555-1221 | 1968-01-21 |    0.00
           4 | Wonderland, Alice N.  | 555-1122 | 1969-03-05 |    3.00

movies=# INSERT INTO customers VALUES
movies-# (
movies-#    1,
movies-#    'John Gomez',
movies-#    '555-4272',
movies-#    '1982-06-02',
movies-#    0.00
movies-# );

ERROR:  Cannot insert a duplicate key into unique
        index customers_customer_id_key
```

When you create a UNIQUE column, PostgreSQL will ensure that an index exists for that column. If you don't create one yourself, PostgreSQL will create one for you. We'll talk more about indexes in Chapter 3.

PRIMARY KEY

Almost every table that you create will have one column (or possibly a set of columns) that uniquely identifies each row. For example, each tape in the tapes table is uniquely identified by its tape_id. Each customer in your customers table is identified by a UNIQUE customer_id. In relational database lingo, the set of columns that act to identify a row is called the *primary key*.

Quite often, you will find that a table has more than one unique column. For example, a table holding employee information might have an employee_id column and a social_security_number (SSN) column. You could argue that either of these would be a reasonable primary key. The employee_id would probably be the better choice for at least three reasons. First, you are likely to refer to an employee record in other tables (for example, withholdings and earnings)—an employee_id is (most likely) shorter than an SSN. Second, an SSN is considered private information, and you don't want to expose an employee's SSN to everyone who has access to one of the related files. Third, it is entirely possible that some of your employees may not have Social Security numbers (they may not be U.S. citizens)—you can't define a column as the PRIMARY KEY if that column allows NULL values.

PostgreSQL provides a constraint, PRIMARY KEY, that you can use to define the primary key for a table. Practically speaking, identifying a column (or a set of columns) as a PRIMARY KEY is the same as defining the column to be NOT NULL and UNIQUE. But the PRIMARY KEY constraint does offer one advantage over NOT NULL and UNIQUE: documentation. When you create a PRIMARY KEY, you are stating that the columns that comprise the key should be used when you need to refer to a row in that table. Each row in the rentals table, for example, contains a reference (rentals.tape_id) to a tape and a reference (rentals.customer_id) to a customer. You should define the customers.customer_id column as the PRIMARY KEY of the customers table:

```
CREATE TABLE customers (
        customer_id    INTEGER PRIMARY KEY,
        name           VARCHAR(50)    NOT NULL,
        phone          CHAR(8),
        birth_date     DATE,
        balance        DECIMAL(7,2)
);
```

You should also define the tapes.tape_id column as the primary key of the tapes table:

```
CREATE TABLE tapes (
        tape_id        CHARACTER(8) PRIMARY KEY,
        title          CHARACTER VARYING(80)
);
```

Now, let's look at the other half of the equation: the REFERENCES constraint.

REFERENCES

A foreign key is a column (or group of columns) in one table that refers to a row in another table. Usually, but not always, a foreign key refers to the primary key of another table.

The REFERENCES constraint tells PostgreSQL that one table refers to another table (or more precisely, a foreign key in one table refers to the primary key of another). Let's look at an example:

```
CREATE TABLE rentals (
        tape_id      CHARACTER(8) REFERENCES tapes,
        customer_id INTEGER       REFERENCES customers,
        rental_date DATE
);
```

I've now defined rentals.tape_id and rentals.customer_id to be foreign keys. In this example, the rentals.tape_id column is also called a *reference* and the tapes.tape_id column is called the *referent*.

There are a few implications to the REFERENCES constraint that you will need to consider. First, the REFERENCES constraint is a *constraint*: PostgreSQL does not allow you to change the database in such a way that the constraint would be violated. You cannot add a `rentals` row that refers to a nonexistent tape (or to a nonexistent customer):

```
movies=# SELECT * FROM tapes;
 tape_id  |     title
----------+---------------
 AB-12345 | The Godfather
 AB-67472 | The Godfather
 MC-68873 | Casablanca
 OW-41221 | Citizen Kane
 AH-54706 | Rear Window

movies=# INSERT INTO rentals VALUES
movies-# (
movies(#       'OW-00000',
movies(#       1,
movies(#       '2002-02-21'
movies(# );
ERROR:  <unnamed> referential integrity violation -
             key referenced from rentals not found in tapes
```

The next thing to consider is that you cannot (normally) DELETE a referent—doing so would violate the REFERENCES constraint:

```
movies=# SELECT * FROM rentals;
 tape_id  | customer_id | rental_date
----------+-------------+-------------
 AB-12345 |           1 | 2001-11-25
 AB-67472 |           3 | 2001-11-25
 OW-41221 |           1 | 2001-11-25
 MC-68873 |           3 | 2001-11-20
(4 rows)

movies=# DELETE FROM tapes WHERE tape_id = 'AB-12345';
ERROR:  <unnamed> referential integrity violation -
             key in tapes still referenced from rentals
```

Sometimes, it's not appropriate for a REFERENCES constraint to block the deletion of a referent. You can specify the action that PostgreSQL should take when the referent is deleted. The default action (also known as NO ACTION and RESTRICT) is to prevent the deletion of a referent if there are still any references to it. The next alternative, CASCADE, deletes all rows that refer to a value when the referent is deleted. The final two choices break the link between the reference and the referent: SET NULL updates any references to NULL whenever a referent is deleted, whereas SET DEFAULT updates any references to their default values when a referent is deleted.

If you want to specify one of the alternatives, you would use the following syntax when you create the REFERENCES constraint:

```
REFERENCES table [ (column) ] ON DELETE
     NO ACTION | RESTRICT | CASCADE | SET NULL | SET DEFAULT
```

By default, a REFERENCES constraint also prevents you from changing data in such a way that the constraint would be violated. You can use the ON UPDATE clause to relax the constraint a little, much the same as the ON DELETE clause.

The syntax required for ON UPDATE is

```
REFERENCES table [ (column) ] ON UPDATE
    NO ACTION | RESTRICT | CASCADE | SET NULL | SET DEFAULT
```

There is a subtle difference between the *ON UPDATE* clause and *ON DELETE* clause. When you *DELETE* a referent, the entire row disappears, so the behavior of the *ON DELETE* clause is obvious. When you *UPDATE* a referent row, you may change values other than the referent column(s). If you *UPDATE* a referent row, but you don't update the referent column, you can't introduce a constraint violation, so the *ON UPDATE* action doesn't come into play. If you do change the referent column, the *ON UPDATE* action is triggered.

The NO ACTION and RESTRICT actions simply prevent a constraint violation—this is identical to the ON DELETE clause. The CASCADE action causes all references to be updated whenever a referent changes. SET NULL and SET DEFAULT actions work the same for ON UPDATE as for ON DELETE.

CHECK()

By defining a CHECK() constraint on a column, you can tell PostgreSQL that any values inserted into that column must satisfy an arbitrary Boolean expression. The syntax for a CHECK() constraint is

```
[CONSTRAINT constraint-name] CHECK( boolean-expression )
```

For example, if you want to ensure that the customer_balance column is a positive value, but less than $10,000.00, you might use the following:

```
CREATE TABLE customers
(
        customer_id    INTEGER UNIQUE,
        customer_name  VARCHAR(50),
        phone          CHAR(8),
        birth_date     DATE,
        balance        DECIMAL(7,2)
           CONSTRAINT invalid_balance
           CHECK( balance > 0 AND balance < 10000 )
);
```

[17] You may also see the terms dyadic (meaning two-valued) and monadic (meaning single-valued). These terms have the distinct advantage that you will never have to worry about accidentally saying "urinary operator" in polite company.

[18] A type conversion that is automatically provided by PostgreSQL is called a coercion. A type conversion caused explicitly by the programmer (using the CAST() or '::' operator) is called a cast.

Now, if you try to INSERT an invalid value into the customer_balance table, you'll cause an error:

```
INSERT INTO customers VALUES
(
  10,
  'John Smallberries',
  '555-8426',
  '1970-JAN-02',
  20000
);
```

```
ERROR:  ExecAppend: rejected due to CHECK constraint invalid_balance
```

Expression Evaluation and Type Conversion

Now that you have seen all the standard PostgreSQL data types, it's time to talk about how you can combine values of different types into complex expressions.

First, you should understand that an expression represents a value. In a well-designed language, you can use an expression anywhere you can use a value. An expression can be as simple as a single value: 3.14159 is an expression. A complex expression is created by combining two simple expressions with an operator. An operator is a symbol that represents some sort of operation to be applied to one or two operands. For example, the expression "customer_balance * 1.10" uses the multiplication operator (*) to multiply customer_balance by 1.10. In this example, customer_balance is the left operand, * is the operator, and 1.10 is the right operand. This expression combines two different kinds of values: customer_balance is (presumably) a column in one of your tables; whereas 1.10 is a literal value (informally called a constant). You can combine column values, literal values, function results, and other expressions to build complex expressions.

Most operators (such as *, +, and <) require two operands: these are called *binary operators*. Other operators (such as !!, the factorial operator) work with a single value: these are called *unary operators*[17]. Some operators (such as -) can function as either.

For some expressions, particularly those expressions that mix data types, PostgreSQL must perform implicit type conversions[18]. For example, there is no predefined operator that allows you to add an INT2 to a FLOAT8. PostgreSQL can convert the INT2 into a FLOAT8 before performing the addition, and there *is* an operator that can add two FLOAT8 values. Every computer language defines a set of rules[19] that govern automatic type conversion; PostgreSQL is no exception.

PostgreSQL is rather unique in its depth of support for user-defined data types. In most RDBMSs, you can define new data types, but you are really just providing a different name for an existing data type (although you might be able to constrain the set of legal values in the new type). With PostgreSQL, you can add new data types that are not

---

[19] A given language might simply prohibit automatic type conversion, but most languages try to help out the programmer a bit.

necessarily related to the existing data types. When you add a new data type to PostgreSQL, you can also define a set of operators that can operate on the new type. Each operator is implemented as an operator function; usually, but not necessarily, written in C. When you use an operator in an expression, PostgreSQL must find an operator function that it can use to evaluate the expression. The point of this short digression is that although most languages can define a static set of rules governing type conversion, the presence of user-defined data types requires a more dynamic approach. To accommodate user-defined data types, PostgreSQL consults a table named pg_operator. Each row in the pg_operator contains an operator name (such as + or #), the operand data types, and the data type of the result. For example, (in PostgreSQL version 7.1.2) there are 31 rows in pg_operator that describe the + operator: One row describes the + operator when applied to two POINT values, another row describes the + operator when applied to two INTERVAL values, and a third row describes the + operator when applied to an INT2 and an INT4.

You can see the complete list of operators using the "\do" command in the psql query tool.

When searching for an operator function, PostgreSQL first searches the pg_operator table for an operator that exactly matches data types involved in the expression. For example, given the expression:

```
CAST( 1.2 AS DECIMAL ) + CAST( 5 AS INTEGER )
```

PostgreSQL searches for a function named '+' that takes a DECIMAL value as the left operand and an INTEGER value as right operand. If it can't find a function that meets those criteria, the next step is to determine whether it can coerce one (or both) of the values into a different data type. In our example, PostgreSQL could choose to convert either value. The DECIMAL value could be converted into an INTEGER, or the INTEGER value could be converted into a DECIMAL. Now we have *two* operator functions to choose from: One function can add two DECIMAL values and the other can add two INTEGER values. If PostgreSQL chooses the INTEGER + INTEGER operator function, it will have to convert the DECIMAL value into an INTEGER—this will result in loss of precision (the fractional portion of the DECIMAL value will be rounded to the nearest whole number). Instead, PostgreSQL will choose the DECIMAL + DECIMAL operator, coercing the INTEGER value into a DECIMAL.

So to summarize, PostgreSQL first looks for an operator function in which the operand types exactly match the expression being evaluated. If it can't find one, PostgreSQL looks through the list of operator functions that could be applied by coercing one (or both) operands into a different type. If type coercion would result in more than one alternative, PostgreSQL tries to find the operator function that will maintain the greatest precision.

The process of selecting an operator function can get complex and is described more fully in Chapter 5 of the *PostgreSQL User's Guide*.

Table 2.30 lists the type conversion functions supplied with a standard PostgreSQL distribution.

Table 2.30 **Explicit Type Conversion Functions**

Result Type	Source Type
BOX	CIRCLE, POLYGON
DATE	TIMESTAMPTZ, DATE, TEXT
INTERVAL	INTERVAL, TEXT, TIME
LSEG	BOX
MACADDR	TEXT
NUMERIC	BIGINT, SMALLINT, INTEGER, REAL, DOUBLE PRECISION
OID	TEXT
PATH	POLYGON
POINT	PATH, LSEG, BOX, POLYGON, CIRCLE
POLYGON	PATH, CIRCLE, BOX
TEXT	INET, DOUBLE PRECISION, NAME, OID, SMALLINT, INTEGER, INTERVAL, TIMESTAMP WITH TIME ZONE, TIME WITH TIME ZONE, TIME, BIGINT, DATE, MACADDR, CHAR, REAL
TIME	TEXT, TIME, TIMESTAMP WITH TIME ZONE, INTERVAL

Creating Your Own Data Types

PostgreSQL allows you to create your own data types. This is not unique among relational database systems, but PostgreSQL's depth of support *is* unique. In other RDBMSs, you can define one data type in terms of another (predefined) data type. For example, you might create a new numeric data type to hold an employee's age, with valid values between 18 and 100. This is still a numeric data type—you must define the new type as a subset of an existing type. PostgreSQL calls such a "refined" data type a *domain*. Starting with PostgreSQL version 8.0, you can also create *composite* data types. A composite type is a single data type made up of multiple fields. For example, you might define a composite type named address that contains a street number, city, state/province, and postal code. When you define a composite type, each component has a separate name and data type.

With PostgreSQL, you can create entirely new types that have no relationship to existing types. When you define a custom data type (in PostgreSQL), you determine the syntax required for literal values, the format for internal data storage, the set of operators supported for the new type, and the set of (predefined) functions that can operate on values of that type.

There are a number of contributed packages that add new data types to the standard PostgreSQL distribution. For example, the PostGIS project (http://postgis.refractions.net) adds geographic data types based on specifications produced by the Open GIS Consortium. The /contrib directory of a standard PostgreSQL distribution contains a cube data type as well as an implementation of ISBN/ISSN (International

Standard Book Number/International Standard Serial Number) data types.

Creating a new data type is too advanced for this chapter. If you are interested in defining a new data type, see Chapter 6, "Extending PostgreSQL." In the next two sections, we'll show you how to create and work with domains and composite data types.

Refining Data Types with CREATE DOMAIN

A *domain* is a user-defined data type that refines an existing data type. You typically create a domain when you need to store the same kind of data in many tables (or many times within the same table). For example, if you create a phone_number domain, you can store a phone number in a customer table (in fact, you may store many phone numbers per customer), in a salesman table, a vendor table, and so on. At first glance, you may think that you could simply add a CHARACTER(13) column to each table, but a phone number isn't simply a collection of 13 characters—it has a specific format. Here in the U.S., a phone number is often written as

```
(800)555-1212
```

The three-digit area code is surrounded by parentheses, then you see the prefix, a dash, and the last four digits of the phone number. To create a phone_number domain that enforces these constraints, you could execute the command

```
CREATE DOMAIN phone_number AS CHAR(13)
    CHECK( VALUE ~ '\\([[:digit:]]{3}\\)[[:digit:]]{3}-[[:digit:]]{4}' );
```

The first part of this command is straightforward—you're creating a domain named phone_number as a constrained version of a 13-character CHAR field. The second part of the command (the CHECK() clause) is a constraint. In this case, you're telling PostgreSQL that the VALUE stored in a phone_number field must match the given regular expression (if you're not accustomed to reading complex regular expressions, this one specifies that VALUE must be an open parenthesis followed by three digits, followed by a close parenthesis, followed by three digits, a dash, and then four digits).

Once you've created a domain, you can define columns of that type. For example, to add a home phone number to the customers table, use the command:

```
ALTER TABLE customers ADD COLUMN home_phone phone_number;
```

Now here's the payoff. Once you've defined a domain (and all of the constraints you want to apply to the domain), you can use the domain in multiple tables, or many times in the same table. To add two more phone numbers to the customers table, use this command:

```
ALTER TABLE customers ADD COLUMN cell_phone phone_number, work_phone phone_number;
```

You've defined the constraints once, but you've created three columns that enforce those constraints. If you *don't* define a phone_number domain, you'll have to specify the constraints every time you add a phone number to a table.

When should you define a domain? Any time you store the same kind of object in multiple tables (or many times in the same table). You should also define a domain for any column that participates in a PRIMARY/FOREIGNKEY relationship. For example, the rentals table contains two foreign keys: The rentals.customer_id column refers to customer.customer_id and rentals.tape_id refers to tapes.tape_id (for the sake of simplicity, we haven't actually defined PRIMARY/FOREIGN KEY constraints in the sample data for this book). Given these relationships, it's clear that the data type of rentals.customer_id must be identical to the data type of customer.customer_id (and that rentals.tape_id and tapes.tape_id must have the same type). The safest way to ensure that the data types match is to create a customer_id domain and a tape_id domain and define the key columns using those types, as shown in the following sequence of commands:

```
movies=# CREATE DOMAIN tape_id AS CHARACTER(8);
CREATE DOMAIN
movies=# CREATE DOMAIN customer_id AS INTEGER;
CREATE DOMAIN
movies=# ALTER TABLE customers ALTER COLUMN customer_id TYPE customer_id;
ALTER TABLE
movies=# ALTER TABLE rentals ALTER COLUMN customer_id TYPE customer_id;
ALTER TABLE
movies=# ALTER TABLE tapes ALTER COLUMN tape_id TYPE tape_id;
ALTER TABLE
movies=# ALTER TABLE rentals ALTER COLUMN tape_id TYPE tape_id;
ALTER TABLE
```

Notice that the tape_id and customer_id domains are *unconstrained*. You don't have to attach constraints to a domain—an unconstrained domain is still useful because it defines a *logical* data type. In fact, you can attach new constraints to a domain later (or change existing constraints) using the ALTER DOMAIN command and PostgreSQL will ensure that existing data conforms to the new constraints (you'll be rewarded with an error message if you have any data that fails to satisfy the new constraints).

The complete syntax for CREATE DOMAIN is shown here:

```
CREATE DOMAIN name [AS] data_type
    [ DEFAULT expression ]
    [ constraint [ ... ] ]

where constraint is one or more of the following:
    [ CONSTRAINT constraint_name ] NULL
    [ CONSTRAINT constraint_name ] NOT NULL
    [ CONSTRAINT constraint_name ] CHECK( expression )
```

If you include a DEFAULT expression clause, the given value becomes the default for any columns of type name. In other words, if you omit a column of type name in an INSERT command, PostgreSQL inserts expression instead of the usual NULL value. The default value should satisfy any constraints that you attach to the domain.

Once you've created a column whose type is defined by a domain, you can treat that column in the same way you would treat any other column of the base data type. For example, if you define a domain whose base type is CHARACTER, you can insert string values using the same syntax you would use for values of type CHARACTER. You can also create indexes that include domain values. A domain is a refinement of some other data type.

Creating and Using Composite Types

One of the new and powerful features introduced in PostgreSQL version 8.0 is the composite data type. A composite type is a data type composed of one or more named fields. For example, you might want to create a composite type named address composed of a street number, city, state/province, and postal code. The following command will do just that:

```
movies=# CREATE TYPE address AS
movies-# (
movies(#     street_number   VARCHAR,
movies(#     city            VARCHAR,
movies(#     state           CHAR(2),
movies(#     postal_code     VARCHAR
movies(# );
```

Once you've defined a composite type, you can create columns based on the new type. When you add a column of composite type, you're adding a single field that happens to be composed of multiple fields. For example, to add an address to the customers table, execute the following command:

```
movies-# ALTER TABLE customers ADD COLUMN home_address address;
ALTER TABLE
```

Now take a look at the definition of the customers table:

```
movies=# \d customers;
            Table "public.customers"
    Column      |          Type          | Modifiers
----------------+------------------------+-----------
 customer_id    | integer                | not null
 customer_name  | character varying(50)  | not null
 phone          | character(8)           |
 birth_date     | date                   |
 balance        | numeric(7,2)           |
 home_address   | address                |
Indexes:
    "customers_customer_id_key" UNIQUE, btree (customer_id)
```

The ALTER TABLE command added a single field named home_address. So what happened to the street_number, city, state, and postal_code fields? They're *inside* the home_address column. Let's fill in the home_address for one of your customers:

```
movies=# UPDATE customers
movies-#   SET home_address = ( '200 Main Street', 'Springfield', 'CA', '90210' )
movies-#   WHERE customer_id = 3;
```

Notice that the composite value that you're inserting is enclosed in parentheses. There are three ways that you can write a composite literal. The easiest method is the one you've just seen—simply enclose the component values in a set of parentheses. If you only have a single component to INSERT (that is, you're inserting default values for the other components), you must use the *row constructor* form instead:

```
ROW( '200 Main Street' )
```

You can also write the composite value as a string:

```
'(200 Main Street,Springfield,CA,90210)'
```

The row constructor form is typically the easiest way to build a composite literal because you don't have to worry about doubling-up any embedded quotes.

Now take a look at what PostgreSQL stored in the row you just added:

```
movies=# SELECT customer_name, home_address FROM customers;
    customer_name     |                home_address
----------------------+-------------------------------------------
 Jones, Henry         |
 Wonderland, Alice N. |
 Rubin, William       |
 Panky, Henry         | ("200 Main Street",Springfield,CA,90210)
(4 rows)
```

You see a single column (home_address) with four values in it. How do you get to the individual components in the home_address column? Simply refer to (*columnName*).*fieldname*, like this:

```
movies=# SELECT customer_name, (home_address).postal_code FROM customers;
    customer_name     | postal_code
----------------------+-------------
 Jones, Henry         |
 Wonderland, Alice N. |
 Rubin, William       |
 Panky, Henry         | 90210
(4 rows)
```

That command retrieved the postal_code component of the home_address column. The parentheses are required because the PostgreSQL parser can't tell if home_address.postal_code refers to a column (postal_code) within a table (home_address) or a field (postal_code) within a composite column (home_address).

Of course you can UPDATE a single component in a composite column as well:

```
movies=# UPDATE customers
movies-#   SET home_address.postal_code = '94404'
```

---

[20] You can create an index on a composite column, but you'll have to define an index operator class for each composite type—it's much easier to create an index on each component instead.

```
movies-#   WHERE customer_id = 3;
```

Notice that you *can't* include the parentheses around home_address in this case. Why? Because the parser would never expect to see a table name following the word SET and therefore can't mistake home_address as the name of a table.

You can't easily[20] create an index on a composite column, but you can create an index on an individual component (or on multiple components) even though the syntax is a bit mysterious. To create an index on home_address.city plus home_address.state, use the following command:

```
movies=# CREATE INDEX customer_location ON customers
movies-# (
movies(#    (( home_address ).city ),
movies(#    (( home_address ).state )
movies(# );
```

Take careful note of the parentheses—when you create an index on a field within a composite column, you must use the syntax '((*columnName*).*fieldname*)'. If you ask psql to display the layout of a table that contains a composite column, you won't see the component fields listed:

```
movies=# \d customers;
            Table "public.customers"
    Column     |         Type          | Modifiers
---------------+-----------------------+-----------
 customer_id   | integer               | not null
 customer_name | character varying(50) | not null
 phone         | character(8)          |
 birth_date    | date                  |
 balance       | numeric(7,2)          |
 home_address  | address               |
Indexes:
    "customers_customer_id_key" UNIQUE, btree (customer_id)
    "customer_location" btree (((home_address).city), ((home_address).state))
```

To see the definition of a composite type, use the command \d *typename*:

```
movies=# \d address
  Composite type "public.address"
    Column     |       Type
---------------+-------------------
 street_number | character varying
 city          | character varying
 state         | character(2)
 postal_code   | character varying
```

There are a few restrictions on composite types in PostgreSQL version 8.0. You can't attach constraints to a composite type. That's really not a problem because you can attach constraints to a domain and define a composite type that uses the domain. You can't create a domain whose base type is a composite type, but you can create a composite type that includes a domain. You *can* create a composite type that contains fields of composite type (meaning that you can nest one composite type within another). Nesting composite types can cause some confusion when you need to create a literal value of the outermost type (you need a *lot* of parentheses).

Overall, composite types take you one step closer to modeling complex real-world objects inside of a PostgreSQL database. When you combine composite types and domains, you have a powerful mechanism for enforcing constraints on complex objects.

Summary

As you can see, PostgreSQL offers a data type to fit almost every need. In this chapter, I've described each data type included in a standard PostgreSQL distribution. The syntax for literal values may seem a bit contrived for some of the data types, but the fact that PostgreSQL allows you to define new data types requires a few concessions (fortunately, very few).

I've listed all the standard operators in this chapter because they are a bit under-documented in the *PostgreSQL User's Guide*. Functions, on the other hand, are well documented (as well as constantly changing)—refer to Chapter 4 of the *PostgreSQL User's Guide* for an up-to-date list of functions.

In Chapter 3, we'll explore a variety of topics that should round out your knowledge of PostgreSQL from the perspective of a user. Later chapters will cover PostgreSQL programming and PostgreSQL administration.

3

PostgreSQL SQL Syntax
and Use

The first two chapters explored the basics of the SQL language and looked at the data types supported by PostgreSQL. This chapter covers a variety of topics that should round out your knowledge of PostgreSQL.

We'll start by looking at the rules that you have to follow when choosing names for tables, columns, indexes, and such. Next, you'll see how to create, destroy, and view PostgreSQL databases. In Chapter 1, "Introduction to PostgreSQL and SQL," you created a few simple tables; in this chapter, you'll learn all the details of the CREATE TABLE command. I'll also talk about indexes. I'll finish up by talking about transaction processing and locking. If you are familiar with Sybase, DB2, or Microsoft SQL Server, I think you'll find that the locking model used by PostgreSQL is a refreshing change.

PostgreSQL Naming Rules

When you create an object in PostgreSQL, you give that object a name. Every table has a name, every column has a name, and so on. PostgreSQL uses a single data type to define all object names: the name type.

A value of type name is a string of 63 or fewer characters[1]. A name must start with a letter or an underscore; the rest of the string can contain letters, digits, and underscores.

If you examine the entry corresponding to name in the pg_type table, you will find that a name is really 64 characters long. Because the name type is used internally by the PostgreSQL engine, it is a null-terminated string. So, the maximum length of a name value is 63 characters. You can enter more than 63 characters for an object name, but PostgreSQL stores only the first 63 characters.

---

[1] You can increase the length of the name data type by changing the value of the NAMEDATALEN symbol before compiling PostgreSQL.

Both SQL and PostgreSQL reserve certain words and normally, you cannot use those words to name objects. Examples of reserved words are

```
ANALYZE
BETWEEN
CHARACTER
INTEGER
CREATE
```

You cannot create a table named INTEGER or a column named BETWEEN. A complete list of reserved words can be found in Appendix B of the *PostgreSQL User's Guide*.

If you find that you need to create an object that does not meet these rules, you can enclose the name in double quotes. Wrapping a name in quotes creates a quoted identifier. For example, you could create a table whose name is "3.14159"—the double quotes are required, but are not actually a part of the name (that is, they are not stored and do not count against the 63-character limit). When you create an object whose name must be quoted, you have to include the quotes not only when you create the object, but every time you refer to that object. For example, to select from the table mentioned previously, you would have to write

```
SELECT filling, topping, crust FROM "3.14159";
```

Here are a few examples of both valid and invalid names:

```
my_table        -- valid
my_2nd_table    -- valid
échéanciers     -- valid: accented and non-Latin letters are allowed
"2nd_table"     -- valid: quoted identifier
"create table"  -- valid: quoted identifier
"1040Forms"     -- valid: quoted identifier
2nd_table       -- invalid: does not start with a letter or an underscore
```

Quoted names are case-sensitive. "1040Forms" and "1040FORMS" are two distinct names. Unquoted names are converted to lowercase, as shown here:

```
movies=# CREATE TABLE FOO( BAR INTEGER );
CREATE
movies=# CREATE TABLE foo( BAR INTEGER );
ERROR: Relation 'foo' already exists
movies=# \d
            List of relations
      Name        | Type  |    Owner
------------------+-------+---------------
 1040FORMS        | table | bruce
 1040Forms        | table | sheila
 customers        | table | bruce
 foo              | table | bruce
 rentals          | table | bruce
 tapes            | table | bruce
 (6 rows)
```

The names of all objects must be unique within some scope. Every database must have a unique name; the name of a schema must be unique within the scope of a single database, the name of a table must be unique within the scope of a single schema, and column names must be unique within a table. The name of an index must be unique within a database.

The Importance of the COMMENT Command

If you've been a programmer (or database developer) for more than, say, two days, you understand the importance of commenting your code. A comment helps new developers understand how your program (or database) is structured. It also helps *you* remember what you were thinking when you come back to work after a long weekend. If you're writing procedural code (in C, Java, PL/pgSQL, or whatever language you prefer), you can intersperse comments directly into your code. If you're creating objects in a PostgreSQL database, where do you store the comments? In the database, of course. The COMMENT command lets you associate a comment with just about any object that you can define in a PostgreSQL database. The syntax for the COMMENT command is very simple:

```
COMMENT ON object-type object-name IS comment-text;
```

where `object-type` and `object-name` are taken from the following:

```
DATABASE database-name
SCHEMA schema-name
TABLE table-name
COLUMN table-name.column-name
INDEX index-name
DOMAIN domain-name
TYPE data-type-name
VIEW view-name
CONSTRAINT constraint-name ON table-name
SEQUENCE sequence-name
TRIGGER trigger-name ON table-name
```

You can also define comments for other object types (functions, operators, rules, even languages), but the object types that we've shown here are the most common (see the PostgreSQL reference documentation for a complete list).

To add a comment to a table, for example, you would execute a command such as

```
COMMENT ON TABLE customers IS 'List of active customers';
```

You can only store one comment per object—if you COMMENT ON an object twice, the second comment replaces the first. To drop a comment, execute a COMMENT command, but specify NULL in place of the *comment-text* string, like this:

```
COMMENT ON TABLE customers IS NULL;
```

Once you have added a comment to an object, you can view the comment (in `psql`) using the command \dd object-name-pattern, like this:

```
movies=# \dd customers
                Object descriptions
 Schema |    Name    | Object |         Description
--------+------------+--------+----------------------------
 public | customers  | table  | List of active customers
(1 row)
```

The \dd command will show you any commented object whose name matches the *object-name-pattern*. The \dd command will *not* show comments that you've assigned to a column within a table. To see column-related comments, use the command \d+ [table-name]. To see the comment assigned to each database, use the command \l+.

Creating, Destroying, and Viewing Databases

Before you can do anything else with a PostgreSQL database, you must first create the database. Before you get too much further, it might be a good idea to see where a database fits into the overall scheme of PostgreSQL. Figure 3.1 shows the relationships between clusters, databases, schemas, and tables.

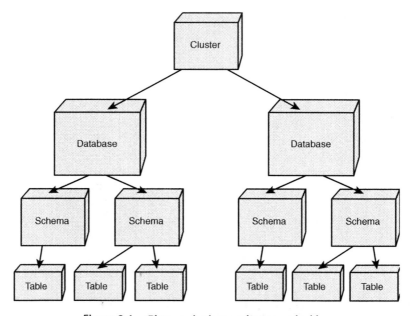

Figure 3.1   Clusters, databases, schemas, and tables.

At the highest level of the PostgreSQL storage hierarchy is the *cluster*. A cluster is a collection of databases. Each cluster exists within a single directory tree, and the entire cluster is serviced by a single postmaster. A cluster is not named—there is no way to refer to a cluster within PostgreSQL, other than by contacting the postmaster servicing that cluster. The $PGDATA environment variable should point to the root of the cluster's directory tree. A cluster is serviced by a single postmaster process. The postmaster listens for connection requests coming from client applications. When a connection request is received (and the user's credentials are authenticated), the postmaster starts a new server process and connects the client to the server. A single client connection can only interact with a single database at any given time (but a client application can certainly open multiple connections if it needs to interact with several databases simultaneously). A postmaster process can connect a client application to any of the databases in the cluster serviced by that postmaster.

Four system tables are shared between all databases in a cluster: pg_group (the list of user groups), pg_database (the list of databases within the cluster), pg_shadow (the list of valid users), and pg_tablespace (the list of tablespaces).

Each cluster contains one or more databases. Every database has a name that must follow the naming rules described in the previous section. Database names must be unique within a cluster. A database is a collection of schemas.

A *schema* is a named collection of tables (as well as functions, data types, and operators). The schema name must be unique within a database. Table names, function names, index names, type names, and operators must be unique within the schema. A schema exists primarily to provide a naming context. You can refer to an object in any schema within a single database by prefixing the object name with schema-name. For example, if you have a schema named bruce, you can create a table within that schema as

```
CREATE TABLE bruce.ratings ( ... );
SELECT * FROM bruce.ratings;
```

Each connection has a schema search path. If the object that you are referring to is found on the search path, you can omit the schema name. However, because table names are not required to be unique within a database, you may find that there are two tables with the same name within your search path (or a table may not be in your search path at all). In those circumstances, you can include the schema name to remove any ambiguity.

To view the schema search path, use the command SHOW SEARCH_PATH:

```
movies=# SHOW SEARCH_PATH;
search_path
--------------
 $user,public
(1 row)
```

The default search path, shown here, is $user,public. The $user part equates to your PostgreSQL user name. For example, if I connect to psql as user bruce, my search path is bruce,public. If a schema named bruce does not exist, PostgreSQL will just ignore that part of the search path and move on to the schema named public. To change the search path, use SET SEARCH_PATH TO:

```
movies=# SET SEARCH_PATH TO 'bruce','sheila','public';
SET
```

You create a new schema with the CREATE SCHEMA command and destroy a schema with the DROP SCHEMA command:

```
movies=# CREATE SCHEMA bruce;
CREATE SCHEMA

movies=# CREATE TABLE bruces_table( pkey INTEGER );
CREATE TABLE

movies=# \d
      List of relations
 Name            | Schema | Type  | Owner
-----------------+--------+-------+-------
 bruces_table    | bruce  | table | bruce
 tapes           | public | table | bruce
(2 rows)

movies=# DROP SCHEMA bruce;
ERROR:  Cannot drop schema bruce because other objects depend on it
        Use DROP ... CASCADE to drop the dependent objects too

movies=# DROP SCHEMA bruce CASCADE;
NOTICE:  Drop cascades to table bruces_table
DROP SCHEMA
```

Notice that you won't be able to drop a schema that is not empty unless you include the CASCADE clause. Schemas are a relatively new feature that first appeared in PostgreSQL version 7.3. Schemas are *very* useful. At many sites, you may need to keep a "development" system and a "production" system. You might consider keeping both systems in the same database, but in separate schemas. Another (particularly clever) use of schemas is to separate financial data by year. For example, you might want to keep one year's worth of data per schema. The table names (invoices, sales, and so on) remain the same across all schemas, but the schema name reflects the year to which the data applies. You could then refer to data for 2001 as FY2001.invoices, FY2001.sales, and so on. The data for 2002 would be stored in FY2002.invoices, FY2002.sales, and so on. This is a difficult problem to solve without schemas because PostgreSQL does not support cross-database access. In other words, if you are connected to database movies, you can't access tables stored in another database. Starting with PostgreSQL 7.3, you can keep all your data in a single database and use schemas to partition the data.

When you create a schema, you can specify an optional tablespace—by default, tables created within the schema will be stored in the schema's tablespace. We discuss tablespaces in more detail in the nextwith the CREATE SCHEMA section.

Tablespaces

Starting with PostgreSQL version 8.0, you can store database objects (tables and indexes) in alternate locations using a new feature called a *tablespace*. A tablespace is a name that you give to some directory within your computer's filesystem. Once you create a tablespace (we'll show you how in a moment), you can create schemas, tables, and indexes within that tablespace. A tablespace is defined within a single cluster—all databases within a cluster can refer to the same tablespace.

To create a new tablespace, use the CREATE TABLESPACE command:

```
CREATE TABLESPACE tablespacename
  [ OWNER username ]
  LOCATION 'directory'
```

The *tablespacename* parameter must satisfy the normal rules for all identifiers; it must be 63 characters or shorter and must start with a letter (or the name must be quoted). In addition, you can't create a tablespace whose name begins with the characters 'pg_' since those names are reserved for the PostgreSQL development team. If you omit the OWNER username clause, the new tablespace is owned by the user executing the CREATE TABLESPACE command. By default, you can't create an object in a tablespace unless you are the owner of that tablespace (or you are a PostgreSQL superuser). You can grant CREATE privileges to other users with the GRANT command (see Chapter 23, "Security" for more information on the GRANT command).

The interesting part of a CREATE TABLESPACE command is the *LOCATION 'directory'* clause. The LOCATION clause includes a directory—objects created within the tablespace are stored in that directory. There are a few rules that you must follow before you can create a tablespace:

- You must be a PostgreSQL superuser
- PostgreSQL must be running on a system that supports symbolic links (that means you can't create tablespaces on a Windows host)
- The *directory* must already exist (PostgreSQL won't create the directory for you)
- The *directory* must be empty
- The *directory* name must be shorter than 991 characters
- The *directory* must be owned by the owner of the postmaster process (typically a user named postgres)

If all of those conditions are satisfied, PostgreSQL creates the new tablespace.

When you create a tablespace, the PostgreSQL server performs a number of actions behind the scenes. First, the permissions on the *directory* are changed to 700 (read, write, and execute permissions for the directory owner, all other permissions denied). Next, PostgreSQL creates a single file named PG_VERSION in the given directory (the PG_VERSION file stores the version number of the PostgreSQL server that created the tablespace—if the PostgreSQL developers change the structure of a tablespace in a future version, PG_VERSION will help any conversion tools understand the structure of an existing tablespace). If the permission change succeeds, PostgreSQL adds a new row to the pg_tablespace table (a cluster-wide table) and assigns a new OID (object-id) to that row. Next, the server uses the OID to create a symbolic link between your cluster and the given *directory*. For example, consider the following scenario:

```
movies# CREATE TABLESPACE mytablespace LOCATION '/fastDrive/pg';
CREATE TABLESPACE

movies# SELECT oid, spcname, spclocation
movies-#    FROM
movies-#      pg_tablespace
movies-#    WHERE
movies-#      spcname = 'mytablespace';
  oid  |   spcname    |  spclocation
-------+--------------+--------------
 34281 | mytablespace | /fastDrive/pg
```

In this case, PostgreSQL assigned the new tablespace (mytablespace) an OID of 34281.
PostgreSQL creates a symbolic link that points from $PGDATA/pg_tblspc/34281 to
/fastDrive/pg. When you create an object (a table or index) inside of this tablespace,
the object is *not* created directly inside of the /fastDrive/pg directory. Instead,
PostgreSQL creates a subdirectory in the tablespace and then creates the object within
that subdirectory. The name of the subdirectory corresponds to the OID of the database
(that is, the object-id of the database's entry in the pg_database table) that holds the
new object. If you create a new table within the mytablespace tablespace, like this:

```
movies# CREATE TABLE foo ( data VARCHAR ) TABLESPACE mytablespace;
CREATE TABLE
```

Then find the OID of the new table and the OID of the database (movies):

```
movies# SELECT oid FROM pg_class WHERE relname = 'foo';
  oid
-------
 34282
(1 row)

movies# SELECT oid FROM pg_database WHERE datname = 'movies';
  oid
-------
 17228
(1 row)
```

You can see the relationships between the tablespace, the database subdirectory, and the
new table:

```
$ ls -l $PGDATA/pg_tblspc
total 0
lrwxrwxrwx    1 postgres postgres      12 Nov  9 19:31 34281 -> /fastDrive/pg

$ ls -l /fastDrive/pg
total 8
drwx------    2 postgres postgres    4096 Nov  9 19:50 17228
-rw-------    1 postgres postgres       4 Nov  9 19:31 PG_VERSION
```

```
$ ls -l /fastDrive/pg/17228
total 0
-rw-------    1 postgres postgres        0 Nov  9 19:50 34282
```

Notice that $PGDATA/pg_tblspc/34281 is a symbolic link that points to /fastDrive/pg (34281 is the OID of mytablespace's entry in the pg_tablespace table), PostgreSQL has created a subdirectory (17228) for the movies database, and the table named foo was created in that subdirectory (in a file whose name, 34282, corresponds to the table's OID). By creating a subdirectory for each database, PostgreSQL ensures that you can safely store objects from multiple databases within the same tablespace without worrying about OID collisions.

When you create a cluster (which is done for you automatically when you install PostgreSQL), PostgreSQL silently creates two tablespaces for you: pg_default and pg_global. PostgreSQL creates objects in the pg_default tablespace when it can't find a more appropriate tablespace. The pg_default tablespace is always located in the $PGDATA/base directory. The pg_global tablespace stores cluster-wide tables like pg_database, pg_group, and pg_tablespace—you can't create objects in the pg_global tablespace.

The name of the pg_default tablespace can be a bit misleading. You may think that PostgreSQL always creates an object in pg_default if you omit the TABLESPACE *tablespacename* clause, but that's not the case. Instead, PostgreSQL follows an inheritance hierarchy to find the appropriate tablespace. If you specify a TABLESPACE *tablespacename* clause when you execute a CREATE TABLE or CREATE INDEX command, the server creates the object in the given *tablespacename*. If you don't specify a tablespace and you're creating an index, the index is created in the tablespace of the parent table (that is, the table that you are indexing). If you don't specify a tablespace and you're creating a table, the table is created in the tablespace of the parent schema. If you are creating a schema and you don't specify a tablespace, the schema is created in the tablespace of the parent database. If you are creating a database and you don't specify a tablespace, the database is created in the tablespace of the template database (typically, template1). So, an index inherits its tablespace from the parent table, a table inherits its tablespace from the parent schema, a schema inherits its tablespace from the parent database, and a database inherits its database from the template database.

To view the databases defined in a cluster, use the \db (or \db+) command in psql:

```
movies=# \db+
                    List of tablespaces
      Name     |   Owner   |    Location      |  Access privileges
---------------+-----------+------------------+-------------------
 mytablespace  | postgres  | /fastDrive/pg    |
 pg_default    | postgres  |                  |
 pg_global     | postgres  |                  | {pg=C/pg}
(4 rows)
```

To see a list of objects defined with a given tablespace, use the following query:

```
SELECT relname FROM pg_class
   WHERE reltablespace =
   (
     SELECT oid FROM pg_tablespace WHERE spcname = 'tablespacename'
   );
```

Don't confuse schemas and tablespaces—they both provide organization for the tables and indexes in your cluster, but they are definitely not the same thing. A tablespace affects the *physical* organization of data within a cluster (that is, it a tablespace defines *where* your data is stored). A schema affects the *logical* organization of data within a database—a schema affects name resolution; a tablespace does not. A schema acts as a part of a name; once you've created an object, you can ignore its physical location (its tablespace).

Creating New Databases

Now let's see how to create a new database and how to remove an existing one.

The syntax for the CREATE DATABASE command is

```
CREATE DATABASE database-name
     [ WITH [ OWNER     [=] {username|DEFAULT} ]
            [ TEMPLATE  [=] {template-name|DEFAULT} ]
            [ ENCODING  [=] {encoding|DEFAULT} ]
            [ TABLESPACE [=] tablespace ]]
```

As I mentioned earlier, the database-name must follow the PostgreSQL naming rules described earlier and must be unique within the cluster.

If you don't include the OWNER=username clause or you specify OWNER=DEFAULT, you become the owner of the database. If you are a PostgreSQL superuser, you can create a database that will be owned by another user using the OWNER=username clause. If you are not a PostgreSQL superuser, you can still create a database if you have the CREATEDB privilege, but you cannot assign ownership to another user. Chapter 21, "PostgreSQL Administration," describes the process of defining user privileges.

The TEMPLATE=template-name clause is used to specify a *template* database. A *template* defines a starting point for a database. If you don't include a TEMPLATE=template-name or you specify TEMPLATE=DEFAULT, the database named template1 is copied to the new database. All tables, views, data types, functions, and operators defined in the template database are duplicated into the new database. If you add objects (usually functions, operators, and data types) to the template1 database, those objects will be propagated to any new databases that you create based on template1. You can also trim down a template database if you want to reduce the size of new databases. For example, you might decide to remove the geometric data types (and the functions and operators that support that type) if you know that you won't need them. Or, if you have a set of functions that are required by your application, you can define the functions in the template1 database and all new databases will automatically include those functions. If you want to create an *as-distributed* database, you can use template0 as your template database. The template0 database is the starting point for template1 and contains only the standard objects included in a

PostgreSQL distribution. You should not make changes to the template0 database, but you can use the template1 database to provide a site-specific set of default objects.

You can use the ENCODING=character-set clause to choose an encoding for the string values in the new database. An *encoding* determines how the bytes that make up a string are interpreted as characters. For example, specifying ENCODING=SQL_ASCII tells PostgreSQL that characters are stored in ASCII format, whereas ENCODING=ISO-8859-8 requests ECMA-121 Latin/Hebrew encoding. When you create a database, all characters stored in that database are encoded in a single format. When a client retrieves data, the client/server protocol automatically converts between the database encoding and the encoding being used by the client. Chapter 22, "Internationalization and Localization," discusses encoding schemes in more detail.

The TABLESPACE=tablespace-name clause tells PostgreSQL that you want to create the database in an alternate location (that is, the database should not be created in the usual $PGDATA/base directory). You must create a tablespace before you can use it. If you don't include a TABLESPACE clause in the CREATE DATABASE command, the new database is created in the same tablespace as the template database.

If you're using an older version of PostgreSQL (older than 8.0), you can't use table-spaces to create a database in a non-standard location. Instead, you must use a feature known as a *location*. In versions of PostgreSQL older than 8.0, the last option for the CREATE DATABASE command is the LOCATION=path clause. In most cases, you will never have to use the LOCATION option, which is good because it's a little strange.

If you do have need to use an alternate location, you will probably want to specify the location by using an environment variable. The environment variable must be known to the postmaster processor at the time the postmaster is started and it should contain an absolute pathname.

The LOCATION=path clause can be confusing. The path might be specified in three forms:

- The path contains a /, but does not begin with a /—this specifies a relative path

- The path begins with a /—this specifies an absolute path

- The path does not include a /

Relative locations are not allowed by PostgreSQL, so the first form is invalid.

Absolute paths are allowed only if you defined the C/C++ preprocessor symbol "ALLOW_ABSOLUTE_DBPATHS" at the time you compiled your copy of PostgreSQL. If you are using a prebuilt version of PostgreSQL, the chances are pretty high that this symbol was *not* defined and therefore absolute paths are not allowed.

So, the only form that you can rely on in a standard distribution is the last—a path that does not include any "/" characters. At first glance, this may look like a relative path that is only one level deep, but that's not how PostgreSQL sees it. In the third form, the path must be the *name* of an environment variable. As I mentioned earlier, the environment variable must be known to the postmaster processor at the time the postmaster is started, and it should contain an absolute pathname. Let's look at an example:

```
$ export PG_ALTERNATE=/bigdrive/pgdata
$ initlocation PG_ALTERNATE
$ pg_ctl restart -l /tmp/pg.log -D $PGDATA
...
$ psql -q -d movies
movies=# CREATE DATABASE bigdb WITH LOCATION=PG_ALTERNATE;
...
```

First, I've defined (and exported) an environment variable named PG_ALTERNATE. I've defined PG_ALTERNATE to have a value of /bigdrive/pgdata—that's where I want my new database to reside. After the environment variable has been defined, I need to initialize the directory structure—the initlocation script will take care of that for me. Now I have to restart the postmaster so that it can see the PG_ALTERNATE variable. Finally, I can start psql (or some other client) and execute the CREATE DATABASE command specifying the PG_ALTERNATE environment variable.

This all sounds a bit convoluted, and it is. The PostgreSQL developers consider it a security risk to allow users to create databases in arbitrary locations. Because the postmaster must be started by a PostgreSQL administrator, only an administrator can choose where databases can be created. So, to summarize the process:

1. Create a new environment variable and set it to the path where you want new databases to reside.

2. Initialize the new directory using the initlocation application.

3. Stop and restart the postmaster.

4. Now, you can use the environment variable with the LOCATION=path clause.

createdb

The CREATE DATABASE command creates a new database from within a PostgreSQL client application (such as psql). You can also create a new database from the operating system command line. The createdb command is a shell script that invokes psql for you and executes the CREATE DATABASE command for you. For more information about createdb, see the *PostgreSQL Reference Manual* or invoke createdb with the --help flag:

```
$ createdb --help
createdb creates a PostgreSQL database.

Usage:
  createdb [OPTION]... [DBNAME] [DESCRIPTION]

Options:
  -D, --tablespace=TABLESPACE  default tablespace for the database
  -E, --encoding=ENCODING      encoding for the database
  -O, --owner=OWNER            database user to own the new database
  -T, --template=TEMPLATE      template database to copy
  -e, --echo                   show the commands being sent to the server
  -q, --quiet                  don't write any messages
```

```
    --help                          show this help, then exit
    --version                       output version information, then exit

Connection options:
    -h, --host=HOSTNAME             database server host or socket directory
    -p, --port=PORT                 database server port
    -U, --username=USERNAME         user name to connect as
    -W, --password                  prompt for password
```

By default, a database with the same name as the current user is created.

Report bugs to <pgsql-bugs@postgresql.org>.

Dropping a Database

Getting rid of an old database is easy. The DROP DATABASE command will delete all of the data in a database and remove the database from the cluster.

For example:

```
movies=# CREATE DATABASE redshirt;
CREATE DATABASE
movies=# DROP DATABASE redshirt;
DROP DATABASE
```

There are no options to the DROP DATABASE command; you simply include the name of the database that you want to remove. There *are* a few restrictions. First, you must own the database that you are trying to drop, or you must be a PostgreSQL superuser. Next, you cannot drop a database from within a transaction block—you cannot roll back a DROP DATABASE command. Finally, the database must not be in use, even by you. This means that before you can drop a database, you must connect to a different database (template1 is a good candidate). An alternative to the DROP DATABASE command is the dropdb shell script. dropdb is simply a wrapper around the DROP DATABASE command; see the *PostgreSQL Reference Manual* for more information about dropdb.

Viewing Databases

Using psql, there are two ways to view the list of databases. First, you can ask psql to simply display the list of databases and then exit. The -l option does this for you:

```
$ psql -l
      List of databases
   Name     |   Owner   | Encoding
-----------+-----------+----------
 template0 | postgres  | UNICODE
 template1 | postgres  | UNICODE
 movies    | bruce     | UNICODE
(3 rows)
$
```

From within `psql`, you can use the `\l` or `\l+` meta-commands to display the databases within a cluster:

```
movies=# \l+
                      List of databases
    Name    |   Owner   | Encoding |        Description
------------+-----------+----------+--------------------------
 template0  | postgres  | UNICODE  |
 template1  | postgres  | UNICODE  | Default template database
 movies     | bruce     | UNICODE  | Virtual Video database
(3 rows)
```

Creating New Tables

The previous section described how to create and drop databases. Now let's move down one level in the PostgreSQL storage hierarchy and talk about creating and dropping tables.

You've created some simple tables in the first two chapters; it's time to talk about some of the more advanced features of the `CREATE TABLE` command. Here is the command that you used to create the `customers` table:

```
CREATE TABLE customers (
        customer_id    INTEGER UNIQUE,
        customer_name  VARCHAR(50),
        phone          CHAR(8),
        birth_date     DATE,
        balance        DECIMAL(7,2)
);
```

This command creates a *permanent* table named `customers`. A table name must meet the naming criteria described earlier in this chapter. When you create a table, PostgreSQL automatically creates a new data type[2] with the same name as the table. This means that you can't create a table whose name is the same as an existing data type.

When you execute this command, the `customers` table is created in the database that you are connected to. If you are using PostgreSQL 7.3 or later, the `customers` table is created in the first schema in your search path. (If you are using a version older than 7.3, your copy of PostgreSQL does not support schemas). If you want the table to be created in some other schema, you can prefix the table name with the schema qualifier, for example:

```
CREATE TABLE joes_video.customers( ... );
```

The new table is owned by you. You can't give ownership to another user at the time you create the table, but you can change it later using the `ALTER TABLE...OWNER TO` command (described later).

When you create a table (or an index), you can tell PostgreSQL to store the object in a specific tablespace by including a `TABLESPACE` *tablespacename* clause, like this:

---

[2] This seems to be a holdover from earlier days. You can't actually do anything with this data type.

```
CREATE TABLE joes_video.customers( ... ) TABLESPACE mytablespace;
```

If you don't specify a tablespace, PostgreSQL creates the table in the tablespace assigned to the schema (if you're creating an index without specifying a tablespace, the index is created in the tablespace of the parent table).

Temporary Tables

I mentioned earlier that the customers table is a permanent table. You can also create *temporary* tables. A permanent table persists after you terminate your PostgreSQL session; a temporary table is automatically destroyed when your PostgreSQL session ends. Temporary tables are also local to your session, meaning that other PostgreSQL sessions can't see temporary tables that you create. Because temporary tables are local to each session, you don't have to worry about colliding with the name of a table created by another session.

If you create a temporary table with the same name as a permanent table, you are effectively *hiding* the permanent table. For example, let's create a temporary table that hides the permanent customers table:

```
CREATE TEMPORARY TABLE customers (
        customer_id    INTEGER UNIQUE,
        customer_name VARCHAR(50),
        phone          CHAR(8),
        birth_date     DATE,
        balance        DECIMAL(7,2)
);
```

Notice that the only difference between this command and the command that you used to create the permanent customers table is the TEMPORARY keyword[3]. Now you have two tables, each named customers. If you now SELECT from or INSERT into the customers table, you will be working with the temporary table. Prior to version 7.3, there was no way to get back to the permanent table except by dropping the temporary table:

```
movies=# SELECT * FROM customers;
 customer_id |    customer_name    |  phone   | birth_date | balance
-------------+---------------------+----------+------------+---------
           1 | Jones, Henry        | 555-1212 | 1970-10-10 |    0.00
           2 | Rubin, William      | 555-2211 | 1972-07-10 |   15.00
           3 | Panky, Henry        | 555-1221 | 1968-01-21 |    0.00
           4 | Wonderland, Alice N. | 555-1122 | 1969-03-05 |    3.00
           8 | Wink Wankel         | 555-1000 | 1988-12-25 |    0.00
(5 rows)

movies=# CREATE TEMPORARY TABLE customers
movies-# (
movies(#   customer_id    INTEGER UNIQUE,
movies(#   customer_name VARCHAR(50),
```

[3] You can abbreviate TEMPORARY to TEMP.

```
movies(#    phone          CHAR(8),
movies(#    birth_date     DATE,
movies(#    balance        DECIMAL(7,2)
movies(#    );
CREATE

movies=# SELECT * FROM customers;
 customer_id |    customer_name    |  phone  | birth_date | balance
-------------+---------------------+---------+------------+---------
(0 rows)


movies=# DROP TABLE customers;
DROP

movies=# SELECT * FROM customers;
 customer_id |    customer_name    |  phone   | birth_date | balance
-------------+---------------------+----------+------------+---------
           1 | Jones, Henry        | 555-1212 | 1970-10-10 |    0.00
           2 | Rubin, William      | 555-2211 | 1972-07-10 |   15.00
           3 | Panky, Henry        | 555-1221 | 1968-01-21 |    0.00
           4 | Wonderland, Alice N. | 555-1122 | 1969-03-05 |    3.00
           8 | Wink Wankel         | 555-1000 | 1988-12-25 |    0.00
(5 rows)
```

Starting with release 7.3, you can access the permanent table by including the name of the schema where the permanent table resides.

A temporary table is like a scratch pad. You can use a temporary table to accumulate intermediate results. Quite often, you will find that a complex query can be formulated more easily by first extracting the data that interests you into a temporary table. If you find that you are creating a given temporary table over and over again, you might want to convert that table into a view. See the section titled "Using Views" in Chapter 1 for more information about views.

Table Constraints

In Chapter 2, "Working with Data in PostgreSQL," we explored the various constraints that you can apply to a column: NOT NULL, UNIQUE, PRIMARY KEY, REFERENCES, and CHECK(). You can also apply constraints to a table as a whole or to groups of columns within a table.

First, let's look at the CHECK() constraint. The syntax for a CHECK() constraint is

```
[CONSTRAINT constraint-name] CHECK( boolean-expression )
```

When you define a CHECK() constraint for a table, you are telling PostgreSQL that any insertions or updates made to the table must satisfy the boolean-expression given within the constraint. The difference between a column constraint and a table constraint is that a column constraint should refer only to the column to which it relates. A table constraint can refer to any column in the table.

For example, suppose that you had an orders table to track customer orders:

```
CREATE TABLE orders
(
    customer_number     INTEGER,
    part_number         CHAR(8),
    quantity_ordered    INTEGER,
    price_per_part      DECIMAL(7,2)
);
```

You could create a table-related CHECK() constraint to ensure that the extended price (that is, quantity_ordered times price_per_part) of any given order is at least $5.00:

```
CREATE TABLE orders
(
    customer_number     INTEGER,
    part_number         CHAR(8),
    quantity_ordered    INTEGER,
    price_per_part      DECIMAL(7,2),

    CONSTRAINT verify_minimum_order
      CHECK (( price_per_part * quantity_ordered) >= 5.00::DECIMAL )
);
```

Each time a row is inserted into the orders table (or the quantity_ordered or price_per_part columns are updated), the verify_minimum_order constraint is evaluated. If the expression evaluates to FALSE, the modification is rejected. If the expression evaluates to TRUE or NULL, the modification is allowed.

You may have noticed that a table constraint looks very much like a column constraint. PostgreSQL can tell the difference between the two types by their placement within the CREATE TABLE statement. A column constraint is placed *within* a column definition—after the column's data type and before the comma. A table constraint is listed *outside* of a column definition. The only tricky spot is a table constraint that follows the last column definition; you normally would not include a comma after the last column. If you want a constraint to be treated as a table constraint, be sure to include a comma following the last column definition. At the moment, PostgreSQL does not treat table constraints and column constraints differently, but in a future release it may.

Each of the table constraint varieties is related to a type of column constraint.

The UNIQUE table constraint is identical to the UNIQUE column constraint, except that you can specify that a group of columns must be unique. For example, here is the rentals table as currently defined:

```
CREATE TABLE rentals
(
    tape_id     CHARACTER(8),
    customer_id INTEGER,
    rental_date DATE
);
```

Let's modify this table to reflect the business rule that any given tape cannot be rented twice on the same day:

```
CREATE TABLE rentals
(
    tape_id     CHARACTER(8),
    customer_id INTEGER,
    rental_date DATE,

    UNIQUE( rental_date, tape_id )

);
```

Now when you insert a row into the `rentals` table, PostgreSQL will ensure that there are no other rows with the same combination of `rental_date` and `tape_id`. Notice that I did not provide a constraint name in this example; constraint names are optional.

The PRIMARY KEY table constraint is identical to the PRIMARY KEY column constraint, except that you can specify that the key is composed of a group of columns rather than a single column.

The REFERENCES table constraint is similar to the REFERENCES column constraint. When you create a REFERENCES column constraint, you are telling PostgreSQL that a column value in one table refers to a row in another table. More specifically, a REFERENCES column constraint specifies a relationship between two columns. When you create a REFERENCES table constraint, you can relate a group of columns in one table to a group of columns in another table. Quite often, you will find that the unique identifier for a table (that is, the PRIMARY KEY) is composed of multiple columns. Let's say that the Virtual Video Store is having great success and you decide to open a second store. You might want to consolidate the data for each store into a single database. Start by creating a new table:

```
CREATE TABLE stores
(
    store_id    INTEGER PRIMARY KEY,
    location    VARCHAR
);
```

Now, change the definition of the `customers` table to include a `store_id` for each customer:

```
CREATE TABLE customers (
        store_id        INTEGER REFERENCES stores( store_id ),
        customer_id     INTEGER,
        customer_name   VARCHAR(50),
        phone           CHAR(8),
        birth_date      DATE,
        balance         DECIMAL(7,2),

        PRIMARY KEY( store_id, customer_id )
);
```

The `store_id` column in the `customers` table refers to the `store_id` column in the stores table. Because `store_id` is the primary key to the `stores` table, you could have written the REFERENCES constraint in either of two ways:

```
store_id INTEGER REFERENCES stores( store_id )
```

or

```
store_id INTEGER REFERENCES stores
```

Also, notice that the primary key for this table is composed of two columns: `store_id` and `customer_id`. I can have two customers with the same `customer_id` as long as they have different `store_ids`.

Now you have to change the `rentals` table as well:

```
CREATE TABLE rentals
(
    store_id     INTEGER,
    tape_id      CHARACTER(8),
    customer_id INTEGER,
    rental_date DATE,

    UNIQUE( rental_date, tape_id )
    FOREIGN KEY( store_id, customer_id ) REFERENCES customers
);
```

The `customers` table has a two-part primary key. Each row in the rentals table refers to a row in the customers table, so the FOREIGN KEY constraint must specify a two-part foreign key. Again, because foreign key refers to the primary key of the customers table, I can write this constraint in either of two forms:

```
FOREIGN KEY( store_id, customer_id )
  REFERENCES customers( store_id, customer_id )
```

or

```
FOREIGN KEY( store_id, customer_id )
  REFERENCES customers
```

Now that I have the referential integrity constraints defined, they will behave as described in the "Column Constraints" section of Chapter 2. Remember, a table constraint functions the same as a column constraint, except that table constraints can refer to more than one column.

Dropping Tables

Dropping a table is much easier than creating a table. The syntax for the DROP TABLE command is

```
DROP TABLE table-name [, ...];
```

If you are using PostgreSQL 7.3 or later, you can qualify the table name with a schema. For example, here is the command to destroy the `rentals` table:

```
DROP TABLE rentals;
```

If the `rentals` table existed in some schema other than your current schema, you would qualify the table name:

```
DROP TABLE sheila.rentals;
```

You can destroy a table only if you are the table's owner or if you are a PostgreSQL superuser. Notice that I used the word *destroy* here rather than *drop*. It's important to realize that when you execute a `DROP TABLE` command, you are destroying all the data in that table.

PostgreSQL has a nice feature that I have not seen in other databases: You can roll back a `DROP TABLE` command. Try the following experiment. First, let's view the contents of the `tapes` table:

```
movies=# SELECT * FROM tapes;

tape_id   |    title       | duration
----------+----------------+----------
 AB-12345 | The Godfather  |
 AB-67472 | The Godfather  |
 MC-68873 | Casablanca     |
 OW-41221 | Citizen Kane   |
 AH-54706 | Rear Window    |
(5 rows)
```

Now, start a multistatement transaction and destroy the `tapes` table:

```
movies=# BEGIN WORK;
BEGIN

movies=# DROP TABLE tapes;

NOTICE: DROP TABLE implicitly drops referential integrity trigger
        from table "rentals"
DROP
```

If you try to `SELECT` from the `tapes` table, you'll find that it has been destroyed:

```
movies=# SELECT * FROM tapes;
ERROR:  Relation "tapes" does not exist
```

If you `COMMIT` this transaction, the table will permanently disappear; let's `ROLLBACK` the transaction instead:

```
movies=# ROLLBACK;
ROLLBACK
```

The `ROLLBACK` threw out all changes made since the beginning of the transaction, including the `DROP TABLE` command. You should be able to `SELECT` from the `tapes` table again and see the same data that was there before:

```
movies=# SELECT * FROM tapes;
tape_id  |     title      | duration
---------+----------------+----------
 AB-12345 | The Godfather |
 AB-67472 | The Godfather |
 MC-68873 | Casablanca    |
 OW-41221 | Citizen Kane  |
 AH-54706 | Rear Window   |
(5 rows)
```

This is a *very* nice feature. You can roll back CREATE TABLE, DROP TABLE, CREATE VIEW, DROP VIEW, CREATE INDEX, DROP INDEX, and so on. I'll discuss transactions a bit later in this chapter. For now, I'd like to point out a few details that I glossed over in the previous example. You may have noticed that the DROP TABLE command produced a NOTICE.

```
movies=# DROP TABLE tapes;
NOTICE: DROP TABLE implicitly drops referential integrity trigger
        from table "rentals"
DROP
```

When you drop a table, PostgreSQL will automatically DROP any indexes defined for that table as well as any triggers or rules. If other tables refer to the table that you dropped (by means of a REFERENCE constraint), PostgreSQL will automatically drop the constraints in the other tables. However, any *views* that refer to the dropped table will not be removed—a view can refer to many tables and PostgreSQL would not know how to remove a single table from a multitable SELECT.

Inheritance

Another PostgreSQL feature that is uncommon in relational database systems is *inheritance*. Inheritance is one of the foundations of the object-oriented programming paradigm. Using inheritance, you can define a hierarchy of related data types (in PostgreSQL, you define a hierarchy of related tables). Each layer in the inheritance hierarchy represents a *specialization* of the layer above it[4].

Let's look at an example. The Virtual Video database defines a table that stores information about the tapes that you have in stock:

```
movies=# \d tapes
  Column  |         Type         | Modifiers
----------+----------------------+-----------
 tape_id  | character(8)         | not null
 title    | character varying(80)| not null
 duration | interval             |
```

---

[4] We'll view an inheritance hierarchy with the most general types at the top and the most specialized types at the bottom.

For each tape, you store the `tape_id`, `title`, and `duration`. Let's say that you decide to jump into the twenty-first century and rent DVDs as well as videotapes. You *could* store DVD records in the `tapes` table, but a tape and a DVD are not really the same thing. Let's create a new table that defines the characteristics common to both DVDs and videotapes:

```
CREATE TABLE video
(
  video_id        CHARACTER(8) PRIMARY KEY,
  title           VARCHAR(80),
  duration        INTERVAL
);
```

Now, create a table to hold the DVDs. For each DVD you have in stock, you want to store everything in the `video` table plus a `region_id` and an array of `audio_tracks`. Here is the new table definition:

```
movies=# CREATE TABLE dvds
movies-# (
movies(#   region_id    INTEGER,
movies(#   audio_tracks VARCHAR[]
movies(# ) INHERITS ( video );
```

Notice the last line in this command: You are telling PostgreSQL that the `dvds` table *inherits from* the `video` table. Now let's INSERT a new DVD:

```
movies=# INSERT INTO dvds VALUES
movies=# (
movies(#   'ASIN-750',                -- video_id
movies(#   'Star Wars',               -- title
movies(#   '121 minutes',             -- duration
movies(#   1,                         -- region_id
movies(#   '{English,Spanish}'        -- audio_tracks
movies(# );
```

Now, if you SELECT from the `dvds` table, you'll see the information that you just inserted:

```
video_id |   title   | duration | region_id |   audio_tracks
---------+-----------+----------+-----------+-------------------
ASIN-750 | Star Wars | 02:01:00 |         1 | {English,Spanish}
```

At this point, you might be thinking that the INHERITS clause did nothing more than create a row template that PostgreSQL copied when you created the `dvds` table. That's not the case—if you simply want to create a table that has the same structure as another table, use the LIKE *table-name* clause instead of the INHERITS *table-name* clause. When we say that `dvds` inherits from `video`, we are not simply saying that a DVD is *like* a video, we are saying that a DVD *is* a video. Let's SELECT from the `video` table now; remember, you haven't explicitly inserted any data into the `video` table, so you might expect the result set to be empty:

```
movies=# SELECT * FROM video;
 video_id |   title   | duration
----------+-----------+----------
 ASIN 750 | Star Wars | 02:01:00
```

A DVD is a video. When you SELECT from the video table, you see only the columns that comprise a video. When you SELECT from the dvds table, you see all the columns that comprise a DVD. In this relationship, you say that the dvds table *specializes*[5] the more general video table.

If you are using a version of PostgreSQL older than 7.2, you must code this query as SELECT * FROM video* to see the DVD entries. Starting with release 7.2, SELECT will include descendent tables and you have to say SELECT * FROM ONLY video to suppress descendents.

You now have a new table to track your DVD inventory; let's go back and redefine the tapes table to fit into the inheritance hierarchy. For each tape, we want to store a video_id, a title, and a duration. This is where we started: the video table already stores all this information. You should still create a new table to track videotapes—at some point in the future, you may find information that relates to a videotape, but not to a DVD:

```
movies=# CREATE TABLE tapes ( ) INHERITS( video );
CREATE
```

This CREATE TABLE command creates a new table identical in structure to the video table. Each row in the tapes table will contain a video_id, a title, and a duration. Insert a row into the tapes table:

```
movies=# INSERT INTO tapes VALUES
movies-# (
movies(#    'ASIN-8YD',
movies(#    'Flight To Mars(1951)',
movies(#    '72 min'
movies(# );
INSERT
```

When you SELECT from the tapes table, you should see this new row:

```
movies=# SELECT * FROM tapes;
 tape_id  |        title         | duration
----------+----------------------+----------
 ASIN-8YD | Flight To Mars(1951) | 01:12:00
(1 row)
```

And because a tape *is* a video, you would also expect to see this row in the video table:

```
movies=# SELECT * FROM video;
```

[5] Object-oriented terminology defines many different phrases for this inheritance relationship: specialize/generalize, subclass/superclass, and so on. Choose the phrase that you like.

```
video_id |             title            | duration
---------+-----------------------------+----------
ASIN-750 | Star Wars                   | 02:01:00
ASIN-8YD | Flight To Mars(1951)        | 01:12:00
(2 rows)
```

Now here's the interesting part. A DVD is a video—any row that you add to the dvds table shows up in the video table. A tape is a video—any row that you add to the tapes table shows up in the video table. But a DVD is *not* a tape (and a tape is *not* a DVD). Any row that you add to the dvds table will *not* show up in the tapes table (and vice versa).

If you want a list of all the tapes you have in stock, you can SELECT from the tapes table. If you want a list of all the DVDs in stock, SELECT from the dvds table. If you want a list of all videos in stock, SELECT from the videos table.

In this example, the inheritance hierarchy is only two levels deep. PostgreSQL imposes no limit to the number of levels that you can define in an inheritance hierarchy. You can also create a table that inherits from *multiple* tables—the new table will have all the columns defined in the more general tables.

I should caution you about two problems with the current implementation of inheritance in PostgreSQL. First, indexes are not shared between parent and child tables. On one hand, that's good because it gives you good performance. On the other hand, that's bad because PostgreSQL uses an index to guarantee uniqueness. That means that you could have a videotape and a DVD with the same video_id. Of course, you can work around this problem by encoding the type of video in the video_id (for example, use a T for tapes and a D for DVDs). But PostgreSQL won't give you any help in fixing this problem. The other *potential* problem with inheritance is that triggers are not shared between parent and child tables. If you define a trigger for the topmost table in your inheritance hierarchy, you will have to remember to define the same trigger for each descendant.

We have redefined some of the example tables many times in the past two chapters. In a real-world environment, you probably won't want to throw out all your data each time you need to make a change to the definition of an existing table. Let's explore a better way to alter a table.

ALTER TABLE

Now that you have a video table, a dvds table, and a tapes table, let's add a new column to all three tables that you can use to record the rating of the video (PG, G, R, and so on).

You could add the rating column to the tapes table and to the dvds table, but you really want the rating column to be a part of every video. The ALTER TABLE ... ADD COLUMN command adds a new column for you, leaving all the original data in place:

```
movies=# ALTER TABLE video ADD COLUMN rating VARCHAR;
ALTER
```

Now, if you look at the definition of the video table, you will see the new column:

```
movies=# \d video
               Table "video"
  Column  |          Type          | Modifiers
----------+------------------------+-----------
 video_id | character(8)           | not null
 title    | character varying(80)  |
 duration | interval               |
 rating   | character varying      |
Indexes:
    "video_pkey" PRIMARY KEY, btree (video_id)
```

After the ALTER TABLE command completes, each row in the video table has a new column; the value of every rating column will be NULL. Because you have changed the definition of a video, and a DVD is a video, you might expect that the dvds table will also contain a rating column:

```
movies=# \d dvds
                  Table "dvds"
    Column     |          Type          | Modifiers
---------------+------------------------+-----------
 video_id      | character(8)           | not null
 title         | character varying(80)  |
 duration      | interval               |
 region_id     | integer                |
 audio_tracks  | character varying[]    |
 rating        | character varying      |
Inherits: video
```

Similarly, the tapes table will also inherit the new rating column:

```
movies=# \d tapes
               Table "tapes"
  Column  |          Type          | Modifiers
----------+------------------------+-----------
 video_id | character(8)           | not null
 title    | character varying(80)  |
 duration | interval               |
 rating   | character varying      |
Inherits: video
```

Starting with PostgreSQL version 8.0, you can change the data type of an existing column using ALTER TABLE. For example, to change the data type of the customers.customer_id column from INTEGER to NUMERIC(7, 2), you could execute the command:

```
ALTER TABLE customers ALTER COLUMN customer_id TYPE NUMERIC( 7,2 )
```

As long as PostgreSQL knows how to convert a value from the old data type to the new data type, you can freely change data types. If PostgreSQL doesn't know how to convert between the old and new types, you can include a USING expression clause to tell

PostgreSQL how to perform the conversion. The *expression* following the USING keyword typically refers to the original column value. For example, if you want to change the data type of customers.customer_id and multiply each customer_id by 100 at the same time, use the following command:

```
ALTER TABLE customers ALTER COLUMN customer_id TYPE NUMERIC( 7,2 ) USING cus-
tomer_id * 100
```

You can also refer to *other* columns in the USING *expression*. For example, say that you are currently storing each customer name in two columns, last_name and first_name, and you've decided to combine them into a single column named customer_name. You can do that with the following commands:

```
movies=# ALTER TABLE customers
movies-#     ALTER COLUMN last_name
movies-#         TYPE VARCHAR USING ( last_name || ',' || first_name ),
movies-#     DROP COLUMN first_name;
ALTER TABLE


movies=# ALTER TABLE customers
movies-#     RENAME COLUMN last_name TO customer_name;
ALTER TABLE
```

The first ALTER TABLE command performs two alterations. First, for each row in the table, it evaluates the expression last_name || ',' || first_name and assigns that value to the last_name column (converting the result into type VARCHAR along the way). Next, the (first) ALTER TABLE command removes the first_name column from each row. You're left with a single column called last_name that contains the concatenation of the original last_name and first_name columns (with a comma in between). The second ALTER TABLE command renames the last_name column to customer_name.

Keep in mind that some ALTER TABLE commands will take longer to execute than others. It takes very little time to change the name of a column. It can take quite a while to change the data type of a column (because PostgreSQL has to traverse every row in the table and write out a new version). If you use ALTER TABLE ... SET TABLESPACE to move a table from one tablespace to another, the server must physically copy each block in the table. In most cases, it's faster to execute a series of ALTER TABLE commands than it is to read the old data into a client application, change each row, and then write the result back to the server. When you use an ALTER TABLE command, the entire transformation occurs within the server; if you modify the structure of a table using a custom-written client application, you have to send every row to the client, perform the transformation, and then send every row back to the server.

The ALTER TABLE command is useful when you are in the development stages of a project. Using ALTER TABLE, you can add new columns to a table, define default values, rename columns (and tables), add and drop constraints, change the data type of a column, and transfer ownership. The capabilities of the ALTER TABLE command seem to grow with each new release—see the *PostgreSQL Reference Manual* for more details.

Adding Indexes to a Table

Most of the tables that you have created so far have no indexes. An index serves two purposes. First, an index can be used to guarantee uniqueness. Second, an index provides quick access to data (in certain circumstances).

Here is the definition of the `customers` table that you created in Chapter 1:

```
CREATE TABLE customers (
        customer_id   INTEGER UNIQUE,
        customer_name VARCHAR(50),
        phone         CHAR(8),
        birth_date    DATE,
        balance       DECIMAL(7,2)
);
```

When you create this table, PostgreSQL will display a rather terse message:

```
NOTICE:  CREATE TABLE / UNIQUE will create implicit
    index 'customers_customer_id_key' for table 'customers'
```

What PostgreSQL is trying to tell you here is that even though you didn't explicitly ask for one, an index has been created on your behalf. The implicit index is created so that PostgreSQL has a quick way to ensure that the values that you enter into the `customer_id` column are unique.

Think about how you might design an algorithm to check for duplicate values in the following list of names:

Grumby, Jonas

Hinkley, Roy

Wentworth, Eunice

Floyd, Heywood

Bowman, David

Dutton, Charles

Poole, Frank

Morbius, Edward

Farman, Jerry

Stone, Jeremy

Dutton, Charles

Manchek, Arthur

A first attempt might simply start with the first value and look for a duplicate later in the list, comparing `Grumby, Jonas` to `Hinkley, Roy`, then `Wentworth, Eunice`, and so on. Next, you would move to the second name in the list and compare `Hinkley, Roy` to `Wentworth, Eunice`, then `Floyd, Heywood`, and so on. This algorithm would certainly work, but it would turn out to be slow as the list grew longer. Each time you add a new name to the list, you have to compare it to every other name already in the list.

A better solution would be to first sort the list:

Bowman, David

Dutton, Charles

Dutton, Charles

Farman, Jerry

Floyd, Heywood

Grumby, Jonas

Hinkley, Roy

Manchek, Arthur

Morbius, Edward

Poole, Frank

Stone, Jeremy

Wentworth, Eunice

After the list is sorted, it's easy to check for duplicates—any duplicate values appear next to each other. To check the sorted list, you start with the first name, `Bowman, David` and compare it to the second name, `Dutton, Charles`. If the second name is not a duplicate of the first, you know that you won't find any duplicates later in the list. Now when you move to the second name on the list, you compare it to the third name—now you can see that there is a duplicate. Duplicate values appear next to each other after the list is sorted. Now when you add a new name to the list, you can stop searching for duplicate values as soon as you encounter a value that sorts after the name you are adding.

An index is similar in concept to a sorted list, but it's even better. An index provides a quick way for PostgreSQL to find data within a range of values. Let's see how an index can help narrow a search. First, let's assign a number to each of the names in the sorted list, just for easy reference (I've removed the duplicate value):

1 Bowman, David

2 Dutton, Charles

3 Farman, Jerry

4 Floyd, Heywood

5 Grumby, Jonas

6 Hinkley, Roy

7 Manchek, Arthur

8 Morbius, Edward

9 Poole, Frank

10 Stone, Jeremy

11 Wentworth, Eunice

Now let's build a (simplistic) index (see Figure 3.2). The English alphabet contains 26 letters—split this roughly in half and choose to keep track of where the "Ms" start in the list. In this list, names beginning with an M start at entry number 7. Keep track of this pair (M,7) and call it the *root* of your index.

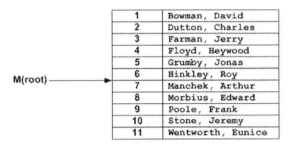

Figure 3.2   One-level index.

Now when you insert a new name, Tyrell, Eldon, you start by comparing it to the root. The root of the index tells you that names starting with the letter M are found starting at entry number 7. Because the list is sorted, and you know that Tyrell will sort after M, you can start searching for the insertion point at entry 7, skipping entries 1 through 6. Also, you can stop searching as soon as you encounter a name that sorts later than Tyrell.

As your list of names grows, it would be advantageous to add more levels to the index (see Figure 3.3). The letter M splits the alphabet (roughly) in half. Add a second level to the index by splitting the range between A and M (giving you G), and splitting the range between M and Z (giving you T).

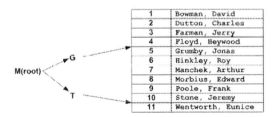

Figure 3.3   Two-level index.

Now when you want to add Tyrell, Eldon to the list, you compare Tyrell against the root and find that Tyrell sorts later than M. Moving to the next layer of the index, you find that Tyrell sorts later than T, so you can jump straight to slot number 11 and insert the new value.

You can see that you can add as many index levels as you need. Each level divides the parent's range in half, and each level reduces the number of names that you have to search to find an insertion point[6].

Using an index is similar in concept to the way you look up words in a dictionary. If you have a dictionary handy, pull it off the shelf and take a close look at it. If it's like my dictionary, it has those little thumb-tab indentations, one for each letter of the alphabet. If I want to find the definition of the word "polyglot," I'll find the thumb-tab labeled "*P*" and start searching about halfway through that section. I know, because the dictionary is sorted, that "polyglot" won't appear in any section prior to "P" and it won't appear in any section following "P." That little thumb-tab saves a lot of searching.

You also can use an index as a quick way to check for uniqueness. If you are inserting a new name into the index structure shown earlier, you simply search for the new name in the index. If you find it in the index, it is obviously a duplicate.

I mentioned earlier that PostgreSQL uses an index for two purposes. You've seen that an index can be used to search for unique values. But how does PostgreSQL use an index to provide faster data access?

Let's look at a simple query:

```
SELECT * FROM characters WHERE name >= 'Grumby' AND name < 'Moon';
```

Now assume that the list of names that you worked with before is actually a table named `characters` and you have an index defined for the `name` column, as in Figure 3.4.

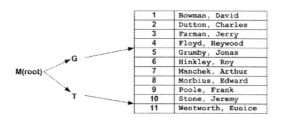

Figure 3.4   Two-level index (again).

When PostgreSQL parses through the SELECT statement, it notices that you are constraining the result set to a *range* of names and that you have an index on the `name` column. That's a convenient combination. To satisfy this statement, PostgreSQL can use the index to start searching at entry number 5. Because the rows are already sorted, PostgreSQL can stop searching as soon as it finds the first entry greater than "Moon" (that is, the search ends as soon as you hit entry number 8). This kind of operation is called a *partial index scan*.

[6] Technically speaking, the index diagrams discussed here depict a clustered index. In a clustered index, the leaf nodes in the index tree are the data rows themselves. In a non-clustered index, the leaf nodes are actually row pointers—the rows are not kept in sorted order. PostgreSQL does not support clustered indexes. I've diagrammed the index trees in clustered form for clarity. A clustered index provides fast, sequential access along one index path, but it is very expensive to maintain.

Think of how PostgreSQL would process this query if the rows were *not* indexed. It would have to start at the beginning of the table and compare each row against the constraints; PostgreSQL can't terminate the search without processing every row in the table. This kind of operation is called a *full table scan*, or *table scan*.

Because this kind of index can access data in sorted order, PostgreSQL can use such an index to avoid a sort that would otherwise be required to satisfy an ORDER BY clause.

In these examples, we are working with small tables, so the performance difference between a full table scan and an indexed range read is negligible. As tables become larger, the performance difference can be huge. Chapter 4, "Performance," discusses how the PostgreSQL query optimizer chooses when it is appropriate to use an index.

PostgreSQL actually supports several kinds of indexes. The previous examples show how a B-Tree index works[7]. Another type of index is the Hash index. A Hash index uses a technique called *hashing* to evenly distribute keys among a number of *hash buckets*. Each key value added to a hash index is run through a hashing function. The result of a hashing function is a bucket number. A simplistic hashing function for string values might sum the ASCII value of each character in the string and then compute the sum modulo the number of buckets to get the result. In C, you might write this function as

```
int hash_string( char * key, int bucket_count )
{
    int hash = 0;
    int i;

    for( i = 0; i < strlen( key ); i++ )
        hash = hash + key[i];

    return( hash % bucket_count );
}
```

Let's run each of the names in the characters table through this function to see what kind of numbers you get back (I've used a bucket_count of 5):

hash_string( ) Value	Name
1	Grumby, Jonas
2	Hinkley, Roy
3	Wentworth, Eunice
4	Floyd, Heywood
4	Bowman, David
3	Dutton, Charles
3	Poole, Frank

[7] The "B" in B-Tree stands for "Balanced." A balanced tree is a type of data structure that retains its performance characteristics even in the face of numerous insertions and deletions. The most important feature of a B-Tree is that it takes about the same amount of time to find any given record.

hash_string( ) Value	Name
0	Morbius, Edward
0	Farman, Jerry
0	Stone, Jeremy
4	Manchek, Arthur

The numbers returned don't really have any intrinsic meaning, they simply serve to distribute a set of keys amongst a set of buckets.

Now let's reformat this table so that the contents are grouped by bucket number:

Bucket Number	Bucket Contents
0	Morbius, Edward
	Farman, Jerry
	Stone, Jeremy
1	Grumby, Jonas
2	Hinkley, Roy
3	Wentworth, Eunice

Bucket Number	Bucket Contents
	Dutton, Charles
	Poole, Frank
4	Floyd, Heywood
	Bowman, David
	Manchek, Arthur

You can see that the hash function (hash_string()) did a respectable job of distributing the names between the five hash buckets. Notice that we did not have to assign a unique hash value to each key—hash keys are seldom unique. The important feature of a good hash function is that it distributes a set of keys fairly evenly. Now that you have a Hash index, how can you use it? First, let's try to insert a new name: Lowell, Freeman. The first thing you do is run this name through your hash_string() function, giving you a hash value of 4. Now you know that if Lowell, Freeman is already in the index, it will be in bucket number 4; all you have to do is search that one bucket for the name you are trying to insert.

There are a couple of important points to note about Hash indexes.

First, you may have noticed that each bucket can hold many keys. Another way to say this is that each key does not have a unique hash value. If you have too many collisions (that is, too many keys hashing to the same bucket), performance will suffer. A good hash function distributes keys evenly between all hash buckets.

Second, notice that a hash table is not sorted. The name Floyd, Heywood hashes to bucket 4, but Farman, Jerry hashes to bucket 0. Consider the SELECT statement that we looked at earlier:

```
SELECT * FROM characters WHERE name >= 'Grumby' AND name < 'Moon';
```

To satisfy this query using a Hash index, you have to read the entire contents of each bucket. Bucket 0 contains one row that meets the constraints (Farman, Jerry), bucket 2 contains one row, and bucket 4 contains one row. A Hash index offers no advantage to a range read. A Hash index is good for searches based on equality. For example, the SELECT statement

```
SELECT * FROM characters WHERE name = 'Grumby, Jonas';
```

can be satisfied simply by hashing the string that you are searching for. A Hash index is also useful when you are joining two tables where the join constraint is of the form table1-column = table2-column[8]. A Hash read cannot be used to avoid a sort required to satisfy an ORDER BY clause.

PostgreSQL supports two other types of index structures: the R-Tree index and the GiST index. An R-Tree index is best suited for indexing spatial (that is, geometric or geographic) data. A GiST index is a B-Tree index that can be extended by defining new query predicates[9]. More information about GiST indexes can be found at http://gist.cs.berkeley.edu/.

Tradeoffs

The previous section showed that PostgreSQL can use an index to speed the process of searching for data within a range of values (or data with an exact value). Most queries (that is, SELECT commands) in PostgreSQL include a WHERE clause to limit the result set. If you find that you are often searching for results based on a range of values for a specific column or group of columns, you might want to consider creating an index that covers those columns.

However, you should be aware that an index represents a performance tradeoff. When you create an index, you are trading read performance for write performance. An index can significantly reduce the amount of time it takes to retrieve data, but it will also *increase* the amount of time it takes to INSERT, DELETE, and UPDATE data. Maintaining an index introduces substantial overhead when you modify the data within a table.

You should consider this tradeoff when you feel the need to add a new index to a table. Adding an index to a table that is updated frequently will certainly slow the updates. A good candidate for an index is a table that you SELECT from frequently but seldom update. A customer list, for example, doesn't change often (possibly several times each day), but you probably query the customer list frequently. If you find that you often query the customer list by phone number, it would be beneficial to index the phone number column. On the other hand, a table that is updated frequently, but seldom queried, such as a transaction history table, would be a poor choice for an index.

---

[8] This type of join is known as an equi-join.

[9] A predicate is a test. A simple predicate is the less-than operator (<). An expression such as a < 5 tests whether the value of a is less than 5. In this expression, < is the predicate and it is called the less-than predicate. Other predicates are =, >, >=, and so on.

Creating an Index

Now that you have seen what an index can do, let's look at the process of adding an index to a table. The process of creating a new index can range from simple to somewhat complex.

Let's add an index to the `rentals` table. Here is the structure of the rentals table for reference:

```
CREATE TABLE rentals
(
        tape_id        CHARACTER(8) REFERENCES tapes,
        customer_id    INTEGER REFERENCES customers,
        rental_date    DATE
);
```

The syntax for a simple `CREATE INDEX` command is

```
CREATE [UNIQUE] INDEX index-name ON table-name( column [,...] );
```

You want to index the `rental_date` column in the `rentals` table:

```
CREATE INDEX rentals_rental_date ON rentals ( rental_date );
```

You haven't specified any optional information in this command (I'll get to the options in a moment), so PostgreSQL creates a B-Tree index named `rentals_rental_date`. PostgreSQL considers using this whenever it finds a `WHERE` clause that refers to the `rental_date` column using the <, <=, =, >=, or > operator. This index also can be used when you specify an `ORDER BY` clause that sorts on the `rental_date` column.

Multicolumn Indexes

A B-Tree index (or a GiST index) can cover more than one column. Multicolumn indexes are usually created when you have many values on the second column for each value in the first column. For example, you might want to create an index that covers the `rental_date` and `tape_id` columns—you have many different tapes rented on any given date. PostgreSQL can use multicolumn indexes for selection or for ordering. When you create a multicolumn index, the order in which you name the columns is important. PostgreSQL can use a multicolumn index when you are selecting (or ordering by) a prefix of the key. In this context, a prefix may be the entire key or a leading portion of the key. For example, the command `SELECT * FROM rentals ORDER BY rental_date` could not use an index that covers `tape_id` plus `rental_date`, but it could use an index that covers `rental_date` plus `tape_id`.

The `index-name` must be unique within the database: You can't have two indexes with the same name, even if they are defined on different tables. New rows are indexed as they are added, and deleted rows are removed. If you change the `rental_date` for a given row, the index will be updated automatically. If you have any data in the `rentals` table, each row will be included in the index.

Indexes and NULL Values

Earlier, I mentioned that an index includes a pointer for every row in a table. That statement isn't 100% accurate. PostgreSQL will not index NULL values in R-Tree, Hash, and GiST indexes. Because such an index will never include NULL values, it cannot be used to satisfy the ORDER BY clause of a query that returns all rows in a table. For example, if you define a GiST index covering the phone column in the customers table, that index would not include rows where phone was NULL. If you executed the command SELECT * FROM customers ORDER BY phone, PostgreSQL would have to perform a full table scan and then sort the results. If PostgreSQL tried to use the phone index, it would not find all rows. If the phone column were defined as NOT NULL, then PostgreSQL could use the index to avoid a sort. Or, if the SELECT command included the clause WHERE phone IS NOT NULL, PostgreSQL could use the index to satisfy the ORDER BY clause. An R-Tree, Hash, or GiST index that covers an optional (that is, NULLs-allowed) column will not be used to speed table joins, either.

A B-Tree index (the default index type) *does* include NULL values.

If you don't specify an index type when creating an index, you'll get a B-Tree index. Let's change the rentals_rental_date index into a Hash index. First, drop the original index:

```
DROP INDEX rentals_rental_date;
```

Then you can create a new index:

```
CREATE INDEX rentals_rental_date ON rentals USING HASH ( rental_date );
```

The only difference between this CREATE INDEX command and the previous one is that I have included a USING clause. You can specify USING BTREE (which is the default), USING HASH, USING RTREE, or USING GIST.

This index cannot be used to satisfy an ORDER BY clause. In fact, this index can be used only when rental_date is compared using the = operator.

I dropped the B-Tree index before creating the Hash index, but that is not strictly necessary. It is perfectly valid (but unusual) to have two or more indexes that cover the same column, as long as the indexes are uniquely named. If we had both a B-Tree index and a Hash index covering the rental_date column, PostgreSQL could use the Hash index for = comparisons and the B-Tree index for other comparisons.

Functional Indexes and Partial Indexes

Now let's look at two variations on the basic index types: functional indexes and partial indexes.

A column-based index catalogs the values found in a column (or a set of columns). A functional index (or more precisely a function-valued index) catalogs the values returned by a given function. This might be easiest to understand by looking at an example. Each row in the customers table contains a phone number. You can use the exchange[10] portion of the phone number to determine whether a given customer is located close to your store. For example, you may know that the 555, 556, and 794 exchanges are within five miles of your virtual video store. Let's create a function that extracts the exchange from a phone number:

[10] In the U.S., a phone number is composed of an optional three-digit area code, a three-digit exchange, and a four digit?ummm, number.

```
-- exchange_index.sql
--
CREATE OR REPLACE FUNCTION get_exchange( CHARACTER )
  RETURNS CHARACTER AS '

  DECLARE
    result                CHARACTER(3);
  BEGIN

    result := SUBSTR( $1, 1, 3 );

    return( result );
  END;
' LANGUAGE 'plpgsql' WITH ( ISCACHABLE );
```

Don't be too concerned if this looks a bit confusing; I'll cover the PL/pgSQL language in more detail in Chapter 7, "PL/pgSQL." This function (get_exchange()) accepts a single argument, presumably a phone number, and extracts the first three characters. You can call this function directly from psql:

```
movies=# SELECT customer_name, phone, get_exchange( phone )
movies-#   FROM customers;
```

```
    customer_name      |  phone   | get_exchange
-----------------------+----------+--------------
 Jones, Henry          | 555-1212 | 555
 Rubin, William        | 555-2211 | 555
 Panky, Henry          | 555-1221 | 555
 Wonderland, Alice N.  | 555-1122 | 555
 Wink Wankel           | 555-1000 | 555
```

You can see that given a phone number, get_exchange() returns the first three digits. Now let's create a function-valued index that uses this function:

```
CREATE INDEX customer_exchange ON customers ( get_exchange( phone ));
```

When you insert a new row into a column-based index, PostgreSQL will index the values in the columns covered by that index. When you insert a new row into a *function-valued* index, PostgreSQL will call the function that you specified and then index the return value.

After the customer_exchange index exists, PostgreSQL can use it to speed up queries such as

```
SELECT * FROM customers WHERE get_exchange( phone ) = '555';
SELECT * FROM customers ORDER BY get_exchange( phone );
```

Now you have an index that you can use to search the customer list for all customers that are geographically close. Let's pretend that you occasionally want to send advertising flyers to those customers closest to you: you might never use the customer_exchange index for any other purpose. If you need the `customer_exchange` index for only a small set of customers, why bother maintaining that index for customers outside of your vicinity? This is where a *partial* index comes in handy. When you create an index, you can include a WHERE clause in the CREATE INDEX command. Each time you insert (or update) a row, the WHERE clause is evaluated. If a row satisfies the constraints of the WHERE clause, that row is included in the index; otherwise, the row is not included in the index. Let's DROP the `customer_exchange` index and replace it with a partial, function-valued index:

```
movies=# DROP INDEX customer_exchange;
DROP
movies=# CREATE INDEX customer_exchange
movies-#   ON customers ( get_exchange( phone ))
movies-#   WHERE
movies-#     get_exchange( phone ) = '555'
movies-#      OR
movies-#     get_exchange( phone ) = '556'
movies-#      OR
movies-#     get_exchange( phone ) = '794';
CREATE
```

Now the `customer_exchange` partial index contains entries only for customers in the 555, 556, or 794 exchange.

There are three performance advantages to a partial index:

- A partial index requires less disk space than a full index.
- Because fewer rows are cataloged in a partial index, the cost of maintaining the index is lower.
- When a partial index is used in a query, PostgreSQL will have fewer index entries to search.

Partial indexes and function-valued indexes are variations on the four basic index types. You can create a function-valued Hash index, B-Tree index, R-tree index, or GiST index. You can also create a partial variant of any index type. And, as you have seen, you can create partial function-valued indexes (of any type). A function-valued index doesn't change the organization of an index—just the values that are actually included in the index. The same is true for a partial index.

Creating Indexes on Array Values

Most indexes cover scalar-valued columns (columns that store a single value). PostgreSQL also allows you to define indexes that cover index values. In fact, you can create an index that covers the entire array or (starting with PostgreSQL version 7.4) an index that covers individual elements within an array. In Chapter 2 we showed you a modified version of the `customers` table that included an array column (`monthly_balances`). You can add this column to your working copy of the `customers` table with the following command:

```
movies=#  ALTER TABLE customers
movies-#     ADD COLUMN
movies-#        monthly_balances DECIMAL( 7, 2 )[ 12 ];
ALTER TABLE
```

To create an index that covers a single element of monthly_balances array (say, the element corresponding to the month of February), you could execute the following command:

```
movies=# CREATE INDEX customers_feb
movies-#   ON customers(( monthly_balances[2] ));
CREATE INDEX
```

Notice that you need an extra set of parentheses around monthly_balances[2]. Once you've created the customers_feb index, PostgreSQL can use it to satisfy queries such as

```
movies=# SELECT * FROM customers WHERE monthly_balances[2] = 10;
movies=# SELECT * FROM customers ORDER BY monthly_balances[2];
```

To create an index that covers the entire monthly_balances array, execute the command

```
movies=# CREATE INDEX customers_by_monthly_balance
movies-#   ON customers( monthly_balances );
CREATE INDEX
```

When you create an index that covers an array column, the syntax is the same as you would use to cover a scalar (single-valued) column. The PostgreSQL optimizer can use the customers_by_monthly_balance index to satisfy an ORDER BY clause such as

```
movies=# SELECT * FROM customers ORDER BY monthly_balances;
```

However, you may be surprised to find that the optimizer will *not* use customers_by_monthly_balance to satisfy a WHERE CLAUSE such as

```
movies=# SELECT * FROM customers WHERE monthly_balances[1] = 10;
```

The PostgreSQL optimizer *will* use the customers_by_monthly_balance index to satisfy a WHERE_CLAUSE that compares the entire monthly_balances array against another array, like this:

```
movies=# SELECT * FROM customers WHERE monthly_balances = '{10}';
```

But be aware that these queries are not equivalent. The first WHERE clause (monthly_balances[1] = 10) selects any row where monthly_balances[1] is equal to 10, regardless of the other monthly_balances in that row. The second WHERE clause (monthly_balances = '{10}') selects only those rows where monthly_balances[1] = 10 and all other monthly_balances values are NULL.

Indexes and Tablespaces

When you create an index, you can tell PostgreSQL to store the index in a specific tablespace by including a TABLESPACE *tablespacename* clause, like this:

```
CREATE INDEX rentals_rental_date
   ON rentals ( rental_date ) TABLESPACE mytablespace;
```

If you don't specify a tablespace, PostgreSQL creates the index in the tablespace assigned to the table that you are indexing. You can move an existing index to a different tablespace using the `ALTER INDEX` command. For example, to move the `rentals_rental_date` index to `mytablespace`, you would execute the command

```
ALTER INDEX rentals_rental_date SET TABLESPACE mytablespace;
```

You may want to store a table and its indexes in different tablespaces in order to spread the workload among multiple physical disk drives.

Getting Information About Databases and Tables

When you create a table, PostgreSQL stores the definition of that table in the system catalog. The system catalog is a collection of PostgreSQL tables. You can issue `SELECT` statements against the system catalog tables just like any other table, but there are easier ways to view table and index definitions.

When you are using the psql client application, you can view the list of tables defined in your database using the \d meta-command:

```
movies=# \d
            List of relations
      Name        | Type  |    Owner
------------------+-------+---------------
 customers        | table | bruce
 rentals          | table | bruce
 tapes            | table | bruce
```

To see the detailed definition of a particular table, use the \d *table-name* meta-command:

```
movies=# \d tapes
              Table "tapes"
  Column  |         Type         | Modifiers
----------+----------------------+-----------
 tape_id  | character(8)         | not null
 title    | character varying(80)| not null
 duration | interval             |
```

You can also view a list of all indexes defined in your database. The \di meta-command displays indexes:

```
movies=# \di
                List of relations
 Schema  |           Name            | Type  | Owner  |   Table
---------+---------------------------+-------+--------+-----------
 public  | customers_customer_id_key | index | korry  | customers
```

You can see the full definition for any given index using the \d *index-name* meta-command:

```
movies=# \d customers_customer_id_key
Index "public.customers_customer_id_key"
   Column    | Type
-------------+---------
 customer_id | integer
UNIQUE, btree, for table "public.customers"
```

Table 3.1 shows a complete list of the system catalog-related meta-commands in psql:

Table 3.1 **System Catalog Meta-Commands**

Command	Result
\dd *object-name*	Display comments for *object-name*
\db	List all tablespaces
\dn	List all schemas
\d_\dt	List all tables
\di	List all indexes
\ds	List all sequences
\dv	List all views
\dS	List all PostgreSQL-defined tables
\d table-name	Show table definition
\d index-name	Show index definition
\d view-name	Show view definition
\d sequence-name	Show sequence definition
\dp	List all privileges
\dl	List all large objects
\da	List all aggregates
\df	List all functions
\dc	List all conversions
\dC	List all casts
\df function-name	List all functions with given name
\do	List all operators
\do operator-name	List all operators with given name
\dT	List all types
\dD	List all domains
\dg	List all groups
\du	List all users
\l	List all databases in this cluster

Alternative Views (Oracle-Style Dictionary Views)

One of the nice things about an open-source product is that code contributions come from many different places. One such project exists to add Oracle-style dictionary views to PostgreSQL. If you are an experienced Oracle user, you will appreciate this feature. The orapgsqlviews project contributes Oracle-style views such as `all_views`, `all_tables`, `user_tables`, and so on. For more information, see http://gborg.post-gresql.org.

PostgreSQL version 8.0 introduced a set of views known as the INFORMATION_SCHEMA. The views defined in the INFORMATION_SCHEMA give you access to the information stored in the PostgreSQL system tables. The INFORMATION_SCHEMA is defined as part of the SQL standard and you'll find an INFORMATION_SCHEMA in most commercial (and a few open-source) database systems. If you become familiar with the views defined in the INFORMATION_SCHEMA, you'll find it much easier to move from one RDBMS system to another—every INFORMATION_SCHEMA contains the same set of views, each containing the same set of columns. For example, to see a list of the tables defined in your current database, you could execute the command:

```
SELECT table_schema, table_name, table_type FROM information_schema.tables;
```

You can execute that same query in DB2, MS SQL Server, or Informix (sadly, Oracle doesn't support the INFORMATION_SCHEMA standard at the time we are writing this). So what can you find in the INFORMATION_SCHEMA?

- `schemata`—Lists the schemas (in the current database) that are owned by you
- `tables`—Lists all tables in the current database (actually, you only see those tables that you have the right to access in some way)
- `columns`—Lists all columns in all tables that you have the right to access
- `views`—Lists all of the views you have access to in the current database
- `table_privileges`—Shows the privileges you hold (or that you granted) for each accessible object in the current database
- `domains`—Lists all of the domains defined in the current database
- `check_constraints`—Lists all of the CHECK constraints defined for the accessible tables (or domains) in the current database

There are more views in the INFORMATION_SCHEMA than we've described here (in fact, there are a total of 39 INFORMATION_SCHEMA views in PostgreSQL 8.0). See Chapter 30, "The Information Schema," of the PostgreSQL user guide for a complete list.

Why would you want to use the INFORMATION_SCHEMA instead of psql's \d commands? We can think of three reasons. First, you can use the INFORMATION_SCHEMA inside of your own client applications—you can't do that with the \d commands because they are part of the psql console application (itself a PostgreSQL client) instead of the PostgreSQL server. Second, by using the views defined in the INFORMATION_SCHEMA, you can read the PostgreSQL system tables using the same queries that you would use to read the DB2 system tables (or Sybase or SQL Server). That makes your client applications a bit more portable. Finally, you can write *custom queries* against the views defined in the INFORMATION_SCHEMA—you can't customize the \d commands. For example, if you need to find all of the date columns in your database, just look inside of INFORMA-TION_SCHEMA.columns, like this:

```
SELECT DISTINCT table_name
    FROM information_schema.columns WHERE data_type = 'date';
```

Need to know which columns can hold a NUMERIC value of at least seven digits? Use this query:

```
SELECT table_name,column_name, numeric_precision
    FROM information_schema.columns
    WHERE data_type = 'numeric' AND numeric_precision >= 7;
```

Of course, you can find all the information exposed by the INFORMATION_SCHEMA in the PostgreSQL system tables (pg_class, pg_index, and so on), but the INFORMATION_SCHEMA is often much easier to work with. The INFORMATION_SCHEMA views usually contain human-readable names for things like data type names, table names, and so on—the PostgreSQL system tables typically contain OIDs that you have to JOIN to another table in order to come up with a human-readable name.

Transaction Processing

Now let's move on to an important feature in any database system: transaction processing.

A *transaction* is a group of one or more SQL commands treated as a unit. PostgreSQL promises that all commands within a transaction will complete or that none of them will complete. If any command within a transaction does not complete, PostgreSQL will roll back all changes made within the transaction.

PostgreSQL makes use of transactions to ensure database consistency. Transactions are needed to coordinate updates made by two or more concurrent users. Changes made by a transaction are not visible to other users until the transaction is *committed*. When you commit a transaction, you are telling PostgreSQL that all the changes made within the transaction are logically complete, the changes should be made permanent, and the changes should be exposed to other users. When you roll back a transaction, you are telling PostgreSQL that the changes made within the transaction should be discarded and not made visible to other users.

To start a new transaction, execute a BEGIN command. To complete the transaction and have PostgreSQL make your changes permanent, execute the COMMIT command. If you want PostgreSQL to revert all changes made within the current transaction, execute the ROLLBACK command[11].

It's important to realize that *all* SQL commands execute within a transaction. If you don't explicitly BEGIN a transaction, PostgreSQL will automatically execute each command within its own transaction.

---

[11] BEGIN can also be written as BEGIN WORK or BEGIN TRANSACTION. COMMIT can also be written as COMMIT WORK or COMMIT TRANSACTION. ROLLBACK can also written as ROLLBACK WORK or ROLLBACK TRANSACTION.

Persistence

I used to think that single-command transactions were pretty useless: I was wrong. Single-command transactions are important because a single command can access multiple rows. Consider the following: Let's add a new constraint to the `customers` table.

```
movies=# ALTER TABLE customers ADD CONSTRAINT
movies-#   balance_exceeded CHECK( balance <= 50 );
```

This constraint ensures that no customer is allowed to have a balance exceeding $50.00. Just to prove that it works, let's try setting a customer's balance to some value greater than $50.00:

```
movies=# UPDATE CUSTOMERS SET balance = 100 where customer_id = 1;
ERROR:  ExecReplace: rejected due to CHECK constraint balance_exceeded
```

You can see that the UPDATE is rejected. What happens if you try to update more than one row? First, let's look at the data already in the `customers` table:

```
movies=# SELECT * FROM customers;
 customer_id |    customer_name     |   phone   | birth_date | balance
-------------+----------------------+-----------+------------+---------
           1 | Jones, Henry         | 555-1212  | 1970-10-10 |    0.00
           2 | Rubin, William       | 555-2211  | 1972-07-10 |   15.00
           3 | Panky, Henry         | 555-1221  | 1968-01-21 |    0.00
           4 | Wonderland, Alice N. | 555-1122  | 1969-03-05 |    3.00
           8 | Wink Wankel          | 555-1000  | 1988-12-25 |    0.00
(5 rows)
```

Now, try to UPDATE every row in this table:

```
movies=# UPDATE customers SET balance = balance + 40;
ERROR:  ExecReplace: rejected due to CHECK constraint balance_exceeded
```

This UPDATE command is rejected because adding $40.00 to the balance for Rubin, William violates the `balance_exceeded` constraint. The question is, were any of the customers updated before the error occurred? The answer is: probably. You don't really know for sure because any changes made before the error occurred are rolled back. The net effect is that no changes were made to the database:

```
movies=# SELECT * FROM customers;
 customer_id |    customer_name     |   phone   | birth_date | balance
-------------+----------------------+-----------+------------+---------
           1 | Jones, Henry         | 555-1212  | 1970-10-10 |    0.00
           2 | Rubin, William       | 555-2211  | 1972-07-10 |   15.00
           3 | Panky, Henry         | 555-1221  | 1968-01-21 |    0.00
           4 | Wonderland, Alice N. | 555-1122  | 1969-03-05 |    3.00
           8 | Wink Wankel          | 555-1000  | 1988-12-25 |    0.00
(5 rows)
```

If some of the changes persisted while others did not, you would have to somehow find the persistent changes yourself and revert them. You can see that single-command transactions are far from useless. It took me awhile to learn that lesson.

What about multicommand transactions? PostgreSQL treats a multicommand transaction in much the same way that it treats a single-command transaction. A transaction is *atomic*, meaning that all the commands within the transaction are treated as a single unit. If any of the commands fail to complete, PostgreSQL reverts the changes made by other commands within the transaction.

Transaction Isolation

I mentioned earlier in this section that the changes made within a transaction are not visible to other users until the transaction is committed. To be a bit more precise, uncommitted changes made in one transaction are not visible to other transactions[12].

Transaction isolation helps to ensure consistent data within a database. Let's look at a few of the problems solved by transaction isolation.

Consider the following transactions:

User: bruce	Time	User: sheila
BEGIN TRANSACTION	T1	BEGIN TRANSACTION
UPDATE customers	T2	
SET balance = balance - 3		
WHERE customer_id = 2;		
	T3	SELECT SUM(balance)
		FROM customers;
	T4	COMMIT TRANSACTION;
ROLLBACK TRANSACTION;	T5	

At time T1, bruce and sheila each begin a new transaction. bruce updates the balance for customer 3 at time T1. At time T3, sheila computes the SUM() of the balances for all customers, completing her transaction at time T4. At time T5, bruce rolls back his transaction, discarding all changes within his transaction. If these transactions were not isolated from each other, sheila would have an incorrect answer: Her answer was calculated using data that was rolled back.

This problem is known as the *dirty read* problem: without transaction isolation, sheila would read uncommitted data. The solution to this problem is known as READ COMMITTED. READ COMMITTED is one of the two transaction isolation levels supported by

---

[12] This distinction is important when using (or developing) a client that opens two or more connections to the same database. Transactions are not shared between multiple connections. If you make an uncommitted change using one connection, those changes will not be visible to the other connection (until committed).

PostgreSQL. A transaction running at the READ COMMITTED isolation level is not allowed to read uncommitted data. I'll show you how to change transaction levels in a moment.

There are other data consistency problems that are avoided by isolating transactions from each other. In the following scenario, sheila will receive two different answers within the same transaction:

User: bruce	Time	User: sheila
BEGIN TRANSACTION;	T1	BEGIN TRANSACTION;
	T2	SELECT balance
FROM customers		
WHERE customer_id = 2;		
UPDATE customers		
SET balance = 20		
WHERE customer_id = 2;	T3	
COMMIT TRANSACTION;	T4	
	T5	SELECT balance
		FROM customers
		WHERE customer_id = 2;
	T6	COMMIT TRANSACTION;

Again, bruce and sheila each start a transaction at time T1. At T2, sheila finds that customer 2 has a balance of $15.00. bruce changes the balance for customer 2 from $15.00 to $20.00 at time T3 and commits his change at time T4. At time T5, sheila executes the same query that she executed earlier in the transaction, but this time she finds that the balance is $20.00. In some applications, this isn't a problem; in others, this interference between the two transactions is unacceptable. This problem is known as the *non-repeatable read*.

Here is another type of problem:

User: bruce	Time	User: sheila
BEGIN TRANSACTION;	T1	BEGIN TRANSACTION;
	T2	SELECT * FROM customers;
INSERT INTO customers VALUES	T3	
(		
6,		
'Neville, Robert',		
'555-9999',		
'1971-03-20',		
0.00		
);		

User: bruce	Time	User: sheila
COMMIT TRANSACTION;	T4	
	T5	SELECT * FROM customers;
	T6	COMMIT TRANSACTION;

In this example, sheila again executes the same query twice within a single transaction. This time, bruce has inserted a new row in between the sheila's queries. Notice that this is not a case of a *dirty read*—bruce has committed his change before sheila executes her second query. At time T5, sheila finds a new row. This is similar to the non-repeatable read, but this problem is known as the *phantom read* problem.

The answer to both the non-repeatable read and the phantom read is the SERIALIZABLE transaction isolation level. A transaction running at the SERIALIZABLE isolation level is only allowed to see data committed before the transaction began.

In PostgreSQL, transactions usually run at the READ COMMITTED isolation level. If you need to avoid the problems present in READ COMMITTED, you can change isolation levels using the SET TRANSACTION command. The syntax for the SET TRANSACTION command is

```
SET TRANSACTION ISOLATION LEVEL { READ COMMITTED | SERIALIZABLE };
```

The SET TRANSACTION command affects only the current transaction (and it must be executed before the first DML[13] command within the transaction). If you want to change the isolation level for your session (that is, change the isolation level for future transactions), you can use the SET SESSION command:

```
SET SESSION CHARACTERISTICS AS
    TRANSACTION ISOLATION LEVEL { READ COMMITTED | SERIALIZABLE }
```

PostgreSQL version 8.0 introduces a new transaction processing feature called a SAVEPOINT. A SAVEPOINT is a named marker that you define within the stream of commands that make up a transaction. Once you've defined a SAVEPOINT, you can ROLLBACK any changes that you've made since that point without discarding changes made prior to the SAVEPOINT—in other words, you can ROLLBACK part of a transaction (the trailing part) without rolling back the entire transaction. To create a SAVEPOINT, execute a SAVEPOINT command within a transaction. The syntax for a SAVEPOINT command is very simple:

```
SAVEPOINT savepoint-name
```

The *savepoint-name* must follow the normal rules for an identifier; it must be unique within the first 64 characters and must start with a letter or underscore (or it must be a quoted identifier). A SAVEPOINT gives a name to a point in time; in particular, a point between two SQL commands. Consider the following sequence:

---

[13] A DML (data manipulation language) command is any command that can update or read the data within a table. SELECT, INSERT, UPDATE, FETCH, and COPY are DML commands.

```
movies=# SELECT customer_id, customer_name FROM customers;
 customer_id |    customer_name
-------------+----------------------
           3 | Panky, Henry
           1 | Jones, Henry
           4 | Wonderland, Alice N.
           2 | Rubin, William
(4 rows)

movies=# START TRANSACTION;
START TRANSACTION

movies=# INSERT INTO customers VALUES( 5, 'Kemp, Hans' );
INSERT 44272 1

movies=# SELECT * FROM customers;
 customer_id |    customer_name     |  phone   | birth_date | balance
-------------+----------------------+----------+------------+---------
           3 | Panky, Henry         | 555-1221 | 1968-01-21 |    0.00
           1 | Jones, Henry         | 555-1212 | 1970-10-10 |    0.00
           4 | Wonderland, Alice N. | 555-1122 | 1969-03-05 |    3.00
           2 | Rubin, William       | 555 2211 | 1972-07-10 |   15.00
           5 | Kemp, Hans           |          |            |
(5 rows)
```

At this point, you've started a new transaction and inserted a new row, but you haven't committed your changes yet. Now define a SAVEPOINT named p1 and insert a second row:

```
movies=# SAVEPOINT P1;
SAVEPOINT

movies=# INSERT INTO customers VALUES( 6, 'Falkstein, Gerhard' );
INSERT 44273 1
```

The SAVEPOINT command inserted a marker into the transaction stream. If you execute a ROLLBACK command at this point, both of the newly inserted rows will be discarded (in other words, *all* of the changes you've made in this transaction will be rolled back):

```
movies=# ROLLBACK;
ROLLBACK
movies=# SELECT * FROM customers;
 customer_id |    customer_name     |  phone   | birth_date | balance
-------------+----------------------+----------+------------+---------
           3 | Panky, Henry         | 555-1221 | 1968-01-21 |    0.00
           1 | Jones, Henry         | 555-1212 | 1970-10-10 |    0.00
           4 | Wonderland, Alice N. | 555-1122 | 1969-03-05 |    3.00
           2 | Rubin, William       | 555-2211 | 1972-07-10 |   15.00
(4 rows)
```

Now repeat the same sequence of commands, but this time around, execute a qualified ROLLBACK command, like this:

```
movies=# ROLLBACK TO SAVEPOINT P1;
ROLLBACK
movies=# SELECT * FROM customers;
 customer_id |    customer_name     |  phone   | birth_date | balance
-------------+----------------------+----------+------------+---------
           3 | Panky, Henry         | 555-1221 | 1968-01-21 |    0.00
           1 | Jones, Henry         | 555-1212 | 1970-10-10 |    0.00
           4 | Wonderland, Alice N. | 555-1122 | 1969-03-05 |    3.00
           2 | Rubin, William       | 555-2211 | 1972-07-10 |   15.00
           5 | Kemp, Hans           |          |            |
(5 rows)
```

When you ROLLBACK to a SAVEPOINT, changes made since the SAVEPOINT are discarded, but not changes made before the SAVEPOINT. So, you see that the customers table retains the first row that you inserted, but not the second row. When you ROLLBACK to a SAVEPOINT, you are still in the middle of a transaction—you must complete the transaction with a COMMIT or ROLLBACK command.

Here are a few important points to keep in mind when you're working with SAVEPOINTs:

- You can nest SAVEPOINTs. For example, if you create a SAVEPOINT named P1, then create a second SAVEPOINT named P2, you have created a nested SAVEPOINT (P2 is nested within P1). If you ROLLBACK TO SAVEPOINT P2, PostgreSQL discards any changes made since P2, but preserves changes made between P1 and P2. On the other hand, if you ROLLBACK TO SAVEPOINT P1, PostgreSQL discards all changes made since P1, including all changes made since P2. Nested SAVEPOINTs are handy when you are working with a multilevel table structure such as ORDERS and LINEITEMS (where you have multiple line items per order). If you define a SAVE-POINT prior to modifying each order, and a second, nested SAVEPOINT prior to modifying each line item, you can ROLLBACK changes made to a single line item, changes made to a single order, or an entire transaction.

- You can use the same SAVEPOINT name as often as you like within a single transaction—the new SAVEPOINT simply replaces the old SAVEPOINT[14]. Again, this is useful when you are working with a multilevel table structure. If you create a SAVE-POINT prior to processing each line item and you give each of those SAVEPOINTs the same name, you can ROLLBACK changes made to the most recently processed line item.

---

[14] PostgreSQL doesn't follow the SQL standard when you create two SAVEPOINTs within the same transaction. PostgreSQL simply hides the old SAVEPOINT—the SQL standard states that the old SAVEPOINT should be destroyed. If you need the SQL-prescribed behavior, you can destroy the old SAVEPOINT with the command RELEASE SAVEPOINT savepoint-name.

- If you ROLLBACK to a SAVEPOINT, the SAVEPOINT is not destroyed—you can make more changes in the transaction and ROLLBACK to the SAVEPOINT again. However, any SAVEPOINTs nested within that SAVEPOINT will be destroyed. To continue the ORDERS and LINEITEMS example, if you ROLLBACK the changes made to an ORDERS row, you also discard changes made to the LINEITEMS for that ORDER and you are destroying the SAVEPOINT that you created for the most recent line item.

- If you make a mistake (such as a typing error), PostgreSQL rolls back to the most recent SAVEPOINT. That's a very nice feature. If you've used PostgreSQL for any length of time, you've surely exercised your vocabulary after watching PostgreSQL throw out a long and complex transaction because you made a simple typing error. If you insert SAVEPOINTs in your transaction, you won't lose as much work when your fingers fumble a table name.

Multi-Versioning and Locking

Most commercial (and open-source) databases use *locking* to coordinate multiuser updates. If you are modifying a table, that table is locked against updates and queries made by other users. Some databases perform page-level or row-level locking to reduce contention, but the principle is the same—other users must wait to read the data you have modified until you have committed your changes.

PostgreSQL uses a different model called *multi-versioning*, or *MVCC* for short (locks are still used, but much less frequently than you might expect). In a multi-versioning system, the database creates a new copy of the rows you have modified. Other users see the original values until you commit your changes—they don't have to wait until you finish. If you roll back a transaction, other users are not affected—they did not have access to your changes in the first place. If you commit your changes, the original rows are marked as obsolete and other transactions running at the READ COMMITTED isolation level will see your changes. Transactions running at the SERIALIZABLE isolation level will continue to see the original rows. Obsolete data is not automatically removed from a PostgreSQL database. It is hidden, but not removed. You can remove obsolete rows using the VACUUM command. The syntax of the VACUUM command is

```
VACUUM [ VERBOSE ] [ ANALYZE ] [ table ]
```

I'll talk about the VACUUM command in more detail in the next chapter.

The MVCC transaction model provides for much higher concurrency than most other models. Even though PostgreSQL uses multiple versions to isolate transactions, it is still necessary to lock data in some circumstances.

Try this experiment. Open two psql sessions, each connected to the movies database. In one session, enter the following commands:

```
movies=# BEGIN WORK;
BEGIN
movies=# INSERT INTO customers VALUES
movies-#  ( 5, 'Manyjars, John', '555-8000', '1960-04-02', 0 );
INSERT
```

In the other session, enter these commands:

```
movies=# BEGIN WORK;
BEGIN
movies=# INSERT INTO customers VALUES
movies-#  ( 6, 'Smallberries, John', '555-8001', '1960-04-02', 0 );
INSERT
```

When you press the `Enter` (or `Return`) key, this `INSERT` statement completes immediately. Now, enter this command into the second session:

```
movies=# INSERT INTO customers VALUES
movies-#  ( 5, 'Gomez, John', '555-8000', '1960-04-02', 0 );
```

This time, when you press `Enter`, `psql` hangs. What is it waiting for? Notice that in the first session, you already added a customer whose `customer_id` is 5, but you have not yet committed this change. In the second session, you are also trying to insert a customer whose `customer_id` is 5. You can't have two customers with the same `customer_id` (because you have defined the `customer_id` column to be the unique `PRIMARY KEY`). If you commit the first transaction, the second session would receive a *duplicate value* error. If you roll back the first transaction, the second insertion will continue (because there is no longer a constraint violation). PostgreSQL won't know which result to give you until the transaction completes in the first session.

Summary

Chapter 1, "Introduction to PostgreSQL and SQL," showed you some of the basics of retrieving and modifying data using PostgreSQL. In Chapter 2, "Working with Data in PostgreSQL," you learned about the many data types offered by PostgreSQL. This chapter has filled in some of the scaffolding—you've seen how to create new databases, new tables, and new indexes. You've also seen how PostgreSQL solves concurrency problems through its multi-versioning transaction model.

The next chapter, Chapter 4, "Performance," should help you understand how the PostgreSQL server decides on the fastest way to execute your SQL commands.

4

Performance

In the previous three chapters, you have seen how to create new databases and tables. You have also seen a variety of ways to retrieve data. Inevitably, you will run into a performance problem. At some point, PostgreSQL won't process data as quickly as you would like. This chapter should prepare you for that situation—after reading this chapter, you'll have a good understanding of how PostgreSQL executes a query and what you can do to make queries run faster.

How PostgreSQL Organizes Data

Before you can really dig into the details of performance tuning, you need to understand some of the basic architecture of PostgreSQL.

You already know that in PostgreSQL, data is stored in tables and tables are grouped into databases. At the highest level of organization, databases are grouped into clusters—a cluster of databases is serviced by a postmaster.

Let's see how this data hierarchy is stored on disk. You can see all databases in a cluster using the following query:

```
perf=# SELECT datname, oid FROM pg_database;
  datname   |  oid
------------+-------
 perf       | 16556
 template1  |     1
 template0  | 16555
```

From this list, you can see that I have three databases in this cluster. You can find the storage for these databases by looking in the $PGDATA directory:

```
$ cd $PGDATA
$ ls
base     pg_clog     pg_ident.conf   pg_xlog         postmaster.opts
global   pg_hba.conf  PG_VERSION     postgresql.conf  postmaster.pid
```

The $PGDATA directory has a subdirectory named base. The base subdirectory is where your databases reside:

```
$ cd ./base
$ ls -l
total 12
drwx------    2 postgres pgadmin      4096 Jan 01 20:53 1
drwx------    2 postgres pgadmin      4096 Jan 01 20:53 16555
drwx------    3 postgres pgadmin      4096 Jan 01 22:38 16556
```

Notice that there are three subdirectories underneath $PGDATA/base. The name of each subdirectory corresponds to the oid of one entry in the pg_database table: the subdirectory named 1 contains the template1 database, the subdirectory named 16555 contains the template0 database, and the subdirectory named 16556 contains the perf database.

Let's look a little deeper:

```
$ cd ./1
$ ls
1247   16392   16408   16421   16429   16441   16449   16460   16472
1249   16394   16410   16422   16432   16442   16452   16462   16474
1255   16396   16412   16423   16435   16443   16453   16463   16475
1259   16398   16414   16424   16436   16444   16454   16465   16477
16384  16400   16416   16425   16437   16445   16455   16466   pg_internal.init
16386  16402   16418   16426   16438   16446   16456   16468   PG_VERSION
16388  16404   16419   16427   16439   16447   16457   16469
16390  16406   16420   16428   16440   16448   16458   16471
```

Again, you see a lot of files with numeric filenames. You might guess that these numbers also correspond to oids, and (by chance) you would often be correct. Every table (and index) in a database is catalogued in the pg_class system table. To find a table in pg_class, search for a row where the relname column is equal to the name of the table. For example, to find the pg_class entry for the pg_group table, execute the command

```
SELECT * FROM pg_class WHERE relname = 'pg_group';
```

The pg_class.relfilenode value for a table determines the name of the file that stores the table (likewise, the pg_class.relfilenode value for an index determines the name of the file that stores in the index). In most cases, the OID of a table's pg_class entry matches the table's relfilenode, but that's not always the case. If you ALTER a table in such a way that PostgreSQL must first make a new copy of the table and then drop the original, the table's relfilenode will change. The relfilenode may also change if you CLUSTER the table (PostgreSQL makes a new copy of the table in the desired order and then drops the original). The relfilenode value for an index may change if you rebuild in the index with a REINDEX command, or if you ALTER the data type of a column covered by the index.

To see the correspondence between a table's relfilenode and its filename, simply compare the output from the following SELECT command to the filesystem directory that contains the database

```
test=# SELECT relfilenode, relname FROM pg_class ORDER BY relfilenode;
 relfilenode |            relname
-------------+-------------------------------
           0 | pg_xactlock
        1247 | pg_type
        1249 | pg_attribute
        1255 | pg_proc
        1259 | pg_class
         ... | ...
```

Each table is stored in its own disk file and the name of the file is determined by the oid relfilenode of the table's entry in the pg_class table.

There are two more columns in pg_class that might help explain PostgreSQL's storage structure:

```
perf=# SELECT relname, oid, relpages, reltuples FROM pg_class
perf-#    ORDER BY oid
    relname   | oid  | reltuples | relpages
--------------+------+-----------+----------
 pg_type      | 1247 |       143 |        2
 pg_attribute | 1249 |       795 |       11
 pg_proc      | 1255 |      1263 |       31
 pg_class     | 1259 |       101 |        2
 pg_shadow    | 1260 |         1 |        1
 pg_group     | 1261 |         0 |        0
    ...       | ...  |    ...    |    ...
```

The reltuples column tells you how many tuples are in each table. The relpages column shows how many *pages* are required to store the current contents of the table. How do these numbers correspond to the actual on-disk structures? If you look at the table files for a few tables, you'll see that there is a relationship between the size of the file and the number of relpages columns:

```
$ ls -l 1247 1249
-rw-------    1 postgres pgadmin        16384 Jan 01 20:53 1247
-rw-------    1 postgres pgadmin        90112 Jan 01 20:53 1249
```

The file named 1247 (pg_type) is 16,384 bytes long and consumes two pages. The file named 1249 (pg_attribute) is 90,122 bytes long and consumes 11 pages. A little math will show that $16,384/2 = 8,192$ and $90,122/11 = 8,192$: each page is 8,192 (8K) bytes long. In PostgreSQL, all disk I/O is performed on a page-by-page basis[1]. When you select a single row from a table, PostgreSQL will read at least one page—it may read many pages if the row is large. When you update a single row, PostgreSQL will write the new version of the row at the end of the table and will mark the original version of the row as invalid.

---

[1] Actually, *most* disk I/O is performed on a page-by-page basis. Some configuration files and log files are accessed in other forms, but all table and index access is done in pages.

The size of a page is fixed at 8,192 bytes. You can increase or decrease the page size if you build your own copy of PostgreSQL from source, but all pages within a database will be the same size. The size of a row is *not* fixed—different tables will yield different row sizes. In fact, the rows within a single table may differ in size if the table contains variable-length columns. Given that the page size is fixed and the row size is variable, it's difficult to predict exactly how many rows will fit within any given page.

The `perf` database and the `recalls` Table

The sample database that you have been using so far doesn't really hold enough data to show performance relationships. Instead, I've created a new database (named `perf`) that holds some large tables. I've downloaded the `recalls` database from the U.S. National Highway Traffic Safety Administration[2]. This database contains a single table with 39,241 rows. Here is the layout of the `recalls` table:

```
perf=# \d recalls
                    Table "recalls"
    Column    |          Type           | Modifiers
--------------+-------------------------+-----------
 record_id    | numeric(9,0)            |
 campno       | character(9)            |
 maketxt      | character(25)           |
 modeltxt     | character(25)           |
 yeartxt      | character(4)            |
 mfgcampno    | character(10)           |
 compdesc     | character(75)           |
 mgftxt       | character(30)           |
 bgman        | character(8)            |
 endman       | character(8)            |
 vet          | character(1)            |
 potaff       | numeric(9,0)            |
 ndate        | character(8)            |
 odate        | character(8)            |
 influenced   | character(4)            |
 mfgname      | character(30)           |
 rcdate       | character(8)            |
 datea        | character(8)            |
 rpno         | character(3)            |
 fmvss        | character(3)            |
 desc_defect  | character varying(2000) |
 con_defect   | character varying(2000) |
 cor_action   | character varying(2000) |
Indexes: recall_record_id
```

Notice that there is only one index and it covers the `record_id` column.

---

[2] This data (ftp://ftp.nhtsa.dot.gov/rev_recalls/) is in the form of a flat ASCII file. I had to import the data into my `perf` database.

The `recalls` table in the `perf` database contains 39,241 rows in 4,413 pages:

```
perf=# SELECT relname, reltuples, relpages, oid FROM pg_class
perf-#   WHERE relname = 'recalls';
 relname | reltuples | relpages |  oid
---------+-----------+----------+-------
 recalls |     39241 |     4413 | 96409
```

Given that a page is 8,192 bytes long, you would expect that the file holding this table (`$PGDATA/base/16556/96409`) would be 36,151,296 bytes long:

```
$ ls -l $PGDATA/base/16556/96409
-rw-------   1 postgres pgadmin  36151296 Jan 01 23:34 96409
```

Figure 4.1 shows how the `recalls` table might look on disk. (Notice that the rows are not sorted—they appear in the approximate order of insertion.)

Page 1

record_id	campno	maketxt	...	cor_action
42009	02E009000	NXT	...	Nexl will remove the...
13621	82E018000	CATERPILLAR	...	The Dealer will inspect...
42010	02E010000	NEXL	...	Next will notify its custom...
35966	99E039000	APC	...	APS will replace these...
42011	02E010000	NEXL	...	Nexl will notify its custom...
12927	81T009000	HERCULES	...	Tires will be replaced,...
42012	02E010000	NEXL	...	Nexl will notify its custom...
35974	99E039000	APC	...	APS will replace these...

Page 2

record_id	campno	maketxt	...	cor_action
42013	02E010000	NEXT	...	Nexl will notify its custom...
13654	82T014000	GOODYEAR	...	The Dealer will replace all...
42014	02E010000	NXT	...	Nexl will notify its custom...
35133	99E018000	D	...	Dealers will inspect their...
42005	02E009000	NEXL	...	Nexl will remove the...
12924	81T008000	NANKANG	...	Defective tires will be...
41467	01X003000	BRITAX	...	Customers will receive a...
35131	99E017000	MERITOR	...	Meritor will inspect and...

. . .

Page 4412

record_id	campno	maketxt	...	cor_action
42054	02V074002	PONTIAC	...	Dealers will properly tight...
41863	02V044000	HYUNDAI	...	Dealers will inspect the ...
42139	02V095000	INTERNATIONAL	...	Dealers will inspect the ...
41926	02V065000	COUNTRY COACH	...	Dealers will replace the...
42138	02V095000	INTERNATIONAL	...	Dealers will inspect the ...
41927	02V065000	COUNTRY COACH	...	Dealers will replace the...
42140	02V095000	INTERNATIONAL	...	Dealers will inspect the ...
41930	02V065000	COUNTRY COACH	...	Dealers will replace the...

Figure 4.1   The `recalls` table as it might look on disk.

If a row is too large to fit into a single 8K block[3], PostgreSQL will write part of the data into a *TOAST*[4] table. A TOAST table acts as an extension to a normal table. It holds values too large to fit *inline* in the main table.

Indexes are also stored in page files. A page that holds row data is called a *heap* page. A page that holds index data is called an *index* page. You can locate the page file that stores an index by examining the index's entry in the `pg_class` table. And, just like tables, it is difficult to predict how many index entries will fit into each 8K page[5]. If an index entry is too large, it is moved to an index TOAST table.

In PostgreSQL, a page that contains row data is a *heap block*. A page that contains index data is an *index block*. You will never find heap blocks and index blocks in the same page file.

Page Caching

Two of the fundamental performance rules in any database system are:

- Memory access is fast; disk access is slow.
- Memory space is scarce; disk space is abundant.

Accordingly, PostgreSQL tries very hard to minimize disk I/O by keeping frequently used data in memory. When the first server process starts, it creates an in-memory data structure known as the *buffer cache*. The buffer cache is organized as a collection of 8K pages—each page in the buffer cache corresponds to a page in some page file. The buffer cache is shared between all processes servicing a given database.

When you select a row from a table, PostgreSQL will read the heap block that contains the row into the buffer cache. If there isn't enough free space in the cache, PostgreSQL will move some other block out of the cache. If a block being removed from the cache has been modified, it will be written back out to disk; otherwise. it will simply be discarded. Index blocks are buffered as well.

In the "Gathering Performance Information" section, you'll see how to measure the performance of the cache and how to change its size.

Summary

This section gave you a good overview of how PostgreSQL stores data on disk. With some of the fundamentals out of the way, you can move on to more performance issues.

Gathering Performance Information

With release 7.2, the PostgreSQL developers introduced a new collection of performance-related system views. These views return two distinct kinds of information. The

---

[3] PostgreSQL tries to store at least four rows per heap page and at least four entries per index page.

[4] The acronym TOAST stands for "the oversized attribute storage technique."

[5] If you want more information about how data is stored inside a page, I recommend the `pg_filedump` utility from Red Hat.

pg_stat views characterize the frequency and type of access for each table in a database. The pg_statio views will tell you how much physical I/O is performed on behalf of each table.

Let's look at each set of performance-related views in more detail.

The pg_stat_all_tables contains one row for each table in your database. Here is the layout of pg_stat_all_tables:

```
perf=# \d pg_stat_all_tables
        View "pg_stat_all_tables"
    Column       |  Type    | Modifiers
-----------------+----------+-----------
 relid           | oid      |
 schemaname      | name     |
 relname         | name     |
 seq_scan        | bigint   |
 seq_tup_read    | bigint   |
 idx_scan        | numeric  |
 idx_tup_fetch   | numeric  |
 n_tup_ins       | bigint   |
 n_tup_upd       | bigint   |
 n_tup_del       | bigint   |
```

The seq_scan column tells you how many sequential (that is, table) scans have been performed for a given table, and seq_tup_read tells you how many rows were processed through table scans. The idx_scan and idx_tup_fetch columns tell you how many index scans have been performed for a table and how many rows were processed by index scans. The n_tup_ins, n_tup_upd, and n_tup_del columns tell you how many rows were inserted, updated, and deleted, respectively.

Query Execution

If you're not familiar with the terms "table scan" or "index scan," don't worry—I'll cover query execution later in this chapter (see "Understanding How PostgreSQL Executes a Query").

The real value in pg_stat_all_tables is that you can find out which tables in your database are most heavily used. This view does *not* tell you how much disk I/O is performed against each table file, nor does it tell you how much time it took to perform the operations.

The following query finds the top 10 tables in terms of number of rows read:

```
SELECT relname, idx_tup_fetch + seq_tup_read AS Total
  FROM pg_stat_all_tables
  WHERE idx_tup_fetch + seq_tup_read != 0
  ORDER BY Total desc
  LIMIT 10;
```

Here's an example that shows the result of this query in a newly created database:

```
perf=# SELECT relname, idx_tup_fetch + seq_tup_read AS Total
```

```
perf-#    FROM pg_stat_all_tables
perf-#    WHERE idx_tup_fetch + seq_tup_read != 0
perf-#    ORDER BY Total desc
perf-#    LIMIT 10;
```

```
    relname   | total
--------------+-------
 recalls      | 78482
 pg_class     | 57425
 pg_index     | 20901
 pg_attribute |  5965
 pg_proc      |  1391
```

It's easy to see that the recalls table is heavily used—you have read 78,482 tuples from that table.

There are two variations on the pg_stat_all_tables view. The pg_stat_sys_tables view is identical to pg_stat_all_tables, except that it is restricted to showing system tables. Similarly, the pg_stat_user_tables view is restricted to showing only user-created tables.

You can also see how heavily each index is being used—the pg_stat_all_indexes, pg_stat_user_indexes, and pg_stat_system_indexes views expose index information.

Although the pg_stat view tells you how heavily each table is used, it doesn't provide any information about how much physical I/O is performed on behalf of each table. The second set of performance-related views provides that information.

The pg_statio_all_tables view contains one row for each table in a database. Here is the layout of pg_statio_all_tables:

```
perf=# \d pg_statio_all_tables
```

```
        View "pg_statio_all_tables"
      Column       |  Type   | Modifiers
-------------------+---------+-----------
 relid             | oid     |
 schemaname        | name    |
 relname           | name    |
 heap_blks_read    | bigint  |
 heap_blks_hit     | bigint  |
 idx_blks_read     | numeric |
 idx_blks_hit      | numeric |
 toast_blks_read   | bigint  |
 toast_blks_hit    | bigint  |
 tidx_blks_read    | bigint  |
 tidx_blks_hit     | bigint  |
```

This view provides information about heap blocks (heap_blks_read, heap_blks_hit), index blocks (idx_blks_read, idx_blks_hit), toast blocks (toast_blks_read, toast_blks_hit), and index toast blocks (tidx_blks_read, tidx_blks_hit). For each of these block types, `pg_statio_all_tables` exposes two values: the number of blocks read and the number of blocks that were found in PostgreSQL's cache. For example, the `heap_blks_read` column contains the number of heap blocks read for a given table, and `heap_blks_hit` tells you how many of those pages were found in the cache.

PostgreSQL exposes I/O information for each index in the `pg_statio_all_indexes`, `pg_statio_user_indexes`, and `pg_statio_sys_indexes` views.

Let's try a few examples and see how you can use the information exposed by `pg_statio_all_tables`.

I've written a simple utility (called timer) that makes it a little easier to see the statistical results of a given query. This utility takes a snapshot of `pg_stat_all_tables` and `pg_statio_all_tables`, executes a given query, and finally compares the new values in `pg_stat_all_tables` and `pg_statio_all_tables`. Using this utility, you can see how much I/O was performed on behalf of the given query. Of course, the database must be idle except for the query under test.

Execute this simple query and see what kind of I/O results you get:

```
$ timer "SELECT * FROM recalls"
```

	SEQUENTIAL I/O				INDEXED I/O			
	scans	tuples	heap_blks	cached	scans	tuples	idx_blks	cached
pg_aggregate	0	0	1	0	1	1	2	0
pg_am	1	1	1	0	0	0	0	0
pg_amop	0	0	2	10	10	24	4	16
pg_amproc	0	0	1	5	6	6	2	10
pg_attribute	0	0	8	14	21	65	6	57
pg_cast	0	0	2	6	60	8	2	118
pg_class	4	740	5	32	18	17	7	34
pg_database	1	1	1	0	0	0	0	0
pg_index	2	146	3	11	8	12	4	12
pg_namespace	2	10	1	2	2	1	2	2
pg_opclass	0	0	2	11	5	73	4	6
pg_operator	0	0	4	6	10	10	4	26
pg_proc	0	0	6	8	14	14	12	31
pg_rewrite	0	0	1	1	2	2	2	2
pg_shadow	0	0	1	2	3	3	4	2
pg_statistic	0	0	3	5	33	8	2	64
pg_trigger	0	0	1	1	2	2	2	2
pg_type	0	0	2	5	7	7	2	12
recalls	1	39241	4413	0	0	0	0	0
Totals	11	40139	4458	119	202	253	61	394

The `timer` utility shows that a simple query generates a lot of buffer traffic. The PostgreSQL server must parse and plan the query and it consults a number of system tables to do so—that explains the buffer interaction incurred on behalf of all of the tables that start with `pg_`. The `recalls` table generates most of the buffer traffic.

> You can invoke the `timer` utility with one argument or two. The first argument contains the text of the query that you want to measure. The second argument, if present, is the name of the table that you're interested in. If you omit the second argument, you'll see I/O measurements for every table that was hit during the query (including the PostgreSQL system tables). If you include the second argument, you'll only see the I/O measurements for that table. In most of the discussion that follows, we'll filter out the I/O performed against the system tables.

This query retrieved 39,241 rows in a single table scan. This scan read 4,413 heap blocks from disk and found none in the cache. Normally, you would hope to see a cache ratio much higher than 4,413 to 0! In this particular case, I had just started the postmaster so there were few pages in the cache and none were devoted to the `recalls` table. Now, try this experiment again to see if the cache ratio gets any better:

```
$ timer "SELECT * FROM recalls" recalls
```

```
+-------------+------------------------------------+-------------------------------+
|             |         SEQUENTIAL I/O             |         INDEXED I/O           |
|             |scans |tuples |heap_blks |cached|scans |tuples |idx_blks |cached|
+-------------+------+-------+----------+------+------+-------+---------+------+
|recalls      |    1 | 39241 |     4413 |    0 |    0 |     0 |       0 |    0 |
+-------------+------+-------+----------+------+------+-------+---------+------+
```

You get exactly the same results for the `recalls` table—no cache hits. Why not? We did not include an `ORDER BY` clause in this query so PostgreSQL returned the rows in (approximately) the order of insertion. When we execute the same query a second time, PostgreSQL starts reading at the beginning of the page file and continues until it has read the entire file. Because my cache is only 512 blocks in size, the first 512 blocks have been forced out of the cache by the time I get to the end of the table scan. The next time I execute the same query, the final 512 blocks are in the cache, but you are looking for the leading blocks. The end result is no cache hits.

Just as an experiment, try to increase the size of the cache to see if you can force some caching to take place.

The PostgreSQL cache is kept in a segment of memory shared by all backend processes. You can see this using the `ipcs -m` command[6]:

---

[6] In case you are curious, the key value uniquely identifies a shared memory segment. The key is determined by multiplying the postmaster's port number by 1,000 and then incrementing until a free segment is found. The shmid value is generated by the operating system (key is generated by PostgreSQL). The `nattach` column tells you how many processes are currently using the segment.

```
$ ipcs -m
------ Shared Memory Segments --------
key         shmid     owner    perms    bytes      nattch    status
0x0052e2c1 1409024    postgres 600      5021696    3
```

The shared memory segment contains more than just the buffer cache: PostgreSQL also keeps some bookkeeping information in shared memory. With 512 pages in the buffer cache and an 8K block size, you see a shared memory segment that is 5,021,696 bytes long. Let's increase the buffer cache to 513 pages and see what effect that has on the size of the shared memory segment. There are two ways that you can adjust the size of the cache. You could change PostgreSQL's configuration file ($PGDATA/postgresql.conf), changing the shared_buffers variable from 512 to 513. Or, you can override the shared_buffers configuration variable when you start the postmaster:

```
$ pg_ctl stop
waiting for postmaster to shut down......done
postmaster successfully shut down
$ #
$ # Note:  specifying -o "-B 513" is equivalent
$ #        to setting shared_buffers = 513 in
$ #        the $PGDATA/postgresql.conf file
$ #
$ pg_start -o "-B 513" -l /tmp/pg.log
postmaster successfully started
```

Now you can use the ipcs -m command to see the change in the size of the shared memory segment.

```
$ ipcs  m
------ Shared Memory Segments --------
key         shmid     owner    perms    bytes      nattch    status
0x0052e2c1 1409024    postgres 600      5038080    3
```

The shared memory segment increased from 5,021,696 bytes to 5,038,080 bytes. That's a difference of 16,384 bytes, which happens to be the size of *two* blocks. Why two? Because PostgreSQL keeps some bookkeeping information in shared memory in addition to the buffer cache—the amount of extra space required depends on the number of shared buffers. PostgreSQL won't add two blocks each time you increment shared_buffers by 1; it just happens that when you increase from 512 to 513, you cross a threshold that requires an extra page in the bookkeeping system.

Now, let's get back to the problem at hand. We want to find out if doubling the buffer count will result in more cache hits and therefore fewer I/O operations. Remember, a table scan on the recalls table resulted in 4,413 heap blocks read and 0 cache hits. Let's double the size of the shared buffer cache (from 512 to 1,024 blocks). Try the same query again and check the results:

```
$ pg_ctl stop

waiting for postmaster to shut down......done
```

```
postmaster successfully shut down
$ pg_start -o "-B 1024" -l /tmp/pg.log
postmaster successfully started
$ ipcs -m
------ Shared Memory Segments --------
key         shmid     owner    perms   bytes     nattch    status
0x0052e2c1  1409024   postgres 600     9338880   3

$ timer "SELECT * FROM recalls" recalls
```

```
+----------------------------------+----------------------------------+
|           SEQUENTIAL I/O         |           INDEXED I/O            |
| scans | tuples | heap_blks |cached| scans | tuples | idx_blks |cached|
+-------+--------+-----------+------+-------+--------+----------+------+
|   1   | 39241  |    4413   |   0  |   0   |   0    |    0     |   0  |
+-------+--------+-----------+------+-------+--------+----------+------+
```

You have to run this query twice because you shut down and restarted the postmaster to adjust the cache size. When you shut down the postmaster, the cache is destroyed (you can use the ipcs -m command to verify this).

```
$ timer "SELECT * FROM recalls" recalls
```

```
+----------------------------------+----------------------------------+
|           SEQUENTIAL I/O         |           INDEXED I/O            |
| scans | tuples | heap_blks |cached| scans | tuples | idx_blks |cached|
+-------+--------+-----------+------+-------+--------+----------+------+
|   1   | 39241  |    4413   |   0  |   0   |   0    |    0     |   0  |
+-------+--------+-----------+------+-------+--------+----------+------+
```

Still the same results as before—PostgreSQL does not seem to buffer any of the data blocks read from the recalls table. Actually, each block *is* buffered as soon as it is read from disk; but as before, the blocks read at the beginning of the table scan are pushed out by the blocks read at the end of the scan. When you execute the same query a second time, you start at the beginning of the table and find that the blocks that you need are not in the cache.

You could increase the cache size to be large enough to hold the entire table (somewhere around 4,413 + 120 blocks should do it), but that's a large shared memory segment, and if you don't have enough physical memory, your system will start to thrash.

Let's try a different approach. PostgreSQL has enough room for 1,024 pages in the shared buffer cache. The entire recalls table consumes 4,413 pages. If you use the LIMIT clause to select a subset of the recalls table, you should see some caching. I'm going to lower the cache size back to its default of 512 pages before we start:

```
$ pg_ctl stop
waiting for postmaster to shut down......done
postmaster successfully shut down
```

```
$ pg_start -o "-B 512" -l /tmp/pg.log
postmaster successfully started
```

You know that it takes 4,413 pages to hold the 39,241 rows in recalls, which gives
you an average of about 9 rows per page. We have 512 pages in the cache; let's assume
that PostgreSQL needs about 180 of them for its own bookkeeping, leaving us 332
pages. So, you should ask for 9 * 332 (or 2,988) rows:

```
$ ./timer "SELECT * FROM recalls LIMIT 2988" recalls
+-------------+------------------------------------+-----------------------------+
|             |          SEQUENTIAL I/O            |         INDEXED I/O         |
|             |scans |tuples |heap_blks |cached|scans |tuples |idx_blks |cached|
|-------------+------+-------+----------+------+------+-------+---------+------+
|recalls      |    1 | 2988  |      208 |    0 |    0 |    0  |       0 |    0 |
+-------------+------+-------+----------+------+------+-------+---------+------+
```

PostgreSQL read 208 heap blocks. If everything worked, those pages should still be in
the cache. Let's run the query again:

```
$ ./timer "SELECT * FROM recalls LIMIT 2988" recalls
+-------------+------------------------------------+-----------------------------+
|             |          SEQUENTIAL I/O            |         INDEXED I/O         |
|             |scans |tuples |heap_blks |cached|scans |tuples |idx_blks |cached|
|-------------+------+-------+----------+------+------+-------+---------+------+
|recalls      |    1 | 2988  |        0 |  208 |    0 |    0  |       0 |    0 |
+-------------+------+-------+----------+------+------+-------+---------+------+
```

Now you're getting somewhere. PostgreSQL read 208 heap blocks and found all 208 of
them in the cache.

Dead Tuples

Now let's look at another factor that affects performance. Make a simple update to the
recalls table:

```
perf=# UPDATE recalls SET potaff = potaff + 1;
UPDATE
```

This command increments the potaff column of each row in the recalls table. (Don't
read too much into this particular UPDATE. I chose potaff simply because I needed an
easy way to update every row.) Now, after restarting the database, go back and SELECT all
rows again:

```
$ timer "SELECT * FROM recalls" recalls

+-------------+------------------------------------+-----------------------------+
|             |          SEQUENTIAL I/O            |         INDEXED I/O         |
|             |scans |tuples |heap_blks |cached|scans |tuples |idx_blks |cached|
|-------------+------+-------+----------+------+------+-------+---------+------+
|recalls      |    1 | 39241 |     8803 |    0 |    0 |    0  |       0 |    0 |
+-------------+------+-------+----------+------+------+-------+---------+------+
```

That's an interesting result—you still retrieved 39,241 rows, but this time you had to read 8,803 pages to find them. What happened? Let's see if the `pg_class` table gives any clues:

```
perf=# SELECT relname, reltuples, relpages
perf-#    FROM pg_class
perf-#    WHERE relname = 'recalls';
 relname | reltuples | relpages
---------+-----------+----------
 recalls |     39241 |     4413
```

No clues there—pg_class still thinks you have 4,413 heap blocks in this table. Let's try counting the individual rows:

```
perf=# SELECT count(*) FROM recalls;
 count
-------
 39241
```

At least that gives you a consistent answer. But why does a simple update UPDATE cause you to read twice as many heap blocks as before?

When you UPDATE a row, PostgreSQL performs the following operations:

1. The new row values are written to the table.
2. The old row is deleted from the table.
3. The deleted row *remains* in the table, but is no longer accessible.

This means that when you executed the statement "UPDATE recalls SET potaff = potaff + 1", PostgreSQL inserted 39,241 new rows and deleted 39,241 old rows. We now have 78,482 rows, half of which are inaccessible.

Why does PostgreSQL carry out an UPDATE command this way? The answer lies in PostgreSQL's MVCC (multi-version concurrency control) feature. Consider the following commands:

```
perf=# BEGIN WORK;
BEGIN
perf=# UPDATE recalls SET potaff = potaff + 1;
UPDATE
```

Notice that you have started a new transaction, but you have not yet completed it. If another user were to SELECT rows from the recalls table at this point, he *must* see the old values—you might roll back this transaction. In other database systems (such as DB2, Sybase, and SQL Server), the other user would have to wait until you either committed or rolled back your transaction before his query would complete. PostgreSQL, on the other hand, keeps the old rows in the table, and other users will see the original values until you commit your transaction. If you roll back your changes, PostgreSQL simply hides your modifications from all transactions (leaving you with 78,482 rows, half of which are inaccessible).

When you DELETE rows from a table, PostgreSQL follows a similar set of rules. The deleted rows remain in the table, but are hidden. If you roll back a DELETE command, PostgreSQL will simply make the rows visible again.

Now you also know the difference between a *tuple* and a *row*. A tuple is some version of a row.

When you make a change to a table, the tuples that you've changed are hidden from other users until you COMMIT your changes. If you INSERT 100,000 new rows into a table that previously contained only a few rows, another user might suddenly see a decrease in query performance even though he can't see the new rows. If you roll back your changes, other users will never see the new rows, but the dead tuples that you've created will continue to affect performance until someone VACUUMs the table.

You can see that these hidden tuples can dramatically affect performance—updating every row in a table doubles the number of heap blocks required to read the entire table.

There are at least three ways to remove dead tuples from a database. One way is to export all (visible) rows and then import them again using pg_dump and pg_restore. Another method is to use CREATE TABLE ... AS to make a new copy of the table, drop the original table, and rename the copy. The preferred way is to use the VACUUM command. I'll show you how to use the VACUUM command a little later (see the section "Table Statistics").

Index Performance

You've seen how PostgreSQL batches all disk I/O into 8K blocks, and you've seen how PostgreSQL maintains a buffer cache to reduce disk I/O. Let's find out what happens when you throw an index into the mix. After restarting the postmaster (to clear the cache), execute the following query:

```
$ timer "SELECT * FROM recalls ORDER BY record_id;" recalls
```

```
+--------------------------------+-------------------------------+
|       SEQUENTIAL I/O           |        INDEXED I/O            |
| scans | tuples | heap_blks |cached| scans | tuples | idx_blks |cached|
+-------+--------+-----------+------+-------+--------+----------+------+
|   0   |    0   |   26398   |12843 |   1   | 39241  |   146    |  0   |
+-------+--------+-----------+------+-------+--------+----------+------+
```

You can see that PostgreSQL chose to execute this query using an index scan (remember, you have an index defined on the record_id column). This query read 146 index blocks and found none in the buffer cache. You also processed 26,398 heap blocks and found 12,843 in the cache. You can see that the buffer cache helped the performance a bit, but you still processed over 26,000 heap blocks, and you need only 4,413 to hold the entire recalls table. Why did you need to read each heap block (approximately) five times?

Think of how the recalls table is stored on disk (see Figure 4.2).

Notice that the rows are not stored in record_id order. In fact, they are stored in order of insertion. When you create an index on the record_id column, you end up with a structure like that shown in Figure 4.3.

Page 1	record_id	campno	maketxt	...	cor_action
	42009	02E009000	NXT	...	Nexl will remove the...
	13621	82E018000	CATERPILLAR	...	The Dealer will inspect...
	42010	02E010000	NEXL	...	Next will notify its custom...
	35966	99E039000	APC	...	APS will replace these...
	42011	02E010000	NEXL	...	Nexl will notify its custom...
	12927	81T009000	HERCULES	...	Tires will be replaced,...
	42012	02E010000	NEXL	...	Nexl will notify its custom...
	35974	99E039000	APC	...	APS will replace these...

Page 2	record_id	campno	maketxt	...	cor_action
	42013	02E010000	NEXT	...	Nexl will notify its custom...
	13654	82T014000	GOODYEAR	...	The Dealer will replace all...
	42014	02E010000	NXT	...	Nexl will notify its custom...
	35133	99E018000	D	...	Dealers will inspect their...
	42005	02E009000	NEXL	...	Nexl will remove the...
	12924	81T008000	NANKANG	...	Defective tires will be...
	41467	01X003000	BRITAX	...	Customers will receive a...
	35131	99E017000	MERITOR	...	Meritor will inspect and...

• • •

Page 4412	record_id	campno	maketxt	...	cor_action
	42054	02V074002	PONTIAC	...	Dealers will properly tight...
	41863	02V044000	HYUNDAI	...	Dealers will inspect the ...
	42139	02V095000	INTERNATIONAL	...	Dealers will inspect the ...
	41926	02V065000	COUNTRY COACH	...	Dealers will replace the...
	42138	02V095000	INTERNATIONAL	...	Dealers will inspect the...
	41927	02V065000	COUNTRY COACH	...	Dealers will replace the...
	42140	02V095000	INTERNATIONAL	...	Dealers will inspect the...
	41930	02V065000	COUNTRY COACH	...	Dealers will replace the...

Figure 4.2 The recalls table on disk.

Consider how PostgreSQL uses the record_id index to satisfy the query. After the first block of the record_id index is read into the buffer cache, PostgreSQL starts scanning through the index entries. The first index entry points to a recalls row on heap block 2, so that heap block is read into the buffer cache. Now, PostgreSQL moves on to the second index entry—this one points to a row in heap block 1. PostgreSQL reads heap block 1 into the buffer cache, throwing out some other page if there is no room in the cache. Figure 4.2 shows a partial view of the recalls table: remember that there are actually 4,413 heap blocks and 146 index blocks needed to satisfy this query. It's the random ordering of the rows within the recalls table that kills the cache hit ratio.

Let's try reordering the recalls table so that rows are inserted in record_id order. First, create a work table with the same structure as recalls:

record_id
12924
12927
13621
13654
35131
35133
35966
35974

record_id	campno	maketxt	...	cor_action
42009	02E009000	NXT	...	Nexl will remove the...
13621	82E018000	CATERPILLAR	...	The Dealer will Inspect...
42010	02E010000	NEXL	...	Nexl will notify its custom...
35966	99E039000	APC	...	APS will replace these...
42011	02E010000	NEXL	...	Nexl will notify its custom...
12927	81T009000	HERCULES	...	Tires will be replaced, ...
42012	02E010000	NEXL	...	Nexl will notify its custom...
35974	99E039000	APC	...	APS will replace these....

record_id
41467
42005
42009
42010
42011
42012
42013
42014

record_id	campno	maketxt	...	cor_action
42013	02E010000	NEXL	...	Nexl will notify its custom...
13654	82T014000	GOODYEAR	...	The Dealer will replace all ..
42014	02E010000	NXT	...	Nexl will notify its custom...
35133	99E018000	D	...	Dealers will inspect their...
42005	02E009000	NEXL	...	Nexl will remove the...
12924	81T008000	NANKANG	...	Defective tires will be ...
41467	01X003000	BRITAX	...	Customers will receive a ...
35131	99E017000	MERITOR	...	Meritor will inspect and....

Figure 4.3 The `recalls` table structure after creating an index.

```
perf=# CREATE TABLE work_recalls AS
perf-#   SELECT * FROM recalls ORDER BY record_id;
SELECT
```

Then, drop the original table, rename the work table, and re-create the index:

```
perf=# DROP TABLE recalls;
DROP
perf=# ALTER TABLE work_recalls RENAME TO recalls;
ALTER
perf=# CREATE INDEX recalls_record_id ON recalls( record_id );
CREATE
```

At this point, you have the same data as before, consuming the same amount of space:

```
perf=# SELECT relname, relpages, reltuples FROM pg_class
perf-#   WHERE relname IN ('recalls', 'recalls_record_id' );
      relname       | relpages | reltuples
--------------------+----------+-----------
 recalls_record_id  |      146 |     39241
 recalls            |     4422 |     39241
(2 rows)
```

After restarting the `postmaster` (again, this clears out the buffer cache so you get consistent results), let's re-execute the previous query:

```
$ timer "SELECT * FROM recalls ORDER BY record_id;" recalls
```

```
+--------------------------------+--------------------------------+
|        SEQUENTIAL I/O          |         INDEXED I/O            |
| scans | tuples | heap_blks |cached| scans | tuples | idx_blks |cached|
+-------+--------+-----------+------+-------+--------+----------+------+
|   0   |    0   |   4423    |34818 |   1   | 39241  |   146    |   0  |
+-------+--------+-----------+------+-------+--------+----------+------+
```

That made quite a difference. Before reordering, you read 26,398 heap blocks from disk and found 12,843 in the cache for a 40% cache hit ratio. After physically reordering the rows to match the index, you read 4,423 heap blocks from disk and found 34,818 in the cache for hit ratio of 787%. This makes a huge performance difference. Now as you read through each index page, the heap records appear next to each other; you won't be thrashing heap pages in and out of the cache. Figure 4.4 shows how the recalls table looks after reordering.

record_id		record_id	campno	maketxt	...	cor_action
12924	→	12924	81T008000	NANKANG	...	Defective tires will...
12927	→	12927	81T009000	HERCULES	...	Tires will be replaced,...
13621	→	13621	82E018000	CATERPILLAR	...	The Dealer will inspect...
13654	→	13654	82T014000	GOODYEAR	...	The Dealer will replace all...
35131	→	35131	99E017000	MERITOR	...	Meritor will inspect and...
35133	→	35133	99E018000	D	...	Dealers will inspect their...
35966	→	35966	99E039000	APC	...	APS will replace these...
35974	→	35974	99E039000	APC	...	APS will replace these...

record_id		record_id	campno	maketxt	...	cor_action
41467	→	41467	01X003000	BRITAX	...	Customers will receive a...
42005	→	42005	02E009000	NEXL	...	Nexl will remove the...
42009	→	42009	02E009000	NXT	...	Nexl will notify its custom...
42010	→	42010	02E010000	NEXL	...	Nexl will notify its custom...
42011	→	42011	02E010000	NEXL	...	Nexl will notify its custom...
42012	→	42012	02E010000	NEXL	...	Nexl will notify its custom...
42013	→	42013	02E010000	NEXL	...	Nexl will notify its custom...
42014	→	42014	02E010000	NXT	...	Nexl will notify its custom...

Figure 4.4   The recalls table on disk after reordering.

We reordered the recalls table by creating a copy of the table (in the desired order), dropping the original table, and then renaming the copy back to the original name. You can also use the CLUSTER command—it does exactly the same thing.

Understanding How PostgreSQL Executes a Query

Before going much further, you should understand the procedure that PostgreSQL follows whenever it executes a query on your behalf.

After the PostgreSQL server receives a query from the client application, the text of the query is handed to the *parser*. The parser scans through the query and checks it for syntax errors. If the query is syntactically correct, the parser will transform the query text into a *parse tree*. A parse tree is a data structure that represents the *meaning* of your query in a formal, unambiguous form.

Given the query

```
SELECT customer_name, balance FROM customers WHERE balance > 0 ORDER BY balance
```

the parser might come up with a parse tree structured as shown in Figure 4.5.

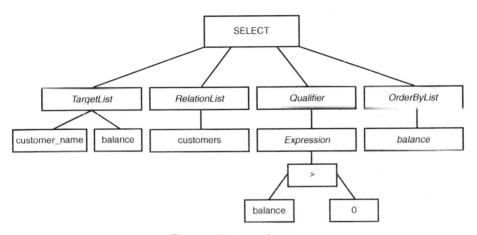

Figure 4.5   A sample parse tree.

After the parser has completed parsing the query, the parse tree is handed off to the planner/optimizer.

The planner is responsible for traversing the parse tree and finding all possible plans for executing the query. The plan might include a sequential scan through the entire table and index scans if useful indexes have been defined. If the query involves two or more tables, the planner can suggest a number of different methods for joining the tables. The execution plans are developed in terms of query operators. Each query operator transforms one or more *input sets* into an intermediate result set. The Seq Scan operator, for example, transforms an input set (the physical table) into a result set, filtering out any rows that don't meet the query constraints. The Sort operator produces a result set by reordering the input set according to one or more sort keys. I'll describe each of the query operators in more detail a little later. Figure 4.6 shows an example of a simple execution plan (it is a new example; it is *not* related to the parse tree in Figure 4.5).

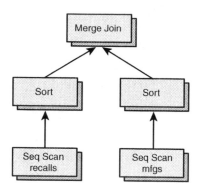

Figure 4.6 A simple execution plan.

You can see that complex queries are broken down into simple steps. The input set for a query operator at the bottom of the tree is usually a physical table. The input set for an upper-level operator is the result set of a lower-level operator.

When all possible execution plans have been generated, the optimizer searches for the least-expensive plan. Each plan is assigned an estimated execution cost. Cost estimates are measured in units of disk I/O. An operator that reads a single block of 8,192 bytes (8K) from the disk has a cost of one unit. CPU time is also measured in disk I/O units, but usually as a fraction. For example, the amount of CPU time required to process a single tuple is assumed to be $1/100^{th}$ of a single disk I/O. You can adjust many of the cost estimates. Each query operator has a different cost estimate. For example, the cost of a sequential scan of an entire table is computed as the number of 8K blocks in the table, plus some CPU overhead.

After choosing the (apparently) least-expensive execution plan, the query executor starts at the beginning of the plan and asks the topmost operator to produce a result set. Each operator transforms its input set into a result set—the input set may come from another operator lower in the tree. When the topmost operator completes its transformation, the results are returned to the client application.

EXPLAIN

The EXPLAIN statement gives you some insight into how the PostgreSQL query planner/optimizer decides to execute a query.

First, you should know that the EXPLAIN statement can be used only to analyze SELECT, INSERT, DELETE, UPDATE, and DECLARE...CURSOR commands.

The syntax for the EXPLAIN command is

```
EXPLAIN [ANALYZE] [VERBOSE] query;
```

Let's start by looking at a simple example:

```
perf=# EXPLAIN ANALYZE SELECT * FROM recalls;
NOTICE:  QUERY PLAN:
```

```
Seq Scan on recalls  (cost=0.00..9217.41 rows=39241 width=1917)
                     (actual time=69.35..3052.72 rows=39241 loops=1)
Total runtime: 3144.61 msec
```

The format of the execution plan can be a little mysterious at first. For each step in the execution plan, EXPLAIN prints the following information:

- The type of operation required.
- The estimated cost of execution.
- If you specified EXPLAIN ANALYZE, the actual cost of execution. If you omit the ANALYZE keyword, the query is planned but not executed, and the actual cost is not displayed.

In this example, PostgreSQL has decided to perform a sequential scan of the recalls table (Seq Scan on recalls). There are many operators that PostgreSQL can use to execute a query. I'll explain the operation type in more detail in a moment.

There are three data items in the cost estimate. The first set of numbers (cost=0.00..9217.41) is an estimate of how "expensive" this operation will be. "Expensive" is measured in terms of disk reads. Two numbers are given: The first number represents how quickly the first row in the result set can be returned by the operation; the second (which is usually the most important) represents how long the entire operation should take. The second data item in the cost estimate (rows=39241) shows how many rows PostgreSQL expects to return from this operation. The final data item (width=1917) is an estimate of the width, in bytes, of the average row in the result set.

If you include the ANALYZE keyword in the EXPLAIN command, PostgreSQL will execute the query and display the *actual* execution costs.

Cost Estimates

I will remove the cost estimates from some of the EXPLAIN results in this chapter to make the plan a bit easier to read. Don't be confused by this—the EXPLAIN command will always print cost estimates.

This was a simple example. PostgreSQL required only one step to execute this query (a sequential scan on the entire table). Many queries require multiple steps and the EXPLAIN command will show you each of those steps. Let's look at a more complex example:

```
perf-# EXPLAIN ANALYZE SELECT * FROM recalls ORDER BY yeartxt;
NOTICE:  QUERY PLAN:

Sort (cost=145321.51..145321.51 rows=39241 width=1911)
     (actual time=13014.92..13663.86 rows=39241 loops=1)

  ->Seq Scan on recalls (cost=0.00..9217.41 rows=39241 width=1917)
                        (actual time=68.99..3446.74 rows=39241 loops=1)
Total runtime: 16052.53 msec
```

This example shows a two-step query plan. In this case, the first step is actually listed at the end of the plan. When you read a query plan, it is important to remember that each step in the plan produces an intermediate result set. Each intermediate result set is fed into the next step of the plan.

Looking at this plan, PostgreSQL first produces an intermediate result set by performing a sequential scan (Seq Scan) on the entire recalls table. That step should take about 9,217 disk page reads, and the result set will have about 39,241 rows, averaging 1,917 bytes each. Notice that these estimates are identical to those produced in the first example—and in both cases, you are executing a sequential scan on the entire table.

After the sequential scan has finished building its intermediate result set, it is fed into the next step in the plan. The final step in this particular plan is a sort operation, which is required to satisfy our ORDER BY clause[7]. The sort operation reorders the result set produced by the sequential scan and returns the final result set to the client application.

The Sort operation expects a single operand—a result set. The Seq Scan operation expects a single operand—a table. Some operations require more than one operand. Here is a join between the recalls table and the mfgs table:

```
perf=# EXPLAIN SELECT * FROM recalls, mfgs
perf-#   WHERE recalls.mfgname = mfgs.mfgname;
NOTICE:  QUERY PLAN:

Merge Join
  -> Sort
      -> Seq Scan on recalls
  -> Sort
      -> Seq Scan on mfgs
```

If you use your imagination, you will see that this query plan is actually a tree structure, as illustrated in Figure 4.7.

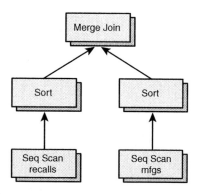

Figure 4.7 Execution plan viewed as a tree.

[7] An ORDER BY clause does not require a Sort operation in all cases. The planner/optimizer may decide that it can use an index to order the result set.

When PostgreSQL executes this query plan, it starts at the top of the tree. The `Merge Join` operation requires two result sets for input, so PostgreSQL must move down one level in the tree; let's assume that you traverse the left child first. Each `Sort` operation requires a single result set for input, so again the query executor moves down one more level. At the bottom of the tree, the `Seq Scan` operation simply reads a row from a table and returns that row to its parent. After a `Seq Scan` operation has scanned the entire table, the left-hand `Sort` operation can complete. As soon as the left-hand `Sort` operation completes, the `Merge Join` operator will evaluate its right child. In this case, the right-hand child evaluates the same way as the left-hand child. When both `Sort` operations complete, the `Merge Join` operator will execute, producing the final result set.

So far, you've seen three query execution operators in the execution plans. PostgreSQL currently has 19 query operators. Let's look at each in more detail.

Seq Scan

The `Seq Scan` operator is the most basic query operator. Any single-table query can be carried out using the `Seq Scan` operator.

`Seq Scan` works by starting at the beginning of the table and scanning to the end of the table. For each row in the table, `Seq Scan` evaluates the query constraints[8] (that is, the `WHERE` clause); if the constraints are satisfied, the required columns are added to the result set.

As you saw earlier in this chapter, a table can include dead (that is, deleted) rows and rows that may not be visible because they have not been committed. `Seq Scan` does not include dead rows in the result set, but it must read the dead rows, and that can be expensive in a heavily updated table.

The cost estimate for a `Seq Scan` operator gives you a hint about how the operator works:

```
Seq Scan on recalls (cost=0.00..9217.41 rows=39241 width=1917)
```

The startup cost is always `0.00`. This implies that the first row of a `Seq Scan` operator can be returned immediately and that `Seq Scan` does not read the entire table before returning the first row. If you open a cursor against a query that uses the `Seq Scan` operator (and no other operators), the first `FETCH` will return immediately—you won't have to wait for the entire result set to be materialized before you can `FETCH` the first row. Other operators (such as `Sort`) *do* read the entire input set before returning the first row.

The planner/optimizer chooses a `Seq Scan` if there are no indexes that can be used to satisfy the query. A `Seq Scan` is also used when the planner/optimizer decides that it would be less expensive (or just as expensive) to scan the entire table and then sort the result set to meet an ordering constraint (such as an `ORDER BY` clause).

---

[8] The entire `WHERE` clause may not be evaluated for each row in the input set. PostgreSQL evaluates only the portions of the clause that apply to the given row (if any). For a single-table `SELECT`, the entire `WHERE` clause is evaluated. For a multi-table join, only the portion that applies to the given row is evaluated.

Index Scan

An Index Scan operator works by traversing an index structure. If you specify a starting value for an indexed column (WHERE record_id >= 1000, for example), the Index Scan will begin at the appropriate value. If you specify an ending value (such as WHERE record_id < 2000), the Index Scan will complete as soon as it finds an index entry greater than the ending value.

The Index Scan operator has two advantages over the Seq Scan operator. First, a Seq Scan must read every row in the table—it can only remove rows from the result set by evaluating the WHERE clause for each row. Index Scan may not read every row if you provide starting and/or ending values. Second, a Seq Scan returns rows in table order, not in sorted order. Index Scan will return rows in index order.

Not all indexes are scannable. The B-Tree, R-Tree, and GiST index types can be scanned; a Hash index cannot.

The planner/optimizer uses an Index Scan operator when it can reduce the size of the result set by traversing a range of indexed values, or when it can avoid a sort because of the implicit ordering offered by an index.

Sort

The Sort operator imposes an ordering on the result set. PostgreSQL uses two different sort strategies: an in-memory sort and an on-disk sort. You can tune a PostgreSQL instance by adjusting the value of the sort_mem runtime parameter. If the size of the result set exceeds sort_mem, Sort will distribute the input set to a collection of sorted work files and then merge the work files back together again. If the result set will fit in sort_mem*1024 bytes, the sort is done in memory using the QSort algorithm.

A Sort operator never reduces the size of the result set—it does not remove rows or columns.

Unlike Seq Scan and Index Scan, the Sort operator must process the entire input set before it can return the first row.

The Sort operator is used for many purposes. Obviously, a Sort can be used to satisfy an ORDER BY clause. Some query operators require their input sets to be ordered. For example, the Unique operator (we'll see that in a moment) eliminates rows by detecting duplicate values as it reads through a sorted input set. Sort will also be used for some join operations, group operations, and for some set operations (such as INTERSECT and UNION).

Unique

The Unique operator eliminates duplicate values from the input set. The input set must be ordered by the columns, and the columns must be unique. For example, the following command

```
SELECT DISTINCT mfgname FROM recalls;
```

might produce this execution plan:

```
Unique
  -> Sort
      -> Seq Scan on recalls
```

The Sort operation in this plan orders its input set by the mfgname column. Unique works by comparing the unique column(s) from each row to the previous row. If the values are the same, the duplicate is removed from the result set.

The Unique operator removes only rows—it does not remove columns and it does not change the ordering of the result set.

Unique can return the first row in the result set before it has finished processing the input set.

The planner/optimizer uses the Unique operator to satisfy a DISTINCT clause. Unique is also used to eliminate duplicates in a UNION.

LIMIT

The LIMIT operator is used to limit the size of a result set. PostgreSQL uses the LIMIT operator for both LIMIT and OFFSET processing. The LIMIT operator works by discarding the first x rows from its input set, returning the next y rows, and discarding the remainder. If the query includes an OFFSET clause, x represents the offset amount; otherwise, x is zero. If the query includes a LIMIT clause, y represents the LIMIT amount; otherwise, y is at least as large as the number of rows in the input set.

The ordering of the input set is not important to the LIMIT operator, but it is usually important to the overall query plan. For example, the query plan for this query

```
perf=# EXPLAIN SELECT * FROM recalls LIMIT 5;
NOTICE: QUERY PLAN:

Limit (cost=0.00..0.10 rows=5 width=1917)
  -> Seq Scan on recalls (cost=0.00..9217.41 rows=39241 width=1917)
```

shows that the LIMIT operator rejects all but the first five rows returned by the Seq Scan. On the other hand, this query

```
perf=# EXPLAIN ANALYZE SELECT * FROM recalls ORDER BY yeartxt LIMIT 5;
NOTICE:  QUERY PLAN:


Limit (cost=0.00..0.10 rows=5 width=1917)
  ->Sort (cost=145321.51..145321.51 rows=39241 width=1911)
    ->Seq Scan on recalls (cost=0.00..9217.41 rows=39241 width=1917)
```

shows that the LIMIT operator returns the first five rows from an ordered input set.

The LIMIT operator never removes columns from the result set, but it obviously removes rows.

The planner/optimizer uses a LIMIT operator if the query includes a LIMIT clause, an OFFSET clause, or both. If the query includes only a LIMIT clause, the LIMIT operator can return the first row before it processes the entire set.

Aggregate

The planner/optimizer produces an `Aggregate` operator whenever the query includes an aggregate function. The following functions are aggregate functions: `AVG()`, `COUNT()`, `MAX()`, `MIN()`, `STDDEV()`, `SUM()`, and `VARIANCE()`.

`Aggregate` works by reading all the rows in the input set and computing the aggregate values. If the input set is not grouped, `Aggregate` produces a single result row. For example:

```
movies=# EXPLAIN SELECT COUNT(*) FROM customers;
Aggregate (cost=22.50..22.50 rows=1 width=0)
  -> Seq Scan on customers  (cost=0.00..20.00 rows=1000 width=0)
```

If the input set *is* grouped, `Aggregate` produces one result row for each group:

```
movies=# EXPLAIN
movies-#   SELECT COUNT(*), EXTRACT( DECADE FROM birth_date )
movies-#     FROM customers
movies-#     GROUP BY EXTRACT( DECADE FROM birth_date );
NOTICE:  QUERY PLAN:

Aggregate (cost=69.83..74.83 rows=100 width=4)
  -> Group (cost=69.83..72.33 rows=1000 width=4)
    -> Sort (cost=69.83..69.83 rows=1000 width=4)
      -> Seq Scan on customers  (cost=0.00..20.00 rows=1000 width=4)
```

Notice that the row estimate of an ungrouped aggregate is always 1; the row estimate of a group aggregate is $1/10^{th}$ of the size of the input set.

Append

The `Append` operator is used to implement a `UNION`. An `Append` operator will have two or more input sets. `Append` works by returning all rows from the first input set, then all rows from the second input set, and so on until all rows from all input sets have been processed.

Here is a query plan that shows the `Append` operator:

```
perf=# EXPLAIN
perf-#   SELECT * FROM recalls WHERE mfgname = 'FORD'
perf-#     UNION
perf-#   SELECT * FROM recalls WHERE yeartxt = '1983';

Unique
  ->Sort
    ->Append
      ->Subquery Scan *SELECT* 1
        ->Seq Scan on recalls
      ->Subquery Scan *SELECT* 2
        ->Seq Scan on recalls
```

The cost estimate for an `Append` operator is simply the sum of cost estimates for all input sets. An `Append` operator can return its first row before processing all input rows.

The planner/optimizer uses an `Append` operator whenever it encounters a `UNION` clause. `Append` is also used when you select from a table involved in an inheritance hierarchy. In Chapter 3, "PostgreSQL SQL Syntax and Use," I defined three tables, as shown in Figure 4.8.

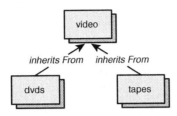

Figure 4.8   Inheritance hierarchy.

The `dvds` table inherits from `video`, as does the `tapes` table. If you `SELECT` from `dvds` or `video`, PostgreSQL will respond with a simple query plan:

```
movies=# EXPLAIN SELECT * FROM dvds;
  Seq Scan on dvds (cost=0.00..20.00 rows=1000 width=122)
```

```
movies=# EXPLAIN SELECT * FROM tapes;
  Seq Scan on tapes (cost=0.00..20.00 rows=1000 width=86)
```

Remember, because of the inheritance hierarchy, a dvd *is a* video and a tape *is a* video. If you `SELECT` from `video`, you would expect to see all `dvds`, all `tapes`, and all `videos`. The query plan reflects the inheritance hierarchy:

```
movies=# EXPLAIN SELECT * FROM video;
```

```
Result(cost=0.00..60.00 rows=3000 width-86)
  ->Append(cost=0.00..60.00 rows=3000 width=86)
    ->Seq Scan on video  (cost=0.00..20.00 rows=1000 width=86)
    ->Seq Scan on tapes video  (cost=0.00..20.00 rows=1000 width=86)
    ->Seq Scan on dvds video  (cost=0.00..20.00 rows=1000 width=86)
```

Look closely at the `width` clause in the preceding cost estimates. If you `SELECT` from the `dvds` table, the `width` estimate is 122 bytes per row. If you `SELECT` from the `tapes` table, the `width` estimate is 86 bytes per row. When you `SELECT` from `video`, all rows are expected to be 86 bytes long. Here are the commands used to create the `tapes` and `dvds` tables:

```
movies=# CREATE TABLE tapes ( ) INHERITS( video );
```

```
movies=# CREATE TABLE dvds
movies-# (
```

```
movies(#   region_id    INTEGER,
movies(#   audio_tracks VARCHAR[]
movies(# ) INHERITS ( video );
```

You can see that a row from the tapes table is identical to a row in the video table—you would expect them to be the same size (86 bytes). A row in the dvds table contains a video plus a few extra columns, so you would expect a dvds row to be longer than a video row. When you SELECT from the video table, you want all videos. PostgreSQL discards any columns that are not inherited from the video table.

Result

The Result operator is used in three contexts.

First, a Result operator is used to execute a query that does not retrieve data from a table:

```
movies=# EXPLAIN SELECT timeofday();
  Result
```

In this form, the Result operator simply evaluates the given expression(s) and returns the results.

Result is also used to evaluate the parts of a WHERE clause that don't depend on data retrieved from a table. For example:

```
movies=# EXPLAIN SELECT * FROM tapes WHERE 1 <> 1;
  Result
    ->Seq Scan on tapes
```

This might seem like a silly query, but some client applications will generate a query of this form as an easy way to retrieve the metadata (that is, column definitions) for a table.

In this form, the Result operator first evaluates the constant part of the WHERE clause. If the expression evaluates to FALSE, no further processing is required and the Result operator completes. If the expression evaluates to TRUE, Result will return its input set.

The planner/optimizer also generates a Result operator if the top node in the query plan is an Append operator. This is a rather obscure rule that has no performance implications; it just happens to make the query planner and executor a bit simpler for the PostgreSQL developers to maintain.

Nested Loop

The Nested Loop operator is used to perform a join between two tables. A Nested Loop operator requires two input sets (given that a Nested Loop joins two tables, this makes perfect sense).

Nested Loop works by fetching each row from one of the input sets (called the *outer table*). For each row in the outer table, the other input (called the *inner table*) is searched for a row that meets the join qualifier.

Here is an example:

```
perf=# EXPLAIN
perf-#   SELECT * FROM customers, rentals
perf-#   WHERE customers.customer_id = rentals.customer_id;

Nested Loop
  -> Seq Scan on rentals
  -> Index Scan using customer_id on customers
```

The outer table is always listed first in the query plan (in this case, rentals is the outer table). To execute this plan, the Nested Loop operator will read each row[9] in the rentals table. For each rentals row, Nested Loop reads the corresponding customers row using an indexed lookup on the customer_id index.

A Nested Loop operator can be used to perform inner joins, left outer joins, and unions.

Because Nested Loop does not process the entire inner table, it can't be used for other join types (full, right join, and so on).

Merge Join

The Merge Join operator also joins two tables. Like the Nested Loop operator, Merge Join requires two input sets: an outer table and an inner table. Each input set must be ordered by the join columns.

Let's look at the previous query, this time executed as a Merge Join:

```
perf=# EXPLAIN
perf-#   SELECT * FROM customers, rentals
perf-#   WHERE customers.customer_id = rentals.customer_id;

Merge Join
  -> Sort
    -> Seq Scan on rentals
  -> Index Scan using customer_id on customers
```

Merge Join starts reading the first row from each table (see Figure 4.9).

rentals

tape_id	rental_date	customer_id
AB-12345	2001-11-25	1
OW-41221	2001-11-25	1
AB-67472	2001-11-25	3
MC-68873	2001-11-20	4

◄ outer ►
inner

customers

customer_id	customer_name
1	Jones, Henry
1	Rubin, William
3	Panky, Henry
4	Wonderland, Alice N.
8	Wankel, Wink

Figure 4.9 Merge Join—Step 1.

---

[9] Actually, Nested Loop reads only those rows that meet the query constraints.

If the join columns are equal (as in this case), `Merge Join` creates a new row containing the necessary columns from each input table and returns the new row. `Merge Join` then moves to the next row in the outer table and joins it with the corresponding row in the inner table (see Figure 4.10).

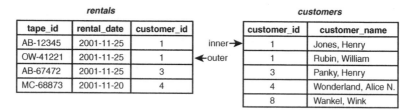

Figure 4.10 `Merge Join`—Step 2.

Next, `Merge Join` reads the third row in the outer table (see Figure 4.11). Now `Merge Join` must advance the inner table twice before another result row can be created (see Figure 4.12).

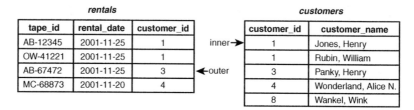

Figure 4.11 `Merge Join`—Step 3.

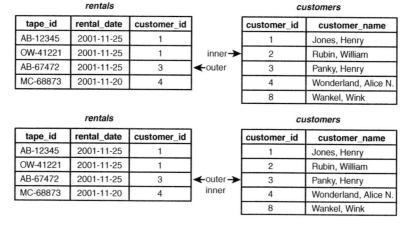

Figure 4.12 `Merge Join`—Step 4.

After producing the result row for `customer_id = 3`, `Merge Join` moves to the last row in the outer table and then advances the inner table to a matching row (see Figure 4.13).

tape_id	rental_date	customer_id
AB-12345	2001-11-25	1
OW-41221	2001-11-25	1
AB-67472	2001-11-25	3
MC-68873	2001-11-20	4

inner→
←outer

customer_id	customer_name
1	Jones, Henry
2	Rubin, William
3	Panky, Henry
4	Wonderland, Alice N.
8	Wankel, Wink

tape_id	rental_date	customer_id
AB-12345	2001-11-25	1
OW-41221	2001-11-25	1
AB-67472	2001-11-25	3
MC-68873	2001-11-20	4

←outer→
inner

customer_id	customer_name
1	Jones, Henry
2	Rubin, William
3	Panky, Henry
4	Wonderland, Alice N.
8	Wankel, Wink

Figure 4.13   `Merge Join`—Step 5.

`Merge Join` completes by producing the final result row (`customer_id = 4`).

You can see that `Merge Join` works by walking through two sorted tables and finding matches—the trick is in keeping the pointers synchronized.

This example shows an *inner join*, but the `Merge Join` operator can be used for other join types by walking through the sorted input sets in different ways. `Merge Join` can do inner joins, outer joins, and unions.

Hash **and** Hash Join

The `Hash` and `Hash Join` operators work together. The `Hash Join` operator requires two input sets, again called the outer and inner tables. Here is a query plan that uses the `Hash Join` operator:

```
movies=# EXPLAIN
movies-#   SELECT * FROM customers, rentals
movies-#     WHERE rentals.customer_id = customers.customer_id;

Hash Join
   -> Seq Scan on customers
   -> Hash
       -> Seq Scan on rentals
```

Unlike other join operators, `Hash Join` does not require either input set to be ordered by the join column. Instead, the inner table is *always* a hash table, and the ordering of the outer table is not important.

The `Hash Join` operator starts by creating its inner table using the `Hash` operator. The `Hash` operator creates a temporary Hash index that covers the join column in the inner table.

Once the hash table (that is, the inner table) has been created, `Hash Join` reads each row in the outer table, hashes the join column (from the outer table), and searches the temporary Hash index for a matching value.

A `Hash Join` operator can be used to perform inner joins, left outer joins, and unions.

Group

The `Group` operator is used to satisfy a `GROUP BY` clause. A single input set is required by the `Group` operator, and it must be ordered by the grouping column(s).

`Group` can work in two distinct modes. If you are computing a grouped aggregate, `Group` will return each row in its input set, following each group with a `NULL` row to indicate the end of the group (the `NULL` row is for internal bookkeeping only, and it will not show up in the final result set). For example:

```
movies=# EXPLAIN
movies-#   SELECT COUNT(*), EXTRACT( DECADE FROM birth_date )
movies-#     FROM customers
movies-#     GROUP BY EXTRACT( DECADE FROM birth_date );
NOTICE:  QUERY PLAN:

Aggregate (cost=69.83..74.83 rows=100 width=4)
  -> Group (cost=69.83..72.33 rows=1000 width=4)
    -> Sort (cost=69.83..69.83 rows=1000 width=4)
      -> Seq Scan on customers  (cost=0.00..20.00 rows=1000 width=4)
```

Notice that the row count in the `Group` operator's cost estimate is the same as the size of its input set.

If you are *not* computing a group aggregate, `Group` will return one row for each group in its input set. For example:

```
movies=# EXPLAIN
movies-#   SELECT EXTRACT( DECADE FROM birth_date ) FROM customers
movies-#     GROUP BY EXTRACT( DECADE FROM birth_date );

Group (cost=69.83..69,83 rows=100 width=4)
  -> Sort (cost=69.83..69.83 rows=1000 width=4)
      -> Seq Scan on customers  (cost=0.00..20.00 rows=1000 width=4)
```

In this case, the estimated row count is $1/10^{th}$ of the `Group` operator's input set.

Subquery Scan **and** Subplan

A `Subquery Scan` operator is used to satisfy a `UNION` clause; `Subplan` is used for subselects. These operators scan through their input sets, adding each row to the result set. Each of these operators are used for internal bookkeeping purposes and really don't affect the overall query plan—you can usually ignore them.

Just so you know when they are likely to be used, here are two sample query plans that show the Subquery Scan and Subplan operators:

```
perf=# EXPLAIN
perf-#   SELECT * FROM recalls WHERE mfgname = 'FORD'
perf-#     UNION
perf-#   SELECT * FROM recalls WHERE yeartxt = '1983';

Unique
  ->Sort
    ->Append
      ->Subquery Scan *SELECT* 1
        ->Seq Scan on recalls
      ->Subquery Scan *SELECT* 2
        ->Seq Scan on recalls

movies=# EXPLAIN
movies-#   SELECT * FROM customers
movies-#     WHERE customer_id IN
movies-#       (
movies(#           SELECT customer_id FROM rentals
movies(#       );
NOTICE:  QUERY PLAN:

Seq Scan on customers  (cost=0.00..3.66 rows=2 width=47)
  SubPlan
    ->  Seq Scan on rentals  (cost=0.00..1.04 rows=4 width=4)
```

Tid Scan

The Tid Scan (tuple ID scan) operator is rarely used. A tuple is roughly equivalent to a row. Every tuple has an identifier that is unique within a table—this is called the tuple ID. When you select a row, you can ask for the row's tuple ID:

```
movies=# SELECT ctid, customer_id, customer_name FROM customers;
ctid  | customer_id |    customer_name
-------+-------------+----------------------
 (0,1) |           3 | Panky, Henry
 (0,2) |           1 | Jones, Henry
 (0,3) |           4 | Wonderland, Alice N.
 (0,4) |           2 | Rubin, William
(4 rows)
```

The "ctid" is a special column (similar to the OID) that is automatically a part of every row. A tuple ID is composed of a block number and a tuple number within the block. All the rows in the previous sample are stored in block 0 (the first block of the table file). The customers row for "Panky, Henry" is stored in tuple 3 of block 0.

After you know a row's tuple ID, you can request that row again by using its ID:

```
movies=# SELECT customer_id, customer_name FROM customers
movies-#   WHERE ctid = '(0,3)';
customer_id |    customer_name
-------------+----------------------
          4 | Wonderland, Alice N.
(1 row)
```

The tuple ID works like a bookmark. A tuple ID, however, is valid only within a single transaction. After the transaction completes, the tuple ID should not be used.

The `Tid Scan` operator is used whenever the planner/optimizer encounters a constraint of the form `ctid = expression` or `expression = ctid`.

The fastest possible way to retrieve a row is by its tuple ID. When you `SELECT` by tuple ID, the `Tid Scan` operator reads the block specified in the tuple ID and returns the requested tuple.

Materialize

The `Materialize` operator is used for some subselect operations. The planner/optimizer may decide that it is less expensive to materialize a subselect once than to repeat the work for each top-level row.

`Materialize` will also be used for some merge-join operations. In particular, if the inner input set of a `Merge Join` operator is not produced by a `Seq Scan`, an `Index Scan`, a `Sort`, or a `Materialize` operator, the planner/optimizer will insert a `Materialize` operator into the plan. The reasoning behind this rule is not obvious—it has more to do with the capabilities of the other operators than with the performance or the structure of your data. The `Merge Join` operator is complex; one requirement of `Merge Join` is that the input sets must be ordered by the join columns. A second requirement is that the inner input set must be *repositionable*; that is, `Merge Join` needs to move backward and forward through the input set. Not all ordered operators can move backward and forward. If the inner input set is produced by an operator that is not repositionable, the planner/optimizer will insert a `Materialize`.

Setop (Intersect, Intersect All, Except, Except All)

There are four `Setop` operators: `Setop Intersect`, `Setop Intersect All`, `Setop Except`, and `Setop Except All`. These operators are produced only when the planner/optimizer encounters an `INTERSECT`, `INTERSECT ALL`, `EXCEPT`, or `EXCEPT ALL` clause, respectively.

All `Setop` operators require two input sets. The `Setop` operators work by first combining the input sets into a sorted list, and then groups of identical rows are identified. For each group, the `Setop` operator counts the number of rows contributed by each input set. Finally, each `Setop` operator uses the counts to determine how many rows to add to the result set.

I think this will be easier to understand by looking at an example. Here are two queries; the first selects all customers born in the 1960s:

```
movies=# SELECT * FROM customers
movies-#   WHERE EXTRACT( DECADE FROM birth_date ) = 196;
 customer_id |   customer_name     | phone    | birth_date | balance
-------------+---------------------+----------+------------+---------
           3 | Panky, Henry        | 555-1221 | 1968-01-21 |    0.00
           4 | Wonderland, Alice N. | 555-1122 | 1969-03-05 |    3.00
```

The second selects all customers with a balance greater than 0:

```
movies=# SELECT * FROM customers WHERE balance > 0;
 customer_id |   customer_name     | phone    | birth_date | balance
-------------+---------------------+----------+------------+---------
           2 | Rubin, William      | 555-2211 | 1972-07-10 |   15.00
           4 | Wonderland, Alice N. | 555-1122 | 1969-03-05 |    3.00
```

Now, combine these two queries with an INTERSECT clause:

```
movies=# EXPLAIN
movies-#   SELECT * FROM customers
movies-#     WHERE EXTRACT( DECADE FROM birth_date ) = 196
movies-#   INTERSECT
movies-#     SELECT * FROM customers WHERE balance > 0;
SetOp Intersect
  -> Sort
    -> Append
      -> Subquery Scan *SELECT* 1
        > Seq Scan on customers
      -> Subquery Scan *SELECT* 2
        -> Seq Scan on customers
```

The query executor starts by executing the two subqueries and then combining the results into a sorted list. An extra column is added that indicates which input set contributed each row:

```
 customer_id |   customer_name     | birth_date | balance | input set
-------------+---------------------+------------+---------+----------
           2 | Rubin, William      | 1972-07-10 |   15.00 | inner
           3 | Panky, Henry        | 1968-01-21 |    0.00 | outer
           4 | Wonderland, Alice N. | 1969-03-05 |    3.00 | outer
           4 | Wonderland, Alice N. | 1969-03-05 |    3.00 | inner
```

The SetOp operator finds groups of duplicate rows (ignoring the input set pseudo-column). For each group, SetOp counts the number of rows contributed by each input set. The number of rows contributed by the outer set is called count(outer). The number of rows contributed by the inner result set is called count(inner).

Here is how the sample looks after counting each group:

```
customer_id |     customer_name      | birth_date | balance | input set
------------+------------------------+------------+---------+----------
          2 | Rubin, William         | 1972-07-10 |   15.00 | inner
                           count(outer) = 0
                           count(inner) = 1
          3 | Panky, Henry           | 1968-01-21 |    0.00 | outer
                           count(outer) = 1
                           count(inner) = 0
          4 | Wonderland, Alice N.   | 1969-03-05 |    3.00 | outer
          4 | Wonderland, Alice N.   | 1969-03-05 |    3.00 | inner
                           count(outer) = 1
                           count(inner) = 1
```

The first group contains a single row, contributed by the inner input set. The second group contains a single row, contributed by the outer input set. The final group contains two rows, one contributed by each input set.

When SetOp reaches the end of a group of duplicate rows, it determines how many copies to write into the result set according to the following rules:

- INTERSECT—If count(outer) > 0 and count(inner) > 0, write one copy of the row to the result set; otherwise, the row is not included in the result set.
- INTERSECT ALL—If count(outer) > 0 and count(inner) > 0, write n copies of the row to the result set; where n is the greater count(outer) and count(inner).
- EXCEPT—If count(outer) > 0 and count(inner) = 0, write one copy of the row to the result set.
- EXCEPT ALL—If count(inner) >= count(outer), write n copies of the row to the result set; where n is count(outer) - count(inner).

Execution Plans Generated by the Planner

The EXPLAIN command only shows you the execution plan that PostgreSQL considered to be the least expensive. Unfortunately, you can't convince PostgreSQL to show the *other* execution plans that it considered. The most common performance question that we hear is "why didn't the database use my index?" If you could see all the alternatives, you could usually (but not always) answer that question.

When the optimizer generates a set of execution plans for a query, it starts by generating a set of plans that traverse each base table involved in the query. For a single-table query, there is only one base table and the planner generates a single set of execution plans. For a multitable query (a join), the planner starts by generating a set of traversal plans for each table.

There are only three ways that PostgreSQL can scan an individual table: a table scan (Seq Scan), an Index Scan, or a tuple-ID scan (TID Scan). For each table involved in the query, the planner generates one plan that makes a pass over the table using a Seq Scan operator. If the WHERE clause of the query selects one or more rows by ctid value, the planner generates a TID Scan. Next, the planner examines each index defined for the table. In theory, any single-table query can be satisfied by making a complete scan of a B-Tree index (assuming that the index is not a partial index), but the planner knows that a complete Index Scan is always more expensive than a complete Seq Scan and won't consider an Index Scan unless it offers some advantage.

An index is useful if it can reduce the number of tuples read from the table. If the WHERE clause for a query contains an expression of the form *indexCol operator constant-expression* or *constant-expression operator indexCol*, PostgreSQL may be able to use the index to read a subset of the table. For example, the recalls table has a B-Tree index that covers the record_id column. If you execute the query

```
perf=# SELECT * FROM recalls WHERE record_id > 8000;
```

the planner examines the expression record_id > 8000 and finds that it is written in the form *indexCol operator constant-expression*—the record_id column is an *indexCol*. Notice that PostgreSQL looks for a *constant-expression*, not just a constant. That means that an expression such as record_id > (800 * 10) is acceptable as well. You can also include function calls in the *constant-expression* as long as the functions are not volatile. A volatile function (such as random()) can change value from row to row as PostgreSQL scans through the table. A *constant-expression* can include any operator that is not implemented by a volatile function.

Prior to version 8.0, PostgreSQL would only use an index if the data type of the indexed value exactly matched the data type of the *constant-expression*. Starting with 8.0, PostgreSQL will use an index if *constant-expression* can be coerced (that is, converted) to the same type as the indexed value.

An index is also useful if it can produce rows in a desired order. If an index produces rows in the sequence required by the ORDER BY clause, the planner will generate an Index Scan plan for the table. Some of the query operators (MergeJoin, Unique, Group, and Setop) require an ordered input set. For example, the Unique operator requires its input set to be ordered by the set of columns required to be unique. If an index can produce rows in the order required by one of these operators, the planner will generate an Index Scan plan for the table. A Hash index cannot produce rows in any particular order and therefore can't contribute to the ordering of a table.

What happens if you have two (or more) indexes that are useful to a given query? The planner generates a plan for each index and the optimizer chooses the least expensive plan among all of the alternatives.

Once the planner has generated a set of plans for each base table, it generates a set of plans to join the tables together according to the WHERE clause. PostgreSQL can join two tables together using any of three query operators: Merge Join, Hash Join, or Nested Loop. Consider a simple two-table query such as

```
movies=# SELECT * FROM rentals, customers
    WHERE rentals.customer_id = customers.customer_id;
```

Assuming that you have a B-Tree indexes that cover `rentals.customer_id` and `customers.customer_id`, the planner would generate the following plans to traverse each table individually:

```
SeqScan( rentals )
IndexScan( rentals.customer_id )
SeqScan( customers )
IndexScan( customers.customer_id )
```

To join these two tables together, the planner produces a set of execution plans.

First, the planner joins `rentals` and `customers` using the `MergeJoin` operator. Given that there are two paths through each table, the planner produces four `MergeJoin` plans for the combination of `rentals` and `customers`:

```
MergeJoin( IndexScan( rentals.customer_id ), IndexScan( customers.customer_id ))
MergeJoin(Sort( SeqScan( rentals )), Sort( SeqScan( customers )))
MergeJoin( IndexScan( rentals.customer_id ) , Sort( SeqScan( customers )))
MergeJoin( Sort( SeqScan( rentals )), IndexScan( customers.customer_id ))
```

Notice that the `MergeJoin` operator requires both input set to be ordered by the join column—because a `SeqScan` operator does not produce rows in any particular order, the planner inserts a `Sort` operator where needed.

Next, the planner produces a set of four `NestedLoop` plans:

```
NestedLoop( IndexScan( rentals.customer_id ), IndexScan( customers.customer_id ))
NestedLoop( SeqScan( rentals ), SeqScan( customers ))
NestedLoop( IndexScan( rentals.customer_id ) , SeqScan( customers ))
NestedLoop( SeqScan( rentals ), IndexScan( customers.customer_id ))
```

Then, the planner considers a set of four `HashJoin` plans:

```
HashJoin
(
    IndexScan( rentals.customer_id ),
    Hash( IndexScan( customers.customer_id ))
)

HashJoin
(
    SeqScan( rentals ),
    Hash( SeqScan( customers ))
)

HashJoin
(
    IndexScan( rentals.customer_id ) ,
    Hash( SeqScan( customers ))
)

HashJoin
```

```
(
    SeqScan( rentals ),
    Hash( IndexScan( customers.customer_id ))
)
```

The `HashJoin` operator requires the inner input set to be a hash table so the planner inserts a `Hash` operator in front of each of the inner tables.

For a simple join, the planner has considered 12 plans. But it's not finished yet. The planner generates a second set of plans using `customers` as the outer table and `rentals` as the inner table (in the first set of join plans, `rentals` served as the outer table and `customers` served as the inner table):

```
MergeJoin( IndexScan( customers.customer_id ), IndexScan( rentals.customer_id ))
MergeJoin(Sort( SeqScan( customers )), Sort( SeqScan( rentals )))
MergeJoin( IndexScan( customers.customer_id ) , Sort( SeqScan( rentals )))
MergeJoin( Sort( SeqScan(customers )), IndexScan( rentals.customer_id ))
NestedLoop( IndexScan( customers.customer_id ), IndexScan( rentals.customer_id ))
NestedLoop( SeqScan(customers ), SeqScan( rentals ))
NestedLoop( IndexScan(customers.customer id ) , SeqScan( rentals ))
NestedLoop( SeqScan(customers ), IndexScan( rentals.customer_id ))
HashJoin(IndexScan(customers.customer_id), Hash(IndexScan(rentals.customer_id)))
HashJoin( SeqScan(customers ), Hash( SeqScan( rentals )))
HashJoin( IndexScan(customers.customer_id ) , Hash( SeqScan( rentals )))
HashJoin( SeqScan( customers ), Hash( IndexScan( rentals.customer_id )))
```

Once it's finished, the planner has considered 24 plans to join these two tables. In general, the planner will consider

```
joinOperatorCount x (( pathCount( table1 ) x pathCount( table2 )) x 2 )
```

plans to join any two tables, where `pathCount( table )` is the number of possible paths (`SeqScans`, `Index Scans`, and `TID Scans`) through a given table and `joinOperatorCount` is always 3 in PostgreSQL (`MergeJoin`, `NestedLoop`, and `HashJoin`).

As you've seen, a two-table join will result in 24 possible plans (assuming that there are two paths through each table). Add a third table and the number of possible plans skyrockets. So how does the planner generate plans for a three-table join? It first generates a set of plans to join two of the three tables into a single result set then generates a set of plans to join the intermediate result set to the remaining table. With three tables (a, b, and c), you find the following combinations (note — I've abbreviated `MergeJoin` and `HashJoin` here to better fit the printed page):

```
Merge( a, Join( b, c ))   NestedLoop( a, Join( b, c ))  Hash( a, Join( b, c ))
Merge( a, Join( c, b ))   NestedLoop( a, Join( c, b ))  Hash( a, Join( c, b ))
Merge( b, Join( a, c ))   NestedLoop( b, Join( a, c ))  Hash( b, Join( a, c ))
Merge( b, Join( c, a ))   NestedLoop( b, Join( c, a ))  Hash( b, Join( c, a ))
Merge( c, Join( a, b ))   NestedLoop( c, Join( a, b ))  Hash( c, Join( a, b ))
Merge( c, Join( c, b ))   NestedLoop( c, Join( c, b ))  Hash( c, Join( c, b ))
```

```
Merge( Join( a, b ), c )  NestedLoop( Join( a, b ), c )  Hash( Join( a, b ), c )
Merge( Join( a, c ), b )  NestedLoop( Join( a, c ), b )  Hash( Join( a, c ), b )
Merge( Join( b, a ), c )  NestedLoop( Join( b, a ), c )  Hash( Join( b, a ), c )
Merge( Join( b, c ), a )  NestedLoop( Join( b, c ), a )  Hash( Join( b, c ), a )
Merge( Join( c, a ), b )  NestedLoop( Join( c, a ), b )  Hash( Join( c, a ), b )
Merge( Join( c, b ), a )  NestedLoop( Join( c, b ), a )  Hash( Join( c, b ), a )
```

And considering that any of these two-table join results in 24 possible plans, you're suddenly looking at 864 possible plans! If you add a fourth table, the planner considers the plans needed to join three of the four tables into an intermediate result, then joins the fourth table to that.

In practice, the planner won't take the time to generate every possible plan—the planner contains a number of heuristics that avoid generating plans that are known to be more expensive than plans already seen. For example, the planner knows that a complete Index Scan is more expensive than a complete Seq Scan and it won't generate a plan that includes a complete Index Scan unless the ordering of the result set is important.

In fact, when you reach a certain point, the plan generator switches from a near-exhaustive search to an algorithm known as the genetic query optimizer. The genetic optimizer *evolves* a plan by mutating and recombining possible join plans and then evaluating each generation for its "fitness." As each generation emerges, the genetic optimizer selects those mutations and recombinations that result in lower execution plans. The plan that eventually evolves is not guaranteed to be the best possible plan, but it is typically a "good" plan. By default, PostgreSQL uses the genetic query optimizer when the FROM clause of a query refers to 12 or more tables.

The ARC Buffer Manager

It's important to keep a few points in mind when you're trying to tune a PostgreSQL database. First, the shared buffer cache is *shared*. All of the examples in this chapter were built using a single-session database—if you try to reproduce these experiments, be sure you're the only one using the database or your results will vary widely. Second, the important part of a buffer management scheme isn't the part that determines what goes into the cache, it's the part that determines what gets thrown out of the cache. When PostgreSQL reads data from a table, it first checks to see if the required page is in the cache. If PostgreSQL finds it in the cache, it stops looking. If the required page isn't in the cache, PostgreSQL must read it in from disk. That means that *every page* in *every table* is read into the cache as soon as a query (or other command) refers to the page. If your buffer cache is large enough, PostgreSQL will never evict a page from the cache (although it will write modified pages to disk).

When PostgreSQL adds a page to the shared cache and finds that the cache is already full, it must evict some other page. Prior to release 8.0, PostgreSQL would always evict the least-recently-used page. Pretend that you have a very small buffer cache (say three pages). When you execute a command that causes a table scan (a scan of every page from beginning to end), the server starts by reading the first page into the cache. Next, the server processes every tuple on that page (ignoring dead and uncommitted tuples as it goes).

Once it has finished processing the first page, it *unpins* that page in the cache (meaning that that page is no longer in use and can be evicted if necessary). The server then moves on to the second page. Because there are still two free pages in the cache, PostgreSQL just reads the second page from disk, stores that page in the cache, processes each tuple in that page, and then unpins that page. The server repeats this sequence for the third page. When PostgreSQL comes to the fourth page, it finds that the cache is full and evicts the least-recently-used page (page one) from the cache, replacing it with page four. That leaves you with pages two, three, and four in the cache. When the server reads in page five, it evicts page two (the least-recently-used page) from the cache, leaving you with pages three, four, and five in the cache. That sequence continues until the server has finished reading the entire table—when you're finished, the cache contains the last three pages from the table. If you execute the same command again, the sequence is the same except that PostgreSQL will have to evict one of the last three pages before it can add the first page to the cache. If instead you execute a command that can be satisfied by looking at the last three pages of the table, PostgreSQL will find those pages in the cache and won't read them from disk.

Of course, if another user is running a command at the same time, he's using the same buffer cache and the eviction sequence will be completely different.

As you've seen earlier in this chapter, a table scan can evict all of the pages from an LRU cache.

Starting with version 8.0, PostgreSQL uses a new caching mechanism that constantly adapts itself to a changing workload. The ARC (adaptive replacement cache) scheme effectively uses two caches: One is a traditional LRU cache and the other is a LFU cache. LFU stands for "least-frequently-used" as opposed to "least-recently-used." PostgreSQL divides the shared memory segment into one cache that buffers recently used pages and a second cache that buffers frequently used pages. That means that if your shared buffer cache contains 1,024 pages, some pages will contain recently used pages and some will contain frequently used pages. How many pages does PostgreSQL devote to each cache? It depends on your workload: PostgreSQL adjusts the relative size of each cache as it runs. If the server sees a period of high "locality of reference" (meaning that the current workload is frequently accessing a small set of pages), it devotes more space to the LFU cache (taking pages away from the LRU cache). If the server sees a request for a page that was recently evicted from the LRU cache, it devotes more space to the LRU cache (taking pages away from the LFU cache). To see how ARC affects the shared buffer cache, we'll show you two simple queries—we'll run the queries first in PostgreSQL version 7.4.2, then again in version 8.0.

```
$ timer  \
>   "SELECT * FROM recalls WHERE record_id > 8000 AND record_id < 8050" recalls
```

| | | SEQUENTIAL I/O | | | INDEXED I/O | | |
	scans	tuples	heap_blks	cached	scans	tuples	idx_blks	cached
recalls	0	0	4	45	1	49	3	0

To satisfy this query, PostgreSQL uses the index that covers the `record_id` column. Because we just restarted the 7.4 server (and we have enough room for 512 pages in the shared buffer cache), PostgreSQL had to read all three of the index blocks that we hit from disk.

```
$ timer \
>   "SELECT * FROM recalls WHERE record_id > 8000 AND record_id < 8050" recalls
+-------------+-----------------------------------+-----------------------------------+
|             |          SEQUENTIAL I/O           |           INDEXED I/O             |
|             |scans |tuples |heap_blks |cached|scans |tuples |idx_blks  |cached|
|-------------+------+-------+----------+------+------+-------+----------+------+
|recalls      |   0  |   0   |      0   |  49  |  1   |  49   |     0    |   3  |
+-------------+-----------------------------------+-----------------------------------+
```

When we execute the same query again, PostgreSQL reads the same three index blocks, but this time, it finds them in the cache. Now we'll execute a query that causes a table scan:

```
$ timer "SELECT * FROM recalls" recalls
+-------------+-----------------------------------+-----------------------------------+
|             |          SEQUENTIAL I/O           |           INDEXED I/O             |
|             |scans |tuples |heap_blks |cached|scans |tuples |idx_blks  |cached|
|-------------+------+-------+----------+------+------+-------+----------+------+
|recalls      |   1  | 39241 |   4400   |   0  |  0   |   0   |     0    |   0  |
+-------------+-----------------------------------+-----------------------------------+
```

This query made a complete pass through the table, shuffling all 4,400 heap blocks through a cache that can only hold 512 blocks. When the query completes, the last 512 or so heap blocks that we read are still in the cache. Now go back and execute the first query (the one that causes a partial index scan):

```
$ timer \
>   "SELECT * FROM recalls WHERE record_id > 8000 AND record_id < 8050" recalls
+-------------+-----------------------------------+-----------------------------------+
|             |          SEQUENTIAL I/O           |           INDEXED I/O             |
|             |scans |tuples |heap_blks |cached|scans |tuples |idx_blks  |cached|
|-------------+------+-------+----------+------+------+-------+----------+------+
|recalls      |   0  |   0   |      4   |  45  |  1   |  49   |     3    |   0  |
+-------------+-----------------------------------+-----------------------------------+
```

Notice that PostgreSQL had to read the same three index blocks again, but the intervening table scan has evicted them from the cache and they must be read from disk.

Now here is the same sequence running in a version 8.0 server. Again, we'll execute the same query that caused a partial index scan:

```
$ timer \
>   "SELECT * FROM recalls WHERE record_id > 8000 AND record_id < 8050" recalls
+-------------+-----------------------------------+-----------------------------------+
|             |          SEQUENTIAL I/O           |           INDEXED I/O             |
|             |scans |tuples |heap_blks |cached|scans |tuples |idx_blks  |cached|
|-------------+------+-------+----------+------+------+-------+----------+------+
|recalls      |   0  |   0   |      5   |   0  |  1   |  49   |     4    |   0  |
+-------------+-----------------------------------+-----------------------------------+
```

And we'll execute it again just to make sure that the index blocks did in fact stay in the cache:

```
$ timer \
>    "SELECT * FROM recalls WHERE record_id > 8000 AND record_id < 8050" recalls
+-------------+--------------------------------------+----------------------------+
|             |          SEQUENTIAL I/O              |         INDEXED I/O        |
|             |scans |tuples |heap_blks |cached|scans |tuples |idx_blks |cached|
|-------------+------+-------+----------+------+------+-------+---------+------+
|recalls      |    0 |    0 |         0 |    5 |    1 |    49 |        0 |    4 |
+-------------+--------------------------------------+----------------------------+
```

Now we'll execute a query that, in version 7.4.2, threw the index blocks out of the cache:

```
$ timer "SELECT * FROM recalls" recalls
+-------------+--------------------------------------+----------------------------+
|             |          SEQUENTIAL I/O              |         INDEXED I/O        |
|             |scans |tuples |heap_blks |cached|scans |tuples |idx_blks |cached|
|-------------+------+-------+----------+------+------+-------+---------+------+
|recalls      |    1 | 39241 |     4400 |    5 |    0 |     0 |        0 |    0 |
+-------------+--------------------------------------+----------------------------+
```

And finally, we'll repeat the partial index scan query:

```
$ timer \
>    "SELECT * FROM recalls WHERE record_id > 8000 AND record_id < 8050" recalls
+-------------+--------------------------------------+----------------------------+
|             |          SEQUENTIAL I/O              |         INDEXED I/O        |
|             |scans |tuples |heap_blks |cached|scans |tuples |idx_blks |cached|
|-------------+------+-------+----------+------+------+-------+---------+------+
|recalls      |    0 |    0 |         0 |    5 |    1 |    49 |        0 |    4 |
+-------------+--------------------------------------+----------------------------+
```

This time, the 8.0 server has retained the frequently used index blocks in the LFU cache.

Table Statistics

You've seen all the operators that PostgreSQL can use to execute a query. Remember that the goal of the optimizer is to find the plan with the least overall expense. Each operator uses a different algorithm for estimating its cost of execution. The cost estimators need some basic statistical information to make educated estimates.

Table statistics are stored in two places in a PostgreSQL database: pg_class and pg_statistic.

The pg_class system table contains one row for each table defined in your database (it also contains information about views, indexes, and sequences). For any given table, the pg_class.relpages column contains an estimate of the number of 8KB pages required to hold the table. The pg_class.reltuples column contains an estimate of the number of tuples currently contained in each table.

Note that `pg_class` holds only estimates—when you create a new table, the `relpages` estimate is set to 10 pages and reltuples is set to 1,000 tuples. As you INSERT and DELETE rows, PostgreSQL does *not* maintain the `pg_class` estimates. You can see this here:

```
movies=# SELECT * FROM tapes;

 tape_id  |     title      | duration
----------+----------------+----------
 AB-12345 | The Godfather  |
 AB-67472 | The Godfather  |
 MC-68873 | Casablanca     |
 OW-41221 | Citizen Kane   |
 AH-54706 | Rear Window    |
(5 rows)


movies=# CREATE TABLE tapes2 AS SELECT * FROM tapes;
SELECT
movies=# SELECT reltuples, relpages FROM pg_class
movies-#   WHERE relname = 'tapes2';
 reltuples | relpages
-----------+----------
      1000 |       10
```

Create the `tapes2` table by duplicating the `tapes` table. You know that `tapes2` really holds five tuples (and probably requires a single disk page), but PostgreSQL has not updated the initial default estimate.

There are three commands that you can use to update the `pg_class` estimates: VACUUM, ANALYZE, and CREATE INDEX.

The VACUUM command removes any dead tuples from a table and recomputes the `pg_class` statistical information:

```
movies=# VACUUM tapes2;
VACUUM
movies=# SELECT reltuples, relpages FROM pg_class WHERE relname = 'tapes2';
 reltuples | relpages
-----------+----------
         5 |        1
(1 row)
```

The `pg_statistic` system table holds detailed information about the data in a table. Like `pg_class`, `pg_statistic` is *not* automatically maintained when you INSERT and DELETE data. The `pg_statistic` table is not updated by the VACUUM or CREATE INDEX command, but it is updated by the ANALYZE command:

```
movies=# SELECT staattnum, stawidth, stanullfrac FROM pg_statistic
movies-#   WHERE starelid =
movies-#     (
movies(#        SELECT oid FROM pg_class WHERE relname = 'tapes2'
```

```
movies(#      );
 staattnum | stawidth | stanullfrac
-----------+----------+-------------
 (0 rows)


movies=# ANALYZE tapes2;
ANALYZE


movies=# SELECT staattnum, stawidth, stanullfrac FROM pg_statistic
movies-#   WHERE starelid =
movies-#     (
movies(#        SELECT oid FROM pg_class WHERE relname = 'tapes2'
movies(#     );
 staattnum | stawidth | stanullfrac
-----------+----------+-------------
        1 |       12 |           0
        2 |       15 |           0
        3 |        4 |           0
(3 rows)
```

PostgreSQL defines a view (called pg_stats) that makes the pg_statistic table a little easier to deal with. Here is what the pg_stats view tells us about the tapes2 table:

```
movies-# SELECT attname, null_frac, avg_width, n_distinct FROM pg_stats
movies-#   WHERE tablename = 'tapes2';

 attname | null_frac | avg_width | n_distinct
---------+-----------+-----------+------------
 tape_id |         0 |        12 |         -1
 title   |         0 |        15 |       -0.8
(2 rows)
```

You can see that pg_stats (and the underlying pg_statistics table) contains one row for each column in the tapes2 table (except for the duration column where every value happens to be NULL). The null_frac value tells you the percentage of rows where a given column contains NULL. In this case, there are no NULL values in the tapes2 table, so null_frac is set to 0 for each column. avg_width contains the average width (in bytes) of the values in a given column. The n_distinct value tells you how many distinct values are present for a given column. If n_distinct is positive, it indicates the actual number of distinct values. If n_distinct is negative, it indicates the percentage of rows that contain a distinct value. A value of –1 tells you that every row in the table contains a unique value for that column.

pg_stats also contains information about the actual values in a table:

```
movies=# SELECT attname, most_common_vals, most_common_freqs
movies-#   FROM pg_stats
movies-#   WHERE tablename = 'tapes2';
```

```
attname | most_common_vals   | most_common_freqs
--------+--------------------+-------------------
tape_id |                    |
title   | {"The Godfather"}  | {0.4}
(2 rows)
```

The `most_common_vals` column is an array containing the most common values in a given column. The `most_common_freqs` value tells you how often each of the most common values appear. By default, `ANALYZE` stores the 10 most common values (and the frequency of those 10 values). You can increase or decrease the number of common values using the `ALTER TABLE ... SET STATISTICS` command.

Looking back at the `recalls` table, you can see that the `datea` column contains 825 distinct values:

```
perf=# \x
Expanded display is on.
perf=# SELECT
perf-#   n_distinct, most_common_vals, most_common_freqs
perf-#   FROM
perf-#   pg_stats
perf-#   WHERE
perf-#    tablename = 'recalls' AND attname = 'datea';
-[ RECORD 1 ]-----+-----------------------------------------------------------
n_distinct        | 825
most_common_vals  | {19791012,19921230,20001129,19980814,19950524,19950901,...}
most_common_freqs | {0.319667,0.005,0.005,0.00466667,0.00433333,0.00433333,...}
```

(We've turned on psql's expanded display (with the \x command) and trimmed the results a bit to make them easier to read.) The most commonly found `datea` value is `19791012` and it occurs in approximately 32% of all rows. The second most common value is `19921230` and that value is found in .5% of all rows. Go ahead and create an index that covers the `datea` column and then `ANALYZE` the `recalls` table:

```
perf=# CREATE INDEX recalls_by_datea ON recalls( datea );
CREATE INDEX
perf=# ANALYZE recalls;
ANALYZE
```

You might expect PostgreSQL to use this index in a query that selects rows based on datea values, and sometimes it does:

```
perf=# EXPLAIN SELECT * FROM recalls WHERE datea = '19921230';
                             QUERY PLAN
-----------------------------------------------------------------------
 Index Scan using recalls_by_datea (cost=0.00..31.44 rows=31 width=1908)
   Index Cond: (datea = '19921230'::bpchar)
```

You can see that the optimizer chose a partial index scan (using the `recalls_by_datea` index) to satisfy this query. Now try to select a different set of rows:

```
perf=# EXPLAIN SELECT * FROM recalls WHERE datea = '19791012';
                          QUERY PLAN
----------------------------------------------------------------
 Seq Scan on recalls  (cost=0.00..9015.09 rows=10690 width=1908)
   Filter: (datea = '19791012'::bpchar)
```

In this case, the optimizer thinks it would be faster to perform a complete table scan on the recalls table, ignoring the rows that fail to satisfy the WHERE clause.

The only thing that's changed between the two queries is the value that you're searching for. The recalls table hasn't changed; the statistics haven't changed. Why would PostgreSQL use an index to retrieve the second most-frequently-found value, but not the most-frequently-found value? Because the optimizer knows (based on the pg_stats.most_common_vals and pg_stats.most_common_freqs) that it must process 32% of the recalls table in the second case and reading a table via an index is more expensive than reading it via a sequential scan. To retrieve the second most-frequently-found value, the optimizer knows that it will only read .5% of the table via the index.

Another statistic exposed by pg_stat is called histogram_bounds. The histogram_bounds column contains an array of values for each column in your table. These values are used to partition your data into approximately equally sized chunks. For example, here are the histogram_bounds values for the recalls.potaff column:

```
perf=# SELECT histogram_bounds FROM pg_stats
perf-#    WHERE tablename = 'recalls' and attname = 'potaff';
                     histogram_bounds
----------------------------------------------------------------
 {3,104,305,700,1503,3203,6503,15263,48003,210003,32000003}
```

Because there are 11 values shown, the histogram_bounds show that 10% of the potaff values fall between 3 and 104, 10% of the potaff values fall between 104 and 305, 10% fall between 305 and 700, and so on. The optimizer uses the histograms_bounds to decide how much of an index it will need to traverse in order to search for a specific value. For example, if you search for a potaff value of 32000004 (which fits into the last histogram "bucket"), PostgreSQL knows that it will only have to traverse the last 10% of the recalls_by_potaff index to satisfy the query. On the other hand, if you search for the value 210003, PostgreSQL must traverse the last 20% of the index. Here's how the optimizer handles a search over the last 10% of the index:

```
perf=# EXPLAIN SELECT * FROM recalls WHERE potaff >= 14500003;
                          QUERY PLAN
----------------------------------------------------------------
 Index Scan using recalls_by_potaff (cost=0.00..17.99 rows=4 width=1908)
   Index Cond: (potaff >= 14500003::numeric)
```

The optimizer has chosen an index scan to satisfy this query because traversing 10% of the index is less expensive than a complete table scan. Now consider a similar query, but this time, you're searching for a value known to fall within the last 20% of the index:

```
perf=# EXPLAIN SELECT * FROM recalls WHERE potaff >= 210003;
                          QUERY PLAN
-----------------------------------------------------------------
 Seq Scan on recalls  (cost=0.00..9015.09 rows=3928 width=1908)
   Filter: (potaff >= 210003::numeric)
```

This time, the optimizer has chosen a table scan. The structure of this query is identical the previous query—only the search value has changed.

The last statistic stored in pg_stats is an indication of whether the rows in a table are stored in column order:

```
movies=# SELECT attname, correlation FROM pg_stats
movies-#  WHERE tablename = 'tapes2';
 attname | correlation
---------+-------------

 attname | correlation
---------+-------------
 tape_id |         0.7
 title   |        -0.5
(2 rows)
```

A correlation of 1 means that the rows are sorted by the given column. In practice, you will see a correlation of 1 only for brand new tables (whose rows happened to be sorted before insertion) or tables that you have reordered using the CLUSTER command.

Performance Tips

That wraps up the discussion of performance in PostgreSQL. Here are few tips that you should keep in mind whenever you run into an apparent performance problem:

- VACUUM and ANALYZE your database after any large change in data values. This will give the query optimizer a better idea of how your data is distributed.

- Use the CREATE TABLE AS or CLUSTER commands to cluster rows with similar key values. This makes an index traversal *much* faster.

- If you think you have a performance problem, use the EXPLAIN command to find out how PostgreSQL has decided to execute your query.

- You can influence the optimizer by disabling certain query operators. For example, if you want to ensure that a query is executed as a sequential scan, you can disable the Index Scan operator by executing the following command: "SET ENABLE_INDEX_SCAN TO OFF;". Disabling an operator does not guarantee that the optimizer won't use that operator—it just considers the operator to be much more expensive. The *PostgreSQL User Manual* contains a complete list of runtime parameters.

- You can also influence the optimizer by adjusting the relative costs for certain query operations. See the descriptions for CPU_INDEX_TUPLE_COST, CPU_OPERATOR_COST,

CPU_TUPLE_COST, EFFECTIVE_CACHE_SIZE, and RANDOM_PAGE_COST in the *PostgreSQL User Manual*.

- Minimize network traffic by doing as much work as possible in the server. You will usually get better performance if you can filter data on the server rather than in the client application.

- One source of extra network traffic that might not be so obvious is metadata. If your client application retrieves 10 rows using a single SELECT, one set of metadata is sent to the client. On the other hand, if you create a cursor to retrieve the same set of rows, but execute 10 FETCH commands to grab the data, you'll also get 10 (identical) sets of metadata.

- Use server-side procedures (triggers and functions) to perform common operations. A server-side procedure is parsed, planned, and optimized the first time you use it, not every time you use it.

II

Programming with PostgreSQL

Introduction to PostgreSQL Programming

Postgre SQL is a client/server database. When you use PostgreSQL, there are at least two processes involved—the client and the server. In a client/server environment, the server provides a service to one or more clients. The PostgreSQL server provides data storage and retrieval services. A PostgreSQL client is an application that receives data storage and retrieval services from a PostgreSQL server. Quite often, the client and the server exist on different physical machines connected by a network. The client and server can also exist on a single host. As you will see, the client and the server do not have to be written in the same computer language. The PostgreSQL server is written in C; many client applications are written in other languages.

In this chapter, I'll introduce you to some of the concepts behind client/server programming for PostgreSQL. I'll also show you options you have for server-side programming languages and for client-side programming interfaces. I also discuss the basic structure of a PostgreSQL client application, regardless of which client-side language you choose. Finally, I explore the advantages and disadvantages of server-side versus client-side code.

Server-Side Programming

The task of programming for PostgreSQL falls into two broad categories: server-side programming and client-side programming.

Server-side code (as the name implies) is code that executes within a PostgreSQL server. Server-side code executes the same way regardless of which language was used to implement any given client. If the client and server are running on different physical hosts, all server-side code executes on the server machine and within the server process. If the client and server are running on the same machine, server-side code still runs within the server process. In most cases, server-side code is written in one of the procedural languages distributed with PostgreSQL.

PostgreSQL version 7.1 ships with three procedural languages: PL/pgSQL, PL/Tcl, and PL/Perl. Release 7.2 adds PL/Python to the mix. You can also write server-side procedures in SQL. Later versions of PostgreSQL add support for PL/Java. You can even write server-side procedures in the form of bash shell-scripts using PL/bash.

You can use procedural languages to create functions that execute within the server. A *function* is a named sequence of statements that you can use within an SQL expression. When you write a function in a server-side language, you are extending the server. These server extensions are also known as *stored procedures*.

PL/pgSQL

If you have ever used a commercial database system—Oracle, Sybase, or SQL Server, for example—you have probably used a SQL-based procedural language. Oracle's procedural language is called PL/SQL; Sybase and SQL Server use TransactSQL. PL/pgSQL is very similar to these procedural languages.

PL/pgSQL combines the declarative nature of SQL commands with structures offered by other languages. When you create a PL/pgSQL function, you can declare local variables to store intermediate results. PL/pgSQL offers a variety of loop constructs (FOR loops, WHILE loops, and cursor iteration loops). PL/pgSQL gives you the capability to conditionally execute sections of code based on the results of a test. You can pass parameters to a PL/pgSQL function, making the function reusable. You can also invoke other functions from within a PL/pgSQL function.

Chapter 7, "PL/pgSQL," provides an in-depth description of PL/pgSQL.

Other Procedural Languages Supported by PostgreSQL

One of the more unusual aspects of PostgreSQL (compared to other database systems) is that you can write procedural code in more than one language. As noted previously, the standard distribution of PostgreSQL includes PL/pgSQL, PL/Perl, PL/Tcl, and, as of release 7.2, PL/Python.

The latter three languages each enable you to create stored procedures using a subset of the host language. PostgreSQL restricts each to a subset of the language to ensure that a stored procedure can't do nasty things to your environment.

Specifically, the PostgreSQL procedural languages are not allowed to perform I/O external to the database (in other words, you can't use a PostgreSQL procedural language to do anything outside of the context of the server). If you find that you need to affect your external environment, you can load an untrusted procedural language, but be aware that you will be introducing a security risk when you do so.

When you install PostgreSQL from a standard distribution, none of the server-side languages are installed. You can pick and choose which languages you want to install in the server. If you don't use a given language, you can choose not to install it. I'll show you how to install server-side languages in Chapter 7.

You can see which languages are currently installed in your database server with the following query:

```
movies=# select * from pg_language;
 lanname  | lanispl | lanpltrusted | lanplcallfoid | lanvalidator | lanacl
----------+---------+--------------+---------------+--------------+---------
 internal | f       | f            |             0 |         2246 |
 c        | f       | f            |             0 |         2247 |
 sql      | f       | t            |             0 |         2248 | {=U/pg}
(3 rows)
```

You can see that my server currently supports three languages: internal, C, and sql. The
lanispl column tells us that none of these are considered to be procedural languages. You
may be thinking that C should be considered a procedural language, but in this context a
procedural language is one that can be installed and de-installed from the server. You can
determine whether a language is trusted by examining the lanpltrusted column. A *trusted
language* promises not to provide elevated privileges to a user. If a language is not a trusted language, only PostgreSQL superusers can create a new function in that language.

Extending PostgreSQL Using External Languages

PostgreSQL-hosted procedural languages are not the only tools available for extending
the server. You can also add extensions to a PostgreSQL server by creating custom data
types, new functions, and new operators written in an external language (usually C or
C++).

When you create procedural-language extensions, the source code (and the object
code, if any) for those functions is stored in tables within the database. When you create
a function using an external language, the function is not stored in the database. Instead,
it is stored in a shared library that is linked into the server when first used.

You can find many PostgreSQL extensions on the Web. For example, the PostGIS
project adds a set of data types and supporting functions for dealing with geographic
data. The contrib directory of a PostgreSQL distribution contains an extension for dealing with ISBNs and ISSNs.

In Chapter 6, "Extending PostgreSQL," I'll show you a few simple examples of how
to add custom data types and functions written in C.

Client-Side APIs

When you want to build applications that access a PostgreSQL database, you use one (or
more) of the client application programming interfaces (or APIs for short). PostgreSQL
has a rich variety of APIs that support a number of programming languages.

PostgreSQL supports the APIs shown in Table 5.1.

Table 5.1 **PostgreSQL Client APIs**

Interface Name	Supported Languages	Described In
libpq	C/C++	Chapter 8
libpgeasy	C/C++	Chapter 9

Table 5.1 **Continued**

libpq++	C++	Chapter 10
ecpg	C/C++	Chapter 11
ODBC	C/C++	Chapter 12
JDBC	Java	Chapter 13
Perl	Perl	Chapter 14
PHP[1]	PHP	Chapter 15
pgtcl	TCL	Chapter 16
PyGreSQL	Python	Chapter 17
pg.el1	Emacs Lisp	Not covered

Table 5.1 is not all-inclusive. You can write PostgreSQL clients using languages not mentioned in Table 5.1. For example, Kylix (Borland's Pascal offering for Linux) offers a PostgreSQL interface. Also, many other languages (such as Microsoft Access and Visual Basic) provide access to PostgreSQL through the ODBC interface. In recent versions, the PostgreSQL development team has removed some interfaces from the core PostgreSQL distribution. If the language that you want to use is not directly supported in the core distribution, surf the gborg.postgresql.org website to find the interface you need.

General Structure of Client Applications

This is a good time to discuss, in general terms, how a client application interacts with a PostgreSQL database. All the client APIs have a common structure, but the details vary greatly from language to language.

Figure 5.1 illustrates the basic flow of a client's interaction with a server.
An application begins interacting with a PostgreSQL database by establishing a connection.

Because PostgreSQL is a client/server database, some sort of connection must exist between a client application and a database server. In the case of PostgreSQL, client/server communication takes the form of a network link. If the client and server are on different systems, the network link is a TCP/IP socket. If the client and server are on the same system, the network link is either a Unix-domain socket or a TCP/IP connection. A Unix-domain socket is a link that exists entirely within a single host—the network is a logical network (rather than a physical network) within the OS kernel.

Connection Properties

Regardless of whether you are connecting to a local server or a remote server, the API uses a set of properties to establish the connection. Connection properties are used to identify the server (a network port number and host address), the specific database that you want to connect to, your user ID (and password if required), and various debugging

---

[1] The standard PostgreSQL distribution does not include the PHP or Emacs interfaces, but they are available separately on the Web.

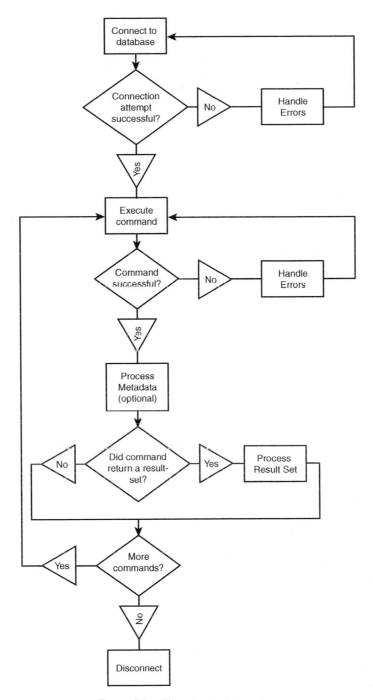

Figure 5.1   Client/server interaction.

and logging options. Each API allows you to explicitly specify connection properties, but you can also use default values for some (or all) of the properties. Most of the client-side APIs let you specify connection properties in the form of a string of `keyword=value` pairs. For example, to connect to a database named `accounting` on a host named `jersey`, you would use a property string such as

```
"dbname=accounting host=jersey"
```

Each `keyword=value` defines a single connection property. If you omit a connection property, PostgreSQL checks for an environment variable that corresponds to the property and, if the environment variable doesn't exist, PostgreSQL uses a hard-coded default value. See Table 5.2.

Table 5.2 **Keywords and Environment Variables**

Keyword	Environment Variable	Description
dbname	PGDATABASE	Specifies the name of the database that you want to connect to. If not specified, the client application tries to connect to a database with the same name as your username.
user	PGUSER	Specifies the PostgreSQL username you want to connect as. If not specified, the client uses your operating system identity.
host	PGHOST	Specifies the name (or IP address) of the computer that hosts the database you want to connect to. If the value starts with a '/', the client assumes that you want to connect to a Unix-domain socket located in that directory. If not specified, the client connects to a Unix-domain socket in /tmp.
hostaddr	PGHOSTADDR	Specifies the IP address of the computer that hosts the database you want to connect to. When you specify hostaddr (instead of host), you avoid a name lookup (which can be slow on some networks). If not specified, the client uses the value of the host property to find the server.
port	PGPORT	Specifies the TCP/IP port number to connect to (or, if you're connecting to a Unix-domain socket, the socket filename extension). If not specified, the default PGPORT is 5432.
connect_timeout	PGCONNECT_TIMEOUT	Specifies the maximum amount of time (in seconds) to wait for the connection process to complete. If not specified (or if you specify a value of 0), the client will wait forever.

Table 5.2 **Continued**

Keyword	Environment Variable	Description
slmode	PGSSLMODE	Specifies whether the client will attempt (or accept) an SSL-secured connection. Possible values are disable, allow, prefer, and require. disable and require are obvious, but allow and prefer seem a bit mysterious. If sslmode is allow, the client first attempts an insecure connection, but *allows* an SSL connection if an insecure connection can't be built. If sslmode is preferred, the client first attempts a *secure* connection, but accepts an insecure connection if a secure connection can't be built. If not specified, the default sslmode is prefer.
service	PGSERVICE	Specifies the name of a service as defined in the pg_service.conf file (see next section).

A more convenient way to encode connection parameters is to use the pg_service.conf file. When you specify a service name (with the PGSERVICE environment variable or the service=*service-name* connection property), the client application (actually the libpq library) opens a file named $PREFIX/etc/pg_service.conf and searches for a section that matches the *service-name* that you provided. If libpq locates the section that you named, it reads connection properties from that section. A typical pg_service.conf file might look similar to the following:

```
[accounting]
dbname=accounting
host=jersey
sslmode=required

[development]
dbname=accounting
host=guernsey
sslmode=prefer
```

Each service begins with the service name (enclosed in square brackets) and continues until the next section (or the end of the file). A service is simply a collection of connection properties in the usual *keyword=value* format. The sample above defines two services (one named accounting and the other named development).

The nice thing about using a service name is that you can consolidate all your connection properties in a single location and then give only the service name to your database users. When you connect to a database using a service name, the client application loads the service definition first then processes the connection string. That means that you can specify both a service name and a connection string (properties found in the connection string will override the properties specified in the service). Environment variables are only consulted in a last-ditch effort to find missing values.

After a server connection has been established, the API gives you a handle. A *handle* is nothing more than a chunk of data that you get from the API and that you give back to the API when you want to send or receive data over the connection. The exact form of a handle varies depending on the language that you are using (or more precisely, the data type of a handle varies with the API that you use). For example, in libpq (the C API), a handle is a void pointer—you can't do anything with a void pointer except to give it back to the API. In the case of libpq++ and JDBC, a handle is embedded within a class.

After you obtain a connection handle from the API, you can use that handle to interact with the database. Typically, a client will want to execute SQL queries and process results. Each API provides a set of functions that will send a SQL command to the database. In the simplest case, you use a single function; more complex applications (and APIs) can separate command execution into two phases. The first phase sends the command to the server (for error checking and query planning) and the second phase actually carries out the command; you can repeat the execution phase as many times as you like. The advantage to a two-phase execution method is performance. You can parse and plan a command once and execute it many times, rather than parsing and planning every time you execute the command. Two-phase execution can also simplify your code by factoring the work required to generate a command into a separate function: One function can generate a command and a separate function can execute the command.

After you use an API to send a command to the server, you get back three types of results. The first result that comes back from the server is an indication of success or failure—every command that you send to the server will either fail or succeed. If your command fails, you can use the API to retrieve an error code and a translation of that code into some form of textual message.

If the server tells you that the command executed successfully, you can retrieve the next type of result: metadata. Metadata is data about data. Specifically, *metadata* is information about the results of the command that you just executed. If you already know the format of the result set, you can ignore the metadata.

When you execute a command such as INSERT, UPDATE, or DELETE, the metadata returned by the server is simply a count of the number of rows affected by the command. Some commands return no metadata. For example, when you execute a CREATE TABLE command, the only results that you get from the server are success or failure (and an error code if the command fails). When you execute a SELECT command, the metadata is more complex. Remember that a SELECT statement can return a set of zero or more rows, each containing one or more columns. This is called the *result set*. The metadata for a SELECT statement describes each of the columns in the result set.

Field Versus Column in Result Sets

When discussing a result set, the PostgreSQL documentation makes a distinction between a *field* and a *column*. A column comes directly from a table (or a view). A field is the result of a computation in the SELECT statement. For example, if you execute the command SELECT customer_name,

> `customer_balance * 1.05 FROM customers`, `customer_name` is a column in the result set and `customer_balance * 1.05` is a field in the result set. The difference between a field and a column is mostly irrelevant and can be ignored; just be aware that the documentation uses two different words for the same meaning.

When the server sends result set metadata, it returns the number of rows in the result set and the number of fields. For each field in the result set, the metadata includes the field name, data type information, and the size of the field (on the server).

I should mention here that most client applications don't really need to deal with all the metadata returned by the server. In general, when you write an application you already know the structure of your data. You'll often need to know how many rows were returned by a given query, but the other metadata is most useful when you are processing ad-hoc commands—commands that are not known to you at the time you are writing your application.

After you process the metadata (if you need to), your application will usually process all the rows in the result set. If you execute a SELECT statement, the result set will include all the rows that meet the constraints of the WHERE clause (if any). In some circumstances, you will find it more convenient to DECLARE a cursor for the SELECT statement and then execute multiple FETCH statements. When you execute the DECLARE statement, you won't get metadata. However, as you execute FETCH commands, you are constructing a new result set for each FETCH and the server has to send metadata describing the resulting fields—that can be expensive.

After you have finished processing the result set, you can execute more commands, or you can disconnect from the server.

LISTEN/NOTIFY

Sometimes, you might want a client application to wait for some server-side event to occur before proceeding. For example, you might need a queuing system that writes a work order into a PostgreSQL table and then expects a client application to carry out that work order. The most obvious way to write a client of this sort is to put your client application to sleep for a few seconds (or a few minutes), then, when your application awakens, check for a new record in the work-order table. If the record exists, do your work and then repeat the whole cycle.

There are two problems with this approach. First, your client application can't be very responsive. When a new work order is added, it may take a few seconds (or a few minutes) for your client to notice (it's fast asleep after all). Second, your client application might spend a lot of time searching for work orders that don't exist.

PostgreSQL offers a solution to this problem: the LISTEN/NOTIFY mechanism. A PostgreSQL server can signal client applications that some event has occurred by executing a NOTIFY *eventName* command. All client applications that are listening for that event are notified that the event has occurred. You get to choose your own event names. In a work-order application, you might define an event named workOrderReceived. To inform the server that you are interested in that event, the client application executes a LISTEN workOrderReceived command (to tell the server that you are no longer interested in an event, simply UNLISTEN workOrderReceived). When a work order arrives at the server (via some other client application), executing the command NOTIFY workOrderReceived will inform all clients that a workOrderReceived event has occurred (actually, PostgreSQL will only notify those clients listening for that specific event).

Each client-side API offers a different LISTEN mechanism and you rarely execute a LISTEN command yourself—instead, you call an API function that executes the LISTEN command for you (after arranging to intercept the event in a language-specific way).

Regardless of the language that you choose, you should be aware that notifications are only sent at the end of a successful transaction. If you ROLLBACK a transaction, any NOTIFY commands executed within that transaction are ignored. That makes sense if you think about it: If your application adds a work order record, but then aborts the transaction, you don't want to wake client applications with a false alarm.

Choosing an Application Environment

When you choose an environment for your code, there are a number of issues to consider. To start with, you have to decide whether the feature that you want to build should be server-side code, client-side code, or a combination of both.

Server-Side Code

There are several advantages to adding functionality as server-side code.

The first consideration is performance. If you are creating an application that needs to access many rows of data, it will execute faster on the server. You won't have to send the data across the network to the client (network traffic is very expensive in terms of performance).

Next, you should consider code reuse. If you add a feature in the form of a server-side function, that feature can be used by *any* client application. You can also use server-side functions within SQL queries.

Another advantage to creating server-side functions is that you can use a server function as a trigger. A *trigger function* is executed whenever a particular condition occurs. For example, you can define a trigger that executes whenever a row is deleted from a particular table.

Finally, server-side code is portable. Any function that you write in a server-side procedural language runs on any platform that supports PostgreSQL. Of course, if you write a server-side function that requires specific server-side features (such as other functions or data types), those features must be installed in each server.

Client-Side Code

Client-side code is useful for building the user interface. You can't build a user interface using one of the server-side procedural languages—they execute within the context of the server and the server has no user interface.

One of the interesting things to note about the client APIs is that most of them are implemented using the libpq API (ODBC and JDBC are not). This means, for example, that if you are using libpq++ from a C++ application and you call a member function of the PgDatabase class, it will be translated into one or more calls to the libpq library.

The ODBC and JDBC interfaces are not implemented using libpq. Instead, they talk directly to the backend database using the same network protocol as libpq. If you ever decide to implement your own client API, you can choose either method: implement your API in terms of libpq (or one of the other APIs), or talk directly to the server using the same underlying network protocol.

Mixing Server-Side and Client-Side Code

A particularly powerful strategy is to create an application using a mixture of client-side code and stored-procedures. Many commercial applications are shipped with two types of code. When you use one of these packages, you install a set of stored-procedures into the database; then you install external client applications that make use of the custom procedures.

This arrangement gives you all the advantages of server-side code (performance, portability, and reusability) plus the capability to create a pleasant user interface in the client.

Summary

This chapter discussed the options available to you when you create applications to work with PostgreSQL. With PostgreSQL, you can write client-side applications in a variety of languages and you can also choose between many server-side languages.

When you write an application that uses PostgreSQL, you have to decide whether you want to implement server-side code, client-side code, or a combination of both. I've explained some of the advantages and disadvantages of each approach. Personally, I prefer to mix server-side and client-side code so that I can realize the advantages offered by each.

The next few chapters describe in greater detail PL/pgSQL (server-side programming) and many of the client APIs.

6

Extending PostgreSQL

PostgreSQL is an extensible database. You can add new functions, new operators, and custom data types to the PostgreSQL server.

In this chapter, I'll show you how to add two simple functions, a new data type, and a set of operators that work with the new type. The examples build on each other, so it would be a good idea to read this chapter in sequence rather than skipping around too much. The sample code used in this chapter was developed using PostgreSQL release 8.0.

We'll start by adding a new function to the PostgreSQL server. The details are important, but the process is not difficult. After you know how to add one function to the server, it's easy to add others.

Extending the PostgreSQL Server with Custom Functions

An extension function is loaded into a running PostgreSQL server process as needed. If you don't actually use an extension, it will not be loaded. Extension functions must be created in the form of a dynamically loadable object module. In the Windows world, an extension is contained within a DLL. In the Linux/Unix environment, an extension is contained within a shared object module.

There are two phases to the process of adding an extension function to the PostgreSQL server. First, you create the extension function in the language of your choice, compiling it into a dynamic object module (.dll or .so). Next, tell the PostgreSQL server about the function. The CREATE FUNCTION command adds a new function to a database.

I'll show you two examples that should help clarify this process.

PostgreSQL and Portability

Some of the steps required to write a PostgreSQL extension function in C may seem rather odd at first. You may feel more comfortable with the process if you understand the problem that the PostgreSQL authors were trying to fix.

When you call a function in a typical C program, you know at the time you write your code how to call that function. You know how many arguments are required and you know the data type of each argument. If you provide an incorrect number of parameters or incorrect data types, it is highly likely that your program will crash. For example, the `fopen()` function (from the C Runtime Library) requires two parameters:

```
FILE * fopen( const char * filename, const char * mode )
```

If you omit the `mode` parameter or send a numeric data type instead of a pointer, your program will fail in some way.

Now, suppose that your program prompts the user for the name of a dynamic object module and the name of a function within that module. After you load the given module into your program, you have to call the named function. If you know which function the user will select, you can formulate your function call properly at the time you write your code. What happens if the user selects some other function that takes a completely different argument list? How can you formulate the function call if you don't know the parameter list? There is no portable way to do that, and PostgreSQL aims to be extremely portable.

So, the PostgreSQL authors decided to change the way you pass arguments to an extension function. Rather than declaring a separate formal parameter for each value passed to the function, PostgreSQL marshals all the arguments into a separate data structure and passes the address of the marshaled form to your extension. When you need to access function parameters, you get to them through the marshaled form.

This is similar in concept to the way the `main()` function of a C program behaves. You can't know, at the time you write the `main()` function, how many command-line parameters you will receive. (You might know how many parameters you should receive, but how many you will receive is not quite the same animal.) The startup routine on the C Runtime Library marshals the command-line arguments into a data structure (the `argv[]` array) and passes you the address of that structure. To find the actual values specified on the command line, you must use the data structure rather than formal parameters.

Older versions of PostgreSQL used a strategy that became less portable as operating systems advanced into the 64-bit arena. The old strategy is known as the "version-0 calling convention." The new strategy is called the "version-1 calling convention." PostgreSQL still supports both calling conventions, but you should stick to the version-1 convention for better portability.

For more information on the difference between the version-0 and version-1 conventions, see section 12 of the PostgreSQL Programmer's Guide.

There are two important consequences to the version-1 convention. First, all version-1 functions return the same data type: a `Datum`. A `Datum` is a sort of universal data type. Any PostgreSQL data type can be accessed through a `Datum`. PostgreSQL provides a set of macros that make it easy to work with `Datum`s. Second, a version-1 function makes use of a set of macros to access function arguments. Every version-1 function is declared in the same way:

```
Datum function-name(PG_FUNCTION_ARGS);
```

As you read through the examples in this chapter, keep in mind that the PostgreSQL authors had to solve the portability problem.

The first example adds a simple function, named `filesize`, to the PostgreSQL server. Given the name of a file, it returns the size of the file (in bytes). If the file does not exist, cannot be examined, or is not a regular[1] file, this function returns NULL. You might find this function (and the `filelist()` function shown later) useful for performing system administration tasks from within a PostgreSQL application. After you have created the `filesize` function, you can call it like this:

```
movies=# SELECT filesize( '/bin/bash' );
 filesize
----------
   512668
```

We'll develop the `filesize` function in C (see Listing 6.1).

The `filesize` function takes a single argument—a pathname in the form of a TEXT value. This function returns the size of the named file as an INTEGER value.

Listing 6.1   `filesize.c`

```
 1 /*
 2 ** Filename: filesize.c
 3 */
 4
 5 #include "postgres.h"
 6 #include "fmgr.h"
 7 #include <sys/stat.h>
 8
 9 PG_FUNCTION_INFO_V1(filesize);
10
11 Datum filesize(PG_FUNCTION_ARGS)
12 {
13     text * fileNameText = PG_GETARG_TEXT_P(0);
14     size_t fileNameLen  = VARSIZE( fileNameText ) - VARHDRSZ;
15     char * fileName      = (char *)palloc( fileNameLen + 1 );
16     struct stat statBuf;
17
18     memcpy( fileName, VARDATA( fileNameText ), fileNameLen );
19     fileName[fileNameLen] = '\0';
20
21     if( stat(fileName, &statBuf) == 0 && S_ISREG(statBuf.st_mode))
22     {
23       pfree( fileName );
24
25       PG_RETURN_INT32((int32)statBuf.st_size );
26     }
```

[1] In this context, a file is considered "regular" if it is not a directory, named pipe, symbolic link, device file, or socket.

Listing 6.1   **Continued**

```
27    else
28    {
29      pfree( fileName );
30
31      PG_RETURN_NULL();
32    }
33 }
```

Lines 5 and 6 #include two header files supplied by PostgreSQL. These files (post-gres.h and fmgr.h) provide data type definitions, function prototypes, and macros that you can use when writing extensions. The <sys/stat.h> file included at line 7 defines the layout of the struct stat object used by the stat() function (described later).

Line 9 uses the PG_FUNCTION_INFO_V1() to tell PostgreSQL that the function (file-size()) uses the version-1 calling convention.

At line 11, you see the signature used for all version-1 functions. The filesize() function returns a Datum and expects a single argument. PG_FUNCTION_ARGS is a pre-processor symbol that expands to declare a consistently named parameter. So, your function definition expands from this:

```
Datum filesize(PG_FUNCTION_ARGS)
```

to this:

```
Datum filesize( FunctionCallInfo fcinfo )
```

This might seem a little strange at first, but the version-1 argument accessor macros are written so that the single function argument must be named fcinfo.

At line 13, you create a variable of type text. text is one of the data types defined in the postgres.h header file (or in a file included by postgres.h). Whenever you write an extension function, you will be working with two sets of data types. Each function parameter (and the return value) will have a SQL data type and a C data type. For example, when you call the filesize function from within PostgreSQL, you pass a TEXT parameter: TEXT is the SQL data type. When you implement the filesize function in C, you receive a text value: text is the C data type. The name for the C data type is usually similar to the name of the corresponding SQL data type. For clarity, I'll refer to the PostgreSQL data types using uppercase letters and the C data types using lowercase letters.

Notice that a macro is used to retrieve the address of the TEXT value. I mentioned earlier that an extension function must use macros to access parameters, and this is an example of such a macro. The PG_GETARG_TEXT_P(n) macro returns the nth parameter, which must be of type TEXT. The return value of PG_GETARG_TEXT_P(n) is of type text. There are many argument-accessor functions, each corresponding to a specific parameter type: PG_GETARG_INT32(n), PG_GETARG_BOOL(n), PG_GETARG_OID(n), and so on. See the fmgr.h PostgreSQL header file for a complete list.

We'll be using the stat() function (from the C Runtime library) to find the size of a given file. stat() expects to find the pathname in the form of a null-terminated string.

PostgreSQL has given you a text value, and text values are not null-terminated. You will need to convert fileNameText into a null-terminated string.

If fileNameText is not null-terminated, how do you know the length of the pathname? Let's take a peek at the definition of the text data type (from the c.h PostgreSQL header file):

```
struct varlena
{
    int32   vl_len;
    char    vl_data[1];
};


typedef struct varlena text;
```

You can see that a text value is defined by the struct varlena structure. The vl_len member tells you how many bytes are required to hold the entire structure. The characters that make up the text value start at the address of the vl_data[0] member. PostgreSQL supplies two macros that make it easy to work with variable-length data structures. The VARHDRSZ symbol contains the size of the fixed portion of a struct varlena. The VARSIZE() macro returns the size of the entire data structure. The VARDATA() macro returns a pointer to first byte of the TEXT value. The length of the TEXT value is VARSIZE() - VARHDRSZ. You store that length in the fileNameLen variable.

At line 15, you allocate enough space to hold a copy of the null-terminated string. The palloc() function is similar to malloc(): It allocates the requested number of bytes and returns a pointer to the new space. You should use palloc() and pfree() when you write extension functions rather than malloc() and free(). The palloc() and pfree() functions ensure that you can't create a memory leak in an extension function, which is something you *can* do if you use malloc() instead.

Lines 18 and 19 create a null-terminated copy of the TEXT value, and line 21 passes the null-terminated string to the stat() function. If the stat() function succeeds, it fills in the statBuf structure and returns 0.

If you succeeded in retrieving the file status information and the file is a regular file, free the null-terminated string (using pfree()) and return the file size. Notice that you must use a macro to translate the return value (an int32) into a Datum.

If the stat() function failed (or the file is not a regular file), you free the null-terminated string and return NULL. Again, you use a macro to produce the return value in the form of a Datum.

Now that you have crafted the filesize function, you need to compile it into a shared object module. You usually compile a C source file into a standalone executable program, but PostgreSQL expects to find the filesize function in a shared object module. The procedure for producing a shared object module is different for each compiler; section 31.9 of the PostgreSQL reference documentation describes the process for a number of compilers. Listing 6.2 shows the makefile that I've used to compile the filesize function using Fedora Core (Linux):

Listing 6.2 `makefile`

```
# File name: makefile
SERVER_INCLUDES += -I $(shell pg_config --includedir)
SERVER_INCLUDES += -I $(shell pg_config --includedir-server)

CFLAGS += -g $(SERVER_INCLUDES)

.SUFFIXES:       .so

.c.so:
        $(CC) $(CFLAGS) -fpic -c $<
        $(CC) $(CFLAGS) -shared -o $@ $(basename $<).o
```

To compile `filesize` using this `makefile`, you would issue the following command:

```
$ make -f makefile filesize.so
```

After the compile step is completed, you are left with a file named `filesize.so` in your current directory. The preferred location for a PostgreSQL extension can be found using the `pg_config` command:

```
$ pg_config --pkglibdir
/usr/local/pg800/lib/postgresql
```

You can copy the `filesize.so` file to this directory, but I prefer to create a symbolic link pointing back to my development directory instead. After an extension is completely debugged, I delete the symbolic link and copy the final version into the preferred location. To create a symbolic link, use the following command:

```
$ ln -s `pwd`/filesize.so `pg_config --pkglibdir`
```

At this point, you have a shared object module, but you still have to tell PostgreSQL about the function that you want to import into the server.

The CREATE FUNCTION command tells PostgreSQL everything it needs to know to call your function:

```
movies=# CREATE OR REPLACE FUNCTION
movies-#   filesize( TEXT ) RETURNS INTEGER AS
movies-#   'filesize.so', 'filesize' LANGUAGE 'C'
movies-#   STRICT;
CREATE
```

This command defines a function named `filesize( TEXT )`. This function returns an INTEGER value. The function is written in C and can be found in the file `filesize.so` in the preferred extension directory. You can specify a complete pathname to the shared object module if you want to, but in most cases it's easier to just put it where PostgreSQL expects to find it, as I've done here. You can also omit the filename extension (the `.so` part), as long as you follow the shared object module-naming rules imposed by your host operating system.

I've defined `filesize()` as a *strict* function. The STRICT attribute tells PostgreSQL that this function will always return NULL if any argument is NULL. If PostgreSQL knows that a function is STRICT, it can avoid calling the function with a NULL argument (again, a performance optimization). STRICT makes it easier for you to implement your extension functions; you don't have to check for NULL arguments if you declare your functions to be STRICT.

Now you can call the function from within a PostgreSQL session:

```
movies=# SELECT filesize( '/bin/bash' );
 filesize
----------
   512668
(1 row)
movies=# SELECT filesize( 'non-existent file' );
 filesize
----------

(1 row)
```

Debugging PostgreSQL Extensions

One of the challenges you'll face in creating PostgreSQL extensions is figuring out how to debug them. Relax, it's easy. First, remember that the extension function that you create is loaded into the server (not the client). That means that when you fire up a debugger, you want to attach it to the *server* process. How do you *find* the server process? Call the `pg_backend_pid()` function once the server is up and running—`pg_backend_pid()` returns the process ID of the server that your client is connected to. Next, load the shared-object file (the file that contains your extension function) into the server with the LOAD command. At this point, your server is waiting for you—it's time to attach the debugger. If you're using the gdb debugger, you can attach to a running process with the command:

```
gdb postgres server-process-id
```

But remember, the PostgreSQL server process is owned by user `postgres`: If you try to attach without the proper privileges, gdb will just laugh at you. Make sure you `su postgres` before you run gdb. When you ask gdb to attach to a running process, the second argument is ignored—it has to be there, but it really doesn't matter what you string you use.

If you have the proper privileges, gdb should now be waiting for you to enter a command. Now you can set a breakpoint at your extension function and gdb will interrupt the server when that function is invoked. Notice that the server process is suspended until you tell the debugger to `continue` (if you try to execute a command from your PostgreSQL client application, the client will hang until the server wakes up again). Once you've told gdb to continue, you can go back to your client application and issue a command that invokes the function that you're interested in.

If you're debugging an extension function on a Windows host, the procedure is similar: Find the process ID of the server and attach a Windows debugger to that process.

To summarize:

- Start a client application (such as psql)
- From within the client: `SELECT pg_backend_pid();`
- From within the client: `LOAD 'extension-file.so';`
- Start another terminal session and `su postgres`
- Fire up the debugger: `$ gdb postgres server-process-id`
- Set a breakpoint: `(gdb) break my-function`
- Tell gdb to continue: `(gdb) cont`
- Go back to the client application and execute a command that will call your extension function

Returning Multiple Values from an Extension Function

The second extension that you will add works well with the `filesize` function. Given the name of a directory, the `filelist` function returns a list of all files (and subdirectories) contained in that directory. The `filesize` function (from the previous example) returns a single value; `filelist` will return multiple rows. An extension function that can return multiple results is called a *set-returning function*, or SRF.

PostgreSQL's SRF Interface

Before you read too much further, I should tell you that there's an easy way to write set-returning functions and another method that's *almost* as easy. I'll describe both methods, starting with the slightly more difficult approach. Starting with version 7.3, the PostgreSQL developers introduced a set of wrapper functions (and macros) that put a friendlier face on top of the original method. Under the hood, your SRF is doing the same thing whether you use the new approach or the old approach, but it's a little easier to understand the new SRF interface if you can peek under the covers.

When you are finished creating the `filelist` function, you can use it like this:

```
movies=# SELECT filelist( '/usr' );
  filelist
------------
  .
  ..
  bin
  dict
  etc
  games
  html
  include
  kerberos
  lib
```

```
libexec
local
sbin
share
src
tmp
X11R6
(17 rows)
```

In this example, the user has invoked the `filelist` function only once, but 17 rows were returned. A SRF is actually called multiple times. In this case, the `filelist()` function is called 18 times. The first time through, `filelist()` does any preparatory work required and then returns the first result. For each subsequent call, `filelist()` returns another row until the result set is exhausted. On the 18th call, `filelist()` returns a status that tells the server that there are no more results available.

Like the `filesize` function, `filelist` takes a single argument; a directory name in the form of a `TEXT` value. This function returns a `SETOF TEXT` values. Listing 6.3 shows the first part of the `filelist.c` source file:

Listing 6.3 `filelist.c` **(Part 1)**

```
 1 /*
 2 **  Filename:  filelist.c
 3 */
 4
 5 #include "postgres.h"
 6 #include "fmgr.h"
 7 #include "nodes/execnodes.h"
 8
 9 #include <dirent.h>
10
11 typedef struct
12 {
13   int             dir_ctx_count;
14   struct dirent ** dir_ctx_entries;
15   int             dir_ctx_current;
16 } dir_ctx;
17
18 PG_FUNCTION_INFO_V1(filelist);
19
```

`filelist.c` #includes four header files, the first three of which are supplied by PostgreSQL. `postgres.h` and `fmgr.h` provide data type definitions, function prototypes, and macros that you will need to create extensions. The `nodes/execnodes.h` header file defines a structure (`ReturnSetInfo`) that you need because `filelist` returns a set of values. You will use the `scandir()` function to retrieve the directory contents from the operating system. The fourth header file defines a few data types that are used by `scandir()`.

Line 11 defines a structure that keeps track of your progress. In the first invocation, you will set up a context structure (dir_ctx) that we can use for each subsequent call. The dir_ctx_count member indicates the number of files and subdirectories in the given directory. The dir_ctx_entries member is a pointer to an array of struct dirent structures. Each member of this array contains a description of a file or subdirectory. dir_ctx_current keeps track of the current position as you traverse the dir_ctx_entries array.

Line 18 tells PostgreSQL that filelist() uses the version-1 calling convention. Listing 6.4 shows the filelist() function:

Listing 6.4 filelist.c **(Part 2)**

```
20 Datum filelist(PG_FUNCTION_ARGS)
21 {
22   FmgrInfo       * fmgr_info = fcinfo->flinfo;
23   ReturnSetInfo * resultInfo = (ReturnSetInfo *)fcinfo->resultinfo;
24   text          * startText  = PG_GETARG_TEXT_P(0);
25   int             len        = VARSIZE( startText ) - VARHDRSZ;
26   char          * start      = (char *)palloc( len+1 );
27   dir_ctx       * ctx;
28
29   memcpy( start, startText->vl_dat, len );
30   start[len] = '\0';
31
32   if( fcinfo->resultinfo == NULL )
33     elog(ERROR, "filelist: context does not accept a set result");
34
35   if( !IsA( fcinfo->resultinfo, ReturnSetInfo ))
36     elog(ERROR, "filelist: context does not accept a set result");
37
38   if( fmgr_info->fn_extra == NULL )
39   {
40     dir_ctx     * new_ctx;
41
42     fmgr_info->fn_extra = MemoryContextAlloc( fmgr_info->fn_mcxt,
43                                               sizeof( dir_ctx ));
44
45     new_ctx = (dir_ctx *)fmgr_info->fn_extra;
46
47     new_ctx->dir_ctx_count   = scandir( start,
48                                         &new_ctx->dir_ctx_entries,
49                                         NULL,
50                                         alphasort );
51     new_ctx->dir_ctx_current = 0;
52   }
53
54   ctx = (dir_ctx *)fmgr_info->fn_extra;
55
```

Listing 6.4   **Continued**

```
56   if( ctx->dir_ctx_count == -1 )
57   {
58     pfree( fmgr_info->fn_extra );
59
60     fmgr_info->fn_extra = NULL;
61
62     resultInfo->isDone = ExprEndResult;
63
64     PG_RETURN_NULL();
65   }
66
67   if( ctx->dir_ctx_current < ctx->dir_ctx_count )
68   {
69     struct dirent * entry;
70     size_t          nameLen;
71     size_t          resultLen;
72     text          * result;
73
74     entry     = ctx->dir_ctx_entries[ctx->dir_ctx_current];
75     nameLen   = strlen( entry->d_name );
76     resultLen = nameLen + VARHDRSZ;
77
78     result = (text *)palloc( resultLen );
79
80     VARATT_SIZEP( result ) = resultLen;
81
82     memcpy( VARDATA( result ), entry->d_name, nameLen );
83
84     resultInfo->isDone = ExprMultipleResult;
85
86 /*
87 **  Advance to the next entry in our array of
88 **  filenames/subdirectories
89 */
90     ctx->dir_ctx_current++;
91
92     PG_RETURN_TEXT_P( result );
93   }
94   else
95   {
96     free( ctx->dir_ctx_entries );
97
98     pfree( fmgr_info->fn_extra );
99
100    fmgr_info->fn_extra = NULL;
101
```

Listing 6.4   **Continued**

```
102     resultInfo->isDone = ExprEndResult;
103
104     PG_RETURN_NULL();
105   }
106 }
```

Line 20 declares `filelist()` using the standard version-1 calling convention (remember, a version-1 function always returns a `Datum` and uses the `PG_FUNCTION_ARGS` preprocessor symbol as an argument list).

The C preprocessor translated line 20 into

```
Datum filesize( FunctionCallInfo fcinfo )
```

As you can see, you can access the single argument to `filesize()` through the variable `fcinfo`. All version-1 extension functions expect a `FunctionCallInfo` structure. Here is the definition of the `FunctionCallInfo` data type:

```
typedef struct FunctionCallInfoData
{
  FmgrInfo    *flinfo;     /* ptr to lookup info used for this call  */
  struct Node *context;    /* pass info about context of call        */
  struct Node *resultinfo; /* pass or return extra info about result */
  bool        isnull;      /* true if result is NULL                 */
  short       nargs;       /* # arguments actually passed            */
  Datum       arg[FUNC_MAX_ARGS];    /* Function arguments           */
  bool        argnull[FUNC_MAX_ARGS]; /* T if arg[i] is NULL         */
} FunctionCallInfoData;
```

There is quite a bit of information in this structure. For now, you need to know about only two of the structure members; the rest of the members are manipulated using macros, so you should pretend that you don't see them. The two members that you are interested in are `flinfo` and `resultInfo`. The `flinfo` member points to a structure of type `FmgrInfo`. The `FmgrInfo` structure looks like this:

```
typedef struct FmgrInfo
{
  PGFunction  fn_addr;   /* function or handler to be called        */
  Oid         fn_oid;    /* OID of function (NOT of handler, if any) */
  short       fn_nargs;  /* 0..FUNC_MAX_ARGS, or -1 if variable arg */
  bool        fn_strict; /* func. is "strict" (NULL in = NULL out)  */
  bool        fn_retset; /* func. returns a set (multiple calls)    */
  void        *fn_extra; /* extra space for use by handler          */
  MemoryContext fn_mcxt; /* memory context to store fn_extra in     */
} FmgrInfo;
```

Look closely at the `FmgrInfo` and `FunctionCallInfo` structures. Why would you need two structures to represent a function call? The `FmgrInfo` function contains information about the *definition* of a function; in other words, the stuff you tell PostgreSQL in the

CREATE FUNCTION command can be found in the FmgrInfo structure. The FunctionCallInfo structure represents a single invocation of a function. If you call the same function 20 times, you'll have 20 different FunctionCallInfo structures, each pointing to a single FmgrInfo structure. You can see the difference by comparing FmgrInfo.fn_nargs with FunctionCallInfo.nargs. FmgrInfo.fn_nargs tells you how many arguments were listed in the CREATE FUNCTION command; FmgrInfo.fn_nargs tells you how many arguments were passed to this particular invocation.

Line 23 declares a variable called fmgr_info; you'll use this to get to the FmgrInfo structure for this function. Line 24 declares a variable that you will use to get to the ReturnSetInfo structure. I'll describe the ReturnSetInfo structure in a moment.

Lines 24 through 30 turn the text argument into a null-terminated string. This is basically the same procedure you used in the filesize() function.

Lines 32 through 36 perform some sanity checks. It's possible to call the filelist() function in an inappropriate context. We know that filelist() returns multiple rows, so it makes sense to call that function as a target of a SELECT command. You could also call filelist() in the WHERE clause of a SELECT command, but that would be an inappropriate context (because of that multiple-row problem). When you write a function that returns a set of values, you should ensure that your function is being called in an appropriate context the way we do here.

Line 38 is where the interesting stuff starts. fmgr_info->fn_extra is a pointer that you can use for your own purposes; PostgreSQL doesn't do anything with this structure member except to provide for your use. The first time filelist() is called, the fmgr_info->fn_extra member is NULL. In each subsequent call, fmgr_info->fn_extra is equal to whatever you set it to in the previous call. Sounds like a great place to keep context information. Remember the dir_ctx structure you looked at earlier? That structure holds the information that you use to keep track of your progress as you walk through the array of file entries in a given directory.

At line 42, you know that fmgr_info->fn_extra is NULL: That implies that you have not yet started traversing a directory list. So, you allocate a dir_ctx structure and point fmgr_info->fn_extra to the new structure. The next time you are called, fmgr_info->fn_extra will point to the same dir_ctx structure (remember, there is only one FmgrInfo structure, regardless of how many times this function is called).

You may be thinking that I should have used palloc() to allocate the dir_ctx structure. In most extension functions, that is precisely what you should do. But in the case of an SRF, you want to allocate information related to the FmgrInfo structure in a different memory context[2], the context pointed to in the fmgr_info structure.

---

[2] You can think of a memory context as a pool of memory. Unlike malloc(), the MemoryContextAlloc() function allocates memory from a specific pool (malloc() allocates all memory from the same pool). A memory context has lifetime (or scope). When the scope completes, all memory allocated within that scope is automatically released. The palloc() function is just a wrapper around MemoryContextAlloc(). The memory context used by palloc() is destroyed at the end of a transaction (or possibly sooner).

Lines 47 through 50 do the real grunt work. You use the `scandir()` function to create an array of `struct dirent` structures. Each element in this array (`new_ctx->dir_ctx_entries`) describes a file or subdirectory. The `scandir()` function expects four parameters. The first parameter is the name of the directory that you are interested in; you pass the null-terminated string (`start`) that you crafted earlier in this function. The second parameter is a bit complex—it's a pointer to a pointer to an array of `struct dirent` structures. You know that your `dir_ctx.dir_ctx_entries` member is a pointer to an array of structures, so you pass the *address* of `dir_ctx_entries` and `scandir()` points `dir_ctx_entries` to the new array. The third parameter is a pointer to a structure. If you want to choose which files and subdirectories to include in the result set, you can write your own selection function and pass its address to `scandir()`. You want all files and subdirectories so you just pass in a `NULL` to tell `scandir()` not to filter the result set. The final `scandir()` parameter is a pointer to a comparison function. If you *don't* provide a comparison function, `scandir()` won't sort the result set. Use the `alphasort` function from the C Runtime Library—it's already written, and you aren't too concerned about performance here. For more information on `scandir()` and `alphasort()`, see the `scandir()` man page.

Finish initializing the `dir_ctx` structure by setting `dir_ctx_current` to zero. `dir_ctx_current` is incremented as you walk through the `dir_ctx_entries`.

Now that the initialization is complete, you can return your first result. But first, a quick review. You know that PostgreSQL calls this function many times and it continues to call `filelist()` until you set `resultInfo->isDone` to `ExprEndResult`. You can detect the initial call to `filelist()` by the fact that `fmgr_info->fn_extra` is `NULL`. In the initial call, you allocate a context structure and point `fmgr_info->fn_extra` to the new structure; the next time that `filelist()` is called, `fmgr_info->fn_extra` will *not* be `NULL`, so you know that you can skip the initialization step. Next, populate the context structure by calling the `scandir()` function: `scandir()` allocates an array of `struct dirent` structures and gives you a pointer to that array.

Line 54 retrieves the address of your context structure from `fmgr_info->fn_extra`.

Lines 56 through 65 take care of the case where the `scandir()` function fails to return any directory entries. The `scandir()` function returns the number of directory entries retrieved—it returns -1 on failure.

The details in this section of code are important. First, you must free the context structure that you allocated in the initial call (using `pfree()`). You also set `fmgr_info->fn_extra` to `NULL`; if you forget this step, the next call to `filelist()` will find a stale context structure and won't reinitialize. Remember, there is one FunctionCallInfo structure for each invocation, but there is never more than one FmgrInfo structure; you'll get the same FmgrInfo structure each time `filelist()` is invoked. Line 62 tells PostgreSQL that you have reached the end of the result set and line 64 returns a `NULL` Datum.

Lines 67 through 93 take care of returning a single result to the caller.

Lines 74 through 82 create a `text` value from a null-terminated directory entry (actually, ignore most of the `struct dirent` structure and just return the name portion). You first allocate a new `text` structure using `palloc()`; then set the structure size and copy the directory entry name into place. Notice that you don't copy the null-terminator: A text value should not be null-terminated. At line 84, you tell PostgreSQL that you are returning a result and there may be more results, so keep calling. Next, you increment the array index so that the next call to `filelist()` will return the next directory entry. Finally, you return the directory entry to the caller in the form of a text value.

Notice that the context structure in this section of code has not been freed. You need to preserve the `dir_ctx` structure until you have processed the last directory entry.

You reach Lines 96 through 104 once you have returned all directory entries. This section is nearly identical to the code that deals with a `scandir()` failure (lines 58-64). In fact, the only difference is that you have one more thing to clean up. When you called the `scandir()` function, it allocated an array of `struct dirent` structures using `malloc()`. You have to `free()` that array before you finish up.

That completes the C part of this function; now you have to compile it into a shared object module and tell PostgreSQL where to find it. You can use the same `makefile` that you used to compile the `filesize` function:

```
$ make -f makefile filelist.so
```

As before, you'll create a symbolic link between `filelist.so` and PostgreSQL's preferred package directory:

```
$ ln -s `pwd`/filelist.so `pg_config --pkglibdir`
```

Now the only thing remaining is to tell PostgreSQL about the new function:

```
movies=# CREATE FUNCTION filelist( TEXT )
movies-#   RETURNS SETOF TEXT
movies-#   AS 'filelist.so' LANGUAGE 'C';
CREATE
```

Now, let's call `filelist()` to see how it works:

```
movies=# SELECT filelist( '/usr' );
  filelist
-----------
  .

  ..
  bin
  dict
  etc
  games
  html
  include
  kerberos
  lib
  libexec
  local
  sbin
  share
  src
```

```
tmp
X11R6
(17 rows)
```

Notice that the results appear in sorted order. The ordering comes because you used the
`alphasort()` function when you called `scandir()`. If you don't care about the ordering,
you can specify a NULL comparison function instead. Of course, we can ask PostgreSQL
to order the data itself:

```
movies=# SELECT filelist( '/usr' ) ORDER BY filelist DESC;
  filelist
------------
 X11R6
 tmp
 src
 share
 sbin
 local
 libexec
 lib
 kerberos
 include
 html
 games
 etc
 dict
 bin
 ..
 .
(17 rows)
```

Now that you know how to create an SRF the hard way, I'll describe the new SRF
interface that was introduced with PostgreSQL version 7.3.

The PostgreSQL SRF Interface

First off, you should know that the new SRF interface is simply a wrapper around the
old method. Set-returning functions are still invoked multiple times. The first time
through, an SRF initializes its own context structure and stores that structure away so
that each subsequent invocation can find it. In the old approach, an SRF examined
`fmgr_info->fn_extra` to determine whether it was being invoked for the first time (if
`fmgr_info->fn_extra` is NULL, this is the first call). In the new approach, you call the
`SRF_IS_FIRSTCALL()` macro instead. You can probably guess what this macro does: It
returns TRUE if `fmgr_info->fn_extra` is NULL (implying that this is the first call). In fact,
here's the definition of the `SRF_IS_FIRSTCALL()` macro:

```
#define SRF_IS_FIRSTCALL()  ( fcinfo->flinfo->fn_extra == NULL )
```

No great surprises there.

Once you know that you're looking at the first invocation of an SRF, you typically allocate a context structure of some sort and store the address of the structure in fmgr_info->fn_extra. In the new approach, you call the SRF_FIRSTCALL_INIT() macro. This macro allocates *its own* context structure (a structure of type FuncCallContext), records the address of the structure in fmgr_info->fn_extra, and returns the address back to your SRF. A FuncCallContext structure looks like this:

```
typedef struct FuncCallContext
{
    uint32          call_cntr;
    uint32          max_calls;
    TupleTableSlot * slot;
    void           * user_fctx;
    AttInMetadata  * attinmeta;
    MemoryContext    multi_call_memory_ctx;
    TupleDesc        tuple_desc;
} FuncCallContext;
```

If the SRF_FIRSTCALL_INIT() macro stores its own pointer in fmgr_info->fn_extra, where are you supposed to store the address of your context structure? In the user_fctx field—that pointer is reserved for your own personal use, just like fmgr_info->fn_extra was reserved for your use in the old SRF mechanism. I'll explain the other members of the FuncCallContext structure in a moment.

Now that you have a pointer to a spanking new FuncCallContext (remember, SRF_FIRSTCALL_INIT() returns the address of the structure), you can allocate your own context structure and store its address in user_fctx:

```
...
FuncCallContext * srf = SRF_FIRSTCALL_INIT();
dir_ctx               * ctx;

ctx = (dir_ctx *) MemoryContextAlloc( srf->multi_call_memory_ctx,
                                      sizeof( dir_ctx ));

srf->usr_fctx = ctx;
...
```

Notice that the FuncCallContext structure holds a MemoryContext named multi_call_memory_ctx. Any data that you need to save from one invocation to the next must be allocated from the multi_call_memory_ctx or PostgreSQL will discard that data as soon as the first invocation completes (multi_call_memory_ctx is equivalent to fmgr_info->fn_mctx in the old SRF mechanism).

Each time your SRF is invoked (even the first time), you should call the SRF_PER-CALL_SETUP() macro. Like SRF_FIRSTCALL_INIT(), SRF_PERCALL_SETUP() returns a pointer to the FuncCallContext structure. The context pointer that you saved in user_fctx is still there. You can use that pointer to get to the context structure that you allocated (and initialized) the first time through.

The new SRF mechanism provides two more macros: SRF_RETURN_NEXT() and SRF_RETURN_DONE(). As you might expect, these macros return information to the caller. The SRF_RETURN_NEXT() macros returns a value (a Datum) to the caller and tells the server to call you again to retrieve the next value in the result set (remember, you're writing a set-returning function; the server will call your function until you indicate that you have no more results to add to the set). The SRF_RETURN_DONE() macros returns a NULL value to the caller and tells the server that you have no more results to add to the result set. SRF_RETURN_DONE() also deallocates the FullCallContext structure so you should perform any cleanup work before you call SRF_RETURN_DONE()—you won't get another chance.

To show you how all of these macros fit together, Listing 6.5 shows the filelist() function again, this time created with the new SRF mechanism:

Listing 6.5 filelistSRF.c

```
 1 /*
 2 **  Filename:  filelistSRF.c
 3 */
 4
 5 #include "postgres.h"
 6 #include "funcapi.h"
 7
 8 #include <dirent.h>
 9 #include <sys/stat.h>
10
11 typedef struct
12 {
13   struct dirent ** dir_ctx_entries;
14 } dir_ctx;
15
16 PG_FUNCTION_INFO_V1(filelist);
17
18 Datum filelist(PG_FUNCTION_ARGS)
19 {
20   text            * startText = PG_GETARG_TEXT_P(0);
21   int               len       = VARSIZE( startText ) - VARHDRSZ;
22   char            * start     = (char *)palloc( len+1 );
23   dir_ctx         * ctx;
24   FuncCallContext * srf;
25
26   memcpy( start, startText->vl_dat, len );
27   start[len] = '\0';
28
29   if( SRF_IS_FIRSTCALL())
30   {
31     srf = SRF_FIRSTCALL_INIT();
```

Listing 6.5 **Continued**

```
32
33     srf->user_fctx = MemoryContextAlloc( srf->multi_call_memory_ctx,
34                                          sizeof( dir_ctx ));
35
36     ctx = (dir_ctx *)srf->user_fctx;
37
38     srf->max_calls = scandir(start,&ctx->dir_ctx_entries,NULL,alphasort);
39     srf->call_cntr = 0;
40   }
41
42   srf = SRF_PERCALL_SETUP();
43   ctx = (dir_ctx *)srf->user_fctx;
44
45   if( srf->max_calls == -1 )
46     SRF_RETURN_DONE( srf );
47
48   if( srf->call_cntr < srf->max_calls )
49   {
50     struct dirent * entry;
51     size_t          nameLen;
52     size_t          resultLen;
53     text          * result;
54
55     entry     = ctx->dir_ctx_entries[srf->call_cntr];
56     nameLen   = strlen( entry->d_name );
57     resultLen = nameLen + VARHDRSZ;
58
59     result = (text *)palloc( resultLen );
60
61     VARATT_SIZEP( result ) = resultLen;
62
63     memcpy( VARDATA( result ), entry->d_name, nameLen );
64
65     SRF_RETURN_NEXT( srf, (Datum) result );
66   }
67   else
68   {
69     SRF_RETURN_DONE( srf );
70   }
71 }
```

I'll point out a few of the differences. First, notice that you don't need quite as many
#include files when you use the new mechanism (the new funcapi.h header takes care
of including any required headers). Next, take a look at the dir_ctx structure at line 11.

If you compare that to the original version, you'll notice that the new version is much shorter. The `FuncCallContext` structure already contains placeholders for some of the data that used to be in `dir_ctx`. I'll explain more in a moment.

The next significant change appears at line 29. The new version of `filelist()` calls the `SRF_IS_FIRSTCALL()` macro to decide whether to initialize itself or return the next value in the result set. At line 31 you see a call to the `SRF_FIRSTCALL_INIT()` macro. That macro returns a pointer to the `FuncCallContext` structure that you're supposed to use for this invocation and for future invocations. The call to `MemoryContextAlloc()` (line 33) allocates space for a `dir_ctx` from the `srf->multi_call_memory_ctx` context. `srf->multi_call_memory_ctx` is a memory pool that survives from invocation to invocation.

Now take a look at lines 38 and 39. The call to `scandir()` returns the number of files that it finds in the given directory. In the previous version, you stored the file count in `dir_ctx->dir_ctx_count`. In the new version, you don't need an extra field (`dir_ctx_count`) to hold the file count; the `FuncCallContext` structure already has a field that serves the same purpose: `max_calls`. The SRF mechanism doesn't actually *do* anything with `max_calls`, it just gives you a place to store a number. At line 38, `filelist()` stores the file count in `srf->max_calls`. The `FuncCallContext` structure also has a replacement for the `dir_ctx_current` field that you saw in the original version of this function. Each time PostgreSQL calls your function, it increments the `call_cntr` field in the `FuncCallContext` structure. `call_cntr` starts at 0 and is incremented each time you call `SRF_RETURN_NEXT()`. To summarize, the new version of `filelist()` stores the file count in `srf->max_calls` and uses `srf->call_cntr` to index into the array of filenames.

Every time the server calls this function, `filelist()` calls `SRF_PERCALL_SETUP()` to retrieve a pointer to the `FuncCallContext` structure (see line 42). If `filelist()` decides that it has no more filenames to add to the result set, it calls `SRF_RETURN_DONE()` to tell PostgreSQL that it has finished its work (lines 46 and 69). If `filelist()` *does* have another result, it creates a text structure and calls `SET_RETURN_NEXT()` (see the previous version of this function for a more complete explanation). `SET_RETURN_NEXT()` increments `srf->call_cntr`, returns the `Datum` (`result`) to the server, and tells the server that it should call this function again to retrieve the next result.

You can see that the new version of this function is very similar to the old version. The SRF macros simply hide a few of the quirks imposed by the PostgreSQL calling convention. Which approach should you use? The down-and-dirty approach or the new SRF-macro–based approach? That depends on your goals. If you need to write an extension function that will work in an older version of PostgreSQL (older than version 7.3), use the original approach (the SRF macros were added in version 7.3). If not, consider the new approach. It's possible that the SRF calling convention may change in the future and it seems safer to assume that the PostgreSQL developers will hide as many changes as possible behind the SRF macros. If you choose to use the old approach, you may find that you have to change your source code when you upgrade to a future release.

Returning Complete Rows from an Extension Function

If you've read through the first few sections in this chapter, you know how to write an extension function that returns a single scalar value (that's what the `filesize()` function does). You also know how to return a set of scalar values (that's what the `filelist()` function does). In this section, I'll show you how to return a set of *rows* (or, as the PostgreSQL developers prefer to call them, tuples).

To illustrate the sequence that you must follow to return multiple tuples from an extension function, I'll create a new function, `fileinfo()`, that combines `filesize()` and `filelist()`. You call `fileinfo()` with the name of a directory and it returns a `SETOF` tuples. Each tuple contains three columns: a filename, the size of the file (or `NULL` if the size is not known), and the file type (or `NULL` if the type is not known). When you've finished, you can call the `fileinfo()` function like this:

```
movies=# SELECT * FROM fileinfo( '/dev' );
    filename    |  filesize  | filetype
----------------+------------+----------
 .              |       9380 | d
 ..             |       4096 | d
 adsp           |          0 | c
 agpgart        |          0 | c
 aipd           |          0 | c
 audio          |          0 | c
 cdrom          |          0 | b
 console        |          0 | c
 core           | 1073156096 | -
 cpu            |        360 | d
 ...
```

To start, you must define a data type that describes each row returned by the fileinfo() function:

```
movies=# CREATE TYPE _fileinfo AS ( filename TEXT, filesize INTEGER, filetype
CHAR(1));
CREATE TYPE
```

I'll create a few helper functions that will simplify the fileinfo() function. Listing 6.6 shows the getFileInfo(), getFileType(), and text2cstring() functions:

Listing 6.6 `fileinfo.c` **(Part 1)**

```
1 /*
2 ** Filename:  fileinfo.c
3 */
4 #include "postgres.h"
5 #include "funcapi.h"
6
```

Listing 6.6   **Continued**

```
 7 #include <dirent.h>
 8 #include <sys/stat.h>
 9
10 typedef struct
11 {
12   struct dirent ** dir_ctx_entries;
13   char           * dir_ctx_name;
14 } dir_ctx;
15
16 static bool getFileInfo(struct stat * buf, char * dirName, char * fileName)
17 {
18   char * pathName = (char *) palloc(strlen(dirName)+1+strlen(fileName)+1);
19
20   strcpy( pathName, dirName );
21   strcat( pathName, "/" );
22   strcat( pathName, fileName );
23
24   if( stat( pathName, buf ) == 0 )
25     return( true );
26   else
27     return( false );
28 }
29
30 static char getFileType( mode_t mode )
31 {
32   if( S_ISREG(mode))
33     return( '-' );
34   if( S_ISDIR(mode))
35     return( 'd' );
36   if( S_ISCHR(mode))
37     return( 'c' );
38   if( S_ISBLK(mode))
39     return( 'b' );
40   if( S_ISFIFO(mode))
41     return( 'p' );
42   if( S_ISLNK(mode))
43     return( 'l' );
44   if( S_ISSOCK(mode))
45     return( 's' );
46
47   return( '?' );
48
49 }
50
51 static char *  text2cstring( text * src )
52 {
```

Listing 6.6   **Continued**

```
53    int     len = VARSIZE( src ) - VARHDRSZ;
54    char  * dst = (char *)palloc( len+1 );
55
56    memcpy( dst, src->vl_dat, len );
57    dst[len] = '\0';
58
59    return( dst );
60 }
61
```

The getFileInfo() helper function (lines 16 through 28) calls stat() to retrieve metadata that describes the given file. The caller provides three parameters: the address of a struct stat structure that getFileInfo() fills in, the name of the directory where the target file resides, and the name of the target file itself. If the stat() function succeeds, getFileInfo() returns true and the caller can find the metadata for the file in the struct stat structure. If the stat() function fails, getFileInfo() returns false.

The second helper function, getFileType(), translates a mode_t (returned by the stat() function) into a single character that represents a file type. getFileType() returns one of the following values:

- d (directory)
- c (character device)
- b (block device)
- p (named pipe)
- l (symbolic link)
- s (socket)
- ? (unknown)
- - (a "regular" file—that is, not one of the above)

The last helper function is text2cstring() (see lines 51 through 60). This function converts a TEXT value into a dynamically allocated, null-terminated string. The fileinfo() function (which I'll describe next) calls text2cstring() to convert its TEXT argument into the form expected by scandir().

The fileinfo() function is shown in Listing 6.7:

Listing 6.7   fileinfo.c **(Part 2)**

```
62 PG_FUNCTION_INFO_V1(fileinfo);
63
64 Datum fileinfo(PG_FUNCTION_ARGS)
65 {
66    char             * start = text2cstring( PG_GETARG_TEXT_P(0));
67    dir_ctx          * ctx;
```

Listing 6.7 **Continued**

```
68    FuncCallContext * srf;
69
70    if( SRF_IS_FIRSTCALL())
71    {
72      TupleDesc          tupdesc;
73      MemoryContext      oldContext;
74
75      srf = SRF_FIRSTCALL_INIT();
76
77      oldContext = MemoryContextSwitchTo( srf->multi_call_memory_ctx );
78
79      ctx = (dir_ctx *) palloc( sizeof( dir_ctx ));
80
81      tupdesc = RelationNameGetTupleDesc( "_fileinfo" );
82
83      srf->user_fctx = ctx;
84      srf->max_calls = scandir( start, &ctx->dir_ctx_entries, NULL, alphasort );
85      srf->attinmeta = TupleDescGetAttInMetadata( tupdesc );
86
87      ctx->dir_ctx_name = start;
88
89      MemoryContextSwitchTo( oldContext );
90
91    }
92
93    srf = SRF_PERCALL_SETUP();
94    ctx = (dir_ctx *)srf->user_fctx;
95
96    if( srf->max_calls == -1 )
97      SRF_RETURN_DONE( srf );
98
99    if( srf->call_cntr < srf->max_calls )
100   {
101     struct dirent * entry;
102     char          * values[3];
103     struct stat     statBuf;
104     char            fileSizeStr[10+1] = {0};
105     char            fileTypeStr[1+1]  = {0};
106     HeapTuple       tuple;
107
108     entry    = ctx->dir_ctx_entries[srf->call_cntr];
109     values[0] = entry->d_name;
110
111     if( getFileInfo( &statBuf, ctx->dir_ctx_name, entry->d_name ))
112     {
113       snprintf( fileSizeStr, sizeof( fileSizeStr ), "%d", statBuf.st_size );
```

Listing 6.7   **Continued**

```
114        fileTypeStr[0] = getFileType( statBuf.st_mode );
115
116        values[1] = fileSizeStr;
117        values[2] = fileTypeStr;
118      }
119    else
120      {
121        values[1] = NULL;
122        values[2] = NULL;
123      }
124
125      tuple = BuildTupleFromCStrings( srf->attinmeta, values );
126
127      SRF_RETURN_NEXT( srf, HeapTupleGetDatum( tuple ));
128    }
129    else
130      {
131        SRF_RETURN_DONE( srf );
132      }
133 }
```

The fileinfo() function calls scandir() to generate an array that contains the names of all files in the given directory and then calls getFileInfo() (which in turn calls stat()) to retrieve the metadata for each file. The server calls fileinfo() until it stops returning values. Each invocation returns a single tuple (of type _fileinfo) that contains a filename and the size and type of that file.

fileinfo() starts by converting its argument from a TEXT value into a null-terminated string (the scandir() function that fileinfo() calls at line 84 requires a null-terminated string). At line 70, fileinfo() calls the SRF_IS_FIRSTCALL() macro to decide whether it should create and initialize a new context structure or use a structure created by a prior invocation.

The fileinfo() function has to do a little more memory-management work than the other functions you've seen in this chapter. The earlier functions allocated memory from the srf->multi_call_memory_ctx (or fmgr_info>fn_mcxt) pool. fileinfo() also allocates memory from that pool, but fileinfo() calls other PostgreSQL functions that allocate memory as well. For example, at line 81, you see a call to RelationNameGetTupleDesc(). That function allocates memory using the server's palloc() function. You must ensure that RelationNameGetTupleDesc() (and any function called by RelationNameGetTupleDesc()) allocates memory from the correct MemoryContext. Each MemoryContext has its own lifetime (or *scope*). If RelationNameGetTupleDesc() allocates memory from a MemoryContext with a lifetime that's too short (that is, a lifetime that ends before that last call to fileinfo()), you'll find that the data created by RelationNameGetTupleDesc() is de-allocated out from under you. On the other hand, if `RelationNameGetTupleDesc()` allocates memory from a `MemoryContext` with a lifetime that's too long, you'll create a memory leak. Take a look at line 81. Notice that you call `RelationNameGetTupleDesc()` with a single argument (the name of tuple type). Since you can't pass a `MemoryContext` to `RelationNameGetTupleDesc()`, how do you tell that function *which* `MemoryContext` to use? The answer is deceptively simple. Look closely at the call to `palloc()` at line 79. `palloc()` is the most commonly used memory allocation function in the PostgreSQL server. `palloc()` allocates memory from the `MemoryContext` pointed to by the `CurrentMemoryContext` global variable. If you want to talk `RelationNameGetTupleDesc()` into using a specific `MemoryContext`, you have to point `CurrentMemoryContext` to that context. That's what the code at line 77 does. Call `MemoryContextSwitchTo()` whenever you need to change the lifetime of data allocated by `palloc()`. Notice that the call at line 77 selects `srf->multi_call_memory_ctx` (which is a `MemoryContext` that survives as long as `fileinfo()` has more tuples to return). After `MemoryContextSwitchTo()` returns, `palloc()` will allocate memory from that `MemoryContext` until somebody calls `MemoryContextSwitchTo()` again. `MemoryContextSwitchTo()` switches to a new `MemoryContext` and returns the previous value. You should *restore* the original `MemoryContext` when you're finished with the new one (see line 89).

Once the correct `MemoryContext` is in place, `fileinfo()` allocates a new `dir_ctx` context structure (see line 79). Next, `fileinfo()` calls the `RelationNameGetTupleDesc()` function to retrieve the `TupleDesc` that defines the `_fileinfo` type (remember, the `_fileinfo` type describes the layout of the tuples returned by `fileinfo()`; you created the `_fileinfo` type earlier with a CREATE TYPE command). A `TupleDesc` is a structure that describes the shape of a tuple. It contains (among other things) the number of columns in the tuple and a description of each column. You don't have to peek inside of a `TupleDesc` (unless you want to) but `fileinfo()` needs the descriptor to build a return value.

After retrieving the tuple descriptor, `fileinfo()` records the address of its new context structure so it can find the structure in future invocations (line 83). Next, `fileinfo()` calls the `scandir()` function to generate an array that contains the name of each file in the given directory (start). `scandir()` records the address of the array in `ctx->dir_ctx_entries`.

When the `fileinfo()` function returns a value to the caller, it does so by building a tuple out of a collection of null-terminated strings; each string corresponds to one of the columns in the tuple. The `TupleDesc` that `fileinfo()` retrieved at line 81 doesn't contain quite enough information to convert C strings into a tuple. Fortunately, PostgreSQL provides a function that translates a `TupleDesc` into a new structure that contains all of the data you'll need: `TupleDescGetAttInMetaData()`. The code at line 85 calls this function and stores the address of the resulting structure in `srf->attinmeta` (which the PostgreSQL developers conveniently included for just this purpose). A little later, `fileinfo()` will use the new structure to create the return tuple.

The initialization phase completes by storing a copy of the directory name (line 87) and restoring the `MemoryContext` that was in place when `fileinfo()` was first called (line 89).

The code at lines 93 through 99 should be familiar by now—see the previous section ("The PostgreSQL SRF Interface") if you need a refresher. Every time `fileinfo()` is called, it calls the `SRF_PERCALL_SETUP()` macro to find the appropriate `FuncCallContext` structure and then extracts the address of the `dir_ctx` structure created by the initial invocation.

I mentioned earlier that `fileinfo()` creates a return tuple out of a collection of null-terminated strings. Each tuple contains three columns: a filename, the size of the file, and the file type. Accordingly, `fileinfo()` creates three null-terminated strings (one for each column). The `values[]` array (see line 102) contains a pointer to each null-terminated string. After filling in `values[]`, `fileinfo()` will call `BuildTupleFromCStrings()` to convert the strings into a tuple.

The first null-terminated string (`values[0]`) contains the name of one file found in the `dir_ctx_entries[]` array. The assignment statement at line 109 copies the address of the file name into `values[0]`.

The other null-terminated strings (`values[1]` and `values[2]`) contain the file size and the file type (respectively). To find the size of the file, `fileinfo()` calls the `getFileInfo()` function you saw earlier. If successful, `getFileInfo()` returns true and fills in the `statBuf` structure with (among other things), the file size and type. After converting the file size into a null-terminated string (line 113) and translating the file mode into a human-readable file type (line 114), `fileinfo()` fills in the rest of the `values[]` array.

If `getFileInfo()` fails for some reason, the return tuple should contain a NULL `filesize` and a NULL `filetype` to indicate that those values are "unknown." Setting a column to NULL is easy Just set the corresponding entry in the `values[]` array to NULL (see lines 121 and 122).

By the time it reaches line 125, `fileinfo()` has gathered all of the information it needs to create the return tuple. The `values[]` array contains three string pointers (or one string pointer and two NULL's). To convert the null-terminated strings into a tuple, `fileinfo()` calls PostgreSQL's `BuildTupleFromCStrings()`. That function uses the tuple description produced by the earlier call to `TupleDescGetAttInMetadata()` and the pointers in `values[]` to create a tuple in the form expected by the PostgreSQL server. `fileinfo()` returns the tuple to the server by invoking the `SRF_RETURN_NEXT()` macro that I described earlier (see "The PostgreSQL SRF Interface" for more information).

When `fileinfo()` has finished processing all of the file names found in `dir_ctx_entries[]`, it invokes the `SRF_RETURN_DONE()` macro instead to tell the server that it has finished building the result set.

If you want to try this function yourself, compile and install it (as described earlier) and execute the following command to tell the PostgreSQL server how to find and invoke the function:

```
CREATE OR REPLACE FUNCTION fileinfo(TEXT)
    RETURNS SETOF _fileinfo
    AS 'filelist.so','fileinfo' LANGUAGE C
    STRICT;
```

If you are rewarded with a message that states type _fileinfo is not yet defined, you forgot to execute the CREATE TYPE command that I mentioned at the beginning of this section.

You can call the fileinfo() function in any context where you would normally SELECT from a table. For example, to find the names of all files in the /dev directory:

```
movies=# SELECT * FROM fileinfo( '/dev' );
   filename     |   filesize   | filetype
---------------+------------+----------
      .         |      9380    | d
      ..        |      4096    | d
  adsp          |         0    | c
  agpgart       |         0    | c
  arpd          |         0    | c
  audio         |         0    | c
  cdrom         |         0    | b
  console       |         0    | c
  core          | 1073156096   | -
  cpu           |       360    | d
  ...
```

One of the cool things about PostgreSQL functions is that you can mix functions that are written in different languages. For example, you can call fileinfo() (which is written in C) from a function written in PL/pgSQL (one of PostgreSQL's procedural language). In fact, Listing 6.8 shows a PL/pgSQL function that returns a SETOF _fileinfo tuples (just like the fileinfo() function). This function calls fileinfo() to recursively descend through an entire directory tree, returning one tuple for each file (and subdirectory) that it finds.

Listing 6.8 dirtree.sql

```
 1 -- File: dirtree.sql
 2
 3 CREATE OR REPLACE FUNCTION dirtree( TEXT ) RETURNS SETOF _fileinfo AS $$
 4 DECLARE
 5   file  _fileinfo%rowtype;
 6   child _fileinfo%rowtype;
 7 BEGIN
 8
 9   FOR file IN SELECT * FROM fileinfo( $1 ) LOOP
10     IF file.filename != '.' and file.filename != '..' THEN
11       file.filename = $1 || '/' || file.filename;
12
13       IF file.filetype = 'd' THEN
14         FOR child in SELECT * FROM dirtree( file.filename ) LOOP
15           RETURN NEXT child;
16         END LOOP;
17       END IF;
```

Listing 6.8 **Continued**

```
18      RETURN NEXT file;
19    END IF;
20  END LOOP;
21
22  RETURN;
23
24 END
25 $$ LANGUAGE 'PLPGSQL';
```

Don't worry if you don't understand the dirtree() function yet. I'll describe the PL/pgSQL language in full detail in Chapter 7, "PL/pgSQL." The important thing to note here is that dirtree(), a function written in PL/pgSQL can call fileinfo(), a function written in C. Adding useful extension functions to PostgreSQL is not too difficult (assuming that you are comfortable working in C). Now that you understand the mechanism for creating new functions, I'd like to turn your attention to the process of creating a new data type. When you add a new data type to PostgreSQL, you must create a few supporting extension functions, so be sure you understand the material covered so far.

Extending the PostgreSQL Server with Custom Data Types

The customers table in this sample application contains a column named balance. I've made the assumption that the values in the balance column are expressed in local currency (that is, U.S. dollars in the U.S., British pounds in the U.K.). This assumption serves us well until our corner video store opens a web site and starts accepting orders from foreign customers.

PostgreSQL doesn't have a predefined data type that represents a foreign currency value, so let's create one. You want to store three pieces of information for each foreign currency value: the name of the currency (pounds, dollars, drachma, and so on), the number of units, and the exchange rate at the time the foreign currency value was created. Call your new data type FCUR (Foreign Currency). After you have fully defined the FCUR data type, you can create tables with FCUR columns, enter and display FCUR values, convert between FCUR values and other numeric types, and use a few operators (+,-,*,/) to manipulate FCUR values.

Internal and External Forms

Before going much further, it is important to understand the difference between the external form of a value and the internal form.

The *external* form of a data type defines how the user enters a value and how a value is displayed to the user. For example, if you enter a numeric value, you might enter the characters 7218942. If you enter these characters from a client that uses an ASCII encoding, you have entered the character values 37, 32, 31, 38, 39, 34, and 32 (in hexadecimal notation). The external form of a data type is used to interact with the user.

The *internal* form of a data type defines how a value is represented inside the database. The preceding numeric value form might be translated from the string 7218942 into the four-byte integer value 00 6E 26 FE (again in hexadecimal notation). The internal form of a data type is used within the database.

Why have two forms? Most programming languages can deal with numeric values implicitly (that is, without requiring the *programmer* to implement simple arithmetic operations). For example, the C programming language defines a built-in data type named int. An int value can store integer (that is, whole) numbers within some range determined by the compiler. The C compiler knows how to add, subtract, multiply, and divide int values. A C programmer is not required to perform the bit manipulations himself; the compiler emits the code required to perform the arithmetic.

Most programmers share a common understanding of what it means to add two integer values. When you add two integer values, you expect the result to be the arithmetic sum of the values. Another way to state this is to say that the + operator, when applied to two integer operands, should return the arithmetic sum of the operands, most likely in the form of an integer.

What would you expect the result to be if you applied the + operator to two string values? If each string contained only a sequence of one or more digits, such as '1' + '34', you might expect the result to be the string '35'. What would happen if you tried adding '1' + 'red'? That's pretty hard to predict. Because it is difficult to come up with a good *arithmetic* definition of the + operator when applied to strings, many programming languages define + to mean concatenation when applied to string operands. So, the expression '1' + 'red' would evaluate to the string '1red'.

So, to summarize a bit, the external form of a numeric value is a string of numeric digits, sign characters, and a radix point. When you choose the internal form for a numeric value, you want to choose a representation that makes it easy to define and implement mathematical operations.

You've already seen the external and internal form of the TEXT data type. The external form of a TEXT value is a string of characters enclosed in single quotes (the quotes are not part of the value; they just mark the boundaries of the value). If you need to include single quotes in a TEXT value, the external form defines a set of rules for doing so. The internal form of a TEXT value is defined by the TEXT data type. The TEXT structure contains a length and an array of characters.

Defining a Simple Data Type in PostgreSQL

Now that you understand the difference between internal and external forms, it should be obvious that PostgreSQL needs to convert values between these forms. When you define a new data type, you tell PostgreSQL how to convert a value from external form to internal form and from internal form to external form.

Let's create a simple type that mimics the built-in TEXT data type. Data type descriptions are stored in the pg_type system table. We are interested in three of the columns:

```
movies=# SELECT typinput, typoutput, typlen
movies-#   FROM pg_type
movies-#   WHERE typname = 'text';
 typinput | typoutput | typlen
----------+-----------+--------
 textin   | textout   |     -1
```

The `typinput` column tells you the name of the function that PostgreSQL uses to convert a TEXT value from external form to internal form; in this case, the function is named `textin`. The `typoutput` column contains the name of the function (`textout`) that PostgreSQL uses to convert from internal to external form. Finally, `typlen` specifies how much space is required to hold the internal form of a TEXT value. TEXT values are of variable length, so the space required to hold the internal form is also variable (–1 in this column means *variable length*). If TEXT were a fixed-length type, the `typlen` column would contain the number of bytes required to hold the internal form.

Now you have enough information to create a new data type. Here is the command that you'll use to create a type named `mytexttype`:

```
movies=# CREATE TYPE mytexttype
movies-# (
movies-#   INPUT=textin,
movies-#   OUTPUT=textout,
movies-#   INTERNALLENGTH=VARIABLE
movies-# );
```

The `INPUT=textin` clause tells PostgreSQL which function to call when it needs to convert a `mytexttype` value from external to internal form. The `OUTPUT=textout` clause tells PostgreSQL which function converts a `mytexttype` value from internal to external form. The final clause, `INTERNALLENGTH=VARIABLE`, tells PostgreSQL how much space is required to hold the internal form of a `mytexttype` value; you specify VARIABLE here to tell PostgreSQL that you are not defining a fixed length data type.

You have essentially cloned the TEXT[3] data type. Because you are using the same input and output functions as the TEXT type, the internal and external form of a `mytexttype` value is identical to the internal and external form of a TEXT value.

After you execute this CREATE TYPE command, you can use the `mytexttype` data type to create new columns:

```
movies=# CREATE TABLE myTestTable
movies-# (
movies(#   pkey  INTEGER,
movies(#   value mytexttype
movies(# );
CREATE
```

---

[3] You have created an extremely limited clone. At this point, you can enter and display `mytext-type` values, but you can't do anything else with them. You have not defined any operators that can manipulate `mytexttype` values.

You can also enter `mytexttype` values. Because you borrowed the `textin` and `textout` functions, you have to enter values according to the rules for a TEXT value:

```
movies=# INSERT INTO myTestTable
movies-#  VALUES ( 1, 'This is a mytexttype value in external form' );
```

Now, let's define a new data type from scratch.

Defining the Data Type in C

We'll start out by defining the internal form for an FCUR value. As I mentioned before, you want to store three pieces of information for each value: the name of the currency (dollars, euros, yen, and so on), the number of units, and the exchange rate at the time the value was created. Why do you need to store the exchange rate with each value? Because exchange rates vary over time, and you need to know the rate at the time the value is created.

Because you are going to use the C programming language to implement the required conversion functions, you need to define a structure[4] containing the three components. Listing 6.9 shows the first few lines of the implementation file:

Listing 6.9 `fcur.c` **(Part 1)**

```
 1 /*
 2 **   File name: fcur.c
 3 */
 4
 5 #include "postgres.h"
 6 #include "fmgr.h"
 7
 8 typedef struct
 9 {
10     char     fcur_name[4];    /* Currency name   */
11     float4   fcur_units;      /* Units of currency  */
12     float4   fcur_xrate;      /* Exchange rate   */
13 } fcur;
14
15 static char * baseCurrencyName    = "US$";
16 static char * unknownCurrencyName = "???";
17
```

Start by #including the `postgres.h` and `fmgr.h` header files, just like you did for the earlier examples. The `fcur` structure defines the internal form for your `fcur` data type. Store the currency name (`fcur_name`) as a three-character, null-terminated string. The

---

[4] This is not necessarily the most efficient (or even realistic) way to store a foreign currency value, but it works well for purposes of illustration. In a real-world implementation, you would not want to store monetary values using floating-point data types because of their inherent lack of precision. You would also want more control over the format of the currency name.

`fcur_units` member stores the number of currency units as a floating-point number. The exchange rate is stored as a floating-point number in `fcur_xrate`.

At lines 15 and 16, you define two currency names. The `baseCurrencyName` is the name of the local currency. When the `fcur_name` of a value is equal to `baseCurrencyName`, the value is said to be *normalized*. A normalized value will always have an exchange rate (`fcur_xrate`) of `1.0`: One U.S. dollar always equals one U.S. dollar. The `unknownCurrencyName` is used when the user enters a value containing a number of units and an exchange rate, but fails to provide the currency name. We'll use each of these variables in a moment.

Defining the Input and Output Functions in C

Now you will create the input and output functions for this data type. At this point, you have to decide what your external form will look like. You know that you need to deal with three components: the number of units, an optional exchange rate, and an optional currency name. You want the typical case (units only) to be easy to enter, so you will accept input in any of the following forms:

```
units
units(exchange-rate)
units(exchange-rate/currency-name)
```

If you see a number (and nothing else), assume that you have a number of units of the base currency. If you see a number followed by an open parenthesis, you will expect an exchange rate to follow. If the exchange rate is followed by a slash character, expect a currency name. Of course, we expect a closed parenthesis if we see an open one.

Table 6.1 shows a few valid FCUR external values (assuming that `baseCurrencyName` is "US$"):

Table 6.1   **Sample** FCUR **Values (in External Form)**

External Form	Meaning
`'1'`	1 U.S. dollar
`'1(.5)'`	1 unit of `unknownCurrencyName` with an exchange rate of 0.5
`'3(1/US$)'`	3 U.S. dollars
`'5(.687853/GPB)'`	-5 British pounds with an exchange rate of .687853 Pounds per 1 U.S. dollar
`'10(7.2566/FRF)'`	-10 French francs with an exchange rate of 7.2566 Francs per 1 U.S. dollar
`'1.52(1.5702/CA$)'`	-1.52 Canadian dollars with an exchange rate of 1.5702 Canadian dollars per 1 U.S. dollar

The input function is named `fcur_in` (see Listing 6.10), and it converts from external (FCUR) form to internal (fcur) form. This function expects a single parameter: a pointer to a null-terminated string containing the external form of an `fcur` value.

Listing 6.10   `fcur.c` **(Part 2)**

```
18 /*
19 **  Name: fcur_in()
20 **
21 **        Converts an fcur value from external form
22 **      to internal form.
23 */
24
25 PG_FUNCTION_INFO_V1(fcur_in);
26
27 Datum fcur_in(PG_FUNCTION_ARGS)
28 {
29     char  * src     = PG_GETARG_CSTRING(0);
30     char  * workStr = pstrdup( src );
31     char  * units   = NULL;
32     char  * name    = NULL;
33     char  * xrate   = NULL;
34     fcur  * result  = NULL;
35     char  * endPtr  = NULL;
36
37     /* strtok() will find all of the components for us */
38
39     units = strtok( workStr, "(" );
40     xrate = strtok( NULL, "/)" );
41     name  = strtok( NULL, ")" );
42
43     result = (fcur *)palloc( sizeof( fcur ));
44
45     memset( result, 0x00, sizeof( fcur ));
46
47     result->fcur_units = strtod( units, &endPtr );
48
49     if( xrate )
50     {
51         result->fcur_xrate = strtod( xrate, &endPtr );
52     }
53     else
54     {
55         result->fcur_xrate = 1.0;
56     }
57
58     if( name )
59     {
60         strncpy( result->fcur_name,
61                  name,
62                  sizeof( result->fcur_name ));
63     }
64     else
```

Listing 6.10   **Continued**

```
65      {
66            strncpy( result->fcur_name,
67                    unknownCurrencyName,
68                  sizeof( result->fcur_name ));
69      }
70
71      PG_RETURN_POINTER( result );
72  }
73
```

Notice that this looks suspiciously similar to the extension functions you saw earlier in this chapter. In particular, fcur_in() returns a Datum and uses PG_FUNCTION_ARGS to declare the parameter list. This similarity exists because fcur_in() *is* an extension function, so everything that you already know about writing extension functions applies to this discussion as well.

You use the strtok() function (from the C Runtime Library) to parse out the external form. strtok() is a destructive function; it modifies the string that you pass to it. So the first thing you need to do in this function is to make a copy of the input string. Use the pstrdup() function to make the copy. pstrdup() is similar to the strdup() function from the C Runtime Library, except that the memory that holds the copy is allocated using palloc() and must be freed using pfree(). You use pstrdup() to avoid any memory leaks should you forget to clean up after yourself.

Lines 39, 40, and 41 parse the input string into three components. Remember, you will accept input strings in any of the following forms:

```
units
units(exchange-rate)
units(exchange-rate/currency-name)
```

The units component must be a string representing a floating-point number. You will use the strtod() runtime function to convert units into a float4, so the format of the input string must meet the requirements of strtod(). Here is an excerpt from the Linux strtod() man page that describes the required form:

```
The expected form of the string is optional leading  white
space  as  checked by isspace(3), an optional plus (``+'')
or minus sign (``-'') followed by  a  sequence  of  digits
optionally  containing  a decimal-point character, option-
ally followed by an exponent.  An exponent consists of  an
``E''  or  ``e'',  followed  by  an optional plus or minus
sign, followed by a non-empty sequence of digits.  If  the
locale  is  not  "C"  or "POSIX", different formats may be
used.
```

The optional exchange-rate component is also converted to a float4 by strtod().

The `currency-name` component is simply a three-character string. Values such as "US$" (U.S. dollar), "GPB" (British pound), and "CA$" (Canadian dollar) seem reasonable. In your sample data type, you won't do any validation on this string. In a real-world implementation, you would probably want to match the currency name with a table of valid (and standardized) spellings.

The first call to `strtok()` returns a null-terminated string containing all characters up to (but not including) the first (in `workStr`. If `workStr` doesn't contain a (character, `units` will contain the entire input string. The second call to `strtok()` picks out the optional `exchange-rate` component. The final call to `strtok()` picks out the optional `currency-name`.

After you have tokenized the input string into units, exchange rate, and currency name, you can allocate space for the internal form at line 43. Notice that `palloc()` is used here.

The rest of this function is pretty simple. You use `strtod()` to convert the units and exchange rate into the `fcur` structure. If the user didn't provide you with an exchange rate, assume that it must be 1.0. You finish building the `fcur` structure by copying in the first three characters of the currency name, or `unknownCurrencyName` if you didn't find a currency name in the input string.

Line 71 returns the `Datum` to the caller.

That's pretty simple! Of course, I omitted all the error-checking code that you would need in a real-world application.

Now, let's look at the output function. `fcur_out()`, shown in Listing 6.11, converts an `fcur` structure from internal to external form.

Listing 6.11   `fcur.c` **(Part 3)**

```
74 /*
75 **  Name: fcur_out()
76 **
77 **        Converts an fcur value from internal form
78 **        to external form.
79 */
80
81 PG_FUNCTION_INFO_V1(fcur_out);
82
83 Datum fcur_out(PG_FUNCTION_ARGS)
84 {
85     fcur  * src  = (fcur *)PG_GETARG_POINTER( 0 );
86     char  * result;
87     char    work[16+sizeof(src->fcur_name)+16+4];
88
89     sprintf( work, "%g(%g/%s)",
90         src->fcur_units,
91         src->fcur_xrate,
92         src->fcur_name );
```

Listing 6.11   **Continued**

```
 93
 94    result = (char *)palloc( strlen( work ) + 1 );
 95
 96    strcpy( result, work );
 97
 98    PG_RETURN_CSTRING( result );
 99
100 }
101
```

This function is much shorter than the input function. That's typically the case because your code has far fewer decisions to make.

You format the `fcur` components into a work buffer at lines 89 through 92: `sprintf()` takes care of all the grunt work. Notice that you are formatting into an array of characters large enough to hold the largest result that you can expect (two 16-digit numbers, a function name, two parentheses, a slash, and a null terminator). Some of you might not like using a fixed-size buffer with `sprintf()`; use `snprintf()` if you have it and you are worried about buffer overflows.

After you have a formatted string, use `palloc()` to allocate the result string. (In case you were wondering, you format into a temporary buffer first so that you can allocate a result string of the minimum possible size.) At line 96, you copy the temporary string into the result string and then return that string at line 98.

I should point out an important consideration about the input and output functions that you have just written. It's *very* important that the format of the string produced by the output function match the format understood by the input function. When you back up a table using `pg_dump`, the archive contains the external form of each column. When you restore from the archive, the data must be converted from external form to internal form. If they don't match, you won't be able to restore your data.

Defining the Input and Output Functions in PostgreSQL

Now that you have created the input (external to internal) and output (internal to external) functions in C, you must compile them into a shared object module:

```
$ make -f makefile fcur.so
```

Next, create a symbolic link between `fcur.so` and PostgreSQL's preferred package directory so that PostgreSQL knows how to find out code:

```
$ ln -s `pwd`/fcur.so `pg_config --pkglibdir`
```

Now you can define the input and output functions in PostgreSQL:

```
movies=# CREATE OR REPLACE FUNCTION fcur_in( opaque )
movies-#   RETURNS opaque
```

```
movies-#    AS 'fcur.so' LANGUAGE 'C'
movies=# IMMUTABLE STRICT
CREATE
movies=# CREATE OR REPLACE FUNCTION fcur_out( opaque )
movies-#    RETURNS opaque
movies-#    AS 'fcur.so' LANGUAGE 'C'
movies=# IMMUTABLE STRICT
```

Notice that each of these functions expects an opaque parameter and returns an opaque value. You might be thinking that fcur_in() should take a null-terminated string and return a FCUR. That makes sense except for two minor problems: PostgreSQL doesn't have a SQL data type that represents a null-terminated string and PostgreSQL doesn't know anything about the FCUR data type yet. Okay, those aren't exactly *minor* problems. PostgreSQL helps you out a little here by letting you define these functions in terms of opaque. The opaque data type tells PostgreSQL that a SQL data type doesn't define the data that you are working with. One of the special properties of an opaque function is that you can't call it directly:

```
movies=# SELECT fcur_in( '5(1.3/GPB)' );
ERROR:  getTypeOutputInfo: Cache lookup of type 0 failed
```

This error message means, "don't try that again."

We've defined each of these functions with two additional attributes. The IMMUTABLE attribute tells PostgreSQL that calling this function twice with the same argument(s) is guaranteed to return the same result. If PostgreSQL knows that a function IMMUTABLE, it can optimize certain operations by computing the return value once and caching the result (hence the clever name).

Defining the Data Type in PostgreSQL

At this point, PostgreSQL knows about your input and output functions. Now you can tell PostgreSQL about your data type:

```
CREATE TYPE FCUR ( INPUT=fcur_in, OUTPUT=fcur_out, INTERNALLENGTH=12 );
```

This command creates a new data type (how exciting) named FCUR. The input function is named fcur_in, and the output function is named fcur_out. The INTERNAL-LENGTH=12 clause tells PostgreSQL how much space is required to hold the internal value. I computed this value by hand—just add up the size of each member of the fcur structure and be sure that you account for any pad bytes. The safest way to compute the INTERNALLENGTH is to use your C compiler's sizeof() operator.

Let's create a table that uses this data type and insert a few values:

```
movies=# CREATE TABLE fcur_test( pkey INT, val FCUR );
CREATE
movies=# INSERT INTO fcur_test VALUES( 1, '1' );
INSERT
movies=# INSERT INTO fcur_test VALUES( 2, '1(.5)' );
```

```
INSERT
movies=# INSERT INTO fcur_test VALUES( 3, '3(1/US$)' );
INSERT
movies=# INSERT INTO fcur_test VALUES( 4, '5(.687853/GBP)' );
INSERT
movies=# INSERT INTO fcur_test VALUES( 5, '10(7.2566/FRF)' );
INSERT
movies=# INSERT INTO fcur_test VALUES( 6, '1(1.5702/CA$)' );
INSERT
movies=# INSERT INTO fcur_test VALUES( 7, '1.5702(1.5702/CA$)' );
INSERT
```

Now let's see what those values look like when you retrieve them:

```
movies=# SELECT * FROM fcur_test;
 pkey |         val
------+--------------------
    1 | 1(1/???)
    2 | 1(0.5/???)
    3 | 3(1/US$)
    4 | 5(0.687853/GBP)
    5 | 10(7.2566/FRF)
    6 | 1(1.5702/CA$)
    7 | 1.5702(1.5702/CA$)
```

Not bad. The question marks are kind of ugly, but the data that you put in came back out.

At this point, you officially have a new data type. You can put values in and you can get values out. Let's add a few functions that make the FCUR type a little more useful.

It would be nice to know if two FCUR values represent the same amount of money expressed in your local currency. In other words, you want a function, fcur_eq, which you can call like this:

```
movies=# SELECT fcur_eq( '1', '1.5702(1.5702/CA$)' );
 fcur_eq
---------
 t
(1 row)


movies=# SELECT fcur_eq( '1', '3(1.5702/CA$)' );
 fcur_eq
---------
 f
(1 row)
```

The first call to fcur_eq tells you that 1.5702 Canadian dollars is equal to 1 U.S. dollar. The second call tells you that 3 Canadian dollars are *not* equal to 1 U.S. dollar.

To compare two FCUR values, you must convert them into a common currency. The normalize() function shown in Listing 6.12 does just that.

Listing 6.12 `fcur.c` **(Part 4)**

```
102 /*
103 **   Name: normalize()
104 **
105 **        Converts an fcur value into a normalized
106 **        double by applying the exchange rate.
107 */
108
109 static double normalize( fcur * src )
110 {
111     return( src->fcur_units / src->fcur_xrate );
112 }
```

The `normalize()` function converts a given FCUR value into our local currency. You can use `normalize()` to implement the `fcur_eq()` function, shown in Listing 6.13.

Listing 6.13 `fcur.c` **(Part 5)**

```
115 /*
116 **   Name: fcur_eq()
117 **
118 **        Returns true if the two fcur values
119 **        are equal (after normalization), otherwise
120 **        returns false.
121 */
122
123 PG_FUNCTION_INFO_V1(fcur_eq);
124
125 Datum fcur_eq(PG_FUNCTION_ARGS)
126 {
127     fcur  * left    = (fcur *)PG_GETARG_POINTER(0);
128     fcur  * right   = (fcur *)PG_GETARG_POINTER(1);
129
130     PG_RETURN_BOOL( normalize( left ) == normalize( right ));
131 }
132
```

This function is straightforward. You normalize each argument, compare them using the C == operator, and return the result as a BOOL Datum. You declare this function as STRICT so that you don't have to check for NULL arguments.

Now you can compile your code again and tell PostgreSQL about your new function (`fcur_eq()`):

```
$ make -f makefile fcur.so
$ psql -q
movies=# CREATE OR REPLACE FUNCTION fcur_eq( fcur, fcur )
movies-#   RETURNS bool
```

```
movies-#   AS 'fcur.so' LANGUAGE 'C'
movies=#   IMMUTABLE STRICT
```

Now you can call this function to compare any two FCUR values:

```
movies=# SELECT fcur_eq( '1', '1.5702(1.5702/CA$)' );
 fcur_eq
---------
 t
(1 row)


movies=# SELECT fcur_eq( '1', NULL );
 fcur_eq
---------

(1 row)
```

The fcur_eq function is nice, but you really want to compare FCUR values using the = operator. Fortunately, that's easy to do:

```
movies=# CREATE OPERATOR =
movies-# (
movies-#   leftarg   = FCUR,
movies-#   rightarg  = FCUR,
movies-#   procedure = fcur_eq,
movies-# );
```

This command creates a new operator named =. This operator has a FCUR value on the left side and a FCUR value on the right side. PostgreSQL calls the fcur_eq function whenever it needs to evaluate this operator.

Now you can evaluate expressions such as

```
movies=# SELECT * FROM fcur_test WHERE val = '1';
 pkey |         val
------+--------------------------
    1 | 1(1/???)
    7 | 1.5702(1.5702/CA$)
(2 rows)
```

The operator syntax is much easier to read than the functional syntax. Let's go ahead and add the other comparison operators: <>, <, <=, >, and >= (see Listing 6.14). They all follow the same pattern as the = operator: You normalize both arguments and then compare them as double values.

Listing 6.14   fcur.c **(Part 6)**

```
133 /*
134 **  Name: fcur_ne()
135 **
136 **        Returns true if the two fcur values
```

Listing 6.14 **Continued**

```
137 **        are not equal (after normalization),
138 **        otherwise returns false.
139 */
140
141 PG_FUNCTION_INFO_V1(fcur_ne);
142
143 Datum fcur_ne(PG_FUNCTION_ARGS)
144 {
145     fcur * left     = (fcur *)PG_GETARG_POINTER(0);
146     fcur * right    = (fcur *)PG_GETARG_POINTER(1);
147
148     PG_RETURN_BOOL( normalize( left ) != normalize( right ));
149 }
150
151 /*
152 **  Name: fcur_lt()
153 **
154 **        Returns true if the left operand
155 **        is less than the right operand.
156 */
157
158 PG_FUNCTION_INFO_V1(fcur_lt);
159
160 Datum fcur_lt(PG_FUNCTION_ARGS)
161 {
162     fcur * left     = (fcur *)PG_GETARG_POINTER(0);
163     fcur * right    = (fcur *)PG_GETARG_POINTER(1);
164
165     PG_RETURN_BOOL( normalize( left ) < normalize( right ));
166 }
167
168 /*
169 **  Name: fcur_le()
170 **
171 **        Returns true if the left operand
172 **        is less than or equal to the right
173 **        operand.
174 */
175
176 PG_FUNCTION_INFO_V1(fcur_le);
177
178 Datum fcur_le(PG_FUNCTION_ARGS)
179 {
180     fcur * left     = (fcur *)PG_GETARG_POINTER(0);
181     fcur * right    = (fcur *)PG_GETARG_POINTER(1);
```

Listing 6.14   **Continued**

```
182
183     PG_RETURN_BOOL( normalize( left ) <= normalize( right ));
184 }
185
186 /*
187 **  Name: fcur_gt()
188 **
189 **      Returns true if the left operand
190 **    is greater than the right operand.
191 */
192
193 PG_FUNCTION_INFO_V1(fcur_gt);
194
195 Datum fcur_gt(PG_FUNCTION_ARGS)
196 {
197     fcur * left    = (fcur *)PG_GETARG_POINTER(0);
198     fcur * right   = (fcur *)PG_GETARG_POINTER(1);
199
200     PG_RETURN_BOOL( normalize( left ) > normalize( right ));
201 }
202
203 /*
204 **  Name: fcur_ge()
205 **
206 **      Returns true if the left operand
207 **      is greater than or equal to the right operand.
208 */
209
210 PG_FUNCTION_INFO_V1(fcur_ge);
211
212 Datum fcur_ge(PG_FUNCTION_ARGS)
213 {
214     fcur * left    = (fcur *)PG_GETARG_POINTER(0);
215     fcur * right   = (fcur *)PG_GETARG_POINTER(1);
216
217     PG_RETURN_BOOL( normalize( left ) >= normalize( right ));
218 }
```

Now you can tell PostgreSQL about these functions:

```
movies=# CREATE OR REPLACE FUNCTION fcur_ne( fcur, fcur )
movies-#   RETURNS boolean
movies-#   AS 'fcur.so' LANGUAGE 'C'
movies=#   IMMUTABLE STRICT
CREATE
```

```
movies=# CREATE OR REPLACE FUNCTION fcur_lt( fcur, fcur )
movies-#   RETURNS boolean
movies-#   AS 'fcur.so' LANGUAGE 'C'
movies=#   IMMUTABLE STRICT
CREATE
movies=# CREATE OR REPLACE FUNCTION fcur_le( fcur, fcur )
movies-#   RETURNS boolean
movies-#   AS 'fcur.so' LANGUAGE 'C'
movies=#   IMMUTABLE STRICT
CREATE
movies=# CREATE OR REPLACE FUNCTION fcur_gt( fcur, fcur )
movies-#   RETURNS boolean
movies-#   AS 'fcur.so' LANGUAGE 'C'
movies=#   IMMUTABLE STRICT
CREATE
movies=# CREATE OR REPLACE FUNCTION fcur_ge( fcur, fcur )
movies-#   RETURNS boolean
movies-#   AS 'fcur.so' LANGUAGE 'C'
movies=#   IMMUTABLE STRICT
CREATE
```

And you can turn each of these functions into an operator:

```
movies=# CREATE OPERATOR <>
movies-# (
movies-#   leftarg    = fcur,
movies-#   rightarg   = fcur,
movies-#   procedure  = fcur_ne,
movies-#   commutator = <>
movies-# );
CREATE

movies=# CREATE OPERATOR <
movies-# (
movies-#   leftarg    = fcur,
movies-#   rightarg   = fcur,
movies-#   procedure  = fcur_lt,
movies-#   commutator = >
movies-#);
CREATE

movies=# CREATE OPERATOR <=
movies-# (
movies-#   leftarg    = fcur,
movies-#   rightarg   = fcur,
movies-#   procedure  = fcur_le,
movies-#   commutator = >=
movies-# );
CREATE
```

```
movies=# CREATE OPERATOR >
movies-# (
movies-#   leftarg   = fcur,
movies-#   rightarg  = fcur,
movies-#   procedure = fcur_gt,
movies-#   commutator = <
movies-# );
CREATE

movies=# CREATE OPERATOR >=
movies-# (
movies-#   leftarg   = fcur,
movies-#   rightarg  = fcur,
movies-#   procedure = fcur_ge,
movies-#   commutator = <=
movies-#);
CREATE
```

Notice that there is a commutator for each of these operators. The commutator can help PostgreSQL optimize queries that involve the operator.

For example, let's say that you have an index that covers the balance column. With a commutator, the query

```
SELECT * FROM customers WHERE balance > 10 and new_balance > balance;
```

can be rewritten as

```
SELECT * FROM customers WHERE balance > 10 and balance < new_balance;
```

This allows PostgreSQL to perform a range scan using the balance index. The commutator for an operator is the operator that PostgreSQL can use to swap the order of the operands. For example, > is the commutator for < because if x > y, y < x. Likewise, < is the commutator for >. Some operators are commutators for themselves. For example, the = operator is a commutator for itself. If x = y is true, then y = x is also true.

There are other optimizer hints that you can associate with an operator. See the CREATE OPERATOR section of the *PostgreSQL Reference Manual* for more information.

I'll finish up this chapter by defining one more operator (addition) and two functions that extend the usefulness of the FCUR data type.

First, let's look at a function that adds two FCUR values (see Listing 6.15):

Listing 6.15   fcur.c **(Part 7)**

```
259 /*
260 **  Name: fcur_add()
261 **
262 **       Adds two fcur values, returning the result
263 **    If the operands are expressed in the same
264 **    currency (and exchange rate), the result
265 **    will be expressed in that currency,
```

Listing 6.15 **Continued**

```
266 **          otherwise, the result will be in normalized
267 **      form.
268 */
269
270 PG_FUNCTION_INFO_V1(fcur_add);
271
272 Datum fcur_add(PG_FUNCTION_ARGS)
273 {
274     fcur * left   = (fcur *)PG_GETARG_POINTER(0);
275     fcur * right  = (fcur *)PG_GETARG_POINTER(1);
276     fcur * result;
277
278     result = (fcur *)palloc( sizeof( fcur ));
279
280     if( left->fcur_xrate == right->fcur_xrate )
281     {
282        if( strcmp( left->fcur_name, right->fcur_name ) == 0 )
283        {
284 /*
285 **   The two operands have a common currency - preserve
286 **   that currency by constructing a new fcur with the
287 **    same currency type.
288 */
289            result->fcur_xrate = left->fcur_xrate;
290            result->fcur_units = left->fcur_units + right->fcur_units;
291            strcpy( result->fcur_name, left->fcur_name );
292
293            PG_RETURN_POINTER( result );
294        }
295     }
296
297     result->fcur_xrate = 1.0;
298     result->fcur_units = normalize( left ) + normalize( right );
299     strcpy( result->fcur_name, baseCurrencyName );
300
301     PG_RETURN_POINTER( result );
302
303 }
304
```

This function returns a FCUR datum; at line 278, we use palloc() to allocate the return value. fcur_add() has a nice feature: If the two operands have a common currency and a common exchange rate, the result is expressed in that currency. If the operands are not expressed in a common currency, the result will be a value in local currency.

Lines 289 through 291 construct the result in a case where the operand currencies are compatible. If the currencies are not compatible, construct the result at lines 297 through 299.

Let's tell PostgreSQL about this function and make an operator (+) out of it:

```
movies=# CREATE OR REPLACE FUNCTION fcur_add( fcur, fcur )
movies-#    RETURNS fcur
movies-#    AS 'fcur.so' LANGUAGE 'C'
movies=#    IMMUTABLE STRICT
CREATE
movies-# CREATE OPERATOR +
movies-# (
movies-#    leftarg    = fcur,
movies-#    rightarg   = fcur,
movies-#    procedure  = fcur_add,
movies-#    commutator = +
movies-# );
CREATE
```

Now, try it:

```
movies=# SELECT *, val + '2(1.5702/CA$)' AS result FROM fcur_test;
 pkey |        val         |       result
------+--------------------+--------------------
    1 | 1(1/???)           | 2.27372(1/US$)
    2 | 1(0.5/???)         | 3.27372(1/US$)
    3 | 3(1/US$)           | 4.27372(1/US$)
    4 | 5(0.687853/GBP)    | 8.54272(1/US$)
    5 | 10(7.2566/FRF)     | 2.65178(1/US$)
    6 | 1(1.5702/CA$)      | 3(1.5702/CA$)
    7 | 1.5702(1.5702/CA$) | 3.5702(1.5702/CA$)
(7 rows)
```

Notice that the result values for rows 6 and 7 are expressed in Canadian dollars.

Creating other arithmetic operators for the FCUR type is simple. If the operands share a common currency (and exchange rate), the result should be expressed in that currency. I'll let you add the rest of the arithmetic operators.

The last two functions that I wanted to show you (see Listing 6.16) will convert FCUR values to and from REAL values. Internally, the REAL data type is known as a float4.

Listing 6.16   fcur.c **(Part 8)**

```
220 /*
221 **  Name: fcur_to_float4()
222 **
223 **        Converts the given fcur value into a
224 **        normalized float4.
225 */
226
```

Listing 6.16   **Continued**

```
227 PG_FUNCTION_INFO_V1(fcur_to_float4);
228
229 Datum fcur_to_float4(PG_FUNCTION_ARGS)
230 {
231     fcur * src = (fcur *)PG_GETARG_POINTER(0);
232
233     PG_RETURN_FLOAT4( normalize( src ));
234
235 }
```

The fcur_to_float4() function converts an FCUR value into a normalized FLOAT4 (that is, REAL) value. There isn't anything fancy in this function; let normalize() do the heavy lifting.

Listing 6.17 shows the float4_to_fcur() function:

Listing 6.17   fcur.c **(Part 9)**

```
237 /*
238 **  Name: float4_to_fcur()
239 **
240 **        Converts the given float4 value into an
241 **        fcur value
242 */
243
244 PG_FUNCTION_INFO_V1(float4_to_fcur);
245
246 Datum float4_to_fcur(PG_FUNCTION_ARGS)
247 {
248     float4  src    = PG_GETARG_FLOAT4(0);
249     fcur  * result = (fcur *)palloc( sizeof( fcur ));
250
251     result->fcur_units = src;
252     result->fcur_xrate = 1.0;
253
254     strcpy( result->fcur_name, baseCurrencyName );
255
256     PG_RETURN_POINTER( result );
257 }
```

The float4_to_fcur() function is a bit longer, but it's not complex. You allocate space for the result using palloc(); then create the result as a value expressed in your local currency.

When you tell PostgreSQL about these functions, you won't follow the same form that you have used in earlier examples:

```
movies=# CREATE OR REPLACE FUNCTION FCUR( FLOAT4 )
movies-#    RETURNS FCUR
movies-#    AS 'fcur.so','float4_to_fcur'
movies-#    LANGUAGE 'C'
movies=#    IMMUTABLE STRICT
CREATE
```

Notice that the internal (C) name for this function is `float4_to_fcur()`, but the external (PostgreSQL) name is FCUR. Older versions of PostgreSQL (release 7.2 or older) know that the FCUR function can be used to implicitly convert a FLOAT4 (or REAL) value into a FCUR value. PostgreSQL considers a function to be a conversion function if all of the following are true:

- The name of the function is the same as the name of a data type.
- The function returns a value whose type is the same as the function's name.
- The function takes a single argument of some other data type.

You can see that the FCUR function meets these criteria. Let's create the FLOAT4 function along the same pattern:

```
movies=# CREATE OR REPLACE FUNCTION FLOAT4( FCUR )
movies-#    RETURNS FLOAT4
movies-#    AS 'fcur.so','fcur_to_float4'
movies-#    LANGUAGE 'C'
movies=#    IMMUTABLE STRICT
CREATE
```

If you're using PostgreSQL version 7.3 or later, you must explicitly tell the PostgreSQL server that FLOAT4(FCUR) and FCUR(FLOAT4) are conversion functions. To create a CAST that will convert a FLOAT4 value to an FCUR value, execute the following command:

```
movies=#  CREATE CAST( FLOAT4 AS FCUR )  WITH FUNCTION FCUR( float4 ) AS IMPLICIT;
```

The CREATE CAST command specified the source type (FLOAT4), the target type (FCUR) and the signature of the conversion function (FCUR(float4)). The AS IMPLICIT clause tells PostgreSQL that it can silently convert FLOAT4 values to FCUR values whenever it needs to; you don't have to write things like CAST(4.0 AS FCUR) once you've defined an IMPLICIT CAST.

Don't forget to create a CAST that will convert values in the other direction:

```
movies=#  CREATE CAST( FCUR AS FLOAT4)  WITH FUNCTION FLOAT4( FCUR ) AS IMPLICIT;
```

Now PostgreSQL knows how to (implicitly) convert between FLOAT4 values and FCUR values. Why is that so important? You can now use a FCUR value in any context in which a FLOAT4 value is allowed. If you haven't defined a particular function (or operator), PostgreSQL will implicitly convert the FCUR value into a FLOAT4 value and then choose the appropriate function (or operator).

For example, you have not defined a multiplication operator for your FCUR data type, but PostgreSQL knows how to multiply FLOAT4 values:

```
movies=# SELECT *, (val * 5) as "Result" FROM fcur_test;
 pkey |         val         |      Result
------+---------------------+------------------
    1 | 1(1/???)            |                5
    2 | 1(0.5/???)          |               10
    3 | 3(1/US$)            |               15
    4 | 5(0.687853/GBP)     | 36.3449764251709
    5 | 10(7.2566/FRF)      | 6.89027905464172
    6 | 1(1.5702/CA$)       | 3.18430781364441
    7 | 1.5702(1.5702/CA$)  |                5
```

You can now multiply FCUR values. Notice that the Result column does not contain FCUR values. PostgreSQL converted the FCUR values into FLOAT4 values and then performed the multiplication. Of course, you can cast the result back to FCUR form. Here, we use the @ (absolute value) operator to convert from FCUR to FLOAT4 form and then cast the result back into FCUR form:

```
movies=# SELECT *, CAST( abs(val) AS FCUR ) FROM fcur_test;
 pkey |         val         |       fcur
------+---------------------+------------------
    1 | 1(1/???)            | 1(1/US$)
    2 | 1(0.5/???)          | 2(1/US$)
    3 | 3(1/US$)            | 3(1/US$)
    4 | 5(0.687853/GBP)     | 7.269(1/US$)
    5 | 10(7.2566/FRF)      | 1.37806(1/US$)
    6 | 1(1.5702/CA$)       | 0.636862(1/US$)
    7 | 1.5702(1.5702/CA$)  | 1(1/US$)
(7 rows)
```

Notice that all the result values have been normalized into your local currency.

Indexing Custom Data Types

At this point, you have a reasonably complete custom data type. You can create and display FCUR values, store them in a table, compare two FCUR values, and convert them to (and from) other data types. But you're missing one important feature: You can't create an index that includes an FCUR value. Once you have all of the comparison operators (<, <=, =, >=, and so on) in place you are two short steps away.

To index values of a given data type, you must create an *operator class* that tells PostgreSQL which operators it should use for that type. You may recall from Chapter 3, "PostgreSQL Syntax and Use," that PostgreSQL supports a number of index types (B-tree, hash, R-tree, and GiST). Each index type requires a different set of operators. For example, to build a B-tree index, PostgreSQL can make use of five different operators: <, <=, =, >=, and >. Before you can create an operator class that PostgreSQL can use to build B-tree indexes over FCUR values, you'll need one more function.

Listing 6.18 shows the `fcur_cmp()` function that compares two FCUR values:

Listing 6.18 `fcur.c` **(Part 10)**

```
305 PG_FUNCTION_INFO_V1(fcur_cmp);
306
307 Datum fcur_cmp(PG_FUNCTION_ARGS)
308 {
309     fcur * left      = (fcur *)PG_GETARG_POINTER(0);
310     fcur * right     = (fcur *)PG_GETARG_POINTER(1);
311     double left_dbl  = normalize( left );
312     double right_dbl = normalize( right );
313
314     if( left_dbl > right_dbl )
315       PG_RETURN_INT32( 1 );
316     else if( left_dbl < right_dbl )
317       PG_RETURN_INT32 ( -1 );
318     else
319       PG_RETURN_INT32 ( 0 );
320 }
```

PostgreSQL will call `fcur_cmp()` repeatedly as it builds a B-tree index. `fcur_cmp()` expects two arguments, both of type `fcur`. After normalizing the values, `fcur_cmp()` returns +1 if the first argument is greater than the second, -1 if the second argument is greater than the first, or 0 if the arguments are equal.

Don't forget to tell PostgreSQL how to find this function:

```
CREATE OR REPLACE FUNCTION FCUR_CMP( FCUR, FCUR )
    RETURNS INT4
    AS 'fcur.so'
    LANGUAGE 'C'
    IMMUTABLE STRICT;
```

Now you have all of the pieces in place; you can create an operator class with the following command:

```
CREATE OPERATOR CLASS fcur_ops
  DEFAULT FOR TYPE fcur USING BTREE as
    OPERATOR 1 <,
    OPERATOR 2 <=,
    OPERATOR 3 =,
    OPERATOR 4 >=,
    OPERATOR 5 >,
    FUNCTION 1 fcur_cmp( fcur, fcur );
```

That's it; once you've created an operator class for type FCUR, you can create an index that includes values of that type. To create an operator class for the other index types (hash, R-tree, and GiST), you'll have to create a few more support functions. See section 31 ("Extending SQL") of the PostgreSQL reference documentation for more details.

Summary

I hope I've convinced you that adding new functions, operators, and data types is not a complex task. If you follow the rules that I've described in this chapter, you should be able to extend PostgreSQL to meet your specific needs. I encourage you to explore Open Source extensions, which you can find on the Web. You might also consider contributing your extensions to the PostgreSQL community—if you need it, someone else probably needs it, too.

7

PL/pgSQL

PL/pgSQL (Procedural Language/PostgreSQL) is a language that combines the expressive power of SQL with the more typical features of a programming language. PL/pgSQL adds control structures such as conditionals, loops, and exception handling to the SQL language. When you write a PL/pgSQL function, you can include any and all SQL commands, as well as the procedural statements added by PL/pgSQL.

Functions written in PL/pgSQL can be called from other functions. You can also define a PL/pgSQL function as a *trigger*. A trigger is a procedure that executes when some event occurs. For example, you might want to execute a PL/pgSQL function that fires when a new row is added to a table—that's what a trigger is for. You can define triggers for the INSERT, UPDATE, and DELETE commands.

Installing PL/pgSQL

PostgreSQL can support a variety of procedural languages. Before you can use a procedural language, you have to install it into the database. Fortunately, this is a simple procedure.

The createlang shell script installs PL/pgSQL into a database. If you install PL/pgSQL in the template1 database, it will automatically be installed in all databases created from that template. The format for createlang is

```
createlang plpgsql database-name
```

To install PL/pgSQL in the movies database, execute the following command:

```
$ createlang plpgsql movies
```

Notice that this is a command-line utility, not a psql command.

Language Structure

PL/pgSQL is termed a block-structured language. A *block* is a sequence of statements between a matched set of DECLARE/BEGIN and END statements. Blocks can be nested—meaning that one block can entirely contain another block, which in turn can contain other blocks, and so on. For example, here is a PL/pgSQL function:

```
1  --
2  -- ch07.sql
3  --
4
5  CREATE OR REPLACE FUNCTION my_factorial(value INTEGER) RETURNS INTEGER AS $$
6    DECLARE
7      arg INTEGER;
8    BEGIN
9
10     arg := value;
11
12     IF arg IS NULL OR arg < 0 THEN
13         RAISE NOTICE 'Invalid Number';
14         RETURN NULL;
15     ELSE
16        IF arg = 1 THEN
17          RETURN 1;
18        ELSE
19          DECLARE
20            next_value INTEGER;
21          BEGIN
22            next_value := my_factorial(arg - 1) * arg;
23            RETURN next_value;
24          END;
25        END IF;
26     END IF;
27   END;
28 $$ LANGUAGE 'plpgsql';
```

The body of my_factorial() is actually the string between the opening dollar quotes (following the word AS) and the closing dollar quotes (just before the word LANGUAGE).

This function contains two blocks of code. The first block starts at line 6 and ends at line 27. The second block, which is nested inside the first, starts at line 19 and ends at line 24. The first block is called an *outer* block because it contains the *inner* block.

I'll talk about variable declarations in more detail in a moment, but I want to point out a few things here. At line 7, we declare a variable named arg. This variable has a well-defined lifetime. arg comes into existence when the function reaches the first DECLARE statement and goes out of existence as soon as the function reaches the END statement at line 27. The lifetime of a variable is also referred to as its *scope*. You can refer to a variable in any statement within the block that defines the scope of the variable. If you try to refer to a variable outside of its scope, you will receive a compilation error. Remember that you have two (nested) blocks in this function: the outer block and the inner block. Variables declared in an outer block can be used in inner blocks, but the reverse is not true. At line 22 (which is in the inner block), we use the arg variable, which was declared in the outer block. The variable next_value is declared within the inner block: If you try to use next_value in the outer block, you'll get an error.

This function (`my_factorial()`) contains two blocks, one nested within the other. You can nest blocks as deeply as you need to. You can also define blocks that are not nested. Here is the `my_factorial()` function again, but this time, I've included a few more blocks:

```
1  --
2  -- ch07.sql
3  --
4
5  CREATE FUNCTION my_factorial( value INTEGER ) RETURNS INTEGER AS $$
6    DECLARE
7      arg INTEGER;
8    BEGIN
9
10     arg := value;
11
12     IF arg IS NULL OR arg < 0 THEN
13       BEGIN
14         RAISE NOTICE 'Invalid Number';
15         RETURN NULL;
16       END;
17     ELSE
18         IF arg = 1 THEN
19           BEGIN
20             RETURN 1;
21           END;
22         ELSE
23           DECLARE
24             next_value INTEGER;
25           BEGIN
26             next_value := my_factorial(arg - 1) * arg;
27             RETURN next_value;
28           END;
29         END IF;
30     END IF;
31   END;
32 $$ LANGUAGE 'plpgsql';
```

This version still has an outer block (lines 6 through 31), but you have multiple inner blocks: lines 13 through 16, lines 19 through 21, and lines 23 through 28. As I said earlier, variables declared in an outer block can be used in inner blocks but the reverse is not true. If you had declared any variables in the block starting at line 19, you could not use any of those variables past the end of the block (at line 21).

Notice that you can indicate the beginning of a block with a DECLARE statement or with a BEGIN statement. If you need to declare any variables within a block, you must include a DECLARE section. If you don't need any local variables within a block, the DECLARE section is optional (an empty DECLARE section is perfectly legal).

Quoting Embedded Strings

Prior to version 8.0, including string literals in a PL/pgSQL function was difficult and error prone. Because the body of a PL/pgSQL function is itself a string, you had to double up the quote characters around any string literals within the function.
Take a close look at line 14 in the previous example:

```
RAISE NOTICE 'Invalid Number';
```

Notice that the string literal Invalid Number is surrounded by a set of single quotes. You can write an embedded string value that way because the body of the function is defined in a string delimited by PostgreSQL's new *dollar-quoting* mechanism. If you don't use dollar-quoting to define function body, you must double up the quotes, like this:

```
RAISE NOTICE ''Invalid Number'';
```

If you're using a version of PostgreSQL older than 8.0, you can't use dollar-quoting and you'll have to write embedded string literals in one of the other forms described in Chapter 2, "Working with Data in PostgreSQL." You could have written the embedded string in any of the three following forms:

```
RAISE NOTICE ''Invalid Number'';

RAISE NOTICE \'Invalid Number\';

RAISE NOTICE \047Invalid Number\047;
```

CREATE FUNCTION

Now, let's go back and look at the components of a function in more detail.

You define a new PL/pgSQL function using the CREATE FUNCTION command. The CREATE FUNCTION command comes in two forms. The first form is used for language interpreters that are embedded into the PostgreSQL server—PL/pgSQL functions fall into this category:

```
CREATE [OR REPLACE] FUNCTION name ( [[argname] argtype [, ...] ] )
    RETURNS return_type
    AS $$definition$$
    LANGUAGE langname
    [ WITH ( attribute [, ...] ) ]
```

The second form is used to define functions that are defined in an external language and compiled into a dynamically loaded object module:

```
CREATE [OR REPLACE] FUNCTION name ( [[argname] argtype [, ...] ] )
    RETURNS return_type
    AS $$obj_file$$, $$link_symbol$$
    LANGUAGE langname
    [ WITH ( attribute [, ...] ) ]
```

I covered compiled functions in more detail in Chapter 6, "Extending PostgreSQL." For this chapter, I'll focus on the first form. Don't forget, if you're using a version of PostgreSQL older than 8.0, you can't use $$ to delimit string values and you'll have to carefully quote embedded strings as described earlier in this chapter.

Each function has a name. However, the name alone is not enough to uniquely identify a PostgreSQL function. Instead, the function name and the data types of each argument (if any) are combined into a *signature*. A function's signature uniquely identifies the function within a database. This means that you can define many my_factorial() functions:

```
CREATE FUNCTION my_factorial( INTEGER )...
CREATE FUNCTION my_factorial( REAL )...
CREATE FUNCTION my_factorial( NUMERIC )...
```

Each of these functions is uniquely identified by its signature. When you call one of these functions, you provide the function name and an argument; PostgreSQL determines which function to use by comparing the data type of the arguments that you provide with the function signatures. If an exact match is found, PostgreSQL uses that function. If PostgreSQL can't find an exact match, it tries to find the closest match.

When you create a new function, you specify a list of arguments required by that function. In most programming languages, you would declare a name and a type for each function argument. In PL/pgSQL, you declare only the data type. The first argument is automatically named "$1", the second argument is named "$2", and so forth, up to a maximum of 32 arguments (if you're using a version of PostgreSQL older than 8.0, you're limited to 16 arguments per function). Starting with PostgreSQL version 8.0, you can include argument names in the CREATE FUNCTION command. That means that you can define the my_factorial() function like this:

```
CREATE FUNCTION my_factorial( inputArgument INTEGER )...
CREATE FUNCTION my_factorial( inputArgument REAL )...
CREATE FUNCTION my_factorial( inputArgument NUMERIC )...
```

Inside of my_factorial(), you can refer to the first argument as $1 or as inputArgument. If you include argument names in the CREATE FUNCTION command, the names are not considered to be part of the function signature. If you define a function such as

```
CREATE FUNCTION my_factorial( inputArgument INTEGER )...
```

the function's signature is my_factorial(INTEGER)—you can DROP the function without specifying argument names (in fact, if you *do* specify argument names in a DROP FUNCTION command, the names are ignored).

You can use predefined data types, user defined data types, and arrays of those types in a PL/pgSQL function.

It is important to remember that PL/pgSQL does *not* support default parameters. If you define a function that requires three parameters, you cannot call that function with fewer (or more) parameters. If you find that you need a function with a variable argument list, you can usually *overload* your function to obtain the same effect. When you overload a function, you define two (or more) functions with the same name but different argument lists. For example, let's define a function to compute the due date for a tape rental:

```
1  --
2  -- ch07.sql
3  --
4
5  CREATE FUNCTION compute_due_date(DATE) RETURNS DATE AS $$
6    DECLARE
7
8      due_date        DATE;
9      rental_period   INTERVAL := '7 days';
10
11   BEGIN
12
13     due_date := $1 + rental_period;
14
15     RETURN due_date;
16
17   END;
18 $$ LANGUAGE 'plpgsql';
```

This function takes a single parameter, a DATE value, and returns the date one week later. You might want a second version of this function that expects the rental date and a rental period:

```
20 -- ch07.sql
21 --
22 CREATE FUNCTION compute_due_date(DATE, INTERVAL) RETURNS DATE AS $$
23   BEGIN
24
25     RETURN( $1 + $2 );
26
27   END;
28 $$ LANGUAGE 'plpgsql';
```

Now you have two functions named compute_due_date(). One function expects a DATE value, and the other expects a DATE value and an INTERVAL value. The first function compute_due_date(DATE), provides the equivalent of a default parameter. If you call compute_due_date() with a single argument, the rental_period defaults to seven days.

I'd like to point out two things about the compute_due_date(DATE, INTERVAL) function.

First, a stylistic issue—the RETURN statement takes a single argument, the value to be returned to the caller. You can RETURN any expression that evaluates to the *return_type* of the function (we'll talk more about a function's *return_type* in a moment). I find it easier to read a RETURN statement if the expression is enclosed in parentheses (see line 25).

Second, you'll notice that I did not DECLARE any local variables. You can treat parameter variables just like any other variable—I used them in an expression in line 25. It's a rare occasion when you should settle for the automatic variable names supplied for function parameters. The name "$1" doesn't convey much meaning beyond telling you that this variable happens to be the first parameter. You should really provide a meaningful name for each parameter; this gives the reader some idea of what you intended to do with each parameter.

If you're using an older version of PostgreSQL (or you're writing code that must work on an older version), you can use the ALIAS statement to give a second, more meaningful name to a parameter. Here is the compute_due_date(DATE, INTERVAL) function again, but this time I have given alternate names to the parameters:

```
20 -- ch07.sql
21 --
22 CREATE FUNCTION compute_due_date(DATE, INTERVAL) RETURNS DATE AS '
23   DECLARE
24     rental_date    ALIAS FOR $1;
25     rental_period  ALIAS FOR $2;
26   BEGIN
27
28     RETURN( rental_date + rental_period );
29
30   END;
31 ' LANGUAGE 'plpgsql';
```

ALIAS gives you an alternate name for a parameter; you can still refer to an aliased parameter using the $n form, but I don't recommend it. Why bother to give a meaningful name to a parameter and then ignore it?

Starting with PostgreSQL version 8.0, you can skip the ALIAS commands and simply name the arguments in the CREATE FUNCTION command, like this:

```
CREATE FUNCTION compute_due_date(rental_date DATE, rental_period INTERVAL)
    RETURNS DATE AS ...
```

When you create a function, you must declare the data type of the return value. Our compute_due_date() functions return a value of type DATE. A value is returned from a function using the RETURN expression statement. Keep in mind that PL/pgSQL will try to convert the returned expression into the type that you specified when you created the function. If you tried to RETURN(''Bad Value'') from the compute_due_date() function, you would get an error (Bad Date External Representation). We'll see a special data type a little later (TRIGGER, or in versions older than 8.0, OPAQUE) that can be used only for trigger functions.

If you're writing a PL/pgSQL function that you want to run in a version of PostgreSQL older than 7.3, you must ensure that the function returns a value, even it if it only returns NULL. Starting with version 7.3, you can define functions that return type void. A function that returns type void doesn't actually return a value—you would call such a function for the side effects provided by the function.

I'll skip over the function body[1] for the moment and look at the final component[2] required to define a new function. PostgreSQL functions can be written in a variety of languages. When you create a new function, the last component that you specify is the name of the language in which the body of the function is written. All the functions that you will see in this chapter are written in PL/pgSQL, which PostgreSQL knows as LANGUAGE 'plpgsql'.

DROP FUNCTION

Before you experiment much more with PL/pgSQL functions, it might be useful for you to know how to replace the definition of a function.

If you are using PostgreSQL 7.2 or later, you can use the CREATE OR REPLACE FUNC-TION ... syntax. If a function with the same signature already exists, PostgreSQL will silently replace the old version of the function; otherwise, a new function is created.

If you are using a version of PostgreSQL older than 7.2, you will have to DROP the old function before you can create a new one. The syntax for the DROP FUNCTION command is

```
DROP FUNCTION name( [[argname] argtype [, ...] ] );
```

Notice that you have to provide the complete signature when you drop a function; otherwise, PostgreSQL would not know which version of the function to remove.

Of course, you can use the DROP FUNCTION command to simply remove a function—you don't have to replace it with a new version.

Function Body

Now that you have an overview of the components of a PL/pgSQL function, let's look at the function body in greater detail. I'll start by showing you how to include documentation (that is, comments) in your PL/pgSQL functions. Next, I'll look at variable declarations. Finally, I'll finish up this section by describing the different kinds of statements that you can use inside of a PL/pgSQL function.

Comments

There are two comment styles in PL/pgSQL. The most frequently seen comment indicator is the double dash: --. A double dash introduces a comment that extends to the end of the current line. For example:

---

[1] The function body is everything between the AS keyword and the LANGUAGE keyword. The function body is specified in the form of a string.

[2] When you create a function, you can also specify a set of optional attributes that apply to that function. These attributes tell PostgreSQL about the behavior of the function so that the query optimizer can know whether it can take certain shortcuts when evaluating the function. See the CREATE FUNCTION section in the *PostgreSQL Programmer's Guide* for more information.

```
-- This line contains a comment and nothing else
DECLARE
    customer_id  INTEGER;       -- This is also a comment

-- due_date     DATE;          -- This entire line is a comment
                               -- because it begins with a '--'
```

PL/pgSQL understands C-style comments as well. A C-style comment begins with the characters /* and ends with the characters */. A C-style comment can span multiple lines:

```
/*
    NAME: compute_due_date()

    DESCRIPTION:  This function will compute the due date for a tape
                  rental.

    INPUT:
                  $1 -- Date of original rental

    RETURNS:      A date indicating when the rental is due.
*/

CREATE FUNCTION compute_due_date( DATE ) RETURNS DATE
...
```

Choosing a comment style is purely a matter of personal preference. Of course, the person choosing the style may not be you—you may have to conform to coding standards imposed by your customer (and/or employer). I tend to use only the double dash comment style in PL/pgSQL code. If I want to include a multi-line comment, I start each line with a double dash:

```
-----------------------------------------------------------------
-- NAME: compute_due_date()
--
-- DESCRIPTION:  This function will compute the due date for a tape
--               rental.
--
-- INPUT:
--               $1 -- Date of original rental
--
-- RETURNS:      A date indicating when the rental is due.

CREATE FUNCTION compute_due_date( DATE ) RETURNS DATE
...
```

I find that the double-dash style looks a little cleaner.

Variables

The variable declarations that you've seen up to this point have all been pretty simple. There are actually five ways to introduce a new variable (or at least a new variable name) into a PL/pgSQL function.

- Each parameter defines a new variable.
- You can declare new variables in the DECLARE section of a block.
- You can create an alternate name for a function parameter using the ALIAS statement.
- You can define a new name for a variable (invalidating the old name) using the RENAME statement.
- The iterator variable for an integer-based FOR loop is automatically declared to be an integer.

Let's look at these variables one at a time.

Function Parameters

I mentioned earlier in this chapter that each parameter in a PL/pgSQL function is automatically assigned a name. The first parameter (in left-to-right order) is named $1, the second parameter is named $2, and so on. You define the data type for each parameter in the function definition-for example:

```
CREATE FUNCTION write_history( DATE, rentals )...
```

This function expects two parameters. The first parameter is named $1 and is of type DATE. The second parameter is named $2 and is of type rentals. If you're using a newer version of PostgreSQL (8.0 or later), you can also define your own names for function parameters:

```
CREATE FUNCTION write_history( historyDate DATE, rentalRecord rentals )...
```

In this case, you've given two names to each parameter. You can refer to the first parameter as historyDate or as $1 and the second parameter as rentalRecord or $2. When you include parameter names in a CREATE FUNCTION command, you're assigning aliases for the parameters without explicitly writing ALIAS commands.

Notice that the write_history() function (in the preceding code line) expects an argument of type rentals. In the sample database, 'rentals' is actually the name of a table. Inside of the write_history() function, you can use the rentalRecord parameter (also known as $2) as if it were a row in the rentals table. That means that you can work with rentalRecord.tape_id, rentalRecord.customer_id, rentalRecord.rental_date, or $2.tape_id, $2.customer_id, and $2.rental_date.

When you call this function, you need to pass a row from the rentals table as the second argument. For example:

```
SELECT write_history( CURRENT_DATE, rentals ) FROM rentals;
```

DECLARE

The second way to introduce a new variable into a PL/pgSQL function is to list the variable in the DECLARE section of a block. The name of a non-parameter variable can include alphabetic characters (A-Z), underscores, and digits. Variable names must begin with a letter (A-Z or a-z) or an underscore. Names are case-insensitive: my_variable can also be written as My_Variable, and both still refer to the same variable.

The PL/pgSQL documentation mentions that you can force a variable name to be case-sensitive by enclosing it in double quotes. For example, "pi". As of PostgreSQL 7.1.3, this does not seem to work. You *can* enclose a variable name within double quotes if you need to start the name with a digit.

Oddly enough, you can actually DECLARE a variable whose name starts with a '$', $3, for example, but I wouldn't recommend it; I would expect that this feature (bug?) may be removed (fixed?) at some point in the future.

The complete syntax for a variable declaration is

```
var-name [CONSTANT] var-type [NOT NULL] [{ DEFAULT | := } expression];
```

Some of the examples in this chapter have declared variables using the most basic form:

```
due_date       DATE;
rental_period  INTERVAL := ''7 days'';
```

The first line creates a new variable named due_date. The data type of due_date is DATE. Because I haven't explicitly provided an initial value for due_date, it will be initialized to NULL.

The second line defines a new INTERVAL variable named rental_period. In this case, I *have* provided an initial value, so rental_period will be initialized to the INTERVAL value '7 days'. I could have written this declaration as

```
rental_period  INTERVAL DEFAULT ''7 days'';
```

In the DECLARE section of a block, DEFAULT is synonymous with ':='.

The initializer expression must evaluate to a value of the correct type. If you are creating an INTEGER variable, the initializer expression must evaluate to an INTEGER value or to a type that can be coerced into an INTEGER value.

In newer versions of PostgreSQL, you can declare array variables by writing a set of square brackets (and an optional element count) following the data type. For example, the declaration

```
montly_balances NUMERIC(7.2)[12] := '{}';
```

defines a variable named monthly_balances as an array of 12 numeric values. There is one counter-intuitive quirk that you should know about when you declare an array variable. If you define an array without an initializer, the array is NULL—apparently, that's not the same thing as saying that the array is full of NULL values. You can't insert individual values into a NULL array. That means that code such as the following will silently fail:

```
DECLARE
  monthly_balances NUMERIC(7.2)[12];
BEGIN
  monthly_balances[1] := 10;
  monthly_balances[2] := monthly_balances[1] * 1.10;
    ...
```

You can't insert a value into a NULL array, but you *can* copy an entire array over the top of a NULL array:

```
DECLARE
  new_balances   NUMERIC(7.2)[12];
  old_balances   NUMERIC(7,2)[12] := '{}';
BEGIN
  new_balances := old_balances;
    ...
```

So you can only put a value into an array by initializing it or by copying another array over the top of it.

You can define PL/pgSQL functions that take array values as arguments, and you can return array values from PL/pgSQL functions.

Prior to PostgreSQL version 8.0, the DECLARE section had a couple of surprises up its sleeve. First, you could use any of the function parameters in the initializer expression, even if you ALIASed them. The following is illegal:

```
CREATE FUNCTION compute_due_date(DATE) RETURNS DATE AS '
  DECLARE
    due_date  DATE := $1 + ''7 days''::INTERVAL;
    ...
```

```
ERROR: Parameter $1 is out of range
```

The second issue was that once you created a variable in a DECLARE section, you could not use that variable later within the same DECLARE section. That meant that you couldn't do something like

```
CREATE FUNCTION do_some_geometry(REAL) RETURNS REAL AS '
  DECLARE
    pi        CONSTANT REAL := 3.1415926535;
    radius          REAL := 3.0;
    diameter        REAL := pi * ( radius * radius );
    ...
```

```
ERROR: Attribute 'pi' not found
```

Both of these problems have been fixed in release 8.0.

Notice in the previous example that I declared pi to be a 'CONSTANT REAL'. When you define a variable as CONSTANT, you prevent assignment to that variable. You must provide an initializer for a CONSTANT.

The final modifier for a variable declaration is NOT NULL. Defining a variable to be NOT NULL means that you will receive an error if you try to set that variable to NULL. You must provide an initializer when you create a NOT NULL variable[3].

Now you can put all these pieces together. The following declarations are identical in function:

```
pi CONSTANT REAL NOT NULL DEFAULT 3.1415926535;
pi CONSTANT REAL NOT NULL := 3.1415926535;
pi CONSTANT REAL := 3.1415926535;
```

Each declares a REAL variable named pi, with an initial value of 3.14159265. The NOT NULL clause is superfluous here because we have declared pi to be a constant and we have given it a non-null initial value; it's not a bad idea to include NOT NULL for documentation purposes.

The default value for a variable is computed each time you enter the block that declares it. If you define a default value in terms of an expression, the variables and functions within that expression can change value from one execution to the next. For example, if an inner block declares a variable whose default value is defined by a variable in an outer block, the default value will vary with the outer variable.

Pseudo Data Types—%TYPE and %ROWTYPE

When you create a PL/pgSQL variable, you must declare its data type. Before moving on to the ALIAS command, there are a few *pseudo* data types that you should know about.

%TYPE lets you define one variable to be of the same type as another. Quite often, you will find that you need to temporarily store a value that you have retrieved from a table, or you might need to make a copy of a function parameter. Let's say that you are writing a function to process a rentals record in some way:

```
CREATE FUNCTION process_rental( rentals ) RETURNS BOOLEAN AS $$
  DECLARE
    original_tape_id        CHAR(8);
    original_customer_id    INTEGER;
    original_rental_row     ALIAS FOR $1;

  BEGIN

    original_tape_id     := original_rental_row.tape_id;
    original_customer_id := original_rental_row.customer_id;
    ...
```

In this snippet, you are making a local copy of the rentals.tape_id and rentals.customer_id columns. Without %TYPE, you have to ensure that you use the correct data types when you declare the original_tape_id and original_customer_id variables.

---

[3] This makes perfect sense if you think about it. If you don't provide an initializer, PL/pgSQL will initialize each variable to NULL—you can't do that if you have declared the variable to be NOT NULL.

That might not sound like such a big deal now, but what about six months later when you decide that eight characters isn't enough to hold a tape ID?

Instead of doing all that maintenance work yourself, you can let PL/pgSQL do the work for you. Here is a much better version of the process_rental() function:

```
CREATE FUNCTION process_rental( rentals ) RETURNS BOOLEAN AS $$
  DECLARE
    original_tape_id        rentals.tape_id%TYPE;
    original_customer_id    rentals.customer_id%TYPE;
    original_rental_row     ALIAS FOR $1;

  BEGIN

    original_tape_id     := original_rental_row.tape_id;
    original_customer_id := original_rental_row.customer_id;
    ...
```

By using %TYPE, I've told PL/pgSQL to create the original_tape_id variable using whatever type rentals.tape_id is defined to be. I've also created original_customer_id with the same data type as the rentals.customer_id column.

This is an extremely powerful feature. At first blush, it may appear to be just a simple timesaving trick that you can use when you first create a function. The real power behind %TYPE is that your functions become self-maintaining. If you change the data type of the rentals.tape_id column, the process_rentals() function will automatically inherit the change. You won't have to track down all the places where you have made a temporary copy of a tape_id and change the data types.

You can use the %TYPE feature to obtain the type of a column or type of another variable (as shown in the code that follows). You cannot use %TYPE to obtain the type of a parameter. Starting with PostgreSQL version 7.2, you can use %TYPE in the argument list for a function. For example:

```
CREATE FUNCTION process_rental( rentals, rentals.customer_id%TYPE )
 RETURNS BOOLEAN AS '
  DECLARE
    original_tape_id        rentals.tape_id%TYPE;
    original_customer_id    rentals.customer_id%TYPE;
    original_rental_row     ALIAS FOR $1;
    ...
```

%TYPE lets you access the data type of a column (or variable). %ROWTYPE provides similar functionality. You can use %ROWTYPE to declare a variable that has the same structure as a row in the given table. For example:

```
CREATE FUNCTION process_rental( rentals ) RETURNS BOOLEAN AS $$
  DECLARE
    original_tape_id        rentals.tape_id%TYPE;
    original_customer_id    rentals.customer_id%TYPE;
    original_rental_row     rentals%ROWTYPE;
    ...
```

The `original_rental_row` variable is defined to have the same structure as a row in the `rentals` table. You can access columns in `original_rental_row` using the normal dot syntax: `original_rental_row.tape_id`, `original_rental_row.rental_date`, and so on.

Using `%ROWTYPE`, you can define a variable that has the same structure as a row in a specific table. A bit later in this chapter, I'll show you how to process dynamic queries (see the section "`EXECUTE`"); that is, a query whose text is not known at the time you are writing your function. When you are processing dynamic queries, you won't know which table to use with `%ROWTYPE`.

Other Pseudo Types

The `RECORD` data type is used to declare a composite variable whose structure will be determined at execution time. I'll describe the `RECORD` type in more detail a bit later (see the section "Loop Constructs").

PostgreSQL version 7.3 introduced a new pseudo type named `TRIGGER`. A function defined with a return type of `TRIGGER` can only be used as a trigger function. I'll describe trigger functions later in this chapter (see the section titled "Triggers").

The final pseudo data type is `OPAQUE`. The `OPAQUE` type can be used only to define the return type of a function[4]. You cannot declare a variable (or parameter) to be of type `OPAQUE`. In fact, you can use `OPAQUE` only to define the return type of a trigger function *only*. `OPAQUE` is an obsolete name; you should define trigger functions using the `TRIGGER` type instead.

ALIAS and RENAME

Now, let's move on to the next method that you can use to define a new variable, or a least a new name for an existing variable. You've already seen the `ALIAS` statement earlier in this chapter. The `ALIAS` statement creates an alternative name for a function parameter. You cannot `ALIAS` a variable that is not a function parameter. Using `ALIAS`, you can define any number of names that equate to a parameter:

```
CREATE FUNCTION foo( INTEGER ) RETURNS INTEGER AS '
  DECLARE
    param_1  ALIAS FOR $1;
    my_param ALIAS FOR $1;
    arg_1    ALIAS FOR $1;
  BEGIN
    $1 := 42;
    -- At this point, $1, param_1, my_param and arg_1
    -- are all set to 42.
    . . .
```

As we've mentioned already, if you're using PostgreSQL version 8.0 or later, you can skip the `ALIAS` commands and simply name each parameter in the argument list.

---

[4] You *can* use OPAQUE to define the data type of a function argument, but not when you are creating a PL/pgSQL function. Remember, functions can be defined in a number of different languages.

The RENAME statement is similar to ALIAS; it provides a new name for an existing variable. Unlike ALIAS, RENAME invalidates the old variable name. You can RENAME any variable, not just function parameters. The syntax for the RENAME statement is

```
RENAME old-name TO new-name
```

Here is an example of the RENAME statement:

```
CREATE FUNCTION foo( INTEGER ) RETURNS INTEGER AS '
  DECLARE
    RENAME $1 TO param1;
  BEGIN
  ...
```

Important Note

The RENAME statement does not work in PostgreSQL versions 7.1.2 through at least 7.4, but it appears to function correctly in version 8.0.

RENAME and ALIAS can be used only within the DECLARE section of a block.

FOR **Loop Iterator**

So far, you have seen four methods for introducing a new variable or a new variable name. In each of the preceding methods, you explicitly declare a new variable (or name) in the DECLARE section of a block and the scope of the variable is the block in which it is defined. The final method is different.

One of the control structures that you will be looking at soon is the FOR loop. The FOR loop comes in two flavors—the first flavor is used to execute a block of statements some fixed number of times; the second flavor executes a statement block for each row returned by a query. In this section, I will talk only about the first flavor.

Here is an example of a FOR loop:

```
FOR i IN 1 .. 12 LOOP
  balance := balance + customers.monthly_balances[i];
END LOOP;
```

In this example, you have defined a loop that will execute 12 times. Each statement within the loop (you have only a single statement) will be executed 12 times. The variable i is called the *iterator* for the loop (you may also see the term *loop index* to describe the iterator). Each time you go through this loop, the iterator (i) is incremented by 1.

The iterator for an integer FOR loop is automatically declared for you. The type of the iterator is INTEGER. It is important to remember that the iterator for an integer FOR loop is a *new* variable. If you have already declared a variable with the same name as the iterator, the original variable will be hidden for the remainder of the loop. For example:

```
...
  DECLARE
    i REAL = 0;
    balance NUMERIC(9,2) = 0;
```

```
BEGIN

  --
  -- At this point, i = 0
  --

  FOR i IN 1 .. 12 LOOP

    --
    -- we now have a new copy of i, it will vary from 1 to 12
    --

    balance := balance + customers.monthly_balances[i];
  END LOOP;

  --
  -- Now, if we access i, we will find that it is
  -- equal to 0 again
  --
```

Notice that while you are inside the loop, there are two variables named i—the inner variable is the loop iterator, and the outer variable was declared inside of this block. If you refer to i inside the loop, you are referring to the inner variable. If you refer to i outside the loop, you are referring to the outer variable. A little later, I'll show you how to access the outer variable from within the loop.

Now that you have seen how to define new variables, it's time to move on. This next section explains each type of statement that you can use in the body of a PL/pgSQL function.

PL/pgSQL Statement Types

At the beginning of this chapter, I said that PL/pgSQL adds a set of procedural constructs to the basic SQL language. In this next section, I'll examine the statement types added by PL/pgSQL. PL/pgSQL includes constructs for looping, exception and error handling, simple assignment, and conditional execution (that is, IF/THEN/ELSE). Although I don't describe them here, it's important to remember that you can also include any SQL command in a PL/pgSQL function.

Assignment

The most commonly seen statement in many programs is the assignment statement. Assignment lets you assign a new value to a variable. The format of an assignment statement should be familiar by now; you've already seen it in most of the examples in this chapter:

```
target := expression;
```

target should identify a variable, a function parameter, a column, or in some cases, a row. If target is declared as CONSTANT, you will receive an error. When PL/pgSQL executes an assignment statement, it starts by evaluating the expression. If expression evaluates to a value whose data type is not the same as the data type of target, PL/pgSQL will convert the value to the target type. (In cases where conversion is not possible, PostgreSQL will reward you with an error message.)

The expression is actually evaluated by the PostgreSQL server, not by PL/pgSQL. This means that expression can be any valid PostgreSQL expression. Chapter 2, "Working with Data in PostgreSQL," describes PostgreSQL expressions in more detail.

SELECT INTO

The assignment statement is one way to put data into a variable; SELECT INTO is another. The syntax for a SELECT INTO statement is

```
SELECT INTO destination [, ...] select-list FROM ...;
```

A typical SELECT INTO statement might look like this:

```
...
DECLARE
  customer    customers%ROWTYPE;
BEGIN
  SELECT INTO customer * FROM customers WHERE customer_id = 10;
...
```

When this statement is executed, PL/pgSQL sends the query "SELECT * FROM customers WHERE customer_id = 10" to the server. This query should not return more than one row. The results of the query are placed into the customer variable. Because I specified that customer is of type customers%ROWTYPE, the query must return a row shaped exactly like a customers row; otherwise, PL/pgSQL signals an error.

I could also SELECT INTO a list of variables, rather than into a single composite variable:

```
DECLARE
  phone    customers.phone%TYPE;
  name     customers.customer_name%TYPE;
BEGIN
  SELECT INTO name, phone
    customer_name, customers.phone FROM customers
    WHERE customer_id = 10;
...
```

Notice that I had to explicitly request customers.phone in this query. If I had simply requested phone, PL/pgSQL would have assumed that I really wanted to execute the query:

```
SELECT customer_name, NULL FROM customers where customer_id = 10;
```

Why? Because I have declared a local variable named phone in this function, and PL/pgSQL would substitute the current value of phone wherever it occurred in the query. Because phone (the local variable) is initialized to NULL, PL/pgSQL would have stuffed NULL into the query. You should choose variable names that don't conflict with column names, or fully qualify column name references.

Of course, you can also SELECT INTO a RECORD variable and the RECORD will adapt its shape to match the results of the query.

I mentioned earlier that the query specified in a SELECT INTO statement must return no more than one row. What happens if the query returns no data? The variables that you are selecting into are set to NULL. You can also check the value of the predefined variable FOUND (described later in this chapter) to determine whether a row was actually retrieved. What happens if the query returns more than one row? If you're using an older version of PostgreSQL, PL/pgSQL will throw an error at you. If you're using PostgreSQL version 8.0 or later, the target variables are filled in with values from the first row returned by the SELECT command.

A bit later in this chapter, you'll see the FOR-IN-SELECT loop that can handle an arbitrary number of rows (see the section "Loop Constructs").

Conditional Execution

Using the IF statement, you can conditionally execute a section of code. The most basic form of the IF statement is

```
IF expression THEN
  statements
END IF;
```

The expression must evaluate to a BOOLEAN value or to a value that can be coerced into a BOOLEAN value. If expression evaluates to TRUE, the *statements* between THEN and END IF are executed. If expression evaluates to FALSE or NULL, the statements are not executed.

Here are some sample IF statements:

```
IF ( now() > rentals.rental_date + rental_period ) THEN
   late_fee := handle_rental_overdue();
END IF;

IF ( customers.balance > maximum_balance ) THEN
    PERFORM customer_over_balance( customers );
    RETURN( FALSE );
END IF;
```

In each of these statements, the condition expression is evaluated by the PostgreSQL server. If the condition evaluates to TRUE, the statements between THEN and END IF are executed; otherwise, they are skipped and execution continues with the statement following the END IF.

You can also define a new block within the IF statement:

```
IF ( tapes.dist_id IS NULL ) THEN
  DECLARE
    default_dist_id CONSTANT integer := 0;
  BEGIN
    ...
  END;
END IF;
```

The obvious advantage to defining a new block within an IF statement is that you can declare new variables. It's usually a good idea to declare variables with the shortest possible scope; you won't pollute the function's namespace with variables that you need in only a few places, and you can assign initial values that may rely on earlier computations.

The next form of the IF statement provides a way to execute one section of code if a condition is TRUE and a different set of code if the condition is not TRUE. The syntax for an IF-THEN-ELSE statement is

```
IF expression THEN
  statements_1
ELSE
  statements_2
END IF;
```

In this form, statements_1 will execute if expression evaluates to TRUE; otherwise, statements_2 will execute. Note that statements_2 will not execute if the expression is TRUE. Here are some sample IF-THEN-ELSE statements:

```
IF ( now() > rentals.rental_date + rental_period ) THEN
  late_fee := handle_rental_overdue();
ELSE
  late_fee := 0;
END IF;


IF ( customers.balance > maximum_balance ) THEN
  PERFORM customer_over_balance( customers );
  RETURN( FALSE );
ELSE
  rental_ok = TRUE;
END IF;
```

An IF-THEN-ELSE is *almost* equivalent to two IF statements. For example, the following

```
IF ( now() > rentals.rental_date + rental_period ) THEN
  statements_1
ELSE
  statements_2
END IF;
```

is nearly identical to

```
IF ( now() > rentals.rental_date + rental_period ) THEN
  statements_1
END IF;


IF ( now() <= rentals.rental_date + rental_period ) THEN
  statements_2
END IF;
```

The difference between these two scenarios is that using IF-THEN-ELSE, the condition expression is evaluated once; but using two IF statements, the condition expression is evaluated twice. In many cases, this distinction won't be important; but in some circumstances, the condition expression may have side effects (such as causing a trigger to execute), and evaluating the expression twice will double the side effects.

You can nest IF-THEN-ELSE statements:

```
IF ( today > compute_due_date( rentals )) THEN
  --
  --  This rental is past due
  --
  ...
ELSE
  IF ( today = compute_due_date( rentals )) THEN
    --
    --  This rental is due today
    --
    ...
  ELSE
    --
    -- This rental is not late and it's not due today
    --
    ...
  END IF;
END IF;
```

PostgreSQL versions 7.2 and later support a more convenient way to nest IF-THEN-ELSE IF statements:

```
IF ( today > compute_due_date( rentals )) THEN
  --
  --  This rental is past due
  --
  ...
ELSIF ( today = compute_due_date( rentals )) THEN
  --
  --  This rental is due today
  --
  ...
ELSE
  --
  -- This rental is not late and it's not due today
  --
  ...
END IF;
```

The ELSIF form is functionally equivalent to a nested IF-THEN-ELSE-IF but you need only a single END IF statement. Notice that the spelling is ELSIF, not ELSE IF. You can include as many ELSIF sections as you like.

Loop Constructs

Next, let's look at the loop constructs offered by PL/pgSQL. Using a loop, you can repeat a sequence of statements until a condition occurs. The most basic loop construct is the LOOP statement:

```
[<<label>>]
LOOP
  statements
END LOOP;
```

In this form, the statements between LOOP and END LOOP are repeated until an EXIT or RETURN statement exits the loop. If you don't include an EXIT or RETURN statement, your function will loop forever. I'll explain the optional <<label>> in the section that covers the EXIT statement.

You can nest loops as deeply as you need:

```
 1 row := 0;
 2
 3 LOOP
 4   IF( row = 100 ) THEN
 5     EXIT;
 6   END IF;
 7
 8   col := 0;
 9
10   LOOP
11     IF( col = 100 ) THEN
12       EXIT;
13     END IF;
14
15     PERFORM process( row, col );
16
17     col := col + 1;
18
19   END LOOP;
20
21   row := row + 1;
22 END LOOP;
23
24 RETURN( 0 );
```

In the preceding code snippet, there are two loops. Because the inner loop is completely enclosed within the outer loop, the inner loop executes each time the outer loop repeats. The statements in the outer loop execute 100 times. The statements in the inner loop (lines 10 through 19) execute 100 × 100 times.

The EXIT statement at line 5 causes the outer LOOP to terminate; when you execute that statement, execution continues at the statement following the END LOOP for the enclosing loop (at line 24). The EXIT statement at line 12 will change the point of execution to the statement following the END LOOP for the enclosing loop (at line 21).

I'll cover the EXIT statement in more detail in the next section.

The next loop construct is the WHILE loop. The syntax for a WHILE loop is

```
[<<label>>]
WHILE expression LOOP
  statements
END LOOP;
```

The WHILE loop is used more frequently than a plain LOOP. A WHILE loop is equivalent to

```
[<<label>>]
LOOP

  IF( NOT ( expression )) THEN
    EXIT;
  END IF;

  statements

END LOOP;
```

The condition expression must evaluate to a BOOLEAN value or to a value that can be coerced to a BOOLEAN. The expression is evaluated each time execution reaches the top of the loop. If expression evaluates to TRUE, the statements within the loop are executed. If expression evaluates to FALSE or NULL, execution continues with the statement following the END LOOP.

Here is the nested loop example again, but this time, I have replaced the IF tests with a WHILE loop:

```
1 row := 0;
2
3 WHILE ( row < 100 ) LOOP
4
5   col := 0;
6
7   WHILE ( col < 100 ) LOOP
8
9     PERFORM process( row, col );
10
11     col := col + 1;
12
13   END LOOP;
14
15   row := row + 1;
16 END LOOP;
17
18 RETURN( 0 );
```

You can see that the WHILE loop is much neater and easier to understand than the previous form. It's also a lot easier to introduce a bug if you use a plain LOOP and have to write the IF tests yourself.

The third loop construct is the FOR loop. There are two forms of the FOR loop. In the first form, called the integer-FOR loop, the loop is controlled by an integer variable:

```
[<<label>>]
FOR iterator IN [ REVERSE ] start-expression .. end-expression LOOP
    statements
END LOOP;
```

In this form, the statements inside the loop are repeated while the iterator is less than or equal to end-expression (or greater than or equal to if the loop direction is REVERSE). Just before the first iteration of the loop, iterator is initialized to start-expression. At the bottom of the loop, iterator is incremented by 1 (or –1 if the loop direction is REVERSE); and if within the end-expression, execution jumps back to the first statement in the loop.

An integer-FOR loop is equivalent to:

```
[<<label>>]
DECLARE
    Iterator  INTEGER;
    increment INTEGER;
    end_value INTEGER;
BEGIN
  IF( loop-direction = REVERSE ) THEN
    increment := -1;
  ELSE
    increment := 1;
  END IF;

  iterator  := start-expression;
  end_value := end-expression;

  LOOP
    IF( iterator >= end_value ) THEN
      EXIT;
    END IF;

    statements

  iterator := iterator + increment;

  END LOOP;
END;
```

The start-expression and end-expression are evaluated once, just before the loop begins. Both expressions must evaluate to an INTEGER value or to a value that can be coerced to an INTEGER.

Here is the example code snippet again, this time written in the form of an integer-FOR loop:

```
 1 FOR row IN 0 .. 99 LOOP
 2
 3   FOR col in 0 .. 99 LOOP
 4
 5     PERFORM process( row, col );
 6
 8     END LOOP;
 9
10 END LOOP;
11
12 RETURN( 0 );
```

This version is more readable than the version that used a WHILE loop. All the information that you need in order to understand the loop construct is in the first line of the loop. Looking at line 1, you can see that this loop uses a variable named row as the iterator; and unless something unusual happens inside the loop, row starts at 0 and increments to 99.

There are a few points to remember about the integer-FOR loop. First, the iterator variable is automatically declared—it is defined to be an INTEGER and is local to the loop. Second, you can terminate the loop early using the EXIT (or RETURN) statement. Third, you can change the value of the iterator variable inside the loop: Doing so can affect the number of iterations through the loop.

You can use this last point to your advantage. In PL/pgSQL, there is no way to explicitly specify a loop increment other than 1 (or 1 if the loop is REVERSEd). But you can change the effective increment by modifying the iterator within the loop. For example, let's say that you want to process only odd numbers inside a loop:

```
1 ...
2 FOR i IN 1 .. 100 LOOP
3   ...
4   i := i + 1;
5   ...
6 END LOOP;
7 ...
```

The first time you go through this loop, i will be initialized to 1. At line 4, you increment i to 2. When you reach line 6, the FOR loop will increment i to 3 and then jump back to line 3 (the first line in the loop). You can, of course, increment the loop iterator in whatever form you need. If you fiddle with the loop iterator, be sure to write yourself a comment that explains what you're doing.

The second form of the FOR loop is used to process the results of a query. The syntax for this form is

```
[<<label>>]
FOR iterator IN query LOOP
  statements
END LOOP;
```

In this form, which I'll call the FOR-IN-SELECT form, the statements within the loop are executed once for each row returned by the query. query must be a SQL SELECT command. Each time through the loop, iterator will contain the next row returned by the query. If the query does not return any rows, the statements within the loop will not execute.

The iterator variable must either be of type RECORD or of a %ROWTYPE that matches the structure of a row returned by the query. Even if the query returns a single column, the iterator must be a RECORD or a %ROWTYPE.

Here is a code snippet that shows the FOR statement:

```
1 DECLARE
2   rental    rentals%ROWTYPE;
3 BEGIN
4
5   FOR rental IN SELECT * FROM rentals ORDER BY rental_date LOOP
6     IF( rental_is_overdue( rental )) THEN
7        PERFORM process_late_rental( rental );
8     END IF;
9   END LOOP;
10
11 END;
```

A %ROWTYPE iterator is fine if the query returns an entire row. If you need to retrieve a partial row, or you want to retrieve the result of a computation, declare the iterator variable as a RECORD. Here is an example:

```
1 DECLARE
2   my_record  RECORD;
3 BEGIN
4
5 FOR my_record IN
6   SELECT tape_id, compute_due_date(rentals) AS due_date FROM rentals
7 LOOP
8   PERFORM
9     check_for_late_rental( my_record.tape_id, my_record.due_date );
10 END LOOP;
11
12 END;
```

A RECORD variable does not have a fixed structure. The fields in a RECORD variable are determined at the time that a row is assigned. In the previous example, you assign a row returned by the SELECT to the my_record RECORD. Because the query returns two columns, my_record will contain two fields: tape_id and due_date. A RECORD variable can change its shape. If you used the my_record variable as the iterator in a second FOR-IN-SELECT loop in this function, the field names within the RECORD would change. For example:

```
1 DECLARE
2   my_record  RECORD;
```

```
 3 BEGIN
 4
 5   FOR my_record IN SELECT * FROM rentals LOOP
 6     -- my_record now holds a row from the rentals table
 7     -- I can access my_record.tape_id, my_record.rental_date, etc.
 8   END LOOP;
 9
10   FOR my_record IN SELECT * FROM tapes LOOP
11     -- my_record now holds a row from the tapes table
12     -- I can now access my_record.tape_id, my_record.title, etc.
13   END LOOP;
12 END;
```

You also can process the results of a dynamic query (that is, a query not known at the time you write the function) in a FOR loop. To execute a dynamic query in a FOR loop, the syntax is a bit different:

```
[<<label>>]
FOR iterator IN EXECUTE query-string LOOP
  statements
END LOOP;
```

Notice that this is nearly identical to a FOR-IN loop. The EXECUTE keyword tells PL/pgSQL that the following string may change each time the statement is executed. The *query-string* can be an arbitrarily complex expression that evaluates to a string value; of course, it must evaluate to a valid SELECT statement. The following function shows the FOR-IN-EXECUTE loop.

```
 1 CREATE OR REPLACE FUNCTION my_count( VARCHAR ) RETURNS INTEGER AS '
 2   DECLARE
 3     query          ALIAS FOR $1;
 4     count          INTEGER := 0;
 5     my_record      RECORD;
 6   BEGIN
 7     FOR my_record IN EXECUTE query LOOP
 8       count := count + 1;
 9     END LOOP;
10   RETURN count;
11   END;
12 ' LANGUAGE 'plpgsql';
```

EXIT

An EXIT statement (without any operands) terminates the enclosing block, and execution continues at the statement following the end of the block.

The full syntax for the EXIT statement is

```
EXIT [label] [WHEN boolean-expression];
```

All the EXIT statements that you have seen in this chapter have been simple EXIT statements. A simple EXIT statement unconditionally terminates the most closely nested block.

If you include WHEN boolean-expression in an EXIT statement, the EXIT becomes conditional—the EXIT occurs only if boolean-expression evaluates to TRUE. For example:

```
1 FOR i IN 1 .. 12 LOOP
2   balance := customer.customer_balances[i];
3   EXIT WHEN ( balance = 0 );
4   PERFORM check_balance( customer, balance );
5 END LOOP;
6
7 RETURN( 0 );
```

When execution reaches line 3, the WHEN expression is evaluated. If the expression evaluates to TRUE, the loop will be terminated and execution will continue at line 7.

This statement should really be named EXIT...IF. The EXIT...WHEN expression is not evaluated after each statement, as the name might imply.

Labels—EXIT Targets and Name Qualifiers

Now let's turn our attention to the subject of labels. A label is simply a string of the form

```
<<label>>
```

You can include a label prior to any of the following:

- A DECLARE section
- A LOOP
- A WHILE loop
- An integer FOR loop
- A FOR...SELECT loop

A label can perform two distinct functions. First, a label can be referenced in an EXIT statement. For example:

```
1 <<row_loop>>
2 FOR row IN 0 .. 99 LOOP
3
4   <<column_loop>>
5   FOR col in 0 .. 99 LOOP
6
7     IF( process( row, col ) = FALSE ) THEN
8       EXIT row_loop;
9     END IF;
10
11   END LOOP;
12
13 END LOOP;
15
15 RETURN( 0 );
```

Normally, an EXIT statement terminates the most closely nested block (or loop). When you refer to a label in an EXIT statement, you can terminate more than one nested block. When PL/pgSQL executes the EXIT statement at line 8, it will terminate the <<column_loop>> block *and* the <<row_loop>> block. You can't EXIT a block unless it is active: In other words, you can't EXIT a block that has already ended or that has not yet begun.

The second use for a label has to do with variable scoping. Remember that an integer-FOR loop creates a new copy of the iterator variable. If you have already declared the iterator variable outside of the loop, you can't directly access it within the loop. Consider the following example:

```
1 <<func>>
2 DECLARE
3   month_num  INTEGER := 6;
4 BEGIN
5   FOR month_num IN 1 .. 12 LOOP
6     PERFORM compute_monthly_info( month_num );
7   END LOOP;
8 END;
```

Line 2 declares a variable named month_num. When execution reaches line 4, PL/pgSQL will create a second variable named month_num (and this variable will vary between 1 and 12). Within the scope of the new variable (between lines 4 and 6), any reference to month_num will refer to the new variable created at line 4. If you want to refer to the outer variable, you can qualify the name as func.month_num. In general terms, you can refer to any variable in a fully qualified form. If you omit the label qualifier, a variable reference refers to the variable with the shortest lifetime (that is, the most recently created variable).

RETURN

Every PL/pgSQL function must terminate with a RETURN statement. There are two forms for the RETURN statement:

```
RETURN expression;
RETURN;
```

Use the first form when you're writing a PL/pgSQL function that returns a simple value and the second form when you're writing a function returns a SETOF values. If your function returns a SETOF values, you'll use the RETURN NEXT statement (described in the next section) to build up a result set as you go.

When a RETURN statement executes, four things happen:

1. The expression (if any) is evaluated and, if necessary, coerced into the appropriate data type. The RETURN type of a function is declared when you create the function. In the example "CREATE FUNCTION func() RETURNS INTEGER ...", the RETURN type is declared to be an INTEGER. If the RETURN expression does not evaluate to the declared RETURN type, PL/pgSQL will try to convert it to the required type. If you are writing a function that returns a SETOF values, you should omit the expression.

2. The current function terminates. When a function terminates, all code blocks within that function terminate, and all variables declared within that function are destroyed.

3. The return value (obtained by evaluating *expression* or executing some number of RETURN NEXT statements) is returned to the caller. If the caller assigns the return value to a variable, the assignment completes. If the caller uses the return value in an expression, the caller uses the return value to evaluate the expression. If the function was called by a PERFORM statement, the return value is discarded.

4. The point of execution returns to the caller.

If you fail to execute a RETURN statement, you will receive an error (control reaches end of function without RETURN). You can include many RETURN statements in a function, but only one will execute: whichever RETURN statement is reached first.

RETURN NEXT

If you've defined a function that returns a SETOF values, you don't use the RETURN statement to give a value to the caller. Instead, you execute a series of zero or more RETURN NEXT statements. The syntax for a RETURN NEXT statement is

```
RETURN NEXT expression;
```

Each time you execute a RETURN NEXT statement, PL/pgSQL evaluates the *expression* and adds the result to the function's result set. If you are returning a SETOF rows, *expression* must evaluate to a row value. If you are returning a SETOF arrays, each *expression* must evaluate to an array (of the proper type). If you are returning a SETOF simple values, each *expression* must evaluate to a simple value of the appropriate type. If you are returning a SETOF anyarray or anyelement, see the discussion of polymorphic functions later in this chapter.

When you have finished building the result set, simply RETURN from the function. The following example defines a function that returns the monthly balances for a given customer in the form of a SETOF NUMERIC values:

```
CREATE OR REPLACE FUNCTION getBalances( id INTEGER ) RETURNS SETOF NUMERIC AS $$
  DECLARE
    customer    customers%ROWTYPE;
  BEGIN

    SELECT * FROM customers INTO customer WHERE customer_id = id;

    FOR month IN 1..12 LOOP

      IF customer.monthly_balances[month] IS NOT NULL THEN
        RETURN NEXT customer.monthly_balances[month];
      END IF;

    END LOOP;
```

```
    RETURN;

  END;
$$ LANGUAGE 'plpgsql';
```

Notice that this function will execute the RETURN NEXT statement anywhere from 0 to 12 times—that means that the result set built by this function may contain anywhere from 0 to 12 rows. If you don't execute a RETURN NEXT statement, the result set built by the function will be empty.

A function that returns a SETOF values acts like a table. That means that a SETOF function is typically written to the right of the FROM in a SELECT command. For example, to call the getBalances() function you just saw, you would write a query such as the following. (Note: These queries won't work for you unless you've added a monthly_balances array to the customers table):

```
movies=# SELECT customer_id, customer_name, balance, monthly_balances
movies-#   FROM customers;
customer_id |    customer_name     | balance | monthly_balances
------------+----------------------+---------+------------------
          1 | Jones, Henry         |    0.00 |
          4 | Wonderland, Alice N. |    3.00 |
          2 | Rubin, William       |   15.00 |
          3 | Panky, Henry         |    0.00 | {5.00,52.20}
(4 rows)

movies=# SELECT * FROM getBalances( 3 );
getbalances
-------------
        5.00
       52.20
(2 rows)

movies=# SELECT * FROM getBalances( 2 );
getbalances
-------------
(0 rows)
```

Notice that the first call to getBalances(3) returned two rows because there are two entries in the monthly_balances column for customer number 3. The second call returned zero rows.

PERFORM

A function written in PL/pgSQL can contain SQL commands intermingled with PL/pgSQL-specific statements. Remember, a SQL command is something like CREATE TABLE, INSERT, UPDATE, and so on; whereas PL/pgSQL adds procedural statements such as IF, RETURN, or WHILE. If you want to create a new table within a PL/pgSQL function, you can just include a CREATE TABLE command in the code:

```
CREATE FUNCTION process_month_end( ) RETURNS BOOLEAN AS '
  BEGIN
    ...
    CREATE TABLE temp_data ( ... );
    ...
    DROP TABLE temp_data;
    ...
  END;
' LANGUAGE 'plpgsql';
```

You can include *almost* any SQL command just by writing the command inline. The exception is the SELECT command. A SELECT command retrieves data from the server. If you want to execute a SELECT command in a PL/pgSQL function, you normally provide variables to hold the results:

```
DECLARE
  Customer    customers%ROWTYPE;
BEGIN
  ...
  SELECT INTO customer * FROM customers WHERE( customer_id = 1 );
  --
  -- The customer variable will now hold the results of the query
  --
  ...
END;
```

On rare occasions, you may need to execute a SELECT statement, but you want to ignore the data returned by the query. Most likely, the SELECT statement that you want to execute will have some side effect, such as executing a function. You can use the PERFORM statement to execute an arbitrary SELECT command without using the results. For example:

```
...
  PERFORM SELECT my_function( rentals ) FROM rentals;
...
```

You can also use PERFORM to evaluate an arbitrary expression, again discarding the results:

```
...
  PERFORM record_timestamp( timeofday() );
...
```

EXECUTE

The EXECUTE statement is similar to the PERFORM statement. Although the PERFORM statement evaluates a SQL expression and discards the results, the EXECUTE statement executes a *dynamic* SQL command, and then discards the results. The difference is subtle but important. When the PL/pgSQL processor compiles a PERFORM expression statement, the query plan required to evaluate the expression is generated and stored along with the function. This means that expression must be known at the time you write your function. The EXECUTE statement, on the other hand, executes a SQL statement that is *not* known at the time you write your function. You may, for example, construct the text of a SQL statement within your function, or you might accept a string value from the caller and then execute that string.

Here is a function that uses the EXECUTE command to time the execution of a SQL command:

```
1 CREATE FUNCTION time_command( VARCHAR ) RETURNS INTERVAL AS '
2  DECLARE
3    beg_time   TIMESTAMP;
4    end_time   TIMESTAMP;
5  BEGIN
6
7    beg_time := timeofday( );
8    EXECUTE $1;
9    end_time := timeofday( );
10
11   RETURN( end_time - beg_time );
12  END;
13 ' LANGUAGE 'plpgsql';
```

You would call the time_command() function like this:

```
movies=# SELECT time_command( 'SELECT * FROM rentals' );
time_command
--------------
 00:00:00.82
(1 row)
```

With the EXECUTE statement, you can execute any SQL command (including calls to PL/pgSQL functions) and the results will be discarded, except for the side effects.

GET DIAGNOSTICS

PL/pgSQL provides a catch-all statement that gives you access to various pieces of result information: GET DIAGNOSTICS. Using GET DIAGNOSTICS, you can retrieve a count of the rows affected by the most recent UPDATE or DELETE command and the object-ID of the most recently inserted row. The syntax for the GET DIAGNOSTICS statement is

```
GET DIAGNOSTICS variable = [ROW_COUNT|RESULT_OID], ...;
```

ROW_COUNT is meaningless until you have executed an UPDATE or DELETE command. Likewise, RESULT_OID is meaningless until you execute an INSERT command.

Error Handling

PostgreSQL version 8.0 introduced a new error-handling scheme to PL/pgSQL. Prior to version 8.0, any error that occurred during a PL/pgSQL function would abort the function and the transaction that called the function. Beginning with version 8.0, you can intercept error conditions (PL/pgSQL calls them *exceptions*) and handle them gracefully.

To trap an exception, include an EXCEPTION section just before the END of a block. The syntax for an EXCEPTION section is

```
EXCEPTION
  WHEN condition [OR condition...] THEN
      statements
  [ WHEN condition [OR condition...] THEN
      statements
      ...
    ]
```

The condition is derived from the error descriptions listed in Appendix A of the PostgreSQL reference documentation. Table 7.1 shows an excerpt from Appendix A. To convert one of these errors into a condition, just find the error code that you want to trap and write the error description, replacing each space with an underscore.

Table 7.1   **Sample PostgreSQL Error Codes**

Error Code	Description
Class 08	Connection Exception
08000	CONNECTION EXCEPTION
08003	CONNECTION DOES NOT EXIST
08006	CONNECTION FAILURE
08001	SQLCLIENT UNABLE TO ESTABLISH SQLCONNECTION
08004	SQLSERVER REJECTED ESTABLISHMENT OF SQLCONNECTION
08007	TRANSACTION RESOLUTION UNKNOWN
08P01	PROTOCOL VIOLATION

For example, to trap error 08006, you would write an EXCEPTION section like this:

```
BEGIN
  ...
EXCEPTION
    WHEN connection_failure THEN
        RAISE ERROR 'Connection To Server Lost';
  END;
```

If any of the statements between BEGIN and EXCEPTION throws a connection_failure error, PL/pgSQL immediately jumps to the first statement in the exception handler (in this case, the RAISE ERROR statement), bypassing the rest of the statements in the block.

You can't trap every condition listed in Appendix A; in particular, you can't trap successful_completion, any of the conditions listed in the WARNING category, or any of the conditions listed in the NO DATA category.

You can trap a whole category of error conditions by writing an EXCEPTION handler for that category. You can distinguish between errors and categories by looking at the last digit of the error code. If the last digit is a 0, you're looking at a category. To trap any of the errors in the connection_exception class, just write an EXCEPTION section like this:

```
BEGIN
    ...
EXCEPTION
    WHEN connection_exception THEN
        RAISE ERROR 'Something went wrong with the server connection';
    END;
```

That sequence is equivalent to:

```
BEGIN
    ...
EXCEPTION
    WHEN
        connection_does_not_exist OR
        connection_failure OR
        sql_client_unable_to_establish_sql_connection OR
        sql_server_rejected_establishment_of_sql_connection OR
        transaction_resolution_unkown OR
        protocol_violation
    RAISE ERROR 'Something went wrong with the server connection';
    END;
```

PL/pgSQL defines a catch-all condition, named others, that you can use to trap any exceptions not trapped by another handler.

A single exception may match multiple exception handlers. For example, consider the following EXCEPTION section:

```
BEGIN
    ...
EXCEPTION
    WHEN connection_failure THEN
        RAISE ERROR 'Connection Lost;
    WHEN connection_exception THEN
        RAISE ERROR 'Something went wrong with the server connection';
    WHEN others THEN
        RAISE ERROR 'Something broke';
    END;
```

If a connection_failure occurs, all three handlers match the exception: The connection_failure handler matches exactly; the connection_exception handler matches because a connection_failure is a member of the connection_exception category; and the others handler matches because others will match any exception. Which handler executes? The first one that matches. That means that you should always list the handlers from most-specific to most-general. If you were to write the others handler first, the connection_failure and connection_exception handlers could never execute.

Remember that you can nest blocks within a single PL/pgSQL function. Each block can have its own EXCEPTION section. When an exception occurs, PL/pgSQL searches through the currently active blocks to find a handler for that exception. If the first (most deeply nested) block hasn't defined a handler for the exception, PL/pgSQL aborts the first block and looks at the surrounding block. If that block hasn't defined a handler for the exception, PL/pgSQL aborts the second block as well and continues to the next block. If PL/pgSQL can't find a handler, it aborts the entire function and reports the exception to the caller of the function.

When a PL/pgSQL function enters a block that includes an EXCEPTION section, it creates a "subtransaction" by executing the internal equivalent of a SAVEPOINT command. If you have one block nested within another (and each block defines exception handlers), you have two subtransactions, one nested within the other. If an exception occurs, PL/pgSQL rolls back nested subtransactions as it searches for an exception handler. When PL/pgSQL finds an exception handler, it executes the handler and rolls back that subtransaction as well. Consider the following code snippet:

```
...
FOR tape IN SELECT * FROM tapes LOOP
  BEGIN

    update_tape( tape );

    FOR rental IN SELECT * FROM rentals WHERE rentals.tape_id = tape.tape_id LOOP

      BEGIN

        update_rental_1( rental );
        update_rental_2( rental );

      EXCEPTION
        WHEN insufficient_privilege THEN
          RAISE NOTICE 'Privilege denied';
      END;

    END LOOP;
  EXCEPTION
    WHEN others THEN
      RAISE NOTICE 'Unable to process all tapes';
  END;
END LOOP;
...
```

This snippet contains two loops, one nested within the other. The outer loop reads through the tapes table and, for each tape, calls a function named update_tape() (presumably another PL/pgSQL function). The inner loop reads each rentals record for the current tape and calls two functions with each rental.

Every time the PL/pgSQL interpreter executes the first BEGIN statement, it creates a new subtransaction which we'll call T_{outer}. Likewise, every time PL/pgSQL executes the second BEGIN statement, it creates a new subtransaction, T_{inner}, nested within T_{outer}. Now consider what happens when an exception occurs.

If the update_rental_2() function throws an exception, PL/pgSQL aborts T_{inner} (rolling back any changes made by update_rental_1() and update_rental_2()) and then searches for a handler that matches the exception. If update_rental_2() throws an insufficient_privilege exception, PL/pgSQL finds the inner-most exception handler, jumps to the first RAISE NOTICE statement, and then moves on to the statement following the inner-most block. If update_rental_2() throws any other exception, PL/pgSQL ignores the inner-most exception handler (because it doesn't match the exception), aborts T_{outer} (rolling back any changes made by update_tape(), update_rental_1(), and update_rental_2()), jumps to the second RAISE NOTICE statement, and moves on to the statement following the outer-most block.

If the update_tape() function throws an exception, PL/pgSQL aborts T_{outer} (rolling back any changes made by update_tape()), jumps to the second RAISE NOTICE statement, and then moves on to the statement following the outer-most block.

Notice that an exception *always* aborts the inner-most subtransaction. PL/pgSQL will continue aborting nested subtransactions until it finds a handler for the exception. If no handler is found, the entire transaction is aborted. By using nested subtransactions (and nested exception handlers) in this way, the inner subtransaction contains all of the updates for a single rental. If the inner subtransaction aborts, only those changes made to the current rental are rolled back. The outer subtransaction contains all of the updates for a single tape (including all of the updates for all rentals of that tape). If you abort the outer subtransaction all changes made to the tape are rolled back and all changes made to the rentals of that tape are rolled back as well.

RAISE

Even though PL/pgSQL doesn't offer a way to intercept errors, it does provide a way to generate an error: the RAISE statement. Exceptions are usually generated when an error occurs while executing an SQL (or PL/pgSQL) statement, but you can *explicitly* raise an exception using the RAISE statement. The syntax for a RAISE statement is

```
RAISE severity 'message' [, variable [...]];
```

The severity determines how far the error message will go and whether the error should abort the current transaction.

Valid values for severity are

- DEBUG—The message is written to the server's log file and otherwise ignored. The function runs to completion, and the current transaction is not affected.

- NOTICE—The message is written to the server's log file and sent to the client application. The function runs to completion, and the current transaction is not affected.

- EXCEPTION—The message is written to the server's log file and PL/pgSQL throws a raise_exception exception that you can trap with an EXCEPTION handler as described in the previous section.

The message string must be a literal value—you can't use a PL/pgSQL variable in this slot, and you cannot include a more complex expression. If you need to include variable information in the error message, you can sneak it into the message by including a % character wherever you want the variable value to appear. For example:

```
rentals.tape_id := ''AH-54706'';
RAISE DEBUG ''tape_id = %'', rentals.tape_id;
```

When these statements are executed, the message tape_id = AH-54706 will be written to the server's log file. For each (single) % character in the message string, you must include a variable. If you want to include a literal percent character in the message, write it as %%. For example:

```
percentage := 20;
RAISE NOTICE ''Top (%)%%'', percentage;
```

translates to Top (20)%.

The RAISE statement is useful for debugging your PL/pgSQL code; it's even better for debugging someone else's code. I find that the DEBUG severity is perfect for leaving evidence in the server log. When you ship a PL/pgSQL function to your users, you might want to leave a few RAISE DEBUG statements in your code. This can certainly make it easier to track down an elusive bug (remember, users *never* write down error messages, so you might as well arrange for the messages to appear in a log file). I use the RAISE NOTICE statement for interactive debugging. When I am first building a new PL/pgSQL function, the chances are *very* slim that I'll get it right the first time. (Funny, it doesn't seem to matter how trivial or complex the function is.) I start out by littering my code with RAISE NOTICE statements; I'll usually print the value of each function parameter as well as key information from each record that I SELECT. As it becomes clearer that my code is working, I'll either remove or comment out (using "--") the RAISE NOTICE statements. Before I send out my code to a victim, er, user, I'll find strategic places where I can leave RAISE DEBUG statements. The RAISE DEBUG statement is perfect for reporting things that should never happen. For example, because of the referential integrity that I built into the tapes, customers, and rentals tables, I should never find a rentals record that refers to a nonexistent customer. I'll check for that condition (a missing customer) and report the error with a RAISE DEBUG statement. Of course, in some circumstances, a missing customer should really trigger a RAISE EXCEPTION—if I just happen to notice the problem in passing and it really doesn't affect the current function, I'll just note it with a RAISE DEBUG. So, the rule I follow is: if the condition prevents further processing, I RAISE an EXCEPTION; if the condition should never happen, I RAISE a DEBUG message; if I am still developing my code, I RAISE a NOTICE.

Cursors

Direct cursor support is new in PL/pgSQL version 7.2. Processing a result set using a cursor is similar to processing a result set using a FOR loop, but cursors offer a few distinct advantages that you'll see in a moment.

You can think of a cursor as a name for a result set. You must declare a cursor variable just as you declare any other variable. The following code snippet shows how you might declare a cursor variable:

```
...
DECLARE
  rental_cursor      CURSOR FOR SELECT * FROM rentals;
...
```

rental_cursor is declared to be a cursor for the result set of the query SELECT * FROM rentals. When you declare a variable of type CURSOR, you must include a query. The cursor variable is said to be *bound* to this query, and the variable is a *bound* cursor variable.

Before you can use a bound cursor, you must open the cursor using the OPEN statement:

```
...
DECLARE
  rental_cursor      CURSOR FOR SELECT * FROM rentals;
BEGIN

    OPEN rental_cursor;

...
```

If you try to OPEN a cursor that is already open, you will receive an error message (cursor "name" already in use). If you try to FETCH (see the section that follows) from a cursor that has not been opened, you'll receive an error message (cursor "name" is invalid). When you use a cursor, you first DECLARE it, then OPEN it, FETCH from it, and finally CLOSE it, in that order. You can repeat the OPEN, FETCH, CLOSE cycle if you want to process the cursor results again.

FETCH

After a bound cursor has been opened, you can retrieve the result set (one row at a time) using the FETCH statement. When you fetch a row from a cursor, you have to provide one or more destination variables that PL/pgSQL can stuff the results into. The syntax for the FETCH statement is

```
FETCH cursor-name INTO destination [ , destination [...]];
```

The destination (or destinations) must match the shape of a row returned by the cursor. For example, if the cursor SELECTs a row from the rentals table, there are three possible destinations:

- A variable of type rentals%ROWTYPE
- Three variables: one of type rentals.tape_id%TYPE, one of type rentals.customer_id%TYPE, and the last of type rentals.rental_date%TYPE
- A variable of type RECORD

Let's look at each of these destination types in more detail.

When you FETCH into a variable of some %ROWTYPE, you can refer to the individual columns using the usual variable.column notation. For example:

```
...
DECLARE
  rental_cursor        CURSOR FOR SELECT * FROM rentals;
  rental               rentals%ROWTYPE;
BEGIN

  OPEN rental_cursor;

  FETCH rental_cursor INTO rental;
  --
  -- I can now access rental.tape_id,
  -- rental.customer_id, and rental.rental_date
  --
  IF ( overdue( rental.rental_date )) THEN
     ...
```

Next, I can FETCH into a comma-separated list of variables. In the previous example, the rental_cursor cursor will return rows that each contain three columns. Rather than fetching into a %ROWTYPE variable, I can declare three separate variables (of the appropriate types) and FETCH into those instead:

```
...
DECLARE
  rental_cursor        CURSOR FOR SELECT * FROM rentals;
  tape_id              rentals.tape_id%TYPE;
  customer_id          rentals.customer_id%TYPE;
  rental_date          rentals.rental_date%TYPE;
BEGIN

  OPEN rental_cursor;

  FETCH rental_cursor INTO tape_id, customer_id, rental_date;

  IF ( overdue( rental_date )) THEN
     ...
```

You are not required to use variables declared with %TYPE, but this is the perfect place to do so. At the time you create a function, you usually know which columns you will be interested in, and declaring variables with %TYPE will make your functions much less fragile in cases where the referenced column types might change.

You *cannot* combine composite variables and scalar variables in the same FETCH statement[5]:

[5] This seems like a bug to me. You may be able to combine composite and scalar variables in a future release.

```
...
DECLARE
  rental_cursor  CURSOR FOR SELECT *, now() - rental_date FROM rentals;
  rental         rentals%ROWTYPE;
  elapsed        INTERVAL;
  BEGIN

  OPEN rental_cursor;

  FETCH rental_cursor INTO rental, elapsed;  -- WRONG! Can't combine
                                             -- composite and scalar
                                             -- variables in the same
                                             -- FETCH

  IF ( overdue( rental.rental_date )) THEN
    ...
```

The third type of destination that you can use with a FETCH statement is a variable of
type RECORD. You may recall from earlier in this chapter that a RECORD variable is something of a chameleon—it adjusts to whatever kind of data that you put into it. For
example, the following snippet uses the same RECORD variable to hold two differently
shaped rows:

```
...
DECLARE
  rental_cursor   CURSOR FOR SELECT * FROM rentals;
  customer_cursor CURSOR FOR SELECT * FROM customers;
  my_data         RECORD;
BEGIN
  OPEN rental_cursor;
  OPEN customer_cursor;

  FETCH rental_cursor INTO my_data;
  --  I can now refer to:
  --      my_data.tape_id
  --      my_data.customer_id
  --      my_data.rental_date

  FETCH customer_cursor INTO my_data;
  --  Now I can refer to:
  --      my_data.customer_id
  --      my_data.customer_name
  --      my_data.phone
  --      my_data.birth_date
  --      my_data.balance
...
```

After you have executed a FETCH statement, how do you know whether a row was actually retrieved? If you FETCH after retrieving the entire result, no error occurs. Instead, each PL/pgSQL function has an automatically declared variable named FOUND. FOUND is a BOOLEAN variable that is set by the PL/pgSQL interpreter to indicate various kinds of state information. Table 7.2 lists the points in time where PL/pgSQL sets the FOUND variable and the corresponding values.

Table 7.2   FOUND **Events and Values**

Event	Value
Start of each function	FALSE
Start of an integer—FOR loop	FALSE
Within an integer—FOR loop	TRUE
Start of a FOR...SELECT loop	FALSE
Within a FOR...SELECT loop	TRUE
Before SELECT INTO statement	FALSE
After SELECT INTO statement	TRUE (if rows are returned)
Before FETCH statement	FALSE
After FETCH statement	TRUE (if a row is returned)

So, you can see that FOUND is set to TRUE if a FETCH statement returns a row. Let's see how to put all the cursor related statements together into a single PL/pgSQL function:

```
...
DECLARE
  next_rental  CURSOR FOR SELECT * FROM rentals;
  rental       rentals%ROWTYPE;
BEGIN
  OPEN next_rental;

  LOOP
    FETCH next_rental INTO rental;
    EXIT WHEN NOT FOUND;
    PERFORM process_rental( rental );
  END LOOP;

  CLOSE next_rental;
END;
...
```

The first thing you do in this code snippet is OPEN the cursor. Next, you enter a LOOP that will process every row returned from the cursor. Inside of the LOOP, you FETCH a single record, EXIT the loop if the cursor is exhausted, and call another function (process_rental())if not. After the loop terminates, close the cursor using the CLOSE statement.

So far, it looks like a cursor loop is pretty much the same as a FOR-IN-SELECT loop. What else can you do with a cursor?

Parameterized Cursors

You've seen that you must provide a SELECT statement when you declare a CURSOR. Quite often, you'll find that you don't know the exact values involved in the query at the time you're writing a function. You can declare a *parameterized* cursor to solve this problem.

A parameterized cursor is similar in concept to a parameterized function. When you define a function, you can declare a set of parameters (these are called the *formal* parameters, or *formal arguments*); those parameters can be used within the function to change the results of the function. If you define a function without parameters, the function will always return the same results (unless influenced by global, external data). Each language imposes restrictions on where you can use a parameter within a function. In general, function parameters can be used anywhere that a value-yielding expression can be used. When you make a call to a parameterized function, you provide a value for each parameter: The values that you provide (these are called the *actual* parameters, or *actual arguments*) are substituted inside of the function wherever the formal parameters appear.

When you define a cursor, you can declare a set of formal parameters; those parameters can be used with the cursor to change the result set of the query. If you define a cursor without parameters, the query will always return the same result set, unless influenced by external data. PL/pgSQL restricts the places that you can use a parameter within a cursor definition. A cursor parameter can be used anywhere that a value-yielding expression can be used. When you open a cursor, you must specify values for each formal parameter. The actual parameters are substituted inside of the cursor wherever the formal parameters appear.

Let's look at an example:

```
1  ...
2 DECLARE
3    next_customer    CURSOR (ID INTEGER) FOR
4                        SELECT * FROM customers WHERE
5                        customer_id = ID;
6    customer         customers%ROWTYPE;
7    target_customer  ALIAS FOR $1;
8 BEGIN
9
10   OPEN next_customer( target_customer );
11 ...
```

Lines 3, 4, and 5 declare a parameterized cursor. This cursor has a single formal parameter; an INTEGER named ID. Notice (at the end of line 5), that I have used the formal parameter within the cursor definition. When I open this cursor, I'll provide an INTEGER value for the ID parameter. The actual parameter that I provide will be substituted into the query wherever the formal parameter is used. So, if `target_customer` is equal to, say, 42, the cursor opened at line 10 will read:

```
SELECT * FROM customers WHERE customer_id = 42;
```

The full syntax for a cursor declaration is

```
variable-name CURSOR
    [ (param-name param-type [, param-name param-type ...] ) ]
  FOR select-query;
```

The full syntax for an OPEN statement is

```
OPEN cursor-name [ ( actual-param-value [, actual-param-value...] ) ];
```

You would parameterize a cursor for the same reasons that you would parameterize a function: you want the results to depend on the actual arguments. When you parameterize a cursor, you are also making the cursor more reusable. For example, I might want to process all the rentals in my inventory, but I want to process the rentals one customer at a time. If I don't use a parameterized cursor, I have to declare one cursor for each of my customers (and I have to know the set of customers at the time I write the function). Using a parameterized cursor, I can declare the cursor once and provide different actual arguments each time I open the cursor:

```
1  CREATE OR REPLACE FUNCTION process_rentals_by_customer( ) RETURNS void AS $$
2    DECLARE
3      next_customer     CURSOR FOR SELECT * FROM customers;
4      next_rental       CURSOR( ID integer ) FOR
5                          SELECT * FROM rentals WHERE customer_id = ID;
6      customer          customers%ROWTYPE;
7      rental            rentals%ROWTYPE;
8    BEGIN
9
10     OPEN next_customer;
11
12     LOOP
13       FETCH next_customer INTO customer;
14         EXIT WHEN NOT FOUND;
15
16       OPEN next_rental( customer.customer_id );
17
18       LOOP
19         FETCH next_rental INTO rental;
20           EXIT WHEN NOT FOUND;
21
22         PERFORM process_rental( customer, rental );
23
24       END LOOP;
25
26       CLOSE next_rental;
```

```
27     END LOOP;
28
29     CLOSE next_customer;
30
31     RETURN;
32
33   END;
34
35 $$ LANGUAGE 'plpgsql';
```

Notice that you can OPEN and CLOSE a cursor as often as you like. A cursor must be closed before it can be opened. Each time you open a parameterized cursor, you can provide new actual parameters.

Cursor References

Now, let's turn our attention to another aspect of cursor support in PL/pgSQL—cursor references.

When you declare a CURSOR variable, you provide a SELECT statement that is bound to the cursor. You can't change the text of the query after the cursor has been declared. Of course, you can parameterize the query to change the results, but the shape of the query remains the same: If the query returns rows from the tapes table, it will always return rows from the tapes table.

Instead of declaring a CURSOR, you can declare a variable to be of type REFCURSOR. A REFCURSOR is not actually a cursor, but a *reference* to a cursor. The syntax for declaring a REFCURSOR is

```
DECLARE
  ref-name REFCURSOR;
  ...
```

Notice that you do *not* specify a query when creating a REFCURSOR. Instead, a cursor is bound to a REFCURSOR at runtime. Here is a simple example:

```
 1 ...
 2 DECLARE
 3   next_rental CURSOR FOR SELECT * FROM rentals;
 4   next_tape   CURSOR FOR SELECT * FROM tapes;
 5   rental      rentals%ROWTYPE;
 6   tape        tape%ROWTYPE;
 7   next_row    REFCURSOR;
 8 BEGIN
 9   OPEN next_rental;
10   next_row := next_rental;
11   FETCH next_rental INTO rental;
12   FETCH next_row INTO rental;
13   CLOSE next_rental;
14
```

```
15    next_row := next_tape;
16    OPEN next_tape;
17    FETCH next_row  INTO tape;
18    CLOSE next_row;
19 ...
```

In this block, I've declared two cursors and one cursor reference. One of the cursors returns rows from the `rentals` table, and the other returns rows from the `tapes` table.

At line 9, the `next_rental` cursor opens. At line 10, I give a value to the `next_row` cursor reference. We now have two ways to access the `next_rental` cursor: through the `next_rental` cursor variable and through the `next_row` cursor reference. At this point, `next_row` *refers to* the `next_rental` cursor. You can see (at lines 11 and 12) that you can FETCH a row using either variable. Both FETCH statements return a row from the `rentals` table.

At line 14, the `next_row` cursor reference points to a different cursor. Now, when you FETCH from `next_row`, you'll get a row from the `tapes` table. Notice that you can point `next_row` to a cursor that has not yet been opened. You can CLOSE a cursor using a cursor reference, but you can't OPEN a cursor using a cursor reference.

Actually, you *can* open a cursor using a REFCURSOR; you just can't open a *named* cursor. When you declare a CURSOR variable, you are really creating a PostgreSQL cursor whose name is the same as the name of the variable. In the previous example, you created one cursor (not just a cursor variable) named `next_rental` and a cursor named `next_tape`. PL/pgSQL allows you to create anonymous cursors using REFCURSOR variables. An anonymous cursor is a cursor that doesn't have a name[6]. You create an anonymous cursor using the OPEN statement, a REFCURSOR, and a SELECT statement:

```
1 ...
```

```
2 DECLARE
3    next_row REFCURSOR;
4 BEGIN
5    OPEN next_row FOR SELECT * FROM customers;
6 ...
```

At line 5, you are creating an anonymous cursor and binding it to the `next_row` cursor reference. After an anonymous cursor has been opened, you can treat it like any other cursor. You can FETCH from it, CLOSE it, and lose it. That last part might sound a little fishy, so let me explain further. Take a close look at the following code fragment:

```
1 CREATE FUNCTION leak_cursors( INTEGER ) RETURNS INTEGER AS '
2    DECLARE
3    next_customer CURSOR FOR SELECT * FROM customers;
4      next_rental  REFCURSOR;
5      customer        customers%ROWTYPE;
```

---

[6] An anonymous cursor does in fact have a name, but PostgreSQL constructs the name, and it isn't very reader-friendly. An anonymous cursor has a name such as `<unnamed cursor 42>`.

```
 6     rental          rentals%ROWTYPE;
 7     count           INTEGER := 0;
 8   BEGIN
 9
10     OPEN next_customer;
11
12     LOOP
13     FETCH next_customer INTO customer;
14     EXIT WHEN NOT FOUND;
15     OPEN next_rental FOR
16       SELECT * FROM rentals
17         WHERE rentals.customer_id = customer.customer_id;
18
19     LOOP
20     FETCH next_rental INTO rental;
21     EXIT WHEN NOT FOUND;
22
23     RAISE NOTICE ''customer_id = %, rental_date = %'',
24          customer.customer_id, rental.rental_date;
25
26      count := count + 1;
27     END LOOP;
28
29     next_rental := NULL;
30
31   END LOOP;
32     CLOSE next_customer;
33     RETURN( count );
34   END;
35 ' LANGUAGE 'plpgsql';
```

This function contains two loops: an outer loop that reads through the customers table and an inner loop that reads each rental for a given customer. The next_customer cursor is opened (at line 10) before the outer loop begins. The next_rental cursor is bound and opened (at lines 15, 16, and 17) just before the inner loop begins. After the inner loop completes, I set the next_rental cursor reference to NULL and continue with the outer loop. What happens to the cursor that was bound to next_rental? I didn't explicitly close the cursor, so it must remain open. After executing the assignment statement at line 29, I have no way to access the cursor again—remember, it's an anonymous cursor, so I can't refer to it by name. This situation is called a *resource leak*. A resource leak occurs when you create an object (in this case, a cursor) and then you lose all references to that object. If you can't find the object again, you can't free the resource. Avoid resource leaks; they're nasty and can cause performance problems. Resource leaks will also cause your code to fail if you run out of a resource (such as memory space). We can avoid the resource leak shown in this example by closing the next_rental before setting it to NULL.

You've seen what *not* to do with a cursor reference, but let's see what cursor references are really good for. The nice thing about a cursor reference is that you can pass the reference to another function, or you can return a reference to the caller. These are powerful features. By sharing cursor references between functions, you can factor your PL/pgSQL code into reusable pieces.

One of the more effective ways to use cursor references is to separate the code that processes a cursor from the code that creates the cursor. For example, you may find that we need a function to compute the total amount of money that we have received from a given customer over a given period of time. I might start by creating a single function that constructs a cursor and processes each row in that cursor:

```
. . .
  OPEN next_rental FOR
    SELECT * FROM rentals WHERE
      customer_id = $1 AND
      rental_date BETWEEN $2 AND $3;

  LOOP
    FETCH next_rental INTO rental
    -- accumulate rental values here
    . . .
```

This is a good start, but it works only for a single set of conditions: a given customer and a given pair of dates. Instead, you can factor this one function into three separate functions.

The first function creates a cursor that, when opened, will return all `rentals` records for a given customer within a given period; the cursor is returned to the caller:

```
CREATE FUNCTION
select_rentals_by_customer_interval( INTEGER, DATE, DATE )
 RETURNS REFCURSOR AS '
  DECLARE
    next_rental  REFCURSOR;
  BEGIN
    OPEN next_rental FOR
      SELECT * FROM RENTALS WHERE
        customer_id = $1 AND
        rental_date BETWEEN $2 AND $3;
    RETURN( next_rental );
  END;
' LANGUAGE 'plpgsql';
```

The second function, given a cursor that returns `rentals` records, computes the total value of the `rentals` accessible through that cursor:

```
CREATE FUNCTION
compute_rental_value( REFCURSOR )
 RETURNS NUMERIC AS '
  DECLARE
    total        NUMERIC(7,2) := 0;
```

```
  rental       rentals%ROWTYPE;
  next_rental ALIAS FOR $1;
BEGIN
  LOOP
    FETCH next_rental INTO rental;
    EXIT WHEN NOT FOUND;
    -- accumulate rental values here
    --
    -- pretend that this is a complex
    -- task which requires loads of amazingly
    -- clever code
    ...
  END LOOP;
  RETURN( total );
END;
' LANGUAGE 'plpgsql';
```

The last function invokes the first two:

```
CREATE FUNCTION
compute_value_by_customer_interval( INTEGER, DATE, DATE )
RETURNS NUMERIC AS '
  DECLARE
    curs  REFCURSOR;
    total NUMERIC(7,2);
  BEGIN
    curs  := select_rentals_by_customer_interval( $1, $2, $3 );
    total := compute_rental_value( curs );
    CLOSE curs;
    RETURN( total );
  END;
' LANGUAGE 'plpgsql';
```

The advantage to this approach is that you can construct a cursor using *different* selection criteria and call compute_total_value(). For example, you might want to compute the total values of all rentals of a given tape:

```
CREATE FUNCTION compute_tape_value( VARCHAR )
RETURNS NUMERIC AS '
  DECLARE
    curs  REFCURSOR;
    total NUMERIC(7,2);
  BEGIN
    OPEN curs FOR SELECT * FROM rentals WHERE tape_id = $1;
    total := compute_rental_value( curs );
    CLOSE curs;
    RETURN( total );
  END;
' LANGUAGE 'plpgsql';
```

Triggers

So far, all the functions that defined in this chapter have been called explicitly, either by using a SELECT function() command or by using the function within an expression. You can also call certain PL/pgSQL functions automatically. A *trigger* is a function that is called whenever a specific event occurs in a given table. An INSERT command, an UPDATE command, or a DELETE command can cause a trigger to execute.

Let's look at a simple example. You currently have a customers table defined like this:

```
CREATE TABLE customers
(
        customer_id     integer primary key,
        customer_name   character varying(50) not null,
        phone           character(8),
        birth_date      date,
        balance         decimal(7,2)
);
```

You want to create a new table that you can use to archive any rows that are deleted from the customers table. You also want to archive any updates to the customers table. Name this table customer_archive:

```
CREATE TABLE customer_archive
(
    customer_id     integer,
    customer_name   character varying(50) not null,
    phone           character(8),
    birth_date      date,
    balance         decimal(7,2),
    user_changed    varchar,
    date_changed    date,
    operation       varchar
);
```

Each row in the customer_archive table contains a complete customers record plus a few pieces of information about the modification that took place.

Now, let's create a trigger function that executes whenever a change is made to a row in the customers table. A trigger function is a function that takes no arguments and returns a special data type—TRIGGER. (I'll talk more about the information returned by a trigger in a moment.)

```
CREATE FUNCTION archive_customer() RETURNS TRIGGER AS '
  BEGIN
    INSERT INTO customer_archive
      VALUES
      (
        OLD.customer_id,
        OLD.customer_name,
        OLD.phone,
```

```
        OLD.birth_date,
        OLD.balance,
        CURRENT_USER,
        now(),
                TG_OP
        );
    RETURN NULL;
  END;
' LANGUAGE 'plpgsql';
```

Notice that I am using a variable in this function that I have not declared: OLD. Trigger functions have access to several predefined variables that make it easier to find information about the context in which the trigger event occurred. The OLD variable contains a copy of the original row when a trigger is executed because of an UPDATE or DELETE command. The NEW variable contains a copy of the new row when a trigger is executed for an UPDATE or INSERT command.

When this trigger executes, it creates a new row in the customer_archive() table. The new row will contain a copy of the original customers row, the name of the user making the modification, the date that the modification was made, and the type of operation: TG_OP will be set to 'UPDATE', 'INSERT', or 'DELETE'.

Table 7.3 contains a complete list of the predefined variables that you can use inside of a trigger function:

Table 7.3   **Predefined Trigger Variables**

Name	Type	Description
NEW	%ROWTYPE	New values (for UPDATE and INSERT)
OLD	%ROWTYPE	Old values (for UPDATE and DELETE)
TG_NAME	name	Name of trigger
TG_WHEN	text	BEFORE or AFTER
TG_LEVEL	text	ROW or STATEMENT
TG_OP	text	INSERT, UPDATE, or DELETE
TG_RELID	oid	Object ID of trigger table
TG_RELNAME	name	Name of trigger table
TG_NARGS	integer	Count of the optional arguments given to the CREATE TRIGGER command
TG_ARGV[]	text[]	Optional arguments given to the CREATE TRIGGER command

Now that you have created a function, you have to define it as a trigger function. The CREATE TRIGGER command associates a function with an event (or events) in a given table. Here is the command that you use for the archive_customer() function:

```
1 CREATE TRIGGER archive_customer
2   AFTER DELETE OR UPDATE
3   ON customers
4   FOR EACH ROW
5     EXECUTE PROCEDURE archive_customer();
```

This is a rather unwieldy command, so let's look at it one line at a time.

The first line tells PostgreSQL that you want to create a new trigger—each trigger has a name—in this case, `archive_customer`. Trigger names must be unique within each table (in other words, I can have two triggers named `foo` as long as the triggers are defined for two different tables). Inside the trigger function, the `TG_NAME` variable holds the name of the trigger.

Line 2 specifies the event (or events) that cause this trigger to fire. In this case, I want the trigger to occur `AFTER` a `DELETE` command or an `UPDATE` command. Altogether, PostgreSQL can fire a trigger `BEFORE` or `AFTER` an `UPDATE` command, an `INSERT` command, or a `DELETE` command. In the trigger function, `TG_WHEN` is set to either `BEFORE` or `AFTER`, and `TG_OP` is set to `INSERT`, `UPDATE`, or `DELETE`.

Line 3 associates this trigger with a specific table. This is not an optional clause; each trigger must be associated with a specific table. You can't, for example, define a trigger that will execute on every `INSERT` statement regardless of the table involved. You can use the `TG_RELNAME` variable in the trigger function to find the name of the associated table. `TG_RELOID` holds the object-ID (`OID`) of the table.

A single `DELETE` or `UPDATE` statement can affect multiple rows. The `FOR EACH` clause determines whether a trigger will execute once for each row or once for the entire statement. PostgreSQL supports statement-level triggers starting with release 7.4—prior to release 7.4, the only choice is `FOR EACH ROW`. Inside of the trigger function, `TG_LEVEL` can contain either `ROW` or `STATEMENT`.

Line 5 finally gets around to telling PostgreSQL which function you actually want to execute when the specified events occur.

The full syntax for the `CREATE TRIGGER` command is

```
CREATE TRIGGER trigger-name
  [BEFORE | AFTER] [ INSERT | DELETE | UPDATE [OR ...]]
    ON table-name FOR EACH ROW
    EXECUTE PROCEDURE function-name [(args)];
```

TRIGGER Return Values

A trigger function can return a value just like any other function, but the value that you return can have far-reaching consequences. If you return `NULL` from a row-level `BEFORE` trigger, PostgreSQL cancels the rest of the operation for that row—that means that PostgreSQL won't fire any subsequent triggers and the `INSERT`, `UPDATE`, or `DELETE` won't occur for that row. If you return a non-`NULL` value from a row-level `BEFORE` trigger, the value that you return must match the structure of the table that you're modifying. If PostgreSQL is executing an `UPDATE` or `INSERT` command, the row value that you return from the trigger function is used in place of the original value.

PostgreSQL ignores the return value of an AFTER trigger. PostgreSQL also ignores the return value of a statement-level BEFORE trigger.

TRIGGER **Function Arguments**

Notice that the CREATE TRIGGER command allows you to specify optional arguments (indicated by args in the preceding syntax diagram). You can include a list of string literals when you create a trigger (any arguments that are not of string type are converted into strings). The arguments that you specify are made available to the trigger function through the TG_NARGS and TG_ARGV variables. TG_NARGS contains an integer count of the number of arguments. TG_ARGV contains an array of strings corresponding to the values that you specified when you created the trigger: TG_ARGV[0] contains the first argument, TG_ARGV[1] contains the second argument, and so on. You can use the optional trigger arguments to pass extra information that might help the trigger function know more about the context in which the trigger has executed. You might find this useful when using the same function as a trigger for multiple tables; although in most situations, the TG_NAME, TG_RELNAME, and TG_OP variables provide enough context information.

Polymorphic Functions

Starting with PostgreSQL version 8.0, you can write *polymorphic* functions in PL/pgSQL. A polymorphic function is a function with at least one parameter of type ANYELEMENT or ANYARRAY. The types ANYELEMENT and ANYARRAY are called polymorphic types because they can assume different "shapes" at run-time.

Here's a simple polymorphic function that will return the greater of two arguments:

```
-- ch07.sql
CREATE OR REPLACE FUNCTION max( arg1 ANYELEMENT, arg2 ANYELEMENT )
    RETURNS ANYELEMENT AS $$
  BEGIN

    IF( arg1 > arg2 ) THEN
      RETURN( arg1 );
    ELSE
      RETURN( arg2 );
    END IF;

  END;
$$ LANGUAGE 'plpgsql';
```

When you call this function with two INTEGER values, PL/pgSQL treats the function as if you had defined it as

```
CREATE OR REPLACE FUNCTION max( arg1 INTEGER, arg2 INTEGER )
    RETURNS INTEGER AS $$
```

The polymorphic arguments arg1 and arg2 are assumed to be of type INTEGER.

If you call this function with two TEXT values, arg1 and arg2 are considered to be of type TEXT and the return value is also assumed to be of type TEXT. In fact, you can call this function with two arguments of almost any type. The only restriction is that the function must compile properly for a given type. In the case of the max() function, that means that there must be a > operator that compares two values of that type (since the function compares arg1 and arg2 using the > operator).

When you call a polymorphic function, the actual values that you provide for polymorphic parameters must all be of the same type. You can't call the max() function with an INTEGER and a TEXT argument because arg1 and arg2 are both defined as ANYELEMENT parameters. You can mix polymorphic arguments with other data types, you just have to ensure that all polymorphic arguments are of the same type. If you define ANYARRAY arguments, the elements within those arrays must match the type of other polymorphic parameters.

You can also write functions that return a value of type ANYELEMENT or ANYARRAY. When you call such a function, PostgreSQL infers the date type of the return value from the data type of the polymorphic arguments. You can't write a function that returns a polymorphic value unless the function expects at least one ANYELEMENT (or ANYARRAY) argument.

Here's a function that returns a polymorphic value. firstSmaller() finds the first element in arg2 that's smaller than arg1. arg2 must be a one-dimensional array:

```
-- ch07.sql
CREATE OR REPLACE FUNCTION firstSmaller( arg1 ANYELEMENT, arg2 ANYARRAY )
    RETURNS ANYELEMENT AS $$
  BEGIN

    FOR i IN array_lower( arg2, 1 ) .. array_upper( arg2, 1 ) LOOP

      IF arg2[i] < arg1 THEN
        RETURN( arg2[i] );
      END IF;

    END LOOP;

    RETURN NULL;

  END;
$$ LANGUAGE 'plpgsql';
```

You can call this function with an INTEGER value and array of INTEGERS, or a TEXT value and array of TEXT values, or a NUMERIC value and an array of NUMERIC values, and so on. If the polymorphic arguments (arg1 and arg2) are of type INTEGER, the return value will be of type INTEGER. If you call firstSmaller() with NUMERIC values, the return value will be of type NUMERIC.

A function that returns a polymorphic value automatically inherits an extra variable named $0. You can ALIAS $0 to a more descriptive name, such as result, to make it easier to read your code. The type of $0 is the same as the type of the return value; in other words, the data type of $0 matches the data type of the polymorphic arguments.

The sum() function, shown here, returns a polymorphic value.

```
-- ch07.sql
CREATE OR REPLACE FUNCTION sum( arg1 ANYARRAY ) RETURNS ANYELEMENT AS $$
  DECLARE
    result ALIAS FOR $0;
  BEGIN

    result := 0;

    FOR i IN array_lower( arg1, 1 ) .. array_upper( arg1, 1 ) LOOP

      IF arg1[i] IS NOT NULL THEN
        result := result + arg1[i];
      END IF;

    END LOOP;

    RETURN( result );

  END;

$$ LANGUAGE 'plpgsql';
```

The data type for $0 is inferred from the type of arg1. PL/pgSQL always initializes the return value to NULL—because this function accumulates result as it progresses through the arg1 array, you must re-initialize result to 0 before you can add to it (remember, NULL + 5 is not the same as 0 + 5—NULL+ 5 = NULL).

Note that you can't call the sum() function with an array of TEXT values because PostgreSQL doesn't define a TEXT + TEXT operator. You *can* call sum() with an array of any numeric type (INTEGER, REAL, NUMERIC, and so on).

PL/pgSQL and Security

By default, a PL/pgSQL function executes with the privileges of the user that calls it. That's safe because an unprivileged user won't gain extra privileges simply by calling a PL/pgSQL function. However, there are times when you may *want to* convey extra privileges to a function. For example, you might hide sensitive information (such as payroll data) from a clerical user, but you want that user to "close the books" at the end of each month. Presumably, the close_the_books() function can do its work without exposing secret data to the user. If that's the case, you can tell PostgreSQL that you want the close_the_books() function to inherit the privileges of the author of the function. To convey extra privileges to a function, just add a SECURITY clause to the function definition. The SECURITY clause follows the function body and can precede or follow the LANGUAGE clause:

```
CREATE [OR REPLACE] FUNCTION name ( [[argname] argtype [, ...] ] )
    RETURNS return_type
    AS $$definition$$
    LANGUAGE langname |   [ SECURITY INVOKER | SECURITY DEFINER ]
```

For example:

```
CREATE OR REPLACE FUNCTION close_the_books( ) RETURNS void AS $$
  BEGIN
    ...
  END;
$$ LANGUAGE 'plpgsql' SECURITY DEFINER;
```

If you don't include a SECURITY clause, PostgreSQL assumes SECURITY INVOKER (meaning that the function executes with the privileges of the invoker). Be aware that when you convey extra privileges to close_the_books(), you are also conveying extra privileges to any SECURITY INVOKER functions *called by* close_the_books().

Summary

In this chapter, you've seen that PL/pgSQL provides a way for you to execute procedural code on the server. PL/pgSQL is not the only procedural language that you can use for server-side programming. The standard PostgreSQL distribution includes PL/perl, PL/python, and PL/tcl. You can also add functionality to the server using the Server Programming Interface. For more information on these features, refer to the *PostgreSQL Programmer's Guide*.

The next several chapters will describe the client-side programming interfaces included with PostgreSQL.

The PostgreSQL C API—libpq

A user interacts with a PostgreSQL database by using an application, but how does an application interact with PostgreSQL? PostgreSQL provides a number of *application programming interfaces* (or APIs for short). Three of these APIs are designed to be used by applications written in C-libpq, libpgeasy, and ODBC (the ODBC API can easily be used from other languages as well). Each API has advantages and disadvantages. libpgeasy, for example, is very easy to use, but doesn't offer much flexibility. If your application uses the ODBC API, you gain portability at the cost of complexity.

Table 8.1 compares the three C-language APIs offered by PostgreSQL.

Table 8.1 **Comparison of C Language APIs for PostgreSQL**

API	Complexity	Flexibility	RDBMS Portability
libpq	Medium	Medium to high	PostgreSQL only
libpgeasy	Low	Low	PostgreSQL only
ODBC	Medium to high	High	Multiple database systems

Notice that an application that uses ODBC to connect to PostgreSQL can connect to other database systems as well.

In this chapter, I'll explain the libpq API. libpq is a set of functions that you can call from a C program to interact with a PostgreSQL server. In later chapters, I will cover libpgeasy and ODBC, as well as a few APIs designed for languages other than C.

The libpq API is used to implement most of the other client APIs. After you understand how to interact with a PostgreSQL server using libpq, you will find that most of the other APIs simply wrap up the libpq API in different flavors. For example, the libpgeasy API combines some of the more common libpq operations into a set of higher-level functions. The libpgeasy functions are easier to use, but you don't have quite as much power and flexibility as you would with a libpq application.

Prerequisites

When you write a client application using libpq, you'll need a C compiler. I'll assume that you have the GNU C compiler (gcc) installed and ready to use. I'll also assume that you have GNU make available, and I'll use that tool to actually invoke the compiler (and linker).

APIs that are used within a C application are usually made up of two components: a set of header files and an object code library.

The header files contain data type definitions and function prototypes (in other words, the header files *describe* the API to your C compiler). The object code library contains the actual implementation for each function contained in the API. When you use libpq, you will need to include the libpq-fe.h header file within your C code (using the #include directive). You will also need to link your program against the libpq object library.

Client 1—Connecting to the Server

Our first client is very simple—it connects to a server, disconnects, and then exits.

There are two sets of functions that you can use to connect to a PostgreSQL server: the simple form uses the PQconnectdb() function, whereas the more complex form uses PQconnectStart() and PQconnectPoll(). PQconnectdb() is easier to use because it is a *synchronous* function; when you call PQconnectdb(), your program will not continue until the connection attempt succeeds or fails. The PQconnectStart() and PQconnectPoll() functions give your application a way to connect to a server *asynchronously*. A call to PQconnectStart() returns immediately—it won't wait for the connection attempt to complete. The PQconnectPoll() function can be used to monitor the progress of a connection attempt started by PQconnectStart(). I use the synchronous form in this chapter:

```
/*
** File: client1.c
*/

#include "libpq-fe.h"

int main( void )
{
    PGconn * connection;

    connection = PQconnectdb( "" );

    PQfinish( connection);

    return( 0 );
}
```

`client1.c` starts by including a single header file: `libpq-fe.h`. The `libpq-fe.h` file defines the data types that we need to communicate with libpq. `libpq-fe.h` also contains function prototypes for the libpq API functions.

Connecting to a PostgreSQL database from libpq can be very simple. The `PQconnectdb()` function returns a handle to a connection object. `PQconnectdb()` is synchronous—it will not return to the caller until the connection attempt succeeds or fails. Here is the prototype for `PQconnectdb()`:

```
extern PGconn *PQconnectdb(const char *conninfo);
```

`PQconnectdb()` takes a single argument—a pointer to a null-terminated connection string. A *connection string* is a list of zero or more connection attributes. For example, the connection string `"dbname=accounting user=korry"` specifies that we want to connect to a database named "`accounting`" as user "`korry`". Each option is of the form `keyword=value`. Multiple attributes are separated by whitespace.

Notice that I specified an empty connection string in this example. When `PQconnectdb()` finds an empty connection string, it connects to the default database using a default set of attributes. An empty string is not the same as a NULL pointer. Don't pass a NULL pointer to `PQconnectdb()` unless you want to see libpq (and your application) die a fiery death.

I'll describe connection attributes and their default values in more detail a bit later. When you call `PQconnectdb()`, you get back a pointer to a PGconn. PGconn is considered a handle. A *handle* is an opaque data type, meaning that there is something behind a PGconn pointer, but you can't see it. The information behind a handle is for "internal use only." The libpq library has access to the implementation details, but API users do not. A PGconn object represents a database connection within your application. You will use this object when you call other libpq functions.

Compiling the Client

Now let's compile `client1.c` and try to run it. You will use a simple `makefile` to drive the C compiler and linker. Here is the `makefile` you will use throughout this chapter—as you add new clients, you will just add new targets to the `makefile`:

```
## File: Makefile
##
##        Rules to create libpq sample applications

CPPFLAGS  += -I/usr/local/pgsql/include
CFLAGS    += -g
LDFLAGS   += -g
LDLIBS    += -L/usr/local/pgsql/lib -lpq

client1:  client1.o
```

If you have installed PostgreSQL into a directory other than `/usr/local/pgsql`, you should substitute your directory names in the `makefile`.

To build `client1` with this `makefile`, you can use the following command:

```
$ make client1
cc -g -I/usr/local/pgsql/include  -c -o client1.o client1.c
cc -g  client1.o -L/usr/local/pgsql/lib -lpq -o client1
$
```

The `client1` application doesn't expect any command-line parameters so you can run it like this:

```
$ ./client1
```

Using GNU `make` to Build libpq Applications

The make utility is used to perform the operations required to turn a source file (such as `client1.c`) into an application. make does two (extremely useful) things for you. First, make determines the minimum set of operations required to build an application. Second, make invokes the various preprocessors, compilers, and linkers to actually carry out minimum required operations.

The make utility learns how to build an application by consulting two sources of information. make has a huge collection of built-in rules that describe how to convert one type of file into another type of file. For example, make knows how convert a ".c" file into an executable. First, make converts a source file into a ".o" (object) module by asking the C compiler to compile the source file. Then, make converts the ".o" into an executable by invoking the linker.

The second information source that make uses is known as a `makefile` (probably because the file is usually named "makefile"—clever huh?). A makefile is a set of rules that define how to build your specific application (or applications). makefiles are usually written in terms of targets and prerequisites. A *target* is something that you want to build. A *prerequisite* is a file that the target depends on. In this case, you want to build an application named `client1`—that's your target. The prerequisite for your target is `client1.c`. The makefile rule that describes this relationship is "`client1:    client1.c`". This line is read as "`client1` depends on `client1.c`". When make sees this rule, it looks through its database of built-in rules to find a way to convert `client1.c` into `client1`. It finds the rule (or actually, rules) to perform this conversion, invokes the C compiler to produce `client1.o` from `client1.c`, and then invokes the linker to convert `client1.o` into the `client1` executable.

The makefile that you will use for the examples in this chapter is a little more complex than the single rule that I just described.

The built-in rule that produces an object module (`.o`) from a C source file (`.c`) looks like this:

```
$(CC)  -c $(CPPFLAGS) $(CFLAGS)
```

This command invokes the C compiler, passing it the command-line flags `-c`, `$(CPPFLAGS)`, and `$(CFLAGS)`. `$(CPPFLAGS)` and `$(CFLAGS)` are variables that you can modify within the makefile. To build a libpq application, you have to tell the C compiler how to find the PostgreSQL header files. You can do that by modifying the `$(CPPFLAGS)` variable:

```
CPPFLAGS += -I/usr/local/pg800/include
```

To find the correct directory name, execute the command

```
$ pg_config --includedir
```

If you want the C compiler to produce debuggable code, you can modify the $(CFLAGS) variable to include the -g flag:

```
CFLAGS += -g
```

Now when make invokes the C compiler to compile client1.c, the command will look like this:

```
cc -c -I/usr/local/pg800/include -g -o client1.o client1.c
```

If the compiler does not find any serious errors in client1.c, you will end up with an object module named client1.o. Your target is not client1.o, but client1: client1.o is just an intermediate target. To build client1 from client1.o, make will invoke the linker using the following built-in rule:

```
$(CC) $(LDFLAGS) prerequisite.o $(LOADLIBES) $(LDLIBS)
```

You want to link client1.o with the libpq library to produce client1. The libpq library is found in /usr/local/pg800/lib on my system, so I'll tell make to include libpq by modifying $(LDLIBS). I want debugging symbols in my executable, so I also will add the -g flag to $(LDFLAGS):

```
LDLIBS += -L/usr/local/pg800/lib -lpq
LDFLAGS += -g
```

Again, you can use the pg_config command to find the directory that contains the libpq library:

```
$ pg_config --libdir
```

The final command produced by make is

```
cc -g client1.o -L/usr/local/pg800/lib -lpq -o client1
```

The complete makefile looks like this:

```
CPPFLAGS += -I$(shell pg_config --includedir)
CFLAGS   += -g
LDFLAGS  += -g
LDLIBS   += -L$(shell pg_config --libdir) -lpq

client1:  client1.o
```

Identifying the Server

If you provide an empty connection string to PQconnectdb(), how does it find a database server? libpq uses a hierarchy of default values to decide which server to try to connect to.

The libpq library uses three different sources when trying to find each connection attribute.

First, the connection string (given to PQconnectedb()) can contain a set of keyword=value pairs.

Next, libpq looks for a set of specifically named environment variables. Each environment variable corresponds to one of the keyword=value pairs that you can use in the connection string.

Finally, libpq uses a set of values that are hard-wired into the library at build-time.

Table 8.2 shows how the keywords and environment variables correspond to each other.

Table 8.2 **Connection Attributes**

Connect-String Keyword	Environment Variable	Example
user	PGUSER	user=korry
password	PGPASSWORD	password=cows
dbname	PGDATABASE	dbname=accounting
host	PGHOST	host=jersey
hostaddr	PGHOSTADDR	hostaddr=127.0.0.1
service	PGSERVICE	service=accounting
port	PGPORT	port=5432

You can use the PQconndefaults() function to find the default value for each connection attribute.

```
1 /*
2 ** File: get_dflts.c
3 */
4
5 #include <stdio.h>
6 #include <libpq-fe.h>
7
8 int main( void )
9 {
10   PQconninfoOption * d;
11   PQconninfoOption * start;
12 /*
13 **  Get the default connection attributes
14 */
15   start = d = PQconndefaults( );
16
17   while( d->keyword != NULL )
18   {
19     printf( "keyword = %s\n", d->keyword  ? d->keyword  : "null" );
20     printf( "envvar  = %s\n", d->envvar   ? d->envvar   : "null" );
21     printf( "label   = %s\n", d->label    ? d->label    : "null" );
22     printf( "compiled = %s\n", d->compiled ? d->compiled : "null" );
23     printf( "val     = %s\n", d->val      ? d->val      : "null" );
24     printf( "\n" );
```

```
25
26    d++;
27    }
28
29 /*
30 **   Free up the memory that lipq allocated on our behalf
31 */
32
33    PQconninfoFree( start );
34
35    return( 0 );
```

When you call the PQconndefaults() function, you get back a pointer to the first member of an array of PQconninfoOption structures. Each structure contains (among other things) a keyword, the name of an environment variable, a hard-wired (or compiled-in) value, and a current value. If you iterate through the members of this array, you can recognize the end of the list by looking for a member where the keyword pointer is NULL.

You can compile this program by adding another entry to the makefile and then typing make get_dflts:

```
$ cat makefile
##
##  File:  Makefile
##
##         Rules for building libpq sample applications
##

CPPFLAGS += I$(shell pg_config --includedir)
CFLAGS   += -g
LDFLAGS  += -g
LDLIBS   += -L$(shell pg_config --libdir) -lpq

client1:   client1.o
get_dflts: get_dflts.o


$ make get_dflts
cc -g -I/usr/local/pg800/include  -c -o get_dflts.o get_dflts.c
cc -g  get_dflts.o  -L/usr/local/pg800/lib -lpq -o get_dflts
```

Running the get_dflts program on my system results in the following:

```
$ ./get_dflts
keyword  = authtype
envvar   = PGAUTHTYPE
label    = Database-Authtype
compiled =
val      =
```

```
keyword  = service
envvar   = PGSERVICE
label    = Database-Service
compiled = (null)
val      = (null)

keyword  = user
envvar   = PGUSER
label    = Database-User
compiled = (null)
val      = bruce

keyword  = password
envvar   = PGPASSWORD
label    = Database-Password
compiled =
val      =

keyword  = dbname
envvar   = PGDATABASE
label    = Database-Name
compiled = (null)
val      = Administrator

keyword  = host
envvar   = PGHOST
label    = Database-Host
compiled = (null)
val      = (null)

keyword  = hostaddr
envvar   = PGHOSTADDR
label    = Database-Host-IPv4-Address
compiled = (null)
val      = (null)

keyword  = port
envvar   = PGPORT
label    = Database-Port
compiled = 5432
val      = 5432

keyword  = tty
envvar   = PGTTY
label    = Backend-Debug-TTY
compiled =
val      =
```

```
keyword    = options
envvar     = PGOPTIONS
label      = Backend-Debug-Options
compiled   =
val        =
```

You can see that each `keyword` member corresponds to a `keyword` accepted by the `PQconnectdb()` function. You may have noticed that `PQconndefaults()` returned more connection attributes than are shown in Table 8.2. Some of the connection attributes are obsolete but still supported for compatibility with older clients. Some attributes are reserved for future use and are not fully supported. Other attributes exist for debugging purposes and are not normally used. If you stick to the connection attributes listed in Table 8.2, you should be safe.

Each connection parameter is computed from a sequence of default values, in the absence of explicitly specified values in the connection string.

For example, if you omit the `port` keyword from your `PQconnectdb()` connection string, libpq will look for an environment variable named `PGPORT`. If you have defined the `PGPORT` environment variable, libpq will use the value of that variable for the port; if not, a hard-wired (or compiled-in) value is used. In this case, the hard-wired port number is `5432`. (Compiled-in values are defined when the libpq object-code library is built from source code.) The default hierarchy works like this:

If the keyword is found in the connection string, the value is taken from the connection string, else

If the associated environment variable is defined, the value is taken from the environment variable, else

The hard-wired value is used.

The `user` and `dbname` parameters are treated a little differently—instead of using hard-wired values, the last default for the `user` parameter is your login name and the `dbname` parameter is copied from the `user` parameter. For example, if I am logged in (to my Linux operating system) as user `korry`, both `user` and `dbname` will default to `korry`. Of course, I can override the default `user` and `dbname` attributes using environment variables or explicit connect-string attributes.

Client 2—Adding Error Checking

The `client1.c` application discussed has a fundamental flaw—there is no way to tell whether the connection attempt was successful. This next program attempts a connection and displays an error message if the attempt fails:

```
1 /*
2 ** File: client2.c
3 */
4
5 #include <stdlib.h>
```

```
 6 #include <libpq-fe.h>
 7
 8 int main( int argc, char * argv[] )
 9 {
10   PGconn * connection;
11
12   if( argc != 2 )
13   {
14     printf( "usage  : %s \"connection-string\"\n", argv[0] );
15     printf( "example: %s \"user=myname password=cows\"\n", argv[0]);
16     exit( 1 );
17   }
18
19   if(( connection = PQconnectdb( argv[1] )) == NULL )
20   {
21     printf( "Fatal error - unable to allocate connection\n" );
22     exit( 1 );
23   }
24
25   if( PQstatus( connection ) != CONNECTION_OK )
26     printf( "%s\n", PQerrorMessage( connection ));
27   else
28     printf( "Connection ok, disconnecting\n" );
29
30   PQfinish( connection );
31
32   exit( 0 );
33
34 }
```

You can specify a connection string on the command line when you run this program. If you want to include more than one connection attribute, enclose the entire connection string in double quotes. For example:

```
$ ./client2 user=korry
Connection ok, disconnecting

$ ./client2 "user=korry password=cows"
Connection ok, disconnecting
```

I recommend that you run this program a few times, feeding it a variety of invalid connect strings so you become familiar with the error messages that you might receive when things go wrong. For example:

```
$ ./client2 host=badhost
connectDBStart() --  unknown hostname: badhost

$ ./client2 port=1000
```

```
connectDBStart() -- connect() failed: No such file or directory
        Is the postmaster running locally
        and accepting connections on Unix socket '/tmp/.s.PGSQL.1000'?

$ ./client2 badparameter
ERROR: Missing '=' after 'badparameter' in conninfo

$ ./client2 badparameter=1000
ERROR: Unknown conninfo option 'badparameter'
```

Viewing Connection Attributes

In the get_dflts application I showed you how to use the PQconndefaults() function
to view the default connection attributes that will be used to establish a connection.

libpq also provides a number of functions that you can use to retrieve the *actual* connection attributes after you have a PGconn object. These functions are useful because in
most situations, you won't explicitly specify every connection attribute. Instead, many
(perhaps all) of the connection attributes will be defaulted for you.

PQconnectdb() will return a PGconn pointer in almost every case (PQconnectdb()
will return a NULL pointer only if libpq runs out of memory).

The following program attempts to make a connection and then print the set of connection parameters. I've modified client2.c to show the complete set of final connection parameters after a connection attempt. The new application is called client2b:

```
 1 /*
 2 ** File: client2b.c
 3 */
 4
 5 #include <stdlib.h>
 6 #include <libpq-fe.h>
 7
 8 static void show_connection_attributes( const PGconn * conn );
 9 static const char * check( const char * value );
10
11 int main( int argc, char * argv[] )
12 {
13   PGconn * connection;
14
15   if( argc != 2 )
16   {
17     printf( "usage  : %s \"connection-string\"\n", argv[0] );
18     printf( "example: %s \"user=myname password=cows\"\n", argv[0]);
19     exit( 1 );
20   }
21
22   if(( connection = PQconnectdb( argv[1] )) == NULL )
23   {
```

```
24       printf( "Fatal error - unable to allocate connection\n" );
25       exit( 1 );
26     }
27
28     if( PQstatus( connection ) != CONNECTION_OK )
29       printf( "%s\n", PQerrorMessage( connection ));
30     else
31       printf( "Connection ok\n" );
32
33     show_connection_attributes( connection );
34
35     PQfinish( connection );
36
37     exit( 0 );
38
39   }
40
41  static const char * check( const char * value )
42  {
43       if( value )
44       return( value );
45       else
46       return( "(null)" );
47  }
48
49  static void show_connection_attributes( const PGconn * c )
50  {
51     printf( "dbname   = %s\n", check( PQdb( c )));
52     printf( "user     = %s\n", check( PQuser( c )));
53     printf( "password = %s\n", check( PQpass( c )));
54     printf( "host     = %s\n", check( PQhost( c )));
55     printf( "port     = %s\n", check( PQport( c )));
56     printf( "tty      = %s\n", check( PQtty( c )));
57     printf( "options  = %s\n", check( PQoptions( c )));
58  }
```

Take a look at the `show_connection_attributes()` function (lines 49-58). Given a PGconn pointer, you can find the connection attributes that result after all the defaults are applied by calling `PQdb()`, `PQuser()`, and so on. In some cases, one or more of these functions may return a NULL pointer, so I wrapped each function invocation in a call to `check()` (lines 41-47) to avoid giving any bad pointers to `printf()`.

If, for some reason, you need to know the process ID of the server that you're connected to, you can retrieve that value by calling the `PQbackendPID()` function. `PQbackendPID()` is particularly useful if you're debugging or exploring the PostgreSQL server. You can find the version number of the server using the `PQserverVersion()` function. `PQserverVersion()` returns an integer value that encodes the server's version number—version 7.3.2 is encoded as 70302, version 8.0.0 is encode as 80000, and so forth.

Remember that `PQconnectdb()` returns a `PGconn` pointer even when a connection attempt fails; it is often instructive to see the final connection attributes for a failed connection attempt. Here are the results when I try to connect to a nonexistent database on my system:

```
$ ./client2b user=korry
FATAL 1:  Database "korry" does not exist in the system catalog.

dbname    = korry
user      = korry
password =
host      = (null)
port      = 5432
tty       =
options   =
```

In this case, I can see that libpq chose an invalid database name (defaulted from my username).

Client 3—Simple Processing—`PQexec()` and `PQprint()`

Now let's turn our attention to the task of processing a query. I'll start by showing a simple example—you'll connect to a database, execute a hard-wired query, process the results, clean up, and exit.

```
1  /*
2  ** File: client3.c
3  */
4
5  #include <stdlib.h>
6  #include <libpq-fe.h>
7
8  void process_query( PGconn * connection, const char * query_text )
9  {
10   PGresult  *       result;
11   PQprintOpt        options = {0};
12
13   if(( result = PQexec( connection, query_text )) == NULL )
14   {
15     printf( "%s\n", PQerrorMessage( connection ));
16     return;
17   }
18
19   options.header   = 1;    /* Ask for column headers              */
20   options.align    = 1;    /* Pad short columns for alignment     */
21   options.fieldSep = "|";  /* Use a pipe as the field separator   */
22
```

```
23   PQprint( stdout, result, &options );
24
25   PQclear( result );
26 }
27
28 int main( int argc, char * argv[] )
29 {
30   PGconn * connection;
31
32   if( argc != 2 )
33   {
34     printf( "usage   : %s \"connection-string\"\n", argv[0] );
35     printf( "example: %s \"user=myname password=cows\"\n", argv[0]);
36     exit( 1 );
37   }
38
39   if(( connection = PQconnectdb( argv[1] )) == NULL )
40   {
41     printf( "Fatal error - unable to allocate connection\n" );
42     exit( 1 );
43   }
44
45   if( PQstatus( connection ) != CONNECTION_OK )
46     printf( "%s\n", PQerrorMessage( connection ));
47   else
48   {
49     process_query( connection, "SELECT * FROM rentals" );
50   }
51
52   PQfinish( connection );
53
54   exit( 0 );
55 }
```

The interesting part of this program is the process_query() function (lines 8-26).
client3.c starts by calling PQexec(). This function is used to execute a query in a synchronous (that is, blocking) fashion. (Like the connection API, there are two methods to
execute a query: synchronous and asynchronous. I'll show you the asynchronous query
functions later.) When you call PQexec(), you provide a connection object(a PGconn
pointer) and a command string. PQexec() returns a pointer to a PGresult object. A
PGresult is similar to a PGconn—it is an opaque handle and you can query the object
for different pieces of information (such as "Did my query succeed or fail?"). A
PGresult object represents the result of executing a command. When you execute a
query (as opposed to an INSERT command), the entire result set (including meta-data) of
the query is accessible through the object. A PGresult object also provides access to any
error messages that may result from executing a command.

I'm going to cheat here. libpq provides a handy function called PQprint() that does all the dirty work required to print the results of a query.

I'll use PQprint() here because it is such a simple way to print a result set. Later, I'll show you how to produce much of the same functionality yourself.

Before you can call PQprint(), you must construct a PQprintOpt object. At line 11, you initialize the PQprintOpt object and then set the three members that you care about (header, align, and fieldSep) at lines 19-21. PQprint() requires three arguments: a FILE pointer (in this case, specify stdout), a PGresult pointer (returned from PQexec()), and a pointer to a PGprintOpt object. PQprint() formats the results of the query and prints them to the file that you specified. If the query fails, PQprint() will print an appropriate error message.

Remember that PQexec() returned a pointer to a PGresult object—you need to free that object because PQclear() will destroy a PGresult object.

When you are finished processing the result set, free the PGresult resources using PQclear() (see line 25). It's important to PQclear() all PGresult objects when you are done with them. When libpq executes a query on your behalf, the entire result set of the query is accessible through a PGresult object. That means that if you execute a query that returns 100,000 rows, the PGresult object will consume enough memory to hold all 100,000 rows.

Results Returned by PQexec()

Many client applications need to do more than just print column values. After executing a command, you can obtain a lot of information about the results of the command through the PGresult object returned by PQexec().

The most obvious piece of information that you can obtain from a PGresult pointer is whether the command succeeded or failed. If the command succeeded, PQresultStatus() will return either PGRES_COMMAND_OK or PGRES_TUPLES_OK. PGRES_TUPLES_OK means that you successfully executed a query and there are zero or more rows available for processing. PGRES_COMMAND_OK means that you successfully executed some command other than SELECT; an INSERT command for example. If the query causes an error, you will get back a result of PGRES_FATAL_ERROR or PGRES_NONFATAL_ERROR. (There are other values that PQresultStatus() can return; see the *PostgreSQL Programmer's Guide* for more information.) It's possible that PQexec() will return a NULL PGresult pointer if libpq runs out of memory—you should treat that as a PGRES_FATAL_ERROR.

If a command fails, you can use PQresultErrorMessage() to find the reason for failure. To call PQresultErrorMessage(), pass the PGresult pointer that was returned by PQexec(). PQresultErrorMessage() returns a pointer to the null-terminated string containing the reason for failure (if you call PQresultErrorMessage() for a successful query, you'll get back a pointer to an empty string).

I'll modify the process_query() function from the previous example (client3.c) to show how to use PQresultStatus() and PQresultErrorMessage():

```
 1 /*
 2 ** File: client3b.c
 3 */
 4
 5 #include <stdlib.h>
 6 #include <libpq-fe.h>
 7
 8 void process_query( PGconn * connection, const char * query_text )
 9 {
10   PGresult  *        result;
11
12   if(( result = PQexec( connection, query_text )) == NULL )
13   {
14     printf( "%s\n", PQerrorMessage( connection ));
15     return;
16   }
17
18   if(( PQresultStatus( result ) == PGRES_COMMAND_OK ) ||
19      ( PQresultStatus( result ) == PGRES_TUPLES_OK ))
20   {
21     PQprintOpt            options = {0};
22
23     options.header   = 1;   /* Ask for column headers          */
24     options.align    = 1;   /* Pad short columns for alignment */
25     options.fieldSep = "|"; /* Use a pipe as the field separator*/
26
27     PQprint( stdout, result, &options );
28
29   }
30   else
31   {
32     printf( "%s\n", PQresStatus( PQresultStatus( result )));
33     printf( "%s\n", PQresultErrorMessage( result ));
34
35   }
36
37   PQclear( result );
38 }
39
40 int main( int argc, char * argv[] )
41 {
42   PGconn * connection;
43
44   if( argc != 2 )
45   {
46     printf( "usage  : %s \"connection-string\"\n", argv[0] );
```

```
47      printf( "example: %s \"user=myname password=cows\"\n", argv[0] );
48      exit( 1 );
49    }
50
51    if(( connection = PQconnectdb( argv[1] )) == NULL )
52    {
53      printf( "Fatal error - unable to allocate connection\n" );
54      exit( 1 );
55    }
56
57    if( PQstatus( connection ) != CONNECTION_OK )
58      printf( "%s\n", PQerrorMessage( connection ));
59    else
60    {
61      process_query( connection, "SELECT * FROM rentals" );
62    }
63
64    PQfinish( connection );
65
66    exit( 0 );
67  }
```

At lines 18 and 19, this application checks to see whether the command succeeded. If so, it calls PQprint() to print the result set just like you did in client3.c.

If the command failed, you want to tell the user what went wrong. Look closely at line 32. client3b is calling the PQresultStatus() function again, but this time around it calls PQresStatus() with the return value. PQresultStatus() returns the command status in the form of an integer[1]. The PQresStatus() function translates a value returned by PQresultStatus() into a human-readable string.

At line 33, the call to PQresultErrorMessage() retrieves the text of the error message.

After you have successfully executed a query (that is, PQresultStatus() has returned either PGRES_COMMAND_OK or PGRES_TUPLES_OK), you are ready to process the actual results. There are three types of information that you can access through a PGresult object. You've already seen the first type of information: success or failure and an error message. The second type of information is metadata, or data *about* your data. We'll look at metadata next. Finally, you can access the values returned by the command itself—the rows returned by a query or the OID of an affected row in the case of an INSERT or UPDATE.

First, I'll show you how to find the metadata for your query. libpq provides a number of functions that let you find information about the *kind* of data returned by your query. For example, the PQntuples() function tells you how many rows (or tuples) will be returned from your query.

---

[1] More precisely, PQresultStatus() returns a value of type enum ExecStatusType.

The following function prints (most of) the metadata returned for a command:

```
 1 void print_meta_data( PGresult * result )
 2 {
 3   int    col;
 4
 5   printf( "Status: %s\n", PQresStatus( PQresultStatus( result )));
 6   printf( "Returned %d rows ", PQntuples( result ));
 7   printf( "with %d columns\n\n", PQnfields( result ));
 8
 9   printf( "Column Type TypeMod Size Name       \n" );
10   printf( "------ ---- ------- ---- -----------\n" );
11
12   for( col = 0; col < PQnfields( result ); col++ )
13   {
14     printf( "%3d     %4d %7d %4d %s\n",
15             col,
16             PQftype( result, col ),
17             PQfmod( result, col ),
18             PQfsize( result, col ),
19             PQfname( result, col ));
20   }
21 }
```

If you want to try this function, it is included in `client3c.c` in the sample code for this book. I won't show the complete application here because it is largely the same as `client3b.c`.

At line 5, client3b prints the success/failure status from the given PQresult object. It uses the same PQresStatus() and PQresultStatus() functions described earlier, but I've included them in this example because they really do return metadata information.

At line 6, the call to PQntuples() retrieves the number of rows returned by the command. PQntuples() returns zero if the command was not a query. PQntuples() also returns zero if the command *was* a query, but the query happened to return zero rows in the result set. libpq does not consider it an error for a query to return zero rows. In fact, the PQresult object contains all the usual metadata even when a query does not return any rows.

The PQnfields() function (line 7) returns the number of columns in the result set. Line PQntuples(), PQnfields() returns zero for commands other than SELECT.

The naming convention for the metadata functions is a little confusing at first. PQntuples() returns the number of *rows* in the result set. PQnfields() returns the number of *columns* in the result set. A tuple is the same thing as a row. A field is the same thing as a column[2].

---

[2] Technically speaking, a tuple is a version of a row. PostgreSQL uses a concurrency system known as multi-version concurrency control (MVCC). In MVCC, the database can contain multiple versions of the same row. There is also a slight difference between a field and a column. A column is stored in a table. A field is the result of an expression. A column is a valid expression, so a column can be considered a field, but a field is not necessarily a column.

At line 16, the call to PQftype() returns the data type for a given column. The PQftype(), PQfmod(), and PQfsize() functions work together to tell you about the format of the data in a given column.

PQftype() returns a value of type OID. The value returned by PQftype() corresponds to the object-id (OID) of a row in the pg_type system table. (In Chapter 6, "Extending PostgreSQL," you learned that data type descriptions are stored in pg_type.) You can find the OIDs for predefined data types in the catalog/pg_type.h PostgreSQL header file. PQfmod() returns a value that, in theory, gives you more detailed information about a data type. The values returned by PQfmod() are type-specific and are not documented. You can use the format_type()[3] function to convert values returned by PQftype() and PQfmod() into a human-readable string. PQfsize() returns the number of bytes required to hold a value on the server. For variable-length data types, PQfsize() returns –1.

It turns out that the information returned by PQftype(), PQfmod(), and PQfsize() is not all that useful in most applications. In most cases, the field values returned to your application will be null-terminated strings. For example, if you SELECT a date column, the date values will be converted into string form before it gets to your application. The same is true for numeric values. It *is* possible to request raw data values (that is, values that have not been converted into string form). I'll show you how to do that a little later.

You can also find information about the table (if any) that each column belongs to. If a given column comes from a table, you can find the OID of that table by calling the PQftable() function. If, instead, the column is a computed value, PQftable() returns the value InvalidOid. If a given column comes directly from a table, you can find the column number (within the table) by calling PQftablecol(). PQftablecol() returns 1 for the first column in a table, 2 for the second column, and so on. The order of the columns within a table (as defined by PQftablecol()) matches what you would see if you executed a SELECT * from that table. PQftablecol() returns zero for computed columns.

The last two metadata functions are PQfname() and PQfnumber(). PQfname() returns the name of the given column in the result set. PQfnumber() returns the column number of the named column.

Now that you know how to retrieve the metadata for a query, let's see how to actually retrieve the data. In this example, we'll replace the earlier calls to PQprint() with our own function.

```
1 /*
2 ** File: client3d.c
3 */
4
5 #include <stdlib.h>
6 #include <string.h>
7 #include <libpq-fe.h>
8
```

---

[3] format_type() is not a libpq function. It is a server function that you can call from a SELECT command. For example, SELECT format_type(atttpyid, atttypmod) FROM pg_attribute.

```
 9 #define MAX_PRINT_LEN       40
10
11 static char separator[MAX_PRINT_LEN+1];
12
13 void print_result_set( PGresult * result )
14 {
15   int         col;
16   int         row;
17   int          * sizes;
18
19 /*
20 **   Compute the size for each column
21 */
22   sizes = (int *)calloc( PQnfields( result ), sizeof( int ));
23
24   for( col = 0; col < PQnfields( result ); col++ )
25   {
26     int    len = 0;
27
28     for( row = 0; row < PQntuples( result ); row++ )
29     {
30       if( PQgetisnull( result, row, col ))
31         len = 0;
32       else
33         len = PQgetlength( result, row, col );
34
35       if( len > sizes[col] )
36         sizes[col] = len;
37     }
38
39     if(( len = strlen( PQfname( result, col ))) > sizes[col] )
40       sizes[col] = len;
41
42     if( sizes[col] > MAX_PRINT_LEN )
43       sizes[col] = MAX_PRINT_LEN;
44   }
45
46 /*
47 **   Print the field names.
48 */
49   for( col = 0; col < PQnfields( result ); col++ )
50   {
51     printf( "%-*s ", sizes[col], PQfname( result, col ));
52   }
53
54   printf( "\n" );
55
```

```
56 /*
57 **  Print the separator line
58 */
59   memset( separator, '-', MAX_PRINT_LEN );
60
61   for( col = 0; col < PQnfields( result ); col++ )
62   {
63     printf( "%*.*s ", sizes[col], sizes[col], separator );
64   }
65
66   printf( "\n" );
67
68 /*
69 **  Now loop through each of the tuples returned by
70 **  our query and print the results.
71 */
72   for( row = 0; row < PQntuples( result ); row++ )
73   {
74     for( col = 0; col < PQnfields( result ); col++ )
75     {
76       if( PQgetisnull( result, row, col ))
77         printf( "%*s", sizes[col], "" );
78       else
79         printf( "%*s ", sizes[col], PQgetvalue( result, row, col ));
80     }
81
82     printf( "\n" );
83
84   }
85   printf( "(%d rows)\n\n", PQntuples( result ));
86   free( sizes );
87 }
```

This function (print_result_set()) replaces PQprint().

The real work in this function is finding the width of each column. For each column in the result set, you must search through all rows to find the widest value in that column. At line 22, print_result_set() allocates an array (sizes[]) of integers to hold the column widths. Lines 24 through 44 fill in the sizes[] array. The PQgetisnull() function tells you whether a given column is NULL in the current row. If you find a NULL field, consider it to have a length of 0. Use the PQgetlength() function to find the length of each value.

Notice that we ensure that each column is wide enough to hold the column name. The limit to each column is MAX_PRINT_LEN characters. This is a rather arbitrary decision that you can certainly change.

After computing the column widths the code at lines 46-55 will print the name of each column followed by a line of separator characters.

At lines 68 through 84, you loop through every row in the result set and print each column value. The PQgetvalue() function returns a pointer to the value for a given row and column. Because this client has not requested a BINARY cursor (I'll talk about those soon), each data value comes to you in the form of a null-terminated string.

Finally, at line 86, print_result_set() frees up the resource that it allocated (sizes[]) and returns.

```
89 void process_query( PGconn * connection, const char * query_text )
90 {
91   PGresult  *        result;
92
93   if(( result = PQexec( connection, query_text )) == NULL )
94   {
95     printf( "%s\n", PQerrorMessage( connection ));
96     return;
97   }
98
99   if( PQresultStatus( result ) == PGRES_TUPLES_OK )
100  {
101    print_result_set( result );
102  }
103  else if( PQresultStatus( result ) == PGRES_COMMAND_OK )
104  {
105    printf( "%s", PQcmdStatus( result ));
106
107    if( strlen( PQcmdTuples( result )))
108      printf( " - %s rows\n\n", PQcmdTuples( result ));
109    else
110      printf( "\n\n" );
111  }
112  else
113  {
114      printf( "%s\n\n", PQresultErrorMessage( result ));
115  }
116
117  PQclear( result );
118 }
```

This function (process_query()) is not very complex. It executes the given command and prints the results. If an error occurs, process_query() uses PQerrorMessage() or PQresultErrorMessage() to display an error message to the user. You should call PQerrorMessage() if PQexec() fails to return a PQresult pointer; otherwise, you call PqresultErrorMessage().

If the command is successful, you need to decide whether it was a SELECT or some other type of command. If PQresultStatus() returns PGRES_TUPLES_OK, you know that the command was a query and you can call print_result_set() to do the grunt work.

If PQresultStatus() returns PGRES_COMMAND_OK, you know that some other command has executed. PQcmdStatus() tells you the name of the command that just completed. You've probably noticed that when you execute a command (other than SELECT) in psql, the name of the command is echoed if the command succeeded—that's what PQcmdStatus() gives you. PQcmdTuples() tells you how many rows were affected by the command. PQcmdTuples() is meaningful for the INSERT, UPDATE, or DELETE command. For any other command, PQcmdTuples() returns a string of zero length. If you've just executed an INSERT command (that inserted exactly one row), you can retrieve the OID of the new row by calling the PQoidValue() function. Note that some tables may not contain an OID column—in that case, PQoidValue() returns InvalidOid. process_query() finishes by freeing up the PGresult object and all the resources (that is, memory) managed by that object.

The main() function for client3d.c is the same as for client3.c:

```
117 int main( int argc, char * argv[] )
118 {
119   PGconn * connection;
120
121   if( argc != 2 )
122   {
123     printf( "usage  : %s \"connection-string\"\n", argv[0] );
124     printf( "example: %s \"user=myname password=cows\"\n", argv[0]);
125     exit( 1 );
126   }
127
128   if(( connection = PQconnectdb( argv[1] )) == NULL )
129   {
130     printf( "Fatal error - unable to allocate connection\n" );
131     exit( 1 );
132   }
133
134   if( PQstatus( connection ) != CONNECTION_OK )
135     printf( "%s\n", PQerrorMessage( connection ));
136   else
137     process_query( connection, "SELECT * FROM rentals" );
138
139   PQfinish( connection );
140
141   exit( 0 );
142 }
```

Now let's compile this client and run it:

```
$ make client3d
cc -g -I/usr/local/pg800/include  -c -o client3d.o client3d.c
cc -g  client1.o -L/usr/local/pg800/lib -lpq -o client3
```

```
$ ./client3d "dbname=movies"
tape_id   rental_date customer_id
--------  ----------- -----------
AB-12345  2002-07-01            1
AB-67472  2002-07-01            3
OW-41221  2002-07-01            1
(3 rows)
```

Let's compare that with the output from client3:

```
$ ./client3 "dbname=movies"
tape_id  |rental_date|customer_id
---------+-----------+-----------
AB-12345| 2002-07-01|           1
AB-67472| 2002-07-01|           3
OW-41221| 2002-07-01|           1
(3 rows)
```

Pretty similar—the only differences are in the vertical separator characters. Remember, client3 uses the PQprint() function (from the libpq library) to format the result set. In client3d, you did all of the hard work yourself.

The Prepare/Execute Model

One of the newer features in PostgreSQL is the prepare/execute model (introduced in version 7.3). When you execute a SELECT command, the PostgreSQL server parses the command, generates a set of possible execution plans, optimizes the query (by selecting the best plan), and then executes the command right away. If you execute the same command a second time, the server goes through the same process of parsing, planning, and optimizing the command. If you execute that command 1,000 times, the server parses, plans, and optimizes the command 1,000 times. It's very likely to come up with the same plan each time.

The prepare/execute model gives you more control over the process. To use the prepare/execute model, you first PREPARE a command, then you EXECUTE the command. If you want to execute the same command over and over again, you skip the PREPARE part and simply EXECUTE the prepared command. When you PREPARE a command, the server parses, plans, and optimizes the command and saves the data structures that it needs in order to execute the command later. The syntax for the PREPARE command is

```
PREPARE plan-name [ (datatype [, ...] ) ] AS statement
```

Once the server has parsed, planned, and optimizes the statement, it associates the resulting execution plan with the given plan-name. For example:

```
movies=# PREPARE getCustomerNames AS SELECT customer_name FROM customers;
PREPARE
```

To execute the getCustomers plan, use the EXECUTE command:

```
movies=# EXECUTE getCustomerNames;
    customer_name
----------------------
 Panky, Henry
 Jones, Henry
 Wonderland, Alice N.
 Rubin, William
(4 rows)
```

You can EXECUTE a plan as many times as you like. The server remembers prepared execution plans until your session ends but you can force it to forget a plan with the DEALLOCATE *plan-name* command (you must DEALLOCATE a plan before you can reuse the name). If you look closely at the syntax for the PREPARE command, you'll notice that you can include a list of (optional) data types after the *plan-name*. When you PREPARE a command that you intend to reuse, you can include *parameter markers* in the command and then substitute actual values each time you EXECUTE the command. For example, to PREPARE a parameterized query that expects a customer_id each time you execute it:

```
movies=# PREPARE getCustomers( INTEGER, INTEGER ) AS
movies-#  SELECT customer_name FROM customers
movies-#    WHERE customer_id >= $1 AND customer_id <= $2;
PREPARE
```

Notice the $1 and $2 things in the WHERE clause—those are parameter markers. You can include as many parameter markers as you need, but you can only place a parameter marker where PostgreSQL expects to find a value (or an expression). You can't, for example, PREPARE a command such as SELECT * FROM $1, hoping to provide a table name each time you EXECUTE the command. When you PREPARE a parameterized command, you must tell PostgreSQL the approximate data type for each parameter. I say "approximate" because, as long as the value that you provide at EXECUTE—time can be converted into the required type, you'll be OK. Be aware that the query optimizer will often find a better execution plan if you can *exactly* match parameter types to column types. To execute a parameterized plan, use the EXECUTE command, but include the parameter values, like this:

```
movies=# EXECUTE getCustomers( 2, 3 );
customer_name
---------------
 Panky, Henry
(1 row)
```

Of course, if you EXECUTE a prepared command a second time, the server will skip the parsing, planning, and optimizing steps, even if you provide different values for the command parameters. You can only use the prepare/execute model to execute SELECT, INSERT, or UPDATE commands.

There are two ways to use the prepare/execute model in a libpq application. First, you can simply create command strings that PREPARE and EXECUTE and then use one of the typical libpq functions to execute those commands. That method certainly works and you'll often increase performance in those cases where you execute the same commands over and over again. The second method involves using a new set of libpq functions.

To prepare a SELECT, INSERT, or UPDATE command from a libpq application, call the PQprepare() function:

```
PGresult *PQprepare( PGconn     * connection,
                     const char * planName,
                     const char * queryText,
                     int          typeCount,
                     const Oid  * paramTypes );
```

The PQprepare() function expects a pointer to a PGconn object, a name for the plan, the text of the query, and an array of parameter data types (along with a count (typeCount) of the number of elements in the paramTypes array). Unlike the PREPARE command, you *don't* have to declare the type of each parameter in the query. If you don't declare the type of a given parameter, the server infers the type by treating the parameter as an un-typed literal string. If you decide to declare parameter types, the paramTypes parameter should point to an array of typeCount OID values. Each element in the paramTypes array corresponds to a parameter (paramTypes[0] declares the data type for parameter $1, paramTypes[1] declares the data type for parameter $2, and so on). So what do you put in the paramTypes array? The OID (object id) of the pg_class entry for the server-side data type. For example, if you want to declare the first parameter as an int4, you would set paramTypes[0] = 23. To find the correct OID value, use the query: SELECT oid FROM pg_type WHERE typnam = 'type' (that's not a typo—there's only one 'e' in typname). If you prefer, you can find symbolic names for the predefined data types (that is, the data types included in a standard PostgreSQL distribution) in the postgresql/server/catalog/pg_type.h header file. For example, the pg_type.h header defines the symbol:

```
#define INT4OID   23
```

Here's a code snippet that prepares the getCustomers query you saw earlier:

```
...

Oid paramTypes[2] = { 23, 23 };

result = PQprepare( connection,
                    "getCustomers",
                    "SELECT * FROM customers WHERE customer_id BETWEEN $1 AND $2"
                    2,
                    paramTypes );

...
```

If PQprepare() returns successfully, the server has created an execution plan named getCustomers. The result object that you get back from PQprepare() will tell you whether the PREPARE succeeded or failed, but it (obviously) won't contain the result set from the SELECT command. Remember that you don't have to provide types for each command parameter. The fourth argument (typeCount) to PQprepare() specifies how many OIDs are present in the paramTypes array, not the number of parameters in the command. If typeCount is less than the number of parameters in the prepared command, the server infers the type of each remaining parameter. If you want to declare the data types for trailing parameters and skip some of the leading parameters, just set the missing data types to InvalidOid, like this:

```
Oid paramTypes[3] = { InvalidOid, InvalidOid, 23 };
```

Once you've prepared a command, you can execute that command by calling the PQexecPrepared() function:

```
PGresult *PQexecPrepared( PGconn              * connection,
                          const char          * planName,
                          int                   paramCount,
                          const char * const  * paramValues,
                          const int           * paramLengths,
                          const int           * paramFormats,
                          int                   resultFormat );
```

The meaning of the first two arguments should be obvious: connection points to a PGconn connection object and planName points to a null-terminated string containing the name of the command that you prepared earlier. The last five arguments take a bit of explanation.

I'll start with the last argument because it's the easiest to explain. If resultFormat is 0, libpq returns each value in the result set in the form of a null-terminated string. That's typically what you find in a libpq application. If you retrieve a numeric value from the server, you'll get the result as a null-terminated string that you must convert into binary form (say an int or float) using a function such atoi() or strtof(). If you retrieve a date value, you'll get a null-terminated string (and you'll have to convert it to the binary form you require). If resultFormat is 1, libpq returns every value in the result set in binary form. What exactly is *binary form?* It varies with the server-side data type. If you retrieve an int4 value in binary form, you'll get back a four-byte value that looks suspiciously like an int. In fact, on some systems, an int4 value is exactly the same as an int value, but only if the byte-ordering of your CPU matches "network" byte ordering. The PostgreSQL server transfers integer values in network byte order as defined by the ntohs(), ntohl(), htons(), and htonl() functions. In a multibyte network-ordered value, the first byte transferred across a network (or the byte with the lowest address in memory) is the most significant byte. Most RISC processors (such as Sun's SPARC and HP's PA-RISC) store multibyte integer values in network byte order. Network byte ordering is also known as *big-endian* or RISC ordering. Intel processors use *little-endian* ordering (or simply, Intel ordering). If your client application is running on a little-endian CPU, you must convert integer values from network order to host order. That's what the ntohs() (network-to-host short) and ntohl() (network-to-host long) functions do. Table 8.3 shows the relationships between server data types and their corresponding C data types.

Table 8.3 **Equivalent C Types for Built-In PostgreSQL Types**

SQL Type	C Type	Defined In
abstime	AbsoluteTime	utils/nabstime.h
boolean	bool	postgres.h (maybe compiler built-in)
box	BOX*	utils/geo_decls.h
bytea	bytea*	postgres.h
"char"	char	(compiler built-in)
character	BpChar*	postgres.h
cid	CommandId	postgres.h
date	DateADT	utils/date.h
smallint (int2)	int2 or int16	postgres.h
int2vector	int2vector*	postgres.h
integer (int4)	int4 or int32	postgres.h
real (float4)	float4*	postgres.h
double precision	float8*	postgres.h_(float8)
interval	Interval*	utils/timestamp.h
lseg	LSEG*	utils/geo_decls.h
name	Name	postgres.h
oid	Oid	postgres.h
oidvector	oidvector*	postgres.h
path	PATH*	utils/geo_decls.h
point	POINT*	utils/geo_decls.h
regproc	regproc	postgres.h
reltime	RelativeTime	utils/nabstime.h
text	text*	postgres.h
tid	ItemPointer	storage/itemptr.h
time	TimeADT	utils/date.h
time with time zone	TimeTzADT	utils/date.h
timestamp	Timestamp*	utils/timestamp.h
tinterval	TimeInterval	utils/nabstime.h
varchar	VarChar*	postgres.h
xid	TransactionId	postgres.h

*(Source: PostgreSQL Documentation, Section 31.7.2)

What Table 8.3 does *not* tell you is how to convert a binary value as delivered to your client application into the proper byte ordering. In fact, PostgreSQL doesn't document which pieces are stored in network order and which are stored in host order. To find that information, you have to look at the *type*_recv() and *type*_send() functions in the PostgreSQL source code. For example, to find the network format of a DATE field (stored in a DateADT), you'd have to read through the date_recv() and date_send() functions. And since the format is officially undocumented, it may change with the next release.

We can't recommend using binary format for two reasons. First, it's difficult to find the exact binary representation of each value and the representation may change from release to release. Second, the primary benefit of binary format values is performance—if a value arrives in your application in the format you need, you don't have to convert it from string form first. However, because binary values are *not* guaranteed to be stored in client-host order, you'll have to convert them anyway (unless you happen to be running the client application on a RISC cpu). In general, binary values are rarely worth the hassle.

Now back to the PQexecPrepared() function. As we mentioned before this short diversion, the last argument to PQexecPrepared() determines whether the query results are returned in string form or in binary form. The paramFormats argument tells libpq whether you've provided the *parameter values* (the values that get substituted into the query) in string form or binary form. The paramFormats argument points to an array of (int) indicators—each indicator corresponds to one of the parameter values pointed to by the paramValues array. paramFormats[0] determines the format of paramValues[0] (which corresponds to $1), paramFormats[1] determines the format of paramValues[1] (which corresponds to $2), and so on. If paramFormats[n] is 0, paramValues[n] must point to a null-terminated string. If paramFormats[n] is 1, paramValues[n] must point to a value in binary format. Notice that paramValues[n] must point to a value in either case—it never contains a data value, just a pointer to a value. The rules for supplying binary parameter values are the same as the rules for receiving binary values in the result set—the data type of the binary value must match the network-ordered format of the server-side data type. Again, we don't recommend using binary parameter values—they are error-prone and subject to change.

At this point, the purpose of each argument should be clear. paramCount determines how many entries are in the paramValues, paramLengths, and paramFormats arrays. Each element in paramValues points to a parameter value. paramValues[0] points to the value for parameter $1, paramValues[1] points to the value for parameter $2, and so on. If paramValues[n] contains a null pointer, then parameter $n+1 is assumed to be NULL (likewise, if paramCount is less than the number of parameters in the prepared command, the remaining parameters are assumed to be NULL). If you are providing parameter values in string form, paramLengths and paramFormats should both be null pointers. If you are providing (at least some) parameters in binary form, paramFormats should point to an array of (int) indicators (as described earlier) and paramLengths should point to an array of paramCount lengths (also of type int). If you are providing parameter $n+1 in binary format, paramFormats[n] should set be set to 1 and paramLengths[n] should contain the length of the binary value of the parameter.

Here's a code snippet that shows how to execute the getCustomers command (described earlier) using string-form parameters:

```
...

const char * values[2];

values[0] = "2";      // Start with customer number 2
values[1] = "3";      // End with customer number 3
```

```
result = PQexecPrepared( connection,      // connection object
                         "getCustomers",  // planName
                         2,               // paramCount
                         values,          // paramValues
                         NULL,            // paramLengths
                         NULL,            // paramFormats
                         0 );             // resultFormat
```

PostgreSQL assumes that each parameter value is provided in string form because the
paramFormats argument is NULL. The following snippet shows how to execute the
getCustomers command using binary-form parameters:

```
...
int4     firstCustomer = (int4) htonl( 2 );   // Start with customer number 2
int4     lastCustomer  = (int4) htonl( 3 );   // End with customer number 3
int4  *  valuePointers[2];
int      valueLengths[2];
int      valueFormats[2];

valuePointers[0] = &firstCustomer;
valuePointers[1] = &lastCustomer;

valueLengths[0] = sizeof( firstCustomer );
valueLengths[1] = sizeof( lastCustomer );

valueFormats[0] = 1;                     // Indicate that $1 is in binary format
valueFormats[1] = 1;            // Ditto for $2

result = PQexecPrepared( connection,      // connection object
                         "getCustomers",  // planName
                         2,               // paramCount
                         valuePointers,   // paramValues
                         valueLengths,    // paramLengths
                         valueFormats,    // paramFormats
                         0 );             // resultFormat
```

As you can see, providing parameter values in binary form is much more complex. Don't
forget to convert multibyte integer values into network order first or you'll be sending
the wrong values to the server.

libpq provides another function that combines the PREPARE and EXECUTE steps into a
single function: PQexecParams().

```
PGresult *PQexecParams(PGconn          * connection,
               const char              * command,
               int                       paramCount,
               const Oid               * paramTypes,
               const char * const      * paramValues,
               const int               * paramLengths,
               const int               * paramFormats,
               int                       resultFormat )
```

Notice that this function combines the arguments of the PQprepare() and PQexecPrepared() functions and the arguments work the same way. You may be wondering why libpq provides this function if the whole point behind the PREPARE/EXECUTE model is to separate the two steps. PREPARE/EXECUTE can improve performance if you execute the same command over and over again, but it can also simplify your client application. In most client applications, you execute a fixed set of commands and you know what those commands will be at the time you write the application. What you generally don't know at the time you write a client application is the exact set of values that you'll be working with when you run your program. For example, if you're writing a program that you will use to add tapes to the movies database, you know what a typical INSERT command will look like:

```
INSERT INTO tapes( tape_id, title, duration )
  VALUES( 'MC-68873', 'The Godfather', NULL );
```

but you don't know the actual data values. If you were writing a libpq application using an older version of PostgreSQL (older than 7.3), you had to generate the entire INSERT command each time you wanted to add a new row. Before the PREPARE/EXECUTE model, you would typically generate the INSERT command using the sprintf() function, like this:

```
...
char       insertCommand[MAX_COMMAND_LEN+1];

sprintf( insertCommand,
         "INSERT INTO tapes(tape_id,title,duration) VALUES('%s', '%s', '%s')",
         tapeID, title, duration );
```

At first glance, the sprintf() approach doesn't seem too bad, but there are a number of gotchas lurking in that code. First, what happens if the formatted command won't fit into the insertCommand buffer? That's a stack overflow waiting to happen (of course you can avoid the stack overflow by using the snprintf() function instead, but that merely truncates the command before it overflows—you still end up with an invalid command). Next, you have to take care of NULL values in some fashion. For example, if the duration value is unknown, you should really insert NULL instead of 0. That makes the code more complex. Finally, any string values (like the tapeID and title values) must be properly quoted. What happens if you try to add a tape whose title is "The Sorcerer's Apprentice"? That apostrophe will result in a syntax error unless you take steps to quote it properly first. Finally, if you've gathered any of these values from an untrusted source, a devious user could destroy data simply by supplying a carefully crafted movie title. Consider what would happen if you blindly inserted a movie titled "Bye Bye Data', '5 hours'); DROP DATABASE movies;" into the previous command.

You can avoid all of those problems using PREPARE/EXECUTE. Even if you don't need to execute the same command over and over again, you can still use PQexecParams() to simplify your application.

Client 4—An Interactive Query Processor

At this point, you should have a pretty good understanding of how to use many of the libpq functions. There are two other issues I want to explore in this chapter: processing multiple result sets and asynchronous operations. Before we get to those, let's convert the previous client application (client3d) into an interactive query processor. After you've done that, you will have a good example of why you need to consider multiple result sets and asynchronous processing.

The next client that we want to build connects to a database and prompts you for a SQL command. client4 sends the command to the server and display the results. The program repeats this cycle (prompt, execute, display) until you enter the command quit.

You've already seen most of the code in this application—it builds on the client3d application. The important difference between client3d and client4 is that you'll use the GNU readline library to prompt the user for multiple commands (in client3d, the command text was hard-coded).

```
 1 /*
 2 ** File:  client4.c
 3 */
 4
 5 #include <stdlib.h>
 6 #include <string.h>
 7 #include <libpq-fe.h>
 8 #include <readline/readline.h>
 9 #include <readline/history.h>
10
11 typedef enum { FALSE, TRUE } bool;
```

Notice the two extra header files in this application. The readline/readline.h header file defines the interface to the GNU readline library. You may not be familiar with the name of the readline library; but if you are a Linux (or bash) user, you probably know the user interface that it provides. When you use the readline library in your application, your users can enter SQL commands *and* correct their typing errors. I don't know about you, but I type faster backward than I do forward—I hate using tools that don't let me correct typing mistakes.

The readline/history.h header file defines the interface to the GNU history library. readline and history work well together. The history library gives you an easy way to record SQL commands and recall them later.

I'll show you how to use readline and history a bit later.

```
13 #define MAX_PRINT_LEN        40
14
15 static char separator[MAX_PRINT_LEN+1];
16
17 void print_result_set( PGresult * result )
18 {
```

```
19   int          col;
20   int          row;
21   int           * sizes;
22
23 /*
24 ** Compute the size for each column
25 */
26   sizes = (int *)calloc( PQnfields( result ), sizeof( int ));
27
28   for( col - 0; col < PQnfields( result ); col++ )
29   {
30     int    len = 0;
31
32     for( row = 0; row < PQntuples( result ); row++ )
33     {
34       if( PQgetisnull( result, row, col ))
35         len = 0;
36       else
37         len = PQgetlength( result, row, col );
38
39       if( len > sizes[col] )
40         sizes[col] - len;
41     }
42
43     if(( len = strlen( PQfname( result, col ))) > sizes[col] )
44       sizes[col] = len;
45
46     if( sizes[col] > MAX_PRINT_LEN )
47       sizes[col] = MAX_PRINT_LEN;
48   }
49
50 /*
51 ** Print the field names.
52 */
53   for( col = 0; col < PQnfields( result ); col++ )
54   {
55     printf( "%-*s ", sizes[col], PQfname( result, col ));
56   }
57
58   printf( "\n" );
59
60 /*
61 ** Print the separator line
62 */
63   memset( separator, '-', MAX_PRINT_LEN );
64
65   for( col = 0; col < PQnfields( result ); col++ )
```

```
66    {
67      printf( "%*.*s ", sizes[col], sizes[col], separator );
68    }
69
70    printf( "\n" );
71
72  /*
73  ** Now loop through each of the tuples returned by
74  ** our query and print the results.
75  */
76    for( row = 0; row < PQntuples( result ); row++ )
77    {
78      for( col = 0; col < PQnfields( result ); col++ )
79      {
80        if( PQgetisnull( result, row, col ))
81          printf( "%*s", sizes[col], "" );
82        else
83          printf( "%*s ", sizes[col], PQgetvalue( result, row, col ));
84      }
85
86      printf( "\n" );
87
88    }
89    printf( "(%d rows)\n\n", PQntuples( result ));
90    free( sizes );
91  }
92
93  void process_query( PGconn * connection, const char * query_text )
94  {
95    PGresult  *        result;
96
97    if(( result = PQexec( connection, query_text )) == NULL )
98    {
99      printf( "%s\n", PQerrorMessage( connection ));
100     return;
101   }
102
103   if( PQresultStatus( result ) == PGRES_TUPLES_OK )
104   {
105     print_result_set( result );
106   }
107   else if( PQresultStatus( result ) == PGRES_COMMAND_OK )
108   {
109     printf( "%s", PQcmdStatus( result ));
110
111     if( strlen( PQcmdTuples( result )))
112       printf( " - %s rows\n\n", PQcmdTuples( result ));
```

```
113    else
114       printf( "\n\n" );
115    }
116    else
117    {
118       printf( "%s\n\n", PQresultErrorMessage( result ));
119    }
120
121    PQclear( result );
122 }
```

The print_result_set() and process_query() functions in client4 are identical to those used in client3d. If you need a refresher on how these functions operate, look back to the previous example.

```
124 int main( int argc, char * argv[] )
125 {
126    PGconn  * connection;
127    char    * buf;
128
129
130    connection = PQconnectdb( argc > 1 ? argv[1] : "" );
131
132    if( connection == NULL )
133    {
134      printf( "Fatal error - unable to allocate connection\n" );
135      exit( EXIT_FAILURE );
136    }
137
138    if( PQstatus( connection ) == CONNECTION_OK )
139    {
140
141      using_history();
142      read_history( ".pg_history" );
143
144      while(( buf = readline( "-->" )) != NULL )
145      {
146        if( strncmp( buf, "quit", sizeof( "quit" ) - 1  ) == 0 )
147        {
148          break;
149        }
150        else
151        {
152          if(strlen( buf ) != 0 )
153          {
154            add_history( buf );
155            process_query( connection, buf );
156          }
```

```
157          free( buf );
158        }
159      }
160
161    err = write_history( ".pg_history" );
162
163  }
164  else
165  {
166    printf( "%s\n", PQerrorMessage( connection ));
167  }
168
169  PQfinish( connection );
170
171  exit( EXIT_SUCCESS );
172 }
```

The main() function differs significantly from client3d. The first change you might
notice is how we handle command-line arguments. In previous examples, you had to
enter a connection string on the command line. Now we are trying to be a bit more
user-friendly, so the command-line argument is optional. If you provide a command-line
argument, we assume that it is a connection string. If you don't, you'll call
PQconnectdb() with an empty string (see line 130) to indicate that you want to connect
using the default connection attributes (either the compiled-in values or values derived
from the connection-related environment variables).

The most significant change is the processing loop starting at line 141 and continuing
through line 158. At line 141, client4 calls a function named using_history() to initialize the GNU history library.

Just before exiting this application, client4 will call the write_history() function
to write your command history to the $PWD/.pg_history file. The call to read_histo-
ry() reads in any history records from previous invocations. Using write_history()
and read_history(), you can maintain a command history across multiple invocations
of client4. The read_history() and write_history() functions are part of the GNU
history library.

At line 144, this application prompts the user for a command using the readline()
function. readline() is the primary function in the GNU readline library (no big sur-
prise there). This function prints the prompt (-->) and waits for you to enter a complete
command. You can use the normal editing keys (backspace, left and right arrows, and so
on) to correct typing errors. You can also use the up- and down-arrow keys to scroll
through command history. (See the readline man page for a complete list of editing
options.) readline() returns a pointer to the null-terminated command string entered
by the user. readline() will return a NULL pointer if the user presses the end-of-file key
(usually Ctrl-D).

client4 checks for the quit command at line 146 and breaks out of the command-
processing loop when it finds it.

If you enter a non-blank command, the command is added to the history list `process_query()` is called to execute and display the results. You should `free()` the buffer returned by `readline()` after you have finished processing the command.

At line 161, `client4` writes the history list to the `.pg_history` file. The next time you run this application, it will read the `.pg_history` file at startup.

This function finishes up by handling connection errors (at line 166), disconnecting from the server (line 166), and exiting.

You have to make a couple of minor changes to the `makefile` before you can build this application:

```
##
##  File:  Makefile
##
##         Rules for building libpq sample applications
##


INCLUDES  += -I/usr/local/pgsql/include

CPPFLAGS  += $(INCLUDES)
CFLAGS    += -g

LDLIBS    += -L/usr/local/pgsql/lib -lpq
LDFLAGS   += -g

client1:       client1.o
get_dflts:     get_dflts.o

client4:       LDLIBS += -lreadline ltermcap
client4:       client4.o
```

The last two lines tell `make` to link `client4.o` against the `readline` (and `termcap`) libraries to build the `client4` application (`termcap` is required by the `readline` library).

Now let's build `client4` and test it:

```
$ make client4
cc -g -I/usr/local/pgsql/include -c -o client4.o client4.c
cc -g client4.o -L/usr/local/pgsql/lib -lpq -lreadline -ltermcap -o client4

$ ./client4
-->SELECT * FROM rentals;
tape_id   rental_date customer_id
--------  ----------- -----------
AB-12345  2002-07-01            1
AB-67472  2002-07-01            3
OW-41221  2002-07-01            1
(3 rows)
-->quit
$
```

Go ahead and play around with `client4` a little. Try the editing keys; use the up-arrow key and down-arrow key to scroll through your history list. Notice that when you quit and reinvoke `client4`, you can recall the commands entered in the previous session[4].

Processing Multiple Result Sets

Now try an experiment. Run `client4` and enter two commands on the same line, terminating the first command with a semicolon:

```
$ client4 "dbname=movies"
-->SELECT * FROM tapes; SELECT * FROM rentals
tape_id   rental_date customer_id
--------  ----------- -----------
AB-12345  2002-07-03            1
AB-67472  2002-07-03            3
OW-41221  2002-07-03            1
(3 rows)
-->
```

Hmmm, there's a problem here. We executed two SELECT commands, but we only see the results of the last command.

This demonstrates a problem with the `PQexec()` function. `PQexec()` discards all result sets except for the last one.

Fortunately, it's not too difficult to fix this problem. Here is a replacement for the `process_query()` function that will correctly handle multiple result sets (this function appears in `client4b.c` in the sample source code):

```
 1 void process_query( PGconn * connection, const char * query_text )
 2 {
 3   PGresult  *        result;
 4
 5   if( PQsendQuery( connection, query_text ) == 0 )
 6   {
 7     printf( "%s\n", PQerrorMessage( connection ));
 8     return;
 9   }
10
11   while(( result = PQgetResult( connection )) != NULL )
12   {
13     if( PQresultStatus( result ) == PGRES_TUPLES_OK )
14     {
15       print_result_set( result );
16     }
17     else if( PQresultStatus( result ) == PGRES_COMMAND_OK )
```

---

[4] If you find that your command history is not saved between sessions, it is probably because you don't have the permissions required to create the `.pg_history` file in your current directory.

```
18      {
19        printf( "%s", PQcmdStatus( result ));
20
21        if( strlen( PQcmdTuples( result )))
22          printf( " - %s rows\n", PQcmdTuples( result ));
23        else
24          printf( "\n" );
25      }
26      else
27      {
28        printf( "%s\n", PQresultErrorMessage( result ));
29      }
30
31      PQclear( result );
32    }
33 }
```

In this version of process_query(), you split the command-processing effort into two steps. First, send the command string to the server using the PQsendQuery() function. PQsendQuery() returns immediately after queuing the command—it will not wait for results from the server. If PQsendQuery() cannot send the command string, it will return 0 and you can find the error message by calling PQerrorMessage().

The second step starts at line 11. You call PQgetResult() to obtain a result set from the server. Notice that you invoke PQgetResult() within a loop. PQgetResult() returns one result set for each command in the command string and returns NULL when there are no more result sets to process. The PQgetResult() function returns a pointer to a PGresult object—we already know how to work with a PGresult, so the rest of this function remains unchanged.

Now let's try to run this version (client4b):

```
$ client4b "dbname=movies"
-->SELECT * FROM tapes; SELECT * FROM rentals
tape_id  title
-------- --------------
AB-12345 The Godfather
AB-67472 The Godfather
MC-68873  Casablanca
OW-41221  Citizen Kane
AH-54706  Rear Window
(5 rows)

tape_id  rental_date customer_id
-------- ----------- -----------
AB-12345 2002-07-03           1
AB-67472 2002-07-03           3
OW-41221 2002-07-03           1
(3 rows)
```

```
-->quit
$
```

This time, you get the results that you would expect: one result set for each command.

Asynchronous Processing

In the previous section, I mentioned that the PQsendQuery() function will not wait for a result set to be returned by the server. That can be an important feature for certain applications, particularly graphical (GUI) applications. In a GUI application, your code must remain responsive to the user even if you are waiting for results from a long-running SQL command. If you use PQexec() in a GUI application, you will find that the screen will not repaint while waiting for server results. The PQexec() function (and in fact most of the libpq functions) is *synchronous*—the function will not return until the work has been completed.

In a GUI application, you need *asynchronous* functions, like PQsendQuery() (or, you can write a multithreaded client application, but that can be much more difficult). Things get a little more complex when you use asynchronous functions. Simply using PQsendQuery() is not enough to make your application responsive while waiting for results. Without doing some extra work, your application will still pause when you call the PQgetResult() function.

Here is a revised version of the process_query() function:

```
 1 void process_query( PGconn * connection, const char * query_text )
 2 {
 3   PGresult  *       result;
 4
 5   if( PQsendQuery( connection, query_text ) == 0 )
 6   {
 7     printf( "%s\n", PQerrorMessage( connection ));
 8     return;
 9   }
10
11   do
12   {
13     while( is_result_ready( connection ) == FALSE )
14     {
15       putchar( '.' );
16       fflush( stdout );
17     }
18     printf( "\n" );
19
20     if(( result = PQgetResult( connection )) != NULL )
21     {
22       if( PQresultStatus( result ) == PGRES_TUPLES_OK )
23       {
24         print_result_set( result );
```

```
25        }
26        else if( PQresultStatus( result ) == PGRES_COMMAND_OK )
27        {
28          printf( "%s", PQcmdStatus( result ));
29
30          if( strlen( PQcmdTuples( result )))
31            printf( " - %s rows\n", PQcmdTuples( result ));
32          else
33            printf( "\n" );
34        }
35        else
36        {
37          printf( "%s\n", PQresultErrorMessage( result ));
38        }
39        PQclear( result );
40      }
41    } while( result != NULL );
42 }
```

The important change to this version of process_query() starts at line 13. After sending
the command to the server, process_query() enters a loop that calls
is_result_ready(). The is_result_ready() function waits for a result set to appear
from the server. is_result_ready() will wait no longer than one second—if a result set
is not ready within one second, is_result_ready() will return FALSE. This client simu-
lates normal GUI processing by printing a "." for every second that we wait. (Okay,
that's a pretty cheap imitation of a GUI don't you think?)

Now let's look at the is_result_ready() function:

```
44 bool is_result_ready( PGconn * connection )
45 {
46     int            my_socket;
47     struct timeval timer;
48     fd_set         read_mask;
49
50     if( PQisBusy( connection ) == 0 )
51       return( TRUE );
52
53     my_socket = PQsocket( connection );
54
55     timer.tv_sec  = (time_t)1;
56     timer.tv_usec = 0;
57
58     FD_ZERO( &read_mask );
59     FD_SET( my_socket, &read_mask );
60
61     if( select(my_socket + 1, &read_mask, NULL, NULL, &timer) == 0)
62     {
```

```
63          return( FALSE );
64        }
65        else if( FD_ISSET( my_socket, &read_mask ))
66        {
67          PQconsumeInput( connection );
68
69          if( PQisBusy( connection ) == 0 )
70            return( TRUE );
71          else
72            return( FALSE );
73        }
74        else
75        {
76          return( FALSE );
77        }
78  }
```

This is one of the most complex functions that we've seen in this chapter. We start (at line 50) by calling a the PQisBusy() function. PQisBusy() returns 0 if a result set is ready for processing, and 1 if not.

If you find that a result set is not ready, you have more work to do. It might help to understand the details to come if you have a quick overview of where you are heading.

When you connect to a PostgreSQL server, the connection is represented by a PGconn object. You know that a PGconn object is opaque—you can't look at the internals of the object to see what's inside. libpq provides one function that enables you to peek under the covers: PQsocket(). The PQsocket() returns the network socket that libpq uses to communicate with the server. We will use that socket to determine when data from the server becomes available.

Although server data is available it does *not* mean that a result set is ready. This is an important point. You may find that a single byte has been received from the server, but the result set is many megabytes in size. Once you know that *some* data is available, you have to let libpq peek at it. The PQconsumeInput() function (from libpq) reads all available server data and assembles it into a partial result set. After libpq has processed the available data, you can ask if an entire result set is ready for you.

That's the overview, now the details.

At line 53, is_result_ready() retrieves the client/server socket by calling PQsocket(). Remember, this is the socket that libpq uses to communicate with the server.

Next, is_result_ready() prepares to wait for data to become available from the server. At lines 55 and 56, we set up a timer structure. You want to wait, at most, one second for data to become available from the server so you initialize the timer structure to indicate one second and zero microseconds. This is an arbitrary value—if you want to be a bit more responsive, you can choose a shorter interval. If you want to consume fewer CPU cycles, you can choose a longer interval.

At lines 58 and 59, you initialize an fd_set structure. An fd_set is a data structure that represents a set of file (or, in our case, socket) descriptors. When you call select(), you must tell it which file descriptors (or socket descriptors) you are interested in. You want to listen for data on the socket you retrieved from PQsocket(), so turn on the corresponding entry in the fd_set[5].

At line 61, you see a call to the select() function. This function waits until any of the following occurs:

- Data is ready on one of the file descriptors indicated in the read_mask.

- The timer expires (that is, one second elapses).

- A Unix signal is intercepted.

In other words, the select() function returns after waiting one second for data to become available on the my_socket socket. If data is ready before the timer expires, select() will return immediately.

When select() finally returns, you have to figure out which of the three previously mentioned events actually occurred.

If select() returns zero, it's telling you that the timer expired without any activity on my_socket. In that case, you know that a result set can't possibly be ready so is_result_ready() returns FALSE to your caller.

If select() returns something other than zero, you know that one of the file descriptors specified in read_mask has some data available. We'll be good little programmers here and use the FD_ISSET() macro to make sure that data is available on the my_socket socket. Practically speaking, there is only one descriptor enabled in read_mask, so you know that if any of the descriptors has data, it must be your descriptor.

At line 66, you know that *some* data is available from the server, but you don't know if an entire result set is ready: call PQconsumeInput(). PQconsumeInput() reads all data available from the server and stuffs that data into the result set that is being accumulated.

After that's done, you can call PQisBusy() again. PQisBusy() tells you whether a complete result set has been assembled. If PQisBusy() returns 0 (meaning, no, the connection is not busy), you tell the caller that a result set is ready for processing. Otherwise, you return FALSE to indicate that more data is needed.

Lines 74 through 77 handle the case where a Unix signal interrupted the call to select(). There really isn't much to do in this case, so just tell the caller that a result set is *not* ready for processing.

---

[5] This description might sound a bit mysterious. We programmers aren't supposed to know how an fd_set is implemented. The developers of the socket library want to hide the implementation so they can change it without our permission. We are only supposed to use a prescribed set of macros and functions to manipulate an fd_set. Think of an fd_set as a big set of bits. Each bit corresponds to a file/socket descriptor. When you call PQsocket(), it gives you back a number— you want to turn on the bit corresponding to that number to tell select() that you are interested in activity on that socket. The FD_SET() macro turns on one bit. FD_ZERO() turns off all the bits. Now, if anyone asks, pretend that you don't know any of this stuff.

If you want to try this code, you will find it in the `client4c.c` source file. Here is a sample session:

```
$ ./client4c dbname=movies
-->SELECT COUNT(*) FROM pg_class, pg_attribute;
.........
count
-----
96690
(1 rows)
-->
```

Notice that it took nine seconds to execute this query (nine dots printed while we were waiting for the result set to come back from the server).

libpq provides three functions that you can use to asynchronously execute *parameterized* commands (using the `PREPARE`/`EXECUTE` model). `PQsendPrepare()` is analogous to the `PQprepare()` function, except it executes in an asynchronous fashion. Call the `PQsendQueryPrepared()` function to execute a previously prepared command without waiting for the result set. The `PQsendQueryParams()` function combines the `PREPARE` and `EXECUTE` steps into a single non-blocking function. See the section titled "The Prepare/Execute Model" earlier in this chapter for more information about processing parameterized commands.

Besides the asynchronous command processing functions, libpq offers a way to make asynchronous connection attempts. I find that the asynchronous connection functions are overly complex for the limited benefits that they offer. In general, database connections are established in such a short period of time that I am willing to wait for the attempt to complete. If you find that a connection attempt is taking an excessive amount of time, you probably have a name server problem and I would rather fix that problem. If you do find that you need to make asynchronous connection attempts, see the *PostgreSQL Programmer's Guide*.

Summary

The libpq library is very well designed. I've used many other database APIs (OCI from Oracle, DBLibrary and OpenClient from Sybase, and ODBC) and none have compared to the simplicity offered by libpq. Other database APIs may offer a few more features, but these generally come at the cost of greatly increased complexity.

I encourage you to try the sample applications in this chapter. Feel free to experiment. I haven't covered all the libpq functions in this chapter, only the ones you are most likely to need in your own applications. Explore the library; as you will see in the next few chapters, libpq is the foundation on which most of the other PostgreSQL APIs are built. The better you understand libpq, the easier it will be to work with other APIs.

A Simpler C API—libpgeasy

The libpq library is very powerful. In fact, libpq is the basis for most of the other PostgreSQL APIs—the other APIs translate a high-level request into a set of calls to the libpq library. The power behind libpq comes at the price of complexity. libpgeasy lets you avoid that complexity by acting as a lightweight wrapper around the more commonly used libpq functions. The simplicity afforded by the use of libpgeasy often comes at the expense of functionality.

The functions provided by the libpgeasy library use the same data structures used by libpq. For example, when you connect to a database using libpgeasy, you get back a PGconn * ; that's the same data type that you get when you connect to a database using libpq. This means that you can mix and match calls to libpq and libpgeasy, taking advantage of the power of libpq and the simplicity of libpgeasy.

Although the data types of libpq and libpqeasy may be similar, the design philosophies of libpq and libpgeasy are very different. libpq is designed to provide access to all the features of the PostgreSQL server. Libpgeasy, on the other hand, is designed to provide a simple interface to the most commonly used PostgreSQL features.

Prerequisites

As mentioned previously, libpgeasy is a wrapper around libpq. The basic requirements for building a libpq client were described in Chapter 8, "The PostgreSQL C API—libpq," and so I won't repeat them here.

libpgeasy is no longer included in the core PostgreSQL distribution. If you want to try out libpgeasy, you can download it from the official PostgreSQL Projects website, gborg.postgresql.org (search for "pgeasy"). Once you've downloaded the most recent (stable) version, unpack the archive (it will be named something like libpgeasy-version.tgz) into a temporary directory and then do the typical GNU two-step to configure and compile the library. Once you've unpacked the archive, move into the newly created directory and browse through the README file—note that you have to tell the configure script how to find the libpq header files and library. If you're running a relatively recent version of PostgreSQL, you can use the pg_config utility to do the hard work for you; just run the command:

```
$ export CPPFLAGS=-I$(pg_config --includedir)
$ export LDFLAGS=-L$(pg_config --libdir)
./configure
```

If you're using an older version of PostgreSQL (a version that does not include the pg_config utility), follow the directions in the README file to configure the libpgeasy source code. When the configure script completes, execute the following command to compile and install libpgeasy:

```
$ make && make install
```

That's it. You should be ready to compile and link your own libpgeasy applications. In addition to the libpq header files and object libraries, you will need to #include the libpgeasy.h file and link to the libpgeasy object library (-lpgeasy).

Client 1—Connecting to the Server

Connecting to a database using libpgeasy is simple. libpgeasy provides a single connection function:

```
PGconn * connectdb( char * options );
```

The single argument to connectdb() is a connection string in the same form expected by the libpq PQconnectdb() function. An example connection string might look like this:

```
char * connectString = "dbname=movies user=sheila";
```

Let's look at a simple client that uses the connectdb() function:

```
/* client1.c */

#include <stdlib.h>
#include <libpq-fe.h>
#include <libpgeasy.h>

int main( int argc, char * argv[] )
{
  connectdb( argv[1] ? argv[1] : "" );
  disconnectdb();
  exit( EXIT_SUCCESS );

}
```

You can use the following makefile to compile and link all samples in this chapter (see the section titled "Using GNU make to Build libpq applications" in Chapter 8 for more information about makefiles).

```
# Filename: makefile

INCLUDES = -I$(shell pg_config --includedir)
```

```
CFLAGS  += $(INCLUDES) -g

LDFLAGS += -g -L $(shell pg_config --libdir) -lpgeasy -lpq

ALL  = client1.o
ALL += client2a.o client2b.o
ALL += client3a.o client3b.o client3c.o
ALL += client4.o

all:    $(ALL)

client4:       client4.o -lreadline -ltermcap
```

client1.c shows the minimum required code for a libpgeasy application. You must #include two files: libpq-fe.h and libpgeasy.h, and you must #include them in that order[1].

In the call to connectdb(), I've passed in the first command-line argument (or an empty string if there are no command-line arguments). When you run this program, you should provide a connection string as the only argument. If you need to specify more than one connection property, enclose the list in double quotes and separate the properties with a space. Here are two examples:

```
$ ./client1 dbname=movies
$ ./client1 "dbname=movies user=sheila"
```

After the connectdb() function returns, I call disconnectdb(). The function prototype for disconnectdb() is

```
void disconnectdb( void );
```

Notice that disconnectdb() does not expect any arguments. You may have also noticed that I did not capture any return value from the call to connectdb().

How does libpgeasy know which connection I want to terminate? In keeping with the goal of simplicity, libpgeasy remembers the database connection for me. When I call connectdb(), libpgeasy stores (in a private variable) the PGconn pointer. When I call disconnectdb(), it uses the stored connection pointer. Although libpgeasy has the capacity to remember the database connection, it will remember only one connection at a time. This is one example of the tradeoffs made when using libpgeasy versus libpq— you have gained simplicity, but lost some flexibility.

If you want, you can capture the return value from connectdb() in a PGconn pointer variable and use it in the same ways that you could use a PGconn * through libpq.

Now let's run this client application to see what it does:

```
$ ./client1 dbname=movies
$
```

---

[1] libpqeasy refers to items in libqp-fe, so they must be #included in that order.

Exciting, don't you think? Let's try that again, feeding it an erroneous database name this time:

```
$ ./client1 dbname=foofoo
Connection to database using 'dbname=foofoo' failed.
FATAL 1:  Database "foofoo" does not exist in the system catalog.
$
```

This time, you can see that libpgeasy produced an error message. The `client1.c` source code doesn't include any error handling at all—you didn't include any code to check for errors or to print error messages. Again, this is consistent with the goal of simplicity. Of course, in a sophisticated application, you probably want a little more control over the handling of error conditions.

Client 2—Adding Error Checking

Now let's add a little error-handling code to the client:

```
/* client2a.c    */

#include <stdlib.h>
#include <libpq-fe.h>
#include <libpgeasy.h>

int main( int argc, char * argv[] )
{
  PGconn *  connection;

  connection = connectdb( argv[1] ? argv[1] : "" );

  if( PQstatus( connection ) != CONNECTION_OK )
    printf( "Caught an error: %s\n", PQerrorMessage( connection ));
  else
    printf( "connection ok\n" );

  disconnectdb();

  exit( EXIT_SUCCESS );
}
```

This time around, I captured the `PGconn *` returned by `connectdb()`. Remember that this `PGconn *` is the same type of object that you would find in a libpq application. Call the `PQstatus()` function to determine whether the connection attempt succeeded or failed. If a failure occurs, this function prints an error message; otherwise, it prints "connection ok".

Let's run this a couple of times to see how it behaves:

```
$ ./client2a dbname=movies
connection ok
```

As expected, you see a friendly little confirmation that the connection attempt was successful. Now let's feed in an error and see what happens:

```
$ ./client2a dbname=foofoo
Connection to database using 'dbname=foofoo' failed.
FATAL 1:  Database "foofoo" does not exist in the system catalog.
```

This time, you see an error message. But look closely and you'll see that the error message doesn't match your source code—the error message should start with the text Caught an error:.

What happened? If you don't make any other arrangements, connectdb() will print an error message and terminate the calling program if it encounters a failure. So, this program didn't even get to the point where it could call PQstatus()—the program terminated before connectdb() ever returned.

So, how do you make these "other arrangements?" libpgeasy provides two functions that you can use to control the error-handling mode:

```
void on_error_stop( void );
void on_error_continue( void );
```

The on_error_stop() function tells libpgeasy that you want it to handle error conditions. Calling on_error_continue() tells libpgeasy that you want to handle error conditions yourself. on_error_stop() is the default error-handling mode.

I should point out here that calling on_error_continue() has no effect on the connectdb() function. If the connection attempt fails, connectdb() will terminate the program regardless of which error-handling mode is in effect.

In the next section, you will see that libpgeasy does in fact let you construct your own error-handling code once a connection has been established.

Client 3—Processing Queries

Query processing is simple in libpgeasy. To execute a SQL command, you call the doquery() function. The function prototype for doquery() is

```
PGresult * doquery( char * query );
```

Notice that doquery() does not expect a PGconn *—libpgeasy can deal with only a single database connection and it implicitly uses the one returned by connectdb(). doquery() returns a PGresult *. This is the same data structure you saw in the previous chapter—it represents the result set of the query.

After you have executed a command, you will need to process the result set. libpgeasy provides a number of functions for dealing with a result set—of course, you can use any of the libpq functions as well.

If you are reasonably sure that your query succeeded, you can use the fetch() function to retrieve a single row from the result set. Here is the function prototype for fetch():

```
int fetch( void * param, ... );
```

The fetch() function returns the index of the row that you just fetched. The first row returned is row 0, the second row is row 1, and so on. When the result set is exhausted, fetch() will return END_OF_TUPLES. If the query returns zero rows, the first call to fetch() will return END_OF_TUPLES. When you call fetch(), you pass a list of pointers.

Each argument should point to a buffer large enough to hold the corresponding field from the result set. You must pass one pointer for each column returned by the query. If you aren't interested in the value of a column, you can pass a NULL pointer.

This might be a good point to see an example:

```
/* client3a.c */

#include <stdlib.h>
#include <libpq-fe.h>
#include <libpgeasy.h>

int main( int argc, char * argv[] )
{
  char      tape_id[8+1];
  char      title[80+1];
  char      duration[80+1];
  PGconn *  connection;

  connection = connectdb( argv[1] ? argv[1] : "" );

  on_error_stop( );

  doquery( "SELECT * FROM tapes" );

  while( fetch( tape_id, title, duration ) != END_OF_TUPLES )
  {
    printf( "%s - %-40s - %s\n", tape_id, title, duration );
  }

  disconnectdb();

  exit( EXIT_SUCCESS );

}
```

In client3a.c, I select all columns (and all rows) from the tapes table. Here is the definition of tapes:

```
movies=# \d tapes
               Table "tapes"
 Attribute  |         Type          | Modifier
-----------+-----------------------+----------
 tape_id    | character(8)          | not null
 title      | character varying(80) | not null
 duration   | interval              |
```

---

[2] I tend to declare my string buffers using this n+1 format. I could obviously declare the tape_id variable as "char tape_id[9];". When I see [9], I wonder if I forgot to include space for the null terminator. When I see [8+1], I know I did the right thing.

I've allocated three buffers; one for each column in the table. The `tape_id` column is eight characters long. The buffer that I allocated for `tape_id` is `8+1` bytes[2] long—the extra byte is for the null terminator (remember that C strings are terminated with a zero, or null, byte). `title` is a varchar with a maximum of 80 characters; my buffer is 80+1 bytes long. The duration column is an `interval`; it will be automatically converted into a null-terminated character string. You don't know exactly how long the text form of an `interval` will be, but 80+1 bytes should be enough.

I haven't included any error-handling code in this program, so I'll ask libpgeasy to intercept any error conditions by calling `on_error_stop()`. As I mentioned earlier, `on_error_stop()` is the default error-handling mode, but including an explicit call makes the behavior obvious to anyone reading your code.

Next, I'll call `doquery()` to send the command to the server.

When `doquery()` returns, it has assembled the result set and I can call `fetch()` repeatedly to process each row. When I call the `fetch()` function, I pass in three addresses. `fetch()` matches each buffer that I provide with a column in the result set. The `tape_id` column is placed in my `tape_id` buffer, the `title` column is placed in my `title` buffer, and the duration column is placed in my duration buffer. If I am not interested in retrieving a field, I can pass in a `NULL` pointer for that field.

Some readers might find my call to `fetch()` a little confusing at first. It may clarify things to rewrite the call to `fetch()` as follows:

```
while( fetch( &tape_id[0], &title[0], &duration[0] ) != END_OF_TUPLES )
```

Writing the code this way makes it a little more obvious that I am passing the address of the first byte of each buffer to `fetch()`.

After `fetch()` returns, I print the row. In case you aren't too familiar with the syntax, "`%-40s`" tells `printf()` to print the `title` within a left-justified 40-character column[3]. Let's run this program:

```
$ ./client3a dbname=movies
AB-12345 - The Godfather                         -
AB-67472 - The Godfather                         -
MC-68873 - Casablanca                            -
OW-41221 - Citizen Kane                          -
AH-54706 - Rear Window                           -
```

There is one very important point to understand when you use the `fetch()` function. When you call `fetch()`, you are passing in buffer pointers—`fetch()` has no way to know how large those buffers are. If you give `fetch()` a pointer to a four-byte buffer, but you really need 80 bytes to hold a value, `fetch()` will happily copy 80 bytes. The most likely effect of this is that your program will immediately crash—if you are lucky. If you aren't lucky, your program will exhibit random failures that are really hard to track down. Sometimes, ignorance is not bliss.

---

[3] The title column is 80 characters wide but I am only printing the first 40 characters to conserve screen real estate.

Working with Binary Cursors

You can use the libpgeasy library to retrieve binary[4] data as well as text-form data. Using binary data can give you a performance boost in a few cases, but you usually use binary cursors to retrieve, well...binary data (such as JPEG files, audio files, and so on). Let's modify this simple application a little to see how binary data is handled (the examples are getting a little longer now, so I'll start including line numbers):

```
 1 /* client3b.c */
 2
 3 #include <stdlib.h>
 4 #include <libpq-fe.h>
 5 #include <libpgeasy.h>
 6
 7 int main( int argc, char * argv[] )
 8 {
 9   int        customer_id;
10   char       customer_name[80+1];
11   PGconn *   connection;
12
13   connection = connectdb( argv[1] ? argv[1] : "" );
14
15   on_error_stop( );
16
17   doquery( "BEGIN WORK" );
18   doquery( "DECLARE customer_list BINARY CURSOR FOR "
19            "SELECT customer_id, customer_name FROM customers" );
20
21
22   doquery( "FETCH ALL FROM customer_list" );
23
24   while( fetch( &customer_id, customer_name ) != END_OF_TUPLES )
25   {
26     printf( "%d: %-40s\n", customer_id, customer_name );
27   }
28
29   doquery( "COMMIT" );
30
31   disconnectdb();
32   exit( EXIT_SUCCESS );
33 }
```

This example is a little more complex than the previous one. To retrieve binary values, I have to DECLARE a BINARY CURSOR within the context of a transaction block. At line 17,

---

[4] Binary is really a misnomer. Declaring a binary cursor really means that you will get results in the form used to store the data in PostgreSQL. If you don't use a binary cursor, PostgreSQL will convert all values into null-terminated strings.

I create a new transaction; the transaction will end at line 29. At line 18, I declare a binary cursor. Rather than processing the (direct) results of a SELECT statement, I loop through the results of a FETCH ALL.

In the previous example (client3a.c), I used the fetch() function to retrieve the text form for each value. In client3b.c, I am retrieving binary values. The fetch() function doesn't know anything about data types—it just copies bytes from the result set into the buffer that was provided.

If you compare the call that I made to printf() in client3b to the corresponding call in client3a, you will see that the difference between text and binary form is reflected in the format string. With text format data, you can always use %s to print result values. With binary data, the format string depends on the underlying column types.

The customer_id column is defined as an int. You want fetch() to copy the customer_id column into the customer_id variable. Because this is a binary cursor, the customer_id column will come to us in binary (or int) form; therefore, customer_id is declared as an int. The customer_name column is defined as a VARCHAR(50)—a character column comes to you as a null terminated string regardless of whether you are retrieving from a binary or text-form cursor.

Now let's run this client:

```
$ ./client3b dbname=movies
16777216: Jones, Henry
67108864: Wonderland, Alice N.
33554432: Rubin, William
50331648: Panky, Henry
```

Not what you expected to see? Why does client3b display the wrong customer_id for each row? Read on to learn why binary cursors aren't as easy to use as they first appear.

Byte Ordering and NULL Values

There are two more things you have to worry about when working with a binary cursor.

If the client application is not on the same host as the server, you must be concerned about byte ordering. As I mentioned in the previous chapter, different processors (CPUs) order the bytes within numeric data types in different ways. The PostgreSQL client/server protocol always sends numeric data in "network byte order." If you are running a client application on a machine whose CPU uses some other byte ordering, you'll see the wrong values (actually, they are the correct values, the bytes are just in the wrong order). Intel CPUs do *not* use network byte ordering—if you run client3b on a system that uses an Intel processor, you'll see the wrong customer_id values. If you run client3b on a Sun, HP, or IBM system, you'll see the customer_id values that you expect. The next problem that you will encounter when using a binary cursor is the NULL value. If you are using a text-form cursor, PostgreSQL simply returns an empty string whenever it encounters a NULL value in the result set. That won't work if you are

retrieving an int value (or any of the noncharacter data types). You should really use the
fetchwithnulls() function whenever you use a binary cursor. The function prototype
for fetchwithnulls() is

```
int fetchwithnulls( void * param, ... );
```

When you call fetchwithnulls(), you provide two buffers for each field in the result set.
The first buffer receives the field value; the second receives a NULL indicator (in the form
of an int). If the field in question contains a NULL value, the NULL indicator will be set to 1
and the value returned (in the first buffer) is meaningless. If the field contains a non-NULL
value, the NULL indicator is set to 0 and you can use the value returned in the first buffer.

```
 1  /* client3c.c */
 2
 3  #include <stdlib.h>
 4  #include <libpq-fe.h>
 5  #include <libpgeasy.h>
 6
 7  int main( int argc, char * argv[] )
 8  {
 9    int        id;              /* customer_id column   */
10    char       name[80+1];      /* customer_name column */
11    float      balance;         /* balance column       */
12    int        nulls[3];        /* NULL indicators      */
13    PGconn *   connection;
14
15    connection = connectdb( argv[1] ? argv[1] : "" );
16
17    on_error_stop( );
18
19    doquery( "BEGIN WORK" );
20
21    doquery( "DECLARE customer_list BINARY CURSOR FOR "
22             "SELECT "
23             " customer_id, customer_name, CAST(balance AS real) "
24             "FROM customers" );
25
26    doquery( "FETCH ALL FROM customer_list" );
27
28    while( fetchwithnulls( &id,       &nulls[0],
29                           &name[0], &nulls[1],
30                           &balance, &nulls[2] )
31           != END_OF_TUPLES )
32    {
33      if( nulls[2] )
34        printf( "%4d: %-40s   NULL\n", id, name );
35      else
36        printf( "%4d: %-40s %6.2f\n", id, name, balance );
37    }
```

```
38
39    doquery( "COMMIT" );
40
41    disconnectdb();
42    exit( EXIT_SUCCESS );
43 }
```

In this client application (`client3.c`), you are retrieving data using a binary cursor. At line 12, you allocate an array of three null indicators. At lines 28–31, you pass a pointer to each null indicator (and the value buffers) to the `fetchwithnulls()` function.

By the time `fetchwithnulls()` has returned, it has set each of the null indicators—`1` if the corresponding field is NULL, `0` if the corresponding field is non-NULL.

In this example, you know that the `customer_id` and `customer_name` columns cannot be NULL; when you created the customers table, you specified that these two columns were *not null*. You must provide `fetchwithnulls()` with the address of a null indicator, even if a result field cannot possibly contain a NULL value.

Working with Result Sets in libpgeasy

In this chapter, you may have noticed that I never bother to free any of the query result sets when I have finished with them. When you use the libpq API, you have to be sure to call `PQclear()` when you are finished processing a result set—if you don't, your application will have a memory leak. The libpgeasy library manages the result set for you. Each time you execute a new query (by calling `doquery()`), the previous result set is cleared.

libpgeasy provides a few functions that you can use to manipulate the result set. If you call the `reset_fetch()` function, the result set will be "rewound" to the beginning. If you fetch after calling `reset_fetch()`, you will find yourself back at the first row in the result set.

libpgeasy provides three more (poorly documented) functions that you can use to manage multiple result sets.

The `get_result()` function returns a pointer to the current result set (that is, `get_result()` returns a `PGresult *`). When you call `get_result()`, you are telling libpgeasy that you are going to manage the result set and it will not be automatically cleared the next time you call `doquery()`. When you want to use a result set that you have saved, pass the `PGresult *` to `set_result()`. After calling `set_result()`, any calls to `fetch()` (or `fetchwithnulls()`) will use the new result set.

When you want libpgeasy to manage its own result sets again, call `unset_result()` with the pointer you got from the first call to `get_result()`. Don't forget to clear the other result sets using `PQclear()`.

Client 4—An Interactive Query Processor

To wrap up this chapter, you'll convert the interactive query processor from the previous chapter into a libpgeasy client.

Most of the code remains the same, so I'll point out only the differences. The most important change is that you no longer have to pass the `PGconn *` (connection handle) to every function-libpgeasy is managing the connection handle for you.

```
 1 /*
 2 ** File: client4.c
 3 */
 4
 5 #include <stdlib.h>
 6 #include <string.h>
 7 #include <libpq-fe.h>
 8 #include <libpgeasy.h>
 9 #include <readline/readline.h>
10 #include <readline/history.h>
11
12 typedef enum { FALSE, TRUE } bool;
13
14 #define MAX_PRINT_LEN40
15
16 static char separator[MAX_PRINT_LEN+1];
17
18 void print_result_set( PGresult * result )
19 {
20   int       col;
21   int       row;
22   int       * sizes;
23
24 /*
25 ** Compute the size for each column
26 */
27   sizes = (int *)calloc( PQnfields( result ), sizeof( int ));
28
29   for( col = 0; col < PQnfields( result ); col++ )
30   {
31     int   len = 0;
32
33     for( row = 0; row < PQntuples( result ); row++ )
34     {
35       if( PQgetisnull( result, row, col ))
36         len = 0;
37       else
38         len = PQgetlength( result, row, col );
39
40       if( len > sizes[col] )
41         sizes[col] = len;
42     }
43
44     if(( len = strlen( PQfname( result, col ))) > sizes[col] )
45       sizes[col] = len;
46
47     if( sizes[col] > MAX_PRINT_LEN )
```

```
48       sizes[col] = MAX_PRINT_LEN;
49   }
50
51 /*
52 ** Print the field names.
53 */
54   for( col = 0; col < PQnfields( result ); col++ )
55   {
56     printf( "%-*s ", sizes[col], PQfname( result, col ));
57   }
58
59   printf( "\n" );
60
61 /*
62 ** Print the separator line
63 */
64   memset( separator, '-', MAX_PRINT_LEN );
65
66   for( col = 0; col < PQnfields( result ); col++ )
67   {
68     printf( "%*.*s ", sizes[col], sizes[col], separator );
69   }
70
71   printf( "\n" );
72
73 /*
74 ** Now loop through each of the tuples returned by
75 ** our query and print the results.
76 */
77   for( row = 0; row < PQntuples( result ); row++ )
78   {
79     for( col = 0; col < PQnfields( result ); col++ )
80     {
81       if( PQgetisnull( result, row, col ))
82         printf( "%*s", sizes[col], "" );
83       else
84         printf( "%*s ", sizes[col], PQgetvalue(result, row, col));
85     }
86
87     printf( "\n" );
88
89   }
90   printf( "(%d rows)\n", PQntuples( result ));
91
92   free( sizes );
93 }
```

You can't use the `fetch()` or `fetchwithnulls()` in the `print_result_set()` function. There is no way to construct a call to these functions because you can't know (at the time the program is compiled) how many columns will be returned by a query.

The `process_query()` function is very simple. The call to `doquery()` sends the command to the server and returns a pointer to the result set.

```
 95 void process_query( char * buf )
 96 {
 97   PGresult *  result;
 98
 99   result = doquery( buf );
100
101   if( PQresultStatus( result ) == PGRES_TUPLES_OK )
102   {
103     print_result_set( result );
104   }
105   else if( PQresultStatus( result ) == PGRES_COMMAND_OK )
106   {
107     printf( "%s", PQcmdStatus( result ));
108
109     if( strlen( PQcmdTuples( result )))
110       printf( " - %s rows\n", PQcmdTuples( result ));
111     else
112       printf( "\n" );
113   }
114   else
115   {
116       printf( "%s\n", PQresultErrorMessage( result ));
117   }
118 }
```

The `main()` function is largely unchanged. I don't bother to save the connection handle returned by `connectdb()` because libpgeasy remembers it for me. The only other change in `main()` is that you set the error-handling mode calling `on_error_continue()`. If you don't set the error-handling mode, libpgeasy assumes that it should terminate your application if an error is encountered.

```
120 int main( int argc, char * argv[] )
121 {
122   char    * buf;
123
124   connectdb( argc > 1 ? argv[1] : "" );
125
126   on_error_continue();
127
128   using_history();
129   read_history( ".pg_history" );
130
```

```
131    while(( buf = readline( "->" )) != NULL )
132    {
133      if( strncmp( buf, "quit", sizeof( "quit" ) - 1  ) == 0 )
134      {
135        break;
136      }
137      else
138      {
139        if( strlen( buf ) != 0 )
140        {
141          add_history( buf );
142          process_query( buf );
143        }
144        free( buf );
145      }
146    }
147
148    write_history( ".pg_history" );
149
150    disconnectdb();
151
152    exit( EXIT_SUCCESS );
153  }
```

Summary

The libpgeasy library is a nice addition to libpq. You can mix and match libpgeasy and libpq functions. libpgeasy makes it easy to write simple utility applications, but it is not well suited to writing applications that need a lot of user input. If your application needs to execute commands that are not known at compile time, you should probably use libpq instead—libpgeasy won't offer you many advantages.

The source code for libpgeasy is available in the PostgreSQL source distributions. I recommend that you read through the code—you'll see some good sample code that will help in your libpq programming efforts. You will also gain a better understanding of some of the limitations of libpgeasy.

10

The New PostgreSQL C++
API—libpqxx

libpqxx is PostgreSQL's next-generation interface for programs written in C++. From its inception, libpqxx was designed to provide an object-oriented, STL-compatible approach to client-side programming. The author (and contributors) of libpqxx have done a remarkable job of creating a rich and familiar framework for accessing PostgreSQL servers from a program written in STL style. As you explore libpqxx, you'll find well-designed classes that transform libpq objects into STL-compatible containers. You can use standard STL iterators and algorithms to walk through command results and, using `transactors<>` (described later in this chapter), you can create objects that encapsulate database interaction into simple objects.

If you're a seasoned C++ programmer, you'll find that libpqxx feels very natural. If you're new to C++, libpqxx is a great place to start.

Prerequisites

I'll assume that you have a working knowledge of general C++ programming. All the examples in this chapter were tested using the GNU C++ compiler and GNU `make`. libpqxx requires a modern C++ compiler and you may have to upgrade your compiler (or even the OS) if you're running an older version: See the libpqxx website for compatibility information. The libpqxx library is distributed separately from the PostgreSQL distribution: You can find it at http://gborg.postgresql.org/project/libpqxx. Click the Downloads link (look closely, it's there in the upper-right corner of the page) and download the most recent (stable) version. When the download completes, unpack the source tarball with the command:

```
$ tar -zxvf libpqxx-version.tgz
$ cd libpqxx-version
```

(Be sure to plug the correct `version` into those commands.)

Now, before you run the `configure` command, there's one important step that you don't want to forget. The libpqxx `configure` script examines your computer and creates configuration files that ensure libpqxx will compile and install without any problems. Because libpqxx is a wrapper around PostgreSQL's libpq library, it needs to know where the libpqx header and library files are installed on your system. libpqxx uses the `pg_config` command to find what it needs. `pg_config` is a small script that displays the location of various bits of your PostgreSQL installation, and it was custom-created when you installed PostgreSQL. For libpqxx's `configure` script to work properly, the `pg_config` script must in your shell's search path. To find out whether you're ready to go, simply type **`pg_config --help`** at the command line—if you see a `command not found` message, you have to find `pg_config` (it's usually in the same directory that holds `psql`) and add it to your `$PATH` environment variable. For example, if you find `pg_config` in the directory `/usr/local/bin`, execute the following command to add `/usr/local/bin` to your search path:

```
$ export PATH=$PATH:/usr/local/bin
```

The export command works in the `bash` and `korn` shells; if you're using a different shell, check the documentation to find out how to adjust `$PATH`. Once you know that `pg_config` is in your search path, do the usual `configure/make/make install` three-step:

```
$ ./configure
checking for a BSD-compatible install... /usr/bin/install -c
checking whether build environment is sane... yes
checking for gawk... gawk
...
$ make
Making all in include
make[1]: Entering directory '/usr/local/src/libpqxx-2.3.0/include'
Making all in pqxx
make[2]: Entering directory '/usr/local/src/libpqxx-2.3.0/include/pqxx'
...
$ make install
Making install in include
make[1]: Entering directory '/usr/local/src/libpqxx-2.3.0/include'
Making install in pqxx
make[2]: Entering directory '/usr/local/src/libpqxx-2.3.0/include/pqxx'
make[3]: Entering directory '/usr/local/src/libpqxx-2.3.0/include/pqxx'
...
```

After the `make` (and `make install`) has finished, you have a new set of `#include` files, some new documentation, and a new library to link against. If you chose the default prefix when you configured libpqxx (that is, if you did *not* include a `--prefix=location` argument), you'll find the header files in `/usr/local/include/pqxx`, the object library in `/usr/local/lib`, and the documentation in `./doc` (the documentation isn't copied anywhere—it stays in the directory where you unpacked the source tarball).

Client 1—Connecting to the Server

The libpqxx class library includes a number of public classes you use to interact with the PostgreSQL server. libpqxx also includes a number of private classes you aren't supposed to peek at. All the public components are defined in the pqxx namespace (private classes are defined in a separate namespace). That means you must prefix all libpqxx class names with pqxx:: or include a using namespace pqxx; directive near the top of your source files.

Every libpqxx client includes at least one object of class connection (or a class derived from connection). The connection class, as you might expect, represents a connection to a server. Class connection offers three constructors:

```
connection();
connection( const std::string & options );
connection( const char options[] );
```

The first constructor builds a connection using default values and environment variables (see Table 5.2 for details). The second and third constructors let you specify connection properties with a string (either a std::string or a C-style null-terminated string) of the form:

$keyword_1=value_1\ keyword_2=value_2\ \ldots$

For example, to connect to a database named accounting on a host named jersey, construct a connection object like this:

```
connection myConnection( "dbname=accounting host=jersey" );
```

Or, if you've defined a service named accountingService, (see the section titled "Connection Properties" in Chapter 5, "Introduction to PostgreSQL Programming," for more information about services), you could create a connection object like this:

```
connection myConnection( "service=accountingService" );
```

If you don't supply a full set of connection properties in the constructor, libpqxx will search for the missing values using the environment variables (and hard-wired defaults) shown in Table 5.2.

Listing 10.1 shows a simple client that establishes a connection to a server and then exits.

Listing 10.1 client1.cc

```
 1 /* client1.cc */
 2
 3 #include <stdlib.h>        // Required for exit()
 4 #include <iostream>      // Required for cerr
 5 #include <pqxx/pqxx>   // libpqxx definitions
 6
 7 using namespace pqxx;
 8 using namespace std;
 9
10 int main( int argc, const char * argv[] )
11 {
12
```

Listing 10.1   **Continued**

```
13   try
14   {
15     connection     myConnection( argv[1] );
16
17     myConnection.activate();
18   }
19   catch( ... )
20   {
21     cerr << "Unknown exception caught" << endl;
22     exit( EXIT_FAILURE );
23   }
24
25   exit( EXIT_SUCCESS );
26
27 }
```

Any C++ program that uses the libpqxx library should #include <pqxx/pqxx> (see line 5). (Or, if you are a minimalist, you can selectively #include the bits and pieces you need; I'll show you how to find the header files in a moment.) Remember that all the libpqxx public classes are defined in namespace pqxx, so line 8 tells the compiler to search that namespace for unqualified classnames. At line 15 you see a call to the connection constructor. In this case, myConnection is built using the first command-line argument, which should be a connection string such as "service=accountingService".

Contrary to the current version of the libpqxx documentation, the connection constructors do *not* complete the connection to the server. Instead, the connection object connects to the server (or at least makes the attempt) the first time you use it to interact with the server. If you don't want to wait that long (maybe you want to report a connection error right away), you can call the connection::activate() member function (see line 17) to force the connection attempt.

You've probably noticed that the calls to the connection constructor and connection::activate() are wrapped in a try/catch block. libpqxx follows the STL philosophy that an error should be reported by throwing an exception. See the section "Client 2—Adding Error Checking" later in this chapter for detailed information about the exceptions defined by libpqxx.

Using pqxx-config to Create a Simple Makefile

The libpqxx package includes a handy utility that makes short work of the usually tedious (and error-prone) task of creating Makefiles. The pqxx-config program is currently a shell script and can display the compiler and linker flags required to build a libpqxx client application. pqxx-config is built and installed when you run the configure/make/make install three-step described earlier (see the section titled "Prerequisites" earlier in this chapter). If you chose the default install prefix at that time, pqxx-config ends up in /usr/local/bin; if you chose a different prefix, you'll find pqxx-config in $prefix/bin.

To see a summary of the command-line options supported by pqxx-config, type
/usr/local/bin/pqxx-config --help. You'll see a list similar to the following:

```
$ /usr/local/bin/pqxx-config --help
Usage: pqxx-config [OPTION]

Known values for OPTION are:

  --prefix=DIR          change libpqxx prefix [default /usr/local/pg800b2/]
  --libs                print library linking information
  --cflags              print pre-processor and compiler flags
  --help                display this help and exit
  --version             output version information
```

To see the preprocess/compiler flags required to build a libpqxx client application, use
the command pqxx-config --cflags, like this:

```
$ /usr/local/bin/pqxx-config --cflags
-I/usr/local/include -I/usr/local/postgresql/include
```

To see the linker flags required to build a libpqxx client application, use the --libs option:

```
$ /usr/local/bin/pqxx-config --libs
-L/usr/local/lib -lpqxx -L/usr/local/postgresql/lib -lpq
```

Don't bother writing down the information displayed by pqxx-config because you can
invoke it directly from your Makefile to ensure that the flags are always up-to-date
(even if you install a new version of PostgreSQL or libpqxx). Listing 10.2 shows a
Makefile that compiles and links the client1.cc client application.

Listing 10.2   **libpqxx Client** Makefile

```
1 # Filename: Makefile
2
3 CXXFLAGS  = $(shell /usr/local/bin/pqxx-config --cflags)
4 LDLIBS        = $(shell /usr/local/bin/pqxx-config --libs)
5
6 client1:  client1.cc
```

Because the GNU make program knows how to build an executable from a .cc (C++)
source code file, this Makefile is very simple. Line 3 uses pqxx-config to define the
CXXFLAGS variable. make uses CXXFLAGS to build the C++ compiler command line. Line 4
defines LDLIBS, which make uses to build the linker command line. Line 6 simply states
that the client1.cc is the one and only prerequisite for client1. After you have the
Makefile in place, simply type **make client1** to compile and link the client1 program:

```
$ make client1
g++ -I/usr/local/include -I/usr/local/postgresql/include client1.cc \
    -L/usr/local/lib -lpqxx -L/usr/local/postgresql/lib -lpq
```

When you run `client1`, you won't see much in the way of interesting and exciting output. In fact, unless something goes wrong, you won't see any output at all:

```
$ ./client1 "dbname=test"
$
```

If `client1` can't connect to the database you've specified, you'll see an error message:

```
$ ./client1 "dbname=neverland"
Unknown exception caught
```

`connection` Member Functions

After you have a `connection` object, you can use a number of member functions to interrogate the status of the `connection`. The `connection::is_open()` function returns TRUE if the connection is up and running and FALSE if the connection has been broken or is not yet established. To find the process ID of the server process (see the section titled "LISTEN/NOTIFY" later in this chapter for an example of why you might want to know this), call the `connection::backedpid()` function. You can also retrieve the database name, username, hostname, port number, and connection options from a `connection` object using the functions shown here:

```
const char * connection::dbname();
const char * connection::username();
const char * connection::hostname();
const char * connection::port();
const char * connection::options();
```

Client 2—Adding Error Checking

As mentioned earlier, libpqxx follows the STL philosophy that an error condition should be reported by throwing an exception. libpqxx defines three exception types, all derived from `std::runtime_error`:

- `sql_error`—Thrown when the PostgreSQL server reports an error
- `broken_connection`—Thrown when the libpqxx library detects that the connection to the server has been broken
- `in_doubt_error`—Thrown when you COMMIT a transaction but the connection to the server fails before libpqxx has received an acknowledgement that the COMMIT completed

Because these exception classes are ultimately derived from `std::exception`, each provides a member function named `what()` that returns a description of the error that occurred. In addition, the `sql_error` class includes a member function named `query()` that returns the text of the query that produced the error.

Other Exceptions Thrown by libpqxx

An `sql_error` exception is thrown when the PostgreSQL server reports an error, but libpqxx throws other exception types when client-side errors occur (or when an error occurs in the client/server protocol):

- `logic_error`—Indicates a design error. Typically, a `logic_error` indicates a problem with the design of your client code, such as trying to COMMIT a transaction after you've already aborted it. A `logic_error` can also indicate a problem with the internal design of the libpqxx library. Think of a `logic_error` as some condition that "should never happen." A user should never be able to induce a `logic_error`.

- `out_of_range`—Thrown when you try to access a nonexistent element in an array (or array-like collection) or a string. libpqxx throws an `out_of_range` exception when you call `result::at()`, `tuple::at()`, `result::column_name()`, or `binarystring::at()` with an invalid index.

- `invalid_argument`—Thrown when you call a libpqxx function with an invalid argument. For example, `result:column_number()`, which maps a column name to a its corresponding column number, throws an `invalid_argument` if you search for a column name that doesn't exist in the result set.

- `runtime_error`—Sort of a catch-all for other errors that can occur in a libpqxx client application. Most notably, whenever libpqxx receives an unexpected result from the PostgreSQL server (or the client/server protocol stack), it translates the result into text form and throws a `runtime_error` to report the problem. You can retrieve the text of the PostgreSQL error message from the exception.

Listing 10.3 shows a simple client that establishes a connection to a server and then exits, this time reporting error messages in a more meaningful manner.

Listing 10.3   `client2.cc`

```
 1 /* client2.cpp */
 2
 3 #include <stdlib.h>        // Required for exit()
 4 #include <iostream>        // Required for cerr
 5 #include <pqxx/pqxx>       // libpqxx definitions
 6
 7 using namespace pqxx;
 8 using namespace std;
 9
10 int main( int argc, const char * argv[] )
11 {
12
13   try
14   {
15     connection   myConnection( argc > 1 ? argv[1] : "" );
```

Listing 10.3 **Continued**

```
16
17     myConnection.activate();
18  }
19  catch( runtime_error & e )
20  {
21    cerr << "Connection failed: " << e.what();
22    exit( EXIT_FAILURE );
23  }
24  catch( exception & e )
25  {
26    cerr << e.what();
27    exit( EXIT_FAILURE );
28  }
29  catch( ... )
30  {
31    cerr << "Unknown exception caught" << endl;
32    exit( EXIT_FAILURE );
33  }
34
35  exit( EXIT_SUCCESS );
36
37 }
```

client2.cc is nearly identical to client1.cc—we've added two new catch clauses to distinguish between runtime_error exceptions, other standard exceptions (all derived from std::exception), and unknown exceptions. The handler for runtime_error exceptions (lines 19–23) displays a meaningful error message followed by the text of the exception, obtained by calling e.what(). The handler for exception-derived exceptions (line 24–28) is a bit more generic—it simply displays the text message carried within the exception object. The catch-all handler (lines 29–33) displays a less satisfying message because the type of the exception is unknown.

In general, the handler for a runtime_error can be called with a broken_connection object, an sql_error object, an in_doubt_error object, or any other object derived from runtime_error (in client2.cc, the runtime_error handler will never receive an sql_error or in_doubt_error because the code simply connects to a server and exits). Of course, you could write a separate handler for each class derived from runtime_error if you needed to do something other than report the text of the error message. A broken_connection is often fatal, but you can continue processing after an sql_error exception).

Listing 10.4 shows a bonus function that returns the demangled name of a type (just in case you want to include the exception type in your error messages). This function works when compiled with the GCC g++ compiler and many other compilers that produce code compatible with the Itanium C++ ABI (application binary interface) described at http://www.codesourcery.com/cxx-abi/abi.html.

Listing 10.4   **The** demangled_name() **Function**

```
#include <typeinfo>
#include <string>
#include <cxxabi.h>      // C++ name demangler functions

using namespace std;

string demangled_name( type_info const & typeinfo )
{
  int      status;
  char * name = abi::__cxa_demangle( typeinfo.name(), NULL, NULL, &status );

  if( name )
  {
    string result( name );

    free( name );

    return( result );
  }
  else
  {
    return( "can't demangle typename" );
  }
}
```

To print the name of an exception type, call demangled_name() like this:

```
...
catch( runtime_error & e )
{
   cerr << "Caught exception of type " << demangled_name( typeid( e )) << endl;
   cerr << "Connection failed: " << e.what();
   exit( EXIT_FAILURE );
}
...
```

Handling Informational/Warning Messages with Notice Processor Objects

libpqxx throws an exception whenever an error is detected, but the PostgreSQL server occasionally sends other messages that are not classified as errors. For example, when you type the following command into psql:

```
test=# CREATE TABLE myTestTable
test-# (
```

```
test(#      pkey INTEGER primary key,
test(#      value INTEGER
test(# );
```

the `psql` client displays two messages:

```
NOTICE:  CREATE TABLE / PRIMARY KEY will create implicit
    index "mytesttable_pkey" for table "mytesttable"
CREATE TABLE
```

The first message is a *notice*; the second message simply shows that the CREATE TABLE command completed successfully. A notice is an informational message or a warning message that the server sends to the client outside the normal metadata/data channel. There is an important but subtle difference between an error and a notice: An error interrupts the normal flow of a program (that is, the program cannot continue until the error is handled in some way); a notice is simply extra information you can ignore if you're not interested. Another, more important, distinction is that an error aborts the current transaction, whereas a notice does not.

The PostgreSQL server defines six error severities (plus a few more used for logging debugging information):

- INFO—Extra information you might be interested in but that implies no negative consequences. For example, if you define an unrecognized configuration option in your server configuration file, you'll see an INFO message stating that the option is unrecognized and therefore has no effect.

- NOTICE—Extra information that tells you that a command has had (possibly) surprising, but not negative, consequences. For example, when you create a column defined as a PRIMARY KEY, the server produces a NOTICE stating that an index has automatically been created to support the primary key.

- WARNING—Implies that a command succeeded but found a problem along the way. For instance, if you try to remove a user from a group and that user isn't a member of the group, you'll see a WARNING. Technically speaking, the command succeeds because, when it's finished, the user will not be a member of the group, but you'll see a WARNING to tell you that something unexpected occurred.

- ERROR—A command has failed. When an ERROR is generated, the server aborts the current transaction. All further commands are ignored until you execute a ROLLBACK or COMMIT command. If you execute a COMMIT in an aborted transaction, the server automatically translates the command into a ROLLBACK. An error implies that the command was not able to complete but that the server can continue to process commands in future transactions.

- FATAL—A FATAL error means the server cannot continue to process commands. A FATAL error aborts the current transaction and terminates your server process. FATAL errors are rarely seen except for one particular type: authentication failures. If you try to connect to a server with an invalid username or password, the authentication failure is reported as a FATAL error.

- PANIC—A PANIC is similar to a FATAL error in that the server process cannot continue to execute commands. A PANIC is more severe than a FATAL error because it forces *all* server processes to terminate (a FATAL error terminates only *your* server process). PANICs are extremely rare. In fact, there is nothing that a client application can do to cause a PANIC. A PANIC represents a programming error made by a PostgreSQL designer or a failure in the PostgreSQL environment, such as corrupted memory or a failed disk drive.

libpqxx reports ERROR, FATAL, and PANIC messages by throwing an exception. libpqxx delivers INFO, NOTICE, and WARNING messages to a noticer object. The libpqxx noticer class is very simple: It defines a single member function, operator(), that takes a null-terminated character string (the info/notice/warning/ message) as its only argument. Every connection object holds a (possibly NULL) pointer to a single noticer object. When libpqxx wants to report an INFO, NOTICE, or WARNING message, it calls the operator() member function of the connection's current noticer. If a connection doesn't own a noticer (that is, if the connection's noticer pointer is NULL), the text of the message is written to the applications stderr stream.

Don't confuse *notice* with *notification*. Notifications are generated by the NOTIFY command and are handled (in libpqxx applications) by trigger objects. We cover NOTIFY, LISTEN, and trigger objects later in the section titled "LISTEN/NOTIFY."

To create your own notice processor, simply derive a class from pqxx::noticer, override the operator() member function with your own code, create an object of the new class, and assign the object to your connection. Listing 10.5 shows an implementation of a noticer-derived class that simply echoes any messages to the std::cerr stream.

Listing 10.5   myNoticer **Class Definition**

```
class myNoticer : public pqxx::noticer
{
  public:
    virtual void operator()( const char message[] ) throw()
    {
        cerr << message;
    }
};
```

Notice that you don't have to append any end-of-line characters to the message; libpqxx ensures that every message is terminated with a newline character. Attaching a noticer-derived object to a connection is a little tricky because the connection wants to take ownership of the noticer. You can infer this change in ownership from set_noticer()'s complex function prototype:

```
auto_ptr< pqxx::noticer >
    pqxx::connection_base::set_noticer( auto_ptr< noticer > N ) throw ()
```

When you see a function that requires an `auto_ptr<>` argument (as opposed to a simple pointer), you know that the function will take ownership of the object pointed to. The use of `auto_ptr<>` has two important consequences for how you manage `noticer` objects in your own application. First, after you've attached a `noticer` object to a connection, you can forget about it—the `connection` object automatically deletes its `noticer` when the `connection` is destroyed. Second, because a `connection` uses `delete` to destroy its `noticer`, you must use `new` to allocate `noticer` objects. So, the process of allocating and attaching a `noticer` looks like this:

```
...
static void attachNoticer( connection & conn )
{
    noticer * noticeProcessor = new myNoticer;

    conn.set_noticer( auto_ptr<noticer>( noticeProcessor ));
}
...
```

The `connection_base::set_noticer()` function returns an `auto_ptr<>` to the connection's previous notice processor (if any). If you capture the return value in another `auto_ptr<>`, you own the old `noticer`, meaning you decide when to `delete` the old `noticer`. If you don't capture the old `noticer`, it's automatically `deleted` when your function returns because the implicit `auto_ptr<>` created for the return value goes out of scope at the end of your function.

libpqxx offers two ways to detach a `noticer` from a connection. First, you can replace a connection's `noticer` by creating a new `noticer` object and calling `set_noticer()` with the new object (and wrapping it in an `auto_ptr<>`). Second, you can detach a `noticer` without replacing it with a new one by calling `set_noticer( auto_ptr<noticer>( NULL ))`.

If you want to send a message to your own client application, you could retrieve a pointer to a connection's `noticer` by calling the `connection_base::get_noticer()` function, but libpqxx offers a better way. The `connection_base::process_notice()` function routes a message through the connection's current `noticer`. `process_notice()` comes in two flavors:

```
connection_base::process_notice( const char message[] ) throw()
connection_base::process_notice( const std::string & message ) throw()
```

The first flavor expects a null-terminated C-style string, and the second expects a reference to a `std::string` object. Any notices you generate in your own application should end with a newline character, just to be consistent with the messages generated by libpqxx (or by the PostgreSQL server).

Why would you want to send your own messages through `process_notice()`? Because libpqxx routes all informational messages through a notice processor, you can use the same mechanism to route debugging information or progress messages to the same destination. That way, any debug messages you generate in your own application are interspersed with informational messages generated by PostgreSQL.

Now that you know how to connect to a database server, catch error conditions, and intercept informational messages generated by the server, it's time to get to the interesting stuff: query processing.

Client 3—Processing Queries

libpqxx defines a small group of interrelated classes you use to execute commands and retrieve results. You already know about the connection class, which represents a connection to a server. In a libpqxx application, all commands are executed using an object derived from class transaction_base, which represents a server-side transaction. When you execute a command, the result set (that is, the data returned by the server) is stored in an object of class result—libpqxx creates a result object each time you execute a command. Inside a result object you'll find a collection of zero or more objects of class tuple. A tuple represents a single row in the result set and is a collection of one or more objects of type field. Each field represents a single data value. You can access the metadata returned by a command through the result, tuple, and field classes as well. In this section, we'll show you how all the pieces fit together.

Working with Transactions

To execute a query or object>> object>other command in a libpqxx, you must use a transaction<> object (or an object derived from transaction<>). The transaction<> constructor expects either one or two arguments:

```
transaction( connection_base & conn, const std::string & transactionName );
transaction( connection_base & conn );
```

Each transaction<> is attached to a single connection object—the transaction<> uses the connection to send commands to the server and to retrieve results from the server. If you provide a transactionName[1] when you call the constructor, error messages thrown by the transaction include the name you provide; that makes it a little easier to figure out where an exception is coming from in a complex application.

The transaction<> type is a template class, parameterized on the transaction isolation level you want to enforce. Because the PostgreSQL server offers only two transaction isolation levels, you can choose from read_committed or serializable (see the section titled "Transaction Processing" in Chapter 3, "PostgreSQL SQL Syntax and Use," for more information about isolation levels). The default isolation level is read_committed so all three of the following definitions are equivalent:

```
transaction<read_committed>  myTransaction( myConnection );
transaction<>  myTransaction( myConnection );
work myTransaction( myConnection );
```

---

[1] The libpqxx documentation states that a transaction<> name must start with a letter and contain only letters and digits.

libpqxx defines a class named work as a convenient synonym for transaction<read_committed>.

After you have a transaction<> object, call the exec() member function to execute a command on the server. transaction<> defines three flavors of the exec() member function:

```
result exec( const char queryText[], const std::string & description );
result exec( const std::string queryText, const std::string & description );
result exec(const std::stringstream queryText, const std::string & description);
```

You can execute a command using whatever object>> object>form of query string you happen to have (a null-terminated C-style string, an std::string, or an std::stringstream). The description argument is optional—if you provide a description, libpqxx includes it in some (but not all) error messages generated by the command.

To execute a command on the server, simply call exec() with the text of the command and capture the return value in a result object:

```
...
    std::string         myCommand( "SELECT * FROM customers" );

    try
    {
        result myResult = myTransaction.exec( myCommand. "Get Customer List" );
    }
    catch( runtime_error & e )
    {
        cerr << "Error detected: << e.what();
    }
    catch( exception & e )
    {
        cerr << e.what();
    }
    catch( ... )
    {
        cerr << "Unknown exception caught" << endl;
    }
...
```

The call to exec() blocks until the command completes and the entire result set has been received (or until an exception is thrown). libpqxx does not provide a nonblocking exec() variant at this time.

Use sqlesc() to Quote Strings That You Get from Outside Sources

Let's say you're writing object>> object>an interactive program that any customer can use to find his current account balance. You prompt the customer for his *name* and then create and execute a query similar to the following:

```
SELECT balance FROM customers WHERE customer_name = 'name';
```

That looks innocuous enough. But what happens if a customer types in something like this:

```
Panky, Henry'; DELETE  FROM customers; COMMIT;
```

Now you append this suspicious *name* to the end of your SELECT command and you end up with:

```
SELECT balance FROM c3ustomers
     WHERE name = 'Panky, Henry'; DELETE FROM customers; COMMIT;'
```

That's probably not what you want. How do you prevent that kind of attack? You simply run any string you get from the outside world through the sqlesc() function before using it in a command. sqlesc() makes outside strings safe. In this example, sqlesc() would have changed *name* into

```
Panky, Henry'';DELETE FROM customer; COMMIT;
```

Notice that the single quotation mark in the original *name* has been doubled—that makes it safe to use inside of a query. When the server sees the properly quoted string, it thinks you're looking for a customer whose name happens to include a single quote and simply returns an empty result set.

Completing a Transaction

Because a libpqxx object>> object>application executes all commands within the context of a transaction<>, you must complete the transaction<> by calling either transaction<>::commit() or transaction::abort(). It's important to remember that if you don't explicitly commit a transaction by calling transaction<>::commit(), the transaction is automatically aborted when the transaction<> object is destroyed.

When you complete a transaction, the result set data and metadata are still available, but be aware that a result set that comes from an aborted transaction should be treated with suspicion.

Other Transaction Types (nontransaction and robusttransaction)

The transaction<> template class is one of three transaction-like classes defined by libpqxx. The robusttransaction<>> class class>has the same interface as transaction<>—you use a robusttransaction<> object in exactly the same way that you use a transaction<> object. The difference between the two classes becomes apparent when you lose the connection to a server at exactly the wrong time. Regardless of which transaction type you use, libpqxx tries to reconnect to a server if your connection breaks down—you don't have to do anything because it happens automatically. What happens if your connection drops immediately after you execute a COMMIT, but before the server has a chance to send you an acknowledgement? Did the COMMIT execute? Without some extra work, you have no way to know. A robusttransaction takes care of that extra work for you. When you start a robusttransaction, libpqxx writes a record into a special log table in the server. When you COMMIT a robusttransaction the log record is committed as well. If the connection drops out before the COMMIT is acknowledged, robusttransaction simply looks for the log record (after reconnecting). If the log record is there, the COMMIT succeeded; if it's not there, the entire transaction aborted and you can execute the transaction again. Or better yet, you can use a transactor object to automate the whole process (see "Client 4—Working with `transactors`" later in this chapter for more details). If you are executing read-only queries, you can use the class `nontransaction` instead of `transaction<>`. When you execute commands through a `nontransaction` object, you don't need to commit or abort the transaction when you're finished because each command is automatically object>> object> committed as soon as it completes.

Working with Result Sets

The `transaction<>::exec()` functions all return an object of type `class result`. A `result` is a very rich, STL-compatible container that holds both the data and metadata returned by a command. Because `result` is a standard container, it provides the usual container-related member functions such as `size()`, which returns the number of rows in the result set; `empty()`, which returns TRUE if the `size()` is zero; and `clear()`, which discards the result set.

If a `result` is a container, what exactly does it contain? A `result` object contains all the `tuples` (that is, rows) returned by a command. A `tuple` is a container, too—it contains all the `fields` in a single row of the result set. So, a `result` is a collection of `tuples` and a `tuple` is a collection of `fields`.

Working with Tuples (Rows)

The `result` class offers three methods for getting at the `tuples` inside. First, you can use the `operator[]` function to retrieve a `tuple` by its zero-based index:

```
...
    result myResult = myTransaction.exec( myCommand, "Get Customer List" );

    tuple  firstRow   = myResult[0];
    tuple  secondRow = myResult[1];
...
```

Like any container class, calling `result::operator[]()` with an out-of-range index results in undefined, but generally nasty, behavior (I'll show you how to find the number of rows contained inside a `result` in a moment). Second, you can use the `at()` member function:

```
...
    result myResult = myTransaction.exec( myCommand, "Get Customer List" );

    try
    {
        tuple  firstRow   = myResult.at( 0 );
        tuple  secondRow = myResult.at( 1 );
    }
    catch( out_of_range e )
    {
        // Handle out_of_range error here
    }
...
```

If you call `result::at()` with an out-of-range index, it throws an `out_of_range` exception. Finally, you can use the `result::begin()` and `result::end()` member functions to process tuples using an iterator:

```
...
    result myResult = myTransaction.exec( myCommand, "Get Customer List" );

    result::const_iterator  I;

    for( I = myResult.begin(); I != myResult.end(); ++I )
    {
        const tuple tup = *I;

        processTuple( tup );
    }
...
```

Calling `result::begin()` gives you an iterator that points to the first tuple in the result set. `result::end()` returns an iterator that points just past the last `tuple` in the result set. An iterator acts suspiciously like a pointer. If you de-reference an iterator with the `*` operator—for example, `*myIterator`—you get a copy of the `tuple` to which the iterator currently points. If you de-reference an iterator with the `->`—for example, `myIterator->member`—you access a member of the object to which the iterator currently points.

Because a `result::const_iterator` is an STL-compatible iterator, you can use it with most of the STL algorithms. I say "most" because libpqxx provides a const iterator, but not a non const iterator. That means you can't use libpqxx iterators with algorithms that modify the object pointed to; that is, you can't use algorithms like `sort()`, `transform()`, `fill()`, `replace_if()`, `remove()`, and `random_shuffle()`. You *can* use a const_iterator with nonmodifying algorithms.

Most, if not all, of the STL algorithms expect at least two iterators that define a range of elements within the collection. For example, one of the most useful STL algorithms, `for_each()`, expects two iterators and a functor[2]. `for_each()` applies the functor to each element in the range between the first and second iterator.
Consider the following code snippet:

```
...
    result myResult = myTransaction.exec( myCommand, "Get Customer List" );
    for_each( myResult.begin(), myResult.end(), printTuple );
...
```

The call to `myResult.begin()` returns an iterator that points to the first `tuple` in `myResult`. The call to `myResult.end()` returns an iterator that points just past the last `tuple` in `myResult`. The two iterators define a range—in this case, the range consists of

---

[2] A *functor* is a function pointer or an object that defines the `operator()` member function.

all elements (tuples) in the collection (myResult). for_each() walks through the range and calls printTuple()[3] for each tuple it encounters.

Of course, you can fine-tune the range seen by for_each() if you want to process a subset of the tuples in a result set. Because an iterator acts like a pointer, you can perform pointer arithmetic with iterators. For example, to advance an iterator by two elements, simply add 2 to the iterator, like this:

```
...
    result::const_iterator i = myResult.begin();

    i = i + 2;
...
```

To back up by two elements (that is, to move an iterator two elements toward the beginning of the collection), just subtract 2 from the iterator:

```
...
    result::const_iterator i = myResult.end();

    i = i - 2;
...
```

You can subtract one iterator from another to find the distance (the number of tuples) between the two. For example, to find the number of tuples in a result set, you could use the following code:

```
int    tupleCount = myResult.end() - myResult.beg();
```

You *could* compute tupleCount that way, but we'll show you a much more intuitive method in a moment.

libpqxx also defines a reverse iterator (result::const_reverse_iterator) that walks through a result set starting with the last tuple and moving toward the first tuple. To print a result set in reverse order, use the following:

```
...
    result myResult = myTransaction.exec( myCommand, "Get Customer List" );

    for_each( myResult.rbegin(), myResult.rend(), printTuple );
...
```

When you call rbegin() (as opposed to begin()), you get an iterator that points just past the last tuple in the result set. Calling rend(), as opposed to end(), returns an iterator that points to the first tuple in the result set. When you increment a reverse itera-

---

[3] There are two ways you could define the printTuple() function: printTuple(tuple) or printTuple(const tuple &). In the first case, for_each() makes a copy of every tuple it finds in the range. In the second case, for_each() simply passes a reference to each tuple (which is a bit less expensive). Note that if you try to define both variants, your compiler will complain about an ambiguous overloaded function.

tor, you move toward the beginning of the collection (when you increment a forward iterator, you move towards the end).

Avoiding the find() and count() Algorithms

You might be tempted to use the find(), find_if(), count(), and count_if() STL algorithms to search through the tuples in a result. If possible, you should avoid using those functions—if you need to know whether a particular value exists within the result set, refine your WHERE clause and ask the server to find the value you're interested in. If you ask the server to find the value(s) you are interested in or to count data values, you won't suffer the performance hit required to send a large result set over the client/server connection.

Working with Fields (Columns)

Now that you know how to access the rows in a result set, it's time to turn your attention to the columns (libpqxx calls them *fields*) within a tuple. First off, you can find out how many fields are found within a tuple by calling the tuple::size() member function:

```
...
    const result::tuple   & myTuple = myResult[0];

    cout << "This tuple holds " << myTuple.size() << " columns" << endl;
...
```

Note that tuple::size() returns the same number of fields for every tuple in a result regardless of whether the tuple contains NULL values.

There are two mechanisms and six member functions you can use to get a field value from a tuple. To access a field by its zero-based column number, you can call the tuple::operator[]() member function or tuple::at(). Like other STL containers, tuple::operator[]() with an invalid index causes undefined behavior (but you can bet you won't like the behavior). tuple::at throws an out_of_range exception instead. The following calls are equivalent (assuming that index is valid):

```
...
    result::field    myField;

    myField = myTuple[index];
    myField = myTuple.at( index );
...
```

Of course, you should call tuple::at() within a try/catch block because it can throw an exception.

If you know the name of a field in the result set, you can access that field by name. tuple overloads both the [] operator and the at() member function to retrieve a field by its name. You can specify a field name as a std::string or as a C-style null-terminated string. To access a field by name using a C-style string, use code similar to the following:

```
...
    result::field     myField;

    myField = myTuple[ "customer_name"];
    myField = myTuple.at( "customer_name" );
...
```

To access a field, by name, using a std::string:

```
...
    result::field     myField;
    std::string       fieldName( "customer_name" );

    myField = myTuple[ fieldName ];
    myField = myTuple.at( fieldName );
...
```

As you might expect, calling operator[]() with an invalid field name results in undefined behavior. However, if you call at() with an invalid name, you get an invalid_argument exception instead of the usual out_of_range exception.

All together, tuple defines six member functions that return a field:

```
field operator[]( size_type index) const throw()
field operator[]( const char fieldName[] ) const
field operator[]( const std::string & fieldName ) const
field at( size_type index ) const throw( std::out_of_range )
field at( const char fieldName[] ) const throw()
field at( const std::string & fieldName ) const throw()
```

You might have noticed that a tuple—which is an STL-compatible container in most other respects—does *not* provide an iterator you can use to walk through the fields within the tuple. The author of libpqxx might add a column iterator at a later day, but for now you'll have to use operator()[] or at() (or write your own iterators).

Because result defines an operator[]() function that returns a tuple and tuple defines an operator[]() function that returns a field, you can treat a result as a two-dimensional array. For example, to process every field in every tuple in a result, you could use a code snippet similar to the following:

```
...
    for( row = 0; row < myResult.size(); ++row )
        for( col = 0; col < myResult[0].size(); ++col )
            processField( myResult[row][col] );
...
```

A field object can tell you a lot about itself. If you want to know the name of a field, call the field::name() member function (which returns a C-style null-terminated string):

```
...
    for( col = 0; col < myResult[0].size(); ++col )
        cout << "Column " << col <<
            " is named " << myResult[0][col].name() << endl;
...
```

To retrieve the data type of a `field`, call the `field::type()` member function:

```
oid columnType = myField.type();
```

Notice that `field::type()` returns an OID. The OID you get back from `field::type()` corresponds to an entry in the server's pg_type table. To map an OID back into a type name, simply execute the following query:

```
SELECT typname FROM pg_type WHERE oid = value;
```

Plugging in the return value from `field::type()` in place of `value`. libpqxx does not currently provide a way to retrieve the type modifiers associated with a `field`. That means, for example, that you can't query a DECIMAL field for its precision or scale.

You can call the `field::is_null()` function (which returns a `bool`) to determine whether a given field is NULL. `is_null()` returns `true` if the field is NULL and returns `false` if the field is non-NULL.

Finally, you can find the size of a `field`'s value (in bytes) by calling `field::size()`.

Which brings us around to two important questions: How do you get to the *value* of a `field`, and how is that value represented? All `field` values are stored internally as C-style null-terminated strings, which we'll refer to as "`c_str()` form". To get to the null-terminated string, call the `field::c_str()` member function—`c_str()` returns a pointer to the first character in the string. Here's a code snippet that prints every column in every row returned by a query[4]:

```
...
    for( row = 0; row < myResult.size(); ++row )
    {
        for( col = 0; col < myResult[0].size(); ++col )
            cout << myResult[row][col].c_str() << ' ';
        cout << endl;
    }
...
```

The `field` class defines a number of template functions you can use to convert values from `c_str()` form into some other data type—namely, the type of the template parameter. The conversion functions can seem a little mysterious at first, but after you've seen a few examples, they make perfect sense. The `template<T> bool field::to( T & obj )` conversion function (or `field::to()` for short) is the easiest to understand. This function converts a field value from its normal `c_str()` form into some other type (T). `field::to()` returns `true` if the conversion succeeded, returns `false` if the field is NULL, or throws an `std::domain_error` if the conversion fails (a conversion might fail if, for example, you try to convert a string that contains letters into an `int`). Here's an example:

---

[4] libpqxx defines an `operator<<` function that makes this code snippet even easier: You can omit the call to `c_str()` when you write a `field` to a `stream`. `cout << myResult[row][col]` will do the job nicely.

```
...
   const result::field  & myField = myResult[0]["balance"];
   float                   fldValue( 0.0F );

   try
   {
       if( myField.to( fldValue ))
           cout << "Customer balance: " << fldValue << endl;
       else
           cout << "Customer balance: NULL" << endl;
   }
   catch( std::domain_error )
   {
       cerr << "Can't convert customer_balance into float form" << endl;
   }
....
```

Look closely at the call to `myField.to( fldValue )`. If the conversion succeeds, `fldValue` contains the value of the `field`, converted from `c_str()` form to `float` form. If the value of `myField` happens to be `NULL`, `fldValue` remains untouched—that is, `fldValue` retains its initial value of `0.0F`. If the conversion fails, `field::to()` throws an exception.

If you prefer, you can use the second variant of `field::to()` to provide an explicit value to use in place of `NULL`; the first form of `field::to()` leaves the destination object untouched if the `field` contains a `NULL` value. The second form of `field::to()` expects two arguments: a reference to the destination object and a default value. Here's the same code snippet you just saw, rewritten to use the second form of `field::to()`:

```
...
   const result::field  & myField = myResult[0]["balance"];
   float                   fldValue;

   try
   {
         myField.to( fldValue, float( 0.0F )))

         cout << "Customer balance: " << fldValue << endl;
   }
   catch( std::domain_error )
   {
       cerr << "Can't convert customer_balance into float form" << endl;
   }
....
```

Notice that you don't have to check the return code from `myField::to()`—if the function returns (that is, if it doesn't throw an exception) `fldValue` returns a predictable value. If `myField` contains `NULL`, `fldValue` is explicitly set to `0.0F`. The data type of the default value must match the data type of the destination object—in this example, the default value and destination object are both of type `float`.

`field:to()` knows how to convert a `c_str()` value into any of the following data types:

- `long`
- `unsigned long`
- `int`
- `unsigned int`
- `short`
- `unsigned short`
- `float`
- `double`
- `long double`
- `bool`
- `std::string`
- `std::stringstream`

The `field` class defines two more conversion (template) functions that you might find useful. The `template<T> T field::as( const T & defaultValue )` function (or `field::as( defaultValue )` for short) converts a `field` value from `c_str()` form into type `T`, substituting `defaultValue` if the `field` happens to contain NULL. Like `field::to()`, `field::as( defaultValue )` throws an `std::domain_error` if the conversion fails. `field::as( defaultValue )` can convert into the same set of data types that `field::to()` knows how to deal with (long, unsigned long, int, and so on). So what's the difference between `field::to()` and `field::as( defaultValue )`? When you call `field::to()`, it converts the `field` value into an object (you provide a reference to the target object) and `field::to()` returns a Boolean value to indicate whether the `field` contains a NULL value. When you call `field::as( defaultValue )`, *it* creates an object of the desired type and returns a copy of that object. Here's a snippet that shows `field::as( defaultValue )` in action:

```
...
  const result::field  & myField = myResult[0]["balance"];

  try
  {
    cout << "New customer balance: " <<  myField.as( float(0.0F))+10.0F << endl;
  }
  catch( std::domain_error )
  {
    cerr << "Can't convert customer_balance into float form" << endl;
  }
....
```

Notice that you don't have to create a temporary float object here; `field::as(` `defaultValue )` does that for you. Using `field::as( defaultValue )` instead of `field::to()` can make your code more understandable.

You might be wondering how `field::as( defaultValue )` decides which type of object to produce (C++ compilers can't infer the data type based on the return value). The answer is devilishly simple: `field::as( defaultValue )` produces an object whose type matches the type of `defaultValue`, which brings us around to the last conversion function defined by class `field`. The second variant of `field::as()` is similar to `field::as( defaultValue )` except that it doesn't let you specify a `defaultValue`. When you call the second variant, it throws an `std::domain_error` exception if the field contains a NULL value. In addition, it throws an `std::domain_error` if the conversion fails. If you can't define a `defaultValue` when you call this variant of `field::as()`, how does the function know what kind of object to return? You have to tell it—and if you're not a hard-core C++ hacker, the syntax looks a little strange. Here's the same code snippet you saw earlier, this time rewritten to use the second form of `field::as()`:

```
...
  const result::field  & myField = myResult[0]["balance"];

  try
  {
    cout << "New customer balance: " <<  myField.as<float>() + 10.0F << endl;
  }
  catch( std::domain_error )
  {
    cerr << "Can't convert customer_balance into float (or balance is NULL)"
         << endl;
  }
....
```

A call to this variant of `field::as()` is written `myField.as<typename>()`, where typename indicates the kind of object you want.

A Few Words About Qualified Data Type Names

All the libpqxx data types are defined in the `pqxx` namespace to help segregate libpqxx names from other libraries. That's good, but it can result in a lot of typing if you include `pqxx::` at the beginning of every data type name. Instead, you can add a `using namespace pqxx;` directive near the top of your C++ source file (just after the `#include` directives). Likewise, libpqxx defines a few classes *inside* the `result` class. For example, the complete name of the `tuple` data type is really `pqxx::result::tuple`. Again, this involves a lot of extra typing. Make your source code a little easier to read and define a few new type names to make it easier to deal with libpqxx's well-structured nesting:

```
typedef pqxx::result::tuple  tuple;  // a synonym for 'pqxx::result::tuple'
typedef pqxx::result::field  field;  // a synonym for 'pqxx::result::field'
typedef pqxx::result::const_iterator result_iterator;  // You get the idea...
```

Summary of Metadata Stored in `result`, `tuple`, **and** `field` **Objects**

That's a lot of information to digest—the `result`, `tuple`, and `field` classes are very rich. Here's a quick summary of the metadata and data-access functions you'll find in these three classes.

A result set is represented by an object of class `result`. You get a `result` object when you call `transaction<>::exec()` to execute a command on the server.

A `result` is a collection of zero or more rows, each represented by an object of class `tuple`. You can access the `tuple`s within a `result` by calling `result::at()` or `result::operator[]()`, as shown here:

```
const tuple result::operator[]( size_type rowNumber ) throw();
const tuple result::at( size_type rowNumber ) throw( std::out_of_range );
```

Or, you can call `result::begin()` or `result::rbegin()` to obtain an iterator (or reverse iterator) you can use to walk through the `tuple`s in a `result`. The prototypes for the iterator factories are

```
const_iterator          result::begin();
const_iterator          result::end();
const_reverse_iterator  result::rbegin();
const_reverse_iterator  result::rend();
```

A `result` object contains a wealth of metadata as well. To determine whether the command returned any `tuple`s, call `result::empty()`. To find the number of `tuple`s in the result set, call `result::size()`, and to find the number of columns, call `result::columns()`. The prototypes for these three functions are shown here:

```
size_type          result::size();
bool               result::empty();
tuple::size_type   result::columns() throw();
```

You can also retrieve the name and data type of each column within a result using these functions:

```
const char * result::column_name( tuple::size_type columnNumber );
oid          result::column_type( tuple::size_type columnNumber );
oid          result::column_type( const std::string & columnName );
oid          result::column_type( const char columnName[]);
```

Notice that you can retrieve the data type of a column by column name or column number.

You can find the column number of a column, if you know its name, by calling either of these two functions:

```
tuple::size_type result::column_number( const char columnName[]);
tuple::size_type result::column_number( const std::string & columnName);
```

Finally, the `result` class provides two functions you can call after you execute a command other than `SELECT`. The `result::affected_rows()` function returns the number of rows affected by an `INSERT`, `UPDATE`, or `DELETE` command. If you've just executed an

INSERT command, you can call result::inserted_oid() to find the object id of the new row.

```
size_type result::affected_rows();
oid        result::inserted_oid();
```

result::inserted_oid() returns the constant InvalidOid if you've just executed a command other than INSERT, if you've added more than one row, or if you've added a row to a table that does not store OIDs.

A tuple is a collection of one or more values, each represented by an object of class field. You can access the fields within a tuple by calling field::at() or field::operator[](), as shown here:

```
field tuple::operator[]( size_type columnNumber ) throw();
field tuple::operator[]( const char columnName[] );
field tuple::operator[]( const std::string & columnName );
field tuple::at( size_type columnNumber ) throw( std::out_of_range );
field tuple::at( const char columnName[] );
field tuple::at( const std::string & columnName );
```

You can use tuple::at() and tuple::operator[]() to find a column by its zero-based columnNumber or its columnName. If you try to find a column by name and the result set contains two or more columns with that name, the results are unpredictable (currently, you'll find the first column with the given name, but that behavior is undocumented and might change in the future).

If you want to retrieve the row number of a tuple (that is, the offset from the first tuple), call tuple::rownumber(). To find the number of columns in a tuple, use the tuple::size() function. These two functions are defined as follows:

```
result::size_type tuple::rownumber() throw();
size_type          tuple::size() throw();
```

Like the result class, tuple provides a number of ways to find the column number and data type of a given column:

```
size_type tuple::column_number( const std::string & columnName );
size_type tuple::column_number( const char columnName[] );
oid       tuple::column_type( size_type columnNumber );
oid       tuple::column_type( const std::string & columnName );
oid       tuple::column_type( const char columnName[] );
```

Unlike the result class, tuple does not provide a function that returns a column's name given its column number—that seems like an oversight and might be corrected in a future version.

Finally, an object of type field represents the value of one column in one row of a result set. The field class defines four functions that expose the metadata associated with a value:

```
const char * field::name();
oid           field::type();
```

```
bool        field::is_null();
size_type   field::size();
```

To access the value stored within a `field` as a C-style null-terminated string, call the `field::c_str()` function. To convert a field value into a different data type, call any of the `field::to()` or `field::as()` functions. The prototypes for these functions are shown here:

```
                const char *field::c_str();
template<typename T>  bool  field::to( T & destination );
template<typename T>  bool  field::to( T &destination, const T & defaultValue );
t emplate<typename T>  T     field::as( const T & defaultValue );
template<typename T>  T     field::as();
```

The Relationship Between libpqxx and libpq

Like most of the client-side APIs, libpqxx is a wrapper around the libpq interface, which is often used direct-ly by PostgreSQL applications written in C. libpqxx is a lightweight wrapper. When you make a copy of a `result` object, you aren't duplicating the entire result set of a command; you're duplicating a pointer to libpq's copy of the result set. When you make a copy of a `tuple`, you're not duplicating all the values within that `tuple`—you're duplicating a pointer to the result set plus a row number. The same holds true for a `field` object: It's simply a pointer (of some sort) into the libpq result set. That means that libpqxx is an inexpensive wrapper. libpqxx uses a reference-counting scheme to ensure that the libpq result set is not discarded until all the pointers have been destroyed.

Now that you know how to access all the data and metadata stored inside a `result` and how to execute a command on the server, it's time to put everything together into a simple client application. Listings 10.6–10.9 show a simple client that uses libpqxx to execute a hard-wired query and print the results.

Listing 10.6   `client3.cc` **(Part 1)**

```
 1 /* client3.cc */
 2
 3 #include <iostream>
 4 #include <iomanip>
 5 #include <pqxx/pqxx>
 6
 7 using namespace std;
 8 using namespace pqxx;
 9
10 typedef pqxx::result::tuple        tuple;
11 typedef vector<string::size_type> widthVector;
12
13 // Forward function declarations
14 static void getColumnWidths(const result & res, widthVector & widths);
15 static void printColumnHdrs(const result & res, const widthVector & widths);
16 static void printColumnVals(const result & res, const widthVector & widths);
```

Listing 10.6   **Continued**

```
17
18 int main( int argc, char * argv[] )
19 {
20   try
21   {
22     connection      myConnection( argc > 1 ? argv[1] : "" );
23     transaction<>  myTransaction( myConnection, "Get Customer List" );
24     const result & customerList =
25                             myTransaction.exec( "SELECT * FROM customers" );
26     widthVector    columnWidths( customerList.columns());
27
28     getColumnWidths( customerList, columnWidths );
29     printColumnHdrs( customerList, columnWidths );
30     printColumnVals( customerList, columnWidths );
31
32     myTransaction.commit();
33
34   }
35   catch( ... )
36   {
37     cerr << "Unknown exception caught" << endl;
38     exit( EXIT_FAILURE );
39   }
40
41   exit( EXIT_SUCCESS );
42 }
43
```

Lines 3–5 #include the header files required for this application. The only unusual header here is <iomanip>—you need that header to use the stream manipulators you'll use to set column widths and justifications. Line 10 defines a shorthand synonym for result::tuple, and line 11 defines a class named widthVector you'll use to collect the maximum required width for each column.

Next you see the forward declarations for the three workhorse functions (in lines 14–16). getColumnWidths() walks through a result set, finds the longest value in each column, and stores the required column widths in a widthVector. The printColumnHdrs() function uses the column widths computed by getColumnWidths() and the column names stored in the result to format and print column headers. printColumnVals() prints each value in every tuple in the result set (again, using the column widths computed by getColumnWidths() to format the values into tabular form).

Lines 21–43 show the main() function for this application. client3 starts by creating a connection (myConnection) to a server. If you invoke client3 with any command-line arguments, the first argument is assumed to be a connection string and myConnection uses the properties in that string to find the server. If you invoke client3 without any command-line arguments, myConnection uses the built-in default connection properties and environment variables listed in Table 5.2 to connect to the server. If the connection attempt fails, myConnection throws an exception and the program jumps to the catch() clause at lines 35–39. (Note: we've omitted most of the error handling code in the application for the sake of clarity.)

When the connection is up and running, client3 creates a transaction<> object named myTransaction. myTransaction is assigned a descriptive name of "Get Customer List" so any error messages that show up will be a little easier to track down. At line 24 you see a call to myTransaction.exec()—exec() sends the text of the query (SELECT * FROM customers) to the server and waits for the entire result set to accumulate within the customerList object.

When myTransaction.exec() returns, the result set (customerList) is ready for use. At line 26, client3 creates a widthVector, named columnWidths, that holds the maximum width of each column in the result set. Notice that you can create a widthVector with exactly the right number of elements by initializing it with the number of columns returned by customerList.columns().

At lines 28–30, client3 calls three helper functions (which I'll show you in a moment) to compute the width of each column, print column headers, and print the data values stored in result. The call to myTransaction.commit() (see line 32) completes the transaction and commits any changes to the database.

Listing 10.7   client3.cc **(Part 2)**

```
44 static void getColumnWidths( const result & res, widthVector & widths )
45 {
46   result::size_type row;
47   tuple::size_type  col;
48
49   // Compute width of widest value in each column
50   for( row = 0; row < res.size(); ++row )
51     for( col = 0; col < res.columns(); ++col )
52       if( res[row][col].size() > widths[col] )
53         widths[col] = res[row][col].size();
54
55   // Make room for any column name which happens to be
56   // longer than the widest value in that column
57   for( col = 0; col < res.columns(); ++col )
58     if( strlen( res.column_name( col )) > widths[col] )
59       widths[col] = strlen( res.column_name( col ));
60 }
61
```

Listing 10.7 shows the getColumnWidths() function. This function expects a (const) reference to a result object and a reference to a widthVector. It finds the longest value in each column in the result and stores the maximum length in the corresponding element in the widthVector. You'll need this vector to print column names and data values in tabular form.

Lines 50 and 51 traverse every row and column in the result set. You could use any of the tuple enumeration methods here: `result::at()`, `result::operator[]()`, or a pair of iterators. Lines 52 and 53 hunt down the longest string in a given column and store the width in `widths[col]`. When the loop (lines 50–53) completes, `widths[n]` holds the length of the longest string found in column n.

Lines 55–59 walk through the column names stored in the `result`. If any given column name is longer than the longest value in that column, the `widths[]` element corresponding to that column is adjusted to reflect the length of the column name. When this loop completes, `widths[n]` holds the length of the longest string found in column n or the length of the column name, whichever is longer.

Listing 10.8 `client3.cc` **(Part 3)**

```
62 static void printColumnHdrs(const result & res, const widthVector & widths)
63 {
64
65   std::ostream out( cout.rdbuf());  // Construct a new stream so we can
66                                      // change the format flags and
67                                      // options without mucking up cout
68
69   for( tuple::size_type col = 0; col < res.columns(); ++col )
70     out << setw( widths[ col ] ) << left << res.column_name( col ) << " ";
71
72   out << endl;
73
74   for( tuple::size_type col = 0; col < res.columns(); ++col )
75     out << setw( widths[ col ] ) << setfill( '-' ) << "" << " ";
76
77   out << endl;
78
79 }
80
```

Listing 10.8 shows the `printColumnHdrs()` function. This function prints the name of each column in the given `result` (res) and then, on the next line, prints a line of separator characters (dashes) to show the width of each column. Here's a sample of the output generated by `printColumnHdrs()`:

```
id customer_name        phone    birth_date balance
-- -------------------- -------- ---------- -------
```

`printColumnHdrs()` does its work by changing the formatting options of an output stream using stream manipulators. To avoid making permanent changes to the output stream, `printColumnHdrs()` clones `std::cout` (see line 65) and applies the necessary changes to the clone. That way, the formatting options for `std::cout` remain unchanged.

The loop at lines 69 and 70 prints the name of each column found in res. Before writing the column name (res.column_name(col)), printColumnHdrs() calls the setw() stream manipulator to set the field width to match the column width computed earlier by getColumnWidths(). The left manipulator tells the output stream to left-justify the column name—if the column name happens to be shorter than the column width, the name \ appears at the left side of the column.

The loop at lines 74 and 75 prints a sequence of dashes under each column name. Again, the setw() manipulator adjusts the field width for each column. The setfill() manipulator sets the stream's fill character to -. The fill character is used to pad the next value to the field width defined by setw(). Next, printColumnHdrs() writes an empty string to the output stream; because the empty string has a length of zero, you end up with a string of fill characters of just the right length.

Listing 10.9 client3.cc **(Part 4)**

```
81 static void printColumnVals(const result & res, const widthVector & widths)
82 {
83     result::const_iterator      i;
84
85     for( i = res.begin(); i != res.end(); ++i )
86     {
87         const tuple      & tup = *i;
88
89         for( tuple::size_type col = 0; col < tup.size(); ++col )
90         {
91             // Note:  because of a bug in some STL implementations,
92             //        setw() doesn't work as expected when followed
93             //        by a std::string so we convert to a const char *
94             //        instead
95             cout << setw( widths[ col ] ) << tup[col].c_str() << " ";
96         }
97
98         cout << endl;
99     }
100 }
```

The printColumnVals() function in Listing 10.9 completes client3. printColumnVals() uses a result::const_iterator to walk through the tuples in the given result set (res). Take a close look at line 87—notice that when you de-reference a result::const_iterator, you get a tuple (in this case, you don't need a copy of the tuple so printColumnVals() captures a tuple reference instead). Like printColumnHdrs(), this function changes the field width of the output stream (cout) just before printing each column value. You might be thinking that you could rewrite line 95 to look like this:

```
cout << setw( widths[ col ] ) << tup[col] << " ";
```

That should work because libpqxx defines an operator<< function that writes a field directly onto a stream. But, as the code comment says, a bug in some STL implementations (most notably, GNU's libstdc++ library) makes it impossible to set a stream's field width before printing an std::string.

Working with Large-Objects

Most of the tables you create are defined in terms of simple data types. You already know that PostgreSQL provides numeric, textual, date-time, geometric, and logical data types. But what data type should you use to store photographs? Or MP3 audio files?

One answer is a *large-object* (you might also see the term *binary-large-object [BLOB]*). A large-object is just an entry in the pg_largeobject system table. PostgreSQL provides a few predefined functions that make working large-objects easy. When you store a large-object in a PostgreSQL database, it's saved in one or more rows in the pg_largeobject table. Each row in pg_largeobject stores a 2KB chunk of your object. How do you store a large-object (say, a photograph) on your *own* table? You don't. You add a pointer to a large-object instead—that is, you store the large-object's OID in your table.

A second alternative is the BYTEA data type. A column of type BYTEA can store an arbitrarily sized string of octets (also known as *bytes*). The BYTEA data type is similar to the VARCHAR data type, but some important differences exist. First, a VARCHAR value cannot hold a character whose value is 0—I'm not talking about the character 0 whose value is actually 48 (see http://www.asciitable.com); I mean the character often called NULL. A BYTEA value can hold any 8-bit character. Second, a VARCHAR value is defined in terms of some specific character set (usually US ASCII). This means the collation sequence used when you compare two VARCHAR values might be based on something other than just the numeric value of each byte. When you compare two BYTEA values, the relationship between the two values is determined by comparing the numeric value of each character.

Whether you choose to use the large-object interface or the BYTEA data type depends mostly on how large your data is and what you need to do with it. A BYTEA column can hold up to 1GB; a large-object can hold values larger than 1GB. PostgreSQL provides a few functions that make loading binary data from an external file into a large-object easy. Loading external data into a BYTEA column isn't quite so easy, though. When you insert data into a BYTEA column, you must translate the data into a quoted (also called *escaped*) form (see Chapter 2, "Working with Data in PostgreSQL"). When you SELECT data from a BYTEA column, it comes back in quoted form, and that's not always easy to work with because you have to parse through the result and unquote it yourself. When you retrieve data from a large-object, you get the same binary data you put into it, but you have to get at the data using some special functions, described in this section. For more information on the BYTEA data type, refer to Chapter 2. This section describes how to work with large-objects using libpqxx.

Let's say you want to add a picture to the tapes table and for each tape, you want to store a photograph of the box that was shipped with the tape. Currently, the tapes table looks like this:

```
CREATE TABLE tapes
(
    tape_id     character(8),
    title       character varying(80)
);
```

Because you aren't actually storing a photograph in this table (remember that large-objects are stored in the `pg_largeobject` table), you add a large-object identifier instead. A large-object identifier has a data type of OID. Here's what the new `tapes` table looks like after adding the row reference:

```
CREATE TABLE tapes
(
    tape_id     character(8),
    title       character varying(80),
    photo_id    oid
);
```

It's important to remember that the `photo_id` column doesn't actually hold a photograph; it holds the address of a row in the `pg_largeobjects` table.

To store a photo in PostgreSQL, you might use the `lo_import()` function. `lo_import()` takes a filename as an argument and returns an OID as a result. Here's an example:

```
INSERT INTO tapes VALUES
(
    'AA-55892',
    'Casablanca',
    lo_import('/tmp/casablanca.jpg' )
);
```

The call to `lo_import()` opens the /tmp/Casablanca.jpg file, imports the contents of that file into the `pg_largeobjects` table, and returns the OID of the new large-object. You insert the OID into the `photo_id` column.

After you have a photo in your database, what can you do with it? It doesn't make a lot of sense to SELECT the photo from a text-based client because you would just see a lot of binary garbage.

You could use the `lo_export()` function to copy a photo back out to the filesystem. For example

```
SELECT lo_export( photo_id, '/tmp/casa2.jpg' )
WHERE tape_id = 'AA-5892';
```

libpqxx defines four interrelated classes that let you manipulate large-objects from within your own client applications:

- `largeobject`—A `largeobject` object stores a large-object ID (or `loid`)
- `largeobjectaccess`—Provides low-level access to a large-object
- `olostream`—An STL-compatible `ostream` you can use to write objects into a large-object

- ilostream—An STL-compatible istream you can use to read object from a large-object

You can create a large-object (that is, create an empty entry in the pg_largeobjects table) using an object of type largeobject or largeobjectaccess. Each class defines a constructor that will create an empty large-object:

```
largeobject( dbtransaction & transaction );
largeobjectaccess( dbtransaction & transaction,
                   openmode mode = ios::in | ios::out );
```

The mode argument determines what you can do with the largeobjectaccess object. If mode is std::ios::in, you can read data from the large-object into other objects. If mode is std::ios::in, you can write data into the large-object. If mode is std::ios::in | std::ios::out (which is the default value), you can read data from or write data to the large-object.

You can also create a large-object and fill it with a copy of an existing file (such as a photograph or MP3 file) by calling a different constructor:

```
largeobject( dbtransaction & transaction, std::string fileName );
largeobjectaccess( dbtransaction & transaction, std::string fileName,
                   openmode mode = ios::in | ios::out );
```

When you call one of these constructors, it creates a new large-object, opens the given file, and copies the content of the file into the new large-object. If libpqxx can't open the file you've named, the constructor throws a runtime_error exception.

If you've retrieved a large-object ID from the server, you can convert it into a largeobject object using this constructor:

```
largeobject( oid largeObjectID );
```

Or you can convert it into a largeobjectaccess object using this constructor:

```
largeobjectaccess( dbtransaction & transaction, oid largeObjectID );
```

After you have an object of type largeobject (or largeobjectaccess), you can retrieve the loid (large-object ID) with the id() member function:

```
oid largeobject::id();
oid largeobjectaccess::id();
```

In most cases, you'll store the loid in some other table (the tapes.photo_id column, for example). But you might want to write a large-object into a file. You can do that with the to_file() member functions:

```
void largeobject::to_file( dbtransaction & transaction, std::string fileName );
void largeobjectaccess::to_file( std::string fileName );
```

If libpqxx can't write to the file you've named, the constructor throws a runtime_error exception.

At this point, you're probably wondering about the distinction between largeobject and largeobjectaccess. They both provide access to server-side large-objects; they can both import an existing (client-side) file into a large-object; and they can both export a large-object to a client-side file. In fact, that's just about all they have in common. Think of a `largeobject` as a way to work with large-object identifiers. The `largeobject` class defines operators you can use to compare two large-object IDs (`operator==()`, `operator!=()`, `operator<()`, and so on). A `largeobjectaccess` object, on the other hand, lets you manipulate the *content* of a large-object.

The `largeobjectaccess` class defines three member functions that write a chunk of data to a large-object:

```
off_type cwrite( const char data[], size_type byteCount ) throw();
void     write( const char data[], size_type byteCount );
void     write( const std::string & data );
```

The `cwrite()` function writes, at most, `byteCount` bytes worth of `data` to the large-object, returning the number of bytes actually written, or `-1` if an error occurs. The `write()` functions copy data into the large-object as well, but they throw a `runtime_error` exception if something goes wrong.

`largeobjectaccess` defines two member functions you can use to read data from a large-object:

```
off_type  cread( char destination[], size_type byteCount ) throw();
size_type read( char destination[], size_type byteCount );
```

`cread()` reads, at most, `byteCount` bytes worth of data from the large-object into the buffer pointed to by `destination`, returning the number of bytes read, or `-1` if an error occurs. The `read()` function does the same except that it throws a `runtime_error` exception if an error occurs.

Finally, `largeobjectaccess` provides two member functions you can use to "move around" inside of a large-object:

```
pos_type  cseek( off_type offset, seekdir origin ) throw();
size_type seek ( size_type offset, seekdir origin );
```

To understand the `cseek()` and `seek()` functions, you have to know that a `largeobjectaccess` object maintains a pointer within the data stored in a large-object. This pointer always starts out by pointing to the first byte in the large-object. When you read data from a large-object, you start reading at the pointer and the pointer moves to a position just past the last byte that you've read. When you write data to a large object, the data is written starting at the pointer and the pointer moves to a position just past the last byte you write. The `cseek()` and `seek()` functions move the pointer. The first argument (`offset`) specifies how many bytes you want to move. The second argument (`origin`) specifies the starting point. If `origin` is `ios::cur`, the pointer moves by `offset` bytes; if `offset` is positive, the pointer moves toward the end of the large-object; and if `offset` is negative, the pointer moves toward the beginning of the large-object. If `origin` is `ios::beg`, the pointer is positioned exactly `offset` bytes into the large-object (if you want to move to the beginning of the object, call `seek( 0, ios::beg )`). If `origin` is `ios::end`, the pointer is positioned exactly `offset` bytes before the end of the large-object (if you want to move to the end of the object, call `seek( 0, ios::end )`).

We said earlier that `largeobjectaccess` provides low-level access to a large-object. We said that because, when you use a `largeobjectaccess`, you're dealing with a sequence of raw bytes. libpqxx provides two more classes that provide high-level (that is, object-oriented) access: `olostream` and `ilostream`.

Both `olostream` and `ilostream` are derived from `std::iostream`. Therefore, you can use an `olostream` or `ilostream` anywhere you can use an `std::iostream`. To create an `olostream` or `ilostream`, you can call any of the following constructors:

```
olostream( dbtransaction & transaction, largeobject & obj );
olostream( dbtransaction & transaction, oid objectID );
ilostream( dbtransaction & transaction, largeobject & obj );
ilostream( dbtransaction & transaction, oid objectID );
```

An `olostream` is a stream you can use to append a C++ object onto a large-object. An `ilostream` is a stream you can use to create a C++ object from the content of a large-object.

To write an object to an `olostream`, use the `<<` operator, just like you would with a standard `ostream`:

```
...
  myStream << "This string is written to the large object";
  myStream << 10.0F;
  myStream << int( 42 );
...
```

To read an object from an `ilostream`, use the `>>` operator, just like you would with a standard `istream`:

```
...
  std::string  myString;
  float        myFloat;
  int          myInt;

  myStream >> myString;
  myStream >> myFloat;
  myStream >> myInt;
...
```

LISTEN/NOTIFY

Sometimes you want a client application to wait for some server-side event to occur before proceeding. You might, for example, need to write a queuing system that writes a work order into a PostgreSQL table and then expects a client application to carry out that work order. The most obvious way to write a client of this sort is to put your client application to sleep for a few seconds or minutes and then, when your application awakens, check for a new record in the work order table. If the record exists, go do your work and then repeat the whole cycle.

There are two problems with this approach, however. First, your client application can't be very responsive. When a new work order is added, it can take a few seconds or minutes for your client to notice (it's fast asleep after all). Second, your client application might spend a lot of time searching for work orders that don't exist.

PostgreSQL offers a solution to this problem: the LISTEN/NOTIFY mechanism (not to be confused with the notice mechanism you read about earlier in this chapter). A PostgreSQL server can signal client applications that some event has occurred by executing a NOTIFY *eventName* command. All client applications that are listening for that event are notified that the event has occurred. You get to choose your own event names (something like workOrderReceived might be a good choice). To inform the server that you are interested in an event, execute a LISTEN *eventName* command; to tell the server you are no longer interested in an event, simply use UNLISTEN *eventName*.

A libpqxx application can put itself to sleep until an event is signaled. To tell libpqxx that you are interested in an event, you create an object derived from pqxx::trigger—which is not related to a server-side procedural-language trigger—and attach that object to a connection. A trigger-derived object is very simple to build: You need only one constructor and an operator() function (of course, you'll need a destructor for nontrivial classes).

Here's a simple trigger that simply displays a message when its event is signaled:

```
...
class myTrigger : public trigger
{

public:

    explicit myTrigger( connection & conn, string eventName )
    : trigger( conn, eventName )
    {
    }

    virtual void operator()(int backendPid )
    {
      cout << "Notification: " << name() << " received from process "
          << backendPid << endl;
    }

};
...
```

The constructor is trivial—it simply initializes the parent class with a connection and eventName. When libpqxx is notified that event eventName has occurred, it calls the operator() function, passing it the process ID of the server process that generated the event. If you're only interested in events generated by *your* server process, compare backendPid with the value returned by conn.backendpid().

To create a myTrigger object, just give it a reference to the connection you're using and the name of the event you're interested in, like this:

```
...
connection conn( argv[1] );
myTrigger  trigger( conn, "workOrderReceived" );
...
```

This code snippet creates a trigger object that fires whenever a workOrderReceived event is signaled.

Here's the final piece of the puzzle. To put your application to sleep until an event occurs—specifically, an event you're interested in—just call connection::await_notification(). await_notification() won't return until an interesting event is signaled by the server. If you prefer, you can call an alternative form of await_notification():

```
int connection::await_notification( );
int connection::await_notification( long seconds, long microseconds );
```

The second form waits no longer than the specified period of time. Both forms return the number of notifications (events) received.

set_variable() **and** get_variable()

The PostgreSQL server keeps track of a number of configuration parameters that affect the way the server works (see the section titled "Configuring Your PostgreSQL Runtime Environment" in Chapter 21, "PostgreSQL Administration," for a complete list). For example, the search_path variable determines how objects, such as tables, functions, and so on, are located if you don't provide a fully qualified name. search_path defines the list of schemas to search and the order in which they are searched.

The connection and transaction<> classes both provide member functions you can and should use to modify and interrogate these runtime variables. The set_variable() function changes the value of a variable, and get_variable() returns the current value of a variable. The prototype for each function is shown here:

```
void connection::set_variable(std::string variableName, std::string newValue);
void transaction<>::set_variable(std::string variableName, std::string newValue);
std::string connection::get_variable(std::string variableName);
std::string transaction<>::get_variable(std::string variableName);
```

In each case, the function throws an sql_error exception if variableName refers to a nonexistent variable. There's an important difference between connection::set_variable() and transaction<>::set_variable(): When you modify a variable with transaction<>::set_variable(), the variable is restored to its original value if your transaction aborts. If, on the other hand, the transaction commits, the variable retains its new value. Variables you modify with connection::set_variable() retain their values for the life of the connection object. If the physical connection to the server is lost and reestablished behind the scenes, connection::set_variable() restores the values you've given to each variable. That's why you should use set_connection() function(s) to modify runtime variables instead of executing SET commands. If you modify a variable with a SET command, libpqxx won't notice and can't restore the desired value if the connection is lost and reestablished.

Client 4—Working with transactors

libpqxx strives to provide a robust connection to a PostgreSQL server, and the transactor<> class reflects that effort. The transactor<> class defines four important member functions:

```
void operator()( TRANSACTION & trans );
void OnAbort( const char errorMessage[] ) throw();
void OnCommit( void ) throw();
void OnDoubt( void ) throw();
```

When you derive a class from transactor<>, you must provide your own implementation for the operator() member function: That's where all the real work is done. To execute a transaction, you create an object derived from transactor<> and then pass that object to the connection_base::perform() member function. connection_base::perform() calls the operator() function in your transactor<> object and then calls OnAbort(), OnCommit(), or OnDoubt() to complete the transaction. transactor<> has a rather surprising but convenient quirk: If your operator() function throws an exception, transactor<> aborts the transaction, creates a new transaction, and re-invokes the operator() function. In fact, transactor<> repeats this cycle until it stops throwing exceptions or until a maximum retry count is reached. That's convenient because you don't have to litter *your* code with complex retry logic to handle connection failures.

Listings 10.10–10.14 show a simple application (client4.cc) that updates a table using a transactor<>.

Listing 10.10　client4.cc **(Part 1)**

```
 1  /* client4.cc */
 2
 3  #include <string>
 4  #include <iostream>
 5
 6  #include <pqxx/pqxx>
 7
 8  using namespace std;
 9  using namespace pqxx;
10
11  class updateBalance : public transactor<>
12  {
13  public:
14     updateBalance( float increment = 10.0F );
15
16     void operator()( argument_type & T );
```

Listing 10.10 **Continued**

```
17    void OnCommit( void );
18
19 private:
20    float          m_increment;
21    result         m_totalResult;
22 };
23
```

The interesting part of this listing starts with the definition of the updateBalance class at line 11. updateBalance derives from the transactor<> template class. The transactor<> template class is parameterized by a transaction<>, which itself is a template class parameterized by a transaction isolation type. Class updateBalance derives from the default parameter type and is equivalent to

```
class updateBalance : public transactor< transaction<read_committed> >
```

You can use any transaction<> type to parameterize a transactor<>, although it seems silly to derive a class from transactor< nontransaction >. Any of the following choices are valid:

```
transactor<>
transactor< transaction<> >
transactor< transaction< read_committed > >
transactor< transaction< serializable > >
transactor< robusttransaction< read_committed > >
transactor< robusttransaction< serializable > >
```

The updateBalance class increases or decreases the balance in every row in the customers table by some amount. The only public constructor for updateBalance expects a single argument—the amount to add to each balance. The operator() function (declared at line 16) is the function that is called repeatedly to carry out the work of the transaction.

operator() takes a single parameter of argument_type. When the transactor<> framework calls your operator() function, it passes a reference a transaction<>, and you use that transaction<> to execute commands on the server. You choose the type of transaction (transaction<> or robusttransaction<>, read_committed or serializable) when you specify the parent for your own transactor<>-derived class. If you've derived a class from transactor< transaction< serializable > >, operator() is called with a reference to a transaction< serializable >. If you've derived a class from transactor< transaction< read_committed > >, operator() is called with a reference to a transaction< read_committed >. The transactor<> class provides a typedef (argument_type) that specifies the exact transaction<> type.

Remember that the real work performed by a transactor<> happens when the transactor<> framework calls your operator() function. Inside operator() (which we'll show you in a moment), you use a transaction<> to execute commands on the server and process the result set of each command. Where does the transaction<> come from? The transactor<> framework creates a new transaction<> for you every time it calls operator(). When you commit the transaction, the transactor<> framework calls your OnCommit() function. If you abort the transaction<> or throw an exception, the transactor<> framework calls your OnAbort() function, passing in the reason for failure.

Lines 20 and 21 declare the two data members for updateBalance. m_increment holds a copy of the increment value given to the constructor, and m_increment is added to the balance column of every row in the customers table. After updating the customers table, the operator() function asks the server to compute the total of customer balances, and m_totalResult stores the result set for that query.

Listing 10.11   client4.cc **(Part 2)**

```
24 int main( int argc, const char * argv[] )
25 {
26
27   try
28   {
29     connection  conn( argv[1] );
30
31     conn.perform( updateBalance( 3.0F ));
32   }
33   catch( runtime_error & err )
34   {
35     cerr << err.what();
36   }
37   catch( ... )
38   {
39     cerr << "Unexpected exception" << endl;
40     return( EXIT_FAILURE );
41   }
42
43   return( EXIT_SUCCESS );
44 }
45
```

Listing 10.11 shows the main() function for client4. Line 29 creates a connection to the server using the first command-line parameter, if present, to specify connection properties. Line 31 creates a new object of type updateBalance and then calls connection::perform() with that object. connection::perform() is the magic framework we've been talking about all along—it creates a transaction<> (of the appropriate type), invokes your operator() function, and then commits the transaction<> if everything worked. If the operator() function throws an exception (or calls the transaction<>::abort() function), connection::perform() repeats the cycle until it succeeds. If you call connection::perform() with two arguments, the second argument limits the number of retries; by default, connection::perform() calls your operator() function a maximum of three times.

Each time `connection::perform()` calls your `operator()` function, it creates a new `transaction<>` and a new copy of your `transactor<>`. Because `connection::perform()` always makes a copy of your `transactor<>`, you must ensure that your class defines a *public* copy constructor. You can let the compiler generate the copy constructor for you—you just have to make sure it's public. Also, take a look at the prototype for `connection::perform()` (we've tidied it up a bit for the sake of readability):

```
void connection::perform( const transactor<> & T, int Attempts = 3 );
```

Notice that it expects a *const* `transactor<>` reference. The const qualifier does *not* mean you're prohibited from changing the `transactor<>` inside your `operator()` function; it just means `connection::perform()` won't modify the `transactor<>` you give to it. It modifies a copy of your `transactor<>` instead. That means you can't interrogate the `transactor<>` you give to `connection::perform()` after it returns and it can't be changed within the call to `connection::perform()`. So, how do you get information back out of the `transactor<>`? You simply add a reference or pointer to your `transactor<>`. Initialize the reference when you create a `transactor<>` object and all copies of the `transactor<>` will refer to the same object. For example, if you want to extract a `float` value from your `transactor<>`, add a `float` reference to your `transactor<>`, make sure the reference points to an object *outside* your `transactor<>`, and then interrogate the referenced object after `connection::perform()` completes. Of course, you could store query results in a set of global variables, but using a reference or pointer to a local object is usually a better idea.

`client4` is rather simple-minded (it just writes the result to `cout`), so you won't find a `float` reference in the `updateBalance` class.

Listing 10.12 `client4.cc` **(Part 3)**

```
46 updateBalance::updateBalance( float increment )
47   : transactor< argument_type >( "updating balance" ),
48     m_increment( increment )
49 {
50 }
51
```

The `updateBalance` constructor in Listing 10.12 is very simple. It expects a single argument (`increment`) and stores that value in the `m_increment` member variable. The funny-looking code at line 47 calls the constructor for the `updateBalance`'s parent class. Notice that we've used `argument_type` here to locate the exact data type of `updateBalance`'s parent. The constructor for `transactor<>` expects a single argument—a `const char[]` that provides descriptive name for the work performed by the `operator()` function.

Listing 10.13 `client4.cc` **(Part 4)**

```
52 void updateBalance::operator()( argument_type & trans )
53 {
54
55    string command( "UPDATE customers SET balance = balance + " );
```

Listing 10.13 **Continued**

```
56
57   command += to_string( m_increment );
58
59   result  updateResult( trans.exec( command ));
60
61   m_totalResult = trans.exec( "SELECT SUM( balance ) FROM customers" );
62
63 }
64
```

Listing 10.13 shows the updateBalance::operator() function. operator() is where all the database interaction occurs in a transactor<>. When the transactor<> framework calls operator(), it creates a new transaction<> of type argument_type and provides a reference to that transaction<>. This function executes two commands on the server. The first command adds m_increment to the balance column in every customers row. The second command asks the server to compute the SUM() of all customer balances.

operator() stores the result object in m_totalResult for use in the OnCommit() member function. This illustrates an important concept you must keep in mind when you write your own transactor<>-derived classes. Because the operator() function can be called an unpredictable number of times, you should not modify any values *outside* the transactor<> in operator(). Instead, you should modify your program's state in the OnCommit() function because OnCommit() will never be called more than once and won't be called at all if the transactor<> exceeds its retry limit.

Listing 10.14 client4.cc **(Part 5)**

```
65 void updateBalance::OnCommit( void )
66 {
67   cout << "Total Balance = " << m_totalResult[0][0] << endl;
68 }
69
```

The updateBalance::OnCommit() function in Listing 10.14 is straightforward. It simply extracts a value from the m_totalResult result set and writes that value to cout (the standard output stream). OnCommit() is called only if the transactor<> completes successfully.

You can also define OnAbort() and OnDoubt() functions for your own transactor<>-derived classes.

connection::perform() calls OnAbort() each time the operator() function fails. That means OnAbort() might not be the best place to report error messages. For example, if your transaction fails 50 times, you'll see 50 copies of the same error message. Instead, you can report any error messages in the try/catch handler that wraps the call to connection::perform()—the runtime_error you catch will contain a copy of the most recent error message.

The OnDoubt() function is called if the connection to the server is lost and can't be recovered after executing a COMMIT but before an acknowledgement is received. There isn't much useful work that you can do in an OnDoubt() function other than tell the user that something nasty just happened.

Designing transactor<>-based Applications

The overall architecture of your application changes when you design around transactors<>. Every transaction becomes an object, and the transaction might execute many times behind the scenes. Here's a strategy you can use when designing transactor<>-based applications.

First, define two classes.

The first class (which we'll call *input*) carries data into the transaction. Any values that act as input to the commands within the transactor<> should be stored in an input object. Then, add an input, a reference to an input, or a pointer to an input to your transactor<>. Don't forget that libpqxx might make multiple copies of your transactor<>, so you might prefer to store an input reference in the transactor<> instead of a copy of input. In the client4 application, the m_increment value goes into the input class.

The second class (*output*) carries result values out of the transaction. Remember that it can't store results inside the transactor<> because libpqxx gets a const copy of the object. Instead, add a reference to output to the transactor<>. That way, the operator() function can store result values somewhere other than the transactor<> itself. If you were to add an output object to your transactor<> (as opposed to a reference to an output), it wouldn't do any good because libpqxx will never let you modify the transactor<> object that you give to connection::perform(). In the client4 sample application, you would store the SUM(balances) result in class output.

Now, define a transactor<> class. It should contain a reference to an input and a reference to an output. The constructor should expect a const input reference and a non-const output reference. Interact with the server in the transactor<>'s operator() function, but don't modify the output object there. Instead, store any results in the output object when the OnCommit() function is called.

When you're ready to execute the transactor<>, create an input object and an output object. Fill the input object with the data values required by the transactor<>. Now create an instance of your transactor<> object, passing references to the input and output objects to the constructor.

Call the connection::perform() function with a reference to your new transactor<> and wait for it to finish—the result values can be found in the output object.

Summary

libpqxx is a relatively new addition to PostgreSQL, so it will surely evolve in the future. But, libpqxx is a well-designed interface that makes writing client applications that fit into the STL style of programming easy. If you're a seasoned C++ programmer, libpqxx should seem very familiar. If you're new to C++, libpqxx is a terrific way to learn about the STL style.

11

Embedding SQL Commands in C Programs—ecpg

In the three previous chapters, you've seen how to connect a C or C++ application to a PostgreSQL database by making function calls into a PostgreSQL API. Now you're going to look at a different method for interfacing C applications with PostgreSQL. The ecpg preprocessor and runtime library enable you to embed SQL commands directly into the source code of your application. Rather than making explicit function calls into PostgreSQL, you include specially tagged SQL statements in your C code. The ecpg preprocessor examines your source code and translates the SQL statements into the function calls required to carry out the operations that you request. When you run the ecpg preprocessor, you feed it a source file that includes both C source code and SQL commands; the preprocessor produces a file that contains only C source code (it translates your SQL commands into function calls) and you then compile the new C file. Using ecpg, you can retrieve PostgreSQL data directly into C variables, and the ecpg runtime library takes care of converting between PostgreSQL data types and C data types.

The ecpg package is great for developing static applications—applications whose SQL requirements are known at the time you write your source code. ecpg can also be used to process *dynamic SQL*. Dynamic SQL is an accepted standard (part of the ANSI SQL3/SQL99 specification) for executing SQL statements that may not be known until the application is actually executing. I'll cover the dynamic SQL features at the end of this chapter, but I don't think that ecpg offers many advantages (over libpq) when dealing with ad hoc queries.

Prerequisites

Because an ecpg application is written in C, you will need a C compiler, the GNU make utility, and the ecpg preprocessor and library on your system before you can try the examples in this chapter.

The `makefile` for this chapter follows:

```
1 INCLUDES = -I$(shell pg_config --includedir)
2
3 LIBPATH  = -L $(shell pg_config --libdir)
4
5 CFLAGS    += $(INCLUDES) -g
6 LDFLAGS   += -g
7 LDLIBS    += $(LIBPATH) -lecpg -lpq
8 ECPGFLAGS += -c $(INCLUDES)
9 ECPG       = ecpg
10
11 .SUFFIXES: .pgc
12
13 .pgc.c:
14          $(ECPG) $(ECPGFLAGS) $?
15
16 ALL  = client1a client1b client2a client2b client2c
17 ALL += client3a client3b client3c client3d client3e client3f
18 ALL += client4.pgc
19
20 all: $(ALL)
21
22 clean:
23          rm -f $(ALL) *~
24
```

The examples in this chapter follow the normal PostgreSQL convention of naming ecpg source files with the extension `.pgc`. The `makefile` rules on lines 11 through 14 tell make that it can convert a `.pgc` file into a `.c` file by running the ecpg preprocessor.

Assuming that you have the prerequisites in place, let's start out by developing a simple client that will connect to a database using ecpg.

Client 1—Connecting to the Server

If you have read the previous three chapters, you know that there are two schemes for managing PostgreSQL connections.

In libpq and ODBC, you ask the API to create a connection object (a handle) and then your application keeps track of the connection. When you need to interact with the database, you call an API function and pass the connection object to the API. When you are finished interacting with the database, you ask the API to tear down the connection and destroy the connection object. When you use libpgeasy, the API keeps track of the connection object for you. You still have to ask the API to create a connection and, when you are finished, you must ask the API to tear down the connection, but libpgeasy stores the connection object itself and you never need to worry about it.

The ecpg interface gives you a mixture of these two schemes. Most ecpg applications use a single database connection. If you only need one connection, ecpg will keep track of it for you. If your application needs to work with multiple connections, you can switch between them.

In the libpq and ODBC APIs, a database connection is represented by a handle of some type. In an ecpg application, a database connection is simply a name[1].

Let's start by building a simple client application that connects to a database and then disconnects:

```
/* client1a.pgc */

int main( )
{
    EXEC SQL CONNECT TO movies AS myconnection;

    EXEC SQL DISCONNECT myconnection;

    return( 0 );
}
```

In client1a, you create a database connection named myconnection. Assuming that the connection attempt is successful, myconnection can be used to access the movies database. You will notice that you did not have to declare any C variables to keep track of the connection; the ecpg API does that for you—all you have to do is remember the name of the connection. Just like normal C statements, EXEC SQL statements are terminated with a semicolon.

If your application doesn't need more than one database connection, you can omit the AS database clause when you create the connection. You can also omit the name in the DISCONNECT statement:

```
/* client1b.pgc */

int main(  )
{
    EXEC SQL CONNECT TO movies;

    EXEC SQL DISCONNECT;

    return( 0 );
}
```

client1a.pgc and client2a.pgc are functionally equivalent applications.

You can associate a SQL statement with a named connection using an extended form of the EXEC SQL prefix:

```
EXEC SQL AT connection_name sql_statement;
```

[1] Later in this chapter, I'll show you how to use C variables (called host variables in ecpg) within EXEC SQL statements. If you use a host variable to specify a connection name, the variable should be a pointer to a null-terminated string.

If you don't specify an AT connection_name clause, ecpg will execute statements using the current connection. When you create a new connection, that connection becomes the current one. You can change the current connection using the SET CONNECTION TO command:

```
SET CONNECTION TO connection_name;
```

When you close a connection, you can specify any of the statements shown in Table 11.1.

Table 11.1 **Various Approaches to** DISCONNECT

Statement	Explanation
EXEC SQL DISCONNECT connection-name;	Closes the named connection
EXEC SQL DISCONNECT;	Closes the current connection
EXEC SQL DISCONNECT CURRENT;	Closes the current connection
EXEC SQL DISCONNECT ALL;	Closes all connections

The ecpg Preprocessor

The C compiler obviously won't understand the EXEC SQL statements that you must include in an ecpg application. To fix this problem, you have to run the source code for your applications through a preprocessor named ecpg.

You can view the syntax expected by the ecpg preprocessor using the --help option:

```
$ ecpg --help
ecpg is the PostgreSQL embedded SQL preprocessor for C programs.

Usage:
  ecpg [OPTION]... FILE...

Options:
  -c            automatically generate C code from embedded SQL code;
                currently this works for EXEC SQL TYPE
  -C MODE       set compatibility mode;
                MODE may be one of "INFORMIX", "INFORMIX_SE"
  -D SYMBOL     define SYMBOL
  -h            parse a header file, this option includes option "-c"
  -i            parse system include files as well
  -I DIRECTORY  search DIRECTORY for include files
  -o OUTFILE    write result to OUTFILE
  -r OPTION     specify runtime behaviour;
                OPTION may only be "no_indicator"
  -t            turn on autocommit of transactions
  --help        show this help, then exit
  --version     output version information, then exit
```

If no output file is specified, the name is formed by adding .c to the
input file name, after stripping off .pgc if present.

Report bugs to <pgsql-bugs@postgresql.org>.

Let's take a quick peek under the hood to see what the ecpg preprocessor is doing with
our source code. I'll run the client1b.pgc program through ecpg:

```
$ ecpg client1b.pgc
$ cat client1b.c
/* Processed by ecpg (3.2.0) */
/* These include files are added by the preprocessor */
#include <ecpgtype.h>
#include <ecpglib.h>
#include <ecpgerrno.h>
#include <sqlca.h>
/* End of automatic include section */
#line 1 "client1b.pgc"

/* client1b.pgc */

int main( )
{
    { ECPGconnect( __LINE__, "movies" , NULL,NULL , NULL, 0); }
#line 6 "client1b.pgc"


    { ECPGdisconnect( __LINE__, "CURRENT"); }
#line 8 "client1b.pgc"


    return( 0 );
}
```

The ecpg preprocessor converts client1b.pgc into client1b.c. You can see that ecpg
has inserted quite a bit of code into our application.

First, ecpg has inserted some comments and a few #include statements. You can usually ignore the #include files—they declare the functions and data types that are
required by the ecpg library.

Following the #includes, ecpg has inserted a C preprocessor directive that you might
not have seen before. The #line directive tells the C compiler to pretend that it is compiling the given line (and source file)—ecpg inserts these directives so that any error
messages produced by the C compiler correspond to the correct line numbers in your
original source file. For example, consider what would happen if you had a syntax error
in your declaration of the main() function. In your original source file (client1b.pgc),
main() is declared at line 4. In the post-processed file, main() is declared at line 12.
Without the #line directives, the C compiler would tell you that an error occurred at
line 12 of client1b.c. With the #line directives, the C compiler will report the error at
line 4 of client1b.pgc.

> **Debugging ecpg Applications**
>
> Unfortunately, the #line directives inserted by the ecpg preprocessor can really confuse most source-level debuggers. If you find that you need to debug an ecpg application, you should run the ecpg preprocessor over your source code, strip the #line directives from the resulting .c file, and then compile the .c file into an executable. At that point, you will have a program in which the debug symbols correspond to the .c file and your debugger should behave properly.

The interesting part of clientlb.c starts where the preprocessor translated

```
EXEC SQL CONNECT TO movies;
```

into

```
{ ECPGconnect(__LINE__, "movies" , NULL,NULL , NULL, 0); }
```

You can see that ecpg parsed out the EXEC SQL CONNECT command into a simple function call. This is really what ecpg is all about—translating EXEC SQL statements into function calls. The resulting code calls functions defined in the ecpg library.

Connection Strings

When you create a client application using libpq or libpgeasy, you specify a connection string as a series of *keyword=value* properties. Connecting to a database using ecpg is a bit different. When you connect to a database using ecpg, you can use any of three forms. The first form is considered obsolete but is still accepted by the most recent releases of PostgreSQL:

```
database[@host][:port][AS conn-name][USER username]
```

In this form, you must specify the name of the database to which you want to connect. You can also specify the hostname (or network address), port number (as an integer value), connection name, and username. The username can be in any of the following formats:

```
userid
userid/password
userid IDENTIFIED BY password
userid USING password
```

Each of the next two forms is similar to a URL (Uniform Resource Locator):

```
TCP:POSTGRESQL://host [:port] /database [AS conn-name] [USER username]
UNIX:POSTGRESQL://host [:port] /database [AS conn-name] [USER username]
```

In each of these forms, you specify the type of socket to which you want to connect (either TCP or Unix). If you specify a Unix socket type, the only valid value for the host component is localhost, or 127.0.0.1.

The documentation distributed with PostgreSQL says that the /database component is optional. In releases 7.1 and 7.2, an apparent bug in the preprocessor makes the /database component mandatory. The 7.1 and 7.2 documentation also suggests that you can specify TO DEFAULT or a username after EXEC SQL CONNECT; these features do not seem to be implemented and, in fact, will cause your client to crash if you try to use them.

Here are a few sample connection strings, first in the old (obsolete) format:

```
EXEC SQL CONNECT TO movies;

EXEC SQL CONNECT TO movies AS movie_conn;

EXEC SQL CONNECT TO movies USER bruce/cows;

EXEC SQL CONNECT TO movies@arturo:1234 AS remote_movies USER sheila;
```

and now in the new (URL-based) format:

```
EXEC SQL CONNECT TO UNIX:POSTGRESQL://localhost/movies;

EXEC SQL CONNECT TO UNIX:POSTGRESQL://localhost/movies AS movie_conn;

EXEC SQL CONNECT TO UNIX:POSTGRESQL://localhost/movies USER bruce/cows;

EXEC SQL CONNECT TO TCP:POSTGRESQL://arturo:1234/movies
              AS remote_movies USER sheila;
```

Client 2—Adding Error Checking

Now let's move on to see how you can detect and respond to errors. When you create an application that works by calling API functions, you can usually tell whether an operation succeeded or failed by examining the return value. In an ecpg application, your program is not calling PostgreSQL functions (at least at the source code level), so you can't just examine a return code.

The `sqlca` Structure

Instead, the ecpg library uses a special data structure, the `sqlca`, to communicate failure conditions. Here is the definition of the `sqlca` structure (from `sqlca.h`):

```
struct sqlca
{
   char      sqlcaid[8];
   long      sqlabc;
   long      sqlcode;
   struct
   {
      int    sqlerrml;
      char   sqlerrmc[SQLERRMC_LEN];
   } sqlerrm;
   char      sqlerrp[8];
   long      sqlerrd[6];
   char      sqlwarn[8];
   char      sqlext[8];
};
```

The `sqlca` structure differs slightly in newer versions of PostgreSQL:

```
struct sqlca
{
    char       sqlcaid[8];
    long       sqlabc;
    long       sqlcode;
    struct
    {
        int    sqlerrml;
        char   sqlerrmc[SQLERRMC_LEN];
    } sqlerrm;
    char       sqlerrp[8];
    long       sqlerrd[6];
    char       sqlwarn[8];
    char       sqlstate[5];
};
```

Notice that the last member of the original structure has been replaced by `sqlstate[]`. The (obsolete) `sqlext[]` member was never used. The new member, `sqlstate[]`, provides a modern, standard-compliant way for ecpg to report error conditions to your application. In this chapter, we'll show you how to use both the old and new error-handling schemes. If you're writing an ecpg application that needs to run with older PostgreSQL servers, use the old scheme (which stores error codes in the sqlcode member). The `sqlstate[]` scheme is more powerful, more flexible, and complies with SQL standards. The new scheme was introduced to PostgreSQL in version 7.4.

You don't #include this file as you would with most header files. The ecpg pre-processor offers a special directive that you should use[2]:

`EXEC SQL INCLUDE sqlca;`

The difference between a #include and an `EXEC SQL INCLUDE` is that the ecpg pre-processor can see files that are included using the second form. The C preprocessor can see header files imported by #include or `EXEC SQL INCLUDE`, but the ecpg preprocessor can only see headers imported by `EXEC SQL INCLUDE`. That doesn't mean that you can't use #include files, but if you need to import a structure (or other definition) that the ecpg preprocessor must see, you should `EXEC SQL INCLUDE` it instead. Just remember that the #include inclusion occurs *after* the ecpg preprocess has finished its work.

The contents of the `sqlca` structure might seem a bit weird. Okay, they don't just seem weird—they are weird.

Let's walk through the members of the `sqlca` structure. PostgreSQL won't use many of the fields in the `sqlca` structure—that structure was inherited from the SQL standard.

First, we'll look at the fields that never change. The `sqlaid` array always contains the string 'SQLCA'. Why? I don't know—history, I suppose. The `sqlabc` member always contains the size of the `sqlca` structure. `sqlerrp` always contains the string 'NOT SET'.

---

[2] Starting with PostgreSQL release 7.2, `sqlca` is automatically included in every ecpg program. You don't have to include it yourself.

[3] The symbolic names for `sqlcode` values (such as ECPG_NOT_FOUND) are automatically #defined for you by the ecpg preprocessor.

Now let's look at the interesting parts of a `sqlca`.

The `sqlcode` member is an error indicator (`sqlcode` is the basis of the older error handling scheme). If the most recent (ecpg library) operation was completely successful, `sqlcode` will be set to zero. If the most recent operation succeeded, but it was a query that returned no data, `sqlcode` will contain the value `ECPG_NOT_FOUND`[3] (or 100). `sqlcode` will also be set to `ECPG_NOT_FOUND` if you execute an `UPDATE`, `INSERT`, or `DELETE` that affects zero rows. If an error occurs, `sqlcode` will contain a negative number. The `sqlstate` member (not present in versions of PostgreSQL older than 7.4) also functions as an error indicator. If the most recent (ecpg library) operation was completely successful, `sqlstate` will contain the characters `00000`. Note that `sqlstate` is *not* a null-terminated string; it's an array containing five ASCII characters. That means that you cannot use `strcmp()` to test the value of `sqlstate`; you have to use `strncmp()` instead. If `sqlstate` contains a value other than `00000`, an error *may* have occurred. Appendix A of the PostgreSQL reference documentation contains a list of the values you may find in the `sqlstate` member. Most `sqlstate` values indicate that an error has occurred, but two values indicate success: `00000` means that the previous operation succeeded and `02000` means that the previous command returned zero rows. The ecpg library sets `sqlcode` every time it puts a value into `sqlstate` so you can use either structure member to check for errors—just remember that `sqlstate` is designed to be standards-compliant and `sqlcode` is specific to PostgreSQL.

If `sqlca.sqlstate` contains a value other than `00000` (or `sqlca.sqlcode` contains a non-zero value), the `sqlerrm` structure will contain a printable error message. `sqlerrm.sqlerrmc` will contain the null-terminated text of the message and `sqlerrm.sqlerrml` will contain the length of the error message.

The `sqlerrd` array also contains useful information. After executing a `SELECT` statement, `sqlerrd[2]` will contain the number of rows returned by the query. After executing an `INSERT`, `UPDATE`, or `DELETE` statement, `sqlerrd[1]` will contain the OID (object ID) of the most recently affected row, and `sqlerrd[2]` will contain the number of rows affected.

The `sqlwarn` array is used to tell you about warnings. When you retrieve data from PostgreSQL, `sqlwarn[1]` will be set to `W` if any of the data has been truncated. Truncation can occur, for example, when you retrieve a `varchar` column into a buffer too small to contain the actual value. `sqlwarn[2]` is set to `W` whenever a non-fatal error (such as executing a `COMMIT` outside of the context of a transaction) occurs. If any member of the `sqlwarn` array contains a `W`, `sqlwarn[0]` will contain a `W`.

I've modified the previous client application (`client1b.pgc`) so that it prints an error message if the connection attempt fails. Here is `client2a.pgc`:

```
1   /* client2a.pgc */
2
3   EXEC SQL INCLUDE sqlca;
4
5   #include <stdio.h>
6
7   int main( )
8   {
9       EXEC SQL CONNECT TO movies;
```

```
10
11     if( strncmp( sqlca.sqlstate, "00000", sizeof( sqlca.sqlstate )) == 0 )
12         printf( "Connected to 'movies'\n" );
13     else
14         printf( "Error: %s\n", sqlca.sqlerrm.sqlerrmc );
15
16     EXEC SQL DISCONNECT;
17
18     return( 0 );
19 }
```

At line 11, this application checks `sqlca.sqlstate`. If it contains `00000`, your connection attempt was successful. If sqlca.sqlstate contains any other value, an error has occurred and you find the error message in `sqlca.sqlerrm.sqlerrmc`. If you want to try this code, you can induce an error by shutting down your PostgreSQL server and then running `client2a`.

Now let's modify this client slightly so that you can experiment with different error-processing scenarios:

```
 1 /* client2b.pgc */
 2
 3 EXEC SQL INCLUDE sqlca;
 4
 5 #include <stdio.h>
 6
 7 void dump_sqlca( void )
 8 {
 9     int     i;
10
11     printf( "sqlca\n" );
12     printf( "sqlaid                    - %s\n",    sqlca.sqlcaid );
13     printf( "sqlabc                    - %d\n",    sqlca.sqlabc );
14     printf( "sqlcode                   - %d\n",    sqlca.sqlcode );
15     printf( "sqlstate                  - %5.5s\n", sqlca.sqlstate );
16     printf( "sqlerrml                  - %d\n",    sqlca.sqlerrm.sqlerrml );
17     printf( "sqlerrmc                  - %s\n",    sqlca.sqlerrm.sqlerrmc );
18     printf( "sqlerrp                   - %s\n",    sqlca.sqlerrp );
19     printf( "sqlerrd[1] (oid)          - %d\n",    sqlca.sqlerrd[1] );
20     printf( "sqlerrd[2] (rows)         - %d\n",    sqlca.sqlerrd[2] );
21     printf( "sqlwarn[0]                - %c\n",    sqlca.sqlwarn[0] );
22     printf( "sqlwarn[1] (truncation)   - %c\n",    sqlca.sqlwarn[1] );
23     printf( "sqlwarn[2] (non-fatal)    - %c\n",    sqlca.sqlwarn[2] );
24 }
25
26 int main( int argc, char * argv[] )
27 {
28     EXEC SQL BEGIN DECLARE SECTION;
29     char * url;
```

```
30      EXEC SQL END DECLARE SECTION;
31
32      url = argv[1] ? argv[1] : "";
33
34      EXEC SQL CONNECT TO :url;
35
36      if( sqlca.sqlcode == 0 )
37          printf( "Connected to '%s'\n", url );
38      else
39      {
40          printf( "Error: %s\n", sqlca.sqlerrm.sqlerrmc );
41          dump_sqlca( );
42      }
43
44      EXEC SQL DISCONNECT;
45
46      return( 0 );
47 }
```

In client2b.pgc, I've added a new function, dump_sqlca(), which simply prints the contents of the sqlca structure. I've also changed the main() function so that you can include a connection URL on the command line. We haven't talked about the EXEC SQL BEGIN DECLARE SECTION and EXEC SQL END DECLARE SECTION directives yet, so don't worry if they aren't familiar—I'll cover that topic in a moment. I'll also show you how to refer to host variables (that :url thing in line 34) in EXEC SQL statements.

Compile this program and run it a few times, feeding it connection URLs that will result in errors. Here is an example of what you might see:

```
$ ./client2b foo
Error: Could not connect to database  in line 34.
sqlca
sqlaid                    - SQLCA
sqlabc                    - 140
sqlcode                   - -402
sqlstate                  - 08001
sqlerrml                  - 42
sqlerrmc                  - Could not connect to database  in line 34.
sqlerrp                   - NOT SET
sqlerrd[1] (oid)          - 0
sqlerrd[2] (rows)         - 0
sqlwarn[0]                -
sqlwarn[1] (truncation) -
sqlwarn[2] (non-fatal)  -
```

Table 11.1 shows some of the error messages you might encounter. This list is not exhaustive. Some of the messages in this table may not make sense to you until later in this chapter.

Table 11.1 **ECPG Runtime Errors**

Error	SQLSTATE	Explanation
ECPG_NOT_FOUND	02000	No data found
ECPG_OUT_OF_MEMORY	YE001	Out of memory
ECPG_UNSUPPORTED	YE000	Unsupported type typename
ECPG_TOO_MANY_ARGUMENTS	07001 or 07002	Too many arguments
ECPG_TOO_FEW_ARGUMENTS	07001 or 07002	Too few arguments
ECPG_TOO_MANY_MATCHES	21000	You selected more rows than will fit into the space you allocated
ECPG_INT_FORMAT	42804	Incorrectly formatted int type typename
ECPG_UINT_FORMAT	42804	Incorrectly formatted unsigned int type typename
ECPG_FLOAT_FORMAT	42804	Incorrectly formatted floating point type typename
ECPG_CONVERT_BOOL	42804	Unable to convert to bool
ECPG_EMPTY	YE000	Empty query
ECPG_MISSING_INDICATOR	22002	NULL value encountered without a corresponding indicator
ECPG_NO_ARRAY	42804	Variable is not an array
ECPG_DATA_NOT_ARRAY	42804	Data read from server is not an array
ECPG_NO_CONN	08003	No such connection connection_name
ECPG_NOT_CONN	YE000	Not connected to 'database'
ECPG_INVALID_STMT	26000	Invalid statement name statement_name
ECPG_UNKNOWN_DESCRIPTOR	33000	Descriptor name not found
ECPG_INVALID_DESCRIPTOR_INDEX	07009	Descriptor index out of range
ECPG_UNKNOWN_DESCRIPTOR_ITEM	YE000	Unknown descriptor item
ECPG_VAR_NOT_NUMERIC	07006	Variable is not a numeric type
ECPG_VAR_NOT_CHAR	07006	Variable is not a character type
ECPG_TRANS	08007	Error in transaction processing
ECPG_CONNECT	08001	Could not connected to database database_name
ECPG_PSQL	*no equivalent*	Generic PostgreSQL error

The ecpg preprocessor provides an alternative method for detecting and handling errors: the EXEC SQL WHENEVER directive. The general form for a WHENEVER directive is

```
EXEC SQL WHENEVER condition action;
```

where *condition* can be any of the following:

- SQLERROR—Occurs whenever sqlca.sqlcode is less than zero
- SQLWARNING—Occurs whenever sqlca.sqlwarn[0] contains W
- NOT FOUND—Occurs whenever sqlca.sqlcode is ECPG_NOT_FOUND (that is, when a query returns no data)

When you use the EXEC SQL WHENEVER directive, you are telling the ecpg preprocessor to insert extra code into your program. Each time ecpg emits an ecpg library call that might raise a condition (at runtime), it follows that function call with code to detect and handle the condition that you specify. The exact format of the error-handling code depends on the action that you use. You can specify any of the following actions:

- SQLPRINT—Calls the sqlprint() function to display an error message to the user; the sqlprint() function simply prints "sql error " followed by the contents of the sqlca.sqlerrm.sqlerrmc string
- STOP—Calls exit(1); this will cause your application to terminate whenever the specified condition arises
- GOTO label-name—Causes your application to goto the label specified by label-name whenever the specified condition arises
- GO TO label-name—Same as GOTO
- CALL function-name(arguments)—Causes your application to call the given function-name with the given arguments whenever the specified condition arises
- DO function-name(arguments)—Same as CALL
- CONTINUE—Causes your application to execute a continue statement whenever the specified condition arises; this should be used only inside of a loop
- BREAK—Causes your application to execute a break statement whenever the specified condition arises; this should be used only inside loops or a switch statement

You may find it useful to examine the sqlca structure, even when you use EXEC SQL WHENEVER to intercept errors or warnings. EXEC SQL WHENEVER is a convenient way to detect error conditions, but sometimes you will find it overly broad—different error conditions can produce the same result. By interrogating the sqlca structure, you can still use EXEC SQL WHENEVER to trap the errors, but treat each condition differently.

Here is client2c.pgc. I've modified the first client in this section (client2a.pgc) so that it uses the EXEC SQL WHENEVER directive to intercept a connection error.

```
1
2 /* client2c.pgc */
3
4 EXEC SQL INCLUDE sqlca;
5
6 #include <stdio.h>
7
8 int main( int argc, char * argv[] )
```

```
 9  {
10      EXEC SQL BEGIN DECLARE SECTION;
11        char * url;
12      EXEC SQL END DECLARE SECTION;
13      url = argv[1] ? argv[1] : "";
14
15      EXEC SQL WHENEVER SQLERROR SQLPRINT;
16
17      EXEC SQL CONNECT TO :url;
18
19      EXEC SQL DISCONNECT;
20
21      return( 0 );
22  }
```

Let's run this program in such a way that a connection error occurs:

```
$ ./client2c foo
sql error Could not connect to database foo in line 17.
sql error No such connection CURRENT in line 19.
```

Notice that I received two error messages. The first error occurred when my connection attempt failed; the second occurred when I tried to tear down a nonexistent connection. That's an important thing to remember—the EXEC SQL WHENEVER directive continues to affect your epcg code until you change the action associated with a given condition.

It's important to understand that EXEC SQL WHENEVER is a preprocessor directive, not a true C statement. A directive affects the actions of the ecpg preprocessor from the point at which it is encountered in the source code. This means, for example, that if you include an EXEC SQL WHENEVER directive within an if statement, you probably won't get the results you were hoping for. Consider the following code:

```
if( TRUE )
{
EXEC SQL WHENEVER SQLERROR SQLPRINT;
}
else
{
EXEC SQL WHENEVER SQLERROR STOP;
}


EXEC SQL CONNECT TO movies;
```

Looking at this code, you might expect that a connection failure would result in a call to the sqlprint() function. That's not what you'll get. Instead, the ecpg preprocessor will arrange for the exit() function to be called if the connection attempt fails. Preprocessor directives are not executable statements; they affect the code produced by the preprocessor. As the preprocessor reads through your source code, it keeps track of the action that you choose for each condition. Each time the preprocessor encounters an EXEC SQL WHENEVER directive, it remembers the new action and applies it to any EXEC SQL statements further down the source code. So, with EXEC SQL WHENEVER, the order of appearance (within the source file) is important, but the order of execution is not.

I recommend compiling a few ecpg programs that include the various EXEC SQL WHENEVER directives and then examining the resulting C code to better understand how they will affect your programs.

Client 3—Processing SQL Commands

Now let's turn our attention to the task of executing SQL commands and interpreting the results. To start with, I'll show you how to execute simple SQL statements in an ecpg application:

```
1
2 /* client3a.pgc */
3
4 EXEC SQL INCLUDE sqlca;
5
6 #include <stdio.h>
7
8 int main( )
9 {
10
11   EXEC SQL WHENEVER SQLERROR   SQLPRINT;
12   EXEC SQL WHENEVER SQLWARNING SQLPRINT;
13   EXEC SQL WHENEVER NOT FOUND  SQLPRINT;
14
15   EXEC SQL CONNECT TO movies;
16
17   EXEC SQL
18     INSERT INTO tapes
19       VALUES
20       (
21         'GG-44278',
22         'Strangers On A Train',
23         '1 hour 3 minutes'
24       );
25
26   EXEC SQL
27     DELETE FROM tapes WHERE tape_id = 'GG-44278';
28
29   EXEC SQL
30     DELETE FROM tapes WHERE tape_id IS NULL;
31
32   EXEC SQL DISCONNECT;
33
34     return( 0 );
35 }
```

You can see from this example that executing *simple* SQL statements with ecpg is easy—
you just insert the text of the statement after EXEC SQL. I've used the EXEC SQL WHEN-
EVER statement that you saw in the previous section to show how easy it can be to handle errors. The DELETE command on lines 29 and 30 will produce an error message; and
at the beginning of the program, I told ecpg to SQLPRINT whenever a NOT FOUND condition occurs.

The three SQL statements executed in client3a.pgc are considered simple for two
reasons:

- They don't require any data to be provided at runtime (the values involved are
  hard-coded).

- No data is returned to the client application (other than error conditions).

Things get a bit more complex if you need to provide (or retrieve) data at runtime. The
first thing that changes when you need to provide C data to ecpg is that you have to tell
the ecpg preprocessor about the variables in your code. You may remember from earlier
in this chapter that I used the EXEC SQL BEGIN DECLARE SECTION and EXEC SQL END
DECLARE SECTION directives. These ecpg directives tell the preprocessor that it should pay
close attention to the variable declarations in between because you will use those variables when interacting with ecpg. A quick example should make this a little clearer:

```
 1 /* client3b.pgc */
 2
 3 EXEC SQL INCLUDE sqlca;
 4
 5 #include <stdio.h>
 6
 7 int main( int argc, char * argv[] )
 8 {
 9   EXEC SQL BEGIN DECLARE SECTION;
10     char  * tape_id  = argc > 1 ? argv[1] : NULL;
11     char  * title    = argc > 2 ? argv[2] : NULL;
12     char  * duration = argc > 3 ? argv[3] : NULL;
13   EXEC SQL END DECLARE SECTION;
14
15   EXEC SQL WHENEVER SQLERROR   SQLPRINT;
16   EXEC SQL WHENEVER SQLWARNING SQLPRINT;
17   EXEC SQL WHENEVER NOT FOUND  SQLPRINT;
18
19   EXEC SQL CONNECT TO movies;
20
21   EXEC SQL
22     INSERT INTO tapes
23       VALUES
24       (
25          :tape_id,
```

```
26          :title,
27          :duration
28       );
29
30   EXEC SQL DISCONNECT;
31
32   return( 0 );
33 }
```

At line 9, I've included an EXEC SQL BEGIN DECLARE SECTION directive. This tells the ecpg preprocessor that I'm about to declare one or more variables—the variable declarations end with an EXEC SQL END DECLARE SECTION directive. Once I have told ecpg about my variables, I can use them in future EXEC SQL commands.

At lines 25, 26, and 27, I've told ecpg that it should find the values that I want to insert in the tape id, title, and duration variables. When you want ecpg to substitute a C variable within a SQL statement, you prefix the variable name with a colon (:).

When you run this program, you should provide three strings on the command line (enclose each string in double quotes). For example:

```
$ ./client3b "SP-00001" "Young Einstein" "91 minutes"
```

If you run this program with fewer than three command-line arguments, it will crash because one (or more) of the host variables will be set to NULL. To handle NULL values correctly, you must pair each host variable with an *indicator variable*. An indicator variable is a value that determines whether the related host variable is NULL. Indicator variables can be any of the following types: unsigned short, unsigned int, unsigned long, unsigned long long, short, int, long, or long long. As you'll see a little later, you should avoid using the unsigned variants because PostgreSQL uses negative values to return useful information to your application.

You match a host variable to its indicator by appending a colon and then the indicator name to the host variable name. I've rewritten client3b.pgc a bit (now client3c.pgc) to handle NULL values better:

```
 1 /* client3c.pgc */
 2
 3 EXEC SQL INCLUDE sqlca;
 4
 5 EXEC SQL WHENEVER SQLERROR   SQLPRINT;
 6 EXEC SQL WHENEVER SQLWARNING SQLPRINT;
 7 EXEC SQL WHENEVER NOT FOUND  SQLPRINT;
 8
 9 #include <stdio.h>
10
11 int main( int argc, char * argv[] )
12 {
13   EXEC SQL BEGIN DECLARE SECTION;
14
```

```
15      char   * tape_id  = argc > 1 ? argv[1] : "ignored";
16      char   * title    = argc > 2 ? argv[2] : "ignored";
17      char   * duration = argc > 3 ? argv[3] : "ignored";
18
19      short    tape_id_ind  = argc > 1 ? 0 : -1;
20      short    title_ind    = argc > 2 ? 0 : -1;
21      short    duration_ind = argc > 3 ? 0 : -1;
22
23  EXEC SQL END DECLARE SECTION;
24
25  EXEC SQL CONNECT TO movies;
26
27  EXEC SQL INSERT INTO tapes
28    VALUES
29    (
30      :tape_id   :tape_id_ind,
31      :title     :title_ind,
32      :duration  :duration_ind
33    );
34
35  EXEC SQL DISCONNECT;
36
37  return( 0 );
38 }
```

You can see that at lines 19, 20, and 21, I've created three indicator variables—one for each host variable. If I want to tell the ecpg library that a column value should be set to NULL, I set its corresponding indicator variable to a negative number (0 means NOT NULL, any other value means NULL). Notice that if an indicator variable is set to indicate a NULL value, the matching host variable is completely ignored.

Indicator variables are also used when you retrieve data from the database. The following client application (client3d.pgc) requests a single row from the tapes table and displays the values:

```
1 /* client3d.pgc */
2
3 EXEC SQL INCLUDE sqlca;
4
5 EXEC SQL WHENEVER SQLERROR   SQLPRINT;
6 EXEC SQL WHENEVER SQLWARNING SQLPRINT;
7 EXEC SQL WHENEVER NOT FOUND  SQLPRINT;
8
9 #include <stdio.h>
10
11 int main( int argc, char * argv[] )
12 {
13   EXEC SQL BEGIN DECLARE SECTION;
```

```
14
15      char  * desired_tape = argv[1];
16
17      char     tape_id[8+1];
18      varchar title[80+1];
19      varchar duration[30+1];
20
21      short    duration_ind;
22
23  EXEC SQL END DECLARE SECTION;
24
25  EXEC SQL CONNECT TO movies;
26
27  EXEC SQL
28     SELECT * INTO
29        :tape_id,
30        :title,
31        :duration :duration_ind
32     FROM tapes
33     WHERE
34        tape_id = :desired_tape;
35
36  printf( "tape_id  = %s\n", tape_id );
37  printf( "title    = %s\n", title.arr );
38  printf( "duration = %s\n", duration_ind < 0
39                                  ? "null" : duration.arr );
40
41  EXEC SQL DISCONNECT;
42
43     return( 0 );
44 }
```

At line 21, I've declared a single indicator—I don't need an indicator variable for
tape_id or title because those columns are declared as NOT NULL. In the SELECT command that starts at line 27, I've asked ecpg to return the value of the tape_id column
into the tape_id variable, the title column into the title variable, and the duration
column into the duration variable and duration_ind indicator. If you SELECT a row
where the duration column is NULL, the duration_ind variable will be set to a negative
number.

Take a close look at the definitions of the title and duration variables—each is defined
as an array of type varchar. varchar has special meaning to the ecpg preprocessor.
Whenever the preprocessor sees a variable defined as varchar (within the declaration
section), it translates the variable into a structure. The title variable is defined as varchar title[80+1]; the ecpg preprocessor will translate that definition into

```
struct varchar_title { int len; char arr[80+1]; } title;
```

When you SELECT a column into a varchar variable, ecpg will set the len member to the length of the data actually retrieved (the array is also null-terminated if the null character will fit).

You might be wondering what happens if the data that you ask for won't fit into the space that you have allocated. That's the second use for an indicator variable. Whenever ecpg has to truncate a value, it sets the indicator to the number of bytes actually retrieved (that is, a positive indicator contains the number of bytes that would be required to hold the entire value). ecpg will only truncate char[], unsigned char[], and varchar values. If you retrieve a *numeric* value into a host variable that's too small to hold the value, ecpg will corrupt the host variable. For example, if you retrieve the value 65536 (which is too large to fit in a typical short int) into a host variable of type short int, your host variable will contain some value other than 65536. Unfortunately, ecpg doesn't provide a way to detect integer overflow so your best strategy is to avoid them by ensuring that host variables are large enough to hold the values you expect to receive.

To summarize, when you retrieve a value from the database, an indicator variable can hold any of the values shown in Table 11.2.

Table 11.2 **Indicator Variable Values**

Indicator Value	**Meaning**
indicator < 0	Value was NULL
indicator = 0	Value was NOT NULL and fit into the associated host variable without being truncated
indicator > 0	Value was NOT NULL, but was truncated

ecpg Data Types

I mentioned the varchar data type earlier, but what other data types are understood by ecpg? The ecpg preprocessor needs to know some basic information about each of the data types that you use. When you interact with a database using ecpg, the ecpg library can convert between the C data types used in your application and the PostgreSQL data types stored in the database. When you supply data *to* the database, the ecpg library will convert from your C data type into the format required by the database. When you retrieve data *from* the database, the ecpg library will convert from PostgreSQL format into the format required by your application.

The ecpg library includes implicit support for the C data types shown here:

- unsigned
- unsigned short
- unsigned int
- unsigned long
- unsigned long int
- unsigned long long

- unsigned long long int
- unsigned char
- short
- short int
- int
- long
- long int
- long long
- long long int
- bool
- float
- double
- char
- varchar
- struct
- union
- enum

Note that the char and varchar data types will be null terminated if the null character will fit within the allotted space. If the null terminator will *not* fit, the indicator variable will *not* reflect the fact that the string was truncated.

Sometimes, we C programmers find that it's a good idea to introduce artificial data types. For example, if your application must deal with account numbers, you might introduce an acct_no data type that is defined in terms of one of the basic C data types:

```
typedef unsigned int acct_no;
```

You can use the contrived data type with ecpg, but you must use the EXEC SQL TYPE directive. Here's a code snippet that shows how you might use EXEC SQL TYPE:

```
EXEC SQL TYPE acct_no IS unsigned int;
typedef unsigned int acct_no;

EXEC SQL BEGIN DECLARE SECTION;
    acct_no payroll_acct;
EXEC SQL END DECLARE SECTION;

EXEC SQL
    SELECT payroll_acct
    INTO :payroll_acct
    FROM employees
    WHERE employee_id = 133;
```

Notice that you must tell both ecpg and the C compiler what an acct_no is (in other words, you need both the EXEC SQL TYPE and the typedef). In later releases of ecpg (newer than 7.2), you can use the -c flag to tell the ecpg preprocessor to generate the typedefs for you.

In the preceding list you saw that the ecpg preprocessor supports the struct data type. When you ask ecpg to retrieve data into a struct, it will place each result column in a separate member of the structure. Let's modify client3d.pgc to SELECT into a structure:

```
 1 /* client3e.pgc */
 2
 3 EXEC SQL INCLUDE sqlca;
 4
 5 EXEC SQL WHENEVER SQLERROR   SQLPRINT;
 6 EXEC SQL WHENEVER SQLWARNING SQLPRINT;
 7 EXEC SQL WHENEVER NOT FOUND  SQLPRINT;
 8
 9 #include <stdio.h>
10
11 int main( int argc, char * argv[] )
12 {
13   EXEC SQL BEGIN DECLARE SECTION;
14
15     char  * desired_tape = argv[1];
16
17     struct
18     {
19        char    tape_id[8+1];
20        varchar title[80+1];
21        varchar duration[30+1];
22     } tape;
23
24     struct
25     {
26        short    tape_id_ind;
27        short    title_ind;
28        short    duration_ind;
29     } tape_ind;
30
31   EXEC SQL END DECLARE SECTION;
32
33   EXEC SQL CONNECT TO movies;
34
35   EXEC SQL
36     SELECT * INTO
37       :tape :tape_ind
38     FROM tapes
39     WHERE
```

```
40        tape_id = :desired_tape;
41
42    printf( "tape_id  = %s\n", tape_ind.tape_id_ind < 0
43                                ? "null" : tape.tape_id );
44    printf( "title    = %s\n", tape_ind.title_ind < 0
45                                ? "null" : tape.title.arr );
46    printf( "duration = %s\n", tape_ind.duration_ind < 0
47                                ? "null" : tape.duration.arr );
48
49    EXEC SQL DISCONNECT;
50
51    return( 0 );
52 }
```

At lines 17-22, I've defined a structure to hold a single row from the tapes table. At lines 24-29, I've defined a structure that holds the indicator variables for a tapes row.

When I SELECT a row from the tapes table, I've asked ecpg to place the resulting data into the tape structure and to set the indicators in the tape_ind structure.

If the data that you retrieve into a structure cannot be matched up with the structure members, you will receive a runtime error. For example, if you SELECT four columns of data into a structure that contains three members, you will receive an ECPG_TOO_FEW_ARGUMENTS error (at runtime). Likewise, if your indicator structure doesn't match the data returned by the query, you may get an ECPG_MISSING_INDICATOR error if you run into a NULL value.

To wrap up this discussion of ecpg data types, I should mention that you can ask ecpg to retrieve multiple rows into an array of host (and indicator) variables. I've modified the previous client application to show you how to use arrays with ecpg:

```
 1 /* client3f.pgc */
 2
 3 #include <stdio.h>
 4
 5 EXEC SQL INCLUDE sqlca;
 6
 7 EXEC SQL WHENEVER SQLERROR   SQLPRINT;
 8 EXEC SQL WHENEVER SQLWARNING SQLPRINT;
 9 EXEC SQL WHENEVER NOT FOUND  SQLPRINT;
10
11 EXEC SQL TYPE tape IS
12     struct tape
13     {
14         char    tape_id[8+1];
15         varchar title[80+1];
16         varchar duration[10+1];
17     };
18
19 EXEC SQL TYPE ind IS
```

```
20     struct ind
21     {
22         short   id_ind;
23         short   title_ind;
24         short   duration_ind;
25     };
26
27 int main( )
28 {
29   EXEC SQL BEGIN DECLARE SECTION;
30
31     tape    tapes[5];
32     ind     inds[5];
33
34   EXEC SQL END DECLARE SECTION;
35
36   int       r;
37
38   EXEC SQL CONNECT TO movies;
39
40   EXEC SQL
41     SELECT * INTO :tapes:inds
42     FROM tapes
43     LIMIT 5;
44
45   for( r = 0; r < 5; r++ )
46   {
47     printf( "tape_id  = %s\n", inds[r].id_ind < 0
48                          ? "null" : tapes[r].tape_id );
49     printf( "title    = %s\n", inds[r].title_ind < 0
50                          ? "null" : tapes[r].title.arr );
51     printf( "duration = %s\n\n",inds[r].duration_ind < 0
52                          ? "null" : tapes[r].duration.arr );
53   }
54
55   EXEC SQL DISCONNECT;
56
57   return( 0 );
58 }
```

At line 30 and 31, I've defined an array of five tape structures and five indicator structures.[4] When I SELECT data into these variables, the ecpg library will place the first row

---

[4] In this example, I've taken advantage of the -c flag to let the ecpg preprocessor generate structure typedefs for me. The -c flag offers more than mere convenience—it lets you include varchar members in a structure. Without the -c flag, you can't include varchar members with a structure; the ecpg preprocessor can't handle it.

in the first array element, the second row in the second array element, and so on. Likewise, the indicators for the first row will be placed in the first member of the `inds` array, the second set of indicators will be placed in the second member, and so on. In this example, I've allocated enough space to hold five rows and I've limited the query to return no more than five rows. If you try to retrieve more rows than will fit into the space you've allocated, ecpg will trigger an `ECPG_TOO_MANY_MATCHES` error.

Client 4—An Interactive Query Processor

Following the pattern set in the previous few chapters, I'll wrap up the discussion of ecpg by developing an interactive query processor. Because of the complexity of using ecpg to handle dynamic queries, I'll take a few shortcuts in this client, and I'll try to point to them as I go.

Let's start by looking at the `main()` function for the final client application in this chapter:

```
 1 /* client4.pgc */
 2
 3 #include <stdio.h>
 4 #include <stdlib.h>
 5
 6 EXEC SQL INCLUDE sql3types;
 7 EXEC SQL INCLUDE sqlca;
 8
 9 EXEC SQL WHENEVER SQLERROR DO print_error();
10
11 static int  is_select_stmt( char * stmt );
12 static void process_other_stmt( char * stmt_text );
13 static void process_select_stmt( char * stmt_text );
14 static void print_column_headers( int col_count );
15 static void print_meta_data( char * desc_name );
16 static void print_error( void );
17 static int  usage( char * program );
18
19 char * sep = "-----------------------------------------";
20 char * md1 = "col field               data           ret";
21 char * md2 = "num name                type           len";
22 char * md3 = "--- -------------------- -------------- ---";
23
24 int    dump_meta_data = 0;
25
26 int main( int argc, char * argv[] )
27 {
28   EXEC SQL BEGIN DECLARE SECTION;
29     char * db   = argv[1];
30     char * stmt = argv[2];
```

```
31    EXEC SQL END DECLARE SECTION;
32
33    FILE * log = fopen( "client4.log", "w" );
34
35    ECPGdebug( 1, log );
36
37    if( argc < 3 )
38      exit( usage( argv[0] ));
39    else if( argc > 3 )
40      dump_meta_data = 1;
41
42    EXEC SQL CONNECT TO :db;
43
44    if( is_select_stmt( stmt ))
45      process_select_stmt( stmt );
46    else
47      process_other_stmt( stmt );
48
49    exit( 0 );
50  }
```

You've already seen most of this code. I've included an extra EXEC SQL INCLUDE statement: sql3types provides symbolic names for the data types returned by a dynamic
SQL statement. I'll show you where to use these a little later.

The only other new feature in main() is the call to ECPGdebug(). Debugging
dynamic SQL can be pretty tricky, and it's always helpful to have a record of the
sequence of events that your application follows. When you call ECPGdebug(), you provide an integer and a FILE *. The first argument turns logging on or off: A 0 disables
logging and any other value tells the ecpg library to write trace information to the file
indicated by the second argument.

Here is the first shortcut that I've taken (for clarity). Rather than prompting you for
multiple commands, client4 expects you to provide a single command (on the command line). This client expects either two or three command-line arguments. The first
argument should be the name of the database to which you want to connect. The second argument is an SQL command. The third argument is optional. If you provide a
third command-line argument (it doesn't matter *what* you provide), client4 will print
out meta-data for a SELECT command. A typical invocation of this application might
look like this:

```
$ ./client4 movies "select * from tapes" true
```

Notice that at line 44, I am calling the is_select_stmt() function. The processing
required to handle a SELECT statement is considerably different from that required to
handle other command types, so let's defer it for a while and first look instead at the
code required execute commands other than SELECT:

```
52 static void process_other_stmt( char * stmt_text )
```

```
53 {
54   EXEC SQL BEGIN DECLARE SECTION;
55     char  * stmt = stmt_text;
56   EXEC SQL END DECLARE SECTION;
57
58   EXEC SQL EXECUTE IMMEDIATE :stmt;
59
60   if( sqlca.sqlcode >= 0 )
61   {
62     printf( "ok\n" );
63     EXEC SQL COMMIT;
64   }
65 }
```

The `process_other_stmt()` function is actually pretty simple. Line 55 defines a variable to hold the statement text (inside of a DECLARE SECTION so that you can use it as a host variable). At line 50, this function executes the command using the host variable. Using this form of the EXEC SQL EXECUTE command, you don't get back any result information other than what's found in the `sqlca` structure. In the next section, I'll show you how to get more result information.

If the command succeeds, `process_other_stmt()` executes a COMMIT command to commit any changes.

ecpg and Autocommit

When you compile this program, do not use the -t flag. The -t flag tells the ecpg preprocessor to arrange for each statement to be committed as soon as it completes (in other words, the -t flag enables auto-commit). Because we aren't using autocommit in this example, you must COMMIT or ROLLBACK your changes to complete the transaction. If you forget to COMMIT your changes (and you don't use the -t flag), your changes will automatically be rolled back when your application completes. If you invoke the ecpg preprocessor with the -t flag, each change will be committed as soon as it completes.

If you're using a newer version of ecpg (8.0 or later), you can change the autocommit flag at runtime using the command EXEC SQL SET AUTOCOMMIT = [on|off].

Now let's look at the `process_select_stmt()` function—it is much more complex.

```
67 static void process_select_stmt( char * stmt_text )
68 {
69   EXEC SQL BEGIN DECLARE SECTION;
70     char  * stmt = stmt_text;
71   EXEC SQL END DECLARE SECTION;
72     int    row;
73
74     EXEC SQL ALLOCATE DESCRIPTOR my_desc;
75     EXEC SQL PREPARE query FROM :stmt;
76
77     EXEC SQL DECLARE my_cursor CURSOR FOR query;
```

```
78      EXEC SQL OPEN my_cursor;
79
80      for( row = 0; ; row++ )
81      {
82        EXEC SQL BEGIN DECLARE SECTION;
83          int     col_count;
84          int     i;
85        EXEC SQL END DECLARE SECTION;
86
87        EXEC SQL FETCH IN my_cursor INTO SQL DESCRIPTOR my_desc;
88
89        if( sqlca.sqlcode != 0 )
90          break;
91
92        EXEC SQL GET DESCRIPTOR my_desc :col_count = count;
93
94        if( row == 0 )
95        {
96          print_meta_data( "my_desc" );
97          print_column_headers( col_count );
98        }
99
100       for( i = 1; i <= col_count; i++ )
101       {
102         EXEC SQL BEGIN DECLARE SECTION;
103           short   ind;
104         EXEC SQL END DECLARE SECTION;
105
106         EXEC SQL GET DESCRIPTOR my_desc VALUE
107           :i :ind = INDICATOR;
108
109         if( ind == -1 )
110         {
111           printf( "null " );
112         }
113         else
114         {
115           EXEC SQL BEGIN DECLARE SECTION;
116             varchar val[40+1];
117             int     len;
118           EXEC SQL END DECLARE SECTION;
119
120           EXEC SQL GET DESCRIPTOR my_desc VALUE
121             :i :len = RETURNED_LENGTH;
122
123           EXEC SQL GET DESCRIPTOR my_desc VALUE :i :val = DATA;
124
```

```
125              if( len > 40 )
126                len = 40;
127
128              printf( "%-*s ", len, val.arr );
129            }
130          }
131
132      printf( "\n" );
133
134      }
135
136      printf( "%d rows\n", row );
137
138 }
```

If you've read the previous few chapters, you know that the most stubborn problem in ad-hoc query processing is that you don't know, at the time you write the program, what kind of data will be returned by any given query. The bulk of the code that you need to write involves discovering and interpreting the meta-data associated with a query.

When you use ecpg to process dynamic SQL commands, the meta-data comes back in the form of a descriptor (or, more precisely, a group of descriptors). A *descriptor* is a data structure, much like libpq's PGresult, that contains information about the data returned by a SQL command.

Before you can use a descriptor, you must tell the ecpg library to allocate one. The following statement will create a new descriptor named my_desc:

```
EXEC SQL ALLOCATE DESCRIPTOR my_desc;
```

At line 75, process_select_stmt() prepares the command for execution. When you prepare a command, you are giving ecpg a chance to peek at the command and do whatever bookkeeping it needs to execute it. After a command has been prepared, ecpg will remember it for you and you can refer to that statement by name (query, in this case).

After you have a prepared the statement, declare a cursor (named my_cursor) for the statement and then open the cursor. (You can execute singleton[5] SELECTs without preparing them, but there is a no way to tell that a dynamic query is a singleton SELECT.)

At line 80, process_select_stmt() enters a loop to process all the rows returned by the cursor.

Line 87 shows the magic that occurs in a dynamic SQL application. When you execute the EXEC SQL statement at line 87, you are fetching the next row from my_cursor and putting the results into the my_desc descriptor. The my_desc descriptor now contains all the meta-data for this SQL command (FETCH).

I mentioned earlier that a descriptor is a data structure. Although that is a true statement, you can't access the members of the data structure using the normal C structure

___
[5] A singleton SELECT is a SELECT command that returns either zero rows or one row, never more.

reference syntax. Instead, you use the EXEC SQL GET DESCRIPTOR directive. The general form of the GET DESCRIPTOR directive is

```
EXEC SQL GET DESCRIPTOR
descriptor_name [column_number] host_variable = item;
```

The item specifies what kind of information you want to retrieve from the descriptor. The returned information is placed into the host_variable. The column_number is optional, but there is only one piece of information that you can retrieve without specifying a column_number—a count of the columns in the result set.

The EXEC SQL GET DESCRIPTOR directive at line 72 retrieves the column count from my_desc and places the result into the col_count host variable.

After you know how many columns are in the result set, you can (optionally) print the meta-data and the column headers. I'll show you those functions in a moment.

At line 100, process_select_stmt() enters a loop that processes each column from the most recently fetched row.

To display a column value, the first thing you need to know is whether that column value is NULL. Each column in the result set has an associated indicator variable, and you can retrieve the value of that indicator through the descriptor. Notice (at line 107) that you have to tell ecpg which column you are interested in: for any descriptor item other than COUNT, you must include a column number after the word VALUE.

If the column contains NULL, process_select_stmt() just prints the word "null". This is another shortcut that I've taken in this client; to properly maintain the alignment of the columns when you print the result set, you have to know the maximum length of each value within a column and that information is not available using dynamic SQL and ecpg. So, instead of printing null and then padding it with spaces to the proper length, we'll just print "null". This means that you lose vertical alignment of the columns if your data includes NULL values.

If a column contains a value other than NULL, process_select_stmt() prints the value (or at most the first 40 characters of the value).

At line 120, this function retrieves the length of the character form of the value from the RETURNED_LENGTH member of the my_desc descriptor. I say the "length of the character form" here because there are other length-related items that you can retrieve from a descriptor. I'll include a description of all the descriptor items a little later.

Finally, at line 123, process_select_stmt() retrieves the actual data value from the descriptor. When you ask for a DATA item, you have to provide a host variable where ecpg can return the value. If the data value that you retrieve is longer than the host variable, ecpg will truncate the value and set sqlca.sqlwarn[1] to tell you that truncation has occurred.

After processing all the columns for all rows, process_select_stmt() prints a message indicating how many rows were retrieved.

Now let's move on to the print_meta_data() function. The first thing I'll point out about this function is that it expects the descriptor name to be passed in as the one and only argument. This isn't really important to the structure of this particular application, but I wanted to point out that you can use a host variable to specify a descriptor.

```
140 static void print_meta_data( char * desc_name )
141 {
142   EXEC SQL BEGIN DECLARE SECTION;
143     char  * desc = desc_name;
144     int     col_count;
145     int     i;
146   EXEC SQL END DECLARE SECTION;
147
148   static char * types[] =
149   {
150     "unused             ",
151     "CHARACTER          ",
152     "NUMERIC            ",
153     "DECIMAL            ",
154     "INTEGER            ",
155     "SMALLINT           ",
156     "FLOAT              ",
157     "REAL               ",
158     "DOUBLE             ",
159     "DATE_TIME          ",
160     "INTERVAL           ",
161     "unused             ",
162     "CHARACTER_VARYING  ",
163     "ENUMERATED         ",
164     "BIT                ",
165     "BIT_VARYING        ",
166     "BOOLEAN            ",
167     "abstract           "
168   };
169
170   if( dump_meta_data == 0 )
171     return;
172
173   EXEC SQL GET DESCRIPTOR :desc :col_count = count;
174
175   printf( "%s\n", md1 );
176   printf( "%s\n", md2 );
177   printf( "%s\n", md3 );
178
179   for( i = 1; i <= col_count; i++ )
180   {
181     EXEC SQL BEGIN DECLARE SECTION;
182       int     type;
```

```
183        int     ret_len;
184        varchar name[21];
185     EXEC SQL END DECLARE SECTION;
186     char *  type_name;
187
188     EXEC SQL GET DESCRIPTOR :desc VALUE
189        :i :name = NAME;
190
191     EXEC SQL GET DESCRIPTOR :desc VALUE
192        :i :type = TYPE;
193
194     EXEC SQL GET DESCRIPTOR :desc VALUE
195        :i :ret_len = RETURNED_OCTET_LENGTH;
196
197     if( type > 0 && type < SQL3_abstract )
198       type_name = types[type];
199     else
200       type_name = "unknown";
201
202     printf( "%02d: %-20s %-17s %04d\n",
203        i, name.arr, type_name, ret_len );
204   }
205
206   printf( "\n" );
207 }
```

This function pulls a few more meta-data items out of the descriptor. The first thing this function does is to check the dump_meta_data flag—if you don't want to see meta-data, this function will simply return without printing anything. The dump_meta_data flag will be set to TRUE if you include a third argument on the command line when you run this program.

At line 173, print_meta_data() retrieves a count of the number of columns in the descriptor. Lines 175 through 177 print column headers for the meta-data (md1, md2, and md3 are defined at the top of client4.pgc).

At line 179, this function enters a loop that prints the meta-data for each column. Lines 188 through 195 retrieve the NAME, (data) TYPE, and RETURNED_OCTET_LENGTH for each column.

The TYPE item returns an integer that *may* correspond to one of the data type names defined in the sql3types.h header file. Not all data types are defined in sql3types.h—there are many PostgreSQL data types that don't exactly map to a SQL3 data type. If you encounter an unknown data type, this function will just print unknown instead of a real type name.

This is probably a good place to show you all the descriptor items that you can retrieve using ecpg (see Table 11.3).

Table 11.3 **Descriptor Item Types**

Item Type	Meaning
CARDINALITY	Number of rows in result set (usually one and therefore not particularly useful)
DATA	Actual data value
DATETIME_INTERVAL_CODE	SQL3_DDT_DATE, SQL3_DDT_TIME, SQL3_DDT_TIMESTAMP, SQL3_DDT_TIMESTAMP_WITH_TIME_ZONE, SQL3_DDT_TIME_WITH_TIME_ZONE
DATETIME_INTERVAL_PRECISION	Not currently used
INDICATOR	Indicator variable
KEY_MEMBER	Always returns FALSE
LENGTH	Length of data as stored in server
NAME	Name of field
NULLABLE	Always returns TRUE
OCTET_LENGTH	Length of data as stored in server
PRECISION	Precision (for numeric values)
RETURNED_LENGTH	Length of actual data item
RETURNED_OCTET_LENGTH	Synonym for RETURNED_LENGTH
SCALE	Scale (for numeric values)
TYPE	SQL3 data type or PostgreSQL data type

The rest of client4.pgc is pretty mundane; I'll include the remainder of the source code here and offer a few quick explanations:

```
209 static void print_column_headers( int col_count )
210 {
211   EXEC SQL BEGIN DECLARE SECTION;
212     char    name[40];
213     int     len;
214   EXEC SQL END DECLARE SECTION;
215   int     i;
216
217   for( i = 1; i <= col_count; i++ )
218   {
219     EXEC SQL GET DESCRIPTOR my_desc VALUE
220       :i :name = NAME;
221
222     EXEC SQL GET DESCRIPTOR my_desc VALUE
223       :i :len  = RETURNED_OCTET_LENGTH;
224
225     if( len > 40 )
226       len = 40;
```

```
227
228    printf( "%-*s ", len, name );
229    }
230
231    printf( "\n" );
232
233    for( i = 1; i <= col_count; i++ )
234    {
235      EXEC SQL GET DESCRIPTOR my_desc VALUE
236        :i :len  = RETURNED_OCTET_LENGTH;
237
238      if( len > 40 )
239        len = 40;
240
241      printf( "%*.*s ", len, len, sep );
242    }
243
244    printf( "\n" );
245  }
```

The `print_column_headers()` function does a half-hearted job of trying to print properly aligned column headers. This function can't do a perfect job because ecpg doesn't expose enough information. For example, to properly align column headers, you have to know the longest value in any given column. Because you process SELECT statements one record at a time, you would have to do a lot of work to be able to find this information. If you are not a purist, you can mix ecpg and libpq code in the same application.

```
247 static int is_select_stmt( char * stmt )
248 {
249   char * token;
250
251   for( token = stmt; *token; token++ )
252     if( *token != ' ' && *token != '\t' )
253       break;
254
255   if( *token == '\0' )
256     return( 0 );
257
258   if( strncasecmp( token, "select", 6 ) == 0 )
259     return( 1 );
260   else
261     return( 0 );
262 }
```

The `is_select_stmt()` function represents another shortcut—you have to look at the first word of a SQL command to determine whether it is a SELECT statement or some other command. With other dynamic SQL packages (such as Oracle's Pro*C product), you can obtain this information from the descriptor, but not with PostgreSQL.

```
264 static void print_error()
265 {
266   printf( "#%ld:%s\n", sqlca.sqlcode, sqlca.sqlerrm.sqlerrmc );
267 }
268
269 static int usage( char * program )
270 {
271   fprintf( stderr, "usage: %s <database> <query>\n", program );
272   return( 1 );
273 }
```

The print_error() and usage() functions are simple utility functions. print_error() is called whenever a SQL error occurs. The usage() function is called by main() if there is an improper number of arguments on the command line.

Summary

This chapter should have given you a good feel for how to build C applications using ecpg. Don't let the last section throw you off too much—ecpg isn't all that well suited to processing dynamic SQL (at least in comparison to libpq or libpgeasy).

The ecpg preprocessor and library are remarkably well designed for building complete PostgreSQL applications quickly.

If you don't need to process dynamic queries, I think that ecpg is the quickest and easiest way to connect a C application to a PostgreSQL database. If you do need to handle dynamic queries, you should consider coding the static parts of your application using ecpg and using libpq (or libpgeasy) for the dynamic parts.

Most of the features in ecpg come from the SQL3 standard and you should find that it is reasonably easy to move embedded SQL applications among various databases (assuming that you haven't used too many "special" features).

12

Using PostgreSQL from an ODBC Client Application

ODBC (open database connectivity) is an API (application programming interface) that provides an application with a consistent database interface. To understand the architecture of ODBC, it helps to understand the problem that ODBC was designed to solve.

Let's say that you are an independent software vendor and you have just finished developing an accounting package that you intend to sell to as many users as possible. Your accounting application was designed to store its data in Sybase. Your original application uses the Sybase OpenClient interface to interact with the database. One day, a potential customer tells you that he is very interested in buying your application, but his corporate standard mandates that all data must be stored in PostgreSQL. If you want to sell your product to this customer, you have two options.

First, you could add a second interface to your application and somehow arrange things so that your application would use whichever database is available. That would leave you with a Sybase-specific interface and a PostgreSQL-specific interface. The downside to this approach is that you now have twice as much code to maintain (not to mention having to learn both interfaces). If you encounter another customer who requires Oracle support, you'll have to learn and maintain three interfaces.

Your other choice is to use a database-independent interface from the start. That's ODBC. ODBC gives your application a single API that can interact with PostgreSQL, Oracle, Sybase, SQL Server, MySQL, and many other databases.

The ODBC interface is based on the X/Open CLI (call-level interface) standard. The X/Open CLI standard is compatible with the ISO/IEC SQL/CLI standard. This means that an application that is written to use the ODBC standard API will also be compatible with the X/Open CLI standard and the ISO/IEC SQL/CLI standard. There are two important consequences to all this: An ODBC application can interact with many databases, and the standard is not likely to change at the whim of a single database vendor.

ODBC won't solve all your database portability problems. It provides an industry-standard API for establishing database connections, sending commands to a server, and retrieving the results. ODBC does *not* provide a standard language. If your application sends commands that are specific to PostgreSQL, that application won't automatically work with an Oracle backend. For example, in PostgreSQL, END WORK is a synonym for the more common COMMIT. If you are trying to build a portable application, you should use COMMIT rather than END WORK. In practice, most applications can use a common subset of SQL to achieve database portability. ODBC provides API portability, and SQL provides language portability. With this combination, your application can be *very* portable.

In this chapter, I'll focus on using ODBC from an application written in C or C++. ODBC would be a very useful API if it only provided a consistent database interface to C programs. However, ODBC offers another important feature—you can use ODBC to access databases from languages such as Visual Basic, Microsoft Access, FoxPro, Delphi, and others. You can also use ODBC to connect a web server to an ODBC-compliant database. I'll talk more about the PostgreSQL/Web server connection in Chapter 15, "Using PostgreSQL with PHP."

ODBC Architecture Overview

In a typical ODBC application, there are five components: the client application, the ODBC driver manager, a database-specific driver, an ODBC-compliant database server, and a data source.

The ODBC Client Application

The client application is the component that you have to write. Typically, an ODBC client is written in C or C++. The client interacts with a database by opening a data source (which I will describe in a moment), sending requests to the data source, and processing results.

The ODBC Driver Manager

The ODBC driver manager gets involved when the client application opens a data source. The driver manager is responsible for converting a data source name into a data source handle. After the client has provided the name of a data source, the driver manager searches a configuration file for the definition of that data source. One of the properties contained in a data source is the name of an ODBC driver.

The ODBC Driver

An ODBC driver is a shared library (or DLL on the MS Windows platform). A driver provides access to a specific type of database (for example, PostgreSQL or Oracle). The driver is responsible for translating ODBC requests into whatever form is expected by the backend database. The driver also translates database-specific results back into ODBC form for the client application.

The ODBC-Compliant Database

The backend database processes requests and provides results. By the time the database receives a request from the client application, the driver has already translated the request from ODBC form into a form understood by the server. In the case of PostgreSQL, the PostgreSQL ODBC driver translates requests into the PostgreSQL client/server protocol.

The Data Source

A *data source* is a named set of connection properties.

Each data source has a unique name (in the following examples, I use a data source named MoviesDSN). This name is used by a client application to represent the connection properties needed to connect to a particular database.

Here is a simple data source definition (later, I'll tell you how to actually build a data source definition):

```
[MoviesDSN]
Driver          = PostgreSQLDriver
Description     = Movie Database
```

(Don't worry—you rarely have to build a data source definition by hand. In most cases, you construct a data source using a nice graphical user interface.)

The first line specifies the name of the data source (in this case, the data source is named MoviesDSN). The data source name is followed by a set of "keyword=value" pairs—each pair defines a connection property. The Driver property tells the ODBC driver manager which driver should be used to connect to this particular data source. The Description property is a human-friendly description of the data source (this property is displayed in ODBC configuration utilities).

Each ODBC driver supports a different set of connection properties (the Driver and Description properties are used by the driver manager, not by the driver). The PostgreSQL driver enables you to specify the database name, host address, port number, and a number of other properties.

Why does ODBC use a data source instead of letting you specify the connection properties each time you connect? It is much easier for an application (and a human) to work with a data source name than with a huge set of connection properties (I've shown you two properties here—most drivers support 10 or more properties). Separating the connection properties from the application also makes it much easier for a client to achieve database portability. Rather than embedding the properties in each client, you can use an external configuration tool to define a data source for each database that you might want to use.

Setting Up a Data Source on Unix Systems

Many people think that ODBC exists only in the world of Microsoft Windows—that's not the case at all. If you are working in a Linux or Unix environment, there are two open-source ODBC implementations: unixODBC (www.unixODBC.org) and iODBC (www.iodbc.org). You can also find commercially supported ODBC implementations for Unix, Linux, and other environments.

Installing unixODBC and the PostgreSQL ODBC Driver

Before you can use unixODBC, you must ensure that it is installed on your system. You'll also need the PostgreSQL ODBC driver. As in previous chapters, I'll assume that you are running a Red Hat Linux (or Fedora) host. You'll need two RPM (Red Hat Package Manager) files: unixODBC and unixODBC-kde. Assuming that your host is connected to the Internet, you can use either the apt or rpmfind program to download the latest versions:

```
# rpmfind --latest --auto unixODBC unixODBC-kde
Installing unixODBC will require 2345 KBytes
Installing unixODBC-kde will require 244 KBytes


### To Transfer:
ftp://ftp.redhat.com/pub/.../RPMS/unixODBC-kde-2.2.0-5.i386.rpm
ftp://ftp.redhat.com/pub/.../RPMS/readline-4.2a-4.i386.rpm
ftp://ftp.redhat.com/pub/.../RPMS/unixODBC-2.2.0-5.i386.rpm
transferring ...
```

The rpmfind utility has located and downloaded all the packages that you need and saved them in the /tmp directory. Notice that you asked for two packages, but rpmfind downloaded three. The rpmfind utility checks for dependencies: It found that unixODBC requires the readline package and downloaded that for you as well.

Now that you have the packages downloaded, let's install them:

```
# cd /tmp
# rpm -ihv *.rpm
Preparing...      ########################### [100%]
1: readline       ########################### [ 33%]
2: unixODBC       ########################### [ 66%]
3: unixODBC-kde ########################### [100%]
```

If you want to view the list of files installed for a given package, you can use the rpm command in query mode. For example:

```
$ rpm -q -l unixODBC-kde
/etc/X11/applnk/System/DataManager.desktop
/etc/X11/applnk/System/ODBCConfig.desktop
/usr/bin/DataManager
/usr/bin/ODBCConfig
```

The unixODBC package includes the PostgreSQL ODBC driver.

If you install unixODBC from the Red Hat package files, unixODBC will store configuration information in the /etc directory. If you decide to build and install unixODBC from source, the default configuration will store information in the /usr/local/etc directory, but you can override the location at compile time. The remainder of this discussion assumes that you installed from the Red Hat package files and will expect configuration files to be located in /etc.

The unixODBC implementation stores data source information in a set of configuration files (in Windows, ODBC configuration information is stored in the Registry). For any given user, there are three configuration files: a systemwide list of data sources, a systemwide list of drivers, and a user-specific list of data sources.

Each configuration file is organized as a flat text file, divided into sections, starting with a name surrounded by square brackets ([]). Each section contains a list of property = value pairs.

The /etc/odbcinst.ini file contains a list of ODBC drivers that are available on your system. Here is a sample odbcinst.ini entry:

```
[PostgreSQLDriver]
Description     = PostgreSQL driver
Driver          = /usr/local/lib/libodbcpsql.so
Setup           = /usr/local/lib/libodbcpsqlS.so
FileUsage       - 1
```

The first line defines a driver named PostgreSQLDriver. When you define a data source, you use this name to connect a data source to a driver. An ODBC driver is usually composed of two shared libraries: a setup library and the driver itself. The ODBC administrator (ODBCConfig) uses the setup library to prompt the user for driver-specific configuration information. The driver library contains a set of functions that provide a client application with access to the database. The Driver property contains the name of the driver-shared library. The Setup property contains the name of the setup-shared library. The final property (FileUsage) is an enumerated value that describes how a driver maps files into relational tables.[1] See the ODBC reference documentation (msdn.microsoft.com/library) for more information.

The /etc/odbc.ini file contains a list of ODBC data sources. Remember that a data source is a named set of properties. Here is a sample entry:

```
[PostgreSQL]
Description         = PostgreSQL Accounting Database
Driver              = PostgreSQLDriver
```

The first line defines a data source named PostgreSQL. The Description property provides a human-friendly description of the data source (you will see both the description and the data source name in the ODBCConfig program). The Driver property contains the name of an ODBC driver, as defined in the /etc/odbcinst.ini file. Most of the entries

---

[1] The FileUsage property can be set to one of three predefined values: 0, 1, or 2. FileUsage provides a hint to the client application about how the database stores data in the OS filesystem. Some databases, such as Oracle, can store an entire installation in a single file or in a collection of files—the actual organization of the data is not important (and is not discernable) to the client application. An Oracle data source has a FileUsage value of 0. Other databases, such as Paradox, store each table in a separate file. A Paradox data source has a FileUsage value of 1. Finally, a data source whose FileUsage is set to 2 stores an entire database in a single file. This is different from type 0 in that a type 0 data source can store multiple databases in a single file.

in /etc/odbc.ini are more complex than this example. The unixODBC driver manager understands a few more properties, and each driver supports its own set of properties.

Fortunately, you don't have to edit any of the configuration files by hand. The unixODBC package includes a GUI configuration tool named ODBCConfig. When you first run ODBCConfig, you will see a list of all the data sources defined on your system (see Figure 12.1).

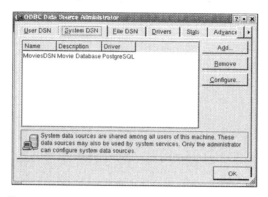

Figure 12.1 unixODBC Data Source Administrator.

If you installed unixODBC from the unixODBC and unixODBC-kde packages as previously described, you should find the ODBCConfig application on the KDE Start menu in the System folder. Click the ODBCConfig entry to invoke the program, or run ODBCConfig from a command line. The first time you run this program, you may get a warning that you don't have an .ODBCConfig subdirectory in your home directory—you can just click the OK button and ignore this warning: ODBCConfig creates the required configuration files automatically.

To add a new data source, press the Add button and you will see a list of installed drivers (see Figure 12.2).

Select one of the drivers and press OK (Note: If you're like me, you'll press the Add button by mistake. If you do that, ODBCConfig will assume that you want to add a new driver.)

After you have selected a driver, you will be asked to define the rest of the connection properties (see Figure 12.3). Remember that each driver understands a different set of connection properties, so the Data Source Properties dialog will look different if you are using a different driver.

You can leave most of these properties set to their default values—you really need to provide only the Name, Description, and Database properties. (This dialog is a little confusing. Where's the OK button? To accept the changes that you have made, click the check mark in the upper-left corner of the window. To cancel, click the X.)

You can see that using the ODBCConfig utility is much easier than configuring a data source by hand. When you create a new data source using ODBCConfig, the data source properties are stored in the odbc.ini file.

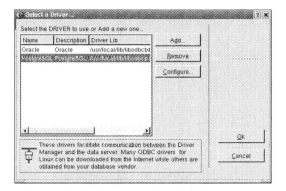

Figure 12.2   Adding a new data source.

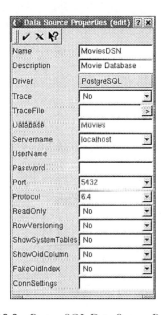

Figure 12.3   PostgreSQL Data Source Properties.

Setting Up a Data Source in Windows

MS Windows also provides a graphical configuration tool, almost identical to
ODBCConfig. On most Windows systems, you will find the ODBC administrator in the
Control Panel or in the Administrative Tools applet within the Control Panel. Double-
click whichever ODBC icon is present on your system, and you should see something
similar to what is shown in Figure 12.4.

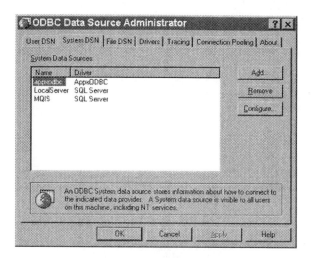

Figure 12.4   Windows ODBC Data Source Administrator.

The procedure for creating a data source using the Windows ODBC Data Source
Administrator is identical to the procedure you would following using the unixODBC
Data Source Administrator.

If you're using a recent version of the PostgreSQL ODBC driver, the data source
configuration screens will look a bit different. Figure 12.5 shows the initial configuration
dialog.

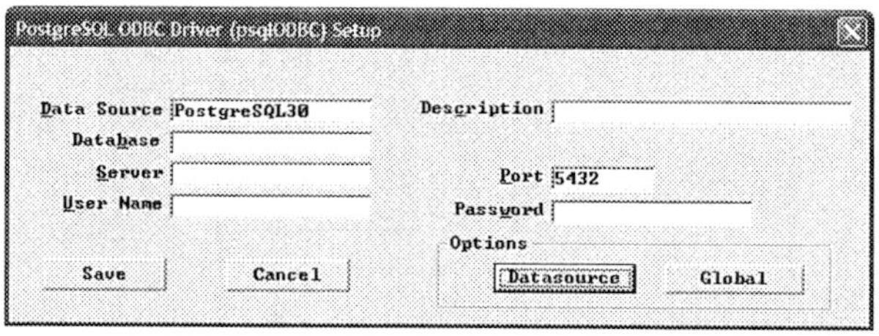

Figure 12.5   Windows Data Source Configuration.

To fine-tune the data source, click the button labeled Datasource (in the Options
group). A dialog similar to the one shown in Figure 12.6 will appear.

I'll explain the configuration options in more detail in the next section. Click Page 2
to get to the second page of data source options, shown in Figure 12.7.

If you click the button labeled Global (from the dialog shown in Figure 12.5), you'll
see the dialog shown in Figure 12.8.

Check the first box (labeled CommLog) if you want a complete log of the client/server
communication stream. Check the second box (labeled Mylog) to record a detailed log of
the internals of the psqlodbc driver. In most cases, you'll never need to record either log.

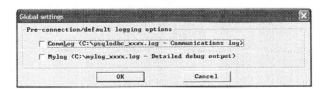

Figure 12.6   Advanced Options—Page 1

Figure 12.7   Advanced Options—Page 2

Figure 12.8   Windows Data Source Configuration—Global Settings.

Datasource Connection Properties

The psqlodbc driver supports a number of connection properties. If you're using psqlodbc on a Windows host, you can configure the driver using a graphical interface (see Figures 12.5, 12.6, 12.7, and 12.8). If you're using psqlodbc on a Linux/Unix host, you'll have to edit the odbc.ini file by hand.

Table 12.1 shows the connection properties supported by psqlodbc version 8.0. In the first column, you see the label that appears in the Windows configuration dialogs (Figures 12.5, 12.6, and 12.7). The second column shows the corresponding name as it must appear in the odbc.ini file. The third column lists the default value for each property.

Table 12.1 **PostgreSQL/ODBC Connection Properties**

Property Label (Windows)	odbc.ini name	Default Value
Database	Database	*None*
Server	Servername	*None*
User Name	Username	*None*
Description	Description	*None*
Port	Port	5432
Password	Password	*None*
Disable Genetic Optimizer	Optimizer	On
KSQO (Keyset Query Optimization)	Ksqo	On
Recognize Unique Indexes	UniqueIndex	On
Use Declare/Fetch	UseDeclareFetch	Off
CommLog	CommLog	Off
Parse Statements	Parse	Off
Cancel as FreeStmt	CancelAsFreeStmt	Off
MyLog	Debug	Off
Unknown Sizes	UnknownSizes	Maximum
Text as LongVarChar	TextAsLongVarChar	On
Uknowns as LongVarChar	UnknownAsLongVarchar	Off
Bools as Char	BoolsAsChar	On
Max Varchar	MaxVarcharSize	254
Max LongVar	Char MaxLongVarcharSize	8190
Cache Size	Fetch	100
SysTable Prefixes	ExtraSysTablePrefixes dd_;	
Read Only	ReadOnly	Off
Show System Tables	ShowSystemTables	Off
LF <-> CR/LF conversion	LFConversion	On for Windows, Off for others
Updatable Cursors	UpdatableCursors	Off
bytea as LO	ByteaAsLongVarBinary	Off
Row versioning	RowVersioning	Off
Disallow Premature	DisallowPremature	Off
True is -1	TrueIsMinus1	Off
Server side prepare	UseServerSidePrepare	Off
Int8 As	BI	Default

Table 12.1 **Continued**

Protocol	Protocol	Latest
OID Options: Show Column	ShowOidColumn	Off
OID Options: Fake Index	FakeOidIndex	Off
Connect Settings	ConnSettings	None
	Socket	4096
	Lie	Off
	LowerCaseIdentifier	Off

In the list below, I describe each property:

- Database—The name of the PostgreSQL database that you want to connect to with this data source.

- Server—The name (or IP address) of the server that you want to connect to.

- Username—The dedicated username that this data source will use to connect to the PostgreSQL server—leave this field blank if you want the client application to prompt for a username.

- Description—A descriptive name for the data source (some client applications display the description when you browse through the list of data sources).

- Port—The TCP/IP port number where the postmaster is listening in the PostgreSQL server (you only need to change this if your postmaster is listening on a port other than the usual 5432).

- Password—The password used to connect to the PostgreSQL server—leave this field blank if you want the client application to prompt for a password.

- Optimizer—Disables PostgreSQL's genetic query optimizer (the genetic optimizer is responsible for selecting a reasonably good execution plan when you join many tables in a single query).

- Ksqo—Enables server-side support for keyset queries generated by the Microsoft Jet database engine. Disable this property if you are using a PostgreSQL server newer than version 7.1.

- UniqueIndex—If enabled, the ODBC's SQLStatistics() function will report unique indexes (including a "fake" index on each table's OID column). If Off, the SQLStatistics() function will report that all indexes allow duplicate values. You may want to disable UniqueIndex if you are reading PostgreSQL-hosted data from a Microsoft Access application.

- UseDeclareFetch—If enabled, the driver will automatically use server-side cursors (via DECLARE and FETCH) whenever your application executes a SELECT command. Instead of retrieving the entire result set, the driver will fetch a small number of rows as needed. The number of rows fetched is controlled by the Fetch property.

- Fetch—Determines the number of rows fetched by the driver when UseDeclareFetch is enabled.

- CommLog—If defined, the driver records all client/server traffic in a log file. The log file is named `C:\psqlodbc_<process-id>` on Windows systems and `/tmp/psqlodbc _<user-name><process-id>.log` on Linux/Unix systems.

- Parse—If enabled, the *driver* (not the server) will parse simple SELECT statements when you call the SQLNumResultCols(), SQLDescribeCol(), or SQLColAttributes() function. The driver reads through the SELECT statement to identify individual columns and *then* asks the server to return type information for each column that it found.

- CancelAsFreeStmt—If enabled, the driver's SQLCancel() function will call SQLFreeStmt(SQL_CLOSE) on your behalf. Applications designed around ODBC 2.x may expect the SQLCancel() function to behave the same as SQLFreeStmt(SQL_CLOSE). If you're using such an application, you can enable this property (or better yet, upgrade the application to conform to ODBC 3.x specifications).

- Debug—If enabled, the driver records a detailed record of its work in a log file. The log file is named `C:\mylog_<process-id>` on Windows systems and `/tmp/mylog_<user-name><process-id>.log` on Linux/Unix systems.

- UnknownSizes—This property determines how the SQLDescribeCol() and SQLColAttributes() functions compute the size of a column of unknown type. You can specify *Maximum* (0) to force the driver to report the maximum size allowed for the type, *Don't Know* (1) to force the driver to report an *unknown* length (-1), or *Longest* (2) to force the driver to search through the current result set to find the longest value. You should not specify *Longest* if you have enabled UseDeclareFetch.

  As of psqlodbc version 8.0, the driver has built in support for the following data types: CHAR, NAME, BPCHAR, VARCHAR, TEXT, BYTEA, SMALLINT (INT2), OID, XID, INTEGER (INT or INT4), BIGINT (INT8), NUMERIC (or DECIMAL), REAL (FLOAT or FLOAT4), DOUBLE PRECISION (FLOAT8), DATE, TIME, ABSTIME, TIMESTAMPTZ, TIMETZ, MONEY, BOOL, and large objects. Any other type is considered "unknown." Arrays are viewed as "unknown" data types as well.

- TextAsLongVarChar—If enabled, the driver treats PostgreSQL TEXT columns as if they are of type SQL_LONGVARCHAR (or SQL_WLONGVARCHAR if you are using the Unicode-enabled driver). If disabled, the driver treats TEXT column as SQL_VARCHAR (or SQL_WVARCHAR) values.

- UnknownAsLongVarChar—If enabled, the driver treats columns of unknown type as SQL_LONGVARCHAR values. If disabled, the driver treats columns of unknown type as SQL_VARCHAR values.

- BoolsAsChar—If enabled, the driver treats PostgreSQL BOOL columns as SQL_CHAR values. If disabled, BOOL columns are treated as SQL_BIT values.

- MaxVarcharSize—The driver treats VARCHAR and BPCHAR values longer than MaxVarCharSize as SQL_LONGVARCHAR (or SQL_WLONGVARCHAR) values.

- MaxLongVarcharSize—If TextAsLongVarChar is enabled, the driver reports that TEXT values are MaxLongVarcharSize bytes long; otherwise TEXT values are reported to be MaxVarcharSize bytes long. Also, if UnknownAsLongVarChar is enabled, columns of unknown type are reported to be MaxLongVarcharSize bytes long, otherwise they are reported to be MaxVarcharSize bytes in length.

- ReadOnly—If defined, the driver prevents you from executing any of the following commands: INSERT, UPDATE, DELETE, CREATE, ALTER, DROP, GRANT, REVOKE, or LOCK. The driver also prohibits procedure calls that use ODBC's procedure call escape syntax {call=procedure-name?}.

- ShowSystemTables—If enabled, the driver will report PostgreSQL system tables when you call the SQLTables() function. The SQLTables() function will also report system tables if you specifically ask for them by specifying a table type of SYSTEM TABLE. The driver considers any table whose name starts with pg_ to be a system table. The driver will also consider any table whose prefix matches one of the strings specified in ExtraSysTablePrefixes (see the next property) to be a system table.

- ExtraSysTablePrefixes—If defined, this property specifies a semicolon-separated list of prefixes. A table whose name starts with one of these prefixes is considered to be a system table (see the previous property).

- LFConversion—If enabled, the driver converts line-feed characters to carriage-return/line-feed pairs when retrieving character values *from* the server and converts carriage-return/line-feed pairs to line-feed characters when sending character values *to* the server.

- UpdatableCursors—If enabled, the driver permits positioned UPDATE and DELETE operations using the SQLSetPos() or SQLBulkOperations() function.

- ByteaAsLongVarBinary—If enabled, the driver treats PostgreSQL BYTEA columns as if they are of type SQL_LONGVARBINARY. If disabled, BYTEA columns are treated as SQL_VARBINARY values.

- RowVersioning—If enabled, the driver includes the xmin column when reporting the columns defined for a given table. Well-designed applications can use the xmin column to avoid updating rows that have been modified by another transaction. The SQLSpecialColumns() function treats xmin as an SQL_ROWVER column.

- DisallowPremature—This property determines how the driver behaves if you try to retrieve information about a query (such as the number of columns in the result set or the type of each column) without actually executing the command. If DisallowPremature is enabled, the cursor declares a cursor for the query and fetches the meta-data from the cursor (without actually fetching a row). If DisallowPremature is disabled, the driver executes the command as soon as you request any meta-data.

- UseServerSidePrepare—If enabled, the driver will use the PREPARE and EXECUTE commands to implement the Prepare/Execute model (explained later in this chapter). UseServerSidePrepare is ignored if you connect to a server running PostgreSQL version 7.2 or older.

- BI—This property determines how the driver treats BIGINT (INT8) values. BI can be set to any of the following values: -5 (SQL_BIGINT), 2 (SQL_NUMERIC), 8 (SQL_DOUBLE), 4 (SQL_INTEGER), 12 (SQL_VARCHAR), or 0. If BI is set to 0, the driver treats BIGINT values as SQL_NUMERIC when connected to an MS Jet client and SQL_BIGINT when connected to any other client.

- Protocol—If defined, forces the driver to interact with the server using a specific protocol version. If not defined, the driver negotiates with the server to find a suitable protocol.

- ShowOidColumn—If defined, the SQLColumns() function reports the OID column (if present). If not defined, the OID column is hidden from SQLColumns().

- FakeOidIndex—If defined, the SQLStatistics() function reports that a unique index exists on each OID column.

- ConnSettings—A semicolon-separated list of SQL commands that are executed when the driver first connects to the server. Typically, this property contains a list of SET statements that initialize the server's runtime parameters (CLIENT_ENCODING, DATESTYLE, and so on) to fit your needs.

- Socket—Determines the size of the buffer that the driver uses when communicating with the client. You can increase the buffer size to improve performance if you are shuffling large fields between the client and the server.

- Lie—If defined, the driver (when asked) claims to support a number of ODBC features that it does not in fact support. For example, if Lie is defined, the driver claims to support positioned UPDATE's and DELETE's, dynamic and mixed scrolling within cursors, the SQLBrowseConnect() function, SQLColumnPrivileges(), and more. Presumably, this property exists to satisfy client applications that check for advanced features but don't actually use them.

- LowerCaseIdentifier—If enabled, the driver will translate identifiers (column names, table names, schema names, etc.) to lowercase. If disabled, the driver reports identifiers in the form delivered by the server.

Prerequisites

The examples in this chapter assume that you have installed and configured the unixODBC or iODBC driver manager. I'll also assume that you have installed the PostgreSQL ODBC driver and created an ODBC data source.

Most of the examples in this chapter were developed with the GNU C/C++ compiler and GNU make. The final example uses the Qt library described in Chapter 10, "The PostgreSQL C++ API\u2014libpq++."

Client 1—Connecting to the Server

Now that you understand the basic architecture of the ODBC API and you have defined a PostgreSQL data source, let's look at some sample code. This first client application connects to a database and then exits. Listing 12.1 provides an example that is much more complex than the sample clients in earlier chapters—ODBC is a complex API.

Listing 12.1 odbc/client1.c

```
1 /* client1.c */
2
3 #include <sql.h>
4 #include <sqlext.h>
5
6 #include <stdio.h>
7
8 typedef enum { FALSE, TRUE } bool;
9
10 int main( int argc, char * argv[] )
11 {
12   SQLRETURN   result;
13   SQLHENV     envHandle;
14   SQLHDBC     conHandle;
15
16   SQLAllocHandle( SQL_HANDLE_ENV,
17                   SQL_NULL_HANDLE,
18                   &envHandle );
19
20   SQLSetEnvAttr( envHandle,
21                  SQL_ATTR_ODBC_VERSION,
22                  (SQLPOINTER)SQL_OV_ODBC2,
23                  0 );
24
25   SQLAllocHandle( SQL_HANDLE_DBC,
26                   envHandle,
27                   &conHandle );
28
29   result = SQLConnect( conHandle,  // connection handle
30                  argv[1], SQL_NTS,   // data source name
31                  argv[2], SQL_NTS,   // user name
32                  argv[3], SQL_NTS ); // password
33
34
35   if( result == SQL_SUCCESS || result == SQL_SUCCESS_WITH_INFO )
36   {
37     printf( "connection ok...\n" );
38     return( 0 );
39   }
40   else
41   {
42     printf( "connection failed...\n" );
43     return( -1 );
44   }
45 }
```

If you want to run this program, you will need to provide three arguments: the name of a data source, a valid username, and a password. Here is an example:

```
$ ./client1 MoviesDSN korry cows
connection ok...
```

Now, let's look through the code.

The first thing you'll notice when you work with ODBC is that you have to create a lot of handles. Remember that a handle is an opaque data type—there is a data structure behind a handle, but you can't get to it. There are only three things that you can do with a handle: You can create it, you can destroy it, and you can pass it to a function.

ODBC Handle Types

ODBC defines four different types of handles:

- A SQLHENV is an environment handle—it functions as the top-level handle to the ODBC API. You must create an environment handle before you can do anything else with ODBC.

- A SQLHDBC is a handle to a database connection. When you connect to a database, you initialize a SQLHDBC handle. After you have a valid database connection handle, you can allocate a statement handle.

- A statement handle has the type SQLHSTMT. You must create a statement handle before you can send a command to the database. Result set information is returned through a SQLHSTMT handle.

- The last handle type defined by ODBC is SQLHDESC. A SQLHDESC handle is a descriptor handle. Descriptor handles are used when you are writing an ODBC driver (as opposed to a client application) and may be used in sophisticated error-handling code. I've never needed to allocate a SQLHDESC myself; you probably won't need to either.

You create an environment handle at line 13 and initialize it by calling SQLAllocHandle_(SQL_HANDLE_ENV, ...). There are three arguments to the SQLAllocHandle() function. The first argument specifies what type of handle you are trying to create. The second argument specifies the parent of the new handle. The final argument is a pointer to the handle that you want to initialize. Table 12.2 shows how to allocate different types of handles using SQLAllocHandle(). Notice that an environment handle doesn't have a parent, so you pass SQL_NULL_HANDLE as the second argument.

Table 12.2 SQLAllocHandle() **Arguments**

Data Type of Symbolic Name	New Handle	Type of Parent	Description
SQL_HANDLE_ENV	SQLHENV	No parent	Environment handle
SQL_HANDLE_DBC	SQLHDBC	SQLHENV	Database connection handle
SQL_HANDLE_STMT	SQLHSTMT	SQLHDBC	Statement handle
SQL_HANDLE_DESC	SQLHDESC	SQLHDBC	Descriptor handle

After you have an initialized environment handle, you need to tell the ODBC library what version of ODBC you expect to find. Use the SQLSetEnvAttr() function to tell

ODBC that you are going to interact using the ODBC 2.x protocol. The PostgreSQL ODBC driver is written to the ODBC 2.5 specification, so you can't call any of the driver-supplied functions that were added in ODBC 3.0. (Note: The driver manager translates many 3.0 functions into 2.x requests, but I find that the results generally are not reliable.)

At line 25, you allocate a connection handle (a SQLHDBC). Compare this function call with your earlier call to SQLAllocHandle():

```
SQLAllocHandle( SQL_HANDLE_ENV, SQL_NULL_HANDLE, &envHandle );
SQLAllocHandle( SQL_HANDLE_DBC, envHandle,       &conHandle );
```

You can see in Table 12.2 that an environment handle does not have a parent. When you allocate an environment handle, you pass SQL_NULL_HANDLE instead of a parent. When you allocate a connection handle, you allocate it within the context of an environment; you provide an environment handle as the second parameter to SQLAllocHandle().

At this point in the example code, you have allocated an environment handle, declared which ODBC protocol you want to use, and allocated a connection handle. You still have not connected to a data source. There are three functions that we can use to connect to a data source: SQLConnect(), SQLDriverConnect(), and SQLBrowseConnect(). The simplest connection function is SQLConnect(). Here is the function prototype for SQLConnect():

```
SQLRETURN SQLConnect( SQLHDBC      ConnectionHandle,
                      SQLCHAR    * DataSourceName,
                      SQLSMALLINT DataSourceLength,
                      SQLCHAR    * UserName,
                      SQLSMALLINT UserNameLength,
                      SQLCHAR    * Password,
                      SQLSMALLINT PasswordLength );
```

When you call SQLConnect(), you provide a connection handle, a data source name, a username, and a password. In this sample code, you use command-line arguments for the data source name, username, and password. Notice that you don't actually compute the length of each string that you pass to SQLConnect()—instead, you pass SQL_NTS to tell ODBC that you are sending NULL-terminated strings.

The other connection functions—(SQLDriverConnect() and SQLBrowseConnect())—are more complex. I'll show you how to use SQLDriverConnect() in a later example, but the PostgreSQL ODBC driver does not support SQLBrowseConnect().

SQLConnect() returns a SQLRETURN value. One of the things that complicates ODBC programming is that ODBC defines two different SUCCESS values, SQL_SUCCESS and SQL_SUCCESS_WITH_INFO, and you have to check for either of these values. I'll discuss the difference between these two values in the next section.

In the sample code, you just print a message to tell the user whether he could connect to the requested data source. I'm cheating a little in this example—a well-behaved application would tear down the database connection and properly discard the environment and connection handles. In this case, the application exits immediately after finishing its interaction with the database. If you still had more work to do and no longer needed the database connection, it would be a good idea to free up the resources required to maintain the connection.

Client 2—Adding Error Checking

In the previous example, I omitted a lot of code that would normally appear in a real-world application. In this section, I'll add some simple error-handling functions and show you how to properly free up the resources (handles) that you create. I'll also use a more complex and more flexible connection function: SQLDriverConnect().

In the previous section, I mentioned that most ODBC functions return two different values to indicate a successful completion: SQL_SUCCESS and SQL_SUCCESS_WITH_INFO. To make your ODBC programming life a little easier, you can use the following function to check for success or failure:

```
static bool SQL_OK( SQLRETURN result )
{
  if( result == SQL_SUCCESS || result == SQL_SUCCESS_WITH_INFO )
    return( TRUE );
  else
    return( FALSE );
}
```

A typical call to SQL_OK() might look like this:

```
if( SQL_OK( SQLAllocHandle( SQL_HANDLE_ENV, SQL_NULL_HANDLE, &handle ))
{
  ...
}
```

So what's the difference between SQL_SUCCESS and SQL_SUCCESS_WITH_INFO? The simple answer is that SQL_SUCCESS implies that a function succeeded; SQL_SUCCESS_WITH_INFO also means that a function succeeded, but more information is available. For example, if you try to REVOKE a privilege from a user, but the user did not have the privilege to begin with, you'll get a SQL_SUCCESS_WITH_INFO result. The request is completed successfully, but you might want to know the extra information.

In an ODBC 2.x application, you call the SQLError() to retrieve any extended return information. If you call SQLError() after receiving a SQL_SUCCESS result, the SQLError() function will fail. Here is the function prototype for the SQLError() function:

```
SQLRETURN SQLError(
    SQLHENV       envHandle,
    SQLHDBC       conHandle,
    SQLHSTMT      stmtHandle,
    SQLCHAR     * sqlState,
    SQLINTEGER  * nativeError,
    SQLCHAR     * messageText,
    SQLSMALLINT   messageTextLength,
    SQLSMALLINT * requiredLength );
```

Notice that the SQLError() function can accept three different handles—when you call SQLError(), you provide only one of the three. For example, if you receive an error status on a statement handle, you would call SQLError(), as follows:

```
SQLError( SQL_NULL_HENV, SQL_NULL_HDBC, stmtHandle, ... );
```

Table 12.3 shows how you would call SQLError() given each handle type.

Table 12.3   Handle Types and SQLError() **Parameters**

Handle Type	SQLError() Parameters
SQLHENV	envHandle, SQL_NULL_HDBC, SQL_NULL_HSTMT, ...
SQLHDBC	SQL_NULL_HENV, conHandle, SQL_NULL_HSTMT, ...
SQLHSTMT	SQL_NULL_HENV, SQL_NULL_HDBC, stmtHandle, ...

If the SQLError() function succeeds[2], it returns three pieces of status information.

The first is called the SQLSTATE. The sqlState parameter should point to a six-byte SQLCHAR array. SQLError() will fill in the sqlState array with a five-character code (and a NULL-terminator). ODBC uses the SQLSTATE as a way to provide status information in a database-independent format. A SQLSTATE code is composed of a two-character *class* followed by a three-character *subclass*. SQLSTATE code '00000' means 'successful completion' and is equivalent to SQL_SUCCESS. SQLSTATE values that begin with the class '01' are warnings. Any other SQLSTATE class indicates an error. Table 12.4 shows a few common SQLSTATE values.

Table 12.4   Common SQLState Values

SQLState	Meaning
00000	Successful completion
01004	Warning string data, right truncation (that is, you tried to select 20 bytes into a 10-byte buffer)
23000	Integrity constraint violation (for example, you tried to add a duplicate key value into a unique index)
42000	Syntax error or access rule violation
HY010	Function sequence error
42S02	Base table (or view) not found

The second piece of information returned by SQLError() is a native error number. The driver returns the native error number—you have to know what kind of database your application is connected to before you can make sense of the native error numbers. Not all drivers return native error numbers.

The most useful information returned by SQLError() is the text of an error message. The last three parameters to SQLError() are used to retrieve the error message. The messageText parameter points to an array of SQLCHARs. This array should be SQL_MAX_MESSAGE_LENGTH+1 bytes long. messageTextLength tells SQLError() how many bytes it can write into *messageText. SQLError() writes the number of bytes required to contain the message text into the SQLSMALLINT pointed to by the requiredLength[3] parameter.

---

[2] The SQLError() will fail if you give it a bad handle or if there are no more messages to report to the application.

Listing 12.2 shows the `client1.c` example, fleshed out with some error-handling code.

Listing 12.2   odbc/`client2.c`

```
 1 /* client2.c */
 2
 3 #include <sql.h>
 4 #include <sqlext.h>
 5 #include <sqltypes.h>
 6 #include <stdio.h>
 7
 8 typedef enum { FALSE, TRUE } bool;
 9
10 static bool SQL_OK( SQLRETURN result )
11 {
12   if( result == SQL_SUCCESS || result == SQL_SUCCESS_WITH_INFO )
13     return( TRUE );
14   else
15     return( FALSE );
16 }
17
```

You've already seen the `SQL_OK()` function—it simply checks for the two success codes returned by ODBC.

```
18 static bool printErrors( SQLHENV   envHandle,
19                          SQLHDBC   conHandle,
20                          SQLHSTMT  stmtHandle )
21 {
22   SQLRETURN    result;
23   SQLCHAR      sqlState[6];
24   SQLINTEGER   nativeError;
25   SQLSMALLINT  requiredLength;
26   SQLCHAR      messageText[SQL_MAX_MESSAGE_LENGTH+1];
27
28   do
29   {
30     result = SQLError( envHandle,
31                        conHandle,
32                        stmtHandle,
```

[3] Many API functions need to return variable-length information—somehow, the caller must know how much space to allocate for the return information. A common solution to this problem is to call a function twice. When you make the first call, you tell the function that you allocated 0 bytes for the variable-length information. The function tells you how much space is required by setting something like the `requiredLength` parameter described previously. After you know how much space is required, you allocate the required number of bytes and call the function a second time. In the case of `SQLError()`, the `requiredLength` parameter is pretty pointless. We can't call `SQLError()` more than once per diagnostic because the diagnostic is discarded as soon as `SQLError()` retrieves it from the given handle.

```
33                        sqlState,
34                        &nativeError,
35                        messageText,
36                        sizeof( messageText ),
37                        &requiredLength );
38
39      if( SQL_OK( result ))
40        {
41          printf( "SQLState    = %s\n", sqlState );
42          printf( "Native error = %d\n", nativeError );
43          printf( "Message text = %s\n", messageText );
44        }
45    } while( SQL_OK( result ));
46  }
47
```

The printErrors() function is new. You call SQLError() until it returns a failure code. Why would you call SQLError() multiple times? Because each ODBC function can return multiple errors. Remember, each time SQLError() returns successfully, it removes a single diagnostic from the given handle. If you don't retrieve all the errors from a handle, they will be discarded (and lost) the next time you use that handle.

```
48  int main( int argc, char * argv[] )
49  {
50    SQLRETURN    res;
51    SQLHENV      env;
52    SQLHDBC      con;
53    SQLCHAR      fullConnectStr[SQL_MAX_OPTION_STRING_LENGTH];
54    SQLSMALLINT requiredLength;
55
56    res = SQLAllocHandle( SQL_HANDLE_ENV, SQL_NULL_HANDLE, &env );
57
58    if( SQL_OK( res ))
59    {
60      res = SQLSetEnvAttr( env,
61                           SQL_ATTR_ODBC_VERSION,
62                           (SQLPOINTER)SQL_OV_ODBC2,
63                           0 );
64      if( !SQL_OK( res ))
65      {
66        printErrors( env, SQL_NULL_HDBC, SQL_NULL_HSTMT );
67        exit( -1 );
68      }
69
70      res = SQLAllocHandle( SQL_HANDLE_DBC, env, &con );
71      if( !SQL_OK( res ))
72      {
73        printErrors( env, SQL_NULL_HDBC, SQL_NULL_HSTMT );
74        exit( -2 );
75      }
76
```

```
77      res = SQLDriverConnect( con,
78                              (SQLHWND)NULL,
79                              argv[1], SQL_NTS,
80                              fullConnectStr,
81                              sizeof( fullConnectStr ),
82                              &requiredLength,
83                              SQL_DRIVER_NOPROMPT );
84
85
86      if( !SQL_OK( res ))
87      {
88        printErrors( SQL_NULL_HENV, con, SQL_NULL_HSTMT );
89        exit( -3 );
90      }
91
92      printf( "connection ok...disconnecting\n" );
93
94      res = SQLDisconnect( con );
95      if( !SQL_OK( res ))
96      {
97        printErrors( SQL_NULL_HENV, con, SQL_NULL_HSTMT );
98        exit( -4 );
99      }
100
101     res = SQLFreeHandle( SQL_HANDLE_DBC, con );
102     if( !SQL_OK( res ))
103     {
104       printErrors( SQL_NULL_HENV, con, SQL_NULL_HSTMT );
105       exit( -5 );
106     }
107
108     res = SQLFreeHandle( SQL_HANDLE_ENV, env );
109     if( !SQL_OK( res ))
110     {
111       printErrors( env, SQL_NULL_HDBC, SQL_NULL_HSTMT );
112       exit( -6 );
113     }
114   }
115
116   exit( 0 );
117
118 }
```

There are three new features in the main() function.

First, you'll notice that I have littered the code with calls to printErrors(). You call printErrors() any time an ODBC function returns a failure status. You could also call printErrors() when you get a SQL_SUCCESS_WITH_INFO status, but in most cases, the extra information is uninteresting.

Notice that you exit as soon an error is encountered. Each call to exit() specifies a different value: If the program succeeds, you return 0; in all other cases, you return a unique negative number. The return value is given to the calling program (usually a shell) and is used to check for success or failure.

The other thing that's different between this version of *main()* and the version that I included in *client1.c* is that you use the *SQLDriverConnect()* function instead of *SQLConnect()*. The *SQLDriverConnect()* function is a more powerful version of *SQLConnect()*. Whereas *SQLConnect()* allows you to specify three connection properties (the data source name, user id, and password), *SQLDriverConnect()* can accept an arbitrary number of properties. In fact, the following two calls are (roughly) equivalent:

```
SQLConnect( con, "MoviesDSN", SQL_NTS, "korry", SQL_NTS, "cows", SQL_NTS );
SQLDriverConnect( con, (SQLHWND)NULL,
                  "DSN=MoviesDSN;UID=korry;PWD=cows", SQL_NTS, ... );
```

Here is the function prototype for SQLDriverConnect():

```
SQLRETURN SQLDriverConnect(
    SQLHDBC        connectionHandle,
    SQLHWND        windowHandle,
    SQLCHAR      * connectStrIn,
    SQLCHAR      * connectStrOut,
    SQLSMALLINT    connectStrOutMax,
    SQLSMALLINT  * requiredBytes,
    SQLUSMALLINT   driverCompletion )
```

The purpose of the first argument is pretty obvious—you provide the connection handle that you want to connect.

The second argument might seem a bit mysterious—what's a SQLHWND, and why would I need one to connect to a database? One of the differences between SQLDriverConnect() and SQLConnect() is that SQLDriverConnect() can prompt the user for more connection parameters. If you are running a graphical client application, you would expect to see a pop-up dialog if the database that you are connecting to requires more information. The SQLHWND parameter is used to provide a parent window handle that the driver can use to display a dialog. Under Windows, a SQLHWND is really a window handle (that is, a HWND). There is no clear winner in the Unix GUI wars, so there is no standard data type that represents a window handle. The driver manager ignores the windowHandle parameter and just passes it along to the driver. Very few Unix-hosted ODBC drivers support a connection dialog when using SQLDriverConnect(). One driver that does support a connection dialog is the IBM DB2 driver. If you are calling SQLDriverConnect() to connect to a DB2 database, you would pass in a Motif widget handle as the windowHandle parameter (if you are connecting to a DB2 database under Windows, you would pass in a HWND). Drivers that don't provide a connection dialog return an error if the connectStrIn parameter doesn't contain all the required information.

The third argument to SQLDriverConnect() is an ODBC connection string (this is *not* the same as a libpq connection string). An ODBC connection string is a semicolon-delimited collection of keyword=value properties. The ODBC driver manager looks for the DSN property to determine which data source you want to connect to. After the driver is loaded, the driver manager passes all the properties to the driver. The PostgreSQL driver understands the following properties shown in Table 12.5.

Table 12.5 **PostgreSQL/ODBC Connection String Properties**

Property	Description
DSN	Data source name
UID	User ID
PWD	Password
SERVER	Server's IP address or hostname
PORT	TCP port number on server
DATABASE	PostgreSQL database name

(The PostgreSQL ODBC driver supports other connection properties. See the documentation that comes with the driver for a complete list.)

The next three arguments (connectStrOut, connectStrOutMax, and requiredBytes) are used to return a complete connection string to the client application. If you successfully connect to a database, the driver will populate *connectStrOut with a null-terminated string that contains all the connection properties that the driver used. For example, if you call SQLDriverConnect() with the following connection string:

```
"DSN=MoviesDSN; UID=korry; PWD=cows"
```

the driver will return a string such as

```
DSN=MoviesDsn;
DATABASE=movies;
SERVER=localhost;
PORT=5432;
UID=korry;
PWD=;
READONLY=No;
PROTOCOL=6.4;
FAKEOIDINDEX=No;
SHOWOIDCOLUMN=No;
ROWVERSIONING=No;
SHOWSYSTEMTABLES=No;
CONNSETTINGS=';
```

This is assuming that the video-store data source uses a PostgreSQL driver. You may have noticed that the complete connection string is composed from the set of connection properties that this driver understands—most of the properties are defaulted from the data source.

If the buffer that you provide is too short for the entire connection string, SQLDriverConnect() will truncate the string and will return the required length in *requiredBytes.

You use the final parameter to SQLDriverConnect() to indicate how much assistance you want if the connection string is incomplete. Acceptable values for driverCompletion are shown in Table 12.6.

Table 12.6   **Values for** `SQLDriverConnect().driverCompletion`

Value	Description
`SQL_DRIVER_PROMPT`	The user sees a connection dialog, even if it is not required.
`SQL_DRIVER_COMPLETE`	The user sees a connection dialog if the connection string does not contain all required information. The connection dialog prompts the user for required and optional connection properties.
`SQL_DRIVER_COMPLETE_REQUIRED`	The user sees a connection dialog if the connection string does not contain all required information. The connection dialog only prompts the user for required connection properties.
`SQL_DRIVER_NOPROMPT`	If the connection string does not contain all required information, `SQLDriverConnect()` will return `SQL_ERROR`, and the user will not be prompted (by the driver).

Most open-source ODBC drivers support only the `SQL_DRIVER_NOPROMPT` option. If you ask for a different completion type, it will be treated like `SQL_DRIVER_NOPROMPT`.

The last thing that I'll explain about this client is the teardown code. To properly clean up the client application, you have to disconnect the connection handle (using `SQLDisconnect()`) and then free the connection and environment handles using `SQLFreeHandle()`. The order in which you tear down connections is important. You won't be able to free the connection handle until you disconnect it. You won't be able to free an environment handle until all the connection handles have been disconnected and freed.

If you want to run this program, the single command-line argument is a `SQLDriverConnect()` connection string. For example:

```
$ ./client2 "DSN=MoviesDSN; UID=korry; PWD=cows"
```

In the next section, I'll introduce a new handle type—the `SQLHSTMT` statement handle. The parent of a `SQLHSTMT` is a connection handle. You must free all child statement handles before you can free a connection handle.

This section was rather long, but now you know how to connect to a database, how to detect errors, and how to properly tear down an ODBC connection. The next section describes how to process a simple query in an ODBC client.

Client 3—Processing Queries

When you execute a query using ODBC, your client will first send the query to the server, and then process the results.

The ODBC result-processing model is more complex than other PostgreSQL APIs. In the libpq, libpq++, and libpgeasy APIs, you send a query to the server and then call a function to access each field (in each row) in the result set.

An ODBC application generally uses a different scheme. After you send the query to the server, you *bind* each field in the result set to a variable in your application. After all the result fields are bound, you can fetch the individual rows in the result set—each time you fetch a new row, the bound variables are populated by ODBC.

Listing 12.3 shows you how to execute a query and display the results.

Listing 12.3 odbc/client3.c

```
 1 /* client3.c */
 2
 3 #include <sql.h>
 4 #include <sqlext.h>
 5 #include <sqltypes.h>
 6 #include <stdio.h>
 7
 8 typedef enum { FALSE, TRUE } bool;
 9
10 typedef struct
11 {
12   char          name[128+1];
13   SQLSMALLINT   nameLength;
14   SQLSMALLINT   dataType;
15   SQLUINTEGER   fieldLength;
16   SQLSMALLINT   scale;
17   SQLSMALLINT   nullable;
18   SQLINTEGER    displaySize;
19   int           headerLength;
20   SQLINTEGER    resultLength;
21   char        * value;
22 } resultField;
23
24 static void printResultSet( SQLHSTMT stmt );
25
```

The only thing that is new here is the resultField structure. I'll use an array of resultFields to process the result set. A note on terminology here: PostgreSQL documentation makes a minor distinction between a field and a column. Column refers to a column in a database, whereas field can refer to a column or a computed value. ODBC does not make this distinction. I tend to use the terms interchangeably.

```
26 static bool SQL_OK( SQLRETURN result )
27 {
28   if( result == SQL_SUCCESS || result == SQL_SUCCESS_WITH_INFO )
29     return( TRUE );
30   else
31     return( FALSE );
32 }
33
34 static bool printErrors( SQLHENV   envHandle,
35                          SQLHDBC   conHandle,
```

```
36                          SQLHSTMT stmtHandle )
37 {
38   SQLRETURN    result;
39   SQLCHAR      sqlState[6];
40   SQLINTEGER   nativeError;
41   SQLSMALLINT  requiredLength;
42   SQLCHAR      messageText[SQL_MAX_MESSAGE_LENGTH+1];
43
44   do
45   {
46     result = SQLError( envHandle,
47                        conHandle,
48                        stmtHandle,
49                        sqlState,
50                        &nativeError,
51                        messageText,
52                        sizeof( messageText ),
53                        &requiredLength );
54
55     if( SQL_OK( result ))
56       {
57         printf( "SQLState    = %s\n", sqlState );
58         printf( "Native error = %d\n", nativeError );
59         printf( "Message text = %s\n", messageText );
60       }
61   } while( SQL_OK( result ));
62 }
63
```

You've already seen SQL_OK() and printErrors() in the previous example, so I won't bother explaining them here.

```
64 static void executeStmt( SQLHDBC con, char * stmtText )
65 {
66   SQLHSTMT  stmt;
67
68   SQLAllocHandle( SQL_HANDLE_STMT, con, &stmt );
69
70   if( SQL_OK( SQLExecDirect( stmt, stmtText, SQL_NTS )))
71     printResultSet( stmt );
72   else
73     printErrors( SQL_NULL_HENV, SQL_NULL_HDBC, stmt );
74 }
```

The executeStmt() function is responsible for sending a query to the server. You start by allocating a new type of handle—a SQLHSTMT. A SQLHSTMT is a statement handle. The parent of a statement handle is always a connection handle (or a SQLHDBC).

After you have a statement handle, send the query to the server using SQLExecDirect(). SQLExecDirect() is pretty simple—you provide a statement handle, the text of the query that you want to send to the server, and the length of the query string (or SQL_NTS to indicate that the query text is a null-terminated string).

If SQLExecDirect() returns a success value, you call printResultSet() to process the result set.

```
75
76  static void printResultSet( SQLHSTMT stmt )
77  {
78    SQLSMALLINT   i;
79    SQLSMALLINT   columnCount;
80    resultField * fields;
81
82    //  First, examine the metadata for the
83    //  result set so that we know how many
84    //  fields we have and how much room we need for each.
85
86    SQLNumResultCols( stmt, &columnCount );
87
88    fields = (resultField *)calloc( columnCount+1,
89               sizeof( resultField ));
90
91    for( i = 1; i <= columnCount; i++ )
92    {
93      SQLDescribeCol( stmt,
94            i,
95            fields[i].name,
96            sizeof( fields[i].name ),
97            &fields[i].nameLength,
98            &fields[i].dataType,
99            &fields[i].fieldLength,
100           &fields[i].scale,
101           &fields[i].nullable );
102
103     SQLColAttribute( stmt,
104           i,
105           SQL_DESC_DISPLAY_SIZE,
106           NULL,
107           0,
108           NULL,
109           &fields[i].displaySize );
110
111
112     fields[i].value = (char *)malloc( fields[i].displaySize + 1 );
113
114     if( fields[i].nameLength > fields[i].displaySize )
115       fields[i].headerLength = fields[i].nameLength;
116     else
117       fields[i].headerLength = fields[i].displaySize;
118   }
119
```

```
120    //  Now print out the column headers
121
122    for( i = 1; i <= columnCount; i++ )
123    {
124      printf( "%-*s ", fields[i].headerLength, fields[i].name );
125    }
126    printf( "\n" );
127
128    //  Now fetch and display the results...
129
130    while( SQL_OK( SQLFetch( stmt )))
131    {
132      for( i = 1; i <= columnCount; i++)
133      {
134        SQLRETURN result;
135
136        result = SQLGetData( stmt,
137              i,
138              SQL_C_CHAR,
139              fields[i].value,
140              fields[i].displaySize,
141              &fields[i].resultLength );
142
143        if( fields[i].resultLength == SQL_NULL_DATA )
144          printf( "%-*s ", fields[i].headerLength, "" );
145        else
146          printf( "%-*s ", fields[i].headerLength, fields[i].value );
147      }
148      printf( "\n" );
149    }
150
151    for( i = 1; i <= columnCount; i++ )
152      free( fields[i].value );
153
154    free( fields );
155
156 }
157
```

The printResultSet() function is somewhat complex. It starts by building up an array
of resultField structures to keep track of the metadata for the query that was just executed.

You first call SQLNumResultCols() to determine how many fields (or columns) will
appear in the result set. After you know how many fields you will be processing, you
allocate an array of resultField structures—one structure for each field (and one extra
to simplify the code).

Next, you call two metadata functions so that you know what kind of information is
being returned for each field. The SQLDescribeCol() function returns the column
name, data type, binary field length, scale (used for numeric data types), and nullability

for a given field. Notice that field indexes start with 1, not 0—so, the loop goes from 1 to `columnCount` rather than the usual 0 to `columnCount-1`; I won't use `fields[0]` for the sake of simplicity.

The `SQLColAttribute()` function returns a specific metadata attribute for the given column (i). You will retrieve each field in the form of a null-terminated string, so you need to know the maximum display length for each field. The `SQL_DESC__DISPLAY_SIZE` attribute is just what you need.

The `SQLDescribeCol()` and `SQLColAttribute()` functions both return column-related metadata. `SQLDescribeCol()` is a convenient function that returns the most commonly used metadata properties. Calling `SQLDescribeCol()` is equivalent to

```
SQLColAttribute( stmt, column, SQL_DESC_NAME, ... );
SQLColAttribute( stmt, column, SQL_DESC_TYPE, ... );
SQLColAttribute( stmt, column, SQL_DESC_LENGTH, ... );
SQLColAttribute( stmt, column, SQL_DESC_SCALE, ... );
SQLColAttribute( stmt, column, SQL_DESC_NULLABLE, ... );
```

After retrieving and storing the metadata for a column, this function allocates a buffer large enough to hold the data for the column in the form of a null-terminated string. It also computes the header length. You want to print each column in a horizontal space large enough to hold either the column name or the column contents, whichever is longer.

After printing out the column headings (lines 122-126), we start processing the contents of the result set. The `SQLFetch()` function will fetch the next row within the result set associated with the given `SQLHSTMT`. `SQLFetch()` will return the value `SQL_NO_DATA` when you have exhausted the result set.

ODBC Metadata Types

So far, we have looked only at metadata that describes a result set. Because ODBC is designed as a portability layer between your application and the backend database, ODBC provides a rich set of metadata functions. First, you can retrieve a list of the data sources defined on your system using the `SQLDataSources()` function. The `SQLDrivers()` function will retrieve a list of installed drivers.

After you have connected to a data source, you can retrieve a list of supported data types by calling `SQLGetTypeInfo()`. This function returns the list as a result set—you use `SQLFetch()` and `SQLGetData()` (described later) to obtain the list.

You can use `SQLFunctions()` to determine which of the ODBC API functions are supported by a given driver. The PostgreSQL ODBC Driver is (currently) an ODBC 2.5 driver and does not directly support ODBC 3.0 functions. The PostgreSQL driver does not support a few of the ODBC 2.5 functions (such as `SQLProcedures()`, `SQLProcedureColumns()`, and `SQLBrowseConnect()`).

You can also ask the driver whether it supports various SQL syntax features. For example, if you call `SQLGetInfo( ..., SQL_CREATE_TABLE, ... )`, you can determine which CREATE TABLE clauses are supported by the database's CREATE TABLE statement. The `SQLGetInfo()` function also returns version information, as shown in Table 12.7.

You can use `SQLGetInfo(..., SQL_TXN_CAPABLE, ...)` to find out about the transaction-processing capabilities of a database.

Table 12.7   **Version Information Returned by** SQLGetInfo()

SQLGetInfo() InfoType **Argument**	**Return Information**
SQL_DBMS_VER	Database version (for example, PostgreSQL 8.0)
SQL_DM_VER	Driver manager version
SQL_DRIVER_NAME	Driver name
SQL_DRIVER_ODBC_VER	ODBC version that driver conforms to
SQL_DRIVER_VER	Driver version
SQL_SERVER_NAME	Name of server

If SQLFetch() succeeds, you retrieve each column in the current row using the SQLGetData() function, which has the following prototype:

```
SQLRETURN SQLGetData( SQLHSTMT     stmtHandle,
                      SQLUSMALLINT columnNumber,
                      SQLSMALLINT  desiredDataType,
                      SQLPOINTER   destination,
                      SQLINTEGER   destinationLength,
                      SQLINTEGER * resultLength );
```

When you call SQLGetData(),you want ODBC to put the data into your fields[i].value buffer so you pass that address (and the displaySize). Passing in a desiredDataType of SQL_C_CHAR tells ODBC to return each column in the form of a null-terminated string. SQLGetData() returns the actual field length in fields[i].resultLength—if the field is NULL, you will get back the value SQL_NULL_DATA.

Lines 143-146 print each field (left-justified within a fields[i].headerLength space).

Finally, clean up after yourself by freeing the value buffers and then the resultField array:

```
158 int main( int argc, char * argv[] )
159 {
160     SQLRETURN    res;
161     SQLHENV      env;
162     SQLHDBC      con;
163     SQLCHAR      fullConnectStr[SQL_MAX_OPTION_STRING_LENGTH];
164     SQLSMALLINT requiredLength;
165
166     res = SQLAllocHandle( SQL_HANDLE_ENV, SQL_NULL_HANDLE, &env );
167
168     if( SQL_OK( res ))
169     {
170       res = SQLSetEnvAttr( env,
171                            SQL_ATTR_ODBC_VERSION,
172                            (SQLPOINTER)SQL_OV_ODBC2,
173                            0 );
174       if( !SQL_OK( res ))
175       {
176         printErrors( env, SQL_NULL_HDBC, SQL_NULL_HSTMT );
177         exit( -1 );
178       }
```

```
179
180     res = SQLAllocHandle( SQL_HANDLE_DBC, env, &con );
181     if( !SQL_OK( res ))
182     {
183       printErrors( env, SQL_NULL_HDBC, SQL_NULL_HSTMT );
184       exit( -2 );
185     }
186
187     res = SQLDriverConnect( con,
188                             (SQLHWND)NULL,
189                             argv[1], SQL_NTS,
190                             fullConnectStr,
191                             sizeof( fullConnectStr ),
192                             &requiredLength,
193                             SQL_DRIVER_NOPROMPT );
194
195
196     if( !SQL_OK( res ))
197     {
198       printErrors( SQL_NULL_HENV, con, SQL_NULL_HSTMT );
199       exit( -3 );
200     }
201
202     printf( "connection ok\n" );
203
204     executeStmt( con, argv[2] );
205
206     res = SQLDisconnect( con );
207     if( !SQL_OK( res ))
208     {
209       printErrors( SQL_NULL_HENV, con, SQL_NULL_HSTMT );
210       exit( -4 );
211     }
212
213     res = SQLFreeHandle( SQL_HANDLE_DBC, con );
214     if( !SQL_OK( res ))
215     {
216       printErrors( SQL_NULL_HENV, con, SQL_NULL_HSTMT );
217       exit( -5 );
218     }
219
220     res = SQLFreeHandle( SQL_HANDLE_ENV, env );
221     if( !SQL_OK( res ))
222     {
223       printErrors( env, SQL_NULL_HDBC, SQL_NULL_HSTMT );
224       exit( -6 );
225     }
226   }
227
228   exit( 0 );
229
230 }
```

The main() function for client3.c is identical to that in client2.c.

When you run this program, the single command-line argument should be a SQLDRIVERCONNECT() connection string:

```
$ ./client3 "DSN=MoviesDSN; UID=korry; PWD=cows"
```

This example has shown you the easiest way to execute a query and process results in an ODBC application, but using SQLExecDirect() and SQLGetData() will not always give you the best performance. The next client shows a method that is more complex, but performs better.

Client 4—An Interactive Query Processor

I'll finish this chapter by developing a general purpose, interactive query processor. In this example, I'll describe the SQLPrepare()/SQLExec() query execution method. Finally, I'll show you a way to process result sets more efficiently.

This example is based on the libpq++/qt-sql.cpp client from Chapter 10, "The New PostgreSQL C++ API—libpqxx." Rather than showing you the entire application again, I'll just explain the differences—refer to Chapter 10 for a complete explanation of the original application.

In this application, you can enter arbitrary SQL commands; the result set for SELECT statements appears in a table and the results for other commands display in a status bar.

The first thing that you need to change in this client is the MyTable class. The new MyTable class includes an environment handle (env) and a connection handle (db).

```
1 /* qt-sql.h */
2
3 class MyTable : public QTable
4 {
5 public:
6
7     MyTable( QWidget * parent );
8
9     SQLHDBC     db;
10    SQLHENV     env;
11
12    void buildTable( SQLHSTMT stmt );
13    void displayErrors( SQLSMALLINT type, SQLHANDLE handle );
14
15 };
```

Next, I'll borrow the resultField structure from the previous example. This structure contains metadata for a field and a pointer to a buffer (value) that holds the field data as you retrieve each row.

```
// File qt-sql.cpp (partial listing - see downloads for complete text)
22 typedef struct
23 {
24   char          name[128+1];
25   SQLSMALLINT   nameLength;
26   SQLSMALLINT   dataType;
```

```
27    SQLUINTEGER    fieldLength;
28    SQLSMALLINT    scale;
29    SQLSMALLINT    nullable;
30    SQLINTEGER     displaySize;
31    int            headerLength;
32    SQLINTEGER     resultLength;
33    char        * value;
34  } resultField;
```

Now let's look at the MyTable constructor:

```
// File qt-sql.cpp (partial listing - see downloads for complete text)
109 MyTable::MyTable( QWidget * parent )
110   : QTable( parent )
111 {
112   //
113   //  Create a database connection...
114   //
115   SQLRETURN  res;
116
117   res = SQLAllocHandle( SQL_HANDLE_ENV,
118           SQL_NULL_HANDLE,
119           &env );
120   if( !SQL_OK( res ))
121   {
122     displayErrors( SQL_HANDLE_ENV, env );
123     exit( -1 );
124   }
125
126   SQLSetEnvAttr( env,
127       SQL_ATTR_ODBC_VERSION,
128       (SQLPOINTER)SQL_OV_ODBC2,
129       0 );
130
131   res = SQLAllocHandle( SQL_HANDLE_DBC,
132         env,
133         &db );
134
135   if( !SQL_OK( res ))
136   {
137     displayErrors( SQL_HANDLE_ENV, env );
138     exit( -1 );
139   }
140
141   res = SQLConnect( db,
142           (SQLCHAR *)qApp->argv()[1], SQL_NTS,
143           (SQLCHAR *)qApp->argv()[2], SQL_NTS,
144           (SQLCHAR *)qApp->argv()[3], SQL_NTS );
145
146   if( !SQL_OK( res ))
147   {
148     displayErrors( SQL_HANDLE_DBC, db );
```

```
149    exit( -1 );
150  }
151
152
153  // We don't have any table-oriented results to
154  // show yet, so hide the table.
155  //
156  setNumRows( 0 );
157  setNumCols( 0 );
158 }
```

The MyTable constructor should be familiar by now. You initialize an environment handle, inform ODBC that you are an ODBC version 2 (SQL_OV_ODBC2) application, and then try to connect to the database identified on the command line. When this application is invoked, it expects three command-line arguments: a data source name, a username, and a password. The qApp->argv() function returns a pointer to the array of command-line arguments. If the connection attempt fails, you call the displayErrors() function to display any error messages. displayErrors() is shown here:

```
// File qt-sql.cpp (partial listing - see downloads for complete text)
160 void MyTable::displayErrors( SQLSMALLINT type, SQLHANDLE handle )
161 {
162   SQLHDBC   dbc  = SQL_NULL_HDBC;
163   SQLHENV   env  = SQL_NULL_HENV;
164   SQLHSTMT  stmt = SQL_NULL_HSTMT;
165
166   switch( type )
167   {
168     case SQL_HANDLE_ENV:  env  = (SQLHENV)handle; break;
169     case SQL_HANDLE_DBC:  dbc  = (SQLHENV)handle; break;
170     case SQL_HANDLE_STMT: stmt = (SQLHSTMT)handle; break;
171   }
172
173   SQLRETURN    result;
174   SQLCHAR      sqlState[6];
175   SQLINTEGER   nativeError;
176   SQLSMALLINT  requiredLength;
177   SQLCHAR      messageText[SQL_MAX_MESSAGE_LENGTH+1];
178
179   QDialog     * dlg  = new QDialog( this, 0, TRUE );
180   QVBoxLayout * vbox = new QVBoxLayout( dlg );
181   QPushButton * ok   = new QPushButton( "Ok", dlg );
182
183   setCaption( "Error" );
184   QMultiLineEdit * edit = new QMultiLineEdit( dlg );
185
186   vbox->addWidget( edit );
187   vbox->addWidget( ok );
188
189   connect( ok, SIGNAL( clicked()), dlg, SLOT( accept()));
190
```

```
191   edit->setReadOnly( TRUE );
192
193   do
194   {
195     result = SQLError( env,
196                        dbc,
197                        stmt,
198                        sqlState,
199                        &nativeError,
200                        messageText,
201                        sizeof( messageText ),
202                        &requiredLength );
203
204     if( SQL_OK( result ))
205     {
206       edit->append((char *)messageText );
207       edit->append( "\n" );
208     }
209   } while( SQL_OK( result ));
210
211   dlg->adjustSize();
212   dlg->exec();
213
214 }
```

The `displayErrors()` function is complicated by the fact that you may get multiple error messages from ODBC—you can't use the usual QT `MessageBox` class to display multiple errors. Instead, we construct a dialog that contains an edit control (to contain the error messages) and an OK button. Figure 12.9 shows a typical error message.

Figure 12.9 Sample error message.

After the dialog object has been built, you call `SQLError()` to retrieve the error messages and append each message into the edit control. When you have retrieved the final error message, you display the dialog by calling the `dlg->exec()` function.

Now let's look at the code that used to execute a command:

```
// File qt-sql.cpp (partial listing - see downloads for complete text)
216 void MyMain::execute( void )
217 {
218   //  This function is called whenever the user
219   //  presses the 'Execute' button (or whenever
220   //  the user presses the Return key while the
221   //  edit control has the keyboard focus)
222   SQLHDBC   db = table->db;
```

```
223    SQLHSTMT   stmt;
224    SQLRETURN  res;
225    QString    qcmd = edit->text();
226    SQLCHAR * cmd;
227
228    // Convert the query command from Unicode
229    // into an 8-bit, SQLCHAR format
230
231    cmd = (SQLCHAR *)qcmd.latin1();
232
233    SQLAllocHandle( SQL_HANDLE_STMT, db, &stmt );
234
235    res = SQLPrepare( stmt, (SQLCHAR *)cmd, SQL_NTS );
236
237    if( !SQL_OK( res ))
238    {
239      table->displayErrors( SQL_HANDLE_STMT, stmt );
240    }
241    else
242    {
243
244      if( SQL_OK( SQLExecute( stmt )))
245      {
246        SQLSMALLINT  columnCount;
247
248        SQLNumResultCols( stmt, &columnCount );
249
250        if( columnCount == 0 )
251        {
252          SQLINTEGER  rowCount;
253          SQLRowCount( stmt, &rowCount );
254
255          if( rowCount == -1 )
256            status->message( "Ok" );
257          else
258          {
259            QString m( "Ok, %1 rows affected" );
260
261            status->message( m.arg((int)rowCount ));
262          }
263        }
264        else
265        {
266          status->message( "Ok..." );
267          table->buildTable( stmt );
268        }
269      }
270      else
271        table->displayErrors( SQL_HANDLE_STMT, stmt );
272
273    }
```

```
274
275    SQLFreeHandle( SQL_HANDLE_STMT, stmt );
276  }
```

`MyMain::execute()` starts by making a copy of the query (`edit->text()`) and converts the string from Unicode (Qt's native character encoding) into ASCII (the format expected by ODBC).

Next, you initialize a statement handle.

In the previous example (`client3.c`), I used the `SQLExecDirect()` function to execute a SQL command. In this function, I am using a different execution model—the Prepare/Execute model.

You should use the Prepare/Execute model if you are expecting to execute the same SQL command multiple times, possibly substituting different values for each execution. Some ODBC-compliant databases support "parameter markers" within a SQL command. You generally use parameter markers when you are using the Prepare/Execute model. Here is an example of a command that contains parameter markers:

```
insert into customers values ( ?, ?, ? );
```

Each question mark in this command represents a parameter whose value is provided each time the command is executed. (The parameters are numbered—the leftmost question mark is parameter number 1, the next mark is parameter number 2, and so on.)

The advantage to the Prepare/Execute model is that you send the command to the server only once, but you can execute the command as many times as needed. Most ODBC-compliant databases parse the command and create an execution plan when you call `SQLPrepare()`. When you want to execute the statement, you *bind* each parameter to a memory address, place the appropriate value at that address, and then call `SQLExecute()` to execute the command. When you use the Prepare/Execute model with a database that supports parameter markers, you can gain a huge performance boost.

It's not really appropriate to use the Prepare/Execute model to process ad hoc queries. Prepare/Execute is useful when you plan to execute the same SQL command multiple times. You can also use Prepare/Execute to simplify your code: Factor the code that generates a command into a function separate from the code that generates data.

The Prepare/Execute model has been part of the ODBC architecture for quite a while, but it's a recent addition to the PostgreSQL server. In older versions of PostgreSQL, the ODBC driver simulated the Prepare/Execute process. If you're using a recent version of the ODBC driver (version 1.45 or later) and a recent PostgreSQL server (7.3 or later), and you have enabled the `UseServerSidePrepare` option, the ODBC driver implements the Prepare/Execute model by executing a PREPARE command followed by an EXECUTE command.

After you have successfully prepared and executed the command entered by the user, you are ready to process the results.

The first thing you need to know is whether the command could have returned any rows. (In other words, was this a SELECT command.) ODBC version 2.x does not provide a function that tells you what kind of SQL command you just executed, but you can use the `SQLNumResultCols()` to infer that information. If `SQLNumResultCols()` tells you that there are no columns in the result set, you can assume that you have not executed a SELECT command. In that case, you use `SQLRowCount()` to determine how many rows (if any) were

affected by the command. For UPDATE, INSERT, and DELETE statements, SQLRowCount()
returns a value (greater than or equal to zero) indicating how many rows were affected. For
other types of statements (such as BEGIN WORK or CREATE TABLE), SQLRowCount() returns -
1. Use the value returned by SQLRowCount() to determine how to update the status bar.

When you execute a SELECT command, you call the MyTable::buildtable() function to copy the result set into a table:

```
// File qt-sql.cpp (partial listing - see downloads for complete text)
278 void MyTable::buildTable( SQLHSTMT stmt )
279 {
280   // This function is called to fill in
281   // the table control.  We want to fill
282   // the table with the result set.
283   SQLSMALLINT   i;
284   SQLSMALLINT   columnCount;
285   resultField * fields;
286
287   setNumRows( 0 );
288   setNumCols( 0 );
289
290   // First, examine the metadata for the
291   // result set so that we know how much
292   // room we need for each column.
293
294   SQLNumResultCols( stmt, &columnCount );
295
296   fields = new resultField[ columnCount+1 ];
297
298   setNumCols( columnCount );
299
300   for( i = 1; i <= columnCount; i++ )
301   {
302     SQLDescribeCol( stmt,
303           i,
304           (SQLCHAR *)fields[i].name,
305           sizeof( fields[i].name ),
306           &fields[i].nameLength,
307           &fields[i].dataType,
308           &fields[i].fieldLength,
309           &fields[i].scale,
310           &fields[i].nullable );
311
312     SQLColAttribute( stmt,
313           i,
314           SQL_DESC_DISPLAY_SIZE,
315           NULL,
316           0,
317           NULL,
318           &fields[i].displaySize );
```

```
319
320     fields[i].value = (char *)malloc( fields[i].displaySize+1 );
321
322     // Build the column headers as we go
323     horizontalHeader()->setLabel( i-1, fields[i].name );
324
325   }
326
327   //  Bind the fields to our buffers
328   for( i = 1; i <= columnCount; i++ )
329   {
330     SQLRETURN res;
331
332     res = SQLBindCol( stmt,
333                 i,
334                 SQL_C_CHAR,
335                 fields[i].value,
336                 fields[i].displaySize+1,
337                 &fields[i].resultLength );
338
339     if( !SQL_OK( res ))
340       displayErrors( SQL_HANDLE_STMT, stmt );
341   }
342
343   //
344   //  Now, put the data into the table...
345   //
346   int       row = 0;
347   SQLRETURN res;
348
349   while( SQL_OK(( res =  SQLFetch( stmt ))))
350   {
351     if( res == SQL_SUCCESS_WITH_INFO )
352       displayErrors( SQL_HANDLE_STMT, stmt );
353
354     setNumRows( row+1 );
355
356     for( int col = 1; col <= columnCount; col++ )
357     {
358       setText( row, col-1, fields[col].value );
359     }
360
361     row++;
362
363   }
364 }
```

`buildTable()` starts by initializing the table to zero rows and zero columns. Next, you use `SQLNumResultCols()` to determine how many columns are in the result set. You allocate a `resultField` structure for each column.

Then, you build an array of `resultField` structures (the same way you did in the `odbc/client3.c` example) using `SQLDescribeCol()` and `SQLColAttribute()`. You also populate the table's column headers as you process the metadata.

Rather than using `SQLGetData()` to retrieve field values, I'm going to bind each column to a memory buffer. Then, as you fetch each row from the server, ODBC automatically copies the data values into your bind buffers. Here is the function prototype for `SQLBindCol()`:

```
SQLRETURN SQLBindCol( SQLHSTMT      stmtHandle,
                      SQLUSMALLINT  columnNumber,
                      SQLSMALLINT   bindDataType,
                      SQLPOINTER    bindBuffer,
                      SQLINTEGER    bindBufferLength,
                      SQLLEN      * resultLength )
```

When you call `SQLBindCol()`, you are binding a column (`columnNumber`) to a memory address (`bindBuffer` and `bindBufferLength`) and asking ODBC to convert the field data into a specific data type (`bindDataType`). You can also provide a pointer to a result length – after you fetch a row, the result length will contain the length of the data value (or `SQL_NULL_DATA` if the field is NULL). In general, you will get better performance results if you bind each column rather than using `SQLGetData()`. You have to call `SQLGetData()` for each column in *each row*, but you have to bind each column only once regardless of the number of rows you actually fetch.

After you have bound all the columns in the result set, you can start fetching. For each row that you fetch, you increase the table size by one row (this isn't very efficient, but ODBC does not give you a way to determine the size of the result set without fetching each row).

Finally, use the `QTable::setText()` member function to insert each column into the table.

Figure 12.10 shows you an example of what you would see when you run the `odbc/qt-sql` sample.

That's it! The rest of the `qt-sql` application is explained in Chapter 10.

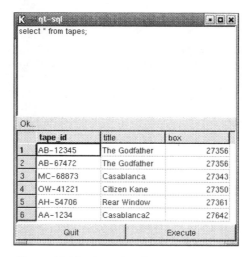

Figure 12.10 Running the `qt-sql` application.

Summary

ODBC is a complex API. I have covered only the basics of ODBC programming in this chapter. If you decide to write a client application using ODBC, I strongly recommend that you obtain one (or more) of the books in the "Resources" section that follows. Several of these books are devoted entirely to ODBC programming, whereas this chapter gives a short introduction aimed at writing simple applications against the PostgreSQL ODBC driver.

Resources

1. Stinson, Barry. *PostgreSQL Essential Reference*. New Riders Publishing, 2002.

   Chapter 13 provides a brief description of how to install unixODBC and create a PostgreSQL data source.

2. Gulutzan, Peter and Pelzer, Trudy. *SQL-99 Complete, Really*. R&D Books, 1999.

   The ODBC standard is paralleled by the SQL-99 standard. This book provides a complete description of SQL-99. Most of the information in this book applies directly to an ODBC application.

3. Sanders, Roger E. *DB2 Universal Database Call Level Interface Developer's Guide*. McGraw-Hill, 1999.

   The DB2 Call Level Interface is nearly identical to the ODBC API; as in the previous reference, this book translates almost entirely into ODBC.

4. Geiger, Kyle. *Inside ODBC*. Microsoft Press, 1995.

   This book is currently out of print, but if you can find a copy, I highly recommend it. *Inside ODBC* includes an interesting history of ODBC development within Microsoft and describes how ODBC works from the inside.

Using PostgreSQL from a Java Client Application

If you read the previous chapter, you know that ODBC is a technology that can connect a single application to different databases without making any changes to the application. ODBC is popular in the C, C++, Visual Basic, and VBA worlds. The folks at Sun Microsystems developed a similar technology for Java applications: JDBC. Many people will tell you that JDBC is an acronym for "Java Database Connectivity," but according to Sun, "*JDBC is the trademarked name and is not an acronym.*"

JDBC is an API that makes it easy for Java applications to connect to a database, send commands to the database, and retrieve the results. JDBC is packaged as a collection of classes[1]. To start working with JDBC, you use the `DriverManager` class to obtain a `Driver` object. After you have a `Driver`, you make a connection to the database, which results in a `Connection` object. Using a `Connection`, you can create a `Statement`. When you execute a command (using a `Statement` object), you get back a `ResultSet`. JDBC also provides classes that let you retrieve `ResultSetMetaData` and `DatabaseMetaData`.

In this chapter, I won't try to explain all the features of Java's JDBC technology—covering that topic thoroughly would easily require another book. Instead, I'll show you how to use the PostgreSQL JDBC driver. I'll briefly discuss each of the classes I mentioned earlier and show you how to use them.

JDBC Architecture Overview

JDBC is similar in structure to ODBC. A JDBC application is composed of multiple layers, as shown in Figure 13.1.

---

[1] I use the term class rather loosely in this chapter. JDBC is actually a collection of classes and interfaces. The distinction is not important to JDBC application developers—we use interfaces as if they were classes. Programmers who are building new JDBC drivers will need to understand the distinction.

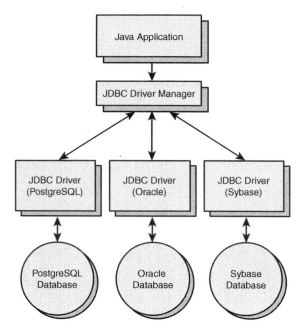

Figure 13.1 JDBC architecture.

The topmost layer in this model is the Java application. Java applications are portable—you can run a Java application without modification on any system that has a Java run-time environment installed. A Java application that uses JDBC can talk to many databases with few, if any, modifications. Like ODBC, JDBC provides a consistent way to connect to a database, execute commands, and retrieve the results. Also like ODBC, JDBC does not enforce a common command language—you can use Oracle-specific syntax when connected to an Oracle server and PostgreSQL-specific syntax when connected to a PostgreSQL server. If you stick to a common subset, you can achieve remarkable portability for your applications.

The JDBC `DriverManager`

The JDBC `DriverManager` class is responsible for locating the JDBC driver that your application requires. When a client application requests a database connection, the request is expressed in the form of a URL (Uniform Resource Locator). A typical URL might look like `jdbc:postgresql:movies`. A JDBC URL is similar to the URLs that you use with a web browser (http://www.postgresql.org, for example). I'll explain the JDBC URL syntax in detail a bit later.

The JDBC `Driver`

As each driver is loaded into a Java Virtual Machine (VM), it registers itself with the JDBC `DriverManager`. When an application requests a connection, the `DriverManager` asks each `Driver` whether it can connect to the database specified in the given URL. As soon as it finds an appropriate `Driver`, the search stops and the `Driver` attempts to make a connection to the database. If the connection attempt fails, the `Driver` will throw an `SQLException` to the application. If the connection completes successfully, the `Driver` creates a `Connection` object and returns it to the application.

The JDBC 2.0 architecture introduced another method for establishing database connections: the `DataSource`. A `DataSource` is a named collection of connection properties that can be used to load a `Driver` and create a `Connection`. I'll briefly discuss the `DataSource` class a bit later in this chapter.

The JDBC-Compliant Database

The bottom layer of the JDBC model is the database. The PostgreSQL `Driver` class (and other JDBC classes) translates application commands into PostgreSQL network requests and translates the results back into JDBC object form.

Prerequisites

If you want to build the sample applications in this chapter, you will need a Java compiler and a Java runtime environment. If you are using Windows, Linux, or Solaris, you can obtain the Java SDK (software development kit) and runtime environment from Sun Microsystems (http://java.sun.com). For other environments, search the web or contact your vendor.

I'll use a simple `makefile` to build the JDBC sample applications, so you will need the `make` utility as well.

Listing 13.1 shows the `makefile` that I'll use:

Listing 13.1   `makefile`

```
#
# Filename: makefile
#
JAVAC      = javac
JFLAGS     = -g


.SUFFIXES: .class .java


.java.class:
        $(JAVAC) $(JFLAGS) $<
```

This `makefile` states that, to turn a `.java` (Java source code) file into a `.class` (Java executable) file, you must run the `javac` compiler. I like all my applications to be debuggable, so I set `JFLAGS` to `-g` (the `-g` flag tells the compiler to include symbolic debugger information in the `.class` file); you can replace `-g` with `-O` if you want better performance and less debugability.

The last piece that you will need is the PostgreSQL JDBC driver itself. You can find a precompiled version of the PostgreSQL JDBC driver at http://jdbc.postgresql.org. The Java runtime environment will need to know where your driver is located. The driver is typically named `postgresql.jar`, and the easiest way to tell Java about the driver is to add the jar file's location to the end of your CLASSPATH environment variable. For example, if you are connected to a Unix/Linux host and find `postgresql.jar` in the `/usr/local/pgsql/share` directory, execute the following command:

```
$ export CLASSPATH=$CLASSPATH:/usr/local/pgsql/share/postgresql.jar
```

If you are connected to a Windows host and find `postgresql.jar` in the `C:\WINDOWS\CLASSES` directory, use the following command:

```
C:\>  set CLASSPATH=%CLASSPATH%;C:\WINDOWS\CLASSES\postgresql.jar
```

Client 1—Connecting to the Server

Before you can connect to a database, you have to tell JDBC to which server you want to connect. JDBC uses a paradigm that you are undoubtedly already familiar with: A database is identified using a URL (Uniform Resource Locator). Every time you use your web browser, you use URLs.

A URL is composed of at least two parts, sometimes more. For example, the URL http://www.postgresql.org has two components. The http part specifies the protocol to use (in this case, hypertext transport protocol). Everything following the colon is used by the protocol to find the resource you want.

JDBC URLs

A JDBC URL is composed of three parts. We'll be using the URL jdbc:postgresql:movies in many of the examples for this chapter.

The protocol component for a JDBC URL is always `jdbc`. Following the protocol (and the : delimiter), is the *subprotocol*. The subprotocol is usually the name of a JDBC driver, but it can also identify a naming service that will provide a specific name, given an alias[2]. In the case of PostgreSQL, the subprotocol is `postgresql`. Finally, you can include a string that identifies a specific data source that the driver should use (Sun's JDBC documentation calls this the *subname*). In our example, the subname is `movies`. The format of the subname string is determined by the author of the JDBC driver. In the case of the PostgreSQL JDBC driver, the URL can take any of the following forms:

```
jdbc:postgresql:database
jdbc:postgresql://host/database
jdbc:postgresql://host:port/database
jdbc:org.postgresql://host:port/database?param1=val1&...
```

---

[2] See the JDBC documentation for more information about naming services.

If you don't provide a port, the standard PostgreSQL port (5432) is assumed. Notice that in all cases, you must provide the database name. Unlike the other PostgreSQL APIs, JDBC will not look for any environment variables when you omit required connection parameters, so you must include the database name in the URL. In the last form, you can include other connection parameters. For example:

```
jdbc:org:postgresql?user=korry&password=cows
```

You can include any of the parameters shown in Table 13.1 after the question mark in the URL:

```
user=user-name
password=password
loglevel={0|1|2}
```

Table 13.1 **PostgreSQL Connection Parameters**

Parameter Name	Description
user=*user-name*	Username sent to the PostgreSQL server
password=*password*	Password used to authenticate the user
ssl	If present, requests an SSL-secured connection
sslfactory—*class-name*	Specifies an alternate SSL factory class (see the PostgreSQL JDBC driver manual for more information)
protocolVersion={2|3}	Specifies which client/server protocol to use when connecting to the server
loglevel={0|1|2}	Determines how much debugging information to write the standard error stream (0 disables logging, 1 writes information messages, 2 writes detailed information)
charSet=*character-set-name*	Specifies which character encoding to use when connecting to the server (only useful when connecting to a PostgreSQL server older than version 7.3)
prepareThreshold=*count*	Determines how many times the driver will execute the same command before it decides to switch over to the Prepare/Execute model.

Listing 13.2 shows a simple JDBC client application. This application connects to a database (using a URL), prints a completion message, disconnects, and then exits.

Listing 13.2 `client1.java`

```
1 //
2 // File: client1.java
3 //
4
5 import java.sql.*;
6
7 public class client1
```

Listing 13.2 **Continued**

```
 8 {
 9   public static void main( String args[] )
10     throws ClassNotFoundException, SQLException
11   {
12     String  driver = "org.postgresql.Driver";
13     String  url    = "jdbc:postgresql:movies";
14     String  user   = "korry";
15     String  pwd    = "cows";
16
17     Class.forName( driver );
18
19     Connection con = DriverManager.getConnection( url, user, pwd );
20
21     System.err.println( "Connection complete" );
22
23     con.close();
24
25   }
26 }
```

At line 5, `client1.java` imports the `java.sql` package. Most of the JDBC interface is defined in this package, with a few extensions residing in the `javax.sql` package[3]. I won't do any error checking in this client, so you have to declare that the `main()` method can throw two exceptions (at line 10). In the next client application (`client2.java`), I'll show you how to intercept these exceptions and handle them a bit more gracefully.

Lines 12 through 15 define a few `String` objects that should make the code more descriptive. The `driver` string tells the JVM the fully qualified name of the driver class. The JDBC driver distributed with PostgreSQL is named `org.postgresql.Driver`[4]. The `url` string specifies the URL to which you want to connect.

The `user` and `pwd` (password) strings will be passed to the `DriverManager` and then to the `Driver` when you actually get around to making a connection attempt.

Line 17 loads the PostgreSQL `Driver` class. A lot of things happen with this simple method call. First, the `Class.forName()`[5] method locates and loads the object file that

---

[3] The `javax.sql` package was an optional feature introduced in the JDBC 2.0 specification. In the JDBC 3.0 specification, `javax.sql` has been moved from the JDBC 2.0 Optional Package (included in the J2EE) into J2SE.

[4] If you use a JDBC driver obtained from another source, the driver name will be different. For example, the PostgreSQL driver from the jxDBCon project is named org.sourceforge.jxdbcon.JXDBConDriver.

[5] In some versions of Java, you may need to call `Class.forName().newInstance()` to load the driver correctly. If you have trouble with `Class.forName()`, append `.newInstance()` to the end of the string.

implements the `org.postgresql.Driver` class. Normally, a reference to another class is compiled into your class. Using `Class.forName()`, you can dynamically load classes into your VM at runtime. This is roughly equivalent to

```
org.postgresql.Driver Driver = new org.postgresql.Driver();
```

The important difference between this method (creating an instance of an `org.post-gresql.Driver` object) and using `Class.forName()` is that you can use the latter method to select the driver that you want at *runtime*, rather than at compile time. If you arrange the code properly, you can load different drivers based on an external value, such as a command-line parameter or an environment variable. That might not be important if you simply want code that can talk only to PostgreSQL, but JDBC was designed to provide database portability. After `Class.forName()` loads the `Driver` class into your VM, the `Driver`'s static initializer is invoked to register the driver with the JDBC `DriverManager` class.

After the `DriverManager` knows about the PostgreSQL JDBC driver, you can ask it to create a `Connection` object for you.

There are three `DriverManager.getConnection()` methods:

```
getConnection( String url, String user, String password );
getConnection( String url, Properties props );
getConnection( String url );
```

Each form uses a different strategy for getting the username and password to the driver. In the first form, the username and password are passed as extra parameters. In the second form, the username and password are expected to be in the `props` property list. In the last form, the URL should contain the username and password as separate properties.

In the following code fragment, the three calls to `getConnection()` are equivalent:

```
...
Properties     connectionProps;
String         url = "jdbc:postgresql:movies";

connectionProps.put( "user", "korry" );
connectionProps.put( "password", "cows" );

DriverManager.getConnection( url, "korry", "cows" );
DriverManager.getConnection( url, connectionProps );
DriverManager.getConnection( url + "?user=korry&password=cows" );
...
```

Looking back at `client1.java`, you see the first form of `getConnection()`. If `getConnection()` returns successfully, `client1` prints a message, closes the connection (at line 23), and runs to completion. If `getConnection()` fails to connect to the database, it will throw an exception. You'll see how to intercept errors in the next section.

Let's compile and run this client:

```
$ make client1.class
javac -g client1.java
```

```
$ java client1
Connection complete
$
```

Sorry, that's not very exciting is it? Shut down the `postmaster` just so you know what an error might look like:

```
$ pg_ctl stop
waiting for postmaster to shut down......done
postmaster successfully shut down

$ java client1
Exception in thread "main" Connection refused. Check that the
hostname and port is correct, and that the postmaster is
running with the -i flag, which enables TCP/IP networking.
        at org.postgresql.Connection.openConnection(Unknown Source)
        at org.postgresql.Driver.connect(Unknown Source)
        at java.sql.DriverManager.getConnection(DriverManager.java:517)
        at java.sql.DriverManager.getConnection(DriverManager.java:177)
        at client1.main(client1.java:19)
$
```

You can almost feel the heat as `client1` crashes and burns. That error message isn't very friendly. Let's move on to `client2`, in which we will try to intercept the failure and provide a little insulation to the end users.

Client 2—Adding Error Checking

In the previous section, I mentioned that the `DriverManager.getConnection()` method will throw an exception whenever it fails. Listing 13.3 shows the second JDBC client. This version is nearly identical to `client1.java`, except that `client1`, ignored any exceptions and in `client2`, you will intercept them and produce friendlier error messages.

Listing 13.3 `client2.java`

```
1 //
2 // File: client2.java
3 //
4
5 import java.sql.*;
6
7 public class client2
8 {
9   public static void main( String args[] )
10   {
11     String driver = "org.postgresql.Driver";
12     String url   = "jdbc:postgresql:movies";
13     String user   = "korry";
14     String pwd   = "cows";
```

Listing 13.3 **Continued**

```
15
16     try
17     {
18       Class.forName( driver );
19     }
20     catch( ClassNotFoundException e )
21     {
22       System.err.println( "Can't load driver" + e.getMessage());
23       System.exit( 1 );
24     }
25
26     try
27     {
28       Connection con = DriverManager.getConnection(url, user, pwd);
29
30       System.out.println( "Connection attempt successful" );
31
32       con.close();
33
34     }
35     catch( Exception e )
36     {
37       System.err.println( "Connection attempt failed" );
38       System.err.println( e.getMessage());
39     }
40   }
41 }
```

The first difference between client1 and client2 appears at line 10. In the client1 version, you had to declare that main() could throw ClassNotFoundException and SQLException. You'll be intercepting those exceptions now, so main() should not throw any exceptions.

At lines 17 through 24, client2 wraps the call to Class.forName() in a try/catch block. Remember that forName() dynamically loads the implementation of a class into your VM—it is entirely possible that forName() may not be able to load the class file that you need. You may have misspelled the class name, or the class file might not be in your $CLASSPATH search path. You may also find that you don't have the permissions required to load the class file, or you could even find that the class file has been corrupted. If client2 catches an exception, it prints a suitable error message and exits.

After the Driver class has been loaded into your VM, you can attempt to make a connection. Wrap the connection attempt in a try/catch block so that you can intercept any exceptions. The call to DriverManager.getConnection() throws a SQLException if something goes wrong. Let's compile this application and give it a try:

```
$ make client2.class
javac -g client2.java
```

```
$ java client2
Connection attempt failed
Connection refused. Check that the hostname and port is correct,
and that the postmaster is running with the -i flag, which
enables TCP/IP networking.
$
```

I haven't restarted the postmaster yet, so I encounter the same error as before, but this time the error message is less intimidating.

DriverManager.getConnection() can throw two kinds of exceptions: SQLException and PSQLException (PSQLException is derived from SQLException). PSQLExceptions are specific to the PostgreSQL driver; SQLExceptions indicate errors that might be common to many drivers. Let's modify client2.java so that you can see which type of exception you catch. The new client is shown in Listing 13.4.

Listing 13.4   client2a.java

```
 1 //
 2 // File: client2a.java
 3 //
 4
 5 import java.sql.*;
 6 import org.postgresql.util.PSQLException;
 7
 8 public class client2a
 9 {
10   public static void main( String args[] )
11   {
12     String  driver = "org.postgresql.Driver";
13
14     try
15     {
16       Class.forName( driver );
17     }
18     catch( ClassNotFoundException e )
19     {
20       System.err.println( "Can't load driver " + e.getMessage());
21       System.exit( 1 );
22     }
23     catch( Exception e )
24     {
25       System.err.println( "Can't load driver " + e.toString());
26       System.exit( 1 );
27     }
28
29     try
30     {
31       Connection con = DriverManager.getConnection( args[0] );
```

Listing 13.4 **Continued**

```
32
33       System.out.println( "Connection attempt successful" );
34
35       con.close();
36
37     }
38     catch( PSQLException e)
39     {
40       System.err.println( "Connection failed(PSQLException)" );
41       System.err.println( e.getMessage());
42     }
43     catch( SQLException e )
44     {
45       System.err.println( "Connection failed(SQLException)" );
46       System.err.println( e.getMessage());
47     }
48   }
49 }
```

I've made a few minor changes in client2a.java. First off, you want to distinguish between SQLException and PSQLException, so at line 6, import the appropriate pack age. I've also removed most of the string variables used in the previous version. In this version, you supply a URL on the command line rather than hard-coding the connection parameters. At line 31, client2a calls a different flavor of the getConnection() method; this one expects a single argument (the URL to which you want to connect). Notice that I have removed the hard-coded URL from this client. When you invoke client2a, you provide a connection URL on the command line (see the next example). Finally, client2a catches PSQLException explicitly.

Compile this client and reproduce the same error that you saw earlier:

```
$ make client2a.class
javac -g client2a.java

$ java client2a "jdbc:postgresql:movies?user=korry&password=cows"
Connection failed(PSQLException)
Connection refused. Check that the hostname and port is correct,
and that the postmaster is running with the -i flag, which
enables TCP/IP networking.
$
```

Okay, that message comes from a PSQLException. Now, let's restart the postmaster and try connecting with an invalid password:

```
$ pg_ctl start -l /tmp/pg.log -o -i
postmaster successfully started
$ java client2a "jdbc:postgresql:movies?user=korry&password=oxen"
```

```
Connection failed(PSQLException)
Something unusual has occurred to cause the driver to fail.
Please report this exception:
Exception: java.sql.SQLException:
  FATAL 1:  Password authentication failed for user "korry"

Stack Trace:

java.sql.SQLException: FATAL 1:  Password authentication failed
for user "korry"

        at org.postgresql.Connection.openConnection(Unknown Source)
        at org.postgresql.Driver.connect(Unknown Source)
        at java.sql.DriverManager.getConnection(DriverManager.java:517)
        at java.sql.DriverManager.getConnection(DriverManager.java:199)
        at client2a.main(client2a.java:31)
End of Stack Trace
```

We're back to the intimidating error messages again. This is still a PSQLException, but the PostgreSQL JDBC Driver feels that an invalid password is unusual enough to justify this kind of error. You can see the importance of catching exceptions—you may want to translate this sort of message into something a little less enthusiastic rather than attacking your users with the raw error message text, as we've done here.

It's a little harder to generate a SQLException when the only thing you are doing is connecting and disconnecting. If you try hard enough, you can break just about anything:

```
$ java client2a "jdbc:postgres:movies?user=korry&password=cows"
Connection failed(SQLException)
No suitable driver
```

In this example, I've misspelled the subprotocol portion of the connection URL (postgres should be postgresql).

JNDI and the DataSource Class

So far, all of the JDBC client applications that you've seen in this chapter connect to a PostgreSQL server using a URL. Every time you connect to the server, you have to craft a URL that contains all of the connection properties required by the server. Creating a URL by hand doesn't seem too onerous if you're writing one or two client applications that interact with a single database, but it can become quite burdensome as you add more clients and more databases.

Fortunately, Java provides a better way to scale JDBC applications: the DataSource. If you've read through Chapter 12, "Using PostgreSQL from an ODBC Client Application," you're already familiar with the concept of a DataSource. A DataSource is a *named* collection of connection properties (and you get to choose the name). In an ODBC application, each DataSource is stored in the Windows registry (or in

/etc/odbc.ini for Linux/Unix hosts). In a JDBC application, a `DataSource` is typically stored in a JNDI (Java Naming and Directory Interface) repository. The JNDI package is an interface that maps a name into an object. Using JNDI, you can store `DataSource` objects in an LDAP directory or a Java RMI registry (or any JNDI-enabled repository).

When you connect to a PostgreSQL server using a `DataSource` (as opposed to a URL), you typically ask the JNDI (the Java Naming and Directory Interface) to create the `DataSource` object for you. The JNDI searches through its repository to find a `DataSource` object whose name matches the name that you provide. If the JNDI finds such an object, it creates a Java `DataSource` object and returns the object to you. The `DataSource` object contains all of the properties required to connect to a PostgreSQL server. In fact, the `DataSource` object can connect to the server on your behalf and return a reference to a `Connection` object. For example, to connect to a `DataSource` named `accounting`, you might write code similar to the following:

```
...
    DataSource acctg = (DataSource) new InitialContext().lookup("accounting");
    Connection conn  = acctg.getConnection();
...
```

When you invoke `InitialContext().lookup("accounting")`, the JNDI starts searching its repository (which may be an LDAP directory, an RMI registry, or some other JNDI service provider) for an object with the name `accounting`. If the JNDI can't find such an object, it throws a `NameNotFound` exception. If the `lookup()` method *does* find an object with that name, it returns a copy of that object. The call to `acctg.getConnection()` tries to connect to the PostgreSQL server using the connection properties defined in the `DataSource`.

In between the call to `lookup()` and the call to `getConnection()`, you may want to modify the properties in your copy of the `DataSource` object. For example, you may not want to store a plain-text password in an insecure repository. Instead, you can create an *incomplete* `DataSource` in the repository and set the password property in your copy. You can modify any of the `DataSource` properties shown in Table 13.2.

Table 13.2 **PostgreSQL DataSource Properties**

Property Name	Description
setUser()	Username sent to the PostgreSQL server
setPassword()	Password used to authenticate the user
setServerName()	Host name (or IP address) of server
setPortNumber()	Port number that postmaster is servicing
setDatabaseName()	Name of the database you want to access

Now that you know how to connect to a PostgreSQL database (using a URL or a `DataSource`), I'll show you how to execute a PostgreSQL command from a JDBC application. I'll also explain how to retrieve data from a `ResultSet` and how to find the metadata exposed by the server.

Client 3—Processing Queries

The next client executes a hard-coded query, intercepts any errors, and prints the result set. I've factored most of the code into separate methods to make it easier to follow. Listing 13.5 shows `client3.java`.

Listing 13.5 `client3.java` **(Part 1)**

```
 1 //
 2 //  File: client3.java
 3 //
 4
 5 import java.sql.*;
 6
 7 public class client3
 8 {
 9   public static void main( String args[] )
10   {
11     Class driverClass = loadDriver( "org.postgresql.Driver" );
12
13     if( driverClass == null )
14       return;
15
16     if( args.length != 1 )
17     {
18       System.err.println( "usage: java client3 <url>" );
19       return;
20     }
21
22     Connection con = connectURL( args[0] );
23
24     if( con != null )
25     {
26       ResultSet result = execQuery( con, "SELECT * FROM tapes;" );
27
28       if( result != null )
29         printResults( result );
30     }
31   }
```

The `main()` method for `client3` should be much easier to read now that the details have been factored out (see Listing 13.6). Start by loading the `Driver` class. If that fails, the call to `loadDriver()` will print an error message and exit. Next, `main()` verifies that the user provided a URL on the command line and connects to the database using that URL. If the connection succeeds, `client3` executes a hard-coded query and prints the result set.

Listing 13.6   `client3.java` **(Part 2)**

```
33    static Class loadDriver( String driverName )
34    {
35      try
36      {
37        return( Class.forName( driverName ));
38      }
39      catch( ClassNotFoundException e )
40      {
41        System.err.println( "Can't load driver - " + e.getMessage());
42        return( null );
43      }
44    }
45
46    static Connection connectURL( String URL )
47    {
48      try
49      {
50        return( DriverManager.getConnection( URL ));
51      }
52      catch( SQLException e )
53      {
54        System.err.println( "Can't connect - " + e.getMessage());
55        return( null );
56      }
57    }
```

You should be familiar with most of the code in the `loadDriver()` and `connectURL()` methods[6].

`loadDriver()` uses `Class.forName()` to load the named `Driver` into your VM. If the load is successful, `loadDriver()` returns the `Class` object for the `Driver`; otherwise, `loadDriver()` prints an error message and returns `null` to inform the caller that something went wrong.

The `connectURL()` method is similar in structure. It attempts to connect to the requested URL, returning a `Connection` object or `null` if the connection attempt fails (see Listing 13.7).

Listing 13.7   `client3.java` **(Part 3)**

```
59    static ResultSet execQuery( Connection con, String query )
60    {
61      try
```

---

[6] These methods show a personal design preference. I try to intercept exceptions as early as possible rather than throwing them back up the call stack. I find the resulting mainline code a little easier to read without the `try/catch` blocks.

Listing 13.7 **Continued**

```
62    {
63        Statement stmt = con.createStatement();
64
65        System.out.println( query );
66
67        return( stmt.executeQuery( query ));
68    }
69    catch( SQLException e )
70    {
71        System.err.println( "Query failed - " + e.getMessage());
72        return( null );
73    }
74 }
```

execQuery() shows how to execute a query using JDBC. When this method is invoked, the caller gives you a Connection. Before you can execute a query, you must create a Statement object. A Statement object gives you a way to send a command to the server. After the command has been sent to the server, you can ask the Statement for a ResultSet. Some database servers (PostgreSQL included) support multiple Statement objects for each Connection. This means that you can execute multiple commands and process the results concurrently.

The Statement.executeQuery() method throws a SQLException if something (a syntax error, for example) goes wrong.

If the call to executeQuery() succeeds, this function returns the ResultSet to the caller, which passes it to printResults() to be displayed to the user.

The final method (see Listing 13.8) in this application is printResults().

Listing 13.8 client3.java **(Part 4)**

```
76    static void printResults( ResultSet res )
77    {
78        System.out.println( " tape_id | title" );
79        System.out.println( "---------+-------------------------" );
80
81        try
82        {
83            while( res.next())
84            {
85                System.out.print( res.getString( 1 ));
86                System.out.print( " | ");
87                System.out.print( res.getString( 2 ));
88                System.out.println( "" );
89            }
90        }
91        catch( SQLException e )
92        {
```

Listing 13.8 **Continued**

```
93        System.err.println( "Fetch failed: " + e.getMessage());
94    }
95  }
96 }
```

The printResults() method fetches every row in the given ResultSet and prints each column. Lines 78 and 79 print the column headings for the result set. Because you are working with a hard-coded query in this client, you can take a few shortcuts— if you don't know the shape of the result set, you would have to interrogate the metadata for this ResultSet to find the column headings. You'll do that in the next client (client4.java).

The loop at lines 83 through 89 iterates through each row in the result set. Each ResultSet maintains a pointer[7] to the current row. ResultSet offers a number of methods for navigating through a result set. The ResultSet.next() method moves you forward through the result set. Table 13.3 lists all the navigation methods.

Table 13.3 ResultSet **Navigation Methods**

Navigation Method	**Related Accessor Method**	**Description**
absolute(n)	getRow()	Moves to the nth row in the result set if n is positive or to the last $|n|$ row if n is negative
afterLast()	isAfterLast()	Moves past the last row in the result set
beforeFirst()	isBeforeFirst()	Moves to just before the first row
first()	isFirst()	Moves to the first row
last()	isLast()	Moves to the last row
next()	getRow()	Moves to the next row
previous()	getRow()	Moves to the previous row
relative(n)	getRow()	Moves forward n rows if n is positive or back n rows if n is negative

The first column in Table 13.3 lists the methods you can call to move through the result set. Each entry in the second column shows the related accessor method. The isAfterLast(), isBeforeLast(), isFirst(), and isLast() methods return true or false to indicate whether you are pointed to the named position within the result set. The getRow() function returns the current row number with the result set.

first() differs from beforeFirst() in that you can retrieve column values if you are positioned on the first row, but not if you are positioned before the first row. Similarly, you can retrieve column values if you are positioned on the last row, but not if you are positioned after the last row.

[7] The JDBC documentation refers to this pointer as a cursor; to avoid confusion with database cursors (a similar concept), I'll use the term *pointer*.

Scrollable Result Sets

JDBC makes a distinction between a scrollable result set and a non-scrollable result set. If you have a non-scrollable `ResultSet`, the only navigation method you can use is `next()`. If you look back to line 63 (in Listing 13.7), you'll see a call to the `Connection::createStatement()` method. If you call `createStatement()` with an empty argument list, you get a non-scrollable `Statement` (that's a bit of a misnomer—you are actually telling the `Statement` that it should produce non-scrollable a `ResultSet`).

To create a scrollable `ResultSet`, you must provide two extra parameters when you create the `Statement` that returns the `ResultSet`. The first argument specifies a scroll type and can be any of the following values: `ResultSet.TYPE_SCROLL_FORWARD_ONLY`, `ResultSet.TYPE_SCROLL_INSENSITIVE`, or `ResultSet.TYPE_SCROLL_SENSITIVE`. If you specify `ResultSet.TYPE_SCROLL_FORWARD_ONLY`, `createStatement()` returns a non-scrollable `Statement` (which will create non-scrollable `ResultSets`). If you specify `ResultSet.TYPE_SCROLL_INSENSITIVE`, `createStatement()` returns a scrollable `Statement`—you can scroll through the `ResultSet` using any of the navigation methods shown in Table 13.3. The PostgreSQL JDBC driver treats `ResultSet.TYPE_SCROLL_SENSITIVE` as if you had specified `ResultSet.TYPE_SCROLL_INSENSITIVE` (other databases may make a distinction between the two, but PostgreSQL does not). In general, you should specify `ResultSet.TYPE_SCROLL_INSENSITIVE` when you create a scrolling `Statement` using the PostgreSQL JDBC driver. The second argument determines whether the given `Statement` will produce updateable `ResultSets` or read-only `ResultSets`. Specify `ResultSet.CONCUR_READ_ONLY` to create a read-only `ResultSet` or `ResultSet.CONCUR_UPDATABLE` to create a `ResultSet` that you can modify with the `Statement::executeUpdate()` method.

When you call `Connection::createStatement()` with an empty argument list, JDBC assumes you want a `FORWARD_ONLY`, `READ_ONLY` `ResultSet`.

You use the `ResultSet.getString()` method to retrieve a column from the current row. When you call `getString()`, you provide an integer argument that specifies which column you are interested in; column numbers start at 1.

After printing the two column values, `printResults()` continues looping until `res.next()` returns `false` (meaning that there are no more rows in the result set).

This example shows that it's easy to process a query and a result set using JDBC. Now, let's go back and fill in a few of the details that I avoided.

Statement **Classes**

In `client3.java`, you used the `Statement.executeQuery()` method to execute a query. `Statement` is one of three interfaces that you can use to execute a SQL command. `Statement` is the most general interface and can be used to execute any SQL command. Let's look at the other `Statement` interfaces.

PreparedStatement

The `PreparedStatement` interface provides a way to *precompile* a command and execute it later. `PreparedStatement` inherits from (extends) `Statement`, so anything that you can do with a `Statement`, you can also do with a `PreparedStatement`. If you read the previous chapter, you may recognize `PreparedStatement` as the JDBC implementation of the ODBC Prepare/Execute execution model. When you use a `PreparedStatement`, you can parameterize your SQL commands. Let's say you are writing an application that repeatedly queries the `tapes` table, providing a different `tape_id` for each query. Rather than constructing a new command for each query, you can create a `PreparedStatement` like this:

```
...
PreparedStatement stmt;

stmt = con.prepareStatement( "SELECT * FROM tapes WHERE tape_id = ?" );
...
```

Notice that the text of this query doesn't specify an actual `tape_id` in the `WHERE` clause; instead, you include a parameter marker (?). Using a parameter marker, you can substitute different values each time you execute the `PreparedStatement`. You can include as many parameter markers as you like[8].

The `PreparedStatement` object returned by `prepareStatement()` can be executed many times. Each time you execute the query, you can provide a different substitution value for each parameter marker. For example, to substitute a `tape_id` value in the previous query:

```
PreparedStatement stmt;

stmt = con.prepareStatement( "SELECT * FROM tapes WHERE tape_id = ?" );

stmt.setString( 1, "AA-55281" );

ResultString result = stmt.executeQuery();
...
```

The call to `setString()` substitutes the value `"AA-55281"` in place of the first parameter marker (parameter markers are numbered starting with 1). The net effect is that `executeQuery()` executes the string `"SELECT * FROM tapes WHERE tape_id = 'AA-55281'"`. Notice that `setString()` automatically includes the single quotes required around a string literal, so you don't have to include them in the string.

`PreparedStatement` supports a number of parameter-substitution methods. We've used the `setString()` method in this example, but there are also methods for setting Boolean values (`setBoolean()`), numeric values (`setInt()`, `setFloat()`, `setDouble()`, `setLong()`,

---

[8] The JDBC documentation suggests that you can include a parameter marker *anywhere* within a SQL command. For example, the following command is allowed `SELECT ? FROM customers`, implying that you could substitute a list of column names at runtime. I recommend that you only use parameter markers where *values* are expected (and use one marker for each value). The PostgreSQL driver and many other drivers will not function correctly if you try to use a parameter marker in a context in which a value is not allowed.

setBigDecimal()), temporal values (setDate(), setTime(), setTimestamp()), large objects (setBlob(), setClob()), and generic objects (setObject()). You can also assign a set of arbitrary bytes to a parameter using the setBytes() method. You can even copy the content of a file (or even a web page) into a parameter with the setBinaryStream() method. Each of these methods expect a parameter number and a value of the appropriate type. You use the setNull() method to substitute a null value.

Each time you execute a PreparedStatement, you can substitute new values for some or all the parameter markers. If you don't supply a new value for a given marker, the previous value is retained.

Why would you want to use a PreparedStatement instead of a Statement? The Prepare/Execute model makes it easy to factor the code required to generate a command into a separate method. You may also experience a performance boost by preparing a command and then reusing it many times.

CallableStatement

The CallableStatement interface inherits from PreparedStatement, so anything that you can do with a PreparedStatement, you can also do with a CallableStatement. The CallableStatement provides a way to call a function or stored-procedure using a database-independent syntax.

The following code fragment illustrates CallableStatement:

```
...
CallableStatement stmt;
boolean         result;

stmt = con.prepareCall( "{?= call has_table_privilege(?,?)}" );

stmt.registerOutParameter( 1, Types.BIT );

stmt.setString( 2, "customers" );
stmt.setString( 3, "UPDATE" );

stmt.execute();

result = stmt.getBoolean( 1 );
...
```

This example calls PostgreSQL's has_table_privilege() function. has_table_privilege() expects two parameters: a table name and an access type. It returns a Boolean value that indicates whether the current user holds the given privilege on the named table. The query string contains three parameter markers. The first marker tells JDBC that the function that you want to call will return a value. The second and third markers specify the IN parameters. Each function parameter can be an input value (IN), a return value (OUT), or both (IN/OUT).

Before you can execute the CallableStatement, you use the setString() method (inherited from PreparedStatement) to substitute the two input parameters. You also have to tell JDBC about the type of all OUT parameters; the call to registerOutParameter() does that for you. After executing the statement, you can retrieve the result using getBoolean().

Metadata

Metadata is another issue that I glossed over in describing client3. There are two types of metadata that you can retrieve using JDBC: database metadata and result set metadata.

The DatabaseMetaData interface provides information about the database at the other end of a Connection. To access a DatabaseMetaData object, you call the Connection.getMetaData() method. Here is a snippet that shows how to retrieve the JDBC driver name and version information:

```
...
Connection        con  = DriverManager.getConnection( args[0] );
DatabaseMetaData dbmd = con.getMetaData();

System.out.println( "Driver name:     " + dbmd.getDriverName());
System.out.println( "Driver version: " + dbmd.getDriverVersion());
...
```

At last count, DatabaseMetaData exposes more than 120 items of database information.

In most applications, you will probably be more interested in the other type of metadata. The ResultSetMetaData interface exposes information about the data contained within a result set. You obtain a ResultSetMetaData object by calling the ResultSet.getMetaData() method. For example:

```
...
ResultSet          rs   = stmt.executeQuery();
ResultSetMetaData  rsmd = rs.getMetaData();
...
```

After you have a ResultSetMetaData object, you can query it for all sorts of information. The getColumnCount() method returns the number of columns in the result set. Because all ResultSetMetaData methods (except getColumnCount()) return information about a given column, you will probably want to process metadata in a loop:

```
...
int   colCount = rsmd.getColumnCount();

for( int column = 1; column <= colCount; column++ )
{
  System.out.println( "Column #" + column );
  System.out.println( "  Name: " + rsmd.getColumnName( column ));
  System.out.println( "  Type: " + rsmd.getTypeName( column ));
}
...
```

This code snippet uses getColumnName() to retrieve the name of each column and getTypeName() to retrieve the type of each column.

Client 4—An Interactive Query Processor

Now, let's move on to the final JDBC client. As in previous chapters, we'll wrap up by looking at an application that processes arbitrary commands entered by the user.

Listing 13.9 shows the `client4.main()` method.

Listing 13.9   `client4.java` **(Part 1)**

```
 1 //
 2 //  File: client4.java
 3 //
 4
 5 import java.sql.*;
 6 import java.io.*;
 7
 8 public class client4
 9 {
10   static String blanks = "                                    ";
11   static String dashes = "----------------------------------";
12
13   public static void main( String args[] )
14     throws SQLException
15   {
16     Class driverClass = loadDriver( "org.postgresql.Driver" );
17
18     if( driverClass == null )
19       return;
20
21     if( args.length != 1 )
22     {
23       System.err.println( "usage: java client4 <url>" );
24       return;
25     }
26
27     Connection con = connectURL( args[0] );
28
29     if( con != null )
30     {
31       DatabaseMetaData dbmd = con.getMetaData();
32
33       System.out.print( "Connected to " );
34       System.out.print( dbmd.getDatabaseProductName());
35       System.out.println( " " + dbmd.getDatabaseProductVersion());
36
37       processCommands( con );
38
39       con.close();
40     }
41   }
```

client4.main() is similar to client3.main(); it loads the PostgreSQL driver and then connects to the database using the URL provided by the user. At line 31, client4 obtains a DatabaseMetaData object so you can print a welcome message that includes the product name and version.

main() finishes by calling processCommands(). Now, let's look at the processCommands() method (Listing 13.10).

Listing 13.10   client4.java **(Part 2)**

```
43    static void processCommands( Connection con )
44    {
45      try
46      {
47        Statement stmt = con.createStatement(ResultSet.TYPE_SCROLL_INSENSITIVE,
48                                             ResultSet.CONCUR_READ_ONLY);
49        String      cmd = "";
50        BufferedReader in;
51        in = new BufferedReader( new InputStreamReader( System.in ));
52
53        while( true )
54        {
55          System.out.print( "--> " );
56
57          cmd = in.readLine();
58
59          if( cmd == null )
60              break;
61
62          if( cmd.equalsIgnoreCase( "quit" ))
63            break;
64
65          processCommand( stmt, cmd );
66
67        }
68
69        System.out.println( "bye" );
70
71      }
72      catch( Exception e )
73      {
74          System.err.println( c );
75      }
76    }
```

The processCommands() method prompts the user for a command and then executes that command. Because this is not a graphical application, you need a way to read input from the user. Java's BufferedReader class lets you read user input one line at a time, so processCommands() creates a new BufferedReader object at line 51.

Lines 53 through 67 comprise the main processing loop in this application. At the top of the loop, `processCommands()` prints a prompt string and then reads the user's response using `BufferedReader`'s `readline()` method.

Three things can cause you to break out of this loop. First, one of the methods that you call can throw an exception. `processCommands()` catches any exceptions at line 72 and simply prints the error message contained in the exception. Next, the user can close the input stream (usually by pressing Ctrl+D). In that case, `readline()` returns a `null` `String` reference and you break out of the loop at line 60. Finally, you break out of this loop if the user enters the string `quit`.

When you reach line 65, you call the `processCommand()` method to execute a single command. Listing 13.11 shows the `processCommand()` method.

Listing 13.11   `client4.java` **(Part 3)**

```
78    static void processCommand( Statement stmt, String cmd )
79      throws SQLException
80    {
81
82      if( stmt.execute( cmd ))
83          printResultSet( stmt.getResultSet());
84      else
85      {
86        int count = stmt.getUpdateCount();
87
88        if( count == -1 )
89          System.out.println( "No results returned" );
90        else
91          System.out.println( "(" + count + " rows)" );
92      }
93    }
```

The `processCommand()` method is a little difficult to understand at first. Here's some background information that might help.

There are three[9] ways to execute a command using a `Statement` object. I've used the `executeQuery()` method in most of the examples in this chapter. Calling `executeQuery()` is only appropriate if you know that you are executing a SELECT command. `executeQuery()` returns a `ResultSet`. If you know that you are executing some other type of command (such as CREATE TABLE, INSERT, or UPDATE), you should use the `executeUpdate()` method instead of `executeQuery()`. `executeUpdate()` returns the number of rows affected by the command (or 0 for DDL commands).

If you don't know whether you are executing a query or a command, which is the case in this client, you can call the `execute()` method. `execute()` returns a Boolean

[9] Actually, there is a fourth way to execute a SQL command. You can call the `addBatch()` method repeatedly to build up a batch of commands, and then execute the whole batch using `executeBatch()`.

value: true means that the command returned a result set; false means that the command returned the number of rows affected by the command (or 0 for DDL commands)[10].

Because you don't know what kind of command the user entered, you use execute(). If the command returns a result set (that is, if execute() returns true), you can call printResultSet() to display the results. If the command does not return a result set, you have to call getUpdateCount() to determine whether the command modified any rows. Note that the 7.2 version of the PostgreSQL JDBC driver seems to contain a small bug: the getUpdateCount() method returns 1, even for commands such as CREATE TABLE, GRANT, and CREATE INDEX.

Now let's look at the methods that display result sets to the user. The first one is pad(), shown in Listing 13.12.

Listing 13.12 `client4.java` **(Part 4)**

```
95     static String pad( String in, int len, String fill )
96     {
97         String result = in;
98
99         len -= in.length();
100
101        while( len > 0  )
102        {
103            int l;
104
105            if( len > fill.length())
106                l = fill.length();
107            else
108                l = len;
109
110            result = result + fill.substring( 0, l );
111
112            len -= l;
113        }
114
115        return( result );
116    }
```

The pad() method is a helper method used by printResultSet(). It returns a string padded with fill characters to the given length.

Next, let's look at the printResultSet() method, shown in Listing 13.13.

---

[10] This is not entirely accurate. Some JDBC drivers (but not the PostgreSQL driver) can execute multiple commands in a single call to execute(). In that case, the return code from execute() indicates the type of the first result. To get subsequent results, you call the getMoreResults() method. See the JDBC documentation for more information.

Listing 13.13 `client4.java` **(Part 5)**

```
118   static void printResultSet( ResultSet rs )
119     throws SQLException
120   {
121     int[]              sizes;
122     ResultSetMetaData rsmd     = rs.getMetaData();
123     int               colCount = rsmd.getColumnCount();
124     int               rowCount = 0;
125
126     sizes = new int[colCount+1];
127
128     //
129     // Compute column widths
130     //
131     while( rs.next())
132     {
133       rowCount++;
134
135       for( int i = 1; i <= colCount; i++ )
136       {
137         String val = rs.getString(i);
138
139         if(( rs.wasNull() == false ) && ( val.length() > sizes[i] ))
140           sizes[i] = val.length();
141       }
142     }
143
144     //
145     // Print column headers
146     //
147     for( int i = 1; i <= colCount; i++ )
148     {
149       if( rsmd.getColumnLabel(i).length() > sizes[i] )
150         sizes[i] = rsmd.getColumnLabel(i).length();
151
152       System.out.print( pad( rsmd.getColumnLabel( i ),
153                              sizes[i],
154                              blanks ));
155
156       if( i < colCount )
157         System.out.print( " | " );
158       else
159         System.out.println();
160     }
161
162     for( int i = 1; i <= colCount; i++ )
163     {
```

Listing 13.13 **Continued**

```
164        if( i < colCount )
165            System.out.print( pad( "", sizes[i], dashes ) + "-+-" );
166        else
167            System.out.println( pad( "", sizes[i], dashes ) );
168        }
169
170    //
171    //  Rewind the result set and print the contents
172    //
173    rs.beforeFirst();
174
175    while( rs.next())
176    {
177      for( int i = 1; i <= colCount; i++ )
178      {
179        String val = rs.getString(i);
180
181        if( rs.wasNull())
182          val = "";
183
184        if( i < colCount )
185            System.out.print( pad( val, sizes[i], blanks ) + " | " );
186        else
187            System.out.println( pad( val, sizes[i], blanks ) );
188        }
189      }
190    }
```

The printResultSet() method is easily the most complex method in this application.

It starts by computing the width of each column header. Each column should be as wide as the widest value in that column. You have to read through the entire result set to find the widest value. The code at lines 147 through 168 prints the column headers. If getColumnLabel() returns a string longer than the widest value in the column, line 150 adjusts the width to accommodate the label.

After you have printed the column headers, you have to rewind the result set so that you are positioned just before the first row. Remember, you processed the entire result set earlier when you were computing column widths.

The loop covering lines 175 through 189 processes every row in the result set. For each column in the result set, printResultSet() retrieves the value in String form. Line 181 shows an oddity in the JDBC package: There is no way to determine whether a value is NULL without first retrieving that value. So, you must first call rs.getString() to retrieve a column from the current row and then call rs.wasNull() to detect NULL values. You may be wondering what the getXXXX() methods will return if the value is NULL. The answer depends on which getXXXX() method you call. In this chapter, you have retrieved most result values in the form of a Java `String`, but you can also ask for values to be returned in other data types. `getString()` returns a `null` reference if the column value is `NULL`. `getBoolean()` will return `false` if the column value is `NULL`. Of course, `getBoolean()` will also return `false` if the column value is `false`. Likewise, `getInt()` returns `0` if the value is `NULL` or if the value is `0`. You *must* call `wasNull()` to detect `NULL` values.

After fixing up any `NULL` values, lines 184 through 187 print the result, padded to the width of the column.

The last two methods in `client4.java` are identical to those included in `client3.java`. `loadDriver()` is shown in Listing 13.14.

Listing 13.14 `client4.java` **(Part 6)**

```
192    static Class loadDriver( String driverName )
193    {
194      try
195      {
196        return( Class.forName( driverName ));
197      }
198      catch( ClassNotFoundException e )
199      {
200        System.err.println( "Can't load driver - " + e.getMessage());
201        return( null );
202      }
203    }
204
205    static Connection connectURL( String URL )
206    {
207      try
208      {
209        return( DriverManager.getConnection( URL ));
210      }
211      catch( SQLException e )
212      {
213        System.err.println( "Can't connect - " + e.getMessage());
214        return( null );
215      }
216    }
217 }
```

The `loadDriver()` method tries to load the named JDBC driver, and `connectURL()` attempts to connect to the given JDBC URL.

Now, let's compile and run this application:

```
$ make client4.class
javac -g client4.java
```

```
$ java client4 "jdbc:postgresql:movies?user=korry&password=cows"
Connected to PostgreSQL 8.0.0

--> SELECT * FROM tapes
tape_id  | title
---------+--------------
AB-12345 | The Godfather
AB-67472 | The Godfather
MC-68873 | Casablanca
OW-41221 | Citizen Kane
AH-54706 | Rear Window

--> SELECT * FROM customers
id | customer_name       | phone    | birth_date
---+---------------------+----------+-----------
1  | Jones, Henry        | 555-1212 | 1970-10-10
2  | Rubin, William      | 555-2211 | 1972-07-10
3  | Panky, Henry        | 555-1221 | 1968-01-21
4  | Wonderland, Alice N. | 555-1122 | 1969-03-05
5  | Funkmaster, Freddy  | 555-FUNK |
7  | Gull, Jonathan LC   | 555-1111 | 1984-02-05
8  | Grumby, Jonas       | 555-2222 | 1984-02-21
```

Now, I'd like to show you a problem with this application.

```
--> SELECT * FROM tapes; SELECT * FROM customers
Cannot handle multiple result groups.
```

In this example, I tried to execute two SQL commands on one line. As the message suggests, the PostgreSQL JDBC driver cannot handle multiple result groups (this message comes from an exception thrown by the PostgreSQL driver). Note that this is not a limitation of the JDBC package, but of this particular driver. The PostgreSQL source distribution includes an example application (`src/interfaces/jdbc/example/psql.java`) that gets around this problem by parsing user input into individual commands.

Summary

The JDBC package is a large piece of technology. This chapter described the basic techniques for connecting a Java application to PostgreSQL using JDBC and the PostgreSQL JDBC driver. It does not cover a few of the more advanced JDBC topics.

The Connection class includes methods that can commit and roll back transactions—of course, you can do that yourself by executing COMMIT and ROLLBACK commands.

The examples in this chapter intercept database errors by catching exceptions. JDBC also throws exceptions for database *warnings*.

One of the more interesting features added to the JDBC 2.0 specification is the updateable ResultSet. This feature lets you update, insert, and delete rows in a result set by directly modifying the ResultSet, rather than executing the corresponding commands yourself.

Finally, JDBC gives you a way to map PostgreSQL data types into Java data types. In this chapter, you used `String` values (and an occasional Boolean) to communicate between Java and PostgreSQL, but JDBC can map between other data types as well. You can even map user-defined PostgreSQL types into Java.

JDBC is a powerful and well-designed technology. If you are interested in Java programming, you will want to learn more about JDBC. Sun has done a great job of documenting the JDBC package. For more information, I suggest reading the "JDBC Technology Guide: Getting Started" at http://java.sun.com/j2se/1.3/_docs/guide/jdbc/.

Using PostgreSQL with Perl

The Perl language has been called the "toolbox for Unix." If you are an experienced Perl programmer, you already know three things about the language: It's extremely useful, it's notoriously difficult to master, and it gives you a new way to write completely incomprehensible code. If you are *not* already a Perl programmer, you should be forewarned that I won't try to teach you the basics of Perl programming in this chapter. But that doesn't mean that you won't be able to get anything useful from this chapter. If you don't already know Perl, read this chapter once without paying too much attention to the syntactical details—they won't make a lot of sense the first time through. Then, read through the client applications again, trying them out as you go. You'll be surprised at how quickly you can make sense of the examples if you don't get too hung up on the unusual syntax.

There are two ways to connect to a PostgreSQL database from a Perl application[1]: pgsql_perl5 (also known as the Pg module) and the DBI module.

The pgsql_perl5 interface is a Perl binding for the libpq API. If you are already comfortable with the libpq API, you will find pgsql_perl5 very familiar.

In this chapter, I'll focus on the DBI module. DBI provides a portable interface to a variety of database systems. When you use the DBI module within a Perl application, you can move from database to database with few if any changes to your code. The architecture of the DBI module is similar in structure to JDBC (the Java database API) and ODBC.

DBI Architecture Overview

The DBI module, like other portable database interfaces, is layered. Figure 14.1 shows the structure of a Perl/DBI application.

---

[1] I'll use the terms' application, script, and program interchangeably in this chapter. They all mean the same thing in Perl: a series of statements that does something—hopefully something useful.

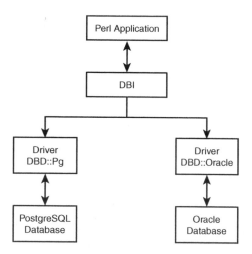

Figure 14.1 DBI architecture.

The topmost layer is the Perl application. A Perl application uses the DBI module to interact with one or more database drivers in a driver-independent (and therefore, database-independent) fashion. *DBI* is an acronym for "database interface." *DBD* is an acronym for "database driver." You can think of the DBI module as "database independent" and the DBD module as "database dependent."

The DBI

The DBI class is responsible for loading DBI drivers into the Perl runtime. The DBI can return a list of available drivers as well as a list of data sources available through a given driver. The DBI class is also responsible for creating database connections.

The DBD Driver

The DBD driver is the component that interfaces with the database. Notice that I've changed spelling here: DBI is the interface seen by the application; DBD is the interface seen by DBI.

The PostgreSQL DBI driver is known as DBD::Pg. DBD::Pg is a combination of Perl code and C code. In the future, you may see a pure Perl driver for PostgreSQL. Pure Perl drivers are much easier to install because you don't have to worry about finding a binary (that is, precompiled) distribution or compiling the driver yourself.

The DBI-Compliant Database

At the bottom of the heap, you'll find the actual database. The DBD driver translates client requests into the form required by the backend database and translates results into the form expected by the client application. The PostgreSQL driver connects to a PostgreSQL database using the libpq API.

Prerequisites

If you want to try out the examples in this chapter, you will need to install and configure the following components (in addition to a running PostgreSQL installation):

- Perl5 or later (www.perl.org)
- The DBI module (www.cpan.org/modules/by-module/DBI)
- The DBD::Pg driver (www.cpan.org/modules/by-module/DBD)

Client 1—Connecting to the Server

Before you try to connect to a PostgreSQL server, take a moment to examine the basic components of a typical Perl/DBI script.

Listing 14.1 shows a Perl script that will print the list of available DBD drivers.

Listing 14.1 `get_drivers.pl`

```
 1 #!/usr/bin/perl -W
 2 #
 3 #  Filename: get_drivers.pl
 4 #
 5 use strict;
 6 use DBI;
 7
 8 # Get the list of drivers from the DBI
 9 #
10 my @driver_names = DBI->available_drivers();
11
12 # Print the name of each driver
13 #
14 foreach my $driver ( @driver_names ) {
15     print( "Driver: $driver\n" );
16 }
```

The first line of the script identifies this file as an executable. When you run a program on Unix/Linux systems, or if you are using Cygwin in the Windows environment, a script file is (directly) executable when the first line of the file contains the characters #! followed by the name of the script interpreter (of course, you must hold *execute* privileges for the script, too). For example, a bash shell script would start with the line #!/bin/bash. For Perl scripts, the interpreter is named perl and is usually found in the /usr/bin directory. So, the first line of each of our Perl scripts will be #!/usr/bin/perl -W[2]. The -W flag is passed to the perl interpreter and tells perl to display all warnings—this is useful when you are trying to debug new scripts.

---

[2] You can also run a Perl script without including the magic first line—just type **perl** followed by a space and then the name of the script file. So you can invoke this program as ./get_drivers.pl or as perl get_drivers.pl.

The next feature common to all our Perl applications is seen at line 5. If you don't include use strict, Perl will be happy to let you misspell variable names and it will just assume that a misspelled name is a variable that it has never seen before. The use strict directive tells the Perl interpreter to catch this kind of mistake by requiring that you declare all variables before they are used.

The use DBI directive (at line 6) tells Perl that you want to use features defined in the DBI module. You must include a use DBI directive in every application that uses the DBI module.

This application calls the DBI->available_drivers() method to retrieve the names of all drivers currently installed on your host. available_drivers() returns an array of driver names. The loop at lines 14 through 16 iterates through the array and prints each driver name.

To run this script, you first have to be sure that its "x" (executable) permission is turned on:

```
$ chown a+x get_drivers.pl
$ ./get_drivers.pl
Driver: ExampleP
Driver: Pg
Driver: Proxy
```

You can see that there are three DBD drivers installed on my system: ExampleP, Pg, and Proxy.

The DBI class also can give you a list of the data sources accessible through a driver. Let's pick one of these drivers (Pg is the PostgreSQL driver) and print the list of data sources. Listing 14.2 shows the required code:

Listing 14.2 get_datasources.pl

```
 1 #!/usr/bin/perl -W
 2 #
 3 #  Filename: get_datasources.pl
 4 #
 5 use strict;
 6 use DBI;
 7
 8 foreach my $data_source ( DBI->data_sources( "Pg" )) {
 9     print $data_source . "\n";
10 }
```

This script calls the DBI->data_sources() method to obtain a list of the data sources accessible through the Pg driver. Each driver is free to define a data source however it sees fit; the PostgreSQL driver considers a data source to be equivalent to a database. The PostgreSQL driver connects to the template1 database to obtain a list of valid database names. When you run this program, you will see a list of all databases in your database cluster:

```
$ ./get_datasources.pl
dbi:Pg:dbname=movies
dbi:Pg:dbname=perf
dbi:Pg:dbname=template0
dbi:Pg:dbname=template1
```

If you don't see a list of database names when you run this program, you may have to define the DBI_USER and DBI_PASS environment variables. DBI_USER should hold your PostgreSQL user name, and DBI_PASS should hold your PostgreSQL password. In the next two sections, you'll see a better way to supply a username and password to PostgreSQL.

The list returned by get_datasources.pl shows the same set of databases that would be returned using the psql -l command:

```
$ psql -l
        List of databases
  Name      | Owner | Encoding
------------+-------+-----------
 movies     | brucc | SQL_ASCII
 perf       | bruce | SQL_ASCII
 template0  | bruce | SQL_ASCII
 template1  | bruce | SQL_ASCII
```

Notice that these two lists are not identical. The list produced by psql includes the owner and encoding[3] of each database. The list produced from DBI->data_sources() is actually a list of data source names, or DSNs. A DSN is similar in concept to the connection strings that you have seen in earlier chapters.

DBI URLs

A DBI data source name is encoded in the form of a URL (Uniform Resource Locator). A DBI URL is composed of three parts: a protocol (always dbi), a driver name, and a driver-specific string of connection options. For example, the URL for the movies database is dbi:Pg:dbname=movies. The PostgreSQL driver can work with connection URLs of the following form:

```
dbi:Pg:option=value[;option=value]...
```

Where option=value can be any of the values shown in Table 14.1.

Table 14.1 **PostgreSQL DBI URL Options**

Option	Environment Variable Used as Default
service=*service name*	PGSERVICE
dbname=*database name*	PGDATABASE

[3] You won't see the Encoding column on your system if you have not enabled multibyte support.

Table 14.1 **Continued**

host=*host name*	PGHOST
hostaddr=*IP address*	PGHOSTADDR
port=*port number*	PGPORT
username=*user name*	PGUSER
password=*password*	PGPASSWORD
options=*options*	PGOPTIONS
sslmode={disable}allow|prefer|require}	PGSSLMODE

To connect to the movies database, you could use any of the following URLs:

```
dbi:Pg:dbname=movies
dbi:Pg:dbname=movies;host=arturo;port=8234
dbi:Pg:
```

That last URL doesn't include any connection options. DBD::Pg uses the environment variables shown in Table 14.1 to default any values missing from the connection URL.

At this point, you know how to obtain the list of installed drivers, how to get the list of data sources accessible through a given driver, and how to construct a connection URL. Now, let's try to connect to a database (see Listing 14.3).

Listing 14.3 `client1.pl`

```
1 #!/usr/bin/perl -W
2 #
3 #  Filename: client1.pl
4 #
5
6 use strict;
7 use DBI;
8
9 my $dbh = DBI->connect( "dbi:Pg:" );
```

The `DBI->connect()` method tries to connect to the URL that you provide (`dbi:Pg:`). If successful, `connect()` will return a database handle. If `connect()` fails, things get complicated. The `connect()` method can perform a number of different actions, depending on the attributes that you specify. In `client1.pl`, you didn't supply any attributes—I'll get to attributes in a moment.

Let's run this script to see how it reacts to error conditions:

```
$ chmod a+x client1.pl  # Make sure the script is executable
$ ./client1.pl
DBI->connect() failed: FATAL 1:  Database "korry" does not exist
   in the system catalog. at ./client1.pl line 9
```

This error is telling you that client1 tried to connect to a database named korry and I don't have a database named korry. Why did client1 try to connect to that database? Take a look at line 9 in Listing 14.3. When client1 asked DBI to create a connection, it didn't provide a database name. According to Table 14.1, the DBD::Pg driver looks to the PGDATABASE environment variable if you don't specify a database name in the connection URL. If you don't supply a database name in the connection URL and you haven't defined PGDATABASE, how does DBD::Pg decide which database to connect to? To find this answer, you have to look to libpq (the PostgreSQL C API); DBD::Pg is implemented using the libpq library. It's actually libpq that looks for the environment variables shown in Table 14.1. If you don't supply an explicit database in the connection URL and you haven't defined PGDATABASE, libpq will try to connect to a database whose name matches your username; I'm logged in as user korry so libpq (and therefore DBD::Pg) tries to connect to a database named korry.

Now let's run this script again, supplying a value for PGDATABASE:

```
$ PGDATABASE=movies ./client1.pl
Database handle destroyed without explicit disconnect.
```

That's a little better (take my word for it). This message means that you did make a successful connection, but you didn't clean up after yourself as the script ended. Fixing that problem is easy—you need to call the $dbh->disconnect() function before you exit. You'll do that in the next client.

Client 2—Adding Error Checking

client1.pl didn't do any error checking at all. The error messages that you saw were produced by DBI or DBD::Pg, not by the script. For simple applications, it might be sufficient to let DBI handle errors, but in more complex cases, you probably want some other options.

Let's start by modifying the previous client so that it prints its own error message if something goes wrong. Listing 14.4 shows the resulting code.

Listing 14.4   client2a.pl

```perl
 1 #!/usr/bin/perl -W
 2 #
 3 #  Filename: client2a.pl
 4 #
 5
 6 use strict;
 7 use DBI;
 8
 9 my $dbh = DBI->connect( "dbi:Pg:" )
10   or die "Can't connect to PostgreSQL: $DBI::errstr ($DBI::err)\n";
11
12 $dbh->disconnect();
```

This script detects `connect()` failures by examining the return value. `DBI::connect()` returns `undef` (instead of a database handle) when it fails. The error message that prints (see line 10) includes an error message (`$DBI::errstr`) and an error number (`$DBI::err`).

At line 12, `client2a` disconnects the database handle if the connection attempt was successful. This should prevent the error message that you saw with client1 (`Database handle destroyed without explicit disconnect`). Notice that you will never reach line 12 if the connection attempt fails because the script `dies` (at line 10) if `connect()` encounters an error.

Now, let's run this client:

```
$ chmod a+x client2a.pl
$ ./client2a.pl
DBI->connect() failed: FATAL 1:  Database "korry" does not exist
    in the system catalog. at ./client2a.pl line 9
Can't connect to PostgreSQL: FATAL 1:  Database "korry" does not
    exist in the system catalog. (1)
```

There's the error message, but you are still getting the automatic error message delivered by DBI and/or DBD::Pg, too. Listing 14.5 shows how to turn off DBI's automatic error messages.

Listing 14.5   `client2b.pl`

```perl
 1 #!/usr/bin/perl -W
 2 #
 3 #  Filename: client2b.pl
 4 #
 5
 6 use strict;
 7 use DBI;
 8
 9 my $dbh = DBI->connect( "dbi:Pg:", undef, undef, {PrintError => 0} )
10   or die "Can't connect to PostgreSQL: $DBI::errstr ($DBI::err)\n";
11
12 $dbh->disconnect();
```

`client2b` uses another form of the `DBI->connect()` method (actually, it's the same method, just a different number of arguments). The full prototype for the `DBI->connect()` method is

```
DBI->connect( $url, $username, $password, \%attributes )
```

The `$url` parameter specifies to which data source you want to connect. The `$username` and `$password` parameters specify the username and password, respectively (I'll come back to those in a moment). The final parameter is a list of attributes. Every DBI-related handle has a set of attributes that control how the handle behaves.

There are two attributes that control the way a handle responds when an error occurs. client2b.pl sets the PrintError attribute to 0. PrintError controls whether error messages should be printed by the driver (or the DBI class). When PrintError is enabled (which is the default), the driver (or DBI) prints an error message any time an error is encountered—that's where the extra message came from when you ran client2a.pl. If PrintError is disabled (by setting it to 0), the driver will not print any error messages. In either case, the DBI will set $DBI::err and $DBI::errstr. The next error-control attribute is RaiseError. When RaiseError is enabled, the DBI or driver throws an exception (by calling the die() method) whenever an error is encountered. Unless you catch the exception (using eval{}), your application will terminate when an error is raised. RaiseError is disabled by default. If you want a really quick way to handle DBI-related errors, enable RaiseError (that is, set it to 1 using {RaiseError => 1}), and your application will die if any errors occur. We'll leave RaiseError disabled in the examples shown in this chapter.

When you run this client, you'll see that you have disabled the automatic error messages and intercepted any error conditions with your own code:

```
$ chmod a+x client2b.pl
$ ./client2b.pl
Can't connect to PostgreSQL: FATAL 1:  Database "korry" does not
    exist in the system catalog. (1)
```

This time, you only see the error message that you explicitly printed.

If you're using a recent version of DBD::Pg and you're connected to a PostgreSQL server newer than version 7.4, you can examine $DBI::state to find the SQLSTATE value returned by the most recent command. You can find a list of SQLSTATE values in Appendix A, "PostgreSQL Error Codes," of the PostgreSQL reference manual. SQLSTATE values are short strings (such as 40P01, the uncooperative 42846, or the dreaded 42601) that are a little easier to handle if you need to interpret an error result within a program. If you're just displaying an error message to the user, use $DBI::errstr; if you're making some sort of programmatic decision based on an error condition, use $DBI::state.

Client 3—Processing Queries

Now, let's turn our attention to query processing. DBI treats SELECT commands and non-SELECT commands differently. Commands other than SELECT require less-complex processing, so let's look at those first. Listing 14.6 shows the source code for client3a:

Listing 14.6 client3a.pl

```
1 #!/usr/bin/perl -W
2 #
3 #  Filename: client3a.pl
4 #
5
6 use strict;
```

Listing 14.6   **Continued**

```
 7 use DBI;
 8
 9 my $dbh = DBI->connect( "dbi:Pg:", undef, undef, {PrintError => 0} )
10   or die "Can't connect to PostgreSQL: $DBI::errstr ($DBI::err)\n";
11
12 my $rows = $dbh->do( $ARGV[0] );
13
14 if( !defined( $rows )) {
15     print( $dbh->errstr."(".$dbh->err().")\n" );
16 }
17 else {
18     print( "Ok: $rows rows affected\n" );
19 }
20
21 $dbh->disconnect();
```

After successfully connecting to the database (lines 9 and 10), you can use the $dbh->do() method to execute a command. In this example, the command that client3a executes is specified on the command line. The do() method executes a single SQL command and returns *something*. I know that sounds a little vague, but do() encodes a lot of information in its return value—let's see what kinds of information you can discern from the return code.

If the command fails, do() returns undef, and you can interrogate the $dbh->errstr and $dbh->err values to find out what went wrong.

If you execute a command such as CREATE TABLE, ANALYZE, or GRANT, do() will return -1 to indicate success.

If you use do() to execute a command such as DELETE or UPDATE, do() will return the number of rows affected by the command. However, if the command affects zero rows, do() will return the string 0E0. I'll tell you why in just a moment. First, let's run this program and see what happens when you execute a few commands:

```
$ chmod a+x ./client3a.pl
$ ./client3a.pl "GRANT SELECT ON tapes TO bruce"
Ok: -1 rows affected
```

That behaves as advertised. No data rows were affected, so do() returns -1.

If you are following along with me, be sure you have a backup before you execute the next command—it deletes all rows from the tapes table.

```
./client3a.pl "DELETE FROM tapes"
Ok: 5 rows affected
```

In this case, you deleted five rows from the tapes table, so do() returned 5. Now, let's see what happens when an error occurs:

```
./client3a.pl "DELETE FROM ship"
ERROR: Relation "ship" does not exist(7)
```

This time, the table name is misspelled, so the do() method returned undef. We catch this condition at line 14 of client3a.pl, and print the error message (and error code) at line 15.

Now, let's see what the 0E0 business is all about:

```
./client3a.pl "DELETE FROM tapes where tape_id <> tape_id"
Ok: 0E0 rows affected
```

This time, I've fed do() a command that can't possibly affect any rows (it is impossible for tape_id to not be equal to tape_id in any given row). It is not considered an error for a DELETE command (or an UPDATE command) to affect zero rows, so we don't want do() to return undef. Instead, do() returns the mysterious string 0E0. If you haven't figured it out yet, 0E0 is the same thing as $0x10^0$. In other words, 0E0 is 0 written in Perl's dialect of exponential notation. Why doesn't do() just return 0? Because the string 0 is interpreted as False in a logical expression. If you wrote code like this:

```
...
$row_count = $dbh->do("DELETE * FROM tapes WHERE tape_id <> tape_id");

if( $row_count ) {
  print( "Ok, $row_count rows affected\n" );
}
else {
  print( "Yeow! Something bad just happened\n" );
}
...
```

you would be reporting an error if the command affected zero rows. So instead, do() returns 0E0, which is not interpreted as False. In this way, do() returns False only when an error occurs. Perl programmers think a *little* differently?

It's easy to translate the 0E0 into a more palatable 0: just add 0. For example:

```
...
$row_count = $dbh->do("DELETE * FROM tapes WHERE tape_id <> tape_id");

if( $row_count ) {
  print( "Ok, " . $row_count+0 . " rows affected\n" );
}
else {
  print( "Yeow! Something bad just happened\n" );
}
...
```

Be sure that you add 0 *after* checking for undef (undef+0 equals 0).

Enough of that. Let's move on to SELECT execution now.

Executing a SELECT command is more complex than executing other commands because you need a way to process the result set. The DBI package uses a two-step, prepare/execute model for processing SELECT commands. Listing 14.7 shows the basic steps required to process a SELECT command.

Listing 14.7 client3b.pl

```
 1 #!/usr/bin/perl -W
 2 #
 3 #  Filename: client3b.pl
 4 #
 5 use strict;
 6 use DBI;
 7
 8 my $dbh = DBI->connect("dbi:Pg:", undef, undef, {PrintError => 1})
 9  or die "Can't connect to PostgreSQL: $DBI::errstr ($DBI::err)\n";
10
11 my $sth = $dbh->prepare( $ARGV[0] );
12
13 if( defined( $sth )) {
14     if( $sth->execute()) {
15         $sth->dump_results();
16     }
17 }
18
19 $dbh->disconnect();
```

Line 11 prepares a command for execution (the command is taken from the first command-line argument). The prepare() method returns a statement handle, or undef if an error is encountered. Note that I have enabled PrintError in this example to simplify the code a little. If the command is successfully prepared, client3b calls the $sth->execute() method to actually carry out the query. At line 15, client3b takes a real short shortcut. The dump_results() method prints the result set associated with your statement handle. I call this a shortcut because you probably won't want to use this method except in quick-and-dirty programs or as an aid to debugging. If you run this application, I think you'll see what I mean:

```
$ chmod a+x client3b.pl
$ ./client3b.pl "SELECT * FROM customers"
'1', 'Jones, Henry', '555-1212', '1970-10-10'
'2', 'Rubin, William', '555-2211', '1972-07-10'
'3', 'Panky, Henry', '555-1221', '1968-01-21'
'4', 'Wonderland, Alice N.', '555-1122', '1969-03-05'
'5', 'Funkmaster, Freddy', '555-FUNK', undef
'7', 'Gull, Jonathan LC', '555-1111', '1984-02-05'
'8', 'Grumby, Jonas', '555-2222', '1984-02-21'
7 rows
```

All the data shows up, but dump_results() didn't do a very nice job of formatting the results. I'll show you how to fix that a little later. For now, let's go back and talk about some of the things that you can do between the call to prepare() and the call to execute().

The Prepare/Execute Model

In earlier chapters, I explained that the prepare/execute model is useful for two different reasons: performance and simplicity.

Some database systems (including recent versions of PostgreSQL) gain a performance boost by using prepare/execute. In the prepare phase, the client application constructs a query (or other command) that includes placeholders[4] for actual data values. For example, the command INSERT INTO tapes VALUES(?,?) contains two placeholders (the question marks). This parameterized command is sent to the server. The server parses the command, prepares an execution plan, and returns any error messages to the client.

Before a prepared command can be executed, you must *bind* each placeholder. Binding a parameter creates a connection between a placeholder and a value—in other words, binding gives a value to a placeholder. After all the placeholders have been bound, you can execute the command.

The performance gain is realized from the fact that you can execute a prepared command over and over again, possibly providing different placeholder values each time. The server may not have to parse the command and formulate an execution plan once the command has been prepared.

The second advantage offered by the prepare/execute model is applicable to PostgreSQL. By splitting command processing into multiple pieces, you can factor your code for greater simplicity. For example, you may want to place the code that *generates* a command into one method, the code to compute and bind parameter values in a second method, and the code to process results in a third method—for example:

```
. . .

prepare_insert_tapes_command( $sth );

while( defined( $line = <STDIN> )) {
  bind_tape_values( $sth, chomp( $line ));
  execute_insert_tapes( $sth );
}
. . .
```

In this code snippet, you prepare an INSERT command once, and bind and execute it multiple times.

Listing 14.8 shows client3c.pl. When you run this client, you can include a parameterized command on the command line, and it will prompt you to supply a value for each placeholder.

Listing 14.8   client3c.pl
```
1 #!/usr/bin/perl -W
2 #
```

---

[1] Placeholders are also known as parameter markers.

Listing 14.8 **Continued**

```
 3 #  Filename: client3c.pl
 4 #
 5 use strict;
 6 use DBI;
 7
 8 my $dbh = DBI->connect("dbi:Pg:", undef, undef, {PrintError => 1})
 9   or die "Can't connect to PostgreSQL: $DBI::errstr ($DBI::err)\n";
10
11 $dbh->do( "SET TRANSFORM_NULL_EQUALS TO ON" );
12
13 my $sth = $dbh->prepare( $ARGV[0] );
14
15 if( defined( $sth )) {
16
17     get_params( $sth );
18
19     if( $sth->execute()) {
20         $sth->dump_results();
21     }
22 }
23
24 $dbh->disconnect();
25
26 #
27 #  subroutine: get_params( $sth )
28 #
29 sub get_params
30 {
31     my $sth            = shift;
32     my $parameter_count = $sth->{NUM_OF_PARAMS};
33     my $line           = undef;
34
35     for( my $i = 1; $i <= $parameter_count; $i++ ) {
36         print( "Enter value for parameter $i: " );
37
38         chomp( $line = <STDIN> );
39
40         if( length( $line )) {
41             $sth->bind_param( $i, $line );
42         }
43         else {
44             $sth->bind_param( $i, undef );
45         }
46     }
47 }
```

After connecting to the database, client3c executes the command SET TRANSFORM_
NULL_EQUALS TO ON. This command allows you to write WHERE ... = NULL when
you should really write WHERE ... IS NULL. I know that sounds a little mysterious
right now, but I'll show you why you want to do that in a moment. At line 13,
client3c prepares the statement entered on the command line. If that succeeds, you
can call the get_params() method (described next) to prompt the user for parameter
values. Then, client3c wraps up by executing the prepared command and dumping
the results.

The get_params() method (line 29) prompts the user for a value for each placeholder in the command. How do you know how many placeholders appear in the command? The statement handle has a number of attributes that you can query once the
command has been prepared. One of these attributes (NUM_OF_PARAMS) contains the
number of placeholders on the command. The for loop starting at line 35 executes once
for each placeholder. After printing a prompt, get_params() reads one line from STDIN
and strips off the terminator (new-line). If the user enters something, get_params()
calls bind_param() to bind the string entered by the user to the current parameter. If
the user doesn't enter anything (that is, he just presses the Return key), get_params()
binds undef to the current parameter. When you bind undef to a placeholder, you are
effectively setting the parameter to NULL.

Let's run this script a few times. First, execute a command that does not include any
placeholders.

```
$ chmod a+x client3c.pl
$ $ ./client3c.pl "SELECT * FROM customers WHERE customer_id = 2"
'2', 'Rubin, William', '555-2211', '1972-07-10'
1 rows
```

Now, try one that includes a parameter marker:

```
$ ./client3c.pl "SELECT * FROM customers WHERE customer_id = ?"
Enter value for parameter 1: 2
'2', 'Rubin, William', '555-2211', '1972-07-10'
1 rows
```

Finally, see what happens when you *don't* enter a parameter value:

```
$ ./client3c.pl "SELECT * FROM customers WHERE birth_date = ?"
Enter value for parameter 1:
'5', 'Funkmaster, Freddy', '555-2132', undef
1 rows
```

Because get_params() binds undef to this parameter (see line 44), you are executing
the command SELECT * FROM customers WHERE birth_date = NULL. Normally, that
would not be considered a valid command (NULL is never *equal* to anything), but at the
beginning of this script, you enabled PostgreSQL's TRANSFORM_NULL_EQUALS runtime
parameter.

Metadata and Result Set Processing

Now, I'd like to revisit the issue of result set processing. In earlier examples, you've been using `dump_results()` to avoid dealing with too many details at once.

After you call the `execute()` method, you can access the result set and metadata about the result set through the statement handle.

You can use any of three methods to process individual rows within the result set: `fetchrow_arrayref()`, `fetchrow_array()`, or `fetchrow_hashref()`. A fourth method, `fetchall_arrayref()`, returns a reference to an array that contains a reference to each row.

Let's look at each of these methods in detail.

`fetchrow_arrayref()` returns a reference to an array containing the values for the next row in the result set. When you reach the end of the result set, `fetchrow_arrayref()` returns undef. `fetchrow_arrayref()` will also return undef if an error occurs—you have to check `$sth->err()` to distinguish between an error and the end of the result set.

Each element of the array returned by `fetchrow_arrayref()` contains a value that corresponds to a column in the result set. If a row contains NULL values, they are represented by undef values in the array. Listing 14.9 shows a script that processes a result set using the `fetchrow_arrayref()` method.

Listing 14.9   `client3d.pl`

```
 1 #!/usr/bin/perl
 2 #
 3 #  Filename: client3d.pl
 4 #
 5 use strict;
 6 use DBI;
 7
 8 my $dbh = DBI->connect("dbi:Pg:", undef, undef, {PrintError => 1})
 9   or die "Can't connect to PostgreSQL: $DBI::errstr ($DBI::err)\n";
10
11 my $sth = $dbh->prepare( $ARGV[0] );
12
13 if( defined( $sth )) {
14     if( $sth->execute()) {
15         print_results( $sth );
16     }
17 }
18
19 $dbh->disconnect();
20
21 #
22 #  subroutine: print_results( $sth )
23 #
24 sub print_results
```

Listing 14.9   **Continued**

```
25 {
26     my $sth = shift;
27
28     while( my $vals = $sth->fetchrow_arrayref()) {
29         foreach my $val ( @$vals ) {
30             print( $val . "\t" );
31         }
32         print( "\n" );
33     }
34 }
```

The interesting part of this script is the print_results() subroutine (lines 24 through 34). This method loops through the result set by calling fetchrow_arrayref() to retrieve one row at a time. print_results() loops through each value in the array and print the contents. When you run this script, you will see the result set printed in a format similar to that produced by the dump_results() method:

```
$ chmod a+x client3d.pl
$ ./client3d.pl "SELECT * FROM customers"
1       Jones, Henry      555-1212         1970-10-10
2       Rubin, William   555-2211         1972-07-10
3       Panky, Henry     555-1221         1968-01-21
4       Wonderland, Alice N.     555-1122         1969-03-05
7       Gull, Jonathan LC        555-1111         1984-02-05
8       Grumby, Jonas    555-2222         1984-02-21
```

It's important to understand that fetchrow_arrayref() does *not* return an array; it returns a reference to an array. In fact, fetchrow_arrayref() happens to return a reference to the same array each time you call it. This means that each time you call fetchrow_arrayref(), the values from the previous call are overwritten by the next row.

You can see this by modifying the print_results() subroutine to save each reference returned by fetchrow_arrayref(), as shown in Listing 14.10.

Listing 14.10   print_results_and_saved_references

```
...
sub print_results_and_saved_references
{
    my $sth = shift;
    my @saved_refs;

    while( my $vals = $sth->fetchrow_arrayref()) {
        foreach my $val ( @$vals ) {
            print( $val . "\t" );
        }
        print( "\n" );
```

Listing 14.10 **Continued**

```
        push( @saved_refs, $vals );
    }

    print( "Saved References:\n" );

    foreach my $vals ( @saved_refs ) {
        foreach my $val( @$vals ) {
            print( $val . "\t" );
        }
        print( "\n" );
    }
}
...
```

In this version of print_results(), you add each reference returned by fetchrow__
arrayref() to your own @saved_refs array. After you finish processing the result set,
go back and print the contents of @saved_refs. Now the output looks like this:

```
1       Jones, Henry     555-1212        1970-10-10
2       Rubin, William   555-2211        1972-07-10
3       Panky, Henry     555-1221        1968-01-21
4       Wonderland, Alice N.     555-1122        1969-03-05
7       Gull, Jonathan L         1984-02-05
8       Grumby, Jonas    555-2222        1984-02-21
Saved References:
8       Grumby, Jonas    555-2222        1984-02-21
8       Grumby, Jonas    555-2222        1984-02-21
8       Grumby, Jonas    555-2222        1984-02-21
8       Grumby, Jonas    555-2222        1984-02-21
8       Grumby, Jonas    555-2222        1984-02-21
8        Grumby, Jonas       555-2222            1984-02-21
```

You can see that there were six rows in this result set, so you saved six references in
@saved_refs. When you print the contents of @saved_refs, you can see that all prior
results have been overwritten by the last row in the result set. This is because
fetchrow_arrayref() uses a single array *per statement handle*, no matter how many rows
are in the result set.

   In contrast, fetchrow_array() returns a new array each time you call it (except, of
course, when you encounter an error or the end of the result set; then
fetchrow_array() returns undef). Listing 14.11 shows how to process a result set using
the fetchrow_array() method.

Listing 14.11 print_results_using_fetchrow_array

```
...
sub print_results_using_fetchrow_array
{
```

Listing 14.11   **Continued**

```
    my $sth = shift;

    while( my @vals = $sth->fetchrow_array()) {
        foreach my $val ( @vals ) {
            print( $val . "\t" );
        }
        print( "\n" );
    }
}
...
```

In some circumstances, it's easier to work with a hash than with an array. The `fetchrow_hashref()` method fetches the next result set row into a hash and returns a reference to the hash. Listing 14.12 shows how to process a result set using `fetchrow_hashref()`.

Listing 14.12   `print_results_using_fetchrow_hashref`

```
...
sub print_results_using_fetchrow_hashref
{
    my $sth = shift;

    while( my $vals = $sth->fetchrow_hashref()) {
        foreach my $key ( keys( %$vals )) {
            print( $vals->{$key} . "\t" );
        }
        print( "\n" );
    }
}
...
```

Each key in the hash is a column name. For example, if you execute the command SELECT * FROM customers, you will find the following keys:

```
customer_name
birth_date
id
phone
```

There are a couple of points to be aware of when using `fetchrow_hashref()`. First, the order of the column names returned by `keys()` is random[5]. If you feed the same result

---

[5] Random, but consistent. It is extremely likely that the column names will appear in the same order during the processing of the entire result set. If the ordering is important, you should really be using an array in the first place, not a hash.

set to print_results_using_fetchrow_hashref() and print_results_using_
fetchrow_array(), you will see the same values, but the columns are not likely to be
displayed in the same left-to-right order. Second, if a result set contains two or more
columns with the same name, all but one value will be discarded. This makes a lot of
sense because a hash cannot contain duplicate keys. You might encounter this problem
when a query includes computed columns and you forget to name the columns (using
AS). This problem can also occur when you join two or more tables and SELECT the
common columns. For example:

```
./client3d_hashref.pl "
> SELECT
>    datname, blks_read*8192, blks_hit*8192
> FROM
>    pg_stat_database"
0          perf
0          template1
0          template0
235732992  movies
```

Notice that you requested three values, but you see only two of them. The column name
for blks_read*8192 and blks_hit*8192 is the same:

```
?column?
```

So, one of the columns is discarded by fetchrow_hashref(), and you can't predict
which one will be thrown out. If you give a unique name to each column, you will see
all three results:

```
./client3d_hashref.pl "
> SELECT
>    datname, blks_read*8192 AS Read, blks_hit*8192 AS Hit
> FROM
>    pg_stat_database"
perf      0          0
template1 0          0
template0 0          0
movies    243728384        3661824
```

That fixes one bug, but now you have a new problem. This table is difficult to read; it
doesn't have column headers and there is no vertical alignment. Let's fix both of those
problems.

Listings 14.13 through 14.18 show the client3e.pl script. This client is (almost)
capable of executing an arbitrary query and printing a nicely formatted result set. There's
still one problem left in this client, and I'll show you how to fix it in a moment.

Listing 14.13 shows the mainline code for client3e.pl:

Listing 14.13   client3e.pl

```
 1 #!/usr/bin/perl
 2 #
```

Listing 14.13   **Continued**

```perl
3 #  Filename: client3e.pl
4 #
5 use strict;
6 use DBI;
7
8 my $dbh = DBI->connect("dbi:Pg:", undef, undef, {PrintError => 1})
9   or die "Can't connect to PostgreSQL: $DBI::errstr ($DBI::err)\n";
10
11 my $sth = $dbh->prepare( $ARGV[0] );
12
13 if( defined( $sth )) {
14   if( $sth->execute()) {
15     my($widths, $row_values) = compute_column_widths( $sth );
16     print_column_headings( $sth, $widths );
17     print_results( $row_values, $widths );
18   }
19 }
20
21 $dbh->disconnect();
```

After connecting to the database, preparing the command, and executing it, you are ready to print the results. First, call compute_column_widths() (see Listing 14.14) to figure out how wide each column should be. Next, print the column headings, and finally print the results.

Listing 14.14   client3e.pl-compute_column_widths

```perl
23 #
24 #  subroutine: compute_column_widths( $sth )
25 #
26 sub compute_column_widths
27 {
28   my $sth   = shift;
29   my $names = $sth->{NAME};
30   my @widths;
31
32   for( my $col = 0; $col < $sth->{NUM_OF_FIELDS}; $col++ ) {
33     push( @widths, length( $names->[$col] ));
34   }
35
36   my $row_values = $sth->fetchall_arrayref();
37
38   for( my $col = 0; $col < $sth->{NUM_OF_FIELDS}; $col++ ) {
39     for( my $row = 0; $row < $sth->rows(); $row++ ) {
40       if( defined( $row_values->[$row][$col] )) {
41         if( length( $row_values->[$row][$col] ) > $widths[$col] ) {
42           $widths[$col] = length( $row_values->[$row][$col] );
```

Listing 14.14   **Continued**

```
43              }
44            }
45          }
46        }
47
48      return( \@widths, $row_values );
49  }
```

Listing 14.14 shows the compute_column_widths() subroutine. There's a lot of new stuff going on in this subroutine. First, you use the statement handle to retrieve two pieces of metadata. At line 29, compute_column_widths() uses the {NAME} attribute to find column names. {NAME} is a reference to an array of column names[6]. DBI also provides the {NAME_lc} and {NAME_uc} attributes, in case you want the column names to appear in lowercase or uppercase, respectively. The {NUM_OF_FIELDS} attribute returns the number of columns (or fields, if you prefer) in the result set. {NUM_OF_FIELDS} will return 0 for commands other than SELECT.

At lines 32 through 34, compute_columns_widths() loops through each column in the result set and inserts the length of the column name into the widths array. When it finishes the loop, you have an array with {NUM_OF_FIELDS} entries, and each entry in this array contains the length of the corresponding column name.

I mentioned earlier that there are four methods that you can use to walk through a result set. The first three, fetchrow_array(), fetchrow_arrayref(), and fetchrow_hashref(), process a result set one row at a time. The fourth method, fetchall_arrayref(), gives us access to the entire result set at once. We use fetchall_arrayref() at line 36. This method returns a reference to an array of references: one reference for each row in the result set. Think of fetchall__arrayref() as returning a two-dimensional array. For example, to get the value returned in the fourth column of the third row, you can use the syntax $row__values->[3][4].

After you have a reference to the entire result set, compute_column_widths() loops through every row and every column (lines 38 through 46), finding the widest value for each column.

There's another piece of metadata buried in this loop. At line 39, this script calls $sth->rows() method to determine how many rows are in the result set.

Calling $sth->rows()

The DBI reference guide discourages calls to $sth->rows() rows() method, calling>rows();calling>rows>, except in cases where you know that you have executed a command *other than* SELECT. The DBD::Pg driver always returns a meaningful value when you call $sth->rows(). If you are concerned with the portability of your Perl application, you should compute the number of rows in a result set using some other method (such as finding the size of the array returned by fetchall_arrayref()).

---

[6] Some database drivers may include undef column names in the {NAME} array. The DBD::Pg never includes undefined column names.

compute_column_widths() returns two values. The first value is a reference to the @widths array. The second value returned by this method is the reference to the result set.

You may be thinking that it's kind of silly to return the result set reference from this subroutine; why not just call fetchall_arrayref() again when you need it? You can't. After a command has been executed, you can *fetch* the results only once. Of course, you can *access* the result set as many times as you like; you just can't fetch any given row more than once.

Now, let's look at the pad() subroutine (see Listing 14.15).

Listing 14.15   client3e.pl-pad

```
51 #
52 #  subroutine: pad( $val, $col_width, $pad_char )
53 #
54 sub pad
55 {
56   my( $val, $col_width, $pad_char ) = @_;
57   my $pad_len;
58
59   $val      = "" if ( !defined( $val ));
60   $pad_char = " " if( !defined( $pad_char ));
61   $pad_len  = $col_width - length( $val );
62
63   return( $val . $pad_char x $pad_len . " " );
64
65 }
```

The pad() subroutine simply pads the given value ($val) to $col_width characters. If the given value is undef, meaning that it is a NULL value from the result set, pad() translates it into an empty string for convenience. The optional $pad_char parameter determines the pad character. If the caller does not provide a $pad_char, pad() will pad with spaces.

Listing 14.16 shows the print_column_headings() subroutine.

Listing 14.16   client3e.pl-print_column_headings

```
67 #
68 #  subroutine: print_column_headings( $sth )
69 #
70 sub print_column_headings
71 {
72   my $sth    = shift;
73   my $widths = shift;
74   my $names  = $sth->{NAME};
75
76   for( my $col = 0; $col < $sth->{NUM_OF_FIELDS}; $col++ ) {
77     print( pad( $names->[$col], $widths->[$col] ));
78   }
```

Listing 14.16 **Continued**

```
79
80   print( "\n" );
81
82   for( my $col = 0; $col < $sth->{NUM_OF_FIELDS}; $col++ ) {
83     print( pad( "-", $widths->[$col], "-" ));
84   }
85
86   print( "\n" );
87 }
```

The print_column_headings() subroutine prints properly aligned column headings.
The first loop (lines 76 through 78) prints each column name, padded with spaces to the
width of the column. The second loop (lines 82 through 84) prints a string of dashes
under each column name.

The print_results() subroutine is shown in Listing 14.17.

Listing 14.17 client3e.pl-print_results

```
89 #
90 #   subroutine: print_results( )
91 #
92 sub print_results
93 {
94   my( $rows, $widths ) = @_;
95
96   for( my $row = 0; $row < $sth->rows(); $row++ ) {
97     for( my $col = 0; $col < $sth->{NUM_OF_FIELDS}; $col++ ) {
98       print( pad( $rows->[$row][$col], $widths->[$col] ));
99     }
100    print( "\n" );
101  }
102 }
```

Finally, print_results() prints the entire result set. Use the widths array (constructed
by compute_column_widths()) to pad each value to the appropriate width.

Now let's run this script a few times:

```
$ chmod a+x ./client3e.pl
$ ./client3e "SELECT * FROM customers";
id customer_name        phone    birth_date
-- -------------------- -------- ----------
1  Jones, Henry         555-1212 1970-10-10
2  Rubin, William       555-2211 1972-07-10
3  Panky, Henry         555-1221 1968-01-21
4  Wonderland, Alice N. 555-1122 1969-03-05
```

```
8  Grumby, Jonas        555-2222 1984-02-21
7  Gull, Jonathan LC             1984-02-05
```

That looks much better; all the columns line up nicely and you can finally see the column names.

Now how does this client react when you give it a bad table name?

```
$ ./client3e.pl "SELECT * FROM ship"
DBD::Pg::st execute failed: ERROR:  Relation "ship" does not
exist at ./client3e.pl line 14.
```

That's not the prettiest error message, but it certainly does tell you what's wrong and even where in your code the error occurs.

What happens if you try to execute a command other than SELECT?

```
$ ./client3e.pl "INSERT INTO tapes VALUES( 'JS-4820', 'Godzilla' )"
DBD::Pg::st fetchall_arrayref failed: no statement executing at
 ./client3e.pl line 36.
```

That's not so good. You can't use fetchall_arrayref() or any of the fetch() methods, unless the command that you execute returns a result set. Notice that you got all the way to line 36 before you ran into an error. That's an important point—you can still use prepare() and execute() to executed non-SELECT commands, you just can't fetch from a nonexistent result set.

Listing 14.18 presents a new version of the client3e.pl mainline that fixes the problem.

Listing 14.18 client3e.pl-modified mainline

```perl
 1 #!/usr/bin/perl -W
 2 #
 3 #  Filename: client3e.pl
 4 #
 5 use strict;
 6 use DBI;
 7
 8 my $dbh = DBI->connect("dbi:Pg:", undef, undef, {PrintError => 1})
 9   or die "Can't connect to PostgreSQL: $DBI::errstr ($DBI::err)\n";
10
11 my $sth = $dbh->prepare( $ARGV[0] );
12
13 if( defined( $sth )) {
14   if( $sth->execute()) {
15     if( $sth->{NUM_OF_FIELDS} == 0 ) {
16         print($sth->{pg_cmd_status} . "\n" );
17     }
18     else {
19       my($widths, $row_values) = compute_column_widths( $sth );
20       print_column_headings( $sth, $widths );
```

Listing 14.18 **Continued**

```
21         print_results( $row_values, $widths );
22     }
23   }
24 }
25
26 $dbh->disconnect();
```

You distinguish between SELECT commands and other commands by interrogating $sth->{NUM_OF_FIELDS}. If {NUM_OF_FIELDS} returns 0, you can safely assume that you just executed some command other than SELECT. If {NUM_OF_FIELDS} returns anything other than 0, you know that you just executed a SELECT command.

You can't use $sth->rows() to determine the command type. When you execute a SELECT command, $sth->rows() returns the number of rows in the result set. When you execute an INSERT, UPDATE, or DELETE command, $sth->rows() returns the number of rows affected by the command. For all other command types, $sth->rows() will return -1.

If you've just executed an INSERT or UPDATE command, you can call $dbh->last_insert_id() to retrieve the value of the sequence assigned to the new row (assuming that the row does in fact contain a sequence column). $dbh->last_insert_id() comes in two flavors. Use the first variant if you know the name of the sequence:

```
$lastID = $dbh->last_insert_id( undef, undef, undef, undef, {sequence=>name } );
```

The first four arguments are ignored by DBD::Pg (but may be used by other drivers). The last argument must be an attribute that specifies the name of the sequence.

Use the second variant when you know the name of the table but not the name of the sequence:

```
$lastID = $dbh->last_insert_id( undef, $schema, $table, undef );
```

The first and last arguments are always ignored by DBD::Pg. The $schema and $table arguments ($schema by be undef) specify the table that you're interested in. DBD::Pg tries to find a UNIQUE, NOT NULL column in that table whose default value is based on a sequence. If it finds such a column, last_insert_id() returns the value of the sequence. If the given table contains two or more sequences, last_insert_id() returns the sequence used by the PRIMARY KEY (assuming that it can find a sequence-based PRIMARY KEY).

In general, you should use the first form of last_insert_id() when you can. The second form forces DBD::Pg to search through the PostgreSQL dictionary to find the correct sequence and that can really slow things down (the second form can also produce an unexpected result when it encounters a table that contains two or more sequence-based columns).

Other Statement and Database Handle Attributes

At line 16, client3e uses a nonstandard extension to the DBI statement handle: pg_cmd_status. The PostgreSQL DBI driver adds four PostgreSQL-specific attributes to the statement handle. pg_cmd_status returns the standard PostgreSQL command status. For example, when you INSERT a new row, the command status is the word INSERT, followed by the OID of the new row, and then the number of rows affected:

```
$ psql -d movies
movies=# INSERT INTO tapes VALUES
movies-# (
movies(#    'KL-24381', 'The Day The Earth Stood Still'
movies(# );
INSERT 510735 1
```

Now, when you run client3e.pl (with the new code in place), you see that non-SELECT commands are handled properly:

```
$ ./client3e.pl "INSERT INTO tapes VALUES( 'JS-4820', 'Godzilla' )"
INSERT 510736 1

$ ./client3e.pl "DELETE FROM tapes WHERE tape_id = 'JS-4820'"
DELETE 1
```

The other three statement handle extensions are pg_size, pg_type, and pg_oid_status.

The pg_size attribute returns a reference to an array that contains the size of each column in the result set. The size of a variable-length column is returned as -1. In most cases, this information is not terribly useful because it represents the size of each column *on the server*, not the actual amount of data sent to the client. If you need to know the width of a column, you'll have to compute it by hand as you did in the compute_column_widths() function.

pg_type is a little more useful than pg_size. pg_type returns a reference to an array that contains the name of the data type of each column in the result set. Note that pg_type does not understand user-defined data types and will return the string "unknown" for such columns.

The pg_oid_status attribute returns the OID (object-ID) of the new row after an INSERT command is executed. This attribute uses the libpq PQoidstatus() function and has the same limitations (namely, pg_oid_status returns a meaningful value only when an INSERT command creates a single new row).

The DBI API supports a few more statement handle attributes that are not well-supported (or not supported at all) by the PostgreSQL driver.

The {TYPE} attribute returns a reference to an array containing data type codes (one entry per result set column). The values returned by {TYPE} are intended to provide database-independent data type mappings. Currently, the DBD::Pg module maps PostgreSQL data types into the symbolic values shown in Table 14.2. All other PostgreSQL data types map to a number—the OID (object id) for the type as defined in the pg_type system table. For example, the OID for the BOX data type is 603—the {TYPE} value for a BOX column is 603.

Table 14.2 {TYPE} **Mappings**

PostgreSQL Data Type	Symbolic Name
BYTEA	SQL_BINARY
INT8	SQL_DOUBLE
INT2	SQL_SMALLINT
INT4	SQL_INTEGER
FLOAT4	SQL_NUMERIC
FLOAT8	SQL_REAL
BPCHAR	SQL_CHAR
VARCHAR	SQL_VARCHAR
DATE	SQL_DATE
TIME	SQL_TIME
TIMESTAMP	SQL_TIMESTAMP

The {PRECISION}, {SCALE}, and {NULLABLE} attributes are not supported by DBD::Pg.
{PRECISION} returns the same value as {pg_size}, {SCALE} will return undef, and
{NULLABLE} will return 2 (meaning *unknown*).

Another statement handle attribute not supported by DBD::Pg is {CursorName}.
Other drivers return the name of the cursor associated with statement handle (if any):
the {CursorName} attribute in DBD::Pg returns undef. You *can* use cursors with the
PostgreSQL driver, but you must do so explicitly by executing the DECLARE ...
CURSOR, FETCH, and CLOSE commands.

As you know, PostgreSQL cursors can be used only within a transaction block. By
default, a DBI database handle starts out in AutoCommit mode. When the {AutoCommit}
attribute is set to 1 (meaning *true*), all changes are committed as soon as they are made. If
you want to start a transaction block, simply set {AutoCommit} to 0 (meaning *false*), and the
DBD::Pg driver will automatically execute a BEGIN command for you. When you want to
complete a transaction block, you can call $dbh->commit() or $dbh->rollback(). You
should not try to directly execute COMMIT or ROLLBACK commands yourself—the DBD::Pg
driver will intercept those commands and reward you with an error message. The next
client (client4.pl) lets you explore DBI transaction processing features interactively.

Client 4—An Interactive Query Processor

The final client application for this chapter will be a general purpose interactive command processor. Perl makes it easy for you to create a feature-rich application with a
minimum of code: You don't need a lot of scaffolding just to use the basic DBI features.
Accordingly, I'll use this application as a way to explain some of the remaining DBI features that haven't really fit in anywhere else.

client4.pl (see Listing 14.19) accepts two kinds of commands from the user.
Commands that start with a colon are meta-commands and are processed by the application. Commands that don't begin with a colon are PostgreSQL commands and are sent
to the server.

Listing 14.19   client4.pl-mainline

```perl
 1 #!/usr/bin/perl -W
 2 #
 3 #  Filename: client4.pl
 4 #
 5
 6 use DBI;
 7 use Term::ReadLine;
 8
 9 my $dbh = DBI->connect("dbi:Pg:", undef, undef, {PrintError => 1})
10   or die "Can't connect to PostgreSQL: $DBI::errstr ($DBI::err)\n";
11
12 my $term = new Term::ReadLine( 'client4' );
13
14 print( "\nEnter SQL commands or :help for assistance\n\n" );
15
16 while( my $command = $term->readline( "--> " )) {
17     if( $command =~ /^:(\w+)\s*(.*)/ ) {
18         eval {
19             my $subr_name = "do_$1";
20             my @args      = split '\s', $2||'';
21
22             &$subr_name( $dbh, @args );
23         }
24     }
25     else {
26         do_sql_command( $dbh, $command );
27     }
28 }
29
30 do_quit( $dbh );
```

The mainline code for this client is a little different from the earlier clients in this chapter. Because this client is interactive, you will need to accept queries and other commands from the user. The Term::ReadLine module (which you use at line 7) offers the
Perl equivalent of the GNU ReadLine and History libraries.

The main loop in this application (lines 16 through 28) prompts the user for a command, executes the command, and displays the results (if any).

When you call the $term->readline() method (at line 16), the user is presented
with the prompt (-->) and can compose a command string using the editing and history
features offered by the Term::ReadLine module. $term->readline() returns the fully
composed command string.

This client application handles two different command types. If a command starts
with a colon character (:), it is treated as a meta-command and is handled by subroutines
that I'll explain in a moment. If a command docs *not* start with a colon, assume that it is

a PostgreSQL command, and call the `do_sql_command()` method to execute the command and display the results.

We will support the following meta-commands:

- `:help`
- `:autocommit [0|1]`
- `:commit`
- `:rollback`
- `:trace [0|1|2|3|4] [tracefile]`
- `:show_tables`
- `:show_table table-name`
- `:show_types`

Meta-commands are detected and dispatched starting at line 17. If you're not used to reading Perl regular expression strings, the `if` command at line 17 can look pretty daunting. The `=~` operator determines whether the string on the left side (`$command`) matches the regular-expression on the right side. I'll interpret the regular-expression for you: You want to match a pattern that starts at the beginning of the string (`^`) and is immediately followed by a colon (`:`). Next, you expect to see one or more *word* characters (`\w+`). A *word* character is an alphanumeric character or an underscore. I'll explain the extra parenthesis in a moment. Following the leading word, you expect zero or more whitespace characters (that is, tabs or spaces). Anything else on the command line is gobbled up by the last subpattern (`.*`).

Two of these subpatterns (`\w+` and `.*`) are enclosed in parentheses. Enclosing a subpattern like this tells Perl that you want it to *remember* the characters that match that subpattern in a special variable that you can use later. We have two enclosed subpatterns: the characters that match the first subpattern will be remembered in variable `$1` and the characters that match the second subpattern will be remembered in `$2`.

The effect here is that you detect meta-commands by looking for strings that start with a colon immediately followed by a word[7]. If you find one, the first word (the meta-command itself) will show up in `$1`, and any arguments will show up in `$2`. That regular-expression operator is pretty powerful, huh?

After you have parsed out the meta-command and the optional arguments, use a little more Perl magic to call the subroutine that handles the given command. If the user enters the meta-command `:help`, you want to call the subroutine `do_help()`. If the user enters the meta-command `:commit`, you want to call the subroutine `do_commit()`. You probably see a pattern developing here; to find the subroutine that handles a given meta-command, you simply glue the characters `do` to the front of the command name. That's what line 19 is doing. At line 19, you are splitting any optional arguments (which are all stored in `$2`) into an array.

---

[7] You could, of course, change the regular-expression to look for a string that starts with a colon, followed by optional whitespace, followed by a word.

Now to call the appropriate command handler, you call the subroutine, *by name*, at
line 22. Don't let the funky looking expression at line 22 confuse you. This is just a plain
old subroutine call, but Perl determines *which* subroutine to call by evaluating the contents of the $subr_name variable. Note that you can't defer the name resolution until
runtime like this if you are in strict mode—I have omitted the use strict directive
from this script. Another approach that you can take is to use strict in most of your
code, but specify no strict in the cases that would otherwise cause an error.

I have wrapped the subroutine invocation in an eval{} block. This is roughly equivalent to a try{}/catch{} block in Java—it catches any errors thrown by the code inside
of the block. If the user enters an invalid meta-command (that is, a command that starts
with a colon but doesn't match any of the do_xxx() subroutines), the eval{} block will
silently catch the exception rather than aborting the entire application.

All of the command handler subroutines expect to receive a database handle as the
first parameter, and then an array of optional parameters.

If the command entered by the user does not match your meta-command regular-
expression, client4 assumes that the command should be sent to the PostgreSQL server
and calls the do_sql_command() subroutine (see Listing 14.20).

Listing 14.20   client4.pl-do_sql_command

```
32 sub do_sql_command
33 {
34    my $dbh     = shift;
35    my $command = shift;
36
37    my $sth = $dbh->prepare( $command );
38
39    if( defined( $sth )) {
40        if( $sth->execute()) {
41            process_results( $dbh, $sth );
42        }
43    }
44 }
```

The do_sql_command() subroutine is called whenever the user enters a PostgreSQL
command. We expect two arguments in this subroutine: a database handle and the text of
the command. There are no surprises in this subroutine: do_sql_command() simply prepares the command, executes it, and calls process_results() to finish up.

```
46 sub do_ping
47 {
48    my( $dbh, @args ) = @_;
49
50    print( $dbh->ping() ? "Ok\n" : "Not On" );
51 }
```

This subroutine, do_ping(), is called whenever the user enters the command :ping. The $dbh->ping() subroutine is designed to test the validity of a database handle. The DBD::Pg implementation of this method executes an empty query to ensure that the database connection is still active.

The do_autocommit() subroutine shown in Listing 14.21 is used to enable or disable AutoCommit mode. By default, every command executed through DBI is committed as soon as it completes. If you want to control transaction boundaries yourself, you must disable AutoCommit mode. To disable AutoCommit, execute the command :autocommit 0. To enable AutoCommit, use :autocommit 1. The $dbh->{AutoCommit} attribute keeps track of the commit mode for a database handle.

Listing 14.21   client4.pl-do_autocommit

```
53 sub do_autocommit
54 {
55   my( $dbh, @args ) = @_;
56
57   $dbh->{AutoCommit} = $args[0];
58
59 }
```

Listing 14.22 shows the do_commit() and do_rollback() subroutines.

Listing 14.22   client4.pl-do_commit, do_rollback

```
61 sub do_commit
62 {
63   my( $dbh, @args ) = @_;
64
65   $dbh->commit();
66 }
67
68 sub do_rollback
69 {
70     my( $dbh, @args ) = @_;
71
72     $dbh->rollback();
73 }
```

After you have disabled AutoCommit mode, you can commit and roll back transactions using :commit and :rollback. If you try to :commit or :rollback while AutoCommit is enabled, you will be rewarded with an error message (commit ineffective with AutoCommit enabled.).

Next, you have the do_quit() subroutine (see Listing 14.23).

Listing 14.23   client4.pl-do_quit

```
75 sub do_quit
76 {
77     my( $dbh, @args ) = @_;
78
79     if( defined( $dbh )) {
80         $dbh->disconnect();
81     }
82
83     exit( 0 );
84 }
```

The do_quit() subroutine is simple—if the database handle is defined (that is, is not undef), disconnect it. The call to exit() causes this application to end.

In Listing 14.24, you see the do_trace() subroutine.

Listing 14.24   client4.pl-do trace

```
86 sub do_trace
87 {
88     my( $dbh, @args ) = @_;
89
90     $dbh->trace( @args );
91
92 }
```

This subroutine gives you a way to adjust the DBI tracing mechanism. The $dbh_trace() method expects either one or two arguments: a trace level (0 through 4) and an optional filename. Every DBI application starts at trace level 0, meaning that no trace output is generated. If you don't supply a trace filename, trace output is sent to STDOUT (your terminal).

If you want a *little* information about what's going on under the hood, set the trace level to 1. Here's an example of what you'll see:

```
--> :trace 1
    DBI::db=HASH(0x8208020) trace level set to 1 in DBI 1.30-nothread

--> SELECT * FROM customers LIMIT 1;
dbd_st_prepare: statement = >SELECT * FROM customers LIMIT 1;<
dbd_st_preparse: statement = >SELECT * FROM customers LIMIT 1;<
    <- prepare('SELECT * FROM customers LIMIT 1;')= DBI::st=HASH(0x82081a0) at
Âclient4.pl line 37
dbd_st_execute
    <- execute= 1 at client4.pl line 39
...
```

Okay, you actually get a *lot* of information at trace level 1, but not as much as you do for higher trace levels. Tracing is useful for debugging and for understanding how DBI and the PostgreSQL driver are carrying out your requests.

Listing 14.25 shows the do_help subroutine.

Listing 14.25 `client4.pl-do_help`

```
 94 sub do_help
 95 {
 96     print( "Commands\n" );
 97     print( "   :help\t\t\t\tShow help text\n" );
 98     print( "   :autocommit [0|1]\t\tSet AutoCommit\n" );
 99     print( "   :commit\t\t\tCOMMIT TRANSACTION\n" );
100     print( "   :rollback\t\t\tROLLBACK TRANSACTION\n" );
101     print( "   :trace [0|1|2|3|4] [tracefile]\tSet Trace level\n" );
102     print( "   :show_tables\t\t\tShow all table names\n" );
103     print( "   :show_table table_name\tDescribe table\n" );
104     print( "   :show_types\t\t\tList Data Types\n" );
105 }
```

`do_help()` is called whenever the user enters the command `:help`.

This subroutine (`do_show_tables()`, Listing 14.26) shows how to call the `$dbh->table_info()` method.

Listing 14.26 `client4.pl-do_show_tables`

```
107 sub do_show_tables
108 {
109   my( $dbh, @args ) = @_;
110
111   process_results( $dbh, $dbh->table_info());
112
113 }
```

`$dbh->table_info()` returns a result set containing a list of tables accessible through the database handle. Here is an example:

```
--> :show_tables
TABLE_CAT TABLE_SCHEM TABLE_NAME TABLE_TYPE REMARKS
--------- ----------- ---------- ---------- -------
          bruce       customers  TABLE
          bruce       rentals    TABLE
          bruce       returns    TABLE
          bruce       tapes      TABLE
```

The author of each DBD driver can interpret the `$dbh->table_info()` request in a different way. The DBD::Pg driver returns all table and view definitions owned by the current user; other drivers may give different results. In some cases, you may find it easier to call the $dbh->tables() method, which returns an array of table names rather than a result set.

The do_show_types() subroutine, shown in Listing 14.27, displays a list of server data types.

Listing 14.27   client4.pl-do_show_types

```
115 sub do_show_types
116 {
117   my( $dbh, @args ) = @_;
118
119   print("Type            Type        SQL Col.  Prefix  \n");
120   print("Name            Parameters  Type Size    Suffix\n");
121   print("--------------- ------------ ---- ----- - ------\n" );
122
123   foreach my $type ( $dbh->type_info( undef )) {
124       printf( "%-15s %-12s %-3d  %-5d %s %s\n",
125               $type->{TYPE_NAME},
126               $type->{CREATE_PARAMS} || "",
127               $type->{DATA_TYPE},
128               $type->{COLUMN_SIZE},
129               $type->{LITERAL_PREFIX} || " ",
130               $type->{LITERAL_SUFFIX} || " " );
131   }
132 }
```

At line 123, do_show_types() calls the $dbh->type_info() method. This method returns an array of hash references. Each hash corresponds to a single data type and contains a number of key/value pairs. do_show_types() prints the {TYPE_NAME}, {CREATE_PARAMS}, {DATA_TYPE}, and {COLUMN_SIZE} attributes as well as the prefix and suffix characters. Here is an example:

```
--> :show_types
Type            Type        SQL Col.  Prefix
Name            Parameters  Type Size    Suffix
--------------- ------------ ---- ----- - ------
bytea                        -2   4096  ' '
bool                         0    1     ' '
int8                         8    20
int2                         5    5
int4                         4    10
text                         12   4096  ' '
float4          precision    6    12
float8          precision    7    24
abstime                      10   20    ' '
reltime                      10   20    ' '
tinterval                    11   47    ' '
```

```
money                       0    24
bpchar       max length     1    4096     ' '
bpchar       max length     12   4096     ' '
varchar      max length     12   4096     ' '
date                        9    10       ' '
time                        10   16       ' '
datetime                    11   47       ' '
timespan                    11   47       ' '
timestamp                   10   19       ' '
```

You may notice that this list is not a complete list of PostgreSQL data types. It is also not entirely accurate. For example, you know that a VARCHAR column has no maximum length, but it is reported to have a length of 4096 bytes.

The $dbh->type_info() method is implemented by the DBD::Pg driver, not by the DBI package, so the DBD::Pg author chose the data types that he used most often. My recommendation would be to ignore the information returned by this method, at least when you are connected to a PostgreSQL database. You may find this method more useful if you are exploring *other* database systems.

Listing 14.28 shows the do_show_table() subroutine.

Listing 14.28 client4.pl-do_show_table

```
134 sub do_show_table
135 {
136   my( $dbh, @args ) = @_;
137
138   my $sth = $dbh->prepare( "SELECT * FROM $args[0] WHERE 1 <> 1" );
139
140   if( defined( $sth )) {
141       if( $sth->execute()) {
142           print_meta_data( $dbh, $sth );
143           $sth->finish();
144       }
145   }
146 }
```

I wanted to include a subroutine that would display the layout of a named table, similar to the \d meta-command in psql. Older versions of the DBI package do not provide a method that exposes this information, but you can certainly trick it into providing enough metadata that you can build such a method yourself.

The do_show_table() method is called whenever the user enters a command such as :show_table customers. The trick is to construct a query that returns all columns, but is guaranteed to return 0 rows. At line 138, do_show_table() creates and executes a query of the following form:

SELECT * FROM table-name WHERE 1 <> 1;

The WHERE clause in this command can never evaluate to True so it will never return any rows. When you execute this query, you get a result set, even though no rows are returned. You can examine the metadata from this result set to determine the layout of the table. After displaying the metadata, do_show_table() calls $sth->finish() to tell DBI that you are finished with this result set.

If you're using a recent version of DBI and DBD::Pg, you can obtain similar information by calling the $dbh->column_info() method.

The print_meta_data subroutine is shown in Listing 14.29.

Listing 14.29   client4.pl-print_meta_data

```
148 sub print_meta_data
149 {
150   my $dbh = shift;
151   my $sth = shift;
152
153   my $field_count = $sth->{NUM_OF_FIELDS};
154   my $names       = $sth->{NAME};
155   my $pg_types    = $sth->{pg_type};
156
157   print( "Name                          | Type  \n" );
158   print( "------------------------------+--------\n" );
159
160   for( my $col = 0; $col < $field_count; $col++ ) {
161     printf( "%-30s| %-8s\n", $names->[$col], $pg_types->[$col] );
162   }
163 }
```

This subroutine prints the metadata associated with a result set. print_meta_data() is called from the do_show_table() subroutine.

This subroutine shows how to obtain the number of fields in a result set ($sth->{NUM_OF_FIELDS}), the name of each column ($sth->{NAME}), and the PostgreSQL data type name for each column ($sth->{pg_type}).

As I mentioned earlier, the DBD::Pg driver adds three PostgreSQL-specific attributes to a statement handle: {pg_type}, {pg_oid_status}, and {pg_ctl_status}.

Here is a sample showing print_meta_data() in action:

```
--> :show_table customers
Name                          | Type
------------------------------+--------
id                            | int4
customer_name                 | varchar
phone                         | bpchar
birth_date                    | date
```

The process_results() subroutine (see Listing 14.30) prints the result of a PostgreSQL command.

Listing 14.30 `client4.pl-process_results`

```
165 sub process_results
166 {
167   my $dbh = shift;
168   my $sth = shift;
169
170   if( defined( $sth )) {
171       if( $sth->{NUM_OF_FIELDS} == 0 ) {
172         print( $sth->{pg_cmd_status} . "\n" );
173       }
174       else {
175         my($widths, $row_values) = compute_column_widths( $sth );
176         print_column_headings( $sth, $widths );
177         print_results( $sth, $row_values, $widths );
178       }
179   }
180 }
```

You've already seen most of this code in earlier clients. `process_results()` begins by deciding whether it's processing a SELECT command or some other type of command. If the number of fields in the result set is 0 (that is, this is a non-SELECT command), `process_results()` simply prints the `$sth->{pg_cmd_status}` attribute. If `process_results()` decide that you *are* processing a SELECT command, it computes the column widths, prints the column headings, and then prints the entire result set.

The `compute_column_widths()`, `print_column_headings()`, and `print_results()` subroutines are identical to those used in `client3e.pl` earlier in this chapter, so I won't describe them here.

Let's run this client and exercise it a bit:

```
$ chmod a+x client4.pl
$ ./client4.pl

Enter SQL commands or :help for assistance

--> :help
Commands
  :help                          Show help text
  :autocommit [0|1]              Set AutoCommit
  :commit                        COMMIT TRANSACTION
  :rollback                      ROLLBACK TRANSACTION
  :trace [0|1|2|3|4] [filename]  Set Trace level
  :show_tables                   Show all table names
  :show_table table_name         Describe table
  :show_types                    List Data Types
```

So far, so good. This help text was generated by the do_help() subroutine. Now, let's see a list of the tables in this database:

```
--> :show_tables
TABLE_CAT TABLE_SCHEM TABLE_NAME TABLE_TYPE REMARKS
--------- ----------- ---------- ---------- -------
          bruce       customers  TABLE
          bruce       rentals    TABLE
          bruce       returns    TABLE
          bruce       tapes      TABLE
```

Next, I'll turn off AutoCommit mode, create a new table, and show the layout of the new table:

```
--> :autocommit 0

--> CREATE TABLE foobar( pkey INTEGER, data VARCHAR );
CREATE TABLE

--> :show_table foobar
Name                            | Type
--------------------------------+--------
pkey                            | int4
data                            | varchar
```

Now, let's roll back this transaction and try to view the table layout again:

```
--> :rollback
--> :show_table foobar
DBD::Pg::st execute failed: ERROR:  Relation "foobar" does not exist at
Â./client4.pl line 141.
```

The :rollback meta-command apparently worked (we don't see any error messages), but the :show_table meta-command has failed. We expect this :show_table command to fail because we have rolled back the CREATE TABLE command.

You may have noticed that I haven't included any error-handling code in this application. When it makes the initial connection to the database (way back at line 9 of this script), client4 sets the {PrintError} attribute to 1 so DBI and the DBD::Pg driver print any error messages that you may encounter.

Summary

The first time I looked at a Perl program, my reaction was "that is some *ugly* code." I still think Perl is an ugly language, but it sure is useful! I am amazed at how quickly you can construct a useful application with Perl.

After reading this chapter, you may think that Perl is great for quick-and-dirty programs, but not for serious applications. I would disagree—like any programming language, you can write incomprehensible code in Perl. But you can also write Perl scripts that are easy to understand and not too difficult to maintain. Include comments in your code. Avoid constructs that are difficult to understand. Perl often offers many ways to do any one thing: Use the most descriptive form, not the most cryptic.

One of the real benefits to the combination of Perl and PostgreSQL is that you can execute Perl scripts (accessing a PostgreSQL database) from within a web server. When you write Perl scripts intended to run within a web server, the script produces a new web page each time it executes. Because a Perl script can interface with PostgreSQL, you can generate dynamic web content on-the-fly.

I haven't covered web interfacing in this chapter, but Chapter 15, "Using PostgreSQL with PHP," shows you how to use PostgreSQL with the PHP web server scripting language.

15

Using PostgreSQL with PHP

PHP is a general-purpose programming language, but PHP is most commonly used to build dynamic web pages. A *dynamic* web page is a document that is regenerated each time it is displayed. For example, each time you point your web browser to cnn.com, you see the latest news. PHP is useful for building dynamic web pages because you can embed PHP programs within HTML documents. In fact, you can *produce* HTML documents from a PHP script.

PHP Architecture Overview

The job of a web server (such as Apache or Microsoft's IIS) is to reply to requests coming from a client (usually a web browser). When a browser connects to a web server, it requests information by sending a URL (Uniform Resource Locator). For example, if you browse to the URL http://www.postgresql.org/software.html, your web browser connects to the server at www.postgresql.org and requests a file named software.html.

After the web server has received this request, it must decide how to reply. If the requested file cannot be found, you'll see the all too familiar HTTP 404 - File not found. Most web servers will choose a response based on the extension of the requested file. A filename ending with .html (or .htm) is usually associated with a text file containing a HTML document.

Occasionally, you'll see a URL that ends in the suffix .php. A .php file is a script that is executed by a PHP processor embedded within the web server. The script is executed each time a client requests it. The web *browser* never sees the .php script; only the web server sees it. As the .php script executes, it sends information back to the browser (usually in the form of an HTML document).

Listing 15.1 shows a simple PHP script.

Listing 15.1 `Simple.php`

```
1  <?php
2    # Filename: Simple.php
3    echo "Hey there, I'm a PHP script!";
4  ?>
```

When you run this script (I'll show you how in a moment), the PHP interpreter will send the string "Hey there, I'm a PHP script!" to the browser.

PHP syntax might look a little strange at first, so here's a quick explanation. The script starts with the characters `<?php`: This tells the web server that everything that follows, up to the next `?>`, is a PHP script and should be interpreted by the PHP processor. The next line is treated as a comment because it starts with a `#` character (PHP understands other comment characters, such as "`//`" as well). The third line is where stuff happens—this is a call to PHP's `echo()` function. `echo()` is pretty easy to understand; it just sends a string to the web browser. The characters on line 4 (`?>`) mark the end of the script.

Web *browsers* don't understand how to interpret PHP scripts; they prefer HTML documents. If you can use PHP to send textual data from the server to the browser, you can also send HTML documents (because an HTML document is textual data). This next PHP script (see Listing 15.2) will create an HTML document (and send it to the browser) as it executes.

Listing 15.2 `SimpleHTML.php`

```
1  <?php
2    # Filename: SimpleHTML.php
3    echo "<HTML>\n";
4    echo   "<HEAD>\n";
5    echo     "<TITLE>SimpleHTML</TITLE>\n";
6    echo   "<BODY>\n";
7    echo     "<CENTER>I'm another simple PHP script</CENTER>\n";
8    echo   "</BODY>\n";
9    echo "</HTML>";
10 ?>
```

When you use a web browser to request this file (`SimpleHTML.php`), the server will execute the script and send the following text to the browser:

```
<HTML>
<HEAD>
<TITLE>SimpleHTML</TITLE>
<BODY>
<CENTER>I'm another simple PHP script</CENTER>
</BODY>
</HTML>
```

The web browser interprets this as an HTML document and displays the result, as shown in Figure 15.1.

Figure 15.1   `SimpleHTML.php` in a browser.

Of course, if you want to display static HTML pages, PHP doesn't really offer any advantages—we could have produced this HTML document without PHP's help. The power behind a PHP script is that it can produce a different page each time it executes. Listing 15.3 shows a script that displays the current time (in the server's time zone).

Listing 15.3   `Time.php`

```
 1 <?php
 2    //Filename: Time.php
 3
 4    $datetime = date( "Y-m-d H:i:s (T)" );
 5
 6    echo "<HTML>\n";
 7    echo   "<HEAD>\n";
 8    echo     "<TITLE>Time</TITLE>\n";
 9    echo   "<BODY>\n";
10    echo     "<CENTER>";
11    echo       "The current time " . $datetime;
12    echo     "</CENTER>\n";
13    echo   "</BODY>\n";
14    echo "</HTML>";
15 ?>
```

Line 4 retrieves the current date and time, and assigns it to the variable `$datetime`. Line 11 appends the value of `$datetime` to a string literal and echoes the result to the browser. When you request this PHP script from within a browser, you see a result such as that shown in Figure 15.2.

If you request this document again (say by pressing the `Refresh` button), the web server will execute the script again and display a different result.

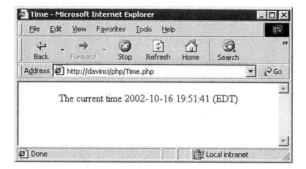

Figure 15.2   `Time.php` in a browser.

Prerequisites

To try the examples in this chapter, you will need access to a web server that understands PHP. I'll be using the Apache web server with PHP installed, but you can also use PHP with Microsoft's IIS, Netscape's web server, and many other servers. To find out if the PostgreSQL interface is available in your copy of PHP, call the `phpinfo()` function and look for a section titled "PostgreSQL Support." If you see that section, you're ready to go. If you don't you might have to compile PHP from source code. You can learn how to compile PHP for your platform at the Zend website (http://www.zend.com). Be sure to add the `--with-pgsql` option when you configure the PHP source code.

I'll assume that you are comfortable reading simple HTML documents and have some basic familiarity with PHP in general. Most of this chapter focuses on the details of interacting with a PostgreSQL database from PHP. If you need more information regarding general PHP programming, visit http://www.zend.com.

Client 1—Connecting to the Server

The first PHP/PostgreSQL client establishes a connection to a PostgreSQL server and displays the name of the database to which you connect. Listing 15.4 shows the `client1a.php` script.

Listing 15.4   `client1a.php`

```
1 <?php
2    //Filename: client1a.php
3
4    $connect_string = "dbname=movies user=bruce";
5
6    $db_handle = pg_connect( $connect_string );
7
8    echo "<HTML>\n";
9    echo   "<HEAD>\n";
```

Listing 15.4   **Continued**

```
10   echo     "<TITLE>client1</TITLE>\n";
11   echo   "<BODY>\n";
12   echo     "<CENTER>";
13   echo       "Connected to " . pg_dbname( $db_handle );
14   echo     "</CENTER>\n";
15   echo   "</BODY>\n";
16   echo "</HTML>";
17 ?>
```

This script connects to a database whose name is hard-coded in the script (at line 4). At line 6, you attempt to make a connection by calling the pg_connect() function. pg_connect() returns a database handle (also called a database *resource*). Many of the PostgreSQL-related functions require a database handle, so you need to capture the return value in a variable ($db_handle).

When you call pg_connect(), you supply a connection string that contains a list of *property=value* pairs[1]. Table 15.1 lists some of the properties that can appear in a pg_connect() connection string. In client1.php, you specified two properties: dbname=movies and user=bruce.

Table 15.1   **Connection Attributes**

Connect-string Property	Environment Variable	Example
user	PGUSER	user=korry
password	PGPASSWORD	password=cows
dbname	PGDATABASE	dbname=accounting
host	PGHOST	host=jersey
hostaddr	PGHOSTADDR	hostaddr=127.0.0.1
port	PGPORT	port=5432

If you don't specify one or more of the connect-string properties, default values are derived from the environment variables shown in Table 15.1. If necessary, pg_connect() will use hard-coded default values for the host (localhost) and port (5432) properties. See the section titled "Connection Properties" in Chapter 5, "Introduction to PostgreSQL Programming," for a complete description of the connection properties that you can use when you call pg_connect().

I'm not very comfortable with the idea of leaving usernames and passwords sitting around in the web server's document tree. It's just too easy to make a configuration error that will let a surfer grab your PHP script files in plain-text form. If that happens, you've suddenly exposed your PostgreSQL password to the world.

---

[1] When you call pg_connect() with a single argument, PHP calls the PQconnectdb() function from PostgreSQL's libpq API. PHP is yet another PostgreSQL API implemented in terms of libpq.

A better solution is to factor the code that establishes a database connection into a separate PHP script and then move that script outside the web server's document tree. Listing 15.5 shows a more secure version of your basic PostgreSQL/PHP script.

Listing 15.5   `client1b.php`

```
 1 <?php
 2   //Filename: client1b.php
 3
 4   include( "secure/my_connect_pg.php" );
 5
 6   $db_handle = my_connect_pg( "movies" );
 7
 8   echo "<HTML>\n";
 9   echo  "<HEAD>\n";
10   echo   "<TITLE>client1</TITLE>\n";
11   echo  "<BODY>\n";
12   echo   "<CENTER>";
13   echo    "Connected to " . pg_dbname( $db_handle );
14   echo   "</CENTER>\n";
15   echo  "</BODY>\n";
16   echo "</HTML>";
17 ?>
```

If you compare this to `client1a.php`, you'll see that I've replaced the call to `pg_con-nect()` with a call to `my_connect_pg()`. I've also added a call to PHP's `include()` directive. The `include()` directive is similar to the `#include` directive found in most C programs: `include(filename)` inlines the named file into the PHP script (`.php`). Now let's look at the `my_connect_pg.php` file (see Listing 15.6).

Listing 15.6   `connect_pg.php`

```
 1 <?php
 2   // File:  my_connect_pg.php
 3
 4   function my_connect_pg( $dbname )
 5   {
 6     $connect_string  = "user=korry password=cows dbname=";
 7     $connect_string .= $dbname;
 8
 9     return( pg_connect( $connect_string ));
10   }
11 ?>
```

This script defines a function, named `my_connect_pg()`, which you can call to create a PostgreSQL connection. `my_connect_pg()` expects a single string argument, which must specify the name of a PostgreSQL database.

Notice that the username and password are explicitly included in this script. Place this script *outside* of the web server's document tree so that it can't fall into the hands of a web surfer. The question is: Where should you put it? When you call the `include()` directive (or the related `require()` function), you can specify an absolute path or a relative path. An absolute path starts with a / (or drive name or backslash in Windows). A relative path does not. The PHP interpreter uses a search path (that is, a list of directory names) to resolve relative pathnames. You can find the search path using PHP's `ini_get()` function:

```
...
echo "Include path = " . ini_get( "include_path" );
...
```

The `ini_get()` function returns a variable defined in PHP's initialization file[2]; in this case, the value of `include_path`. On my system, `ini_get("include_path")` returns ".:/usr/local/php". PHP searches for `include` files in the current directory (that is, the directory that contains the including script), and then in `/usr/local/php`. If you refer back to Listing 15.5, you'll see that I am including `secure/my_connect_pg.php`. Combining the search path and relative pathname, PHP will find my `include` file in `/usr/local/php/secure/my_connect_pg.php`. The important detail here is that `/usr/local/php` is outside the web server's document tree (`/usr/local/htdocs`).

The `my_connect_pq.php` script not only secures the PostgreSQL password, it also gives you a single connection function that you can call from any script—all you need to know is the name of the database that you want.

If everything goes well, the user will see the message "Connected to movies."

Let's see what happens when you throw a few error conditions at this script. First, try to connect to a nonexistent database (see Figure 15.3).

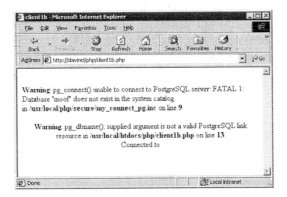

Figure 15.3   Connecting to a nonexistent database.

---

[2] You can find the PHP's initialization file using echo `get_cfg_var( "cfg_file_path" )`.

That's not a friendly error message. Let's see what happens when you try to connect to a database that *does* exist, but where the PostgreSQL server has been shut down (see Figure 15.4).

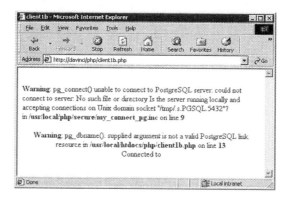

Figure 15.4 Connecting to a database that has been shut down.

Again, not exactly the kind of message that you want your users to see. In the next section, I'll show you how to intercept this sort of error and respond a little more gracefully.

Client 2—Adding Error Checking

You've seen that PHP will simply dump error messages into the output stream sent to the web browser. That makes it easy to debug PHP scripts, but it's not particularly kind to your users.

There are two error messages displayed in Figure 15.4. The first error occurs when you call the pg_connect() function. Notice that the error message includes the name of the script that was running at the time the error occurred. In this case, my_connect__pg.php encountered an error on line 9—that's the call to pg_connect(). The second error message comes from line 13 of client1b.php, where you try to use the database handle returned by my_connect_pg(). When the first error occurred, pg_connect() returned an invalid handle and my_connect_pg() returned that value to the caller.

Listing 15.7 shows a new version of the client script that intercepts both error messages.

Listing 15.7   `client2a.php`

```php
1 <?php
2   //Filename: client2a.php
3
4   include( "secure/my_connect_pg.php" );
5
6   $db_handle = @my_connect_pg( "movies" );
7
```

Listing 15.7   **Continued**

```
 8    echo "<HTML>\n";
 9    echo    "<HEAD>\n";
10    echo     "<TITLE>client1b</TITLE>\n";
11    echo    "<BODY>\n";
12    echo     "<CENTER>";
13
14    if( $db_handle == FALSE )
15      echo "Sorry, can't connect to the movies database";
16    else
17      echo "Connected to " . pg_dbname( $db_handle );
18
19    echo      "</CENTER>\n";
20    echo     "</BODY>\n";
21    echo "</HTML>";
22 ?>
```

If you compare this script with client1b.php, you'll see that they are very similar. The
first change is at line 6—I've added a @ character in front of the call to my_connect_pg().
The @ character turns off error reporting for the expression that follows. The next change
is at line 14. Rather than blindly using the database handle returned by my_connect_pg(),
you should first ensure that it is a valid handle. pg_connect() (and therefore my_con-
nect_pg()) will return FALSE to indicate that a connection could not be established. If you
find that $db_handle is FALSE, client2a displays a friendly error message; otherwise, it
displays the name of the database to which you are connected (see Figure 15.5).

Figure 15.5   A friendlier error message.

This looks much nicer, but now we've lost the details that we need to debug connection
problems. What we really want is a friendly error message for the user, but details for the
administrator.

You can achieve this using a custom-written error handler. Listing 15.8 shows a custom error handler that emails the text of any error messages to your administrator.

Listing 15.8 `my_error_handler.php`

```php
1 <?php
2
3  // Filename: my_handler.inc
4
5  function my_handler( $errno, $errmsg, $fname, $lineno, $context )
6  {
7
8    $err_txt  = "At " . date("Y-m-d H:i:s (T)");
9    $err_txt .= " an error occured at line " . $lineno;
10   $err_txt .= " of file " . $fname . "\n\n";
11   $err_txt .= "The text of the error message is:\n";
12   $err_txt .= $errmsg;
13
14   mail( "administrator", "Website error", $err_txt );
15  }
16 ?>
```

In a moment, you'll modify the `client2a.php` script so that it installs this error handler before connecting to PostgreSQL.

An error handler function is called whenever a PHP script encounters an error. The default error handler writes error messages into the output stream sent to the web browser. The custom error handler shown in Listing 15.8 builds an email message from the various error message components and then uses PHP's `mail()` function to send the message to an address of your choice.

Now, let's modify the client so that it uses `my_handler()` (see Listing 15.9).

Listing 15.9 `client2b.php`

```php
1 <?php
2  //Filename: client2b.php
3
4  include( "secure/my_connect_pg.php" );
5  include( "my_handler.php" );
6
7  set_error_handler( "my_handler" );
8
9  $db_handle = my_connect_pg( "movies" );
10
11  echo "<HTML>\n";
12  echo  "<HEAD>\n";
13  echo   "<TITLE>client2b</TITLE>\n";
14  echo  "<BODY>\n";
15  echo   "<CENTER>";
```

Listing 15.9   **Continued**

```
16
17   if( $db_handle == FALSE )
18     echo "Sorry, can't connect to the movies database";
19   else
20     echo "Connected to " . pg_dbname( $db_handle );
21
22   echo     "</CENTER>\n";
23   echo     "</BODY>\n";
24   echo "</HTML>";
25
26   restore_error_handler();
27 ?>
```

You'll make four minor changes to client2a.php. First, include() my_handler.php. Next, call set_error_handler() to direct PHP to call my_handler() rather than the default error handler (see line 7). Third, remove the @ from the call to my_connect_pg()—you want errors to be reported now; you just want them reported through my_handler(). Finally, at line 26, restore the default error handler (because this is the last statement in your script, this isn't strictly required).

Now, if you run client2b.php, you'll see a user-friendly error message, *and* you should get a piece of email similar to this:

```
From daemon  Sat Jan 12 09:15:59 2002
Date: Sat, 12 Jan 2002 09:15:59 -0400
From: daemon <daemon@davinci>
To: bruce@virtual_movies.com
Subject: Website error

At 2002-02-12 09:15:59 (EDT) an error occurred at line 9
of file /usr/local/php/secure/my_connect_pg.php

The text of the error message is:
   pg_connect() unable to connect to PostgreSQL server: could
   not connect to server: No such file or directory

   Is the server running locally and accepting
   connections on Unix domain socket "/tmp/.s.PGSQL.5432"?
```

Now, you know how to suppress error messages (using the @ operator) and how to intercept them with your own error handler.

In the remaining samples in this chapter, I will omit most error handling code so that you can see any error messages in your web browser; that should make debugging a little easier.

Now, it's time to move on to the next topic-query processing.

Client 3—Query Processing

The tasks involved in processing a query (or other command) using PHP are similar to those required in other PostgreSQL APIs. The first step is to execute the command; then you can (optionally) process the metadata returned by the command; and finally, you process the result set.

We're going to switch gears here. So far, we have been writing PHP scripts that are procedural—one PHP command follows the next. We've thrown in a couple of functions to factor out some repetitive details (such as establishing a new connection). For the next example, you'll create a PHP *class*, named my_table, that will execute a command and process the results. You can reuse this class in other PHP scripts; and each time you extend the class, all scripts automatically inherit the changes.

Let's start by looking at the first script that uses the my_table class and then we'll start developing the class. Listing 15.10 shows client3a.php.

Listing 15.10   client3a.php

```
 1 <HTML>
 2   <HEAD>
 3     <TITLE>client3a</TITLE>
 4   <BODY>
 5
 6 <?php
 7   //Filename: client3a.php
 8
 9   include( "secure/my_connect_pg.php" );
10   include( "my_table_a.php" );
11
12   $db_handle = my_connect_pg( "movies" );
13
14   $table = new my_table( $db_handle, "SELECT * FROM customers;" );
15   $table->finish();
16
17   pg_close( $db_handle );
18
19 ?>
20
21   </BODY>
22 </HTML>
```

I rearranged the code in this client so that the static (that is, unchanging) HTML code is separated from the PHP script; that makes it a little easier to discern the script.

At line 10, client3a includes() the my_table_a.php file. That file contains the definition of the my_table class, and we'll look at it in greater detail in a moment. Line 14 creates a new my_table object named $table. The constructor function for the my_table class expects two parameters: a database handle and a command string. my_table()

executes the given command and formats the results into an HTML table. At line 15, the call to my_table->finish() completes the HTML table. Finally, you call pg_close() to close the database connection; that's not strictly necessary, but it's good form.

Listing 15.11 shows my_table_a.php.

Listing 15.11 my_table_a.php

```php
 1  <?php
 2
 3    // Filename: my_table_a.php
 4
 5    class my_table
 6    {
 7      var $result;
 8      var $columns;
 9
10      function my_table( $db_handle, $command )
11      {
12        $this->result  = pg_query( $db_handle, $command );
13        $this->columns = pg_num_fields( $this->result );
14        $row_count     = pg_num_rows( $this->result );
15
16        $this->start_table();
17
18        for( $row = 0; $row < $row_count; $row++ )
19            $this->append_row( $this->result, $row );
20      }
21
22      function start_table()
23      {
24        echo '<TABLE CELLPADDING="2" CELLSPACING="0" BORDER=1>';
25        echo "\n";
26      }
27
28      function finish()
29      {
30        print( "</TABLE>\n" );
31
32        pg_free_result( $this->result );
33      }
34
35      function append_row( $result, $row )
36      {
37        echo( "<TR>\n" );
38
39        for( $col = 0; $col < $this->columns; $col++ )
40        {
```

Listing 15.11 **Continued**

```
41          echo "  <TD>";
42          echo pg_fetch_result( $result, $row, $col );
43          echo "</TD>\n";
44        }
45
46        echo( "</TR>\n" );
47      }
48    }
49
50 ?>
```

`my_table.php` defines a single class named `my_table`. At lines 7 and 8, you see the two instance variables for this class. `$this->$result` contains a handle to a result set. `$this->columns` stores the number of columns in the result set.

The constructor for `my_table` (lines 10 through 20) expects a database handle and a command string. At line 12, the constructor calls the `pq_query()` function to execute the given command. `pg_query()` returns a result set handle if successful, and returns FALSE if an error occurs. You'll see how to intercept `pg_query()` errors in a moment. After you have a result set, you can call `pg_num_fields()` to determine the number of columns in the result set and `pg_num_rows()` to find the number of rows.

pg_query() in Earlier PHP Versions

In older versions of PHP, the `pg_query()` function was named `pg_exec()`, `pg_num_fields()` was named `pg_numfields()`, and `pg_num_rows()` was named `pg_numrows()`. If you run into complaints about invalid function names, try the old names.

At line 16, the call to the `start_table()` member function prints the HTML table header. Finally, at lines 18 and 19, the constructor iterates through each row in the result set and calls `append_row()` to create a new row in the HTML table. We'll look at `append_row()` shortly.

The `start_table()` and `finish_table()` member functions create the HTML table header and table footer, respectively. `finish_table()` also frees up the resources consumed by the result set by calling `pg_free_result()`.

The `append_row()` member function starts at line 35. `append_row()` expects two parameters: a result set handle (`$result`) and a row number (`$row`). At line 37, `append_row()` writes the HTML table-row tag (`<TR>`). The loop at lines 39 through 44 processes each column in the given row. For each column, `append_row()` writes the HTML table-data tag (`<TD>`) and the table-data closing tag (`</TD>`). In-between these tags, you see a call to `pg_fetch_result()` that retrieves a single value from the result set. When you call `pg_fetch_result()`, you provide three parameters: a result set handle, a row number, and a column number. `pg_fetch_result()` returns NULL if the requested value is NULL[3]. If not NULL, pg_fetch_result() will return the requested value in the form of a string. Note that the PHP/PostgreSQL documentation states numeric values are returned as float or integer values. This appears not to be the case; all values are returned in string form.

Now if you load client3a.php in your web browser, you'll see a table similar to that shown in Figure 15.6.

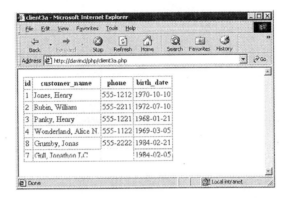

Figure 15.6 client3a.php loaded into your web browser.

Other Ways to Retrieve Result Set Values

Besides pg_fetch_result(), PHP provides a number of functions that retrieve result set values.

The pg_fetch_row() function returns an array of values that correspond to a given row. pg_fetch_row() requires two parameters: a result resource (also known as a result set handle) and a row number.

```
pg_fetch_row( resource result, int row_number )
```

Listing 15.12 shows the my_table.append_row() member function implemented in terms of pg_fetch_row().

Listing 15.12   append_row() **Using** pg_fetch_row()

```
...
1 function append_row( $result, $row )
2 {
3   echo( "<TR>\n" );
4
```

---

[3] In PHP 4.0 and above, NULL is equal to FALSE, but not identical to FALSE. This means that NULL == FALSE evaluates to TRUE, but NULL === FALSE does not.

Listing 15.12 **Continued**

```
5   $values = pg_fetch_row( $result, $row );
6
7   for( $col = 0; $col < count( $values ); $col++ )
8   {
9     echo "  <TD>";
10    echo $values[$col];
11    echo "</TD>\n";
12  }
13  echo( "</TR>\n" );
14 }
...
```

In this version, you fetch the requested row at line 5. When the call to pg_fetch_row()
completes, $values will contain an array of column values. You can access each array
element using an integer index, starting at element 0.

The next function, pg_fetch_array(), is similar to pg_fetch_row(). Like
pg_fetch_row(), pg_fetch_array() returns an array of columns values. The difference
between these functions is that pg_fetch_array() can return a normal array (indexed
by column *number*), an associative array (indexed by column *name*), or both.
pg_fetch_array() expects one, two, or three parameters:

pg_fetch_array(resource result [, int row [, int result_type]])

The third parameter can be PGSQL_NUM, PGSQL_ASSOC, or PGSQL_BOTH. When you specify
PGSQL_NUM, pg_fetch_array() operates identically to pg_fetch_row(); the return value is
an array indexed by column number. When you specify PGSQL_ASSOC, pg_fetch_array()
returns an associative array indexed by column name. If you specify PGSQL_BOTH, you will
get back an array that can be indexed by column number as well as by column name.
Listing 15.13 shows the append_row() function rewritten to use pg_fetch_array().

Listing 15.13 append_row() **Using** pg_fetch_array()

```
...
1   function append_row( $result, $row )
2   {
3     echo( "<TR>\n" );
4
5     $values = pg_fetch_array( $result, $row, PGSQL_ASSOC );
6
7     foreach( $values as $column_value )
8     {
9       echo "  <TD>";
10      echo $column_value;
11      echo "</TD>\n";
12    }
```

Listing 15.13 **Continued**

```
13
14    echo( "</TR>\n" );
15    }
...
```

You should note that this version of append_row() misses the point of using PGSQL_ASSOC. It ignores the fact that pg_fetch_array() has returned an *associative* array. Associative arrays make it easy to work with a result set if you know the column names ahead of time (that is, at the time you write your script), but they really don't offer much of an advantage for ad hoc queries. To really take advantage of pg_fetch_array(), you would write code such as

```
...
  $result   = pg_query( $dbhandle, "SELECT * FROM customers;" );

  for( $row = 0; $row < pg_num_rows( $result ); $row++ )
  {
      $customer = pg_fetch_array( $result, $row, PGSQL_ASSOC );

      do_something_useful( $customer["customer_name"] );

      do_something_else( $customer["id"], $customer["phone"] );
  }
...
```

You can also obtain an associative array by calling pg_fetch_assoc(resource result [, int row]). Calling pg_fetch_assoc() is equivalent to calling pg_fetch_array(..., PGSQL_ASSOC).

Another function useful for static queries is pg_fetch_object(). pg_fetch_object() returns a single row in the form of an object. The object returned has one field for each column, and the name of each field will be the same as the name of the column. For example:

```
...
  $result   = pg_query( $dbhandle, "SELECT * FROM customers;" );

  for( $row = 0; $row < pg_num_rows( $result ); $row++ )
  {
      $customer = pg_fetch_object( $result, $row, PGSQL_ASSOC );

      do_something_useful( $customer->customer_name );

      do_something_else( $customer->id, $customer->phone );
  }
...
```

There is no significant difference between an object returned by `pg_fetch_object()` and an associative array returned by `pg_fetch_array()`. With `pg_fetch_array()`, you reference a value using `$array[$column]` syntax. With `pg_fetch_object()`, you reference a value using `$object->$column` syntax. Choose whichever syntax you prefer.

One warning about `pg_fetch_object()` and `pg_fetch_array( ..., PGSQL_ASSOC)`—if your query returns two or more columns with the same column name, you will lose all but one of the columns. You can't have an associative array with duplicate index names, and you can't have an object with duplicate field names.

Metadata Access

You've seen that `pg_fetch_object()` and `pg_fetch_array()` expose column names to you, but the PHP/PostgreSQL API lets you get at much more metadata than just the column names.

The PHP/PostgreSQL interface is written using libpq (PostgreSQL's C-language API). Most of the functions available through libpq can be called from PHP, including the libpq metadata functions. Unfortunately, this means that PHP shares the limitations that you find in libpq.

In particular, the `pg_field_size()` function returns the size of a field. `pg_field_size()` expects two parameters:

```
int pg_field_size( resource $result, int $column_number )
```

The problem with this function is that the size reported is the number of bytes required to store the value *on the server*. It has nothing to do with the number of bytes seen by the client (that is, the number of bytes seen by your PHP script). For variable-length data types, `pg_field_size()` will return –1. If you're using a newer version of PHP (at least version 4.2.0) you can call `pg_field_prtlen()` to find the string length of a given value. You can call `pg_field_prtlen()` in either of the following forms:

```
int pg_field_prtlen( resource $result, int $row_number, int $column_number )
int pg_field_prtlen( resource $result, int $row_number, string $column_name )
```

The `pg_field_type()` function returns the name of the data type for a given column. `pg_field_type()` requires two parameters:

```
int pg_field_type( resource $result, int $column_number )
```

The problem with `pg_field_type()` is that it is not 100% accurate. `pg_field_type()` knows nothing of user-defined types or domains. Also, `pg_field_type()` won't return details about parameterized data types. For example, a column defined as NUMERIC(7,2) is reported as type NUMERIC. *Note*: `pg_field_type()` has been improved in PHP version 5; it now queries the server to retrieve the name of the column's data type so it will return the correct name for user-defined types and domains (but it still doesn't return details about parameterized types).

Having conveyed the bad news, let's look at the metadata functions that are a little more useful for most applications.

You've already seen `pg_num_rows()` and `pg_num_fields()`. These functions return the number of rows and columns (respectively) in a result set.

The pg_field_name() and pg_field_num() functions are somewhat related. pg_field_name() returns the name of a column, given a column number index. pg_field_num() returns the column number index of a field given the field's name.

Let's enhance the my_table class a bit by including column names in the HTML table that we produce. Listing 15.14 shows a new version of the start_table() member function.

Listing 15.14 my_table.start_table()

```
 1 function start_table()
 2 {
 3   echo '<TABLE CELLPADDING="2" CELLSPACING="0" BORDER=1>';
 4
 5   for( $col = 0; $col < $this->columns; $col++ )
 6   {
 7     echo "  <TH>";
 8     echo pg_field_name( $this->result, $col );
 9     echo "</TH>\n";
10   }
11   echo "\n";
12 }
```

I used the <TH> tag here instead of <TD>, so that the browser knows that these are table header cells (table header cells are typically bolded and centered).

Now when you browse to client3a.php, you see a nice set of column headers as shown in Figure 15.7.

Let's fix one other problem as long as we are fiddling with metadata. You may have noticed that the last row in Figure 15.7 looks a little funky—the phone number cell has not been drawn the same as the other cells. That happens when we try to create a table cell for a NULL value. If you look at the code that you built for the HTML table, you'll see that the last row has an empty <TD></TD> cell. For some reason, web browsers draw an empty cell differently.

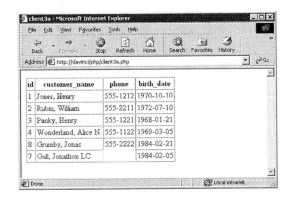

Figure 15.7 client3a.php—with column headers.

To fix this problem, you can modify append_row() to detect NULL values (see Listing 15.15).

Listing 15.15 my_table.append_row()

```
 1  function append_row( $result, $row )
 2  {
 3    echo( "<TR>\n" );
 4
 5    for( $col = 0; $col < $this->columns; $col++ )
 6    {
 7      echo "  <TD>";
 8
 9      if( pg_field_is_null( $result, $row, $col ) == 1 )
10        echo " ";
11      elseif( strlen( pg_result( $result, $row, $col )) == 0 )
12        echo " "
13      else
14        echo pg_result( $result, $row, $col );
15      echo "</TD>\n";
16    }
17
18    echo( "</TR>\n" );
19  }
```

At line 9, you detect NULL values using the pg_field_is_null() function. If you encounter a NULL, you echo a non-breaking space character ( ) instead of an empty string. You have the same problem (a badly drawn border) if you encounter an empty string, and you fix it the same way (lines 11 and 12). Now, when you display a table, all the cells are drawn correctly, as shown in Figure 15.8.

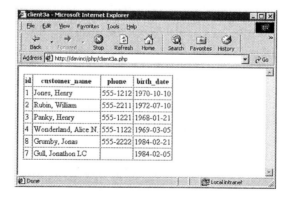

Figure 15.8 client3a.php—final version.

There are a few more metadata functions that you can use in PHP, and you will need those functions in the next client that you write.

PHP, PostgreSQL, and Associative Functions

One of the more interesting abstractions promised (but not yet offered) by PHP and the PHP/PostgreSQL API is the *associative function*. An associative function gives you a way to execute a SQL command without having to construct the entire command yourself. Let's say that you need to INSERT a new row into the customers table. The most obvious way to do this in PHP is to build up an INSERT command by concatenating the new values and then executing the command using pg_query(). Another option is to use the pg_insert() function. With pg_insert(), you build an associative array. Each element in the array corresponds to a column. The key for a given element is the name of the column, and the value for the element is the value that you want to insert. For example, you can add a new row to the customers table with the following code:

```
...
$customer["id"]            = 8;
$customer["customer_name"] = "Smallberries, John";
$customer["birth_date"]    = "1985-05-14";

pg_insert( $db_handle, "customers", $customer );
...
```

In this code snippet, you have created an associative array with three entries. When you execute the call to pg_insert(), PHP will construct the following INSERT command:

```
INSERT INTO customers
  (
    id,
    customer_name,
    birth_date
  )
  VALUES
  (
    8,
    'Smallberries, John',
    '1985-05-14'
  );
```

PHP knows the name of the table by looking at the second argument to pg_insert(). The column names are derived from the keys in the $customers array, and the values come from the values in the associative array.

Besides pg_insert(), you can call pg_delete() to build and execute a DELETE command. When you call pg_delete(), you provide a database handle, a table name, and an associative array. The associative array is used to construct a WHERE clause for the DELETE command. The values in the associative array are ANDed together to form the WHERE clause.

You can also use pg_select() to construct and execute a SELECT * command. pg_select() is similar to pg_delete()—it expects a database handle, a table name, and an associative array. Like

> pg_delete(), the values in the associative array are ANDed together to form a WHERE clause.
>
> Finally, the pg_update() function expects two associative arrays. The first array is used to form a WHERE clause, and the second array should contain the data (column names and values) to be updated.
>
> As of PHP version 5.0, the associative functions are documented as experimental and are likely to change. Watch for these functions in a future release.

Client 4—An Interactive Query Processor

You now have most of the pieces that you need to build a general-purpose query processor within a web browser. Our next client simply prompts the user for a SQL command, executes the command, and displays the results.

If you want to try this on your own web server, be sure that you understand the security implications. If you follow the examples in this chapter, your PHP script will use a hard-coded username to connect to PostgreSQL. Choose a user with *very* few privileges. In fact, most PHP/PostgreSQL sites should probably define a user account specifically designed for web access. If you're not careful, you'll grant John Q. Hacker permissions to alter important data.

We'll start out with a simple script and then refine it as we discover problems.

First, you need an HTML page that displays a welcome and prompts the user for a SQL command. Listing 15.16 shows the client4.html document.

Listing 15.16 client4.html

```
 1 <HTML>
 2
 3 <!-- Filename: client4.html>
 4
 5   <HEAD>
 6     <TITLE>client4a</TITLE>
 7   <BODY>
 8     <CENTER>
 9     <FORM ACTION="client4a.php" METHOD="POST">
10       <I>Enter SQL command:</I><br>
11
12       <INPUT TYPE="text"
13              NAME="query"
14              SIZE="80"
15              ALIGN="left"
16              VALUE="">
17
18       <BR><BR>
19       <INPUT TYPE="submit" VALUE="Execute command">
20     </FORM>
21   </CENTER></BODY>
22 </HTML>
```

This HTML document defines a form that will be *posted* to the server (see line 9). After the user enters a command and presses the `Execute Command` button, the browser will request the file `client4a.php`. We'll look at `client4a.php` in a moment. When you request this page in a web browser, you will see a form similar to that shown in Figure 15.9.

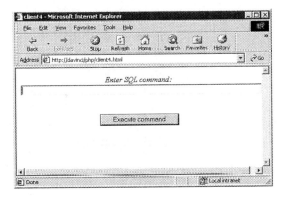

Figure 15.9 `client4.html`.

Now let's look at the second half of the puzzle—`client4a.php` (see Listing 15.17)

Listing 15.17 `client4a.php`

```
1  <HTML>
2    <HEAD>
3      <TITLE>Query</TITLE>
4    <BODY>
5      <?php
6
7        # Filename: client4a.php
8
9        include( "secure/my_connect_pg.php" );
10       include( "my_table_e.php" );
11
12       $command_text = $HTTP_POST_VARS[ "query" ];
13
14       if( strlen( $command_text ) == 0 )
15       {
16         echo "You forgot to enter a command";
17       }
18       else
19       {
20         $db_handle = my_connect_pg( "movies" );
21
22         $table = new my_table( $db_handle, $command_text );
```

Listing 15.17 **Continued**

```
23          $table->finish();
24
25          pg_close( $db_handle );
26      }
27  ?>
28  </BODY>
29  </HTML>
```

Most of this script should be pretty familiar by now. You include `secure/my_con-nect__pg.php` to avoid embedding a username and password inline. Next, include `my_table_e.php` so that you can use the `my_table` class (`my_table_e.php` includes all the modifications you made to the original version of `my_table_a.php`).

At line 12, `client4a` retrieves the command entered by the user from the `$HTTP_POST__VARS[]` variable. Look back at lines 12 through 16 of Listing 15.16 (`client4.html`). You are defining an `INPUT` field named `query`. When the user enters a value and presses the `Execute Command` button, the browser *posts* the `query` field to `client4a.php`. PHP marshals all the posted values into a single associative array named `$HTTP_POST__VARS[]` (also known as `$_POST` starting in PHP version 5). The key for each value in this array is the name of the posted variable. So, you defined a field named `query`, and you can find the value of that field in `$HTTP_POST__VARS["query"]`.

If you try to execute an empty command using `pg_query()`, you'll be rewarded with an ugly error message. You can be a little nicer to your users by intercepting empty commands at lines 14 through 16 and displaying a less intimidating error message.

The remainder of this script is straightforward: simply establish a database connection and use the `my_table` class to execute the given command and display the result.

Let's run this script to see how it behaves (see Figures 15.10 and 15.11).

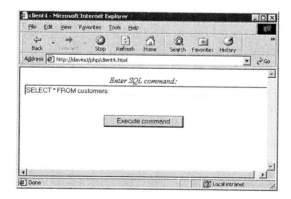

Figure 15.10 Submitting a query with `client4.html`.

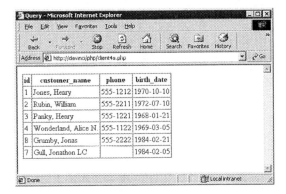

Figure 15.11 Submitting a query with `client4.html`—result.

That worked nicely. Let's try another query (see Figures 15.12 and 15.13).

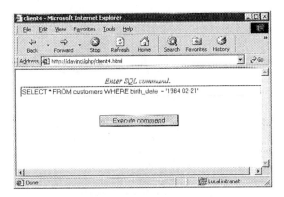

Figure 15.12 Causing an error with `client4.html`.

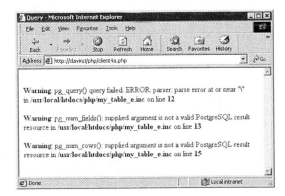

Figure 15.13 Causing an error with `client4.html`—result.

Hmmm…that's not what we were hoping for. What went wrong? Actually, there are several problems shown here. First, PHP is reporting that we have an erroneous backslash on line 12 of my_table_e.php. Line 12 is inside of the my_table constructor and it sends the following command to the server:

```
$this->result  = pg_query( $db_handle, $command );
```

There are no backslashes on that line; there are no backslashes in the command that you entered. Where are the backslashes coming from? If you echo $HTTP_POST_VARS_["query"], you'll see that PHP has added escape characters to the command entered by the user. You entered SELECT * FROM customers WHERE birth_date = '1984-02-21', and PHP changed this to SELECT * FROM customers WHERE birth_date = \'1984-02-21\'. According to the PHP manual, all single-quotes, double-quotes, backslashes, and NULLs are escaped with a backslash when they come from a posted value.[4]

This is easy to fix. You can simply strip the escape characters when you retrieve the command text from $HTTP_VARS[]. Changing client4a.php, line 12, to

```
if( get_magic_quotes_gpc())
    $command_text = stripslashes( $HTTP_POST_VARS[ "query" ] );
```

will make it possible to execute SQL commands that contain single-quotes.

That was the first problem. The second problem is that you don't want the end-user to see these nasty-looking PHP/PostgreSQL error messages. To fix this problem, you need to intercept the error message and display it yourself. Listing 15.18 shows a new version of the my_table constructor.

Listing 15.18 my_table.my_table()

```
 1 function my_table( $db_handle, $command )
 2 {
 3   $this->result  = @pg_query( $db_handle, $command );
 4
 5   if( $this->result == FALSE )
 6   {
 7     echo pg_last_error( $db_handle );
 8   }
 9   else
10   {
11     $this->columns = pg_num_fields( $this->result );
12     $row_count     = pg_num_rows( $this->result );
13
14     $this->start_table( $command );
15
16     for( $row = 0; $row < $row_count; $row++ )
17       $this->append_row( $this->result, $row );
```

[4] You can disable the automatic quoting feature by setting the magic_quote_gpc configuration variable to no. I would not recommend changing this value—you're likely to break many PHP scripts.

Listing 15.18   **Continued**

```
18    }
19  }
```

We've restructured this function a bit. Because the goal is to intercept the default error message, we suppress error reporting by prefixing the call to pg_query() with an @. At line 5, determine whether pg_query() returned a valid result set resource. If you are used to using PostgreSQL with other APIs, there is an important difference lurking here. In other PostgreSQL APIs, you get a result set even when a command fails—the error message is part of the result set. In PHP, pg_query() returns FALSE when an error occurs. You must call pg_last_error() to retrieve the text of the error message (see line 7).

If you have succeeded in executing the given command, you can build an HTML table from the result set as before.

Now, if you run into an error condition, the result is far more palatable (see Figures 15.14 and 15.15).

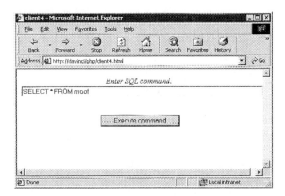

Figure 15.14   Causing an error with client4.html—part 2.

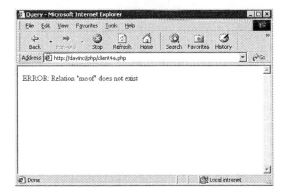

Figure 15.15   Causing an error with client4.html—part 2, result.

Notice that you see only one error message this time. In Figure 15.13, you saw multiple error messages. Not only had `client4a` failed to intercept the original error, but it went on to use an invalid result set handle; when you fix the first problem, the other error messages go away.

At this point, you can execute queries and intercept error messages. Let's see what happens when you execute a command other than `SELECT`. First, enter the command shown in Figure 15.16.

After clicking on the `Execute Command` button, you see the result displayed in Figure 15.17.

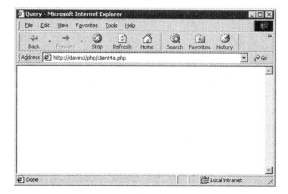

Figure 15.16   Executing an `INSERT` command.

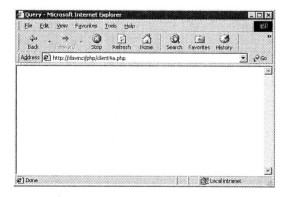

Figure 15.17   Executing an `INSERT` command—result.

Hmmm…that's a bit minimalist for my taste. You should at least see a confirmation that *something* has happened. When you execute a non-`SELECT` command, the `pg_query()` function will return a result set resource, just like it does for a `SELECT` command. You can differentiate between `SELECT` and other commands by the fact that `pg_num_fields()` always returns 0 for non-`SELECT` commands.

Let's make one last modification to the my_table constructor, in Listing 15.19, so that it gives feedback regardless of which type of command executed.

Listing 15.19 `my_table.my_table()`—**Final Form**

```
 1 function my_table( $db_handle, $command )
 2 {
 3   $this->result  = @pg_query( $db_handle, $command );
 4
 5   if( $this->result == FALSE )
 6   {
 7     echo pg_last_error( $db_handle );
 8   }
 9   else
10   {
11     $this->columns = pg_num_fields( $this->result );
12
13     if( $this->columns == 0 )
14     {
15       echo $command;
16       echo "<BR>";
17       echo pq_affected_rows( $this->result );
18       echo " row(s) affected";
19
20       if( pg_last_oid( $this->result ) != 0 )
21         echo ", OID =  ". pg_last_oid( $this->result );
22     }
23     else
24     {
25       $row_count      = pg_num_rows( $this->result );
26
27       $this->start_table( $command );
28
29       for( $row = 0; $row < $row_count; $row++ )
30         $this->append_row( $this->result, $row );
31     }
32   }
33 }
```

This version checks the result set column count at line 13. If you find that the result set contains 0 columns, echo the command text and the number of rows affected by the command (that gives you feedback similar to what you would see using the psql client). You can also call the pg_last_oid() function. pg_last_oid() returns the OID (object ID) of the most recently inserted row. pg_last_oid() returns 0 if the command was not an INSERT or if more than one row was inserted.

The final results are shown in Figure 15.18.

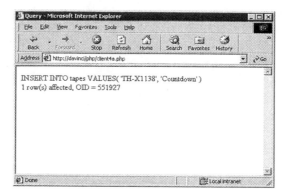

Figure 15.18 Executing an INSERT command—final result.

Now that you know how to write an interactive query processor using PHP, don't forget the security implications of doing so. Make sure that you connect to the PostgreSQL server using an account with *very* few privileges: If you give a visitor lots of privileges and a way to execute any command he wants, you're inviting disaster.

More typically, you ask a visitor to your site to type in a value that you use to construct an SQL command. For example, you may prompt the user for a "Customer Name" and retrieve the matching record with a query such as

```
$query  = "SELECT * FROM customers WHERE customer_name = '";
$query .= $_POST['customer_name'] . "'";
```

That works, sometimes. What happens if the user types in a value such as "Freddy's Fudge Factory"? Then your query becomes

```
SELECT * FROM customers WHERE customer_name = 'Freddy's Fudge Factory'.
```

See the problem? As far as PostgreSQL is concerned, a string literal is enclosed in a pair of single quotes. The PostgreSQL parser thinks the customer name ends at Freddy—the rest of the customer name is just a syntax error. To fix that sort of problem, just quote any string values with the pg_escape_string() function, like this:

```
$customer_name = pg_escape_string( $_POST['customer_name'] );
$query = "SELECT * FROM customers WHERE customer_name = '$customer_name'";
```

Other Features

There are a number of PostgreSQL-related PHP functions that I have not covered in this chapter.

Newer versions of PHP have added support for asynchronous query processing (see pg_send_query(), pg_connection_busy(), and pg_get_result()). Asynchronous query processing probably won't be of much use when you are constructing dynamic web pages, but clever coders can use asynchronous queries to provide intermediate feedback for long-running operations (sorry, I'm not that clever).

PHP offers a set of functions that can give you information about a database connection. We used the pg_dbname() function in the first client (see Listing 15.4) to display the name of the database to which we were connected. You can also use the pg_port() and pg_options() function to retrieve the port number and options associated with a database connection. PHP provides a pg_host() function that is supposed to return the name of the host where the server resides. Be very careful calling pg_host(); if you have established a local connection (that is, using a Unix-domain socket), calling pg_host() may crash your web server because of a bug in the PHP/PostgreSQL interface.

Another function offered by PHP is pg_pconnect(). The pg_pconnect() function establishes a *persistent* connection to a PostgreSQL database. Persistent connections are cached by the web server and can be reused the next time a browser requests a document that requires access to the same database. See the PHP manual for information about the pros and cons of persistent connections.

Finally, PHP supports the PostgreSQL large-object interface. You can use the large-object interface to read (or write) large data items such as images or audio files.

Summary

If you have never used PHP before, I think you'll find it a delightfully easy language to learn. As a long-time C/C++ programmer, I found PHP very familiar when I first started to explore the language. (Don't let that scare you off if you aren't a fan of C—PHP is *much* easier to learn than C.)

One of the things I like most about developing with PHP is the fact that all error messages appear in-line, right inside my web browser. This feature makes debugging easy.

PHP and PostgreSQL combine with your web server to create a system that delivers dynamic content to your users.

16

Using PostgreSQL with Tcl and Tcl/Tk

Tcl is an interpreted scripting language. Tcl is an acronym for *Tool Command Language* and is often pronounced as "tickle." The original goal of Tcl's creator (John Ousterhout) was to create an *embeddable* interpreted language that could be included in many small applications. His idea was to create a language that could be embedded in applications that might not normally justify having their own language. Another example of this sort of embeddable language is Microsoft's VBA (Visual Basic for Applications). With an embedded language, you can make any application programmable (or *scriptable*). For example, you might have a spiffy terminal emulator that you've developed for your own use. It would be nice if you could add a scripting capability to the emulator, but that would require a ton of work. This is a perfect fit for Tcl. By embedding Tcl in your terminal emulator, you are incorporating an entire programming language in your application with very little work.

Tcl is also a general purpose programming language. In fact, I think Tcl might just be the simplest language ever invented. (But beware, a simple language doesn't *always* imply simple programs; it just means the language won't get in your way.)

There are only a few rules that you have to remember:

- Everything in Tcl is a string—*everything.*
- A variable reference ($variable) is replaced by the variable value anywhere it occurs within a string.
- A command reference ([command]) is replaced by the command value anywhere it occurs within a string.
- If you want to suppress variable and command substitution, surround a string with curly braces.
- If you don't want to suppress substitution, surround a string with double quotes.

If you remember those simple rules (and suspend your disbelief—it really is that simple), you'll be fluent in Tcl in no time. When you start writing Tcl applications, you'll probably use the Tcl shell as an execution environment. The Tcl shell (tclsh) is a simple shell (like bash or sh) that has been combined with the Tcl interpreter. Using tclsh, you can do all the things you would normally do in a Unix shell (such as run a program, change directories, redirect output, and so on) *in addition* to all the things you can do in a Tcl program.

Tcl is often combined with Tk. *Tk* is a graphical toolkit. Using Tk, you can create windows and widgets (graphical controls), and interact with the user in a graphical interface. You can use Tk with many different languages, but it was originally designed as a companion to Tcl. The Tcl/Tk environment includes a graphical shell called wish. The wish shell is similar to tclsh, except that it has Tk thrown in so you can build graphical shell scripts.

Tcl applications (and therefore Tcl/Tk applications) can interact with PostgreSQL database servers. The Tcl-to-PostgreSQL interface is contained in a library named libpgtcl. libpgtcl provides a small number (17) of procedures that you can call from a Tcl script. In this chapter, I'll describe each of these procedures, and you'll build a few client applications that show you how to use libpgtcl to build PostgreSQL client applications.

Prerequisites

If you want to try the examples in this chapter, you will need to install and configure Tcl/Tk (version 8.0 or later) and libpgtcl.

If you are running on a Linux host, the chances are good that you already have Tcl/Tk installed on your system. To find out whether Tcl is ready to use, enter the command tclsh, as shown here:

```
$ tclsh
% exit
$
```

If you see the % prompt, you have Tcl installed on your system. If instead, you see an error such as "tcl: command not found," you may still have a copy of Tcl installed on your system, but it's not in your search path ($PATH)—ask your system administrator whether Tcl is available.

If you find that you need to install Tcl, you can find it at http://tcl._activestate.com. ActiveState distributes Tcl/Tk in binary (precompiled) form for Linux, Solaris, and Windows. You can also find the source code for Tcl/Tk at ActiveState.

The second component that you need is libpgtcl. libpgtcl is a package of Tcl extension functions that enable a Tcl script to interact with PostgreSQL. This component can be a little hard to find. libpgtcl was distributed with PostgreSQL up until release 8.0. If you are building a copy of PostgreSQL from pre-8.0 source code, adding the --with-tcl flag to configure should build libpgtcl for you. If you have installed PostgreSQL using a RPM package, be sure to install the postgresql-tcl package. If you are using Tcl on a Windows host, the easiest way to obtain the libpgtcl library is to install PgAccess (http://www.pgaccess.org). If all else fails, you can find the source code for libpgtcl at PostgreSQL's GBorg website (http://gborg.postgresql.org).

Finally, some of the examples in this chapter require the TkTable extension to Tk. TkTable provides a table widget that you will use to display query results. If you have already installed Tcl and Tk, you may find that TkTable came with the distribution that you loaded. If not, you can find TkTable at http://tktable.sourceforge.net.

Client 1—Connecting to the Server

The first step to interacting with a PostgreSQL server is to establish a connection; in this section, you'll use Tcl and Tk to build a simple graphical client that establishes a connection to a PostgreSQL server. The libpgtcl library is implemented on top of the libpq, so many of the features that you see in libpgtcl will seem familiar if you've read through Chapter 8, "The PostgreSQL C API—libpq." To connect to a PostgreSQL server, use the pg_connect procedure. pg_connect comes in two flavors:

```
pg_connect -conninfo connection-string
```

or

```
pg_connect database-name
           [-host host-name]
           [-port port-number]
           [-tty tty-name]
           [-options option-string]
```

The second form is considered obsolete, and I've included it here only for completeness.

The preferred form uses a connection string similar to those used in libpq applications. A *connection string* is a list of keyword=value pairs, separated by whitespace. Each pair in the connection string specifies the value for a connection property. A typical connection string might look something like this:

```
host=davinci user=bruce password=koalas dbname=movies
```

This particular connection string provides four connection properties: a hostname, a username and password, and a database name. Table 16.1 lists the properties that may appear in a connection string.

Table 16.1 **Connection Properties**

Connect-String Property	Environment Variable	Example
user	PGUSER	user=korry
password	PGPASSWORD	password=cows
dbname	PGDATABASE	dbname=accounting
host	PGHOST	host=jersey
hostaddr	PGHOSTADDR	hostaddr=127.0.0.1
port	PGPORT	port=5432

The second column in Table 16.1 shows the environment variable that libpgtcl will use if you omit the property shown in the first column. For example, if you omit the `host` property from your connection string, libpgtcl will use the value of the `PGHOST` environment variable. If you don't supply a particular property in the connection string, and you haven't defined the corresponding environment variable, libpgtcl will use hard-wired default values. To see the hard-wired values, you can use the `pg_conndefaults`[1] procedure:

```
$ tclsh
% package require Pgtcl
1.4
% foreach prop [pg_conndefaults] { puts $prop }
authtype    Database-Authtype          D 20 {}
service     Database-Service           {} 20 {}
user        Database-User              {} 20 korry
password    Database-Password          * 20 {}
dbname      Database-Name              {} 20 korry
host        Database-Host              {} 40 {}
hostaddr    Database-Host-IPv4-Address {} 15 {}
port        Database-Port              {} 6  5432
tty         Backend-Debug-TTY          D 40 {}
options     Backend-Debug-Options      D 40 {}
requiressl  Require-SSL                D 1  0
sslmode     SSL-Mode                   {} 8  prefer
```

The first column lists property names; the last column displays the final default values that will be used if you don't provide overrides.

The `pg_conndefaults` procedure returns a list of sublists. The values returned by `pg_conndefaults` might seem a little confusing until you understand the problem that this procedure was trying to solve. From time to time, the PostgreSQL authors need to introduce new connection properties. How can you support new connection properties without rewriting every PostgreSQL client application? The client application can ask `pg_conndefaults` for a list of supported properties and then ask the user to provide a value for each of those properties. A robust client application will not have to be recompiled each time a new connection property is introduced; it just prompts the user for more information.

Having said that, you probably won't let me off the hook unless we build a "robust" client application (or at least make an attempt).

The first client application in this chapter does little more than connect to a PostgreSQL server, but does so using a self-adjusting login dialog. This particular client application is rather long—building a graphical login dialog from barebones Tcl/Tk is not a trivial task. In a real-world application, you might want to explore add-on toolkits that make it easier to do this sort of work.

Let's dive into the code for `client1.tcl`—I'll explain how to use `pg_conndefaults` as we go. You'll also see how to call the `pg_connect` procedure. Listing 16.1 shows the start of the `client1.tcl` application.

---

[1] I've cleaned up the listing returned by `pg_conndefaults` to make it easier to read.

Listing 16.1 `client1.tcl`—**main**

```
 1 #!/usr/local/bin/wish
 2 #
 3 # Filename: client1.tcl
 4
 5 proc main { } {
 6
 7   package require Pgtcl
 8
 9   wm withdraw .
10
11   set result "retry"
12
13   while { $result == "retry" } {
14     set connstr [connect_dialog]
15
16     if { [catch {pg_connect -conninfo $connstr} conn] } {
17       set result [tk_messageBox \
18                 -message $conn \
19                 -title "Connection failed" \
20                 -type retrycancel]
21     } else {
22       tk_messageBox \
23         -message "Connection is: $conn" \
24         -title "Connection Ok"
25
26       set result "ok"
27     }
28   }
29 }
```

The first line specifies the name of the interpreter that should be used to run this script: wish is the graphical Tcl/Tk shell[2]. Line 5 defines a procedure named main. Unlike many other languages, a function with the name of main is *not* the default entry point for Tcl script—I'll call this function main just so that it is easily recognizable. In Tcl, the entry point for a program is the first executable line of code outside of a proc definition. In fact, the first few executable lines of code in this program are right at the end of the script (the end of this script is *not* shown in Listing 16.1; you still have four more listings to get through).

The main function expects no arguments (you can tell that because the braces immediately following the function name are empty).

---

[2] The magic string at the beginning of a shell script such as this is called the shebang line: "she" is for shell and "bang" is how some people pronounce the exclamation point. A shebang line tells the operating system which program should be used to execute the script. Shebang lines are supported on Unix and Linux hosts, but not on Windows systems (except when using the Cygwin environment).

The first thing that you do in this function is load the libpgtcl library into the Tcl interpreter—that's what the `package require` statement on line 7 does (if you're using a version of PostgreSQL older than 8.0, use the command `load libpgctl` instead). Before you can call *any* PostgreSQL-related functions, you must load the libpgtcl library.

Next, *withdraw* the root window. If you are not a seasoned Tk programmer, that probably sounds a little ominous. When the `wish` interpreter starts up, it automatically creates an empty window for you. That window is called a *root* window, and its name is simply the period character (.). You withdraw the window now so that you can make your own window a little later.

Lines 13 through 28 form a loop. Inside this loop, you create a dialog that prompts the user for connection properties. Figure 16.1 shows the dialog that appears when you run `client1.tcl` (you may see a slightly different dialog than the one shown in Figure 16.1 depending on which version of libpgtcl you are using).

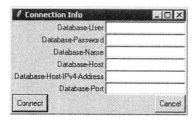

Figure 16.1   The Connection Info dialog.

If the user clicks the `Cancel` button, the entire application will end. If the user clicks the `Connect` button, it tries to connect to a PostgreSQL server using the information provided. If the connect attempt succeeds, a message displays and the application terminates. If a connection attempt fails, you want the user to see a Retry/Cancel dialog that displays the error message and offers a chance to try again.

Repeat the loop at lines 13 through 28 until you establish a connection or until the user presses the `Cancel` button.

At line 14, call the `connect_dialog` procedure (you'll see that procedure in a moment) to display the connection dialog and wait for user input. `connect_dialog` returns a connection string, which is awfully handy because you need a connection string before you can talk to PostgreSQL.

After you have a connection string, call the `pg_connect` function to attempt a connection. When `pg_connect` is called, it either establishes a connection or it throws an error. You want to intercept any error messages, so you call `pg_connect` within a `catch{}` block. If the call to `pg_connect` succeeds, `catch{}` will return 0 (also known as `TCL_OK`). If `pg_connect` throws an error, the `catch{}` command will return a value other than zero. In either case, the `conn` variable (the third argument to the `catch{}` command) is modified. In the case of a connection failure, `conn` will contain the text of the error message. If the connection attempt is successful, `conn` will contain a connection *channel*. A channel is similar to a handle (handles are used in many programming language/API combinations). A channel is simply a unique identifier returned by the API—you give the identifier back to the API when you want to do something with that connection (like execute a command). Like everything else in Tcl, a channel is a string.

If you were not able to establish a connection, display a message to the user by using the tk_messageBox function (see line 17). A typical error message is shown in Figure 16.2.

Figure 16.2   The Connection dialog, Connection failed error message.

After displaying the error message, tk_messageBox waits for the user to click either the Retry button or the Cancel button. tk_messageBox returns a string telling you which option the user selected (either retry or cancel). You store that string in the result variable, which controls the loop. So, if the user clicks the Retry button, you repeat the loop; otherwise, end the loop and terminate the application.

If the connection attempt succeeds, use tk_messageBox again. In this case, display the channel (not really useful but mildly interesting), as shown in Figure 16.3.

Figure 16.3   The Connection dialog, Connection OK message.

That covers the main() function; now let's see how to build a dialog using Tcl/Tk. (I should warn you; it's not pretty.)

Listing 16.2 shows the connect_dialog procedure. This procedure constructs a dialog that prompts the user for connection properties, displays the dialog, and assembles a connection string with the values supplied by the user.

Listing 16.2   client1.tcl-connect_dialog

```
31 proc connect_dialog { } {
32
33    global next_row
34
35    set next_row 0
36    set set_focus true
37
```

Listing 16.2   **Continued**

```
38   #  Create a new window with the title
39   #      "Connection Info"
40   #
41   set w [toplevel .dlg]
42   wm title .dlg "Connection Info"
43
44   #  Create the labels and entry fields for this dialog
45   #
46
47   foreach prop [pg_conndefaults] {
48
49      set varname     [lindex $prop 0]
50      set label_text  [lindex $prop 1]
51      set type        [lindex $prop 2]
52      set length      [lindex $prop 3]
53      set default     [lindex $prop 4]
54
55      if { $type != "D" } {
56
57        global $varname
58
59        set $varname $default
60
61        set entry [add_label_field .dlg $label_text $varname]
62
63        if { $type == "*" } {
64          $entry configure -show "*"
65        }
66
67        if { $set_focus == "true" } {
68           focus -force $entry
69        set set_focus false
70        }
71      }
72   }
73
74   #  Create the "Connect" and "Cancel" buttons
75   add_button .dlg.default "Connect" {set result Ok} 1
76   add_button .dlg.cancel  "Cancel"  {exit}          2
77
78   .dlg.default configure -default active
79
80   vwait result
81
82   set result ""
83
```

Listing 16.2 **Continued**

```
84    foreach prop [pg_conndefaults] {
85
86      set type [lindex $prop 2]
87
88      if { $type != "D" } {
89
90        set varname "$[lindex $prop 0]"
91        set varval [subst $varname]
92
93        if { $varval != "" } {
94          append result "[lindex $prop 0]=$varval "
95        }
96      }
97    }
98
99    destroy .dlg
100
101   return $result
102 }
```

You can find Tk extension libraries that make dialogs easier to build, but we'll build our own so you can stick to plain vanilla Tcl/Tk code.

Lines 33, 35, and 36 initialize a few variables that you will be using in this procedure; I'll explain the purpose of each variable as we go.

To construct the dialog shown in Figure 16.1, you will create a new toplevel widget named .dlg (at line 41). The toplevel widget automatically resizes as you add more widgets to it. To manage the placement of child widgets within .dlg, you will use the grid layout manager. The grid layout manager arranges child widgets in a grid (makes sense so far). You build a grid with two columns: A text label goes in the left column and the corresponding text entry widget goes in the right column. You use the next_row global variable to keep track of which grid row you are working on.

At line 47, enter a loop that iterates through each connection property returned by pg_conndefaults. Remember, pg_conndefaults returns a list of connection properties and enough information about each property so that you can construct a connection dialog. pg_conndefaults returns a list of sublists: Each sublist corresponds to a single connection property. There are five items in each sublist, and you pick apart the items at lines 49 through 53. The first item is the property name; for example, authtype, user, and password. You will create a variable that holds the value of each connection property; the name of the variable is the same as the name of the property. The second item is a descriptive name such as Database-User or Database-Name. The descriptive name displays as a prompt. The third item in the sublist is a property type. There are three possible values for the property type: an empty string, the character "D", and the character "*". If the property type is set to D, the property is meant for debugging purposes and should not normally be displayed to a casual user. If the property type is set to *, the property holds secret information (such as a password) and should not be echoed to the screen. If the property type is an empty string, it needs no special handling. You will ignore debug properties and arrange for any password fields to be displayed as * characters. The fourth sublist item returned by `pg_conndefaults` is the suggested length of the property value—you will ignore this item for now. The final item in each sublist is the default value for the property. The default value reflects the environment variable associated with the property, or it reflects the hard-wired value if the environment variable has not been defined.

After picking apart the property sublist, you start processing it at line 55. The `if` statement at line 55 ensures that you ignore debug properties. I mentioned earlier that you will create a new variable for each connection property—that happens at line 57. For example, if `[lindex $prop 0]` evaluates to `password`, you will create a new global variable named `password`. At line 57, you assign the default value (if any) to the new variable.

Next, add a `label` widget and an `entry` widget for each value that you want. The `add_label_field` procedure expects three parameters: a parent widget (`.dlg`), the text to display, and a variable that holds the value entered by the user.

When you call `add_label_field` (which you will examine next), two widgets are created. The first, a `label` widget, displays the text that was provided. The second, an `entry` widget, holds a value entered by the user. `add_label_field` returns the name of the new `entry` widget—you'll need that name to customize the widget.

At lines 63 and 64, you configure any "secret" properties (that is, passwords) to show asterisks rather than the actual characters entered by the user.

Next, at lines 67 through 70, you force the *focus* to the first entry widget in the dialog. When a widget has focus, keyboard and mouse events are sent to that widget and that widget holds the text cursor. You force the focus to the first modifiable widget on the dialog so that it lands in a useful, predictable place.

At lines 75 and 76, you create the two buttons that appear at the bottom of your dialog. When the user clicks on the first button (labeled `Connect`), Tcl will execute the command `{set result Ok}`. If the user clicks on the second button (labeled `Cancel`), Tcl will execute the command `{exit}`, terminating the entire application.

If the user presses the `Return` key, the default widget will be activated. You want the `Return` key to trigger the `Connect` button, so make that the default widget (see line 78).

At this point, you have created all the widgets that you want to display to the user. You have a `toplevel` widget that contains a collection of labels and text entry widgets, and you have a pair of buttons so the user can make something happen. Now, you want to display the complete dialog to the user and wait for him to click the `Connect` button or the `Cancel` button. That's what the `vwait` procedure does (line 80). The argument for `vwait` is the name of a variable; in this case, `result`. The `vwait` procedure waits for the `result` variable to change. `result` changes when the user clicks the `Connect` button because the code executed by the `Connect` button is `{set result 1}`.

Remember, if the user clicks the `Cancel` button, the `exit` procedure is invoked, terminating the entire application.

After the user has clicked the `Connect` button, you construct a connection string from the values the user had entered. To do this, loop through each non-debug property and extract the property name. You use the property name to reconstruct the name of the variable that holds the property value (line 90). After you know the variable name, you can extract the value (line 91). If the property value is non-null, you construct a *property=value* pair and append it to the result string.

Finally, destroy the toplevel window (.dlg) and return the connection string to the caller.

This procedure (connect_dialog) gives you a self-adjusting procedure that prompts the user for connection properties, even if you run a newer (or older) version of PostgreSQL that supports a different set of properties.

Now, let's look at the helper functions: add_label_field and add_button. The add_label_field procedure is shown in Listing 16.3.

Listing 16.3 client1.tcl-add_label_field

```
104 proc add_label_field { w text textvar } {
105
106     global next_row
107
108     set next_row    [expr $next_row + 1]
109     set label_path "$w.label_$textvar"
110     set entry_path "$w.$textvar"
111
112     label $label_path  text $text
113     grid  $label_path -row $next_row  column 1  sticky e
114
115     entry $entry_path -textvariable $textvar
116     grid  $entry_path -row $next_row -column 2 -sticky w
117
118     bind $entry_path <Return> "$w.default invoke"
119
120     return $entry_path
121 }
```

This procedure creates two new widgets: a label widget and a text entry widget. The caller provides three arguments: a parent widget (w), the text to appear in the label widget (text), and the name of a variable that will hold the value that the user types into the entry widget (textvar).

We use the next_row global variable to determine where the label and entry widgets will be located. If you refer to line 35 of the previous listing (Listing 16.2), you'll see that next_row to zero was initialized before building the dialog.

Lines 109 and 110 construct the name that you will use for the label widget and for the entry widget. The widget names are constructed from the name of the text variable provided by the caller.

At line 112, you create the label widget and place the given text on the label. At line 113, you position the label widget using Tcl's grid layout manager. Always position the label widget in the first (leftmost) column and entry widget in the second (rightmost) column.

The `-sticky` option is used to position a widget within the grid cell. Specifying `-sticky e` means that the east (right) side of the widget sticks to the edge of the grid cell. The widget is right-justified within the cell.

At lines 115 and 116, you create the `entry` widget and position it within the `grid`.

Line 118 creates a *binding* for the `Return` key. If the user clicks the `Return` key while the `entry` widget is in focus, you want to trigger (or *invoke*) the `$w.default` button (that is, the `Connect` button). To accomplish this, bind the `Return` key to the code fragment `$w.default invoke`.

Finally, return the name of the `entry` widget to the caller.

The final procedure in `client1.tcl` is `add_button` (shown in Listing 16.4).

Listing 16.4 `client1.tcl-add_button`

```
123 proc add_button { path text command column } {
124
125     global next_row
126
127     if { $column == 1 } {
128       set next_row  [expr $next_row + 1]
129       set sticky "w"
130     } else { set sticky "e"   }
131
132     button $path -text $text -command $command
133     grid   $path -row $next_row -column $column -sticky $sticky
134
135     bind $path <Return> "$path invoke"
136 }
```

The caller provides four parameters: the name of the widget (path), the text to display on the button (text), a command to execute when the button is pressed (command), and a column number (column). The column number, along with the next_row global variable, determines which grid cell will hold the new button.

Line 132 creates and configures the `button` widget, and line 133 positions the button within the `grid` layout manager. Finally, you bind the command `$path invoke` to the `Return` key. It's a little odd, but Tk doesn't do that automatically—pressing the `Return` key doesn't trigger a `button` widget unless you explicitly configure the `button` to do so.

Listing 16.5 shows the mainline code for `client1.tcl`. When the Tcl interpreter runs this script, it begins execution at line 140 (the first command outside of a procedure body). The mainline code is simple; you invoke the procedure `main` (refer to Listing 16.1) and `exit` when that procedure completes.

Listing 16.5 `client1.tcl-mainline`

```
138 #  Mainline code follows
139 #
140 main
141 exit
```

Making the Connection Dialog Reusable

The `connect_dialog` procedure that you just finished turns out to be rather handy. Let's rearrange the code a little to make this procedure more reusable.

The easiest way to share code among Tcl applications is to factor the desired procedures into a separate source file and `source` that file into your applications. When you source a file, you are copying the contents of that file into your application at runtime. If you are familiar with C or C++, source is identical to `#include`.

We'll create a new file named `pgconnect.tcl` that contains only the code that you want to share among various applications. Listing 16.6 shows the outline of `pgconnect.tcl`.

Listing 16.6 `pgconnect.tcl-outline`

```
# Filename: pgconnect.tcl

proc connect_dialog { } {
...
}

proc add_label_field { w text textvar } {
...
}

proc add_button { path text command column } {
...
}

proc connect { } {
...
}
```

You can see that the `connect_dialog`, `add_label_field`, and `add_button` procedures are copied into `pgconnect.tcl`. I've also removed the mainline code and the `main` procedure—that code will be provided by the calling application. I've added one new procedure: connect. The body of the connect function is shown in Listing 16.7.

Listing 16.7 `pgconnect.tcl-connect`

```
1 proc connect { } {
2
3   package require Pgtcl
4
5   set result "retry"
6
7   while { $result == "retry" } {
8     set connstr [connect_dialog]
9
```

Listing 16.7   **Continued**

```
10    if { [catch {pg_connect -conninfo $connstr} conn] } {
11      set result [tk_messageBox \
12                  -message $conn \
13                  -title "Connection failed" \
14                  -type retrycancel]
15    } else {
16      return $conn
17    }
18  }
19  return {}
20  }
```

The connect procedure is similar to the main procedure from client1.tcl. After loading the libpgtcl library, connect enters a loop that calls the connect_dialog procedure
until a connection is made or the user cancels. If a connection is made, connect will
return the connection handle to the caller; otherwise, it will return an empty string.

Now that you've factored the connection dialog logic into a separate source file, you
can use these procedures in multiple applications. Listing 16.8 shows a new version of
the client1.tcl application, rewritten to take advantage of pgconnect.tcl.

Listing 16.8   client1a.tcl

```
 1 #!/usr/local/bin/wish
 2 #
 3 # Filename: client1a.tcl
 4
 5 proc main { } {
 6
 7   wm withdraw .
 8
 9   set conn [connect]
10
11   if { $conn != {} } {
12     tk_messageBox \
13         -message "Connection is: $conn" \
14             -title "Connection Ok"
15   }
16
17   pg_disconnect $conn
18
19 }
20
21 #  Mainline code follows
22 #
23
```

Listing 16.8   **Continued**

```
24 source pgconnect.tcl
25
26 main
27 exit
```

This new application is much shorter than the original version. I'll point out two changes that I've made to this code. First, at line 24, I replaced the connect_dialog, add_label_field, and add_button procedures with source pgconnect.tcl. Because I haven't included a pathname in the source command, Tcl looks for pgconnect.tcl in the current directory. The other change that I've made is at line 17—you call pg_disconnect to free up the connection handle when you are finished with it. You should call pg_disconnect to gracefully close a connection handle when you no longer need the connection. Closing the connection handle is not strictly required, but it is good form to free up resources as soon as you are done with them.

Now that you know how to connect to a PostgreSQL database from Tcl (and how to disconnect when you're finished), let's look at the steps required to execute a SQL command and process the results.

Client 2—Query Processing

Executing a command with libpgtcl is easy. You invoke the pg_exec procedure and you get back a result handle. pg_exec expects two parameters:

```
pg_exec connection_handle command
```

A typical call to pg_exec might look like this:

```
set result_handle [pg_exec $conn "SELECT * FROM customers"]
```

Calling pg_exec like this captures the result handle in the variable result_handle. A result handle encapsulates many items of information into a single object. You can't get at any of this information directly; instead, you have to use the pg_result procedure.

Result Set Processing

Let's look at some of the things that you can do with a result handle:

```
$ tclsh

% package require Pgtcl

% set connstr "host=davinci user=korry password=cows dbname=movies"
host=davinci user=korry password=cows dbname=movies

% set conn [pg_connect -conninfo $connstr]
pgsql276
```

At this point, you have loaded the libpgtcl library into the Tcl interpreter and established a connection to your database. Next, you will execute a simple query using the pg_exec function:

```
% set result [pg_exec $conn "SELECT * FROM customers"]
pgsql276.0
```

When you call pg_exec, you get back a result handle. You may have noticed that the string you get back from pg_exec is similar to the string returned by pg_connect. In fact, appending a number to the connection handle forms the result handle. If you were to execute another command using the same connection handle, pg_exec would return pgsql276.1. Result handles remain valid until you clear them or close the parent connection handle. I'll show you how to clear result handles and how to close connection handles in a moment. First, let's get back to pg_result:

```
% pg_result $result -status
PGRES_TUPLES_OK
```

The pg_result -status option returns a string that tells you whether the command succeeded or failed. If a command has executed successfully, pg_result -status will return PGRES_TUPLES_OK, PGRES_COMMAND_OK, or PGRES_EMPTY_QUERY[3]. If the command fails, you will see PGRES_NONFATAL_ERROR, PGRES_FATAL_ERROR, or PGRES_BAD_RESPONSE.

If your command fails, you can use the pg_result -error option to retrieve the text of the error message. Let's execute another (erroneous) command so you can see pg_result -error in action:

```
% set result2 [pg_exec $conn "SELECT * FROM moof"]
pgsql276.1

% pg_result $result2 -status
PGRES_FATAL_ERROR

% pg_result $result2 -error
ERROR:  Relation "moof" does not exist
```

Of course, you could capture the error message in a variable using set error [pg_result $result2 -error].

Assuming that the command succeeded, you can determine how many rows and columns are in the result set using pg_result -numTuples and pg_result -numAttrs (respectively):

```
% pg_result $result -numTuples
5
```

---

[3] You may also see PGRES_COPY_IN and PGRES_COPY_OUT if you execute the COPY FROM or COPY TO commands. I won't be covering the COPY command this chapter; the details vary with implementation and seem to be rather unstable.

```
% pg_result $result -numAttrs
4
```

If you call `pg_result -numTuples` (or `-numAttrs`) using a result handle for a failed command, the row count (or column count) will be zero.

You can retrieve the column names from a result handle using `pg_result -attributes`:

```
% pg_result $result -attributes
id customer_name phone birth_date
```

`pg_result -attributes` returns a list of column names. You can pick apart this list using `lindex`:

```
% lindex [pg_result $result -attributes] 0
id
```

```
% lindex [pg_result $result -attributes] 1
customer
```

A related option is `pg_result -lAttributes`. This option returns complete metadata for a result handle. The `-lAttributes` option returns a list of sublists. Each sublist contains three elements: the name of a column, the data type of a column, and the size of a column. Here is the metadata for the `SELECT * FROM customers` query that you have executed:

```
% pg result $result -lAttributes
{id 23 4} {customer_name 1043 -1} {phone 1042 -1} {birth_date 1082 4}
```

This result set holds four columns so the `pg_result -lAttributes` returns four sublists. Notice that the data type for each column is returned in numeric form. The data type values correspond to the OID (object-id) of the corresponding entry in the `pg_type` system table. You can find the type names using the following query (in `psql`):

```
$ psql -d movies -q

movies=# SELECT oid, typname FROM pg_type
movies-#    WHERE oid IN (23, 1043, 1042, 1082);
 oid  | typname
------+---------
   23 | int4
 1042 | bpchar
 1043 | varchar
 1082 | date
(4 rows)
```

Let's compare the results returned by `pg_result -lAttributes` with the output of the `\d` meta-command in `psql`:

```
$ psql -d movies
movies=# \d customers
```

```
                    Table "customers"
     Attribute     |         Type          | Modifier
    ---------------+-----------------------+----------
     customer_id   | integer               |
     customer_name | character varying(50) |
     phone         | character(8)          |
     birth_date    | date                  |
```

We see the same column names, but the column sizes and data types returned by
pg_result don't look right. For example, the customer_name column is defined as a
VARCHAR(50), but pg_result-lAttributes reports a length of -1 and a type of 1043.
The problem is that the -lAttributes option returns the size of each column as stored
on the server. Columns of variable size are reported as being -1 byte long. You probably
won't find too many uses for -lAttributes.

One function that you *will* find useful is pg_result -getTuple. The -getTuple
option returns a row from the result set in the form of a list. Let's retrieve the first row
returned by our query:

```
% set tuple [pg_result $result -getTuple 0]
1 {Jones, Henry} 555-1212 1970-10-10
```

Notice that row numbers start at 0, not 1. With a result set containing five rows, you
can request rows 0 through 4. If you try to retrieve an invalid row, you will see an error
message:

```
% pg_result $result -getTuple 5
argument to getTuple cannot exceed number of tuples - 1
```

As with any other Tcl list, you can pick apart a row using the lindex operator:

```
% puts $tuple
1 {Jones, Henry} 555-1212 1970-10-10

% lindex $tuple 1
Jones, Henry
```

An empty string represents a NULL value. I happen to know that the last row in this result
set contains a NULL phone number:

```
% set tuple [pg_result $result -getTuple 4]
7 {Grumby, Jonas} {} 1984-02-21

% lindex $tuple 2

%
```

Notice that lindex has returned an empty string when you asked for the phone number
value (it's a little hard to see, but it's there).

In addition to -getTuple, pg_result gives you three other ways to get at the rows in
a result set. First, and easiest to understand, is pg_result -tupleArray:

```
% pg_result $result -tupleArray 0 one_row

% parray one_row
one_row(birth_date)     = 1970-10-10
one_row(customer_name)  = Jones, Henry
one_row(customer_id)    = 1
one_row(phone)          = 555-1212
```

The -tupleArray option assigns a single tuple to an array variable. In this example, you asked pg_result to copy the first row (row 0) into an array variable named one_row. In Tcl, every array is an associative array, meaning that you can index into the array using any string value. A nonassociative array forces you to assign a unique number to each array element. Associative arrays are nice. You can see from this example that the -tupleArray option uses the name of each column as a key (array index). If you want to find the customer name in this array, you could write the following:

```
% puts $one_row(customer_name)
Jones, Henry
```

There is a serious *gotcha* waiting in the -tupleArray option. Because -tupleArray produces an associative array, the column names in your result set must be unique. Normally, this isn't an issue, but if you have two or more computed columns in your result set, you must give them unique names using the AS clause. Here is an example that shows the problem:

```
% set result2 [pg_exec $conn "SELECT 2*3, 5*3"]
pgsql276.2

% pg_result $result2  tupleArray 0 missing_fields

% parray missing_fields
missing_fields(?column?) = 15
```

You can see the problem; unless you rename a computed column, it will be named ?column?. If you have two columns with the same name, one of them will vanish from the associative array. Let's fix this:

```
% set result2 [pg_exec $conn "SELECT 2*4 AS first, 5*3 AS second"]
pgsql276.3

% pg_result $result2 -tupleArray 0 all_fields

% parray all_fields
all_fields(first)  = 8
all_fields(second) = 15
```

Much better—now you see both values.

The next pg_result option assigns all the rows in a result set to a single array—for example:

```
% pg_result $result -assign all_rows
all_rows

% parray all_rows
all_rows(0,birth_date)     = 1970-10-10
all_rows(0,customer_name)  = Jones, Henry
all_rows(0,customer_id)    = 1
all_rows(0,phone)          = 555-1212
all_rows(1,birth_date)     = 1972-07-10
all_rows(1,customer_name)  = Rubin, William
all_rows(1,customer_id)    = 2
all_rows(1,phone)          = 555-2211
all_rows(2,birth_date)     = 1968-01-21
all_rows(2,customer_name)  = Panky, Henry
all_rows(2,customer_id)    = 3
all_rows(2,phone)          = 555-1221
all_rows(3,birth_date)     = 1969-03-05
all_rows(3,customer_name)  = Wonderland, Alice N.
all_rows(3,customer_id)    = 4
all_rows(3,phone)          = 555-1122
all_rows(4,birth_date)     = 1984-02-21
all_rows(4,customer_name)  = Grumby, Jonas
all_rows(4,customer_id)    = 7
all_rows(4,phone)          =
```

pg_result -assign copies all rows in the result set into a two-dimensional array. After you execute the command pg_result $result -assign all_rows, the array variable $all_rows will contain 20 elements (five rows times four columns). The first array index is the row number and the second index is the column name (remember, Tcl arrays are associative; you can use any string value as an array index). If you want the phone number value from the third row, you will find it in $all_rows(2,phone):

```
% puts $all_rows(2,phone)
555-1221
```

Because the array produced by -assign is an associative array, you must ensure that each column in the result set has a unique name.

Finally, pg_result can create an associative array from your result set where the key to the array is formed by the values in the first column. I think this option is best understood by looking at an example:

```
% set result3 \
[pg_exec $conn "SELECT customer_id, phone, birth_date FROM customers"]
pgsql276.4

% pg_result $result3 -assignbyidx results
results
```

```
% parray results
results(1,birth_date)  = 1970-10-10
results(1,phone)       = 555-1212
results(2,birth_date)  = 1972-07-10
results(2,phone)       = 555-2211
results(3,birth_date)  = 1968-01-21
results(3,phone)       = 555-1221
results(4,birth_date)  = 1969-03-05
results(4,phone)       = 555-1122
results(7,birth_date)  = 1984-02-05
results(7,phone)       =
```

Like pg_result -assign, the -assignbyidx option creates a two-dimensional array. The difference between -assign and -assignbyidx is in how they create the key values for the array. -assign uses the row number as the first index and the column name as the second dimension. On the other hand, -assignbyidx removes the first column from the result set and uses the first column in each row as the first index.

This result set ($result3) contains five rows and three columns. An array created by -assign would have 15 members, but an array created by -assignbyidx will have 10 members (five rows times two columns). The -assignbyidx option has removed the first column (the customer_id column) from the array and used those values (1, 2, 3, 4, and 7) to index the first dimension in the result array.

When you use -assignbyidx, you have to pay attention to the order in which the columns appear in the result set. The first column is used to index the resulting array. You must also ensure that the values in the first column are unique, or you will lose entire rows from the result set.

Lazy Programmers Are Good Programmers, or pg_select

libpgtcl offers one last procedure that you can use to process the result set of a query: pg_select. The pg_select procedure gives you a quick way to execute a command (usually SELECT) and process the result set all at once. pg_select requires four parameters:

```
pg_select connection_handle command variable procedure
```

When you call pg_select, you supply a connection handle, the text of the command that you want to send to the server, the name of an array variable that will hold each row (one row at a time), and a procedure that will be called once for each row in the result set. Here is an example:

```
% pg_select $conn \
    "SELECT * FROM customers LIMIT 2" \
    one_row \
    {puts "" ; parray one_row }

one_row(.command)    = update
one_row(.headers)    = customer_id customer_name phone birth_date
one_row(.numcols)    = 4
one_row(.tupno)      = 0
```

```
one_row(birth_date)        = 1970-10-10
one_row(customer_name)  = Jones, Henry
one_row(customer_id)      = 1
one_row(phone)             = 555-1212

one_row(.command)          = update
one_row(.headers)          = customer_id customer_name phone birth_date
one_row(.numcols)          = 4
one_row(.tupno)            = 1
one_row(birth_date)        = 1972-07-10
one_row(customer_name)  = Rubin, William
one_row(customer_id)      = 2
one_row(phone)             = 555-2211
```

When you execute this statement, pg_select will send the SELECT command to the server. If the
SELECT command fails, pg_select will throw an error. If the SELECT command completes successfully, pg_select will loop through the result set. After assigning the next row to the one_row variable,
pg_select will execute the string {puts "" ; parray one_row}.

When pg_select assigns a row to the variable that you specify, it creates an associative array indexed by
column name, just like pg_result -tupleArray. You may have noticed that there are a few extra
entries reported for each row. Each time a row is processed, pg_select defines four extra elements in the
associative array that it creates. The .tupno member indicates which row is currently being processed
(starting at 0). The .numcols and .headers members will not change from row to row—they hold the
column count and column names, respectively. The fourth special member is .command; this member is
not only undocumented, it appears to be wrong. Of course, we can only guess what the .command member is supposed to do; but in the latest release, .command is always set to update. My advice is to ignore
.command for now.

Now that you know how to process the result set of a query, let's look at a sample application that will execute a single (hard-wired) query and display the results in tabular form.

Listing 16.9 shows the first few lines of client2.tcl.

Listing 16.9 client2.tcl—main

```
 1 #!/usr/local/bin/wish
 2 #
 3 # Filename: client2.tcl
 4
 5 proc main { } {
 6
 7   wm withdraw .
 8
 9   package require Tktable
10
11   set conn [connect]
12
```

Listing 16.9   **Continued**

```
13    if { $conn != {} } {
14
15        set table [build_dialog $conn]
16
17        process_command $conn $table "SELECT * FROM customers"
18
19        tkwait window .top
20
21        pg_disconnect $conn
22    }
23 }
```

In this application, you use the Tktable extension to Tk. If you don't already have this extension, you can find it at http://tktable.sourceforge.net. Because this is an extension, you have to explicitly load (or `package require`) the Tktable package before you can use it (see line 9).

Next, call the `connect` procedure to establish a connection to the PostgreSQL server. This is the same `connect` procedure that you developed earlier in this chapter (it's imported from `pgconnect.sql` at the bottom of this application). `connect` returns a connection handle if successful, or returns an empty string in the event of a failure.

If you connected, create a dialog that you will use to display the results of a query. The `build_dialog` procedure (shown in Listing 16.10) returns the name of the table widget hosted in the dialog. Next, call the `process_command` procedure (shown later in Listing 16.12) to execute a simple SELECT command. `process_command` expects three parameters: a connection handle, the name of a table widget, and the text of a query.

After you've finished filling in the table widget, display the dialog to the user and wait for him to close that window.

Finally, play nice and disconnect from the server using `pg_disconnect` when you are finished.

Listing 16.10   `client2.tcl—build_dialog`

```
25 proc build_dialog { conn } {
26
27    toplevel .top
28
29    wm title .top "Customers"
30
31    set table [make_table .top]
32
33    button .top.close -text "Close Window" -command {exit}
34
35    scrollbar .top.sy -command [list $table yview]
36    scrollbar .top.sx -command [list $table xview] -orient horizontal
37
```

Listing 16.10 **Continued**

```
38   grid    $table .top.sy       -sticky news
39   grid           .top.sx       -sticky ew
40   grid           .top.close

42   grid columnconfig .top 0 -weight 1
43   grid rowconfig    .top 0 -weight 1
44   grid rowconfig    .top 2 -weight 0

46   return $table
47 }
```

Listing 16.10 shows the `build_dialog` procedure. This procedure creates a `toplevel` window that hosts a table widget, scrollbars, and a `Close Window` button. Figure 16.4 shows the window layout that you are constructing.

After creating a `toplevel` window and configuring its title bar, you call the `make_table` procedure (shown later in Listing 16.11). `make_table` creates a new `table` widget (whose parent is `.top`) and does some initial configuration work. Next you create the `Close Window` button and a vertical and horizontal scrollbar. Finally, arrange all the child widgets (the table widget, button, and scrollbars) using the `grid` layout manager.

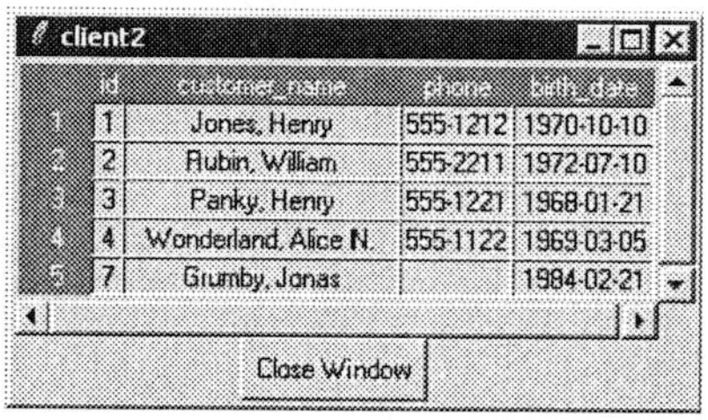

Figure 16.4 The `client2.tcl-results`.

If you look closely at the window layout in Figure 16.4 (and use your imagination), you'll see that the child widgets are arranged in a grid containing three rows and two columns. You have to use your imagination because the grid cells are not equally sized. Be sure to look at the layout of the *child widgets*, not the data values in the table control. The top row in the grid contains a table control in the leftmost column and a vertical scrollbar in the rightmost column. The middle row contains the horizontal scrollbar in the leftmost column and the rightmost column is empty. Finally, the bottom row contains the `Close Window` button in the leftmost column and, again, the rightmost column is empty.

Now, look back to lines 38 through 40 in Listing 16.10. You'll see how the `grid` layout manager arranges everything.

Lines 42 through 44 ensure that the table widget resizes whenever the `toplevel` widget is resized. The easiest way to understand these three lines of code is to comment them out, run the application, and then stretch out the window. You'll see that the vertical scrollbar gets wider and the horizontal scrollbar gets taller. A bit too "Salvador Dali" for my taste. The `grid columnconfig` and `grid rowconfig` procedures fix up everything again.

You finish by returning the name of the table widget to our caller.

Listing 16.11   `client2.tcl—make_table`

```
49 proc make_table { parent } {
50
51    table $parent.table \
52      -titlerows 1 \
53      -titlecols 1 \
54      -roworigin -1 \
55      -colorigin -1 \
56      -variable table_data \
57      -yscrollcommand {.top.sy set} \
58      -xscrollcommand {.top.sx set} \
59      -colstretchmode last -rowstretchmode last
60
61    return $parent.table
62 }
```

This procedure (`make_table`) creates a new table widget and configures it so that it is ready for use.

The name of the table widget is `$parent.table`. You'll use the first row of the table to display column names and the first column to display row numbers: The `-titlerows 1` and `-titlecols 1` options tell the table widget that you want to dedicate one row and one column to hold titles.

Normally, the first row in a table is row 0 (and the first column is column 0). Change the origin of the table to `-1,-1` to make it a little easier to account for the title row and column. That means that the title row is actually row –1 and the first *data* row is row 0 (similar trickery is performed on the column-numbering scheme).

A `table` widget needs a variable to hold all its data—we'll use a variable named `table_data` for that purpose. We won't actually *do* anything with this variable; we just need to provide one. (If you want to see a completely pointless widget, remove the `-variable table_data` line and run this application—the results violate the *Principle Of Least Astonishment*).

The next two options (`-yscrollcommand` and `-xscrollcommand`) connect the table widget to the two scrollbars (`.top.sx` and `.top.sy`) that you will be creating a little later.

The final configuration options tell the table widget how to behave if the container (`.top`) is resized. Setting the column stretch mode to `last` means that the rightmost column in the table will expand to take up any extra real estate. Similarly, setting the row stretch mode to `last` will stretch out the bottom row in the table. See the Tktable documentation for other resizing options.

Finish up by returning the name of the table widget to the caller. Listing 16.12 shows the process_command procedure.

Listing 16.12   `client2.tcl—process_command`

```
64 proc process_command { conn table command } {
65
66   set result_set [pg_exec $conn $command]
67
68   load_table $table $result_set
69 }
```

This procedure is nice and short. It executes a command (passed from the caller in the command parameter) and calls the load_table procedure to load the results of the command into a table widget.

I mentioned earlier that pg_exec executes a PostgreSQL command and returns a result set handle. pg_exec returns a result set, even if something goes wrong. In the next client application, I'll show you how to handle execution errors. For now, just assume that the command will succeed.

The procedure shown in Listing 16.13 (load_table) doesn't do much by itself—it simply calls a few helper procedures in the correct order.

Listing 16.13   `client2.tcl—load_table`

```
71 proc load_table { table result_set } {
72
73   size_table $table $result_set
74
75   set_column_headers $table $result_set
76
77   fill_table $table $result_set
78
79   size_columns $table $result_set
80 }
```

load_table is called whenever you want to copy values from a result set into a table widget. There are four steps to this process. First, you adjust the size of the table (this is the logical size, not the physical, onscreen widget size) to contain the same number of rows and columns as the result set. Next, copy the column names from the result set into the first row of the table. After that, we copy all the data values from the result set into the individual table cells. Finally, you adjust the size of each column in the table widget. You want each column to be wide enough to display the widest value.

The size_table procedure (see Listing 16.14) is responsible for adjusting the number of rows and columns in the table widget to match the size of the result set. We start by extracting the number of columns (libpgtcl calls them *attributes*) and the number of rows (also known as *tuples*) from the result set.

Listing 16.14 `client2.tcl—size_table`

```
82 proc size_table { table result_set } {
83
84   set col_cnt   [pg_result $result_set -numAttrs]
85   set row_cnt   [pg_result $result_set -numTuples]
86
87   $table configure \
88     -rows [expr $row_cnt + 1 ] \
89     -cols [expr $col_cnt + 1 ]
90 }
```

Notice that you add an extra row and column to the table widget. The topmost row holds column names. The leftmost column holds row numbers.

The `set_column_headers` procedure (see Listing 16.15) performs two functions: copying column names from the result set into the title row of the given table widget and storing the width of each column name in the `col_widths` global array.

Listing 16.15 `client2.tcl—set_column_headers`

```
92 proc set_column_headers { table result_set } {
93
94   global col_widths
95
96   set col_cnt   [pg_result $result_set -numAttrs]
97   set col_names [pg_result $result_set -attributes]
98
99   for {set col 0} {$col < $col_cnt} {incr col} {
100    set col_name [lindex $col_names $col]
101    $table set -1,$col $col_name
102    set col_widths($col) [string length $col_name]
103  }
104 }
```

`set_column_headers` begins by retrieving the column count and column names from the given result set. When you call `pg_result -attributes`, you get back a list of column names.

Lines 99 through 102 loop through each column in the result set. In each iteration, you extract a column name from the list, copy the column name into the first row of the table (line 101), and store the length of the column name in `col_widths`.

The `col_widths` array is used by `size_columns` to set each column to its optimal width. You want to stretch each column so that it is wide enough to display the widest value in that column. Note that you can't compute the *final* width of each column in this procedure, only the starting width. You won't know the final width for a column until you have processed every row in the result set.

The `fill_table` procedure (see Listing 16.16) copies data values from the result set into the table.

Listing 16.16   `client2.tcl—fill_table`

```
106 proc fill_table { table result_set } {
107
108   global col_widths
109
110   set col_cnt   [pg_result $result_set -numAttrs]
111   set row_cnt   [pg_result $result_set -numTuples]
112
113   for {set row 0} {$row < $row_cnt} {incr row} {
114     set tuple [pg_result $result_set -getTuple $row]
115
116     $table set $row,-1 [expr $row + 1]
117
118     for {set col 0} {$col < $col_cnt} {incr col} {
119
120       set val [lindex $tuple $col]
121
122       if { $col_widths($col) < [string length $val] } {
123         set col_widths($col) [string length $val]
124       }
125       $table set $row,$col $val
126     }
127   }
128 }
```

First, set up two loop invariants to help improve performance: `col_cnt` contains the number of columns in the result set and `row_cnt` contains the number of rows.

A Quick Word About Quick Words[4]

When we first wrote this procedure, we didn't set up any local variables to hold the row and column counts. Instead, we just plugged [`pg_result $result_set -numAttrs`] or [`pg_result $result_set -numTuples`] into the code wherever we needed it. That gave us code like this:

```
    for {set row 0} {$row < [pg_result $result_set -numTuples] } {incr row}
```

That code works, but it's very wasteful. Each time you iterate through this loop, you have to call a procedure stored in the libpgtcl library. Worse yet, you have nested loops that contain multiple libpgtcl function calls. That means, for example, that a query that returns 10 rows of 20 columns each will require (let me break out my calculator here) more than 200 calls to libpgtcl. By stuffing the loop invariants into local variables, you trim this to 2 function calls. In a compiled C program, that might not make much of a difference, but Tcl is an interpreted language and the difference is noticeable.

---

[4] In Tcl, each command is a *word*. This sidebar talks about writing quick code. Quick words? oh, nevermind.

After computing the column count and row count, iterate through the rows in the result set. To access each row, you use pg_result -getTuple. You may recall from the earlier discussion that libpgtcl gives you a number of ways to get at the data values in a result set. pg_result -getTuple returns a single row in the form of a list of values.

At line 116, you copy the row number into the first column of the table (this is a "title" column).

Next, enter a nested loop to process each column in the current row. First, extract the data value from the list returned by pg_result -getTuple (line 120). Second, update the column width (stored in $col_widths($col)) if this value is wider than any value that you have seen in this column. Remember, you want to size each column to the width of the widest value. Finally, copy the data value into the table (line 125).

size_columns (see Listing 16.17) is responsible for sizing each column in the table widget. The set_column_headers and fill_table procedures built an array of column widths ($col_widths). We use the table -width option to set the size of each column.

Listing 16.17   client2.tcl—size_columns

```
130 proc size_columns { table result_set } {
131
132    global col_widths
133
134    set col_cnt    [pg_result $result_set -numAttrs]
135
136    for {set col 0} {$col < $col_cnt} {incr col} {
137      $table width $col $col_widths($col)
138    }
139
140    $table width -1 5
141 }
```

The final call to table -width adjusts the width of the first column—remember, the first column displays a row counter. A width of 5 is aesthetically pleasing (at least on my screen).

Listing 16.18 shows the mainline code for client2.tcl. You load the pgconnect.tcl source file, call the main procedure, and then exit.

Listing 16.18   client2.tcl—mainline

```
143 #  Mainline code follows
144 #
145 source pgconnect.tcl
146 main
147 exit
```

Try to run this application. It's not very exciting, is it? You really want to change the query and run it again, don't you?

At this point, you have enough information to write an interactive query processor in Tcl/Tk. In fact, you need only a few small changes to `client2.tcl` to process arbitrary commands.

Client 3—An Interactive Query Processor

In this section, we'll build an interactive command processor in Tcl/Tk. Fortunately, we can reuse most of the code that we developed in `client2.tcl`. I'll explain the differences and point out where we can share code with the previous client.

Figure 16.5 presents what we are trying to build.

You can see that this application is similar to the previous application. I've added a few widgets: a label at the top of the window that tells the user what to do, a text entry widget where you enter commands, and a status bar that gives feedback.

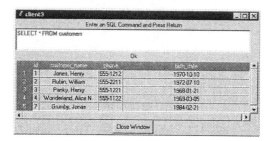

Figure 16.5 The `client3.tcl-results`.

Now, let's look at the code. We have to change three procedures to transform `client2.tcl` into `client3.tcl`. Listing 16.19 shows the `main` procedure for the third client.

Listing 16.19 `client3.tcl—main`

```
 1 #!/usr/local/bin/wish
 2 #
 3 # Filename: client3.tcl
 4
 5 proc main { } {
 6
 7   wm withdraw .
 8
 9   package require Tktable
10
11   set conn [connect]
12
13   if { $conn != {} } {
14
```

Listing 16.19   **Continued**

```
15    build_dialog $conn
16
17    tkwait window .top
18
19    pg_disconnect $conn
20   }
21 }
```

If you compare this to the main procedure from client2.tcl (refer to Listing 16.9), you'll see that the only difference is that I have removed the call to process_command. In the new application, the query is not hard-coded into the application—you prompt the user for a command string instead. So, after connecting to the server, you call build_dialog to construct the user interface and then wait for the dialog window to close.

Listing 16.20 shows the build_dialog procedure.

Listing 16.20   client3.tcl—build_dialog

```
23 proc build_dialog { conn } {
24
25   toplevel .top
26
27   wm title .top "client3"
28
29   set table [make_table .top]
30
31   button .top.close  text "Close Window"  command {exit}
32
33   label .top.label    -text "Enter an SQL Command and Press Return"
34   text  .top.command -height 3
35   label .top.status
36
37   focus -force .top.command
38
39   bind .top.command <Return> \
40       "process_command $conn $table \[.top.command get 1.0 end\]"
41
42   scrollbar .top.sy -command [list $table yview]
43   scrollbar .top.sx -command [list $table xview] -orient horizontal
44
45   grid     .top.label
46   grid     .top.command     -sticky news
47   grid     .top.status
48   grid     $table .top.sy     -sticky news
49   grid     .top.sx           -sticky ew
50   grid     .top.close
```

Listing 16.20 **Continued**

```
51
52   grid columnconfig .top 0 -weight 1
53
54   grid rowconfig     .top 1 -weight 0
55   grid rowconfig     .top 3 -weight 1
56   grid rowconfig     .top 5 -weight 0
57 }
```

The build_dialog procedure is a little longer than it used to be, but not any more complex. I've added a label (line 33) that displays a prompt to the user. I've also added a text widget. The text widget (named .top.command) is where you'll type in your PostgreSQL commands. A text widget is a like a multiline entry widget—you configure it to be three lines tall. We also add a second label widget (.top.status), in which we will display the status of each command. Refer to Figure 16.5; the .top.status widget is positioned between the text entry widget and the table widget.

Line 37 forces the keyboard focus to .top.command (the text entry widget).

Next, you bind a piece of Tcl code to the Return key. This piece of code executes whenever the user presses the Return key while the .top.command widget has the focus.

Line 40 might look a bit cryptic. It might be easier to understand if you walk through the evaluation process that Tcl will use when it executes our code snippet.

When you call the bind procedure, Tcl will evaluate the code segment, performing variable substitution wherever it sees an unquoted dollar sign. So, if $conn contains pg224 and $table contains .top.table, the first iteration translates from

```
process_command $conn $table \[.top.command get 1.0 end\]
```

to

```
process_command pg224 $table \[.top.command get 1.0 end\]
```

Next, Tcl translates the second variable substitution to

```
process_command pg224 .top.table \[.top.command get 1.0 end\]
```

Finally, Tcl removes the escape characters from the string, resulting in

```
process_command pg224 .top.table [.top.command get 1.0 end]
```

At this point, Tcl stops evaluating the code snippet. It binds this final string to the Return key. When the Return key is pressed, Tk will execute this string. The last part of the string ([.top.command get 1.0 end]) extracts the contents of the text entry widget.

The net effect is that the process_command procedure is called whenever the user presses the Return key, and the text of the command is passed as the final parameter.

The rest of the code in build_dialog should be pretty familiar. We create a vertical and horizontal scrollbar and then arrange everything using the grid layout manager.

The final three lines in this procedure ensure that the text entry widget and the Close Window button remain visible if you resize the application window.

Now, let's look at the process_command procedure (see Listing 16.21).

Listing 16.21   `client3.tcl—process_command`

```
75  proc process_command { conn table command } {
76
77    set result_set [pg_exec $conn $command]
78
79    switch [pg_result $result_set -status] {
80
81      PGRES_EMPTY_QUERY {
82        .top.status configure -text ""
83      }
84
85      PGRES_TUPLES_OK {
86        .top.status configure -text "Ok"
87        load_table $table $result_set
88      }
89
90      PGRES_COMMAND_OK {
91        .top.status configure -text "Ok"
92      }
93
94      default
95      {
96        .top.status configure -text ""
97
98        tk_messageBox -title [pg_result $result_set -status] \
99                      -message [pg_result $result_set -error] \
100                      -type ok
101      }
102    }
103  }
```

The process_command procedure has changed considerably. In the previous version
(refer to Listing 16.12), a couple of assumptions were made that need to be corrected
here if you want to process arbitrary commands. First, it was assumed that the command
executed successfully. If you are executing something other than a hard-wired command,
you must expect errors to occur (of course, you really should expect errors, even when
you know which commands are going to execute). The second assumption was that you
were executing only SELECT commands. Again, you have to handle any type of command if you let the user enter arbitrary text.

Like before, call the pg_exec procedure to execute the command provided by the caller.

Next, examine the value returned by pg_result -status to determine what kind of
result set you have. As I mentioned earlier, pg_result -status returns values such as
PGRES_TUPLES_OK, PGRES_COMMAND_OK, PGRES_FATAL_ERROR, and so on. You will handle
three of these values explicitly and assume that anything else is a message that you
should display to the user.

The simplest case occurs when the user presses the Return key without entering a command. When that happens, pg_result -status will return PGGRES_EMPTY_QUERY. In this case, clear the status line (.top.status) and return.

Next, handle PGRES_TUPLES_OK. pg_result -status returns PGRES_TUPLES_OK when you (successfully) execute a SELECT command. Handling the result set from a SELECT command is something you already know how to do; you set the status line to Ok and call the load_table procedure to copy the result set into the table widget. The load_table procedure is unchanged from client2.tcl.

pg_result -status returns PGRES_COMMAND_OK when you successfully execute a command other than SELECT. This one is easy—you just set the status line to read Ok. If you were really energetic, you might also display the OID from the previous command (pg_result -oid).

Finally, assume that any other return code is a message that you should simply display to the user. After clearing the status line, use the tk_messageBox to display the status (pg_result -status) and error message (pg_result -error).

That's it. All the other procedures in client3.tcl are identical to those in client2.tcl.

Run this application a few times to see how it behaves. Be sure to feed it a few errors so you can see the error handling in action (how exciting).

I'll wrap up this chapter by describing how to access large-objects from a Tcl application.

The libpgtcl Large-Object API

The libpgtcl library provides a number of procedures that you can use to interact with PostgreSQL large-objects. A *large-object* is a value that is stored indirectly. When you create a column that will contain a large-object, the column should be of type OID (object-id). When you import a large-object into your database, the bits that make up the object are stored in the pg_largeobject system table and a reference is stored in your table. Large-objects are typically used to hold images, sound files, or large pieces of unstructured data.

There are two ways to create a large-object. First, you can create a large-object using the pg_lo_creat procedure. pg_lo_creat creates a new (empty) entry in the pg_largeobject table and returns the OID of that entry. After you have an empty large-object, you can write data into it using pg_lo_write.

Second, you can import an existing file (such as a JPEG-encoded photograph) into a database using pg_lo_import. The pg_lo_import manual page says that pg_lo_import requires two parameters (a connection handle and a filename) and returns nothing. That documentation is incorrect: pg_lo_import returns the OID of the new large-object.

Here is a code snippet that shows how to use the pg_lo_import procedure:

```
...
pg_result [pg_exec $conn "BEGIN WORK"] -clear # Start a transaction

set large_object_oid [pg_lo_import $conn "/images/happyface.jpg"]
```

```
pg_result [pg_exec $conn "COMMIT WORK"] -clear
...
```

Note that you must call pg_lo_import within a transaction block. In fact, *all* large-object operations must occur within a transaction block.

The inverse of pg_lo_import is pg_lo_export. pg_lo_export copies a large-object into a file:

```
...
pg_result [pg_exec $conn "BEGIN WORK"] -clear # Start a transaction

pg_log_export $conn $large_object_oid "/images/jocularface.jpg"

pg_result [pg_exec $conn "COMMIT WORK"] -clear
...
```

Like pg_lo_import, pg_lo_export must be called within a transaction block. You can also read the contents of a large-object using libpgtcl. To start with, you must open the desired large-object using pg_lo_open:

```
...
set fd [pg_lo_open $conn $large_object_oid "rw"]
...
```

When you call pg_lo_open, you provide a connection handle, the OID of the large-object that you want, and an access mode. libpgtcl is a little fickle when it comes to large-object access modes; pg_lo_open expects "r", "w", or "rw," but pg_lo_create expects "INV_READ," "INV_WRITE," or "INV_READ|INV_WRITE." The value returned by pg_lo_open is a large-object handle; and after you have one of those, you can read from, write to, or move around in the large-object.

First, let's talk about positioning within a large-object. Large-objects can be, well, large. Your application may not need to read (or write) an entire large-object all at once; for really big large-objects, you may want to work with small chunks. To make this possible, libpgtcl lets you *seek* your large-object handle to the part that you are interested in; then, you can read or write from there.

The pg_lo_lseek procedure is modeled after the Unix lseek() function. pg_lo_lseek requires three parameters:

```
pg_lo_lseek connection-handle large-object-handle offset starting-point
```

The *connection-handle* and *large-object-handle* parameters are self-explanatory. *offset* specifies the number of bytes you want to move. *starting-point* specifies which position you want to move *from*. SEEK_CUR means that you want to move *offset* bytes relative to the current position. SEEK_SET means that you want to move *offset* bytes relative to the start of the object. SEEK_END will position your *offset* bytes from the end of the object.

If you specify a *starting-point* of SEEK_CUR or SEEK_END, *offset* can be either positive or negative (a negative offset moves you toward the beginning of the object). With SEEK_SET, *offset* should always be a non-negative number. A *starting-point* of

SEEK_SET and an *offset* of 0 position you to the beginning of the object. A *starting-point* of SEEK_END and an offset of 0 position you to the end of the object. If you specify a *starting-point* of SEEK_CUR and an *offset* of 0, your position within the object remains unchanged.

The pg_lo_tell procedure returns your current position within an object. pg_lo_tell requires two parameters:

```
set current_offset [pg_lo_tell connection-handle large-object-handle]
```

You can determine the number of bytes in a large-object by seeking to the end of the object and then finding the offset:

```
...
pg_lo_lseek $conn $object_handle 0 SEEK_CUR
set object_size [pg_lo_tell $conn $object_handle]
...
```

After you have established a position within a large-object, you can read from or write to the object. To write (or modify) data in a large-object, use the pg_lo_write procedure:

```
pg_lo_write connection-handle large-object-handle string length
```

For example, if you want to append a file onto an existing large-object, you would write code similar to this:

```
...
pg_exec $conn "BEGIN"
set fd [open "/images/sadface.jpg"]
set object_handle [pg_lo_open $conn $large_object_oid "rw"]

pg_lo_lseek $conn $object_handle 0 SEEK_END

while { [eof $fd] != 1 } {
  set val [read $fd 1000]
  pg_lo_write $conn $object_handle val [string length $val]
}

close $fd
pg_lo_close $object_handle
pg_exec $conn "COMMIT"
...
```

After opening the file and the large-object, seek to the end of the large-object and then copy from the file handle to the large-object handle, 1000 bytes at a time. We've also called pg_lo_close to close the large-object handle.

When you write to a large-object, you can create *holes* in the data. For example, if you start out with an empty large-object and then seek 100 bytes into it before calling pg_lo_write, you are creating a 100-byte hole at the beginning of the large-object.

Holes are treated as if they contain zeroes. In other words, when you read back this particular large-object, the first 100 bytes will contain nothing but zeroes[5].

You can also read from a large-object in a piece-by-piece manner using pg_lo_lseek and pg_lo_read:

```
...
pg_exec $conn "BEGIN"

set object_handle [pg_lo_open $conn $large_object_oid "r"]

pg_lo_lseek $conn $object_handle 0 SEEK_END
set len [pg_tell $conn $object_handle]
pg_lo_lseek $conn $object_handle 0 SEEK_SET

pg_lo_read $conn $object_handle img $len

image create photo my_photo

my_photo put $img -format gif

pg_lo_close $object_handle
pg_exec $conn "COMMIT"
...
```

As before, you must start a transaction block before using any of the large-object procedures. After opening the large-object (using pg_lo_open), compute the size of the object. The easiest way to find the size of an existing large-object is to seek to the end and then use pg_lo_tell to find the offset of the last byte. After you know the size, you can read the entire object into a string variable using pg_lo_read. In the preceding example, we read the entire large-object in one call to pg_lo_read, but that is not strictly necessary. You can use pg_lo_lseek to move around within the large-object before you read (or write).

One important point here: When you call pg_lo_read (or pg_lo_write), your position within the object is advanced by the number of bytes read (or written).

The pg_lo_read procedure requires four parameters:

```
pg_lo_read connection-handle object-handle varname length
```

The *connection-handle* and *object-handle* parameters should be familiar by now. The *varname* parameter should contain the name of a variable—be careful with this parameter: You don't want to pass the *contents* of a variable; you want to pass the name. So, the following example will usually be incorrect:

---

[5] In case you are wondering, PostgreSQL stores each large-object in a collection of blocks. Each block is typically 2048 bytes long. When you create a hole in a large-object, PostgreSQL will store the minimal number of blocks required to hold the object. If a block within a large-object contains nothing but a hole, it will not take up any physical space in the pg_largeobject table.

```
pg_lo_read $conn $object_handle $img $len
```

This is likely to be wrong because you are passing the contents of the `$img` variable, not the name. You most likely want[6]

```
pg_lo_read $conn $object_handle img $len
```

There is one more large-object procedure that you might need to know about. If you want to remove a large-object from your database, use the `pg_lo_unlink` procedure:

```
pg_unlink $conn $large_object_id
```

Summary

Tcl is a surprisingly simple language.

Having said that, I should point out that solving complex problems is not necessarily easier in Tcl than in other languages, you just have fewer syntactic rules to remember. Tcl is not a panacea, just a really nice little language.

The libpgtcl library fits into Tcl very nicely. If you want to toss together a PostgreSQL client application quickly, explore Tcl and libpgtcl.

---

[6] The only time you would want to pass the value of a variable (as the third parameter) would be when one variable holds the name of another.

17

Using PostgreSQL with Python

Python is an object-oriented programming language. Like Perl, Tcl, and Java, Python is an interpreted language (as opposed to being a *compiled* language such as C or C++). Python supports a number of high-level data structures (lists, tuples, and sequences) that integrate very nicely into the table-oriented world of PostgreSQL.

Python/PostgreSQL Interface Architecture

If you are writing a Python application that interfaces with PostgreSQL you can choose from a number of different APIs, most of which are compatible with the Python DB-API specification. DB-API is a three-layer interface that lets you build Python applications that can, at least in theory, interact with many different databases. The top layer (the layer that your application deals with) is a database-neutral interface that hides all of the nasty details of writing database-dependent code. The middle layer is an interface that converts requests and responses between DB-API form and the form required by the database. The bottom layer is the database itself (in this case, PostgreSQL). The three most commonly found Python/PostgreSQL interfaces are PyGreSQL, PsycoPg (great name don't you think?), and PoPy. All three libraries can be used as the middle layer in a DB-API stack. Each library offers its own set of extensions to the DB-API library, but I won't cover those here—see the documentation for each library for full details.

The standard PostgreSQL distribution included the PyGreSQL library until a few releases ago. Starting with PostgreSQL version 7.4, you'll have to download a Python/PostgreSQL interface from a separate website. You can find PyGreSQL at http://www.pygresql.org, PsycoPg at http://initd.org/projects/psycopg1, and PoPy at http://popy.sourceforge.net.

The alternate implementations (PyscoPg and PoPy) have been designed to maximize performance in some configurations. The interface distributed with PostgreSQL (PyGreSQL) was implemented as a wrapper, so it probably won't be quite as fast as the other two; but with PyGreSQL, you can pick and choose between the two interface layers.

In this chapter, I'll describe the DB-API interface between Python and PostgreSQL, but not the PyGreSQL extensions. Applications written to the DB-API specification can connect to different databases; applications written using PyGreSQL cannot. See the PyGreSQL Web site (http://www.pygresql.org) for more information about the extensions offered by PyGreSQL.

Prerequisites

If you want to try the examples in this chapter, you'll probably need to install a few extra pieces of software. You will obviously need Python and PostgreSQL. You'll also need the PyGreSQL interface. The easiest way to build PyGreSQL is to download it, unpack it, and run the included `setup.py` program. If you're using Linux (or Unix):

```
$ cd /usr/local/src
$ wget ftp://ftp.pygresql.org/pub/distrib/PyGreSQL.tgz
Length: 45,824 (unauthoritative)

100%[=====================================>] 45,824          32.75K/s

17:12:32 (32.65 KB/s) - 'PyGreSQL.tgz' saved [45,824]

$ tar -zxvf PyGreSQL.tgz
$ cd PyGreSQL-version
```

Make sure that `pg_config` is in your `$PATH` search path before you run the next command. The setup.py program invokes pg_config to find the PostgreSQL components that it needs. pg_config is usually found in PostgreSQL's bin directory (the same directory that holds the psql and `postmaster` programs).

```
$ ./setup.py build
running build
running build_py
running build_ext

$ ./setup.py install
running install
running build
...
```

If you intend to use the Python-DB API (which I would recommend), you will also need the mx extensions package from Egenix (http://www.egenix.com/files/python/).

Some of the examples in this chapter make use of the Tkinter GUI toolkit (more on that later). Tkinter is usually distributed with Python, but you will also need the Tktable module. You can find Tktable.py at http://tktable.sourceforge.net.

Client 1—Connecting to the Server

To interact with a PostgreSQL server using Python's DB-API, you must first import the pgdb module. This module defines a few exception classes (we'll talk about exceptions a little later), two classes (pgdbCnx and pgdbCursor), and a single module function.

The pgdb.connect() function returns a connection object (an instance of class pgdbCnx). This function actually comes in two flavors:

```
pgdb.connect( dsn )
pgdb.connect( dsn      = dsn,
              user     = user,
              password = password,
              host     = host,
              database = dbname )
```

In the first flavor, the dsn is expected to be a string of the form:

```
host:database:user:password:opt:tty
```

The rules for composing a valid dsn are a bit complex. In the simplest case, you can specify all connection properties in the order shown:

```
"davinci:movies:bruce:cows:-fi:/dev/tty"
```

You can omit leading properties, but you must include the proper number of delimiters (that is, colons):

```
"::bruce:cows:-fi:/dev/tty"        # omit host and database
```

You can omit properties in the middle of the dsn, but again, you must include the proper number of colons:

```
"davinci:movies::::-fi:/dev/tty"    # omit user and password
```

You can omit trailing properties, in which case the extra delimiters are optional:

```
"davinci:movies:bruce::: "         # omit password, opt, and tty
"davinci:movies:bruce"             # ditto
```

In the second flavor, you should pass each parameter using Python's named parameter mechanism. For example:

```
pgdb.connect( host='davinci', user='bruce' )
pgdb.connect( host='davinci:5432', user='bruce' )
pgdb.connect( user     = 'bruce',
              password = 'cows',
              host     = 'davinci',
              database = 'movies' )
```

The order in which the parameters appear is unimportant when you use named parameters. Also notice, in the second example, that you can include a port number in the host parameter—just separate the hostname and port number with a colon.

You can also combine the first and second forms:

```
pgdb.connect( dsn = "davinci:movies", user='bruce', password='cows' )
```

In this case, we have used the dsn to specify the hostname and database, and named parameters to specify the username and password. If you have duplicate properties, the named parameters take precedence over the properties specified in the dsn, for example:

```
pgdb.connect( dsn      = "davinci:movies:sheila",
              user     = "bruce",
              password = "cows" )
```

In this case, we specified a username (sheila) in the dsn, but we have also supplied a username (bruce) with the user named parameter; we will connect as user bruce.

The PostgreSQL implementation of the DB-API eventually ends up using the libpq library (PostgreSQL's C language API) to do all the low-level communications work. If you've read some of the previous chapters, you might be thinking that you can use environment variables (such as PGDATABASE) to supply default values for connection properties (refer to Table 8.2 for a description of the connection-related environment variables). You may be able to, but for only three of the connection properties: PGHOST, PGPORT, and PGUSER. An apparent bug in Python prevents you from using PGOPTIONS, PGTTY, PGDATABASE, and PGPASSWORD. This problem may be fixed in newer versions of Python, so be sure to test the feature if you need it.

After you have successfully connected, pgdb.connect() returns a connection object. We'll look at some of the things that you can do with a connection object a bit later. For now, let's develop a simple client that establishes a connection to a PostgreSQL server.

Listing 17.1 shows the file client1.py. The first line tells the operating system which interpreter to use to run this script. If your copy of Python is stored in a different location, you should adjust this line to reflect the correct directory. If you are new to Python, you may be surprised to find that there are no block delimiters (curly braces or BEGIN/END pairs) to mark the boundaries of complex statements. Python uses indentation to indicate block boundaries.

Listing 17.1 client1.py

```
 1 #!/usr/bin/python
 2 #
 3 # Filename: client1.py
 4
 5 import pgdb
 6
 7 connection = pgdb.connect( database = "movies",
 8                            user     = "bruce",
 9                            password = "cows" )
10
11 print connection
```

At line 5, client1 imports the pgdb module. When you import a module, all the classes and functions in that module become available for you to use. Next, at lines 7, 8, and 9 client1 uses the pgdb.connect() function to establish a connection to the movies database. Finally, it prints the connection object returned by pgdb.connect().

Let's run this client application to see what a connection object looks like:

```
$ chmod a+x client1.py
$ ./client1.py
<pgdb.pgdbCnx instance at 810dd98>
$
```

The single line of output really doesn't tell you anything useful other than your program did *something*. Now, shut down the postmaster and run client1.py again so you can see how an error is reported:

```
$ pg_ctl stop
waiting for postmaster to shut down......done
$ ./client1.py
Traceback (innermost last):
  File "./client1.py", line 9, in ?
    password = "cows" )
  File "/usr/lib/python1.5/site-packages/pgdb.py", line 376, in connect
    user = dbuser, passwd = dbpasswd)
    pg.error: could not connect to server: No such file or directory
        Is the server running locally and accepting
        connections on Unix domain socket "/tmp/.s.PGSQL.5432"?
```

Don't you just love being assaulted by error messages like this? If you're a programmer, you probably appreciate the level of detail and a complete context, but our users tend to get upset when they see smoke and flames. Let's clean this up.

Client 2—Adding Error Checking

If you look back to line 7 of Listing 17.1, you'll notice that client1 calls pgdb. connect() to connect to a PostgreSQL server. If anything goes wrong during this function call, Python will print a stack trace and abort the program.

If you want to intercept a connection error, you must wrap the call to pgdb. connect() in a try/except block. The Python DB-API specification defines a hierarchy of exception types that a conforming implementation may throw. The most general exception type is StandardError. All other DB-API exceptions are derived (directly or indirectly) from StandardError.

Listing 17.2 shows client2.py. This client calls pgdb.connect() inside of a try/except block and catches any exceptions derived from StandardError (including StandardError).

Listing 17.2 `client2.py`

```
 1 #!/usr/bin/python
 2 #
 3 # Filename: client2.py
 4
 5 import pgdb
 6 import sys
 7
 8 try:
 9     connection = pgdb.connect( database = "movies",
10                                user     = "bruce",
11                                password = "cows" )
12     print connection
13
14 except StandardError, e:
15     print str( e )
16
17 except:
18     exception = sys.exc_info()
19
20     print "Unexpected exception:"
21     print "  type : %s" % exception[0]
22     print "  value: %s" % exception[1]
```

client2 includes two except clauses that catch *any* exception thrown by `pgdb.con-nect()`. The first except clause will catch any exception derived from `StandardError`. The second catches exceptions derived from any other class. When you catch an exception that has not been derived from `StandardError`, you can use the `sys.exc_info()` function to obtain information about the exception. `sys.exc_info()` returns a tuple with three values: `exception[0]` contains the name of the exception type, `exception[1]` contains the exception parameter (usually an error message), and `exception[2]` contains a traceback object. client2 prints the exception type and parameter:

```
$ ./client2.py

        could not connect to server: No such file or directory
        Is the server running locally and accepting
        connections on Unix domain socket "/tmp/.s.PGSQL.5432"?
```

The Python DB-API describes the exception types shown in Table 17.1.

Table 17.1 **DB-API Exception Types**

Exception Type	Derived From	Thrown By
Warning	StandardError	Not used
Error	StandardError	Not used

Table 17.1 **Continued**

Exception Type	Derived From	Thrown By
InterfaceError	Error	execute() executemany()
DatabaseError	Error	execute() executemany()
DataError	DatabaseError	Not used
OperationalError	DatabaseError	execute() executemany() commit() rollback() cursor() connect()
IntegrityError	DatabaseError	Not used
InternalError	DatabaseError	Not used
ProgrammingError	DatabaseError	Not used
NotSupportedError	DatabaseError	Not used

The first column in Table 17.1 shows the name of each exception. The middle column shows the parent type for each exception. The final column shows the name of each PostgreSQL/DB-API function that throws the exception.

It's important to remember that the DB-API functions can throw exceptions *other* than the ones listed in Table 17.1 (syntax errors, invalid data type errors, and so on). It's usually a good idea to catch specific exceptions that you *expect* to see with a typed except clause and catch unexpected exceptions with an *untyped* except. That's what we've done in client2.py. The first except (at line 14) catches exceptions derived from StandardError. The second, at line 17, catches all other exceptions.

Now, you have a client application that establishes a connection or reports an error if the connection attempt fails. It's time to do something a little more interesting.

Client 3—Query Processing

To execute a SQL command with Python's DB-API, you must first create a cursor. Don't confuse this cursor with a cursor created by PostgreSQL's DECLARE CURSOR command; they have some similarities, but they are certainly not the same thing, as you will see in this section.

You create a cursor object by calling a connection's cursor() function[1]. For example, if you have a connection named connect, you would create a cursor like this:

```
cur = connect.cursor()
```

---

[1] It is possible, but extremely unlikely, that a call to connect.cursor() can throw a pgOperationalError exception. In fact, the only way that can happen is if somebody is messing around with the internals of a connection object; and we would never do that, would we?

Notice that the cursor() function expects no arguments. You can create multiple cursor objects from the same connection; they operate independently, except that a commit() or rollback() executed on the connection will affect all cursors open on that connection.

The next client application (client3.py) shows the steps required to create a cursor, execute a command, and print the results (see Listing 17.3).

Listing 17.3   client3.py—main()

```
 1 #!/usr/bin/python
 2 #
 3 # File: client3.py
 4
 5 import pgdb
 6 import string
 7
 8 ############################################################
 9 def main( ):
10     try:
11         connection = pgdb.connect( database = "movies",
12                                     user     = "bruce",
13                                     password = "cows" )
14
15     except Exception, e:
16         print str( e )
17         exit
18
19     cur = connection.cursor()
20
21     try:
22         cur.execute( "SELECT * FROM customers" )
23         process_results( cur )
24
25     except StandardError, e:
26       print str( e )
27
28     cur.close()
29     connection.close()
30     exit
```

Listing 17.3 shows the main() procedure from client3.py. It starts by calling pgdb.connect() to establish a connection to the movies database. Lines 15 through 17 take care of any exceptions thrown by pgdb.connect(). I'll take a shortcut here by defining a single exception handler that can catch proper DB-API exceptions as well as the (apparently) erroneous exception thrown by the PostgreSQL interface.

At line 19, main() creates a new cursor object by calling connection.cursor(). It is very unlikely that this call to cursor() will fail, so we won't bother catching any exceptions. If cursor() *does* fail, Python will print a stack trace and an error message and abort the application.

Next, main() uses the cursor.execute() function to execute a simple SELECT command. If something goes wrong with this command, execute() will throw an exception. The text of the error message is encapsulated in the exception parameter (specifically, e.args). If the command completes without error, main() calls the process_result() function (see Listing 17.4) to display the result set.

After you have finished with the cursor object, you should close it by calling cur.close(). This is not strictly required because Python closes this object for you during garbage collection, but it's usually a good idea.

You should also close the connection object when you are done with it. Even though you can ignore the cursor.close() function, you should get into the habit of closing connection objects. In fact, before you call connection.close(), you should call connection.commit(). Why? Because the PostgreSQL DB-API interface does not run in "auto-commit" mode. When you first call pgdb.connect() to establish a connection, the connect() function silently executes a BEGIN command for you. That means that all commands that you execute belong to a single multistatement transaction until you either connection.commit() or connection.rollback(). If you fail to commit before you close a connection, any changes made in the most recent transaction are rolled back. Watch out for this-it will bite you if you aren't careful.

Now, let's look at the process_results() function (see Listing 17.4). This function is responsible for formatting and displaying the result of the SELECT command. We don't actually do any of the grunt work in process_results(); instead, I've factored the details into three helper functions.

Listing 17.4   client3.py—process_results()

```
32 ############################################################
33 def process_results( cur ):
34
35     widths = []
36     rows    = cur.fetchall()
37     cols    = cur.description
38
39     compute_widths( cur, widths, rows, cols )
40     print_headers( cur, widths, cols )
41     print_values( cur, widths, rows )
```

process_results() starts by defining an (empty) array that holds the display width for each column in the result set. I'll pass this array to the helper functions, so I'll define it here.

Next, `process_results()` calls the `cursor.fetchall()` function to retrieve all rows from the result set. The `cursor.fetchall()` function returns a sequence of sequences[2]. Each member of this sequence represents a single row. So, to get to the second column in the third row, you would use the following:

```
print rows[2][1] # sequence indexes start at 0, not 1
```

Besides `cursor.fetchall()`, there are two other functions that return all or part of a result set. The `cursor.fetchone()` function fetches the next row in a result set. `fetchone()` returns a sequence or returns `None` if you have exhausted the result set. The `cursor.fetchmany( [size=n] )` function returns the next n rows in the result set. If you omit the `size` parameter, `fetchmany()` will assume that n=5. If there are fewer than n rows remaining in the result set, `fetchmany()` will return all remaining rows. If the result set has been exhausted, `fetchmany()` will return `None`. Like `fetchall()`, `fetchmany()` returns a sequence of one or more sequences.

Notice that there is no way to go *backward* in the result set. You can't re-fetch a row after you have gone past it, nor can you "rewind" the result set to the beginning. If you need to move around in the result set, use `fetchall()` or declare a PostgreSQL cursor (not a DB-API cursor) and execute the FETCH commands yourself.

After you have retrieved all the rows in the result set, `process_results()` nabs the column metadata from `cursor.description`. Notice that `cursor.description` is a public data member, not a function. `cursor.description` is a list of seven-element lists. Table 17.2 shows the meaning of each sublist.

Table 17.2 `cursor.description` **Metadata Values**

Element	Meaning
0	Column name
1	Data type
2	Maximum display size
3	Server size (in bytes)
4	Precision (not used)
5	Scale (not used)
6	Null allowed? (not used)

Currently, the PyGreSQL DB-API implementation does not use the last three elements in the table (precision, scale, and null allowed?); they are always set to `None`. The data type member does not conform to the DB-API specification, but it's probably more useful that way. Data types are reported by their PostgreSQL names (char, oid, float4, and so on). The display size and server size elements are set to -1 for any variable-sized columns.

---

[2] If you're not familiar with Python, think of a "sequence of sequences" as "an array of arrays" or maybe as a "list of lists." They are not completely analogous, but close enough to understand that `fetchall()` returns a collection of collections.

We will be using the column names a little later, so we store them in the local variable cols.

Now that you have access to the data (rows) and the metadata (cols), process_results() calls each of the helper functions in the right order. compute_widths() computes the width of each column name, storing the result in the widths array (see Listing 17.5). Next, print_headers() prints column headings. Finally, print_values() prints the entire result set.

Listing 17.5 client3.py—compute_widths()

```
43 ###########################################################
44 def compute_widths( cur, widths, rows, cols ):
45
46     c = 0
47
48     for col in cols:
49         widths.append( len( col[0] ))
50         c = c + 1
51
52     r = 0
53
54     for row in rows:
55         c = 0
56
57         for col in row:
58             if( len( str( col )) > widths[c] ):
59                 widths[c] = len( str( col ))
60             c = c + 1
61         r = r + 1
```

The compute_widths() function computes the width of each column in the result set.

It starts by walking through the list of column names and appending the length of each name to the widths[] array. Remember, the caller (process_results()) gave you a complete metadata array in the cols parameter. Element 0 of each metadata list is the column name.

Next, compute_widths() has to find the widest value in each column of the result set. The caller gave it a list of all the rows in the result set in the rows parameter. As it processes each column in each row of the result set, compute_widths() increases the corresponding element in the widths[] array to its maximum required width.

Notice (in lines 58 and 59) that this function converts each data value into string form before calling the len() function. The result set can contain integer values, string values, float values, and so on. You can't invoke the len() function on a numeric value so you must convert them into string form first.

You can view the actual Python data types using the `type()` function:

```
>>> cur.execute( "SELECT * FROM pg_class" )
>>> c = 0
>>> for col in cur.fetchone():
...     print cur.description[c][0], '\t', col, '\t', type(col)
...     c = c+1
...
relname          pg_type  <type 'string'>
reltype          71L      <type 'long int'>
relowner         1        <type 'int'>
relam            0L       <type 'long int'>
relfilenode      1247L    <type 'long int'>
relpages         2        <type 'int'>
reltuples        143.0    <type 'float'>
reltoastrelid    0L       <type 'long int'>
reltoastidxid    0L       <type 'long int'>
relhasindex      1        <type 'int'>
relisshared      0        <type 'int'>
relkind          r        <type 'string'>
relnatts         17       <type 'int'>
relchecks        0        <type 'int'>
reltriggers      0        <type 'int'>
relukeys         0        <type 'int'>
relfkeys         0        <type 'int'>
relrefs          0        <type 'int'>
relhasoids       1        <type 'int'>
relhaspkey       0        <type 'int'>
relhasrules      0        <type 'int'>
relhassubclass   0        <type 'int'>
relacl           None     <type 'None'>
```

Listing 17.6 shows the `print_headers()` function.

Listing 17.6 `client3.py`—`print_headers()`

```
63 ##########################################################
64 def print_headers( cur, widths, cols ):
65
66     c = 0;
67
68     for col in cols:
69         print string.center( col[0], widths[c] ),
70         c = c + 1
71     print
72
73     c = 0;
74
75     for col in cur.description:
```

Listing 17.6   **Continued**

```
76          print '-' * widths[c],
77          c = c + 1
78      print
```

print_headers() centers each column name within the width calculated by compute_widths(). You may have noticed that I have a dangling comma at the end of line 69 (and again at the end of line 76). Those aren't typos—a dangling comma suppresses the new-line character that print would otherwise emit. I want all the column names to appear on the same line, so I'll suppress all new-lines until you get to line 71 (or 78 in the case of the second loop).

Following the column names, print_headers() prints a line of separator characters (hyphens). When you apply the multiply operator (*) to a string, as in line 76, the result is a string of repeated characters. I'll create the separator strings my "multiplying" a dash by the width of each column.

Listing 17.7 shows the remaining code in client3.py. The print_values() function loops through each row and column in the result set (rows). At line 89, convert each value to string form, left-justify it within the proper column, and print it.

Listing 17.7   client3.py—print_values() **and mainline**

```
80 ############################################################
81 def print_values( cur, widths, rows ):
82
83      r = 0
84
85      for row in rows:
86          c = 0
87
88          for col in row:
89              print string.ljust( str(col), widths[c] ),
90              c = c + 1
91          r = r + 1
92          print
93
94
95 ############################################################
96
97 main()
```

The mainline code (that is, the entry point for your client application) is at line 97—we just call the main() function and exit when main() returns.

Now, run this application:

```
$ chmod a+x client3.py
$ ./client3.py
```

```
id   customer_name          phone    birth_date
--   --------------------   -------- ----------
1    Jones, Henry           555-1212 1970-10-10
2    Rubin, William         555-2211 1972-07-10
3    Panky, Henry           555-1221 1968-01-21
4    Wonderland, Alice N.   555-1122 1969-03-05
7    Grumby, Jonas          None     1984-02-21
```

At this point, you know how to connect to a PostgreSQL server from Python, how to intercept errors, and how to process SELECT commands. In the next section, we'll develop an interactive command processor using Python and the Tkinter GUI module.

Client 4—An Interactive Command Processor

The next client is an interactive command processor. The basic Python language distribution does not include any tools for building graphical applications. Instead, you can add GUI toolkits to Python based on your needs. If you don't need graphics, you won't have to weigh down your application with extra code. If you *do* need graphics in your application, you can choose the toolkit best suited to your requirements.

We'll use the Tkinter toolkit for our command processor. If you read the previous chapter, you know that Tk is a portable toolkit originally designed for the Tcl language. Tkinter is a Python wrapper around the Tk graphics toolkit. Using Tkinter, you can create and manipulate Tk widgets (buttons, windows, scrollbars, and so on) from Python applications.

The application that we will build should look like Figure 17.1 when you are finished. When you run this program, you can enter an arbitrary PostgreSQL command in the text entry widget, press Return, and then view the results in the table widget below. We'll also place a status line in the middle of the window so you can show error messages and row counts.

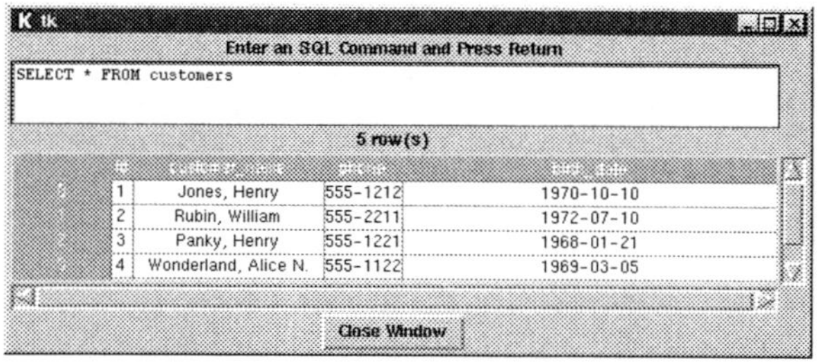

Figure 17.1 The client4.py application.

This application (client4.py) is a bit larger than the other Python clients you have seen so far (see Listing 17.8). It starts by importing the pgdb module (as usual) and two Tk-related modules: Tkinter and Tktable. Tkinter is the basic Tk GUI toolkit. Tktable is an extension to Tkinter that adds a table widget. You can find the source code for Tktable at http://tktable.sourceforge.net.

Listing 17.8   client4.py—PGDialog.init()

```
 1 #!/usr/bin/python
 2 #
 3 # File: client4.py
 4
 5 import pgdb
 6 from Tkinter import *
 7 from Tktable import Table,ArrayVar
 8
 9 class PGDialog:
10 ############################################
11     def _init_( self ):
12         self.widths  = []
13         self.conn    = None
14         # Widgets
15         self.table   = None
16         self.command = None
17         self.status  = None
```

At line 9, client4 declares the PGDialog class. I'll create PGDialog as a single container for all the variables that you would otherwise need to pass between member functions.

It may not be obvious because of the formatting requirements of this book, but all the functions defined in client4.py are members of the PGDialog class.

The _init_() function is called whenever you create an instance of a PGDialog object. C++ and Java programmers will recognize _init_() as a constructor. Inside of this constructor, you initialize all member variables to a known state.

The self.widths[] member variable holds the computed width for each column. self.widths[] is filled by the set_column headers() function, modified by fill_table(), and used by size_columns().

The self.conn variable holds the connection object that we create in main().

self.table, self.command, and self.status are widgets that client4 needs to manipulate. All widgets are created in the build_dialog() function.

Listing 17.9 shows PGDialog.main(). This function is called when you want to display the dialog (refer to Figure 17.1) to the user.

Listing 17.9   client4.py—PGDialog.main()

```
19 ############################################
20     def main( self ):
21
22         self.conn = pgdb.connect( database="movies" )
23
24         self.build_dialog( )
25         self.table.mainloop( )
```

At line 22, main() calls pgdb.connect() to establish a connection to the PostgreSQL server. Notice that main() won't catch any exceptions thrown by pgdb.connect()—if this call fails, your application can't do anything useful, so just let Python print an error message and end. If you want to embed the PGDialog class in a larger application, you'll want to add some error checking here.

Assuming that pgdb.connect() returned successfully, main() calls the build_dialog() function to create all required widgets. Next, call Tk's mainloop() function. mainloop() displays the dialog and waits for user interaction. mainloop() does not return until the user closes the dialog window.

Listing 17.10 shows PGDialog.build_dialog().

Listing 17.10 client4.py—PGDialog.build_dialog()

```
28  ##############################################
29      def build_dialog( self ):
30
31          root = Tk()
32
33          self.make_table( root )
34
35          self.command = Text( root, height=3 )
36          self.status  = Label( root )
37
38          close = Button( root,
39                          text="Close Window",
40                          command=root.destroy )
41
42          label = Label( root,
43                         text="Enter an SQL Command and Press Return")
44
45          self.command.focus_force( )
46
47          self.command.bind( "<Return>", self.execute )
48
49          sy = Scrollbar( root,
50                          command=self.table.yview )
51
52          sx = Scrollbar( root,
53                          command=self.table.xview,
54                          orient="horizontal" )
55
56          self.table.config( xscrollcommand=sx.set,
57                             yscrollcommand=sy.set )
58
59          label.grid( row=0 )
60
61          self.command.grid( row=1, sticky='news' )
```

Listing 17.10 **Continued**

```
62            self.status.grid( row=2 )
63            self.table.grid( row=3, column=0, sticky='news' )
64
65            sy.grid( row=3, column=1, sticky='news' )
66            sx.grid( row=4, sticky='ew' )
67            close.grid( row=5 )
68
69            root.columnconfigure( 0, weight=1 )
70
71            root.rowconfigure( 1, weight=0 )
72            root.rowconfigure( 3, weight=1 )
73            root.rowconfigure( 5, weight=0 )
```

The `build_dialog()` function is responsible for creating and arranging the widgets in your dialog. At line 31, `build_dalog()` constructs a `Tk` object named `root`. `root` will act as the parent window for all the widgets that you create.

Next, `build_dialog()` calls the `make_table()` member function (see Listing 17.11) to create a `Tktable` widget. You won't know how many rows and columns you need in the table until you execute a SELECT command, but you can configure everything else now.

Lines 35 through 42 create a few more child widgets that will display on the dialog. `self.command` is a text entry widget that holds the command text entered by the user. `self.status` is a simple Label widget—client4 will display error messages and row counts in this widget (if you refer to Figure 17.1, `self.status` is the part that says "`5(rows)`").

The `close` widget is a `Button` that displays the text "`Close Window`". When the user clicks on this button, Tk will execute the command `root.destroy`, closing the application.

The `label` widget displays a prompt ("`Enter an SQL Command and Press Return`") to the user.

At line 45, client4 moves the keyboard focus to the `command` (text entry) widget. That way, the cursor is positioned in the right place when this application starts running.

Next, `build_dialog()` *binds* a chunk of Python code to the Return key. When the command widget has the keyboard focus and the user presses Return, client4 calls the `self.execute()` function (see Listing 17.12. The `self.execute()` function grabs any text that the user typed into the `command` widget and sends it to the PostgreSQL server.

The next few lines of code (lines 49 through 57) create a vertical scrollbar (`sy`) and horizontal scrollbar (`sx`) and connect them to the `self.table` widget. The `Tktable` widget won't automatically display scrollbars, so you have to wire them in manually.

Lines 59 through 67 arrange all the widgets using Tk's `grid` layout manager. Refer to Figure 17.1. We lay out the child widgets in a `grid` of unevenly sized cells. The `label` widget appears at the top of the dialog, so we'll place it in row 0 (because you have only a single widget in row 0, the column is irrelevant). Next, place the `command` (text entry) widget in the second row (`row=1`). The third row (`row=2`) contains the `status` widget. The fourth row actually contains two widgets: the `table` widget on the left (`column=0`) and the `sy` vertical scrollbar on the right (`column=1`). The horizontal scrollbar (`sx`) and `close` button are placed in the last two rows.

The "sticky" stuff is taking care of widget placement *within* each grid cell. If you don't specify any sticky options, each widget is centered (vertically and horizontally) within its own cell. sticky=news means that you want the grid layout manager to *stick* a widget to the *n*orth (top), *e*ast (right), *w*est (left), and *s*outh (bottom) side of its cell.

The final four lines in this function tell the layout manager how to stretch or compress the widgets whenever the user resizes the root window. You want the table widget (which is positioned in column 0) to resize, but the vertical scrollbar to remain the same; so give column 0 a resize *weight* of 1. You also want the command widget (row 1) and the close button to stay the same size, so give those rows a weight of 0.

Give yourself a quick break—the next few functions are mercifully short.

Listing 17.11   client4.py—PGDialog.make_table()

```
75 ###########################################
76     def make_table( self, parent ):
77
78         var = ArrayVar( parent )
79
80         self.table = Table( parent,
81                             variable=var,
82                             titlerows=1,
83                             titlecols=1,
84                             roworigin=-1,
85                             colorigin=-1,
86                             colstretchmode='last',
87                             rowstretchmode='last' )
```

The make_table() function creates a Table widget and does some preliminary configuration work. A Table widget requires a variable that it can use to hold the actual data values that you stuff into the table. Fortunately, the Tktable.py module (remember, you imported that module at the beginning of this application) defines a data type custom-made to work with a Tktable. At line 78, make_table() creates an instance of Tktable.ArrayVar().

Next, make_table() creates the table widget and configures a few options. First, make_table() tells the table to use var as its data variable. Next, we'll arrange to reserve the top row for column headers and the leftmost column for row numbering. Normally, the first row in a table is row 0; likewise, the first column is usually column 0. For convenience, we will change the table origin to -1, --1. That way, the title row is row -1 and the first *data* row is row 0. We pull a similar trick with the column-numbering scheme.

make_table() also sets the column stretch mode and row stretch mode. colstretch-mode and rowstretchmode determine how the table will behave when you resize it. A value of 'last' resizes the last row (or column) to fill extra space.

The execute() function is called whenever the table widget holds the focus and the user presses the Return key (see Listing 17.12). You arranged for this behavior back at line 47 (refer to Listing 17.10).

Listing 17.12   `client4.py`—`PGDialog.execute()`

```
89 ############################################
90     def execute( self, event ):
91
92         self.process_command( self.command.get( "1.0", "end" ))
```

This function is simple—first retrieve the contents of the `command` widget and then call `self.process_command()` with that text. If you have trouble seeing the flow in this function, you could have written it as follows:

```
...
text = self.command.get( "1.0", "end" )

self.process_command( text )
...
```

The `process_command()` function (see Listing 17.13) is where things start to get interesting again. This function is called whenever the user wants to execute a command. It starts by creating a new `cursor` object (remember, a DB-API `cursor` is *not* the same as a PostgreSQL cursor).

Listing 17.13   `client4.py`—`PGDialog.process_command()`

```
94 ############################################
95     def process_command ( self, command ):
96
97         cur = self.conn.cursor()
98
99         try:
100            cur.execute( command )
101            self.load_table( cur )
102
103        except Exception, e:
104            from mx.TextTools import collapse
105            self.status.configure( text=collapse( str( e )))
106
```

Next, `process_command()` calls the `cursor.execute()` function to execute the command provided by the caller. If the command completes without error, the call to `load_table()` (see Listing 17.14) displays the results. If anything goes wrong, `cursor.execute()` will throw an exception. `process_command()` catches any exceptions at line 103. You want to display error messages in the `status` widget, which is only one line high. So, you can use the `mx.TextTools.collapse()` function to remove any new-line characters from the text of the error message before copying the message into the `status` widget.

A Few More Ways to Execute PostgreSQL Commands

So far, all the examples in this chapter have used a simple form of the `cursor.execute()` method to execute PostgreSQL commands. When you call `cursor.execute()`, you call it with a complete command.

You can also call `cursor.execute()` with a *parameterized* command and collection of parameter values. A parameterized command contains placeholders (also known as parameter markers) in which you can substitute values. For example, assume that you have a dictionary that holds two values, one named min and one named max:

```
...
>>> min_max = { 'min':2, 'max':4 }
...
```

You can execute a command such as[3]

```
...
>>> cmd="SELECT * FROM customers WHERE customer_id >= %(min)d AND \
>>>      customer_id <= %(max)d"
>>>
>>> cur.execute( cmd % min_max )
>>> cur.fetchall()
[
  [2, 'Rubin, William', '555-2211', '1972-07-10'],
  [3, 'Panky, Henry', '555-1221', '1968-01-21'],
  [4, 'Wonderland, Alice N.', '555-1122', '1969-03-05']
]
...
```

In this example, the `SELECT` command includes two placeholders: `%(min)d` and `%(max)d`. Python replaces the first placeholder with the min value from dictionary `min_max` and the second placeholder with the max value. In effect, you are executing the following command:

```
SELECT * FROM customers WHERE customer_id >= 2 AND customer_id <= 4
```

You can also refer to other variables by name in a parameterized command:

```
...
>>> min = 2
>>> max = 4
>>> cmd="SELECT * FROM customers WHERE customer_id >= %(min)d AND \
>>>      customer_id <= %(max)d"
>>> cur.execute( cmd % vars())
>>> cur.fetchall()

[
  [2, 'Rubin, William', '555-2211', '1972-07-10'],
  [3, 'Panky, Henry', '555-1221', '1968-01-21'],
```

---

[3] The results returned by `cur.fetchall()` have been reformatted for clarity.

```
    [4, 'Wonderland, Alice N.', '555-1122', '1969-03-05']
]
...
```

I don't want to give you the impression that parameterized commands are a feature unique to the Python/PostgreSQL interface. In fact, we are simply using Python's string formatting operator. You still have to be sure that the end result (that is, the result after formatting) is a valid SQL command—you must quote strings properly, and you can't simply bind None where you really want NULL to appear.

Note that finding documentation for Python's string formatting operator is notoriously difficult. You can find this information in the *Python Library Reference Manual:* Built-in Functions, Types, and Exceptions; Built-in Types; Sequence Types; String Formatting Operations.

Besides cursor.execute(), you can use the cursor.executemany() function to execute PostgreSQL commands. The executemany() function executes a command repeatedly, substituting new parameter values with each iteration. For example, let's create a list of tuple values that we want to INSERT into the tapes table:

```
>>> vals = \
... [
...    ( 'TH-X1138', 'This Island Earth' ),
...    ( 'MST-3000', 'Python' ),
...    ( 'B-MOVIE1', 'Frogs' ),
...    ( 'B-MOVIE2', 'Bats' )
... ]
```

Now we can INSERT all four tuples with a single command:

```
>>> cmd = "INSERT INTO tapes VALUES( %s, %s )"
>>> cur.executemany( cmd, vals )
```

You can use cursor.execute() and cursor.executemany() to simplify your code. Using these functions, you can factor the code that executes a command and the code that produces parameter values into two separate functions.

The function in Listing 17.14, load_table(),loads the result of a command into the status widget and the table widget. It starts by setting the status widget: We query cur.rowcount to find the number of rows and format this value into a nice, polite message.

Listing 17.14   client4.py—PGDialog.load_table()

```
108 #############################################
109     def load_table( self, cur ):
110
111         self.status.configure( text= "%d row(s)" % cur.rowcount )
112
113         self.size_table( cur )
114
115         if( cur.description == None ):
```

Listing 17.14 **Continued**

```
117
118          self.set_column_headers( cur )
119
120          self.fill_table( cur )
121
122          self.size_columns( cur )
```

Next, `load_table()` calls the `size_table()` function (see Listing 17.15) to configure the `table` widget to the proper number of rows and columns.

At line 115, `load_table()` decides whether you are processing a SELECT command or some other type of command. A SELECT command is the only type of command that will return column metadata (`cur.description`). If you don't have metadata, `load_table()` is finished. Otherwise, `load_table()` copies the column headers into the table (see Listing 17.16), copies the data values into the table (Listing 17.17), and sizes each column to match the data (Listing 17.18).

Listing 17.15 `client4.py`—`PGDialog.size_table()`

```
124  ##############################################
125      def size_table( self, cur ):
126
127          if( cur.description == None ):
128              self.table.configure( rows=0, cols=0 )
129          else:
130              col_cnt = len( cur.description )
131              row_cnt = cur.rowcount
132
133              self.table.configure( rows=row_cnt+1, cols=col_cnt+1 )
```

The `size_table()` function configures the `table` widget to hold the proper number of rows and columns. If you have no metadata, `size_table()` modifies the table to hold 0 rows and 0 columns (metadata is returned for only a SELECT command).

If you have metadata, you can look into the `cursor` object to find the number of rows and (indirectly) the number columns in the result set. Finding the row count is easy—each `cursor` object contains a data member named `rowcount`. Finding the column count is a bit more complex—you have to count the number of sequences in the metadata list.

After you know how many rows and columns are present in the result set, `size_table()` configures `self.table` to hold one extra row (for the column headers) and one extra column (for row numbers).

Listing 17.16 `client4.py`—`PGDialog.set_column_headers()`

```
135  ##############################################
136      def set_column_headers( self, cur ):
137
```

Listing 17.16   **Continued**

```
138          col_no = 0
139
140          for col in cur.description:
141              self.table.set( "-1," + str(col_no), col[0] )
142              self.widths.append(len( col[0] ))
143              col_no = col_no + 1
144
```

The set_column_headers() function tackles two different problems. First, it copies the name of each column in the result set into the first row of self.table. Second, it initializes the self.widths[] array to hold the width of each column header.

The cur.description data member is a list of tuples—each tuple corresponds to one column in the result set. The first member of each tuple contains the column name. Refer to Table 17.2 for more information on the contents of cur.description.

Listing 17.17   client4.py—PGDialog.fill_table()

```
146  ############################################
147      def fill_table( self, cur ):
148
149          rows = cur.fetchall()
150
151          r = 0
152          for row in rows:
153              c = 0
154
155              for col in row:
156
157                  self.table.set( str(r) + "," + str(c), str( col ))
158
159                  if( col != None ):
160                      if( len( str( col )) > self.widths[c] ):
161                          self.widths[c] = len( str( col ))
162
163                  c = c + 1
164
165              self.table.set( str(r) + ",-1", str(r))
166
167              r = r + 1
```

Listing 17.17 shows the PGDialog.fill_table() function. This function looks complicated, but it's actually very simple. You have a pair of nested loops: The outer loop iterates through each row in the result set and the inner loop iterates through each column in the current row.

In the inner loop, you convert each data value into string form and copy it into the proper cell in the `table` widget (line 157). `fill_table()` also uses the length of each value to update the `self.widths[]` array. We'll use the `widths[]` array to set each column in the table to the proper width. You want each column to be wide enough to display the widest value in the column, so you have to measure each value as you encounter it.

After it has finished processing the data values in each row, `fill_table()` copies the row number into the leftmost column of `self.table`.

Listing 17.18   `client4.py`—`PGDialog.size_columns()`

```
169 #############################################
170    def size_columns( self, cur ):
171        col_cnt = len( cur.description )
172
173        for col in range( 0, col_cnt ):
174            self.table.width( col, self.widths[col] )
```

`size_columns()` is the last function in `client4.py`. This function is responsible for configuring each column in `self.table` to the proper width. You computed the optimal width of each column in the `fill_table()` and `set_column_headers()` functions.

Listing 17.19 shows the mainline code for `client4.py`. These are the first executable commands outside of `PGDialog`, so execution begins at line 178. Getting this program up and running is pretty easy; you create an instance of the `PgDialog` class and then invoke that object's `main()` function (refer to Listing 17.8).

Listing 17.19   `client4.py`—**mainline code**

```
176 #############################################
177
178 obj = PGDialog()
179 obj.main( )
```

Summary

In this chapter, we've shown you the Python DB-API (version 2.0). There are at least three implementations of the PostgreSQL/DB-API interface; we've described the PyGreSQL implementation because that is the one you are most likely to have if you're using an older version of PostgreSQL (it was distributed with PostgreSQL for quite some time). As we mentioned at the beginning of this chapter, all three PostgreSQL/Python APIs are compatible with the Python DB-API so you can choose a different implementation if you find that it offers features that you need.

As we mentioned at the start of this chapter, you can also use the PyGreSQL interface without using the DB-API wrapper. PyGreSQL is a nifty toolkit, but the DB class offers some nice features.

18

Npgsql: The .NET Data Provider

IF YOU'VE BEEN INVOLVED IN THE software industry over the last few years, you've heard of Microsoft's .NET initiative. .NET is a collection of development tools and technologies that implement a portable "virtual operating system" on top of whatever operating system you happen to be running. The idea behind .NET is that you can use the development tools to build applications that run on any computer that has a copy of the .NET framework (in a fashion very similar to the Java virtual machine and Java runtime architecture). The .NET initiative was created by Microsoft and developed chiefly for Microsoft operating systems, but an open-source implementation of the .NET framework (and some of the development tools) is available for many operating systems. The open-source version of .NET is named Mono (you can find more information about Mono at www.go-mono.com).

One component of .NET is the ADO.NET Data Access framework (*ADO* is an acronym for *Active Data Objects*). ADO.NET is a set of classes (and interfaces) that make it possible to write database-independent code at a very high level. When you build an ADO.NET application, you typically interact with a set of "adapters." The adapters, in turn, interact with the database on your behalf. Npgsql is an open-source ADO.NET data provider that gives you an adapter (and other tools) that know how to interact with PostgreSQL.

In this chapter, I'll show you how to use the Npgsql data provider to create PostgreSQL-enabled applications written in Microsoft's Visual Basic (VB). You can use Npgsql with any .NET-compatible language, but VB makes it easy for novice programmers to develop attractive applications in very little time. (Oddly enough, experienced programmers tend to get bogged down with Visual Basic because we just want to write more code and, as you'll see, there's very little coding involved in simple VB applications.)

Prerequisites

To create the Npgsql applications I describe in this chapter, you'll need a copy of Visual Studio .NET (preferably, Visual Studio 2003 or later) and you must install the Visual Basic component. You'll also need a copy of the Npgsql package (which you can find at gborg.postgresql.org or www.pgfoundry.org).

To install Npgsql, open the `Npgsql-version.zip` archive and extract all files into a permanent home. (I recommend saving the archive files in your `Desktop` folder so you can find them easily—you'll need to refer to them often.)

Next, add the `Npgsql.dll` and `Mono.Security.Protocol.Tls.dll` files to the .NET global assembly cache. If you unpacked the Npgsql archive to your `Desktop` folder, you'll find these files in the `Desktop\Npgsql\bin\ms` directory. If you're comfortable with the Windows command line, you can execute the following commands to install the Npgsql assemblies:

```
C:\...\Desktop\Npgsql\bin\ms> gacutil /nologo -i Npgsql.dll
Assembly successfully added to the cache.


C:\...\Desktop\Npgsql\bin\ms > gacutil /nologo -i Mono.Security.Protocol.Tls.dll
Assembly successfully added to the cache.
```

If you prefer the drag-and-drop approach, open two Windows Explorer sessions. In the first session, navigate to the `assembly` folder in the `Windows` directory (typically `C:\WINDOWS\assembly`). In the second session, open the directory that contains the Npgsql package and browse to the `bin\ms` subdirectory. Drag the `Npgsql.dll` and `Mono.Security.Protocol.Tls.dll` files from the `Npgsql\bin\ms` folder and drop them in the `WINDOWS\assembly` folder.

Preparing Visual Studio

Now you're ready to install Npgsql into the Visual Studio development environment. Once you've prepared Visual Studio, the Toolbox window will display a number of Npgsql components that you can add to your own applications. To add the Npgsql components to Visual Studio, open the Data tab (in the Toolbox window), right-click anywhere in the `Data Toolbox`, and choose Add/Remove Items. When the Customize Toolbox dialog appears, click the Browse button, navigate to the directory that holds Npgsql (`Desktop\Npgsql\bin\ms`), and open `Npgsql.dll`. Four new components will appear in the `Data Toolbox`: `NpgsqlCommand`, `NpgsqlCommandBuilder`, `NpgsqlDataAdapter`, and `NpgsqlConnection`.

Understanding the ADO.NET Class Hierarchy

ADO.NET defines a bewildering number of classes, but Microsoft has done a good job of arranging them into a meaningful hierarchy. In this section, I'll briefly describe the most important ADO.NET classes. You'll see them in action in the remainder of this chapter.

NpgsqlConnection

This class represents a connection to a PostgreSQL database. You really can't do much with an NpgsqlConnection object other than give it to some other object. Other ADO.NET objects will use an NpgsqlConnection object to interact with a PostgreSQL database.

The most important property defined by an NpgsqlCommand object is the ConnectionString. The ConnectionString tells Npgsql how to connect to a PostgreSQL database, and it looks similar to a typical libpq connection string. Don't be fooled; Npgsql *is not* based on the libpq client library. Npgsql speaks the same client/server protocol as libpq, but it interacts with the server without getting libpq involved. Instead, the Npgsql developers implemented the PostgreSQL client/server protocol using nothing but .NET managed code.

The NpgsqlCommand class contains a design-time helper dialog that can help you fill in the ConnectionString property. I'll show you how to use the helper (the Data Connection Properties dialog) in the section titled "Client 1—Connecting to the Server." The Data Connection Properties dialog is useful when you know, at design time, how to connect to the database. If you don't have that information at design time, you can still use the helper dialog to try out different connection properties and learn how to assemble them into the format required by the NpgsqlCommand class.

NpqsqlCommand

An NpgsqlCommand object represents a single SQL command that you want to execute in a PostgreSQL server. Before you can execute an NpgsqlCommand object, you must link it to an NpgsqlConnection object. At design time, you can link an NpgsqlCommand to a connection by clicking the Connection property (in the Properties window) and choosing one of the NpgsqlConnection objects that you've defined. At run time, you can link an NpgsqlCommand to a connection by modifying the Connection property.

An NpgsqlCommand object holds the text of the command that you want to execute in its CommandText property. When you ask an NpgsqlCommand property to execute its command, it returns a result set.

DataTable

A DataTable (note that it's not an NpgsqlDataTable—this is an ADO.NET class) is an in-memory copy of a result set. Each DataTable contains a name (the TableName property), a collection of column descriptors, and a collection of rows. Each column descriptor describes a single column and is an object of type DataColumn. Each row contains the values for a single row in the result set and is an object of type DataRow. You typically find DataTable objects inside of a DataSet (another ADO.NET class), but you can also create and populate a DataTable with your own VB code.

DataRow

A DataRow is an in-memory copy of a single row. Each DataRow contains a collection of column values (one Item for each column in the table). A DataRow also contains a

RowState that keeps track of whether you've modified the values in the Item collection. A DataRow can also hold a row-specific error message. You typically find DataRow objects inside of a DataTable's Row collection.

DataColumn

A DataColumn describes a column within a DataTable. Each DataColumn contains a ColumnName property, a DataType property, a MaximumLength property, and so on. DataColumns (and the DataRow that the DataColumns belong to) store the metadata for a result set.

DataSet

The DataSet class is the focus of the ADO.NET class hierarchy. In PostgreSQL terms, a DataSet holds a collection of result sets. In the simplest case, a DataSet contains a single result set—both the data and the metadata returned by a single query. A DataSet can also contain multiple data sets. One of the features that makes a DataSet so useful is that you can use it as the data source for a UI control. When you *bind* a DataSet to a grid control, you end up with a DataGrid that can display the values in the DataSet—no programming required (well, very little anyway). You can also bind a single column within a DataSet to a ListView and display the column values to the user.

If you modify the values in a DataSet, you can ask a DataAdapter object (which I'll tell you about in a moment) to write those changes back to the database. The DataAdapter looks through each row in the data set and executes a series of INSERT, UPDATE, and DELETE commands (as appropriate) to record the changes you've made.

DataSet objects come in two flavors: typed and untyped. A typed DataSet is a class that knows the shape of the data that it holds. A typed DataSet extends the base DataSet class and adds new members (and methods) that provide direct, named access to the tables and columns in the DataSet. For example, if you create a typed DataSet subclass named DSCustomers, based on the customers table, you can write code like this:

```
Dim  dsCustomers  As DSCustomers
Dim  customerName As String
Dim  birthDate    As DateTime

customerName = dsCustomers.customers(3).customer_name
birthDate    = dsCustomers.customers(3).birthDate
```

A typed DataSet creates first-class objects out of the tables and columns that it contains. When you add a typed DataSet to a Visual Studio project, you can use the graphical tools (schema editors, query builders, and so on) provided by Visual Studio to manipulate the tables and columns in the DataSet. Visual Studio also integrates typed DataSets into its code-completion mechanism (IntelliSense) so it's easier to write code that actually compiles without errors.

An untyped DataSet does not provide named access to the tables and columns that it contains. Instead, each result set lives in the DataSet.Tables array. DataSet.Tables is an array of `DataTable` objects. A `DataTable` object contains (among other things) an array of `Columns` and an array of `Rows`. Each member of the `Columns` array is a `DataColumn` object that describes a single column in the result set (the column name, column data type, and so on). The rows in the result set are stored in the `Rows` array as a collection of `DataRow` objects.

In this chapter, I'll show you how to create a VB application that can create a typed `DataSet` for any table in your database.

A `DataSet` can be considerably more complex than I've described so far. If a `DataSet` contains more than one `DataTable`, you can define parent/child relationships between the tables. Each relationship is defined by a `DataRelation` that links a key in one table with a key in a second table. You can use the relationships with a `DataSet` to access the children that belong to a given parent row, or to find the parent row for a given child. You can also ask a `DataSet` to filter and sort the data that it contains (without getting the backing database involved).

NpgsqlDataAdapter

The `NpgsqlDataAdapter` class links a `DataSet` to the database. An `NpgsqlDataAdapter` object contains (references to) a SELECT command, an INSERT command, an UPDATE command, and a DELETE command. An `NpgsqlDataAdapter` object *fills* a `DataSet` by executing its SELECT command. If you've made changes to a `DataSet`, you can call the `NpgsqlDataAdapter.Update` method to copy the changes back to the database. The `Update` method executes the INSERT, UPDATE, and DELETE commands required to store your modifications in the PostgreSQL database.

The `DataSet` class is generic—you can use a `DataSet` object with any database system (you can even use a `DataSet` object *without* a database). `DataAdapters`, on the other hand, are database-specific. The `NpgsqlDataAdapter` class only works with a PostgreSQL database. An `OracleDataAdapter` only works with an Oracle database. That's why they are called *adapters*—they adapt a database to the needs of a `DataSet` (or other database-neutral) object.

NpgsqlCommandBuilder

An `NpgsqlCommandBuilder` object builds the UPDATE, INSERT, and DELETE commands required by an `NpgsqlDataAdapter` object. An `NpgsqlCommandBuilder` object works by examining the metadata in a `DataRow` object that you provide. The `NpgsqlCommandBuilder.GetInsertCommand()` method, for example, creates an `NpgsqlCommand` object that INSERTs every column in the given row. You typically create an `NpgsqlCommandBuilder` object when you want to write `DataSet` modifications back to the database.

NpgsqlDataReader

The `NpgsqlDataReader` class provides a "raw" interface to a PostgreSQL result set. If you invoke an `NpgsqlCommand`'s ExecuteReader method, you'll get back an `NpgsqlDataReader` object that you can use to read through the result set, one row at a time. (You can't skip around in a result set using an `NpgsqlDataReader`.) You'll rarely need to create an `NpgsqlDataReader`, since you can use a `DataSet` to hop around inside of a result set instead.

That gives you a broad overview of the most important ADO.NET classes (and the Npgsql components). ADO.NET defines a number of *other* classes that you may need in some applications, so be sure to read through the ADO.NET documentation at the MSDN website (msdn.microsoft.com).

Creating an Npgsql-enabled VB Project

Creating a PostgreSQL client application is easy with the tools provided by Visual Studio, but before you start, there's one step that you'll need to follow every time you create a new Npgsql-enabled VB project.

When you create a new VB project, Visual Studio automatically links in a number of commonly used .NET framework components (such as `System`, `System.Data`, and `System.Windows.Forms`). If you're going to add Npgsql components to a VB project, you must define a "reference" to the Npgsql assembly. If you're not used to .NET terminology, think of an assembly as an object library, and the process of adding a reference as analogous to adding that library to the link command line.

To create a new VB project, open the File menu and choose New, then Project. When the New Project dialog appears, select Visual Basic Projects (in the box labeled Project Types), then click Windows Application (in the box labeled Templates).

To add an Npgsql reference to your project, open the Project menu and click Add Reference. When the Add Reference dialog appears, click Browse and open the `Npgqsql.dll` file (you'll find it in the `Desktop\Npgsql\bin\ms` directory if you've followed my recommendation). Click the `Ok` button to close the Add Reference dialog.

Client 1—Connecting to the Server

Connecting a VB.NET application to a PostgreSQL database is easy. Simply add an `NpgsqlConnection` object to your application and set the `ConnectionString` property. You can open the connection programmatically, or let another Npgsql object manage the connection as needed.

To create an `NpgsqlConnection` object, open the Data tab (in the Toolbox) and double-click the `NpgsqlConnection` tool—Visual Studio adds an `NpgsqlConnection` object to the form that you're editing. If you see a message that states "`The .NET assembly 'Npgsql' could not be found.`", you forgot to add an Npgsql reference to your project. See the previous section ("Creating an Npgsql-enabled VB.NET Project") to learn how to fix the problem.

To define the `ConnectionString` property, click the `NpgsqlConnection` object (when it appears below the form) and then click the `ConnectionString` property in the Properties window (see Figure 18.1).

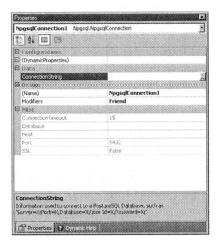

Figure 18.1   VB Properties window.

There are two ways to define the `ConnectionString`. First, you can use a helper dialog (see Figure 18.2) by clicking on the "..." button next to the `ConnectionString` property. After you've filled in the server name, username, and password, you can select a database from the drop-down list box (the `NpgsqlConnection` object connects to the server that you've specified and retrieves a list of database names for you to choose from). When you click Ok, the dialog converts the values that you entered into a connection string and copies that string into the `ConnectionString` property.
The Data Connection Properties dialog is very picky—it does its best to ensure that you create a connection string that actually works. The dialog connects to the server that you specify, verifies the user ID and password, and won't let you connect to a database that doesn't actually exist. That means that you can't use the Data Connection Properties dialog unless your PostgreSQL server is running (and accessible), and you've already created the user account and database that you want to use.

If you don't want to use the Data Connection Properties dialog, or you need to create a connection string at run-time, you can build one by hand. An Npgsql connection string is semicolon separated list of *property=value* pairs. You can include any of the keywords shown in Table 18.1. You must specify a SERVER and USER ID. (Npgsql does *not* search for any environment variables to satisfy missing connection properties.)

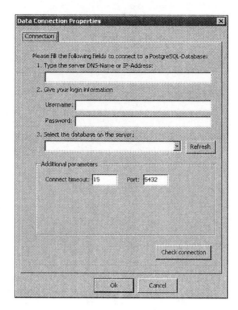

Figure 18.2 PostgreSQL Data Connection Properties.

Table 18.1 **Npgsql Connection String Keywords**

Keyword	Synonyms	Description
SERVER	HOST	Specifies the hostname or IP address of the PostgreSQL server.
PORT		Specifies the TCP port number (typically 5432) where the postmaster is listening for client requests.
PROTOCOL		Determines which version of the client/server proto-col the connection will use when talking to the server. This property is automatically negotiated at the time the NpgsqlConnection object connects to the server.
DATABASE	DB	Specifies the name of the PostgreSQL database that you want to connect to.
USER ID	USER, USERID, USER NAME, USERNAME, UID	Specifies the PostgreSQL user account used by the connection.
PASSWORD	PSW, PWD	Specifies the password provided to the PostgreSQL server (if required by the authentication used by the server). At the time we are writing this (Npgsql version 0.7), Npgsql supports clear-text password authentication and MD5-encrpyted authentication.

Table 18.1 **Continued**

Keyword	Synonyms	Description
SSL		If True, the NpgsqlConnection object tries to create an SSL-secured connection to the server. If the server does not support SSL connections, Npgsql will try to create an insecure connection.
ENCODING		Determines the encoding (character set) reported to the server. This property defaults to SQL_ASCII.
TIMEOUT		Specifies the number of seconds to wait for the connection to complete before throwing an exception.

If you are creating an NpgsqlConnection object at run-time (as opposed to design-time), you can set ConnectionString property by hand or you can pass the connection string to the NpgsqlConnection constructor:

```
...
Dim conn_1 AS Npgsql.NpgsqlConnection
Dim conn_2 AS Npgsql.NpgsqlConnection

conn_1 = New Npgsql.NpgsqlConnection
conn_1.ConnectionString = "SERVER=cows;USER=bruce"

conn_2 = New Npgsql.NpgsqlConnection("SERVER=cows;USER=bruce" )
...
```

When you create an NpgsqlConnection, the object doesn't actually connect to the database until you call the Open() method. In some cases, some other object will invoke Open() for you. For example, when you use a DataAdapter object to fill a DataSet, the DataAdapter will Open() a connection on your behalf. It's not easy to find out which objects automatically Open() a connection—you have to slog through the .NET documentation to know for sure. It's usually safer to Open() the connection yourself.

The Open() method throws an exception if anything goes wrong, so you should only call Open() inside of a try/catch block (if you don't, your program will die a fiery death should something go awry).

To wrap up your first Npgsql client, double-click on the background of the form you're designing and add the code shown in Listing 18.1 to the Form1_Load() method.

Listing 18.1 **The** client1 Form1_Load() **Subroutine**

```
1   Private Sub Form1_Load(...) Handles MyBase.Load
2     Try
3         NpgsqlConnection1.Open()
4         MessageBox.Show(NpgsqlConnection1.ConnectionString, "Connected!")
5     Catch ex As Exception
6         MessageBox.Show(ex.Message, "Can't connect")
```

Listing 18.1 **Continued**

```
7    End Try
8    Application.Exit()
9    End Sub
```

When you build and run this program, you'll see a `MessageBox` appear. If the `NpgsqlConnection` object successfully connects to the server you specify, the code at line 4 displays a `MessageBox` (titled "`Connected!`") that displays the `ConnectionString` property. If the connection attempt fails, the code at line 6 extracts an error message from the `Exception` object thrown by `Open()` and displays that message in a `MessageBox` (titled "`Can't Connect`").

Client 2—An Interactive Query Processor

The second client application that we'll build is an interactive query processor (see Figure 18.3). Enter a PostgreSQL command in the top window, press Ctrl+Return, and the query results appear in the `DataGrid` in the bottom window. VB.NET makes it very easy to build a simple application of this sort.

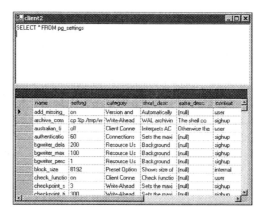

Figure 18.3   The `client2` application.

This application creates an `NpgsqlConnection` object named m_conn, an `NpgsqlCommand` object (named m_cmd) linked to m_conn, an `NpgsqlDataAdapter` (named m_da) linked to m_cmd, and a `DataSet` (m_ds) that gets filled by m_da. The only code that you have to write is the function that fires when the user presses Ctrl+Enter in the text control.

To build this application, create a new VB.NET project (I've named mine `client2`) and make sure that you have `Form1` open in design mode. Be sure to add a reference to `Npgsql.dll` to your project as I described earlier in this chapter (see the section titled "Creating an Npgsql-enabled VB.NET Project"). Next, open the Data tab in the Toolbox window to expose the `Npgsql` tools.

The first object that you'll need in this application is an `NpgsqlConnection`. Double-click the `NpgsqlConnection` tool (on the Data tab of the Toolbox window) and Visual Studio adds an object named `NpgsqlConnection1` to the form. Visual Studio automatically assigns a unique name to each object that you add to a project, but those names can get awfully tedious: Click the `Name` property (in the Design section of the Properties window) and change the name of this `NpgsqlConnection` object to m_conn. Make sure that you set the `ConnectionString` property using either of the methods I described in the previous section (you can use the Data Connection Properties helper dialog or just type in the connection string yourself). `client2` uses this object to interact with the PostgreSQL server.

Next, double-click the `NpgsqlCommand` tool (also in the Data tab) and change the name of the new object to m_cmd. In a typical application, you know the text of the command that you want to execute at the time you write the application and you can set the `CommandText` property accordingly. In this case, the *user* provides the text of each command so you can't set the `CommandText` property now (you'll change the `CommandText` property every time the user types in a new command). When you ask the m_cmd object to execute itself, it needs an `NpgsqlConnection` object in order to communicate with the PostgreSQL server—sounds like a job for m_conn (the `NpgsqlConnection` object you created in the previous step). To link m_cmd to m_conn, change m_cmd's `Connection` property to m_conn.

At this point, you have a connection to the database and a command object that knows how to execute itself using that connection. If you wanted to do things the hard way, you could ask m_cmd to execute itself and then read through the result set, adding each row to the `DataGrid` yourself. Instead, I'll take the easy way out and use a `DataSet` to do the tough work. I mentioned earlier in this chapter that you can *bind* a `DataSet` to a UI control (such as a `DataGrid`) and the control will display (some or all of) the data in the `DataSet`. To add a `DataSet` to the form, double-click the `DataSet` tool (again, in the Data tab). The `DataSet` tool pops up a dialog that asks you to choose one of the typed `DataSets` in the project, or an untyped `DataSet`. You don't have any typed `DataSets` in this project so you'll have to create an untyped `DataSet` (you can't use a typed `DataSet` unless you know, at design-time, which tables you'll use in an application). Change the name of this object to m_ds. (Be sure you change the `Name` property, not the `DataSetName` property.)

So far, none of the objects that you've added present any sort of visible interface to the user (the form looks empty). `client2` displays the result of each query in a `DataGrid` control. To create the `DataGrid`, open the Windows Forms tab (in the Toolbox window), click the `DataGrid` tool, and drag out a rectangle across the bottom half of the form. Change the name of the `DataGrid` object to m_grid. You'll also want to change the `Anchor` property from its default value (Top, Left) to Top, Bottom, Left, Right. That tells the `DataGrid` to resize itself if the user enlarges (or shrinks) the form. You want the `DataGrid` control to display the rows and columns inside of the m_ds `DataSet`, so set m_grid's `DataSource` property to m_ds. That binds the `DataGrid` and the

DataSet together. The binding works in both directions. As you might expect, the values displayed in the DataGrid will change if you modify the content of the DataSet. What you may find surprising is that you can change the values in the DataGrid and the rows and columns in the DataSet reflect those changes. I'll show you how to write those changes back to the database in the next client.

You'll also need a place for the user to type in SQL commands—you could use a multi-line TextBox control for this, but I'll use a RichTextBox instead, since it's a tad bit easier. Click the RichTextBox tool (in the Windows Forms tab) and drag out a rectangle across the top half of the form. Change the name of this object to m_cmdText and set the Dock property to Top. (That tells the RichTextBox to resize itself horizontally, but keep the same height if the user stretches out the form.) You may also want to blank out the Text property (or better yet, set it to SELECT * FROM to give a hint to the user).

Here's a quick review of the objects that you've created so far. You have an NpgsqlCommand object (m_cmd) linked to an NpgsqlConnection object (m_conn). When you execute a command, m_cmd interacts with the database using the m_conn connection. You have a RichTextBox (m_cmdText) where the user can enter PostgreSQL commands. You can't link m_cmdText and m_cmd at design-time, so you'll have to write some code to move the command text from m_cmdText into m_cmd—I'll show that code to you in a moment. You also have a DataGrid (m_grid) bound to a DataSet (m_ds). The DataGrid displays the row and column values inside of the DataSet. You're missing one very important component—you don't have anything that links the DataSet (m_ds) to the NpgsqlCommand (m_cmd). You need an adapter; specifically, an NpgsqlDataAdapter.

As I mentioned earlier in this chapter, an NpgsqlDataAdapter class links a DataSet to the database. An NpgsqlDataAdapter object contains a link to a SELECT command (stored inside of an NpgsqlCommand object). To add an NpgsqlDataAdapter to the form, open the Data tab (in the Toolbox) and double-click the NpgsqlDataAdapter tool. Change the name of this object to m_da. To link m_da to a command object, change the SelectCommand property to m_cmd. When the DataAdapter needs a result set from the database, it executes the SelectCommand.

When the user types in a command and presses Ctrl+Enter, you want to copy the command text from the RichTextBox (m_cmdText) to the NpgsqlCommand (m_cmd) and then ask the DataAdapter (m_da) to fill the DataSet (m_ds). To intercept the Ctrl+Enter event, switch to the Code view (right-click on the form and choose View Code), choose m_cmdText from the Class Name list box (that's up at the very top of the Code View window), and select Key Up in the Method Name list box (also at the top of the Code View window). Visual Studio inserts the code for a skeleton subroutine named m_cmdText.KeyUp() and moves your cursor into that code. Add the following code to the m_cmdTextKey() subroutine:

```
If (e.Control() And e.KeyCode = Keys.Enter) Then
    m_cmd.CommandText = m_cmdText.Text
    m_da.Fill(m_ds)
End If
```

Your subroutine should look like Listing 18.2 (I've trimmed out the argument list to fit on the printed page—don't change the argument list that Visual Studio created for you).

Listing 18.2   **Filling a** DataSet

```
1   Private Sub m_cmdText_KeyUp(...) Handles m_cmdText.KeyUp
2     If (e.Control() And e.KeyCode = Keys.Enter) Then
3       m_cmd.CommandText = m_cmdText.Text
4       m_da.Fill(m_ds)
5     End If
6   End Sub
```

The code at line 3 copies the text that the user entered from the RichTextBox (m_cmdText) into the NpgsqlCommand object (m_cmd). The call to m_da.Fill() (see line 4) fills the DataSet (m_ds) with a result set. When you call the Fill() method, the DataAdapter examines its own SelectCommand property to find the appropriate DataCommand object. In this case, m_da.SelectCommand is a reference to the m_cmd command (which holds a reference to the m_conn connection). The DataAdapter asks m_cmd to execute itself and then loads the result set into the DataSet.

Go ahead and run this program. Type a SELECT command into the RichTextBox and press Ctrl+Enter. After a short pause (the client has to connect to the database, execute the command that you entered, and read the result set), the DataGrid changes its appearance (see Figure 18.4), but it doesn't display the result set. Click the + in the DataGrid and then choose Table to see the result set.

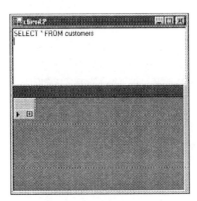

Figure 18.4   A confusing DataGrid.

It's rather annoying that you have to click the DataGrid to see the result set, but there's a good reason that the DataGrid behaves that way. I mentioned earlier that a DataSet can hold *many* result sets, not just one. Since the DataGrid is bound to the DataSet, it doesn't know which result set you want to view. That's why you have to choose. Of course, in this application, this application never adds more than one result set to the `DataSet`, so this behavior isn't very intuitive. Fortunately, this problem is easy to fix. Instead of binding the `DataGrid` to the entire `DataSet`, you can bind the grid to a single result set, but you can't bind the grid until you *have* a result set. That means you have to write some more code: Change the `m_cmdText.KeyUp()` subroutine so that it looks like Listing 18.3.

Listing 18.3   **Binding to a Single Result Set**

```
1  Private Sub m_cmdText_KeyUp(...) Handles m_cmdText.KeyUp
2    If (e.Control() And e.KeyCode = Keys.Enter) Then
3      m_cmd.CommandText = m_cmdText.Text
4      m_da.Fill(m_ds)
5      m_grid.DataSource = m_ds.Tables(0)
6    End If
7  End Sub
```

The only change here is that I've added line 5. By binding the `DataGrid` (`m_grid`) to a single result set (`m_ds.Tables(0)`), the grid knows which result set you want to view and automatically displays that result set as soon as its ready.

Run this client again and you'll see that it behaves better. But there's still one problem. Execute two (or more) queries and the result sets are co-mingled. Figure 18.5 shows the problem—I've executed two commands (`SELECT * FROM customers` and `SELECT * FROM tapes`). The first four grid rows display the first result set and the last five rows display the second result set. When you `Fill()` a `DataSet`, the old data is *not* removed. Instead, the `Fill()` method searches through the `DataSet` to find a result set with the same name and adds the new data to that result set. Since we're creating anonymous (unnamed) result sets in this application, the `DataSet` makes up a name. The problem is that the `DataSet` always comes up with the same name (`Table`), even if the *shape* of the new result set differs. When you `Fill()` the `DataSet` the first time, it ends up in a result set named `Table`. When you add the second result set, it's also named `Table` and the `DataSet` merges the new data into the existing `Table`. If the shape of the new result set differs (in other words, if the columns are different), the `DataSet` adds `NULL` values to each result set to morph them into the same shape.

This problem is easy to fix, too. In fact, you can solve the problem in two different ways. First, you could assign a unique name to each result set by passing the name to the `Fill()` method. For example, the following code snippet increments a counter and assigns the counters current value (in string form) to each result set:

```
...
   m_queryCounter += 1
   m_da.Fill(m_ds, m_queryCounter.ToString())
...
```

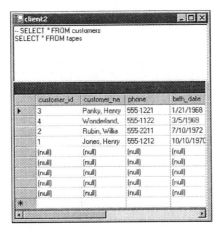

Figure 18.5 Another confusing DataGrid.

That method works, but the DataSet grows and grows as you execute more queries. Instead, you can discard the old DataSet and create a new one as you execute each query. Listing 18.4 shows a slightly modified version of m_cmdText.KeyUp():

Listing 18.4   Creating a New DataSet

```
1   Private Sub m_cmdText_KeyUp(...) Handles m_cmdText.KeyUp
2     If (e.Control() And e.KeyCode = Keys.Enter) Then
3       m_cmd.CommandText = m_cmdText.Text
4       m_ds = New DataSet
4       m_da.Fill(m_ds)
5       m_grid.DataSource = m_ds.Tables(0)
6     End If
7   End Sub
```

This version creates a new DataSet for each query. The old DataSet is simply lost (and eventually reclaimed by the VB garbage collector). When you run this program, you can execute query after query and you get a new DataSet each time. Since you bind the DataGrid to each new DataSet, the grid displays the result set returned by the most recent query.

Client 3—Updating the Database with a DataSet

The third client that I want to show you is based on client2—you can keep all of the work that you put into laying out a nice-looking application and just add a few lines of VB code here and there. client3 looks very much like client2—it's a general purpose interactive query processor—but client3 lets you *change* the result set data displayed in the grid and write those changes back to the database. I'll add two buttons (`Commit` and `Rollback`) but those buttons remain disabled until you change a value in the grid (see Figure 18.6).

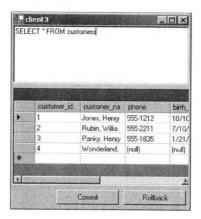

Figure 18.6   The `client3` application.

To start, make room for two buttons near the bottom of the form (you may have to drag the `DataGrid` to a new location before you can get to the bottom of the grid). Now add the `Rollback` button to the lower-right corner of the form: Open the Windows Forms tab (in the Toolbox), click the `Button` tool, and drag out a rectangle where you want the button to live. Change the name of the button to `m_rollback` and change the `Text` property to `Rollback`. When the user clicks the `Rollback` button, `client3` will discard all changes. It's a little misleading to show the user a button named `Rollback` when he hasn't actually made any changes, so set `m_rollback`'s `Enabled` property to `False`. (We'll enable the button as soon as the user makes a change.) Add a second button named `m_commit` and change its `Text` property to `Commit`. When the user clicks this button, `client3` will (try to) save all changes back to the database. Again, we'll enable this button when the user changes a value in the grid, so set `m_commit`'s `Enabled` property to `False`.

When the user clicks the `Rollback` button (and the button has been enabled), `client3` discards all changes made to the `DataSet` (`m_ds`). This would probably be a good time to remind you that the `DataGrid` is bound to the `DataSet` and that the binding works in both directions. If you change a value in the `DataSet`, that change is reflected in the `DataGrid` (that is, the user sees the new value). If the user changes a value in the grid, that change is reflected in the `DataSet`. To discard all changes recorded in the `DataSet`, just call `m_ds.RejectChanges()`. `RejectChanges()` throws out any changes that you've made to the `DataSet` since the most recent call to `RejectChanges()`, `AcceptChanges()`, or `Update()`. You want to invoke

RejectChanges() when the Rollback button fires off a Click event. Double-click the Rollback button and add the code shown in Listing 18.5 to the subroutine that Visual Basic creates for you. (I've trimmed the argument list again to make this subroutine fit on the printed page.)

Listing 18.5   **Rejecting DataSet Modifications**

```
1 Private Sub m_revert_Click(...) Handles m_revertChanges.Click
2   m_ds.RejectChanges()
3 End Sub
```

When the user clicks the Commit button (and the button has been enabled), client3 tries to write all changes back to the database. The code that implements the Commit button is a bit more complex than the code you added for the Rollback function. The Commit button may have to execute INSERT commands (if the user added new rows), DELETE commands (if the user deleted any rows), and UPDATE commands (if the user changed any values). The DataSet keeps track of the modification state for each row in the result set(s) and you can inspect that state by looking at m_ds.Tables(0).Rows(rowNumber).RowState.

Fortunately, you don't have to read through the DataSet yourself—a DataAdapter (m_da) can take care of that for you. You may recall (from the previous client application) that a DataAdapter connects a DataSet to a database. The DataAdapter.Fill() method fills the DataSet each time the user executes a new query. A DataAdapter can move data in the other direction (from the DataSet to the database), too. The DataAdapter.Update() method reads through all of the DataRows in the DataSet, inspects the RowState, and executes an INSERT, DELETE, or UPDATE command (as appropriate) to write the modifications back to the database.

A DataAdapter (specifically, an NpgsqlDataAdapter) can hold a reference to four different DataCommand objects: a SelectCommand, an InsertCommand, an UpdateCommand, and a DeleteCommand. When the user clicks the Commit button, your DataAdapter (m_da) holds a reference to a SelectCommand (the command entered by the user), but the other three command references are empty. Npgsql has a class that can build the INSERT, UPDATE, and DELETE commands for you: the NpgsqlCommandBuilder. An NpgsqlCommandBuilder object performs its magic by examining the layout of a DataRow. For example, if you have an NpgsqlCommandBuilder named builder, you can extract an UPDATE command like this:

```
updateCommand = builder.GetUpdateCommand( m_ds.Tables(0).Rows(0) )
```

GetUpdateCommand() reads through each DataColumn in the given row (m_ds.Tables(0).Rows(0)) and builds an UPDATE command from the column names (and data types) that it finds. If m_ds.Tables(0) contained a row from the customers table, for example, GetUpdateCommand() would build a command similar to the one shown in Listing 18.6[1].

Listing 18.6 **An Automatic** UpdateCommand

```
UPDATE customers SET
    customer_id   = :s_customer_id,
    customer_name = :s_customer_name,
    phone         = :s_phone,
    birth_date    = :s_birth_date,
    balance       = :s_balance
  WHERE
    customer_id   = :w_customer_id AND
    customer_name = :w_customer_name AND
    phone         = :w_phone AND
    birth_date    = :w_birth_date AND
    balance       = :w_balance
```

Now that you have most of the pieces of the puzzle, you're ready to write the commit_Click() subroutine. This subroutine (see Listing 18.7) is called when the user clicks the Commit button.

Listing 18.7 **Committing** DataSet **Modifications**

```
1   Private Sub m_commitChanges_Click(...) Handles m_commitChanges.Click
2     Dim builder As Npgsql.NpgsqlCommandBuilder
3
4     builder = New Npgsql.NpgsqlCommandBuilder(m_da)
5
6     m_da.InsertCommand = builder.GetInsertCommand(m_ds.Tables(0).Rows(0))
7     m_da.DeleteCommand = builder.GetDeleteCommand(m_ds.Tables(0).Rows(0))
8     m_da.UpdateCommand = builder.GetUpdateCommand(m_ds.Tables(0).Rows(0))
9
10    m_da.Update(m_ds)
11    m_commitChanges.Enabled = False
12    m_revertChanges.Enabled = False
13    End Sub
```

There's only one step left to complete this client: Enable the Commit and Rollback buttons when the user changes a value in the DataGrid. An object of type DataSet fires a series of events when you modify one of the values that it holds. We'll create a handler

---

1. The :s_customer_id, :s_customer_name, :w_customer_id, :w_customer_id stuff tells you where the DataAdapter will substitute named parameter values to arrive at the actual command.

for the `Commit_Changed` event and tell VB to call that handler whenever your `DataSet` (`m_ds`) fires that event. The handler (see Listing 18.8) simply sets the `Enabled` property for each button.

Listing 18.8   **Enabling** `Commit` **and** `Rollback` **Buttons**

```
1   Private Sub Column_Changed(...)
2     m_commitChanges.Enabled = True
3     m_revertChanges.Enabled = True
4   End Sub
```

To wire this subroutine into the VB event handling scheme, you must execute an `AddHandler` command, but knowing when to execute that command is a bit tricky. Look back at Listing 18.4 ("Creating a New DataSet"). That subroutine (`m_cmdText_KeyUp`) takes care of creating a new `DataSet` and filling that `DataSet` with a result set built from the command that the user typed in. Because you're creating a new `DataSet` for each command, you'll have to add the `Column_Changed` event handler to each `DataSet`. The new version of `m_cmdText_KeyUp` is shown in Listing 18.9 (the only difference is that I've added an `AddHandler` command at line 7).

Listing 18.9   **Handling** `Column_Changed` **Events**

```
1   Private Sub m_cmdText_KeyUp(...) Handles m_cmdText.KeyUp
2     If (e.Control() And e.KeyCode = Keys.Enter) Then
3       m_cmd.CommandText = m_cmdText.Text
4       m_ds = New Dataset
5       m_da.Fill(m_ds)
6       m_grid.DataSource = m_ds.Tables(0)
7
8       AddHandler m_ds.Tables(0).ColumnChanged, AddressOf Column_Changed
9     End If
10  End Sub
```

That's it. You have a client application that lets you enter SELECT commands, view the results, *change* the results, and write those changes back to the database.

Go ahead and try it out—type in a few queries, change the result set, and check out the `Commit` and `Rollback` buttons. When you've had enough fun, I'll show you a few problems with the way I've designed `client3`, and (better yet) I'll show you how to fix them.

Client 4—A More Robust Query Processor

In `client4`, I'll show you how to handle three different problems that you'll eventually find in the `client3` application:

- If the user executes a command that fails for some reason (syntax error, table doesn't exist, and so on), client3 throws an unhandled exception and the program gets so embarrassed that it terminates.

- If the user executes a command other than SELECT, the command completes, but the application throws another one of those embarrassing unhandled exceptions.

- If the user clicks the Commit button and something goes wrong during the Update(), some changes *may be* recorded to the database and others *may not*.

It's easy to replicate the first problem—just type in a nonsense command and press Ctrl+Enter. It's just as easy to fix: Wrap the code that executes the command in a Try/Catch block. Of course, if something goes wrong (that is, if the Catch clause actually catches an exception), you'll want to display the error message somewhere. I'll add a StatusBar control to the bottom of the client4 window (client4 starts out as a carbon copy of client3) and display the error message there. To add a StatusBar, open the Windows Forms tab (in the Toolbox) and double-click the StatusBar tool. Visual Studio automatically places the StatusBar at the bottom of the form. (You may have to scooch the Commit and Rollback buttons a bit to make room for the StatusBar.) Change the name of the StatusBar to m_statusBar and set the Text property to Ready.

With a StatusBar in place, you're ready to Catch the exception that's thrown when a user executes an invalid command. In this application, you're never executing the user's command directly—instead, a DataAdapter executes the command when you call the Fill() method (to fill up a DataSet). That means that you want to wrap the invocation of the Fill() method (since the exception is thrown from inside of that method). Listing 18.10 shows a new version of the m_cmdText_KeyUp() subroutine.

Listing 18.10   **Intercepting Execution Errors**

```
1  Private Sub m_cmdText_KeyUp(...) Handles m_cmdText.KeyUp
2    If (e.Control() And e.KeyCode = Keys.Enter) Then
3      m_cmd.CommandText = m_cmdText.Text
4      m_ds = New DataSet
5
6      Try
7        m_da.Fill(m_ds)
8        m_grid.DataSource = m_ds.Tables(0)
9        AddHandler m_ds.Tables(0).ColumnChanged, AddressOf Column_Changed
10       m_statusBar.Text = "Ready"
11     Catch ex As Exception
12       m_statusBar.Text = ex.Message
13     End Try
14   End If
15 End Sub
```

I've moved three steps into the Try clause: the call to Fill() (that's the one most likely to throw an exception), binding the DataGrid to the DataSource, and adding an event handler to the DataSet. You want all three steps in the Try clause because you don't want to bind the DataGrid or add an event handler if the Fill() invocation fails. I've also added code (see line 10) to set the StatusBar text to indicate that the command succeeded. That's important because a *previous* command may have placed an error message in the StatusBar. The code inside of the Catch clause (line 12) copies the error message text (it's inside of the ex Exception) into the StatusBar.

That takes care of the first problem without adding too much code. Try it out—if you execute a command that generates an error, you'll see the message appear in the status bar at the bottom of the window.

The second problem is just as easy to replicate and just as easy to fix. As long as you have client4 up and running, try executing a non-query command (ANALYZE customers would be a good choice). When you execute a non-query command, client4 does something very strange: The status bar displays the cryptic message "Cannot find table 0." Where in the world is that message coming from? Take a look at Listing 18.10 again, particularly at line 9. Notice that I'm hooking up an event handler that gets invoked when m_ds.Tables(0) (the first table in the m_ds DataSet) fires off a ColumnChanged event. You see the problem. If you don't execute a SELECT command, the DataSet doesn't *have* a first table (it doesn't hold any tables). It's the code at line 9 that's throwing the exception. Since the exception is thrown within the Try clause, the Catch clause catches it and copies the error message ("Cannot find table 0") to the StatusBar. Makes perfect sense now, doesn't it?

To fix this problem, you'll need a way to differentiate between SELECT commands and all other commands. The Npgsql classes don't provide an obvious way to tell the difference. It would be nice if the NpgsqlCommand object contained a CommandType property that exposed this information that you're looking for, but it doesn't. (Actually, an NpgsqlCommand object *does* have a CommandType property, but it's used for something completely different.) If you think back to the error message we're dealing with, you may see the solution. The error message states "Cannot find table 0" when you've execute a command other than SELECT. That means that, if you execute a command other than SELECT, the DataSet won't contain any tables. If m_ds.Tables.Count > 0, you've executed a SELECT command. If m_ds.Tables.Count = 0, you've executed some other command.

Listing 18.11 shows a modified version of the m_cmdText_KeyUp() subroutine (the last version, I promise).

Listing 18.11 **Intercepting Execution Errors**

```
1   Private Sub m_cmdText_KeyUp(...) Handles m_cmdText.KeyUp
2     If (e.KeyCode = Keys.Enter And e.Control) Then
3       m_cmd.CommandText = m_cmdText.Text
4       m_ds = New DataSet
5
```

Listing 18.11 **Continued**

```
6        Try
7          m_da.Fill(m_ds)
8
9          If (m_ds.Tables.Count = 0) Then
10           m_grid.Hide()
11           m_statusBar.Text = "Ok"
12         Else
13           m_grid.DataSource = m_ds.Tables(0)
14           m_grid.Show()
15           m_statusBar.Text = "Ready"
16           AddHandler m_ds.Tables(0).ColumnChanged, AddressOf Column_Changed
17         End If
18
19         Catch ex As Exception
20           m_statusBar.Text = ex.Message
21         End Try
22    End If
23 End Sub
```

At line 9, this subroutine inspects the m_ds.Tables.Count property. If it finds that there are no tables in the result set, it hides the DataGrid (line 10) and writes Ok into the StatusBar. If the result set *does* contain a table, the Else clause binds the DataGrid to the DataSet, displays the DataGrid (in case it's been hidden by a prior command), writes Ready into the StatusBar, and wires up the ColumnChanged event handler.

The last problem is a bit more complex to replicate and a bit more complex to resolve. To see the problem, fire up client4 and execute the command SELECT * FROM customers. (That command should return at least three or four rows.) Now start another PostgreSQL client application (you could start a second instance of client4 if you like) and execute the command UPDATE customers SET balance = 16.16 WHERE customer_id = 3. The first session is displaying the content of the m_ds DataSet (that is, it's displaying the result of the SELECT * FROM customers query). The second session has just modified *one* of the rows in the customers table. Now go back to the first session, change the phone_number for customer_id 3, and click Commit. The m_commitChanges_Click() subroutine tries to Update() the DataSet based on the contents of the DataGrid. But the DataGrid holds stale data—you've modified the balance for customer_id 3 in another session. If the Update() method succeeds, you'll lose that modification. Instead, the Update() method throws an exception (Concurrency Violation: the UpdateCommand affected 0 rows) when it tries to update customer_id 3. To understand *why* the Update() method fails, look back to the UPDATE command shown in Listing 18.6 ("An Automatic Update Command"). That UPDATE command was generated by an NpgsqlCommandBuilder object and it *fails* because the WHERE clause refers to every column in the table. The WHERE clause looks something like this:

```
WHERE
  customer_id   = 3 AND
  customer_name = 'Panky, Henry' AND
  phone         = '555-1221' AND
  birth_date    = '1968-01-21' AND
  balance       = 0.00
```

The WHERE clause won't match any of the rows in the customers table because you've changed the balance in another session (which explains the message UpdateCommand affected 0 rows).

The obvious way to fix this problem is to wrap the invocation of m_da.Update(m_ds) inside of a Try/Catch block. That works fine if you've only modified a single row in the DataGrid. But what happens if you've modified *two* (or more) rows in the DataGrid and one of the UPDATE statements fails? Some changes are written to the database and others aren't. The obvious way to fix *that* problem is to wrap the call to m_da.Update(m_ds) in a transaction, wrap the transaction in a Try/Catch block, and ROLLBACK the transaction if you catch an exception. That ensures that the database is consistent (all modifications are written to the database or none of the modifications are written to the database), but there's still a problem. The DataSet is keeping track of the modification state of each row in the DataTable. When you call the Update() method, it walks through each row in the DataTable, eyeballs the modification state, and executes an INSERT, UPDATE, or DELETE command if the modification state demands. If the INSERT, UPDATE, or DELETE command succeeds, Update() resets the modification state to indicate that the row is Unchanged and moves on to the next row. If one of the INSERT, UPDATE, or DELETE commands fails, Update() throws an exception and you ROLLBACK the entire transaction. The modification states stored in the DataSet are completely befuddled. Update() has changed *some* modification states to Unchanged even though those rows have not in fact been committed.

As I said earlier, the fix for this problem is a bit complex. The important point is that you must *retain* the modification states stored in the DataSet just in case you have to ROLLBACK an aborted transaction. Listing 18.12 shows a modified version of the m_commitChanges_Click()—I'll walk you through the changes in a moment.

Listing 18.12 **Intercepting Execution Errors**

```
1   Private Sub m_commitChanges_Click(...) Handles m_commitChanges.Click
2     Dim builder As Npgsql.NpgsqlCommandBuilder
3
4     builder = New Npgsql.NpgsqlCommandBuilder(m_da)
5
6     m_da.InsertCommand = builder.GetInsertCommand(m_ds.Tables(0).Rows(0))
7     m_da.UpdateCommand = builder.GetUpdateCommand(m_ds.Tables(0).Rows(0))
8     m_da.DeleteCommand = builder.GetDeleteCommand(m_ds.Tables(0).Rows(0))
9
10    If (m_conn.State <> ConnectionState.Open) Then
```

Listing 18.12 **Continued**

```
11      m_conn.Open()
12   End If
13
14   Dim transact As Npgsql.NpgsqlTransaction
15
16   transact = m_conn.BeginTransaction()
17
18   m_da.InsertCommand.Transaction = transact
19   m_da.UpdateCommand.Transaction = transact
20   m_da.DeleteCommand.Transaction = transact
21
22   Dim changes As DataTable = m_ds.Tables(0).GetChanges()
23
24   Try
25     m_da.Update(changes)
26     transact.Commit()
27
28     m_ds.AcceptChanges()
29     m_commitChanges.Enabled = False
30     m_revertChanges.Enabled = False
31   Catch ex As Exception
32     transact.Rollback()
33     MessageBox.Show(ex.Message, "Update Failed")
34   End Try
35 End Sub
```

The first eight lines of this version are identical to the previous version: You're creating an NpgsqlCommandBuilder object and extracting the required INSERT, UPDATE, and DELETE, commands from it. The first change appears at lines 10–12. If the database connection (m_conn) is not open, the call to m_conn.Open() opens it. (You need an open connection to create a new transaction and there's no guarantee that the connection is still open when you reach this subroutine.)

At line 14, you're creating a new transaction (an object of type NpgsqlTransaction). As you can see, you create a transaction by calling the BeginTransaction() method defined by an open NpgsqlConnection.

The BeginTransaction() method returns a reference to a transaction object and the code at lines 18 through 20 binds the INSERT, UPDATE, and DELETE commands to that transaction. When you invoke the m_da.Update() method, it will execute the INSERT, UPDATE, and DELETE commands within the transaction that you've created.

The transaction part of this subroutine is straightforward. To COMMIT the transaction, you'll call transact.Commit(). To ROLLBACK the transaction, you'll call transact.Rollback(). But we haven't solved the modification state mangling problem yet. Remember, you must retain the modification states stored in the DataSet just in case you have to ROLLBACK the transaction. The easiest way to retain the modification states for each row is to make a copy of each row before you call Update(). You *could* copy the rows by cloning (or copying) the DataTable that you find in the DataSet (m_ds.Tables(0)), but that's actually more than you need. You only need to copy the DataRows that have changed. The DataTable class provides a method, GetChanges(), that returns a new DataTable that contains a copy of all DataRows with a modification state of Added, Deleted, or Modified. The code you see at line 22 invokes the GetChanges() method and assigns the result to a new DataTable named changes.

At line 25, I've changed the call to m_da.Update(). In the previous version, I called the Update() method with a DataSet argument (m_ds). That applied all modifications found in the DataSet. In this version, I'm asking Update() to apply all modifications found in the changes DataTable. If the Update() succeeds, you can COMMIT the transaction (line 26). At this point, the Update() method has reset all of the modification states in the changes DataTable, but the modification states in the DataSet (m_ds) still claim that some rows have been modified. The call to AcceptChanges() (line 28) resets all of the modification states in m_ds. So far, so good.

If the call to Update() fails, you can ROLLBACK the transaction (see line 32). Since the Update() method applied all modifications found in the changes DataTable (as opposed to the m_ds DataSet), the modifications states in the DataSet are still correct. (They still tell you which rows have been modified.) The user can (try to) correct the problem (probably in a concurrent session) and try to COMMIT his changes again.

Client 5—Using a Typed DataSet

The VB clients that you've seen so far have used untyped DataSets to manage data retrieved from a PostgreSQL server. Untyped DataSets are useful when you don't know the structure of the data at the time you create an application. In most cases, you *will* know the layout of the data that you're working with so a typed (or strong) DataSet is more useful. A typed DataSet exposes data in the form of objects. An untyped DataSet exposes data in the form of a group of collections.

For example, if you load a copy of the customers table into an untyped DataSet, you'll find that the DataSet contains a collection of DataTable objects (in this case, the collection contains a single DataTable). That DataTable contains a collection of DataColumn objects (one DataColumn for each column in the customers table) that describe the columns in the DataTable. The DataTable also contains a collection of DataRow objects (one DataRow object for each row read from the customers table). To access the customers table (within the DataSet), you would refer to DataSet.Tables(0). To access a row within the customers table, you would write DataSet.Tables(0).Rows(5). To access a value within a row (within the customers table), you would write DataSet.Tables(0).Rows(5).Items(2).

On the other hand, if you load a copy of the customers table into a (properly) typed DataSet, you would find that the DataSet contains a member named customers.

customers is a an extension (subclass) of the DataTable class. Inside of the customers object, you'll find a DataColumn named columncustomer_id, a DataColumn named columncustomer_name, a DataColumn named columnphone, and so on. Each DataColumn describes the corresponding column. The customers object (inside of the DataSet) also contains a collection of Items. Each member of the Items collection is an object of type customersRow and contains a single row from the database. An object of type customersRow contains (among other things) an Integer member named customer_id, a String member named customer_balance, a Date member named birth_date, and so on.

A typed DataSet is a class derived from DataSet. A typed DataTable is a class derived from DataTable. That means that you can still access the tables within a typed DataSet through the Rows collection, you can still access the DataColumns within a typed DataTable through the Columns collection, and you can still access the DataRows within a typed DataTable through the Rows collection. But your code will be much more readable (and much more resilient in the face of schema changes) if you access the named (and strongly typed) objects instead.

To demonstrate the power offered by typed DataSets, I'll show you one more VB.NET client application. This client (client5) displays a row from the customers table in a form (see Figure 18.7). client5 loads a typed DataSet with the result set of the query SELECT * FROM customers ORDER BY customer_id. The ListBox that you see on the left side of the window is bound to the customer_name member of the DataSet. The other fields, Customer ID, Customer Name, Phone, and so on, are bound to other strongly typed members of the DataSet. As you scroll through the customer names in the ListBox, the other fields follow along. And it only takes six lines of code.

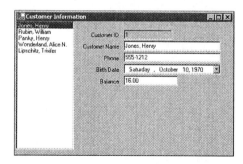

Figure 18.7   The client5 application.

Before you can create this application, you need a typed DataSet. In the last segment of this chapter, I'll show you a tool (included in the source code for this book) that will generate a typed DataSet for any PostgreSQL table. You can skip ahead to that section to generate your own typed DataSet or you can use the DataSet that comes with the source code for this book. You'll find both (the tool and the typed DataSet) in the ch18 subdirectory.

Once you have the typed DataSet loaded on your computer, create a new VB project and add a reference to the Npgsql.dll library (just like you've done for the other clients in this chapter).

Next, add the typed DataSet to the project. The tools that I've used to produce the customers typed DataSet create two separate files, and the project requires both files. The first file is named customers.xsd and it's an XML description of the customers table (in fact, customers.xsd is an XMLSchema). The second file is named customers.vb—it's a VB source file that defines the customers DataTable, the customersRow DataRow, and so on. To add the DataSet files to the project, open the Project menu and click Add Existing Item. When the Add Existing Item finder appears, navigate to the directory that holds the typed DataSet, select the customers.vb file and the customers.xsd file (hold down the Ctrl key to select multiple files), and then click Open. Visual Studio reads through both files and adds the new class descriptions (customers, customersRow, and so on) to the project database. Once you've added the typed DataSet to your project, Visual Studio will incorporate the new classes in its IntelliSense code-completion mechanism.

Now you're ready to create a typed DataSet object. Open the Data tab (in the Toolbox window) and double-click the DataSet tool. When the Add DataSet dialog appears choose Typed DataSet and select customerForm._public from the drop-down list box. Change the name of the new DataSet to m_dsPublic. You may be wondering why the typed DataSet is named public instead of customers. A DataSet can hold more than one table. If you added the rentals and tapes tables to the DataSet, you'd have to come up with a distinct name for the DataSet (distinct from the names of the tables within the DataSet). The tool that I've used to create the typed DataSet assigns the PostgreSQL schema name (public in this case) to the DataSet.

Add a new NpgsqlConnection object, change its name to m_conn, and fill in the ConnectionString property. client5 uses this connection to interact with the PostgreSQL server.

Add a new NpgsqlCommand object, changes its name to m_cmd, and set the Connection property to m_conn. That links the new command object (m_cmd) to the connection object that you created in the previous step (m_conn). In the earlier client applications, the user typed in the text of each query. In this application, you know, at design time, that you want to display all customers, so you can formulate the query now. Set the CommandText property to SELECT * FROM customers ORDER BY customer_id. client5 will execute this command when the form loads.

Add a new NpgsqlDataAdapter object, change its name to m_da, and set the SelectCommand property to m_cmd. That links the new adapter to the command object that you created in the previous step. This DataAdapter will fill the m_dsPublic DataSet by executing the query stored in the m_cmd command object.

Double-click the form background and add the code shown in Listing 18.13 to the Form1_Load() subroutine.

Listing 18.13 **Filling a Typed** DataSet

```
1  Private Sub Form1_Load(...) Handles MyBase.Load
2    Try
3      m_da.Fill(m_dsPublic, "customers")
4    Catch ex As ConstraintException
5
6    Catch ex As Exception
7      MessageBox.Show(ex.Message, "Query Failed")
8    End Try
9 End Sub
```

The Form1_Load() subroutine executes as soon as the client5 application starts. The call to m_da.Fill() fills the m_dsPublic DataSet by executing the query contained in m_da.SelectCommand (which happens to be a reference to m_cmd). You may have noticed that there's an extra argument in this invocation of Fill(). (The invocations you've seen in the previous clients supplied a single argument.) The second argument tells Fill() *which* DataTable to load in the m_dsPublic DataSet. If you don't provide a table name, Fill() makes one up. If you do that, the DataSet will contain *two* DataTables: an empty customers DataTable and an untyped DataTable named Table. (Fill()'s not very original when it comes to making up table names.)

Notice that the call to Fill() is wrapped in a complex Try/Catch block. The first Catch clause will intercept any ConstraintException exceptions thrown by Fill(). Fill() will throw a ConstraintException exception when it finds a NULL value in a column that prohibits NULL values. You may be thinking that you'll never run into that sort of problem because the PostgreSQL server won't let you store a NULL value in a column that prohibits NULL values. Unfortunately, the Npgsql typed DataSet generator isn't smart enough to figure which columns allow NULL values and which columns prohibit NULL values. Instead, Npgsql assumes that every column prohibits NULL values. That means that Fill() will throw an exception if it encounters *any* NULL values. I've included an empty Catch clause so that VB will ignore ConstraintException errors. If you prefer, you can modify the DataColumn objects in the customers DataTable before calling Fill(), like this:

```
...
m_dsPublic.customers.phoneColumn.AllowDBNull      = True
m_dsPublic.customers.birth_dateColumn.AllowDBNull = True
m_dsPublic.customers.balanceColumn.AllowDBNull    = True
m_da.Fill(m_dsPublic, "customers")
...
```

If Fill() throws any other type of exception, the code at line 7 displays an error message to the user.

At this point, you're ready to create the user-interface for this application. Open the Windows Forms tab (in the Toolbox window), select the ListBox tool, and drag out a rectangle that covers the left third of the form. Change the name of the new ListBox to m_customerList. This ListBox will display customer names. You don't have to write any code to manage the ListBox; you simply bind it to the DataSet. Binding a ListBox is a two-step process—you bind the control itself to a DataSet, and then bind the Text property to a particular column within the DataSet. Change the DataSource property (in the DataBindings section of the Properties window) to m_dsPublic. That binds the ListBox to the m_dsPublic DataSet. Now click the DisplayMember property. The drop-down list displays the columns defined in the customers table. Choose customer_name. That tells the ListBox (which is bound to the customers table) to display the customer_column column of each row in the DataSet.

If you run the application at this point, you'll see that the ListBox displays the customer names stored in the customers table. Close the application and you can start painting the rest of the form.

Click the Label tool (in the Windows Forms tab), drag out a rectangle on the form, and change the Text to Customer ID. (You can change the object name too, but you don't define Label names in a typical application unless you have to refer to a Label in the code.)

Click the TextBox tool, drag out a rectangle to the right of the Customer ID label, and change the name of the new control to m_customerID. The m_customerID TextBox will display the customer_id value of the current row (that is, the row selected in the m_customerList ListBox). Change the DataBindings.Text property to m_dsPublic - customers.customer_id. That binds the Text property (that is, the string displayed in the TextBox) to the customer_id column.

Follow the same procedure to add Label and TextBox for the customer_name, phone, birthdate, and balance columns. Be sure to bind each control to the appropriate member of the m_dsPublic.customers DataTable.

You may want to bind the birth_date column to a DateTimePicker instead of binding to a TextBox. Because m_dsPublic.customers.birth_date is strongly typed (it's a Date object), you can wire it up to a DateTimePicker control or to a MonthCalendar control. That's another advantage to using a typed DataSet instead of an untyped DataSet. The values in the DataTables have real data types. You can treat a date/time value as a DateTime object, or a numeric value as a Decimal object (or Integer as appropriate).

Table 18.2 shows how Npgsql maps PostgreSQL data types into .NET data types.

Table 18.2 PostgreSQL to .NET Data Type Mappings

PostgreSQL Data Type	.NET Data Type
varchar	String
text	String
char	String
bpchar	String
bytea	Byte[]

Table 18.2 **Continued**

PostgreSQL Data Type	.NET Data Type
bool	Boolean
int2	Int16
int4	Int32
int8	Int64
float4	Single
float8	Double
numeric	Decimal
money	Decimal
date	DateTime
time	DateTime
timetz	DateTime
timestamp	DateTime
timestamptz	DateTime
point	Npgsql.NpgsqlPoint
box	Npgsql.NpgsqlBox
lseg	Npgsql.NpgsqlLSeg
path	Npgsql.NpgsqlPath
polygon	Npgsql.NpgsqlPolygon
circle	Npgsql.NpgsqlCircle
anything else	String

When you've finished adding labels and control for each column in the customers table, go ahead and run the application. As you scroll through the customers listed on the left side of the window (in the ListBox), you'll see that the other controls follow along. Not too bad for six lines of code. To complete this application, you may want to add Commit and Rollback buttons and wire them up like you did in the previous application (client4).

You can see that typed DataSets add a lot of power to your application. They also add a lot of power to the Visual Studio development environment. In fact, if you have a typed DataSet that contains more than one table, you can define the relationships between the tables using Visual Studio's graphical schema editor (see Figure 18.8).

Creating a Typed DataSet

The sample source code for this book includes a VB.NET project named GenDataSet that you can use to generate a typed DataSet for any PostgreSQL table. Figure 18.9 shows this application in action.

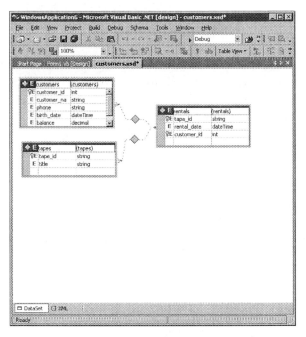

Figure 18.8   The Visual Studio Schema Editor.

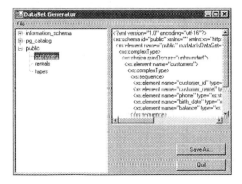

Figure 18.9   The GenDataSet application.

I won't explain the entire application here (it's not very big, but you've seen most of the code already in previous clients). Instead, I'll describe two subroutines that you'll find in the application.

The first subroutine, LoadTree(), loads the TreeView control that you see on the left side of the window. A TreeView control is perfect when you need to display hierarchical information. In this case, the TreeView displays a list of the tables defined in a

PostgreSQL database, grouped into schemas. My database contains three schemas (information_schema, pg_catalog, and public) so you see three *nodes* at the top of the hierarchy. I've expanded the public node to display the child tables defined in that schema.

Listing 18.14 shows the LoadTree() subroutine.

Listing 18.14 **Loading a** TreeView **Control**

```
1  Private Sub LoadTree()
2    Dim tables        As _public.pg_tablesDataTable
3    Dim table         As _public.pg_tablesRow
4    Dim r             As Integer
5    Dim prevSchemaName As String = ""
6    Dim schemaNode    As TreeNode
7    Dim node          As TreeNode
8
9    tables = m_dsPgTables.pg_tables
10
11   For r = 0 To tables.Rows.Count - 1
12
13     table = tables(r)
14
15     If (table.schemaname <> prevSchemaName) Then
16       prevSchemaName = table.schemaname
17       schemaNode      = m_tvPgTables.Nodes.Add(prevSchemaName)
18     End If
19
20     node      = schemaNode.Nodes.Add(table.tablename)
21     node.Tag = table
22   Next r
23 End Sub
```

To load the TreeView (which is named m_tvPgTables), I'll read through a DataSet (m_dsPgTables) built from the the query SELECT * from pg_tables ORDER by schemaname,tablename. At line 9, I extract a reference to the pg_tables member of the DataSet (just so I have a shorter name to type in). The result (tables) is a typed DataTable. The For loop that covers lines 11 through 22 will iterate through each row in tables. At line 13, I extract a reference to the current row and I end up with an object (table). The table object contains a member named schemaname, a member named tablename, a member named tableowner, and so on: Each member corresponds to a column in the pg_tables view. Because I want to group the tables into separate schemas, I'll need to keep track of three different levels in the TreeView hierarchy. As I read through each table in the result set, I'll add a new node to the TreeView root whenever I encounter a new schema. (Remember, I'm reading pg_tables in schemaname order.) The If statement at line 15 takes care of figuring out when the schema name changes, adds a new node for each schema, and stores a reference (schemaNode) to that node. The code at line 20 adds a new node for each table—every table becomes a child of the most recent schemaNode. Line 21 adds a *tag* to the new node. In .NET-speak, a tag is a property that's reserved for your own private use. (In other words, if you have a chunk of data that you want to associate with a node, create an object to hold the data and store a reference to the object in node.Tag.) As you'll see in a moment, the tag that we assign to the TreeView node gives you a way to get back to the DataRow associated with that node.

You can follow a similar procedure to populate any TreeView with a hierarchy of data. Just be sure to sort the result set in the proper order and keep a reference to the most recently added parent node(s).

The last subroutine I'd like to show you takes care of generating an XML DataSet. The m_tvPgTables.AfterSelect() subroutine (shown in Listing 18.15) is invoked when you click on a table name displayed in the TreeView.

Listing 18.15 Creating an XMLSchema (a Typed DataSet)

```
1   Private Sub m_tvPgTables_AfterSelect(...)Handles m_tvPgTables.AfterSelect
2     If (e.Node.Tag Is Nothing) Then
3       Exit Sub
4     End If
6
7     Dim table      As public.pg_tablesRow = e.Node.Tag
8     Dim da         As Npgsql.NpgsqlDataAdapter
9     Dim tableName  As String = table.tablename
10    Dim schemaName As String = table.schemaname
11    Dim query      As String
12
13    query = "SELECT * FROM " + schemaName + "." + tableName + " LIMIT 0"
14    da    = New Npgsql.NpgsqlDataAdapter(query, m_conn)
15
16    m_ds = New DataSet
17    da.FillSchema(m_ds, SchemaType.Source)
18
19    m_ds.DataSetName        = schemaName
20    m_ds.Tables(0).TableName = tableName
21    m_dsXML.Text            = m_ds.GetXmlSchema()
22    m_currentTableName      = tableName
23  End Sub
```

This subroutine translates a pg_tablesRow into an XML schema definition (which .NET abbreviates as XSD). When this subroutine is invoked, e.Node contains a reference to the node that holds the focus in the TreeView. (In other words, e.Node points to the currently selected node.) As you saw in the previous listing, e.Node.Tag points to the pg_tablesRow associated with the selected node. Once you have a reference to the pg_tablesRow, you know the name of the table (table.tablename)and the schema in which the resides (table.schemaname).

The easiest way to discover the layout of the selected table is to construct and execute a query that nabs every column in the table. We don't really need any of the data here, just the metadata. Line 13 constructs a query guaranteed to return zero rows, but it returns the metadata that we need. (The "LIMIT 0" clause ensures that PostgreSQL won't send any rows back to us.)

The code at line 14 creates a new NpgsqlDataAdapter object that uses the query that we just built. Notice that I'm using a new constructor here—in the past, I've always created a NpgsqlDataAdapter using a single-argument constructor. In this case, the constructor turns the query text into an NpgsqlCommand object and stuffs that object into its own SelectCommand property.

Line 16 creates a new (empty) DataSet object. The call to da.FillSchema() (at line 17) executes the SelectCommand and copies the resulting metadata into the m_ds DataSet.

At this point, m_ds is a DataSet that contains the metadata for a single table, but the DataSet name and table name are incorrect. (The DataSet is named "NewDataSet and m_ds.Tables(0) is named "Table".) We want to produce a typed DataSet whose name matches the name of the schema where the table resides. The code at line 19 copies the schemaName into the DataSet. We want the typed DataSet to contain a table whose name matches the table that we're defining, so the code at line 20 copies the tableName into the first table in the DataSet. If you created a typed DataSet for the customers table (which is defined in the public schema), you'll end up with a DataSet named public that contains a single DataTable named customers.

Line 21 is where the real magic occurs. The call to m_ds.GetXmlSchema() returns the XmlSchema for every table in the m_ds DataSet. (There's only one DataTable in there at this point.) Sort of anticlimactic isn't it? You call one function and you get back a complete schema definition. The rest of the GenDataSet application takes care of writing the XmlSchema (it's just a String at this point) to a text file so you can import it into a Visual Studio project.

Just in case you're wondering what an XmlSchema looks like, here's the schema generated for the customers table:

```
<?xml version="1.0" encoding="utf-8"?>
<xs:schema id="public" xmlns="" xmlns:xs="http://www.w3.org/2001/XMLSchema"
  xmlns:msdata="urn:schemas-microsoft-com:xml-msdata">
  <xs:element name="public" msdata:IsDataSet="true">
    <xs:complexType>
      <xs:choice maxOccurs="unbounded">
        <xs:element name="customers">
          <xs:complexType>
            <xs:sequence>
              <xs:element name="customer_id" type="xs:int" />
              <xs:element name="customer_name" type="xs:string" />
              <xs:element name="phone" type="xs:string" />
```

```
            <xs:element name="birth_date" type="xs:dateTime" />
            <xs:element name="balance" type="xs:decimal" />
        </xs:sequence>
      </xs:complexType>
    </xs:element>
  </xs:choice>
</xs:complexType>
</xs:element>
</xs:schema>
```

If you have an XmlSchema stored in a file (XmlSchema filenames typically end with .xsd), you only have half of a solution. You still need a .NET class the defines the DataTable and DataRow extensions. Fortunately, Visual Studio comes with a tool that will generate such a class file for you: xsd. To produce a class file from a .xsd file, run the following command:

```
C:\> xsd /language:vb /dataset data-set-name.xsd
```

For example, to convert the customers.xsd file into a customers.vb class file, execute the following command:

```
C:\> xsd /language:vb /dataset customers.xsd
Microsoft (R) Xml Schemas/DataTypes support utility
[Microsoft (R) .NET Framework, Version 1.1.4322.573]
Copyright (C) Microsoft Corporation 1998-2002. All rights reserved.

Writing file 'C:\customers.vb'.
```

Now you have a schema description (customers.xsd) and a class file (customers.vb) that contains the source code for a typed DataSet extension named public (which contains a single DataRow extension named customers). And just in case you missed in, see the section titled "Client 5—Using a Typed DataSet" earlier in this chapter to learn how to use both components.

Summary

Visual Basic, Visual Studio, .NET, and ADO.NET are powerful tools that work very well together. The Npgsql .NET data provider fits perfectly in the .NET data architecture. If you have Visual Basic .NET and you're building applications that only need to run on Windows, you can use these tools to build robust client applications in very little time.

If you're building applications that must run on platforms other than Windows, you can still use the .NET architecture and the Npgsql data provider. The Mono project is an open-source implementation of the .NET tools and framework. Mono runs on a number of different operating systems (Linux, Apple's OS X, BSD, and Windows) and you can build a .NET application on one platform and run it on all others without recompiling. Mono does not include all of the .NET framework components, but the number of classes packaged with Mono is increasing every day. You can find more information about Mono at www.go-mono.com.

Other Useful Programming Tools

I N THE LAST FEW CHAPTERS, we've described some of the more popular programming interfaces and procedural languages that you can use with PostgreSQL. It seems that new PostgreSQL friendly APIs, tools, and even procedural languages appear almost daily. You can find most of "extras" at the gborg.postgresql.org or pgfoundry.org web sites. In this chapter, we'll give you a short introduction to a few of our favorite development packages. You may not have heard of these packages before, or perhaps you have but haven't had a chance to learn about them. This chapter is by no means exhaustive—there are hundreds of projects hosted at the PostgreSQL incubators.

In this chapter, we'll introduce you to PL/Java, a server-side procedural language that lets you write portable functions and stored procedures in Java. We'll also give you a very short peek at pgcurl, a small collection of functions that you can use to upload and download web documents (using HTTP, FTP, secure HTTP, secure FTP, and so on) from *within* a PostgreSQL server. Finally, we'll show you a replacement for the psql client that combines the convenience of the bash shell with the power of a PostgreSQL server.

PL/Java—Writing Stored Procedures in Java

PL/Java is a procedural language. When you write a PL/Java function, you write normal Java code, compile it to bytecode form (that is, compile the source code into a .class file), store the compiled form in a Java archive file (a .jar file), and then load that archive into the database. When you execute a PL/Java function, the PL/Java call handler creates a Java Virtual Machine (JVM) *within* the PostgreSQL server process and then asks the JVM execute the bytecode form of your function. A PL/Java function corresponds to a method of some Java class. Since a PL/Java function *is a* Java method, you can use Java control structures, Java classes, Java data types, Java functions, and Java interfaces. In fact, a PL/Java function (which runs *within* the PostgreSQL server) can interact with the PostgreSQL database through the standard JDBC interface. (PL/Java includes a "loopback" JDBC driver.)

PL/Java is based on the proposed SQL 2003 standard. That means that you can write stored procedures and functions in PL/Java and use the same code (source code or compiled) with any database system that supports the standard (Oracle, Sybase, and possibly others). The PL/Java package includes a set of deployment aids that makes it easy to install and manage server-side functions written in Java. PL/Java *does not* include a Java compiler or a Java Virtual Machine—you must obtain those components from a separate source.

Installing PL/Java

Installing PL/Java is surprisingly easy, but you have to have a few pieces in place first. The PL/Java developers have written a Java-based installer that will move the required class files into place, define PL/Java as a trusted server-side language, and create a repository for your class files. You have to install PL/Java into each database that you create, but you can install PL/Java into the template1 database to automatically include PL/Java in all databases that you create in the future[1].

Before you install PL/Java, you'll need a properly installed and configured Java virtual machine, the PostgreSQL JDBC driver (see Chapter 13, "Using PostgreSQL from a Java Client Application"), and the PL/Java distribution.

Installing PL/Java is currently a three-step process. First, you install the PL/Java call handler into a cluster. Then you configure the postmaster so that it can find the PL/Java components. Finally, you install the PL/Java language, functions, types, and repository into a database. The installation procedure is likely to change in the near future so be sure to check the release notes before you go any further. I'll outline the steps required to install PL/Java version 1.1 on a Linux host (running PostgreSQL version 8.0).

To install the call handler into a cluster, first unpack the PL/Java tarball (you'll find it at gborg.postgresql.org or pgfoundry.org) into a temporary directory. Next, move the PL/Java call handler into the cluster with the following commands:

```
$ mv libpljava.so $(pg_config –pkglibdir)
$ mv pljava.jar $(pg_config –pkglibdir)
```

To configure the postmaster, edit the $PGDATA/postgresql.conf configuration file and add the following entries:

```
custom_variable_classes = 'pljava'
pljava.classpath        = '$libdir/pljava.jar'
```

Now you can restart the postmaster (pg_ctl restart).

Finally, install the PL/Java into the database like this:

```
$ psql -f install.sql movies
CREATE SCHEMA
```

---

1. Every new database is created by making a clone of template1 (or a database of your choice).

```
GRANT
CREATE FUNCTION
...
```

When the `install.sql` script completes, the PL/Java language is ready to use.

To summarize the PL/Java 1.1 installation process:

- Unpack the PL/Java tarball
- Move `libpljava.so` into the PostgreSQL cluster
- Move `pljava.jar` into the PostgreSQL cluster
- Modify `$PGDATA/postgresql.conf` so the Java VM can find the `pljava.jar` file
- Restart the `postmaster`
- Install the PL/Java components into each database

Writing a Simple PL/Java Function

With all of the prerequisites in place, you're ready to write some code. Listing 19.1 shows a simple Java class that computes the factorial of a given number.

Listing 19.1 `MyMath.java`

```
 1 // FileName: MyMath.java
 2
 3 public class MyMath
 4 {
 5   public static int myFactorial( Integer value )
 6     throws IllegalArgumentException
 7   {
 8     if( value == null )
 9       throw new IllegalArgumentException( "argument must not be NULL" );
10
11     int intValue = value.intValue();
12
13     if( intValue < 0 )
14       throw new IllegalArgumentException( "argument must be >= 0" );
15
16     if( intValue == 1 )
17       return( 1 );
18     else
19     {
20       int result;
21
22       result = myFactorial( new Integer( intValue - 1 ));
23       result = result * intValue;
24
```

Listing 19.1   **Continued**

```
25        return( result );
26    }
27  }
28 }
```

The `MyMath` class exports a single static method: `myFactorial( Integer )`. Once
you've compiled and installed this code, you can call the `myFactorial()` method (from a
PostgreSQL client application) like this:

```
movies=# SELECT myFactorial( 5 );
 myfactorial
------------
        120
(1 row)
```

Take a close look at line 5. Notice that `myFactorial()` returns an `int`, but expects an
`Integer` argument. Why two different data types? There's no way to store a `NULL` value
in a non-reference type (such as `int`). If you want an argument (or a return value) that
can hold a `NULL` value, you must use a reference type such as `Integer`. By looking at the
signature for this method, you can tell that it will never return `NULL` (because the return
type, `int`, is a primitive non-reference type) and that it *should* be able to handle a `NULL`
argument (because the argument type, `Integer`, is a reference type).

You should also note that you can `throw` exceptions from a PL/Java function. The
PL/Java call handler catches any unhandled exceptions and translates them into
PostgreSQL errors. For example, if you call the `myFactorial()` function with a `NULL`
argument, the `throw` at line 9 will be handled like this:

```
movies=# SELECT myFactorial( NULL );
ERROR:  java.lang.IllegalArgumentException: argument must not be NULL
```

To install the `MyMath` class (and the `MyMath.myFactorial()` function), I'll first compile
the `MyMath.java` source code:

```
$ javac MyMath.java
```

The Java compiler translates `MyMath.java` into bytecode form and stores the result in a
file named `MyMath.class`. It's possible to install a `.class` file in PostgreSQL, but I'll
show you in a moment that PL/Java prefers to work with Jar (Java Archive) files instead.
To create a jar file named `MyMath.jar`:

```
$ jar -c -f /tmp/MyMath.jar MyMath.class
```

The syntax for the `jar` command is very similar to the syntax for `tar`. In this case, the
`-c` flags tells `jar` to *create* an archive file. The `-f MyMath.jar` option tells jar to store the
archive in a file named `MyMath.jar` (in the current directory). The last argument specifies the name of the `.class` file that I want to store in the archive. (You can list as many
`.class` files as you want.)

At this point, you should have a Java source code file (MyMath.java), a compiled bytecode file (MyMath.class), and a Java archive (MyMath.jar) that contains a copy of MyMath.class. Now it's time to tell PostgreSQL about the MyMath class.

When you add PL/Java to a database, the installer creates a bytecode repository *inside* of the database. Each entry in the repository contains a copy of a jar file, a record of where the jar file came from, and a symbolic name for the jar file. When you invoke a PL/Java function, the PostgreSQL server loads the Java interpreter and creates a Java VM (the VM runs *within* the PostgreSQL server process). To find the bytecode for the function that you've invoked, the VM searches the bytecode repository in your database. To install a jar file into the bytecode repository, invoke the sqlj.install_jar() function (that is, the install_jar() function in the sqlj schema):

```
$ psql movies
movies=# SELECT sqlj.install_jar( 'file:///tmp/MyMath.jar', 'Math', true );
install_jar
-----------

(1 row)
```

The sql.install_jar() function copies /tmp/MyMath.jar into the repository (specifically, into a table named sql.jar_entry) and assigns the symbolic name Math to that entry (the symbolic name is stored in sqlj.jar_repository). The sqlj.install_jar() function expects three arguments: a URL that resolves to a jar file (typically, you call install_jar() with a URL that begins with file:///), a symbolic name for the jar file, and a boolean value that tells PL/Java whether to process the deployment descriptor contained in the jar file. (I'll explain deployment descriptors a little later in this chapter.) You can delete the MyMath.jar and MyMath.class files at this point if you wish.

PL/Java associates a *classpath* with each schema in a database. A classpath is a colon-separated list of jar filenames. (You can include .class files as well.) When the Java VM needs to find the bytecode for a class, it searches through each jar file (and .class file) listed in the classpath, in order, until it finds a match. To assign a classpath to a schema, call the sqlj.set_classpath() function:

```
movies=# SELECT sqlj.set_classpath( 'public', 'Math' );
set_classpath
-------------

(1 row)
```

Now when you invoke a PL/Java function that's defined in the public schema, the Java VM will search the Math jar file for the bytecode form of the function. If you want the Java VM to search through multiple jar files, just list each one in the call to sqlj.set_classpath(). For example, if you want the VM to search through a jar file named Math, and then a jar file named Movies:

```
movies=# SELECT sqlj.set_classpath( 'public', 'Math:Movies' );
set_classpath
-------------

(1 row)
```

Just remember that the `set_classpath()` function expects a list of symbolic names, not the actual jar filenames. You should also remember that the VM searches through each element of the classpath *in order* until it finds the class that you're invoking. That means that if `Math` and `Movies` both define a class named `VersionInfo`, the VM will stop as soon as it finds the first one.

The last step in the process is easy: Tell the PostgreSQL server which class (and method) to invoke when you call the `myFactorial()` function. To do that, execute a `CREATE FUNCTION` command, like this:

```
movies=# CREATE FUNCTION myFactorial( INT ) RETURNS INT AS
movies-#   'MyMath.myFactorial( java.lang.Integer )'
movies-#   LANGUAGE java;
```

Take careful notice of the data types mentioned in the `CREATE FUNCTION` command. The two data types that you see on the first line of the command (`INT` and `INT`) tell the PostgreSQL server what to expect. When you invoke `myFactorial()`, you call it with a single argument of type `INT` and it returns a value of type `INT`. The data type that you see on the second line (`java.lang.Integer`) tells PL/Java what kind of argument is expected by the Java bytecode. The Java data type serves two purposes. First, it tells the PL/Java call handler how to convert the PostgreSQL `INT` value into the form required by the method that you're defining. (That is, you're telling PL/Java to convert the `INT` argument into a `java.lang.Integer` value.) Second, the Java VM combines the method name (`myFactorial()`) and the argument data types (`java.lang.Integer`) to come up with a *signature* for the method. The signature gives the VM a way to distinguish between two methods that have the same name (but differing argument lists). Because Java searches for a method based on its signature (not just its name), you could create a `myFactorial( java.lang.Integer )` method and a `myFactorial( java.lang.Long )` method in the same class.

Once you've told PostgreSQL about the function by executing a `CREATE FUNCTION` command, you can call it like this:

```
movies=# SELECT myFactorial( 5 )
myfactorial
----------
       120
(1 row)

movies=# SELECT myFactorial( NULL )
ERROR:  java.lang.IllegalArgumentException: argument must not be NULL
```

To summarize the process:

- Write the source code for your Java method
- Compile the source code into a `.class` file
- Store the `.class` file in a Java archive (that is, a jar file)
- Copy the jar file into the PL/Java bytecode repository by calling the `sqlj.install_jar()` function
- Ensure that the new jar file (the one you just added to the bytecode repository) is mentioned in your schema's search path (call the `sqlj.set_classpath()` function)
- Execute a CREATE FUNCTION command for each method that you want to call from PostgreSQL

Accessing the Database from a PL/Java Function

To interact with the PostgreSQL database, a PL/Java function uses the JDBC package. I won't describe JDBC in detail in this chapter, see Chapter 13, "Using PostgreSQL from a Java Client Application," for an introduction to JDBC. Instead, I'll show you how to write some simple JDBC-enabled PL/Java functions that demonstrate a few of the quirks required by the PL/Java JDBC driver.

Listing 19.2 shows a Java source file that defines a single class (`Movies`) and two methods (`getBalance()` and `getTotal()`). The `getBalance()` method returns the current balance for a given customer. The `getTotal()` method returns the total (current) balance for all customers.

Listing 19.2 `Movies.java`

```
 1 // File: Movies.java
 2
 3 import java.sql.Connection;
 4 import java.sql.DriverManager;
 5 import java.sql.PreparedStatement;
 6 import java.sql.Statement;
 7 import java.sql.ResultSet;
 8 import java.sql.SQLException;
 9
10 public class Movies
11 {
12   private static String m_url = "jdbc:default:connection";
13
14   public static double getBalance( int id ) throws SQLException
15   {
16     Connection conn = DriverManager.getConnection( m_url );
17     String     query = "SELECT * FROM customers WHERE customer_id = ?";
```

Listing 19.2 **Continued**

```
18
19      PreparedStatement stmt = conn.prepareStatement( query );
20
21      stmt.setInt( 1, id );
22
23      ResultSet rs = stmt.executeQuery();
24
25      rs.next();
26
27      double balance = rs.getFloat( "balance" );
28
29      stmt.close();
30      conn.close();
31
32      return( balance );
33    }
34
35    public static double getTotal( ) throws SQLException
36    {
37      Connection conn  = DriverManager.getConnection( m_url );
38      Statement   stmt = conn.createStatement();
39
40      ResultSet rs = stmt.executeQuery( "SELECT * FROM customers" );
41
42      double total = 0;
43
44      while( rs.next())
45      {
46        total += rs.getFloat( 5 );
47      }
48
49      stmt.close();
50      conn.close();
51
52      return( total );
53    }
54  }
```

A JDBC client application connects to a database using a JDBC driver. The JDBC package locates the proper driver by examining a URL provided by the client. A typical URL specifies a driver name, database name, username, password, and so on. For example, to connect to a PostgreSQL database from an external JDBC client, you would code an URL that looks like this:

```
jdbc:org.postgresql?user=korry&password=cows
```

The leading part of the URL (the stuff before the question mark) tells JDBC to load the driver provided by `org.postgresql`. The trailing part of the URL (the stuff that follows the question mark) specifies a set of connection properties that are understood by the `org.postgresql` driver. (If you connect to a different database system, say Oracle, the connection properties would look very different.)

The PL/Java procedural language includes a "loopback driver." Rather than connecting to an external database (the way a normal JDBC driver would), the loopback driver connects *back* to the PostgreSQL server. To connect to the loopback driver, you always use the same URL: `jdbc:default:connection` (see Listing 19.2, line 12).

The first method exposed by the Movies class (`getBalance()`), connects to the PostgreSQL server and creates a `PreparedStatement` object. A `PreparedStatement` object prepares an SQL command for later execution. You typically uses a `PreparedStatement` (as opposed to a `Statement`) when you want to execute a command repeatedly, or when the command contains one or more parameters whose values you fill in at a later time. The `SELECT` command (see line 17) managed by the `PreparedStatement` includes a single parameter indicated by the question mark at the end of the `WHERE` clause. The call to `conn.prepareStatement()` (at line 19) sends the query to the server for parsing and planning and returns a handle to the `PreparedStatement`. Before you can execute the query, you must provide a value for the parameter (the question mark in the `WHERE` clause) and that's what the call to `stmt.setInt()` takes care of (see line 21). As I mentioned in the Chapter 13, an object of type `PreparedStatement` supports a variety of parameter-substitution methods. In this case, we're providing a value for the `customer_id` column (which happens to be an `INTEGER` value) so I'll call the `setInt()` method. See the section titled `PreparedStatement` in Chapter 13 for a list of related methods.

At line 23, the call to `stmt.executeQuery()` asks the PostgreSQL server to execute the query that I've prepared. `executeQuery()` returns a reference to a `ResultSet` object. A `ResultSet` contains a copy of all the data and a copy of all the metadata returned by a command. Each `ResultSet` maintains a pointer to the "current row" within the `ResultSet`. Initially, the pointer is positioned just before the first row in the `ResultSet`. To get to the values stored in the first row, I'll call the `rs.next()` method (see line 25).

Result Set Navigation in PL/Java

When you create a `ResultSet` object in a typical JDBC application, you can scroll forward and backward through the rows in the result set. You can also move to the first row or the last row, or to a position just before the first row or just after the last row. At the time we are writing this, PL/Java version 1.1 supports a single navigation method: `ResultSet.next()`. If you try to call any of the other navigation methods (`first()`, `last()`, `previous()`, and so forth), the `ResultSet` will throw an `UnsupportedFeatureException`. You can still call the navigation predicate methods (`isFirst()`, `isLast()`, `isBeforeFirst()`, `isAfterLast()`, and `getRow()`); you just can't move any direction other than forward.

The call to rs.getFloat() (see line 27) extracts the balance column from the current row (the first row) and returns a float value. The remainder of the method closes the PreparedStatement, closes the connection, and returns the balance to the caller.

The second method exposed by the Movies class (getTotal()) is similar to the first. In fact, there are only two significant changes. First, getTotal() creates a Statement object instead of a PreparedStatement. A PreparedStatement offers no advantages in this case because I only need to execute the query once and the query doesn't contain any parameters. I *could* use a PreparedStatement in this method, but a Statement object is easier to work with. Second, getTotal() loops through every row in the ResultSet, accumulating the total value as it goes. As I mentioned earlier, you call the next() method to iterate through the rows in a ResultSet: next() returns FALSE when you've read past the last row.

As you can see, it's easy to interact with the database from within a PL/Java function. It's important to note that the PL/Java loopback driver creates a connection to the caller's PostgreSQL session. When you connect to the loopback driver, the SQL commands that you invoke execute in the same transaction as the function. Your function sees the same user ID, the same search_path, and the same temporary ResultSet object tables as the caller.

Returning Multiple Results from a PL/Java Function

Writing a PL/Java function that returns multiple rows is a bit more complicated. PL/Java provides three different mechanisms for writing a function that returns a SETOF some data type. In the simplest case, you can return a SETOF scalar (simple) values by returning an Iterator. If you want to return a SETOF complex (non-scalar) values, you can return a ResultSet created by a JDBC method or you can create your own ResultSet. In this section, I'll show you all three methods.

Listing 19.3 shows a simple PL/Java function that returns a SETOF string values:

Listing 19.3 Tapes.java

```
 1 // File: Tapes.java
 2
 3 import java.sql.Connection;
 4 import java.sql.DriverManager;
 5 import java.sql.Statement;
 6 import java.sql.ResultSet;
 7 import java.sql.SQLException;
 8 import java.util.Iterator;
 9 import java.util.ArrayList;
10
11 public class Tapes
12 {
13   private static String m_url  = "jdbc:default:connection";
14
```

Listing 19.3 **Continued**

```
15    public static Iterator getTapeIDs( )
16      throws SQLException
17    {
18      Connection conn = DriverManager.getConnection( m_url );
19      Statement  stmt = conn.createStatement();
20      ResultSet  rs   = stmt.executeQuery( "SELECT tape_id FROM tapes" );
21      ArrayList  result = new ArrayList();
22
23      while( rs.next())
24      {
25        result.add( rs.getString( "tape_id" ));
26      }
27
28      return( result.iterator());
29    }
30 }
```

When you call a function defined as RETURNS SETOF *scalarType*, PL/Java expects to find a method that returns a java.util.Iterator. In this case, the getTapeIDs() creates an ArrayList that will hold each tape_id returned by the query that you see at line 20. The while loop (starting at line 23) copies the each row from the result set into the ArrayList. Line 28 creates an Iterator that can read through the ArrayList and returns a reference to that Iterator. When the method completes, PL/Java reads through the Iterator and copies each row into the result set that the PostgreSQL server is assembling.

The getTapeIDs() method shown in Listing 19.3 *materializes* the entire result set before returning to the caller. (That is, it copies all of the result rows into a container and then returns an Iterator that reads from that container.) Materializing a large result set can be somewhat inefficient because you have to copy the entire set into a container and then let PL/Java read through the container. A better approach is to convert a ResultSet into an Iterator *on demand*. Listing 19.4 shows an alternative version of getTapeIDs() that returns a hand-crafted Iterator. I should warn you that this code will *not* work with PL/Java version 1.1 because of a bug that has been fixed (but the fix has not yet been released at the time of this writing).

Listing 19.4 `Tapes2.java`

```
1 // File: Tapes2.java
2
3 import java.sql.Connection;
4 import java.sql.DriverManager;
5 import java.sql.Statement;
6 import java.sql.ResultSet;
7 import java.sql.SQLException;
```

Listing 19.4   **Continued**

```
 8 import java.util.NoSuchElementException;
 9 import java.util.Iterator;
10
11 public class Tapes2 implements Iterator
12 {
13   private static String m_url = "jdbc:default:connection";
14   private ResultSet      m_rs;
15
16   public Tapes2() throws SQLException
17   {
18     Connection conn = DriverManager.getConnection( m_url );
19     Statement   stmt = conn.createStatement();
20
21     m_rs = stmt.executeQuery( "SELECT tape_id FROM tapes" );
22   }
23
24   public static Iterator getTapeIDs( ) throws SQLException
25   {
26     return new Tapes2();
27   }
28
29   public boolean hasNext()
30   {
31     try
32     {
33       return !( m_rs.isLast() );
34     }
35     catch( Exception e )
36     {
37       return( false );
38     }
39   }
40
41   public Object next()
42   {
43     try
44     {
45       m_rs.next();
46
47       return( m_rs.getString( "tape_id" ));
48     }
49     catch( Exception e )
50     {
51       throw new NoSuchElementException( "No more tapes" );
52     }
```

Listing 19.4 **Continued**

```
53    }
54
55    public void remove()
56    {
57      throw new UnsupportedOperationException("No way");
58    }
59  }
```

In this version, the getTapeIDs() method returns a reference to a new Tapes2 object (see line 26). Since Tapes2 implements the Iterator interface (see line 11), returning a reference to a Tapes2 object is the same thing as returning a reference to an Iterator. The Tapes2 constructor (line 16) connects to the database (using the PL/Java loopback driver), executes a simple query, and stores the ResultSet in a member variable (m_rs). Now it's time to implement the Iterator interface. Iterator defines three methods: boolean hasNext(), Object next(), and void remove(). The caller (the PL/Java call handler) invokes hasNext() (line 29) repeatedly to find out whether there are any more values accessible through the Iterator. hasNext() simply calls the m_rs.isLast() method to detect when the ResultSet has been exhausted. If hasNext() returns true, the PL/Java call handler invokes next() (line 41) to retrieve the next value. next() navigates to the next row in the m_rs ResultSet, extracts the tape_id column, and returns it to the caller. The last Iterator method, remove(), is very simple. We can't remove a row from the result set (and PL/Java will never ask us to), so remove() throws an UnsupportedOperationException. As I mentioned earlier, the code shown in Listing 19.4 will *not* work properly with the currently released version of PL/Java (1.1)—if you try to invoke this method, you'll see the first row in the result set, and then the second call to m_rs.isLast() will throw an exception (Stale Handle to native structure). This bug may be fixed by the time you're reading this book, so go ahead and give it a try.

PL/Java provides two different mechanisms for returning a SETOF complex values, but in each case, your code returns a ResultSet. Listing 19.5 shows a Java class (Rentals) that defines a single callable function (getRentals()). The getRentals() method returns a SETOF tuples. When you call getRentals(), you provide a customer_id and it returns information about each tape rented by that customer. For example:

```
movies=# SELECT * FROM getRentals( 3 );
 tape_id  |    title      | rental_date
---------+------------+---------
 AB-67472 | The Godfather | 2001-11-25
 MC-68873 | Casablanca    | 2001-11-20
(2 rows)
```

I'll show you two different implementations for this function. The first method (Listing 19.5) demonstrates the ResultSetHandle interface. The second method (Listing 19.6) shows you how to create a ResultSet on-the-fly.

Listing 19.5 `Rentals.java`

```java
 1 // File: Rentals.java
 2
 3 import java.sql.Connection;
 4 import java.sql.DriverManager;
 5 import java.sql.PreparedStatement;
 6 import java.sql.ResultSet;
 7 import java.sql.SQLException;
 8 import org.postgresql.pljava.ResultSetHandle;
 9
10 public class Rentals implements ResultSetHandle
11 {
12
13   private PreparedStatement m_stmt;
14   private int             m_id;
15   private static String    m_url   = "jdbc:default:connection";
16   private static String    m_query =
17           "SELECT tapes.tape_id, title, rental_date" +
18           " FROM rentals, tapes" +
19           " WHERE rentals.customer_id = ?" +
20           "  AND tapes.tape_id = rentals.tape_id";
21
22   public Rentals( int id )
23   {
24     m_id = id;
25   }
26
27   public static ResultSetHandle getRentals( int id ) throws SQLException
28   {
29     return new Rentals( id );
30   }
31
32   public ResultSet getResultSet() throws SQLException
33   {
34     Connection conn = DriverManager.getConnection( m_url  );
35
36     m_stmt = conn.prepareStatement( m_query );
37     m_stmt.setInt( 1, m_id );
38
39     return( m_stmt.executeQuery( ));
40   }
41
42   public void close() throws SQLException
43   {
44     m_stmt.close();
45   }
46 }
```

One way to return a SETOF complex values is to implement the ResultSetHandle interface. (Note that ResultSetHandle is defined in the org.postgresql.pljava package.) The Rentals class (line 10) defines four methods: a constructor (line 22), the function that you expose to PostgreSQL (line 27), and the two methods required by the ResultSetHandle interface (lines 32 and 42).

When you use this class from within PostgreSQL, you call the getRentals() static method. getRentals() simply creates a new Rentals object and returns a reference to that object. Since Rentals implements the ResultSetHandle interface, returning a reference to a Rentals object is the same thing as returning a reference to a ResultSetHandle. The Rentals constructor (line 22) is equally simple—it just stores a copy of the id argument in the m_id class variable.

getResultSet() is the first of two methods required by the ResultSetHandle interface. When PL/Java invokes the getResultSet() method, it's expecting a ResultSet that it can map into a SETOF of the appropriate type. Where do you get a ResultSet? Just execute a command. In this case, getResultSet() connects to the PostgreSQL server, creates a PreparedStatement, fills in the query parameter (see lines 16 and 37), executes the query, and returns the ResultSet provided by m_stmt.executeQuery(). The second method required by the ResultSetHandle interface is close() (see line 42). The PL/Java call handler calls close() when it has finished mapping the ResultSet into a SETOF values—as you can see, my implementation simply invokes the m_stmt.close() method.

The ResultSetHandle interface works well when you want to return a SETOF values that you can read directly from the PostgreSQL database (or even from some *other* database). But what if you want to build the ResultSet yourself? In that case, you should create a class the implements the ResultSetProvider interface. Listing 19.6 shows an alternate version of the getRentals() function. It returns the same set of rows returned by the original version, but this version creates a ResultSet on the fly.

Listing 19.6   Rentals2.java

```
 1 // File: Rentals2.java
 2
 3 import java.sql.Connection;
 4 import java.sql.DriverManager;
 5 import java.sql.PreparedStatement;
 6 import java.sql.ResultSet;
 7 import java.sql.SQLException;
 8 import org.postgresql.pljava.ResultSetProvider;
 9
10 public class Rentals2 implements ResultSetProvider
11 {
12
13     private PreparedStatement m_stmt;
14     private ResultSet         m_rs;
15     private static String     m_url  = "jdbc:default:connection";
```

Listing 19.6 **Continued**

```
16    private static String      m_query =
17              "SELECT tapes.tape_id, title, rental_date" +
18              " FROM rentals, tapes" +
19              " WHERE rentals.customer_id = ?" +
20              "  AND tapes.tape_id = rentals.tape_id";
21
22    public Rentals2( int id )
23      throws SQLException
24    {
25      Connection conn = DriverManager.getConnection( m_url );
26
27      m_stmt = conn.prepareStatement( m_query );
28      m_stmt.setInt( 1, id );
29
30      m_rs = m_stmt.executeQuery();
31    }
32
33    public static ResultSetProvider getRentals( int id )
34      throws SQLException
35    {
36      return new Rentals2( id );
37    }
38
39    public boolean assignRowValues( ResultSet dst, int rowNum )
40      throws SQLException
41    {
42      if( m_rs.next())
43      {
44        dst.updateString( 1, m_rs.getString( 1 ));
45        dst.updateString( 2, m_rs.getString( 2 ));
46        dst.updateDate( 3, m_rs.getDate( 3 ));
47
48        return( true );
49      }
50      else
51      {
52        return( false );
53      }
54    }
55
56    public void close()
57      throws SQLException
58    {
59      m_stmt.close();
60    }
61 }
```

The `Rentals2` class implements the `org.postgresql.pljava.ResultSetProvider` interface by providing two methods: `assignRowValues()` and `close()`.

When you use this class from within PostgreSQL, you call the `getRentals()` static method. Like the previous version, this version of `getRentals()` simply creates a new `Rentals2` object and returns a reference that object. Since `Rentals` implements the `ResultSetProvider` interface, returning a reference to a `Rentals2` object is the same thing as returning a reference to a `ResultSetProvider`.

The `Rentals2` constructor (line 22) connects to the PostgreSQL server, creates a `PreparedStatement` using the query defined at line 16, fills in the query parameter, and executes the query. Unlike the previous version, this constructor stores the `ResultSet` returned by `m_stmt.executeQuery()` in a member variable (`m_rs`).

After `getRentals()` returns a `ResultSetProvider`, the PL/Java call handler repeatedly invokes the `assignRowValues()` method until it returns `false`. The `assignRowValues()` method expects two arguments: a `ResultSet` and a row number. The `assignRowValues()` fills in the given `ResultSet` (`dst`) one row at a time. When it runs out of results, `assignRowValues()` returns false to tell the PL/Java call handler that the `ResultSet` is complete. In this example, `assignRowValues()` simply reads through one result set (`m_rs`) and copies the column values into the `ResultSet` provided by the caller. In a more realistic scenario, you may compute some (or all) of the values that you store in the caller's `ResultSet`.

When `assignRowValues()` returns false, the PL/Java call handler invokes the `close()` method (the second method required by the `ResultSetProvider` interface).

The `ResultSetHandle` and `ResultSetProvider` mechanisms seem very similar at first glance. Each mechanism returns a `ResultSet` that the PL/Java call handler converts into a `SETOF` rows. Each interface requires two methods. How do you choose the right one? Use the `ResultSetHandle` interface when you already *have* a `ResultSet` that contains the values that you want to return. You obtain a `ResultSet` by executing a command against a database, typically a PostgreSQL database, but you can certainly retrieve a `ResultSet` from any JDBC driver. Use the `ResultSetProvider` interface when you want to construct a `ResultSet` from computed values. The `ResultSetProvider` interface is more flexible than `ResultSetHandle`. (As you've already seen, a `ResultSetProvider` can do anything that a `ResultSetHandle` can, but the reverse is not true.)

Writing PL/Java Trigger Functions

A *trigger* is a function that executes in response to a specific event in a given table. The PostgreSQL server automatically invokes a trigger (if defined) when you execute an `INSERT` command, an `UPDATE` command, or a `DELETE` command. Creating a trigger function in PL/Java is simply a matter of writing a method that expects a single argument: a reference to an object of type `TriggerData`. The PL/Java call handler fills in the `TriggerData` object before calling your code.

A `TriggerData` object contains information about the event that caused the trigger to execute. For example, to determine the type of statement that fired the trigger, you can call the `TriggerData`'s `isFiredByInsert()`, `isFiredByUpdate()`, and `isFiredByDelete()` methods. When you add a trigger to a table (by executing a CREATE TRIGGER command), you can tell PostgreSQL whether to execute the trigger once for each modified row or to execute the trigger when the INSERT, UPDATE, or DELETE statement completes. A `TriggerData` object exposes two methods that you can use to determine how often the trigger executes: `isFiredForEachRow()` and `isFiredForStatement()`. When `isFiredForEachRow()` returns true, the `TriggerData` object holds a copy of the new row (in the case of a trigger fired by an INSERT command), a copy of the old row (in the case of a trigger fired by a DELETE command), or both (when the trigger is fired by an UPDATE command). To access the new row, call the `getNew()` method. To access the old row, call the `getOld()` method. Both methods return a one-row `ResultSet`. Table 19.1 summarizes the information that you can extract from a `TriggerData` object:

Table 19.1 `TriggerData` **Methods**

Method Name	Description
boolean isFiredByInsert()	Returns true if the trigger was fired by an INSERT command.
boolean isFiredByUpdate()	Returns true if the trigger was fired by an UPDATE command.
boolean isFiredByDelete	Returns true if the trigger was fired by a DELETE command.
boolean isFiredForEachRow()	Returns true if the trigger is fired for each row modified by an INSERT, UPDATE, or DELETE command (returns the opposite of isFiredForStatement()).
boolean isFiredForStatement()	Returns true if the trigger is fired when an INSERT, UPDATE, or DELETE command completes (returns the opposite of isFiredForEachRow()).
boolean isFiredBefore()	Returns true if the trigger executes before the command begins (in the case of a statement-level trigger) or before each row is modified (in the case of a row-level trigger).
boolean isFiredAfter()	Returns true if the trigger executes after the command completes (in the case of a statement-level trigger) or after each row is modified (in the case of a row-level trigger).
ResultSet getNew()	Returns the new row for an INSERT or UPDATE command. (You should only call this method when isFiredByInsert() or isFiredByUdate() returns true and isFiredForEachRow() returns true.)

Table 19.1 **Continued**

`ResultSet getOld()`	Returns the new old for a `DELETE` or `UPDATE` command. (You should only call this method when `isFiredByDelete()` or `isFiredByUdate()` returns true and `isFiredForEachRow()` returns true.)
`String getName()`	Returns the name of the trigger.
`String getTableName()`	Returns the name of the modified table.
String[] getArguments()	Returns the (optional) trigger arguments defined by the `CREATE TRIGGER` command.

Listing 19.7 shows a class that will create an audit log of all changes made to the customers table. After you compile and install this PL/Java function (and turn it into a trigger), PostgreSQL will invoke the `archiveCustomer()` method when you modify the customers table. Each time `archiveCustomer()` is invoked, it adds a new row to the customer_archive table. If you `DELETE` a customer, `archiveCustomer()` copies the obsolete data into customer_archive. If you `INSERT` a customer, `archiveCustomer()` copies the *new* data into customer_archive. If you `UPDATE` a customer, `archiveCustomer()` adds two rows to customer_archive—the first row contains the original values and the second row contains the new values. Each row in the customer_archive table contains a complete copy of a customers row plus a few extra audit fields. Here's the complete definition of the customer_archive table:

```
CREATE TABLE customer_archive
(
   customer_id          INTEGER,
   customer_name        VARCHAR(50) NOT NULL,
   phone                CHAR(8),
   birth_date           DATE,
   balance              DECIMAL(7,2),
   user_changed         VARCHAR,
   date_changed         DATE,
   operation            VARCHAR
);
```

The user_changed column contains the name of the user that fired the trigger. The date_changed column contains the modification date. operation will contain `INSERT` or `DELETE` to indicate the type of modification. (An `UPDATE` is recorded as a `DELETE` followed by an `INSERT`.)

Listing 19.7 `Archive.java`

```
1 // File: Archive.java
2
3 import java.sql.Connection;
4 import java.sql.DriverManager;
```

Listing 19.7 **Continued**

```java
5 import java.sql.PreparedStatement;
6 import java.sql.ResultSet;
7 import java.sql.SQLException;
8
9 import org.postgresql.pljava.TriggerData;
10
11 public class Archive
12 {
13   private static String    m_url   = "jdbc:default:connection";
14
15   public static void archiveCustomer( TriggerData td )
16     throws SQLException
17   {
18     if( td.isFiredForStatement())
19       return;
20
21     if( td.isFiredByInsert())
22       addArchive( td.getNew(), "INSERT" );
23     else if( td.isFiredByDelete())
24       addArchive( td.getOld(), "DELETE" );
25     else
26     {
27       addArchive( td.getOld(), "DELETE" );
28       addArchive( td.getNew(), "INSERT" );
29     }
30   }
31
32   private static void addArchive( ResultSet values, String operation )
33     throws SQLException
34   {
35
36     String command =
37       "INSERT INTO customer_archive " +
38       "( " +
39       "  customer_id, " +
40       "  customer_name, " +
41       "  phone, " +
42       "  birth_date, " +
43       "  balance, " +
44       "  user_changed, " +
45       "  date_changed, " +
46       "  operation " +
47       ") " +
48       "VALUES " +
49       "( ?, ?, ?, ?, ?, CURRENT_USER, now(), ? )";
```

Listing 19.7　**Continued**

```
50
51     Connection         conn = DriverManager.getConnection( m_url  );
52     PreparedStatement stmt = conn.prepareStatement( command );
53
54     stmt.setInt(      1, values.getInt( "customer_id" ));
55     stmt.setString(   2, values.getString( "customer_name" ));
56     stmt.setString(   3, values.getString( "phone" ));
57     stmt.setDate(     4, values.getDate( "birth_date" ));
58     stmt.setBigDecimal( 5, values.getBigDecimal( "balance" ));
59     stmt.setString(   6, operation );
60
61     stmt.executeQuery();
62
63     stmt.close();
64     conn.close();
65   }
66 }
```

The archiveCustomer() method begins at line 15. If archiveCustomer() is invoked by
a statement-level trigger, it won't have access to the old and new row values so it simply
returns without doing any work—if you want the old and/or new values in a trigger
function, you must create a row-level trigger. The if/else statement starting at line 21
decides whether to add an INSERT record, a DELETE record, or (in the case of an UPDATE
command), both. Note that each call to the addArchive() method provides a
ResultSet and an operation. The ResultSet contains a copy of the new row values or
a copy of the old row values, depending on whether you call td.getNew() or
td.getOld().

The addArchive() method (line 32) adds a new row to the customer_archive table.
After connecting to the PostgreSQL server, addArchive() creates a PreparedStatement
and fills in the six parameter values. The customers values (customer_id, customer_
name, and so on) are copied straight out of the ResultSet provided by the caller.
The PostgreSQL server computes the values for the audit fields (user_changed,
date_changed).

After compiling and installing this class, you can turn it into a trigger with the following commands:

```
movies=# CREATE FUNCTION archiveCustomer() RETURNS TRIGGER AS
movies-#   'Archive.addArchive';
CREATE FUNCTION

movies=# CREATE TRIGGER archiveCustomer
movies-#   AFTER INSERT OR DELETE OR UPDATE
movies-#   ON customers
```

```
movies-#   FOR EACH ROW
movies-#   EXECUTE PROCEDURE archiveCustomer();
CREATE TRIGGER
```

As you may have noticed by now, it takes quite a bit of tedious work to install a PL/Java function once the Java compiler turned your source code into bytecode form. The PL/Java developers have included a feature that makes it a little bit easier to manage jar files in a PostgreSQL database.

Adding Install/Uninstall Commands to a Jar File

When you create a jar file, you can include an optional *deployment descriptor* that specifies a sequence of SQL commands to execute when the jar file is installed and a sequence of SQL commands to execute when the jar file is uninstalled. A typical deployment descriptor contains one CREATE FUNCTION command (and a corresponding DROP FUNCTION command) for each function defined by the jar file. A deployment descriptor might also contain CREATE TYPE and CREATE TRIGGER commands. When you install the jar file (using the sqlj.install_jar() function), PL/Java executes the install-commands defined by the deployment descriptor. When you uninstall the jar file (using the sqlj.remove_jar() function), PL/Java executes the remove-commands defined by the deployment descriptor. When you add a deployment descriptor to a jar file, you're creating a self-installing archive that will clean up after itself should you remove the jar file from the database.

A deployment descriptor is a text file that contains a list of install-commands and a list of uninstall-commands. Listing 19.8 shows a typical deployment descriptor.

Listing 19.8 Movies.ddr

```
SQLActions[ ] = {
  "BEGIN INSTALL

    BEGIN PostgreSQL SET search_path TO public END PostgreSQL;

    CREATE FUNCTION getBalance(int) RETURNS float8
      AS 'Movies.getTotal(int)' LANGUAGE java;

  END INSTALL",

  "BEGIN REMOVE
    DROP FUNCTION getBalance(int);
  END REMOVE"
}
```

A deployment descriptor begins with the text SQLActions[ ] = { ands ends with a closing brace }. Between the braces you can write a "BEGIN INSTALL ... END INSTALL" section and a "BEGIN REMOVE ... END REMOVE " section. As you've probably guessed, the "BEGIN INSTALL ... END INSTALL" section contains a list of SQL commands that execute when you install the jar that contains the deployment descriptor. Likewise, the "BEGIN REMOVE ... END REMOVE " section contains a list of SQL commands that execute when you remove the jar from the database.

The deployment descriptor shown in Listing 19.8 contains two install-commands. The first command (SET search_path TO public) is wrapped inside of an *implementor block*. To understand implementor blocks, remember that Java's primary goal is portability. When you write a PL/Java class, you can load that class into *other* database systems (Oracle, Sybase, and so on). If you want to execute install-commands specific to a given database system, wrap the commands in an implementor block. When PL/Java sees an install-command (or uninstall-command) wrapped in a BEGIN *implementor*...END *implementor* pair, it only executes those commands where *implementor* is PostgreSQL.

You can create a deployment descriptor for a jar file with any text editor. Just decide which commands you want to execute when the jar file is installed and which commands you want to execute when the jar file is uninstalled. The "BEGIN INSTALL ... END INSTALL" section should (typically) include a CREATE FUNCTION command for each function that you're adding to the database. You may want to include GRANT EXE-CUTE...ON FUNCTION commands as well. The "BEGIN REMOVE ... END REMOVE " section should (typically) include a DROP FUNCTION command for each function. (Or, if you've installed the jar into a specific schema, you can simply DROP SCHEMA *schemaName* CASCADE instead.)

Once you've completed the deployment descriptor, add it to the jar file and add a reference to the descriptor to the jar's manifest. The manifest for a Java archive is stored in a member named META-INF/MANIFEST.MF and it contains meta-data about the other members of the archive. If you don't create a manifest file yourself, the jar command will create an empty one for you. When you store a deployment descriptor in a Java archive, you must build the manifest file by hand. A manifest (like a deployment descriptor) is a text file that you can create with any text editor. Listing 19.9 shows a typical manifest:

Listing 19.9 MANIFEST.MF

```
Manifest-Version: 1.0
Created-By: 0.92-gcc

Name: Movies.ddr
SQLJDeploymentDescriptor: TRUE
```

Each line in the manifest is a keyword : value pair. The first two pairs specify the manifest version (as specified by Sun Microsystems) and a note indicating who created the manifest. The last two pairs specify the name of an archive member and a note that tells PL/Java that the given file (in this case Movies.ddr) is an SQLJDeploymentDescriptor.

If you've saved the manifest in a file named `manifest.txt`, saved the deployment descriptor in a file named `Movies.ddr`, and saved the Java class file in `Movies.class`, you can create a new jar file with the following command:

```
$ jar -cv -f Movies.jar -m manifest.txt Movies.class Movies.ddr
adding: META-INF/ (in=0) (out=0) (stored 0%)
adding: META-INF/MANIFEST.MF (in=104) (out=99) (deflated 4%)
adding: Movies.class (in=1353) (out=783) (deflated 42%)
adding: Movies.ddr (in=283) (out=204) (deflated 27%)
Total:
___
(in = 1740) (out = 1536) (deflated 11%)
```

Notice that the jar command has converted the `manifest.txt` file into `META-INF/MANIFEST.MF` (as required by the Java specification). To view the contents of the new jar file (`Movies.jar`):

```
$ jar -tv -f Movies.jar
     0 Thu Apr 21 01:31:02 UTC 2005 META-INF/
   104 Thu Apr 21 12:52:28 UTC 2005 META-INF/MANIFEST.MF
  1353 Thu Apr 21 10:20:36 UTC 2005 Movies.class
   283 Thu Apr 21 12:16:46 UTC 2005 Movies.ddr
```

Now when you install `Movies.jar`, `sqlj.install_jar()` will execute the install-commands you specified in the deployment descriptor. Likewise, if you uninstall `Movies.jar`, `sqlj.remove_jar()` will execute the uninstall-commands found in the deployment descriptor.

If you're a Java programmer, PL/Java is an easy way to add server-side functionality to a PostgreSQL database. Because PL/Java closely follows industry standards such as JDBC and the SQLJ initiative, you can easily move PL/Java functions between database systems.

SQL—The Other Procedural Language

In this book, I've described the PL/pgSQL and PL/Java procedural languages and mentioned a few others (PL/Perl, PL/tcl, and even PL/bash). You can also write functions and stored procedures in SQL itself (that is, in LANGUAGE SQL). An SQL function is simply a named sequence of SQL commands. PostgreSQL executes each command in the function, in order, and returns any results produced by the last command. Unlike the other procedural languages, you can't "jump around" inside of an SQL function. SQL doesn't support control-of-flow commands like `if`, `while`, or `switch`. You *can* use the CASE, COALESCE, and NULLIF expressions to handle limited decision-making, but for anything more complex you'll need a more complete language. For more information about SQL functions, see the PostgreSQL reference documentation (specifically section 31.4, "Query Language (SQL) Functions" in PostgreSQL version 8.0).

pgcurl—**Web-enabling Your PostgreSQL Server**

The pgcurl package (gborg.postgresql.org/project/pgcurl) adds networking features to a PostgreSQL database. pgcurl wraps the libcurl networking library in a set of five server functions:

- urlencode(TEXT) RETURNS TEXT

  urlencode() translates "special" characters into their URL-escaped form. Specifically, urlencode() converts any character outside of the ranges a–z, A–Z, and 0–9 into the form %*nn* (where *nn* is the two-digit hexadecimal representation of the character according to RFC 2396).

- urldecode(TEXT) RETURNS TEXT

  urldecode() translates an URL-escaped string into a plain-text form. Specifically, urldecode() any sequence of the form %*nn* (where *nn* is the two-digit hexadecimal representation of a character) into the corresponding character.

- urlget(TEXT) RETURNS TEXT

  urlget() downloads a resource (and HTML web page, a file, or whatever) from a web or FTP server and returns the resource as a TEXT value.

- urlpost(TEXT, TEXT) RETURNS TEXT

  urlpost() sends an HTTP POST request (including URL-encoded arguments) to a web server and returns the response as a TEXT value.

- urlhead(TEXT) RETURNS TEXT

  urlhead() is similar to urlget() except that urlhead() returns the meta-data associated with a resource (Content Type, Expires, Transfer Encoding, and such).

The most interesting functions are urlget() and urlpost().

urlget() expects a single argument—a string that specifies a URL that you want to download. When you call urlget(), it downloads the resource that you specify. A typical call to urlget() might look something like this:

```
movies=# INSERT INTO news( source, html ) VALUES (
movies(#   'npr',
movies(#   urlget( 'http://www.npr.org/index.html' ));
INSERT 985949 1
```

urlget() can handle simple HTTP (http://), secure HTTP (https://), simple FTP (ftp://), secure FTP (ftps://), file access (file://), even somewhat obscure protocols such as gopher, telnet, dict, and ldap. If urlget() succeeds, it returns the entire resource as a single TEXT value. Needless to say, urlget() may take a while to complete if you are downloading a large document (or have a slow network connection).

The urlpost() function lets you send an HTTP POST request to a web server. urlpost() expects two arguments—the first argument is the URL that you want to post to and the second argument contains the data that you want to post. For example, say that you are hosting a web site that displays information about the "Movie Of The Week" featured at your video store. You could update the featured title like this:

```
movies=# SELECT urlpost( 'http://virtualVid.example.com/motw.cgi',
movies(#    'name=' || urlencode( title ) ||
movies(#    '&date=' || urlencode( current_date ))
movies-# FROM tapes WHERE tape_id = 'AB-67472';
```

That might be a little difficult to read, so here's a closer look at the call to `urlpost()`:

```
urlpost( 'http://virtualVid.example.com/motw.cgi',
    'name=' || urlencode( title ) '&date=' || urlencode( current_date ))
```

I've used `urlencode()` to translate special characters (such as spaces and dashes) into URL-happy form. PostgreSQL assembles the second argument into a single string that looks like this:

```
'name=The%20Godfather&date=2005%2D04%2D16'
```

The net effect is the same as browsing to the following URL in a web browser:

```
http://virtualVid.example.com/motw.cgi?name=The%20Godfather&date=2005%2D04%2D16
```

`urlpost()` returns the HTML page produced by the web server as a single TEXT value (just like `urlget()` does).

pgbash—**Writing PostgreSQL-enabled Shell Scripts**

pgbash is a set of PostgreSQL-related enhancements for the bash shell. pgbash turns the bash shell into a PostgreSQL client application. When you add pgbash to the bash shell, you can execute PostgreSQL commands without invoking psql (or some other PostgreSQL client application) first—instead of invoking a separate program to execute SQL commands, the pgbash shell interacts directly with the database using the libpq client library. At the time that we are writing this chapter, pgbash is distributed as a set of source-code patches for bash version 2.05a—the current version of bash is 3.0 so pgbash is a few revisions out of sync. Hopefully by the time you read this, pgbash will work with bash version 3.0. The pgbash web site states that pgbash works with PostgreSQL versions 7.3 and above—it works very well with PostgreSQL version 8.0.

When you start a pgbash session, you're running a complete bash shell so you can use any of the bash features that you know and love: redirection, control structures (if/then/else, do/while, ...), filename completion, brace expansion, and so on. pgbash adds a few built-ins to the bash shell. For example, to connect to the movies database and execute a simple query:

```
$ pgbash
Welcome to Pgbash version 7.3 ( bash-2.05a.0(2)-release )
```

```
Type '?' for HELP.
Type 'connect to DB;' before executing SQL.
Type 'SQL;' to execute SQL.
Type 'exit' or 'Ctrl+D' to terminate Pgbash.

pgbash> CONNECT TO movies;
# PostgreSQL 8.0.0 on i686-pc-linux-gnu
# CONNECT TO  movies:5432  AS  movies USER  bruce

pgbash> SELECT * FROM customers;
 customer_id | customer_name      | phone    | birth_date | balance
-------------+--------------------+----------+------------+--------
           2 | Rubin, William     | 555-2211 | 1972-07-10 |  15.00
           1 | Jones, Henry       | 555-1212 | 1970-10-10 |  16.00
           4 | Wonderland, Alice N.| 555-1122 | 1969-03-05 |   3.00
           3 | Panky, Henry       | 555-1835 | 1968-01-21 |  16.16
(4 rows)
```

You may have noticed that I've included a semicolon at the end of each command. pgbash modifies the bash parser to add direct support for SQL commands—to find the end of an SQL command, pgbash looks for a semicolon.

When you execute a CONNECT TO command, pgbash connects to the database that you specify and assigns a symbolic name to that connection. By default, pgbash creates a connection whose name matches the name of the database that you connect to, but you can assign your own name to the connection by including an AS connectionName clause. For example:

```
pgbash> CONNECT TO movies AS movies1;
pgbash> CONNECT TO movies AS movies2;

CONNECT TO { database[@host[:port]] | DEFAULT }
          [AS connectionName]
          [USER userName
          [[{IDENTIFIED BY | USING | /}] password]];
```

Unlike psql, a single pgbash session can maintain any number of open database connections. You can switch from connection to connection by executing SET CONNECTION TO connectionName command. When you switch to a new connection, pgbash does *not* close the previous connection.

The first command creates a connection to the test database. The second command creates a connection to the movies database. When you execute the second CONNECT command, pgbash simply opens a second connection but it does not close the test connection. You can see a list of open connections with the ?m command:

```
pgbash> ?m
# Connected Databases List (C: current database is '*')
+---+--------------+----------+--------------------------+-----------------+
| C | connect_name | user_name | target_name(db@host:port) | client_encoding |
+---+--------------+----------+--------------------------+-----------------+
| * | movies       | korry     | movies:5432               |                 |
|   | test         | korry     | test:5432                 |                 |
+---+--------------+----------+--------------------------+-----------------+
(2 rows)
```

Notice the * in the first column? That tells you which connection is *active*—when you execute an SQL command, pgbash sends the command to the server on the other end of the active connection. You can change the active connection by executing the SET CONNECTION *connectionName* command:

```
pgbash> SET CONNECTION TO test;
pgbash> ?m
# Connected Databases List (C: current database is '*')
+---+--------------+----------+--------------------------+-----------------+
| C | connect_name | user_name | target_name(db@host:port) | client_encoding |
+---+--------------+----------+--------------------------+-----------------+
|   | movies       | korry     | movies:5432               |                 |
| * | test         | korry     | test:5432                 |                 |
+---+--------------+----------+--------------------------+-----------------+
(2 rows)
```

If you open more than one connection, you can interact with many databases at the same time. For example, to copy a table (customers) from one database to another[1]:

```
pgbash> CONNECT TO test;
# PostgreSQL 8.0.0 on i686-pc-linux-gnu
# CONNECT TO  test:5432  AS  movies USER  bruce

pgbash> CONNECT TO movies;
# PostgreSQL 8.0.0 on i686-pc-linux-gnu
# CONNECT TO  movies:5432  AS  movies USER  bruce

pgbash> COPY customers TO STDOUT; |
>          (SET CONNECTION test; && COPY customers FROM STDIN; )
```

After opening two connections (one connected to the test database and one connected to the movies database), the last command copies the customers table (from the

---

1. If the COPY command shown here reports an error message (pgbash: select: command not found), you have an older version of pgbash and you'll need to execute pipelined commands using bash's builtin syntax, like this: COPY customers TO STDOUT; | (exec_sql "SET CONNECTION test"; exec_sql "COPY customers FROM STDIN").

movies database) *to* STDOUT, pipes the result to a subshell that switches to the test database, and then copies the customers table *from* STDIN. You can redirect an SQL command's output stream to another process (using the | operator) or to a file (using the > or >> operators). You can also redirect the standard input stream of the COPY command (using the < or | operators).

To close a connection, execute the command DISCONNECT *connectionName*.

The benefits offered by pgbash become more apparent when you need to interact with a facility *outside* of the database. For example, say you have a whole directory full of photographs that you want to load into a PostgreSQL database. (Each photo should be stored as a large-object.) I'll create a table named wallpapers to hold the photos:

```
pgbash> CREATE TABLE wallpapers ( name VARCHAR, lo_oid );
CREATE TABLE
```

Importing a whole collection of large-objects is not an easy task with most PostgreSQL client applications, but it's trivial with pgbash. The following snippet of code imports all image files found in /usr/share/wallpapers:

```
pgbash> FOR fi IN /usr/share/wallpapers/*.jpg
> DO
>     INSERT INTO wallpapers VALUES
>     (
>       \'$(basename $fi)\',
>       lo_import( \'$fi\' )
>     );
> DONE
```

I've mixed bash features and PostgreSQL features in this example. The FOR...IN loop iterates through each image in the directory (assigning a different filename to $fi for each trip through the loop). Inside of the loop, I'm executing an INSERT command that adds a new row during each iteration. To compute the name column, I'm using bash's command-substitution feature to extract the filename component from $fi. The lo_id column column is filled in by the call to lo_import(). It's important to realize that every INSERT command (in this example) uses the same connection—I'm not opening a new connection, adding a single row, and then closing that connection for each image. That has two important (and beneficial) implications. First, I'm not suffering any performance degradation caused by repeated connection setups and teardowns. Second, I can execute the entire loop within a single transaction. (I just need to execute a BEGIN WORK command before the loop and a COMMIT or ROLLBACK after the loop.)

The previous example showed that you can use bash control structures to control the interaction with a PostgreSQL database. You can also use a PostgreSQL cursor to control bash. For example, you may want to send an email announcing a "Movie of the Week" special to all of your video store customers. First, I'll add an email address column to the customers table and add some sample data:

```
pgbash> ALTER TABLE customers ADD COLUMN email VARCHAR;
ALTER TABLE

pgbash> UPDATE CUSTOMERS SET email='bilirubin@example.com' WHERE customer_id=2;
UPDATE 1
pgbash> UPDATE CUSTOMERS SET email='hankypanky@example.com' WHERE customer_id=3;
UPDATE 1
```

Now I can read through the customers table (using a cursor) and send an email to each recipient as shown in Listing 19.10.

Listing 19.10   sendMOTW.sh

```
 1 #!/usr/local/bin/pgbash
 2 #
 3 # Filename: sendMOTW.sh
 4 #
 5
 6 CONNECT TO movies;
 7
 8 BEGIN WORK;
 9
10 DECLARE cust CURSOR FOR SELECT customer_name, email FROM customers;
11
12 while $(true)
13 do
14
15   FETCH cust INTO :name, :email :email_ind;
16
17   if(( $SQLCODE != $SQL_OK ))
18   then
19     break
20   fi
21
22   if(( $email_ind != $SQL_NULL ))
23   then
24
25         firstName=$(echo $name | cut -d',' -f 2)
26
27     mail -s "Movie of the week" $email <<EOF
28
29 Dear $firstName, our featured movie for this week is $1.
30 Reserve your copy today!
31
32 Sincerely, your friendly neighborhood video store.
33
34 EOF
```

Listing 19.10 **Continued**

```
35
36  fi
37 done
38
39 COMMIT;
```

After connecting to the movies database and starting a new transaction, this script
declares a cursor (named cust) that reads the customer_name and email values from the
customers table. The while loop that covers lines 12 through 37 executes once for each
row returned by the cursor. The FETCH you see at line 15 reads a single row from the
cursor and creates three environment variables: $name, $email, and $email_ind. The
environment variable names are determined by the INTO clause in the FETCH statement:
The name of each variable is prefixed with a colon. Notice that the cursor (see line 10)
retrieves *two* columns but the FETCH creates *three* environment variables. The first two
correspond to the customer_name and email values. The last environment variable
($email ind) is an *indicator variable* and it tells you whether the email address ($email) is
NULL. You can declare an indicator for any value that you FETCH (or SELECT) INTO; just
list the indicator variable after the value variable without a comma in between. If a
value is NULL, its indicator variable is set to $SQL_NULL; otherwise, the indicator is set to 0
(see line 22).

Most of the PostgreSQL-specific pgbash commands modify the $SQLCODE environ-
ment variable to indicate success or failure. At line 17, I'm checking $SQLCODE to
determine when to terminate the while loop—the FETCH command sets $SQLCODE to
$SQL_OK on success and sets $SQLCODE to $SQL_NOT_FOUND when it reaches the end
of the cursor. To see a list of the values you may find in $SQLCODE, execute the ??e
command:

```
pgbash> ??e
+-----------------------+--------------------------------------------------+-----+
|      Value Name       |                    Comment                       | Value |
+-----------------------+--------------------------------------------------+-----+
| SQL_OK                | normal end.                                      | 0     |
| SQL_NOT_FOUND         | EOF(End Of File).                                | 100   |
| SQL_SYSTEM_ERROR      | system error.                                    | -200  |
| SQL_TOO_MANY_ARGUMENTS | too many arguments in fetch_stmt.               | -201  |
| SQL_TOO_FEW_ARGUMENTS | too few  arguments in fetch_stmt.                | -202  |
| SQL_CONNECT_ERROR     | database connection error.                       | -203  |
| SQL_INVALID_STMT      | invalid statements.                              | -230  |
| SQL_READONLY_SHELLVAR | can not set read-only shell variable.            | -231  |
| SQL_DB_NOT_OPEN       | database not open.                               | -232  |
| SQL_CNAME_NOT_FOUND   | connect-name not found.                          | -233  |
| SQL_CNAME_ALREADY_USE | connect-name already exist.                      | -234  |
| SQL_INVALID_COMMAND   | invalid command.                                 | -235  |
```

```
| SQL_INVALID_DATA       | invalid data.                              |-236
| SQL_BAD_RESPONSE       | bad response(backend maybe died).          |-400
| SQL_EMPTY_QUERY        | empty query (backend lost query).          |-401
| SQL_CONNECTION_BAD     | connection bad(disconnect backend)         |-403
| SQL_FATAL_ERROR        | query fatal error    (SQL error on backend)|-403
| SQL_NONFATAL_ERROR     | query nonfatal error(SQL error on backend) |-404
| SQL_NULL               | indicator is NULL.                         |-1
+-----------------------+--------------------------------------------+-----
```

After checking for the end of the result set, the test at line 22 ensures that the current row contains a non-NULL email address. When sendMOTW.sh finds a customer with a non-NULL email address, the code at lines 25 through 34 extracts the customer's first name and sends a message using the mail command. The body of the (admittedly uninspired) message appears in-line in the form of a bash HERE document (that's the stuff between the <<EOF and EOF markers).

pgbash is reasonably complete replacement for the more traditional psql command-line client. For more information about pgbash, see www.psn.co.jp/PostgreSQL/pgbash/index-e.html.

PostgreSQL Administration

20

Introduction to PostgreSQL Administration

This book is divided into three parts. The first part of the book was designed as a guide to new PostgreSQL users. The middle section covered PostgreSQL programming. The third section is devoted to the topic of PostgreSQL administration. These three parts correspond to the real-world roles that we play when using PostgreSQL.

Users are concerned mostly with getting data into the database and getting it back out again. Programmers try to provide users with the functionality that they need. Administrators are responsible for ensuring that programmers and end users can perform their jobs. Quite often, one person will fill two or three roles at the same time.

When you wear the hat of an administrator, you ensure that your users can store their data in a secure, reliable, high availability, high-performance database.

Secure means that your data is safe from intruders. You must ensure that authorized users can do the things they need to do. You also need to ensure that users cannot gain access to data that they should not see.

Reliable means the data that goes into a database can be retrieved without corruption. Any data transformations should be expected, not accidental.

High-availability means that the database is available when needed. Your users should expect that the database is ready to use when they log in. Routine maintenance should follow a predictable schedule and should not interfere with normal use. High-availability may also affect your choice of operating system and hardware. You may want to choose a cluster configuration to prevent problems in the event of a single point of failure.

High-performance means that a user should be able to perform required tasks within an acceptable amount of time. A high-performance database should also feel responsive.

In this chapter, I'll introduce you to some of the tasks that a PostgreSQL administrator must perform. The remaining chapters cover each topic in greater detail.

Security

A PostgreSQL administrator is responsible for ensuring that authorized users can do what they need to do. An administrator is also responsible for making sure that authorized users can do *only* what they need to do. Another critical job is to keep intruders away from the user's data.

There are two aspects to PostgreSQL security—authentication and access. Authentication ensures that a user is in fact who he claims to be. After you are satisfied that a user has proven his identity, you must ensure that he can access the data that he needs.

Each user (or group) requires access to a specific set of resources. For example, an accounting clerk needs access to vendor and customer records, but may not require access to payroll data. A payroll clerk, on the other hand, needs access to payroll data, but not to customer records. One of your jobs as an administrator is to grant the proper privileges to each user.

Another aspect of security in general is the problem of securing PostgreSQL's runtime environment. Depending on your security requirements (that is, the sensitivity of your data), it may be appropriate to install network firewalls, secure routers, and possibly even biometric access controls. Securing your runtime environment is a problem that is not unique to PostgreSQL, and I won't explore that topic further in this book.

Chapter 23, "Security," shows you how to grant and revoke user privileges and also covers how to prevent tampering by intruders. I'll show you how to secure PostgreSQL data, configuration, and program files on Linux/Unix systems and on Windows hosts.

User Accounts

As an administrator, you are responsible for creating, maintaining, and deleting user accounts. Your first challenge will be deciding how to map real people into PostgreSQL identities. One option is to have each user connect to PostgreSQL with a unique identity. That's usually a good policy to start with, but in some circumstances may not be practical. For example, if you are running a web site that uses PostgreSQL as the backend database, you may not want to create a unique user account for every person who connects to your web site. A good way to solve this sort of problem is to create unique identities for the users who you know, and a generic (or anonymous) identity for unknown guests.

You have to know how to create user accounts and user groups. You also need to choose authentication methods. Except in the case of anonymous guest accounts, you will want a user to prove his or her identity in some fashion. PostgreSQL offers many authentication methods, ranging from trust (which means that you trust that the host operating system has already authenticated the user) to password-based authentication to Kerberos authentication. Which authentication method(s) you choose will depend on how sensitive your data is and how secure you feel the host environment is.

Chapter 21, "PostgreSQL Administration," shows you how to maintain user accounts and user groups. Chapter 23 shows you how to choose authentication methods.

Backup and Restore

Okay, I'll admit it. A few years ago I lost two *months'* worth of development work when my hard drive crashed. I had not backed up my source code. That was a painful lesson. Fortunately, software is always better the second time you create it. That is not true for most data. Imagine losing two months' worth of customer transactions.

Database backups are critically important. Some types of data can be re-created, but it's usually easier to load an archive tape than to remanufacture lost data.

You may already have a backup plan in place for archiving filesystem data. That may not be a good solution for backing up data hosted in a PostgreSQL database. For one thing, you must shut down the database server if you choose to archive the filesystem.

PostgreSQL provides a set of utilities that you can use to archive and restore individual tables or entire databases. You can use these utilities on a live server (that is, you don't have to shut down the database first). Using the `pg_dump` and `pg_dumpall` utilities, you can also compress archive data on-the-fly.

Chapter 21 shows you how to use the `pg_dump` and `pg_dumpall` utilities and how to recover data from an archive.

Time for another confession. Not too long ago, I needed to recover some code from an archive that had been created the previous night. (Yes, I did something stupid, and the easiest way to undo it was to restore from backup.) I was surprised to find that, even though an archive had been made the previous night, I could not read from the tape because I had been using the wrong commands to create the archives. It's not enough to have a good backup plan—test your restore procedures as well.

Server Startup and Shutdown

There are a variety of ways to start and stop the PostgreSQL server. In earlier chapters, you used the `pg_ctl` command to perform server startup and shutdown. `pg_ctl` is a shell script that controls the `postmaster`; in some circumstances, you may want to bypass `pg_ctl` and interact directly with the `postmaster`. You'll learn how to do that in the next chapter.

In most cases, you will want the `postmaster` to start when your host system boots. You'll also want the `postmaster` to shut down gracefully whenever the host is powered down. The method you use to accomplish this varies with the host operating system. In Chapter 21, you'll learn how to arrange for boot-time startup and graceful shutdown for a few of the more common operating systems.

Running PostgreSQL on a Windows Host

The PostgreSQL developers reached a major milestone with the release of version 8.0. Starting with that release, PostgreSQL now runs as a native Windows application (in prior releases, PostgreSQL relied on the Cygwin package to provide a Unix-like environment on top of the Win32 subsystem). PostgreSQL version 8.0 runs as a true

Windows application. The PostgreSQL server (that is, the `postmaster`) now runs as a Windows service—you can start and shutdown the PostgreSQL service through the Windows Control Panel.

Installing PostgreSQL version 8 is remarkably easy. If you've ever installed a commercial database on a Windows host, you'll be pleasantly surprised by the simplicity of the new PostgreSQL-for-Windows installer. Once you've installed PostgreSQL on a Windows host, you can manage the server (and your data files) using the same commands and tools that you would use on any other system. With the ODBC interface (see Chapter 12, "Using PostgreSQL from an ODBC Client Application"), the JDBC interface (see Chapter 13, "Using PostgreSQL from a Java Client Application"), and PostgreSQL's new .NET provider (see Chapter 18, "npqsql: The .NET Data Provider"), you can build PostgreSQL-enabled applications using any Windows-friendly programming environment.

In Chapter 21 I'll show you how to install PostgreSQL version 8.0 on a Windows host, and in Chapter 23 you'll learn how to secure PostgreSQL data, configuration, and program files against intruders.

Tuning

Chapter 4, "Performance," covered the basics of performance analysis and query tuning in PostgreSQL. As an administrator, you need to ensure that your users are getting the best possible performance from the database. Application developers are usually responsible for tuning the interaction between their application and the database, but the administrator is responsible for the performance of the database as a whole.

PostgreSQL provides a number of configuration parameters that control the query planner and optimizer. Starting with release 7.2, PostgreSQL also offers performance-monitoring tools that you can use to watch for poor performance before your users complain.

If you are an administrator, it's a good idea to review the material in Chapter 4. Understanding performance monitoring and tuning will help narrow your focus when you are tracking down a performance problem.

You should also formulate a plan for periodic routine maintenance. For example, you decide that you should VACUUM and VACUUM ANALYZE all tables every weekend. You may also want to CLUSTER important tables on a regular basis.

Installing Updates

The PostgreSQL database is constantly evolving. As a PostgreSQL administrator, you will occasionally need to upgrade an existing database to a new release. Fortunately, upgrading an existing database is usually a simple process.

In most cases, the only work required to move to a new release is to dump the entire database cluster (using `pg_dumpall`), install the new software, and restore from the dump. Installing a new release this way is nearly identical to performing a backup and restore operation. For some upgrade paths, you don't even need to dump/restore—the new release includes a `pg_upgrade` utility that upgrades your data in place.

Localization

Localization often involves the administrator. In many organizations, you will find that different users speak different languages. A user who speaks French prefers to see messages and help text in French. A user who speaks German prefers to interact with the database (as much as possible) using the German language. You also might find that you need to store data in character sets other than ASCII.

PostgreSQL can accommodate both of these needs. PostgreSQL can be *localized* into different languages and different cultural preferences. PostgreSQL can also store data using a variety of character encoding. Chapter 22, "Internationalization/Localization," provides an in-depth discussion of the issues involved in providing localized access to your users.

Summary

This short introduction to PostgreSQL administration should give you an overview of the tasks that you might have to perform as a PostgreSQL administrator. The next few chapters fill in the details. I'll start by describing the alternatives for starting and stopping a PostgreSQL server. Next, I'll show you how to manage user accounts. Then I'll move on to the topic of backup and restore procedures. Later chapters will cover internationalization, localization, and security.

21

PostgreSQL Administration

THIS CHAPTER EXPLORES THE ROLE OF the PostgreSQL administrator. You start by looking at the on-disk organization of a typical PostgreSQL installation. Next, you'll see how to install PostgreSQL from source code or from prebuilt binaries on Unix and Windows hosts. After that, you'll learn how to create new database clusters and new databases. We will also talk about managing user accounts and managing user groups. Then, you will see how to arrange for the database server to start up automatically when you boot your system (and how to shut down gracefully when you halt your system). We'll finish this chapter by discussing your options for backup and recovery.

Roadmap (Where's All My Stuff?)

I find it much easier to administer a product if I know where every component is located. With that in mind, let's explore the directory structure for a "standard" PostgreSQL installation.

When you install PostgreSQL, whether from an RPM (Red Hat Package Manager) or from source, it will be configured to install into a particular set of directories. The exact location for any given set of PostgreSQL files is determined when the package is built from source code.

When you build a copy of PostgreSQL from source code (more on that a little later), the —prefix=*directory-name* flag determines the installation directory. The default value for —prefix is /usr/local/pgsql. You can change this by supplying a different prefix directory when you run the configure program:

```
$ ./configure —prefix=/home/bruce/pg801
```

If you want more control over the location of each component, you can add some more options to the configure command line. Table 21.1 shows the location of each component. The leftmost column shows the name of a configure option, the second column lists PostgreSQL components, and the last column shows the component type.

If you want, for example, to place the PostgreSQL shared libraries in a particular directory, you would add `–libdir=location` to the `configure` command line.

Table 21.1   **PostgreSQL Executable, Library, and Header Locations**

Directory Name	Filename	File Type
bindir	clusterdb	shell script
	createdb	shell script
	createlang	shell script
	createuser	shell script
	dropdb	shell script
	droplang	shell script
	dropuser	shell script
	ecpg	executable
	initdb	shell script
	initlocation	shell script
	ipcclean	shell script
	pg_config	shell script
	pg_controldata	executable
	pg_ctl	shell script
	pg_dump	executable
	pg_dumpall	executable
	pg_encoding	executable
	pg_id	executable
	pg_resetxlog	executable
	pg_restore	executable
	postgres	executable
	postmaster	symbolic link
	psql	executable
	vacuumdb	shell script
	sbindir	Not used
	libexecdir	Not used
datadir	conversion_create.sql	SQL script
/postgresql	pg_hba.conf.sample	example
	pg_ident.conf.sample	example
	postgres.bki	server bootstrap
	postgres.description	server bootstrap
	postgresql.conf.sample	example
docdir	postgresql/html/*	Documentation in HTML form

Table 21.1 **Continued**

sysconfdir	Not used	
sharedstatedir	Not used	
localstatedir	Not used	
libdir	libecpg.a	ECPG - library
	libecpg.so	ECPG - shared
	libpq.a	libpq - library
	libpq.so	libpq - shared
	postgresql/plpgsql.so	PL/PGSQL - shared
	postgresql/*	Character mappings
includedir	ecpgerrno.h	CPP include file
	ecpglib.h	CPP include file
	ecpqtype.h	CPP include file
	libpq-fe.h	CPP include file
	pg_config.h	CPP include file
	pg_config_os.h	CPP include file
	postgres_ext.h	CPP include file
	sql3types.h	CPP include file
	sqlca.h	CPP include file
	libpq/libpq-fs.h	CPP include file
	postgresql/*	CPP include file
oldincludedir	Not used	
infodir	Not used	
mandir	man1/*	Manual pages
	man7/*	Manual pages

The directories marked as *not used* are described when you run configure —help (configure is a commonly used generic configuration program), but are not used by PostgreSQL.

Table 21.1 shows where PostgreSQL will install the content of a basic configuration. You also can configure PostgreSQL to install optional packages (such as PL/Perl). Tables 21.2 and 21.3, later in the chapter, show where PostgreSQL will install each of the optional packages.

Installing PostgreSQL

Now that you know how a typical PostgreSQL installation is arranged on disk, it's time to actually *create* a typical installation. In the next few sections, I'll show you how to install PostgreSQL on Unix/Linux hosts and on Windows hosts. In either environment, you can install PostgreSQL from prebuilt installation packages, or you can compile PostgreSQL from source code to create a fully customized installation.

Unix/Linux

PostgreSQL was originally written for Unix, so you will find that installing PostgreSQL on a Unix host is very easy. Installing PostgreSQL on a Linux host is even easier because of the availability of prebuilt distributions.

From Binaries

The easiest way to install PostgreSQL on a Unix (or Linux) system is to use a precompiled package, such as a RPM installer. You can find RPM packages for PostgreSQL at the PostgreSQL web site (`www.postgresql.org` or `ftp.postrgesql.org`).

The process of installing PostgreSQL using a RPM package is described in Chapter 1, "Introduction to PostgreSQL and SQL." Refer to the section titled "Installing PostgreSQL Using a RPM" for more information.

From Source

Given the choice between building a package (such as PostgreSQL) from source and installing a package from a precompiled package, I'll always choose to build from source. When you build from source, you have complete control over the optional features, compiler options, and installation directories for the package. When you install from a precompiled package, you're stuck with the choices made by the person who constructed the package. Of course, using a precompiled package is much simpler. If you want to get up and running as quickly as possible, install from a binary package. If you want more control (as well as a better understanding of the options), build your own copy from source code.

There are four steps to follow when you install PostgreSQL from source code. If you have built other open-source products from source, you're probably comfortable with this procedure. If not, don't be afraid to try the build procedure yourself; it's really not difficult.

We'll walk through the four steps in this section, which are

1. Downloading and unpacking the source code
2. Configuring the source code
3. Compiling the source code
4. Installing the compiled code

Downloading and Unpacking the Source Code

The first step is to load the source code onto your system. PostgreSQL source code is distributed in a set of compressed archive (`tar`) files. The exact content of each archive can vary from release to release, but since release 7.1, the PostgreSQL source code is composed of the following archives:

```
postgresql-base-8.0.1.tar.gz    9.7 MB
postgresql-docs-8.0.1.tar.gz    2.4 MB
postgresql-opt-8.0.1.tar.gz      143.6 KB
```

```
postgresql-test-8.0.1.tar.gz        1 MB
postgresql-8.0.1.tar.gz          13.2 MB
```

The file sizes shown here are for release 8.01.

The "base" archive (`postgresql-base-8.0.1.tar.gz`) contains all the source code necessary to build a PostgreSQL server, the `psql` client, administrative tools, and contributed software. The "docs" archive contains the PostgreSQL documentation in HTML form (the base archive contains the PostgreSQL man pages). Optional features (that is, things that you have to specifically enable when you build from source code) are included in the "opt" archive. The "test" package contains a suite of regression tests that will ensure that your copy of PostgreSQL is functioning as expected.

The last archive (`postgresql-8.0.1.tar.gz`) contains *all* the source code combined into a single archive.

If you want to install as little software as possible, download the base package. If you want to be sure you have everything that you might need, download the combined package.

Table 21.2 shows the detailed contents of each package[1].

Table 21.2 **Source Package Contents**

Package Name	Package Contents
base	server (postgres, postmaster)
	contributed software (contrib)
	include files
	initdb
	ipcclean
	pg_config
	pg_controldata
	pg_ctl
	pg_dump
	pg_resetxlog
	psql
	clusterdb
	createdb
	createlang
	createuser
	dropdb

[1] With release 7.3, some of the optional features of PostgreSQL have been removed from the source distribution and moved to another site (http://gborg.postgresql.org). If you want to build the Perl client interface, for example, you'll have to download the base package (or combined) and the pgperl package from gborg.postgresql.org.

Table 21.2 **Continued**

Package Name	Package Contents
	droplang
	dropuser
	vacuumdb
	cli client interface
	ecpg client interface
	libpq client interface
	PL/pgSQL server-side language
docs	Documentation in SGML form (converted to HTML and man page format during build process)
opt	src/tools (misc. tools for use by PostgreSQL authors)
	CORBA interface
	Tutorial
	PL/Perl server-side language
	PL/Tcl server-side language
	PL/Python server-side language
test	Regression tests

The RPM-based distributions are packaged a bit differently. As of release 8.0, PostgreSQL distributes the RPM packages shown in Table 21.3

Table 21.3 **RPM Package Contents**

RPM Package Name	Package Contents
postgresql	clusterdb
	createdb
	createlang
	createuser
	dropdb
	droplang
	dropuser
	pg_dump
	pg_dumpall
	pg_restore
	psql
	vacuumdb
	documentation

Table 21.3 **Continued**

RPM Package Name	Package Contents
postgresql-server	initdb
	ipcclean
	pg_controldata
	pg_ctl
	pg_resetxlog
	server (postgres, postmaster)
	PL/pgSQL
	server locale files
	timezone information
postgresql-libs	ecpg library
	libpq library
	client locale files
postgresql-contrib	contributed software
postgresql-docs	documentation
postgresql-jdbc	JDBC (Java) interface
postgresql-pl	PL/Perl
	PL/Python
postgresql-python	Python client interface
postgresql-devel	ecpg (embedded SQL C preprocessor)
	pg_config
	header files (for C development)
	ecpg library
	libpq library
	ecpg and pg_config documentation
postgresql-test	regression test suite

In the discussion that follows, I'll assume that you have downloaded the combined package.

Configuring the Source Code

After you have downloaded the source package that you want, you can unpack the archive with the following command[2]:

```
$ tar -zxvf postgresql-version.tgz
```

The source package extracts to a directory named postgresql-version.

---

[2] The -z flag is an extension that is available only if you are using the GNU version of tar. If tar complains about the -z flag, you can achieve the same result using the command: gunzip -c postgresql-8.0.1.tar.gz | tar -xvf -.

The next step is by far the most complex: configuration. Configuration is not *difficult*, it just requires a bit of thought. When you configure source code, you select the set of features that you want and define compiler and linker options. Like most open-source packages, PostgreSQL source code is configured using the configure command. The set of configurable features and options varies from release to release, so you should study the output from the configure −help command carefully. Here is a sample of the output from this command:

```
$ cd postgresql-8.0.1
$ ./configure −help=short
'configure' configures PostgreSQL 8.0.1 to adapt to many kinds of systems.

Usage: ./configure [OPTION]... [VAR=VALUE]...

To assign environment variables (e.g., CC, CFLAGS...), specify them as
VAR=VALUE.  See below for descriptions of some of the useful variables.

Defaults for the options are specified in brackets.

Configuration:
  -h, −help               display this help and exit
      −help=short         display options specific to this package
      −help=recursive     display the short help of all the included packages
  -V, −version            display version information and exit
  -q, −quiet, −silent     do not print 'checking...' messages
      −cache-file=FILE    cache test results in FILE [disabled]
  -C, −config-cache       alias for '−cache-file=config.cache'
  -n, −no-create          do not create output files
      −srcdir=DIR         find the sources in DIR [configure dir or '..']

Installation directories:
  −prefix=PREFIX          install architecture-independent files in PREFIX
                            [/usr/local/pgsql]
  −exec-prefix=EPREFIX    install architecture-dependent files in EPREFIX
                            [PREFIX]

By default, 'make install' will install all the files in
'/usr/local/pgsql/bin', '/usr/local/pgsql/lib' etc.  You can specify
an installation prefix other than '/usr/local/pgsql' using '−prefix',
for instance '−prefix=$HOME'.

For better control, use the options below.

Fine tuning of the installation directories:
  −bindir=DIR             user executables [EPREFIX/bin]
  −sbindir=DIR            system admin executables [EPREFIX/sbin]
  −libexecdir=DIR         program executables [EPREFIX/libexec]
  −datadir=DIR            read-only architecture-independent data [PREFIX/share]
```

```
    —sysconfdir=DIR          read-only single-machine data [PREFIX/etc]
    —sharedstatedir=DIR      modifiable architecture-independent data [PREFIX/com]
    —localstatedir=DIR       modifiable single-machine data [PREFIX/var]
    —libdir=DIR              object code libraries [EPREFIX/lib]
    —includedir=DIR          C header files [PREFIX/include]
     oldincludedir=DIR       C header files for non-gcc [/usr/include]
    —infodir=DIR             info documentation [PREFIX/info]
    —mandir=DIR              man documentation [PREFIX/man]

System types:
    —build=BUILD     configure for building on BUILD [guessed]
    —host=HOST       cross-compile to build programs to run on HOST [BUILD]

Optional Features:
    —disable-FEATURE         do not include FEATURE (same as —enable-FEATURE=no)
    —enable-FEATURE[=ARG]    include FEATURE [ARG=yes]
    —enable-integer-datetimes  enable 64-bit integer date/time support
    —enable-nls[=LANGUAGES]  enable Native Language Support
    —disable-shared          do not build shared libraries
    —disable-rpath           do not embed shared library search path in executables
    —disable-spinlocks       do not use spinlocks
    —enable-debug            build with debugging symbols (-g)
    —enable-depend           turn on automatic dependency tracking
    —enable-cassert          enable assertion checks (for debugging)
    —enable-thread-safety    make client libraries thread-safe
    —enable-thread-safety-force  force thread-safety in spite of test failure
    —disable-largefile       omit support for large files

Optional Packages:
    —with-PACKAGE[=ARG]      use PACKAGE [ARG=yes]
     without-PACKAGE         do not use PACKAGE (same as —with-PACKAGE=no)

    —with-docdir=DIR         install the documentation in DIR [PREFIX/doc]
    —without-docdir          do not install the documentation
    —with-includes=DIRS      look for additional header files in DIRS
    —with-libraries=DIRS     look for additional libraries in DIRS
    —with-libs=DIRS          alternative spelling of —with-libraries
    —with-pgport=PORTNUM     change default port number 5432
    —with-tcl                build Tcl modules (PL/Tcl)
    —with-tclconfig=DIR      tclConfig.sh is in DIR
    —with-perl               build Perl modules (PL/Perl)
    —with-python             build Python modules (PL/Python)
    —with-krb4               build with Kerberos 4 support
    —with-krb5               build with Kerberos 5 support
    —with-krb-srvnam=NAME    name of the service principal in Kerberos [postgres]
    —with-pam                build with PAM support
    —with-rendezvous         build with Rendezvous support
    —with-openssl            build with OpenSSL support
```

```
—without-readline       do not use Readline
—without-zlib           do not use Zlib
—with-gnu-ld            assume the C compiler uses GNU ld [default=no]

Some influential environment variables:
  CC          C compiler command
  CFLAGS      C compiler flags
  LDFLAGS     linker flags, e.g. -L<lib dir> if you have libraries in a
              nonstandard directory <lib dir>
  CPPFLAGS    C/C++ preprocessor flags, e.g. -I<include dir> if you have
              headers in a nonstandard directory <include dir>
  CPP         C preprocessor
  LDFLAGS_SL
  DOCBOOKSTYLE
              location of DocBook stylesheets

Use these variables to override the choices made by 'configure' or to help
it to find libraries and programs with nonstandard names/locations.

Report bugs to <pgsql-bugs@postgresql.org>.
```

If you want to configure your source code to build a plain-vanilla version of PostgreSQL, you can simply run `configure` (without any options) and watch the blinking lights. The `configure` program performs a series of tests to determine what kind of operating system you are using, what kind of CPU you have, which compilers and linkers you have installed, and so forth. `configure` creates a new set of header files and `makefiles` that reflect your configuration choices.

The most interesting configuration options are the *—with-package* options. Using the *—with-package* options, you can build optional features such as the PL/Tcl language and the libpq++ client interface library.

Table 21.4 shows the package-related `configure` options. The second column lists the set of files that result from building each package. If you ever need to know what `configure` options you need to (for example) build the libpq++ shared library or the `pgtclsh` shell, consult Table 21.4.

Table 21.4 `configure` **Options and Resulting Files**

`configure` **Option**	**Files Added to Basic Installation**

—with-tcl
Tcl client API and PL/Tcl
server-side language
	`bindir/pltcl_delmod_`
	`bindir/pltcl_listmod_`
	`bindir/pltcl_loadmod_`
	`datadir/unknown.pltcl`

	`libdir/postgresql/pltcl.so` —with-python
PL/Python server-side language	`libdir/postgresql/plpython.so` —with-perl
PL/Perl server-side language	`libdir/postgresql/plperl.so`

I mentioned earlier that configure runs a number of tests to find a wealth of information about the build environment and runtime environment on your system. This can take quite awhile on a slow or heavily used system. If you want to experiment with different configuration options, you may want to enable configure's cache mechanism:

```
$ ./configure —config-cache
```

This tells configure to record its test results in a cache file (named config.cache) so that the next time you run configure, it won't have to repeat the tests. After you have finished compiling and installing PostgreSQL, you can run the program pg_config to find the set of options used to configure your copy of PostgreSQL:

```
$ pg_config —configure
—prefix=/usr/local/pg801 —enable-debug
```

The easiest way to *add* a configuration to a previously installed copy of PostgreSQL is to feed the result from pg_config back into the configure script. For example, to add PL/Python support to your existing configuration, you can run the following command:

```
$ eval ./configure $(pg_config -configure) —with-python
```

The configure program produces three files that you may be interested in examining.

config.log contains a log of the entire configuration process. This file contains a list of all the configuration tests along with the result of each test. config.log also shows you the changes that the configure program made to your source code (actually, configure leaves the original source code intact and constructs a working copy of each file that it needs to modify). If you run into any configuration or build errors, you may want to examine the config.log file to see how configure arrived at its decisions.

The config.status file is a shell script that you can run to reproduce your original configuration choices. Executing config.status is equivalent to running ./configure 'pg_config —configure'. The advantage that config.status offers is that you can reproduce your configuration choices without having a functional copy of PostgreSQL. The advantage to the second option is that you can *add* configuration options to an existing copy of PostgreSQL.

The src/include/pg_config.h file is modified to reflect many of the configuration options that you select. This file contains a few extra configuration options (such as database block size, default number of buffers, and so on) that you can't adjust using the configure program; to change these options you must edit the include/pg_config.h file (or the template, include/pg_config.h.in) by hand. You will probably never need to change this file, but you may want to glance through it so that you know what your options are.

Compiling the Source Code

After you have configured the PostgreSQL source code, compiling it is easy; just execute the make command:

```
$ make
```

The make program compiles only those portions of the source code requiring recompilation. If you are building PostgreSQL for the first time, make will compile everything. If you have already compiled PostgreSQL a few times, make will compile only the source files that you have changed, or that depend on changes that you have made. If you have made configuration changes, make is likely to recompile everything. If you want to be absolutely sure that make builds *everything*, execute the following command[3]:

```
$ make clean && make
```

After several minutes (or several hours, depending on the speed of your system), the build will complete.

If an error occurs during compilation, you might be able to fix the problem yourself by examining the error message and correcting the cause of the problem. If you're not comfortable wading through the PostgreSQL source code, search for specific error messages at the PostgreSQL web site; you will usually find an answer there.

Installing the Compiled Code

The final step is installation. In most cases, you should be logged into your system with superuser privileges (that is, log in as user root) to ensure that you can write into the installation directories. To install the compiled code, execute the following command:

```
# make install
```

The make utility copies the programs, shell scripts, and data files from your build directories into the install directories.

Completing the Installation Process

At this point, you should have all PostgreSQL components installed into their respective directories. Now, it's time to complete the installation process. When you install PostgreSQL from an RPM script, RPM will create a postgres user account for you. When you build PostgreSQL from scratch, you have to do that yourself. Consult your OS documentation for more information on how to create user accounts.

You'll also want to be sure that the PostgreSQL executables (particularly the client applications, such as psql) appear in your users' search path. The easiest way to accomplish this is to modify the /etc/profile (or equivalent) shell script.

Finally, you will want to create your initial set of databases and arrange for server startup and shutdown. Those topics are covered in other parts of this chapter.

Windows

Prior to release 8.0, you could run the PostgreSQL server on a Windows host, but you had to install a Unix compatibility library (Cygwin) first and then install PostgreSQL. In release 8.0, the PostgreSQL developers introduced a new version of PostgreSQL that

---

[3] make clean deletes the results from previous compilations. make distclean throws out the results from previous runs of the configure program.

runs as a native Windows application. The new version runs much faster than the Cygwin version, operates as a true Windows service application, and includes a spiffy new installer that makes installation a trivial (even gleeful) process. You'll need a modern version of Windows (XP, 2000, 2003, or beyond) and an NTFS filesystem.

From Binaries

To install PostgreSQL on a Windows host, download the `postgresql-version.zip` file from the `win32` section of the PostgreSQL download server (http://www.postgresql.org) and unpack the archive into a work directory (you can delete the work directory when the installer completes its work). Open a copy of Windows Explorer and navigate to the work directory, then click (or double-click if needed) the PostgreSQL installer (there are two installers in this package; choose the smaller of the two).

The installer begins by offering you a choice of (human) languages, as shown in Figure 21.1.

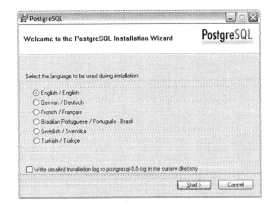

Figure 21.1   Windows Installer—Choose a Language.

Select a language (preferably a language that you understand, but that's up to you) and click Start. After a bit of clicking and whirring, the installer warns you to shut down all other programs before proceeding. Click Next and PostgreSQL displays the window shown in Figure 21.2.

Be sure to read through the installation notes; there's some good (and important) information in there. Click Next and you'll arrive at the Installation Options window (see Figure 21.3).

Select the options that you want to install and click Next.

The next dialog window (see Figure 21.4) gives you a chance to install the postmaster as a Windows service (a service is analogous to a daemon process in the Linux/Unix world).

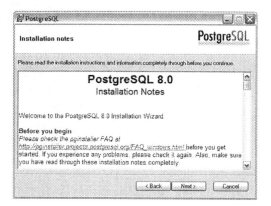

Figure 21.2   Windows Installer—Installation Notes.

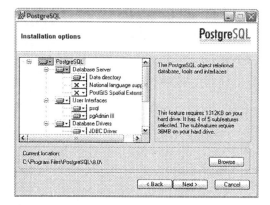

Figure 21.3   Windows Installer—Installation Options.

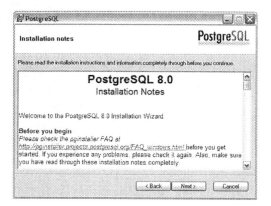

Figure 21.4   Windows Installer—Service Configuration.

If you choose *not* to create a service, you'll have to start the postmaster by hand (but you can use pg_ctl to do the heavy lifting). A Windows service runs with the privileges assigned to a specific user account. You can choose an existing account or the installer will create a new one for you (the PostgreSQL installer won't let you choose an account that holds administrator privileges).

Click Next and the window shown in Figure 21.5 appears.

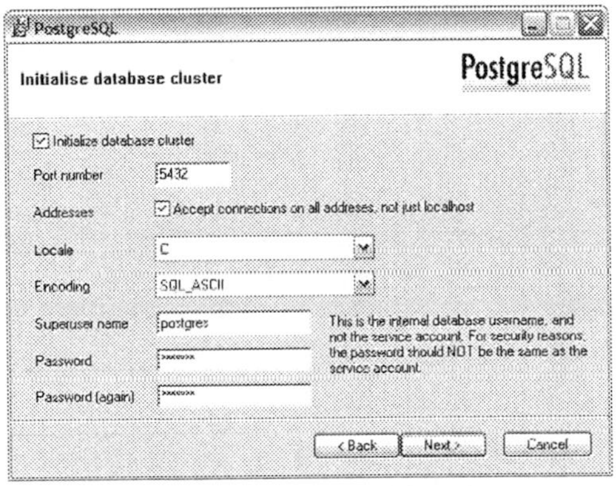

Figure 21.5   Windows Installer—Initialize DatabaseCluster.

On this window, the PostgreSQL installer is asking you to define the cluster superuser (and the superuser's password). Make any changes you deem necessary, fill in the passwords, and click Next.

The next window (Figure 21.6) lets you choose which procedural languages to install.

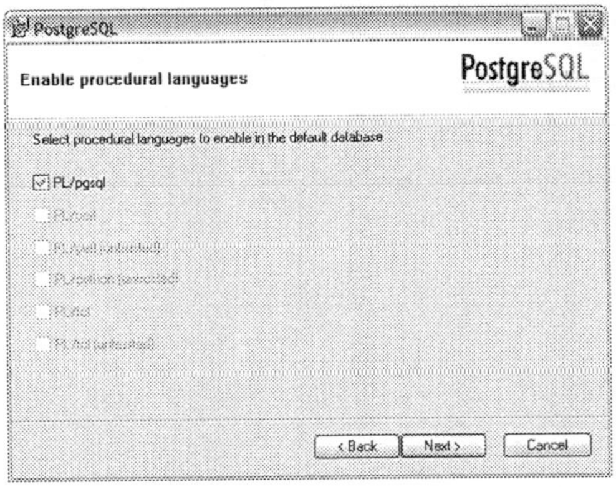

Figure 21.6   Windows Installer—Procedural Languages.

At the time we are writing this, the only choice is PL/pgSQL (which you probably want to install). Make your selection(s), click Next, and the window shown in Figure 21.7 appears.

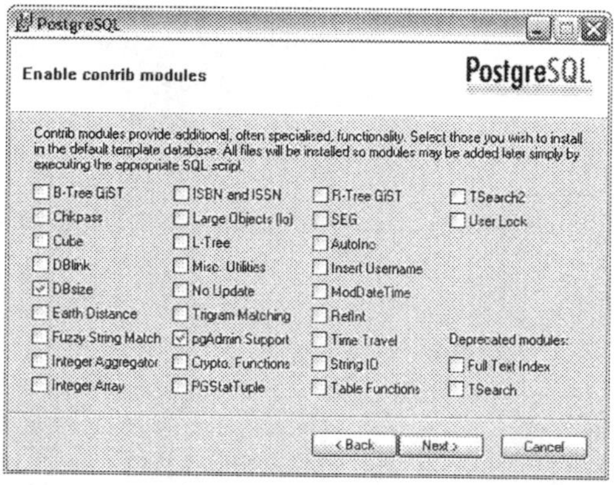

Figure 21.7   Windows Installer—Contributed Modules.

Now you're getting to the fun stuff. From this window, you can choose which contributes software modules you want to install into the template database (anything you install in the template database is automatically copied into each new database as you create it). Unfortunately, the PostgreSQL installer doesn't give you too many clues about what these modules actually do—see the PostgreSQL-related web sites for more information (http://gborg.postgresql.org, http://pgfoundry.org, and http://www.postgresql.org). I can't resist installing the Time Travel module.

Choose the modules you want to install and click Next. The installer gives you one more chance to alter your choices and then it's off and running. When the installation process completes, you have a fully installed, fully configured PostgreSQL server (and a few client applications). If you chose to install the postmaster as a Windows service, PostgreSQL will automatically start each time you boot your computer.

From Source

If you want to compile PostgreSQL from source code in a Windows environment, you'll need to install a number of tools. You can find the list (and the most recent instructions) at http://www.postgresql.org/files/documentation/faqs/FAQ_MINGW.html. After you have installed the necessary tools, you can follow the same procedure described earlier for building PostgreSQL from source on a Unix host.

Completing the Installation Process

Arriving here, you should have all necessary PostgreSQL components installed on your system. To complete the installation, you'll want to make any configuration changes that you require, create a few initial databases, and create PostgreSQL user accounts. These last few steps are described elsewhere in this chapter.

Managing Databases

PostgreSQL stores data in a collection of operating system files. At the highest level of organization, you find a cluster. A *cluster* is a collection of databases (which, in turn, is a collection of schemas).

Creating a New Cluster

You create a new cluster using the initdb program. Note that initdb is an external program, not a command that you would execute in a PostgreSQL client.

When you run initdb, you are creating the data files that define a cluster. The most important command-line argument to initdb is –pgdata=*cluster-location*[4]. The –pgdata argument tells initdb the name of the directory that should contain the new cluster. For example, if you execute the command

```
$ initdb --pgdata=/usr/newcluster
```

initdb creates the directory /usr/newcluster and a few files and subdirectories within /usr/newcluster. It's usually a good idea to let initdb create the directory that contains the cluster so that all the file ownerships and permissions are properly defined. In fact, initdb won't create a cluster in a directory that is not empty.

So, let's see the directory structure that we end up with after initdb has completed its work (see Figure 21.8).

At the top of the directory structure is the cluster directory itself—I'll refer to that as $PGDATA because that is where the $PGDATA environment variable should point.

$PGDATA contains four files and four subdirectories[5]. $PGDATA/pg_hba.conf contains the host-based authentication configuration file. This file tells PostgreSQL how to authenticate clients on a host-by-host basis. We'll look at the pg_hba.conf file in great detail in Chapter 23, "Security." The $PGDATA/pg_ident.conf file is used by the ident authentication scheme to map OS usernames into PostgreSQL user names—again, I'll

---

[4] There are actually three ways to specify the cluster location. The following commands are equivalent:

```
$ initdb --pgdata=/usr/newcluster
$ initdb -D /usr/newcluster
$ export PGDATA=/usr/newcluster ; initdb
```

[5] You are looking at a cluster created with PostgreSQL version 8.0. The exact details may differ if you are using a different version.

describe this file in the chapter dealing with PostgreSQL security. $PGDATA/post-gresql.conf contains a list of runtime parameters that control various aspects of the PostgreSQL server. The fourth file, $PGDATA/PG_VERSION, is a simple text file that contains the version number from initdb.

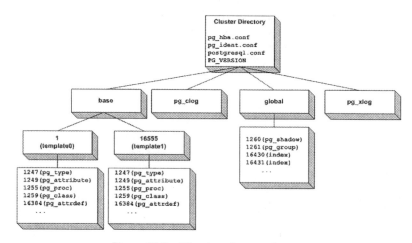

Figure 21.8 The data directory layout.

Now, let's look at each of the subdirectories created by initdb.

The pg_xlog directory contains the write-ahead logs. Write-ahead logs are used to improve database reliability and performance. Whenever you update a row within a table, PostgreSQL will first write the change to the write-ahead log, and at some later time will write the modifications to the actual data pages on disk. The pg_xlog directory usually contains a number of files, but initdb will create only the first one-extra files are added as needed. Each xlog file is 16MB long.

The pg_clog directory contains commit logs. A commit log reflects the state of each transaction (committed, in-progress, or aborted).

The global directory contains three tables that are shared by all databases within a cluster: pg_shadow, pg_group, and pg_database. The pg_shadow table holds user account definitions and is maintained by the CREATE USER, ALTER USER, and DROP USER commands. The pg_group table holds user group definitions and is maintained by the CREATE GROUP, ALTER GROUP, and DROP GROUP commands. pg_database contains a list of all databases within the cluster and is maintained by the CREATE DATABASE and DROP DATABASE commands. The global directory also contains a number of indexes for the pg_shadow, pg_group, and pg_database tables. global contains two other files that are shared by all databases in a cluster: pgstat.stat and pg_control. The pgstat.stat file is used by the statistics monitor (the statistics monitor accumulates performance and usage information for a database cluster). The pg_control file contains a number of cluster parameters, some of which are defined by initdb and will never change. Others are modified each time the postmaster is restarted. You can view the contents of the pg_control file using the pg_controldata utility provided in the contrib directory of a source distribution. Here's a sample of the output from pg_controldata:

```
$ pg_controldata
pg_control version number:              74
Catalog version number:                 200411041
Database system identifier:             4773932360515448816
Database cluster state:                 in production
pg_control last modified:               Tue 22 Jun 2005 02:16:00 PM EST
Current log file ID:                    0
Next log file segment:                  16
Latest checkpoint location:             0/F1AC608
Prior checkpoint location:              0/52EA2B8
Latest checkpoint's REDO location:      0/F1AC608
Latest checkpoint's UNDO location:      0/0
Latest checkpoint's TimeLineID:         1
Latest checkpoint's NextXID:            558
Latest checkpoint's NextOID:            798284
Time of latest checkpoint:              Tue 22 Jun 2005 02:16:00 PM EST
Database block size:                    8192
Blocks per segment of large relation:   131072
Bytes per WAL segment:                  16777216
Maximum length of identifiers:          64
Maximum number of function arguments:   32
Date/time type storage:                 floating-point numbers
Maximum length of locale name:          128
LC_COLLATE:                             en_US.UTF-8
LC_CTYPE:                               en_US.UTF-8
```

The initdb utility also creates two template databases in the new cluster: template0 and template1. The template0 database represents a "stock" database—it contains the definitions for all system tables, as well as definitions for the standard views, functions, and data types. You should never modify template0—in fact, you can't even connect to the template0 database without performing some evil magic. When you run initdb, the template0 database is copied to template1. You *can* modify the template1 database. Just as the template0 database is cloned to create template1, template1 is cloned whenever you create a new database using CREATE DATABASE (or createdb). It's useful to modify the template1 database when you want a particular feature (like a custom data type, function, or table) to exist in every database that you create in the future. For example, if you happen to run an accounting business, you might want to define a set of accounting tables (customers, vendors, accounts, and so on) in the template1 database. Then, when you sign up a new customer and create a new database for that customer, the new database will automatically contain the empty accounting tables.

You may also find it useful to create other template databases. To extend the previous example a bit, let's say that you have a core set of financial applications (general ledger, accounts payable, accounts receivable) that are useful regardless of the type of business your customer happens to run. You may develop a set of extensions that are well suited to customers who own restaurants, and another set of extensions that you use for plumbers. If you create two new template databases, `restaurant_template` and `plumber_template`, you'll be ready to sign up new restaurants and new plumbers with minimal work. When you want to create a database for a new restaurateur, simply clone the `restaurant_template` database.

After you have created a cluster (and the two default template databases), you can create the actual databases where you will do your work.

Creating a New Database

There are two ways to create a new database. You can use the CREATE DATABASE command from within a PostgreSQL client application (such as `psql`), or you can use the `createdb` shell script. The syntax for the CREATE DATABASE command is

```
CREATE DATABASE database-name
    [WITH    [TEMPLATE = template-database-name ]
        [ENCODING = character-encoding ]
            [OWNER = database-owner ]
                [LOCATION = pathname ]]
```

A `database-name` must conform to the usual rules for PostgreSQL identifiers: it should start with an underscore or a letter and should be at most 31 characters long. If you need to include a space (or start the database name with a digit), enclose the `database-name` in double quotes.

When you execute the CREATE DATABASE command, PostgreSQL will copy an existing template database. If you don't include a TEMPLATE=`template-_database-name` clause, CREATE DATABASE will clone the `template1` database. A few restrictions control whether or not you can clone a given database. First, a cluster superuser can clone *any* database. The owner of a database can clone that database. Finally, any user with CREATEDB privileges can clone a database whose `datistemplate` attribute is set to `true` in the `pg_database` system table. Looking at this in the other direction, ordinary users cannot clone a database that is not specifically marked as a template (according to the `datistemplate` attribute).

You can choose an *encoding* for the new database using the ENCODING=`character-encoding` clause. An encoding tells PostgreSQL which character set to use within your database. If you don't specify an encoding, the new database will use the same encoding that the template database uses. Encodings are discussed in detail in Chapter 22, "Internationalization and Localization."

If you don't include the OWNER=`username` clause or if you specify OWNER=DEFAULT, you become the owner of the database. If you are a PostgreSQL superuser, you can create a database that will be owned by another user using the OWNER=`username` clause. If you are not a PostgreSQL superuser, you can still create a database (assuming that you hold the CREATEDB privilege), but you cannot assign ownership to another user.

The final option to the CREATE DATABASE command is LOCATION=*pathname*. This clause is used to control where PostgreSQL places the files that make up the new database. If you don't specify a location, CREATE DATABASE will create a subdirectory in the cluster ($PGDATA) to hold the new database. There are some restrictions to where you can place a new database; see the "Creating New Databases" section of Chapter 3, "PostgreSQL SQL Syntax and Use," for more information.

As I mentioned earlier, there are two ways to create a new database: CREATE DATABASE and createdb. The createdb utility is simply a shell script that invokes the psql client to execute a CREATE DATABASE, command. createdb does not offer any more functionality than CREATE DATABASE so use whichever you find most convenient. For more information on the createdb utility, invoke createdb with the –help flag:

```
$ createdb –help
createdb creates a PostgreSQL database.

Usage:
  createdb [options] dbname [description]

Options:
  -D, –location=PATH       Alternative place to store the database
  -T, –template=TEMPLATE   Template database to copy
  -E, –encoding-ENCODING   Multibyte encoding for the database
  -h, –host=HOSTNAME       Database server host
  -p, –port=PORT           Database server port
  -U, –username-USERNAME   Username to connect as
  W,  password             Prompt for password
  -e, –echo                Show the query being sent to the backend
  -q, –quiet               Don't write any messages

By default, a database with the same name as the current user is created.

Report bugs to <pgsql-bugs@postgresql.org>.
```

Routine Maintenance

Compared to most relational database management systems, PostgreSQL does not require much in the way of routine maintenance, but there are a few things you should do on a regular basis.

Managing Tables (CLUSTER and VACUUM)

When you delete (or update) rows in a PostgreSQL table, the old data is *not* immediately removed from the database. In fact, unlike other database systems, the free space is not even marked as being available for reuse. If you delete or modify a lot of data, your database may become very large very fast. You may also find that performance suffers because PostgreSQL will have to load obsolete data from disk even though it won't use that data.

To permanently free obsolete data from a table, you use the VACUUM command. The VACUUM command comes in four flavors:

```
VACUUM [table-name]
VACUUM FULL [table-name]
VACUUM ANALYZE [table-name]
VACUUM FULL ANALYZE [table-name]
```

The first and third forms are the ones most commonly used.

In the first form, VACUUM makes all space previously used to hold obsolete data available for reuse. This form does not require exclusive access to the table and usually runs quickly. If you don't specify a table-name, VACUUM will process all tables in the database.

In the second form, VACUUM *removes* obsolete data from the table (or entire database). Without the FULL option, VACUUM only marks space consumed by obsolete data as being available for reuse. With the FULL option, VACUUM tries to shrink the data file instead of simply making space available for reuse. A VACUUM FULL requires exclusive access to each table and is generally much slower than a simple VACUUM.

The VACUUM ANALYZE command will first VACUUM a table (or database) and will then compute statistics for the PostgreSQL optimizer. I discussed optimization and statistics in Chapter 4, "Performance." If you will VACUUM a table (or database), you may as well update the per-table statistics as well.

The final form combines a VACUUM FULL with a VACUUM ANALYZE. As you might expect, this shrinks the database by removing obsolete data and then computes new performance-related statistics. Like VACUUM FULL, VACUUM FULL ANALYZE locks each table for exclusive use while it is being processed.

Another command that you may want to execute on a routine basis is the CLUSTER command. CLUSTER rearranges the rows in a given table so that they are physically stored in index order. This is a cheap way to get enormous performance gains—run this command occasionally and you'll look like a hero. See Chapter 4 for more information.

PostgreSQL includes a client application named pg_autovacuum (you'll find it in the contrib source code directory) that you can use to automatically VACUUM tables as required. pg_autovacuum watches for modifications (INSERT, UPDATE, DELETE commands) and VACUUMs the modified tables as soon as the number of changes reaches a certain threshold (you can control the threshold). pg_autovacuum will also update optimizer statistics on your behalf. If you're running an active database server, be sure to consider pg_autovacuum; it can increase performance and decrease the amount of work you put in to managing your system.

Managing Indexes

For the most part, indexes are self-maintaining. Occasionally, you may find that an index has become corrupted and must be rebuilt (actually, you are more likely to *suspect* a corrupted index than to find one). You can also improve performance slightly (and reduce disk space consumption) by rebuilding indexes on an occasional basis.

The easiest way to rebuild an index is with the REINDEX command. REINDEX comes in the following forms:

```
REINDEX INDEX index-name [FORCE]
REINDEX TABLE table-name [FORCE]
REINDEX DATABASE database-name [FORCE]
```

In all three forms, you can force REINDEX to rebuild indexes on system tables (they are normally ignored by REINDEX) by including the keyword FORCE at the end of the command. If you find you need to REINDEX system tables, you should consult the *PostgreSQL Reference Manual* for the gory details. (Warning—this is not for the faint-of-heart.)

Managing Tablespaces

PostgreSQL version 8.0 introduces a new feature that you can use to organize the data files that make up a cluster. A *tablespace* is a name that you give to a directory somewhere in your computer's filesystem. A tablespace can store both tables and indexes. When you CREATE (or ALTER) a table or index, you can tell PostgreSQL to store that object inside of a specific tablespace. A tablespace is defined within a single cluster—all databases within a cluster can refer to the same tablespace.

To create a new tablespace, use the CREATE TABLESPACE command:

```
CREATE TABLESPACE tablespacename
  [ OWNER username ]
  LOCATION 'directory'
```

PostgreSQL reserves all tablespace names that begin with pg_. If you omit the OWNER username clause, the new tablespace is owned by the user executing the CREATE TABLESPACE command. By default, you can't create an object in a tablespace unless you are the owner of that tablespace (or you are a cluster superuser). You can grant CREATE privileges to other users with the GRANT command (see Chapter 23 for more information on the GRANT command).

The LOCATION clause identifies the directory where PostgreSQL will store any objects that you place in the new tablespace. There are a few rules that you must follow before you can create a tablespace:

- You must be a cluster superuser
- PostgreSQL must be running on a system that supports symbolic links (that means you can't create tablespaces on a Windows host)
- The *directory* must already exist (PostgreSQL won't create the directory for you)
- The *directory* must be empty
- The *directory* name must be shorter than 991 characters
- The *directory* must be owned by the owner of the postmaster process (typically a user named postgres)

If all of those conditions are satisfied, PostgreSQL creates the new tablespace.

When you create a tablespace, PostgreSQL changes the permissions on the *directory* to 700 (read, write, and execute permissions for the directory owner, all other permissions denied). PostgreSQL creates a single file named PG_VERSION in the given directory (the PG_VERSION file stores the version number of the PostgreSQL server that created the tablespace—if the PostgreSQL developers change the structure of a tablespace in a future version, PG_VERSION will help any conversion tools understand the structure of an existing tablespace). Next, PostgreSQL adds a new row to the pg_tablespace table (a cluster-wide table) and assigns a new OID (object-id) to that row. Finally, the server uses the OID to create a symbolic link between your cluster and the given *directory*.

To help you understand the details, consider the following scenario:

```
movies# CREATE TABLESPACE mytablespace LOCATION '/fastDrive/pg';
CREATE TABLESPACE

movies# SELECT oid, spcname, spclocation
movies-#    FROM
movies-#       pg_tablespace
movies-#    WHERE
movies-#       spcname = 'mytablespace';
  oid  |   spcname    |  spclocation
-------+--------------+--------------
 34281 | mytablespace | /fastDrive/pg
```

In this case, PostgreSQL assigned the new tablespace (mytablespace) an OID of 34281. PostgreSQL creates a symbolic link that points from $PGDATA/pg_tblspc/34281 to /fastDrive/pg. When you create an object (a table or index) inside of this tablespace, the object is *not* created directly inside of the /fastDrive/pg directory. Instead, PostgreSQL creates a subdirectory in the tablespace and then creates the object within that subdirectory. The name of the subdirectory corresponds to the OID of the database (that is, the object-id of the database's entry in the pg_database table) that holds the new object. If you create a new table within the mytablespace tablespace, like this

```
movies# CREATE TABLE foo ( data VARCHAR ) TABLESPACE mytablespace;
CREATE TABLE
```

then find the OID of the new table and the OID of the database (movies):

```
movies# SELECT oid FROM pg_class WHERE relname = 'foo';
  oid
-------
 34282
(1 row)

movies# SELECT oid FROM pg_database WHERE datname = 'movies';
  oid
-------
```

```
17228
(1 row)
```

You can see the relationships between the tablespace, the database subdirectory, and the new table:

```
$ ls -l $PGDATA/pg_tblspc
total 0
lrwxrwxrwx     1 postgres postgres          12 Nov  9 19:31 34281 -> /fastDrive/pg

$ ls -l /fastDrive/pg
total 8
drwx-----     2 postgres postgres        4096 Nov  9 19:50 17228
-rw------     1 postgres postgres           4 Nov  9 19:31 PG_VERSION

$ ls -l /fastDrive/pg/17228
total 0
-rw------     1 postgres postgres           0 Nov  9 19:50 34282
```

Notice that $PGDATA/pg_tblspc/34281 is a symbolic link that points to /fastDrive/pg (34281 is the OID of mytablespace's entry in the pg_tablespace table), PostgreSQL has created a subdirectory (17228) for the movies database, and the table named foo was created in that subdirectory (in a file whose name, 34282, corresponds to the table's OID). By creating a subdirectory for each database, PostgreSQL ensures that you can safely store objects from multiple databases within the same tablespace without worrying about OID collisions.

When you create a cluster (which is done for you automatically when you install PostgreSQL), PostgreSQL silently creates two tablespaces for you: pg_default and pg_global. PostgreSQL creates objects in the pg_default tablespace when it can't find a more appropriate tablespace. The pg_default tablespace is always located in the $PGDATA/base directory. The pg_global tablespace stores cluster-wide tables like pg_database, pg_group, and pg_tablespace—you can't create objects in the pg global tablespace.

The name of the pg_default tablespace can be a bit misleading. You may think that PostgreSQL always creates an object in pg_default if you omit the TABLESPACE tablespacename clause, but that's not the case. Instead, PostgreSQL follows an inheritance hierarchy to find the appropriate tablespace. If you specify a TABLESPACE tablespacename clause when you execute a CREATE TABLE or CREATE INDEX command, the server creates the object in the given tablespacename. If you don't specify a tablespace and you're creating an index, the index is created in the tablespace of the parent table (that is, the table that you are indexing). If you don't specify a tablespace and you're creating a table, the table is created in the tablespace of the parent schema. If you are creating a schema and you don't specify a tablespace, the schema is created in the tablespace of the parent database. If you are creating a database and you don't specify a tablespace, the database is created in the tablespace of the template database (typically, template1). To summarize: An index inherits its tablespace from the parent table, a table inherits its tablespace from the parent schema, a schema inherits its tablespace from the parent database, and a database inherits its database from the template database.

To view the databases defined in a cluster, use the \db (or \db+) command in psql:
movies=# \db+

```
                        List of tablespaces
     Name      |   Owner   |    Location      |  Access privileges
---------------+-----------+------------------+------------------
 mytablespace  | postgres  | /fastDrive/pg    |
 pg_default    | postgres  |                  |
 pg_global     | postgres  |                  |  {pg=C/pg}
(4 rows)
```

To see a list of objects defined with a given tablespace, use the following query:

```
SELECT relname FROM pg_class
   WHERE reltablespace =
   (
     SELECT oid FROM pg_tablespace WHERE spcname = 'tablespacename'
   );
```

Logfile Rotation

When you start a PostgreSQL server process (either the postmaster or a backend server process), that process typically writes a whole sequence of messages to the server log. If you don't take any special action, PostgreSQL writes the server log to the stderr (standard error) stream of the postmaster process. If you use pg_ctl to control the postmaster, you probably include the -l *logfile* command-line option to redirect the log to a disk file. Starting with PostgreSQL version 8.0, you have a better method at your disposal: rotating log files.

Server logs can grow very quickly, particularly when you're recording a lot of details about how your PostgreSQL cluster is working. At the very least, the server log will tell you when something goes wrong. If you're in a development environment (or if you are trying to solve some sort of problem), the server log can show quite a bit more. You can record the text of every query that causes an error, every query that takes more than, say, two minutes to execute, or the text of every query that your server executes. You can record execution plans, parser and planner statistics, or buffer manager operations.

It's easy to talk PostgreSQL into setting up a rotating log file mechanism for you. First, forget about the -l *logfile* option. Instead, change the REDIRECT_STDERR configuration parameter from its default value (False) to True and restart the postmaster. That's it. As soon as you restart the postmaster, PostgreSQL will create a new log file in the $PGDATA/pg_log directory. The log filename will look something like: postgresql-2005-06-20_102644.log. PostgreSQL will automatically close that file and start a new file when 24 hours have elapsed, or when the log file grows to 10MB in size, whichever occurs first. PostgreSQL will continue to cycle through new log files every 24 hours (or 10MB) as long as the postmaster is running. You can adjust the interval between new log files by changing the configuration parameter (LOG_ROTATION_AGE is measured in minutes). You can also adjust the maximum log file size by changing LOG ROTATION SIZE (measured in kilobytes). If you want to move the log files to a different filesystem (or just move them to a different directory), modify the LOG_DIRECTORY parameter.

At this point, PostgreSQL is creating new log files for you every so often, but it's not actually *rotating* the files. To rotate (or reuse) log files, you have to change the file naming scheme. Take another look at the name of the log file that PostgreSQL created: postgresql-2005-06-20_102644.log. The middle part of the name (the 2005-06-20_102644) looks suspiciously similar to a date/time stamp, and in fact, that's what it is. Unless you tell it to do otherwise, PostgreSQL generates log filenames by splicing together three strings: 'postgresql-', the current date and time, and '.log'. That pattern is defined by the LOG_FILENAME configuration parameter. The default value for LOG_FILENAME is postgresql-%Y-%m-%d_%H%M%S.log. When PostgreSQL creates a new filename, it expands the macros (the %x thingies) in LOG_FILENAME to come up with the actual name. For example, PostgreSQL expands %Y to the current century and year (2005); %m expands to the current two-digit month number (06), and so on. Table 21.5 shows the complete list of macros that you can include in LOG_FILENAME. Obviously, PostgreSQL will never come up with the same filename twice if you include a complete time stamp in LOG_FILENAME (assuming that the granularity of the time stamp is greater than the interval between creating two log files). If it *does* come up with a duplicate filename, we'll all be too old (and too dusty) to care.

To set up a rotating log scheme, you *want* PostgreSQL to generate duplicate filenames on a periodic basis. For example, if you set LOG_FILENAME to a pattern such as postgresql-%a.log, PostgreSQL will generate log filenames like postgresql-Mon.log, postgresql-Tue.log, postgresql-Wed.log, and so on (the %a macro expands to the abbreviated name of the weekday, in the server's locale). If you set LOG_ROTATION_AGE to 10080 (one week), you can see that PostgreSQL will begin generating duplicate log file names as soon as one week has gone by. What happens when PostgreSQL runs into a file with the same name as the log file it wants to record? That depends on the value of the LOG_TRUNCATE_ON_ROTATION configuration parameter. If LOG_TRUNCATE_ON_ROTATION is False (which is the default value), PostgreSQL will simply append new messages to the end of the existing file. In this example, the postgresql-Mon.log file would contain all messages generated on any Monday. If LOG_TRUNCATE_ON_ROTATION is True, you get a true rotation scheme; PostgreSQL deletes the existing file and replaces it with a new log file that contains only the message generated on the most recent Monday. Of course, when PostgreSQL replaces the Monday file, the Tuesday file still contains messages recorded on the *previous* Tuesday. That means that you have one week's worth of history. If you want to keep a year's worth of history, set LOG_FILENAME to postgresql-%b.log

(%b expands to the abbreviated name of the month, in the server's locale). To keep a month's worth of history, include a %d in LOG_FILENAME (%d expands to the two-digit day of the month). You can use the LOG_FILENAME macros to set up just about any rotation scheme you want. In general, you want the date mask in LOG_FILENAME pattern to match the LOG_ROTATION_AGE interval.

The PostgreSQL BGWRITER Process

When a PostgreSQL server process reads data from disk, it first moves the page that contains the data into the shared buffer pool. The shared buffer pool is so named because it's a region of memory that's shared by all server processes that access a given cluster. Another way to look at it is that the shared buffer pool is shared by all processes spawned by a single postmaster. When the shared buffer pool fills, PostgreSQL starts pushing old pages out of the pool to make room for new ones. PostgreSQL uses the ARC algorithm, or, in older versions the LRU (least-recently-used) mechanism to select the page it evicts from the pool (see Chapter 4 for more information). If PostgreSQL chooses a page that has not been modified since it was placed in the pool, that page is simply discarded. On the other hand, if PostgreSQL chooses a page that *has* been modified, it must write the page to disk.

Prior to release 8.0, a modified page would hang around in the shared buffer pool until it was evicted by a server process or by a CHECKPOINT (a CHECKPOINT flushes *all* modified pages from the shared buffer pool). That meant that any given server process might need to wait for a disk write to complete before it could pull a page from disk into the shared buffer pool. That also meant that a CHECKPOINT could cause a flurry of disk activity because it would find many modified pages in the shared buffer pool.

PostgreSQL version 8.0 introduces a new process, the BGWRITER (short for background writer) that lurks in the background and occasionally flushes modified pages out of the shared buffer pool. The BGWRITER spends much of its time sleeping, but every time it wakes, it searches through the shared buffer pool looking for modified pages. After each search, the BGWRITER chooses some number of modified pages, writes them to disk, and evicts those pages from the shared buffer pool.

The BGWRITER improves overall performance in two ways. First, it tries to increase the number of free pages (or at least, the number of unmodified pages) in the shared buffer pool so that individual server processes won't have to wait for disk writes. Second, it decreases the number of modified pages found in the shared buffer pool when a CHECKPOINT occurs—the BGWRITER *smooths out* the I/O spikes caused by CHECKPOINTs.

You can tune the BGWRITER with three configuration parameters: BGWRITER_DELAY, BGWRITER_PERCENT, and BGWRITER_MAXPAGES. The BGWRITER_DELAY parameter controls how long the BGWRITER process sleeps between each round. BGWRITER_PERCENT and BGWRITER_MAXPAGES limit the number of pages that the BGWRITER_PROCESS flushes during each round.

Managing User Accounts

As a PostgreSQL administrator, you may be responsible for creating user accounts and groups. You may also be responsible for granting and revoking privileges.

In most environments, there is a one-to-one mapping between a user's operating system identity and his PostgreSQL identity. In fact, your PostgreSQL username is often identical to your OS username.

In some cases, other configurations are useful. For example, you may want most of your users to identify themselves uniquely while providing an anonymous account for low-privileged guests. You may also have a client application that identifies *itself* rather than identifying the user (this is useful for utility applications that can be executed by *any* user without providing any sort of authentication).

A user account is shared between all databases within a given cluster. User groups are also shared between all databases within a cluster.

CREATE USER

There are two ways to create a new user: you can execute the CREATE USER command from within a client application (such as psql), or you can use the createuser shell script.

The complete syntax for the CREATE USER command is

```
CREATE USER user-name
        [[WITH] option ]...

option := SYSID user-id-number
        | [NO]CREATEDB
        | [NO]CREATEUSER
        | IN GROUP groupname [, ...]
        | [[UN]ENCRYPTED ] PASSWORD 'password'
        | VALID UNTIL 'expiration'
```

A user-name must conform to the usual rules for PostgreSQL identifiers: it should start with a letter (or an underscore) and should be at most 31 characters long. If you need to start a username with a number, just enclose the name in double quotes.

User account definitions are stored in the pg_shadow system table. You can view the layout of the pg_shadow table using the psql \d meta-command:

```
movies=# \d pg_shadow
        Table "pg_shadow"
  Column    |  Type   | Modifiers
------------+---------+----------
 usename    | name    |
 usesysid   | integer |
 usecreatedb| boolean |
 usetrace   | boolean |
 usesuper   | boolean |
```

```
usecatupd   | boolean |
passwd      | text    |
valuntil    | abstime |
Unique keys: pg_shadow_usename_index,
             pg_shadow_usesysid_index
Triggers: pg_sync_pg_pwd
```

You can see the correlation between the pg_shadow table and the CREATE USER options. The *user-name* is stored in the usename column. The *user-id-number* value is stored in usesysid. The usecreatedb column reflects the [NO]CREATEDB option. usetrace is reserved for future use and is not currently used. The usesuper column reflects the value of the [NO]CREATEUSER option. (As you'll see in a moment, a user who is allowed to create new user accounts is considered to be a superuser.) The usecatupd determines whether a user can directly update PostgreSQL's system tables (using the INSERT, UPDATE, and DELETE commands). If usecatupd is false, you can update the system tables only indirectly, using other commands such as CREATE TABLE, CREATE USER, and so on. The only way to change usecatupd is to use the UPDATE command (that is, UPDATE pg_shadow SET usecatupd = true). The passwd and valuntil columns store the *password* and *expiration*, respectively.

Each of the *option* values are, well, optional. I'll describe them all here.

SYSID

Using the SYSID *user-id-number* option, you can assign a specific numeric user-id to a user. The *PostgreSQL Reference Manual* mentions that this option is useful if you want to correlate PostgreSQL user-ids with OS user-ids, but there's a more important use for the SYSID option.

When a user creates a database object (table, view, sequence, and so on), the object owner is not associated with the user's name, but with the user's SYSID. You can see this by looking at the layout of the pg_class system table:

```
movies=# \d pg_class
           Table "pg_class"
    Column       |   Type   | Modifiers
-----------------+----------+----------
 relname         | name     |
 reltype         | oid      |
 relowner        | integer  |
 relam           | oid      |
 ...
 ...
 relhassubclass  | boolean  |
 relacl          | aclitem[]|
Unique keys: pg_class_oid_index,
             pg_class_relname_index
```

Notice that the `relowner` column is defined as an `integer`, not as a `name`. What happens if you delete a user that happens to own a database object? Let's see. First, we'll log in as user bruce and create a new table:

```
$ psql -d movies -q -U bruce
movies=> create table bruces_table ( pkey integer );
CREATE
movies=> SELECT * FROM pg_tables WHERE tablename = 'bruces_table';
  tablename   | tableowner | hasindexes | hasrules | hastriggers
--------------+------------+------------+----------+------------
 bruces_table | bruce      | f          | f        | f
(1 row)
movies=# \q
```

Notice that `bruces_table` is owned by user bruce. Now, let's remove bruce's account:

```
$ psql -q -d movies
movies=# DROP USER bruce;
movies=# SELECT * FROM pg_tables WHERE tablename = 'bruces_table';
  tablename   |    tableowner    | hasindexes | hasrules | hastriggers
--------------+------------------+------------+----------+------------
 bruces_table | unknown (UID=105) | f          | f        | f
(1 row)
```

Now, `bruces_table` is owned by an unknown user (whose `SYSID` is 105). That's not really a problem in itself, but it can certainly lead to confusion. If you *don't* assign a specific `SYSID`, `CREATE USER` will choose the next highest number (starting at 100). That means that eventually, you may create a new user whose `SYSID` turns out to be 105-bruce's old `SYSID`. Suddenly your brand new user owns a whole mess of database objects. You can recover from this sort of problem by adding a new user with a specific `SYSID`[6].

Privileges (CREATEDB and CREATEUSER)

When you create a new user, you can control whether the user is allowed to create new databases. You also can control whether the user is allowed to create new users. Giving a user the right to create new databases will rarely, if ever, pose a security risk, but allowing a user to create new users can. When you grant a user `CREATEUSER` privileges, that user becomes a superuser in your cluster. Let me say that again in a slightly different way: A user who has `CREATEUSER` privileges can bypass *all* security restrictions in your database cluster. You can explicitly deny `CREATEUSER` privileges by specifying `NOCREATEUSER`. `NOCREATEUSER` is assumed if you don't specify either value.

The `CREATEDB` option grants the user the right to create new databases (within the cluster). You can specify `NOCREATEDB` to prohibit the user from creating new databases. If you specify neither `CREATEDB` nor `NOCREATEDB`, `CREATE USER` will assume `NOCREATEDB`.

[6] You can also fix this problem by updating the relowner value in pg_class, but that's living dangerously.

Group Membership (IN GROUP)

You can assign a new user to one or more groups by including the IN GROUP clause. For example, to create a user named bernard as a member of the developers and administrators groups:

```
CREATE USER bernard IN GROUP developers, administrators;
```

If you don't assign the new user to a group, he will be a member of the pseudo-group PUBLIC, but no other groups.

PASSWORD and Password Expiration

The final two options are somewhat related. You can create an initial password for a new user by including the PASSWORD, ENCRYPTED PASSWORD, or UNENCRYPTED PASSWORD option. If you don't specify a password when you create a new user (and you are using passwords to authenticate client connections), the user will not be able to log in. If you choose to create an ENCRYPTED PASSWORD, the password will be stored, in encrypted form, in the pg_shadow system table. If you choose to create an UNENCRYPTED PASSWORD, it will also be stored in pg_shadow, but in cleartext form. If you create a password without specifying ENCRYPTED or UNENCRYPTED, CREATE USER will look to the PASS-WORD_ENCRYPTION server option to decide whether to store the password in cleartext or encrypted form.

Be aware that unencrypted passwords are visible to any PostgreSQL superuser.

The VALID UNTIL 'expiration' option controls password expiration. If you omit VALID UNTIL, the initial password will never expire. If you include VALID UNTIL 'expiration', the password will become invalid after the time and date indicated by expiration.

createuser

The createuser shell script is a bit easier to use than CREATE USER because it prompts you for all required information. Here is sample createuser session:

```
$ createuser
Enter name of user to add: bernard
Shall the new user be allowed to create databases? (y/n) n
Shall the new user be allowed to create more new users? (y/n) n
Password:
CREATE USER
```

There's a serious gotcha that always trips me up when I use createuser. Notice in the previous example that createuser has prompted me for a password. When you see the Password: prompt, createuser is asking for *your* password, not the password to be assigned to the new user. createuser is just a shell script that connects to the server and executes a CREATE USER command on your behalf. You must authenticate yourself to the server, so createdb needs to know your password. If you invoke createuser with the -pwprompt flag (or -P for short), createdb will also prompt you for the new user's password:

```
$ createuser —pwprompt
Enter name of user to add: bernard
Enter password for user "bernard":
Enter it again:
Shall the new user be allowed to create databases? (y/n) n
Shall the new user be allowed to create more new users? (y/n) n
Password:
CREATE USER
```

You can see the difference—when I am supposed to enter bernard's password, createuser is kind enough to use a more descriptive prompt. When I have finished answering all createuser's questions, I am prompted for *my* password.

ALTER USER

You can modify the attributes of existing user accounts with the ALTER USER command. The ALTER USER command is similar to CREATE USER:

```
ALTER USER user-name
      [[WITH] option ]...

option := [NO]CREATEDB
        | [NO]CREATEUSER
        | [[UN]ENCRYPTED ] PASSWORD 'password'
        | VALID UNTIL 'expiration'
```

You can use ALTER USER to change a user's privileges (CREATEDB and CREATEUSER) and password information (PASSWORD and VALID UNTIL). You *cannot* use ALTER TABLE to change a user's SYSID. You can change a user's group membership, but not with ALTER USER; you must use the ALTER GROUP command for that.

DROP USER

Removing obsolete user accounts is easy: use the DROP USER command:

```
DROP USER user-name
```

You must be a PostgreSQL superuser to use DROP USER. When you drop a user, PostgreSQL will not delete any objects (tables, views, sequences) owned by that user— they will be owned by a "mystery" owner. You cannot drop a user who owns a database.

GRANT and REVOKE

After you have created a new user, you must decide which database objects (tables, views, and sequences) that user should be able to access, and what kinds of access they should have. For each user/object combination, you can grant SELECT, INSERT, UPDATE, DELETE, REFERENCES, and TRIGGER privileges. I'll show you how to grant and revoke privileges in Chapter 23.

You can imagine that assigning individual privileges for every user of every table would be rather time-consuming and difficult to maintain. You can reduce the administrative overhead by creating user groups.

Managing Groups

You can define named groups of users to make your administrative life much easier to manage. Every group can include zero or more users. Every user can belong to one or more groups. When you grant or revoke privileges for an object, you can identify a specific user or a group of users.

Every user is automatically a member of the group PUBLIC. PUBLIC is actually a virtual group—you can't add or remove members and you can't drop this group, but you can associate privileges with PUBLIC.

Groups are much easier to manage if they correspond to usage roles in your organization. For example, you might create groups named developers, guests, clerks, and administrators. Laying out groups so that they reflect real-world user groups makes it much easier to assign access privileges to your database objects. Of course, any given user can belong to many groups. For example, a member of the developers group might also be an administrator.

Group definitions are stored in the pg_group system table. Like database users, group definitions are shared by all databases within a cluster.

CREATE GROUP

A PostgreSQL superuser can create a new group using the CREATE GROUP command:

```
CREATE GROUP group-name [[WITH] option [...]]

option :=   SYSID group-id-number
          | USER username, ...
```

The *group-name* must meet the usual rules for PostgreSQL identifiers (31 characters or less, quoted, or starting with an underscore or a letter).

You can include a SYSID value if you want to assign a specific numeric ID for the new group. Like user accounts, a group is referenced by its numeric ID, not by name. We users know each group by name, but any table that refers to a group will refer to the numeric value. You might assign a specific numeric ID to a group for the same reasons that you might assign a specific ID to a user (see the previous section for more information).

You can assign group membership in three ways:

- Use the IN GROUP option in the CREATE USER command
- List the usernames in the USER option of CREATE GROUP
- Change the group membership using the ALTER GROUP command

A typical CREATE GROUP command might look something like this:

```
CREATE GROUP developers USER bernard,lefty;
```

This command creates a new group named developers that initially has two members: bernard and lefty.

ALTER GROUP

Using the ALTER GROUP command, you can add members to a group, or remove users from a group. The format of the ALTER GROUP command is

```
ALTER GROUP group-name {ADD|DROP} USER user-name [, ...]
```

Only PostgreSQL superusers can alter a group.

DROP GROUP

The DROP GROUP command deletes a group. The format of the DROP COMMAND is

```
DROP GROUP group-name
```

You can drop a group only if you are PostgreSQL superuser.

Now let's change focus from security-related issues to another important administrative concern—backup and recovery.

Configuring Your PostgreSQL Runtime Environment

After you have finished installing the PostgreSQL distribution, you may want to review the runtime configuration options.

Permanent configuration options should be defined in the file $PGDATA/postgresql.conf. The postgresql.conf file is a plain text file that you can maintain with your favorite editor (vi, emacs, and so on). When you create a new database cluster, the initdb program will create a default postgresql.conf file for you. postgresql.conf is arranged as a series of *option=value* pairs; blank lines are ignored and any text that follows an octothorpe (#) is treated as a comment. Here is a snippet from a postgresql.conf file created by initdb:

```
#
#       Connection Parameters
#
#tcpip_socket = false
#ssl = false

#max_connections = 32

#port = 5432
#hostname_lookup = false
#show_source_port = false
```

```
#unix_socket_directory = "
#unix_socket_group = "
#unix_socket_permissions = 0777
```

PostgreSQL supports a large number of runtime configuration options (more than 150:
at last count). In the next few sections, you'll see a description of each parameter and the
parameter's default value. Default values can come from four sources: a hard-wired
default value that you can't adjust without changing the source code, a symbolic value
that can be changed only by editing the include/pg_config.h header file, a compile-
time configuration option, or a command-line option to the postmaster.

Some of the options can be modified at runtime using the SET command; others can
be defined only before starting the postmaster. The sections that follow document the
modification time for each parameter.

Parameters with a Modify Time of "Postmaster startup" can be changed only by
modifying the postgresql.conf file and restarting the postmaster.

Parameters labeled SIGHUP can be modified after the postmaster process has started.
To modify a SIGHUP option, edit the postgresql.conf configuration file and send a
SIGHUP signal to the postmaster process. You can use the pg_ctl reload command to
signal the postmaster.

The parameters that you can change with the SET command are labeled with a modification time of "SET command".

File Locations

The PostgreSQL server expects to find data files, configuration files, and authorization/
authentication files in the $PGDATA directory tree. Starting with PostgreSQL version 8.0,
you can move bits and pieces to different locations in your filesystem. For example, you
may have a policy that states that all configuration files must be stored in the /etc directory and all data files must be stored in the /var directory tree. If you're using an older
version of PostgreSQL, you can use symbolic links to relocate PostgreSQL components.
If you're using a PostgreSQL version 8.0 or later, you can customize the placement of
each component by modifying a small collection of runtime parameters: CONFIG_FILE,
HBA_FILE, IDENT_FILE, and EXTERNAL_PID_FILE. You must tell the postmaster how to
find the postgresql.conf file (it can't look in postgresql.conf to find the location of
postgresql.conf).

DATA_DIRECTORY
Default Value: $PGDATA
Modify Time: Postmaster startup
Override: postmaster -D data_directory

DATA_DIRECTORY tells the postmaster how to find your database cluster. If you don't
modify the DATA_DIRECTORY parameters, PostgreSQL expects to find the cluster in the
directory that you specify (following the -D flag) when you start the postmaster, or in
$PGDATA. The directory named by DATA_DIRECTORY should contain the base, global,

pg_clog, pg_subtrans, pg_tblspc, and pg_xlog subdirectories that make up a database cluster.

CONFIG_FILE

Default Value:	$PGDATA/postgresql.conf
Modify Time:	Postmaster startup
Override:	postmaster -c config_file=*file-name*

The CONFIG_FILE parameter tells the postmaster how to find the postgresql.conf configuration file. If you've moved the postgresql.conf file to a location other than $PGDATA/postgresql.conf, you must tell the postmaster the name of the file on the postmaster (or pg_ctl) command line. This is one of the few parameters that you cannot include in the postgresql.conf configuration file (CONFIG_FILE tells the postmaster how to *find* postgresql.conf).

HBA_FILE

Default Value:	$PGDATA/pg_hba.conf
Modify Time:	Postmaster startup
Override:	postmaster -c hba_file=*file-name*

This parameter tells the postmaster how to find the pg_hba.conf file. pg_hba.conf contains the host-based authentication rules that control access to the cluster. See Chapter 23 for more information regarding host-based authentication.

IDENT_FILE

Default Value:	$PGDATA/pg_ident.conf
Modify Time:	Postmaster startup
Override:	postmaster -c ident_file=*file-name*

IDENT_FILE tells the postmaster how to find the ident map file (used by the ident authentication method). See Chapter 23 for more information about the ident authentication method.

EXTERNAL_PID_FILE

Default Value:	"
Modify Time:	Postmaster startup
Override:	

When the postmaster begins servicing a cluster, it records its own process ID in the $PGDATA/postmaster.pid file. The pg_ctl program knows how to find the postmaster by reading the PID file. Other applications (such as the Linux/Unix SysVInit facility) may also use PID files to locate and communicate with a running service (such as the postmaster). To make it easier to interface a third-party service manager with the postmaster, you can ask PostgreSQL to create a second PID file in a separate location by setting EXTERNAL_PID_FILE to the name of the file that you want PostgreSQL to create.

Security-Related Parameters

SSL

Default Value:	`False`
Modify Time:	Postmaster startup
Override:	`postmaster -l`

If true, the `SSL` parameter tells the `postmaster` to negotiate with clients over the use of `SSL`-secured connections. `SSL` is a protocol that encrypts the data stream flowing between the client and the server. If `SSL` is true, and the client supports `SSL`, the data stream will be encrypted; otherwise, PostgreSQL data will be sent in clear-text form. You can override this parameter by invoking the `postmaster` with the `-l` flag.

PASSWORD_ENCRYPTION

Default Value:	`True`
Modify Time:	`SET`
Override:	`SET PASSWORD_ENCRYPTION TO [true|false]`
	`CREATE USER WITH ENCRYPTED PASSWORD...`
	`CREATE USER WITH UNENCRYPTED PASSWORD...`
	`ALTER USER WITH ENCRYPTED PASSWORD...`
	`ALTER USER WITH UNENCRYPTED PASSWORD...`

When you execute a `CREATE USER` (or `ALTER USER ... PASSWORD`) command without an explicit encryption clause, PostgreSQL examines the `PASSWORD_ENCRYPTION` parameter to determine whether it should store the password in encrypted or plain-text form (in other words, `PASSWORD_ENCRYPTION` specifies the default password encryption policy). If `PASSWORD_ENCRYPTION` is `True`, PostgreSQL will store passwords in encrypted form (unless the `CREATE USER` or `ALTER USER` command explicitly requests an `UNENCRYPTED` password). If `PASSWORD_ENCRYPTION` is False, PostgreSQL will store passwords in plain-text form (unless the `CREATE USER` or `ALTER USER` command explicitly requests an `ENCRYPTED` password).

DB_USER_NAMESPACE

Default Value:	`FALSE`
Modify Time:	`SIGHUP`
Override:	None

When you create a user account (with the `createuser` program or the `CREATE USER` command), PostgreSQL stores the account information in a cluster-wide table (`pg_shadow`). That means that a new user can access any database defined within the cluster (subject to the privileges assigned to the database). If you enable `DB_USER_-NAMESPACE`, you can create user accounts specific to each database in addition to creating cluster-wide accounts. To create a database-specific account, specify an account name of the form `"username@database-name"` (`"bruce@movies"` for example). To create a cluster-wide account, use the syntax `"username@"` (in other words, omit the database name). In either case, you must enclose the name in double quotes.

You can only include an @ in an account name if DB_USER_NAMESPACE is TRUE.

It's a little tricky to actually *use* per-database user accounts because you can end up with a mix of cluster-wide and per-database accounts. For example, assume that you've created two accounts: sheila@ and bruce@movies. With DB_USER_NAMESPACE enabled, sheila can only connect to the movies database using the following syntax:

```
$ psql -U "sheila@" movies
```

But user bruce must specify

```
$ psql -U bruce movies
```

With DB_USER_NAMESPACE enabled, PostgreSQL follows a modified procedure to locate the correct user account. If the name that you provide contains an @, PostgreSQL strips off everything that follows the @ and searches for the username in the cluster-wide account table (pg_shadow). If the name that you provide does not include an @, PostgreSQL adds an @ and appends the database name, then searches for the resulting account name in pg_shadow. Note that, in either case, PostgreSQL searches for the account name in pg_shadow (a cluster-wide table).

To summarize, with DB_USER_NAMESPACE enabled

- Add @*database-name* when you create a per-database account
- Add @ to create a cluster-wide account
- Include the trailing @ when you log in to a cluster-wide account
- Omit the @ (and trailing database name) when you log in to a per-database account

The PostgreSQL reference documentation warns that DB_USER_NAMESPACE is an interim solution that may be withdrawn in a future release.

AUTHENTICATION_TIMEOUT

Default Value:	60
Modify Time:	SIGHUP
Override:	None

This parameter defines the maximum amount of time (in seconds) that the postmaster will wait for a client to complete the authentication process. If the timeout period expires, the postmaster will sever the connection with the client.

KRB_SERVER_KEYFILE

Default Value:	/etc/srvtab or $SYSCONFDIR/krb5.keytab
Modify Time:	Postmaster startup
Override:	None

If you are using Kerberos to authenticate clients, the server keyfile is normally located in /etc/srvtab (for Kerberos 4) or $SYSCONFDIR/krb5.keytab (for Kerberos 5). You can specify an alternate (possibly more secure) location using the KRB_SERVER_KEYFILE parameter.

Connection-Related Parameters

This section looks at the connection-related configuration parameters. Notice that most of the connection-related parameters must be defined at the time that the `postmaster` starts.

LISTEN_ADDRESSES

Default Value:	`localhost (127.0.0.1)`
Modify Time:	Postmaster startup
Override:	`postmaster -h address [,address,...]`

The `LISTEN_ADDRESSES` parameter tells the `postmaster` which network interface(s) it should service when listening for client connection requests. By default, the postmaster listens for connection requests arriving on the loopback interface (address 127.0.0.1, typically known as `localhost.localdomain`). If you want to provide service to other computers, set `LISTEN_ADDRESSES` to the IP address (or hostname) of your local network interface. If you are running PostgreSQL on a multi-homed computer (that is, a computer with more than one network interface), you can list multiple IP addresses (or hostnames), separated by commas. To tell the `postmaster` to service all network interfaces, set `LISTEN_ADDRESSES='*'`. Don't forget to configure the `pg_hba.conf` (host-based authentication) file if you service any externally connected network interfaces.

`LISTEN_ADDRESSES` was introduced in release 8.0 and replaces the `VIRTUAL_HOST` and `TCP_IP` parameters used in prior releases.

RENDEZVOUS_NAME

Default Value:	Disabled
Modify Time:	Postmaster startup
Override:	

Rendezvous is Apple's implementation of the ZEROCONF service discovery protocol. ZEROCONF is a protocol that provides service naming and service discovery features to a local area network without the need for manually configured central directory servers. When you use ZEROCONF, you can address computers (and printers and PostgreSQL servers) by name without creating a DNS server or a DHCP server. Instead, each service in your network *advertises* itself on your local area network. Other computers listen for the advertisements and *discover* available services as they appear. PostgreSQL can advertise itself as a ZEROCONF service on computers that support Rendezvous (or the open-source alternative, `howl`, published by http://www.porchdogsoft.com).

To use Rendezvous, you must specify `—with-rendezvous` when you configure the PostgreSQL source code. You must also set `RENDEZVOUS_NAME` to the name that you want your PostgreSQL server to advertise. PostgreSQL will always advertise itself as a service of type "`_postgresql._tcp.`".

TCPIP_SOCKET

Default Value:	`False`
Modify Time:	Postmaster startup
Override:	`postmaster -i`

This parameter determines whether the `postmaster` listens for connection requests coming from a TCP/IP socket. If `TCPIP_SOCKET` is false, the `postmaster` will listen for connection requests coming only from a Unix local domain socket. If `TCPIP__SOCKET` is true, the `postmaster` will listen for connection requests coming from a TCP/IP socket, as well as listening for local connection requests. You can override this variable by invoking the `postmaster` with the `-i` flag.

This parameter has been replaced by `LISTEN_ADDRESSES` starting in PostgreSQL version 8.0.

SUPERUSER_RESERVED_CONNECTIONS

Default Value:	2
Modify Time:	Postmaster startup
Override:	

PostgreSQL reserves at least this many connections (out of the maximum allowed `MAX_CONNECTIONS`) for users that hold superuser privileges within the cluster. With the default value (2), you ensure that your cluster superuser can still connect to the database, even if all other connections have been allocated to non-privileged users. Remember that some maintenance processes (like `pg_autovacuum`) may consume connections that you reserve for superusers so be sure to set `SUPERUSER_RESERVED_CONNECTIONS` to a higher number if you're running those processes.

`postmaster -1`

MAX_CONNECTIONS

Default Value:	100
Modify Time:	Postmaster startup
Override:	`postmaster -n connections`

The `MAX_CONNECTIONS` parameter determines the maximum number of concurrent client connections that the `postmaster` will accept. You can increase (or decrease) the maximum number of connections by invoking the `postmaster` with the `-n connections` parameter. You also can change the default value for `MAX_CONNECTIONS` by invoking `configure` with the `—with-maxbackends=connections` option when you build PostgreSQL from source code.

PORT

Default Value:	5432
Modify Time:	Postmaster startup
Override:	`postmaster -p port`

This parameter determines which TCP/IP port the postmaster should listen to. When a remote client application wants to connect to a PostgreSQL server, it must connect to a TCP/IP port where a postmaster is listening for connection requests. The client and server must agree on the same port number. You can override this parameter by invoking the postmaster with the -p *port* parameter. You can also change the default value for PORT by invoking configure with the —with-pgport=*port* when you build PostgreSQL from source code.

UNIX_SOCKET_DIRECTORY

Default Value:	/tmp
Modify Time:	Postmaster startup
Override:	postmaster -k *directory*

The postmaster always listens for local connection requests using a Unix domain socket. The socket's device file is normally found in the /tmp directory. You can move the socket device file to a different directory by using the UNIX_SOCKET_DIRECTORY configuration parameter or by invoking the postmaster with the -k *directory* parameter. You also can change the default value for this parameter by defining the DEFAULT PGSOCKET_DIR directory when you configure and build PostgreSQL from source code.

UNIX_SOCKET_GROUP

Default Value:	None
Modify Time:	Postmaster startup
Override:	None

This parameter determines the owning group of the Unix local domain socket (see previous entry for more information). If UNIX_SOCKET_GROUP is undefined (or empty), the socket will be created using the default group for the user that starts the postmaster. The *PostgreSQL Administrator's Manual* suggests that you can use this parameter, along with UNIX_SOCKET_PERMISSION, to restrict local connections to a specific group.

UNIX_SOCKET_PERMISSIONS

Default Value:	0777
Modify Time:	Postmaster startup
Override:	None

This parameter determines the permissions assigned to the Unix local domain socket. By default, the socket is created with permissions of 0777 (meaning readable and writable by anyone). By changing the socket permissions, you can restrict local connection requests by user ID or group ID. For example, if you create a group named postgresusers, set UNIX_SOCKET_GROUP to postgresusers, and set UNIX_SOCKET_PERMISSIONS to 0060. Only users in the postgresusers group will be able to connect through the local domain socket.

VIRTUAL_HOST

Default Value:	None
Modify Time:	Postmaster startup
Override:	`postmaster -h host`

If the `postmaster` is running on a host that supports multiple IP addresses (for example, has multiple network adapters), you can use the `VIRTUAL_HOST` parameter to tell the `postmaster` to listen for connection requests on a specific IP address. If you don't specify a `VIRTUAL_HOST`, the postmaster will listen on all network adapters.

This parameter has been replaced by `LISTEN_ADDRESSES` starting in PostgreSQL version 8.0

Operational Parameters

The next set of parameters forms a group of loosely related options that affect how the PostgreSQL server operates. Most of these options affect performance and are therefore related to the options shown in the next section.

BGWRITER_DELAY

Default Value:	`200 (milliseconds)`
Modify Time:	`SIGHUP`
Override:	None

Determines how long the `BGWRITER` process will sleep after writing a collection of modified pages to disk. See the section titled "The PostgreSQL `BGWRITER` Process" (in this chapter) for more information.

BGWRITER_PERCENT

Default Value:	1 (percent)
Modify Time:	`SIGHUP`
Override:	None

When the `BGWRITER` process awakens, it searches through the shared memory pool to find pages that have been modified and, therefore, must be written to disk. `BGWRITER` does not flush *all* modified pages to disk every time it wakes up. Instead, `BGWRITER` chooses a fraction (based on `BGWRITER_PERCENT`) of the least-recently-used (and modified) pages and writes only those pages to disk. `BGWRITER` writes no more than `BGWRITER MAXPAGES` during each cycle (that is, the `BGWRITER` process writes `BGWRITER_MAXPAGES` or `modified_page_count * (BGWRITER_PERCENT/100)`, whichever is smaller).

BGWRITER_MAXPAGES

Default Value:	`100 (pages)`
Modify Time:	`SIGHUP`
Override:	None

The BGWRITER process writes no more than BGWRITER_MAXPAGES pages to disk during each cycle. See the section titled "The PostgreSQL BGWRITER Process" (in this chapter) for more information.

SHARED_BUFFERS

Default Value:	64 or DEF_NBUFFERS=nbuffers
Modify Time:	Postmaster startup
Override:	postmaster -B nbuffers

When PostgreSQL reads data from (or writes data to) disk, it first transfers the data into a cache stored in shared memory. This cache is shared by all clients connected to a single cluster. Disk I/O (and cache I/O) is performed in 8KB chunks (each chunk is called a page). The SHARED_BUFFERS parameter determines how many 8KB pages will be created in the shared cache. The default value, 64, is usually sufficient for a small number of users, but should be increased as your user count grows. See Chapter 4 for more information. You can change the default value for SHARED_BUFFERS by defining the DEF_NBUFFERS environment variable when you configure and build PostgreSQL from source code. You can also override SHARED_BUFFERS by invoking the postmaster with the -B nbuffers command-line parameter.

MAX_FSM_RELATIONS

Default Value:	1000
Modify Time:	Postmaster startup
Override:	None

When PostgreSQL needs to write new data into a table, it searches the table for free space. If free space cannot be found *within* the table, the file holding the table is enlarged. The free-space manager caches free-space information in shared memory for better performance. The MAX_FSM_RELATIONS parameter determines the maximum number of tables that the free-space manager will manage at one time. If the cache becomes full, old free-space information will be removed from the cache to make room. This parameter is related to the MAX_FSM_PAGES parameter.

MAX_FSM_PAGES

Default Value:	120000
Modify Time:	Postmaster startup
Override:	None

This parameter (along with MAX_FSM_RELATIONS) determines the size of the free-space cache used by the free-space manager. The free-space cache contains, at most, MAX_FSM_PAGES worth of data from, at most, MAX_FSM_RELATIONS different tables.

These two parameters have no effect on *read* operations, but can affect the performance of INSERT and UPDATE commands.

WORK_MEM

Default Value:	`1024 kilobytes (1MB)`
Modify Time:	`SET` command
Override:	None

When PostgreSQL processes a query, it transforms the query from string form into an execution plan. An execution plan is a sequence of operations that must be performed in order to satisfy the query. A typical execution plan might include steps to scan through an entire table and sort the results. If an execution plan includes a `Sort` or `Hash` operation, PostgreSQL can use two different algorithm families to perform the sort (or hash). If the amount of memory required to perform the sort (or hash) exceeds `WORK_MEM` KB, PostgreSQL will switch from an in-memory algorithm to a more expensive, disk-based algorithm. You can adjust `WORK_MEM` on a per-command basis using the command `SET WORK_MEM TO maximum_memory`.

This parameter was named `SORT_MEM` prior to PostgreSQL release 8.0.

MAINTENANCE_WORK_MEM

Default Value:	`16384 kilobytes (16MB)`
Modify Time:	`SET` command
Override:	None

`MAINTENANCE_WORK_MEM` specifies the maximum amount of memory PostgreSQL will allocate for maintenance operations (specifically, `VACUUM`, index creation, and foreign key creation).

This parameter was named `VACUUM_MEM` prior to PostgreSQL release 8.0.

MAX_STACK_DEPTH

Default Value:	`2048 kilobytes (2MB)`
Modify Time:	`SET` command (superuser only)
Override:	

This parameter specifies the maximum size of the server execution stack. Your operating system may impose a lower limit, or, in most cases, a higher limit. PostgreSQL checks its own stack size at critical points where complex queries may cause deep recursion (and therefore overflow the stack). If PostgreSQL detects that the size of the stack has exceeded `MAX_STACK_DEPTH` (measure in kilobytes), it will issue an error `54001` (`stack depth limit exceeded`). If you see that error, you may consider increasing `MAX_STACK_DEPTH`. Be aware, however, that if PostgreSQL overflows the operating system-imposed limit before reaching `MAX_STACK_DEPTH`, the most likely result is a nasty crash, smoke, and a few flames.

`MAX_STACK_DEPTH` replaces the (now obsolete) `MAX_EXPR_DEPTH` parameter starting in PostgreSQL release 8.0.

MAX_FILES_PER_PROCESS

Default Value:	1000
Modify Time:	Postmaster startup
Override:	None

This parameter defines maximum number of files that PostgreSQL opens for any given server process. PostgreSQL uses a file-descriptor caching mechanism to extend the number of files that are *logically* open without having to have each file *physically* opened, so if you see any error messages suggesting that you have Too Many Open Files, you should *reduce* this parameter.

FSYNC

Default Value:	True
Modify Time:	SIGHUP
Override:	postmaster -F

When an application (such as the PostgreSQL server) writes data to disk, the operating system usually buffers the modifications to improve performance. The OS kernel flushes modified buffers to disk at some time in the future. If your host operating system (or hardware) experiences a crash, not all buffers will be written to disk. If you set the FSYNC parameter to True, PostgreSQL will occasionally force the kernel to flush modified buffers to disk. Setting FSYNC to True improves reliability with little performance penalty.

VACUUM_COST_LIMIT

Default Value:	200
Modify Time:	SET command
Override:	None

Starting with release 8.0, you can reduce the performance hit that you suffer while VACUUM or ANALYZE commands are executing. When you fire off a VACUUM or ANALYZE command, the server keeps track of the cost of executing that command. The cost is estimated based on the number of pages found in the shared memory buffer, the number of pages found on-disk, and the number of pages modified. When the cost exceeds VACUUM_COST_LIMIT, the server forces the VACUUM (or ANALYZE) command to take a short nap before continuing. The nap lasts for VACUUM_COST_DELAY milliseconds. When the command wakes up again, the server resets the execution cost to zero. By napping from time to time, the VACUUM and ANALYZE commands reduce contention with other (presumably more important) processes.

When PostgreSQL computes the cost of executing a VACUUM or ANALYZE command, is assigns an estimated cost to each type of operation. For example, when PostgreSQL reads a page from disk (on behalf of a VACUUM or ANALYZE command), it adds 10 units (the default value for VACUUM_COST_PAGE_MISS) to the cost of executing the command. When a VACUUM or ANALYZE command writes a modified page back to disk, PostgreSQL adds 20 units (the default value for VACUUM_COST_PAGE_DIRTY) to the cost of executing the command. Assuming the default cost estimates, a VACUUM command would nap for VACUUM_COST_DELAY milliseconds after reading 20 pages from disk or reading 200 pages from the shared memory buffer, or writing 10 modified pages back to disk, or any combination that adds up to VACUUM_COST_LIMIT units.

By default, VACUUM_COST_DELAY is set to zero, which means that the lazy VACUUM feature is effectively disabled.

VACUUM_COST_DELAY

Default Value:	0
Modify Time:	SET command
Override:	None

VACUUM_COST_DELAY determines the amount of time (measured in milliseconds) that a VACUUM or ANALYZE command will nap when the cost of executing the command exceeds VACUUM_COST_LIMIT. When the command reawakens, the server resets the execution cost back to zero.

By default, VACUUM_COST_DELAY is set to zero, which means that the lazy VACUUM feature is disabled.

VACUUM_COST_PAGE_HIT

Default Value:	1
Modify Time:	SET command
Override:	None

This parameter determines the estimated cost of finding a required page in the shared memory buffer (as a result of executing a VACUUM or ANALYZE command). VACUUM_COST_PAGE_HIT is used by the lazy VACUUM feature to estimate the cost of executing a VACUUM or ANALYZE command.

VACUUM_COST_PAGE_MISS

Default Value:	10
Modify Time:	SET command
Override:	None

This parameter determines the estimated expense of reading a page from disk (as a result of executing a VACUUM or ANALYZE command). VACUUM_COST_PAGE_MISS is used by the lazy VACUUM feature to estimate the cost of executing a VACUUM or ANALYZE command.

VACUUM_COST_PAGE_DIRTY

Default Value:	20
Modify Time:	SET command
Override:	None

This parameter determines the estimated expense of writing a modified page back to disk (as a result of executing a VACUUM or ANALYZE command). VACUUM_COST_PAGE_DIRTY is used by the lazy VACUUM feature to estimate the cost of executing a VACUUM or ANALYZE command.

PRELOAD_LIBRARIES
Default Value: "
Modify Time: Postmaster startup
Override:

Use the PRELOAD_LIBRARIES parameter to preload shared libraries into the postmaster. PRELOAD_LIBRARIES should contain a comma-separated list of entries of the form:

```
library-name[ : initializer-name ]
```

Each entry in the list specifies a shared library and the name of an initialization function within that library (the initializer name is optional). For example, to preload the PL/pgSQL and PL/Perl language processors, you would include the following entry in the postgresql.conf configuration file:

```
preload_libraries = 'plpgsql.so:plpgsql_init, plperl.so:plperl_init'
```

If the *library-name* does not include a path separator character (that is, a / or \ character), the postmaster searches the directories named by DYNAMIC_LIBRARY_PATH to find the library.

When you preload a library into the postmaster, the postmaster incurs the overhead of loading and initializing that library. When the postmaster spawns a server process to service a new client, the server process inherits the preloaded, fully initialized library from the postmaster. Use PRELOAD_LIBRARIES with caution—it moves initialization overhead out of the server process and into the postmaster, but that means that *every* server process contains a copy of the shared library (and *every* server process becomes a bit larger). If you don't preload a library, the library is only loaded on-demand; if a server process doesn't actually use the library, it's never loaded.

Write-Ahead Log Parameters

The parameters described in this section influence PostgreSQL's write-ahead log (WAL).

WAL_BUFFERS
Default Value: 8
Modify Time: Postmaster startup
Override: None

When a transaction makes a change to a PostgreSQL table, the change is applied to the heap (and/or index) pages that are cached in shared memory. All changes are also logged to a *write-ahead* log. The write-ahead log is also cached in shared memory. When a transaction is committed, the write-ahead log is flushed to disk, but the changes made to the actual data pages may not be transferred from shared memory to disk until some point in the future. The size of the shared write-ahead cache is determined by WAL_BUFFERS. The default value of 8 creates a shared write-ahead cache of eight 8KB pages.

CHECKPOINT_SEGMENTS

Default Value:	3
Modify Time:	SIGHUP
Override:	None

The write-ahead log files are divided into 6MB segments. Every so often, PostgreSQL will need to move all modified data (heap and index) pages from the shared-memory cache to disk. This operation is called a *checkpoint*. Log entries made prior to a checkpoint are obsolete and the space consumed by those stale entries can be recycled. If PostgreSQL never performed a checkpoint, the write-ahead logs would grow without bound. The interval between checkpoints is determined by the CHECKPOINT_SEGMENTS and CHECKPOINT_TIMEOUT parameters. A checkpoint will occur every CHECKPOINT TIMEOUT seconds or when the number of newly filled segments reaches CHECKPOINT_SEGMENTS.

CHECKPOINT_TIMEOUT

Default Value:	300 (seconds)
Modify Time:	SIGHUP
Override:	None

This parameter determines the maximum amount of time that can elapse between checkpoints. You may see a checkpoint occur *before* CHECKPOINT_TIMEOUT seconds has elapsed if the CHECKPOINT_SEGMENTS threshold has been reached.

CHECKPOINT_WARNING

Default Value:	30 (seconds)
Modify Time:	SIGHUP
Override:	None

If PostgreSQL executes a CHECKPOINT more often CHECKPOINT_WARNING (measured in seconds), the BGWRITER processes records a warning (checkpoints are occurring too frequently) to the server log. If you see this message, you should consider increasing CHECKPOINT_SEGMENTS.

COMMIT_DELAY

Default Value:	0 (microseconds)
Modify Time:	SET command
Override:	None

When a transaction is committed, the WAL must be flushed from shared-memory to disk. PostgreSQL pauses for COMMIT_DELAY microseconds so that other server processes can sneak their commits into the same flush operation. The default for this parameter is 0, meaning that the WAL will be flushed to disk immediately after each COMMIT.

COMMIT_SIBLINGS

Default Value:	5 (transactions)
Modify Time:	SET command
Override:	None

The COMMIT_DELAY (described previously) is a waste of time if there are no other transactions active at the time you COMMIT (if there are no other transactions, they can't possibly try to sneak in a COMMIT). The WAL manager will not delay for COMMIT_DELAY microseconds unless there are at least COMMIT_SIBLINGS transactions active at the time you COMMIT your changes.

WAL_SYNC_METHOD

Default Value:	Dependent on host type
Modify Time:	SIGHUP
Override:	None

When the WAL manager needs to flush cached write-ahead pages to disk, it can use a variety of system calls. The legal values for WAL_SYNC_METHOD vary by host type. It's not very likely that you will ever need to adjust this value—the default value is chosen by the configure program at the time PostgreSQL is built from source code. See the *PostgreSQL Administrator's Guide* for more information.

ARCHIVE_COMMAND

Default Value:	"
Modify Time:	SIGHUP
Override:	None

If ARCHIVE_COMMAND is defined, PostgreSQL archives each WAL (write-ahead-log) segment before recycling that segment. ARCHIVE_COMMAND should specify the command that PostgreSQL executes to archive the segment file. The PostgreSQL reference documentation shows the following examples:

```
archive_command = 'cp "%p" /mnt/server/archivedir/"%f"'
archive_command = 'copy "%p" /mnt/server/archivedir/"%f"'   # Windows
```

PostgreSQL replaces %p with the complete pathname of the segment file and replaces %f with the filename component of the segment file. PostgreSQL executes the specified command whenever a WAL segment file fills up. If the command succeeds (that is, the command exists with a status value of zero), PostgreSQL recycles the segment file.

If ARCHIVE_COMMAND is defined, you can use PostgreSQL's PITR (point in time recovery) features to restore a database to the state it was in at an exact point in time. If ARCHIVE_COMMAND is blank (which is the default), PITR is disabled. See the section labeled "Point In Time Recovery" (in this chapter) for more information.

Optimizer Parameters

This section looks at the configuration options that directly influence the PostgreSQL optimizer. The first seven options can be used to enable or disable execution strategies.

Some of these options affect how the optimizer estimates execution costs. The last set of options control the PostgreSQL Genetic query optimizer (GEQO).

DEFAULT_STATISTICS_TARGET

Default Value:	10
Modify Time:	SET command
Override:	None

When you ANALYZE a table, PostgreSQL gathers statistics that describe the distribution of values within each column. By default, PostgreSQL stores the 10 most commonly seen values for each column along with the bounds for 10 histogram buckets (see Chapter 4 for more information). The optimizer uses these statistics to find the least expensive plan for each query. You can adjust the number of sample values that ANALYZE will store on a column-by-column basis (see ALTER TABLE ... SET STATISTICS). If you don't specify a sample size for a given column, ANALYZE stores the number of samples specified by DEFAULT_STATISTICS_TARGET.

In general, you should define per-column statistics targets using ALTER TABLE ... SET STATISTICS instead of increasing DEFAULT_STATISTICS_TARGET. If you increase DEFAULT_STATISTICS_TARGET, it will take longer to ANALYZE the tables in your database, but the optimizer should become accurate and more predictable.

ENABLE_SEQSCAN

Default Value:	True
Modify Time:	SET command
Override:	None

This parameter affects the estimated cost of performing a sequential scan on a table. Setting ENABLE_SEQSCAN to False does not completely disable sequential scans; it simply raises the estimated cost so that sequential scans are not likely to appear in the execution plan. A sequential scan may still appear in the execution plan if there is no other way to satisfy the query (for example, if you have defined no indexes on a table).

This parameter is most often used to force PostgreSQL to use an index that it would not otherwise use. If you are tempted to force PostgreSQL to use an index, you probably need to VACUUM ANALYZE your table instead.

ENABLE_INDEXSCAN

Default Value:	True
Modify Time:	SET command
Override:	None

Setting ENABLE_INDEXSCAN to False increases the estimated cost of performing an index scan so that it is unlikely to appear in an execution plan.

ENABLE_TIDSCAN

Default Value:	True
Modify Time:	SET command
Override:	None

Setting ENABLE_TIDSCAN to False increases the estimated cost of performing a TID scan so that it is unlikely to appear in an execution plan. Because a TID scan is generated only when you have a WHERE clause that specifically mentions the CTID pseudo-column, this parameter is seldom used.

ENABLE_SORT

Default Value:	True
Modify Time:	SET command
Override:	None

The ENABLE_SORT parameter is used to increase the estimated cost of a sort operation so that it is unlikely to appear in an execution plan (set ENABLE_SORT to False to increase the estimated cost). Sort operations are often required (in the absence of a useful index) when intermediate results must appear in a specific order. For example, both input sets to the MergeJoin operator must appear in sorted order. Of course, an ORDER BY clause can be satisfied using a sort operation. When results are required in a specific order, the only alternative to a sort operation is to use an index scan, thus it makes little sense to disable sorts and index scans at the same time.

ENABLE_NESTLOOP

Default Value:	True
Modify Time:	SET command
Override:	None

Setting ENABLE_NESTLOOP to False increases the estimated cost of performing a nested loop operation so that it is unlikely to appear in an execution plan. The Nested Loop operator, described in Chapter 4, is one of three algorithms that PostgreSQL can use to join two tables. Setting ENABLE_NESTLOOP to False makes it more likely that PostgreSQL will choose a MergeJoin or HashJoin operator over a Nested Loop operator.

ENABLE_MERGEJOIN

Default Value:	True
Modify Time:	SET command
Override:	None

Setting ENABLE_MERGEJOIN to False increases the estimated cost of performing a MergeJoin operation so that it is unlikely to appear in an execution plan. Setting ENABLE_MERGEJOIN to False makes it more likely that PostgreSQL will choose a NestedLoop or HashJoin operator over a MergeJoin operator.

ENABLE_HASHJOIN

Default Value:	True
Modify Time:	SET command
Override:	None

Setting ENABLE_HASHJOIN to False increases the estimated cost of performing a HashJoin operation so that it is unlikely to appear in an execution plan. Setting ENABLE_HASHJOIN to False makes it more likely that PostgreSQL will choose a NestedLoop or MergeJoin operator over a HashJoin operator.

ENABLE_HASHAGG

Default Value:	True
Modify Time:	SET command
Override:	None

Setting ENABLE_HASHAGG to False increases the estimated cost of performing a HashAggregate operation so that it is unlikely to appear in an execution plan. Setting ENABLE_HASHAGG to False makes it more likely that PostgreSQL will choose a Sort operator followed by an Aggregate or GroupAggregate operator. The HashAggregate operator makes it possible to GROUP related rows without first sorting them.

KSQO

Default Value:	False
Modify Time:	SET command
Override:	SET KSQO TO [true|false]

Setting KSQO to True (the default value for this parameter is False) gives PostgreSQL permission to rewrite certain WHERE clauses in order to optimize queries that involve many OR operators. The *Key Set Query Optimizer* is largely obsolete as of PostgreSQL release 7.0 so the KSQO parameter is rarely used. See Chapter 3, "Run-time Configuration," of the *PostgreSQL Administrator's Guide* for more information about the Key Set Query Optimizer.

EFFECTIVE_CACHE_SIZE

Default Value:	1000
Modify Time:	SET command
Override:	None

When estimating the cost of an execution plan, PostgreSQL needs to make an educated guess about the cost of reading a random page from disk into the shared buffer cache. To do so, it needs to know the likelihood of finding a given page in the OS cache. The EFFECTIVE_CACHE_SIZE parameter tells PostgreSQL how much of the OS disk cache is likely to be given to your server process.

This parameter is used only when estimating the cost of an IndexScan or Sort operator (when the sort will overflow SORT_MEM bytes and switch from an in-memory sort to an on-disk sort).

Increasing the EFFECTIVE_CACHE_SIZE makes the cost estimator assume that any given page is more likely to be found in the cache. Decreasing the EFFECTIVE_CACHE_SIZE tells PostgreSQL that any given page is less likely to be found in the cache (and will therefore incur more expense).

RANDOM_PAGE_COST

Default Value:	4.0
Modify Time:	SET command
Override:	None

RANDOM_PAGE_COST specifies the cost of loading a random page into the shared buffer cache. A sequential page fetch is assumed to cost 1 unit; the default value for RANDOM_PAGE_COST means that PostgreSQL assumes that it is four times as expensive to load a random page than a sequentially accessed page.

CPU_TUPLE_COST

Default Value:	0.01
Modify Time:	SET command
Override:	None

CPU_TUPLE_COST specifies the cost of processing a single tuple within a heap (data) page. With the default value of 0.01, PostgreSQL assumes that it is 100 times more expensive to load a sequential page from disk than to process a single tuple.

CPU_INDEX_TUPLE_COST

Default Value:	0.001
Modify Time:	SET command
Override:	None

CPU_INDEX_TUPLE_COST specifies the cost of processing a single index entry. With the default value of 0.001, PostgreSQL assumes that it is 1,000 times more expensive to load a sequential page from disk than to process a single tuple.

CPU_OPERATOR_COST

Default Value:	0.0025
Modify Time:	SET command
Override:	None

CPU_OPERATOR_COST specifies the cost of processing a single operator (such as >= or !=) in a WHERE clause. With the default value of 0.0025, PostgreSQL assumes that it is 2,500 times more expensive to load a sequential page from disk than to process a single operator.

The planner/optimizer works in three phases. The first phase examines the query parse tree and builds a set of execution plans. The second phase assigns a cost to the execution plan by estimating the expense of each step of the plan. The final phase chooses the least expensive alternative and discards the other plans.

Many queries can be evaluated by two or more execution plans. For example, if you have defined an index on the tape_id column, the following query:

```
SELECT * FROM tapes ORDER BY tape_id;
```

results in at least two execution plans. One plan scans through the entire table from beginning to end and sorts the results into the desired order (this plan includes a SeqScan operator and a Sort operator). The second plan reads through the entire table using the tape_id index (this plan includes an IndexScan operator). For complex queries, especially queries involving many tables, the number of alternative plans becomes large.

The job of the Genetic Query Optimizer (or GEQO, for short) is to reduce the number of alternatives that must be evaluated by eliminating plans that are likely to be more expensive than plans already seen. The next seven parameters control the GEQO. The GEQO algorithm is too complex to try to describe in the space available, so I will include the descriptions provided in the *PostgreSQL Administrator's Guide* for each of the GEQO-related parameters.

GEQO

Default Value:	True
Modify Time:	SET command
Override:	None

If GEQO is set to True, PostgreSQL will use the Genetic Query Optimizer to eliminate plans that are likely to be expensive. If GEQO is set to False, the planner/optimizer will produce every possible execution plan and find the least expensive among the alternatives.

GEQO_SELECTION_BIAS

Default Value:	2.0
Modify Time:	SET command
Override:	None

GEQO_SELECTION_BIAS is the selective pressure within the population. Values can be from 1.50 to 2.00; the latter is the default.

GEQO_THRESHOLD

Default Value:	12
Modify Time:	SET command
Override:	None

Use genetic query optimization to plan queries with at least GEQO_THRESHOLD FROM items involved. (Note that a JOIN construct counts as only one FROM item.) The default is 11. For simpler queries, it is usually best to use the deterministic, exhaustive planner. This parameter also controls how hard the optimizer will try to merge subquery FROM clauses into the upper query

GEQO_POOL_SIZE

Default Value:	Number of tables involved in each query
Modify Time:	SET command
Override:	None

GEQO_POOL_SIZE is the number of individuals in one population. Valid values are between 128 and 1024. If it is set to 0 (the default), a pool size of 2^(QS+1), where QS is the number of FROM items in the query, is taken.

GEQO_EFFORT
Default Value: 5
Modify Time: SET command
Override: None

GEQO_EFFORT is used to calculate a default for generations. Valid values are between 1 and 80; 40 being the default.

GEQO_GENERATIONS
Default Value: 0
Modify Time: SET command
Override: None

GEQO_GENERATIONS specifies the number of iterations in the algorithm. The number must be a positive integer. If 0 is specified, GEQO_EFFORT * LOG2(GEQO_POOL_SIZE) is used. The runtime of the algorithm is roughly proportional to the sum of pool size and generations.

GEQO_RANDOM_SEED
Default Value: 0.5
Modify Time: SET command
Override: None

GEQO_RANDOM_SEED can be set to get reproducible results from the algorithm. If GEQO_RANDOM_SEED is set to -1, the algorithm behaves nondeterministically.

JOIN_COLLAPSE_LIMIT
Default Value: 8
Modify Time: SET command
Override: None

PostgreSQL's query optimizer usually ignores the order in which you specify tables in a query that inner-joins multiple tables. Instead, the optimizer tries to find the join ordering that produces the best execution plan. For example, when the optimizer encounters a query such as

```
SELECT * FROM table1
    JOIN table2 ON table1.value = table2.value
    JOIN table3 ON table2.value = table3.value
```

It can choose from any of the following join plans:

```
table1 JOIN (table2 JOIN table3)
table1 JOIN (table3 JOIN table2)
table2 JOIN (table1 JOIN table3)
```

```
table2 JOIN (table3 JOIN table1)
table3 JOIN (table1 JOIN table2)
table3 JOIN (table2 JOIN table1)
```

You can force the optimizer to honor the join order specified in each query by setting JOIN_COLLAPSE_LIMIT to 1. You can also reduce the amount of effort that the optimizer puts into evaluating alternative plans by setting JOIN_COLLAPSE_LIMIT to some number greater than 1 (but less than GEQO_THRESHOLD).

FROM_COLLAPSE_LIMIT

Default Value:	8
Modify Time:	SET command
Override:	None

When the PostgreSQL query planner encounters a query that contains a *subquery*, such as

```
SELECT * FROM table1, table2,
  ( SELECT * FROM table3 WHERE table3.column = value )
  WHERE table1.column = table2.column
```

It collapses the subquery (the SELECT * FROM table3 WHERE table3.column = value part) into the parent so that the optimizer can consider the entire package at once instead of planning the subquery in a separate pass. For example, given the previous query, the planner would collapse the subquery into the parent resulting a query that looks like this:

```
SELECT * FROM table1, table2, table3
  WHERE table1.column = table2.column
  AND table3.column = value
```

The optimizer can often come up with a better execution plan by examining a single query than by planning two separate queries. However, if the FROM clause becomes too complex, the planner can spend a great deal of time evaluating alternative join plans. PostgreSQL strikes a balance by collapsing subqueries only when the resulting FROM list contains no more than FROM_COLLAPSE_LIMIT items.

Debugging/Logging Parameters

The next set of configuration parameters relates to debugging and logging. You may notice that the user can change most of the debugging options (using the SET command). You must be a cluster superuser to change any of the logging options.

LOG_DESTINATION

Default Value:	STDERR
Modify Time:	SIGHUP
Override:	None

The LOG_DESTINATION parameter determines where PostgreSQL writes log messages. Valid choices are STDERR, SYSLOG, and EVENTLOG (SYSLOG is only valid on Linux/Unix systems and EVENTLOG is only valid on Windows hosts). You can specify more than one destination (just separate them with commas). By default, PostgreSQL writes log messages to the postmaster's STDERR stream (which you can redirect with the -l path-name command-line argument or the REDIRECT_STDERR configuration parameter). If the postmaster is running on a Linux or Unix host, PostgreSQL can write messages to the syslog facility (see man syslog for more information). If the postmaster is running on a Windows host, PostgreSQL can write messages to the Windows event log.

REDIRECT_STDERR

Default Value:	False
Modify Time:	Postmaster Startup
Override:	None

If LOG_DESTINATION specifies that PostgreSQL should write log messages to STDERR, you can ask redirect the STDERR stream by setting REDIRECT_STDERR to True. When REDIRECT_STDERR is True, PostgreSQL creates a log file (whose name is determined by the LOG_FILENAME configuration parameter) in a directory whose name is determined by the LOG_DIRECTORY configuration parameter.

You can also redirect the postmaster's STDERR stream by including the -l log-filename command-line option when you start the postmaster using pg_ctl, but REDIRECT_STDERR offers a significant advantage. When you use REDIRECT_ERROR, PostgreSQL will automatically *rotate* the server log into a new file when it grows too large (or too old). You can specify the location of the log files with the LOG_DIRECTORY and LOG_FILENAME configuration parameters. You can control the aging of log files with the LOG_ROTATION_AGE, LOG_ROTATION_SIZE, and LOG_TRUNCATE_ON_ROTATION configuration parameters.

SYSLOG_FACILITY

Default Value:	'LOCAL0'
Modify Time:	Postmaster startup
Override:	None

If you are sending server log messages to syslog, you can use the SYSLOG_FACILITY parameter to classify PostgreSQL-related messages. Most syslog implementations let you redirect each message classification to a different destination (to a text file, the system console, a particular user, or a remote system). SYSLOG_FACILITY is used to specify the classification that you want PostgreSQL to use when sending messages to syslog. Your choices for this parameter are LOCAL0, LOCAL1, ... LOCAL7. You want to choose a value other than the default if you already have software that uses LOCAL0.

SYSLOG_IDENT

Default Value:	'postgres'
Modify Time:	Postmaster startup
Override:	None

If you are sending server log messages to syslog, each message is prefixed with the string specified by the SYSLOG_IDENT parameter.

LOG_DIRECTORY

Default Value: '$PGDATA/pg_log'
Modify Time: SIGHUP
Override: None

If you are using REDIRECT_STDERR to create rotating server logs, LOG_DIRECTORY specifies the name of the directory where PostgreSQL will place the log files.

LOG_FILENAME

Default Value: 'postgresql-%Y-%m-%d_%H%M%S.log'
Modify Time: SIGHUP
Override: None

If you are using REDIRECT_STDERR to create rotating server logs, LOG_FILENAME specifies the template that PostgreSQL uses to create log filenames. Note that LOG_FILENAME doesn't define the actual filename, just a pattern from which PostgreSQL will generate the actual name. You can't specify the final filename yourself because PostgreSQL rotates log files as they grow too large (or too old). If LOG_FILENAME does *not* contain a % character, PostgreSQL appends a dot and the current date and time (measured in number of seconds since Jan. 01 1970, 00:00:00 UTC) to the end of the string that you specify. If LOG_FILENAME contains a %, PostgreSQL searches for date/time macros in the string and expands the macros shown in Table 21.5.

Table 21.5 LOG_FILENAME **Macros**

Macro	Description
%A	The name of the weekday (Monday, Tuesday, . . .) in the server's locale.
%a	The abbreviated name of the weekday (Mon, Tue, . . .) in the server's locale.
%B	The name of the month (January, February, . . .) in the server's locale
%b or %h	The abbreviated name of the month (Jan, Feb, . . .) in the server's locale
%C	The two-digit century (19, 20, . . .)
%c	The preferred time and date notation for the server's locale
%D	The date in MM/DD/YY (American) form
%d	The two-digit day of the month (. . ., 08, 09, 10, 11, . . .)
%e	The one- or two-digit day of the month (. . ., 8, 9, 10, 11, . . .)
%F	ISO-8601 date format (YY-MM-DD)
%H	The two-digit hour (00–23)
%I	The two-digit hour (01–12)
%j	The three-digit day of the year (001–365)
%k	The one- or two-digit hour (0–23)
%K	kitchen sink (really)

Table 21.5 **Continued**

Macro	Description
%l	The one- or two-digit hour (1–12)
%M	The two-digit minute (00–59)
%m	The two-digit month number (01–12)
%n	The newline character (not a good idea to use this in LOG_FILENAME)
%p	AM or PM indicator in the server's locale (noon is considered PM, midnight is AM)
%R	The time in %H:%M format
%r	The time in %I:%M:%S %p format
%S	The two-digit second (00–60)
%T	The time in %H:%M:%S format
%tu	The tab character (not a good idea to use this in LOG_FILENAME)
%U	The two-digit week number (00–53) assuming that Sunday is the first day of week 01
%u	The one-digit day of the week (1–7); Monday is considered to be day 1
%V, %G, or %g	The two-digit week number counting from the week that contains the 4th of January (see the ISO 8601:1988 for a thorough explanation of this arcane rule; leave it to a programmer to come up with something like this)
%v	The date in %e-%b-%Y format
%W	The two-digit week number (00–53) assuming that Monday is the first day of week 01
%X	The preferred time format for the server's locale
%x	The preferred date format for the server's locale
%y	The two-digit year (00–99)
%Y	The four-digit century and year
%z	The server's time zone as an offset from GMT.
%Z	The time zone name
%+	The date and time in the default format used by the operating system's date command
%%	The character %

LOG_ROTATION_AGE

Default Value: 1440 (24 hours)
Modify Time: SIGHUP
Override: None

If you are using REDIRECT_STDERR to create rotating server logs, LOG_ROTATION_AGE determines how often PostgreSQL creates a new log and retires the old one. PostgreSQL will create a new log when LOG_ROTATION_AGE minutes have elapsed, or when the log size exceeds `LOG_ROTATION_SIZE`, whichever occurs first. Note that `LOG_ROTATION_AGE` is measured in minutes, not seconds. To disable time-based log rotation, set `LOG_ROTATION_AGE` to 0.

LOG_ROTATION_SIZE
Default Value: `10240  (10MB)`
Modify Time: `SIGHUP`
Override: None

If you are using `REDIRECT_STDERR` to create rotating server logs, `LOG_ROTATION_SIZE` determines the size at which PostgreSQL creates a new log file and retires the old one. PostgreSQL will create a new log file when the size of the current log exceeds `LOG_ROTATION_SIZE` or when `LOG_ROTATION_AGE` minutes have elapsed, whichever occurs first. `LOG_ROTATION_SIZE` is measured in kilobytes (the default, 10240 kilobytes, creates a new log every 10MB).

LOG_TRUNCATE_ON_ROTATION
Default Value: `False`
Modify Time: `SIGHUP`
Override: None

If you are using `REDIRECT_STDERR` to create rotating server logs, `LOG_TRUNCATE_ON_ROTATION` determines when PostgreSQL will overwrite old log files and when PostgreSQL will append to old log files. If this parameter is `FALSE`, PostgreSQL will always append to existing log file. If `LOG_TRUNCATE_ON_ROTATION` is `TRUE`, PostgreSQL will overwrite existing log files when `LOG_ROTATION_AGE` minutes have elapsed. PostgreSQL will not overwrite existing log files when `LOG_ROTATION_SIZE` forces a new log file, even if `LOG_TRUNCATE_ON_ROTATION` is `TRUE`.

LOG_MIN_MESSAGES
Default Value: `NOTICE`
Modify Time: `SET` command (superuser only)
Override: None

This parameter determines which messages are recorded in the server log. Valid values, in *decreasing* order of severity, are `PANIC`, `FATAL`, `LOG`, `ERROR`, `WARNING`, `NOTICE`, `INFO`, `DEBUG1`, `DEBUG2`, `DEBUG3`, `DEBUG4`, and `DEBUG5`. `LOG_MIN_MESSAGES` specifies the least important message that PostgreSQL should write to the server log. For example, the default value (`NOTICE`) tells PostgreSQL to record `NOTICE` messages along with all messages more severe than `NOTICE`. If you want a more detailed (and faster growing) log, set `LOG_MIN_MESSAGES` to a category of lower severity. If you want a less detailed (and slower growing) log, set `LOG_MIN_MESSAGES` to a category of higher severity.

CLIENT_MIN_MESSAGES
Default Value: `NOTICE`
Modify Time: `SET` command
Override: None

This parameter is nearly identical to LOG_MIN_MESSAGES except that CLIENT_MIN_MESSAGES controls which messages are sent to the client.

LOG_MIN_ERROR_STATEMENT
Default Value: PANIC
Modify Time: SET command (superuser only)
Override: None

When the PostgreSQL server decides (based on LOG_MIN_MESSAGES) to record a message in the server log, it examines LOG_MIN_ERROR_STATEMENT to determine whether to include the text of the SQL statement that produced the message. If the severity of the message is at least as high as LOG_MIN_ERROR_STATEMENT, PostgreSQL records the text of the SQL statement in the log. There is a relationship between LOG_MIN_MESSAGES and LOG_MIN_ERROR_STATEMENT. LOG_MIN_MESSAGES determines whether a given message is recorded in the server log; LOG_MIN_ERROR_STATEMENT affects the content of those messages that actually make it to the log. You usually want LOG_MIN_ERROR_STATEMENT to be of equal or higher severity than LOG_MIN_MESSAGES. For example, with LOG_MIN_MESSAGES=WARNING and LOG_MIN_ERROR_STATEMENT=ERROR, the server will record every message of severity WARNING or greater and messages of severity ERROR (or greater) will include the text of the SQL statement that produced the message.

LOG_ERROR_VERBOSITY
Default Value: DEFAULT
Modify Time: SET command (superuser only)
Override: None

Every message reported by the server will contain a variety of components. Each message contains a *severity* (PANIC, FATAL, LOG, ERROR, and so on), an *error message*, and an *error code* (error codes are listed in Appendix A of the PostgreSQL reference documentation). PostgreSQL also records the *location*, in the PostgreSQL source code, where the error occurred. The location includes the name of the source file, the line number within that file, and, on some hosts, the name of the function that threw the error.

Some messages contain extra *detail*. For example, if you try to DROP a USER that happens to own a database, PostgreSQL will report a message (of severity ERROR) that states user *name* cannot be dropped. That message will contain the extra detail The user owns database *database-name*. A few messages will contain a *hint* that gives you a bit of advice about how to solve the problem. Some messages are generated indirectly. For example, when you execute a SELECT statement that calls a function written in PL/pgSQL, that function may generate an error. When PostgreSQL reports a "nested" error, it records the text of the SELECT statement and the *context* of the error (in the case of an error thrown by a PL/pgSQL function, the context indicates the name of the function and the line number where the error occurred).

LOG_ERROR_VERBOSITY determines which message components PostgreSQL will write to the server log. It does *not* affect the number of messages written to the log (see

LOG_MIN_MESSAGES), only the level of detail in each message. PostgreSQL 8.0 defines three levels: TERSE, DEFAULT, and VERBOSE. When LOG_ERROR_VERBOSITY is set to TERSE, PostgreSQL records the error message and severity and discards the rest of the message details. When LOG_ERROR_VERBOSITY is set to DEFAULT, PostgreSQL records the error message, severity, detail, hint, and context. If you set LOG_ERROR_VERBOSITY to VERBOSE, PostgreSQL will record the entire content of the message in the server log. Table 21.6 summarizes LOG_ERROR_VERBOSITY.

Table 21.6   LOG_ERROR_VERBOSITY **Options**

| | LOG_ERROR_VERBOSITY | | |
Message Component	VERBOSE	DEFAULT	TERSE
Message text	X	X	X
Severity	X	X	X
Detail	X	X	
Hint	X	X	
Context	X	X	
Error code	X		
Location	X		

LOG_STATEMENT

Default Value:	'NONE'
Modify Time:	SET command (superuser only)
Override:	None

This option determines which SQL statements PostgreSQL will record in the server log. The default for this option is 'NONE', which means that the server will not write any SQL statements to the server log. You can also choose 'ALL', 'DDL', or 'MOD'. If LOG_STATEMENT is set to 'ALL', PostgreSQL will record the text of every statement in the server log. Set LOG_STATEMENT to 'DDL' to force PostgreSQL to record the text of all DDL statements (CREATE, ALTER, DROP, GRANT, REVOKE, or COMMENT). If LOG_STATEMENT is set to 'MOD', PostgreSQL will record the text of all INSERT, DELETE, UPDATE, TRUNCATE, and COPY FROM statements as well as all DDL statements.

PostgreSQL will only record the text of a statement when it's first evaluated by the query planner. If you PREPARE a statement and then EXECUTE it multiple times, the text of the prepared statement only appears in the log once. The procedural language handlers (PL/pgSQL, PL/Perl, ...) cache query plans as well.

You may see some statements appear in the server log even though it seems that they should have been filtered out by LOG_STATEMENT. If a statement produces an error at least as severe as LOG_MIN_ERROR_STATEMENT, PostgreSQL will record the text of the statement. If a statement takes more than LOG_MIN_DURATION_STATEMENT to execute (measured in milliseconds), PostgreSQL will record the text of the statement (and the duration). That means that some statements will appear in the log two or three times.

LOG_DURATION
Default Value: `False`
Modify Time: `SET` command (superuser only)
Override: None

`LOG_DURATION` works in conjunction with `LOG_STATEMENT`. If `LOG_DURATION` is `TRUE`, PostgreSQL records the amount of time that it takes to execute every statement that makes it through the `LOG_STATEMENT` filter.

LOG_MIN_DURATION_STATEMENT
Default Value: `-1`
Modify Time: `SET` command (superuser only)
Override: None

Use `LOG_MIN_DURATION_STATEMENT` to find long-running queries. PostgreSQL records the text (and duration) of every statement that takes longer than `LOG_MIN_DURATION_STATEMENT` milliseconds to execute. For example, to see queries that take more than 30 seconds to execute, set `LOG_MIN_DURATION_STATEMENT` to `3000`. Set `LOG_MIN_DURATION_STATEMENT` to `-1` to disable duration-dependent logging.

You may see some statements appear in the log multiple times even though you've only executed them once. A statement may be written to the log file by `LOG_MIN_DURATION_STATEMENT`, `LOG_MIN_ERROR_STATEMENT`, or `LOG_STATEMENT`.

LOG_LINE_PREFIX
Default Value: `"`
Modify Time: `SIGHUP`
Override: None

When PostgreSQL writes a message to the server log, it can prefix the message with a string of your choice. To change the prefix (which is blank by default), set `LOG_LINE_PREFIX` to the string you want to appear in the log. PostgreSQL defines a number of macros that you can include in the string. PostgreSQL expands each macro into a specific bit of information as shown in Table 21.7.

Table 21.7 `LOG_LINE_PREFIX` **Macros**

Macro	Description
%u	The name of the user that created the server process. Note that this is the PostgreSQL username, not the operating system assigned username.
%d	The name of the database that the server process is connected to.
%c	The session ID of the server process (the session ID is a hexadecimal number that encodes the server start time and process ID).
%p	The operating system process ID of the server (or postmaster) process.

Table 21.7 **Continued**

Macro	Description
%l	The message number (starting a message 1). Each process (server or postmaster) assigns a sequential number to each message and prints that number in place of the %l macro. Messages produced by different processes are intermingled in the server log and you can use the message number to untangle the log.
%t	The current time and date in the format YY-MM-DD hh:mm:ss timezone (the timezone is omitted if the server or postmaster process is running on a Windows host).
%s	The time and date that the server (or postmaster) process started, in the format YY-MM-DD hh:mm:ss timezone.
%i	The command tag (INSERT, SELECT, ALTER TABLE, and so on).
%r	The client hostname (or IP address) and port, in the form host(port). If LOG_HOSTNAME is TRUE, %r prints the client name, otherwise, %r prints the IP address of the client.
%x	The current transaction id.
%q	Ignored by server processes. For the postmaster (and related processes), %q tells the log creator to ignore the rest of LOG_LINE_PREFIX. For example, given a LOG_LINE_PREFIX such as %p - %q(connected to %r) - server process messages would appear as 17112 - (connected to springfield(5432)) - *message content* but messages originating from the postmaster would appear as 17100 - *message content*
%%	The literal text % (that is, %% expands to a single percent sign).

SILENT_MODE

Default Value:	False
Modify Time:	Postmaster Startup
Override:	postmaster -S

If SILENT_MODE is set to True, all logging and debugging messages are suppressed. If SILENT_MODE is set to True (the default), the postmaster will write log and debug messages to the log destination. You can specify where log messages will be written by invoking the postmaster with the -i *log-file-name* command-line option.

LOG_CONNECTIONS

Default Value:	False
Modify Time:	Backend startup
Override:	None

If LOG_CONNECTIONS is set to True, the postmaster will log each successful client connection. The log message produced by this parameter is of the form:

```
connection: host=client-address user=user database=database
```

If LOG_HOSTNAME is True, the client-address will include the client's hostname and IP address; otherwise, only the client's IP address is shown.

If SHOW_SOURCE_PORT is True, the client-address will also include the port number used by the client side of the connection. (Note: SHOW_SOURCE_PORT shows the client's port number, not the server's port number.)

LOG_DISCONNECTIONS

Default Value:	False
Modify Time:	Backend startup
Override:	None

If LOG_DISCONNECTIONS is set to True, the postmaster will log each successful client disconnect. The log message is of the form:

```
disconnection:
    session time: duration user=name database=db  host=client-addr port=port
```

If LOG_HOSTNAME is True, the client-addr will include the client's hostname and IP address; otherwise, only the client's IP address is shown.

LOG_HOSTNAME

Default Value:	False
Modify Time:	SIGHUP
Override:	None

Every server process examines LOG_HOSTNAME to decide whether to resolve the client IP address into a hostname. If LOG_HOSTNAME is True, client connect and disconnect messages will include the name of the client host. If LOG_HOSTNAME is False, client connect and disconnect message include only the IP address of the client host.

Be aware that LOG_HOSTNAME is a bit of a misnomer—if you set LOG_HOSTNAME to True, PostgreSQL will convert the client IP address into a hostname *even if you've disabled* LOG_CONNECTIONS and LOG_DISCONNECTIONS. If you see a noticeable delay when starting a new server process, check LOG_HOSTNAME. In many configurations, the process of resolving an IP address into a hostname can consume a significant amount of time.

DEBUG_PRINT_PARSE

Default Value:	False
Modify Time:	SET command
Override:	None

If DEBUG_PRINT_PARSE is True, PostgreSQL will write a textual representation of the parse tree of each query to the server log.

DEBUG_PRINT_REWRITTEN

Default Value:	False
Modify Time:	SET command
Override:	None

PostgreSQL implements views using a set of rules that rewrite queries from the point of view seen by the user to the form required to evaluate the view.

If DEBUG_PRINT_REWRITTEN is True, PostgreSQL will write the rewritten form of each query to the server log.

DEBUG_PRINT_PLAN

Default Value:	False
Modify Time:	SET command
Override:	None

If DEBUG_PRINT_PLAN is True, PostgreSQL will write the execution plan of each command to the server log. Turning on DEBUG_PRINT_PLAN is similar to using the EXPLAIN command-DEBUG_PRINT_PLAN gives a much more detailed (and much less readable) plan.

DEBUG_PRETTY_PRINT

Default Value:	False
Modify Time:	SET command
Override:	None

If DEBUG_PRETTY_PRINT is True, the log entries for DEBUG_PRINT_PARSE, DEBUG_PRINT_REWRITTEN, and DEBUG_PRINT_PLAN are formatted for consumption by mere mortals. If DEBUG_PRETTY_PRINT is False, the log entries just mentioned are packed very tightly and can be very difficult to read.

DEBUG_ASSERTIONS

Default Value:	Depends on configuration
Modify Time:	SET command
Override:	None

This parameter enables (or disables) assertion checking in the PostgreSQL server. The PostgreSQL developers sprinkle assertion checks throughout the PostgreSQL source code to *assert* that certain prerequisites are in place. For example, a developer may assert that a particular function was invoked with the correct number of arguments. Assertions check for things that should never happen. If an assertion check fails, something has gone wrong and it's likely to be something out of your control—it may be a bug in PostgreSQL or an unexpected failure in the PostgreSQL environment. If DEBUG_ASSERTIONS is True (and you've configured the PostgreSQL source code with the —enable-cassert flag), PostgreSQL will verify all assertions and report any failures. If DEBUG_ASSERTIONS is False, PostgreSQL ignores any assertion failures. If you did not include the —enable-cassert flag when you built PostgreSQL from source code, the PostgreSQL server won't even verify the assertions (so you won't see any assertion failure messages).

PRE_AUTH_DELAY

Default Value:	0 (disabled)
Modify Time:	SIGHUP
Override:	None

If you are trying to debug the PostgreSQL server (or perhaps a shared library loaded by the server), you may have trouble attaching a debugger (such as GDB) to the backend process at the right point in time. The PRE_AUTH_DELAY parameter can help. If PRE_AUTH_DELAY is non-zero, the backend process sleeps for that number of seconds immediately after it has been spawned by the postmaster and before authenticating the client application. If you attach a debugger to the backend process while it's sleeping, you can step through the authentication code (or set breakpoints on functions invoked later).

If you plan to attach a debugger to a PostgreSQL process, be sure to include the —enable-debug flag when you configure the PostgreSQL source code.

ZERO_DAMAGED_PAGES

Default Value:	False
Modify Time:	SET command (superuser only)
Override:	None

When PostgreSQL detects that page has been damaged (that is, corrupted) it usually reports an error (code XX001, invalid page header in block *block-number* of *relation name*) and aborts the command that you're executing. If you see this error, the safest remedy is to restore the damaged table from an archive. If you don't have a current archive, you can recover some of the data in the table (but not the data in the damaged page) by setting ZERO_DAMAGED_PAGES to True. When ZERO_DAMAGED_PAGES is True, PostgreSQL destroys the data on the damaged page but leaves the rest of the table intact.

TRACE_NOTIFY

Default Value:	False
Modify Time:	SET command
Override:	None

If TRACE_NOTIFY is True, the server will write debug messages regarding the NOTIFY and LISTEN commands to the server log.

TRACE_LOCKS

Default Value:	False
Modify Time:	SET command (cluster superuser only)
Override:	None

If TRACE_LOCKS is True, the server will write debug messages that detail locking operations within the server. This parameter can be set only if the symbol LOCK_DEBUG was defined when your copy of PostgreSQL was built from source code. TRACE_LOCKS is rarely used except by the PostgreSQL developers, but the output can be useful if you want to understand how PostgreSQL manages locking.

TRACE_LOCK_OIDMIN

Default Value: 16384
Modify Time: SET command (cluster superuser only)
Override: None

If TRACE_LOCKS is True, TRACE_LOCK_OIDMIN specifies the set of tables for which lock information is logged. If the OID (object ID) of a table's pg_class entry is less than TRACE_LOCK_OIDMIN, PostgreSQL will not log locking information for that table. The default value (16384) was chosen to prevent log messages about locking performed on system tables (system tables have OIDs less than 16384). This parameter can be set only if the symbol LOCK_DEBUG was defined when your copy of PostgreSQL was built from source code.

TRACE_LOCK_TABLE

Default Value: 0
Modify Time: SET command (cluster superuser only)
Override: None

If TRACE_LOCKS is False, you can tell PostgreSQL that it should still log locking information for a specific table by setting TRACE_LOCK_TABLE to the OID of that table's entry in pg_class. This parameter can be set only if the symbol LOCK_DEBUG was defined when your copy of PostgreSQL was built from source code.

TRACE_USERLOCKS

Default Value: False
Modify Time: SET command (cluster superuser only)
Override: None

If TRACE_USERLOCKS is True, the server will write debug messages concerning the LOCK TABLE command to the server log. This parameter can be set only if the symbol LOCK_DEBUG was defined when your copy of PostgreSQL was built from source code. TRACE_USERLOCKS is rarely used except by the PostgreSQL developers, but the output can be useful if you want to understand how PostgreSQL manages locking.

TRACE_LWLOCKS

Default Value: False
Modify Time: SET command (cluster superuser only)
Override: None

If TRACE_LWLOCKS is True, the server will write debug messages concerning the lightweight locks that PostgreSQL uses to coordinate multiple server processes. This parameter can be set only if the symbol LOCK_DEBUG was defined when your copy of PostgreSQL was built from source code. TRACE_LWLOCKS is rarely used except by the PostgreSQL developers.

DEBUG_DEADLOCKS

Default Value:	False
Modify Time:	SET command (cluster superuser only)
Override:	None

If DEBUG_DEADLOCKS is True, the server will log lock queue information whenever a deadlock is detected. A deadlock occurs when two (or more) transactions need to lock two (or more) resources (such as a row or table), but the transactions are blocking each other from proceeding.

This parameter can be set only if the symbol LOCK_DEBUG was defined when your copy of PostgreSQL was built from source code.

Performance Statistics

Next, let's look at the set of configuration parameters that control how PostgreSQL computes and reports performance statistics.

LOG_PARSER_STATS

Default Value:	False
Modify Time:	SET command (cluster superuser only)
Override:	None

If LOG_PARSER_STATS is True, the server will write parser statistics to the server log file. For each command, PostgreSQL logs parser statistics, parse analysis statistics, and query rewriter statistics.

This parameter is named SHOW_PARSER_STATS in PostgreSQL versions 7.3 and older.

LOG_EXECUTOR_STATS

Default Value:	False
Modify Time:	SET command (cluster superuser only)
Override:	None

If LOG_EXECUTOR_STATS is True, the server will write execution statistics to the server log file.

This parameter is named SHOW_EXECUTOR_STATS in PostgreSQL versions 7.3 and older.

LOG_PLANNER_STATS

Default Value:	False
Modify Time:	SET command (cluster superuser only)
Override:	None

If LOG_PLANNER_STATS is True, the server will write parser statistics to the server log file.

This parameter is named SHOW_PLANNER_STATS in PostgreSQL versions 7.3 and older.

LOG_STATEMENT_STATS

Default Value:	`False`
Modify Time:	`SET` command (cluster superuser only)
Override:	None

If `LOG_STATEMENT_STATS` is `True`, the server will write statement execution statistics to the server log file.

This parameter is named `SHOW_STATEMENT_STATS` in PostgreSQL version 7.4, and `SHOW_QUERY_STATS` in versions 7.3 and older.

STATS_START_COLLECTOR

Default Value:	`True`
Modify Time:	Postmaster startup
Override:	None

Starting with release 7.2, PostgreSQL can gather ongoing, clusterwide usage statistics in a set of system tables and views. These tables are described in detail in Chapter 4. You must set the `STATS_START_COLLECTOR` to true if you want PostgreSQL to maintain the information in these tables.

STATS_RESET_ON_SERVER_START

Default Value:	`True`
Modify Time:	Postmaster startup
Override:	None

If `STATS_RESET_ON_SERVER_START` is `True`, the statistics captured by the performance monitor will be reset (that is, zeroed out) each time the `postmaster` starts. If this parameter is `False`, the performance statistics will accumulate.

STATS_COMMAND_STRING

Default Value:	`False`
Modify Time:	`SET` command (cluster superuser only)
Override:	None

If `STATS_COMMAND_STRING` is `True`, each PostgreSQL server will send the currently executing command string to the performance monitor. This command string is displayed in the `current_query` column of the `pg_stat_activity` view.

STATS_ROW_LEVEL

Default Value:	`False`
Modify Time:	`SET` command (cluster superuser only)
Override:	None

If `STATS_ROW_LEVEL` is `True`, the performance monitor will gather information regarding the number of tuples processed in each table. When you gather row-level statistics, PostgreSQL records the number of sequential scans and index scans performed on each table, as well the number of tuples processed for each type of scan. The performance

monitor also records the number of tuples inserted, updated, and deleted. The row-level
information gathered by the performance monitor is found in the pg_stat views
described in Chapter 4.

> **STATS_BLOCK_LEVEL**
> Default Value: False
> Modify Time: SET command (cluster superuser only)
> Override: None

If STATS_BLOCK_LEVEL is True, the performance monitor will gather information regarding the number of blocks (also known as pages) processed in each table. When you
gather block-level statistics, PostgreSQL records the number of heap blocks read, the
number of index blocks read, the number of TOAST heap blocks read, and the number of
TOAST index blocks read. The performance monitor also records the number of times
each type of block was found in the shared buffer cache.

The block-level information gathered by the performance monitor is found in the
pg_statio views described in Chapter 4. TOAST blocks are also described in Chapter 4.

> **DEBUG_SHARED_BUFFERS**
> Default Value: 0 (disabled)
> Modify Time: Postmaster startup
> Override: None

If DEBUG_SHARED_BUFFERS is non-zero, the ARC shared buffer manager will periodically
write performance and debugging information to the server log. DEBUG_SHARED_
BUFFERS specifies the interval between each report (measured in seconds).

Per-session Parameters

Every client application inherits a set of *per-session* parameters. You can change any per-
session parameter by executing a SET statement. When you modify a per-session statement (at runtime), the change affects only your session. Every session inherits a fresh set
of per-session parameters from the postmaster.

> **EXPLAIN_PRETTY_PRINT**
> Default Value: True
> Modify Time: SET command
> Override: None

This parameter determines whether the EXPLAIN VERBOSE command displays a query
tree in unindented (machine readable) form or indented (wizard readable) form. There
are few people in this world who can make sense of either form, but you'll find them all
on the pgsql_hackers mailing list. Some client applications may change this parameter,
but it's not something a human is likely to need.

CHECK_FUNCTION_BODIES

Default Value: `True`

Modify Time: `SET` command

Override: None

When you create a new function written in a language such as PL/pgSQL, PostgreSQL usually validates the body of the function to check for syntax errors and references to undefined variables. If the procedural language handler finds an error, PostgreSQL refuses to save the function. In most cases, that's a useful feature because you don't want to litter your server with functions that won't compile. However, there are two occasions when it may be useful to suppress the error checking until later. First, if you're restoring function definitions from a backup, you may run into forward references that cause the restore to fail. For example, if you restore a function that refers to the customers table, but you haven't yet restored the definition of the customers table, PostgreSQL will abort the restore. Second, if you're importing data from an external source, you may want to import function definitions before you define any tables (just a matter of convenience), in which case you may also run into forward references. In either case, you can tell PostgreSQL to defer any syntax (and reference) checks until the first time the function is invoked by setting CHECK_FUNCTION_BODIES to False.

SEARCH_PATH

Default Value: `'$user,public'`

Modify Time: `SET` command

Override: None

SEARCH_PATH determines which schemas PostgreSQL will search when you refer to an object without specifying a schema name (SEARCH_PATH is a comma-separated list of schema names). SEARCH_PATH also determines the order in which the search progresses. When you create a new object (an index, a table, or a function) without explicitly specifying a schema, PostgreSQL places the object in the first schema found in SEARCH_PATH.

PostgreSQL defines three special schema names: $user, pg_catalog, and pg_temp_nnn. $user translates into your PostgreSQL username (or, more precisely, the value of the SESSION_USER parameter). PostgreSQL will not search the $user schema unless it appears in your SEARCH_PATH. The PostgreSQL data dictionary (pg_class, pg_attribute, and so on) is defined in the pg_catalog schema: PostgreSQL always searches the pg_catalog schema, even if it does not appear in SEARCH_PATH. If pg_catalog does not appear in SEARCH_PATH, PostgreSQL searches pg_catalog before any of the schemas that do appear in SEARCH_PATH. Temporary tables are defined in a schema named pg_temp_nnn (where nnn is a unique number that identifies your session). PostgreSQL always searches pg_temp_nnn before searching any other schema (which means that PostgreSQL will always find a temporary object before it finds a permanent object of the same name unless you explicitly specify a schema name when you refer to the object).

DEFAULT_TABLESPACE

Default Value:	"
Modify Time:	SET command
Override:	None

When you create a table or an index without explicitly identifying a target tablespace, PostgreSQL stores the object in the DEFAULT_TABLESPACE. If DEFAULT_TABLESPACE is blank (or if it identifies a nonexistent tablespace), PostgreSQL stores the object the in the default tablespace of the current database.

AUSTRALIAN_TIMEZONES

Default Value:	False
Modify Time:	SET command
Override:	None

If AUSTRALIAN_TIMEZONES is True, the time zones ACST (UTC+9.5), CST (UTC+10.5), EST (UTC+10), EAST (UTC+10) and SAT (UTC+9.5) are interpreted as Central Australia Standard Time, Australian Central Standard Time, Australian Eastern Standard Time, Australian Eastern Standard Time, and South Australian Standard Time, respectively.

If AUSTRALIAN_TIMEZONES is False, ACST is interpreted as UTC-4 (Atlantic Summer Time) CST is interpreted as UTC-6 (Central Standard Time), EST is interpreted as UTC-5 (Eastern Standard Time), EAST is interpreted as UTC-6 (Easter Island Time), and SAT is interpreted as an abbreviation for Saturday.

PostgreSQL's support for time zones is described in Chapter 2, "Working with Data in PostgreSQL."

DEFAULT_TRANSACTION_READ_ONLY

Default Value:	False
Modify Time:	SET command
Override:	None

PostgreSQL usually decides whether you can modify a table (or sequence) by checking the permissions granted to your user (and group). You can write-protect your entire database by setting DEFAULT_TRANSACTION_READ_ONLY to True in the postgresql.conf configuration file. You can also write-protect your session by setting DEFAULT_TRANSACTION_READ_ONLY to True with a SET statement. But be aware that this parameter doesn't give you any *real* protection because any given user can SET DEFAULT_TRANSACTION_READ_ONLY TO FALSE. DEFAULT_TRANSACTION_READ_ONLY simply makes it less likely that you'll modify the database when you don't mean to.

STATEMENT_TIMEOUT

Default Value:	0 (disabled)
Modify Time:	SET command
Override:	None

If `STATEMENT_TIMEOUT` is a value other than zero, PostgreSQL will cancel any command that takes longer than `STATEMENT_TIMEOUT` to execute (measured in milliseconds). When PostgreSQL cancels a query, it throws error `57014` (`canceling query due to user request`).

DEFAULT_TRANSACTION_ISOLATION

Default Value:	`'READ COMMITTED'`
Modify Time:	`SET` command
Override:	None

This parameter defines default transaction isolation level for all transactions. The valid choices for this parameter are `'READ COMMITTED'` and `'SERIALIZABLE'`. Transaction isolation levels are described in the section titled "Transaction Isolation" in Chapter 3.

You can modify the transaction isolation level for an individual transaction using the `SET TRANSACTION ISOLATION LEVEL` command. You can also change the *default* isolation level for a PostgreSQL session using the command `SET SESSION CHARACTERISTICS AS TRANSACTION ISOLATION LEVEL [READ COMMITTED | SERIALIZABLE]`, but I've never be able focus my attention long enough to enter that command.

EXTRA_FLOAT_DIGITS

Default Value:	0
Modify Time:	`SET` command
Override:	None

This parameter changes the number of digits that PostgreSQL will display for floating point values (`REAL`, `DOUBLE PRECISION`, `FLOAT4`, `FLOAT8`, `POINT`, `LINE`, `LSEG`, `BOX`, `PATH`, `POLYGON`, and `CIRCLE`). By default, PostgreSQL displays 6 digits for single-precision data types (`REAL` and `FLOAT4`) and 15 digits for double-precision types (`DOUBLE PRECISION`, `FLOAT8`, and the geometric types). To increase the number of digits displayed, set `EXTRA_FLOAT_DIGITS` to a positive number (1 or 2). To decrease the number of digits, set `EXTRA_FLOAT_DIGITS` to a negative value (-1 through -15).

CLIENT_ENCODING

Default Value:	`SERVER_ENCODING`
Modify Time:	`SET` command
Override:	None

The `CLIENT_ENCODING` parameter tells PostgreSQL which character set to use when sending data to (or reading data from) the client application. See Chapter 22 for more information.

LC_MESSAGES

Default Value:	Determined by the operating system
Modify Time:	`SET` command (superuser only)
Override:	None

This parameter determines the (human) language that the PostgreSQL server will use when it generates an error (or other) message. See Chapter 22 for more information.

LC_NUMERIC

Default Value:	Determined by the operating system
Modify Time:	SET command
Override:	None

LC_NUMERIC determines which characters the server uses when it converts numbers to (and from) character form. In particular, LC_NUMERIC defines the decimal point character, the grouping character, and the rules for using the grouping character. See Chapter 22 for more information.

LC_TIME

Default Value:	Determined by the operating system
Modify Time:	SET command
Override:	None

Not currently used by PostgreSQL— see Chapter 22 for more information.

LC_MONETARY

Default Value:	Determined by the operating system
Modify Time:	SET command
Override:	None

LC_MONETARY defines the local currency symbol ($), the international currency symbol (USD), and positive/negative sign conventions used when PostgreSQL converts monetary values to and from character form. LC_MONETARY also defines the decimal point character, grouping character and grouping rules used to convert monetary values. See Chapter 22 for more information.

TIMEZONE

Default Value:	'UNKNOWN' (use OS time zone)
Modify Time:	SET command
Override:	None

The TIMEZONE parameter determines the server's (assumed) offset from UTC. If TIMEZONE is not set (or is set to the string 'UNKNOWN'), PostgreSQL queries the host operating system to find the timezone.

DYNAMIC_LIBRARY_PATH

Default Value:	$libdir (configure option)
Modify Time:	SET command (cluster superuser only)
Override:	None

The DYNAMIC_LIBRARY_PATH determines which directories PostgreSQL searches to find dynamically loaded functions (that is, external functions defined with the CREATE FUNCTION command). This parameter should be defined as a colon-separated list of the absolute directory. The DYNAMIC_LIBRARY_PATH is consulted only when PostgreSQL needs to load a dynamic object module that does not include a directory name. If DYNAMIC_LIBRARY_PATH is defined but empty, PostgreSQL will not use a search path, and each external function must include a directory name.

Miscellaneous Parameters

Finally, we'll look at the configuration parameters that don't fit well into the other categories.

ADD_MISSING_FROM

Default Value:	True
Modify Time:	SET command
Override:	None

If you've written an application that works with old versions of PostgreSQL, you may have a few SELECT commands that are ill-formed. Older versions of PostgreSQL would automatically repair a faulty FROM clause that omitted tables referenced elsewhere in the query. If ADD_MISSING_FROM is True, PostgreSQL will continue to repair faulty FROM clauses. It's a good idea to disable this feature so you don't accidentally write bad SELECT commands.

DEFAULT_WITH_OIDS

Default Value:	True
Modify Time:	SET command
Override:	None

When DEFAULT_WITH_OIDS is True, PostgreSQL automatically adds an OID (object ID) column to every table that you create unless you explicitly specify WITHOUT OID in the CREATE TABLE command. When DEFAULT_WITH_OIDS is False, PostgreSQL does not add an OID column to every table unless you explicitly specify WITH OID.

MAX_LOCKS_PER_TRANSACTION

Default Value:	64
Modify Time:	Postmaster startup
Override:	None

This parameter, along with MAX_CONNECTIONS, determines the size of PostgreSQL's shared lock table. Any given transaction can hold more than MAX_LOCKS_PER_TRANSACTION locks, but the total number of locks cannot exceed MAX_CONNECTIONS * MAX_LOCKS_PER_TRANSACTION. PostgreSQL locking is described in Chapter 9, "Multi-Version Concurrency Control," of the *PostgreSQL User's Manual*.

DEADLOCK_TIMEOUT

Default Value:	1000 (1 second)
Modify Time:	SIGHUP
Override:	None

A deadlock occurs when one transaction holds a lock required by a second transaction and the second transaction holds a lock required by the first. This situation is called a deadlock because neither transaction can move forward (each transaction is waiting for the lock held by the other transaction). There may be more than two transactions involved in a deadlock.

The PostgreSQL lock manager checks for deadlock whenever a server process waits for a lock longer than DEADLOCK_TIMEOUT (measured in milliseconds). Checking for a deadlock is a relatively expensive operation so the lock manager assumes that a blocked lock request will eventually be satisfied. If DEADLOCK_TIMEOUT milliseconds elapses before a lock is satisfied, PostgreSQL searches through all locks to find out whether a deadlock has occurred.

The default value for this parameter is one second—you may want to increase this value on heavily loaded systems (increasing DEADLOCK_TIMEOUT will reduce the load imposed by deadlock checks, but will increase the amount of time that elapses before a real deadlock is detected).

REGEX_FLAVOR

Default Value:	'advanced'
Modify Time:	SET command
Override:	None

REGEX_FLAVOR determines the regular-expression style recognized by the PostgreSQL backend. PostgreSQL supports three different flavors: advanced (the default flavor), extended, and basic. The advanced flavor offers the largest collection of features. See the PostgreSQL reference documentation for more information.

SQL_INHERITANCE

Default Value:	True
Modify Time:	SET command
Override:	None

Prior to release 7.1, a SELECT command would not include data from descendant tables unless an asterisk was appended to the table name. Starting with release 7.1, data is included from all descendant tables unless the keyword ONLY is included in the FROM clause.

In other words, in release 7.1, the default behavior of PostgreSQL's inheritance feature was reversed. If you find that you need the pre-7.1 behavior, set SQL_INHERITANCE to false.

Inheritance is described in Chapter 3.

TRANSFORM_NULL_EQUALS

Default Value:	False
Modify Time:	SET command
Override:	None

If TRANSFORM_NULL_EQUALS is True, the PostgreSQL parser will translate expressions of the form *expression* = NULL to *expression* IS NULL. In most cases, it's a bad idea to set this parameter to true because there is a semantic difference between = NULL and IS NULL. The expression *expression* = NULL should always evaluate to NULL, regardless of the value of *expression*. The only time that you should consider setting this parameter to True is when you are using Microsoft Access as a client application: Access can generate queries that are technically incorrect but are still expected to function.

Read-only Parameters

PostgreSQL defines a number of read-only parameters (also known as preset parameters). The values of some read-only parameters are determined at the time you build PostgreSQL from source code. Other values are fixed when you create a database cluster. You cannot change these parameters, but you will find them in the pg_settings system view.

SERVER_VERSION

Default Value:	Determined at compile time
Modify Time:	Read Only
Override:	None

This parameter reflects the version of the PostgreSQL server that you are connected to.

BLOCK_SIZE

Default Value:	8192 (bytes)
Modify Time:	Read Only
Override:	None

The BLOCK_SIZE parameter reflects the size of a disk block (as seen by the PostgreSQL server). When a PostgreSQL process reads data from (or writes data to) disk, it always reads (or writes) a block at a time. You can set BLOCK_SIZE by modifying src/include/pg_config_manual.h and then rebuilding PostgreSQL from source code.

MAX_INDEX_KEYS

Default Value:	32
Modify Time:	Read Only
Override:	None

MAX_INDEX_KEYS reflects the maximum number of segments (or keys) allowed in an index. You can set MAX_INDEX_KEYS by modifying src/include/pg_config_manual.h (look for INDEX_MAX_KEYS) and then rebuilding PostgreSQL from source code. The PostgreSQL source code states that FUNC_MAX_ARGS and MAX_INDEX_KEYS must be equal to the same value.

MAX_FUNCTION_ARGS

Default Value:	32
Modify Time:	Read Only
Override:	None

MAX_FUNCTION_ARGS reflects the maximum number of arguments allowed in a function. You can set MAX_FUNCTION_ARGS by modifying src/include/pg_config_manual.h (look for FUNC_MAX_ARGS) and then rebuilding PostgreSQL from source code. The PostgreSQL source code states that FUNC_MAX_ARGS and MAX_INDEX_KEYS must be equal to the same value.

MAX_IDENTIFIER_LENGTH

Default Value:	63 (characters)
Modify Time:	Read Only
Override:	None

The MAX_IDENTIFIER_LENGTH parameter determines the maximum number of characters PostgreSQL will store when you create a named object (you can create and refer to objects with longer names, but they must be unique within the first MAX_IDENTIFIER_LENGTH characters). To change this value, modify the NAMEDATALEN symbol in src/include/postgres_ext.h and rebuild PostgreSQL from source code.

INTEGER_DATETIMES

Default Value:	False
Modify Time:	Read Only
Override:	configure —enable-integer-datetimes

If INTEGER_DATETIMES is False, PostgreSQL stores TIMESTAMP, TIME, and INTERVAL values as DOUBLE PRECISION floating point numbers. If INTEGER_DATETIMES is True, PostgreSQL stores TIMESTAMP, TIME, and INTERVAL values as BIGINT numbers. See the PostgreSQL reference documentation (section 8.5, "Date/Time Types") for more information regarding the tradeoffs involved. To enable INTEGER_DATETIMES, include the —enable-integer-datetimes flag when you configure the PostgreSQL source code.

SERVER_ENCODING

Default Value:	Determined by the operating system
Modify Time:	Read Only
Override:	None

This parameter reflects the encoding (character set) of the database that you are connected to. See Chapter 22 for more information.

LC_COLLATE

Default Value:	Determined by the operating system
Modify Time:	Read Only
Override:	None

LC_COLLATE determines the order in which string values are sorted (to satisfy an ORDER BY clause or to create an index). LC_COLLATE is consulted when you create a database cluster using the initdb command. See Chapter 22 for more information.

LC_CTYPE
Default Value: Determined by the operating system
Modify Time: Read Only
Override: None

LC_CTYPE is consulted when the server needs to classify a character as uppercase, lower-case, printable, whitespace, and so on. Like LC_COLLATE, LC_CTYPE is recorded in $PGDATA/global/pg_control when you create a database cluster. See Chapter 22 for more information.

Arranging for PostgreSQL Startup and Shutdown

In most environments, you will probably want to arrange for your PostgreSQL server to start when you boot your operating system. You'll also want to arrange for your PostgreSQL server to terminate gracefully when you power off your system. In this section, I'll show you how to make these arrangements for Windows and Red Hat Linux—the details will vary if you are using a different operating system.

First, let's see how to start and stop a PostgreSQL server *on-demand*.

Using pg_ctl

The easiest way to start a PostgreSQL server (that is, a postmaster) is to use the pg_ctl command. pg_ctl is a shell script that makes it easy to start, stop, restart, reconfigure, and query the status of a PostgreSQL server.

To start a server, use pg_ctl start:

```
$ pg_ctl start -l /tmp/pg.log -o -i
```

pg_ctl start fires up a postmaster. You can use several options with the pg_ctl start command, as shown in Table 21.8.

Table 21.8 pg_ctl **Start Options**

Option	Parameter	Meaning
-D	data-directory	Look for data files in data-directory
-l	logfile-name	Append postmaster output to logfile-name
-o	postmaster-options	Start postmaster with postmaster-options
-p	postmaster-path	Find postmaster in postmaster-path
-s		Report startup errors, but not informational messages
-w		Wait for postmaster to complete

The -D *data-directory* option tells the postmaster where to find your database cluster. If you don't include this option, the postmaster will interrogate the $PGDATA environment variable to find your cluster. If I am starting a postmaster from a shell script, I usually define PGDATA and then use it when I invoke pg_ctl:

```
...
export PGDATA=/usr/local/pgdata
pg_ctl -D $PGDATA
...
```

Arranging things this way makes it a bit more obvious that PGDATA is defined and that the postmaster will use that variable to find the cluster.

The -l *logfile-name* option determines where the postmaster will send error and informational messages. If you include this option, the postmaster's stdout and stderr will be appended to the named file. If you don't, the postmaster will write to the controlling terminal. That can be handy if you're trying to debug a server-related problem, but it's generally a bad idea. The problem with sending server output to the controlling terminal is that the controlling terminal will disappear if you log out—any server output written after you log out is lost.

You use the -o *postmaster-options* to specify options that will be passed along to the new postmaster. Any option supported by the postmaster can be specified after the -o flag. Enclose the *postmaster-options* in single or double quotes if it contains any whitespace. For example:

```
$ pg_ctl start -o "-i -d 5"
```

You will rarely, if ever, need to use the -p *postmaster-path* option. The -p option tells pg_ctl where to find the postmaster. In the normal case, pg_ctl can find the postmaster executable by looking in the directory that contains pg_ctl. If pg_ctl doesn't find the postmaster in its own directory, it will search in the bindir directory. The bindir directory is determined at the time your copy of PostgreSQL is built from source (that is, the -bindir configuration option). You will need to use only pg_ctl's -p option if you move the postmaster away from its normal location (don't do that).

The -s option is used to tell pg_ctl to be *silent*. Without the -s flag, pg_ctl will cheerfully display progress messages as it goes about its work. With the -s flag, pg_ctl will tell you only about problems.

Finally, use the -w flag if you want the pg_ctl program to *w*ait for the postmaster to complete its startup work before returning. If pg_ctl has to wait for more than 60 seconds, it will assume that something has gone wrong and will report an error. At that point, the postmaster may or may not be running: Use pg_ctl status to find out. I recommend including the -w flag whenever you invoke pg_ctl from a script; otherwise, your script will happily continue immediately after the pg_ctl command completes (but before the server has booted). If you want to see what kind of problems you may run into when you don't wait for a complete boot, try this:

```
$ pg_ctl -s stop
$ pg_ctl start -l /tmp/pg.log ; psql -d movies
```

```
postmaster successfully started
psql: could not connect to server: No such file or directory
        Is the server running locally and accepting
        connections on Unix domain socket "/tmp/.s.PGSQL.5432"?
```

See what happened? The `pg_ctl` command returned immediately after spawning the `postmaster`, but the `psql` command started running before the `postmaster` was ready to accept client connections. If you were to try that inside of a shell script, the PostgreSQL client (`psql` in this case) would fail. This kind of problem (apparently random client failures) can be hard to track down and usually results in a dope slap.

Shutdown Modes

You also can use `pg_ctl` to shut down (or restart) the `postmaster`. The `postmaster` honors three different shutdown signals:

- Smart shutdown—When the `postmaster` receives a terminate signal (`SIGTERM`), it performs a *smart* shutdown. In smart shutdown mode, the server prevents new client connections, allows current connections to continue, and terminates only after all clients have disconnected.

- Fast shutdown—If the `postmaster` receives an interrupt signal (`SIGINT`), it performs a *fast* shutdown. In fast shutdown mode, the server tells each server process to abort the current transaction and exit.

- Immediate shutdown—The third shutdown mode is called *immediate*, but it might be better termed *crash*. When you shut down the `postmaster` in this mode, each server process immediately terminates without cleaning up itself. An immediate shutdown is similar to a power failure and requires a WAL (write-ahead-log) recovery the next time you start your database.

To shut down the `postmaster` using `pg_ctl`, use the command

```
$ pg_ctl stop [smart|fast|immediate]
```

If you want to restart the `postmaster` using `pg_ctl`, use the command

```
$ pg_ctl restart [smart|fast|immediate]
```

Now that you know how to start up and shut down a PostgreSQL server on demand, let's see how to make a server start when your computer boots.

Configuring PostgreSQL Startup on Unix/Linux Hosts

Configuring PostgreSQL to automatically start when your Unix/Linux system boots is not difficult, but it is system-specific. Systems derived from BSD Unix will usually store startup scripts in the `/etc/rc.local` directory. Systems derived from System V Unix (including Red Hat Linux) will store startup scripts in the `/etc/rc.d` directory. The PostgreSQL Administrator's Guide contains a number of suggestions for configuring automatic PostgreSQL startup for various Unix/Linux systems. In this section, I'll describe the process for Red Hat Linux systems.

First, let's see the easy way to configure startup and shutdown on a typical Red Hat Linux system. There are only three steps required if you want to do things the easy way:

- Log in as the superuser (root)
- Copy the file `start-scripts/linux` from PostgreSQL's `contrib` directory to `/etc/rc.d/init.d/postgresql`
- Execute the command `/sbin/chkconfig –add postgresql`

That's it. The `chkconfig` command arranges for PostgreSQL to start when your system boots to multiuser mode and also arranges for PostgreSQL to shut down gracefully when you shut down your host system.

Now, let's look at the more complex way to arrange for startup and shutdown. Why might you want to do things the hard way? You may find that the functionality provided by the startup script (and `chkconfig`) don't fit quite right in your environment. You may have customized run levels (described next), or you may want to change the point in time that PostgreSQL starts (or stops) relative to other services. Reading the next section will also give you a good understanding of what `chkconfig` is doing on your behalf if you decide to use it.

When a Linux system boots, it boots to a specific *runlevel*. Each runlevel provides a set of services (such as network, X Windows, and PostgreSQL) . Most Linux distributions define seven runlevels:

- Runlevel 0—Halt
- Runlevel 1—Single-user (maintenance mode)
- Runlevel 2—Not normally used
- Runlevel 3—Multi-user, networking enabled
- Runlevel 4—Not normally used
- Runlevel 5—Multi-user, networking enabled, X Window login
- Runlevel 6—shutdown

In the usual case, your system is running at runlevel 3 or runlevel 5. You can add PostgreSQL to the set of services provided at a particular runlevel by adding a startup script and a shutdown script to the runlevel's directory.

Startup scripts are stored in the `/etc/rc.d` directory tree. `/etc/rc.d` contains one subdirectory for each runlevel. Here is a listing of the `/etc/rc.d` directory for our Red Hat 7.1 system:

```
$ ls /etc/rc.d
init.d  rc0.d  rc2.d  rc4.d  rc6.d     rc.sysinit
rc      rc1.d  rc3.d  rc5.d  rc.local
```

The numbers in the directory names correspond to different runlevels. So, the services provided at runlevel 3, for example, are defined in the `/etc/rc.d/rc3.d` directory. Here is a peek at the `rc3.d` directory:

```
$ ls /etc/rc.d/rc3.d
K03rhnsd        S05kudzu        S14nfslock      S55sshd         S85gpm
K20nfs          S06reconfig     S17keytable     S56rawdevices   S90crond
K20rwhod        S08ipchains     S20random       S56xinetd       S90xfs
K35smb          S08iptables     S25netfs        S60lpd          S95anacron
K45arpwatch     S10network      S26apmd         S80isdn         S99linuxconf
K65identd       S12syslog       S28autofs       S80pppoe        S99local
K74nscd         S13portmap      S40atd          S80sendmail
```

Inside a runlevel subdirectory, you will see *start* scripts and *kill* scripts. The start scripts
begin with the letter S and are executed whenever the runlevel begins. The kill scripts
begin with the letter K and are executed each time the runlevel ends. A start script is
(appropriately enough) used to start a service. A kill script is used to stop a service.

The numbers following the K or S determine the order in which the scripts will
execute. For example, S05kudzu starts with a lower number so it will execute before
S06reconfig.

I'll assume that you want to run PostgreSQL at runlevels 3 and 5 (the most commonly used runlevels). The start and kill scripts are usually quite complex. Fortunately,
PostgreSQL's contrib directory contains a sample startup script that you can use:
contrib/start-scripts/linux. To install this script, copy it to the /etc/rc.d/init.d
directory and fix the ownership and permissions (you'll need superuser privileges to
do this):

```
# cp contrib/start-scripts/linux /etc/rc.d/init.d/postgresql
# chown root /etc/rc.d/init.d/postgresql
# chmod 0755 /etc/rc.d/init.d/postgresql
```

Notice that you are copying the startup file to /etc/rc.d/init.d rather than /etc/
rc.d/rc3.d, as you might expect. Start and kill scripts are usually combined into a
single shell script that can handle startup requests as well as shutdown requests. Because a
single script might be needed in more than one runlevel, it is stored in /etc/rc.d/
init.d and symbolically linked from the required runlevel directories. You want
PostgreSQL to be available in runlevels 3 and 5, so create symbolic links in those
directories:

```
# ln -s /etc/rc.d/init.d/postgresql /etc/rc.d/rc3.d/S75postgresql
# ln -s /etc/rc.d/init.d/postgresql /etc/rc.d/rc3.d/K75postgresql
# ln -s /etc/rc.d/init.d/postgresql /etc/rc.d/rc5.d/S75postgresql
# ln -s /etc/rc.d/init.d/postgresql /etc/rc.d/rc5.d/K75postgresql
```

The numbers that you chose (S75 and K75) are positioned about three quarters through
the range (00-99). You will want to adjust the script numbers so that PostgreSQL starts
after any prerequisite services and ends after any services that depend upon it. Whenever
we reach runlevel 3 (or runlevel 5), the init process will execute all start scripts
numbered less than 75, then your postgresql script, and then scripts numbered higher
than 75.

You also want to ensure that PostgreSQL shuts down gracefully when you reboot or halt your server. The contributed script can handle that for you as well; you just need to create symbolic links from the halt (`rc0.d`) and reboot (`rc6.d`) directories:

```
# ln -s /etc/rc.d/init.d/postgresql /etc/rc.d/rc0.d/K75postgresql
# ln -s /etc/rc.d/init.d/postgresql /etc/rc.d/rc6.d/K75postgresql
```

As before, you will want to review the other scripts in your `rc0.d` and `rc6.d` directories to ensure that PostgreSQL is shut down in the proper order relative to other services.

Backing Up and Copying Databases

There are two ways to back up your PostgreSQL database. The first method is to create an archive containing the filesystem files that comprise your database. The second method is to create a SQL script that describes how to re-create the data in your database.

In the first method, you use an archiving tool, such as `tar`, `cpio`, or `backup`, to back up all the files in your database cluster. There are a number of disadvantages to this method. First, your entire database cluster must be shut down to ensure that all buffers have been flushed to disk. Second, the size of a filesystem archive will often be larger than the size of the equivalent script because the filesystem archive will contain indexes and partially filled pages that do not have to be archived. Finally, it is not possible to restore a single database or table from a filesystem archive. There are, however, two advantages to using a filesystem archive. First, you may already have a backup scheme in place that will back up a file system; including your database cluster in that scheme is probably pretty easy.

The second (and usually preferred) method is to create a SQL script that can reconstruct the contents of your database from scratch. Then, when you need to restore data from an archive, you simply run the script.

PostgreSQL provides two utilities that you can use to create archive scripts: `pg_dump`, and `pg_dumpall`.

Using `pg_dump`

The `pg_dump` program creates a SQL script that re-creates the data and metadata in your database. Before I get into too many details, it might help to see the kind of script that `pg_dump` will create[7]:

```
$ pg_dump —inserts -t customers movies
—
— Selected TOC Entries:
—
```

---

[7] I've changed the formatting of this script slightly so that it fits on a printed page.

In this example, I've asked `pg_dump` to produce a script that re-creates a single table (`-t customers`) using `INSERT` commands rather than `COPY` commands (`—inserts`).

```
\connect - bruce


—
— TOC Entry ID 2 (OID 518934)
—
— Name: customers Type: TABLE Owner: bruce
—
CREATE TABLE "customers" (
        "id" integer,
        "customer_name" character varying(50),
        "phone" character(8),
        "birth_date" date
);


—
— TOC Entry ID 3 (OID 518934)
—
— Name: customers Type: ACL Owner:
—
REVOKE ALL on "customers" from PUBLIC;
GRANT ALL on "customers" to "bruce";
GRANT ALL on "customers" to "sheila";


—
  Data for TOC Entry ID 4 (OID 518934)
—
— Name: customers Type: TABLE DATA Owner: bruce
—
INSERT INTO "customers" VALUES
        (1,'Jones, Henry','555-1212','1970-10-10');
INSERT INTO "customers" VALUES
        (2,'Rubin, William','555-2211','1972-07-10');
INSERT INTO "customers" VALUES
        (3,'Panky, Henry','555-1221','1968-01-21');
INSERT INTO "customers" VALUES
        (4,'Wonderland, Alice N.','555-1122','1969-03-05');
INSERT INTO "customers" VALUES
        (7,'Grumby, Jonas',NULL,'1984-02-21');
INSERT INTO "customers" VALUES
        (8,'Haywood, Rosemary','666-1212','1965-02-03');
```

If we feed this script back into psql (or some other client application), psql will connect to the database as user bruce, CREATE the customers table, assign the proper privileges to the table, and INSERT all the rows that had been committed at the time that we started the original pg_dump command. You can see that this script contains everything that we need to re-create the customers table starting from an empty database. If we had defined triggers, sequences, or indexes for the customers table, the code necessary to re-create those objects would appear in the script as well.

Now let's look at some of the command-line options for pg_dump. Start with pg_dump —help:

```
$ pg_dump —help
pg_dump dumps a database as a text file or to other formats.

Usage:
  pg_dump [options] dbname

Options:
  -a, —data-only       dump only the data, not the schema
  -b, —blobs           include large objects in dump
  -c, —clean           clean (drop) schema prior to create
  -C, —create          include commands to create database in dump
  -d, —inserts         dump data as INSERT, rather than COPY, commands
  -D, —column-inserts  dump data as INSERT commands with column names
  -f, —file=FILENAME   output file name
  -F, —format {c|t|p}  output file format (custom, tar, plain text)
  -h, —host=HOSTNAME   database server host name
  -i, —ignore-version  proceed even when server version mismatches
                        pg_dump version
  -n, —no-quotes       suppress most quotes around identifiers
  -N, —quotes          enable most quotes around identifiers
  -o, —oids            include oids in dump
  -O, —no-owner        do not output \connect commands in plain
                        text format
  -p, —port=PORT       database server port number
  -R, —no-reconnect    disable ALL reconnections to the database in
                        plain text format
  -s, —schema-only     dump only the schema, no data
  -S, —superuser=NAME  specify the superuser user name to use in
                        plain text format
  -t, —table=TABLE     dump this table only (* for all)
  -U, —username=NAME   connect as specified database user
  -v, —verbose         verbose mode
  -W, —password        force password prompt
                           (should happen automatically)
  -x, —no-privileges   do not dump privileges (grant/revoke)
  -X use-set-session-authorization, —use-set-session-authorization
                         output SET SESSION AUTHORIZATION commands
                         rather than \connect commands
  -Z, —compress {0-9}  compression level for compressed formats
```

If no database name is not supplied, then the PGDATABASE environment
variable value is used.

Report bugs to <pgsql-bugs@postgresql.org>.

The most basic form for the pg_dump command is

pg_dump database

In this form, pg_dump archives all objects in the given *database*. You can see that
pg_dump understands quite a number of command-line options. I'll explain the most
useful options here.

If you use large-objects in your database, you may want to include the —blobs (or -b)
option so that large-objects are written to the resulting script. Needless to say, archiving
large-objects increases the size of your archive.

You also might want to include either —clean (-c) or —create (-C) when you are
using pg_dump for backup purposes. The —clean flag tells pg_dump to DROP an object
before it CREATEs the object—this reduces the number of errors you might see when
you restore from the script. The second option, —create, tells pg_dump to include a
CREATE DATABASE statement in the resulting archive. If you want to archive and restore
an entire database, use the —create option when you create the archive and drop the
database before you restore.

In the previous example, I included the —inserts flag. This flag, and the related
—column-inserts flag affect how pg_dump populates each table in your database. If you
don't include either flag, pg_dump will emit COPY commands to put data back into each
table. If you use the —inserts flag, pg_dump will emit INSERT commands rather than
COPY commands. If you use the —column-inserts flag, pg_dump will build INSERT commands, which include column lists, such as

INSERT INTO "customers" ("id","customer_name","phone","birth_date")
    VALUES (1,'Jones, Henry','555-1212','1970-10-10');

Emitting COPY commands causes the restore to execute more quickly than INSERT commands, so you should usually omit both flags (—inserts and —column-inserts). You
might want to build INSERT commands if you intend to use the resulting script for some
other purpose, such as copying data into an Oracle, Sybase, or SQL Server database.

Because pg_dump is a client application, you don't have to be logged in to the server
to create an archive script. A few of the pg_dump options (—port, —host, and —username)
control how pg_dump will connect to your database.

One of the problems that you may encounter when you run pg_dump is that it can
produce scripts that are too large to store as a single file. Many operating systems impose
a maximum file size of 2GB or 4GB. If you are archiving a large database, the resulting
script can easily exceed the file size limit, even though no single table would (remember,
each table is stored in its own file).

There are two (related) solutions to this problem. First, you can decrease the size of the archive script by compressing it. The `pg_dump` program writes the archive script to its standard output so you can pipe the script into a compression program:

```
$ pg_dump movies | gzip -9 > movies.gz
```

or

```
$ pg_dump movies | bzip2 -9 > movies.bz2
```

You also can compress the archive script by telling `pg_dump` to create the archive in *custom* format. The custom format is compressed and is organized so that the `pg_restore` program (described a bit later) can avoid problems caused by order of execution. To choose the custom format, include the —`format` c flag:

```
$ pg_dump —format c movies > movies.bak
```

Using the custom format means that your archive script will be compressed (thus taking less space and possibly fitting within the operating system imposed file size limit). However, you can't restore a custom-format script using `psql`; you must use `pg_restore`. That's not a problem per se; it's just something to be aware of.

Unfortunately, compressing the archive script is not really a solution; it simply delays the inevitable because even in compressed form, you may still exceed your OS file size limit. You may need to *split* the archive script into smaller pieces. Fortunately, the `split` command (a Unix/Linux/Cygwin utility) makes this easy. You can dump an entire database into a collection of smaller archive scripts (20MB each) with the following command:

```
$ pg_dump movies | split —bytes=20m movies.bak.
```

This command causes `pg_dump` to produce a single script, but when you pipe the script to `split`, it will split the script into 20MB chunks. The end result is a collection of one or more files with names such as `movies.bak.aa`, `movies.bak.ab`, … `movies.bak.zz`. When you want to restore data from these archives, you can concatenate them using the `cat` command:

```
$ cat movies.bak.* | psql -d movies
```

See the *PostgreSQL Reference Manual* for complete details on the `pg_dump` command.

Using `pg_dumpall`

The `pg_dump` command can archive individual tables or all the tables in a single database, but it cannot archive multiple databases. To archive an entire cluster, use the `pg_dumpall` command. `pg_dumpall` is similar to `pg_dump` in that it creates SQL scripts that can be used to re-create a database cluster.

`pg_dumpall` is actually a wrapper that invokes `pg_dump` for each database in your cluster. That means that `pg_dumpall` supports the same set of command-line options as `pg_dump`. Well, almost—`pg_dumpall` silently ignores any attempts to produce a custom or `tar` format script. `pg_dumpall` can produce archive scripts only in plain text format. This introduces two problems. First, you cannot compress the archive script by selecting the custom format; you must pipe the script to an external compression program instead. Second, you cannot archive large-objects using `pg_dumpall` (`pg_dump` can archive only large-objects using custom format, which you can't use with `pg_dumpall`).

Using `pg_restore`

When you create an archive script using `pg_dump` or `pg_dumpall`, you can restore the archive using `pg_restore`. The `pg_restore` command processes the given archive and produces a sequence of SQL commands that re-create the archived data. Note that `pg_restore` *cannot* process plain text archive scripts (such as those produced by `pg_dumpall`); you must produce the archive using the `—format=c` or `—format=t` options. If you want to restore a plain text archive script, simply pipe it into `psql`.

A typical invocation of `pg_restore` might look like this:

```
$ pg_restore —clean -d movies movies.bak
```

The `—clean` flag tells `pg_restore` to drop each database object before it is restored. The `-d movies` option tells `pg_restore` to connect to the `movies` database before processing the archive: All SQL commands built from the archive are executed within the given database. If you don't supply a database name, `pg_restore` writes the generated SQL commands to the standard output stream; this can be useful if you want to clone a database.

Like `pg_dump`, `pg_restore` can be used from a remote host. That means that you can provide the hostname, username, and password on the `pg_restore` command line.

The `pg_restore` program allows you to restore specific database objects (tables, functions, and so on); see the *PostgreSQL Reference Manual* for more details.

Point-in-time Recovery

When you make a change to a PostgreSQL database, the PostgreSQL server records your changes in the shared buffer pool, the write ahead log (WAL), and eventually, in the file that holds the table that you've changed. The WAL stores a complete record of every change that you make. PostgreSQL's point-in-time recovery mechanism (PITR) uses the modification history stored in the WAL files to *roll-forward* changes made since the most recent cluster backup. You can think of PITR as an incremental backup scheme. You start with a complete backup and then, periodically, archive the changes. To recover from a crash, you restore the complete backup and then apply the changes, in sequence, until you've recovered all of the data that you want to restore.

Point-in-time recovery (PITR) can seem very intimidating if you start out reading the documentation (not that the documentation is bad, it just assaults you with a lot of detail before you get the big picture). To give you a broad overview of PostgreSQL's PITR, I'll cook up a new database, make it crash, and then recover the data using the

PITR mechanism. You can follow along if you want, but you'll need some spare disk space.

I'll start by creating a new database cluster so I can experiment without harming any real data:

```
$ export PGDATA=/usr/local/pgPITR
$ initdb
The files belonging to this database system will be owned by user "pg".
This user must also own the server process.
...
Success. You can now start the database server using:

    postmaster -D /usr/local/pgPITR/data
or
    pg_ctl -D /usr/local/pgPITR/data -l logfile start
```

Next, I'll change the $PGDATA/postgresql.conf configuration file to enable PITR. The only change that I have to make is to define the archive_command parameter. archive_command tells PostgreSQL how to archive the WAL (write-ahead-log) files generated by the PostgreSQL server. Since I don't really care about the data in this cluster, I'll just squirrel away the WAL files in the /tmp/wals directory:

```
archive_command = 'cp %p /tmp/wals/%f'
```

PostgreSQL will execute the archive_command instead of simply deleting the WAL files as it would normally do. The %p and %f macros expand to the complete pathname of a WAL file (%p) and the filename component of that file (%f).

Now I'll create the archive directory (/tmp/wals), start the postmaster, and create a database that I can work in:

```
$ mkdir /tmp/wals
$ pg_ctl -l /tmp/pg.log start
postmaster starting
$ createdb test
CREATE DATABASE
```

At this point, I have a fully PostgreSQL cluster, based in $PGDATA, with a sacrificial database named test. When I make changes to database, those changes are recorded in the WAL files stored in $PGDATA/pg_xlog (just like any other PostgreSQL cluster). When a WAL file fills, PostgreSQL will copy the file into the /tmp/wals directory for safekeeping (if this were a real live database, I would employ a much more secure archive method). The only difference between a regular PostgreSQL cluster and a PITR-enabled database is that PostgreSQL archives the WAL files instead of deleting them.

Because the PITR mechanism works by applying changes recorded in the WAL files, I'll generate some WAL data by creating some dummy tables. It really doesn't matter what I put in the dummy tables, they just have to generate enough WAL data to overflow a few WAL files (each WAL file is 16MB long). Since the whole point of PITR is to recover to a specific point in time, I'll make note of the time that I COMMIT each transaction:

```
$ psql test
Welcome to psql 8.0.0, the PostgreSQL interactive terminal.
...
test=# BEGIN WORK;
BEGIN
test=# CREATE TABLE dummy1 AS SELECT * FROM pg_class, pg_attribute;
SELECT
test=# COMMIT; — executed at 12:30:00pm
COMMIT
test=# \q
```

The CREATE TABLE command produced a table that holds more than 245,000 records and produced enough WAL data to overflow a few segments. You can see the archived segments by looking in the /tmp/wals directory:

```
$ ls /tmp/wals
000000010000000000000000
000000010000000000000001
000000010000000000000002
000000010000000000000003
000000010000000000000004
```

Next, I'll create a complete backup of my database cluster. To simplify this example, I'll simply create a tarball and save it in the /tmp directory instead of writing the whole thing to tape. Before I start the backup, I'll tell PostgreSQL what I'm about to do by calling the pg_start_backup() function:

```
$ psql test
Welcome to psql 8.0.0, the PostgreSQL interactive terminal.
...
test=# select pg_start_backup( 'full backup - Monday' );
 pg_start_backup
----------------
 0/52EA2B8
(1 row)
test=# \q

$ tar -zxvf /tmp/pgdata.tgz $PGDATA
tar: Removing leading '/' from member names
/usr/local/pgPITR/data/
/usr/local/pgPITR/data/pg_hba.conf
/usr/local/pgPITR/data/pg_subtrans/
...
```

The argument that you give to pg_start_backup() is simply a label that helps you remember where the archive came from—you'll find a file named $PGDATA/backup_label after calling this function and the label is stored inside of that file.

When the backup completes, I'll tell PostgreSQL that I'm finished by calling the pg_stop_backup() function:

```
$ psql test
Welcome to psql 8.0.0, the PostgreSQL interactive terminal.
...
test=# select pg_stop_backup();
 pg_stop_backup
--------------
 0/52EA2F4
(1 row)

test=# \q
```

At this point, I have a complete backup of the database cluster, PostgreSQL is still running (I did not have to stop the postmaster), any database changes are recorded in the WAL files, and the WAL files are still being archived in /tmp/wals. Pretend that I've locked the backup (/tmp/pgdata.tgz) in a safe place somewhere.

To generate a few more WAL files, I'll create another dummy table:

```
$ psql test
Welcome to psql 8.0.0, the PostgreSQL interactive terminal.
...
test=# BEGIN WORK;
BEGIN
test=# CREATE TABLE dummy2 AS SELECT * FROM pg_class, pg_attribute;
SELECT
test=# COMMIT; — executed at 12:38:00pm
```

Now, just to make things more interesting, I'll add a third dummy table and the drop it again. You would expect that table to disappear once I recover:

```
test=# BEGIN WORK;
BEGIN
test=# CREATE TABLE dummy3 AS SELECT * FROM pg_class, pg_attribute;
SELECT
test=# COMMIT; — executed at 12:39:00pm
COMMIT
test=# BEGIN WORK;
BEGIN
test=# DROP TABLE dummy3;
DROP TABLE
test=# COMMIT; — executed at 12:40:00pm
COMMIT
test=# \q
```

As you would expect, PostgreSQL has copied a few more WAL files to /tmp/wals:

```
$ ls /tmp/wals
000000010000000000000000
```

```
000000010000000000000001
000000010000000000000002
000000010000000000000003
000000010000000000000004
000000010000000000000005
000000010000000000000005.002EA2B8.backup
000000010000000000000006
000000010000000000000007
000000010000000000000008
000000010000000000000009
00000001000000000000000A
00000001000000000000000B
00000001000000000000000C
00000001000000000000000D
00000001000000000000000E
```

At this point, disaster strikes. My power goes out, an unexpected hurricane arrives, or my computer bursts into flames (and everything except my /tmp directory is destroyed—hey, we're just pretending). To simulate disaster, I'll kill off the postmaster:

```
$ kill -9 $(head -1 $PGDATA/postmaster.pid)
```

Now it's time to recover the entire cluster. I'll start by renaming the damaged cluster:

```
$ mv $PGDATA $PGDATA.old
```

Next, I'll restore the backup from its archive:

```
$ pushd / && tar zxvf /tmp/pgdata.tgz && popd
```

That leaves me with the damaged cluster in $PGDATA.old and the backup cluster in $PGDATA. I'll clean up the (freshly restored) cluster by removing the old WAL files and the postmaster.pid file:

```
$ rm -f $PGDATA/pg_xlog/0*
$ rm -f $PGDATA/postmaster.pid
```

To ensure that I can recover as much data as possible, I'll copy the WAL files from the damaged cluster into the restored cluster:

```
$ cp $PGDATA.old/pg_xlog/0* $PGDATA/pg_xlog/
```

If the damaged cluster is not available (maybe it burned up when my computer caught fire), I can still recover—I just can't recover as much. I can recover all transactions committed before the most recent WAL file was archived. In a busy database, that's a few minutes. In a quiescent database, the interval is longer, but the *amount* of data is the same (16MB or so).

Now I can start the PostgreSQL recovery process, but before I do, here's another look at the timeline that I've followed:

- 12:30:00pm—I created the dummy1 table and committed the change
- 2:38:00pm—I created the dummy2 table and committed the change

- 12:39:00pm—I created the dummy3 table and committed the change
- 12:40:00pm—I dropped dummy3 and committed the change

Sometime between 12:30 and 12:38, I backed up the entire cluster. When I start the recovery process, I can recover *all* changes, or I can tell PostgreSQL to stop at a certain point in time. If the recovery stops before 12:38, I should find the dummy1 table, but not the dummy2 (or dummy3) table. If the recovery stops before 12:39, I should find dummy1 and dummy2 (but not dummy3). If the recovery stops before 12:40, I should find all three tables. If I let PostgreSQL recover *all* changes, the dummy3 file should disappear (because I dropped that table before the lights went out).

To control the recovery process, I'll create a file named $PGDATA/recovery.conf that tells PostgreSQL how to proceed. recovery.conf looks like this:

```
$ cat $PGDATA/recovery.conf
restore_command = 'cp /tmp/wals/%f %p'
recovery_target_time = '2005-06-22 12:39:01 EST'
```

The restore_command parameter tells PostgreSQL how to restore the WAL files PostgreSQL tucked away in /tmp/wals (in a real-world environment, the restore_command might be a shell script that asks you to mount a specific tape). The recovery_target_time parameter tells PostgreSQL when to stop. If you want to recover all changes, simply omit the recovery_target_time parameter. In this case, I've asked PostgreSQL to stop the recovery process after it restores the 12:39pm change—I expect to find dummy1, dummy2, and dummy3 in the database when recovery completes.

PostgreSQL starts the recovery process as soon as you start the postmaster (the postmaster knows it has extra work to do because it finds the $PGDATA/recovery.conf file):

```
$ pg_ctl -l /tmp/pg.log start
postmaster started
```

If you're running on a Linux/Unix system (or you have the Cygwin tools installed), you can follow the postmaster's progress by watching the server's log file:

```
$ tail -f /tmp/pg.log
LOG:   starting archive recovery
LOG:   restore_command = "cp /tmp/wals/%f %p"
LOG:   recovery_target_time = 2005-06-22 13:05:00-05
...
LOG:   restored log file "000000010000000000000006" from archive
LOG:   restored log file "000000010000000000000007" from archive
LOG:   restored log file "000000010000000000000008" from archive
LOG:   restored log file "000000010000000000000009" from archive
...
LOG:   archive recovery complete
LOG:   database system is ready
```

When the recovery process completes, PostgreSQL has renamed the `recovery.conf` file (to `recovery.done`) to avoid an accidental recovery the next time you start the postmaster.

I can now connect to the database and see that the `dummy1`, `dummy2`, and `dummy3` tables are in place:

```
$ psql test
Welcome to psql 8.0.0, the PostgreSQL interactive terminal.
...
test=# \d
        List of relations
 Schema |  Name  | Type  | Owner
--------+--------+-------+------
 public | dummy1 | table | pg
 public | dummy2 | table | pg
 public | dummy3 | table | pg
(3 rows)
```

If I had omitted the `recovery_target_time` parameter, the `dummy3` table would disappear because I dropped that table (and, most importantly, committed the change) before my system crashed.

You can see that PITR is easy to configure (just define an `archive_command` in the `postgresql.conf` file). The process of actually *recovering* from a crash can be tricky, but as long as you follow the procedure I've outlined, you should be in good shape. I *strongly* encourage you to practice the whole process before you really need it. Just create a sacrificial cluster, configure PITR recovery, create some data, and fake a few crashes. It won't take much time and you'll be happy that you've learned the procedure if your disk drives start making funny noises.

To summarize the setup procedure:

- Configure PITR recovery by defining an `archive_command` in `$PGDATA/postgresql.conf`
- Restart the `postmaster` to start the WAL archive process
- Connect to the database and invoke the `pg_start_backup( label )` function
- Back up the entire cluster (you *don't* have to shutdown the database)

To summarize the recovery procedure:

- If possible, rename the damaged cluster so you can recover as much data as possible
- Restore the complete cluster backup from the archive
- Clean up the restored cluster (remove the `$PGDATA/pg_xlog` files and `$PGDATA/postmaster.pid`)
- If possible, copy the WAL files from the damaged cluster into the freshly restored cluster

- Create the `$PGDATA/recovery.conf` file (at minimum, this file must define a `restore_command`)
- Start the postmaster
- Verify that the data you expect to find in the database is really there

The most important part of the PITR scheme is the `archive_command`. The PostgreSQL reference documentation (Chapter 22) provides a few guidelines regarding the `archive_command` (and the `restore_command`). You'll also find a detailed explanation of the parameters that you can include in the `recovery.conf` file. Be sure to read that chapter before you try to configure a real-world server that contains important data.

Summary

This chapter is intended as a supplement to the *PostgreSQL Administrator's Guide*, not as a replacement. I've tried to cover the basic operations that a PostgreSQL administrator will be required to perform, but you may need to refer to the official PostgreSQL documentation for detailed reference material.

The next chapter covers the internationalization and localization features of PostgreSQL.

22

Internationalization and Localization

Internationalization and localization are two sides of the same coin. *Internationalization* is the process of developing software so that it can be used in a variety of locations. *Localization* is the process of modifying an application for use in a specific location. When you internationalize software, you are making it portable; when you localize software, you are actually performing a port.

In the PostgreSQL world, the topics of internationalization and localization are concerned with the following:

- Viewing PostgreSQL-generated messages in the *language* of your choice
- Viewing PostgreSQL generated messages in the *character set* of your choice
- Viewing user data in the *character set* of your choice
- Producing the correct results when PostgreSQL returns data in sorted order
- Producing the correct results when PostgreSQL needs to classify characters into categories such as uppercase, punctuation, and so on

We can separate these issues into two broad categories: locales and character sets.

Locale Support

A *locale* is a named group of properties that defines culture-specific conventions. Each locale is made up of one or more categories. Each category controls the behavior of a set of features. For example, the LC_MONETARY category contains information about how monetary values are formatted in some specific territory. The ISO and IEEE (POSIX) standards bodies have stated that a locale should include information such as the ordering of date components, the formatting of numbers, and the language preferred for message text.

PostgreSQL makes use of the locale-processing facilities provided by the host operating system. When you log in to your operating system, you are automatically assigned a locale. On a Linux host (and most Unix hosts), you can find your current locale using the `locale` command:

```
$ locale
LANG=en_US
LC_CTYPE="en_US"
LC_NUMERIC="en_US"
LC_TIME="en_US"
LC_COLLATE="en_US"
LC_MONETARY="en_US"
LC_MESSAGES="en_US"
LC_PAPER="en_US"
LC_NAME="en_US"
LC_ADDRESS="en_US"
LC_TELEPHONE="en_US"
LC_MEASUREMENT="en_US"
LC_IDENTIFICATION="en_US"
LC_ALL=
```

You can see that I am using a locale named `en_US`. Locale names are composed of multiple parts. The first component identifies a language. In my case, the language is `en`, meaning English. The second (optional) component identifies a country, region, or territory where the language is used. I am in the U.S., so my country code is set to `US`. You can think of `en_US` as meaning "English as spoken in the U.S.", as opposed to `en_AU`, which means "English as spoken in Australia." The third component of a locale name is an optional codeset. I'll talk more about codesets later in this chapter. Finally, a locale name may include modifiers, such as "`@euro`" to indicate that the locale uses the Euro for currency values.

Language IDs are usually two characters long, written in lowercase, and chosen from the ISO 639 list of country codes. Territories are usually two characters long, written in uppercase, and chosen from the ISO 3166 standard.

The POSIX (and ISO) standards define two special locales named `C` and `POSIX`. The `C` and `POSIX` locales are defined so that they can be used in many different locations.

Table 22.1 shows a few locale names taken from my Linux host.

Table 22.1 **Sample Locale Names**

Locale Name	Language	Region	Codeset	Modifier
sv_FI	Swedish	Finland		
sv_FI@euro	Swedish	Finland		Euro is used in this locale
sv_FI.utf8	Swedish	Finland	UTF-8	
sv_FI.utf8@euro	Swedish	Finland	UTF-8	Euro is used in this locale
sv_SE	Swedish	Sweden		

Table 22.1 **Continued**

Locale Name	Language	Region	Codeset	Modifier
v_SE.utf8	Swedish	Sweden	UTF-8	
en_AU	English	Australia		
en_AU.utf8	English	Australia	UTF-8	
en_IE	English	Ireland		
en_IE@euro	English	Ireland		Euro is used in this locale
en_IE.utf8	English	Ireland	UTF-8	
en_IE.utf8@euro	English	Ireland	UTF-8	Euro is used in this locale

My Fedora Linux system defines 560 locales. Each locale is broken down into a set of categories. Most locale implementations define (at least) the categories shown in Table 22.2. Some environments define additional categories.

Table 22.2 **Locale Information Categories**

Category	Influences	Used By
LC_MESSAGES	Message formatting and message language	Client/Server
LC_MONETARY	Monetary value formatting	Server
LC_NUMERIC	Numeric value formatting	Server
LC_TIME	Date and time formatting	Not used
LC_CTYPE	Character classifications (uppercase, punctuation, and so on)	Server_
LC_COLLATE	Collating order for string values	Cluster
LC_ALL	All of the above	See all of the above

Enabling Locale Support

Starting with PostgreSQL version 7.3, locale support is automatically included in every build. If you're building a version of PostgreSQL older than 7.3, you must specify the `--enable-locale` option when you configure the source code.

If you want to see messages in a language other than English, you should enable NLS (National Language Support). To enable NLS support, specify `--enable-nls` when you configure the PostgreSQL source code:

```
$ ./configure --enable-nls
```

You choose a locale by setting one or more runtime configuration parameters. Like most configuration parameters, you can define the locale-related parameters in the `postgresql.conf` configuration file and you can modify them at runtime with the `SET` command. The locale-related configuration parameters are named `LC_MESSAGES`, `LC_MONETARY`, `LC_NUMERIC`, and `LC_TIME`. If you don't specify a value for a locale parameter, PostgreSQL looks for the corresponding environment variable.

If you specify a locale using environment variables, there are three levels of environment variables that you can define. At the bottom level, you can set the LANG environment variable to the locale that you want to use. For example, if you want all features to run in a French context *unless overridden*, set LANG=fr_FR. You can created a mixed by defining LC_MESSAGES, LC_MONETARY, LC_NUMERIC, LC_CTYPE, and/or LC_COLLATE. The LC_xxx environment variables override LANG. If you are working with a database that stores French values (monetary units perhaps), for example, you may still want to see PostgreSQL messages in English. In this case, you would set LANG=fr_FR and LC_MESSAGES=en_US. At the top level, LC_ALL overrides any other locale-related environment variables: If you want everything to run in German (as spoken in Germany), set LC_ALL=de_DE. Remember that PostgreSQL configuration parameters (specified in postgresql.conf or modified with a SET command) take precedence over environment variables.

Effects of Locale Support

Let's see what happens when you change locales.

The first category in Table 22.2, LC_MESSAGES, determines which language PostgreSQL uses when it displays a message. I've been running with LC_MESSAGES set to en_US when I run psql, so I see messages displayed in English:

```
$ psql -d movies
Welcome to psql, the PostgreSQL interactive terminal.

Type:  \copyright for distribution terms
       \h for help with SQL commands
       \? for help on internal slash commands
       \g or terminate with semicolon to execute query
       \q to quit

movies=#
```

Let's try setting LC_MESSAGES to fr_CA (French as spoken in Canada):

```
$ LC_MESSAGES=fr_CA psql -d movies
Bienvenu à psql, l'interface interactif de PostgreSQL.

Tapez:  \copyright pour l'information de copyright
        \h pour l'aide-mémoire sur les commandes SQL
        \? pour l'aide-mémoire sur les commandes internes
        \g ou point-virgule pour exécuter une requête
        \q pour quitter

movies=#
```

Voilà! The client messages are now in French.

It's important to remember that the client (psql) and server do *not* share an environment. In other words, if you set LC_MESSAGES=fr_CA before running psql, you're only affecting the psql client—messages produced by the client are displayed in French, but messages produced by the server are produced in the server's locale. To see this behavior, try the following:

```
$ LC_MESSAGES=fr_CA psql -d movies
Bienvenu à psql, l'interface interactif de PostgreSQL.

Tapez:  \copyright pour l'information de copyright
        \h pour l'aide-mémoire sur les commandes SQL
        \? pour l'aide-mémoire sur les commandes internes
        \g ou point-virgule pour exécuter une requête
        \q pour quitter

movies=# SELECT junk ;
ERROR: column "junk" does not exist
```

Notice that the greeting printed by the psql client appears in French, but the error message (which is printed by the server) appears in English. To change the server's LC_MESSAGES locale, define the LC_MESSAGES (or more typically, lc_messages) parameter in your server's postgresql.conf file. You can also change the server's LC_MESSAGES locale in the middle of a session using the SET command:

```
movies=# SELECT junk ;
ERROR: column "junk" does not exist
movies=# SET lc_messages = 'fr_CA';
SET
movies=# SELECT junk ;
ERREUR:  la colonne ?junk? n'existe pas
```

When you execute a SET command, you are changing a parameter in *your* session— any new sessions will inherit the parameter from the *postgresql.conf* file. You can only SET LC_MESSAGES if you are a superuser in the cluster that you're connected to.

Some locale properties affect the server, some affect the client, and a few are stored with the database cluster itself (refer to Table 22.2). The LC_MESSAGES category affects both the client and server because each can produce message text.

Now, let's try a few of the other categories.

The server uses the LC_MONETARY category to control the way in which monetary values are formatted. I've modified the customers table in my database to include a balance column (using the MONEY data type). Here is the new column, shown in the en_US locale:

```
movies=# SELECT * FROM customers;
 id |   customer_name    |  phone   | birth_date |  balance
----+--------------------+----------+------------+------------
  4 | Wonderland, Alice N. | 555-1122 | 1969-03-05 |
  1 | Jones, Henry       | 555-1212 | 1970-10-10 |     $10.00
  2 | Rubin, William     | 555-2211 | 1972-07-10 |  $1,000.00
  3 | Panky, Henry       | 555-1221 | 1968-01-21 | $10,000.00
(4 rows)
```

Next, I'll use the SET command to change LC_MONETARY to fr_FR (French as spoken in France).

```
movies=# SET LC_MONETARY = 'fr_FR';
SET
```

Now, when I query the customers table, the monetary values are formatted using the fr_FR locale:

```
movies=# SELECT * FROM customers;
 id |   customer_name      |  phone   | birth_date  |   balance
----+----------------------+----------+-------------+------------
  4 | Wonderland, Alice N. | 555-1122 | 1969-03-05 |
  1 | Jones, Henry         | 555-1212 | 1970-10-10 |     EUR10,00
  2 | Rubin, William       | 555-2211 | 1972-07-10 | EUR1 000,00
  3 | Panky, Henry         | 555-1221 | 1968-01-21 | EUR10 000,00
(4 rows)
```

Notice that MONEY values are now formatted using French preferences.

The LC_NUMERIC category determines which characters will be used for grouping, the currency symbol, positive and negative signs, and the decimal point. Currently, LC_NUMERIC is used only by the TO_CHAR() function. The LC_NUMERIC category affects the only server.

PostgreSQL currently does not use the LC_TIME category (each date/time value can include an explicit time zone).

LC_CTYPE is consulted whenever PostgreSQL needs to categorize a character. The server locale determines which characters are considered uppercase, lowercase, numeric, punctuation, and so on. The most obvious uses of LC_CTYPE are the LOWER(), UPPER(), and INITCAP() string functions. LC_CTYPE is also consulted when the server evaluates regular expressions and the LIKE operator.

LC_COLLATE affects the result of an ORDER BY clause that sorts by a string value. LC_COLLATE also affects how an index that covers a string value is built. Setting LC_COL-LATE ensures that strings are ordered properly for your locale.

Let's look at an example. Create two new database clusters and insert the same values into each one. The first database uses the French locale for collating:

```
$ PGDATA=/usr/local/locale_FR LC_COLLATE=fr_FR initdb
...
Success. You can now start the database server using:
    postmaster -D /usr/local/locale_FR
or
    pg_ctl -D /usr/local/locale_FR -l logfile start

$ PGDATA=/usr/local/locale_FR pg_ctl start
postmaster successfully started

$ PGDATA=/usr/local/locale_FR createdb french_locale
```

```
CREATE DATABASE

$ PGDATA=/usr/local/locale_FR psql -q -d french_locale
french_locale=# CREATE TABLE sort_test ( pkey char );
CREATE TABLE
french_locale=# INSERT INTO sort_test VALUES ('a');
INSERT
french_locale=# INSERT INTO sort_test VALUES ('ä');
INSERT
french_locale=# INSERT INTO sort_test VALUES ('b');
INSERT
french_locale=# SELECT * FROM sort_test;
 pkey
------
 a
 ä
 b
 (3 rows)
french_locale=# \q
```

Now, repeat this procedure but set LC_COLLATE=en_US before creating the database cluster:

```
$ PGDATA=/usr/local/locale_EN LC_COLLATE=en_US initdb
...
Success. You can now start the database server using:
    postmaster -D /usr/local/locale_EN
or
    pg_ctl -D /usr/local/locale_EN -l logfile start

$ PGDATA=/usr/local/locale_EN pg_ctl start
postmaster successfully started

$ PGDATA=/usr/local/locale_EN createdb english_locale
CREATE DATABASE

$ PGDATA=/usr/local/locale_EN psql -q -d locale_test
english_locale=# CREATE TABLE sort_test ( pkey char );
CREATE TABLE
english_locale=# INSERT INTO sort_test VALUES ('a');
INSERT
english_locale=# INSERT INTO sort_test VALUES ('ä');
INSERT
english_locale=# INSERT INTO sort_test VALUES ('b');
INSERT
english_locale=# SELECT * FROM sort_test;
 pkey
```

```
------
 a
 b
 ä
(3 rows)
locale_test=# \q
```

Notice that the collation sequence has, in fact, changed. With LC_COLLATE set to fr_FR, you see a, ä, b. With LC_COLLATE set to en_US, the ORDER BY clause returns a, b, ä.

The LC_COLLATE and LC_CTYPE categories are only honored when you run the initdb command. Imagine what would happen if you were trying to alphabetize a long list of customer names, but the collation rules changed every few minutes. You'd end up with quite a mess—each portion of the final list would be built with a different ordering. If you could change the collating sequence each time you started a client application, indexes would not be built reliably.

PostgreSQL Locale Summary

To summarize:

- LC_COLLATE determines the order in which string values are sorted (to satisfy an ORDER BY clause or to create an index). LC_COLLATE is consulted when you create a database cluster using the initdb command. initdb records the value of LC_COLLATE in the $PGDATA/global/pg_control file and you can't change it later (run the pg_controldata program to see which locale was in effect when you created a cluster). You can't specify a different collating sequence for each database in a cluster. You can't specify a per-table or per-column collating sequence. If you need a per-column collating sequence, you can use a function (such as the one you can find at http://www.fi.muni.cz/~adelton/l10n/postgresql-nls-string) to convert the column values to a directly sortable form.

- LC_CTYPE is consulted when the server needs to classify a character as uppercase, lowercase, printable, whitespace, and so on. Like LC_COLLATE, LC_CTYPE is recorded in $PGDATA/global/pg_control when you create a database cluster. You can't change a cluster's LC_CTYPE once you've created the cluster. The value of LC_CTYPE is inherited by every database within the cluster.

- LC_MESSAGES determines which language is used when a message is produced by the server or by the client. Each client (such as psql) has it's own copy of LC_MES-SAGES—messages generated by the client appear in the language determined by that client's copy of LC_MESSAGES. The client's copy of LC_MESSAGES is typically defined by an environment variable. The client's copy of LC_MESSAGES is *not* propagated to the server (at least not by the psql client—it certainly could be sent to the server by other client applications). The server's copy of LC_MESSAGES is inherited from the postmaster. The postmaster typically finds LC_MESSAGES by looking in the postgresql.conf configuration file, but if it's not defined there, the postmaster will look for LC_MESSAGES, LC_ALL, or LANG environment variables as described earlier. If you're a cluster superuser, you can change a server's copy of LC_MESSAGES with the SET command. LC_MESSAGES is a per-session setting—each time you start a new server, LC_MESSAGES is inherited from the postmaster.

- LC_NUMERIC determines which characters the server uses when it converts numbers to (and from) character form. In particular, LC_NUMERIC defines the decimal point character, the grouping character, and the rules for using the grouping character. LC_NUMERIC is not (typically) used by PostgreSQL clients because they don't need to convert numeric values to/from character form. Each server session maintains its own copy of LC_NUMERIC. The initial value of LC_NUMERIC is inherited from the postmaster. The postmaster typically finds LC_NUMERIC by looking in the postgresql.conf configuration file, but if it's not defined there, the postmaster will look for LC_NUMERIC, LC_ALL, or LANG environment variables as described earlier. You can change the LC_NUMERIC value for your session with the SET command.

- LC_MONETARY is consulted when the server converts monetary values to and from character form. LC_MONETARY defines the local currency symbol ($), the international currency symbol (USD), and positive/negative sign conventions. LC_MONETARY also defines the decimal point character, grouping character, and grouping rules used to convert monetary values (LC_NUMERIC defines the decimal point character, grouping character, and grouping rules used to convert numeric values that are not considered monetary values).

- LC_TIME is not (currently) used by PostgreSQL.

Multi-Byte Character Sets

Most programmers are accustomed to working with single-byte character sets. In the U.S., we like to pretend that ASCII is the only meaningful mapping between characters and numbers. This is not the case. Standard organizations such as ANSI (American National Standards Institute) and the ISO (International Standards Organization) have defined many different encodings that associate a unique number with each character in a given character set. Theoretically, a single-byte character set can encode 256 different characters. In practice, however, most single-byte character sets are limited to about 96 visible characters. The range of values is cut in half by the fact that the most significant bit is sometimes considered off-limits when representing characters. The most significant bit is often used as a parity bit and occasionally as an end-of-string marker. Of the remaining 127 encodings, many are used to represent *control* characters (such as tab, newline, carriage return, and so on). By the time you add punctuation and numeric characters, the remaining 96 values start feeling a bit cramped.

Single-byte character sets work well for languages with a relatively small number of characters. Eventually, most of us must make the jump to multi-byte encodings. Adding a second byte dramatically increases the number of characters that you can represent. A single-byte character set can encode 256 values; a double-byte set can encode 65,536 characters. Multi-byte character sets are *required* for some languages, particularly languages used in East Asia. Again, standards organizations have defined many multi-byte encoding standards.

The Unicode Consortium was formed with the goal of providing a single encoding for all character sets. The consortium published its first proposed standard in 1991 ("The Unicode Standard, Version 1.0"). A two-byte number can represent most of the Unicode encoding values. Some characters require more than two bytes. In practice, many Unicode characters require a single byte.

I've always found that the various forms of the Unicode encoding standard were difficult to understand. Let me try to explain the problem (and Unicode's solution) with an analogy.

Suppose you grabbed a random byte from somewhere on the hard drive in your computer. Let's say that the byte you select has a value of 48. What does that byte mean? It might mean the number of states in the contiguous United States. It might mean the character 'o' in the ASCII character set. It could represent 17 more than the number of flavors you can get at Baskin-Robbins. Let's assume that this byte represents the current temperature. Is that 48° in the Centigrade, Fahrenheit, Kelvin, Réaumur, or Rankine scale? The distinction is important: 48° is a little chilly in Fahrenheit, but mighty toasty in Centigrade.

There are two levels of encoding involved here. The lowest level of encoding tells us that 48 represents a temperature value. The higher level tells us that the temperature is expressed in degrees Fahrenheit. We have to know both encodings before we can understand the meaning of the byte. If we don't know the encoding(s), 48 is just data. After we understand the encodings, 48 becomes information.

Unicode is an encoding system that assigns a unique number to each character. Which characters are included in the Unicode Standard? Version 3.0 of the Unicode Standard provides definitions for 49,194 characters. Version 3.1 added 44,946 character mappings, and Version 3.2 added an additional 1,016 for a total of 95,156 characters. Version 4.0 takes the total 96,832 characters. I'd say that the chances are very high that any character you need is defined in the Unicode Standard.

Just like the temperature encodings I mentioned earlier, there are two levels of encoding in the Unicode Standard.

At the most fundamental level, Unicode assigns a unique number, called a *code point*, to each character. For example, the Latin capital 'A' is assigned the code point 65. The Cyrillic (Russian) capital *de* ('д') is assigned the value 0414. The Unicode Standard suggests that we write these values using the form 'U+xxxx' where 'xxxx' is the code point expressed in hexadecimal notation. So, we should write U+0041 and U+0414 to indicate the Unicode mappings for 'A' and 'д'. The mapping from characters to numbers is called the Universal Character Set, or UCS.

At the next level, each code point is represented in one of several *UCS transformation formats* (UTF). The most commonly seen UTF is UTF-8[1]. The UTF-8 scheme is a

---

[1] Other UTF encodings are UTF-16BE (variable-width, 16 bit, big-endian), UTF-16LE (variable-width, 16 bit, little-endian), UTF-32BE, and UTF-32LE.

variable-width encoding form, meaning that some code points (that is, some characters) are represented by a single byte; and others represented by two, three, or four bytes. UTF-8 divides the Unicode code point space into four ranges, with each range requiring a different number of bytes as shown in Table 22.3.

Table 22.3 **UTF-8 Code Point Widths**

Low Value	High Value	Storage Size	Sample Character	UTF8-Encoding
U+0000	U+007F	1 byte	A(U+0041)	0x41
			0(U+0030)	0x30
U+0080	U+07FF	2 bytes	©(U+00A9)	0xC2 0xA9
			æ(U+00E6)	0xC3 0xA6
U+0800	U+FFFF	3 bytes	ج(U+062C)	0xE0 0x86 0xAC
			(U+20AC)	0xE2 0x82 0xAC
U+10000	U+10FFFF	4 bytes	♪(U+1D160)	0xF0 0x8E 0xA3 0xA0
			Σ(U+1D6F4)	0xF0 0x9D 0x9B 0xB4

The Unicode mappings for the first 127 code points are identical to the mappings for the ASCII character set. The ASCII code point for 'A' is 0x41, the same code point is used to represent 'A' in Unicode. The UTF-8 encodings for values between 0 and 127 are the values 0 through 127. The net effect of these two rules is that all ASCII characters require a single byte in the UTF-8 encoding scheme and the ASCII characters map directly into the same Unicode code points. In other words, an ASCII string is identical to the UTF-8 string containing the same characters. UTF-8 isn't the only transformation format. The disadvantage to UTF-8 is that it is a variable-width encoding form. Variable-width forms can be difficult to handle in some applications. UTF-16 is another common transformation format: Each character requires two bytes in UTF-16. You may be thinking that you can't encode the 95,156 characters defined by Unicode 4.0 in a two-byte value. You're right; you can't. UTF-16 was a fixed-width encoding until Unicode version 3.0. Starting with version 3.1, the Unicode standard defined more than 65,535 mappings (65,535 is the number of different encodings you can store in a two-byte value). To get around this limitation, the Unicode consortium invented the *surrogate pair*. A surrogate pair is simply a way of encoding a single character in *two* two-byte values. That means that UTF-16 is now a variable-width encoding. The only fixed-width encoding currently defined by the Unicode consortium is UTF-32 (aka UCS-4).

PostgreSQL understands how to store and manipulate characters (and strings) expressed in Unicode/UTF-8. PostgreSQL can also work with multibyte encodings other than Unicode/UTF-8. In fact, PostgreSQL understands *single-byte* encodings other than ASCII.

Encodings Supported by PostgreSQL

PostgreSQL does not store a list of valid encodings in a table, but you can create such a table. Listing 22.1 shows a PL/pgSQL function that creates a temporary table (encodings) that holds the names of all encoding schemes supported by our server.

Listing 22.1 get_encodings.sql

```
1  --
2  -- Filename: get_encodings.sql
3  --
4
5  CREATE OR REPLACE FUNCTION get_encodings() RETURNS INTEGER AS
6  '
7    DECLARE
8      enc      INTEGER := 0;
9      name     VARCHAR;
10   BEGIN
11     CREATE TEMP TABLE encodings ( enc_code int, enc_name text );
12     LOOP
13        SELECT INTO name pg_encoding_to_char( enc );
14
15        IF( name = '''' ) THEN
16            EXIT;
17        ELSE
18            INSERT INTO encodings VALUES( enc, name );
19        END IF;
20
21        enc := enc + 1;
22     END LOOP;
23
24     RETURN enc;
25   END;
26
27 ' LANGUAGE 'plpgsql';
```

get_encodings() assumes that encoding numbers start at zero and that there are no gaps. This may not be a valid assumption in future versions of PostgreSQL. We use the pg_encoding_to_char() built-in function to translate an encoding number into an encoding name. If the encoding number is invalid, pg_encoding_to_char() returns an empty string.

When you call get_encodings(), it will return the number of rows written to the encodings table.

```
movies=# select get_encodings();
 get_encodings
---------------
            34
(1 row)

movies=# select * from encodings;
 enc_code |    enc_name
----------+---------------
        0 | SQL_ASCII
        1 | EUC_JP
        2 | EUC_CN
        3 | EUC_KR
        4 | EUC_TW
        5 | JOHAB
        6 | UNICODE
        7 | MULE_INTERNAL
        8 | LATIN1
        9 | LATIN2
       10 | LATIN3
       11 | LATIN4
       12 | LATIN5
       13 | LATIN6
       14 | LATIN7
       15 | LATIN8
       16 | LATIN9
       17 | LATIN10
       18 | WIN1256
       19 | TCVN
       20 | WIN874
       21 | KOI8
       22 | WIN
       23 | ALT
       24 | ISO_8859_5
       25 | ISO_8859_6
       26 | ISO_8859_7
       27 | ISO_8859_8
       28 | WIN1250
       29 | SJIS
       30 | BIG5
       31 | GBK
       32 | UHC
       33 | GB18030
(34 rows)
```

Some of these encoding schemes use single-byte code points: SQL_ASCII, LATIN*, KOI8, WIN, ALT, ISO-8859*. Table 22.4 lists the encodings supported by PostgreSQL version 8.0.0.

Table 22.4 **Supported Encoding Schemes**

Encoding	Defined By	Single or Multibyte	Languages Supported
SQL_ASCII	ASCII	S	
EUC_JP	JIS X 0201-1997	M	Japanese
EUC_CN	RFC 1922	M	Chinese
EUC_KR	RFC 1557	M	Korean
EUC_TW	CNS 11643-1992	M	Traditional Chinese
JOHAB	KS C 5601-1992 annex 3	M	Extended Korean
UNICODE	Unicode Consortium	M	All scripts
MULE_INTERNAL	CNS 116643-1992		
LATIN1	ISO-8859-1	S	Western Europe
LATIN2	ISO-8859-2	S	Eastern Europe
LATIN3	ISO-8859-3	S	Southern Europe
LATIN4	ISO-8859-4	S	Northern Europe
LATIN5	ISO-8859-9	S	Turkish
LATIN6	ISO-8859-10	S	Nordic
LATIN7	ISO-8859-13	S	Baltic Rim
LATIN8	ISO-8859-14	S	Celtic
LATIN9	ISO-8859-15	S	Similar to LATIN1, replaces some characters with French and Finnish characters, adds Euro
LATIN10	ISO-8859-16	S	Romanian
WIN1256	Windows 1256	S	Arabic
TCVN	TCVN 5712:1993	S	Vietnamese
WIN874	Windows 875	S	Thai
KOI8	RFC 1489	S	Cyrillic
WIN	Windows 1251	S	Cyrillic
ALT	IBM866	S	Cyrillic
ISO_8859_5	ISO-8859-5	S	Cyrillic
ISO_8859_6	ISO-8859-6	S	Arabic
ISO_8859_7	ISO-8859-7	S	Greek
ISO_8859_8	ISO-8859-8	S	Hebrew
SJIS	JIS X 0202-1991	M	Japanese
BIG5	RF 1922	M	Chinese for Taiwan
GBK	GB 13000.1-93	M	Extended Chinese
UHC	Windows 949 (and others)	M	Unified Hangul
GB18030	GB 18030-2000	M	Chinese ideograms
WIN1250	Windows 1250	S	Eastern Europe

I've spent a lot of time talking about Unicode. As you can see from Table 22.4, you can use other encodings with PostgreSQL. Unicode has one important advantage over other encoding schemes. A character in any other encoding system can be translated into Unicode and translated back into the original encoding system.

You can use Unicode as a pivot to translate between other encodings. For example, if you want to translate common characters from ISO-646-DE (German) into ISO-646-DK (Danish), you can first convert all characters into Unicode (all ISO-646-DE characters *will* map into Unicode) and then map from Unicode back to ISO-646-DK. Some German characters will not translate into Danish. For example, the DE+0040 character ('§') will map to Unicode U+00A7. There is no '§' character in the ISO-646-DK character set, so this character would be lost in the translation (not dropped, just mapped into a value that means "no translation").

If you don't use Unicode to translate between character sets, you'll have to define translation tables for every language pair that you need. The CREATE CONVERSION command defines a conversion from one encoding to another. PostgreSQL provides a number of pre-defined conversions (114 in version 8.0.0).

If you need to support more than one character set at your site, I would strongly encourage you to encode your data in Unicode. If you store mostly US-ASCII characters, UTF-8 will save you space. If all of the characters that you need to store are defined in a single-byte character set, use that set. If all of the characters that you need to store are defined by a fixed-width, multibyte character set, you need to choose between that character set and Unicode.

Enabling Multi-Byte Support

When you build PostgreSQL from source code, multibyte support is disabled by default. Unicode is a multibyte character set—if you want to use Unicode, you need to enable multibyte support. Starting with PostgreSQL release 7.3, multibyte support is enabled by default. If you are using a version earlier than 7.3, you enable multibyte support by including the --enable-multibyte option when you run configure:

```
./configure --enable-multibyte
```

If you did not compile your own copy of PostgreSQL, the easiest way to determine whether it was compiled with multi-byte support is to invoke psql, as follows:

```
$ psql -l
      List of databases
   Name      | Owner | Encoding
-------------+-------+-----------
 movies      | bruce | SQL_ASCII
 secondbooks | bruce | UNICODE
```

The -l flag lists all databases in a cluster. If you see three columns, multi-byte support is enabled. If the Encoding column is missing, you don't have multi-byte support.

Selecting an Encoding

There are four ways to select the encoding that you want to use for a particular database.

When you create a database using the createdb utility or the CREATE DATABASE command, you can choose an encoding for the new database. The following four commands are equivalent:

```
$ createdb -E latin5 my_turkish_db
$ createdb --encoding=latin5 my_turkish_db

movies=# CREATE DATABASE my_turkish_db WITH ENCODING 'LATIN5';
movies=# CREATE DATABASE my_turkish_db WITH ENCODING 11;
```

If you don't specify an encoding with createdb (or CREATE DATABASE), the cluster's default encoding is used. You specify the default encoding for a cluster when you create the cluster using the initdb command:

```
$ initdb -E EUC_KR
$ initdb --encoding=EUC_KR
```

If you do not specify an encoding when you create the database cluster, initdb uses the encoding specified when you configured the PostgreSQL source code:

```
./configure --enable-multibyte=unicode
```

Finally, if you don't include an encoding name when you configure the PostgreSQL source code, SQL_ASCII is assumed.

So, if you don't do anything special, your database will not support multi-byte encodings, and all character values are assumed to be expressed in SQL_ASCII.

If you enable multi-byte encodings, *all* encodings are available. The encoding name that you can include in the --enable-multibyte flag selects the default encoding; it does not limit the available encodings.

Client/Server Translation

You now know that the PostgreSQL server can deal with encodings other than SQL_ASCII, but what about PostgreSQL clients? That question is difficult to answer. The pgAdmin and pgAdmin II clients do not. pgAccess does not. The psql client supports multi-byte encodings, but finding a font that can display all required characters is not easy.

Assuming that you are using a client application that supports encodings other than SQL_ASCII, you can select a client encoding with the SET CLIENT_ENCODING command:

```
movies=# SET CLIENT_ENCODING TO UNICODE;
SET
```

You can see which coding has been selected for the client using the SHOW CLIENT_ENCODING command:

```
movies=# SHOW CLIENT_ENCODING;
NOTICE:  Current client encoding is 'UNICODE'
SHOW VARIABLE
```

You can also view the server's encoding (but you can't change it):

```
movies=# SHOW SERVER_ENCODING;
NOTICE:  Current server encoding is 'UNICODE'
SHOW VARIABLE
movies=# SET SERVER_ENCODING TO BIG5;
NOTICE:  SET SERVER_ENCODING is not supported
SET VARIABLE
```

If the CLIENT_ENCODING and SERVER_ENCODING are different, PostgreSQL will convert between the two encodings. In many cases, translation will fail. Let's say that you use a multi-byte-enabled client to INSERT some Katakana (that is, Japanese) text, as shown in Figure 22.1.

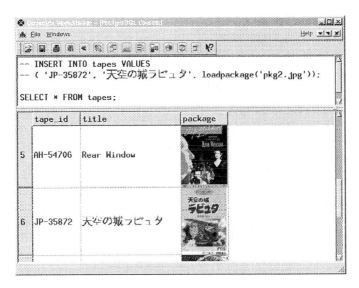

Figure 22.1   A Unicode-enabled client application.

This application (the Conjectrix™ Workstation) understands how to work with Unicode data. If you try to read this data with a different client encoding, you probably won't be happy with the results:

```
$ psql -q -d movies
news=# SELECT tape_id, title FROM tapes WHERE tape_id = 'JP-35872';
tape_id   |                     title
----------+------------------------------------------------------------
 JP-35872 | (bb)(bf)(e5)(a4)(a9)(e7)(a9)(ba)(e3)(81ae)(e5)(9f)(8e)...
(1 row)
```

The values that you see in psql have been translated into the SQL_ASCII encoding scheme. Some characters in the title column can be translated from Unicode into

SQL_ASCII, but most cannot. The SQL_ASCII encoding does not include Katakana characters, so PostgreSQL has given you the hexadecimal values of the Unicode characters instead.

Summary

PostgreSQL is an open-source product, and the core developers come from many different countries. PostgreSQL has been developed to be an international database system. The combination of Unicode and translated message texts mean that PostgreSQL can be used in every region of the world. The biggest challenge to using PostgreSQL in many regions will be the task of finding and installing fonts and input methods for local character sets.

23

Security

The goal of PostgreSQL security is to keep the bad guys out while letting the good guys in.

Security is a balancing act—it is often the case that more secure installations are less convenient for authorized users. Finding the right balance depends primarily on two factors. First, "How much do you trust the people that have access to your machine?" The answer to that question is not as obvious at it may seem—if your system is connected to the Internet, you have to extend your trust to everyone else on the Internet. The second question is "How important is it to keep your data private?" It's probably not very important to keep your personal CD catalog private, but if you are storing customer credit card numbers, you had better put in some extra effort to ensure privacy.

There are three aspects to PostgreSQL security:

- Securing the PostgreSQL data files
- Securing client access
- Granting and denying access to specific tables and specific users

The first aspect is the easiest—the rules are simple and there aren't very many decisions that you have to make. The host operating system enforces file-level security. I'll explain how to ensure that your PostgreSQL installation has the proper ownerships and permissions in the next section.

Securing client access is relatively simple if you are on a secure network and complex if you are not. The main task in securing client access is authentication. *Authentication* is proving that you are who you say you are. PostgreSQL supports a variety of authentication, ranging from complete trust (meaning, "Ok, you say your name is bruce, who am I to argue?") to encryption and message digest protocols. I'll describe each authentication method in this chapter.

The first two aspects of PostgreSQL security are concerned with keeping the wrong people out of your database while letting the right people in. The last aspect determines what you can do once you are allowed inside a PostgreSQL database.

Securing the PostgreSQL Data Files

The first step in securing a PostgreSQL installation is to secure the actual data files that comprise each database. PostgreSQL is typically installed in the `/usr/local/pgsql` directory. Executables (such as `psql`, `initdb`, and the `postmaster`) are often installed in the `/usr/local/pgsql/bin` directory. If you have a typical installation, you can expect to find data files: databases, configuration, and security information in `/usr/local/pgsql/data`. I'll refer to this last directory as `$PGDATA`. PostgreSQL uses the `$PGDATA` environment variable to find its data files.

Let's start by looking at the directory structure of a PostgreSQL installation (see Figure 23.1):

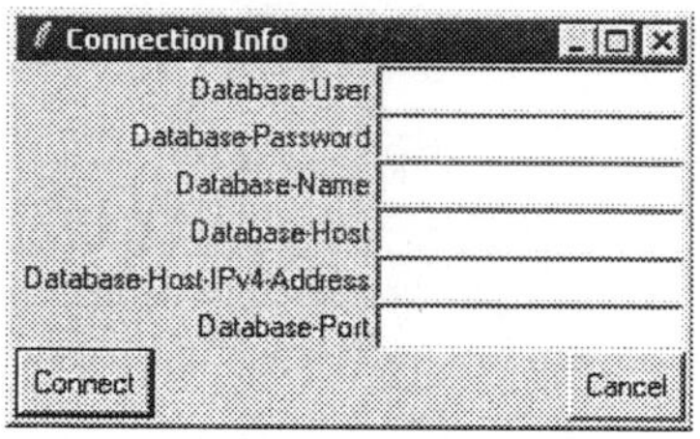

Figure 23.1   The directory structure of a PostgreSQL installation.

The `data` directory contains six subdirectories: `base`, `global`, `pg_xlog`, `pg_clog`, `pg_subtrans`, and `pg_tblspc`[1].

The `data/base` directory is where your databases live. Notice that I have three subdirectories underneath the base directory—that's because I have three databases. If you are curious about the directory naming scheme, the numbers correspond to the OIDs (object ids) of the corresponding rows in the `pg_database` table. You can see the correspondence by executing the following query:

```
psql> select oid, datname from pg_database;

  oid | datname
------+-----------
18721 | movies
    1 | template1
18719 | template0
```

The `data/global` directory contains information that spans all databases; in other words, the information in the `global` directory is independent of any particular database—it contains information that's shared by each database in the cluster. The `global` directory contains the following files (in version 8.0): `1213`, `1260`, `1261`, `1262`, `pg_control`, `pg_pwd`,

---

[1] You may see more files and subdirectories if you are running a different version of PostgreSQL. This snapshot shows a typical installation of PostgreSQL release 7.1.3.

and a number of indexes. If you're running a different version of PostgreSQL, you'll see a different set of files in the `global` directory—you may also see a `pg_pwd` file, `pgstat.stat`, and `pg_fsm.cache` in some releases.

Like the `data/base` directory, the `data/global` directory contains a few files whose names are actually OID values. Table 23.1 shows how the OID values translate into table names.

Table 23.1 **OID to Table Mapping in the `global` Directory**

Filename/OID	Corresponding Table
1213	pg_tablespace
1260	pg_shadow
1261	pg_group
1262	pg_database

Each of these files is explained in Chapter 21, "PostgreSQL Administration," so I won't cover that information here.

The `data/pg_xlog` directory contains the write-ahead transaction log (also described in Chapter 19). `data/pg_clog` contains "commit" logs (which, when used together with `data/pg_xlog`, can provide point-in-time recovery). PostgreSQL keeps track of nested transactions in the `data/pg_subtrans` directory. When you create a new tablespace, PostgreSQL creates a symbolic link to the new location in the `data/pg_tblspc` directory (see Chapter 3, "PostgreSQL Syntax and Use," for more details).

Unix File Permissions and Ownership

In a Unix environment, there are three aspects to filesystem security. Each file (or directory) has an owner, a group, and a set of permissions. You can see all three of these attributes using the `ls -l` command. Here is an example:

```
total 40
drwx------    5 postgres postgresgrp  4096 Oct 22 17:40 base
drwx------    2 postgres postgresgrp  4096 Jan 15 18:58 global
-rw-------    1 postgres postgresgrp  7482 Jan 15 19:26 pg_hba.conf
-rw-------    1 postgres postgresgrp  1118 Oct 22 17:35 pg_ident.conf
-rw-------    1 postgres postgresgrp     4 Oct 22 17:35 PG_VERSION
drwx         2 postgres postgresgrp  4096 Oct 22 17:35 pg_xlog
-rw-------    1 postgres postgresgrp  3137 Oct 22 17:35 postgresql.conf
-rw-------    1 postgres postgresgrp    49 Jan 10 14:18 postmaster.opts
-rw-------    1 postgres postgresgrp    47 Jan 10 14:18 postmaster.pid
```

Each line of output can be divided into seven columns. Starting at the rightmost column, you see the file (or directory) name. Working to the left, you'll see the modification date, file size (in bytes), group name, username, link count, and file permissions.

The file permissions column can be interpreted as follows:

```
drwxrw-r--
```

The first character is a file type indicator and contains a "d" for directories and a "-" for normal files (other values are possible—refer to your OS documentation for more information).

Following the type indicator are three groups of access permissions, and each group contains three characters. The first group (rwx in this example) specifies access permissions for the owner of the file. rwx means that the owner can read, write, and execute the file. The next three characters (rw-) specify access permissions for members of the group. rw- means that members of the group can read and write this file, but cannot execute it. The last three characters in the permissions column control access by other users (you are considered an "other" user if you are not the owner and you are not in the file's group). r-- means that other users can read the file, but cannot write or execute it.

Permissions mean something a little different for directories. If you have read permissions for a directory, you can list the contents of that directory (using ls, for example). If you have write permissions for a directory, you can create files in, and remove files from, that directory. If you have execute permission, you can access the files in a directory (read permission allows you to list the contents of a directory; execute permission allows you to work with the contents of the files in that directory).

When you install PostgreSQL from a standard distribution, such as an RPM package, the installation procedure will automatically apply the correct ownership and permissions to all PostgreSQL components. In rare circumstances, you may find that you need to reset ownerships and permissions back to their correct states. Why? You may find that your system has been "hacked." You may need to recover from an error in a backup/restore procedure. You may have executed a recursive chown, chmod, or chgrp starting in the wrong directory—you're not an experienced system administrator until you have made (and recovered from) this mistake. It's a good idea to understand what the correct ownerships and permissions are, just in case you ever need to put things back the way they are supposed to be.

The entire directory tree (starting at and including the $PGDATA directory) should be owned by the PostgreSQL administrative user (this user is typically named :postgres"). It's easy to correct the file ownerships using the chown command:

```
$ chown -R postgres $PGDATA
```

You can use the following commands to find any files that are *not* owned by user postgres:

```
$ cd $PGDATA
$ find . -not -user postgres -ls
```

The $PGDATA directory tree should be readable and writable by the PostgreSQL administrative user, and should provide no access to the group and other categories. Again, setting the file permissions is easy:

```
$ cd $PGDATA
$ find . -type d -exec chmod 700 '{}' ';'
$ find . -type f -exec chmod 600 '{}' ';'
```

The first find command modifies the directories, and the second modifies the normal files. The numbers (700 and 600) are a portable way to specify access permissions. 700 is equivalent to u=rwx,g=,o=, meaning that the owner of the directory should have read, write, and execute permissions; other users have no rights. 600 is equivalent to u=rw,g=,o= meaning that the owner of the file should have read and write permissions and other users should have no access rights. You can use whichever form you prefer. The numeric form is more succinct and more portable. I prefer the symbolic form, probably because I can't do octal arithmetic in my head.

It's a good idea to verify file and directory permissions occasionally for the reasons I mentioned earlier: You may have an intruder on your system, or you might need to recover from a user mistake. You can also use the find command to find any files or directories with incorrect permissions:

```
$ cd $PGDATA
$ find . -type d -not -perm 700 -print
$ find . -type f -not -perm 600 -print
```

There is one more file that you should consider securing besides the files in the $PGDATA directory tree. When local users (meaning users who are logged in to the system that hosts your PostgreSQL database) connect to the postmaster, they generally use a Unix-domain socket. (A Unix-domain socket is a network interface that doesn't actually use a network. Instead, a Unix-domain socket is implemented entirely within a single Unix operating system.) When you start the postmaster process, it creates a Unix-domain socket, usually in the /tmp directory. If you have a postmaster running on your system, look in the /tmp directory and you will see the socket that your postmaster uses to listen for connection requests:

```
$ ls -la /tmp
total 8095
drwxrwxrwt   12 root     root            1024 Jan 25 18:04 .
drwxr-xr-x   21 root     root            4096 Jan 25 16:23 ..
drwxr-xr-x    2 root     root            1024 Jan 10 10:37 lost+found
srwxrwxrwx    1 postgres postgresgrp        0 Jan 25 18:01 .s.PGSQL.5432
-r--r--r--    1 root     root              11 Jan 24 19:18 .X0 lock
```

(You will likely find other files in the /tmp directory.) The postmaster's socket is named s.PGSQL.5432. You can tell that this is a socket because of the s in the leftmost column. Because the name of the socket starts with a ., I had to use the -a flag on the ls command. Files whose names begin with a period (.) are normally hidden from the ls command.

Notice that the permissions on this socket are rwxrwxrwx. This means that any user (the owner, members of the group, or others) can connect to this socket. You might consider restricting access to this socket. For example, if you change the permissions to rwxrwx---, only user postgres and members of the postgresgrp group could connect.

Unlike normal files, you don't set the socket permissions using the chmod command (the postmaster's socket is created each time the postmaster starts). Instead, you use the UNIX_SOCKET_PERMISSION runtime-configuration option (Chapter 19 discusses runtime-configuration options in more detail).

Note that just because you can connect to the socket does not mean that the postmaster will allow you to access a database—the next section describes how to secure the postmaster.

Securing PostgreSQL Data Files in Windows

In a typical Windows installation, the PostgreSQL installer creates a new account (named postgres) that owns the PostgreSQL service, the executables (psql.exe, postmaster.exe, initdb.exe, and so on), PostgreSQL configuration files, and all PostgreSQL data files. The installer explicitly defines permissions for the $PGDATA directory (and all subdirectories) and the binaries directory (the directory that contains the executables).

For the $PGDATA directory, the installer grants CHANGE privileges to the postgres account. For the binaries directory, the installer first denies all privileges for the postgres account, and then grants READ privileges. Unfortunately, the installer leaves all other (inherited) privileges in place. If you install PostgreSQL in the default location (Program Files), your PostgreSQL server inherits a number of privileges from that directory. For example, on a fresh Win2000 (Professional) system, the Program Files directory grants READ and EXECUTE privileges to all to members of the Users group, CHANGE privileges to the Power Users group, and FULL privileges to Administrators.

If you want to tighten up the security of your PostgreSQL installation, I'd recommend a different strategy: delete all of the ACL entries for the PostgreSQL directory tree and then add back only those privileges that you really want to grant. You can do that with a few simple commands. I'll walk you through the process, assuming that you've installed PostgreSQL in the default location (Program Files) and the PostgreSQL service is owned by the default user (postgres).

First, open a command-prompt window and navigate to the PostgreSQL install directory:

```
CD "Program Files\PostgreSQL\8.0\"
```

To start, delete all ACL entries assigned to the bin and data directory trees:

```
CACLS bin  /T /G Administrators:F
CACLS data /T /G Administrators:F
```

The first command deletes any existing ACL entries and grants FULL privileges to the Administrators group. The /T flag tells CACLS to operate on the entire directory tree. The /G flag grants a privilege (in this case, it grants the F(ull) privilege to the Administrators group). Because you are *not* using the /E flag, CACLS deletes all existing ACL entries before granting new ones (/E stands for *edit*—if you include /E, CACLS edits existing ACLs; if you don't, CACLS replaces any existing ACLs).

The PostgreSQL executables reside in the bin directory so the postgres user must hold READ (and therefore, execute) privileges for that directory. Grant postgres READ privileges for the bin directory tree:

```
CACLS bin  /E /T /G postgres:R
```

That command also grants READ (and execute) privileges to every file in the bin directory, not just the directory itself.

When you create a new database, table, or index, PostgreSQL creates a new file somewhere in the data directory tree. When you UPDATE, DELETE, or INSERT data, the

PostgreSQL server modifies files in the data directory tree. Accordingly, you must grant the postgres account the right to CHANGE (read, write, and create) files in the data directory tree

```
CACLS data /E /T /G postgres:C
```

Your bin and data directories are now protected against tampering. A member of the Administrators group can still mess around with your database, but you shouldn't convey administrator rights to people that you don't trust. You can start the PostgreSQL service at this point and it should be ready to service client requests.

However, most of the PostgreSQL client applications reside in the bin directory and you've just clamped down that directory so tight that a mere user can't see inside of it. To fix that problem, grant READ privileges to the Users group:

```
CACLS bin  /E /G Users:R
```

Notice that I didn't include the /T (tree) flag in that command. Without the /T flag, CACLS only grants READ privileges to the bin directory itself, not to the files within the directory. That means that member of the Users group can see the files in the bin directory (with the DIR command, for example), but he can't execute any of those programs. Look through the bin directory and decide which programs you want your Users to run. In most cases, you don't want Users to run administrative commands such as createuser or dropdb. In fact, the only program needed by most Users is the PostgreSQL command-line client: psql.exe.

To allow your Users to execute the psql.exe command, execute the following:

```
CACLS bin\psql.exe /E /G Users:R
```

If you find other programs that you want to expose to your Users, just grant READ privileges for those programs.

You may want to secure other directories in the PostgreSQL tree as well, but protecting the bin and data directories will ensure that a nefarious intruder can't tamper with your PostgreSQL server or data.

Securing Network Access

The next step in securing a PostgreSQL installation is determining which computers are allowed to access your data.

PostgreSQL uses the $PGDATA/pg_hba.conf file to control client access (hba is an acronym for *host-based authentication*). When a client application (such as psql) tries to connect to a PostgreSQL server, it sends a username and database name to the postmaster (I'll call those the *target user* and the *target database*). For example, if you run psql like this

```
$ psql -U bruce -d sales
```

the target user is bruce and the target database is sales.

When this request arrives, the postmaster searches through pg_hba.conf to find an entry that matches the target user, target database, client address, and connection type. Each entry in the pg_hba.conf file contains a connection type, a database name (or a set

of database names), a username (or a set of usernames), and a client address. The postmaster will rarely find an entry that's an exact match. Instead, an entry may contain
wildcards that match a number of different client requests. For example, the postmaster
may find an entry that matches all users, or perhaps a group of related databases. The
postmaster searches pg_hba.conf from the beginning and stops searching as soon as it
finds an entry that matches all four fields (user, database, client, and connection type). If
the postmaster reaches the end of pg_hba.conf without finding a match, it refuses the
connection request.

If the postmaster finds an entry that matches the connection request, it uses that
entry to decide how to authenticate the user. Each entry specifies an authentication
method (such as trust, reject, or password)—the client application must authenticate
itself (that is, prove its identity) using the method designated in the matching entry. For
example, if the postmaster finds a matching pg_hba.conf entry that requires password
authentication, the client application must supply the correct password. PostgreSQL
supports a number of authentication methods—each method adds a different level of
security to your system. In general, stronger authentication methods are more inconvenient than weaker authentications, but the stronger methods provide better protection
for your data.

Let's start by looking at a short and simple pg_hba.conf file:

```
# Allow all local users to connect without providing passwords

local   all  all   trust

# Allow users on our local network to connect to
# database 'movies' if they have a valid password

host movies 192.168.0.0 255.255.255.0 password
```

First, you should know that lines that begin with a # character are comments, and blank
lines are ignored.

The first field in each record corresponds to a type of connection. PostgreSQL currently supports four types of connections:

- local—A local connection is one that comes in over a Unix-domain socket. By
  definition, a client connecting via a Unix-domain socket is executing on the same
  machine as the postmaster.

- hostssl—A hostssl connection is a TCP/IP connection that uses the SSL
  (secure sockets layer) protocol.

- hostnossl—A hostnossl connection is a TCP/IP connection *not* secured by
  SSL.

- hostmd]A host connection is a TCP/IP connection.

If you're using an older version of PostgreSQL, the pg_hba.conf understands a slightly
different set of connection types:

- local—A local connection is one that comes in over a Unix-domain socket. By definition, a client connecting via a Unix-domain socket is executing on the same machine as the postmaster.
- hostssl—A hostssl connection is a TCP/IP connection that uses the SSL (secure sockets layer) protocol.
- host—A host connection is a TCP/IP connection that does not use SSL.

As the postmaster searches through pg_hba.conf, it compares the connection type field to the method used by the client. For example, if the client contacts the postmaster over an SSL secured TCP/IP connection, the postmaster will examine any entry that begins with hostssl or host— the postmaster will ignore local and hostnossl entries.

TCP/IP Connections with postmaster

By default, the postmaster process will ignore connection requests that arrive from other systems. In the default configuration, the postmaster listens for connection requests that arrive on a Unix-domain socket or requests that arrive on the loopback adapter (127.0.0.1)—if you're using a version of PostgreSQL older than 8.0, the postmaster will only listen to the Unix-domain socket. If you want to provide PostgreSQL service to other computers, you must tell the postmaster to listen to additional ports. To enable networked connections, modify the listen_addresses (or virtual_host in older versions of PostgreSQL) configuration option (see Chapter 21, "PostgreSQL Administration," for more details) or start the postmaster with the -i command-line option.

The second field in each pg_hba.conf record identifies the set of databases controlled by the entry. The postmaster searches through pg_hba.conf to find an entry that matches the target database. You can include the name of a single database in this field, a comma-separated list of database names, or one of three special values. The string all controls access to all databases, and sameuser controls access to a database whose name is identical to the name of the user making the connection. The third special value is samegroup. When the server finds samegroup in the database field, it searches for a group whose name matches the target database. If such a group exists *and* the target user is a member of that group, the entry matches. If the group *does not* exist (or if the target user is not a member of the group), the server continues its search.

For example, if the postmaster encounters a samegroup entry when user bruce tries to connect to a database named sales, the entry matches as long as bruce is a member of the group sales.

The third field in each entry identifies the set of users controlled by the entry. You can enter the name of a single user in this field, the name of a single group (prefix group names with a +), a comma-separated list of user and group names, or the string all (which matches *any* user).

If you're PostgreSQL version 8.0 or later, you can store database names and user/group names in separate files. Just prefix the name of the file with an @ and write that into the pg_hba.conf file in place of the database (or user) field, like this:

```
local @myDatabases.txt @myUsers.txt trust
```

The fourth field identifies the set of client addresses controlled by the entry. You *cannot* include a hostname in this field—you must specify clients by IP address. PostgreSQL prohibits hostnames to deter DNS spoofing attacks. You *can* specify a group of related hosts using a netmask (such as `192.168.0.0 255.255.255.0`) or a CIDR-formatted address (such as `192.168.0.0/24`).

The remainder of the `pg_hba.conf` entry depends on the connection type. I'll look at each one in turn.

`local` **Connections**

The format of a `local` entry is

```
local database user authentication-method [authentication-option]
```

A `local` entry matches any connection attempt that arrives on a Unix-domain socket.

You know that the `database` field contains the name of a database (or `all`, `sameuser`, or `samegroup`). The `user` field contains a list of user (and/or group) names. The `client-address` field is implied for `local` connection types (`local` means that the client resides on the same host as the `postmaster`). The `authentication-method` field determines what method you must use to prove your identity. I'll explain authentication methods and authentication options in a moment.

`host`, `hostssl`, **and** `hostnossl` **Connections**

The format of a `host` or `hostssl` record is

```
host       database user ip-address authentication-method [ option ]
hostnossl database user ip-address authentication-method [ option ]
hostssl    database user ip-address authentication-method [ option ]
```

The `ip-address` field specifies either a TCP/IP host or a TCP/IP network (by numeric address). You can specify the `ip-address` in netmask form or in CIDR form. In netmask form, you provide two pieces of information: an IP-address and a mask (with a space in between). The *mask* tells the `postmaster` how many bits in the `ip-address` are significant. For example, if the `postmaster` sees an address such as

```
192.168.0.0 255.255.255.0
```

the given entry matches any host in the `192.168.0.*` network. To explicitly match a single computer, specify the exact IP address and mask of `255.255.255.255` (for example, `192.168.0.42 255.255.255.255`).

In CIDR form, you provide an IP address and the number of significant bits (with a '/' in between). For example, if the `postmaster` sees an address such as

```
192.168.0.0/24
```

the given entry matches any host in the `192.168.0.*` network. To explicitly match a single computer, specify the exact IP address followed by the number of bits in the address (for example, `192.168.0.42/32` or, for an IPv6 address, `fe80::290:4bff:fe94:7103/64`).

If you try to connect to a postmaster and your client address does not match any of the `pg_hba.conf` records, the connection is rejected.

Now let's look at the authentication methods. Remember that you can specify a different authentication method for each host (or for each network). Some authentication methods are more secure than others, whereas some methods are more convenient than others.

The `trust` Authentication Method

When you use the `trust` authentication method, you allow any user on the client system to access your data. The client application does not have to provide any passwords (beyond what may be required to log in to the client system itself).

`trust` is the least secure of the authentication methods—it relies on the security of the client system.

You should never use `trust` to authenticate a connection attempt in an insecure network.

In most cases, you won't want to use the `trust` method to authenticate local connections. At first glance, it seems reasonable to trust the security on your own host; after all, I have to prove my identity to the operating system before I can start a client application. But the problem is not that I can fool the operating system; the problem is that I can impersonate another user. Consider the following scenario:

```
Welcome to arturo, please login...
login: korry
Password: cows

Last login: Fri Jan 18 10:48:00 from marsalis

[korry]$ psql -U sheila -d movies

Welcome to psql, the PostgreSQL interactive terminal.

movies=>
```

To log in to my host (`arturo`) as user `korry`, I am required to provide an operating system-authenticated password. But, if the `movies` database allows local connection attempts to be trusted, nothing stops me from impersonating another user (possibly gaining elevated privileges).

Given the security problems with `trust`, why would you ever want to use it? The `trust` authentication method is useful on single-user machines (that is, systems with only one user authorized to log in). You may also use `trust` to authenticate `local` connections on development or testing systems.

You *never* want to use `trust` on a multiuser system that contains important data.

The `ident` Authentication Method

The `ident` authentication method (like `trust`) relies on the client system to authenticate the user.

In the previous section, I showed you how easy it is to impersonate another user using the `trust` authentication method. All I have to do to impersonate another user is use the `-U` flag when I fire up the `psql` client application.

`ident` tries to be a bit more secure. Let's pretend that I am currently logged in to host `vivaldi` as user `korry`, and I want to connect to a PostgreSQL server running on host `arturo`:

```
$ whoami
korry
$ psql -h arturo -d movies -U korry

Welcome to psql, the PostgreSQL interactive terminal.

movies=> select user;
 current_user
korry
```

I'll walk through the authentication process for this connection.

First, my local copy of `psql` makes a TCP/IP connection to the `postmaster` process on host `arturo` and sends my username (`korry`). The `postmaster` (on `arturo`) connects back to the `identd` daemon on host `vivaldi` (remember, I am running `psql` on host `vivaldi`). The `postmaster` sends the `psql-to-postmaster` connection information to `identd` and `identd` replies with my username (also `korry`).

Now, the `postmaster` examines the `pg_hba.conf` record that matches my host. Assume that it finds the following:

```
host  all  192.168.0.85 255.255.255.255 ident sameuser
```

The `sameuser` field tells the `postmaster` that if I am trying to connect using a name that matches the `identd` response, I am allowed to connect. (That might sound a little confusing at first. When you use the `ident` authentication method, the `postmaster` works with two different usernames: the name that I provided to the client application and the name returned by the `identd` daemon.)

Now let's see what happens when I try to impersonate another user. Recall from the previous section that I can fool the `trust` authentication method simply by lying about my username. It's a little harder to cheat with `ident`.

Let's say that I am logged in to host `vivaldi` as user `sheila` and I try to impersonate user `korry`. You can assume that because I am logged in to `vivaldi`, I have proven my identity to `vivaldi` by providing `sheila`'s password.

```
$ whoami
sheila
$ psql -h arturo -d movies -U korry
psql: IDENT authentication failed for user 'sheila'
```

As before, my local copy of `psql` makes a TCP/IP connection to the `postmaster` process on host `arturo` and sends the username that I provided on the command line (`korry`). The `postmaster` (on `arturo`) connects back to the `identd` daemon on host `vivaldi`. This time, the `identd` daemon returns my real username (`sheila`).

At this point, the `postmaster` (on `arturo`) is working with two usernames. I have logged in to the client (`vivaldi`) as user `sheila` but when I started `psql`, I specified a username of `korry`. Because my `pg_hba.conf` record specified `sameuser`, I can't connect with two different usernames—my connection attempt is rejected.

Now that you've seen how the `ident` method provides a bit more security than `trust`, I'll show you a few more options that you can use with `ident`.

In the preceding examples, I used the `sameuser` option in my `pg_hba.conf` record. Instead of `sameuser`, I can specify the name of a map. A *map* corresponds to a set of entries in the `$PGDATA/pg_ident.conf` file. `pg_ident.conf` is a text file containing one record per line (as usual, blank lines and lines starting with a '#' character are ignored). Each record in the `pg_ident.conf` file contains three fields:

- `mapname`—Corresponds to the map field in a `pg_hba.conf` record
- `ident-name`—This is a name returned by the `identd` daemon on a client system
- `pguser-name`—PostgreSQL username

Here is an example:

```
# pg_ident.conf
#
#mapname      ident-name       pguser-name
#-----------  -------------    -----------
host-wynton   Administrator    bruce
host-vivaldi  Administrator    sheila
host-vivaldi  sheila           sheila
host-vivaldi  korry            korry


# pg_hba.conf
#
host all 192.168.0.85 255.255.255.255 ident host-vivaldi
host all 192.168.0.22 255.255.255.255 ident host-wynton
```

You can see in this example that I have defined two `ident` maps: `host-vivaldi` and `host-wynton`. The `pg_hba.conf` file specifies that any connection attempts from host `192.168.0.85` should use the `ident` method with the `host-vivaldi` ident map; any connection attempts from host `192.168.0.22` should use the `host-wynton` map.

Now look at the `pg_ident.conf` file—there are three entries in the `host-vivaldi` map and one entry in the `host-wynton` map.

The `host-wynton` map says that if I am logged in to my client machine (192.168.0.22) as user `Administrator`, I can connect to a database as PostgreSQL user `bruce`.

The `host-vivaldi` map says that I can connect as PostgreSQL user `sheila` if I am logged in to my host as `Administrator` or if I am logged in as user `sheila`. Also, if I am logged in as `korry`, I can connect as PostgreSQL user `korry`.

So, why is the `ident` method insecure? Think back to the `trust` method—it is insecure because you trust the user to tell the truth about his or her identity. `ident` is insecure because you are trusting the *client system*. The network protocol used by the `identd` daemon is very simple and easy to impersonate. It's easy to set up a homegrown program to respond to `identd` queries with inaccurate usernames. In fact, I recently downloaded and installed an `ident` server on my Windows laptop, and one of the command-line options allowed me to specify a *fake* username!

I would recommend against using the `ident` authentication method except on closed networks (that is, networks where you control all the connected hosts).

The `password` Authentication Method

The `password` authentication method provides a reasonably high level of security compared to `trust` and `ident`. When you use `password` authentication, the client must prove its identity by providing a valid password.

On a Unix (or Linux) host, OS passwords are usually stored in `/etc/passwd` or `/etc/shadow`. When you log in to a Unix machine, you are prompted for your OS password, and the login program compares the password that you enter with the appropriate entry in the `/etc/passwd` file.

PostgreSQL authentication passwords are not related to the password that you use to log in to your operating system. The PostgreSQL server stores passwords in the `pg_shadow` system table (PostgreSQL servers older than version 7.3 could also store passwords in an external file). You use the `CREATE USER` or `ALTER USER` commands to maintain passwords. For example, to create a new (password-authenticated) user, you would use the following command:

```
CREATE USER bruce WITH PASSWORD 'cricketers';
```

If you want to change `bruce`'s password, you would use the `ALTER USER` command:

```
ALTER USER bruce WITH PASSWORD 'Wooloomooloo';
```

Are `pg_shadow` Passwords Encrypted?

When you assign a password (using `CREATE USER` or `ALTER USER`), you can tell PostgreSQL to store the password in `ENCRYPTED` or `UNENCRYPTED` (that is, plain-text) form. If you are a PostgreSQL superuser (see Chapter 19), you can view any plain-text password by selecting from the `pg_shadow` table. If you are a Unix superuser, you can see any plain-text password by examining the `$PGDATA/global/pg_pwd` file (all passwords are copied from the `pg_shadow` table into the `$PGDATA/global/pg_pwd` every time you change a password). You can only use encrypted password with the `md5` authentication method (which I'll describe in a moment).

The `crypt` Authentication Method

The `crypt` authentication method is nearly identical to `password`. The only difference between the two is that the `password` method sends your password over the network in plain-text form while `crypt` does not. Sending plain-text passwords across the network is always a bad idea—it's just too easy to sniff them out of a network stream.

I mentioned in the last section that you could only use encrypted passwords with the `md5` authentication method. So how does the `crypt` authentication method avoid sending plain-text passwords over the network?

When a client application wants to connect to a crypt-authenticating server, the server sends a random number (called a *salt* value) back to the client. After the client knows what salt value to use, it encrypts the password (entered by the user) with the salt and sends the result to the server. The server reads the plain-text password (stored in the `pg_shadow` table) and encrypts it with the same salt value. If the two encrypted passwords match, the client is successfully authenticated. The result is that passwords are *stored* in plain-text form, but the client sends encrypted passwords across the network.

The `md5` Authentication Method

The third password-based authentication method is `md5`. With `md5` authentication, you store passwords in the `pg_shadow` table in encrypted form. `md5` authentication was not available prior to PostgreSQL release 7.2.

You create encrypted passwords using the `CREATE USER` and `ALTER USER` commands.

```
ALTER USER bruce WITH ENCRYPTED PASSWORD 'Wooloomooloo';
```

Note the keyword `ENCRYPTED`.

`md5` is a cryptographically secure message digest algorithm developed by Ron L. Rivest of RSA Security. A message digest algorithm takes a plain-text message (in our case, a password) and produces a long number, called a *hash* or *digest*, based on the contents of the message. The `md5` algorithm is carefully designed so that no two messages are likely to produce the same digest. It is nearly impossible to recover the original password given an `md5` digest.

How can a message digest be used as a password? If you feed two passwords into the `md5` algorithm, you will get the same digest value if the passwords are identical. When you create an encrypted password, the password itself is not actually stored in `pg_shadow`. Instead, PostgreSQL computes an `md5` digest over the password and stores the digest. When a client attempts to connect using `md5` authentication, the client computes an `md5` digest over the password provided by the user and sends the digest to the server. The server compares the digest stored in `pg_shadow` with the digest provided by the client. If the two digests are identical, it is *extremely* likely that the passwords match.

There are a couple of security holes in the procedure that I just described. Let's say that `bruce` and `sheila` each happened to choose the same password. Two identical passwords will produce the same message digest. If `bruce` happened to notice that his password had the same message digest as `sheila`'s, he would know that he and `sheila` had chosen the same password. To avoid this problem, PostgreSQL combines each password with the user's name before computing the md5 digest. That way, if two users happen to choose the same password, they won't have the same md5 digests. The second problem has to do with network security. If a client sent the same message digest to the server every time a given user logged in, the message digest would essentially function as a plain-text password. A nefarious user could watch the network traffic, capture the plain-text message digest, and impersonate the real user (by providing the same plain-text message digest). Instead, PostgreSQL uses the *salt* strategy that I described earlier. When a client connects to an md5 authenticating server, the server sends a random *salt* to the client. The client computes an md5 digest based on the user ID and password; this digest matches the digest stored in pg_shadow. The client then combines the salt (from the server) with the first md5 digest and computes a second digest. The second digest is sent to the server. The server combines the salt with the digest stored in pg_shadow and computes a new md5 digest. The server then compares the client's digest with its (salted) own—if the digests match, the passwords match.

The pam Authentication Method

The final password-based authentication method is pam (Pluggable Authentication Module). You've probably noticed that PostgreSQL offers many methods for authenticating a user. The authentication problem is not unique to PostgreSQL—many applications need to authenticate users. The goal of pam is to separate the act of authenticating a user from each and every application by placing authentication services in a framework that can be called by any application.

A system administrator can define different authentication methods for each application, depending on how secure the application needs to be. Using pam, an administrator can create a completely open system, requiring no passwords at all, or can choose to authenticate users using passwords, challenge-response protocols, or even more esoteric biometric authentication methods. PostgreSQL can use the pam framework.

Although pam can be ported to many Unix systems, it is most commonly found in Linux and Solaris. Configuring a pam system is not for the faint-of-heart, and the topic deserves an entire book. Because of space considerations, I won't try to describe how to configure a pam installation. Instead, I recommend that you visit the Linux-PAM web site (http://www.kernel.org/pub/linux/libs/pam/) for more information.

The krb4 and krb5 Authentication Methods

The krb4 and krb5 authentication methods correspond to Kerberos version 4 and Kerberos version 5, respectively. Kerberos is a network-secure authentication service developed at MIT.

Kerberos is a complex package (particularly from the administrator's point of view), but it offers a high level of security. After Kerberos is properly installed and configured, it is easy to use.

The easiest way to understand Kerberos is to compare it with a more traditional authentication method.

Let's say that you want to use `telnet` to connect to another host (bach) on your network. You start by issuing the `telnet` command:

```
$ telnet bach
Trying bach...
Connected to bach (192.168.0.56)
Escape character is '^]'.

login: korry
Password: cows

Last login: Thu Jan 24 19:18:44
$
```

After providing your username, the login program (on bach) asks for your password. Your password is compared with the password stored on bach (in the /etc/passwd or /etc/shadow file). If the password that you provide matches, you have proven your identity and bach permits access.

If you log out of bach and log back in, you must again provide your identity and prove that you are who you say you are.

Now let's see how you perform the same operation when using Kerberos.

With Kerberos, you don't have to prove your identity to each server; instead, you authenticate yourself to a trusted server. In this case, *trusted* means that both the client (that's you) and the server will trust the Kerberos authentication agent to verify that you are who you say you are.

Before you telnet using Kerberos, you must first obtain a *ticket*.

```
$ kinit
Password for korry@movies.biz: cows
```

After you enter your password, the `kinit` program contacts the Kerberos authentication server (AS) and asks for a ticket. If your password was correct, the AS returns a chunk of data known as a TGT (ticket-granting ticket). The `kinit` program stores your TGT in a cache file inside of a temporary directory on your system.

At this point, you have proven your identity to the AS, and the AS has given back a certificate that you can use with servers that trust the AS. You can view your TGT using the `klist` command:

```
$ klist
Ticket cache: /tmp/krb5cc_tty1
Default principal: korry@movies.biz

Valid starting     Expires             Service principal
25 Jan 02 01:25:47  25 Jan 02 09:25:42  krbtgt/movies.bi@ movies.biz

$
```

(Notice that the ticket expires in about eight hours—I have to occasionally reauthenticate myself to the AS.)

Now, you can use that TGT by using a Kerberos-enabled `telnet` client to connect to a Kerberos-enabled `telnet` server:

```
$ telnet -a bach
Trying bach...
Connected to bach (192.168.0.56)
Escape character is '^]'.

Last login: Thu Jan 24 19:18:44
$
```

There are two things that you should notice about this login example. First, I used the -a flag when I started `telnet`—that flag asks `telnet` to use Kerberos authentication. Second, I was *not* prompted for a user or for a password. Why not? The `telnet` client (on my local machine) used my TGT to ask the AS for another ticket, specifically a ticket that allows me to connect to the `telnet` server on bach. The AS sent the second ticket back to my local machine, and the new ticket was stored in my ticket cache. This new ticket is specific to `telnet`. My local `telnet` client sends the new ticket to the `telnet` server. The ticket contains enough secure (encrypted) information to satisfy the `telnet` server that I have proven my identity (specifically, I have proven my identity to the AS, and the `telnet` server trusts the AS).

I can view the new ticket with the `klist` command:

```
$ klist
Ticket cache: /tmp/krb5cc_tty1
Default principal: korry@movies.biz

Valid starting       Expires             Service principal
25 Jan 02 01:25:47   25 Jan 02 09:25:42  krbtgt/movies.biz@movies.biz
25 Jan 02 03:01:25   25 Jan 02 13:01:20  host/bach.movies.biz@movies.biz
$
```

So, how does all this fit into PostgreSQL? PostgreSQL client applications (`psql`, for example) and the `postmaster` can be compiled to support Kerberos authentication.

When you specify the `krb4`- or `krb5`-authentication method, you are telling the `postmaster` that client applications must provide a valid Kerberos ticket.

When you connect to a `krb4` or `krb5` authenticated `postmaster` with a Kerberos-enabled client application, you are not required to supply a username or password—instead, the client application sends a Kerberos ticket to the `postmaster`.

The nice thing about Kerberos authentication is that it is secure and convenient at the same time. It is secure because you never send plain-text passwords over an insecure network. It is convenient because you authenticate yourself only once (using the `kinit` program).

As I mentioned earlier, setting up a Kerberos system is not a trivial project. After you have gone through the pain and mystery of installing and configuring Kerberos, you can configure PostgreSQL to use Kerberos to authenticate connection requests. Explaining how to install and configure would require a second book. If you are interested in using Kerberos authentication with PostgreSQL, I recommend you start by reading through the Kerberos web site: http://web.mit.edu/kerberos/www/index.html. The PostgreSQL Administrator's Guide provides the details you will need to connect a PostgreSQL database to an installed Kerberos system.

Kerberos is the second most secure authentication method.

The `reject` Authentication Method

The `reject` authentication method is the easiest to understand and is also the most secure. When a client tries to connect from a system authenticated by the `reject` method, the connection attempt is rejected.

If you try to connect from a system that does not match *any* of the pg_hba.conf records, you are also rejected.

Why might you want to use the `reject` method? Let's say that you have a reasonable amount of trust in most of the machines on your network, but you reserve one host as a demonstration machine (192.168.0.15). The demonstration machine should be allowed to access the `demo` database, but no other databases. Every other host should be allowed to access all databases (using Kerberos 5).

```
# File: pg hba.conf
#
# Type Database Client IP address Netmask          Method
###### ######### ################## ################ ######
  host demo      192.168.0.15       255.255.255.255 trust
  host all       192.168.0.15       255.255.255.255 reject
  host all       192.168.0.0        255.255.255.0   krb5
```

Notice that there are two entries for the demo machine (192.168.0.15). The first entry allows trusted access to the `demo` database. The second entry rejects access to all other databases. This demonstrates an important point: The postmaster starts reading at the beginning of the pg_hba.conf file and stops as soon as it finds a record that matches on connection type, database name, and IP address/mask. When a user tries to connect to the demo database from the demo machine, the postmaster searches for a record of type host with a database of either demo, all, or sameuser (and of course, a match on the IP address/Netmask combination). The first record matches, so the postmaster allows access without requiring any form of authentication other than the IP address of the demo machine. Now suppose that a user (again on the demo machine) tries to connect to a different database (say, accounting). This time, the postmaster searches for a record of type host and a database of accounting, all, or sameuser. The first record no longer matches (wrong database name), so the postmaster moves on. The second record matches and the postmaster rejects the connection attempt. If a user logged in to a different host tries to connect, the postmaster will find the third record (the first two records won't match the IP address) and allow access using Kerberos 5 authentication.

If the postmaster can't find a record that matches a connection attempt, the connection is rejected, so you may be wondering why the reject method is needed.

Consider what would happen if you removed the second record from this file. If a user on the demo machine tries to connect to the accounting database, the postmaster will ignore the first record (wrong database) and move on to the last record. The last record says that anyone in our local network should be allowed to connect to all databases using Kerberos 5 authentication. That is clearly the wrong answer.

Securing Tables

In the preceding sections, I showed you how to keep nefarious intruders out of your database, so you should now know how to keep unauthorized users out of your PostgreSQL data. Now let's look at a different problem: How do you secure your database in such a way that *authorized* users can manipulate database components that they need to work on without gaining access to tables that they should be kept away from?

It's important to recognize a shift in responsibilities here: The operating system enforces the first security component (access to PostgreSQL data files); the postmaster enforces the second component (network access). After you have proven your identity and been granted access to a PostgreSQL database, the database starts enforcing security.

When you set up PostgreSQL internal security, you are controlling the trust relationships between users, groups, database objects, and privileges. First, let's define each of these entities.

Each user who is authorized to access a PostgreSQL database is assigned a unique username. You use the CREATE USER and ALTER USER commands to define (and alter) users. Chapter 19 explains how to maintain the list of PostgreSQL users.

A *group* is a named collection of users. You can use groups to make it easier to assign privileges to a collection of users. There is a special predefined group named PUBLIC—all users are members of the PUBLIC group. Again, see Chapter 19 for information regarding group maintenance.

With PostgreSQL version 8.0, there are eight types of database objects that you can secure:

- Databases (securable starting in version 7.3)
- Schemas (securable starting in version 7.3)
- Tablespaces (securable starting in version 8.0)
- Tables
- Views
- Sequences
- Languages (securable starting in version 7.3)
- Functions (securable starting in version 7.3)

Notice that you cannot secure individual rows within a table. You also cannot secure columns within a table. If you can access any part of table, you can access the entire table. You can, however, use a *view* to control access within a table.

The final piece of the internal-security puzzle is the privilege. Each privilege corresponds to a type of access. If you're using PostgreSQL version 8.0, you can control the privileges shown in Table 23.2.

Table 23.2   **PostgreSQL Privileges**

Privilege Name	Applies To	Description
SELECT	Tables, Views, Sequences	Controls the right to SELECT from any column in a table or view. Also controls the right to interrogate a sequence.
INSERT	Tables, Views, Sequences	Controls the right to INSERT new values into a table, view, or sequence.
UPDATE	Tables, Views, Sequences	Controls the right to UPDATE values in a table, view, or sequence.
DELETE	Tables, Views, Sequences	Controls the right to DELETE values from a table, view, or sequence.
RULE	Tables, Views, Sequences	Controls the right to create new rules on a table or view.
REFERENCES	Tables	Controls the right to link two tables with a foreign key constraint.
TRIGGER	Tables	Controls the right to create triggers on a table.
CREATE	Databases, Tablespaces, Schemas	Controls the right to create new schemas within a database, new objects within a schema, or new indexes (or tables) within a tablespace.
TEMPORARY	Databases	Controls the right to create temporary tables within a database.
EXECUTE	Functions	Controls the right to execute a function.
USAGE	Schemas, Languages	Controls enumeration of objects within a schema, or controls the right to create new functions with a given procedural language.

Let's see how all those components fit together.

First, you should know that when you create a new object, you are considered to be the owner of that object. As the owner of a table (for example), you hold all privileges—you can select, insert, update, or delete rows within that table. Unless you grant privileges to another user, you are the only person that can access that table (actually, the owner of the database can do anything he wants).

Transferring Ownership

You can transfer ownership to another user by using the command ALTER TABLE table OWNER TO new-owner. You must be a PostgreSQL superuser to transfer ownership. To find out who currently owns a table, SELECT from the pg_tables view.

If you want other users to have access to your tables, you need to grant one or more privileges. For example, if you want a user named bruce to be able to select data from the customers table, you would use the following command:

```
GRANT SELECT ON customers TO bruce;
```

If you change your mind, you can deny select privileges to bruce using the REVOKE command, for example:

```
REVOKE SELECT ON customers FROM bruce;
```

As I mentioned earlier, there are seven table-related privileges that you can grant to a user: SELECT, INSERT, UPDATE, DELETE, RULE, REFERENCES, and TRIGGER. The first four of these correspond to the command of the same name. The RULE privilege is used to determine which users can create REWRITE rules. The REFERENCES privilege controls foreign key constraints. For example, the tapes table in the sample database defines two foreign key constraints:

```
CREATE TABLE rentals
(
    tape_id       character(8) references tapes,
    customer_id   integer      references customers,
    rental_date   date
);
```

You must hold the REFERENCES privilege on the tapes and customers tables to create the rentals table. You are not required to hold the REFERENCES privilege to *use* the rentals table, only to create the table. This is an important distinction. If I hold the REFERENCES privilege for a table that you own, I can prevent you from deleting and updating records simply by creating a table that references your table.

The TRIGGER privilege determines which users are allowed to create a TRIGGER. Like the REFERENCES privilege, you can use the TRIGGER privilege to prevent users from interfering with your tables.

You can grant and revoke individual privileges for a user or a group. You can also grant or revoke ALL privileges:

```
GRANT ALL ON customers TO sheila;
REVOKE ALL ON customers FROM bruce;
```

Finding out which users hold privileges for a given table is simple, but the results are a bit hard to interpret. There are two ways to find the list of privilege holders for a table: You can either query the pg_class table, or use the \z command in psql—either way, you get the same results. Here is an example:

```
movies=> \z customers
  Access permissions for database "movies"
 Relation |          Access permissions
-----------+-------------------------------
 customers | {"=","sheila=arwR","bruce=r"}
(1 row)

movies=> select relname, relacl from pg_class where relname = 'customers';
 relname  |             relacl
-----------+-------------------------------
 customers | {"=","sheila=arwR","bruce=r"}
(1 row)
```

The privileges assigned to a table are stored in an array in the `pg_class` system table (in the `relacl` column). Each member of the `relacl` array defines the privileges for a user or a group. The `relacl` column is called an *access control list,* or *ACL*. In the preceding example, user `sheila` holds four privileges and `bruce` holds three. Table 23.3 shows how the codes in a PostgreSQL ACL correspond to privilege names.

Table 23.3   **ACL Code to Privilege Name Mapping**

`relacl` **Code**	**Privilege Name**
a	INSERT
r	SELECT
w	UPDATE
d	DELETE
R	RULES
x	REFERENCES
t	TRIGGER
X	EXECUTE
U	USAGE
C	CREATE
T	TEMPORARY
*	GRANT (can confer privilege to other users)
arwdRxt	ALL

You can see that user `sheila` holds all privileges for the `customers` table and user `bruce` has read-only access.

In the previous example, the ACL for `customers` (`{"=","sheila=arwR","bruce=r"}`) contains three entries. The meaning of the last two entries is obvious, but what does the first entry mean? The first entry corresponds to the `PUBLIC` group (because the username is missing)—the `PUBLIC` group has no privileges (no privileges are listed to the right of the =).

Versions Prior to PostgreSQL 7.2

If you are using a version of PostgreSQL older than release 7.2, you may have noticed that there is no ACL code corresponding to DELETE privileges. Prior to PostgreSQL release 7.2, having DELETE privileges was the same as having UPDATE privileges.

Now let's see how PostgreSQL interprets an ACL to decide whether you have privileges to access a table.

First, I'll start by creating two groups and a new user:

```
CREATE GROUP clerks;
CREATE GROUP managers;

CREATE USER monty;

ALTER GROUP clerks ADD USER bruce;
ALTER GROUP clerks ADD USER sheila;
ALTER GROUP managers ADD USER sheila;
```

Now, let's define some privileges for the customers table:

```
GRANT SELECT ON customers TO PUBLIC;
GRANT INSERT ON customers to GROUP clerks;
GRANT INSERT, UPDATE ON customers to GROUP managers;
```

The ACL for the customers table now looks like this:

```
{=r}
{bruce=r}
{group clerks=ar}
{group managers=arw}
```

Let's look at the simplest case first. User monty holds no explicit privileges to the customers table, but he is (automatically) a member of the PUBLIC group. He can SELECT from customers, but he can't make any changes.

Next, let's see what sheila is allowed to do. User sheila has no explicit privileges to the customers table, but she is a member of two groups: PUBLIC and managers. The PUBLIC group is allowed to select, but the managers group is allowed to modify the customers table. Is sheila allowed to insert new customers? The answer is yes. When deciding whether to allow a given operation, PostgreSQL uses the following set of rules:

- If there is an ACL entry that matches your username, that entry determines whether the operation is allowed.

- If there is not an ACL entry that matches your username, PostgreSQL looks through the ACL entries for all the groups that you belong to. If any of the groups hold the required privilege, you are allowed to perform the operation.

- If the PUBLIC ACL entry holds the required privilege, you are allowed to perform the operation.

- If you are not granted the required privilege by any of the preceding rules, you are prohibited from performing the operation.

So, sheila is allowed to insert new customers, not because she holds the INSERT privilege herself, but because she belongs to two groups that *do* hold that privilege.

Securing Functions

When you call a function (or execute a trigger), that function typically operates with the privileges granted to your user ID or group. That means, for example, that a function can't UPDATE values in a given table unless you hold UPDATE privileges for that table. That's *usually* a good thing—you don't want a user to suddenly gain extra privileges just by calling a function. But it can also be inconvenient.

Say you're storing bookkeeping information in a PostgreSQL database and you've created a number of stored procedures (functions) to manage that data. You're running a large company with its own accounting department and you've created a group named CLERKS that holds limited privileges. In particular, a CLERK can SELECT values from most accounting tables, but can't UPDATE or DELETE rows. At the end of each month, you want a CLERK to execute a CLOSE MONTH procedure that archives old information into a set of history tables. Of course, you must GRANT the CLERK group EXECUTE privileges for the CLOSE MONTH function, but that's not enough—once an "old" record has been copied to the history table, CLOSE MONTH must DELETE the row from the working table. An accounting CLERK doesn't hold DELETE privileges. How do you solve this dilemma? You *could* temporarily GRANT DELETE privileges to the CLERK group at the end of each month, but that's a hassle (and a security hole). Instead, you can convey DELETE privileges (or any required privilege) to the CLOSE MONTH function itself.

When you create the CLOSE MONTH function, you can tell PostgreSQL which set of privileges to enforce at the time the function is invoked. You have two choices: You can tell PostgreSQL to use the privileges assigned to the invoker (SECURITY INVOKER), or to use the privileges assigned to the owner of the function (SECURITY DEFINER). Most functions execute with the privileges assigned to the invoker (SECURITY INVOKER). In this case, you want the CLOSE MONTH function to execute with elevated privileges. When you create the CLOSE MONTH function, be sure to include the SECURITY DEFINER clause and make sure that the function is owned by a user that holds the required privileges (you can use the ALTER FUNCTION ... OWNER TO command to transfer ownership). Problem solved.

Note: prior to version 7.4, *all* functions executed with the privileges assigned to the invoker.

Summary

At this point, you should know how to secure a PostgreSQL installation. There is one more important point that I need to mention. All the security mechanisms provided by PostgreSQL rely on a secure operating environment. If a nefarious user manages to gain superuser access to your system, he or she can bypass all the security measures that you have put into place. Worse yet, he or she can unravel your security in such a way that others can gain access to your private data. PostgreSQL security is not a substitute for a secure operating system.

24

Replicating PostgreSQL Data with Slony

REPLICATION IS THE PROCESS OF DISTRIBUTING data from database to database. Typically, the databases reside on different physical computers. PostgreSQL has supported a number of replication mechanisms over the years, but Slony is emerging as the preferred replication solution. Slony offers asynchronous, one-way, cascading replication of data from one origin to any number of subscribers.

Asynchronous means that the copy of the data that you find at a subscriber may not be the most current data—the subscriber may be "out of sync" with the origin. In fact, you may find different data at each subscriber. Asynchronous replication implies that a subscriber does not need to be up-and-running all the time. You can take a subscriber offline and you won't affect the origin—the subscriber catches up after you bring it back online. Of course, if a subscriber is offline for an extended period of time (and many data changes have occurred at the origin), it can take quite a while for the client to catch up. Bringing a slow subscriber back in sync can also create a heavy load on your network and on the provider database.

One-way replication means that you can only change a replicated table at the origin. Slony copies any changes to the original table to each subscriber node. At each subscriber site, Slony adds a trigger to the replicated table that prevents you from modifying the data. (Replicated tables are modifiable at the origin and read-only at each subscriber.)

A cascading replication mechanism (such as Slony) lets you lighten the load on the origin by *cascading* changes from subscriber to subscriber. Using a cascading topology means that the origin does *not* have to service every subscriber. Instead one subscriber can service another. Every node in a replication cluster can act as a provider for one or more subscribers.

To avoid confusion, Slony documentation doesn't talk about master or slave nodes. Every *node* that participates in a Slony *cluster* can originate tables and subscribe to other tables. (That is, every node can act as both an origin and a subscriber.) Here's a quick preview of the terminology used by the Slony developers:

- Node: A node is a database that acts as an origin, a subscriber, or both.
- Cluster: A cluster (or, more precisely, a replication cluster) is a collection of nodes that share replication data.
- slon: The program (usually run as a background daemon) that copies replication data and configuration information from one node to another.
- Set: The smallest unit of replication; a set defines a collection of tables and sequences that are replicated from node to node.
- Path: The connection properties (hostname, user id, password, and so on) that describe how a slon daemon connects to another node.
- Event: A message sent from one node to other nodes to indicate that replication data or configuration changes are available on the originating node.
- Origin: The node that holds the master copy of a replication set.
- Subscriber: A node that holds a read-only copy of a replication set that has been copied (either directly or through a chain of other subscribers) from the set's origin.
- Provider: A node that provides replication data to a subscriber. (A provider is often an origin, but a provider may be a subscriber that forwards replication data to another subscriber.)

Overview

Slony works by adding an AFTER UPDATE/INSERT/DELETE trigger to the master copy (that is, the origin) of every table that you want to replicate. An AFTER UPDATE/INSERT/DELETE trigger is a function that executes after an UPDATE, INSERT, or DELETE command modifies a table. The new trigger pushes each change from the origin into a history table. When a subscriber comes online, it pulls recent changes from the history table. The history table contains a record of *every* modification. If you UPDATE a row in a replicated table, and then DELETE that row, the history table contains an UPDATE command followed by a DELETE command. When a subscriber pulls the modification history from the provider, it applies each change, in order from earliest change to most recent. Since the original table changed from its earlier form to its current form by executing a sequence of commands (in a specific order), it stands to reason that applying the same changes to an identical copy of the table will produce an exact copy of the new form of the original table.

To illustrate the process, we'll pretend that your video store is expanding. The home office is located in Springfield and you are opening two new stores (one in Boomtown and one in Snoozeville). You have PostgreSQL installed at each site and you've named the hosts springfield, boomtown, and snoozeville (respectively). You want to replicate the customers table to each of the new branches. For the moment, I'll skip over the process of configuring the replication cluster and pretend that your cluster already is up and running. You've created a cluster (named branches) that pushes data from springfield to boomtown, and then from boomtown to snoozeville (in other words, springfield is the *origin* of springfield.customers, boomtown is a *direct subscriber*, and snoozeville is a *chained subscriber*).

I mentioned earlier that every node can act as a provider *and* a subscriber at the same time. If you were running a group of real-world video stores, you would replicate the boomtown and snoozeville databases as well. That way, each store would have a modifiable copy of its own data and a read-only copy of the data for every other store.

Let's say that an existing customer arrives at the springfield branch and tells you that he has a new phone number: You log in to the local server (springfield) and execute the following commands:

```
movies=# BEGIN WORK;
BEGIN
movies=# UPDATE customers SET phone - '555-3322' WHERE customer_id - '1';
UPDATE 1
movies=# COMMIT;
COMMIT
```

When you execute the COMMIT command, the PostgreSQL server running on host springfield executes the AFTER UPDATE trigger that Slony added to the customers table. The AFTER UPDATE trigger builds a *second* UPDATE command[1] and writes the text of the new command to the modification history table. (Specifically, the trigger writes the second UPDATE command to _branches.sl_log_1.) Notice that the trigger does not *push* the new UPDATE command to boomtown itself. Instead, a background process named slon, running on springfield, watches the sl_log_1 table. The slon daemon spends much of its time sleeping, but every 10 seconds, it wakes up and searches for new entries in the sl_log_1 table. If slon finds a new entry (meaning that someone has modified a replicated table), it writes a SYNC *event* into the _branches.sl_event table and executes a NOTIFY command that wakes up any active subscribers (in this case, boomtown).

On the subscriber side, boomtown is also running a slon daemon. boomtown's daemon knows that it subscribes to a SET that originates on springfield and connects to the PostgreSQL server running on springfield. You can see that connection for yourself—when you start the daemon on boomtown, a new listener appears in the pg_listeners table on host springfield. boomtown.slon listens for the notification signaled by

---

[1] In this case, the new UPDATE command is identical to the one that you typed in, but that's not always the case. Consider an UPDATE statement that modifies more than one row. Such a command would generate a new UPDATE command for every row modified (each command would modify a single row).

springfield.slon. When boomtown.slon receives that notification, it searches through springfield's sl_log_1 table to find recent modifications ("recent" meaning a modification that boomtown has not *already* replicated). If it finds any recent modifications, boomtown applies those changes to its *own* copy of the replicated data. In this example, boomtown.slon finds the UPDATE command generated by springfield's AFTER UPDATE trigger and executes that command. When boomtown.slon has applied all of the modifications found in springfield.sl_log_1, it sends a confirmation back to springfield. The confirmation tells springfield that, as far as boomtown is concerned, the modification records in springfield.sl_log_1 are ancient history and may be purged.

If boomtown happens to be offline (that is, if there is no slon daemon servicing boomtown), it won't receive the notification signaled by springfield. When boomtown comes back online, it *eventually* receives a SYNC event from springfield and begins the process of "catching up" with springfield. (springfield sends a SYNC event every so often even if the replication set has not been modified.)

It's also possible that the slon daemon that services springfield may not be running at the time you UPDATE the customers table. In that case, the AFTER UPDATE trigger still pushes the modification record into _branches.sl_log_1, but it remains there until all (direct) subscribers have confirmed that they have applied the changes to their own copies.

You can see that Slony remains robust even when the origin and/or subscribers are offline. If a node doesn't receive a SYNC event immediately, it receives a SYNC event *eventually* and that's sufficient to ensure that modification history is never lost.

Now let's look at the process of creating the branches replication cluster.

Requirements

Before you can create a replication cluster, you must install Slony on every computer that will host a node. You can find Slony at the PostgreSQL's gborg web site (http://gborg.postgresql.org) or at http://slony.info. Currently, you must compile Slony yourself (at the time we are writing this, binary distributions are not available). To build Slony, you must have the following PostgreSQL components on each system:

- PostgreSQL C header files (typically found in /usr/include, you can locate these files with the command pg_config —includedir)
- PostgreSQL Server C header files (typically found in /usr/include/pgsql/server, you can locates these files with the command pg_config —includedir-server)
- PostgreSQL client libraries (typically found in /usr/lib, you can locate the actual directory with the command pg_config -libdir)
- PL/pgSQL (typically found in /usr/lib/pgsql, you can locate the actual directory with the command pg_config —pkglibdir)

Once you've confirmed that you have all of the components that you need, download and unpack the Slony archive. Next `cd` to the directory that holds the freshly unpacked files and then, dance the familiar GNU Tango: `./configure && make && make install`.

If you've installed PostgreSQL in a "standard" location, `configure` should be able to find the PostgreSQL components that it requires. If `configure` complains that it can't find a PostgreSQL component, you may need to add one or more of the following options to the `configure` command line:

- `with pgconfigdir=`*directory*: The given directory must contain the `pg_config` utility (`configure` uses `pg_config` to find most of the other PostgreSQL components)

- `—with-pgbindir=`*directory*: Location of the PostgreSQL postmaster (Slony installs a few programs, such as `slon` and `slonik`, in this directory)

- `—with-pgincludedir=`*directory*: Location of the PostgreSQL headers

- `—with-pgincludeserverdir=`*directory*: Location of the PostgreSQL server headers

- `—with-pglibdir=`*directory*: Location of the PostgreSQL libraries (Slony programs are linked against the libpq object library)

- `—with-pgpkglibdir=`*directory*: Location of the PostgreSQL pkglib directory (specifically, configure searches for the PL/pgSQL shared library)

- `—with-pgsharedir-`*directory*: Location of the PostgreSQL share directory (Slony installs a number of SQL scripts in this directory)

In addition to the Slony package itself, you must prepare each PostgreSQL server for replication. First, the target database (that is, the database that you are originating or subscribing to) must exist on each node. Although not required, you may find it easier to manage the cluster if you use consistent database names on each node. In our video store example, every node contains a database named `movies`. Within `movies`, each node contains one schema for each branch. (You would end up with a schema named `springfield`, a schema named `boomtown`, and a schema named `snoozeville`.) Finally, you must install PL/pgSQL into each node. Many of the triggers and functions that Slony uses are written in PL/pgSQL (others are written in C).

To carry out its work, Slony adds a number of tables, views, sequences, functions, and types to each node. Slony segregates most of its data into a single schema within each node—the name of the schema is formed by adding an underscore to the start of the replication cluster name. For example, if you create a replication cluster named `branches`, Slony creates a schema named `_branches` in each node. Slony will refuse to cooperate if it finds anything in the cluster schema. (Slony prefers to create the cluster schema itself.) Although it's possible to populate the Slony schemas by hand, it's easier to use the `slonik` command. `slonik` is a scripting engine—to create or manage a Slony cluster, you write a script and invoke the `slonik` command to execute that script.

When you execute a script, slonik connects to one or more of the databases in the cluster and executes commands (often stored procedures) in those databases. Each script must contain a *preamble* that tells slonik how to connect to each node. For example, a script that manages the branches cluster would begin like this:

```
cluster name = branches;
node 1 admin conninfo = 'dbname=movies host=springfield user=slony';
node 2 admin conninfo = 'dbname=movies host=boomtown    user=slony';
node 3 admin conninfo = 'dbname=movies host=snoozeville user=slony';
...
```

Symbolic Names and Include Files

The slonik command recently learned how to perform two new tricks that make it much easier to write and, especially, maintain slonik scripts. Starting with release 1.1, you can define symbolic names and refer to those names later in the script. For example, using symbolic names, you could rewrite the preamble like this:

```
define CLUSTER  branches;
define SPRINGFIELD 1;
define BOOMTOWN 2;
define SNOOZEVILLE 3;

cluster = @CLUSTER;
node @SPRINGFIELD admin
        conninfo = 'dbname=movies host=springfield user=slony';
node @BOOMTOWN    admin
        conninfo = 'dbname=movies host=boomtown    user=slony';
node @SNOOZEVILLE admin
        conninfo = 'dbname=movies host=snoozeville user=slony';
```

A define statement assigns a symbolic name to a string. The first define command, for example, creates a symbol named CLUSTER whose value is branches. When slonik sees @*symbol* in a script, it substitutes the value of the symbol. The symbol value may include spaces and can also include references to other symbols.

At first glance, symbolic names may not seem to offer much, but as your slonik scripts become more complex, you'll find that symbolic names make it easier to keep track of node numbers, set numbers, status codes, and so on. In fact, when you combine symbolic names with include files, your slonik scripts become much shorter and much more maintainable. Rather than writing the same cluster and node directives in every slonik script, you can create a separate preamble file and include that file in the other scripts. For the remainder of this chapter, I'll assume that you are using a version of Slony that supports symbolic names and include files. If you're using an older version, I'd encourage you to upgrade.

The first command in the preamble tells slonik the name of the cluster. (slonik needs the cluster name so that it can refer to the proper schema within each database.) The cluster name directive is followed by a series of node declarations. Each node declaration assigns a unique numeric identifier to the node and tells `slonik` how to connect to the database. Since `slonik` is a client application that uses the libpq library to connect to each database, you must provide the connection information in the form of a libpq-style connection string. The `conninfo` string typically specifies a database name, a hostname, a username, and occasionally a port number, but you can include any of the connection properties described in Table 5.2. If you want to consolidate all of your connection properties into a single location, you might consider creating a `pg_service.conf` file and including the service names in your `slonik` script instead. For example, if you have a `pg_service.conf` file that contains the following entries:

```
[springfield-slonik]
dbname=movies
host=springfield
user=slony

[boomtown-slonik]
dbname=movies
host=boomtown
user=slony

[snoozeville-slonik]
dbname=movies
host=snoozeville
user=slony
```

You could write a slonik preamble like this:

```
# File: preamble
cluster name - branches;
node 1 admin conninfo = 'service=springfield-slonik';
node 2 admin conninfo = 'service=boomtown-slonik';
node 3 admin conninfo = 'service=snoozeville-slonik';
...
```

Slony Password Management

You may have noticed that the connection strings shown here do not include a password. Although you *could* include a password in node declarations, it's not a good idea to do so since the passwords would be stored in plain-text form. Instead, you should use one of the more secure authentication methods described in Chapter 23, "Security." The TRUST authentication method is undoubtedly the easiest method to configure (no passwords involved), but that's not particularly secure when you have more than one host in the replication cluster. The md5 authentication method is a reasonably secure choice, but you still have to store your passwords somewhere. Instead of embedding a plain-text password in a script, you should store PostgreSQL passwords in $HOME/.pgpass.

When a libpq application (like `slonik` or `slon`) connects to a database that requires a password, it searches for the password in the connection string. If the connection string does not contain that password (and, in general, it should *not*), it searches for the password in a file named $HOME/.pgpass (note the period at the beginning of the filename). If the client application is running on a Windows host, libpq searches for the password in a file named `\postgresql\pgpass.conf` in the Application Data directory assigned to your account (the `%APPDATA%` environment variable points to your Application Data directory).

For example, if you are logged in to your computer as user `bruce`, libpq reads `~bruce/.pgpass` (which is just another way of writing the `.pgpass` file found in `bruce`'s home directory). Each entry in the `.pgpass` file contains a hostname, port, database name, username, and password (in plain-text form). libpq searches through `.pgpass` until it finds a match on the first four fields (an "*" matches any value for that field). If user `bruce` has created a `.pgpass` file that contains the following entries:

```
# format - hostname:port:database:username:password
# an '*' matches any value in that field
boomtown:*:movies:bruce:cows
boomtown:*:movies:slony:cows-slony
```

He can log in to the `movies` database on host `boomtown` (any port). Since `.pgpass` contains two entries that match host `boomtown` (any port) and database `movies`, `bruce` can log in as user `bruce` or as user `slony`. Either of the following `psql` commands will work without prompting `bruce` for a password:

```
[bruce@springfield ~] psql -h boomtown -U bruce movies
[bruce@springfield ~] psql -h boomtown -U slony movies
```

It's important to remember that libpq reads the `.pgpass` file found in the `$HOME` directory of the user running the client application, even if you connect to a different account in the target database. That means that, given the `slony.preamble` (or `pg_service.conf`) file shown earlier, your `.pgpass` file must contain at least the following entries:

```
springfield:*:movies:slony:cow-slony
boomtown:*:movies:slony:emu-slony
snoozeville:*:movies:slony:penguin-slony
```

Instead of writing the same preamble in *every* `slonik` script, you can save the preamble in a separate file (say, `preamble.sk`) and then `include<>` that file in other scripts. The preamble file is a great place to define symbolic names for values that you'll use in other scripts. Listing 24.1 shows a revised `preamble.sk` file that we'll `include<>` in the rest of the scripts that you'll see in this chapter.

Listing 24.1 `preamble.sk`

```
# File: preamble.sk
define CLUSTER  branches;
define SPRINGFIELD 1;
define BOOMTOWN 2;
define SNOOZEVILLE 3;
define fqn fully qualified name;
define SUCCESS 0;
define FAILURES 1;
```

Listing 24.1   **Continued**

```
cluster = @CLUSTER;
node @SPRINGFIELD admin conninfo = 'dbname=movies host=springfield user=slony';
node @BOOMTOWN    admin conninfo = 'dbname=movies host=boomtown    user=slony';
node @SNOOZEVILLE admin conninfo = 'dbname=movies host=snoozeville user=slony';
```

Once you have the preamble in place, you can add commands to the slonik script. Most commands are composed of a one, two, or three-word verb followed by a comma-separated list of options enclosed in a pair of parentheses.

Creating a Replication Cluster

To create a new preamble.sk replication cluster, you execute an init cluster command targeted at number 1. An init cluster command looks like this:

```
init cluster ( id = node-number, comment = string-literal );
```

The init cluster command connects to the node (which, by the way, must always be node number 1), creates the cluster namespace, and loads a number of tables, sequences, functions, and views into that namespace.

To create the branches replication cluster, you would execute a slonik script that contains the commands shown in Listing 24.2.

Listing 24.2   initCluster.sk

```
#!/usr/local/bin/slonik

# File: initCluster.sk
include <preamble.sk>;

init cluster ( id = @SPRINGFIELD, comment = 'primary node - springfield' );
```

Notice that the script (like every slonik script) must include<> (or begin with) the preamble. After executing this script, you'll find a new schema named _branches in the movies database on host springfield.

Once you've created the replication cluster, you can add the other nodes to the cluster by executing a store node command targeted at each node. The syntax for a store node command is:

```
store node
  (
    id = node-number,
    comment = string-literal
    [ spoolnode = {TRUE|FALSE}, ]
    [event node = node-number ]
  );
```

The `spoolnode` parameter is optional and, if missing, is assumed to be FALSE. (I'll explain spool nodes and log shipping in a moment.) The `event node` parameter is also optional and, if missing, is assumed to specify node 1. When you execute a store node command, `slonik` connects to the node; creates the cluster namespace; loads the same set of tables, sequences, functions, and views that the init cluster command stored on the primary node; and then copies the cluster configuration tables from the event node (usually node 1).

To add the `boomtown` and `snoozeville` nodes to the `branches` cluster, you would execute the script shown in Listing 24.3.

Listing 24.3   `addNodes.sk`

```
#!/usr/local/bin/slonik

# File: addNodes.sk
include <preamble.sk>;

store node ( id = @BOOMTOWN,    comment = 'boomtown' );
store node ( id = @SNOOZEVILLE, comment = 'snoozeville' );
```

After executing the `addNodes.sk` script, you'll find a schema named _branches (in the movies database) on all three nodes.

At this point, each node in the replication cluster knows about every other node, but they don't know how to communicate with each other. You may be thinking that the Slony would use the preamble to connect one node to another, but that's not the case. The preamble (which is part of a `slonik` script) tells the `slonik` administration console how to connect to each node—it *does not* tell the nodes how to connect to each other once the replication servers begin exchanging messages.

To configure node-to-node connection paths, you execute a series of `store path` commands. A `store path` command looks like this:

```
store path
(
    server = node-number,
    client = node-number,
    conninfo = 'connection-string'
);
```

Each `store path` command tells the replication daemon how to connect to the given server node starting from the client node. The *connection-string* parameter is a libpq connection string of the same form that you write in a `slonik` preamble. You typically define connection paths in pairs; the second `store path` command describes the reverse path. (That is, if the first `store path` command defines how to connect to node 2 starting from node 1, the second command describes how to connect to node 1 starting from node 2.) In fact, it's not a bad idea to define a set of paths that describe how to connect every node to every other node. For example, Listing 24.4 shows the commands necessary to connect all of the nodes in the branches replication cluster.

Listing 24.4 addPaths.sk

```
#!/usr/local/bin/slonik

# File: addPaths.sk
include <preamble.sk>;

store path ( server = @SPRINGFIELD, client = @BOOMTOWN,
             conninfo = 'service=springfield-replication' );
store path ( server = @BOOMTOWN,    client = @SPRINGFIELD,
             conninfo = 'service-boomtown-replication' );

store path ( server = @SPRINGFIELD, client = @SNOOZEVILLE,
             conninfo = 'service=springfield-replication' );
store path ( server = @SNOOZEVILLE, client = @SPRINGFIELD,
             conninfo = 'service=snoozeville-replication' );

store path ( server = @BOOMTOWN,    client = @SNOOZEVILLE,
             conninfo = 'service=boomtown-replication' );
store path ( server = @SNOOZEVILLE, client = @BOOMTOWN,
             conninfo = 'service=snoozeville-replication' );
```

It's important to remember that the connection string describes how the client replication daemon should connect to the appropriate database on the server node. If you specify a service name in the connection string, that service must be defined in the client's pg_service.conf file.

Starting the Replication Daemons

Now that you've created all of the replication nodes and defined the paths that connect them, you can start the replication daemons. Every node in the replication cluster must be serviced by a running copy of the slon program. You typically run slon as a background, or daemon, process. The slon program accepts a number of configuration options that you can specify on the command line or in a separate configuration file. I recommend the configuration file approach, since you have a complete record (hopefully, a well-commented record) of the options that you actually used the last time you started the daemon.

Listing 24.5 shows a configuration file that tells `slon` how to service the `springfield` node.

Listing 24.5   `springfield.slon` Configuration File

```
# File: springfield.slon
cluster_name = 'branches'
conn_info = 'service=springfield-replication'
```

At first glance, the syntax for a `slon` configuration file looks similar to the syntax you use to create `slonik` script, but there a few important differences that may trip you up. In a `slonik` script, every command ends with a semicolon—that's not the case for a `slon` configuration file. (If you accidentally terminate a `slon` configuration option with a semicolon, `slon` will taunt you with a rather unfriendly syntax error.) Second, the individual parts of a multi-word command name (such as `cluster name`) are separated by whitespace in a `slonik` script, but you must use an underscore in a `slon` configuration file (`cluster_name`).

You must specify, at least, the `cluster_name` and `conn_info` options to start `slon`. The `cluster_name` option tells `slon` how to find the cluster's schema within the target database. `slon` uses the `conn_info` option to connect to the target database. Once it's up and running, `slon` will use the path that you defined with a `store path` command when it needs to connect to another node.

Remember that you must start one `slon` daemon for *each* node in the replication cluster. That means that you'll need one configuration file for each node. Listing 24.6 shows the configuration files for all three nodes in the `branches` cluster.

Listing 24.6   `slon` Configuration Files

```
#File: springfield.slon
cluster_name = 'branches'
conn_info = 'service=springfield-replication'

#File: boomtown.slon
cluster_name = 'branches'
conn_info = 'service=boomtown-replication'

#File: snoozeville.slon
cluster_nam = 'brances'
conn_info = 'service=snoozeville-replication'
```

To start the three `slon` daemons, execute the following commands:

```
$ slon -f springfield.slon > springfield.log 2>&1 &
$ slon -f boomtown.slon    > boomtown.log 2>&1 &
$ slon -f snoozeville.slon > snoozeville.log 2>&1 &
```

Looking at the first command, the -f flag tells slon to read configuration options from springfield.slon. The > springfield.log part redirects the standard output stream to springfied.log, and the 2>&1 redirects the standard error stream to the same file. (That way, all log information and error messages are recorded in the same file.) The & at the end of the command line tells the Linux/Unix shell to run the entire command in background.

In this example, you're running all three replication daemons on the same computer (even though the daemons are servicing three different nodes). That's a convenient arrangement while you are setting up the replication cluster, but you can also run each slon daemon on the system that hosts the node.

With the slon daemons up and running, you'll see quite a bit of periodic network traffic as the daemons exchange replication messages. You can adjust the frequency of the messages by tuning the sync_interval, sync_interval_timeout configuration options shown in Table 24.1. You can include any of options shown in Table 24.1 in a slon configuration script.

Table 24.1 slon **Configuration Options**

Option	Description	Default Value	Command-line Equivalent
cluster_name	Defines the name of the cluster that slon is servicing.	*none* (required)	first argument
conn_info	Tells slon how to connect to the target database.	*none* (required)	second argument
sync_interval	Interval between checks for replication data. The slon process awakens every sync interval milliseconds and searches for new updates in the *cluster*.sl_log table. If it finds new replication data, it sends a SYNC event to all subscribers. (Each subscriber listens for a SYNC event—when it receives a SYNC event, it pulls the new replication data from the origin.) Valid values are in the range 10–60000 (inclusive).	2000 (2 seconds)	-s *milliseconds*
sync_interval _timeout	In some cases, a subscriber can pull data from the origin before the origin has completed its work. If that happens, the subscriber won't pull all of the replication data from the origin	10000 (10 seconds)	-t *milliseconds*

Table 24.1 **Continued**

Option	Description	Default Value	Command-line Equivalent
sync_interval _timeout	until the next SYNC event is signaled. slon signals a SYNC event every sync_interval timeout milliseconds even if the sync_interval check detects no new replication data. Valid values are in the range 0–1200000, inclusive.		
desired_sync_ time	If a subscriber falls behind, slon groups multiple SYNC events together into increasingly larger events until each event takes desired_sync_time milliseconds to complete. This reduces the number of messages, confirmations, and COMMITs required to "catch up." slon will not create a group that contains more than sync_group maxsize events (see next option). Value values are in the range 10000–600000, inclusive.	60000 (60 seconds)	-o *milliseconds*
sync_group_ maxsize	Specifies the maximum number of SYNC events to coalesce into a single, larger event when a subscriber has fallen behind. Valid values are in the range 0–500, inclusive.	20	-g *count*
log_level	Determines how much information the slon process writes to the debug log (stdout and/or syslog). Valid values range from 0 (minimal output) to 4 (detailed debugging information).	4 (verbose)	-d *level*
syslog	Determines whether slon writes log information to syslog (Linux/Unix hosts only), to the standard output stream (stdout), or both. Valid values are 0—write to stdout only 1—write to syslog and stdout 2—write to syslog only	0	*none*

Table 24.1 **Continued**

Option	Description	Default Value	Command-line Equivalent
syslog_ facility	If slon writes information to syslog daemon (see the previous option), it designates each message as originating from syslog facility. Valid values are LOCAL0, LOCAL1, LOCAL7. See the syslog man page for more information.	LOCAL0	*none*
syslog_ident	If slon writes information to the syslog daemon, it identifies each message originating from the syslog_ident program.	slon	*none*
log_pid	If true, slon includes its process ID in every log message.	false	*none*
log_timestamp	If true, slon includes a timestamp in every log message.	true	*none*
log_timestamp_ format	If log_timestamp is true, this option determines the format of the time stamp included in each log message. See the strftime man page for more details.	'%F %T %Z' (2005-02-28 14:26: 30 GMT)	*none*
pid_file	If present, slon writes its process ID to the named file.	*none*	-p *file-name*
vac_frequency	Determines how frequently slon VACUUMs the Slony configuration and message tables. The slon daemon performs a general cleanup cycle once every 10 minutes. vac_frequency determines the number of cleanup cycles that run before slon VACUUMs its tables. If you are running pg_autovacuum, set vac frequency to 0 to disable the VACUUM feature offered by slon. Valid values range from 0 to 100.	3	-c *cycle-count*
archive_dir	If present slon writes replication data to a "shipping" log in the given directory. See the section titled "Log Shipping" for more information.	*none*	-a *directory-name*

Creating a Replication Set

At this point, you've created a replication cluster (a collection of nodes), defined the paths between the nodes, and you have a daemon (slon) servicing each node in the cluster. The replication daemons are exchanging SYNC messages (and configuration messages), but you're not actually replicating any data yet. To replicate a table (or a collection of tables), you must first define a *set*. A set is a unit of replication—a set can contain one or more tables and one or more sequences. Every set has an origin (a node in the replication cluster).

You create a set by executing a create set command in a slonik script. You add tables to the set by executing a series of set add table commands (likewise, you add a sequence to the set with the set add sequence command). The syntax for these statements is shown here:

```
create set ( id = integer, origin = node-id, comment = 'description' );

set add table ( set id = set-id, origin = node-id, id = integer,
                fully qualified name = 'schema-name.table-name',
                comment = 'description'
                [, key = {'index-name' | SERIAL}] );

set add sequence( set id = set-id, origin = node-id, id = integer,
                  fully qualified name = 'schema-name.sequence-name',
                  comment = 'description' );
```

You must keep a few restrictions in mind when you create a replication set.

First, you cannot add a table (or sequence) to a set once another node has subscribed to that set—instead, you have to create a second set, merge the two sets together, and then re-subscribe all nodes that subscribed to the original. Second, every table that you want to replicate must have a unique identifier. There are three ways that you can convince Slony that a table contains such an identifier. If Slony sees a PRIMARY KEY constraint in the table definition, it's happy. If not, you can include a key=index-name option in the set add table command to tell slonik how to uniquely identify each row in the table. Finally, you can ask slonik to *add* a unique identifier (a BIGINT column whose default value is defined by the _cluster.sl_row_id_seq sequence). Ideally, you should define a PRIMARY KEY for each table or at least a UNIQUE index defined over a set of non-NULL columns. The Slony developers frown upon those who use slonik's table add key command.

Since we want to replicate the customers and tapes tables, you'll have to ensure that each table contains an acceptable unique identifier. Here's the current definition of the customers table:

```
movies=# \d customers
            Table "springfield.customers"
---------------+-----------------------+---------
 customer_id   | integer               | not null
```

```
customer_name | character varying(50) | not null
phone         | character(8)          |
birth_date    | date                  |
balance       | numeric(7,2)          |
Indexes:
    "customers_customer_id_key" UNIQUE, btree (customer_id)
```

You can see that customers already contains an acceptable identifier (the customers_customer_id_key index is a UNIQUE index and it covers a NOT NULL column). You can add the customers table to the replication set without any modifications, but you'll have to tell slonik to use the customers_customer_id_key. The command to do this is

```
set add table ( set id = 1, origin = 1, id = 1,
                fully qualified name = 'springfield.customers',
                comment = 'Springfield customers',
                key = 'customers_customer_id_key' );
```

The tapes table does *not* contain a unique identifier that slonik would find acceptable, but that's easy to fix. You *could* create a UNIQUE index that covers the tape_id column (since, in the real world, each tape is uniquely identified by its tape_id), but you may as well create a PRIMARY KEY constraint instead since slonik prefers a PRIMARY KEY. To add a PRIMARY KEY to the tapes table, you would execute the following command:

```
movies=# ALTER TABLE tapes ADD PRIMARY KEY ( tape_id );
NOTICE:  ALTER TABLE / ADD PRIMARY KEY will create
    implicit index "tapes_pkey" for table "tapes"
ALTER TABLE
```

Now you're ready to complete the replication set. The slonik script shown in Listing 24.7 creates and populates the set.

Listing 24.7   buildSet.sk

```
#!/usr/local/bin/slonik

# File: buildSet.sk
include <preamble.sk>;

create set ( id = 1, origin = @SPRINGFIELD, comment = 'Springfield movies' );

set add table ( set id = 1, origin = @SPRINGFIELD, id = 1,
                fully qualified name = 'springfield.customers',
                comment = 'Springfield customers',
                key = 'customers_customer_id_key' );

set add table ( set id = 1, origin = @SPRINGFIELD, id = 2,
                fully qualified name = 'springfield.tapes',
                comment = 'Springfield tapes' );
```

Notice that the second `set add table` command does *not* specify a key—`slonik` knows that it can use the `PRIMARY KEY` column(s) to uniquely identify each row in the `tapes` table.

Subscribing to a Replication Set

Once you've defined a replication set, the origin node starts pushing a history of every modification to the `_cluster-name.sl_log_1` table and sends `SYNC` events to all subscriber nodes. Subscribing to a replication set is a two-step process. First, you copy the table (and sequence) definitions into the subscriber node. Second, you execute a `subscribe set` command to tell the `slon` daemons to start pulling data out of the `sl_log_1` history file into the subscriber database.

Copying Table and Sequence Definitions

The easiest way to copy the table and sequence definitions to the subscriber node is to talk `pg_dump` and `psql` into doing it for you. First, make sure that the target schema exists on the subscriber node. For example, to create the target schema (`springfield`) on nodes `boomtown` and `snoozeville`, you could execute the following commands:

```
$ psql -h boomtown -c "CREATE SCHEMA springfield"
CREATE SCHEMA
$ psql -h snoozeville -c "CREATE SCHEMA springfield"
CREATE SCHEMA
```

Next, use `pg_dump` to extract the definition of each table (and sequence) in the replication set and pipe the result back into a `psql` command that connects to the subscriber node. For example, to copy the definitions of the `customers` and `tapes` tables from `springfield` to `boomtown` and `snoozeville`:

```
$ pg_dump -s -n springfield -t customers -h springfield |\
>    psql -h boomtown    movies
$ pg_dump -s -n springfield -t tapes     -h springfield |\
>    psql -h snoozeville movies
$ pg_dump -s -n springfield -t customers -h springfield |\
>    psql -h boomtown    movies
$ pg_dump -s -n springfield -t tapes     -h springfield |\
>    psql -h snoozeville movies
```

If you prefer, you can copy the entire `springfield` schema to each subscriber node instead:

```
$ pg_dump -s -n springfield -h springfield | psql -h boomtown    movies
$ pg_dump -s -n springfield -h springfield | psql -h snoozeville movies
```

Note that you don't copy the data itself, just the metadata. (The `-s` flag tells `pg_dump` to extract the definitions, not the data.) If you *do* copy the `customers` and `tapes` table to the subscriber nodes, the `slon` daemons will overwrite the data as soon as replication begins.

Creating a Subscriber

Finally, to subscribe a node to a replication set, you execute a `subscribe set` command (within a `slonik` script). The syntax for the `subscribe set` command is

```
subscribe set
(
    id=set-id,
    provider=node-id,
    receiver=node-id,
    forward={TRUE|FALSE}
);
```

The `id=set-id` option tells `slonik` which replication set you want to subscribe to. (`set-id` corresponds to the `create set` and `set add table` commands that you executed earlier.) The `provider=node-id` option determines which node provides the replication data to the subscriber. If the provider node is the same node as the set's origin, the subscriber pulls replication data straight from the source. If the provider node is *not* the set's origin, the subscriber pulls replication data from another subscriber. The `receiver=node-id` option specifies which node is doing the subscribing. If `forward` is `FALSE` (or if you omit the `forward` option), the subscriber node discards all replication data as soon as it has applied the modifications to the local copy of the database. If `forward` is `TRUE`, the subscriber retains a copy of the replication data so that it can provide the data to other subscribers.

To subscribe nodes `boomtown` and `snoozeville`, you would execute the script shown in Listing 24.8.

Listing 24.8   `subscribeSet.sk`

```
#!/usr/local/bin/slonik

# File: subscribeSet.sk
include <preamble.sk>;

subscribe set ( id = 1, provider = @SPRINGFIELD,
                        receiver = @BOOMTOWN, forward = yes );
subscribe set ( id = 1, provider = @BOOMTOWN,
                        receiver = @SNOOZEVILLE, forward = no );
```

The first `subscribe set` command subscribes node `boomtown`. `boomtown` pulls replication data directly from the set origin (`springfield`). The second `subscribe set` command subscribes node `snoozeville`. `snoozeville` pulls replication data from `boomtown`. When you change the `customers` (or `tapes`) table on `springfield`, the modifications are copied from `springfield` to `boomtown`, and then from `boomtown` to `snoozeville`.

Once you've executed a `subscribe set` command, the `slon` daemons begin replicating data. The first `SYNC` event received by `boomtown` copies the entire `customers` table (and the entire `tapes` table) from `springfield` to `boomtown`. When `boomtown` holds an identical copy of the replication set, it sends a `SYNC` event to `snoozeville` and `snoozeville` pulls the entire replication set from `boomtown`.

Changing the Cluster Topology (Re-mastering and Failover)

Slony makes it very easy to change the topology of a replication cluster. Let's say that business at the Boomtown store is really booming (ouch) and you want to lighten the load on the `boomtown` server. `boomtown` pulls replication data from `springfield` and forwards the data to `snoozeville`. You can tell `snoozeville` to pull its replication data directly from `springfield` by re-subscribing `snoozeville` and specifying a different provider (see Listing 24.9).

Listing 24.9   `changeProvider.sk`

```
#!/usr/local/bin/slonik

# File: changeProvider.sk
include <preamble.sk>;

subscribe set ( id = 1, provider = @SPRINGFIELD,
                               receiver = @SNOOZEVILLE, forward = no );
```

That's nearly identical to the previous `subscribe set` command; the only difference is that you've changed the provider from `@BOOMTOWN` to `@SPRINGFIELD`.

You can also change the *origin* of a replication set—a process known as re-mastering. To move a replication set from its current origin to a different node, you execute two `slonik` commands:

```
lock set ( id = set-id, origin = current-origin );
move set ( id = set-id, old origin = current-origin, new origin = target-origin );
```

When the `move set` command completes, Slony reverses the roles between the old origin (which is now a subscriber) and the new origin (which was formerly a subscriber). The old origin remains a member of the replication set, but it's just another subscriber now.

You can only re-master via the `move set` command if the origin node is healthy. If the origin has experienced a catastrophic failure, you can force another node to assume ownership of the replication set with the `failover` command. The `failover` command moves the replication set to a new origin just like the `move set` command, but it also invalidates the failed node. (Remove the failed node from the cluster with a `drop node` command once the `failover` command completes.) The syntax for the `failover` command is

```
failover ( id = failed-node, backup node = replacement-node );
```

The `failover` command replaces an entire node, not a single set. If the failed node originated more than one set, they're all re-mastered to the replacement node. If the failed node acted as a forwarding provider, `failover` moves all subscribers to the replacement node. If the failed node was a simple (non-forwarding) subscriber, the `failover` command doesn't do much of anything.

Summary

Slony is a powerful, well-designed, and robust replication system. Slony's user interface will surely mature over the next few years to provide a more intuitive installation, configuration, and management structure. The Slony developers are constantly adding new features and performance enhancements so keep an eye on the Slony web site (http://slony.info) for the most recent developments.

25

Contributed Modules

M OST OF THE SOFTWARE THAT I'VE described in this book is considered to be part of the *core* PostgreSQL distribution. The core distribution is managed by the core development team—a small, well-organized, and highly-dedicated team of professional developers and designers. But there are a huge number of developers that contribute software to the PostgreSQL community. Some of the contributed packages are included in the core distribution (in the contrib directory) and you can find many others at the PgFoundry and Gborg web sites (www.pgfoundry.org and gborg.postgresql.org).

Contributed software is a broad term that describes open-source software designed to work with PostgreSQL. That includes everything from graphical SQL client applications and graphical management applications to procedural languages such as PL/Java and PL/perl. You can also find contributed packages that will help you convert data and programs from other systems (such as MySQL, Oracle, and mSQL) into PostgreSQL. At the Gborg web site, you can find an ODBC driver, a JDBC driver (for Java applications), a DBD:: driver (for Perl applications), and interfaces for applications written in C, C++, Visual Basic, C#, Tcl/Tk, Ruby, Python, and maybe even Cobol. You'll find database design tools, monitoring tools, administrator tools, developer tools, even complete business applications.

In this chapter, I'll describe two of the contribute packages that come in the core PostgreSQL distribution: xml2 and tsearch2. The xml2 package lets you store XML documents inside a PostgreSQL database, query those documents using XPath queries, and convert XML documents using XSLT stylesheets. tsearch2 is a full-text indexing and searching package that lets you turn your PostgreSQL server into a search engine.

Exchanging PostgreSQL Data with XML

XML is the wave of the future. Well, it's *a* wave in *some* future anyway. XML was designed to let you and I write applications that can exchange structured data. An XML document is a self-describing textual representation of data, often structured in a hierarchical form. In this section, I'll assume that you have some knowledge of XML, XPath queries, and XSLT stylesheets. If you aren't familiar with those technologies, read on—I'll show you a few examples that should help you understand the basic concepts.

You can store XML data in a PostgreSQL database without any help from third-party software. For example, let's say that one of your distributors offers a new service to the video store that you're running. Every so often the distributor sends you an XML document that describes a number of films. A typical document is shown in Listing 25.1.

Listing 25.1 `films.xml`

```
<films>
  <film>
    <name>Casablanca</name>
    <year>1942</year>
    <writers>
      <writer>Murray Burnett</writer>
      <writer>Joan Alison</writer>
      <writer>Julius J. Epstein</writer>
      <writer>Philip G. Epstein</writer>
      <writer>Howard Koch</writer>
    </writers>
    <leads>
      <lead>Humphrey Bogart</lead>
      <lead>Ingrid Bergman</lead>
      <lead>Peter Lorre</lead>
    </leads>
    <directors>
      <director>Michael Curtiz</director>
    </directors>
  </film>

  <film>
    <name>Rear Window</name>
    <year>1954</year>
    <writers>
      <writer>Cornell Woolrich</writer>
      <writer>John Michael Hayes</writer>
    </writers>
    <leads>
      <lead>James Stewart</lead>
      <lead>Grace Kelly</lead>
      <lead>Raymond Burr</lead>
    </leads>
    <directors>
      <director>Alfred Hitchcock</director>
    </directors>
  </film>
```

Listing 25.1   **Continued**

```
<film>
  <name>The Godfather</name>
  <year>1972</year>
  <writers>
    <writer>Mario Puzo</writer>
    <writer>Francis Ford Coppola</writer>
  </writers>
  <leads>
    <lead>Marlon Brando</lead>
    <lead>Al Pacino</lead>
    <lead>James Caan</lead>
    <lead>Robert Duvall</lead>
    <lead>Diane Keaton</lead>
    <lead>Talia Shire</lead>
  </leads>
  <directors>
    <director>Francis Ford Coppola</director>
  </directors>
</film>
</films>
```

This document (films.xml) describes three films: Casablanca, Rear Window, and
The Godfather. Each description contains a name, a year (the year that the film was
released), a collection of writers, a collection of leads (leading actors and actresses), and
a collection of directors.

To store this document in a PostgreSQL database, you *could* simply INSERT the whole
thing into a TEXT column. In practice, you'd probably want to split the document into
separate records (one for each film) and store each description in a separate row. Let's do
that. First, create a table (filminfo) that will hold the film descriptions like this:

```
$ psql movies
Welcome to psql 8.0.0, the PostgreSQL interactive terminal.
...
movies=# CREATE TABLE filminfo
movies-# (
movies(#    film_name VARCHAR PRIMARY KEY,
movies(#    description TEXT
movies(# );
NOTICE:  CREATE TABLE / PRIMARY KEY will create implicit
  index "filminfo_pkey" for table "filminfo"
CREATE TABLE
```

Now you have a container, but how do you get the XML objects *into* the filminfo
table? The distributor has given you an XML document; you want to split that document into separate objects and then INSERT those objects into the filminfo table.

Sounds like a perfect job for XSLT (Extensible Stylesheet Language Transformations). Listing 25.2 shows an XSLT document (splitFilms.xsl) that will do the trick.

Listing 25.2 splitFilms.xsl

```
1 <xsl:stylesheet
2   xmlns:xsl="http://www.w3.org/1999/XSL/Transform" version="1.0">
3   <xsl:output method="xml" omit-xml-declaration="yes"/>
4
5   <xsl:template match="/">
6     <xsl:for-each select="films/film">
7       <xsl:text>INSERT INTO filminfo VALUES('</xsl:text>
8       <xsl:value-of select="name"/>
9       <xsl:text>','</xsl:text>
10      <xsl:copy-of select="."/>
11      <xsl:text>');
12      </xsl:text>
13    </xsl:for-each>
14  </xsl:template>
15 </xsl:stylesheet>
```

splitFilms.xsl will parse through a list of films and create an INSERT command for each film that it finds. Given the first film described in films.xml (see Listing 25.1), splitFilms.xsl will produce an INSERT command that looks like this:

```
INSERT INTO filminfo VALUES('Casablanca','<film>
  <name>Casablanca</name>
  <year>1942</year>
  <writers>
    <writer>Murray Burnett</writer>
    <writer>Joan Alison</writer>
    <writer>Julius J. Epstein</writer>
    <writer>Philip G. Epstein</writer>
    <writer>Howard Koch</writer>
  </writers>
  <leads>
    <lead>Humphrey Bogart</lead>
    <lead>Ingrid Bergman</lead>
    <lead>Peter Lorre</lead>
  </leads>
  <directors>
    <director>Michael Curtiz</director>
  </directors>
</film>');
```

You can save the INSERT commands to a text file or, better yet, just pipe the output produced by splitFilms.xsl directly into the psql command. If you're using the libxslt package, you can execute splitFilms.xsl like this:

```
$ xsltproc splitFilms.xsl films.xml | psql movies
INSERT 846648 1
INSERT 846649 1
INSERT 846650 1
```

There are three films described in `films.xml` and `psql` reports three `INSERT`
commands—that's a good sign.

Now that you have XML documents in your database, you can use them just like
any other `TEXT` value. You can search inside of an XML document using PostgreSQL's
regular expression operators. For example, to find films starring Jimmy Stewart, you
could execute the following query:

```
movies=# SELECT film_name FROM filminfo
movies-#  WHERE description ~* '<leads>.*James Stewart.*</leads>';
  film_name
------------
 Rear Window
(1 row)
```

You can treat an XML document just like any other `TEXT` value, but you can add a
number of XML-specific features by installing the xml2 contributed module.

XPath Queries

xml2 (also known as pgxml) is a small collection of functions that let you execute XPath
queries against XML documents stored in a PostgreSQL database. xml2 does *not* turn
your database into an XML database—you can't execute XPath queries *in place of* `SELECT`
statements. Instead, xml2 lets you include XPath queries inside of `SELECT` (and other
statements).

xml2 defines three functions that will return a single value from an XPath query:

```
xpath_string( document, query ) RETURNS TEXT
xpath_number( document, query ) RETURNS FLOAT4
xpath_bool( document, query)    RETURNS BOOL
```

When you call one of the xml2 query functions, you provide an XML document and an
XPath query. The query function returns the object (a number, string, Boolean value, list
of values, or a nodeset) identified by the XPath. If that sounds confusing, it may help to
look at an example. Here's a query that extracts the `year` node stored within a film
description:

```
movies=# SELECT film_name, xpath_string( description, 'year' ) FROM filminfo;
   film_name    | xpath_string
----------------+-------------
 Casablanca     | 1942
 Rear Window    | 1954
 The Godfather  | 1972
(3 rows)
```

In this case, the `xpath_string()` function is invoked three times (because there are three rows in the `filminfo` table). In each invocation, the `description` column acts as an XML document and `'year'` is an XPath query that navigates through the document until it finds the `year` element.

You can also use the XPath query functions in other parts of the SELECT command, such as the WHERE clause. For example, to find all films released before 1960:

```
movies=# SELECT film_name FROM filminfo
movies-#   WHERE xpath_number( description, '/film/year' ) < 1960;
  film_name
————-

 Casablanca
 Rear Window
(2 rows)
```

In fact, you can use the result of an XPath query as a table. (I'll show you how to do that in a moment.)

xml2 defines five functions that return multiple values from an XPath query. The first set of functions return a nodeset in the form of a TEXT string (a nodeset is a collection of XML nodes):

```
xpath_nodeset( document, query, topTag, itemTag ) RETURNS TEXT
xpath_nodeset( document, query, itemTag ) RETURNS TEXT
xpath_nodeset( document, query ) RETURNS TEXT
```

Use the nodeset functions when you want to extract a set of values from an XML document and you want the result to retain the XML tags present in the document. For example, to find all `writers` for a given film:

```
movies=# SELECT xpath_nodeset( description, 'writers' ) FROM filminfo
movies-#   WHERE film_name = 'Rear Window';
 xpath_nodeset
--------------
 <writers>
   <writer>Cornell Woolrich</writer>
   <writer>John Michael Hayes</writer>
 </writers>
(1 row)
```

If you include a `topTag` or `itemTag`, `xpath_nodeset()` will wrap the entire nodeset in the `topTag` and wrap each item inside of an `<itemTag> </itemTag>` pair. The extra tags are useful if you are building a new XML document out of data already in the database.

To convert a nodeset into a more conventional (and often more useful form), use the `xpath_list()` function.

```
movies=# SELECT xpath_list( description, 'leads/lead') FROM filminfo
movies-#   WHERE film_name = 'The Godfather';
                            xpath_list
-------------------------------------------------------------------------
 Marlon Brando,Al Pacino,James Caan,Robert Duvall,Diane Keaton,Talia Shire
(1 row)
```

xpath_list() expects two or three arguments. If you call xpath_list() with three arguments, the last argument determines the string that separates each element in the list (the default separator is ",").

The last XPath function provided by xml2 is xpath_table() and it can be somewhat confusing. xpath_table() creates a tabular result set by executing an XPath query (or a series of queries separated by "|") against a table (or view). Here's an example:

```
movies=# SELECT * FROM
movies-#  xpath_table('film_name','description','filminfo','year|leads/*','1=1')
movies-#   AS t(film_name text, year text, leads text);
   film_name   | year |      leads
---------------+------+-----------------
 Casablanca    | 1942 | Humphrey Bogart
 Casablanca    |      | Ingrid Bergman
 Casablanca    |      | Peter Lorre
 Rear Window   | 1954 | James Stewart
 Rear Window   |      | Grace Kelly
 Rear Window   |      | Raymond Burr
 The Godfather | 1972 | Marlon Brando
 The Godfather |      | Al Pacino
 The Godfather |      | James Caan
 The Godfather |      | Robert Duvall
 The Godfather |      | Diane Keaton
 The Godfather |      | Talia Shire
(12 rows)
```

The AS clause tells PostgreSQL the shape of the resulting table. (xpath_table() is defined to a return a SETOF RECORDS—since a RECORD has no predefined shape, you have to tell PostgreSQL what shape to expect.)

xpath_table() expects five arguments:

```
xpath_table( key, document, table, xpathQueries, condition )
```

xpath_table() creates a SELECT command (based on the arguments that you provide) and then executes that command. Next, xpath_table() reads through each row returned by the SELECT command and evaluates the XPath queries against the document column.

The SELECT command is constructed from the key, document, table, and condition arguments. After executing the SELECT command, xpath_table() verifies that the query returned exactly two columns (a key and a document) and then reads through each row in the result set, evaluating each XPath query that you provide. For each XPath query, xpath_table() evaluates that query and, if it returns a value, stores that value in an intermediate tuple. When the tuple is complete, xpath_table() adds its to the final result set. If you invoke xpath_table() with two or more XPath queries that return nodesets of differing sizes, the final result set will contain NULL values.

That's a rather complex description that might be better illustrated by walking through the process one step at a time.

Given the arguments

```
xpath_table('film_name','description','filminfo','year|leads/*','1=1')
```

xpath_table() starts by splitting the xpathQueries argument (year|leads/*) into individual queries. In this case, xpath_table() finds two queries: year and leads/*. Since you've supplied two queries, the result set produced by xpath_table() will contain three columns: the first column will contain the key field (film_name), the second column will contain the result of the first XPath query (year), and the third column will contain the result of the send XPath query (leads/*).

Next, xpath_table() pastes together a SELECT command that looks like this:

```
SELECT film_name, description FROM filminfo WHERE 1=1;
```

xpath_table() always selects two columns from the table: the key and the document. The *condition* argument is tacked on to the end of the command in the form of a WHERE clause—you must provide a *condition* even if you want to process every row in the given table[1].

Next, xpath_table() executes the SELECT command and loops through each row that makes it through the WHERE clause. xpath_table() constructs one or more tuples out of each row returned by the SELECT command. To fill in the first column in each new tuple, xpath_table() simply copies the key column (film_name) from the row returned by the SELECT command. To fill in the remaining columns, xpath_table() evaluates each XPath query against the document column. In this example, the first document (the description column) returned by the SELECT command looks like this:

```
<film>
    <name>Casablanca</name>
    <year>1942</year>
    <writers>
        <writer>Murray Burnett</writer>
        <writer>Joan Alison</writer>
        <writer>Julius J. Epstein</writer>
        <writer>Philip G. Epstein</writer>
```

---

[1] The condition argument is just tacked onto the end of the SELECT command—you can include any text that can legally follow the word WHERE in a SELECT command. In fact, you can force xpath_table() to join two tables by listing them both in the *table* argument and specifying a join in the *condition* argument.

```
        <writer>Howard Koch</writer>
    </writers>
    <leads>
        <lead>Humphrey Bogart</lead>
        <lead>Ingrid Bergman</lead>
        <lead>Peter Lorre</lead>
    </leads>
    <directors>
        <director>Michael Curtiz</director>
    </directors>
</film>
```

The first XPath query (year) nabs a nodeset that contains a single value (1942). The second XPath query (leads/*) returns a nodeset containing three values (Humphrey Bogart, Ingrid Bergman, and Peter Lorre). For each row returned by the SELECT command, xpath_table() produces one or more tuples. The number of new tuples is determined by the largest nodeset returned by the XPath queries. In this case, the largest nodeset contains three nodes, so xpath_table() will add three tuples to the final result set. To form the new tuples, xpath_table() copies the key value ("Casablanca") into the first column of each new tuple, and then starts copying the nodes into the remaining columns. If xpath_table() runs out of nodes for a given column (and it *will* run out when the nodesets differ in length), it writes a NULL value into the tuple instead.

When it finishes with the first row, xpath_table() repeats the process for each of the remaining rows. When it hits the second row (Rear Window), xpath_table() again finds that the nodeset produced by the first XPath query contains a single value (1954) and the second nodeset contains three values—that means three more rows in the final result set. The last row returned by the SELECT command (The Godfather) produces one nodeset that contains a single value (1972) and second nodeset that contains six values, so xpath_table() adds six more rows to the final result set.

You can infer a few rules from this walk-through:

- The number of columns produced by xpath_tables() is always one more than the number of XPath queries that you specify
- The AS clause that you define must contain one more column than the number of XPath queries that you specify
- The first column in the result set always contains values from the *key* column that you specify
- The number of rows produced for any given row in the source table is determined by the largest nodeset extracted from that row
- For any given row in the source table, some columns will contain NULL values if the nodesets extracted from that row differ in size

You can see that the XPath query functions are powerful but they can also be unwieldy. You can simplify the xml2 functions by wrapping them in custom-made views and functions.

For example, you can easily create a view that uses `xpath_table()` to extract leading actors and actresses like this:

```
movies=# CREATE VIEW film_leads AS
movies-#   SELECT * FROM
movies-#   xpath_table('film_name','description','filminfo','leads/*','1=1')
movies-#   AS t(name text, leads text);
CREATE VIEW

test=# SELECT * FROM film_leads WHERE name = 'Casablanca';
    name     |     leads
------------+-----------------
 Casablanca | Humphrey Bogart
 Casablanca | Ingrid Bergman
 Casablanca | Peter Lorre
(3 rows)
```

That's much better. Of course, you can treat a view built from `xpath_table()` just like any other table or view. For example, you could join the `film_leads` view and the tapes table to produce of a list of all leading actors and actresses starring in the films that you have in stock:

```
movies=# SELECT DISTINCT ON( title, leads ) tape_id, title, leads
movies-#   FROM tapes, film_leads WHERE name = title;
 tape_id  |     title      |     leads
----------+----------------+-----------------
 MC-68873 | Casablanca     | Humphrey Bogart
 MC-68873 | Casablanca     | Ingrid Bergman
 MC-68873 | Casablanca     | Peter Lorre
 AH-54706 | Rear Window    | Grace Kelly
 AH-54706 | Rear Window    | James Stewart
 AH-54706 | Rear Window    | Raymond Burr
 AB-67472 | The Godfather  | Al Pacino
 AB-67472 | The Godfather  | Diane Keaton
 AB-67472 | The Godfather  | James Caan
 AB-67472 | The Godfather  | Marlon Brando
 AB-67472 | The Godfather  | Robert Duvall
 AB-67472 | The Godfather  | Talia Shire
(12 rows)
```

(the DISTINCT ON clause weeds out any duplicates in case you have multiple copies of the same video, each with a different `tape_id`.)

You can also simplify the XPath query functions (`xpath_string()`, `xpath nodeset()`, `xpath_list()`, and so on) by wrapping them in more convenient forms. In fact, you don't even have to resort to a procedural language (such as PL/pgSQL or Java)—you can write the wrapper functions in SQL. For example, the script shown in Listing 25.3 creates a function that returns a comma-separated list of the leads actors and actresses starring in a given film.

Listing 25.3 `starring.sql`

```
-
- Filename: starring.sql
-

CREATE FUNCTION starring( title TEXT ) RETURNS TEXT AS
$$
  SELECT xpath_list( description, 'leads/*')
    FROM filminfo
    WHERE film_name = $1
$$
LANGUAGE 'SQL';
```

You can call this function in the select-list part of a SELECT command, in the WHERE clause, or in both parts:

```
movies=# SELECT tape_id, title, starring( title ) FROM tapes
movies-#   WHERE starring( title ) LIKE '%James Stewart%';
 tape_id  |    title     |                starring
----------+--------------+----------------------------------------
 AH-54706 | Rear Window  | James Stewart,Grace Kelly,Raymond Burr
(1 row)
```

That query returns the leading actors and actresses who star in any video that you stock that features James Stewart.

Converting XML Data with XSLT

At the beginning of the previous section, I showed you how to use XSLT to translate an XML document into a sequence of INSERT commands. XSLT can convert any XML document into (just about) any other form.

The xml2 contributed module includes an XSLT processor that you can invoke from within the PostgreSQL server. (Actually, xml2 includes an interface to the libxslt package.) That means that you can use XSLT to convert XML documents stored inside of your database, without ever leaving the comfort of your favorite PostgreSQL client.

XSLT is often used to produce HTML web pages from XML documents, and in this section, I'll show you how to turn the XML documents stored in the filminfo table into user-friendly web pages.

To convert an XML document using an XSLT stylesheet, call the xslt_process() function. xslt_process() expects two arguments:

```
xslt_process( document TEXT, stylesheet TEXT ) RETURNS TEXT
```

It may seem obvious, but it's worth pointing out that you can provide either argument as a TEXT literal, as an expression that evaluates to a TEXT value, or as a reference to a column in the database. The most convenient way to use xslt_process() is to store *both* the XML document and the XSLT stylesheet in a PostgreSQL table (probably in two separate tables).

To start this exercise, I'll create a table that will hold XSLT stylesheets:

```
movies=# CREATE TABLE transforms( name VARCHAR, stylesheet TEXT );
CREATE TABLE
```

Next, I'll create a function named `stylesheet()` that will retrieve a stylesheet from the transforms table, given the name of the desired styelsheet:

```
movies=# CREATE FUNCTION stylesheet( name VARCHAR ) RETURNS TEXT AS
movies-# $$
movies$#   SELECT stylesheet FROM transforms WHERE name = $1
movies$# $$ LANGUAGE 'SQL';
CREATE FUNCTION
```

At this point, the `movies` database stores XML documents inside of the `filminfo` table and stores XSLT stylesheets in the `transforms` table. Listing 25.4 shows a script that will add a new stylesheet to the `transforms` table.

Listing 25.4 `movieOfTheWeek.sql`

```
INSERT INTO transforms VALUES(
'movieOfTheWeek',

$$<xsl:stylesheet
        xmlns:xsl="http://www.w3.org/1999/XSL/Transform"
        version="1.0">

  <xsl:output method="html"/>
  <xsl:template match="/film">
    <HTML>
      <HEAD><TITLE>Movie of the week</TITLE></HEAD>
      <STYLE TYPE="text/css">
        BODY {font-family: sans-serif}
        H1 {font-size: 20pt}
        H2 {font-size: 22pt; font-style: italic}
        LU {font-size: 16pt}
      </STYLE>
      <BODY>
        <H1>This week's movie</H1>
        <H2><xsl:value-of select="name"/></H2>

        <H1>Starring:</H1>

        <UL>
          <xsl:for-each select="leads/lead">
            <LI><xsl:value-of select="."/></LI>
```

Listing 25.4 **Continued**

```
        </xsl:for-each>
      </UL>

      <H1>Directed by:</H1>

      <UL>
        <xsl:for-each select="directors/director">
          <LI><xsl:value-of select="."/></LI>
        </xsl:for-each>
      </UL>

      <P>Released in: <xsl:value-of select="year"/></P>

    </BODY>
  </HTML>
  </xsl:template>
</xsl:stylesheet>$$ );
```

When you execute this script, you're storing an XSLT stylesheet in the transforms
table. I won't walk you through the workings of the stylesheet; XSLT is a powerful but
unfriendly language and I can't really do it justice in this book, so pick up a good XSLT
book if you need more information. I *will* point out a very important rule, though—the
XSLT processor included with xml2 examines the first character in the stylesheet to
decide whether you've given it a real stylesheet or a reference to a remote stylesheet. If
the first character is a "<", the XSLT processor assumes that the string *is* the stylesheet. If
the first character is anything other than a "<", the XSLT processor assumes that you've
given it a URI that identifies the real stylesheet (that is, the string is treated as if it were
something like "http://example.com/the-real-stylesheet.xsl"). When you INSERT (or
UPDATE) a stylesheet into a table, make sure that the opening "<" immediately follows the
quote character(s)—you don't want a newline between the "$$" and the "<" or you'll
spend a great deal of time increasing your four-letter vocabulary.

To apply the stylesheet shown in Listing 25.4, choose a film that you want to feature
(say, Casablanca) and execute the following commands:

```
movies=# \t
Showing only tuples.
movies=# \o movieOfTheWeek.html
movies=# SELECT xslt_process( description, stylesheet( 'movieOfTheWeek' ))
movies-#   FROM filminfo
movies-#   WHERE film_name = 'Casablanca';
movies=# \o
movies=# \t
Tuples only is off
```

The first command (\t) turns on psql's "tuple-only mode." In this mode, psql omits the column headers (and command responses) that you normally see when you execute a query—you only see the data values returned by each query. The second command (\o movieOfTheWeek.html) tells psql to create a new file named movieOfTheWeek .html (in the current directory) and write command results to that file. Once you've executed those two commands, psql will write raw query results (tuples only) to movieOfTheWeek.html.

As I mentioned earlier, xslt_process() expects two arguments. The first argument tells xslt_process() to convert the XML document found in filminfo's description column. The second argument specifies the stylesheet that xslt_process() will use to control the conversion process. The SELECT command calls the stylesheet() function I defined earlier (at the beginning of this section) to retrieve the movieOfTheWeek stylesheet.

When the SELECT command completes, the \o command closes movieOfTheWeek .html and redirects psql output to your screen. The \t command turns tuple-only mode off again so that you'll see column headers (and command tags).

The overall result here is that you've produced an HTML document (movieOfTheWeek.html) by converting the an XML document using an XSLT stylesheet. If you view movieOfTheWeek.html in a web browser, you'll see a page similar to that shown in Figure 25.1.

Figure 25.1 movieOfTheWeek.html.

Using Full-text Search

If you've ever used Google to search for a web site (and who hasn't), you've used a full-text search engine. A full-text search engine catalogs the words and phrases found in a set of documents and then lets you search for documents that match a given pattern. The tsearch2 contributed module adds full-text search features to a PostgreSQL server. When you add the tsearch2 package to a database, you get a small collection of new data types, a large collection of new functions (most of which you'll never invoke directly), and a new search operator. When you use tsearch2, the documents that you catalog and search are the values stored in your database. If you have customers table that stores miscellaneous notes about each customer, the notes column in each row might be a searchable document. If your database includes a parts list, you may want to catalog the description of each part. In tsearch2 terms, a document is a string that you want to catalog and search. A pattern is a logical collection of words that you want to find. A pattern may be as simple as a single word. If a pattern contains multiple words, you can use pattern operators to define how the words relate to the documents that you want to search. For example, you can create a pattern that matches any document that contains *every* word in the pattern, a pattern that matches any document that contains *any of* the words in the pattern, a pattern that matches all documents that contain *none of* the words in the pattern, or any combination.

Before you try out any of the examples in this section, install tsearch2 into your database and then execute the following command:

```
movies=# SELECT set_curcfg( 'default' );
set_curctg
----------

(1 row)
```

If you don't call set_curcfg() first, the queries that I show you will fail with the error:

```
ERROR: could not find tsearch config by locale
```

I'll explain the set_curcfg() function in a moment, but let's look at a few sample queries first.

The @@ operator is similar in concept to LIKE, ILIKE, or the regular-expression operators (~, ~*, and so on): It compares a pattern against a string. To use the @@ operator, you must convert the pattern into an object of type tsquery and the string you want to compare against into an object of type tsvector. For example, to search the tapes table for titles that include the word "Godfather":

```
movies=# SELECT tape_id, title FROM tapes WHERE
movies=#  to_tsvector( title ) @@ to_tsquery( 'Godfather' );
 tape_id  |     title
----------+--------------
 AB-12345 | The Godfather
 AB-67472 | The Godfather
(2 rows)
```

If you want to search for all titles that include Rear and Window, the search pattern should look like this:

```
to_tsquery( 'Rear & Window' )
```

To search for all titles that include Rear *or* Window, separate the words with the | operator, like this:

```
to_tsquery( 'Rear | Window' )
```

To search for all titles that include the word Window, but not the word Rear, use the ! operator:

```
to_tsquery( 'Rear & ! Window' )
```

You can combine operators to create complex patterns. Use parentheses to group expressions. For example, this pattern

```
to_tsquery( 'Island & (Earth | Gilligan)' )
```

will match This Island Earth and Escape From Gilligan's Island, but not Escape From Devil's Island.

It's easy to confuse the tsvector and tsquery data types since they appear to be so similar. They are, in fact, very different. A tsvector contains a *catalog* of the words that appear in a document. A tsquery contains a search pattern, not just a list of words. In fact, if you try to create a tsquery from a string that contains a list of words, tsearch2 will reward you with an error message (ERROR: syntax error). Instead, you have to tell tsearch2 how those words relate to the document that you're searching—you have to separate multiple words with a tsquery operator (&, |, or !).

Of course, if pattern matching was the only feature offered by tsearch2, it wouldn't be very exciting—after all, you can match patterns with LIKE/ILIKE or the regular-expression operators. tsearch2 supports three distinct advantages over the other pattern matching mechanisms offered by PostgreSQL:

- Stop words
- Stemming
- Indexing

A stop word is a word that tsearch2 automatically ignores when searching and indexing. If you've ever Googled for a phrase like the world's best margarita recipe, you may have noticed the following reply:

```
"the" is a very common word and was not included in your search.
```

"The" is a stop word—it's a word that would match just about every (English) document ever searched (other examples include "a," "and," "not," "some," and so on.). Stop words take up extra space (and slow down searches) without contributing to the task of identifying interesting documents. When you convert a search pattern into a tsquery object, tsearch2 strips out any stop words that it finds in the pattern.

Stemming is the process of identifying word variations. When you create a search pattern into a tsquery object, to_tsquery() replaces each word in the pattern with its stem. For example, donate, donation, donating, donates, and donated are all variations of the same word. If to_tsquery() finds one of those variants in a search pattern, it replaces each occurrence with the stem: donat. That means that a search for donate will match documents that contain any variant of donate.

Of course, if you stem a search pattern, you must also stem the documents that you are searching through. to_tsvector() removes stops words and stems word variations using the same set of rules used by to_tsquery().

The process of stemming, stopping, and cataloging the words in a document is expensive. When you execute a query that invokes to_tsvector() like this:

```
SELECT tape_id, title FROM tapes WHERE
    to_tsvector( title ) @@ to_tsquery( 'Godfather' );
```

the PostgreSQL server will stem, stop, and catalog every row in the table. If you execute the same query (or a similar query) again, the server has to stem, stop, and catalog every row a second time. You can greatly improve performance by building a tsvector for each document at the time you add the document to the database.

The movies sample database that we've been using in most of this book doesn't really contain enough data to thoroughly exercise tsearch2, but the recalls table presented in Chapter 4, "Performance," does. The recalls table (in the perf database) contains 39,241 rows of information about automobile recalls. Each row contains three large VARCHAR fields that contain a description of a defect, the possible consequences of the defect, and the corrective action promised by the manufacturer.

To demonstrate the performance benefits offered by tsearch2, I'll use tsearch2 to count the number of recalls that contain the word hydraulic (in the desc_defect column).

It takes my computer approximately 6.4 seconds to execute the following query:

```
SELECT COUNT(*) FROM recalls WHERE
   to_tsvector( desc_defect ) @@ to_tsquery( 'hydraulic' );
```

That query stems, stops, and catalogs every desc_defect in the recalls table, and identifies 808 rows that match the given pattern. If I execute the same query repeatedly, each iteration takes (approximately) the same amount of time.

Just for purposes of comparison, it takes approximately 2.7 seconds to perform a similar query using a regular-expression:

```
SELECT COUNT(*) FROM recalls WHERE
   desc_defect ~* 'hydraulic';
```

Again, if I execute the same query repeatedly, each iteration takes roughly the same amount of time.

Why does a tsearch2-based search take nearly two and a half times longer than a regular-expression search? Because the to_tsvector() function is stemming, stopping, and cataloging every word found in the `desc_defect` column. The regular-expression search simply scans through the `desc_defect` column and stops as soon as it finds the word `hydraulic`. In fact, the tsearch2 and the regular-expression search identify a different set of matches (because of the stemming rules and parsing rules used by tsearch2).

It's usually a waste of time to stem, stop, and catalog every row for each tsearch2 query, because the vast majority of the documents remain unchanged from query to query. Instead, I'll add a `tsvector` column to my recalls table and "precompute" the stem, stop, and catalog information required for a tsearch2 query:

```
perf=# ALTER TABLE recalls
perf-#   ADD COLUMN fts_desc_defect TSVECTOR;
ALTER TABLE

perf=# UPDATE RECALLS SET
perf-#   fts_desc_defect = to_tsvector( desc_defect );
UPDATE 39241

perf=# VACUUM FULL ANALYZE recalls;
VACUUM
```

Now I can run a tsearch2 query again, but this time, I search the new `fts_desc_defect` column instead:

```
SELECT COUNT(*) FROM recalls WHERE
  fts_desc_defect @@ to_tsquery( 'hydraulic' );
```

Notice that I don't have to convert `fts_desc_defect` into a `tsvector` because it already *is* a `tsvector`. This query identifies the same set of rows selected by the first query, but this query runs in 0.22 seconds. That's a considerable improvement over the original query (6.7 seconds). But I can make it faster still.

tsearch2 provides the infrastructure required to index `tsvector` values. To create an index that `@@` can use:

```
perf=# CREATE INDEX fti_desc_defect ON recalls USING GIST( fts_desc_defect );
CREATE INDEX

perf=# VACUUM FULL ANALYZE recalls;
VACUUM
```

Now when I search the `fts_desc_defect` column (using the same query), it takes less than .04 seconds (4/100ths of a second) to identify the same set of rows. PostgreSQL uses the index on `fts_desc_defect` to read only those rows that match the search pattern.

At this point, I've improved performance, but I've introduced a bug. If I search the `desc_defect` column, PostgreSQL has to stem, stop, and catalog every row in the `recalls` table (every time I search) and I get poor performance. If I search the pre-cataloged `fts_desc_defect` column, I get good performance. But what happens if I add a new row to the recalls table? Or UPDATE an existing row (and change the words in the desc_defect column)? Searching against desc_defect guarantees that I'll see the most recent data. Searching against fts_desc_defect guarantees that I'll see obsolete data. Fortunately, this problem is easy to fix—in fact, there are two different solutions.

The most obvious way to keep fts_desc_defect up-to-date is to create a TRIGGER that recomputes the tsvector whenever I add a new row or update an existing row. tsearch2 even comes with a function that you can use to implement the trigger:

```
perf=# CREATE TRIGGER tg_fts_recalls
perf-#    BEFORE UPDATE OR INSERT ON RECALLS
perf-#    FOR EACH ROW
perf=#    EXECUTE PROCEDURE tsearch2( fts_desc_defect, desc_defect );
CREATE TRIGGER
```

The tsearch2() function expects two arguments: the name of a tsvector column and the name of a text (or other string-valued) column. The trigger will effectively call ts_tovector(desc_defect) and copy the result into the fts_desc_defect column.

I can test this trigger pretty easily:

```
perf=# SELECT COUNT(*) FROM recalls fts_desc_defect @@ to_tsquery('hydraulic');
 count
------
   808
(1 row)

perf=# UPDATE recalls
perf-#    SET desc_defect = 'busted hydraulic line'
perf-#    WHERE record_id = 4909;
UPDATE 1

perf=# SELECT COUNT(*) FROM recalls fts_desc_defect @@ to_tsquery('hydraulic');
 count
------
   809
(1 row)
```

Another way to solve this problem is to drop the fts_desc_defect column—you don't need it to gain the benefits offered by pre-cataloging and indexing. Instead of adding an fts_desc_defect column and then creating an index that covers that column, just create a function-based index. First, I'll clean out the tsvector column that I added earlier:

```
perf=# DROP TRIGGER tg_fts_recalls ON recalls;
DROP TRIGGER

perf=# DROP INDEX fti_desc_defect;
DROP INDEX

perf=# ALTER TABLE recalls DROP COLUMN tg_fts_recalls;
ALTER TABLE
```

Now I'll create a new index function-based index:

```
perf=# CREATE INDEX fti_desc_defect ON recalls
perf-#   USING GIST( to_tsvector( desc_defect ));
CREATE INDEX
```

As you might expect, it takes a while to create the function-based index. PostgreSQL reads through every row in the `recalls` table; invokes the `to_tsvector()` function to stem, stop, and catalog the `desc_defect` column; and then stores the result in the new index. Of course, if I add a new row to the `recalls` table (or update an existing row), PostgreSQL ensures that the index is kept up-to-date.

By creating a function-based index (or, more properly, an expression-based index), I eliminate the need for a trigger, I can get rid of the extra `tsvector` column (and save quite a bit of space), and I still get the performance boost offered by a pre-cataloged index.

Searching Multiple Columns

The `recalls` table contains three VARCHAR fields that we might want to search: `desc_defect` (a description of the defect), `con_defect` (possible consequences of the defect), and `cor_action` (the corrective action promised by the manufacturer). I could search all three columns using a query such as

```
perf=# SELECT COUNT(*) FROM recalls WHERE
perf-#   to_tsvector(desc_defect) @@ to_tsquery('hydraulic' )
perf-#     OR
perf-#   to_tsvector(con_defect) @@ to_tsquery('hydraulic' )
perf-#     OR
perf-#   to_tsvector(cor_action) @@ to_tsquery('hydraulic' );
 count
------
   902
(1 row)
```

That works, but it's not a simple query to write. Instead of searching through each column individually, I can string all three columns together and search through the concatenation:

```
perf=# SELECT COUNT(*) FROM recalls WHERE
perf-#   to_tsvector(desc_defect || con_defect || cor_action)
perf-#     @@ to_tsquery('hydraulic' )
 count
------
   902
(1 row)
```

Unfortunately, the simplicity of this query is misleading: It works for the `recalls` table, but it won't produce correct results if your documents contain any NULL values. (The document columns in `recalls` contain no NULL values.) A NULL value wonks out this query because the concatenation operator (||) assumes that any string appended to a NULL results in a NULL. In short: `'hydraulic line' || NULL || 'hydraulic piston'` evaluates to NULL. That means that a NULL value in `desc_defect`, `con_defect`, or `cor_action` would effectively hide the other values in that row. To fix this problem, I can rewrite the query using the `coalesce()` function to map NULL values into some other value (in this case, an empty string):

```
perf=# SELECT COUNT(*) FROM recalls WHERE
perf-#  to_tsvector(
perf(#   COALESCE( desc_defect, '' ) || ' ' ||
perf(#   COALESCE( con_defect,  '' ) || ' ' ||
perf(#   COALESCE( cor_action,  '' ))
perf-#    @@ to_tsquery('hydraulic' )
 count
------
   902
(1 row)
```

This query takes about 15 seconds on my computer. (The OR version takes the same amount of time.) So much for simplicity—the OR version was easier to write and easier to understand.

However, I've been leading you down this tortuous path for a good reason. Remember that in the previous section I showed you how to create an expression-based index? I can create an index defined by the rather complex expression that I wrote in that last query, and PostgreSQL will use that index to search for patterns in `desc_defect`, `con_defect`, and `cor_action`.

```
perf-# CREATE INDEX fti_recalls ON recalls USING GIST(
perf-#  to_tsvector(
perf(#   COALESCE( desc_defect, '' ) || ' ' ||
perf(#   COALESCE( con_defect,  '' ) || ' ' ||
perf(#   COALESCE( cor_action,  '' ));
CREATE INDEX
```

Now, when I run the previous query (the one with all the COALESCE noise in it), I see the results in 0.44 seconds.

Simplifying tsearch2 with Customized Functions

tsearch2 queries tend to be rather unwieldy. You can simply tsearch2 by creating a few wrapper functions that hide the details of the complicated queries. For example, I can create a function named `documents()` that will return the (properly coalesced) concatenation of `desc_defect`, `con_defect`, and `cor_action`:

```
perf=# CREATE FUNCTION documents( recall recalls ) RETURNS TSVECTOR AS
perf-# $$
perf$#   SELECT
```

```
perf$#      COALESCE( $1.desc_defect, '' ) || ' ' ||
perf$#      COALESCE( $1.con_defect,  '' ) || ' ' ||
perf$#      COALESCE( $1.cor_action,  '' );
perf$# $$ LANGUAGE 'SQL' IMMUTABLE;
```

I can also define a function named document() (singular this time) that converts documents() into a tsvector:

```
perf=# CREATE FUNCTION document( recall recalls ) RETURNS TSVECTOR AS
perf-# $$
perf$#   SELECT to_tsvector( documents( $1 ));
perf$# $$ LANGUAGE 'SQL' IMMUTABLE;
```

Now I can use the document() function in conjunction with the @@ operator:

```
perf=# SELECT COUNT(*) FROM recalls r
perf-#   WHERE document(r) @@ to_tsquery( 'hydraulic' );
count
-----
   902
(1 row)
```

That's much easier to type in and much easier to read. I can even create a function-based index based on document():

```
perf=# DROP INDEX fti_recalls;
DROP INDEX

perf=# CREATE INDEX fti_recalls USING GIST( document( recalls ));
CREATE INDEX
```

The document() function returns a tsvector based on desc_defect, con_defect, and cor_action. The only thing that I can do with a tsvector is search it, so I may as well add another function that simplifies the search:

```
perf=# CREATE FUNCTION find_recalls( pattern text ) RETURNS SETOF RECALLS AS
perf-# $$
perf$#   SELECT * FROM recalls WHERE
perf$#     to_tsvector(
perf(#       COALESCE( desc_defect, '' ) || ' ' ||
perf(#       COALESCE( con_defect,  '' ) || ' ' ||
perf(#       COALESCE( cor_action,  '' ))
perf(#     @@ to_tsquery( $1 );
perf$# $$ LANGUAGE 'SQL';
CREATE FUNCTION
```

Now I can simply invoke find_recalls() to search for a pattern in desc_defect, con_defect, or cor_action:

```
perf=# SELECT COUNT(*) FROM find_recalls( 'hydraulic' );
 count
-----
   902
(1 row)
```

Searching for Phrases

You can't use tsearch2 to search for phrases—tsearch2 catalogs the individual words in a document, but doesn't keep enough information to know when one word directly follows another. You can't use tsearch2, for example, to search for a phrase such as hydraulic line. (Enclosing the phrase in quotes won't help.) You *can* search for a pattern such as hydraulic & line, but that will match all documents that contain both words, even if line appears before hydraulic or if hydraulic is separated from line by a number of other words.

To search for a phrase, you have to use LIKE, ILIKE, or a regular-expression operator. For example

```
perf=# SELECT COUNT(*) FROM recalls
perf-#   WHERE documents(recalls) ~* 'hydraulic line';
 count
------
    53
(1 row)
```

But you can still use tsearch2 to speed up a phrase search. It stands to reason that any document that contains the phrase hydraulic line will contain the individual words hydraulic and line, right? Looking at it the other way around, a document cannot contain the phrase hydraulic line unless it contains the individual words hydraulic and line. You already know how to identify the set of rows that contain the words hydraulic and line—just add AND document(recalls) @@ to_tsquery('hydraulic & line') to the WHERE clause.

The original version of this query (regular-expression only) takes about 8.2 seconds to run on my computer. By adding tsearch2 to a regular-expression based phrase search, I can drastically reduce the number of rows that the server will have to search. The new query looks like this:

```
perf=# SELECT COUNT(*) FROM recalls
perf-#   WHERE documents(recalls) ~* 'hydraulic line'
perf-#   AND document(recalls) @@ to_tsquery('hydraulic & line');
 count
------
    53
(1 row)
```

The new version takes 0.12 seconds to identify the same set of rows. I can use the `timer` utility (described in Chapter 4) to see what the server does with each query. Here's the `timer` output from the first (regular-expression only) query:

```
$ timer "SELECT COUNT(*) FROM recalls
>        WHERE documents(recalls) ~* 'hydraulic line'"
+--------+------+--------+-----------+------+------+--------+----------+------+
|        |      SEQUENTIAL I/O        |        INDEXED I/O                    |
|        | scans| tuples | heap_blks |cached| scans| tuples | idx_blks |cached|
|--------+------+--------+-----------+------+------+--------+----------+------+
|recalls |    1| 39241  |      5399 |   0  |    0|     0  |       0  |   0  |
+--------+------+--------+-----------+------+------+--------+----------+------+
```

You can see that the server evaluated this query by scanning every one of the 39,241 rows in the table.

```
$ timer "SELECT COUNT(*) FROM recalls
>        WHERE documents(recalls) ~* 'hydraulic line'"
>        AND document(recalls) @@ to_tsquery('hydraulic & line');
+--------+------+--------+-----------+------+------+--------+----------+------+
|        |      SEQUENTIAL I/O        |        INDEXED I/O                    |
|        | scans| tuples | heap_blks |cached| scans| tuples | idx_blks |cached|
|--------+------+--------+-----------+------+------+--------+----------+------+
|recalls |    0|     0  |        71 |   5  |    1|   126  |     173  | 298  |
+--------+------+--------+-----------+------+------+--------+----------+------+
```

The server first uses an index scan (on `fts_recalls`) to quickly identify the 126 rows that satisfy the tsearch2 criteria and then matches each of those rows against the regular expression.

Configuring tsearch2

Each time you start a new client session, tsearch2 tries to find a configuration that matches the server's locale. tsearch2 configurations are stored in a small collection of tables: `pg_ts_cfg`, `pg_ts_cfgmap`, `pg_ts_parser`, and `pg_ts_dict`. tsearch2 comes with three predefined configurations: `default`, `default_russian`, and `simple`:

```
perf=# SELECT * FROM pg_ts_cfg
    ts_name        | prs_name |   locale
-----------------+----------+-------------
 default         | default  | C
 default_russian | default  | ru_RU.KOI8-R
 simple          | default  |
(3 rows)
```

To find the proper configuration, tsearch2 searches `pg_ts_cfg` for a row where the locale column matches your server's locale. If it can't find a matching configuration, you'll see a message stating `ERROR: could not find tsearch config by locale`. You can find the locale used by your server with the following query:

```
perf=# SELECT setting FROM pg_settings WHERE name = 'lc_ctype';
  setting
------------
 en_US.UTF-8
(1 row)
```

If your server's locale doesn't match any of the locales in pg_ts_cfg, you have four options:

- Specify a configuration on every call to to_tsvector() and to_tsquery()
- Call the set_curcfg() function at the beginning of every client session
- Clone an existing configuration
- Create a new configuration from scratch

The first option is simple, but it complicates your code. The to_tsvector() function comes in two flavors[2]. To use the first flavor, you invoke to_tsvector() with a single string argument and it converts that string into a tsvector using the "current" configuration. To use the second flavor, call ts_vector() with two arguments: the name of a configuration and a string. to_tsvector() will convert the string into a tsvector using the configuration that you specified in the first argument. ts_toquery() comes in two flavors as well.

The second option is inconvenient and somewhat dangerous. You have to call set_curcfg() in every client session that *might* use tsearch2—if you've created a trigger or index based on tsearch2, that means you have to call set_curcfg() in any session that could update a cataloged column.

Cloning an existing configuration is often the easiest and safest choice. Cloning an existing configuration is a two step process. First, you add a new row to the pg_ts_cfg table, then you make a copy of the corresponding entries in the pg_ts_cfgmap table. For example, if your server's locale is en_US.UTF8, you can clone the default configuration with the following commands:

```
perf-# INSERT INTO pg_ts_cfg VALUES( 'default_enUS', 'default', 'en_US.UTF8');
INSERT

perf=# INSERT INTO pg_ts_cfgmap
perf-#    SELECT 'default_enUS', tok_alias, dict_name
pcrf #      FROM pg_ts_cfgmap WHERE ts_name = 'default';
INSERT
```

The first command creates a new (empty) configuration named default_enUS—tsearch2 will select this configuration when the server's locale is en_US.UTF8. The second command clones the default entries in pg_ts_cfgmap, creating an identical set of entries

---

[2] tsearch2 provides a third flavor for to_tsvector() and to_tsquery(). You must know the OID of a pg_ts_cfg row to use the third form.

that belong to `default_enUS`. Once you've created a clone that matches your server's locale, you should be able to use tsearch2 without specifying an explicit configuration in each call to `to_tsquery()` and `to_tsvector()`.

Creating a new configuration from scratch is not too complex, but you'll need an understanding of the stemming, stopping, and cataloging process before you start.

When you create a `tsvector` from a text string, tsearch2 starts by invoking a parser that picks apart the text string into its component parts. tsearch2 comes with a single parser (named `default`), but you can write your own parser if you have special requirements. The `default` parser was designed to parse plain-text and HTML documents: It knows how to process HTML tags, HTTP headers, email and host addresses, and so on. The parser identifies and classifies each *token* in a text string. For example, given the string "`send 42 messages to bruce@example.com`", the default parser will identify four words (`send`, `messages`, and `to`), one unsigned integer (`42`), and an email address (`bruce@example.com`). The `default` parser classifies each token into one (or more) of the categories shown in Table 25.1[3].

Table 25.1 **tsearch2 Lexical Categories**

Category	Description	Examples
`lword`	Any word composed entirely of alphabetic characters	`bruce`
`word`	Any word composed of alphabetic and numeric characters	`bruce42`, `postgres81`
`email`	An Internet email address (user@host)	`bruce@example.com`
`url`	An HTTP or FTP URL	http://www.postgresql. org/index.html ftp://ftp.postgresql.org/ index.html
`host`	An Internet hostname	www.postgresq.org localhost.localdomain
`sfloat`	A floating point number in scientific notation	`325.667E12` `6.626E-34`
`version`	A generic version number (a number with more than one decimal point)	`8.0.0` `2.6.9.1`
`part_hword`	Parts of a hyphenated word	`post-gres-sql8`
`lpart_hword`	Latin parts of a hyphenated word	`post-gre-sql8`
`blank`	Whitespace and any characters not matched by other rules	`(parens are considered blanks)` `$so are other special characters!`

[3] The default parser also defines three categories for words and word fragments composed of Cyrillic characters: `nlword`, `nlhword`, and `part-nlhword`.

Table 25.1 **Continued**

Category	Description	Examples
tag	An HTML tag	`<tr>` `<a href="img.png"/>`
http	The protocol component of an HTTP URL	**http://**www.postgresql.org
hword	A hyphenated word	`postgre-sql8`
lhword	A hyphenated Latin word	`postgre-sql`
uri	A uniform resource identifier (usually the filename component of a URL)	http://www.postgresql.org**/index.html**
file	A relative or absolute Linux/Unix pathname	`/tmp/README.txt../` `README.txt`
float	A floating-point number	`3.14159` `6.626`
int	A signed integer	`-32` `+45`
uint	An unsigned integer	`32` `45`
entity	An HTML entity	` ` `&#044;`

When the parser finishes tokenizing and classifying the text string, it ends up with a collection of token values and each token is assigned to a category. Some of the "words" in the text string may result in multiple tokens. For example, the string http://www.postgresql.org/index.html produces four tokens (you can call the ts_debug() function to see the result of the parsing process):

```
perf=# SELECT token, tok_type
perf-#   FROM ts_debug('http://www.postgresql.org/index.html');
           token                | tok_type
--------------------------------+---------
 http://                        | http
 www.postgresql.org/index.html  | url
 www.postgresql.org             | host
 /index.html                    | uri
(4 rows)
```

Next, the parser iterates through the list of tokens and weeds out any that are deemed uninteresting. To decide which tokens to discard, to_tsvector() uses the token type (and the configuration name) to locate a record in the pg_ts_cfgmap table. If to_tsvector() can't find a matching entry in pg_ts_cfgmap, it discards the token. For example, given the tokens parsed from http://www.postgresql.org/index.html, to_tsvector() finds:

```
perf=# SELECT * FROM pg_ts_cfgmap
perf-#    WHERE ts_name = 'default'
perf-#    AND tok_alias IN( 'http', 'url', 'host', 'uri' );
 ts_name | tok_alias | dict_name
---------+-----------+----------
 default | url       | {simple}
 default | host      | {simple}
 default | uri       | {simple}
(3 rows)
```

Notice that tsearch2 won't find an entry for ts_name = 'default' and tok_alias = 'http', so it discards that token (the http:// header). The default configuration discards blank, tag, http, and entity tokens. Discarding a "word" based on its token classification is similar to *stopping* an entire category of words. Discarded tokens are not cataloged by tsearch2, so you won't be able to search for them. Of course, you can tell tsearch2 that you want it to catalog a given category by adding that category to the pg ts cfgmap table. Similarly, you can tell tsearch2 to ignore a given category (say, the file category) by removing that category from pg_ts_cfgmap.

For each token that makes it through the pg_ts_cfgmap filter, tsearch2 starts the stemming and stopping process. When to_tsvector() finds an entry in pg_ts_cfgmap that matches the configuration name and token type, that entry identifies a *dictionary processor*. ts_tsvector() feeds the token into that dictionary processor and adds the result (if any) to the tsvector. The dictionary processor may *stem* the token by translating it into a new token. The dictionary processor may instead *stop* the word by returning a NULL value. Or, the dictionary processor may pass the token through without modification.

The tsearch2 package comes with five sample dictionary processors.

The simple dictionary processor converts each token into lowercase characters and the searches for the result in a list of stop words—if it finds the (lowercased) token in the list, it returns NULL, otherwise it returns the lowercased token to to_tsvector() (and to_tsvector() adds the token to the tsvector that it's building). tsearch2 installs the simple dictionary processor with an empty stop word list (which means that every token makes it through the simple dictionary after it's been translated to lowercase). To add a stop word list (which is just a newline-separated list of words), save the name of your stop word file in the dict_initoption column of the pg_ts_dict row corresponding to the simple dictionary processor. For example, if you've stored a list of stopwords in a file named /usr/share/stopwords.english, execute the following command:

```
perf=# UPDATE pg_ts_dict SET dict_initoption = '/usr/share/stopwords.english';
UPDATE
```

The en_stem dictionary processor handles stop words and stemming. en_stem searches for the token in a list of stop words and discards the token if found. (Like the simple dictionary processor, en_stem finds the stop word list in its pg_ts_dict.dict initoption.) If the token is *not* found in the stop word list, en_stem tries to convert the token into its root form by stripping off common English prefixes and suffixes. For example, en_stem converts donate, donation, donating, donates, and donated into the stem donat. to_tsvector() stores the stem in the tsvector that it's building. If you search for the word donate, tsearch2 will match donate, donation, donating, donates, and donated.

The ru_stem dictionary processor is identical to the en_stem processor except it stems each token using rules designed for Russian text. (You would most likely use a different list of stop words too.)

The synonym dictionary processor doesn't do any stop word processing (or stemming). When you feed a token to the synonym processor, it searches for a match in a list of word-synonym pairs. If it finds a match, the processor returns the synonym. For example, given the list of synonyms:

```
zaurus    pda
newton    pda
pocketpc  pda
nokia     phone
treo      phone
```

The synonym processor will translate zaurus, newton, and pocketpc into pda, and will translate nokia and treo into phone. If synonym can't find a match in the list, it returns NULL.

The last dictionary processor is named ispell_template. ispell_template is based on the ispell program and it searches for each token in a separate dictionary file (not included with tsearch2). If ispell_template finds the token (or a variant of the token) in the dictionary, it returns the stemmed form of the word to to_tsvector(). If ispell_template can't find the token (or a variant of the token) in the dictionary, it returns NULL (and the token is discarded). ispell_template also uses a stop word list to filter out common words. There's an important difference between ispell_template and en_stem. Both dictionary processors convert tokens into stem form, but ispell_template will discard any token that it can't find in the dictionary: en_stem, on the other hand, simply passes through any token that it can't stem. The ispell_template processor won't work until you connect it to a dictionary—a process described in the "Tsearch Introduction" document that comes with tsearch2.

You can string multiple dictionary processors together by listing each one in the pg_ts_cfgmap.dictname column. For example, to apply the synonym processor and then the en_stem processor to every lword token:

```
perf=# UPDATE pg_ts_cfgmap
perf-#   SET dict_name = '{"synonym","en_stem"}'
perf-#   WHERE ts_name = 'default_enUS' AND tok_alias = 'lword';
UPDATE
```

tsearch2 tries each dictionary processor, in order, and stops as soon as a processor returns a non-NULL value.

Now you know how all of the pieces fit together. tsearch2 uses the server's locale to find a configuration (in the `pg_ts_cfg` table). The configuration identifies a parser. tsearch2 uses that parser to split a text string into a set of tokens and assigns a category to each token. The `pg_ts_cfgmap` maps each configuration/token category combination into the name of a dictionary processor. (If a combination is not found in `pg_ts_cfgmap`, tsearch2 discards all tokens of that category.) The dictionary processor (typically) filters each token through a list of stop words and then stems anything that makes it through the filter.

To create a new configuration, you can write a new parser, change the `pg_ts_cfgmap` to include (or exclude) token categories, modify the `pg_ts_cfgmap` to apply a different dictionary processor to a token category, implement a new dictionary processor, or modify the list of stop words used by a dictionary. If you use the `synonym` dictionary processor, you can also modify the synonym map. In most cases, you won't need to write any code (unless you find that you have to implement a new parser or dictionary processor); just adjust a configuration table (or external file). If you *do* write a new parser or dictionary processor, consider donating it to the PostgreSQL community so other users can benefit from your efforts.

tsearch2 offers a number of other features that I haven't described here. You know that tsearch2 can identify the documents that match a given pattern—tsearch2 can also rank the matches according to relevance. (Check out the `rank()` and `rank_cd()` functions.) When tsearch2 finds a document that matches a pattern, you can ask the `headline()` function to produce a string that highlights the search words in context. See the tsearch2 documentation for more details.

If tsearch2 doesn't have what you need, check out the OpenFTS package. OpenFTS is a user-friendly wrapper around tsearch2. You can use OpenFTS to expose the documents in your database to users that may not know how to formulate SQL queries (and may not understand the results). You can find OpenFTS at openfts.sourceforge.net.

Index

K-L

libpqgeasy, 405
libpqxx, 421–422
  adding error checking, 426-433
  connecting to servers, 423-426
    connection function, 426
    notice processor objects, 429-433
    pqxx-config program, 424-426
    thrown exceptions, 427-429
  processing queries, 433-440, 443-444, 447-459
    get_variable(), 458-459
    large objects, 452-456
    LISTEN/NOTIFY, 456-458
    result sets, 436-451
    set_variable(), 458-459
    transactions, 433-435
  transactors, 459-464
libraries, 392
LIKE, 55–56
LIMIT, 49
Limit operator, 213
Linux
  installing PostgreSQL, 786
  locales, 882-883
  runlevels, 866
  starting PostgreSQL on startup, 865-868
ListBoxes, 735
LISTEN/NOTIFY, 249
  processing queries, 456-458
lists, sorting, 165
-l logfile-name, 864
LoadTree()method, 737–738
local connections, 907–908
locales, 881
  changing, 884
  enabling support, 883-884
  finding current locales, 882
  information categories, 883-888
  language IDs, 882
  names, 882-883
  territories, 882
localization
  administrator's roles, 781
  definition of, 881
location of extensions, finding, 258
LOCATION=path clause, 149
locking, 187
logfiles, rotating, 808–810
logical operators, 39–43, 97
log_level option (slon configuration), 938
log_pid option (slon configuration), 939
log_timestamp option (slon configuration), 939

log_timestamp_format option (slon configuration), 939
logs, config.log, 793
LOOP, PL/pgSQL, 326
loop constructs
  integer-FOR loop, 329
  PL/pgSQL, 326 331
loop index, 320
loopback drivers, 751
loops, 320–321
lo_export() function, 111
lo_import() function, 111
lo_unlink() function, 111
lpart_hword category (tsearch2), 972
LSEG, 98
lword category (tsearch2), 972

M

MACADDR, 112
main(), 418
maintenance
  managing groups. *See* groups
  managing indexes, 804-805
  managing tables, 803-804
  managing user accounts. *See* user accounts
make utility, 364–365
makefiles, 364, 397
managing
  groups, 816-817
  indexes, 804 805
  tables, 803-804
  user accounts, 811
  user accounts. *See* user accounts
manifest files, 765–766
matching patterns, 55–57
Materialize operator, 222
MAX FSM PAGES, 826
MAX FSM RELATIONS, 826
MAX(), 61
md5 authentication method, 913–914
membership (group) creating users, 814
memory (shared), 198–199
Merge Join operator, 211, 217–219
MessageBox classes, 536
meta-commands, 178, 600–602, 611
metadata, 248
  client applications, 249
  JDBC query processing, 563-564
  naming conventions, 378
  PHP, query processing, 630-633
  result set processing, 588-597
  result sets, 249